For Reference

Not to be taken from this room.

THE FOLGER BOOK
OF
SHAKESPEARE QUOTATIONS

THE FOLGER BOOK
OF
Shakespeare Quotations

COMPILED AND ARRANGED
BY
BURTON STEVENSON

FOLGER BOOKS

CONTENTS

CHRONOLOGY OF THE PLAYS AND POEMS   2

THE QUOTATIONS   3

INDEX AND CONCORDANCE   601

THE FOLGER BOOK
OF
SHAKESPEARE QUOTATIONS

CHRONOLOGY OF THE PLAYS

This chronology is that of E. K. Chambers in his *William Shakespeare*, vol. 1, ch. 8. It has been selected because Shakespearean scholars seem to take fewer exceptions to it than to any other. All the plays and poems listed in it are included here with the exception of *The Two Noble Kinsmen*, which is not included in the *Globe Edition* and with which Shakespeare's connection is extremely nebulous.

THE PLAYS

II Henry VI, 1590-1
III Henry VI, 1590-1
I Henry VI, 1591-2
Richard III, 1592-3
The Comedy of Errors, 1592-3
Titus Andronicus, 1593-4
The Taming of the Shrew, 1593-4
The Two Gentlemen of Verona, 1594-5
Love's Labour's Lost, 1594-5
Romeo and Juliet, 1594-5
Richard II, 1595-6
A Midsummer Night's Dream, 1595-6
King John, 1596-7
The Merchant of Venice, 1596-7
I Henry IV, 1597-8
II Henry IV, 1597-8
Much Ado about Nothing, 1598-9
Henry V, 1598-9
Julius Cæsar, 1599-1600
As You Like It, 1599-1600
Twelfth Night, 1599-1600

Hamlet, 1600-1
The Merry Wives of Windsor, 1600-1
Troilus and Cressida, 1601-2
All's Well that Ends Well, 1602-3 *
Measure for Measure, 1604-5
Othello, 1604-5
King Lear, 1605-6
Macbeth, 1605-6
Antony and Cleopatra, 1606-7
Coriolanus, 1607-8
Timon of Athens, 1607-8
Pericles, 1608-9
Cymbeline, 1609-10
The Winter's Tale, 1610-11
The Tempest, 1611-12
Henry VIII, 1612-13
The Two Noble Kinsmen, 1612-13

* The London theatres were closed from March, 1603, to April, 1604, on account of the plague, and during this period Shakespeare is believed to have written no plays.

THE POEMS

Venus and Adonis, 1593
The Rape of Lucrece, 1594
The Passionate Pilgrim, 1599

The Phœnix and the Turtle, 1601
Sonnets, 1609
A Lover's Complaint, 1609?

A

Abraham's Bosom

1 Sweet peace conduct his sweet soul to the bosom
Of good old Abraham!
Richard II, Act iv, sc. 1, l. 103 [BOLINGBROKE]
The sons of Edward sleep in Abraham's bosom.
Richard III, Act iv, sc. 3, l. 38 [KING RICHARD]

2 He's in Arthur's bosom, if ever man went to Arthur's bosom.
Henry V, Act ii, sc. 3, l. 10 [HOSTESS]
(Mistress Quickly, hostess of tavern in Eastcheap, the original
Mrs. Malaprop, means Abraham's bosom. She is referring to
Falstaff. For full quotation see 2515.)

Absence

3 There is no living, none, if Bertram be away.
All's Well that Ends Well, Act i, sc. 1, l. 95 [HELENA]

4 Noblest of men, woo't die?
Hast thou no care of me? shall I abide
In this dull world, which in thy absence is
No better than a sty?
Antony and Cleopatra, Act iv, sc. 15, l. 59 [CLEOPATRA]

5 ORLANDO: For these two hours, Rosalind, I will leave thee.
ROSALIND: Alas! dear love, I cannot lack thee two hours.
As You Like It, Act iv, sc. 1, l. 181 [ORLANDO]
What, keep a week away? seven days and nights?
Eight score eight hours? and lovers' absent hours
More tedious than the dial eight score times?
O weary reckoning!
Othello, Act iii, sc. 4, l. 173 [BIANCA]

6 I am glad this parcel of wooers are so reasonable, for there is not
one among them but I dote on his very absence.
The Merchant of Venice, Act i, sc. 2, l. 117 [PORTIA]

7 O absence, what a torment wouldst thou prove,
Were it not thy sour leisure gave sweet leave
To entertain the time with thoughts of love.
Sonnet xxxix, l. 9

8 How like a winter hath my absence been
From thee, the pleasure of the fleeting year!
What freezings have I felt, what dark days seen!
What old December's bareness every where!
Sonnet xcvii, l. 1

9 O thou that dost inhabit in my breast,
Leave not the mansion so long tenantless,
Lest, growing ruinous, the building fall
And leave no memory of what it was!
The Two Gentlemen of Verona, Act v. sc. 4, l. 7 [VALENTINE]

10 Our absence makes us unthrifty to our knowledge.
The Winter's Tale, Act v. sc. 2, l. 122 [GENTLEMAN]

[3]

Absolute

11 You are too absolute.
>> *Coriolanus,* Act iii, sc. 2, l. 39 [VOLUMNIA]

12 How absolute the knave is!
>> *Hamlet,* Act v, sc. 1, l. 148 [HAMLET]

13 How absolute she's in 't!
>> *Pericles,* Act ii, sc. 5, l. 19 [SIMONIDES]

Abstinence

14   Refrain to-night,
And that shall lend a kind of easiness
To the next abstinence.
>> *Hamlet,* Act iii, sc. 4, l. 165 [HAMLET]

15 Say, can you fast? your stomachs are too young;
And abstinence engenders maladies.
>> *Love's Labour's Lost,* Act iv, sc. 3, l. 294 [BIRON]

16 A man of stricture and firm abstinence.
>> *Measure for Measure,* Act i, sc. 3, l. 12 [DUKE]

17 He doth with holy abstinence subdue
That in himself which he spurs on his power
To qualify in others.
>> *Measure for Measure,* Act iv, sc. 2, l. 84 [DUKE]

18 Be more abstemious, Or else, good night your vow!
>> *The Tempest,* Act iv, sc. 1, l. 53 [PROSPERO]

Abuse

19 The poor abuses of the time want countenance.
>> *I Henry IV,* Act i, sc. 2, l. 174 [FALSTAFF]

20 He . . . Cries out upon abuses, seems to weep
Over his country's wrongs.
>> *I Henry IV,* Act iv, sc. 3, l. 81 [HOTSPUR]

21 PRINCE: I shall drive you then to confess the wilful abuse. . . .
FALSTAFF: No abuse, Hal, o' mine honour; no abuse.
>> *II Henry IV,* Act ii, sc. 4, l. 338 [PRINCE HENRY]

22 GLOUCESTER: In thine own person answer thy abuse.
CARDINAL: Ay, where thou darest not peep.
>> *II Henry VI,* Act ii, sc. 1, l. 41 [GLOUCESTER]

23   They that level
At my abuses reckon up their own.
>> *Sonnet* cxxi, l. 9

Accent

24 Your accent is something finer than you could purchase in so removed a dwelling.
>> *As You Like It,* Act iii, sc. 2, l. 359 [ORLANDO]

25 He speaks . . . like a soldier: do not take
His rougher accents for malicious sounds.
>> *Coriolanus,* Act iii, sc. 3, l. 53 [MENENIUS]

26   Brave soldier, pardon me,
That any accent breaking from thy tongue
Should 'scape the true acquaintance of mine ear.
>> *King John,* Act v, sc. 6, l. 13 [HUBERT]

27 You find not the apostraphas, and so miss the accent.
>> *Love's Labour's Lost,* Act iv, sc. 2, l. 123 [HOLOFERNES]

28 Action and accent did they teach him there;
'Thus must thou speak,' and 'thus thy body bear.'
>> *Love's Labour's Lost,* Act v, sc. 2, l. 99 [BOYET]

Accident

29   All solemn things should answer solemn accidents.
> *Cymbeline,* Act iv, sc. 2, l. 191 [GUIDERIUS]

30   Be not with mortal accidents opprest.
> *Cymbeline,* Act v, sc. 4, l. 99 [JUPITER]

31   The day Was yours by accident.
> *Cymbeline,* Act v, sc. 5, l. 75 (LUCIUS]

32   The accident which brought me to her eye
Upon the moment did her force subdue.
> *A Lover's Complaint,* l. 247

33   O, 'tis an accident that heaven provides!
> *Measure for Measure,* Act iv, sc. 3, l. 81 [DUKE]

34   Think no more of this night's accidents
But as the fierce vexation of a dream.
> *A Midsummer Night's Dream,* Act iv, sc. 1, l. 71 [OBERON]

35   Moving accidents by flood and field.
> *Othello,* Act i, sc. 3, l. 135 [OTHELLO]

Act See also Deed

36   It is no act of common passage, but
A strain of rareness.
> *Cymbeline,* Act iii, sc. 4, l. 94 [IMOGEN]

37   Some act
That has no relish of salvation in 't.
> *Hamlet,* Act iii, sc. 3, l. 91 [HAMLET]

38   QUEEN: What have I done, that thou darest wag thy tongue
In noise so rude against me?
HAMLET: Such an act
That blurs the grace and blush of modesty,
Calls virtue hypocrite, takes off the rose
From the fair forehead of an innocent love
And sets a blister there . . .
QUEEN: Ay me, what act
That roars so loud and thunders in the index?
> *Hamlet,* Act iii, sc. 4, l. 39 [QUEEN]

39   An act hath three branches: it is, to act, to do, and to perform.
> *Hamlet,* Act v, sc. 1, l. 12 [CLOWN]

40   Between the acting of a dreadful thing
And the first motion, all the interim is
Like a phantasma, or a hideous dream:
The Genius and the mortal instruments
Are then in council; and the state of man,
Like to a little kingdom, suffers then
The nature of an insurrection.
> *Julius Cæsar,* Act ii, sc. 1, l. 63 [BRUTUS]

41   This act so evilly born shall cool the hearts
Of all his people and freeze up their zeal,
That none so small advantage shall step forth
To check his reign, but they will cherish it.
> *King John,* Act iii, sc. 4, l. 149 [PANDULPH]

42   This act is as an ancient tale new told,
And in the last repeating troublesome.
> *King John,* Act iv, sc. 2, l. 18 [PEMBROKE]

43   Be great in act, as you have been in thought; . . .
Be stirring as the time; be fire with fire;
Threaten the threatener and outface the brow
Of bragging horror: so shall inferior eyes,

That borrow their behaviours from the great,
Grow great by your example and put on
The dauntless spirit of resolution.
                King John, Act v, sc. 1, l. 45 [BASTARD]

44   [I] did the act of darkness with her.
                King Lear, Act iii, sc. 4, l. 90 [EDGAR]
The blood is made dull with the act of sport.
                Othello, Act ii, sc. 1, l. 230 [IAGO]
She with Cassio hath the act of shame
A thousand times committed.
                Othello, Act v, sc. 2, l. 211 [OTHELLO]
I found you where you did fulfil
The loathsome act of lust.
                The Rape of Lucrece, l. 1635 [TARQUIN]

45   Art thou afeard
To be the same in thine own act and valour
As thou art in desire?
                Macbeth, Act i, sc. 7, l. 39 [LADY MACBETH]

46   I know this act shows horrible and grim.
                Othello, Act v, sc. 2, l. 203 [OTHELLO]

47   O impious act, including all foul harms!
                The Rape of Lucrece, l. 199 [LUCRECE]

48   This act will be
My fame and thy perpetual infamy.
                The Rape of Lucrece, l. 1637 [LUCRECE]

49   The blood of English shall manure the ground,
And future ages groan for this foul act;
Peace shall go sleep with Turks and infidels,
And in this seat of peace tumultuous wars
Shall kin with kin and kind with kind confound.
                Richard II, Act iv, sc. 1, l. 137 [CARLISLE]

50   So smile the heavens upon this holy act
That after hours with sorrow chide us not!
                Romeo and Juliet, Act ii, sc. 6, l. 1 [FRIAR LAURENCE]

51   An act
Whereof what's past is prologue, what to come
In yours and my discharge.
                The Tempest, Act ii, sc. 1, l. 252 [ANTONIO]

52   He finished indeed his mortal act
That day that made my sister thirteen years.
                Twelfth Night, Act v, sc. 1, l. 254 [SEBASTIAN]

53   All your acts are queens.
                The Winter's Tale, Act iv, sc. 4, l. 146 [FLORIZEL]

Acting

54   Speak the speech, I pray you, as I pronounced it to you, trippingly
on the tongue: but if you mouth it, as many of your players do, I
had as lief the town-crier spoke my lines. Nor do not saw the air
too much with your hand, thus, but use all gently; for in the very
torrent, tempest, and, as I may say, the whirlwind of passion, you
must acquire and beget a temperance that may give it smoothness.
O, it offends me to the soul to hear a robustious periwig-pated
fellow tear a passion to tatters, to very rags, to split the ears of
the groundlings, who for the most part are capable of nothing but
inexplicable dumb-shows and noise: I would have such a fellow
whipped for o'erdoing Termagant; it out-herods Herod. . . . Be

not too tame, neither, but let your own discretion be your tutor:
suit the action to the word, the word to the action; with this special observance, that you o'erstep not the modesty of nature: for
any thing so overdone is from the purpose of playing, whose end,
both at the first and now, was and is, to hold as 'twere the mirror
up to nature; to show virtue her own feature, scorn her own
image, and the very age and body of the time his form and pres-
sure. Now this overdone, or come tardy off, though it make the
unskilful laugh, cannot but make the judicious grieve; the censure
of the which one must in your allowance o'erweigh a whole theatre
of others. O, there be players that I have seen play, and heard others
praise, and that highly, not to speak it profanely, that, neither
having the accent of Christians nor the gait of Christian, pagan,
nor man, have so strutted and bellowed that I have thought some
of nature's journeymen had made them and not made them well,
they imitated humanity so abominably. . . . And let those that
play your clowns speak no more than is set down for them; for
there be of them that will themselves laugh, to set on some quantity of barren spectators to laugh too; though, in the mean time,
some necessary question of the play be then to be considered.
Hamlet, Act iii, sc. 2, l. 1 [HAMLET]

55   I must speak in passion, and I will do it in King Cambyses' vein.
I Henry IV, Act ii, sc. 4, l. 424 [FALSTAFF]
(Cambyses was a pompous ranting character in Thomas Pres-
ton's "lamentable tragedy" of that name.)
What scene of death hath Roscius now to act?
III Henry VI, Act v, sc. 6, l. 10 [KING HENRY]
(Quintus Roscius [c. 134-62 B.C.], a slave who became the
greatest comic actor in Rome, is mentioned again in Hamlet,
ii, 2, 410, "When Roscius was an actor.")
My chief humour is for a tyrant: I could play Ercles rarely, or a
part to tear a cat in, to make all split. . . . This is Ercles' vein, a
tyrant's vein.
A Midsummer Night's Dream, Act i, sc. 2, l. 31 [BOTTOM]
(Hercules is always a ranting part.)
56   If I do not act it, hiss me.
The Merry Wives of Windsor, Act iii, sc. 3, l. 40 [MRS. PAGE]
57   Tut, I can counterfeit the deep tragedian;
Speak and look back, and pry on every side,
Tremble and start at wagging of a straw,
Intending deep suspicion: ghastly looks
Are at my service, like enforced smiles;
And both are ready in their offices,
At any time, to grace my stratagems.
Richard III, Act iii, sc. 5, l. 5 [BUCKINGHAM]
58   My dismal scene I needs must act alone.
Romeo and Juliet, Act iv, sc. 3, l. 19 [JULIET]
59   Go, play, boy, play: thy mother plays, and I
Play too, but so disgraced a part, whose issue
Will hiss me to my grave.
The Winter's Tale, Act i, sc. 2, l. 187 [LEONTES]

Acting: The Actor

60   When good-will is show'd, though 't come too short,
The actor may plead pardon.
Antony and Cleopatra, Act ii, sc. 5, l. 8 [CLEOPATRA]
61   The best actors in the world, either for tragedy, comedy, history,

pastoral, pastoral-comical, historical-pastoral, tragical-historical,
. . . Seneca cannot be too heavy, nor Plautus too light.
Hamlet, Act ii, sc. 2, l. 415 [POLONIUS]

62 Good my lord, will you see the players well bestowed? Do you
hear, let them be well used; for they are the abstract and brief
chronicles of the time: after your death you were better have a
bad epitaph than their ill report while you live.
Hamlet, Act ii, sc. 2, l. 546 [HAMLET]

63 Is it not monstrous that this player here,
But in a fiction, in a dream of passion,
Could force his soul so to his own conceit
That from her working all his visage wann'd,
Tears in his eyes, distraction in 's aspect,
A broken voice, and his whole function suiting
With forms to his conceit? And all for nothing!
For Hecuba!
What 's Hecuba to him, or he to Hecuba,
That he should weep for her? What would he do,
Had he the motive and the cue for passion
That I have? He would drown the stage with tears,
And cleave the general ear with horrid speech,
Make mad the guilty, and appal the free,
Confound the ignorant, and amaze indeed
The very faculties of eyes and ears.
Hamlet, Act ii, sc. 2, l. 578 [HAMLET]

64 HAMLET: My lord, you played once i' the university, you say?
POLONIUS: That did I, my lord; and was accounted a good actor.
HAMLET: What did you enact?
POLONIUS: I did enact Julius Cæsar: I was killed i' the Capitol;
Brutus killed me.
HAMLET: It was a brute part of him to kill so capital a calf there.
Hamlet, Act iii, sc. 2, l. 104 [HAMLET]

65 The actors are at hand and by their show
You shall know all that you are like to know.
A Midsummer Night's Dream, Act v, sc. 1, l. 116 [QUINCE]

66 As in a theatre, the eyes of men,
After a well-graced actor leaves the stage,
Are idly bent on him that enters next,
Thinking his prattle to be tedious;
Even so, or with much more contempt, men's eyes
Did scowl on gentle Richard; no man cried 'God save him!'
No joyful tongue gave him his welcome home . . .
Had not God, for some strong purpose, steel'd
The hearts of men, they must perforce have melted
And barbarism itself have pitied him.
Richard II, Act v, sc. 2, l. 23 [YORK]

67   A strutting player, whose conceit
Lies in his hamstring, and doth think it rich
To hear the wooden dialogue and sound
'Twixt his stretch'd footing and the scaffoldage.
Troilus and Cressida, Act i, sc. 3, l. 153 [ULYSSES]

Action

68 In such business Action is eloquence.
Coriolanus, Act iii, sc. 2, l. 75 [VOLUMNIA]

69 If you will make 't an action, call witness to it.
Cymbeline, Act ii, sc. 3, l. 156 [IMOGEN]

I'll bring mine action on the proudest he
That stops my way in Padua.
The Taming of the Shrew, Act iii, sc. 2, l. 236 [PETRUCHIO]
He upon some action
Is now in durance, at Malvolio's suit.
Twelfth Night, Act v, sc. 1, l. 282 [VIOLA]
70   Her pretty action did outsell her gift,
And yet enrich'd it too.
Cymbeline, Act ii, sc. 4, l. 102 [IACHIMO]
71   As many arrows, loosed several ways,
Come to one mark; as many ways meet in one town;
As many fresh streams meet in one salt sea; . .
So may a thousand actions, once afoot,
End in one purpose.
Henry V, Act i, sc. 2, l. 207 [CANTERBURY]
72   We must not stint
Our necessary actions, in the fear
To cope malicious censurers.
Henry VIII, Act i, sc. 2, l. 76 [WOLSEY]
73   Who hath read or heard
Of any kindred action like to this?
King John, Act iii, sc. 4, l. 13 [LEWIS]
74   It is a damned and a bloody work;
The graceless action of a heavy hand.
King John, Act iv, sc. 3, l. 57 [BASTARD]
75   If such actions may have passage free,
Bond-slaves and pagans shall our statesmen be.
Othello, Act i, sc. 2, l. 98 [BRABANTIO]
76   Those men
Blush not in actions blacker than the night,
Will shun no course to keep them from the light.
Pericles, Act i, sc. 1, l. 134 [PERICLES]
77   The rarer action is In virtue than in vengeance.
The Tempest, Act v, sc. 1, l. 27 [PROSPERO]

Adam

78   The Scripture says 'Adam digged': could he dig without arms?
Hamlet, Act v, sc. 1, l. 41 [CLOWN]
79   In the state of innocency Adam fell.
I Henry IV, Act iii, sc. 3, l. 185 [FALSTAFF]
80   Adam was a gardener.
II Henry VI, Act iv, sc. 2, l. 142 [CADE]
81   This gallant pins the wenches on his sleeve;
Had he been Adam, he had tempted Eve.
Love's Labour's Lost, Act v, sc. 2, l. 321 [BIRON]
82   Old Adam's likeness, set to dress this garden.
Richard II, Act iii, sc. 4, l. 73 [QUEEN]

Adder

83   What! art thou, like the adder, waxen deaf?
II Henry VI, Act iii, sc. 2, l. 75 [QUEEN]
84   It is the bright day that brings forth the adder.
Julius Cæsar, Act ii, sc. 1, l. 14 [BRUTUS]
85   An adder did it; for with doubler tongue
Than thine, thou serpent, never adder stung.
A Midsummer Night's Dream, Act iii, sc. 2, l. 72 [HERMIA]
86   The adder hisses where the sweet birds sing.
The Rape of Lucrece, l. 871 [LUCRECE]

87   Guard it, I pray thee, with a lurking adder
     Whose double tongue may with a mortal touch
     Throw death upon thy sovereign's enemies.
                    Richard II, Act iii, sc. 2, l. 20 [KING RICHARD]
88   Is the adder better than the eel,
     Because his painted skin contents the eye?
                The Taming of the Shrew, Act iv, sc. 3, l. 178 [PETRUCHIO]
89   Sometime am I
     All wound with adders who with cloven tongues
     Do hiss me into madness.
                    The Tempest, Act ii, sc. 2, l. 13 [CALIBAN]
90   She starts, like one that spies an adder
     Wreathed up in fatal folds just in his way.
                        Venus and Adonis, l. 878

Admiration See also Wonder

91   Season your admiration for a while
     With an attent ear.
                    Hamlet, Act i, sc. 2, l. 193 [HORATIO]
92   Admiration did not hoop at them.
                    Henry V, Act ii, sc. 2, l. 108 [KING HENRY]
93   With more than admiration he admired
     Her azure veins, her alabaster skin.
                        The Rape of Lucrece, l. 418
94   Admired Miranda! Indeed the top of admiration!
                    The Tempest, Act iii, sc. 1, l. 38 [FERDINAND]

Adultery

95   I pardon that man's life. What was thy cause?
     Adultery? . . . die for adultery? no:
     The wren goes to 't, and the small gilded fly
     Does lecher in my sight.
     Let copulation thrive; . . . for I lack soldiers.
                    King Lear, Act iv, sc. 6, l. 111 [LEAR]
96   Adulterers by an enforced obedience of planetary influence.
                    King Lear, Act i, sc. 2, l. 135 [EDMUND]
         (For full quotation see 6245.)
97   I would divorce me from my mother's womb
     Sepulchring an adultress.
                    King Lear, Act ii, sc. 4, l. 133 [LEAR]
98   They call'd me foul adultress, Lascivious Goth.
                    Titus Andronicus, Act ii, sc. 3, l. 109 [TAMORA]
99   She 's an adultress. . . . She 's an adultress; . . .
     A bed-swerver, even as bad as those
     That vulgars give bold'st titles.
                    The Winter's Tale, Act ii, sc. 1, l. 78 [LEONTES]

Advantage

100   We shall not send
     O'er the vast world to seek a single man,
     And lose advantage, which doth ever cool
     I' the absence of the needer.
                    Coriolanus, Act iv, sc. 1, l. 41 [COMINIUS]
101 Our hands are full of business: let 's away;
     Advantage feeds him fat, while men delay.
                    I Henry IV, Act iii, sc. 2, l. 179 [KING HENRY]
102 Advantage is a better soldier than rashness.
                    Henry V, Act iii, sc. 6, l. 127 [MONTJOY]

103   Make use of time, let not advantage slip.
                              Venus and Adonis, l. 129 [VENUS]

Adversity

104   Sweet are the uses of adversity,
       Which, like the toad, ugly and venomous,
       Wears yet a precious jewel in his head.
                              As You Like It, Act ii, sc. 1, l. 12 [DUKE]
105   A wretched soul, bruised with adversity,
       We bid be quiet when we hear it cry;
       But were we burden'd with like weight of pain,
       As much or more we should ourselves complain.
                              The Comedy of Errors, Act ii, sc. 1, l. 34 [ADRIANA]
106   Let me embrace thee, sour adversity,
       For wise men say it is the wisest course.
                              III Henry VI, Act iii, sc. 1, l. 24 [KING HENRY]
107   A man I am cross'd with adversity.
          The Two Gentlemen of Verona, Act iv, sc. 1, l. 12 [VALENTINE]

Advice

108   When we rage, advice is often seen
       By blunting us to make our wits more keen.
                              A Lover's Complaint, l. 160
109   We should have else desired your good advice,
       Which still hath been both grave and prosperous.
                              Macbeth, Act iii, sc. 1, l. 21 [MACBETH]
110   Take a homely man's advice.
                              Macbeth, Act iv, sc. 2, l. 68 [MESSENGER]
111   Fasten your ear on my advisings.
                              Measure for Measure, Act iii, sc. 1, l. 203 [DUKE]
112   This advice is free I give and honest,
       Probal to thinking.
                              Othello, Act ii, sc. 3, l. 343 [IAGO]
113   How shall I dote on her with more advice,
       That thus without advice begin to love her!
          The Two Gentlemen of Verona, Act ii, sc. 4, l. 207 [PROTEUS]

Affection

114   CELIA: Come, come, wrestle with thy affections.
       ROSALIND: O, they take the part of a better wrestler than myself!
                              As You Like It, Act i, sc. 3, l. 21 [CELIA]
115   My affection hath an unknown bottom, like the bay of Portugal.
                              As You Like It, Act iv, sc. 1, l. 212 [ROSALIND]
116   Out, affection!
       All bond and privilege of nature, break!
                              Coriolanus, Act v, sc. 3, l. 24 [CORIOLANUS]
117   Keep you in the rear of your affection,
       Out of the shot and danger of desire.
                              Hamlet, Act i, sc. 3, l. 34 [LAERTES]
118   Let me wonder, Harry,
       At thy affections, which do hold a wing
       Quite from the flight of all thy ancestors.
                              I Henry IV, Act iii, sc. 2, l. 29 [KING]
119   O, with what wings shall his affections fly
       Towards fronting peril and opposed decay!
                              II Henry IV, Act iv, sc. 4, l. 65 [KING]
120   Some men there are love not a gaping pig;
       Some that are mad if they behold a cat;

And others, when the bagpipe sings i' the nose,
Cannot contain their urine: for affection,
Mistress of passion, sways it to the mood
Of what it likes or loathes.
                    The Merchant of Venice, Act iv, sc. 1, l. 47 [SHYLOCK]

121   His salt and most hidden loose affection.
                    Othello, Act ii, sc. 1, l. 245 [IAGO]

122   Affection is my captain, and he leadeth;
And when his gaudy banner is display'd,
The coward fights and will not be dismay'd.
                    The Rape of Lucrece, l. 271 [TARQUIN]

123   Nothing can affection's course control,
Or stop the headlong fury of his speed.
                    The Rape of Lucrece, l. 500 [TARQUIN]

124   Measuring his affections by my own,
That most are busied when they're most alone.
                    Romeo and Juliet, Act i, sc. 1, l. 133 [BENVOLIO]

125   Had she affections and warm youthful blood,
She would be as swift in motion as a ball.
                    Romeo and Juliet, Act ii, sc. 5, l. 12 [JULIET]

126   Affection is a coal that must be cool'd;
Else, suffer'd, it will set the heart on fire.
                    Venus and Adonis, l. 387 [VENUS]

127   Affection faints not like a pale-faced coward,
But then woos best when most his choice is froward.
                    Venus and Adonis, l. 569

128   Affection! thy intention stabs the centre:
Thou dost make possible things not so held,
Communicatest with dreams.
                    The Winter's Tale, Act i, sc. 2, l. 138 [LEONTES]

Affliction

129   He said he was gentle but unfortunate;
Dishonestly afflicted, but yet honest.
                    Cymbeline, Act iv, sc. 2, l. 39 [GUIDERIUS]

130   He shall be lord of lady Imogen,
And happier much by his affliction made.
                    Cymbeline, Act v, sc. 4, l. 107 [JUPITER]

131   O you mighty gods!
This world I do renounce, and in your sights,
Shake patiently my great affliction off.
                    King Lear, Act iv, sc. 6, l. 34 [GLOUCESTER]

132   Henceforth I'll bear
Affliction till it do cry out itself
'Enough, enough,' and die.
                    King Lear, Act iv, sc. 6, l. 75 [GLOUCESTER]

133   Had it pleased heaven
To try me with affliction; had they rain'd
All kinds of sores and shames on my bare head,
Steep'd me in poverty to the very lips, . . .
I should have found in some place of my soul
A drop of patience: but, alas, to make me
A fixed figure for the time of scorn
To point his slow unmoving finger at!
Yet I could bear that too; well, very well:
But there, where I have garner'd up my heart,
Where either I must live, or bear no life;

The fountain from the which my current runs,
Or else dries up; to be discarded thence!
Or keep it as a cistern for foul toads
To knot and gender in!
Othello, Act iv, sc. 2, l. 48 [OTHELLO]
134 Affliction is enamour'd of thy parts.
Romeo and Juliet, Act iii, sc. 3, l. 2 [FRIAR LAURENCE]
135 I think affliction may subdue the cheek,
But not take in the mind.
The Winter's Tale, Act iv, sc. 4, l. 586 [PERDITA]
136 This affliction has a taste as sweet
As any cordial comfort.
The Winter's Tale, Act v, sc. 3, l. 76 [LEONTES]

Age See also Youth and Age

137 On us both did haggish age steal on.
All's Well that Ends Well, Act i, sc. 2, l. 29 [KING]
138 [Thou hast] the privilege of antiquity upon thee.
All's Well that Ends Well, Act ii, sc. 3, l. 221 [PAROLLES]
I speak not like a dotard nor a fool,
As under privilege of age to brag
What I have done being young, or what would do
Were I not old.
Much Ado about Nothing, Act v, sc. 1, l. 59 [LEONATO]
Prerogative of age.
Troilus and Cressida, Act i, sc. 3, l. 107 [ULYSSES]
139 Though age from folly could not give me freedom,
It does from childishness.
Antony and Cleopatra, Act i, sc. 3, l. 57 [CLEOPATRA]
140 Age cannot wither her, nor custom stale
Her infinite variety: other women cloy
The appetites they feed; but she makes hungry
Where most she satisfies.
Antony and Cleopatra, Act ii, sc. 2, l. 240 [ENOBARBUS]
141 Though I look old, yet I am strong and lusty;
For in my youth I never did apply
Hot and rebellious liquors in my blood,
Nor did not with unbashful forehead woo
The means of weakness and debility;
Therefore my age is as a lusty winter,
Frosty, but kindly.
As You Like It, Act ii, sc. 3, l. 47 [ADAM]
142 Though now this grained face of mine be hid
In sap-consuming winter's drizzled snow
And all the conduits of my blood froze up,
Yet hath my night of life some memory,
My wasting lamps some fading glimmer left,
My dull deaf ears a little use to hear.
The Comedy of Errors, Act v, sc. 1, l. 312 [ÆGEON]
143 The satirical rogue says here that old men have grey beards, that
their faces are wrinkled, their eyes purging thick amber and plum-
tree gum and that they have a plentiful lack of wit, together with
most weak hams: . . . yourself, sir, should be old as I am, if like
a crab you could go backward.
Hamlet, Act ii, sc. 2, l. 198 [HAMLET]
144 HAMLET: That great baby you see there is not yet out of his
swaddling-clouts.

ROSENCRANTZ : Happily he's the second time come to them; for
they say an old man is twice a child.

Hamlet, Act ii, sc. 2, l. 403 [HAMLET]

145   Age, with his stealing steps,
                    Hath claw'd me in his clutch,
                    And hath shipped me intil the land,
                    As if I had never been such.

Hamlet, Act v, sc. 1, l. 79 [CLOWN]

146   Lord, Lord, how subject we old men are to this vice of lying!

II Henry IV, Act iii, sc. 2, l. 324 [FALSTAFF]

147   The old folk, time's doting chroniclers.

II Henry IV, Act iv, sc. 4, l. 126 [CLARENCE]

148   Leaden age,
       Quicken'd with youthful spleen and warlike rage.

I Henry VI, Act iv, sc. 6, l. 12 [TALBOT]

149   O father abbot,
       An old man, broken with the storms of state,
       Is come to lay his weary bones among ye;
       Give him a little earth, for charity.

Henry VIII, Act iv, sc. 2, l. 20 [GRIFFITH, quoting WOLSEY]

150   Look to receive from his age . . . the unruly waywardness that
       infirm and choleric years bring with them.

King Lear, Act i, sc. 1, l. 299 [GONERIL]

151   This policy and reverence of age makes the world bitter to the best
       of our times; keeps our fortunes from us till our oldness cannot
       relish them.

King Lear, Act i, sc. 2, l. 48 [GLOUCESTER, *reading*]

152   Thou shouldst not have been old till thou hadst been wise.

King Lear, Act i, sc. 5, l. 47 [FOOL]

       As you are old and reverend, you should be wise.

King Lear, Act i, sc. 4, l. 261 [GONERIL]

       Why art thou old and yet not wise?

The Rape of Lucrece, l. 1550 [LUCRECE]

153   REGAN : O, sir, you are old;
       Nature in you stands on the very verge
       Of her confine. . . .
       LEAR : Dear daughter, I confess that I am old.
       Age is unnecessary: on my knees I beg
       That you'll vouchsafe me raiment, bed, and food.

King Lear, Act ii, sc. 4, l. 148 [REGAN]

154   You see me here, you gods, a poor old man,
       As full of grief as age; wretched in both.

King Lear, Act ii, sc. 4, l. 275 [LEAR]

155   Here I stand, your slave,
       A poor, infirm, weak, and despised old man.

King Lear, Act iii, sc. 2, l. 19 [LEAR]

156   I am a very foolish fond old man,
       Fourscore and upward, not an hour more nor less;
       And, to deal plainly,
       I fear I am not in my perfect mind.

King Lear, Act iv, sc. 7, l. 60 [LEAR]

157   A good old man, sir; he will be talking: as they say, When the
       age is in, the wit is out.

Much Ado about Nothing, Act iii, sc. 5, l. 36 [DOGBERRY]
       (A play upon the old proverb, "When the wine is in, the wit is
       out.")

158   I am declined Into the vale of years.
                    Othello, Act iii, sc. 3, l. 264 [OTHELLO]
159   Respect and reason, wait on wrinkled age!
                    The Rape of Lucrece, l. 275 [TARQUIN]
160   But old folks, many feign as they were dead;
       Unwieldy, slow, heavy and pale as lead.
                    Romeo and Juliet, Act ii, sc. 5, l. 16 [JULIET]
161   To me, fair friend, you never can be old,
       For as you were when first your eye I eyed,
       Such seems your beauty still.
                                          Sonnet civ, l. 1
162   Let me embrace thine age, whose honour cannot
       Be measured or confined.
                    The Tempest, Act v, sc. 1, l. 121 [PROSPERO]
163   These old fellows
       Have their ingratitude in them hereditary:
       Their blood is caked, 'tis cold, it seldom flows.
                    Timon of Athens, Act ii, sc. 2, l. 223 [TIMON]
164   The faint defects of age
       Must be the scene of mirth; to cough and spit.
                    Troilus and Cressida, Act i, sc. 3, l. 172 [ULYSSES]
165   You have undone a man of fourscore three,
       That thought to fill his grave in quiet, yea,
       To die upon the bed my father died,
       To lie close by his honest bones.
                    The Winter's Tale, Act iv, sc. 4, l. 463 [SHEPHERD]

Age: the Age

166   The age is grown so picked that the toe of the peasant comes so
       near the heel of the courtier, he galls his kibe.
                    Hamlet, Act v, sc. 1, l. 151 [HAMLET]
167   The same breed that I know the drossy age dotes on.
                    Hamlet, Act v, sc. 2, l. 197 [HAMLET]
168   I would . . . excel the golden age.
                    The Tempest, Act ii, sc. 1, l. 168 [GONZALO]

Agincourt

169   Can this cockpit hold
       The vasty fields of France? or may we cram
       Within this wooden O the very casques
       That did affright the air at Agincourt?
                    Henry V, Act i, Prologue, l. 11 [CHORUS]
170   We shall much disgrace . . . the name of Agincourt.
                    Henry V, Act iv, Prologue, l. 49 [CHORUS]
171   KING HENRY: What is this castle call'd that stands hard by?
       MONTJOY: They call it Agincourt.
       KING HENRY: Then call we this the field of Agincourt,
       Fought on the day of Crispin Crispianus.
                    Henry V, Act iv, sc. 7, l. 91 [KING HENRY]

Air

172   The air of paradise did fan the house,
       And angels officed all.
                    All's Well that Ends Well, Act iii, sc. 2, l. 128 [HELENA]
173   Where air comes out, air comes in: there's none abroad so whole-
       some as that you vent.
                    Cymbeline, Act i, sc. 2, l. 3 [LORD]

174 HAMLET: The air bites shrewdly: it is very cold.
HORATIO: It is a nipping and-an eager air.
Hamlet, Act i, sc. 4, l. 1 [HAMLET]
The air is quick there,
And it pierces and sharpens the stomach.
Pericles, Act iv, sc. 1, l. 28 [DIONYZA]

175 But, soft! methinks I scent the morning air.
Hamlet, Act i, sc. 5, l. 58 [GHOST]

176 POLONIUS: Will you walk out of the air, my lord?
HAMLET: Into my grave.
POLONIUS: Indeed, that is out o' the air.
Hamlet, Act ii, sc. 2, l. 209 [POLONIUS]

177 Stand from him, give him air; he'll straight be well.
II Henry IV, Act iv, sc. 4, l. 116 [WARWICK]
I pray you, give her air.
Pericles, Act iii, sc. 2, l. 91 [CERIMON]

178 Welcome, then,
Thou unsubstantial air that I embrace!
The wretch that thou hast blown unto the worst
Owes nothing to thy blasts.
King Lear, Act iv, sc. 1, l. 5 [EDGAR]
To seek the empty, vast, and wandering air.
Richard III, Act i, sc. 4, l. 39 [CLARENCE]

179 This castle hath a pleasant seat; the air
Nimbly and sweetly recommends itself
Unto our gentle senses.
Macbeth, Act i, sc. 6, l. 1 [DUNCAN]

180 ADRIAN: The air breathes upon us here most sweetly.
SEBASTIAN: As if it had lungs and rotten ones.
ANTONIO: Or as 'twere perfumed by a fan.
The Tempest, Act ii, sc. 1, l. 44 [ADRIAN]

181 The climate's delicate, the air most sweet.
The Winter's Tale, Act iii, sc. 1, l. 1 [CLEOMENES]

Ale See also Cakes

182 Would I were in an alehouse in London! I would give all my
fame for a pot of ale and safety.
Henry V, Act iii, sc. 2, l. 12 [BOY]

183 Were he not warm'd with ale,
This were a bed but cold to sleep so soundly.
The Taming of the Shrew, Induction, sc. 1, l. 32 [HUNTSMAN]

184 For God's sake, a pot of small ale. . . .
And once again, a pot o' the smallest ale.
The Taming of the Shrew, Induction, sc. 2, l. 1, 77 [SLY]

185 SPEED: 'Item: She brews good ale.'
LAUNCE: And thereof comes the proverb: 'Blessing of your heart,
you brew good ale.'
The Two Gentlemen of Verona, Act iii, sc. 1, l. 304 [SPEED]

186 The white sheet bleaching on the hedge,
With heigh! the sweet birds, O, how they sing!
Doth set my pugging tooth on edge;
For a quart of ale is a dish for a king.
The Winter's Tale, Act iv, sc. 3, l. 5 [AUTOLYCUS]

Alexander

187 Dost thou think Alexander looked o' this fashion i' the earth? . . .
To what base uses we may return, Horatio! Why may not imagina-

tion trace the noble dust of Alexander, till he find it stopping a
bung-hole?

Hamlet, Act v, sc. 1, l. 218 [HAMLET]

188   FLUELLEN: What call you the town's name where Alexander the
Pig was born? . . .
GOWER: I think Alexander the Great was born in Macedon.

Henry V, Act iv. sc. 7, l. 13 [FLUELLEN]

189   Alexander, God knows, and you know, in his rages, and his furies,
and his wraths, . . . did, in his ales and his angers, look you,
kill his best friend, Cleitus.

Henry V, Act iv, sc. 7, l. 37 [FLUELLEN]

190   When in the world I lived, I was the world's commander;
By east, west, north, and south, I spread my conquering might:
My scutcheon plain declares that I am Alisander.

Love's Labour's Lost, Act v, sc. 2, l. 564 [NATHANIEL]

191   O, sir, you have overthrown Alisander the conqueror!

Love's Labour's Lost, Act v, sc. 2, l. 576 [COSTARD]

Alms

192   That base wretch,
One bred of alms and foster'd with cold dishes.

Cymbeline, Act ii, sc. 3, l. 118 [CLOTEN]

193   Content your lord, who hath received you
At fortune's alms.

King Lear, Act i, sc. 1, l. 280 [GONERIL]

194   So shall I clothe me in a forced content,
And shut myself up in some other course,
To fortune's alms.

Othello, Act iii, sc. 4, l. 120 [CASSIO]

195   Let him have time a beggar's orts to crave,
And time to see one that by alms doth live.

The Rape of Lucrece, l. 985 [LUCRECE]

Alone

196   Alone I did it.

Coriolanus, Act v, sc. 6, l. 117 [CORIOLANUS]

197   You in my respect are all the world:
Then how can it be said I am alone?

A Midsummer Night's Dream, Act ii, sc. 1, l. 224 [HELENA]

198   I myself am best When least in company.

Twelfth Night, Act i, sc. 4, l. 40 [DUKE]

199   VALENTINE: She is alone.
PROTEUS: Then let her alone.

The Two Gentlemen of Verona, Act ii, sc. 4, l. 167 [VALENTINE]

Ambition

200   Ambition,
The soldier's virtue, rather makes choice of loss,
Than gain which darkens him.

Antony and Cleopatra, Act iii, sc. 1, l. 22 [VENTIDIUS]

201   Who doth ambition shun,
And loves to lie i' the sun,
Seeking the food he eats
And pleased with what he gets,
    Come hither, come hither, come hither:
Here shall he see No enemy
    But winter and rough weather.

As You Like It, Act ii, sc. 5, l. 40 [JACQUES]

202 . I hold ambition of so airy and light a quality that it is but a shadow's
shadow.
Hamlet, Act ii, sc. 2, 1. 267 [ROSENCRANTZ]

203 Mark but my fall, and that that ruin'd me.
Cromwell, I charge thee, fling away ambition:
By that sin fell the angels; how can man, then,
The image of his Maker, hope to win by it?
Henry VIII, Act iii, sc. 2, 1. 439 [WOLSEY]

204 Lowliness is young ambition's ladder,
Whereto the climber-upward turns his face;
But when he once attains the upmost round,
He then unto the ladder turns his back,
Looks in the clouds, scorning the base degrees
By which he did ascend.
Julius Cæsar, Act ii, sc. 1, 1. 21 [BRUTUS]

205 Ambition's debt is paid.
Julius Cæsar, Act iii, sc. 1, 1. 83 [BRUTUS]

206   I have no spur
To prick the sides of my intent, but only
Vaulting ambition, which o'erleaps itself
And falls on the other.
Macbeth, Act i, sc. 7, 1. 25 [MACBETH]

207 Thriftless ambition, that wilt ravin up
Thine own life's means.
Macbeth, Act ii, sc. 4, 1. 28 [ROSS]

208 If not to answer, you might haply think
Tongue-tied ambition, not replying, yielded
To bear the golden yoke of sovereignty.
Richard III, Act iii, sc. 7, 1. 144 [GLOUCESTER]

Amen

209 One cried 'God bless us!' and 'Amen' the other;
As they had seen me with these hangman's hands,
Listening their fear, I could not say 'Amen,'
When they did say 'God bless us!' . . .
But wherefore could I not pronounce 'Amen'?
I had most need of blessing, and 'Amen'
Stuck in my throat.
Macbeth, Act ii, sc. 2, 1. 27 [MACBETH]

210 Amen, amen, to that fair prayer, say I.
A Midsummer Night's Dream, Act ii, sc. 2, 1. 62 [LYSANDER]

Amity

211 To hold you in perpetual amity,
To make you brothers, and to knit your hearts
With an unslipping knot, take Antony
Octavia to his wife.
Antony and Cleopatra, Act ii, sc. 2, 1. 127 [AGRIPPA]

212 Surer bind this knot of amity.
I Henry VI, Act v, sc. 1, 1. 16 [GLOUCESTER]

213 I come . . . to crave a league of amity;
And lastly, to confirm that amity
With nuptial knot.
III Henry VI, Act iii, sc. 3, 1. 51 [WARWICK]

214 The amity that wisdom knits not, folly may easily untie.
Troilus and Cressida, Act ii, sc. 3, 1. 110 [ULYSSES]

Ancestor

215   The . . . rotten times that you shall look upon
When I am sleeping with my ancestors.
> *II Henry IV*, Act iv, sc. 4, 1. 60 [KING HENRY]

216   My ancestors did from the streets of Rome
The Tarquin drive, when he was call'd a king.
> *Julius Cæsar*, Act ii, sc. 1, 1. 53 [BRUTUS]

217   SLENDER: All his successors gone before him hath done 't; and
all his ancestors that come after him may: they may give the
dozen white luces in their coat.
SHALLOW: It is an old coat.
EVANS: The dozen white louses do become an old coat well; it
agrees well, passant; it is a familiar beast to man, and signifies
love.
> *The Merry Wives of Windsor*, Act i, sc. 1, 1. 14 [SLENDER]

(The luce is the pike, frequently used in coats-of-arms.)

218   She lies buried with her ancestors,
O, in a tomb where never scandal slept.
> *Much Ado about Nothing*, Act v, sc. 1, 1. 69 [LEONATO]

These that I bring unto their latest home,
With burial amongst their ancestors.
> *Titus Andronicus*, Act i, sc. 1, 1. 83 [TITUS]

219   My derivation was from ancestors
Who stood equivalent with mighty kings.
> *Pericles*, Act v, sc. 1, 1. 91 [MARINA]

Angel

220   An angel! or, if not, An earthly paragon!
> *Cymbeline*, Act iii, sc. 6, 1. 43 [BELARIUS]

VALENTINE: Is she not a heavenly saint?
PROTEUS: No; but she is an earthly paragon.
> *The Two Gentlemen of Verona*, Act ii, sc. 4, 1. 145 [VALENTINE]

221   Angels and ministers of grace defend us!
> *Hamlet*, Act i, sc. 4, 1. 39 [HAMLET]

222   A ministering angel shall my sister be.
> *Hamlet*, Act v, sc. 1, 1. 264 [LAERTES]

223   An angel is like you, Kate, and you are like an angel.
> *Henry V*, Act v, sc. 2, 1. 110 [KING HENRY]

224   'For,' quoth the king, 'an angel shalt thou see;
Yet fear not thou, but speak audaciously.'
The boy replied, 'An angel is not evil;
I should have fear'd her had she been a devil.'
> *Love's Labour's Lost*, Act v, sc. 2, 1. 103 [BOYET]

225   Angels are bright still, though the brightest fell.
> *Macbeth*, Act iv, sc. 3, 1. 22 [MALCOLM]

226   OTHELLO: She's, like a liar, gone to burning hell:
'Twas I that kill'd her.
EMILIA: O, the more angel she,
And you the blacker devil!
> *Othello*, Act v, sc. 2, 1. 129 [OTHELLO]

227   If the angels fight,
Weak men must fall, for heaven still guards the right.
> *Richard II*, Act iii, sc. 2, 1. 61 [KING RICHARD]

228   O, speak again, bright angel! for thou art
As glorious to this night, being o'er my head,
As is a winged messenger of heaven.
> *Romeo and Juliet*, Act ii, sc. 2, 1. 26 [ROMEO]

Angel: Good Angel

229   Go with me, like good angels, to my end;
And, as the long divorce of steel falls on me,
Make of your prayers one sweet sacrifice,
And lift my soul to heaven.
Henry VIII, Act ii, sc. 1, l. 75 [BUCKINGHAM]

230   Now, good angels
Fly o'er thy royal head, and shade thy person
Under their blessed wings!
Henry VIII, Act v, sc. 1, l. 159 [OLD LADY]

231   Let's write good angel on the devil's horn;
'Tis not the devil's crest.
Measure for Measure, Act ii, sc. 4, l. 16 [ANGELO]

232   Poor Desdemona! I am glad thy father's dead: . . .
This sight would make him do a desperate turn,
Yea, curse his better angel from his side,
And fall to reprobation.
Othello, Act v, sc. 2, l. 204 [GRATIANO]

233   Good angels guard thee!
Richard III, Act iv, sc. 1, l. 94 [DUCHESS]
Good angels guard thy battle! live, and flourish!
Richard III, Act v, sc. 3, l. 138 [GHOST OF CLARENCE]

234   Good angels guard thee from the boar's annoy!
Live, and beget a happy race of kings!
Richard III, Act v, sc. 3, l. 156 [GHOSTS OF THE YOUNG PRINCES]

235   God and good angels fight on Richmond's side.
Richard III, Act v, sc. 3, l. 175 [GHOST OF BUCKINGHAM]

236   Two loves I have of comfort and despair,
Which like two spirits do suggest me still:
The better angel is a man right fair,
The worser spirit a woman colour'd ill.
To win me soon to hell, my female evil
Tempteth my better angel from my side,
And would corrupt my saint to be a devil,
Wooing his purity with her foul pride.
But whether that my angel be turn'd fiend
Suspect I may, yet not directly tell;
But being both from me, both to each friend,
I guess one angel in another's hell:
Yet this shall I ne'er know, but live in doubt,
Till my bad angel fire my good one out.
Sonnet cxliv, l. 1
(Repeated in *The Passionate Pilgrim, Sonnet* ii.)

Anger

237   Never anger made good guard for itself.
Antony and Cleopatra, Act iv, sc. 1, l. 10 [MECÆNAS]

238   Anger's my meat; I sup upon myself,
And so shall starve with feeding.
Coriolanus, Act iv, sc. 2, l. 50 [VOLUMNIA]

239   O, I could hew up rocks and fight with flint,
I am so angry at these abject terms.
II Henry VI, Act v, sc. 1, l. 24 [YORK]

240   Anger is like
A full-hot horse, who being allow'd his way,
Self-mettle tires him.
Henry VIII, Act i, sc. 1, l. 132 [NORFOLK]

241   BRUTUS: Be angry when you will, it shall have scope;
        Do what you will, dishonour shall be humour.
        O Cassius, you are yoked with a lamb
        That carries anger as the flint bears fire;
        Who, much enforced, shows a hasty spark,
        And straight is cold again.
        CASSIUS: Hath Cassius lived
        To be but mirth and laughter to his Brutus,
        When grief, and blood ill-temper'd vexeth him?
        BRUTUS: When I spoke that, I was ill-temper'd too. . . .
        CASSIUS: Have you not love enough to bear with me,
        When that rash humour which my mother gave me
        Makes me forgetful?
        BRUTUS: Yes, Cassius; and, from henceforth,
        When you are over-earnest with your Brutus,
        He'll think your mother chides, and leave you so.
                Julius Cæsar, Act iv, sc. 3, l. 108 [BRUTUS]

242   Anger hath a privilege.
                King Lear, Act ii, sc. 2, l. 76 [KENT]

243   Touch me with noble anger.
                King Lear, Act ii, sc. 4, l. 279 [LEAR]

244   They say, my lords, 'ira furor brevis est'; but yond man is ever
        angry.
                Timon of Athens, Act i, sc. 2, l. 28 [TIMON]
        ("Ira furor brevis est," Anger is a brief madness.)

245   To be in anger is impiety;
        But who is man that is not angry?
            Timon of Athens, Act iii, sc. 5, l. 56 [ALCIBIADES]

Answer

246   I have an answer will serve all men. . . . It is like a barber's chair
        that fits all buttocks.
            All's Well that Ends Well, Act ii, sc. 2, l. 15 [CLOWN]

247   Answer me in one word.
             As You Like It, Act iii, sc. 2, l. 237 [ROSALIND]

248   You are full of pretty answers.
             As You Like It, Act iii, sc. 2, l. 287 [JAQUES]

249   HAMLET: Did you not speak to it?
        HORATIO: My lord, I did; But answer made it none.
                 Hamlet, Act i, sc. 2, l. 214 [HAMLET]

250   Your answer, sir, is enigmatical.
          Much Ado about Nothing, Act v, sc. 4, l. 27 [BENEDICK]

251   Is that an answer?
         The Taming of the Shrew, Act v, sc. 2, l. 83 [PETRUCHIO]

252   We cannot take this for an answer.
            Timon of Athens, Act iii, sc. 4, l. 78 [TITUS]

253   A good lenten answer.
             Twelfth Night, Act i, sc. 5, l. 9 [MARIA]

254   A silly answer and fitting well a sheep.
        The Two Gentlemen of Verona, Act i, sc. 1, l. 81 [PROTEUS]

Antony

255   ANTONY: Not Cæsar's valour hath o'erthrown Antony,
        But Antony's hath triumph'd on itself.
        CLEOPATRA: So it should be, that none but Antony
        Should conquer Antony; but woe 'tis so!
          Antony and Cleopatra, Act iv, sc. 15, l. 14 [ANTONY]

256   CLEOPATRA: I dreamed there was an Emperor Antony:
      O, such another sleep, that I might see
      But such another man! . . .
      His face was as the heavens; and therein stuck
      A sun and moon, which kept their course, and lighted
      The little O, the earth. . . .
      His legs bestrid the ocean: his rear'd arm
      Crested the world: his voice was propertied
      As all the tuned spheres, and that to friends;
      But when he meant to quail and shake the orb,
      He was as rattling thunder. . . . his delights
      Were dolphin-like; they show'd his back above
      The element they lived in; in his livery
      Walk'd crowns and crownets; realms and islands were
      As plates dropp'd from his pocket. . . .
      Think you there was, or might be, such a man
      As this I dream'd of?
      DOLABELLA: Gentle madam, no . . .
      CLEOPATRA: But, if there be, or ever were, one such,
      It's past the size of dreaming.
                     Antony and Cleopatra, Act v, sc. 2, l. 76 [CLEOPATRA]

257   See! Antony, that revels long o' nights,
      Is notwithstanding up.
                          Julius Cæsar, Act ii, sc. 2, l. 116 [CÆSAR]

Ape

258   I will be more new-fangled than an ape, more giddy in my desires
      than a monkey.
                     As You Like It, Act iv, sc. 1, l. 153 [ROSALIND]

259   Apes and monkeys
      'Twixt two such shes would chatter this way and
      Contemn with mows the other.
                          Cymbeline, Act i, sc. 6, l. 39 [IACHIMO]

260   No, in despite of sense and secrecy,
      Unpeg the basket on the house's top,
      Let the birds fly, and, like the famous ape,
      To try conclusions, in the basket creep,
      And break your own neck down.
                          Hamlet, Act iii, sc. 4, l. 192 [HAMLET]
         (The fable alluded to by Shakespeare has never been identified.)

261   He keeps them, like an ape, in the corner of his jaw; first mouthed,
      to be last swallowed.
                          Hamlet, Act iv, sc. 2, l. 19 [HAMLET]

262   Out, you mad-headed ape.
      A weasel hath not such a deal of spleen
      As you are toss'd with.
                          I Henry IV, Act ii, sc. 3, l. 80 [LADY PERCY]

263   I will even take sixpence in earnest of the bear-ward, and lead his
      apes into hell.
                     Much Ado about Nothing, Act ii, sc. 1, l. 42 [BEATRICE]
      I must dance barefoot on her wedding day
      And, for your love to her, lead apes in hell.
                     The Taming of the Shrew, Act ii, sc. 1, l. 33 [KATHARINA]
         (Both girls are referring to the old saying that women dying
         maids lead apes in hell.)

264   The ape is dead, and I must conjure him.
      I conjure thee by Rosaline's bright eyes,

By her high forehead and her scarlet lip,
By her fine foot, straight leg, and quivering thigh
And the desmesnes that there adjacent lie,
That in thy likeness thou appear to us!
Romeo and Juliet, Act ii, sc. i, l. 16 [MERCUTIO]

265   We shall all be turned to . . . apes
With foreheads villanous low.
The Tempest, Act iv, sc. i, l. 249 [CALIBAN]

Apothecary

266   Bid the apothecary
Bring the strong poison that I bought of him.
II Henry VI, Act iii, sc. 3, l. 17 [CARDINAL]

267   I do remember an apothecary,—
And hereabouts he dwells—which late I noted
In tatter'd weeds, with overwhelming brows,
Culling of simples; meagre were his looks,
Sharp misery had worn him to the bones:
And in his needy shop a tortoise hung,
An alligator stuff'd, and other skins
Of ill-shaped fishes; and about his shelves
A beggarly account of empty boxes.
Romeo and Juliet, Act v, sc. i, l. 37 [ROMEO]

268   Here's to my love! [Drinks] O true apothecary!
Thy drugs are quick. Thus with a kiss I die.
Romeo and Juliet, Act v, sc. 3, l. 119 [ROMEO]

Appearance

269   Thou hast a grim appearance, and thy face
Bears a command in 't; though thy tackle 's torn,
Thou show'st a noble vessel.
Coriolanus, Act iv, sc. 5, l. 66 [AUFIDIUS]

270   Here's Wart; you see what a ragged appearance it is.
II Henry IV, Act iii, sc. 2, l. 279 [FALSTAFF]

A semblance That very dogs disdain'd.
King Lear, Act v, sc. 3, l. 187 [EDGAR]

271   PANDULPH: You look but on the outside of this work.
LEWIS: Outside or inside, I will not return
Till my attempt so much be glorified.
King John, Act v, sc. 2, l. 109 [PANDULPH]

272   For confirmation that I am much more
Than my out-wall, open this purse and take
What it contains.
King Lear, Act iii, sc. i, l. 44 [KENT]

273   Thy outside looks so fair and warlike.
King Lear, Act v, sc. 3, l. 142 [EDMUND]

274   One by nature's outwards so commended,
That maidens' eyes stuck over all his face.
A Lover's Complaint, l. 80

275   Are ye fantastical, or that indeed
Which outwardly ye show?
Macbeth, Act i, sc. 3, l. 53 [BANQUO]

276   O, what may man within him hide,
Though angel on the outward side!
Measure for Measure, Act iii, sc. 2, l. 285 [DUKE]

277   They have a good cover; they show well outward.
Much Ado about Nothing, Act. i, sc. 2, l. 7 [ANTONIO]

278   God defend the lute should be like the case!
                          Much Ado about Nothing, Act ii, sc. 1, l. 98 [HERO]
279   Sweet prince, the untainted virtue of your years
       Hath not yet dived into the world's deceit:
       Nor more can you distinguish of a man
       Than of his outward show; which, God he knows,
       Seldom or never jumpeth with the heart.
                          Richard III, Act iii, sc. 1, l. 7 [GLOUCESTER]
280   Most putrified core, so fair without,
       Thy goodly armour thus hath cost thy life.
                          Troilus and Cressida, Act v, sc. 8, l. 1 [HECTOR]

Appetite

281   ARVIRAGUS: I am weak with toil, yet strong in appetite.
       GUIDERIUS: There is cold meat i' the cave: we'll browse on that.
                          Cymbeline, Act iii, sc. 6, l. 37 [ARVIRAGUS]
282   She would hang on him,
       As if increase of appetite had grown
       By what it fed on.
                          Hamlet, Act i, sc. 2, l. 143 [HAMLET]
283   O appetite, from judgements stand aloof!
       The one a palate hath that needs will taste,
       Though Reason weep, and cry 'It is thy last.'
                          A Lover's Complaint, l. 166
284   Who riseth from a feast
       With that keen appetite that he sits down?
                          The Merchant of Venice, Act ii, sc. 6, l. 8 [GRATIANO]
285   Doth not the appetite alter? a man loves the meat in his youth that
       he cannot endure in his age.
                          Much Ado about Nothing, Act ii, sc. 3, l. 247 [BENEDICK]
286   To make our appetites more keen,
       With eager compounds we our palate urge.
                          Sonnet cxviii, l. 1
287   Appetite, an universal wolf, . . .
       Must make perforce an universal prey,
       And last eat up himself.
                          Troilus and Cressida, Act i, sc. 3, l. 121 [ULYSSES]
288   [He] pouted in a dull disdain,
       With leaden appetite, unapt to toy.
                          Venus and Adonis, l. 34

Applause

289   I would applaud thee to the very echo,
       That should applaud again.
                          Macbeth, Act v, sc. 3, l. 53 [MACBETH]
290   Hearing applause and universal shout,
       Giddy in spirit, still gazing in a doubt
       Whether those peals of praise be his or no.
                          The Merchant of Venice, Act iii, sc. 2, l. 145 [BASSANIO]
291   This general applause and loving shout
       Argues your wisdoms and your love to Richard.
                          Richard III, Act iii, sc. 7, l. 39 [BUCKINGHAM]
292   The large Achilles, on his press'd bed lolling,
       From his deep chest laughs out a loud applause,
       Cries 'Excellent!'
                          Troilus and Cressida, Act i, sc. 3, l. 162 [ULYSSES]

293   The great Myrmidon Who broils in loud applause.
                    Troilus and Cressida, Act i, sc. 3, l. 379 [ULYSSES]
294   How his silence drinks up this applause!
                    Troilus and Cressida, Act ii, sc. 3, l. 211 [DIOMEDES]

April

295   The April's in her eyes: it is love's spring,
      And these the showers to bring it on.
                    Antony and Cleopatra, Act iii, sc. 2, l. 43 [ANTONY]
296   A day in April never came so sweet,
      To show how costly summer was at hand,
      As this fore-spurrer comes before his lord.
                    The Merchant of Venice, Act ii, sc. 9, l. 93 [SERVANT]
297   Well-apparell'd April on the heel
      Of limping winter treads.
                    Romeo and Juliet, Act i, sc. 2, l. 27 [CAPULET]
298   From you have I been absent in the spring,
      When proud-pied April dress'd in all his trim
      Hath put a spirit of youth in every thing.
                    Sonnet xcviii, l. 1

299   Thy banks with pioned and twilled brims,
      Which spongy April at thy hest betrims,
      To make cold nymphs chaste crowns.
                    The Tempest, Act iv, sc. 1, l. 64 [IRIS]

Arbitrement

300   Put to the arbitrement of swords.
                    Cymbeline, Act i, sc. 4, l. 52 [FRENCHMAN]
      The arbitrement of swords can try it out.
                    Henry V, Act iv, sc. 1, l. 172 [KING HENRY]
301   We of the offering side
      Must keep aloof from strict arbitrement,
      And stop all sight-holes, every loop from whence
      The eye of reason may pry in upon us.
                    I Henry IV, Act iv, sc. 1, l. 69 [WORCESTER]
302   The arbitrement is like to be bloody.
                    King Lear, Act iv, sc. 7, l. 95 [GENTLEMAN]
303   The knight is incensed against you, even to a mortal arbitrement.
                    Twelfth Night, Act iii, sc. 4, l. 286 [FABIAN]

Argument

304   'Tis the rarest argument of wonder that hath shot out in our latter
      times.
                    All's Well that Ends Well, Act ii, sc. 3, l. 8 [PAROLLES]
305   It was much like an argument that fell out last night, where each
      of us fell in praise of our country mistresses.
                    Cymbeline, Act i, sc. 4, l. 60 [FRENCHMAN]
306   It would be argument for a week, laughter for a month and a
      good jest for ever.
                    I Henry IV, Act ii, sc. 2, l. 99 [PRINCE]
      It may prove an argument of laughter.
                    Timon of Athens, Act iii, sc. 3, l. 20 [SEMPRONIUS]
307   [They] sheathed their swords for lack of argument.
                    Henry V, Act iii, sc. 1, l. 21 [KING HENRY]
308   He will maintain his argument as well as any military man in the
      world.
                    Henry V, Act iii, sc. 2, l. 85 [FLUELLEN]

309   If arguing make us sweat,
The proof of it will turn to redder drops.
Julius Cæsar, Act v, sc. 1, l. 48 [OCTAVIUS]

310   You have heard of the news abroad; I mean the whispered ones,
for they are yet but ear-kissing arguments?
King Lear, Act ii, sc. 1, l. 6 [CURAN]

311   ARMADO: How did this argument begin?
MOTH: By saying a costard was broken on a shin.
Love's Labour's Lost, Act iii, sc. 1, l. 106 [ARMADO]

312   He draweth out the thread of his verbosity finer than the staple
of his argument.
Love's Labour's Lost, Act v, sc. 1, l. 18 [HOLOFERNES]

313   DON PEDRO: If thou wilt hold longer argument
Do it in notes.
BALTHASAR: Note this before my notes;
There's not a note of mine that's worth the noting.
Much Ado about Nothing, Act ii, sc. 3, l. 55 [DON PEDRO]

314   For me, I force not argument a straw,
Since that my case is past the help of law.
The Rape of Lucrece, l. 1021 [LUCRECE]

315   How can my Muse want subject to invent,
Whilst thou dost breathe, that pour'st into my verse
Thine own sweet argument, too excellent
For every vulgar paper to rehearse?
Sonnet xxxviii, l. 1

O, know, sweet love, I always write of you;
And you and love are still my argument.
Sonnet lxxvi, l. 9

316   The argument all bare is of more worth
Than when it hath my added praise beside!
Sonnet ciii, l. 3

317   I cannot fight upon this argument;
It is too starved a subject for my sword.
Troilus and Cressida, Act i, sc. 1, l. 95 [TROILUS]

318   All the argument is cuckold and a whore; a good quarrel to draw
emulous factions and bleed to death upon.
Troilus and Cressida, Act ii, sc. 3, l. 78 [THERSITES]

319   The quality of the time and quarrel
Might well have given us bloody argument.
Twelfth Night, Act iii, sc. 3, l. 31 [ANTONIO]

Arithmetic

320   'Tis odds beyond arithmetic.
Coriolanus, Act iii, sc. 1, l. 245 [COMINIUS]

321   Spare your arithmetic: never count the turns.
Cymbeline, Act ii, sc. 4, l. 142 [POSTHUMUS]

322   To divide him inventorially would dizzy the arithmetic of memory.
Hamlet, Act v, sc. 2, l. 119 [HAMLET]

323   And what was he? Forsooth a great arithmetician.
Othello, Act i, sc. 1, l. 18 [IAGO]

324   This counter-caster . . . must his lieutenant be.
Othello, Act i, sc. 1, l. 31 [IAGO]
(Counter-caster, one who counts or reckons with counters: a
term of contempt for an arithmetician.)

325   He . . . ruminates like an hostess that hath no arithmetic but her
brain to set down her reckoning.
Troilus and Cressida, Act iii, sc. 3, l. 252 [THERSITES]

Army

326 For lo! within a ken our army lies,
Upon mine honour, all too confident
To give admittance to a thought of fear.
II Henry IV, Act iv, sc. 1, l. 151 [WESTMORELAND]

327 My lord, our army is dispersed already:
Like youthful steers unyoked, they take their courses
East, west, north, south; or, like a school broke up
Each hurried toward his home and sporting-place.
II Henry IV, Act iv, sc. 2, l. 102 [HASTINGS]

328 From camp to camp through the foul womb of night
The hum of either army stilly sounds . . .
The armourers, accomplishing the knights,
With busy hammers closing rivets up,
Give dreadful note of preparation.
Henry V, Act iv, Prologue, l. 4 [CHORUS]

329 His army is a ragged multitude
Of hinds and peasants, rude and merciless.
II Henry VI, Act iv, sc. 4, l. 32 [MESSENGER]

330 With a puissant and a mighty power
Of gallowglasses and stout kerns
[He] is marching hitherward in proud array.
II Henry VI, Act iv, sc. 9, l. 25 [MESSENGER]

Arrow

331   My arrows,
Too slightly timber'd for so loud a wind,
Would have reverted to my bow again,
And not where I had aimed them.
Hamlet, Act iv, sc. 7, l. 21 [KING]

332 Let my disclaiming from a purposed evil
Free me so far in your most generous thoughts,
That I have shot mine arrow o'er the house,
And hurt my brother.   *Hamlet,* Act v, sc. 2, l. 252 [HAMLET]

333 In my school-days, when I had lost one shaft,
I shot his fellow of the self-same flight
The self-same way with more advised watch,
To find the other forth, and by adventuring both
I oft found both.
The Merchant of Venice, Act i, sc. 1, l. 140 [BASSANIO]

334   An arrow shot
From a well-experienced archer hits the mark
His eye doth level at.   *Pericles,* Act i, sc. 1, l. 163 [ANTIOCHUS]

Art

335 In framing an artist, art hath thus decreed,
To make some good, but others to exceed.
Pericles, Act ii, sc. 3, l. 15 [SIMONIDES]

336 In others' works thou dost but mend the style,
And arts with thy sweet graces graced be;
But thou art all my art and dost advance
As high as learning my rude ignorance.   *Sonnet* lxxviii, l. 11

337 I must obey: his art is of such power,
It would control my dam's god, Setebos,
And make a vassal of him.
The Tempest, Act i, sc. 2, l. 372 [CALIBAN]

Ass

338   DROMIO S.: I am transformed, master, am I not? . . .
ANTIPHOLUS S.: If thou art changed to aught, 'tis to an ass.
DROMIO S.: 'Tis true; she rides me and I long for grass.
'Tis so, I am an ass.
    The Comedy of Errors, Act ii, sc. 2, l. 197 [DROMIO OF SYRACUSE]

339   ANTIPHOLUS E.: I think thou art an ass.
DROMIO E.: Marry, so it doth appear
By the wrongs I suffer, and the blows I bear.
I should kick, being kick'd; and, being at that pass,
You would keep from my heels and beware of an ass.
    The Comedy of Errors, Act iii, sc. 1, l. 15 [ANTIPHOLUS OF EPHESUS]

340   I am an ass, indeed; you may prove it by my long ears.
    The Comedy of Errors, Act iv, sc. 4, l. 30 [DROMIO OF EPHESUS]

341   Why, what an ass am I! This is most brave,
That I, the son of a dear father murder'd,
Prompted to my revenge by heaven and hell,
Must, like a whore, unpack my heart with words,
And fall a-cursing like a very drab!
    Hamlet, Act ii, sc. 2, l. 611 [HAMLET]

342   Your dull ass will not mend his pace with beating.
    Hamlet, Act v, sc. 1, l. 63 [CLOWN]

343   May not an ass know when the cart draws the horse?
    King Lear, Act i, sc. 4, l. 244 [FOOL]

344   MRS. FORD: I will always count you my deer.
FALSTAFF: I do begin to perceive that I am made an ass.
FORD: Ay, and an ox too: both the proofs are extant.
    The Merry Wives of Windsor, Act v, sc. 5, l. 122 [MRS. FORD]
To be an ass were nothing; he is both ox and ass.
    Troilus and Cressida, Act v, sc. 1, l. 65 [THERSITES]

345   I must to the barber's, monsieur; for methinks I am marvelous
hairy about the face; and I am such a tender ass, if my hair do but
tickle me, I must scratch.
    A Midsummer Night's Dream, Act iv, sc. 1, l. 25 [BOTTOM]

346   My Oberon! what visions have I seen!
Methought I was enamour'd of an ass.
    A Midsummer Night's Dream, Act iv, sc. 1, l. 79 [TITANIA]

347   CONRADE: Away! you are an ass, you are an ass. . . .
DOGBERRY: O that he were here to write me down an ass! But,
masters, remember that I am an ass; though it be not written
down, yet forget not that I am an ass. . . . O that I had been
writ down an ass!
    Much Ado about Nothing, Act iv, sc. 2, l. 75 [CONRADE]

348   I'll . . . make the Moor thank me, love me and reward me.
For making him egregiously an ass.
    Othello, Act ii, sc. 1, l. 317 [IAGO]

349   What a thrice-double ass
Was I, to take this drunkard for a god
And worship this dull fool!
    The Tempest, Act v, sc. 1, l. 295 [CALIBAN]

Attempt

350   Impossible be strange attempts to those
That weigh their pains in sense and do suppose
What hath been cannot be.
    All's Well that Ends Well, Act i, sc. 1, l. 239 [HELENA]

351   We pray you, for your own sake, to . . . give over this attempt.
                    As You Like It, Act i, sc. 2, l. 189 [CELIA]
352   A man may, if he were of a fearful heart, stagger in this attempt.
                    As You Like It, Act iii, sc. 3, l. 48 [TOUCHSTONE]
353   This attempt
I am soldier to, and will abide it with
A prince's courage.
                    Cymbeline, Act iii, sc. 4, l. 185 [IMOGEN]
354   The quality and hair of our attempt
Brooks no division.
                    I Henry IV, Act iv, sc. 1, l. 61 [WORCESTER]
355   The attempt and not the deed confounds us.
                    Macbeth, Act ii, sc. 2, l. 11 [LADY MACBETH]

Attendance

356   Last time, I danced attendance on his will
Till Paris was besieged, famish'd, and lost.
                    II Henry VI, Act i, sc. 3, l. 174 [YORK]
357   I had thought
They had parted so much honesty among 'em,
At least, good manners, as not thus to suffer
A man of his place, and so near our favour,
To dance attendance on their lordships' pleasures,
And at the door too, like a post with packets.
                    Henry VIII, Act v, sc. 2, l. 27 [KING HENRY]
358   Welcome, my lord; I dance attendance here;
I think the duke will not be spoke withal.
                    Richard III, Act iii, sc. 7, l. 56 [BUCKINGHAM]

Authority

359   There is no fettering of authority.
                    All's Well that Ends Well, Act ii, sc. 3, l. 251 [PAROLLES]
360   Authority melts from me.
                    Antony and Cleopatra, Act iii, sc. 13, l. 90 [ANTONY]
361   They do prank them in authority
Against all noble sufferance.
                    Coriolanus, Act iii, sc. 1, l. 22 [CORIOLANUS]
362   My soul aches
To know, when two authorities are up,
Neither supreme, how soon confusion
May enter 'twixt the gap of both and take
The one by the other.
                    Coriolanus, Act iii, sc. 1, l. 108 [CORIOLANUS]
363   You have that in your countenance which I would fain call master,
. . . authority.
                    King Lear, Act i, sc. 4, l. 29 [KENT]
364   Thus can the demigod Authority
Make us pay down for our offence by weight
The words of heaven.
                    Measure for Measure, Act i, sc. 2, l. 124 [CLAUDIO]
365   Drest in a little brief authority.
                    Measure for Measure, Act ii, sc. 2, l. 118 [ISABELLA]
      (For full quotation see 4498.)
366   Authority, though it err like others,
Hath yet a kind of medicine in itself,
That skins the vice o' the top.
                    Measure for Measure, Act ii, sc. 2, l. 134 [ISABELLA]

367   Art made tongue-tied by authority,
      And folly doctor-like controlling skill.

                                        Sonnet lxvi, l. 9

368   Though authority be a stubborn bear, yet he is oft led by the
      nose with gold: show the inside of your purse to the outside of
      his hand, and no more ado.

                        The Winter's Tale, Act iv, sc. 4, l. 831 [CLOWN]

Axe

369   An exact command, . . . no leisure bated,
      No, not to stay the grinding of the axe,
      My head should be struck off.

                              Hamlet, Act v, sc. 2, l. 19 [HAMLET]

370   Stir at nothing till the axe of death
      Hang over thee, as, sure, it shortly will.

                          II Henry VI, Act ii, sc. 4, l. 49 [DUCHESS]

371   When we saw our sunshine made thy spring,
      And that thy summer bred us no increase,
      We set the axe to thy usurping root;
      And though the edge hath something hit ourselves,
      Yet, know thou, since we have begun to strike,
      We'll never leave till we have hewn thee down,
      Or bathed thy growing with our heated bloods.

                          III Henry VI, Act ii, sc. 2, l. 163 [GEORGE]

372   Your great goodness, out of holy pity,
      Absolved him with an axe.

                          Henry VIII, Act iii, sc. 2, l. 263 [SURREY]

373   Thou cutt'st my head off with a golden axe,
      And smilest upon the stroke that murders me.

                      Romeo and Juliet, Act iii, sc. 3, l. 22 [ROMEO]

Ay and No

374   LADY GREY: Please you dismiss me, either with 'ay' or 'no.'
      KING EDWARD: Ay, if you wilt say 'ay' to my request;
      No, if thou dost say 'no' to my demand.
      LADY GREY: Then, no, my lord. My suit is at an end.

                        III Henry VI, Act iii, sc. 2, l. 78 [LADY GREY]

375   To say 'ay' and 'no' to every thing that I said!—'Ay' and 'no' too
      was no good divinity.

                              King Lear, Act iv, sc. 6, l. 99 [LEAR]

376   Maids, in modesty, say 'no' to that
      Which they would have the profferer construe 'ay.'

                  The Two Gentlemen of Verona, Act i, sc. 2, l. 55 [JULIA]

B

Babe

377   Holy writ in babes hath judgement shown,
      When judges have been babes.

                  All's Well that Ends Well, Act ii, sc. 1, l. 141 [HELENA]

378   Dost thou not see my baby at my breast,
      That sucks the nurse asleep?

                  Antony and Cleopatra, Act v, sc. 2, l. 312 [CLEOPATRA]

379   Think yourself a baby,
      That you have ta'en these tenders for true pay
      Which are not sterling.

                  Hamlet, Act i, sc. 3, l. 105 [POLONIUS]

380   That great baby you see there is not yet out of his swaddling-
      clouts.
                            Hamlet, Act ii, sc. 2, l. 400 [HAMLET]
381   I have given suck, and know
      How tender 'tis to love the babe that milks me.
                      Macbeth, Act i, sc. 7, l. 54 [LADY MACBETH]
382   Stay, yet look back with me unto the Tower.
      Pity, you ancient stones, these tender babes
      Whom envy hath immured within your walls!
      Rough cradle for such little pretty ones!
      Rude ragged nurse, old sullen playfellow
      For tender princes, use my babies well!
                  Richard III, Act iv, sc. 1, l. 98 [QUEEN ELIZABETH]
383   Ah, my tender babes!
      My unblown flowers, new-appearing sweets!
      If yet your gentle souls fly in the air, . . .
      Hover about me with your airy wings
      And hear your mother's lamentation!
                  Richard III, Act iv, sc. 4, l. 9 [QUEEN ELIZABETH]
384   Thou wast the prettiest babe that e'er I nursed.
                      Romeo and Juliet, Act i, sc. 3, l. 60 [NURSE]
385   Come on, poor babe:
      Some powerful spirit instruct the kites and ravens
      To be thy nurses.
              The Winter's Tale, Act ii, sc. 3, l. 185 [ANTIGONUS]

Bacchus

386   Come, thou monarch of the vine,
      Plumpy Bacchus with pink eyne!
      In thy fats our cares be drown'd,
      With thy grapes our hairs be crown'd:
            Cup us, till the world go round.
              Antony and Cleopatra, Act ii, sc. 7, l. 120 [SONG]

Bachelor

387   As a walled town is more worthier than a village, so is the fore-
      head of a married man more honourable than the bare brow of a
      bachelor.
              As You Like It, Act iii, sc. 3, l. 58 [TOUCHSTONE]
388   CINNA: I am a bachelor.
      CITIZEN: That's as much as to say, they are fools that marry:
      you'll bear me a bang for that, I fear.
                      Julius Cæsar, Act iii, sc. 3, l. 18 [CINNA]
389   Hath not the world one man but he will wear his cap with suspi-
      cion? Shall I never see a bachelor of threescore again?
              Much Ado about Nothing, Act i, sc. 1, l. 200 [BENEDICK]
390   That a woman conceived me, I thank her; that she brought me
      up, I likewise give her most humble thanks: but that I will have
      a recheat winded in my forehead, or hang my bugle in an invisible
      baldrick, all women shall pardon me . . . The fine is, . . . I will
      live a bachelor.
              Much Ado about Nothing, Act i, sc. 1, l. 240 [BENEDICK]
391   When I said I would die a bachelor, I did not think I should live
      till I were married.
              Much Ado about Nothing, Act ii, sc. 3, l. 253 [BENEDICK]

Bacon

392   On, bacons, on!
                      I Henry IV, Act ii, sc. 2, l. 95 [FALSTAFF]

393 'Hang-dog' is Latin for bacon. I warrant you.
 The Merry Wives of Windsor, Act iv, sc. 1, l. 50 [MISTRESS QUICKLY]
(A reference to the famous story told by Sir Francis Bacon in
his *Apothegms*. A thief named Hogg, who was condemned to
death by Bacon, prayed for mercy on the score of kinship. "Ay,
but," replied the judge, "you and I cannot be of kindred unless
you are hanged, for hog is not bacon till it be well hanged.")

Badness

394 He . . . is a thing Too bad for bad report.
 Cymbeline, Act i, sc. 1, l. 16 [GENTLEMAN]
A plague on thee! thou art too bad to curse.
 Timon of Athens, Act iv, sc. 3, l. 365 [APEMANTUS]
395 Thus bad begins and worse remains behind.
 Hamlet, Act iii, sc. 4, l. 179 [HAMLET]
[I count] myself but bad till I be best.
 III Henry VI, Act v, sc. 6, l. 91 [GLOUCESTER]
396 Creating every bad a perfect best.
 Sonnet cxiv, l. 7
397 Things bad begun make strong themselves by ill.
 Macbeth, Act iii, sc. 2, l. 55 [MACBETH]
398 Good night, good night: heaven me such uses send
Not to pick bad from bad, but by bad mend!
 Othello, Act iv, sc. 3, l. 105 [DESDEMONA]
399 Bad is the world; and all will come to nought,
When such bad dealing must be seen in thought.
 Richard III, Act iii, sc. 6, l. 13 [SCRIVENER]

Bag and Baggage

400 Come, shepherd, let us make an honourable retreat; though not
with bag and baggage, yet with scrip and scrippage.
 As You Like It, Act iii, sc. 2, l. 169 [TOUCHSTONE]
401 Let in and out the enemy With bag and baggage.
 The Winter's Tale, Act i, sc. 2, l. 205 [LEONTES]

Ballad

402 A divulged shame Traduced by odious ballads.
 All's Well that Ends Well, Act ii, sc. 2, l. 174 [HELENA]
403 Scald rhymers [will] Ballad us out of tune.
 Antony and Cleopatra, Act v, sc. 2, l. 215 [CLEOPATRA]
404 An I have not ballads made on you all and sung to filthy tunes,
let a cup of sack be my poison.
 I Henry IV, Act ii, sc. 2, l. 49 [FALSTAFF]
405 I will have it in a particular ballad else, with mine own picture on
the top on 't.
 II Henry IV, Act iv, sc. 3, l. 52 [FALSTAFF]
406 ARMADO: Is there not a ballad, boy, of the King and the Beggar?
MOTH: The world was very guilty of such a ballad some three ages
since; but I think now 'tis not to be found.
 Love's Labour's Lost, Act i, sc. 2, l. 114 [ARMADO]
407 SERVANT: O master, if you did but hear the pedlar at the door:
. . . he sings several tunes faster than you'll tell money; he utters
them as he had eaten ballads and all men's ears grew to his
tunes. . . .
CLOWN: He shall come in. I love a ballad but even too well, if it
be doleful matter merrily set down, or a very pleasant thing indeed and sung lamentably.
 The Winter's Tale, Act iv, sc. 4, l. 181 [SERVANT]

408 I love a ballad in print o' life, for then we are sure they are true.
                        The Winter's Tale, Act iv, sc. 4, l. 263 [MOPSA]

Banishment

409 We, even from this instant, banish him our city,
     In peril of precipitation
     From off the rock Tarpeian never more
     To enter our Rome gates.
                        Coriolanus, Act iii, sc. 3, l. 101 [SICINIUS]
410   I banish thee, on pain of death, . . .
     Not to come near our person by ten mile.
                        II Henry IV, Act v, sc. 5, l. 67 [KING HENRY]
411 Be packing, therefore, thou that wast a knight:
     Henceforth we banish thee, on pain of death.
                        I Henry VI, Act iv, sc. 1, l. 46 [KING HENRY]
412 KING RICHARD: We banish you our territories:
     You, cousin Hereford, upon pain of life
     Till twice five summers have enrich'd our fields
     Shall not regreet our fair dominions,
     But tread the stranger paths of banishment.
     BOLINGBROKE: Your will be done: this must my comfort be,
     That sun that warms you here shall shine on me. . . .
     KING RICHARD: Norfolk, for thee remains a heavier doom, . . .
     The hopeless word of 'never to return'
     Breathe I against thee, upon pain of life.
                        Richard II, Act i, sc. 3, l. 139 [KING RICHARD]
413 [I] have sigh'd my English breath in foreign clouds,
     Eating the bitter bread of banishment.
                        Richard II, Act iii, sc. 1, l. 20 [BOLINGBROKE]
414 GLOUCESTER: Wert thou not banished on pain of death?
     QUEEN MARGARET: I was; but I do find more pain in banishment
     Than death can yield me here by my abode.
                        Richard III, Act i, sc. 3, l. 167 [GLOUCESTER]
415 Some word there was, worser than Tybalt's death,
     That murder'd me: I would forget it fain;
     But, O, it presses to my memory,
     Like damned guilty deeds to sinners' minds:
     'Tybalt is dead, and Romeo—banished';
     That 'banished,' that one word 'banished,'
     Hath slain ten thousand Tybalts.
                        Romeo and Juliet, Act iii, sc. 2, l. 108 [JULIET]
416 ROMEO: Exile hath more terror in his look,
     Much more than death: do not say 'banishment.'
     FRIAR LAURENCE: Hence from Verona art thou banished:
     Be patient, for the world is broad and wide.
     ROMEO: There is no world without Verona walls,
     But purgatory, torture, hell itself.
     Hence-banished is banish'd from the world,
     And world's exile is death. . . . Calling death banishment,
     Thou cutt'st my head off with a golden axe,
     And smilest upon the stroke that murders me.
                        Romeo and Juliet, Act iii, sc. 3, l. 13 [ROMEO]
             Banish'd from her
     Is self from self: a deadly banishment.
        The Two Gentlemen of Verona, Act iii, sc. 1, l. 172 [VALENTINE]
417 LUCIUS: The judges have pronounced
     My everlasting doom of banishment.

TITUS: O happy man! they have befriended thee.
Why, foolish Lucius, dost thou not perceive
That Rome is but a wilderness of tigers? . . .
How happy art thou, then,
From these devourers to be banished!

Titus Andronicus, Act iii, sc. 1, l. 50 [LUCIUS]

Banner

418 We shall hardly in our ages see
Their banners wave again.

Coriolanus, Act iii, sc. 1, l. 7 [COMINIUS]

419 The dancing banners of the French, . . .
Triumphantly displayed.

King John, Act ii, sc. 1, l. 308 [HERALD]

France spreads his banners in our noiseless land,
With plumed helm thy state begins to threat.

King Lear, Act iv, sc. 2, l. 56 [GONERIL]

The Norweyan banners flout the sky.

Macbeth, Act i, sc. 2, l. 50 [ROSS]

420 Hang out our banners on the outward walls;
The cry is still 'They come.'

Macbeth, Act v, sc. 5, l. 1 [MACBETH]

Bargain

421 I'll give thrice so much land
To any well-deserving friend;
But in the way of bargain, mark ye me,
I'll cavil on the ninth part of a hair.

I Henry IV, Act iii, sc. 1, l. 137 [HOTSPUR]

422 Your hand; a covenant: we will have these things set down by
lawful counsel, . . . lest the bargain should catch cold and starve.

Cymbeline, Act i, sc. 4, l. 176 [IACHIMO]

423 Clap hands and a bargain.

Henry V, Act v, sc. 1, l. 134 [KING HENRY]

424 Wash our hands
To clap this royal bargain up of peace.

King John, Act iii, sc. 1, l. 234 [KING PHILIP]

425 The boy hath sold him a bargain, a goose, that's flat. . . .
To sell a bargain well is as cunning as fast and loose.

Love's Labour's Lost, Act iii, sc. 1, l. 102 [COSTARD]

426 A time, methinks, too short
To make a world-without-end bargain in.

Love's Labour's Lost, Act v, sc. 2, l. 798 [PRINCESS]

427 Go to, a bargain made: seal it, seal it; I'll be the witness.

Troilus and Cressida, Act iii, sc. 2, l. 204 [PANDAR]

428 Keep this remembrance for thy Julia's sake, . . .
And seal the bargain with a holy kiss.

The Two Gentlemen of Verona, Act ii, sc. 2, l. 5 [JULIA]

Barge

429 The barge she sat in, like a burnish'd throne,
Burn'd on the water: the poop was beaten gold;
Purple the sails, and so perfumed that
The winds were love-sick with them.

Antony and Cleopatra, Act ii, sc. 2, l. 196 [ENOBARBUS]

430 The duke is coming: see the barge be ready;
And fit it with such furniture as suits
The greatness of his person.

Henry VIII, Act ii, sc. 1, l. 98 [VAUX]

Basan

431   O, that I were
Upon the hill of Basan, to outroar
The horned herd! for I have savage cause;
And to proclaim it civilly, were like
A halter'd neck which does the hangman thank
For being yare about him.

Antony and Cleopatra, Act iii, sc. 13, l. 126 [ANTONY]

Bastard

432   We are all bastards;
And that most venerable man which I
Did call my father, was I know not where
When I was stamp'd; some coiner with his tools
Made me a counterfeit: yet my mother seem'd
The Dian of that time.

Cymbeline, Act ii, sc. 5, l. 2 [POSTHUMUS]

That drop of blood that's calm proclaims me bastard,
Cries cuckold to my father, brands the harlot
Even here, between the chaste unsmirched brow
Of my true mother.

Hamlet, Act iv, sc. 5, l. 117 [LAERTES]

433 Thy mother took into her blameful bed
Some stern untutor'd churl, and noble stock
Was graft with crab-tree slip; whose fruit thou art,
And never of the Nevils' noble race.

II Henry VI, Act iii, sc. 2, l. 212 [SUFFOLK]

434 Once he slander'd me with bastardy;
But whether I be true begot or no,
That still I lay upon my mother's head.

King John, Act i, sc. 1, l. 74 [BASTARD]

435   Large lengths of seas and shores
Between my father and my mother lay,
As I have heard my father speak himself,
When this same lusty gentleman was got.

King John, Act i, sc. 1, l. 105 [ROBERT]

436 My boy a bastard! By my soul, I think
His father never was so true begot.

King John, Act ii, sc. 1, l. 129 [CONSTANCE]

437 He is but a bastard to the time
That doth not smack of observation.

King John, Act i, sc. 1, l. 207 [BASTARD]

438 Why bastard? wherefore base? . . . Why brand they us
With base? with baseness? bastardy? base, base?
Who, in the lusty stealth of nature, take
More composition and fierce quality
Than doth, within a dull, stale, tired bed,
Go to the creating a whole tribe of fops,
Got 'tween asleep and wake?

King Lear, Act i, sc. 2, l. 6 [EDMUND]

439 I love bastards: I am a bastard begot, bastard instructed, bastard
in mind, bastard in valour, in every thing illegitimate.

Troilus and Cressida, Act v, sc. 7, l. 16 [THERSITES]

Battle

440   To-morrow the last of many battles
We mean to fight.

Antony and Cleopatra, Act iv, sc. 1, l. 11 [OCTAVIUS CÆSAR]

441   I am afeard there are few die well that die in a battle; for how can
they charitably dispose of any thing, when blood is their argument?
Henry V, Act iv, sc. 1, l. 150 [WILLIAMS]

442   When, without stratagem,
But in plain shock and even play of battle,
Was ever known so great and little loss
On one part and on the other? Take it, God,
For it was none but thine.
Henry V, Act iv, sc. 8, l. 113 [KING HENRY]

443   The battles of the Lord of Hosts he fought.
I Henry VI, Act i, sc. 1, l. 31 [WINCHESTER]

444   Now, by my faith, lords, 'twas a glorious day:
Saint Alban's battle won by famous York
Shall be eternized in all age to come.
II Henry VI, Act v, sc. 3, l. 29 [WARWICK]
We at Saint Alban's met, Our battles join'd.
III Henry VI, Act ii, sc. 1, l. 120 [WARWICK]
              Was not your husband
In Margaret's battle at Saint Alban's slain?
Richard III, Act i, sc. 3, l. 130 [GLOUCESTER]

445   This battle fares like to the morning's war,
What time the shepherd, blowing of his nails,
When dying clouds contend with growing light
Can neither call it perfect day nor night.
III Henry VI, Act ii, sc. 5, l. 1 [KING]

446   The enemy comes on in gallant show;
Their bloody sign of battle is hung out.
Julius Cæsar, Act v, sc. 1, l. 13 [MESSENGER]

Bawcock

447   Good bawcock, bate thy rage; use lenity, sweet chuck!
Henry V, Act iii, sc. 2, l. 25 [PISTOL]
("Bawcock," from the French *beau-coq*, a fine fellow.)
The king's a bawcock.
Henry V, Act iv, sc. 1, l. 44 [PISTOL]

448   Why, how now, my bawcock! how dost thou, chuck?
Twelfth Night, Act iii, sc. 4, l. 125 [SIR TOBY]
Why, that's my bawcock!
The Winter's Tale, Act i, sc. 2, l. 121 [LEONTES]

Bear

449   Thou 'ldst shun a bear;
But if thy flight lay toward the raging sea,
Thou 'ldst meet the bear i' the mouth.
King Lear, Act iii, sc. 4, l. 9 [LEAR]

450   Two bears will not bite one another when they meet.
Much Ado about Nothing, Act iii, sc. 2, l. 80 [CLAUDIO]

451   One bear will not bite another, and wherefore should one bastard?
Troilus and Cressida, Act v, sc. 7, l. 19 [THERSITES]

452   I am gone for ever. [*Exit, pursued by a bear*]
The Winter's Tale, Act iii, sc. 3, l. 58 [ANTIGONUS]
(A much-quoted stage direction.)

Bear-Baiting

453   YORK: Call hither to the stake my two brave bears,
That with the very shaking of their chains
They may astonish these fell-lurking curs. . . .

CLIFFORD: Are these thy bears? we'll bait thy bears to death,
And manacle the bear-ward in their chains.
II Henry VI, Act v, sc. 1, l. 144 [YORK]

454   FABIAN: He brought me out o' favour with my lady about a bear-
baiting here.
SIR TOBY: To anger him, we'll have the bear again.
Twelfth Night, Act ii, sc. 5, l. 9 [FABIAN]

455   Out upon him! prig, for my life, prig: he haunts wakes, fairs and
bear-baitings.
The Winter's Tale, Act iv, sc. 3, l. 108 [CLOWN]

Beard See also **Chin**

456   By my old beard, And every hair that's on't,
Helen, that's dead, was a sweet creature.
All's Well that Ends Well, Act v, sc. 3, l. 76 [LAFEU]

457   TOUCHSTONE: Swear by your beards that I am a knave.
CELIA: By our beards, if we had them, thou art.
As You Like It, Act i, sc. 2, l. 77 [TOUCHSTONE]

458   ROSALIND: Is his head worth a hat, or his chin worth a beard?
CELIA: Nay, he hath but a little beard.
ROSALIND: Why, God will send more, if the man will be thankful.
As You Like It, Act iii, sc. 2, l. 217 [ROSALIND]

459   If e'er again I meet him beard to beard,
He's mine, or I am his.
Coriolanus, Act i, sc. 10, l. 11 [AUFIDIUS]
We might have met them dareful, beard to beard,
And beat them backward home.
Macbeth, Act v, sc. 5, l. 6 [MACBETH]

460   You had more beard when I last saw you.
Coriolanus, Act iv, sc. 3, l. 8 [VOLSCE]
O, my old friend! thy face is valanced since I saw thee last.
Hamlet, Act ii, sc. 2, l. 442 [HAMLET]

461   HAMLET: His beard was grizzled,—no?
HORATIO: It was, as I have seen it in his life,
A sable silver'd.
Hamlet, Act i, sc. 2, l. 240 [HAMLET]

462   His beard was white as snow,
All flaxen was his poll.
Hamlet, Act iv, sc. 5, l. 195 [OPHELIA]

463   Comest thou to beard me in Denmark?
Hamlet, Act ii, sc. 2, l. 442 [HAMLET]
No man so potent breathes upon the ground
But I will beard him.
I Henry IV, Act iv, sc. 1, l. 11 [DOUGLAS]
WINCHESTER: I beard thee to thy face.
GLOUCESTER: What! am I dared and bearded to my face?
I Henry VI, Act i, sc. 3, l. 44 [WINCHESTER]
IDEN: Thou wilt brave me with these saucy terms?
CADE: Brave thee; ay, . . . and beard thee too.
II Henry VI, Act iv, sc. 10, l. 39 [IDEN]

464   You must not think
That we are made of stuff so flat and dull
That we can let our beard be shook with danger
And think it pastime.
Hamlet, Act iv, sc. 7, l. 30 [KING]

465   FALSTAFF: Thy father's beard is turned white with the news: you
may buy land now as cheap as stinking mackerel.

PRINCE: Why, then, it is like . . . we shall buy maidenheads as they buy hob-nails, by the hundreds.

FALSTAFF: By the mass, lad, thou sayest true; it is like we shall have good trading that way.

I Henry IV, Act ii, sc. 4, l. 393 [FALSTAFF]

466   I will sooner have a beard grow in the palm of my hand than he shall get one on his cheek; and yet he will not stick to say his face is a face-royal: God may finish it when he will, 'tis not a hair amiss yet.

II Henry IV, Act i, sc. 2, l. 23 [FALSTAFF]

467   Whose beard the silver hand of peace hath touch'd.

II Henry IV, Act iv, sc. 1, l. 43 [WESTMORELAND]

I'll hide my silver beard in a gold beaver
And in my vantbrace put this wither'd brawn.

Troilus and Cressida, Act i, sc. 3, l. 296 [NESTOR]

468   What a beard of the general's cut . . . will do among foaming bottles and ale-washed wits, is wonderful to be thought on.

Henry V, Act iii, sc. 6, l. 81 [GOWER]

469   Priest, beware your beard;
I mean to tug it and to cuff you soundly.

I Henry VI, Act i, sc. 3, l. 47 [GLOUCESTER]

470   By the kind gods, 'tis most ignobly done
To pluck me by the beard.

King Lear, Act iii, sc. 7, l. 35 [GLOUCESTER]

471   If you did wear a beard upon your chin,
I'd shake it on this quarrel.

King Lear, Act iii, sc. 7, l. 76 [SERVANT]

472   A beard, fair health, and honesty;
With three-fold love I wish you all these three. . . .
I'll mark no words that smooth-faced wooers say.

Love's Labour's Lost, Act v, sc. 2, l. 834 [KATHARINE]

473   What a beard hast thou got! thou hast got more hair on thy chin than Dobbin my fill-horse has on his tail.

The Merchant of Venice, Act ii, sc. 2, l. 99 [GOBBO]

474   QUICKLY: Does he [Slender] not wear a great round beard, like a glover's paring-knife?

SIMPLE: No, forsooth: he hath but a little wee face, with a little yellow beard, a Cain-coloured beard.

The Merry Wives of Windsor, Act i, sc. 4, l. 20 [MRS. QUICKLY]

475   BEATRICE: Lord, I could not endure a husband with a beard on his face: I had rather lie in the woolen.

LEONATO: You may light on a husband that hath no beard.

BEATRICE: What should I do with him? dress him in my apparel and make him my waiting-gentlewoman? He that hath a beard is more than a youth, and he that hath no beard is less than a man.

Much Ado about Nothing, Act ii, sc. 1, l. 31 [BEATRICE]

476   CLAUDIO: The old ornament of his cheek hath already stuffed tennis-balls.

LEONATO: Indeed, he looks younger than he did, by the loss of a beard.

Much Ado about Nothing, Act iii, sc. 2, l. 46 [CLAUDIO]

477   For my Lord Lackbeard there, he and I shall meet.

Much Ado about Nothing, Act v, sc. 1, l. 195 [BENEDICK]

478   White-beards have arm'd their thin and hairless scalps
Against thy majesty.

Richard II, Act iii, sc. 2, l. 122 [SCROOP]

By this white beard, thou'ld fight with thee to-morrow.
Troilus and Cressida, Act iv, sc. 5, l. 211 [NESTOR]
By my white beard, You offer him a wrong.
The Winter's Tale, Act iv, sc. 4, l. 414 [POLIXENES]

479   Jove, in his next commodity of hair, send thee a beard!
Twelfth Night, Act iii, sc. 1, l. 50 [CLOWN]

Beast

480   Nature teaches beasts to know their friends.
Coriolanus, Act ii, sc. 1, l. 6 [SICINIUS]

481   A beast, that wants discourse of reason,
Would have mourn'd longer.
Hamlet, Act i, sc. 2, l. 150 [HAMLET]

482   Let a beast be lord of beasts, and his crib shall stand at the
king's mess.
Hamlet, Act v, sc. 2, l. 86 [HAMLET]

483   DEMETRIUS: I'll leave thee to the mercy of wild beasts.
HELENA: The wildest hath not such a heart as you.
A Midsummer Night's Dream, Act ii, sc. 1, l. 228 [DEMETRIUS]

484   Here come two noble beasts in, a man and a lion.
A Midsummer Night's Dream, Act v, sc. 1, l. 220 [THESEUS]

485   A very gentle beast, and of good conscience.
A Midsummer Night's Dream, Act v, sc. 1, l. 231 [THESEUS]

486   The rough beast that knows no gentle right,
Nor aught obeys but his foul appetite.
The Rape of Lucrece, l. 545

487   Since men prove beasts, let beasts bear gentle minds.
The Rape of Lucrece, l. 1148 [LUCRECE]

488   No beast so fierce but knows some touch of pity.
Richard III, Act i, sc. 2, l. 71 [ANNE]

489   Timon will to the woods, where he shall find
The unkindest beast more kinder than mankind.
Timon of Athens, Act iv, sc. 1, l. 35 [TIMON]

Beating

490   We'll beat 'em into bench-holes: I have yet
Room for six scotches more.
Antony and Cleopatra, Act iv, sc. 7, l. 9 [SCARUS]

491   I'ld have beaten him like a dog, but for disturbing the lords within.
Coriolanus, Act iv, sc. 5, l. 56 [SERVANT]
I'ld beat him like a dog.
Twelfth Night, Act ii, sc. 3, l. 153 [SIR ANDREW]

492   QUICKLY: Mistress Ford, good heart, is beaten black and blue,
that you cannot see a white spot about her.
FALSTAFF: What tellest thou me of black and blue? I was beaten
myself into all the colours of the rainbow.
The Merry Wives of Windsor, Act iv, sc. 5, l. 114 [MRS. QUICKLY]

493   Since I plucked geese, played truant, and whipped top, I knew
not what 'twas to be beaten till lately.
The Merry Wives of Windsor, Act v, sc. 1, l. 28 [FALSTAFF]

Beauty

494   Those [women] that she [Fortune] makes fair she scarce makes
honest, and those that she makes honest she makes very ill-
favouredly.
As You Like It, Act i, sc. 2, l. 40 [CELIA]

HAMLET: If you be honest and fair, your honesty should admit no
discourse to your beauty.

OPHELIA: Could beauty, my lord, have better commerce than with honesty?
HAMLET: Ay, truly; for the power of beauty will sooner transform honesty from what it is to a bawd than the force of honesty can translate beauty into his likeness: this was sometime a paradox, but now the time gives it proof.
Hamlet, Act iii, sc. 1, l. 107 [HAMLET]

495   Beauty provoketh thieves sooner than gold.
As You Like It, Act i, sc. 3, l. 112 [ROSALIND]

496   What though you have no beauty,—
As, by my faith, I see no more in you
Than without candle may go dark to bed.
As You Like It, Act iii, sc. 5, l. 37 [ROSALIND]

497   Since that my beauty cannot please his eye,
I'll weep what's left away, and weeping die.
The Comedy of Errors, Act ii, sc. 1, l. 114 [ADRIANA]

498   Mine eyes
Were not in fault, for she was beautiful.
Cymbeline, Act v, sc. 5, l. 63 [CYMBELINE]

499   Her beauty and her brain go not together: she's a good sign,
but I have seen small reflection of her wit.
Cymbeline, Act i, sc. 2, l. 31 [LORD]

500   All of her that is out of door most rich!
If she be furnish'd with a mind so rare,
She is alone the Arabian bird.
Cymbeline, Act i, sc. 6, l. 15 [IACHIMO]

501   As plays the sun upon the glassy streams,
Twinkling another counterfeited beam,
So seems this gorgeous beauty to mine eyes.
Fain would I woo her, yet I dare not speak: . . .
Ay, beauty's princely majesty is such,
Confounds the tongue and makes the senses rough.
I Henry VI, Act v, sc. 3, l. 62 [SUFFOLK]

502   Beauty that the tyrant oft reclaims
Shall to my flaming wrath be oil and flax.
II Henry VI, Act v, sc. 2, l. 54 [YOUNG CLIFFORD]

503   'Tis beauty that doth oft make women proud;
But, God he knows, thy share thereof is small.
III Henry VI, Act i, sc. 4, l. 128 [YORK]

504   Beauty and honour in her are so mingled
That they have caught the king.
Henry VIII, Act ii, sc. 3, l. 76 [CHAMBERLAIN]

505   Thou art fair, and at thy birth, dear boy,
Nature and Fortune join'd to make thee great:
Of Nature's gifts thou mayst with lilies boast
And with the half-blown rose.
King John, Act iii, sc. 1, l. 51 [CONSTANCE]

506   Good Lord Boyet, my beauty, though but mean,
Needs not the painted flourish of your praise:
Beauty is bought by judgement of the eye,
Not utter'd by base sale of chapmen's tongues.
Love's Labour's Lost, Act ii, sc. 1, l. 13 [PRINCESS OF FRANCE]

507   Where fair is not, praise cannot mend the brow.
Here, good my glass, take this for telling true:
Fair payment for foul words is more than due.
Love's Labour's Lost, Act iv, sc. 1, l. 17 [PRINCESS]

508   By heaven, that thou art fair, is most infallible. . . . More fairer
      than fair, beautiful than beauteous, truer than truth itself.
                          Love's Labour's Lost, Act iv, sc. 1, l. 60 [BOYET, *reading*]
509   As fair as day.
                          Love's Labour's Lost, Act iv, sc. 3, l. 90 [DUMAIN]
      Fairer than tongue can name thee.
                          Richard III, Act i, sc. 2, l. 81 [GLOUCESTER]
510   A wither'd hermit, five-score winters worn,
          Might shake off fifty, looking in her eye:
      Beauty doth varnish age, as if new-born,
          And gives the crutch the cradle's infancy.
                          Love's Labour's Lost, Act iv, sc. 3, l. 242 [BIRON]
511   Look on beauty,
      And you shall see 'tis purchased by the weight;
      Which therein works a miracle in nature,
      Making them lightest that wear most of it:
      So are those crisped snaky golden locks
      Which make such wanton gambols with the wind,
      Upon supposed fairness, often known
      To be the dowry of a second head,
      The skull that bred them in the sepulchre.
                          The Merchant of Venice, Act iii, sc. 2, l. 88 [BASSANIO]
512   HERMIA: God speed, fair Helena! whither away?
      HELENA: Call you me fair? that fair again unsay.
      Demetrius loves your fair: O happy fair!
                          A Midsummer Night's Dream, Act i, sc. 1, l. 180 [HERMIA]
513   She exceeds her as much in beauty as the first of May doth the
      last of December.
                          Much Ado about Nothing, Act i, sc. 1, l. 193 [BENEDICK]
514   She never yet was foolish that was fair,
      For even her folly help'd her to an heir . . .
      She that was ever fair and never proud,
      Had tongue at will and yet was never loud.
                          Othello, Act ii, sc. 1, l. 137 [IAGO]
515   He hath a daily beauty in his life
      That makes me ugly.
                          Othello, Act v, sc. 1, l. 19 [IAGO]
516   Beauty is but a vain and doubtful good;
      A shining gloss that vadeth suddenly;
      A flower that dies when first it 'gins to bud;
      A brittle glass that's broken presently; . . .
          So beauty blemish'd once's for ever lost,
          In spite of physic, painting, pain and cost.
                          The Passionate Pilgrim, Pt. xiii, l. 1
517   Beauty itself doth of itself persuade
      The eyes of men without an orator.
                          The Rape of Lucrece, l. 29
518   All orators are dumb when beauty pleadeth.
                          The Rape of Lucrece, l. 268 [TARQUIN]
519   O, she is rich in beauty, only poor,
      That when she dies with beauty dies her store. . . .
      For beauty starved with her severity
      Cuts beauty off from all posterity.
                          Romeo and Juliet, Act i, sc. 1, l. 221 [ROMEO]
520   Show me a mistress that is passing fair.
                          Romeo and Juliet, Act i, sc. 1, l. 240 [ROMEO]

Is she not passing fair?

The Two Gentlemen of Verona, Act iv, sc. 4, l. 153 [SILVIA]

521 One fairer than my love! the all-seeing sun
Ne'er saw her match since first the world begun.

Romeo and Juliet, Act i, sc. 2, l. 97 [ROMEO]

522 ROMEO: What lady is that, which doth enrich the hand
Of yonder knight?
SERVANT: I know not, sir.
ROMEO: O, she doth teach the torches to burn bright!
It seems she hangs upon the ear of night
Like a rich jewel in an Ethiope's ear;
Beauty too rich for use, for earth too dear!
So shows a snowy dove trooping with crows,
As yonder lady o'er her fellows shows. . . .
Did my heart love till now? forswear it, sight!
For I ne'er saw true beauty till this night.

Romeo and Juliet, Act i, sc. 5, l. 43 [ROMEO]

523 Thy beauty hath made me effeminate
And in my temper soften'd valour's steel!

Romeo and Juliet, Act iii, sc. 1, l. 119 [ROMEO]

524 Her beauty makes
The vault a feasting presence full of light.

Romeo and Juliet, Act v, sc. 3, l. 85 [ROMEO]

525 From fairest creatures we desire increase,
That thereby beauty's rose might never die.

Sonnet i, l. 1

526 Beauty's waste hath in the world an end,
And kept unused, the user so destroys it.

Sonnet ix, l. 11

Beauty within itself should not be wasted.

Venus and Adonis, l. 130 [VENUS]

527 Gentle thou art and therefore to be won,
Beauteous thou art, therefore to be assailed.

Sonnet xli, l. 6

528 Since brass, nor stone, nor earth, nor boundless sea
But sad mortality o'ersways their power,
How with this rage shall beauty hold a plea,
Whose action is no stronger than a flower?

Sonnet lxv, l. 1

529 The ornament of beauty is suspect,
A crow that flies in heaven's sweetest air.

Sonnet lxx, l. 3

530 How like Eve's apple doth thy beauty grow,
If thy sweet virtue answer not thy show!

Sonnet xciii, l. 13

531 When in the chronicle of wasted time
I see descriptions of the fairest wights,
And beauty making beautiful old rhyme
In praise of ladies dead and lovely knights,
Then, in the blazon of sweet beauty's best,
Of hand, of foot, of lip, of eye, of brow,
I see their antique pen would have express'd
Even such a beauty as you master now.

Sonnet cvi, l. 1

532 I have sworn thee fair and thought thee bright
Who art as black as hell, as dark as night.

Sonnet cxlvii, l. 13

I have sworn thee fair; more perjured I,
To swear against the truth so foul a lie.
                                        Sonnet clii, l. 13

533   I saw sweet beauty in her face,
Such as the daughter of Agenor had,
That made great Jove to humble him to her hand,
When with his knees he kiss'd the Cretan strand.
            The Taming of the Shrew, Act i, sc. 1, l. 172 [LUCENTIO]

534   Beauty's a flower.
                        Twelfth Night, Act i, sc. 5, l. 58 [CLOWN]

535   Were beauty under twenty locks kept fast,
Yet love breaks through and picks them all at last.
                                Venus and Adonis, l. 575

536   POLIXENES: This is the prettiest low-born lass that ever
Ran o'er the green-sward. . . .
CAMILLO: Good sooth, she is
The queen of curds and cream.
            The Winter's Tale, Act iv, sc. 4, l. 156 [POLIXENES]

Bed

537   In your bed
Find fairer fortune, if you ever wed!
            All's Well that Ends Well, Act ii, sc. 3, l. 97 [HELENA]

538   When you have conquer'd my yet maiden bed,
Remain there but an hour.
            All's Well that Ends Well, Act iv, sc. 2, l. 57 [DIANA]

539   It is not
Amiss to tumble on the bed of Ptolemy.
            Antony and Cleopatra, Act i, sc. 4, l. 16 [OCTAVIUS]

540   The beds i' the east are soft.
            Antony and Cleopatra, Act ii, sc. 6, l. 51 [ANTONY]
He hides him in . . . soft beds, Sweet words.
                    Cymbeline, Act v, sc. 3, l. 71 [POSTHUMUS]

541   I'll . . . afterward consort you till bed-time.
            The Comedy of Errors, Act i, sc. 2, l. 28 [MERCHANT]
I would 'twere bed-time, Hal, and all well.
                    I Henry IV, Act v, sc. 1, l. 125 [FALSTAFF]

542   Let not the royal bed of Denmark be
A couch for luxury and damned incest.
                        Hamlet, Act i, sc. 5, l. 82 [GHOST]

543   Nay, but to live
In the rank sweat of an enseamed bed,
Stew'd in corruption, honeying and making love
Over the nasty sty.
                        Hamlet, Act iii, sc. 4, l. 91 [HAMLET]

544   If not the face of men,
The sufferance of our souls, the time's abuse,—
If these be motives weak, break off betimes,
And every man hence to his idle bed.
                    Julius Cæsar, Act ii, sc. 1, l. 114 [BRUTUS]

545   You've ungently, Brutus, Stole from my bed.
                    Julius Cæsar, Act ii, sc. 1, l. 237 [PORTIA]

546   I have forsworn his bed and company.
            A Midsummer Night's Dream, Act ii, sc. 1, l. 62 [TITANIA]

547   HERMIA: Lysander, find you out a bed;
For I upon this bank will rest my head.
LYSANDER: One turf shall serve as pillow for us both;
One heart, one bed, two bosoms, and one troth.

HERMIA: Nay, good Lysander; for my sake, my dear,
Lie further off yet, do not lie so near.
LYSANDER: O, take the sense, sweet, of my innocence!
Love takes the meaning in love's conference.
I mean, that my heart unto yours is knit
So that but one heart we can make of it. . . .
Then by your side no bed-room me deny. . . .
HERMIA: But, gentle friend, for love and courtesy,
Lie further off; in human modesty,
Such separation as may well be said
Becomes a virtuous bachelor and a maid.
A Midsummer Night's Dream, Act ii, sc. 2, l. 39 [HERMIA]

548   There's millions now alive
That nightly lie in those unproper beds
Which they dare swear peculiar.
Othello, Act iv, sc. 1, l. 68 [IAGO]

549 Thy bed, lust-stain'd, shall with lust's blood be spotted.
Othello, Act v, sc. 1, l. 36 [OTHELLO]

550 Romeo, good night: I'll to my truckle-bed;
This field-bed is too cold for me to sleep.
Romeo and Juliet, Act ii, sc. 1, l. 39 [MERCUTIO]

551 Weary with toil, I haste me to my bed,
The dear repose for limbs with travel tired.
Sonnet xxvii, l. 1

552   Come, Kate, we'll to bed.
We three are married, but you two are sped.
The Taming of the Shrew, Act v, sc. 2, l. 184 [PETRUCHIO]

553 I will show you a chamber with a bed; which bed, because it shall
not speak of your pretty encounters, press it to death: away!
And Cupid grant all tongue-tied maidens here
Bed, chamber, Pandar to provide this gear!
Troilus and Cressida, Act iii, sc. 2, l. 215 [PANDAR]

554 Not to be abed after midnight is to be up betimes. . . . To be
up after midnight and to go to bed then, is early: so that to go to
bed after midnight is to go to bed betimes.
Twelfth Night, Act ii, sc. 3, l. 1 [SIR TOBY]

Bedfellow

555 Go, you wild bedfellow, you cannot soothsay.
Antony and Cleopatra, Act i, sc. 2, l. 51 [IRAS]

556   He loves your people;
But tie him not to be their bedfellow.
Coriolanus, Act ii, sc. 2, l. 68 [MENENIUS]

557 I'll lie down and sleep. But, soft! no bedfellow!
Cymbeline, Act iv, sc. 2, l. 295 [IMOGEN]

558 Nay, but the man that was his bedfellow,
Whom he hath dull'd and cloy'd with gracious favours,
That he should, for a foreign purse, so sell
His sovereign's life to death and treachery.
Henry V, Act ii, sc. 2, l. 8 [EXETER]

559 Would it not grieve an able man to leave
So sweet a bedfellow?
Henry VIII, Act ii, sc 2, l. 142 [KING HENRY]

560   The beauty of this sinful dame
Made many princes hither frame,
To seek her as a bedfellow,
In marriage-pleasures play-fellow.
Pericles, Act i, Gower, l. 31 [GOWER]

561   Young budding virgin, fair and fresh and sweet,
Whither away, or where is thy abode?
Happy the parents of so fair a child;
Happier the man, whose favourable stars
Allot thee for his lovely bedfellow!
The Taming of the Shrew, Act iv, sc. 5, l. 37 [KATHARINA]

Bee

562   WARWICK: The prince will in the perfectness of time
Cast off his followers. . . .
KING: 'Tis seldom when the bee doth leave her comb
In the dead carrion.
II Henry IV, Act iv, sc. 4, l. 74 [WARWICK]

563   So work the honey-bees,
Creatures that by a rule in nature teach
The act of order to a peopled kingdom.
They have a king and officers of sorts;
Where some, like magistrates, correct at home,
Others, like merchants, venture trade abroad,
Others, like soldiers, armed in their stings,
Make boot upon the summer's velvet buds,
Which pillage they with merry march bring home
To the tent-royal of their emperor;
Who, busied in his majesty, surveys
The singing masons building roofs of gold,
The civil citizens kneading up the honey,
The poor mechanic porters crowding in
Their heavy burdens at his narrow gate,
The sad-eyed justice, with his surly hum,
Delivering o'er to executioners pale,
The lazy yawning drone.
Henry V, Act i, sc. 2, l. 187 [CANTERBURY]

564   The commons, like an angry hive of bees
That want their leader, scatter up and down
And care not who they sting in his revenge.
II Henry VI, Act iii, sc. 2, l. 125 [WARWICK]

565   Is not this a lamentable thing, that of the skin of an innocent
lamb should be made parchment? that parchment, being scribbled
o'er, should undo a man? Some say the bee stings: but I say, 'tis
the bee's wax.
II Henry VI, Act iv, sc. 2, l. 85 [CADE]

566   The honey-bags steal from the humble-bees,
And for night-tapers crop their waxen thighs.
A Midsummer Night's Dream, Act iii, sc. 1, l. 171 [TITANIA]

567   Kill a red-hipped humble-bee on the top of a thistle; and, good
monsieur, bring me the honey-bag.
A Midsummer Night's Dream, Act iv, sc. 1, l. 11 [BOTTOM]

568   The old bees die, the young possess their hive.
The Rape of Lucrece, l. 1769 [LUCRETIUS]

569   Where the bee sucks, there suck I:
In a cowslip's bell I lie;
There I couch when owls do cry.
On the bat's back I do fly
After summer merrily.
Merrily, merrily shall I live now
Under the blossom that hangs on the bough.
The Tempest, Act v, sc. 1, l. 88 [ARIEL]

570   Full merrily the humble-bee doth sing,
Till he hath lost his honey and his sting;
And being once subdued in armed tail,
Sweet honey and sweet notes together fail.
Troilus and Cressida, Act v, sc. 10, l. 42 [PANDARUS]

Beer

571   Doth it not show vilely in me to desire small beer? . . . By my
troth, I do now remember the poor creature, small beer.
II Henry IV, Act ii, sc. 2, l. 7 [PRINCE]

572   There shall be in England seven halfpenny loaves sold for a penny:
the three-hooped pot shall have ten hoops; and I will make it a
felony to drink small beer.
II Henry VI, Act iv, sc. 2, l. 71 [CADE]

573   She that could think and ne'er disclose her mind,
See suitors following and not look behind,
She was a wight, if ever such wight were, . . .
To suckle fools and chronicle small beer.
Othello, Act ii, sc. 1, l. 157 [IAGO]

Beetle

574   Often, to our comfort, shall we find
The sharded beetle in a safer hold
Than is the full-wing'd eagle.
Cymbeline, Act iii, sc. 3, l. 19 [BELARIUS]

575   If I do, fillip me with a three-man beetle.
II Henry IV, Act i, sc. 2, l. 255 [FALSTAFF]
(A three-man beetle was a ram or stomper so heavy it required
three men to handle it.)

576   The poor beetle, that we tread upon,
In corporal sufferance finds a pang as great
As when a giant dies.
Measure for Measure, Act iii, sc. 1, l. 79 [ISABELLA]

Beggar

577   I am not furnished like a beggar, therefore to beg will not become
me: my way is to conjure you.
As You Like It, Epilogue, l. 10 [ROSALIND]

578   Beggary is valiant.
II Henry VI, Act iv, sc. 2, l. 59 [SMITH]

579   The adage must be verified,
That beggars mounted run their horse to death.
III Henry VI, Act i, sc. 4, l. 126 [YORK]

580   Whiles I am a beggar, I will rail
And say there is no sin but to be rich;
And being rich, my virtue then shall be
To say there is no vice but beggary.
King John, Act ii, sc. 1, l. 593 [BASTARD]

581   Is it a beggar-man? . . .
He has some reason, else he could not beg.
I' the last night's storm I such a fellow saw;
Which made me think a man a worm.
King Lear, Act iv, sc. 1, l. 31 [GLOUCESTER]

582   He would mouth with a beggar, though she smelt brown bread
and garlic.
Measure for Measure, Act iii, sc. 2, l. 194 [LUCIO]

583 I see, sir, you are liberal in offers:
You taught me first to beg; and now methinks
You teach me how a beggar should be answer'd.
The Merchant of Venice, Act iv, sc. 1, l. 438 [PORTIA]

584 What fond beggar, but to touch the crown,
Would with the sceptre straight be strucken down?
The Rape of Lucrece, l. 216 [TARQUIN]

585 DUCHESS: Speak with me, pity me, open the door:
A beggar begs that never begg'd before.
BOLINGBROKE: Our scene is alter'd from a serious thing,
And now changed to 'The Beggar and the King.'
Richard II, Act v, sc. 3, l. 77 [DUCHESS]

Begging

586 What, wouldst you have me go and beg my food?
Or with a base and boisterous sword enforce
A thievish living on the common road?
This I must do, or know not what to do:
Yet this I will not do, do how I can.
As You Like It, Act ii, sc. 3, l. 31 [ORLANDO]

587 The gods begin to mock me. I, that now
Refused most princely gifts, am bound to beg.
Coriolanus, Act i, sc. 10, l. 79 [CORIOLANUS]

588 'Twas never my desire yet to trouble the poor with begging.
Coriolanus, Act ii, sc. 3, l. 75 [CORIOLANUS]

589 What! a young knave, and begging! Is there not wars? is there not
employment? doth not the king lack subjects? do not the rebels
need soldiers? Though it be a shame to be on any side but one,
it is worse shame to beg than to be on the worst side.
II Henry IV, Act i, sc. 2, l. 84 [FALSTAFF]

Beginning and End

590   To-night,
When I should take possession of the bride,
[I'll] End ere I do begin.
All's Well that Ends Well, Act ii, sc. 5, l. 28 [BERTRAM]

591 O, make an end Of what I have begun. . . .
Let him that loves me strike me dead.
Antony and Cleopatra, Act iv, sc. 14, l. 106 [ANTONY]

592 I will tell you the beginning; and . . . you may see the end.
As You Like It, Act i, sc. 2, l. 119 [LE BEAU]

593   The other course
Will prove too bloody, and the end of it
Unknown to the beginning.
Coriolanus, Act iii, sc. 1, l. 327 [SENATOR]

594   There to end
Where he was to begin, . . . this admits no excuse.
Coriolanus, Act v, sc. 6, l. 65 [LORD]

595 Orderly to end where I begun.
Hamlet, Act iii, sc. 2, l. 220 [PLAYER KING]

596 Where I did begin, there shall I end.
Julius Cæsar, Act v, sc. 3, l. 24 [CASSIUS]

597 Lo, all these trophies of affections hot, . . .
Nature hath charged me that I hoard them not,
But yield them up where I myself must render,
That is, to you, my origin and ender.
A Lover's Complaint, l. 218

598   To show our simple skill,
      This is the true beginning of our end.
          A Midsummer Night's Dream, Act v, sc. 1, l. 110 [QUINCE]

599   Good uncle, let this end where it begun.
                 Richard II, Act i, sc. 1, l. 158 [KING RICHARD]

600   You always end ere you begin.
         The Two Gentlemen of Verona, Act ii, sc. 4, l. 31 [VALENTINE]

601   Even so she kissed his brow, his cheek, his chin,
      And where she ends she doth anew begin.
                         Venus and Adonis, l. 59

Behaviour

602   Love all, trust a few, Do wrong to none.
           All's Well that Ends Well, Act i, sc. 1, l. 73 [COUNTESS]

603   Your behaviour hath struck her into amazement and admiration.
              Hamlet, Act iii, sc. 2, l. 339 [ROSENCRANTZ]

604   Have more than thou showest,
           Speak less than thou knowest,
           Lend less than thou owest,
           Ride more than thou goest,
           Learn more than thou trowest,
           Set less than thou throwest;
           Leave thy drink and thy whore,
           And keep in-a-door,
           And thou shalt have more
           Than two tens to a score.
                King Lear, Act i, sc. 4, l. 131 [FOOL]

605   All his behaviours did make their retire
      To the court of his eye, peeping through desire.
          Love's Labour's Lost, Act ii, sc. 1, l. 234 [BOYET]

606   If I do not put on a sober habit,
      Talk with respect and swear but now and then,
      Wear prayer-books in my pocket, look demurely,
      Nay more, when grace is saying, hood mine eyes
      Thus with my hat, and sigh and say 'amen,'
      Use all the observance of civility,
      Like one well studied in a sad ostent
      To please his grandam, never trust me more.
          The Merchant of Venice, Act ii, sc. 2, l. 199 [GRATIANO]

607   What an unweighed behaviour hath this Flemish drunkard picked
      —with the devil's name!—out of my conversation, that he dares
      in this manner assay me?
          The Merry Wives of Windsor, Act ii, sc. 1, l. 23 [MRS. PAGE]

608   There is a fair behaviour in thee, captain;
      And thou that nature with a beauteous wall
      Doth oft close in pollution, yet of thee
      I will believe thou hast a mind that suits
      With this thy fair and outward character.
          Twelfth Night, Act i, sc. 2, l. 47 [VIOLA]

609   He has been yonder i' the sun practising behaviour to his own
      shadow this half hour.
          Twelfth Night, Act ii, sc. 5, l. 19 [MARIA]

610   The behaviour of the young gentleman gives him out to be of
      good capacity and breeding.
          Twelfth Night, Act iii, sc. 4, l. 203 [SIR TOBY]

Bell

611   Let's mock the midnight bell.
          Antony and Cleopatra, Act iii, sc. 13, l. 185 [ANTONY]

We have heard the chimes at midnight, Master Shallow.
II Henry IV, Act iii, sc. 2, l. 229 [FALSTAFF]
              The midnight bell
Did, with his iron tongue and brazen mouth,
Sound on into the drowsy race of night.
King John, Act iii, sc. 3, l. 37 [KING JOHN]

612 Why ring not out the bells aloud throughout the town?
Dauphin, command the citizens make bonfires
And feast and banquet in the open streets,
To celebrate the joy that God hath given us.
I Henry VI, Act i, sc. 6, l. 11 [REIGNIER]
Ring, bells, aloud; burn, bonfires, clear and bright,
To entertain great England's lawful king.
Ah! sancta majestas, who would not buy thee dear?
II Henry VI, Act v, sc. 1, l. 3 [YORK]

613   A warning bell
Sings heavy music to thy timorous soul;
And mine shall ring thy dire departure out.
I Henry VI, Act iv, sc. 2, l. 39 [GENERAL]

614   I'll startle you
Worse than the sacring bell, when the brown wench
Lay kissing in your arms, lord cardinal.
Henry VIII, Act iii, sc. 2, l. 294 [SURREY]

615 Bell, book, and candle shall not drive me back,
When gold and silver becks me to come on.
King John, Act iii, sc. 3, l. 12 [BASTARD]
("Bell, book, and candle" refers to a form of excommunication
introduced into the Roman Catholic Church in the 8th century,
which ended with the words, "Doe to the book, quench the
candle, ring the bell!")

616   The bell invites me.
Hear it not, Duncan; for it is a knell
That summons thee to heaven or to hell.
Macbeth, Act ii, sc. 1, l. 62 [MACBETH]

617 Silence that dreadful bell: it frights the isle
From her propriety.
Othello, Act ii, sc. 3, l. 175 [OTHELLO]

Belly

618 There was a time when all the body's members
Rebell'd against the belly, thus accused it:
That only like a gulf it did remain
I' the midst o' the body, idle and inactive,
Still cupboarding the viand, never bearing
Like labour with the rest. . . . The belly answer'd: . . .
'True it is, my incorporate friends,' quoth he,
'That I receive the general food at first,
Which you do live upon; and fit it is,
Because I am the store-house and the shop
Of the whole body: but, if you do remember,
I send it through the rivers of your blood,
Even to the court, the heart, to the seat o' the brain;
And . . . the strongest nerves, and small inferior veins
From me receive that natural competency
Whereby they live.'
Coriolanus, Act i, sc. 1, l. 99 [MENENIUS]

619 An I had but a belly of any indifferency, I were simply the most
active fellow in Europe; my womb, my womb, my womb undoes me.
II Henry IV, Act iv, sc. 3, l. 23 [FALSTAFF]

620 My belly's as cold as if I had swallowed snowballs for pills to cool
the reins.
The Merry Wives of Windsor, Act iii, sc. 5, l. 23 [FALSTAFF]

621 No barricado for a belly.
The Winter's Tale, Act i, sc. 2, l. 204 [LEONTES]

Benedick

622 O Lord, he will hang upon him like a disease: he is sooner caught
than the pestilence, and the taker runs presently mad. God help the
noble Claudio! if he have caught the Benedick, it will cost him a
thousand pound ere a' be cured.
Much Ado about Nothing, Act i, sc. 1, l. 86 [BEATRICE]

623 Let them signify under my sign 'Here you may see Benedick the
married man.'
Much Ado about Nothing, Act i, sc. 1, l. 269 [BENEDICK]

624 DON PEDRO: When shall we set the savage bull's horns on the
sensible Benedick's head?
CLAUDIO: Yea, and text underneath, 'Here dwells Benedick the
married man'?
Much Ado about Nothing, Act v, sc. 1, l. 183 [DON PEDRO]

625 DON PEDRO: How dost thou, Benedick, the married man?
BENEDICK: I'll tell thee what, prince; a college of wit-crackers
cannot flout me out of my humour. Dost thou think I care for a
satire or an epigram?
Much Ado about Nothing, Act v, sc. 4, l. 100 [DON PEDRO]

Benefits

626   Freeze, freeze, thou bitter sky,
        That dost not bite so nigh
          As benefits forgot:
        Though thou the waters warp,
        Thy sting is not so sharp
          As friend remember'd not.
As You Like It, Act ii, sc. 7, l. 184 [AMIENS]

627 When these so noble benefits shall prove
Not well disposed, the mind growing more corrupt,
They turn to vicious forms, ten times more ugly
Than ever they were fair.
Henry VIII, Act i, sc. 2, l. 115 [KING HENRY]

Bermoothes

628 Thou call'dst me up at midnight to fetch dew
From the still-vexed Bermoothes.
The Tempest, Act i, sc. 2, l. 228 [ARIEL]

Besonian

629 Under which king, Besonian? speak, or die.
II Henry IV, Act v, sc. 3, l. 117 [PISTOL]
("Besonian," from the Spanish *bisoño*, raw, undisciplined, or
perhaps from the Italian, *bisogno*, need, want: applied to raw
recruits from Spain who landed in Italy ragged and poverty-
stricken; a needy beggar, a term of contempt.)

630 Great men oft die by vile bezonians:
A Roman sworder and banditto slave
Murder'd sweet Tully; Brutus' bastard hand

Stabb'd Julius Cæsar; savage islanders
Pompey the Great.
> *II Henry VI*, Act iv, sc. 1, l. 134 [SUFFOLK]

Best

631 The best is yet to do.
> *As You Like It*, Act i, sc. 2, l. 122 [LE BEAU]

632 That we did, we did for the best.
> *Coriolanus*, Act iv, sc. 6, l. 144 [CITIZEN]

633 Let's make the best of it.
> *Coriolanus*, Act v, sc. 6, l. 148 [LORD]

634 Let each man do his best.
> *I Henry IV*, Act v, sc. 2, l. 93 [HOTSPUR]

I'll do my best.
> *Pericles*, Act i, sc. 4, l. 20 [DIONYSIA]

635 I hope all's for the best.
> *III Henry VI*, Act iii, sc. 3, l. 170 [PRINCE]

I thought all for the best.
> *Romeo and Juliet*, Act iii, sc. 1, l. 109 [ROMEO]

636 BIRON: This is not so well as I looked for, but the best that ever
I heard.
KING: Ay, the best for the worst.
> *Love's Labour's Lost*, Act i, sc. 1, l. 280 [BIRON]

637 All have done well, But you the best.
> *Pericles*, Act ii, sc. 3, l. 109 [SIMONIDES]

638 LUCETTA: Pardon, dear madam: 'tis a passing shame
That I, unworthy body as I am,
Should censure thus on lovely gentlemen.
JULIA: Why not on Proteus, as of all the rest?
LUCETTA: Then thus: of many good I think him best.
> *The Two Gentlemen of Verona*, Act i, sc. 2, l. 17 [LUCETTA]

639 Great Apollo, Turn all to the best.
> *The Winter's Tale*, Act iii, sc. 1, l. 15 [CLEOMENES]

Better

640 When workmen strive to do better than well,
They do confound their skill in covetousness.
> *King John*, Act iv, sc. 2, l. 28 [PEMBROKE]

641 Striving to better, oft we mar what's well.
> *King Lear*, Act i, sc. 4, l. 369 [ALBANY]

Betters

642 CORIN: Who calls?
TOUCHSTONE: Your betters, sir.
CORIN: Else are they very wretched.
> *As You Like It*, Act ii, sc. 4, l. 68 [CORIN]

643 Our country manners give our betters way.
> *King John*, Act i, sc. 1, l. 156 [BASTARD]

644 When we our betters see bearing our woes,
We scarcely think our miseries our foes.
> *King Lear*, Act iii, sc. 6, l. 109 [EDGAR]

Bird

645 You have simply misused our sex in your love-prate: we must have
your doublet and hose plucked over your head, and show the world
what the bird hath done to her own nest.
> *As You Like It*, Act iv, sc. 1, l. 206 [CELIA]

(A reference to the proverb, "'Tis an ill bird that fouls its own
nest," cited as early as 1400 by Thomas Hoccleve.)

646   Thou art a summer bird,
Which ever in the haunch of winter sings
The lifting up of day.
II Henry IV, Act iv, sc. 4, l. 91 [KING HENRY]

647   I heard a bird so sing,
Whose music, to my thinking, pleased the king.
II Henry IV, Act v, sc. 5, l. 113 [LANCASTER]

648 My ashes, as the phœnix, may bring forth
A bird that will revenge upon you all.
III Henry VI, Act i, sc. 4, l. 35 [YORK]

649 Of their feather many moe proud birds.
III Henry VI, Act ii, sc. 1, l. 170 [WARWICK]

650 Both of you are birds of selfsame feather.
III Henry VI, Act iii, sc. 3, l. 161 [MARGARET]

651 The bird that hath been limed in a bush,
With trembling wings misdoubteth every bush.
III Henry VI, Act v, sc. 6, l. 13 [KING HENRY]

652 Poor bird! thou 'ldst never fear the net nor lime,
The pitfall nor the gin.
Macbeth, Act iv, sc. 2, l. 35 [LADY MACDUFF]
Birds never limed no secret bushes fear.
The Rape of Lucrece, l. 88

653 JULIET: 'Tis almost morning; I would have thee gone:
And yet no further than a wanton's bird;
Who lets it hop a little from her hand,
Like a poor prisoner in his twisted gyves,
And with a silk thread plucks it back again,
So loving-jealous of its liberty.
ROMEO: I would I were thy bird.
JULIET: Sweet, so would I:
Yet I should kill thee with much cherishing.
Romeo and Juliet, Act ii, sc. 2, l. 177 [JULIET]

654 Am I your bird? I mean to shift my bush;
And then pursue me as you draw your bow.
The Taming of the Shrew, Act v, sc. 2, l. 46 [BIANCA]

Birnam Wood

655 APPARITION: Be lion-mettled, proud; and take no care
Who chafes, who frets, or where conspirers are:
Macbeth shall never vanquish'd be until
Great Birnam wood to high Dunsinane hill
Shall come against him.
MACBETH: That will never be:
Who can impress the forest, bid the tree
Unfix his earth-bound root? Sweet bodements! good!
Rebellion's head, rise never till the wood
Of Birnam rise, and our high-placed Macbeth
Shall live the lease of nature, pay his breath
To time and mortal custom.
Macbeth, Act iv, sc. 1, l. 90 [APPARITION]

Birth

656 You were born under a charitable star.
All's Well that Ends Well, Act i, sc. 1, l. 205 [HELENA]
My nativity was under Ursa Major.
King Lear, Act i, sc. 2, l. 140 [EDMUND]
Being, as thou sayest thou art, born under Saturn.
Much Ado about Nothing, Act i, sc. 3, l. 11 [DON JOHN]

Were we not born under Taurus?
Twelfth Night, Act i, sc. 3, l. 147 [Sir Toby]

657 His greatness weigh'd, his will is not his own,
For he himself is subject to his birth:
He may not, as unvalued persons do,
Carve for himself; for on his choice depends
The safety and the health of this whole state.
Hamlet, Act i, sc. 3, l. 17 [Laertes]

658 Their birth—wherein they are not guilty,
Since nature cannot choose his origin.
Hamlet, Act i, sc. 4, l. 25 [Hamlet]

659 Glendower: At my nativity
The front of heaven was full of fiery shapes,
Of burning cressets; and at my birth
The frame and huge foundation of the earth
Shaked like a coward. . . .
Hotspur: The earth was not of my mind,
If you suppose as fearing you it shook.
Glendower: The heavens were all on fire, the earth did tremble.
Hotspur: O, then the earth shook to see the heavens on fire,
And not in fear of your nativity. . . .
Glendower: Give me leave
To tell you once again that at my birth
The front of heaven was full of fiery shapes,
The goats ran from the mountains, and the herds
Were strangely clamorous to the frighted fields.
These signs have mark'd me extraordinary;
And all the courses of my life do show
I am not in the roll of common men. . . .
Hotspur: There's no man speaks better Welsh. I'll to dinner.
I Henry IV, Act iii, sc. 1, l. 13 [Glendower]

660 I was born about three of the clock in the afternoon, with a white
head and something a round belly.
II Henry IV, Act i, sc. 2, l. 210 [Falstaff]

661 There was he born, under a hedge, for his father had never a
house but the cage.
II Henry VI, Act iv, sc. 2, l. 56 [Dick]

662 The owl shriek'd at thy birth,—an evil sign;
The night-crow cried, aboding luckless time;
Dogs howl'd, the hideous tempest shook down trees;
The raven rook'd her on the chimney's top,
And chattering pies in dismal discords sung. . . .
Teeth hadst thou in thy head when thou wast born,
To signify thou camest to bite the world.
III Henry VI, Act v, sc. 6, l. 44 [King Henry]

663 Hence, heap of wrath, foul indigested lump.
As crooked in thy manners as thy shape!
II Henry VI, Act v, sc. 2, l. 157 [Clifford]

664 Thy mother felt more than a mother's pain,
And yet brought forth less than a mother's hope,
To wit, an indigested and deformed lump,
Not like the fruit of such a goodly tree.
III Henry VI, Act v, sc. 6, l. 49 [King Henry]

665 I have often heard my mother say
I came into the world with my legs forward.
III Henry VI, Act v, sc. 6, l. 70 [Gloucester]

666   MACBETH: Let fall thy blade on vulnerable crests;
       I bear a charmed life, which must not yield
       To one of woman born.
       MACDUFF: Despair thy charm;
       And let the angel whom thou still hast served
       Tell thee, Macduff was from his mother's womb
       Untimely ripp'd.
                          Macbeth, Act v, sc. 8, 1. 11 [MACBETH]
                          I, that am . . .
       Deform'd, unfinish'd, sent before my time
       Into this breathing world, scarce half made up.
                          Richard III, Act i, sc. 1, 1. 16 [GLOUCESTER]
667   'Tis better to be lowly born,
       And range with humble livers in content,
       Than to be perk'd up in a glistering grief,
       And wear a golden sorrow.
                          Henry VIII, Act ii, sc. 3, 1. 19 [ANNE BULLEN]
668   We came crying hither:
       Thou know'st the first time that we smell the air,
       We wawl and cry. . . .
       When we are born, we cry that we are come
       To this great stage of fools.
                          King Lear, Act iv, sc. 6, 1. 182 [LEAR]
669   BEATRICE: I was born to speak all mirth and no matter.
       DON PEDRO: Out of question you were born in a merry hour. . . .
       BEATRICE: There was a star danced, and under that was I born.
                          Much Ado about Nothing, Act ii, sc. 1, 1. 343 [BEATRICE]
       I was not born under a rhyming planet.
                          Much Ado about Nothing, Act v, sc. 2, 1. 40 [BENEDICK]
       At their births good stars were opposite.
                          Richard III, Act iv, sc. 4, 1. 215 [KING RICHARD]
670   I have 't. It is engender'd. Hell and night
       Must bring this monstrous birth to the world's light.
                          Othello, Act i, sc. 3, 1. 409 [IAGO]
671   I was born so high,
       Our aery buildeth in the cedar's top,
       And dallies with the wind and scorns the sun.
                          Richard III, Act i, sc. 3, 1. 263 [GLOUCESTER]

Blab

672   Beaufort's red sparkling eyes blab his heart's malice.
                          II Henry VI, Act iii, sc. 1, 1. 154 [GLOUCESTER]
673   O, that delightful engine of her thoughts,
       That blabb'd them with such pleasing eloquence.
                          Titus Andronicus, Act iii, sc. 1, 1. 83 [MARCUS]
674   Why have I blabb'd? who shall be true to us,
       When we are so unsecret to ourselves?
                          Troilus and Cressida, Act iii, sc. 2, 1. 132 [CRESSIDA]
675   When my tongue blabs, then let mine eyes not see.
                          Twelfth Night, Act i, sc. 2, 1. 63 [CAPTAIN]

Blackness

676   [I] am with Phœbus' amorous pinches black.
                          Antony and Cleopatra, Act i, sc. 5, 1. 28 [CLEOPATRA]
677   They'll suck our breath or pinch us black and blue.
       The Comedy of Errors, Act ii, sc. 2, 1. 194 [DROMIO OF SYRACUSE]
       [She] is beaten black and blue.
       The Merry Wives of Windsor, Act iv, sc. 5, 1. 115 [MISTRESS QUICKLY]

We will fool him black and blue.
>   *Twelfth Night,* Act ii, sc. 5, l. 12 [Sir Toby]

678   Black, forsooth; coal-black as jet.
>   *II Henry VI,* Act ii, sc. 1, l. 112 [Simpcox]

As black As if besmear'd in hell.
>   *Henry VIII,* Act i, sc. 2, l. 121 [King Henry]

679   King: By heaven, thy love is black as ebony.
Biron: Is ebony like her? O wood divine!
A wife of such wood were felicity. . . .
King: O paradox! Black is the badge of hell,
The hue of dungeons and the suit of night. . . .
Biron: O, if in black my lady's brows be deck'd,
It mourns that painting and usurping hair
Should ravish doctors with a false aspect;
And therefore is she born to make black fair.
>   *Love's Labour's Lost,* Act iv, sc. 3, l. 247 [King]

680   The starry welkin cover thou anon
With drooping fog as black as Acheron.
>   *A Midsummer Night's Dream,* Act iii, sc. 2, l. 356 [Oberon]

681   If she be black, and thereto have a wit,
She'll find a white that shall her blackness fit.
>   *Othello,* Act ii, sc. 1, l. 133 [Iago]

682   Is black so base a hue? . . .
Coal-black is better than another hue,
In that it scorns to bear another hue;
For all the water in the ocean
Can never turn the swan's black legs to white,
Although she lave them hourly in the flood.
>   *Titus Andronicus,* Act iv, sc. 2, l. 71 [Aaron]

683   Where the bull and cow are both milk-white,
They never do beget a coal-black calf.
>   *Titus Andronicus,* Act v, sc. 1, l. 31 [Goth]

Blemish

684   Read not my blemishes in the world's report:
I have not kept my square; but that to come
Shall all be done by the rule.
>   *Antony and Cleopatra,* Act ii, sc. 3, l. 5 [Antony]

685   In nature there's no blemish but the mind.
>   *Twelfth Night,* Act iii, sc. 4, l. 401 [Antonio]

686   Whilst I remember
Her and her virtues, I cannot forget
My blemishes in them.
>   *The Winter's Tale,* Act v, sc. 1, l. 8 [Leontes]

Blessing

687   Let all the number of the stars give light
To thy fair way!
>   *Antony and Cleopatra,* Act iii, sc. 2, l. 65 [Lepidus]

688   Flow, flow, You heavenly blessings, on her!
>   *Cymbeline,* Act iii, sc. 5, l. 167 [Pisanio]

689   The benediction of these covering heavens
Fall on their heads like dew! for they are worthy
To inlay heaven with stars.
>   *Cymbeline,* Act v, sc. 5, l. 350 [Belarius]

The dews of heaven fall thick in blessings on her!
>   *Henry VIII,* Act iv, sc. 2, l. 133 [Katharine]

690   A double blessing is a double grace.
Hamlet, Act i, sc. 3, l. 53 [LAERTES]

691   The heavens thee guard and keep, most royal imp of fame!
II Henry IV, Act v, sc. 5, l. 45 [PISTOL]

692   Blessings on him: may he live
Longer than I have time to tell his years!
Henry VIII, Act ii, sc. 1, l. 90 [BUCKINGHAM]

693   Upon this land a thousand thousand blessings,
Which time shall bring to ripeness.
Henry VIII, Act v, sc. 5, l. 20 [CRANMER]

694   Bless thee from whirlwinds, star-blasting, and taking!
King Lear, Act iii, sc. 4, l. 60 [EDGAR]

695   A pack of blessings lights upon thy back;
Happiness courts thee in her best array:
But, like a misbehaved and sullen wench,
Thou pout'st upon thy fortune and thy love:
Take heed, take heed, for such die miserable.
Romeo and Juliet, Act iii, sc. 3, l. 142 [FRIAR LAURENCE]

696   JUNO: Honour, riches, marriage-blessing,
Long continuance, and increasing,
Hourly joys be still upon you!
Juno sings her blessings on you.
CERES: Earth's increase and foison plenty,
Barns and garners never empty; . . .
Scarcity and want shall shun you;
Ceres' blessing so is on you.
The Tempest, Act iv, sc. 1, l. 106 [JUNO]

697   The best of happiness,
Honour and fortunes keep with you!
Timon of Athens, Act i, sc. 2, l. 234 [LORD]

698   The gentleness of all the gods go with thee!
Twelfth Night, Act ii, sc. 1, l. 45 [ANTONIO]

699   You gods, look down
And from your sacred vials pour your graces
Upon my daughter's head!
The Winter's Tale, Act v, sc. 3, l. 122 [HERMIONE]

Blindness

700   Forsooth, a blind man at Saint Alban's shrine,
Within this half-hour, hath received his sight;
A man that ne'er saw in his life before.
II Henry VI, Act ii, sc. 1, l. 63 [TOWNSMAN]

701   Now you strike like the blind man: 'twas the boy that stole your
meat, and you'll beat the post.
Much Ado about Nothing, Act ii, sc. 1, l. 205 [BENEDICK]

Blood See also **Flesh and Blood**

702   Does it curd thy blood To say I am thy mother?
All's Well that Ends Well, Act i, sc. 3, l. 155 [COUNTESS]
Come, you spirits, . . . make thick my blood.
Macbeth, Act i, sc. 5, l. 44 [LADY MACBETH]

703   Strange is it that our bloods,
Of colour, weight, and heat, pour'd all together,
Would quite confound distinction, yet stand off
In differences so mighty.
All's Well that Ends Well, Act ii, sc. 3, l. 124 [KING]

There is more difference . . . between your bloods than there is
between red wine and rhenish.

> *The Merchant of Venice,* Act iii, sc. 1, l. 43 [SALARINO]

704   Many will swoon when they do look on blood.

> *As You Like It,* Act iv, sc. 3, l. 159 [OLIVER]

I . . . scarce ever look'd on blood,
Save that of coward hares, hot goats, and venison!

> *Cymbeline,* Act iv, sc. 4, l. 36 [ARVIRAGUS]

705   From face to foot
He was a thing of blood, whose every motion
Was timed with dying cries.

> *Coriolanus,* Act ii, sc. 2, l. 112 [COMINIUS]

Head to foot
Now is he total gules ; horridly trick'd
With blood of fathers, mothers, daughters, sons.

> *Hamlet,* Act ii, sc. 2, l. 478 [HAMLET]

From helmet to the spur all blood he was.

> *Henry V,* Act iv, sc. 6, l. 6 [KING HENRY]

706   For my country I have shed my blood,
Nor fearing outward force.

> *Coriolanus,* Act iii, sc. 1, l. 76 [CORIOLANUS]

The blood he hath lost—
Which, I dare vouch, is more than that he hath,
By many an ounce—he dropp'd it for his country.

> *Coriolanus,* Act iii, sc. 1, l. 299 [MENENIUS]

707   • I do know
When the blood burns, how prodigal the soul
Lends the tongue vows : these blazes, daughter,
Giving more light than heat, extinct in both,
Even in their promise, as it is a-making,
You must not take for fire.

> *Hamlet,* Act i, sc. 3, l. 115 [POLONIUS]

708   At your age
The hey-day in the blood is tame, it 's humble,
And waits upon the judgement. . . . What devil was 't
That thus hath cozen'd you at hoodman-blind?

> *Hamlet,* Act iii, sc. 4, l. 68 [HAMLET]

709   My blood hath been too cold and temperate,
Unapt to stir at these indignities.

> *I Henry IV,* Act i, sc. 3, l. 1 [KING HENRY]

Can sodden water . . .
Decoct their cold blood to such valiant heat?
And shall our quick blood, spirited with wine,
Seem frosty?

> *Henry V,* Act iii, sc. 5, l. 18 [CONSTABLE]

710   I'll empty all these veins,
And shed my dear blood drop by drop in the dust.

> *I Henry IV,* Act i, sc. 3, l. 133 [HOTSPUR]

711   They never prick their finger but they say, 'There 's some of the
king's blood spilt.'

> *II Henry IV,* Act ii, sc. 2, l. 122 [POINS]

Thy fierce hand
Hath with the king's blood stain'd the king's own land.

> *Richard II,* Act v, sc. 5, l. 110 [KING RICHARD]

712   The tide of blood in me
Hath proudly flow'd in vanity till now :
Now doth it turn and ebb back to the sea,

Where it shall mingle with the state of floods
And flow henceforth in formal majesty.
                    II Henry IV, Act v, sc. 2, l. 129 [HENRY V]

713   Never two such kingdoms did contend
Without much fall of blood; whose guiltless drops
Are every one a woe.
                    Henry V, Act i, sc. 2, l. 24 [KING HENRY]

714   One drop of blood drawn from thy country's bosom
Should grieve thee more than streams of foreign gore.
                    I Henry VI, Act iii, sc. 3, l. 54 [PUCELLE]

715   Contaminated, base,
And misbegotten blood I spill of thine,
Mean and right poor, for that pure blood of mine.
                    I Henry VI, Act iv, sc. 6, l. 21 [PUCELLE]

716   In that sea of blood my boy did drench
His over-mounting spirit, and there died.
                    I Henry VI, Act iv, sc. 7, l. 14 [TALBOT]

717   This thy son's blood cleaving to my blade
Shall rust upon my weapon, till thy blood,
Congeal'd with this, do make me wipe off both.
                    III Henry VI, Act i, sc. 3, l. 50 [CLIFFORD]

718   My soul to heaven, my blood upon your heads!
                    III Henry VI, Act i, sc. 4, l. 168 [YORK]

719   Their blood upon thy head.
                    III Henry VI, Act ii, sc. 2, l. 129 [WARWICK]

720   RICHARD: Thy brother's blood the thirsty earth hath drunk. . . .
WARWICK: Then let the earth be drunken with our blood.
                    III Henry VI, Act ii, sc. 3, l. 15 [RICHARD]

721   Blood hath bought blood and blows have answer'd blows;
Strength match'd with strength, and power confronted power.
                    King John, Act ii, sc. 1, l. 329 [CITIZEN]

722   Young blood doth not obey an old decree.
                    Love's Labour's Lost, Act iv, sc. 3, l. 217 [BIRON]

723   Here lay Duncan,
His silver skin laced with his golden blood;
And his gash'd stabs look'd like a breach in nature
For ruin's wasteful entrance.
                    Macbeth, Act ii, sc. 3, l. 117 [MACBETH]

724   Blood hath been shed ere now, i' the olden time,
Ere humane statute purged the gentle weal;
Ay, and since too, murders have been perform'd
Too terrible for the ear: the time has been,
That, when the brains were out, the man would die,
And there an end; but now they rise again,
With twenty mortal murders on their crowns,
And push us from our stools: this is more strange
Than such a murder is.
                    Macbeth, Act iii, sc. 4, l. 76 [MACBETH]

725   They say, blood will have blood:
Stones have been known to move and trees to speak;
Augurs and understood relations have
By maggot pies and choughs and rooks brought forth
The secret'st man of blood.
                    Macbeth, Act iii, sc. 4, l. 122 [MACBETH]

726   I am in blood
Stepp'd in so far that, should I wade no more,

Returning were as tedious as go o'er.
>   *Macbeth,* Act iii, sc. 4, 1. 135 [MACBETH]
>   I am in
> So far in blood that sin will pluck on sin.
>   *Richard III,* Act iv, sc. 2, 1. 64 [KING RICHARD]

727   Who would have thought the old man to have had so much blood
in him?
>   *Macbeth,* Act v, sc. 1, 1. 44 [LADY MACBETH]

728   Lord Angelo; a man whose blood
Is very snow-broth; one who never feels
The wanton stings and motions of the sense.
>   *Measure for Measure,* Act i, sc. 4, 1. 57 [LUCIO]

729   Blood, thou art blood: . . .
Why does my blood thus muster to my heart,
Making both it unable for itself,
And dispossessing all my other parts
Of necessary fitness?
>   *Measure for Measure,* Act ii, sc. 4, 1. 15 [ANGELO]

730   If thou hast slain Lysander in his sleep,
Being o'er shoes in blood, plunge in the deep,
And kill me too.
>   *A Midsummer Night's Dream,* Act iii, sc. 2, 1. 47 [HERMIA]

731   O, my lord, wisdom and blood combating in so tender a body, we
have ten proofs to one that blood hath the victory.
>   *Much Ado about Nothing,* Act ii, sc. 3, 1. 170 [LEONATO]

732   My blood begins my safer guides to rule.
>   *Othello,* Act ii, sc. 3, 1. 205 [OTHELLO]

733   My blood shall wash the slander of mine ill.
>   *The Rape of Lucrece,* 1. 1207 [LUCRECE]

734   Her blue blood changed to black in every vein.
>   *The Rape of Lucrece,* 1. 1454
> Some of her blood still pure and red remain'd,
> And some look'd black, and that false Tarquin stain'd.
>   *The Rape of Lucrece,* 1. 1742

735   Corrupted blood some watery token shows;
And blood untainted still doth red abide.
>   *The Rape of Lucrece,* 1. 1748

736   He did plot the Duke of Gloucester's death, . . .
Sluiced out his innocent soul through streams of blood:
Which blood, like sacrificing Abel's, cries
To me for justice and rough chastisement.
>   *Richard II,* Act i, sc. 1, 1. 100 [BOLINGBROKE]

737   Lords, I protest my soul is full of woe,
That blood should sprinkle me to make me grow.
>   *Richard II,* Act v, sc. 6, 1. 47 [BOLINGBROKE]

738   A knot you are of damned blood-suckers.
>   *Richard III,* Act iii, sc. 3, 1. 6 [GREY]

739   Unlawfully made drunk with innocents' blood!
>   *Richard III,* Act iv, sc. 4, 1. 30 [DUCHESS OF YORK]

740   Civil blood makes civil hands unclean.
>   *Romeo and Juliet,* Prologue, 1. 4

741   Now, these hot days, is the mad blood stirring.
>   *Romeo and Juliet,* Act iii, sc. 1, 1. 4 [BENVOLIO]

742   Friend or brother,
He forfeits his own blood that spills another.
>   *Timon of Athens,* Act iii, sc. 5, 1. 87 [SENATOR]

743　　　　　　　　Is your blood
So madly hot that no discourse of reason,
Nor fear of bad success in a bad cause,
Can qualify the same?
　　　　　　Troilus and Cressida, Act ii, sc. 2, l. 115 [HECTOR]

744　Our bloods are now in calm; and, so long, health!
　　　　　　Troilus and Cressida, Act iv, sc. 1, l. 16 [DIOMEDES]

745　Am I not consanguineous? am I not of her blood? Tillyvally.
　　　　　　Twelfth Night, Act ii, sc. 3, l. 82 [SIR TOBY]

Blow See also Word and Blow

746　Well struck! there was blow for blow.
　　　　　　The Comedy of Errors, Act iii, sc. 1, l. 58 [DROMIO OF EPHESUS]
Blows have answer'd blows.
　　　　　　King John, Act ii, sc. 1, l. 329 [CITIZEN]

747　Come, leave your drinking, and fall to blows.
　　　　　　II Henry VI, Act ii, sc. 3, l. 80 [SALISBURY]

748　Have at thee with a down-right blow.
　　　　　　II Henry VI, Act ii, sc. 3, l. 91 [HORNER]

749　Alas, how many bear such shameful blows,
Which not themselves, but he that gives them knows!
　　　　　　The Rape of Lucrece, l. 832 [LUCRECE]

750　Let thy blows, doubly redoubled,
Fall like amazing thunder on the casque
Of thy adverse pernicious enemy.
　　　　　　Richard II, Act i, sc. 3, l. 80 [GAUNT]

751　Gregory, remember thy swashing blow.
　　　　　　Romeo and Juliet, Act i, sc. 1, l. 68 [SAMPSON]

Blushing

752　The blushes in my cheeks thus whisper me,
'We blush that thou shouldst choose; but, be refused,
Let the white death sit on thy cheek forever;
We'll ne'er come there again.'
　　　　　　All's Well that Ends Well, Act ii, sc. 3, l. 75 [HELENA]

753　Thou blushest, Antony, and that blood of thine
Is Cæsar's homager; else so thy cheek pays shame
When shrill-tongued Fulvia scolds.
　　　　　　Antony and Cleopatra, Act i, sc. 1, l. 30 [CLEOPATRA]

754　　　　　　　　I will go wash,
And when my face is fair, you shall perceive
Whether I blush or no.
　　　　　　Coriolanus, Act i, sc. 9, l. 68 [CORIOLANUS]

755　Thou stolest a cup of sack eighteen years ago, and wert taken
with the manner, and ever since thou hast blushed extempore.
　　　　　　I Henry IV, Act ii, sc. 4, l. 246 [PRINCE]

756　Come, you virtuous ass, you bashful fool, must you be blushing?
wherefore blush you now? What a maidenly man-at-arms are
you become! Is 't such a matter to get a pottle-pot's maidenhead?
　　　　　　II Henry IV, Act ii, sc. 2, l. 79 [BARDOLPH]

757　I would assay, proud queen, to make thee blush, . . .
Wert thou not shameless.
　　　　　　III Henry VI, Act i, sc. 5, l. 118 [YORK]

758　SURREY: If you can blush, . . . You'll show a little honesty. . . .
WOLSEY: If I blush,
It is to see a nobleman want manners.
　　　　　　Henry VIII, Act iii, sc. 2, l. 305 [SURREY]

759   In him a plentitude of subtle matter,
Applied to cautels, all strange forms receives, . . .
To blush at speeches rank, to weep at woes,
Or to turn white and swoon at tragic shows.
A Lover's Complaint, l. 302

760   Lay by all nicety and prolixious blushes,
That banish what they sue for.
Measure for Measure, Act ii, sc. 4, l. 162 [ANGELO]

761   Behold how like a maid she blushes here! . . .
Comes not that blood as modest evidence
To witness simple virtue? Would you not swear
All you that see her, that she were a maid,
By these exterior shows? But she is none:
She knows the heat of a luxurious bed;
Her blush is guiltiness, not modesty.
Much Ado about Nothing, Act iv, sc. 1, l. 35 [CLAUDIO]

762   Their silent war of lilies and of roses.
The Rape of Lucrece, l. 71
Such war of red and white within her cheeks.
The Taming of the Shrew, Act iv, sc. 5, l. 30 [PETRUCHIO]

763   Thou know'st the mask of night is on my face,
Else would a maiden blush bepaint my cheek
For that which thou hast heard me speak to-night.
Fain would I dwell on form, fain, fain deny
What I have spoke: but farewell compliment! . . .
In truth, fair Montague, I am too fond,
And therefore thou mayst think my 'haviour light:
But trust me, gentleman, I'll prove more true
Than those that have more cunning to be strange.
Romeo and Juliet, Act ii, sc. 2, l. 85 [JULIET]

764   Fie, treacherous hue, that will betray with blushing
The close enacts and counsels of the heart!
Titus Andronicus, Act iv, sc. 2, l. 117 [AARON]

765   GOTH : What, canst thou say all this and never blush?
AARON : Ay, like a black dog, as the saying is.
Titus Andronicus, Act v, sc. 1, l. 121 [GOTH]

766   Bid the cheek be ready with a blush
Modest as the morning when she coldly eyes
The youthful Phœbus.
Troilus and Cressida, Act i, sc. 3, l. 228 [ÆNEAS]

767   Come, come, what need you blush? shame 's a baby.
Troilus and Cressida, Act iii, sc. 2, l. 42 [PANDARUS]

768   I think the boy hath grace in him, he blushes.
The Two Gentlemen of Verona, Act v, sc. 4, l. 165 [DUKE]

Boar

769   PRINCE: Is your master here in London?
BARDOLPH : Yes, my lord.
PRINCE: Where sups he? doth the old boar feed in the old frank?
II Henry IV, Act ii, sc. 2, l. 158 [PRINCE]

770   MESSENGER: [My master] dreamt to-night the boar had razed
his helm. . . .
HASTINGS : I wonder he is so fond
To trust the mockery of unquiet slumbers:
To fly the boar before the boar pursues,
Were to incense the boar to follow us
And make pursuit where he did mean no chase.
Richard III, Act iii, sc. 2, l. 11 [MESSENGER]

771   Where is your boar-spear, man?
Fear you the boar, and go so unprovided?
                        Richard III, Act iii, sc. 2, 1. 74 [HASTINGS]

772   That wretched, bloody, and usurping boar,
That spoiled your summer fields and fruitful vines,
Swills your warm blood like wash, and makes his trough
In your embowell'd bosom.
                        Richard III, Act v, sc. 2, 1. 7 [RICHMOND]

773   An angry-chafing boar,
Under whose sharp fangs on his back doth lie
An image like myself.
                        Venus and Adonis, 1. 662 [VENUS]

774   I felt a kind of fear
When as I met the boar, that bloody beast,
Which knows no pity, but is still severe.
                        Venus and Adonis, 1. 998 [VENUS]

775   This foul, grim, and urchin-snouted boar,
Whose downward eye still looketh for a grave.
                        Venus and Adonis, 1. 1105 [VENUS]

Board

776   Certain it is I liked her,
And boarded her i' the wanton way of youth.
                        All's Well that Ends Well, Act v, sc. 3, 1. 210 [BERTRAM]

777   BOYET: I was as willing to grapple as he was to board.
MARIA: Two hot sheeps, marry.
                        Love's Labour's Lost, Act ii, sc. 1, 1. 218 [BOYET]

778   MRS. PAGE: Unless he knew some strain in me, that I know not
myself, he would never have boarded me in this fury.
MRS. FORD: 'Boarding,' call you it? I'll be sure to keep him above
deck.
MRS. PAGE: So will I: if he come under my hatches, I'll never
to sea again.
                        The Merry Wives of Windsor, Act ii, sc. 1, 1. 90 [MRS. PAGE]

779   I will board her, though she chide as loud
As thunder when the clouds in autumn crack.
                        The Taming of the Shrew, Act i, sc. 2, 1. 95 [PETRUCHIO]

780   SIR TOBY: Accost, Sir Andrew, accost. . . .
SIR ANDREW: Good mistress Accost, I desire better acquaintance. . . .
SIR TOBY: You mistake, knight: 'accost' is front her, board her,
woo her, assail her.
                        Twelfth Night, Act i, sc. 3, 1. 52 [SIR TOBY]

Boat

781   My boat sails freely, both with wind and stream.
                        Othello, Act ii, sc. 3, 1. 65 [IAGO]

782   Her boat hath a leak, and she must not speak
Why she dares not come over to thee.
                        King Lear, Act iii, sc. 6, 1. 28 [FOOL]

783   A rotten carcass of a boat; . . . the very rats
Instinctively have quit it.
                        The Tempest, Act i, sc. 2, 1. 146 [PROSPERO]

784   Light boats sail swift, though greater hulks draw deep.
                        Troilus and Cressida, Act ii, sc. 3, 1. 277 [AGAMEMNON]

Body

785   This common body,
Like to a vagabond flag upon the stream,
Goes to and back, lackeying the varying tide,
To rot itself with motion.
Antony and Cleopatra, Act i, sc. 4, l. 44 [OCTAVIUS CÆSAR]

786 We do request your kindest ears, and after,
Your loving motion toward the common body.
Coriolanus, Act ii, sc. 2, l. 56 [SENATOR]

787   Let me twine
Mine arms about that body, where against
My grained ash an hundred times hath broke.
And scarr'd the moon with splinters.
Coriolanus, Act iv, sc. 5, l. 112 [AUFIDIUS]

788   What need I thus
My well-known body to anatomize
Among my household?
II Henry IV, Induction, l. 20 [RUMOUR]

789 Here I commit my body to your mercies.
II Henry IV, Epilogue, l. 16 [DANCER]

790 What is the body when the head is off?
III Henry VI, Act v, sc. 1, l. 41 [KING EDWARD]

791 By my troth, Nerissa, my little body is aweary of this great
world.
The Merchant of Venice, Act i, sc. 2, l. 1 [PORTIA]

792 I never knew so young a body with so old a head.
The Merchant of Venice, Act iv, sc. 1, l. 164 [CLERK]

793 Our bodies are our gardens, to which our wills are gardeners.
. . . Either to have it sterile with idleness, or manured with
industry.
Othello, Act i, sc. 3, l. 323 [IAGO]

794 Who cannot abuse a body dead?
The Rape of Lucrece, l. 1267 [LUCRECE]

Body and Soul

795   My body shall
Pay recompense, if you will grant my suit.
Cannot my body nor blood-sacrifice
Entreat you to your wonted furtherance?
Then take my soul, my body, soul and all.
I Henry VI, Act v, sc. 3, l. 18 [PUCELLE]

796 It were a pity but they should suffer salvation, body and soul.
Much Ado about Nothing, Act iii, sc. 3, l. 2 [VERGES]

797 Thou hadst but power over his mortal body,
His soul thou canst not have.
Richard III, Act i, sc. 2, l. 47 [ANNE]

798 My body or my soul, which was the dearer,
When the one pure, the other made divine?
The Rape of Lucrece, l. 1163 [LUCRECE]

799 Her body sleeps in Capels' monument,
And her immortal part with angels lives.
Romeo and Juliet, Act v, sc. 1, l. 18 [BALTHASAR]

Bohemia

800 A Bohemian born.
Measure for Measure, Act iv, sc. 2, l. 134 [PROVOST]

801   Bohemia. A desert country near the sea.
>   *The Winter's Tale,* Act iii, sc. 3 [STAGE DIRECTION]

802   Our ship hath touch'd upon The deserts of Bohemia.
>   *The Winter's Tale,* Act iii, sc. 3, l. 1 [ANTIGONUS]

Boldness

803   Boldness be my friend!
Arm me, audacity, from head to foot!
Or, like the Parthian, I shall flying fight.
>   *Cymbeline,* Act i, sc. 6, l. 18 [IACHIMO]

804   You call honourable boldness impudent sauciness: if a man will
make courtesy and say nothing, he is virtuous.
>   *II Henry IV,* Act ii, sc. 1, l. 134 [FALSTAFF]

805   That which hath made them drunk hath made me bold;
What hath quench'd them hath given me fire.
>   *Macbeth,* Act ii, sc. 2, l. 1 [LADY MACBETH]

806   Be bloody, bold, and resolute; laugh to scorn
The power of man, for none of woman born
Shall harm Macbeth.
>   *Macbeth,* Act iv, sc. 1, l. 78 [APPARITION]

807   What foolish boldness brought thee to their mercies,
Whom thou, in terms so bloody and so dear,
Hast made thine enemies?
>   *Twelfth Night,* Act v, sc. 1, l. 73 [DUKE]

808   Who is so faint, that dares not be so bold
To touch the fire, the weather being cold?
>   *Venus and Adonis,* l. 401 [VENUS]

Bond

809   SHYLOCK: Antonio, . . . a bankrupt, a prodigal; . . . let him
look to his bond: he was wont to call me usurer; let him look to
his bond: he was wont to lend money for a Christian courtesy;
let him look to his bond.
SALARINO: Why, I am sure, if he forfeit, thou wilt not take his
flesh; what's that good for?
SHYLOCK: To bait fish, withal: if it will feed nothing else, it will
feed my revenge.
>   *The Merchant of Venice,* Act iii, sc. 1, l. 48 [SHYLOCK]

810   I'll have my bond; speak not against my bond:
I have sworn an oath that I will have my bond.
>   *The Merchant of Venice,* Act iii, sc. 3, l. 4 [SHYLOCK]

811   By our holy Sabbath have I sworn
To have the due and forfeit of my bond.
>   *The Merchant of Venice,* Act iv, sc. 1, l. 36 [SHYLOCK]

812   My deeds upon my head! I crave the law,
The penalty and forfeit of my bond.
>   *The Merchant of Venice,* Act iv, sc. 1, l. 206 [SHYLOCK]

Bondage

813   Most welcome, bondage! for thou art a way,
I think, to liberty.
>   *Cymbeline,* Act v, sc. 4, l. 4 [POSTHUMUS]

814   I begin to find an idle and fond bondage in the oppression of
aged tyranny.
>   *King Lear,* Act i, sc. 2, l. 51 [GLOUCESTER, *reading*]

815   Bondage is hoarse, and may not speak aloud.
>   *Romeo and Juliet,* Act ii, sc. 2, l. 161 [JULIET]
(For full quotation see 2284.)

Bones

816 Did these bones cost no more the breeding, but to play at loggats
with 'em? mine ache to think on 't.
Hamlet, Act v, sc. 1, l. 99 [HAMLET]
("Loggats," an old game in which a stake is driven into the
ground and "loggats" or missiles are thrown at it. He that is
nearest the stake wins.)

817 Within my tent his bones to-night shall lie,
Most like a soldier, order'd honourably.
Julius Cæsar, Act v, sc. 5, l. 78 [ANTONY]

818 Beat not the bones of the buried.
Love's Labour's Lost, Act v, sc. 2, l. 666 [ARMADO]

819 Shut me nightly in a charnel-house,
O'er-covered quite with dead men's rattling bones.
Romeo and Juliet, Act iv, sc. 1, l. 81 [JULIET]

820 NURSE: Fie, how my bones ache! . . .
JULIET: I would thou hadst my bones, and I thy news.
Romeo and Juliet, Act ii, sc. 5, l. 26 [NURSE]

821 Is this a poultice for my aching bones?
Romeo and Juliet, Act ii, sc. 5, l. 65 [NURSE]

822 My old bones ache.
The Tempest, Act iii, sc. 3, l. 2 [GONZALO]

823 I feel 't upon my bones.
Timon of Athens, Act iii, sc. 6, l. 130 [LORD]

Book

824   A book? . . .
Be not, as is our fangled world, a garment
Nobler than that it covers.
Cymbeline, Act v, sc. 4, l. 133 [POSTHUMUS]

825 WORCESTER: Now I will unclasp a secret book,
And to your quick-conceiving discontents
I'll read you matter deep and dangerous,
As full of peril and adventurous spirit
As to o'er-walk a current roaring loud
On the unsteadfast footing of a spear.
HOTSPUR: If he fall in, good night! or sink or swim.
I Henry IV, Act i, sc. 3, l. 188 [WORCESTER]
            I have unclasp'd
To thee the book even of my secret soul.
Twelfth Night, Act i, sc. 4, l. 13 [DUKE]

826 A beggar's book Outworths a noble's blood.
Henry VIII, Act i, sc. 1, l. 122 [BUCKINGHAM]

827 You two are book-men.
Love's Labour's Lost, Act iv, sc. 2, l. 35 [DULL]

828 I had rather than forty shillings I had my Book of Songs and
Sonnets here.
The Merry Wives of Windsor, Act i, sc. 1, l. 205 [SLENDER]

829 MESSENGER: I see, lady, the gentleman is not in your books.
BEATRICE: No; an he were, I would burn my study.
Much Ado about Nothing, Act i, sc. 1, l. 78 [MESSENGER]
A herald, Kate? O, put me in thy books.
The Taming of the Shrew, Act ii, sc. 1, l. 225 [PETRUCHIO]

830 This precious book of love, this unbound lover,
To beautify him, only lacks a cover: . . .
That book in many's eyes doth share the glory
That in gold clasps locks in the golden story.
Romeo and Juliet, Act i, sc. 3, l. 87 [LADY CAPULET]

831   Knowing I loved my books, he furnish'd me
       From mine own library with volumes that
       I prize above my dukedom.
                    The Tempest, Act i, sc. 2, l. 166 [PROSPERO]
832   Deeper than did ever plummet sound
       I'll drown my book.
                    The Tempest, Act v, sc. 1, l. 56 [PROSPERO]

Boot

833   Norfolk, throw down, we bid; there is no boot.
                    Richard II, Act i, sc. 1, l. 164 [KING RICHARD]
834   I'll give you boot, I'll give you three for one.
                    Troilus and Cressida, Act iv, sc. 5, l. 40 [MENELAUS]
835   What an exchange had this been without boot! What a boot is
       here with this exchange!
                    The Winter's Tale, Act iv, sc. 4, l. 688 [AUTOLYCUS]

Borrowing and Lending See also Lending

836   Neither a borrower nor a lender be;
       For loan oft loses both itself and friend,
       And borrowing dulls the edge of husbandry.
                    Hamlet, Act i, sc. 3, l. 75 [POLONIUS]
837   Although I neither lend nor borrow
       By taking nor by giving of excess,
       Yet, to supply the ripe wants of my friend,
       I'll break a custom.
                    The Merchant of Venice, Act i, sc. 3, l. 62 [ANTONIO]
838   Methought you said you neither lend nor borrow
       Upon advantage.
                    The Merchant of Venice, Act i, sc. 3, l. 70 [SHYLOCK]
839   They say . . . he borrows money in God's name, the which he
       hath used so long and never paid that now men grow hard-hearted
       and will lend nothing for God's sake.
                    Much Ado about Nothing, Act v, sc. 1, l. 320 [DOGBERRY]
840   Lend to each man enough, that one need not lend to another; for
       were your godheads to borrow of men, men would forsake the
       gods. . . . Stay, I will lend thee money, borrow none.
                    Timon of Athens, Act iii, sc. 6, l. 82 [TIMON]

Bosom

841   Stall this in your bosom.
                    All's Well that Ends Well, Act i, sc. 3, l. 131 [COUNTESS]
842   I am in their bosoms, and I know
       Wherefore they do it.
                    Julius Cæsar, Act v, sc. 1, l. 7 [ANTONY]
843   I know you are of her bosom.
                    King Lear, Act iv, sc. 5, l. 26 [REGAN]
844   He did in the general bosom reign
       Of young, of old.
                    A Lover's Complaint, l. 127
845   The broken bosoms that to me belong
       Have emptied all their fountains in my well.
                    A Lover's Complaint, l. 254
846   Swell, bosom, with thy fraught,
       For 'tis of aspics' tongues!
                    Othello, Act iii, sc. 3, l. 449 [OTHELLO]
847   You have your father's bosom there
       And speak his very heart.
                    The Winter's Tale, Act iv, sc. 4, l. 573 [CAMILLO]

Bounty

848 SOLDIER: Enobarbus, Antony
Hath after thee sent all thy treasure, with
His bounty overplus. . . . Your emperor
Continues still a Jove. . . .
ENOBARBUS: O Antony,
Thou mine of bounty, how wouldst thou have paid
My better service, when my turpitude
Thou dost so crown with gold!
> *Antony and Cleopatra,* Act iv, sc. 6, l. 20 [SOLDIER]

849   For his bounty,
There was no winter in 't; an autumn 'twas
That grew the more by reaping.
> *Antony and Cleopatra,* Act v, sc. 2, l. 86 [CLEOPATRA]

850 I have . . . pared my present havings, to bestow
My bounties upon you. . . . As my hand has open'd bounty to you,
My heart dropp'd love.
> *Henry VIII,* Act iii, sc. 2, l. 159 [KING HENRY]

851 Which of you shall we say doth love us most?
That our largest bounty may extend
Where nature doth with merit challenge.
> *King Lear,* Act i, sc. 1, l. 52 [LEAR]

852 My bounty is as boundless as the sea,
My love as deep; the more I give thee
The more I have, for both are infinite.
> *Romeo and Juliet,* Act ii, sc. 2, l. 133 [JULIET]

853 Magic of bounty! All these spirits thy power
Hath conjured to attend.
> *Timon of Athens,* Act i, sc. 1, l. 6 [POET]

854 'Tis pity bounty had not eyes behind
That man might ne'er be wretched for his mind.
> *Timon of Athens,* Act i, sc. 2, l. 169 [FLAVIUS]

855 No villanous bounty yet hath pass'd my heart;
Unwisely, not ignobly, have I given.
> *Timon of Athens,* Act ii, sc. 2, l. 182 [TIMON]

856 Bounty, that makes gods, does still mar men.
> *Timon of Athens,* Act iv, sc. 2, l. 41 [FLAVIUS]

Bow

857 The bow is bent and drawn, make from the shaft.
> *King Lear,* Act i, sc. 1, l. 145 [LEAR]

858 That fellow handles his bow like a crow-keeper: draw me a
clothier's yard.
> *King Lear,* Act iv, sc. 6, l. 87 [LEAR]

859 He is no woodman that doth bend his bow
To strike a poor unseasonable doe.
> *The Rape of Lucrece,* l. 580 [LUCRECE]

860 Hold or cut bow-strings.
> *A Midsummer Night's Dream,* Act i, sc. 2, l. 114 [BOTTOM]

Bowels See also Guts

861 [He] bids you, in the bowels of the Lord,
Deliver up the crown.
> *Henry V,* Act ii, sc. 4, l. 102 [EXETER]

[He] rushed into the bowels of the battle.
> *I Henry VI,* Act i, sc. 1, l. 129 [MESSENGER]

Thus far into the bowels of the land
Have we march'd on without impediment.
> *Richard III,* Act v, sc. 2, l. 3 [RICHMOND]

862   Thine own bowels, which do call thee sire,
      The mere effusion of thy proper loins,
      Do curse the gout, serpigo, and the rheum,
      For ending thee no sooner.
                   Measure for Measure, Act iii, sc. 1, l. 29 [DUKE]
863   I will begin at thy heel, and tell what thou art by inches, thou thing
      of no bowels, thou!
                   Troilus and Cressida, Act ii, sc. 1, l. 53 [THERSITES]

Boy

864   Proud, scornful boy, unworthy this good gift;
      Thou dost in vile misprison shackle up
      My love and her desert.
                   All's Well that Ends Well, Act ii, sc. 3, l. 158 [KING]
      This is not well, rash and unbridled boy,
      To fly the favours of so good a king.
                   All's Well that Ends Well, Act iii, sc. 2, l. 30 [COUNTESS]
      Go, rate thy minions, proud insulting boy!
      Becomes it thee to be thus bold in terms
      Before thy sovereign and thy lawful king?
                   III Henry VI, Act ii, sc. 2, l. 84 [QUEEN MARGARET]
865   A foolish idle boy, but for all that very ruttish.
                   All's Well that Ends Well, Act iv, sc. 3, l. 243 [PAROLLES]
      'Tis but a peevish boy; yet he talks well.
                   As You Like It, Act iii, sc. 5, l. 110 [PHEBE]
      I scorn thee and thy fashion, peevish boy.
                   I Henry VI, Act ii, sc. 4, l. 76 [PLANTAGENET]
866   On each side her
      Stood pretty dimpled boys, like smiling Cupids.
                   Antony and Cleopatra, Act ii, sc. 3, l. 206 [ENOBARBUS]
867   That blind rascally boy that abuses every one's eyes because his
      own are out.
                   As You Like It, Act iv, sc. 1, l. 218 [ROSALIND]
868   The boy is fair,
      Of female favour, and bestows himself
      Like a ripe sister.
                   As You Like It, Act iv, sc. 3, l. 86 [OLIVER]
      O' my word, the father's son: I'll swear, 'tis a very pretty boy.
                   Coriolanus, Act i, sc. 3, l. 62 [VOLUMNIA]
869   This boy is forest-born,
      And hath been tutor'd in the rudiments
      Of many desperate studies by his uncle.
                   As You Like It, Act v, sc. 4, l. 30 [ORLANDO]
870   Look on the boy,
      And let his manly face . . . steel thy melting heart.
                   III Henry VI, Act ii, sc. 2, l. 39 [CLIFFORD]
871   O boy, thy father gave thee life too soon,
      And hath bereft thee of thy life too late!
                   III Henry VI, Act ii, sc. 5, l. 92 [FATHER]
872   Yon green boy shall have no sun to ripe
      The bloom that promiseth a mighty fruit.
                   King John, Act ii, sc. 1, l. 472 [ELINOR]
873   KING JOHN: Hubert, throw thine eye
      On yon young boy: I'll tell thee what, my friend,
      He is a very serpent in my way;
      And wheresoe'er this foot of mine doth tread,

He lies before me: dost thou understand me?
Thou art his keeper.
HUBERT: And I'll keep him so,
That he shall not offend your majesty.
KING JOHN: Death.
HUBERT: My lord?
KING JOHN: A grave.
HUBERT: He shall not live.
KING JOHN: Enough. I could be merry now.
                    King John, Act iii, sc. 3, l. 59 [KING JOHN]

874   Shall a beardless boy,
A cocker'd silken wanton, brave our fields,
And flesh his spirit in a warlike soil,
Mocking the air with colours idly spread,
And find no check? Let us, my liege, to arms.
                    King John, Act v, sc. 1, l. 69 [BASTARD]

875   The boy was the very staff of my age, my very prop.
                    The Merchant of Venice, Act ii, sc. 2, l. 69 [GOBBO]

876   Scrambling, out-facing, fashion-monging boys,
That lie and cog and flout, deprave and slander.
                    Much Ado about Nothing, Act v, sc. 1, l. 94 [ANTONIO]

877   Boys, with women's voices,
Strive to speak big and clap their female joints
In stiff unwieldy arms against thy crown.
                    Richard II, Act iii, sc. 2, l. 113 [SCROOP]

878   A parlous boy: go to, you are too shrewd.
                    Richard III, Act ii, sc. 4, l. 35 [ELIZABETH]

          O, 'tis a parlous boy;
Bold, quick, ingenious, forward, capable;
He is all the mother's, from the top to toe.
                    Richard III, Act iii, sc. 1, l. 154 [GLOUCESTER]

879   Go to, go to; you are a saucy boy.
                    Romeo and Juliet, Act i, sc. 5, l. 84 [CAPULET]

880   [He is] not yet old enough for a man, nor young enough for a boy;
as a squash is before 'tis a peascod, or a codling when 'tis almost
an apple: 'tis with him in standing water, between boy and man.
. . . One would think his mother's milk were scarce out of him.
                    Twelfth Night, Act i, sc. 5, l. 165 [MALVOLIO]

881   We were, fair queen,
Two lads that thought there was no more behind
But such a day to-morrow as to-day,
And to be boy eternal. . . .
We were as twinn'd lambs that did frisk i' the sun,
And bleat the one at the other: what we changed
Was innocence for innocence; we knew not
The doctrine of ill-doing, nor dream'd
That any did.
                    The Winter's Tale, Act i, sc. 2, l. 62 [POLIXENES]

882   Looking on the lines
Of my boy's face, methought I did recoil
Twenty-three years, and saw myself unbreech'd.
In my green velvet coat, my dagger muzzled,
Lest it should bite its master, and so prove,
As ornaments oft do, too dangerous:
How like, methought, I then was to this kernel,
This squash, this gentleman.
                    The Winter's Tale, Act i, sc. 2, l. 153 [LEONTES]

Brain

883 It's monstrous labour, when I wash my brain,
And it grows fouler.
Antony and Cleopatra, Act ii, sc. 7, l. 105 [CÆSAR]

884 Though grey
Do something mingle with our younger brown, yet ha' we
A brain that nourishes our nerves, and can
Get goal for goal of youth.
Antony and Cleopatra, Act iv, sc. 8, l. 19 [ANTONY]

885 In his brain,
Which is as dry as the remainder biscuit
After a voyage, he hath strange places cramm'd
With observation, the which he vents
In mangled forms.
As You Like It, Act ii, sc. 7, l. 38 [JAQUES]

886 Mine Italian brain
'Gan in your duller Britain operate
Most vilely.
Cymbeline, Act v, sc. 5, l. 196 [IACHIMO]

887 This brain of mine
Hunts not the trail of policy so sure
As it hath used to do.
Hamlet, Act ii, sc. 2, l. 46 [POLONIUS]

888 Cudgel thy brains no more about it.
Hamlet, Act v, sc. 1, l. 63 [CLOWN]

889 My brain more busy than the labouring spider
Weaves tedious snares to trap mine enemies.
II Henry VI, Act iii, sc. 1, l. 339 [YORK]

890 His pure brain,
Which some suppose the soul's frail dwelling-house,
Doth by the idle comments that it makes
Foretell the ending of mortality.
King John, Act v, sc. 7, l. 2 [PRINCE HENRY]

891 If a man's brains were in 's heels, were 't not in danger of kibes?
King Lear, Act i, sc. 5, l. 8 [FOOL]

892 If I be served another such trick, I'll have my brains ta'en out and
buttered, and give them to a dog for a new-year's gift.
The Merry Wives of Windsor, Act iii, sc. 5, l. 7 [FALSTAFF]

893 Have I laid my brain in the sun and dried it, that it wants matter
to prevent so gross o'er-reaching as this?
The Merry Wives of Windsor, Act v, sc. 5, l. 143 [FALSTAFF]

894 If a man will be beaten with brains, a' shall wear nothing handsome about him.
Much Ado about Nothing, Act v, sc. 4, l. 104 [BENEDICK]

895 My brain I'll prove the female to my soul,
My soul the father.
Richard II, Act v, sc. 5, l. 6 [KING RICHARD]

896 His brain as barren As banks of Libya.
Troilus and Cressida, Act i, sc. 3, l. 327 [NESTOR]

897 Thou hast no more brain than I have in mine elbows.
Troilus and Cressida, Act ii, sc. 1, l. 48 [THERSITES]

898 An honest fellow enough, and one that loves quails, but he has not
so much brain as ear-wax.
Troilus and Cressida, Act v, sc. 1, l. 57 [THERSITES]

Brand

899 Methinks the realms of England, France and Ireland
Bear that proportion to my flesh and blood

As did the fatal brand Althæa burn'd
Unto the prince's heart of Calydon.
II Henry VI, Act i, sc. 1, l. 234 [YORK]

900   He that parts us shall bring a brand from heaven,
And fire us hence like foxes.
King Lear, Act v, sc. 3, l. 22 [LEAR]

Breach

901   Once more into the breach, dear friends, once more;
Or close the wall up with our English dead.
Henry V, Act iii, sc. 1, l. 1 [KING HENRY]

902   BARDOLPH: On on! To the breach, to the breach!
NYM: Pray thee, corporal, stay, the knocks are too hot; and for
mine own part, I have not a case of lives. . . .
PISTOL: Knocks go and come; God's vassals drop and die.
Henry V, Act iii, sc. 2, l. 1 [BARDOLPH]

Breakfast

903   I will bestow a breakfast to make you friends.
Henry V, Act ii, sc. 1, l. 12 [BARDOLPH]

904   Thou livedst but as a breakfast to the wolf.
Timon of Athens, Act iv, sc. 3, l. 336 [TIMON]

905   Had I been seized by a hungry lion,
I would have been a breakfast to the beast,
Rather than have false Proteus rescue me.
The Two Gentlemen of Verona, Act v, sc. 4, l. 33 [SILVIA]

Breast

906   Till we call'd
Both field and city ours, he never stood
To ease his breast with panting.
Coriolanus, Act ii, sc. 2, l. 124 [COMINIUS]

907   Take notice, lords, he has a loyal breast,
For you have seen him open 't.
Henry VIII, Act iii, sc. 2, l. 200 [KING HENRY]

908   Who has a breast so pure,
But some uncleanly apprehensions
Keep leets and law-days and in session sit
With meditations lawful?
Othello, Act iii, sc. 3, l. 138 [IAGO]
("Leets," the days on which a manor court was held.)

Breath

909   They say poor suitors have strong breaths: they shall know we have
strong arms too.
Coriolanus, Act i, sc. 1, l. 62 [CITIZEN]

910   You and your apron-men; you that stood so much . . .
Upon . . . the breath of garlic-eaters!
Coriolanus, Act iv, sc. 6, l. 96 [MENENIUS]
Eat no onions nor garlic, for we are to utter sweet breath.
A Midsummer Night's Dream, Act iv, sc. 2, l. 41 [BOTTOM]

911   'Tis her breathing that Perfumes the chamber thus.
Cymbeline, Act ii, sc. 2, l. 18 [IACHIMO]
I saw her coral lips move
And with her breath she did perfume the air.
The Taming of the Shrew, Act i, sc. 1, l. 179 [LUCENTIO]

912   The heaven's breath Smells wooingly here.
Macbeth, Act i, sc. 6, l. 5 [BANQUO]

913 If her breath were as terrible as her terminations, there would be
no living near her ; she would infect to the north star.
> *Much Ado about Nothing,* Act ii, sc. 1, l. 256 [BENEDICK]

914 Ah, balmy breath, that doth almost persuade
Justice to break her sword! . . . So sweet was ne'er So fatal.
> *Othello,* Act v, sc. 2, l. 16 [OTHELLO]

915 Direct not him whose way himself will choose :
'Tis breath thou lack'st, and that breath wilt thou lose.
> *Richard II,* Act ii, sc. 1, l. 29 [YORK]

916 How art thou out of breath, when thou hast breath
To say to me that thou art out of breath?
> *Romeo and Juliet,* Act ii, sc. 5, l. 31 [JULIET]

917 SIR TOBY : A contagious breath.
SIR ANDREW : Very sweet and contagious, i' faith.
SIR TOBY : To hear by the nose, it is dulcet in contagion.
> *Twelfth Night,* Act ii, sc. 3, l. 55 [SIR TOBY]

918 She is not to be kissed fasting in respect of her breath.
> *The Two Gentlemen of Verona,* Act iii, sc. 1, l. 326 [SPEED]

919   Methinks
There is an air comes from her : what fine chisel
Could ever yet cut breath?
> *The Winter's Tale,* Act v, sc. 3, l. 77 [LEONTES]

Breeding

920 COUNTESS : Come on, sir ; I shall now put you to the height of your
breeding.
CLOWN : I will show myself highly fed and lowly taught.
> *All's Well that Ends Well,* Act ii, sc. 2, l. 1 [COUNTESS]

921   Much is breeding,
Which, like the courser's hair, hath yet but life,
And not a serpent's poison.
> *Antony and Cleopatra,* Act i, sc. 2, l. 199 [ANTONY]

922   Consider what is breeding
That changeth thus his manners.
> *The Winter's Tale,* Act i, sc. 2, l. 374 [POLIXENES]

Brevity

923   Since brevity is the soul of wit,
And tediousness the limbs and outward flourishes,
I will be brief.
> *Hamlet,* Act ii, sc. 2, l. 90 [POLONIUS]

I will imitate the honourable Romans in brevity.
> *II Henry IV,* Act ii, sc. 2, l. 134 [POINS]

924 HAMLET : Is this a prologue, or the posy of a ring?
OPHELIA : 'Tis brief, my lord.
HAMLET : As woman's love.
> *Hamlet,* Act iii, sc. 2, l. 162 [HAMLET]

925 It is better to be brief than tedious.
> *Richard III,* Act i, sc. 4, l. 91 [MURDERER]

926 I will be brief, for my short date of breath
Is not so long as is a tedious tale.
> *Romeo and Juliet,* Act v, sc. 3, l. 229 [FRIAR LAURENCE]

Bribery

927 SOLDIER : His qualities being at this poor price, I need not ask you
if gold will corrupt him to revolt.

PAROLLES : Sir, for a quart d'ecu he will sell the fee-simple of his salvation.
All's Well that Ends Well, Act iv, sc. 3, l. 308 [SOLDIER]

928   I cannot make my heart consent to take
A bribe to pay my sword : I do refuse it.
Coriolanus, Act i, sc. 9, l. 37 [MARCIUS]

929   Shall one of us,
That struck the foremost man of all the world
But for supporting robbers, shall we now
Contaminate our fingers with base bribes,
And sell the mighty space of our large honours
For so much trash as may be grasped thus?
I had rather be a dog, and bay the moon,
Than such a Roman.
Julius Cæsar, Act iv, sc. 3, l. 20 [BRUTUS]

930   Know'st thou not any whom corrupting gold
Would tempt unto a close exploit of death?
Richard III, Act iv, sc. 2, l. 33 [RICHARD]

Bridge

931   Jack Cade hath gotten London bridge :
The citizens fly and forsake their houses.
II Henry VI, Act iv, sc. 4, l. 49 [MESSENGER]

932   Go and set London bridge on fire; and if you can, burn down the Tower too.
II Henry VI, Act iv, sc. 6, l. 16 [CADE]

933   What need the bridge much broader than the flood?
The fairest grant is the necessity.
Much Ado about Nothing, Act i, sc. 1, l. 318 [DON PEDRO]
(Quoting an old proverb.)

Britain See also England

934   CLOTEN : Britain is a world by itself. . . .
QUEEN : The natural bravery of your isle, which stands
As Neptune's park, ribbed and paled in
With rocks unscaleable and roaring waters. . . .
CLOTEN : You shall find us in our salt-water girdle.
Cymbeline, Act iii, sc. 1, l. 12 [CLOTEN]

935   Malmutius made our laws,
Who was the first of Britain which did put
His brows within a golden crown and call'd
Himself a king.
Cymbeline, Act iii, sc. 1, l. 59 [CYMBELINE]

936   Hath Britain all the sun that shines? Day, night,
Are they not but in Britain? I' the world's volume
Our Britain seems as of it, but not in 't;
In a great pool, a swan's nest : prithee, think
There 's livers out of Britain.
Cymbeline, Act iii, sc. 4, l. 139 [IMOGEN]

937   Our Britain's harts die flying, not our men.
Cymbeline, Act v, sc. 3, l. 24 [POSTHUMUS]

Brother

938   ARVIRAGUS : Are we not brothers?
IMOGEN :   So man and man should be;
But clay and clay differs in dignity,
Whose dust is both alike.
Cymbeline, Act iv, sc. 2, l. 4 [ARVIRAGUS]

939   O my gentle brothers, . . . you call'd me brother,
      When I was but your sister; I you brothers,
      When ye were so indeed.
                          Cymbeline, Act v, sc. 5, l. 374 [IMOGEN]
940   Better it were a brother died at once,
      Than that a sister, by redeeming him,
      Should die for ever.
                   Measure for Measure, Act ii, sc. 4, l. 106 [ISABELLA]
941   I had rather my brother die by the law than my son should be
      unlawfully born.
                   Measure for Measure, Act iii, sc. 1, l. 195 [ISABELLA]
942   Here lies your brother,
      No better than the earth he lies upon,
      If he were that which now he's like, that's dead;
      Whom I, with this obedient steel, three inches of it,
      Can lay to bed for ever.
                          The Tempest, Act ii, sc. 1, l. 280 [ANTONIO]
943   Twinn'd brothers of one womb,
      Whose procreation, residence, and birth,
      Scarce is dividant.
                     Timon of Athens, Act iv, sc. 3, l. 3 [TIMON]
944   VIOLA: What country, friends, is this?
      CAPTAIN: This is Illyria, lady.
      VIOLA: And what should I do in Illyria?
      My brother he is in Elysium.
                          Twelfth Night, Act i, sc. 2, l. 1 [VIOLA]

Brow

945   'Tis not your inky brows, your black silk hair,
      Your bugle eyeballs, nor your cheek of cream,
      That can entame my spirits to your worship.
                          As You Like It, Act iii, sc. 5, l. 46 [ROSALIND]
946   Yea, this man's brow, like to a title-leaf,
      Foretells the nature of a tragic volume:
      So looks the strand whereon the imperious flood
      Hath left a witness'd usurpation.
                     II Henry IV, Act i, sc. 1, l. 60 [NORTHUMBERLAND]
947   These brows of mine,
      Whose smile and frown, like to Achilles' spear,
      Is able with the change to kill and cure.
                          II Henry VI, Act v, sc. 1, l. 99 [YORK]
948   Thou hast the right arched beauty of the brow that becomes the
      ship-tire, the tire-valiant, or any tire of Venetian admittance.
                   The Merry Wives of Windsor, Act iii, sc. 3, l. 59 [FALSTAFF]
949   Here are the beetle brows shall blush for me.
                          Romeo and Juliet, Act i, sc. 4, l. 32 [MERCUTIO]
950   Black brows, they say,
      Become some women best, so that there be not
      Too much hair there, but in a semicircle,
      Or a half-moon made with a pen.
                          The Winter's Tale, Act ii, sc. 1, l. 8 [MAMILLIUS]
951   MAMILLIUS: What colour are your eyebrows?
      LADY: Blue, my lord.
      MAMILLIUS: Nay, that's a mock; I have seen a lady's nose
      That has been blue, but not her eyebrows.
                          The Winter's Tale, Act ii, sc. 1, l. 13 [MAMILLIUS]

Brutus

952   Brutus' bastard hand Stabb'd Julius Cæsar.
                        II Henry VI, Act iv, sc. 1, l. 136 [SUFFOLK]

953   Poor Brutus, with himself at war,
      Forgets the shows of love to other men.
                        Julius Cæsar, Act i, sc. 2, l. 46 [BRUTUS]

954   CASSIUS: There was a Brutus once that would have brook'd
      The eternal devil to keep his state in Rome
      As easily as a king. . . .
      BRUTUS: Brutus had rather be a villager
      Than to repute himself a son of Rome
      Under these hard conditions as this time
      Is like to lay upon us.
                        Julius Cæsar, Act i, sc. 2, l. 159 [BRUTUS]

955   Well, Brutus, thou art noble; yet, I see,
      Thy honourable metal may be wrought
      From that it is disposed.
                        Julius Cæsar, Act i, sc. 2, l. 312 [CASSIUS]

956   Et tu, Brute! Then fall, Cæsar!
                        Julius Cæsar, Act iii, sc. 1, l. 77 [CÆSAR]

957   Brutus is noble, wise, valiant, and honest;
      Cæsar was mighty, bold, royal, and loving.
                        Julius Cæsar, Act iii, sc. 1, l. 126 [SERVANT]

958   Brutus is an honourable man.
                        Julius Cæsar, Act iii, sc. 2, l. 86, 91 [ANTONY]

959   Brutus, as you know, was Cæsar's angel.
                        Julius Cæsar, Act iii, sc. 2, l. 184 [ANTONY]

Budge

960   Let the first budger die the other's slave,
      And the gods doom him after!
                        Coriolanus, Act i, sc. 8, l. 5 [MARCIUS]

961   Come, come, and sit you down; you shall not budge.
                        Hamlet, Act iii, sc. 4, l. 18 [HAMLET]

962   Here pitch our battle; hence we will not budge.
                        III Henry VI, Act v, sc. 4, l. 66 [OXFORD]

963   'Budge,' says the fiend. 'Budge not,' says my conscience.
                        The Merchant of Venice, Act ii, sc. 2, l. 20 [LAUNCELOT]
               (For fuller quotation see 1510.)

964   He will not budge a foot.
                        I Henry IV, Act ii, sc. 4, l. 388 [FALSTAFF]
      I'll not budge an inch.
                        The Taming of the Shrew, Induction, sc. 1. l. 14 [SLY]
      I will not budge for no man's pleasure, I.
                        Romeo and Juliet, Act iii, sc. 1, l. 59 [MERCUTIO]

Bug

965   Those that would die or ere resist are grown
      The mortal bugs o' the field.
                        Cymbeline, Act v, sc. 3, l. 51 [POSTHUMUS]

966   Ho! Such bugs and goblins in my life.
                        Hamlet, Act v, sc. 2, l. 22 [HAMLET]

967   Die thou, and die our fear;
      For Warwick was a bug that fear'd us all.
                        III Henry VI, Act v, sc. 2, l. 1 [KING EDWARD]

968   Tush, tush! fear boys with bugs.
                        The Taming of the Shrew, Act i, sc. 2, l. 211 [PETRUCHIO]

969   A bugbear take him!
                    Troilus and Cressida, Act iv, sc. 2, l. 34 [PANDARUS]
970   Sir, spare your threats:
       The bug which you would fright me with I seek.
                    The Winter's Tale, Act iii, sc. 2, l. 92 [HERMIONE]

Building

971   When we mean to build,
       We first survey the plot, then draw the model;
       And when we see the figure of the house,
       Then must we rate the cost of the erection;
       Which, if we find outweighs ability,
       What do we do then but draw anew the model
       In fewer offices, or at last desist
       To build at all?
                    II Henry IV, Act i, sc. 3, l. 41 [BARDOLPH]
972   Goodly buildings left without a roof
       Soon fall to ruin.
                    Pericles, Act ii, sc. 4, l. 36 [LORD]

Bull

973   DON PEDRO: 'In time the savage bull doth bear the yoke.'
       BENEDICK: The savage bull may; but if ever the sensible Benedick
       bear it, pluck off the bull's horns and set them in my forehead.
                    Much Ado about Nothing, Act i, sc. 1, l. 263 [DON PEDRO]
974   DON PEDRO: Good morrow, Benedick. Why, what's the matter,
       That you have such a February face,
       So full of frost, of storm and cloudiness?
       CLAUDIO: I think he thinks upon the savage bull.
       Tush, fear not, man; we'll tip thy horns with gold
       And all Europa shall rejoice at thee,
       As once Europa did at lusty Jove,
       When he would play the noble beast in love.
       BENEDICK: Bull Jove, sir, had an amiable low;
       And some such strange bull leap'd your father's cow,
       And got a calf in that same noble feat
       Much like to you, for you have just his bleat.
                    Much Ado about Nothing, Act v, sc. 4, l. 40 [DON PEDRO]

Bum

975   Your bum is the greatest thing about you.
                    Measure for Measure, Act ii, sc. 1, l. 228 [ESCALUS]
976   Then slip I from her bum, down topples she,
       And 'tailor' cries, and falls into a cough.
                    A Midsummer Night's Dream, Act ii, sc. 1, l. 53 [PUCK]
977   What a coil's here!
       Serving of becks and jutting-out of bums!
                    Timon of Athens, Act i, sc. 2, l. 237 [APEMANTUS]
978   Scout me for him at the corner of the orchard like a bum-baily.
                    Twelfth Night, Act iii, sc. 4, l. 193 [SIR TOBY]

Burial

979   FIRST CLOWN: Is she to be buried in Christian burial that wilfully
       seeks her own salvation? . . .
       SECOND CLOWN: Will you ha' the truth on 't? If this had not been
       a gentlewoman, she should have been buried out o' Christian burial.
                    Hamlet, Act v, sc. 1, l. 1 [FIRST CLOWN]

980   But that great command o'ersways the order,
      She should in ground unsanctified have lodged
      Till the last trumpet.
                              Hamlet, Act v, sc. 1, l. 251 [PRIEST]

Burr

981   ROSALIND: O, how full of briars is this working-day world!
      CELIA: They are but burs, cousin, thrown upon thee in holiday
      foolery: if we walk not in the trodden paths, our very petticoats
      will catch them.
      ROSALIND: I could shake them off my coat: these burs are in
      my heart.
                        As You Like It, Act i, sc. 3, l. 12 [ROSALIND]
982   Nay, friar, I am a kind of burr; I shall stick.
                   Measure for Measure, Act iv, sc. 3, l. 189 [LUCIO]
983   They are burs, I can tell you: they'll stick where they are thrown.
                 Troilus and Cressida, Act iii, sc. 2, l. 119 [PANDARUS]

Bush

984   Madam, myself have limed a bush for her,
      And placed a quire of such enticing birds,
      That she will light to listen to the lays,
      And never mount to trouble you again.
                        II Henry VI, Act i, sc. 3, l. 91 [SUFFOLK]
985   [They] have all limed bushes to betray thy wings,
      And, fly thou how thou canst, they'll tangle thee.
                       II Henry VI, Act. ii, sc. 4, l. 54 [DUCHESS]
986   The thief doth fear each bush an officer.
                     III Henry VI, Act v, sc. 6, l. 12 [GLOUCESTER]
987   In the night, imagining some fear,
      How easy is a bush supposed a bear!
             A Midsummer Night's Dream, Act v, sc. 1, l. 22 [THESEUS]
      (For full quotation see 3705.)
988   Let . . . the dire thought of his committed evil
      Shape every bush a hideous shapeless devil.
                            The Rape of Lucrece, l. 972 [LUCRECE]

Business

989   To business that we love we rise betime,
      And go to 't with delight.
                   Antony and Cleopatra, Act iv, sc. 4, l. 20 [ANTONY]
990   The business of this man looks out of him;
      We'll hear him what he says.
                   Antony and Cleopatra, Act v, sc. 1, l. 50 [CÆSAR]
991   'Tis not sleepy business;
      But must be look'd to speedily and strongly.
                            Cymbeline, Act iii, sc. 5, l. 26 [QUEEN]
992   Every man has business and desire,
      Such as it is.
                              Hamlet, Act i, sc. 5, l. 130 [HAMLET]
993   Every man to his business.
                          I Henry IV, Act ii, sc. 2, l. 80 [FALSTAFF]
994   Some heavy business hath my lord in hand,
      And I must know it, else he loves me not.
                       I Henry IV, Act ii, sc. 3, l. 66 [LADY PERCY]
995   This weighty business will not brook delay.
                        II Henry VI, Act i, sc. 1, l. 170 [CARDINAL]

996   It was a gentle business, and becoming
       The action of good women.
               Henry VIII, Act ii, sc. 3, l. 54 [CHAMBERLAIN]

997   Affairs that walk,
       As they say spirits do, at midnight, have
       In them a wilder nature than the business
       That seeks dispatch by day.
               Henry VIII, Act v, sc. 1, l. 13 [GARDINER]

998   What's the business,
       That such a hideous trumpet calls to parley
       The sleepers of the house?
               Macbeth, Act ii, sc. 3, l. 86 [LADY MACBETH]

999   Slubber not business for my sake, Bassanio,
       But stay the very riping of the time.
            The Merchant of Venice, Act ii, sc. 8, l. 39 [ANTONIO]

1000   Full of careful business are his looks.
              Richard II, Act ii, sc. 2, l. 75 [QUEEN]

1001   Thou . . . think'st it much . . .
       To run upon the sharp wind of the north,
       To do me business in the veins o' the earth
       When it is baked with frost.
             The Tempest, Act i, sc. 2, l. 252 [PROSPERO]

But Yet

1002   MESSENGER: But yet, madam,—
       CLEOPATRA: I do not like 'But yet,' it doth allay
       The good precedence; fie upon 'But yet'!
       'But yet' is as a gaoler to bring forth
       Some monstrous malefactor.
         Antony and Cleopatra, Act ii, sc. 5, l. 49 [MESSENGER]

Butterfly

1003   I saw him run after a gilded butterfly; and when he caught it,
       he let it go again.
              Coriolanus, Act i, sc. 3, l. 66 [VALERIA]

1004   There is a differency between a grub and a butterfly; yet your
       butterfly was a grub.
            Coriolanus, Act v, sc. 4, l. 11 [MENENIUS]

1005   Pluck the wings from painted butterflies
       To fan the moonbeams from his sleeping eyes.
       A Midsummer Night's Dream, Act iii, sc. 1, l. 175 [TITANIA]

Buying and Selling

1006   Fair Diomed, you do as chapmen do,
       Dispraise the thing that you desire to buy:
       But we in silence hold this virtue well,
       We'll but commend what we intend to sell.
          Troilus and Cressida, Act iv, sc. 1, l. 75 [PARIS]

1007   Lawn as white as driven snow;
       Cyprus black as e'er was crow;
       Gloves as sweet as damask roses;
       Masks for faces and for noses;
       Bugle bracelet, necklace amber,
       Perfume for a lady's chamber;
       Golden quoifs and stomachers,
       For my lads to give their dears:
       Pins and poking-sticks of steel,
       What maids lack from head to heel:

Come buy of me, come; come buy, come buy;
Buy, lads, or else your lasses cry:
Come buy.
>   *The Winter's Tale,* Act iv, sc. 4, l. 220 [AUTOLYCUS]

By and By

1008   I'll see you by and by.
>   *Antony and Cleopatra,* Act iii, sc. 11, l. 24 [ANTONY]
1009   HAMLET: I will come to my mother by and by. . . . I will come
by and by.
POLONIUS: I will say so.
HAMLET: By and by is easily said.
>   *Hamlet,* Act iii, sc. 2, l. 400 [HAMLET]

C

Cæsar

1010   The scarce-bearded Cæsar.
>   *Anthony and Cleopatra,* Act i, sc. 1, l. 21 [CLEOPATRA]
1011   Broad-fronted Cæsar,
When thou wast here above the ground, I was
A morsel for a monarch.
>   *Antony and Cleopatra,* Act i, sc. 5, l. 29 [CLEOPATRA]
1012   She made great Cæsar lay his sword to bed:
He plough'd her, and she cropp'd.
>   *Antony and Cleopatra,* Act ii, sc. 2, l. 232 [AGRIPPA]
1013   POMPEY: Your fine Egyptian cookery
Shall have the fame. I have heard that Julius Cæsar
Grew fat with feasting there. . . .
And I have heard, Apollodorus carried . . .
ENOBARBUS: A certain queen to Cæsar in a mattress.
>   *Antony and Cleopatra,* Act ii, sc. 6, l. 64 [POMPEY]
1014   ENOBARBUS: Cæsar? Why, he's the Jupiter of men.
AGRIPPA: What's Antony? The god of Jupiter.
ENOBARBUS: Spake you of Cæsar? How! the nonpareil!
AGRIPPA: O Antony! O thou Arabian bird! . . .
ENOBARBUS: Ho! hearts, tongues, figures, scribes, bards, poets,
cannot
Think, speak, cast, write, sing, number, Ho!
His love for Antony. But as for Cæsar,
Kneel down, kneel down, and wonder. . . .
They are his shards, and he their beetle.
>   *Antony and Cleopatra,* Act iii, sc. 2, l. 9 [ENOBARBUS]
1015   'Tis paltry to be Cæsar;
Not being Fortune, he's but Fortune's knave,
A minister of her will.
>   *Antony and Cleopatra,* Act v, sc. 2, l. 2 [CLEOPATRA]
1016   LUCIUS: Julius Cæsar, whose remembrance yet
Lives in men's eyes and will to ears and tongues
Be theme and hearing ever. . . .
CLOTEN: There be many Cæsars Ere such another Julius. . . .
Other of them may have crook'd noses, but to owe such straight
arms, none.
>   *Cymbeline,* Act iii, sc. 1, l. 2 [LUCIUS]

1017 Imperious Cæsar, dead and turn'd to clay,
Might stop a hole to keep the wind away:
O, that that earth, which kept the world in awe,
Should patch a wall to expel the winter's flaw!
Hamlet, Act v, sc. 1, l. 236 [HAMLET]

1018 No bending knee will call thee Cæsar now.
III Henry VI, Act iii, sc. 1, l. 18 [KING HENRY]

1019 When Cæsar says 'do this,' it is performed.
Julius Cæsar, Act i, sc. 2, l. 10 [ANTONY]

1020 Cæsar said to me 'Darest thou, Cassius, now
Leap in with me into this angry flood,
And swim to yonder point?' Upon the word,
Accoutred as I was, I plunged in
And bade him follow; so indeed he did. . . .
But ere we could arrive the point proposed,
Cæsar cried 'Help me, Cassius, or I sink!'
Julius Cæsar, Act i, sc. 2, l. 102 [CASSIUS]

1021 Ye gods, it doth amaze me
A man of such a feeble temper should
So get the start of the majestic world
And bear the palm alone. . . .
Why, man, he doth bestride the narrow world
Like a Colossus, and we petty men
Walk under his huge legs and peep about
To find ourselves dishonourable graves.
Julius Cæsar, Act i, sc. 2, l. 128 [CASSIUS]

1022 Now in the names of all the gods at once,
Upon what meat doth this our Cæsar feed,
That he is grown so great?
Julius Cæsar, Act i, sc. 2, l. 148 [CASSIUS]

1023 Look you, Cassius,
The angry spot doth glow on Cæsar's brow,
And all the rest look like a chidden train.
Julius Cæsar, Act i, sc. 2, l. 182 [BRUTUS]

1024 CASSIUS: What, did Cæsar swound?
CASCA: He fell down in the market-place, and foamed at mouth,
and was speechless.
BRUTUS: 'Tis very like: he hath the falling sickness.
CASSIUS: No, Cæsar hath it not, but you and I
And honest Casca, we have the falling sickness.
Julius Cæsar, Act i, sc. 2, l. 255 [CASSIUS]
(Cæsar was an epileptic.)

1025 Enter Cæsar, in his night-gown.
Julius Cæsar, Act ii, sc. 2 [STAGE DIRECTION]

1026 Cæsar should be a beast without a heart,
If he should stay at home to-day for fear.
No, Cæsar shall not: danger knows full well
That Cæsar is more dangerous than he:
We are two lions litter'd in one day,
And I the elder and more terrible.
Julius Cæsar, Act ii, sc. 2, l. 42 [CÆSAR]

1027 Shall Cæsar send a lie?
Have I in conquest stretch'd mine arm so far,
To be afeard to tell graybeards the truth?
Julius Cæsar, Act ii, sc. 2, l. 65 [CÆSAR]

1028 BRUTUS: Stoop, Romans, stoop,
And let us bathe our hands in Cæsar's blood

Up to the elbows, and besmear our swords:
Then walk we forth, even to the market-place,
And, waving our red weapons o'er our heads,
Let's all cry, 'Peace, freedom and liberty!'
CASSIUS: Stoop, then, and wash. How many ages hence
Shall this our lofty scene be acted over
In states unborn and accents yet unknown!
BRUTUS: How many times shall Cæsar bleed in sport,
That now on Pompey's basis lies along
No worthier than the dust!

Julius Cæsar, Act iii, sc. 1, l. 106 [BRUTUS]

1029   O mighty Cæsar! dost thou lie so low?
Are all thy conquests, glories, triumphs, spoils,
Shrunk to this little measure? Fare thee well.
I know not, gentlemen, what you intend,
Who else must be let blood, who else is rank:
If I myself, there is no hour so fit
As Cæsar's death's hour, nor no instrument
Of half that worth as those your swords, made rich
With the most noble blood of all this world. . . .
No place will please me so, no mean of death,
As here by Cæsar, and by you cut off,
The choice and master spirits of this age.

Julius Cæsar, Act iii, sc. 1, l. 148 [ANTONY]

1030   That I did love thee, Cæsar, O 'tis true:
If then thy spirit look upon us now,
Shall it not grieve thee dearer than thy death,
To see thy Antony making his peace,
Shaking the bloody fingers of thy foes,
Most noble! in the presence of thy corse?
Had I as many eyes as thou hast wounds,
Weeping as fast as they stream forth thy blood,
It would become me better than to close
In terms of friendship with thine enemies.
Pardon me, Julius! Here wast thou bay'd, brave hart;
Here didst thou fall; and here thy hunters stand,
Sign'd in thy spoil, and crimson'd in thy lethe.

Julius Cæsar, Act iii, sc. 1, l. 194 [ANTONY]

1031   O, pardon me, thou bleeding piece of earth,
That I am meek and gentle with these butchers!
Thou art the ruins of the noblest man
That ever lived in the tide of times,
Woe to the hand that shed this costly blood!
Over thy wounds now do I prophesy,—
Which, like dumb mouths, do ope their ruby lips,
To beg the voice and utterance of my tongue—
A curse shall light upon the limbs of men;
Domestic fury and fierce civil strife
Shall cumber all the parts of Italy; . . .
And Cæsar's spirit, ranging for revenge,
With Ate by his side come hot from hell,
Shall in these confines with a monarch's voice
Cry 'Havoc,' and let slip the dogs of war.

Julius Cæsar, Act iii, sc. 1, l. 254 [ANTONY]

1032   BRUTUS: Romans, countrymen, and lovers! hear me for my cause,
and be silent, that you may hear: believe me for mine honour,
and have respect to mine honour, that you may believe: censure

me in your wisdom, and awake your senses, that you may the better judge. If there be any in this assembly, any dear friend of Cæsar's, to him I say that Brutus' love to Cæsar was no less than his. If then that friend demand why Brutus rose against Cæsar, this is my answer:—Not that I loved Cæsar less, but that I loved Rome more. Had you rather Cæsar were living and die all slaves, than that Cæsar were dead, to live all free men? As Cæsar loved me, I weep for him; as he was fortunate, I rejoice at it; as he was valiant, I honour him; but, as he was ambitious, I slew him. There is tears for his love; joy for his fortune; honour for his valour; and death for his ambition. Who is here so base that would be a bondman? If any, speak; for him have I offended. Who is here so rude that would not be a Roman? If any, speak; for him have I offended. Who is here so vile that will not love his country? If any, speak; for him have I offended. I pause for a reply.

ALL: None, Brutus, none.

BRUTUS: Then none have I offended. I have done no more to Cæsar than you shall do to Brutus. The question of his death is enrolled in the Capitol; his glory not extenuated, wherein he was worthy, nor his offences enforced, for which he suffered death. . . . With this I depart—that, as I slew my best lover for the good of Rome, I have the same dagger for myself, where it shall please my country to need my death.

Julius Cæsar, Act iii, sc. 2, l. 14 [BRUTUS]

1033   Friends, Romans, countrymen, lend me your ears;
I come to bury Cæsar, not to praise him.
The evil that men do lives after them;
The good is oft interred with their bones;
So let it be with Cæsar. The noble Brutus
Hath told you Cæsar was ambitious:
If it were so, it was a grievous fault,
And grievously hath Cæsar answer'd it.
Here, under leave of Brutus and the rest—
For Brutus is an honourable man;
So are they all, all honourable men—
Come I to speak in Cæsar's funeral.
He was my friend, faithful and just to me:
But Brutus says he was ambitious;
And Brutus is an honourable man,
He hath brought many captives home to Rome,
Whose ransoms did the general coffers fill:
Did this in Cæsar seem ambitious?
When that the poor have cried, Cæsar hath wept:
Ambition should be made of sterner stuff:
Yet Brutus says he was ambitious;
And Brutus is an honourable man.
You all did see that on the Lupercal
I thrice presented him a kingly crown,
Which he did thrice refuse: was this ambition?
Yet Brutus says he was ambitious;
And, sure, he is an honourable man.
I speak not to disprove what Brutus spoke,
But here I am to speak what I do know.
You all did love him once, not without cause:
What cause withholds you then, to mourn for him?
O judgement! thou art fled to brutish beasts,

And men have lost their reason. Bear with me;
My heart is in the coffin there with Cæsar,
And I must pause till it come back to me. . . .
But yesterday the word of Cæsar might
Have stood against the world; now lies he there,
And none so poor to do him reverence. . . .
If you have tears, prepare to shed them now.
You all do know this mantle: I remember
The first time ever Cæsar put it on;
'Twas on a summer's evening, in his tent,
That day he overcame the Nervii:
Look, in this space ran Cassius' dagger through:
Look what a rent the envious Casca made:
Through this the well-beloved Brutus stabb'd;
And as he pluck'd his cursed steel away,
Mark how the blood of Cæsar follow'd it,
As rushing out of doors, to be resolved
If Brutus so unkindly knock'd or no;
For Brutus, as you know, was Cæsar's angel:
Judge, O you gods, how dearly Cæsar loved him!
This was the most unkindest cut of all;
For when the noble Cæsar saw him stab,
Ingratitude, more strong than traitors' arms,
Quite vanquish'd him: then burst his mighty heart;
And, in his mantle muffling up his face,
Even at the base of Pompey's statua,
Which all the while ran blood, great Cæsar fell.
O, what a fall was there, my countrymen!
Then I, and you, and all of us fell down,
Whilst bloody treason flourish'd over us. . . .
I am no orator, as Brutus is;
But, as you know me all, a plain blunt man,
That love my friend: . . . I only speak right on;
I tell you that which you yourselves do know;
Show you sweet Cæsar's wounds, poor, poor dumb mouths,
And bid them speak for me: but were I Brutus,
And Brutus Antony, there were an Antony
Would ruffle up your spirits and put a tongue
In every wound of Cæsar that should move
The stones of Rome to rise and mutiny.
                    Julius Cæsar, Act iii, sc. 2, l. 78 [ANTONY]

1034   O Julius Cæsar, thou art mighty yet!
       Thy spirit walks abroad, and turns our swords
       In our own proper entrails.
                    Julius Cæsar, Act v, sc. 3, l. 94 [BRUTUS]

1035   Thou 'rt an emperor, Cæsar, Keisar, and Pheezar.
                    The Merry Wives of Windsor, Act i, sc. 3, l. 9 [HOST]

1036   That Julius Cæsar was a famous man;
       With what his valour did enrich his wit,
       His wit set down to make his valour live:
       Death made no conquest of this conqueror;
       For now he lives in fame, though not in life.
                    Richard III, Act iii, sc. 1, l. 84 [PRINCE]

Cæsar: Veni, Vidi, Vici

1037   Cæsar's thrasonical brag of 'I came, saw, and overcame.'
                    As You Like It, Act v, sc. 2, l. 34 [ROSALIND]

1038   A kind of conquest
Cæsar made here; but made not here his brag
Of 'Came' and 'saw' and 'overcame.'
Cymbeline, Act iii, sc. 1, l. 22 [QUEEN]

1039   I may justly say, with the hook-nosed fellow of Rome, 'I came, saw, and overcame.'
II Henry IV, Act iv, sc. 3, l. 46 [FALSTAFF]

1040   He it was that might rightly say, Veni, vidi, vici; which to annothanize in the vulgar,—O base and obscure vulgar!—videlicet, He came, saw, and overcame.
Love's Labour's Lost, Act iv, sc. 1, l. 68 [ARMADO]

Cake

1041   Do you look for ale and cakes here, you rude rascals?
Henry VIII, Act v, sc. 4, l. 10 [PORTER]
SIR TOBY: Dost thou think, because thou art virtuous, there shall be no more cakes and ale?
CLOWN: Yes, by Saint Anne, and ginger shall be hot i' the mouth too.
Twelfth Night, Act ii, sc. 3, l. 123 [SIR TOBY]

1042   Our cake's dough on both sides.
The Taming of the Shrew, Act i, sc. 1, l. 110 [GREMIO]

1043   My cake is dough; but I'll be among the rest,
Out of hope of all, but my share of the feast.
The Taming of the Shrew, Act v, sc. 1, l. 143 [GREMIO]

1044   He that will have a cake out of the wheat must needs tarry the grinding.
Troilus and Cressida, Act i, sc. 1, l. 15 [PANDARUS]

Calamity

1045   You are transported by calamity
Thither where more attends you.
Coriolanus, Act i, sc. 1, l. 77 [MENENIUS]

1046   Thou art wedded to calamity.
Romeo and Juliet, Act iii, sc. 3, l. 3 [FRIAR LAURENCE]

1047   There is no true cuckold but calamity.
Twelfth Night, Act i, sc. 5, l. 57 [CLOWN]

Calf's-Skin

1048   He that goes in the calf's-skin that was killed for the Prodigal.
The Comedy of Errors, Act iv, sc. 3, l. 17 [DROMIO OF SYRACUSE]

1049   Hang a calf's-skin on those recreant limbs. . . .
Will not a calf's-skin stop that mouth of thine?
King John, Act iii, sc. 1, l. 131, 299 [BASTARD]

Caliban

1050   No more dams I'll make for fish;
Nor fetch in firing At requiring;
Nor scrape trencher, nor wash dish:
'Ban, ban, Cacaliban
Has a new master: get a new man.
The Tempest, Act ii, sc. 2, l. 154 [CALIBAN]

Calumny

1051   Virtue itself 'scapes not calumnious strokes.
Hamlet, Act i, sc. 3, l. 38 [LAERTES]

1052   Be thou as chaste as ice, as pure as snow, thou shalt not escape calumny.
Hamlet, Act iii, sc. 1, l. 140 [HAMLET]

1053   No might nor greatness in mortality
        Can censure 'scape; back-wounding calumny
        The whitest virtue strikes. What king so strong
        Can tie the gall up in the slanderous tongue?
                    Measure for Measure, Act iii, sc. 2, l. 196 [DUKE]

1054   The shrug, the hum or ha, these petty brands
        That calumny doth use—O, I am out—
        That mercy does, for calumny will sear
        Virtue itself: these shrugs, these hums and ha's.
                    The Winter's Tale, Act ii, sc. 1, l. 71 [LEONTES]

Camel

1055   Of no more soul nor fitness for the world
        Than camels in the war, who have their provand
        Only for bearing burdens, and sore blows
        For sinking under them.
                    Coriolanus, Act ii, sc. 1, l. 267 [BRUTUS]

1056   It is as hard to come as for a camel
        To thread the postern of a small needle's eye.
                    Richard II, Act v, sc. 5, l. 16 [KING RICHARD]

Canary

1057   You have brought her into such a canaries as 'tis wonderful. The
        best courtier of them all, when the court lay at Windsor, could
        never have brought her to such a canary.
                    The Merry Wives of Windsor, Act ii, sc. 2, l. 61 [MISTRESS
                                                                    QUICKLY]

        (Mistress Quickly is thinking of quandary.)

Candle

1058   CHIEF JUSTICE: What! you are as a candle, the better part
        burnt out.
        FALSTAFF: A wassail candle, my lord, all tallow.
                    II Henry IV, Act i, sc. 2, l. 177 [CHIEF JUSTICE]

1059   Here burns my candle out; ay, here it dies,
        Which, whiles it lasted, gave King Henry light.
                    III Henry VI, Act ii, sc. 6, l. 1 [CLIFFORD]

1060   This candle burns not clear; 'tis I must snuff it;
        Then out it goes.
                    Henry VIII, Act iii, sc. 2, l. 96 [WOLSEY]

1061   Out went the candle, and we were left darkling.
                    King Lear, Act i, sc. 4, l. 237 [FOOL]

1062   Dark needs no candles now, for dark is light.
                    Love's Labour's Lost, Act iv, sc. 3, l. 269 [DUMAIN]

1063   There's husbandry in heaven;
        Their candles are all out.
                    Macbeth, Act ii, sc. 1, l. 4 [BANQUO]

1064   Out, out, brief candle!
                    Macbeth, Act v, sc. 5, l. 23 [MACBETH]

1065   Must I hold a candle to my shames?
                    The Merchant of Venice, Act ii, sc. 6, l. 41 [JESSICA]

1066   Thus hath the candle singed the moth.
                    The Merchant of Venice, Act ii, sc. 9, l. 79 [PORTIA]

1067   PORTIA: That light we see is burning in my hall.
        How far that little candle throws his beams!
        So shines a good deed in a naughty world.
        NERISSA: When the moon shone, we did not see the candle.
        PORTIA: So doth the greater glory dim the less.
                    The Merchant of Venice, Act v, sc. 1, l. 89 [PORTIA]

1068　These blessed candles of the night.
　　　　　The Merchant of Venice, Act v, sc. 1, l. 220 [BASSANIO]
1069　Night's candles are burnt out.
　　　　　Romeo and Juliet, Act iii, sc. 5, l. 9 [ROMEO]

Canker

1070　The canker galls the infants of the spring,
　　　　Too oft before their buttons be disclosed,
　　　　And in the morn and liquid dew of youth
　　　　Contagious blastments are most imminent.
　　　　　Hamlet, Act i, sc. 3, l. 39 [LAERTES]
1071　The cankers of a calm world and a long peace, ten times more
　　　　dishonourable ragged than an old faced ancient.
　　　　　I Henry IV, Act iv, sc. 2, l. 32 [FALSTAFF]
1072　O Nell, sweet Nell, if thou dost love thy lord,
　　　　Banish the canker of ambitious thoughts,
　　　　And may that thought, when I imagine ill
　　　　Against my king and nephew, virtuous Henry,
　　　　Be my last breathing in this mortal world!
　　　　　II Henry VI, Act i, sc. 2, l. 17 [GLOUCESTER]
1073　Thus are my blossoms blasted in the bud.
　　　　　II Henry VI, Act iii, sc. 1, l. 89 [YORK]
1074　Now will canker sorrow eat my bud.
　　　　　King John, Act iii, sc. 4, l. 82 [CONSTANCE]
1075　He is to himself . . . so secret and so close, . . .
　　　　As is the bud bit with an envious worm,
　　　　Ere he can spread his sweet leaves to the air,
　　　　Or dedicate his beauty to the sun.
　　　　　Romeo and Juliet, Act i, sc. 1, l. 154 [MONTAGUE]
1076　Roses have thorns, and silver fountains mud,
　　　　Clouds and eclipses stain both moon and sun,
　　　　And loathsome canker lives in sweetest bud.
　　　　　Sonnet xxxv, l. 2
1077　PROTEUS: In the sweetest bud The eating canker dwells.
　　　　VALENTINE: . . . The most forward bud
　　　　Is eaten by the canker ere it blows.
　　　　　The Two Gentlemen of Verona, Act i, sc. 1, l. 42 [PROTEUS]

Cannon

1078　No jocund health that Denmark drinks to-day,
　　　　But the great cannon to the clouds shall tell,
　　　　And the king's rouse the heavens shall bruit again,
　　　　Re-speaking earthly thunder.
　　　　　Hamlet, Act i, sc. 2, l. 125 [KING]
1079　Be thou as lightning in the eyes of France;
　　　　For ere thou canst report I will be there,
　　　　The thunder of my cannon shall be heard.
　　　　　King John, Act i, sc. 1, l. 24 [KING JOHN]
　　　　The cannons have their bowels full of wrath,
　　　　And ready mounted are they to spit forth
　　　　Their iron indignation 'gainst your walls.
　　　　　King John, Act ii, sc. 1, l. 210 [KING JOHN]
　　　　　　Our thunder from the south
　　　　Shall rain their drift of bullets on this town.
　　　　　King John, Act ii, sc. 1, l. 411 [KING PHILIP]
1080　By east and west let France and England mount
　　　　Their battering cannon charged to the mouths,

Till their soul-fearing clamours have brawl'd down
The flinty ribs of this contemptuous city.
King John, Act ii, sc. 1, l. 381 [BASTARD]

1081   I have seen the cannon
When it hath blown his ranks into the air,
And, like the devil, from his very arm
Puff'd his own brother.
Othello, Act iii, sc. 4, l. 134 [IAGO]

Caper

1082   I have seen
Him caper upright like a wild Morisco,
Shaking the bloody darts as he his bells.
II Henry VI, Act iii, sc. 1, l. 365 [YORK]

1083   He offered to cut a caper at the proclamation.
Pericles, Act iv, sc. 2, l. 116 [BOULT]

1084   Faith, I can cut a caper.
Twelfth Night, Act i, sc. 3, l. 129 [SIR ANDREW]

Caps

1085   They threw their caps
As they would hang them on the horns o' the moon.
Coriolanus, Act i, sc. 1, l. 216 [CORIOLANUS]

1086   The commons made
A shower and thunder with their caps and shouts :
I never saw the like.
Coriolanus, Act ii, sc. 1, l. 282 [MESSENGER]

1087   Caps, hands, and tongues, applaud it to the clouds.
Hamlet, Act iv, sc. 5, l. 107 [GENTLEMAN]

Captain

1088   Captain I'll be no more ;
But I will eat and drink, and sleep as soft
As captain shall.
All's Well that Ends Well, Act iv, sc. 3, l. 367 [PAROLLES]

1089   Who does i' the wars more than his captain can
Becomes his captain's captain.
Antony and Cleopatra, Act iii, sc. 1, l. 21 [VENTIDIUS]
She that I spake of, our great captain's captain.
Othello, Act ii, sc. 1, l. 74 [CASSIO]

1090   HOSTESS : No, good Captain Pistol ; not here, sweet captain.
DOLL : Captain ! thou abominable damned cheater, art thou not
ashamed to be called captain ? . . . You a captain ! you slave, for
what ? for tearing a poor whore's ruff in a bawdy-house ? He a
captain ! hang him, rogue ! he lives upon mouldy stewed prunes
and dried cakes. A captain ! God's light, these villains will make
the word as odious as the word 'occupy' ; which was an excellent
word before it was ill sorted.
II Henry IV, Act ii, sc. 4, l. 151 [HOSTESS]

1091   That in the captain's but a choleric word,
Which in the soldier is flat blasphemy.
Measure for Measure, Act ii, sc. 2, l. 130 [ISABELLA]

Cards

1092   She . . . has
Pack'd cards with Cæsar, and false-play'd my glory
Unto an enemy's triumph.
Antony and Cleopatra, Act iv, sc. 14, l. 18 [ANTONY]

1093   Have I not here the best cards for the game,
        To win this easy match play'd for a crown?
                     King John, Act v, sc. 2, l. 105 [LEWIS]

1094   As sure a card as ever won the set.
                  Titus Andronicus, Act v, sc. 1, l. 100 [AARON]

Care

1095   Care is no cure, but rather corrosive,
        For things that are not to be remedied.
                I Henry VI, Act iii, sc. 3, l. 3 [PUCELLE]

1096   What though care killed a cat, thou hast mettle enough in thee
        to kill care.
          Much Ado about Nothing, Act v, sc. 1, l. 132 [CLAUDIO]

1097   My care is loss of care, by old care done;
        Your care is gain of care, by new care won.
            Richard II, Act iv, sc. 1, l. 196 [KING RICHARD]

1098   Care keeps his watch in every old man's eye,
        And where care lodges, sleep will never lie.
           Romeo and Juliet, Act ii, sc. 3, l. 35 [FRIAR LAURENCE]

1099   Care's an enemy to life.
               Twelfth Night, Act i, sc. 3, l. 3 [SIR TOBY]

Cares

1100   His cares are now all ended.
             II Henry IV, Act v, sc. 2, l. 3 [WARWICK]

1101   Thus sometimes hath the brightest day a cloud;
        And after summer evermore succeeds
        Barren winter, with his wrathful nipping cold:
        So cares and joys abound, as seasons fleet.
           II Henry VI, Act ii, sc. 4, l. 1 [GLOUCESTER]

1102   What watchful cares do interpose themselves
        Betwixt your eyes and night?
           Julius Cæsar, Act ii, sc. 1, l. 98 [BRUTUS]

1103   'Tis our fast intent
    To shake all cares and business from our age;
    Conferring them on younger strengths, while we
    Unburthen'd crawl toward death.
             King Lear, Act i, sc. 1, l. 39 [LEAR]

1104   BOLINGBROKE: Part of your cares you give me with your crown.
    KING RICHARD: Your cares set up do not pluck my cares
           down. . . .
    The cares I give, I have, though given away;
    They tend the crown, yet still with me they stay.
          Richard II, Act iv, sc. 1, l. 194 [BOLINGBROKE]

1105   Alas, why would you heap these cares on me?
    I am unfit for state and majesty.
           Richard III, Act iii, sc. 7, l. 204 [GLOUCESTER]

Case

1106   What a case am I in!
             As You Like It, Epilogue, l. 7 [ROSALIND]
    What case stand I in?
            The Winter's Tale, Act i, sc. 2, l. 352 [CAMILLO]

1107   Why, 'tis a plain case.
      The Comedy of Errors, Act iv, sc. 3, l. 22 [DROMIO OF SYRACUSE]
    'Tis too plain a case.
         Troilus and Cressida, Act iv, sc. 4, l. 31 [PANDARUS]

1108   A rotten case abides no handling.
         II Henry IV, Act iv, sc. 1, l. 161 [WESTMORELAND]

1109   Ay, but the case is alter'd.
                        III Henry VI, Act iv, sc. 3, l. 31 [WARWICK]
        (Quoting a proverb.)

Cat

1110   SECOND LORD: This is your devoted friend, sir, the manifold lin-
        guist and the armipotent soldier.
        BERTRAM: I could endure any thing before but a cat, and now he's
        a cat to me. . . . A pox upon him for me, he's more and more a
        cat.
                All's Well that Ends Well, Act iv, sc. 3, l. 264 [SECOND LORD]
1111   If the cat will after kind,
                        So be sure will Rosalind.
                        As You Like It, Act iii, sc. 2, l. 109 [TOUCHSTONE]
1112   Let Hercules himself do what he may,
        The cat will mew and dog will have his day.
                        Hamlet, Act v, sc. 1, l. 314 [HAMLET]
1113   I am as vigilant as a cat to steal cream.
                        I Henry IV, Act iv, sc. 2, l. 64 [FALSTAFF]
1114   FIRST WITCH: Thrice the brinded cat hath mew'd.
        SECOND WITCH: Thrice and once the hedge-pig whined.
                        Macbeth, Act iv, sc. 1, l. 1 [FIRST WITCH]
1115   The cat, with eyen of burning coal,
        Now crouches fore the mouse's hole.
                        Pericles, Act iii, Induction, l. 5 [GOWER]
1116   BENVOLIO: Why, what is Tybalt?
        MERCUTIO: More than prince of cats, I can tell you.
                        Romeo and Juliet, Act ii, sc. 4, l. 19 [BENVOLIO]
1117   MERCUTIO: Tybalt, you rat-catcher, will you walk?
        TYBALT: What wouldst thou have with me?
        MERCUTIO: Good king of cats, nothing but one of your nine lives.
                        Romeo and Juliet, Act iii, sc. 1, l. 78 [MERCUTIO]

Cataian

1118   I will not believe such a Cataian, though the priest o' town com-
        mended him for a true man.
                The Merry Wives of Windsor, Act ii, sc. 1, l. 148 [PAGE]
1119   My lady's a Cataian, we are politicians.
                        Twelfth Night, Act ii, sc. 3, l. 80 [SIR TOBY]
        ("Cataian," a variant of Cathaian, a man of Cathay or China,
        supposed to be dexterous at thieving; hence, a thief, scoundrel,
        blackguard.)

Catastrophe

1120   The catastrophe and heel of pastime.
                        All's Well that Ends Well, Act i, sc. 2, l. 57 [KING]
1121   Away, you scullion! you rampallian! you fustilarian!
        I'll tickle your catastrophe.
                        II Henry IV, Act ii, sc. 1, l. 65 [FALSTAFF]
1122   Pat he comes like the catastrophe of the old comedy.
                        King Lear, Act i, sc. 2, l. 146 [EDMUND]
1123   The catastrophe is a nuptial.
                        Love's Labour's Lost, Act iv, sc. 1, l. 77 [BOYET]
        (Catastrophe in the sense of conclusion or denouement. Falstaff
        uses it in the old sense of posteriors.)

Caterpillar

1124   Whoreson caterpillars! bacon-fed knaves!
                        I Henry IV, Act ii, sc. 2, l. 88 [FALSTAFF]

1125   Caterpillars eat my leaves away.
                    II Henry VI, Act iii, sc. 1, l. 90 [YORK]
1126   All scholars, lawyers, courtiers, gentlemen,
        They call false caterpillars and intend their death.
                    II Henry VI, Act iv, sc. 3, l. 37 [MESSENGER]
1127   The most just gods
        For every graff would send a caterpillar.
                    Pericles, Act v, sc. 1, l. 60 [LYSIMACHUS]
1128   Bushy, Bagot, and their complices,
        The caterpillars of the commonwealth,
        Which I have sworn to weed and pluck away.
                    Richard II, Act ii, sc. 3, l. 165 [BOLINGBROKE]
1129   Our sea-walled garden . . . Is full of weeds, . . .
        Her wholesome herbs Swarming with caterpillars.
                    Richard II, Act iii, sc. 4, l. 43 [SERVANT]

Cattle

1130   Boys and women are for the most part cattle of this colour.
                    As You Like It, Act iii, sc. 2, l. 435 [ROSALIND]
1131   There he blasts the tree and takes the cattle.
                    The Merry Wives of Windsor, Act iv, sc. 4, l. 32 [MRS. PAGE]
1132   I did . . . Make poor men's cattle break their necks.
                    Titus Andronicus, Act v, sc. 1, l. 127 [AARON]

Cause

1133   HAMLET: Horatio, I am dead;
        Thou livest; report me and my cause aright
        To the unsatisfied.
        HORATIO: Never believe it. . . .
        Here's yet some liquor left.
        HAMLET: As thou 'rt a man, Give me the cup. . . .
        If thou didst ever hold me in thy heart,
        Absent thee from felicity awhile,
        And in this harsh world draw thy breath in pain,
        To tell my story.
                    Hamlet, Act v, sc. 2, l. 348 [HAMLET]
1134   God befriend us, as our cause is just!
                    I Henry IV, Act v, sc. 1, l. 120 [KING HENRY]
1135   KING HENRY: Methinks I could not die any where so contented
        as in the king's company; his cause being just and his quarrel
        honourable. . . .
        BATES: If his cause be wrong, our obedience to the king wipes the
        crime of it out of us.
        WILLIAMS: But if the cause be not good, the king himself hath a
        heavy reckoning to make, when all those legs and arms and heads,
        chopped off in a battle, shall join together at the latter day and
        cry all, 'We died at such a place.'
                    Henry V, Act iv, sc. 1, l. 133 [KING HENRY]
1136   CÆSAR: Decius, go tell them Cæsar will not come.
        DECIUS: Most mighty Cæsar, let me know some cause. . . .
        CÆSAR: The cause is in my will: I will not come.
                    Julius Cæsar, Act ii, sc. 2, l. 68 [CÆSAR]
1137   It is the cause, it is the cause, my soul,—
        Let me not name it to you, you chaste stars!—
        It is the cause.
                    Othello, Act v, sc. 2, l. 1 [OTHELLO]

1138   Cousin of Hereford, as thy cause is right,
So be thy fortune in this royal fight!
Richard II, Act i, sc. 3, l. 55 [KING RICHARD]

1139   God and our good cause fight upon our side.
Richard III, Act v, sc. 3, l. 240 [RICHMOND]

1140   I . . . to my fortunes and the people's favour
Commit my cause in balance to be weigh'd.
Titus Andronicus, Act i, sc. 1, l. 54 [BASSIANUS]

1141   'Tis a cause that hath no mean dependence
Upon our joint and several dignities.
Troilus and Cressida, Act ii, sc. 2, l. 192 [HECTOR]

Cause and Effect

1142   Now remains
That we find out the cause of this effect,
Or rather say, the cause of this defect,
For this effect defective comes by cause.
Hamlet, Act ii, sc. 2, l. 100 [POLONIUS]

1143   ANNE: Thou art the cause, and most accursed effect.
GLOUCESTER: Your beauty was the cause of that effect;
Your beauty, which did haunt me in my sleep
To undertake the death of all the world,
So I might lie one hour in your sweet bosom. . . .
As all the world is cheered by the sun,
So I by that; it is my day, my life.
Richard III, Act i, sc. 2, l. 120 [ANNE]

Cedar

1144   From a stately cedar shall be lopped branches.
Cymbeline, Act v, sc. 4, l. 141 [POSTHUMUS]

1145   The lofty cedar, royal Cymbeline,
Personates thee: and thy lopp'd branches point
Thy two sons forth.
Cymbeline, Act v, sc. 5, l. 453 [SOOTHSAYER]

1146   This day I'll wear aloft my burgonet,
As on a mountain top a cedar shows
That keeps his leaves in spite of any storm.
II Henry VI, Act v, sc. 1, l. 205 [WARWICK]

1147   He shall flourish,
And, like a mountain cedar, reach his branches
To all the plains about him.
Henry VIII, Act v, sc. 5, l. 54 [CRANMER]

1148   My blood, my want of strength, my sick heart shows
That I must yield my body to the earth
And, by my fall, the conquest to my foe.
Thus yields the cedar to the axe's edge,
Whose arms gave shelter to the princely eagle,
Under whose shade the ramping lion slept,
Whose top-branch overpeer'd Jove's spreading tree
And kept low shrubs from winter's powerful wind.
III Henry VI, Act v, sc. 2, l. 8 [WARWICK]

1149   The cedar stoops not to the base shrub's foot,
But low shrubs wither at the cedar's root.
The Rape of Lucrece, l. 664 [LUCRECE]

1150   We are but shrubs, no cedars we.
Titus Andronicus, Act iv, sc. 3, l. 45 [TITUS]

Celerity

1151   Celerity is never more admired
        Than by the negligent.
                    Antony and Cleopatra, Act iii, sc. 7, l. 25 [CLEOPATRA]

1152   It was the swift celerity of his death,
        Which I did think with slower foot came on.
                    Measure for Measure, Act v, sc. 1, l. 399 [DUKE]

Censure

1153   Take each man's censure, but reserve thy judgement.
                    Hamlet, Act i, sc. 3, l. 69 [POLONIUS]

1154   Censure me by what you were
        Not what you are.
                    I Henry VI, Act v, sc. 5, l. 97 [KING HENRY]

1155   To that end we wish'd your lordship here,
        To avoid the carping censures of the world.
                    Richard III, Act iii, sc. 5, l. 67 [GLOUCESTER]

1156   How blest am I
        In my just censure, in my true opinion!
                    The Winter's Tale, Act ii, sc. 1, l. 36 [LEONTES]

Ceremony

1157   Use a more spacious ceremony to the noble lords; . . . for they
        wear themselves in the cap of the time, there do muster true gait,
        eat, speak, and move under the influence of the most received star;
        and though the devil lead the measure, such are to be followed.
                    All's Well that Ends Well, Act ii, sc. 1, l. 51 [PAROLLES]

1158   What have kings, that privates have not too,
        Save ceremony, save general ceremony?
        And what art thou, thou idol ceremony?
        What kind of god art thou, that suffer'st more
        Of mortal griefs than do thy worshippers?
        What are thy rents? What are thy comings in?
        O ceremony, show me but thy worth! . . .
        Art thou aught else but place, degree and form,
        Creating awe and fear in other men? . . .
        What drink'st thou oft, instead of homage sweet,
        But poison'd flattery? O, be sick, great greatness,
        And bid thy ceremony give thee cure!
                    Henry V, Act iv, sc. 1, l. 255 [KING HENRY]

1159   I never stood on ceremonies.
                    Julius Cæsar, Act ii, sc. 2, l. 13 [CALPURNIA]

1160   The sauce to meat is ceremony;
        Meeting were bare without it.
                    Macbeth, Act iii, sc. 4, l. 36 [LADY MACBETH]

1161   Ceremony was but devised at first
        To set a gloss on faint deeds, hollow welcomes,
        Recanting goodness, sorry ere 'tis shown;
        But where there is true friendship, there needs none.
                    Timon of Athens, Act i, sc. 2, l. 15 [TIMON]

Certainty

1162   CLEOPATRA: Is this certain?
        MESSENGER: Or I have no observance.
                    Antony and Cleopatra, Act iii, sc. 3, l. 24 [CLEOPATRA]

1163   SICINIUS: Is it most certain?
        MESSENGER: As certain as I know the sun is fire.
                    Coriolanus, Act v, sc. 4, l. 48 [SICINIUS]

1164   Certainties
Either are past remedies, or, timely knowing,
The remedy then born.
        Cymbeline, Act i, sc. 6, l. 96 [IMOGEN]

1165   Thou art not certain;
For thy complexion shifts to strange effects,
After the moon.
      Measure for Measure, Act iii, sc. 1, l. 23 [DUKE]

1166   I was certain o'er incertainty.
           Sonnet cxv, l. 11

Challenge

1167   I never in my life
Did hear a challenge urged more modestly,
Unless a brother should a brother dare
To gentle exercise and proof of arms.
       I Henry IV, Act v, sc. 2, l. 52 [VERNON]

1168   DUMAIN: Hector will challenge him.
BIRON: Ay, if a' have no more man's blood in 's belly than will
sup a flea.
ARMADO: By the north pole, I do challenge thee. . . .
MOTH: Master, let me take you a button-hole lower. . . . What
mean you? You will lose your reputation.
     Love's Labour's Lost, Act v, sc. 2, l. 706 [DUMAIN]

1169   Thou hast so wrong'd mine innocent child and me
That I am forced to lay my reverence by
And, with grey hairs and bruise of many days,
Do challenge thee to trial of a man.
     Much Ado about Nothing, Act v, sc. 1, l. 63 [LEONATO]

1170   BENEDICK: Shall I speak a word in your ear?
CLAUDIO: God bless me from a challenge!
BENEDICK: You are a villain; I jest not; I will make it good how
you dare, with what you dare, and when you dare.
     Much Ado about Nothing, Act v, sc. 1, l. 143 [BENEDICK]

1171   I have a roisting challenge sent amongst
The dull and factious nobles of the Greeks
Will strike amazement to their drowsy spirits.
     Troilus and Cressida, Act ii, sc. 2, l. 208 [HECTOR]

1172   SIR ANDREW: 'Twere as good a deed as to drink when a man's
a-hungry, to challenge him the field. . . .
SIR TOBY: Do 't, knight: I'll write thee a challenge.
      Twelfth Night, Act ii, sc. 3, l. 135 [SIR ANDREW]

1173   Here's the challenge, read it: I warrant there's vinegar and
pepper in 't.
      Twelfth Night, Act iii, sc. 4, l. 157 [SIR ANDREW]

Chameleon

1174   KING: How fares our cousin Hamlet?
HAMLET: Excellent, i' faith; of the chameleon's dish; I eat the
air, promise-crammed: you cannot feed capons so.
        Hamlet, Act iii, sc. 2, l. 97 [KING]
The chameleon . . . can feed on the air.
     The Two Gentlemen of Verona, Act ii, sc. 1, l. 178 [SPEED]

1175   I can add colours to the chameleon.
      III Henry VI, Act iii, sc. 2, l. 191 [GLOUCESTER]

1176   SILVIA: What, angry, Sir Thurio! Do you change colour?
VALENTINE: Give me leave, madam; he is a kind of chameleon.

THURIO: That hath more mind to feed on your blood than live in your air.
> *The Two Gentlemen of Verona*, Act ii, sc. 4, l. 23 [SILVIA]

Champion

1177   A stouter champion never handled sword.
> *I Henry VI*, Act iii, sc. 4, l. 19 [KING]

1178   By my valour, the most complete champion that ever I heard!
> *II Henry VI*, Act iv, sc. 10, l. 58 [CADE]

1179   Threefold renown'd
For hardy and undoubted champions.
> *III Henry VI*, Act v, sc. 7, l. 5 [KING EDWARD]

1180   Thou Fortune's champion that dost never fight
But when her humorous ladyship is by
To teach thee safety!
> *King John*. Act iii, sc. 1, l. 118 [CONSTANCE]

1181   In peace and honour rest you here, my sons;
Rome's readiest champions, repose you here in rest,
Secure from worldly chances and mishaps!
Here lurks no treason, here no envy swells,
Here grow no damned grudges; here are no storms,
No noise, but silence and eternal sleep.
> *Titus Andronicus*, Act i, sc. 1, l. 150 [TITUS]

Chance

1182   ARCHBISHOP: Against ill chances men are ever merry;
But heaviness foreruns the good event.
WESTMORELAND: Therefore be merry, coz; since sudden sorrow
Serves to say thus, 'some good thing comes to-morrow.'
> *II Henry IV*, Act iv, sc. 2, l. 81 [ARCHBISHOP]

1183   SALISBURY: Let's make haste away, and look unto the main.
WARWICK: Unto the main? . . . Main chance, father, you meant.
> *II Henry VI*, Act i, sc. 1, l. 208 [SALISBURY]

1184   If chance will have me king, why, chance may crown me.
> *Macbeth*, Act i, sc. 3, l. 143 [MACBETH]

1185   You must take your chance.
> *The Merchant of Venice*, Act ii, sc. 1, l. 38 [PORTIA]

1186   In the reproof of chance
Lies the true proof of men.
> *Troilus and Cressida*, Act i, sc. 3, l. 33 [NESTOR]

1187   We profess
Ourselves to be the slaves of chance and flies
Of every wind that blows.
> *The Winter's Tale*, Act iv, sc. 4, l. 548 [FLORIZEL]

Change

1188   He changed almost into another man.
> *All's Well that Ends Well*, Act iv, sc. 3, l. 5 [LORD]

1189   Nor the exterior nor the inward man
Resembles that it was.
> *Hamlet*, Act ii, sc. 2, l. 6 [KING]

1190   How . . . changes fill the cup of alteration
With divers liquors!
> *II Henry IV*, Act iii, sc. 1, l. 52 [KING HENRY]

1191   His people shall revolt from him
And kiss the lips of unacquainted change.
> *King John*, Act iii, sc. 4, l. 165 [PANDULPH]

1192   SNOUT: O Bottom, thou art changed! . . .
Quince: Bless thee, Bottom! bless thee! thou art translated. . . .
Starveling: Out of doubt he is transported.
A Midsummer Night's Dream, Act iii, sc. 1, l. 117 [Snout]

1193   All things that we ordained festival,
Turn from their office to black funeral;
Our instruments to melancholy bells,
Our wedding cheer to a sad burial feast,
Our solemn hymns to sullen dirges change,
Our bridal flowers serve for a buried corse,
And all things change them to the contrary.
Romeo and Juliet, Act iv, sc. 5, l. 84 [Capulet]

Chanticleer

1194   My lungs began to crow like chanticleer.
As You Like It, Act ii, sc. 7, l. 30 [Jaques]

1195   Hark, hark!,I hear
The strain of strutting chanticleer
Cry, Cock-a-diddle-dow.
The Tempest, Act i, sc. 2, l. 384 [Ariel]

Character

1196   He's a most notorious coward, an infinite and endless liar, an
hourly promise-breaker.
All's Well that Ends Well, Act iii, sc. 6, l. 10 [Lord]

1197   He will steal, sir, an egg out of a cloister: for rapes and ravish-
ments he parallels Nessus: he professes not keeping of oaths; in
breaking 'em he is stronger than Hercules: he will lie, sir, with
such volubility, that you would think truth were a fool.
All's Well that Ends Well, Act iv, sc. 3, l. 280 [Parolles]

1198   O, that's a brave man! he writes brave verses, speaks brave
words, swears brave oaths and breaks them bravely, quite traverse,
athwart the heart of his lover; as a puisny tilter, that spurs his
horse but on one side, breaks his staff like a noble goose.
As You Like It, Act iii, sc. 4, l. 43 [Celia]

1199   I have trod a measure; I have flattered a lady; I have been politic
with my friend, smooth with mine enemy; I have undone three
tailors; I have had four quarrels, and like to have fought one.
As You Like It, Act v, sc. 4, l. 45 [Touchstone]

1200   Hasty and tinder-like upon too trivial motion; one that converses
more with the buttock of the night than with the forehead of the
morning; what I think I utter, and spend my malice in my
breath.
Coriolanus, Act ii, sc. 1, l. 55 [Menenius]

1201   You are ambitious for poor knaves' caps and legs: you wear out
a good wholesome forenoon in hearing a cause between an orange-
wife and a fosset-seller: and then rejourn the controversy of three
pence to a second day of audience. . . . When you speak best unto
the purpose, it is not worth the wagging of your beards; and your
beards deserve not so honourable a grave as to stuff a botcher's
cushion, or to be entombed in an ass's pack-saddle. . . . God-den
to your worships: more of your conversation would infect my
brain.
Coriolanus, Act ii, sc. 1, l. 75 [Menenius]

1202   His nature is too noble for the world:
He would not flatter Neptune for his trident,
Or Jove for 's power to thunder. His heart's his mouth:

What his breast forges, that his tongue must vent;
And, being angry, does forget that ever
He heard the name of death.
                    Coriolanus, Act iii, sc. 1, l. 255 [MENENIUS]

1203   He is gracious, if he be observed:
He hath a tear for pity and a hand
Open as day for melting charity:
Yet notwithstanding, being incensed, he 's flint,
As humorous as winter, and as sudden
As flaws congealed in the spring of day.
His temper, therefore, must be well observed:
Chide him for faults, and do it reverently,
When you perceive his blood inclined to mirth;
But, being moody, give him line and scope,
Till that his passions, like a whale on ground,
Confound themselves with working.
                    II Henry IV, Act iv, sc. 4, l. 30 [KING]
        (The reference is to the Prince of Wales.)

1204   He was a scholar, and a ripe and good one;
Exceeding wise, fair-spoken and persuading:
Lofty and sour to them that loved him not;
But to those men that sought him sweet as summer. . . .
His overthrow heap'd happiness upon him;
For then, and not till then, he felt himself,
And found the blessedness of being little:
And, to add greater honours to his age
Than man could give him, he died fearing God.
                    Henry VIII, Act iv, sc. 2, l. 51 [GRIFFITH]
        (The reference is to Wolsey.)

1205   [I have been] A serving-man, proud in heart and mind; that curled
my hair; wore gloves in my cap; served the lust of my mistress'
heart, and did the act of darkness with her; swore as many oaths
as I spake words, and broke them in the face of heaven: one that
slept in the contriving of lust, and waked to do it: wine loved I
deeply, dice dearly; and in woman out-paramoured the Turk:
false of heart, light of ear, bloody of hand; hog in sloth, fox in
stealth, wolf in greediness, dog in madness, lion in prey.
                    King Lear, Act iii, sc. 4, l. 86 [EDGAR]
        ("Wore gloves in my cap," imitating the knights who wore
        their lady's gloves in their helmets.)

1206   His humour is lofty, his discourse peremptory, his tongue filed, his
eye ambitious, his gait majestical and his general behaviour vain,
ridiculous, and thrasonical. He is too picked, too spruce, too affected, too odd, as it were, too peregrinate, as I may call it.
                    Love's Labour's Lost, Act v, sc. 1, l. 11 [HOLOFERNES]
        (Referring to Armado. "Thrasonical," boastful.)

1207   I cannot hide what I am: I must be sad when I have cause and
smile at no man's jests, eat when I have stomach and wait for no
man's leisure, sleep when I am drowsy and tend on no man's business, laugh when I am merry and claw no man in his humour.
                    Much Ado about Nothing, Act i, sc. 3, l. 14 [DON JOHN]

1208   I pray you, in your letters,
When you shall these unlucky deeds relate,
Speak of me as I am; nothing extenuate,
Nor set down aught in malice: then must you speak
Of one that loved not wisely but too well;
Of one not easily jealous, but, being wrought,

Perplex'd in the extreme; of one whose hand,
Like the base Indian, threw a pearl away
Richer than all his tribe; of one whose subdued eyes,
Albeit unused to the melting mood,
Drop tears as fast as the Arabian trees
Their medicinal gum.

Othello, Act v, sc. 2, l. 340 [OTHELLO]

1209   KING RICHARD: Came I not at last to comfort you?
DUCHESS OF YORK: No, by the holy rood, thou know'st it well,
Thou camest on earth to make the earth my hell.
A grievous burthen was thy birth to me;
Tetchy and wayward thy infancy;
Thy school-days frightful, desperate, wild and furious,
Thy prime of manhood daring, bold, and venturous,
Thy age confirm'd, proud, subtle, bloody, treacherous,
More mild, but yet more harmful, kind in hatred.

Richard III, Act iv, sc. 4, l. 164 [KING RICHARD]

1210   Upon my life, Petruchio means but well: . . .
Though he be blunt, I know him passing wise;
Though he be merry, yet withal he 's honest.

The Taming of the Shrew, Act iii, sc. 2, l. 22 [TRANIO]

1211   Ajax, . . . a very man per se. . . . This man, lady, hath robbed
many beasts of their particular additions: he is as valiant as the
lion, churlish as the bear, slow as the elephant. . . . He is melancholy without cause, and merry against the hair.

Troilus and Cressida, Act i, sc. 2, l. 15 [ALEXANDER]

1212   A true knight,
Not yet mature, yet matchless, firm of word,
Speaking in deeds and deedless in his tongue;
Not soon provoked nor being provoked soon calm'd;
His heart and hand both open and both free;
For what he has he gives, what thinks he shows;
Yet gives he not till judgement guide his bounty,
Nor dignifies an impair thought with breath;
Manly as Hector, but more dangerous;
For Hector in his blaze of wrath subscribes
To tender objects, but he in heat of action
Is more vindicative than jealous love;
They call him Troilus, and on him erect
A second hope, as fairly built as Hector.

Troilus and Cressida, Act iv, sc. 5, l. 96 [ULYSSES]

1213   SIR TOBY: He plays o' the viol-de-gamboys, and speaks three or
four languages word for word without book, and hath all the good
gifts of nature.
MARIA: He hath indeed, almost natural: for besides that he 's a
fool, he 's a great quarreller; and but that he hath the gift of a
coward to allay the gust he hath in quarrelling, 'tis thought among
the prudent he would quickly have the gift of a grave.

Twelfth Night, Act i, sc. 3, l. 25 [SIR TOBY]

1214   I suppose him virtuous, know him noble,
Of great estate, of fresh and stainless youth;
In voices well divulged, free, learn'd and valiant;
And in dimensions and the shape of nature
A gracious person.

Twelfth Night, Act i, sc. 5, l. 277 [OLIVIA]

1215   A time-pleaser; an affectioned ass, that cons state without book
and utters it by great swarths; the best persuaded of himself, so

crammed, as he thinks, with excellencies, that it is his grounds of
faith that all that look on him love him.

> *Twelfth Night,* Act ii, sc. 3, l. 160 [MARIA]

Charity

1216   Charity itself fulfils the law,
And who can sever love from charity?

> *Love's Labour's Lost,* Act iv, sc. 3, l. 364 [BIRON]

1217   Lady, you know no rules of charity,
Which renders good for bad, blessings for curses.

> *Richard III,* Act i, sc. 2, l. 68 [GLOUCESTER]

1218   Thou hast not so much charity in thee as to go to the ale with a
Christian.

> *The Two Gentlemen of Verona,* Act ii, sc. 5, l. 60 [LAUNCE]

Charms

1219   All the charms of love,
Salt Cleopatra, soften thy waned lip!
Let witchcraft join with beauty, lust with both!

> *Antony and Cleopatra,* Act ii, sc. 1, l. 20 [POMPEY]

1220   This grave charm, . . .
Like a right gipsy, hath, at fast and loose,
Beguiled me to the very heart of loss.

> *Antony and Cleopatra,* Act iv, sc. 12, l. 25 [ANTONY]

1221   Unchain your spirits now with spelling charms
And try if they can gain your liberty.

> *I Henry VI,* Act v, sc. 3, l. 31 [YORK]

1222   Here stood he in the dark, his sharp sword out,
Mumbling of wicked charms.

> *King Lear,* Act ii, sc. 1, l. 40 [EDMUND]

1223   Your vessels and your spells provide,
Your charms and every thing beside.

> *Macbeth,* Act iii, sc. 5, l. 18 [HECATE]

1224   Never harm,
    Nor spell nor charm,
Come our lovely lady nigh.

> *A Midsummer Night's Dream,* Act ii, sc. 2, l. 16 [FAIRIES]

1225   I pray you all, tell me what they deserve
That do conspire my death with devilish plots
Of damned witchcraft, and that have prevail'd
Upon my body with their hellish charms?

> *Richard III,* Act iii, sc. 4, l. 61 [GLOUCESTER]

1226   MISTRESS QUICKLY: Surely I think you have charms, la; yes, in
truth.
FALSTAFF: Not I, I assure thee: setting the attraction of my good
parts aside, I have no other charms.

> *The Merry Wives of Windsor,* Act ii, sc. 3, l. 108 [MISTRESS
> QUICKLY]

1227   Is there not charms
By which the property of youth and maidhood
May be abused?

> *Othello,* Act i, sc. 1, l. 172 [BRABANTIO]

1228   Thou hast practised on her with foul charms.

> *Othello,* Act i, sc. 2, l. 73 [BRABANTIO]

1229   She was a charmer, and could almost read
The thoughts of people.

> *Othello,* Act iii, sc. 4, l. 57 [OTHELLO]

Chastity

1230   The very ice of chastity.
                    As You Like It, Act iii, sc. 4, l. 19 [CELIA]

1231   Chaste as the icicle
That 's curdied by the frost from purest snow
And hangs on Dian's temple.
                    Coriolanus, Act v, sc. 3, l. 65 [CORIOLANUS]

1232   More fair, virtuous, wise, chaste, constant-qualified and less
attemptable than any the rarest of our ladies in France.
                    Cymbeline, Act i, sc. 4, l. 65 [FRENCHMAN]

1233   Should he make me
Live, like Diana's priest, betwixt cold sheets,
While he is vaulting variable ramps,
In your despite? . . . Revenge it.
                    Cymbeline, Act i, sc. 6, l. 132 [IACHIMO]

1234   Our Tarquin thus
Did softly press the rushes, ere he waken'd
The chastity he wounded.
                    Cymbeline, Act ii, sc. 2, l. 12 [IACHIMO]

1235   Me of my lawful pleasure she restrain'd
And pray'd me oft forbearance; did it with
A pudency so rosy the sweet view on 't
Might well have warm'd old Saturn; that I thought her
As chaste as unsunn'd snow.
                    Cymbeline, Act ii, sc. 5, l. 9 [POSTHUMUS]

1236   Your daughter's chastity. . . .
He spake of her, as Dian had hot dreams,
And she alone was cold. . . . I was taught
Of your chaste daughter the wide difference
'Twixt amorous and villanous.
                    Cymbeline, Act v, sc. 5, l. 179 [IACHIMO]

1237   When he most burn'd in heart-wish'd luxury,
He preach'd pure maid, and praised cold chastity.
                    A Lover's Complaint, l. 314

1238   The impression of keen whips I 'ld wear as rubies,
And strip myself to death, . . . ere I 'ld yield
My body up to shame. . . .
Then, Isabel, live chaste, and, brother die:
More than our brother is our chastity.
                    Measure for Measure, Act ii, sc. 4, l. 101 [ISABELLA]

1239   If I live to be as old as Sibylla, I will die as chaste as Diana.
                    The Merchant of Venice, Act i, sc. 2, l. 116 [PORTIA]

1240   To win his heart, she touch'd him here and there,—
Touches so soft still conquer chastity.
                    The Passionate Pilgrim, Sonnet iv, l. 7

1241   Your peevish chastity, which is not worth a breakfast in the
cheapest country under the cope.
                    Pericles, Act iv, sc. 6, l. 131 [BOULT]

1242   Will you not go the way of women-kind? Marry, come up, my
dish of chastity with rosemary and bays!
                    Pericles, Act iv, sc. 6, l. 159 [BAWD]

1243   BENVOLIO: Then she hath sworn that she will still live chaste?
ROMEO: She hath, and in that sparing makes huge waste.
                    Romeo and Juliet, Act i, sc. 1, l. 223 [BENVOLIO]

1244   She will prove a . . . Roman Lucrece for her chastity.
                    The Taming of the Shrew, Act ii, sc. 1, l. 298 [PETRUCHIO]

1245   [Their] vows are, that no bed-right shall be paid
       Till Hymen's torch be lighted.
                    The Tempest, Act iv, sc. 1, l. 96 [IRIS]

1246   She is stubborn-chaste against all suit.
                    Troilus and Cressida, Act i, sc. 1, l. 100 [TROILUS]

1247   My lady was . . . chaste As may be in the world.
                    Troilus and Cressida, Act i, sc. 3, l. 298 [NESTOR]

1248   Thyself hast loved; and I have heard thee say
       No grief did ever come so near thy heart
       As when thy lady and thy true love died,
       Upon whose grave thou vow'dst pure chastity.
                    The Two Gentlemen of Verona, Act iv, sc. 3, l. 18 [SILVIA]

1249   Despite of fruitless chastity,
       Love-lacking vestals and self-loving nuns,
       That on the earth would breed a scarcity
       And barren dearth of daughters and of sons,
       Be prodigal.
                    Venus and Adonis, l. 751 [VENUS]

1250   My past life
       Hath been as continent, as chaste, as true,
       As I am now unhappy.
                    The Winter's Tale, Act iii, sc. 2, l. 34 [HERMIONE]

Chastity: Its Loss

1251   My chastity's the jewel of our house,
       Bequeathed down from many ancestors;
       Which were the greatest obloquy i' the world
       In me to lose.
                    All's Well that Ends Well, Act iv, sc. 2, l. 46 [DIANA]

1252   Weigh what loss your honour may sustain,
       If with too credent ear you list his songs,
       Or lose your heart, or your chaste treasure open
       To his unmaster'd importunity.
                    Hamlet, Act i, sc. 3, l. 29 [LAERTES]

1253   There my white stole of chastity I daff'd,
       Shook off my sober guards and civil fears.
                    A Lover's Complaint, l. 297

1254   You must lay down the treasures of your body.
                    Measure for Measure, Act ii, sc. 4, l. 96 [ANGELO]

1255   Pure Chastity is rifled of her store,
       And Lust, the thief, far poorer than before.
                    The Rape of Lucrece, l. 692

Cheek

1256   His cicatrice, an emblem of war, here on his sinister cheek.
                    All's Well that Ends Well, Act ii, sc. 1, l. 43 [PAROLLES]

1257   His left cheek is a cheek of two pile and a half, but his right
       cheek is worn bare.
                    All's Well that Ends Well, Act iv, sc. 5, l. 102 [CLOWN]
                    My mother's blood
       Runs on the dexter cheek, and this sinister
       Bounds in my father's.
                    Troilus and Cressida, Act iv, sc. 5, l. 127 [HECTOR]

1258   Our veil'd dames
       Commit the war of white and damask in
       Their nicely-gawded cheeks to the wanton spoil
       Of Phœbus' burning kisses.
                    Coriolanus, Act ii, sc. 1, l. 231 [BRUTUS]

1259   PLANTAGENET: Your cheeks do counterfeit our roses,
        For pale they look with fear. . . .
        SOMERSET: No, Plantagenet,
        'Tis not for fear but anger that thy cheeks
        Blush for pure shame to counterfeit our roses.
                        I Henry VI, Act ii, sc. 4, 1. 62 [PLANTAGENET]

1260   This fellow here, . . . Upbraided me about the rose I wear;
        Saying, the sanguine colour of the leaves
        Did represent my master's blushing cheeks.
                        I Henry VI, Act iv, sc. 1, 1. 90 [BASSET]

1261   LYSANDER: How now, my love! Why is your cheek so pale?
        How chance the roses there do fade so fast?
        HERMIA: Belike for want of rain, which I could well
        Beteem them from the tempest of my eyes.
                A Midsummer Night's Dream, Act i, sc. 1, 1. 128 [LYSANDER]

1262   I'll go with thee, cheek by jole.
                A Midsummer Night's Dream, Act iii, sc. 2, 1. 338 [DEMETRIUS]

1263   Come, sit thee down upon this flowery bed,
            While I thy amiable cheeks do coy,
        And stick musk-roses in thy sleek, smooth head,
            And kiss thy fair large ears, my gentle joy.
                A Midsummer Night's Dream, Act iv, sc. 1, 1. 1 [TITANIA]

1264   The brightness of her cheek would shame those stars,
        As daylight doth a lamp. . . .
        See, how she leans her cheek upon her hand:
        O, that I were a glove upon that hand,
        That I might touch that cheek!
                        Romeo and Juliet, Act ii, sc. 2, 1. 19 [ROMEO]

Cheer

1265   I prithee, lady, have a better cheer.
                All's Well that Ends Well, Act iii, sc. 2, 1. 67 [COUNTESS]

1266   Be of good cheer.
                Antony and Cleopatra, Act v, sc. 2, 1. 21 [PROCULEIUS]

1267   Show a merry cheer.
                The Merchant of Venice, Act iii, sc. 2, 1. 315 [PORTIA]

1268   I have not that alacrity of spirit
        Nor cheer of mind, that I was wont to have.
                        Richard III, Act v, sc. 3, 1. 73 [KING RICHARD]

Cheese

1269   You Banbury cheese!
                The Merry Wives of Windsor, Act i, sc. 1, 1. 130 [BARDOLPH]
                (To Slender because of his thinness, referring to the proverb,
                "As thin as a Banbury cheese.")

1270   I will make an end of my dinner; there's pippins and cheese to
        come.
                The Merry Wives of Windsor, Act i, sc. 2, 1. 13 [EVANS]

1271   Why, my cheese, my digestion, why hast thou not served thyself
        in to my table so many meals?
                Troilus and Cressida, Act ii, sc. 3, 1. 44 [ACHILLES]
                (A reference to the proverb, "Cheese digests everything except
                itself.")

1272   That stale old mouse-eaten dry cheese, Nestor.
                Troilus and Cressida, Act v, sc. 4, 1. 11 [THERSITES]

Cherubin

1273   Patience, thou young and rose-lipp'd cherubin.
                        Othello, Act iv, sc. 2, 1. 63 [OTHELLO]

1274 A cherubin thou wast that did preserve us.
The Tempest, Act i, sc. 2, l. 152 [PROSPERO]

Chiding

1275 Better a little chiding than a great deal of heart-break.
The Merry Wives of Windsor, Act v, sc. 3, l. 10 [MRS. PAGE]

1276 Those that do teach young babes
Do it with gentle means and easy tasks:
He might have chid me so; for, in good faith,
I am a child to chiding.
Othello, Act iv, sc. 2, l. 111 [DESDEMONA]

Child

1277 Be a child o' the time.
Antony and Cleopatra, Act ii, sc. 7, l. 106 [ANTONY]

1278 VALERIA: Indeed, la, 'tis a noble child.
VIRGILIA: A crack, madam.
Coriolanus, Act i, sc. 3, l. 73 [VALERIA]
When a' was a crack not thus high.
II Henry IV, Act iii, sc. 2, l. 34 [SHALLOW]
("Crack," a pert boy.)

1279 How sharper than a serpent's tooth it is
To have a thankless child!
King Lear, Act i, sc. 4, l. 310 [LEAR]

1280 VERGES: If you hear a child cry in the night, you must call to
the nurse and bid her still it.
WATCH: How if the nurse be asleep and will not hear us?
DOGBERRY: Why, then, depart in peace, and let the child wake
her with crying; for the ewe that will not hear her lamb when
it baes will never answer a calf when he bleats.
Much Ado about Nothing, Act iii, sc. 3, l. 70 [VERGES]

1281 Grieved I, I had but one?
Chid I for that at frugal nature's frame?
O, one too much by thee! Why had I one?
Why ever wast thou lovely in my eyes?
. . . . Why she, O, she is fallen
Into a pit of ink, that the wide sea
Hath drops too few to wash her clean again.
Much Ado about Nothing, Act iv, sc. 1, l. 129 [LEONATO]
Wife, we scarce thought us blest
That God had lent us but this only child;
But now I see this one is one too much,
And that we have a curse in having her.
Romeo and Juliet, Act iii, sc. 5, l. 165 [CAPULET]

1282 Woe to that land that's govern'd by a child!
Richard III, Act ii, sc. 3, l. 11 [CITIZEN]

1283 My child is yet a stranger in the world;
She hath not seen the change of fourteen years;
Let two more summers wither in their pride,
Ere we may think her ripe to be a bride.
Romeo and Juliet, Act i, sc. 2, l. 8 [CAPULET]

Children

1284 I shall never have the blessing of God till I have issue o' my body;
for they say barnes are blessings.
All's Well that Ends Well, Act i, sc. 3, l. 26 [CLOWN]
What have we here? Mercy on 's, a barne; a very pretty barne!
A boy or a child, I wonder?
The Winter's Tale, Act iii, sc. 3, l. 71 [SHEPHERD]

1285   HAMLET: Good lads, how do you both?
       ROSENCRANTZ: As the indifferent children of the earth. ·
                              Hamlet, Act ii, sc. 2, l. 230 [HAMLET]

1286   There is, sir, an aery of children, little eyases, that cry out on
       the top of question, and are most tyrannically clapp'd for 't.
                           Hamlet, Act ii, sc. 2, l. 354 [ROSENCRANTZ]
           ("Eyases," a term in falconry, meaning a hawk which has
           been brought up from the nest, as distinguished from one
           caught and trained.)

1287   Bring forth men-children only;
       For thy undaunted metal should compose
       Nothing but males.
                              Macbeth, Act i, sc. 7, l. 72 [MACBETH]

1288   'Tis the eye of childhood That fears a painted devil.
                         Macbeth, Act ii, sc. 2, l. 54 [LADY MACBETH]

1289   ROSS: Your castle is surprised; your wife and babes
       Savagely slaughter'd. . . .
       MACDUFF: My children too? . . . My wife kill'd too? . . .
       All my pretty ones? . . .
       Did you say all? O hell-kite! All?
       What, all my pretty chickens and their dam
       At one fell swoop? . . . Did heaven look on,
       And would not take their part?
                              Macbeth, Act iv, sc. 3, l. 204 [ROSS]

1290   'Tis not good that children should know any wickedness: old
       folks, you know, have discretion, as they say, and know the world.
                    The Merry Wives of Windsor, Act ii, sc. 2, l. 133 [MISTRESS
                                                              QUICKLY]

1291   If children pre-decease progenitors,
       We are their offspring, and they none of ours.
                           The Rape of Lucrece, l. 1756 [LUCRETIUS]

1292   Your children were vexation to your youth,
       But mine shall be a comfort to your age.
                         Richard III, Act iv, sc. 4, l. 305 [KING RICHARD]

1293   If you do free your children from the sword,
       Your children's children quit it in your age.
                         Richard III, Act v, sc. 3, l. 261 [RICHMOND]

Chin

1294   With his Amazonian chin he drove
       The bristled lips before him.
                           Coriolanus, Act ii, sc. 2, l. 95 [COMINIUS]
           ("Amazonian," hairless.)

1295   Whose chin is but enrich'd With one appearing hair.
                           Henry V, Act iii, Prologue, l. 22 [CHORUS]

1296   Small show of man was yet upon his chin;
       His phœnix down began but to appear.
                              A Lover's Complaint, l. 92

1297   Alas, poor chin! many a wart is richer.
                     Troilus and Cressida, Act i, sc. 2, l. 148 [CRESSIDA]

Choice

1298   I had rather be in this choice than throw ames-ace for my life.
                     All's Well that Ends Well, Act ii, sc. 3, l. 84 [LAFEU]
           ("Ames-ace," two aces, the lowest throw at dice.)

1299   I stuck my choice upon her, ere my heart
       Durst make too bold a herald of my tongue.
                     All's Well that Ends Well, Act v, sc. 3, l. 44 [BERTRAM]

1300 I shall be well content with any choice
Tends to God's glory and my country's weal.
I Henry VI, Act v, sc. 1, l. 26 [KING HENRY]

1301 There's small choice in rotten apples.
The Taming of the Shrew, Act i, sc. 1, l. 138 [HORTENSIO]

1302 Pedlar, let's have the first choice.
The Winter's Tale, Act iv, sc. 4, l. 319 [CLOWN]

Choler

1303 Put him to choler straight: . . . being once chafed
He cannot be rein'd again to temperance.
Coriolanus, Act iii, sc. 3, l. 25 [BRUTUS]

1304 For me to put him to his purgation would perhaps plunge him
into far more choler.
Hamlet, Act iii, sc. 2, l. 318 [HAMLET]

1305 What, drunk with choler? stay and pause awhile.
I Henry IV, Act i, sc. 3, l. 129 [NORTHUMBERLAND]

1306 I beseek you now, aggravate your choler.
II Henry IV, Act ii, sc. 4, l. 177 [HOSTESS]

1307   I know Fluellen valiant
And, touch'd with choler, hot as gunpowder.
Henry V, Act iv, sc. 7, l. 187 [KING HENRY]

1308 Go cheerfully together and digest
Your angry choler on your enemies.
I Henry VI, Act iv, sc. 1, l. 167 [KING HENRY]

1309 Throw cold water on thy choler.
The Merry Wives of Windsor, Act ii, sc. 3, l. 88 [HOST]

1310 Let's purge this choler without letting blood: . . .
Deep malice makes too deep incision;
Forget, forgive; conclude and be agreed;
Our doctors say this is no month to bleed.
Richard II, Act i, sc. 1, l. 153 [KING RICHARD]

Choleric

1311 Eat none of it, Lest it make you choleric.
The Comedy of Errors, Act ii, sc. 2, l. 61 [DROMIO OF SYRACUSE]

1312 What, what, my lord, are you so choleric
With Eleanor, for telling but her dream?
II Henry VI, Act i, sc. 2, l. 51 [DUCHESS]

1313 Go show your slaves how choleric you are,
And make your bondmen tremble.
Julius Cæsar, Act iv, sc. 3, l. 43 [BRUTUS]

Chorus

1314 You are as good as a chorus, my lord.
Hamlet, Act iii, sc. 2, l. 255 [OPHELIA]

1315 Admit me Chorus to this history.
Henry V, Prologue, l. 32 [CHORUS]

Christ

1316 As far as to the sepulchre of Christ,
Whose soldier now, under whose blessed cross
We are impressed and engaged to fight,
Forthwith a power of England shall we levy;
Whose arms were moulded in their mothers' womb
  To chase these pagans in those holy fields
  Over whose acres walk'd those blessed feet

Which fourteen hundred years ago were nail'd
For our advantage on the bitter cross.
> *I Henry IV*, Act i, sc. 1, l. 19 [KING HENRY]

1317 In the name of Jesu Christ, speak lower.
> *Henry V*, Act iv, sc. 1, l. 65 [FLUELLEN]

You shall sup with Jesu Christ to-night.
> *II Henry VI*, Act v, sc. 1, l. 214 [RICHARD]

1318 Many a time hath banish'd Norfolk fought
For Jesu Christ in glorious Christian field,
Streaming the ensign of the Christian cross
Against black pagans, Turks, and Saracens;
And toil'd with works of war, retired himself
To Italy; and there at Venice gave
His body to that pleasant country's earth,
And his pure soul unto his captain Christ,
Under whose colours he had fought so long.
> *Richard II*, Act iv, sc. 1, l. 92 [CARLISLE]

Christian

1319 Now, as I am a Christian, answer me.
> *The Comedy of Errors*, Act i, sc. 2, l. 77 [ANTIPHOLUS OF SYRACUSE]

As I am a Christians soul now, . . . this is the place appointed.
> *The Merry Wives of Windsor*, Act iii, sc. 1, l. 96 [EVANS]

No, as I am a Christian.
> *Othello*, Act iv, sc. 2, l. 82 [DESDEMONA]

1320 O Father Abram, what these Christians are,
Whose own hard dealings teaches them suspect
The thoughts of others!
> *The Merchant of Venice*, Act i, sc. 3, l. 161 [SHYLOCK]

1321 There will come a Christian by
Will be worth a Jewess' eye.
> *The Merchant of Venice*, Act ii, sc. 5, l. 42 [LAUNCELOT]

1322 JESSICA: I shall be saved by my husband; he hath made me a Christian.
LAUNCELOT: Truly, the more to blame, he: we were Christians enow before. . . . This making of Christians will raise the price of hogs: if we grow all to be pork-eaters, we shall not shortly have a rasher on the coals for money.
> *The Merchant of Venice*, Act iii, sc. 5, l. 21 [JESSICA]

1323 Thou art an Hebrew, a Jew, and not worth the name of a Christian.
> *The Two Gentlemen of Verona*, Act ii, sc. 5, l. 57 [LAUNCE]

1324 She hath more qualities than a water-spaniel; which is much in a bare Christian.
> *The Two Gentlemen of Verona*, Act iii, sc. 1, l. 272 [LAUNCE]

Christian-Like

1325 Plant . . . Christian-like accord In their sweet bosoms.
> *Henry V*, Act v, sc. 2, l. 381 [FRENCH KING]

1326 Although the duke was enemy to him,
Yet he most Christian-like laments his death.
> *II Henry VI*, Act iii, sc. 2, l. 57 [QUEEN]

1327 He . . . undertakes them with a most Christian-like fear.
> *Much Ado about Nothing*, Act ii, sc. 3, l. 200 [DON PEDRO]

1328 A virtuous and a Christian-like conclusion,
To pray for them that hath done scathe to us.
> *Richard III*, Act i, sc. 3, l. 316 [RIVERS]

Chronicle

1329 Whose chronicle thus writ: 'The man was noble,
But with his last attempt he wiped it out.'
Coriolanus, Act v, sc. 3, l. 145 [VOLUMNIA]

1330 Fill up chronicles in time to come.
I Henry IV, Act i, sc. 3, l. 171 [HOTSPUR]
I have read in the chronicles.
Henry V, Act iv, sc. 7, l. 98 [FLUELLEN]
Look in the chronicles.
The Taming of the Shrew, Act i, Induction, l. 4 [SLY]

1331 'Tis a chronicle of day by day,
Not a relation for a breakfast.
The Tempest, Act v, sc. 1, l. 163 [PROSPERO]

1332 Let me embrace thee, good old chronicle,
That hast so long walk'd hand in hand with time.
Troilus and Cressida, Act iv, sc. 5, l. 202 [HECTOR]
(Referring to Nestor.)

Church

1333 An I have not forgotten what the inside of a church is made of,
I am a peppercorn, a brewer's horse.
I Henry IV, Act iii, sc. 3, l. 8 [FALSTAFF]

1334 Ne'er throughout the year to church thou go'st
Except it be to pray against thy foes.
I Henry VI, Act i, sc. 1, l. 42 [GLOUCESTER]

1335 Be champion of our church,
Or let the church, our mother, breathe her curse,
A mother's curse, on her revolting son.
King John, Act iii, sc. 1, l. 255 [PANDULPH]

1336 I tell thee what: get thee to church o' Thursday,
Or never after look me in the face.
Romeo and Juliet, Act iii, sc. 5, l. 162 [CAPULET]

1337 As the custom is,
In all her best array bear her to church.
Romeo and Juliet, Act iv, sc. 5, l. 80 [FRIAR LAURENCE]

Churchman

1338 Who should study to prefer a peace,
If holy churchmen take delight in broils?
I Henry VI, Act iii, sc. 1, l. 110 [KING HENRY]

1339 Churchmen so hot? good uncle, hide such malice.
II Henry VI, Act ii, sc. 1, l. 25 [GLOUCESTER]

1340 Ambitious churchman, leave to afflict my heart:
Sorrow and grief have vanquish'd all my powers.
II Henry VI, Act ii, sc. 1, l. 182 [GLOUCESTER]

1341 The churchman bears a bounteous mind indeed,
A hand as fruitful as the land that feeds us;
His dews fall every where.
Henry VIII, Act i, sc. 3, l. 55 [LOVELL]

1342 Love and meekness, lord,
Become a churchman better than ambition:
Win straying souls with modesty again,
Cast none away.
Henry VIII, Act v, sc. 3, l. 62 [CRANMER]

1343 VIOLA: Dost thou live by thy tabor?
CLOWN: No, sir, I live by the church.
VIOLA: Art thou a churchman?

CLOWN : No such matter, sir : I do live by the church : for I do live
at my house, and my house doth stand by the church.
Twelfth Night, Act iii, sc. 1, l. 2 [VIOLA]

Circumstance

1344   Can you, by no drift of circumstance,
Get from him why he puts on this confusion?
Hamlet, Act iii, sc. 1, l. 1 [KING]

1345   In our circumstance and course of thought,
'Tis heavy with him.
Hamlet, Act iii, sc. 3, l. 83 [HAMLET]

1346   Good fellow, tell us here the circumstance,
That we for thee may glorify the Lord.
II Henry VI, Act ii, sc. 1, l. 74 [KING]
The circumstance I'll tell you more at large.
I Henry VI, Act i, sc. 1, l. 109 [MESSENGER]

1347   A bombast circumstance,
Horribly stuff'd with epithets of war.
Othello, Act i, sc. 1, l. 12 [IAGO]

1348   Do not embrace me till each circumstance
Of place, time, fortune, do cohere and jump.
Twelfth Night, Act v, sc. 1, l. 258 [VIOLA]

Citizens

1349   Sweep on, you fat and greasy citizens ;
'Tis just the fashion.
As You Like It, Act ii, sc. 1, l. 55 [JAQUES]

1350   Awake the snorting citizens with the bell.
Othello, Act i, sc. 1, l. 90 [IAGO]

1351   Ancient citizens
Cast by their grave beseeming ornaments,
To wield old partisans, in hands as old.
Romeo and Juliet, Act i, sc. 1, l. 99 [PRINCE]

City

1352   SICINIUS : What is the city but the people?
CITIZENS : True, The people are the city.
Coriolanus, Act iii, sc. 1, l. 199 [SICINIUS]

1353   That is the way to lay the city flat;
To bring the roof to the foundation,
And bury all . . . In heaps and piles of ruin.
Coriolanus, Act iii, sc. 1, l. 204 [COMINIUS]

1354   SERVANT : Where dwellest thou?
CORIOLANUS : Under the canopy. . . . I' the city of kites and crows.
Coriolanus, Act iv, sc. 5, l. 40 [SERVANT]

1355   This Tarsus, o'er which I have the government,
A city on whom plenty held full hand,
For riches strew'd herself even in the streets.
Pericles, Act i, sc. 4, l. 21 [CLEON]

1356   O, let those cities that of plenty's cup
And her prosperities so largely taste,
With their superfluous riots, hear these tears !
Pericles, Act i, sc. 4, l. 52 [CLEON]

Civility

1357   DUKE : Art thou thus bolden'd, man, by thy distress, . . .
That in civility thou seem'st so empty? . . .

ORLANDO: The thorny point
Of bare distress hath ta'en from me the show
Of smooth civility.
> *As You Like It,* Act ii, sc. 7, l. 91 [DUKE]

1358   The count is neither sad, nor sick, nor merry, nor well; but civil
count, civil as an orange, and something of that jealous complexion.
> *Much Ado about Nothing,* Act ii, sc. 1, l. 303 [BEATRICE]

1359   Where is Malvolio? he is sad and civil,
And suits well for a servant with my fortunes.
> *Twelfth Night,* Act iii, sc. 4, l. 5 [OLIVIA]

Claim

1360   ANTIPHOLUS S.: What claim lays she to you?
DROMIO S.: Marry, sir, such claim as you would lay to your horse;
she would have me as a beast.
> *The Comedy of Errors,* Act iii, sc. 2, l. 84 [ANTIPHOLUS
> OF SYRACUSE]

1361   'Tis no sinister nor no awkward claim,
Pick'd from the worm-holes of long-vanish'd days,
Nor from the dust of old oblivion raked.
> *Henry V,* Act ii, sc. 4, l. 85 [EXETER]

Cleanliness

1362   Bid them wash their faces, And keep their teeth clean.
> *Coriolanus,* Act ii, sc. 3, l. 66 [CORIOLANUS]

1363   Would thou wert clean enough to spit upon.
> *Timon of Athens,* Act iv, sc. 3, l. 364 [TIMON]

1364   We must be neat; not neat, but cleanly, captain:
And yet the steer, the heifer and the calf
Are all call'd neat.
> *The Winter's Tale,* Act i, sc. 2, l. 123 [LEONTES]

Climbing

1365   KING: Man and birds are fain of climbing high. . . .
GLOUCESTER: My Lord, 'tis but a base ignoble mind
That mounts no higher than a bird can soar.
> *II Henry VI,* Act ii, sc. 1, l. 8 [KING]

1366   [He] bought his climbing very dear.
> *II Henry VI,* Act ii, sc. 1, l. 100 [WIFE]

Clip

1367   Enter the city, clip your wives, your friends.
> *Antony and Cleopatra,* Act iv, sc. 8, l. 8 [ANTONY]

1368   O, let me clip ye
In arms as sound as when I woo'd, in heart
As merry as when our nuptial day was done,
And tapers burn'd to bedward!
> *Coriolanus,* Act i, sc. 6, l. 29 [CORIOLANUS]

Cloak

1369   Now happy he whose cloak and cincture can
Hold out this tempest.
> *King John,* Act iv, sc. 3, l. 155 [BASTARD]

1370   An old cloak makes a new jerkin.
> *The Merry Wives of Windsor,* Act i, sc. 3, l. 18 [FALSTAFF]

1371   Take thine auld cloak about thee.
> *Othello,* Act ii, sc. 3, l. 99 [IAGO]
> (For full quotation see 5420.)

1372   [Night's] black all-hiding cloak.
                          The Rape of Lucrece, 1. 801 [Lucrece]
         The cloak of night being pluck'd from off their backs.
                          Richard II, Act iii, sc. 2, l. 45 [King Richard]

Clock

1373   Rosalind: I pray you, what is 't o'clock?
         Orlando: You should ask me what time o' day: there's no clock
         in the forest.
                          As You Like It, Act iii, sc. 2, l. 317 [Rosalind]
1374   The clock hath strucken twelve upon the bell.
                 The Comedy of Errors, Act i, sc. 2, l. 45 [Dromio of Ephesus]
         Now the clock strikes one.
                The Comedy of Errors, Act iv, sc. 2, l. 54 [Dromio of Syracuse]
         The clock hath stricken three.
                          Julius Cæsar, Act ii, sc. 1, l. 192 [Cassius]
         The clock struck nine when I did send the nurse.
                          Romeo and Juliet, Act ii, sc. 5, l. 1 [Juliet]
1375   Unhappy was the clock that struck the hour.
                          Cymbeline, Act v, sc. 5, l. 153 [Iachimo]
1376   The clock upbraids me with the waste of time.
                          Twelfth Night, Act iii, sc. 1, l. 141 [Olivia]

Cloud

1377   I am not a day of season,
         For thou mayst see a sunshine and a hail
         In me at once: but to the brightest beams
         Distracted clouds give way.
                          All's Well that Ends Well, Act v, sc. 3, l. 32 [King]
1378   He has a cloud in 's face.
                          Antony and Cleopatra, Act iii, sc. 2, l. 52 [Agrippa]
1379   Dissolve, thick cloud, and rain; that I may say
         The gods themselves do weep!
                          Antony and Cleopatra, Act v, sc. 2, l. 302 [Charmian]
1380   Sometime we see a cloud that's dragonish;
         A vapour sometime like a bear or lion,
         A tower'd citadel, a pendent rock,
         A forked mountain, or blue promontory
         With trees upon 't, that nod unto the world. . . .
         That which is now a horse, even with a thought
         The rack dislimns, and makes it indistinct,
         As water is in water.
                          Antony and Cleopatra, Act iv, sc. 14, l. 2 [Antony]
1381   Hamlet: Do you see yonder cloud that's almost in shape of a
         camel?
         Polonius: By the mass, and 'tis like a camel, indeed. . . .
         Hamlet: Or like a whale?
         Polonius: Very like a whale. . . .
         Hamlet: They fool me to the top of my bent.
                          Hamlet, Act iii, sc. 2, l. 393 [Hamlet]
1382   He would be above the clouds.
                          II Henry VI, Act ii, sc. 1, l. 15 [Cardinal]
1383   Every cloud engenders not a storm.
                          III Henry VI, Act v, sc. 3, l. 13 [Clarence]
1384   In the midst of this bright-shining day,
         I spy a black, suspicious, threatening cloud.
                          III Henry VI, Act v, sc. 3, l. 3 [King Edward]

1385   When a black-faced cloud the world doth threat, . . .
From earth's dark womb some gentle gust doth get,
Which blows these pitchy vapours from their biding.
The Rape of Lucrece, l. 547

1386   The more fair and crystal is the sky,
The uglier seem the clouds that in it fly.
Richard II, Act i, sc. 1, l. 41 [BOLINGBROKE]

1387   When clouds appear, wise men put on their cloaks.
Richard III, Act ii, sc. 3, l. 32 [CITIZEN]
Why didst thou promise such a beauteous day
And make me travel forth without my cloak,
To let base clouds o'ertake me in my way,
Hiding thy bravery in their rotten smoke?
Sonnet xxxiv, l. 1

1388   Yond same black cloud, yond huge one, looks like a foul bombard
that would shed his liquor. If it should thunder, . . . yond same
cloud cannot choose but fall by pailfulls.
The Tempest, Act ii, sc. 2, l. 20 [TRINCULO]
(A bombard is a leather jug for liquor.)

1389   Coal-black clouds that shadow heaven's light
Do summon us to part and bid good night.
Venus and Adonis, l. 533 [ADONIS]

Clown

1390   My lord, the roynish clown, at whom so oft
Your grace was wont to laugh, is also missing.
As You Like It, Act ii, sc. 2, l. 8 [LORD]
("Roynish," mangy.)

1391   The clown shall make those laugh whose lungs are tickle o' the
sere.
Hamlet, Act ii, sc. 2, l. 337 [HAMLET]

1392   By my soul, a swain! a most simple clown!
Lord, Lord, how the ladies and I have put him down!
Love's Labour's Lost, Act iv, sc. 1, l. 142 [COSTARD]

Cobweb

1393   BOTTOM : I beseech your worship's name.
COBWEB : Cobweb.
BOTTOM : I shall desire you of more acquaintance, good Master
Cobweb: if I cut my finger, I shall make bold with you.
A Midsummer Night's Dream, Act iii, sc. 1, l. 183 [BOTTOM]

Cock

1394   CLOTEN : Every Jack-slave hath his bellyful of fighting, and I must
go up and down like a cock that nobody can match.
LORD (*Aside*) : You are cock and capon too; and you crow, cock,
with your comb on.
Cymbeline, Act ii, sc. 1, l. 22 [CLOTEN]

1395   HORATIO :   I have heard,
The cock, that is the trumpet to the morn,
Doth with his lofty and shrill-sounding throat
Awake the god of day; and, at his warning,
Whether in sea or fire, in earth or air,
The extravagant and erring spirit hies
To his confine. . . .
MARCELLUS : Some say that ever 'gainst that season comes
Wherein our Saviour's birth is celebrated,
The bird of dawning singeth all night long:
And then, they say, no spirit dare stir abroad, . . .

So hallow'd and so gracious is the time.
HORATIO: So have I heard and do in part believe it.

Hamlet, Act i, sc. 1, l. 149 [HORATIO]

1396 The country cocks do crow, the clocks do toll,
And the third hour of drowsy morning name.

Henry V, Act iv, Prologue, l. 15 [CHORUS]

1397 Look thou meet me ere the first cock crow.

A Midsummer Night's Dream, Act ii, sc. 1, l. 267 [OBERON]

Come, stir, stir, stir! the second cock hath crow'd.

Romeo and Juliet, Act iv, sc. 4, l. 3 [CAPULET]

The early village-cock
Hath twice done salutation to the morn.

Richard III, Act v, sc. 3, l. 209 [RATCLIFF]

1398 You will set cock-a-hoop: you'll be the man!

Romeo and Juliet, Act i, sc. 5, l. 83 [CAPULET]

("Cock-a-hoop," boastful, elated.)

Cog

1399   I'll mountebank their loves,
Cog their hearts from them.

Coriolanus, Act iii, sc. 2, l. 132 [CORIOLANUS]

("Cog," to wheedle, to cheat, to deceive.)
Since you can cog, I'll play no more with you.

Love's Labour's Lost, Act v, sc. 2, l. 235 [PRINCESS]

1400 I cannot cog, I cannot prate. . . . Come, I cannot cog and say thou
art this and that, like a many of these lisping hawthorn-buds.

The Merry Wives of Windsor, Act iii, sc. 3, l. 50 [FALSTAFF]

1401 You hear him cog, see him dissemble,
Know his gross patchery.

Timon of Athens, Act v, sc. 1, l. 98 [TIMON]

Coldness See also Heat and Cold

1402 I spoke with her but once And found her wondrous cold.

All's Well that Ends Well, Act iii, sc. 6, l. 120 [BERTRAM]

1403 When you are dead, you should be such a one
As you are now, for you are cold and stern.

All's Well that Ends Well, Act iv, sc. 2, l. 7 [BERTRAM]

1404 DROMIO E.: My master stays in the street.
DROMIO S.: Let him walk from whence he came, lest he catch cold
on's feet.

The Comedy of Errors, Act iii, sc. 1, l. 36 [DROMIO OF EPHESUS]

Catch cold and starve.

Cymbeline, Act i, sc. 4, l. 180 [IACHIMO]

An thou canst not smile as the wind sits, thou'lt catch cold shortly.

King Lear, Act i, sc. 4, l. 113 [FOOL]

You will catch cold and curse me.

Troilus and Cressida, Act iv, sc. 2 l. 15 [TROILUS]

1405 'Tis bitter cold, And I am sick at heart.

Hamlet, Act i, sc. 1, l. 8 [FRANCISCO]

HAMLET: 'Tis very cold; the wind is northerly.
OSRIC: It is indifferent cold, my lord, indeed.

Hamlet, Act v, sc. 2, l. 98 [HAMLET]

Nipping cold.

II Henry VI, Act ii, sc. 4, l. 3 [GLOUCESTER]

Biting cold.

II Henry VI, Act iii, sc. 2, l. 337 [SUFFOLK]

Icy cold.

Richard III, Act iii, sc. 1, l. 176 [BUCKINGHAM]

1406   As cold as any stone.
                                Henry V, Act ii, sc. 3, l. 25 [HOSTESS]
        She sent him away as cold as a snowball.
                                Pericles, Act iv, sc. 6, l. 148 [BOULT]
        As cold as if I had swallowed snowballs.
                The Merry Wives of Windsor, Act iii, sc. 5, l. 24 [FALSTAFF]
1407   Who gives anything to poor Tom? whom the foul fiend hath led
        through fire and through flame, through ford and whirlipool, o'er
        bog and quagmire? . . . Bless thy five wits! Tom's a-cold.
                                King Lear, Act iii, sc. 4, l. 51 [EDGAR]
1408   What freezings have I felt, what dark days seen!
                                Sonnet xcvii, l. 3
1409   GRUMIO: Considering the weather, a taller man than I will take
        cold. . . .
        CURTIS: Come, you are so full of cony-catching!
        GRUMIO: Why, therefore fire; for I have caught extreme cold.
                    The Taming of the Shrew, Act iv, sc. 1, l. 11 [GRUMIO]

Colt

1410   FALSTAFF: What a plague mean ye to colt me thus?
        PRINCE: Thou liest; thou art not colted, thou art uncolted.
                                I Henry IV, Act ii, sc. 2, l. 40 [FALSTAFF]
        ("Colt," to befool, take in.)
        She hath been colted by him.
                                Cymbeline, Act ii, sc. 4, l. 133 [POSTHUMUS]
1411   A wanton herd . . . of youthful and unhandled colts.
                    The Merchant of Venice, Act v, sc. 1, l. 71 [LORENZO]
1412   Young hot colts being raged do rage the more.
                                Richard II, Act ii, sc. 1, l. 69 [YORK]
1413   Like unback'd colts, they prick'd their ears,
        Advanced their eyelids, lifted up their noses
        As they smelt music.
                                The Tempest, Act iv, sc. 1, l. 176 [ARIEL]
1414   The cold that 's back'd and burden'd being young
        Loseth his pride and never waxeth strong.
                                Venus and Adonis, l. 419 [ADONIS]

Comet

1415   Hung be the heavens with black, yield day to night!
        Comets, importing change of time and states,
        Brandish your crystal tresses in the sky,
        And with them scourge the bad revolting stars
        That have consented unto Henry's death!
                                I Henry VI, Act i, sc. 1, l. 1 [BEDFORD]
1416   By being seldom seen, I could not stir
        But like a comet I was wonder'd at.
                                I Henry IV, Act iii, sc. 2, l. 46 [KING]
1417   I . . . have been gazed on like a comet.
                                Pericles, Act v, sc. 1, l. 87 [MARINA]
1418   Wherefore gaze this goodly company,
        As if they saw . . . some comet?
                The Taming of the Shrew, Act iii, sc. 2, l. 98 [PETRUCHIO]

Comfort

1419   All strange and terrible events are welcome,
        But comforts we despise.
                Antony and Cleopatra, Act iv, sc. 15, l. 3 [CLEOPATRA]

1420   He that doth the ravens feed,
Yea, providently caters for the sparrow,
Be comfort to my age!
                    As You Like It, Act ii, sc. 3, l. 43 [ADAM]

1421   Thou art all the comfort
The gods will diet me with.
                    Cymbeline, Act iii, sc. 4, l. 182 [IMOGEN]

1422   SUFFOLK: Comfort, my sovereign! gracious Henry, comfort!
KING: What, doth my Lord of Suffolk comfort me?
                    II Henry VI, Act iii, sc. 2, l. 38 [SUFFOLK]

1423   Is all thy comfort shut in Gloucester's tomb? . . .
Erect his statua and worship it,
And make my image but an alehouse sign.
                    II Henry VI, Act iii, sc. 2, l. 78 [QUEEN]

1424   Is this your comfort?
The cordial that ye bring a wretched lady,
A woman lost among ye, laugh'd at, scorn'd?
                    Henry VIII, Act iii, sc. 1, l. 105 [QUEEN KATHARINE]

1425   CAPUCIUS: The king . . . entreats you take good comfort.
KATHARINE: O my good lord, that comfort comes too late;
'Tis like a pardon after execution:
That gentle physic, given in time, had cured me;
But now I am past all comforts here, but prayers.
                    Henry VIII, Act iv, sc. 2, l. 118 [CAPUCIUS]

1426   Comfort me with cold. I do not ask you much,
I beg cold comfort.
                    King John, Act v, sc. 7, l. 41 [KING JOHN]
Our mistress, whose hand . . . thou shalt soon feel, to thy cold
comfort.
                    The Taming of the Shrew, Act iv, sc. 1, l. 33 [GRUMIO]

1427   Our good old friend, Lay comforts to your bosom.
                    King Lear, Act ii, sc. 1, l. 127 [REGAN]

1428   Good friend, be gone:
Thy comforts can do me no good at all;
Thee they may hurt.
                    King Lear, Act iv, sc. 1, l. 15 [GLOUCESTER]

1429   OTHELLO: Not another comfort like to this
Succeeds in unknown fate.
DESDEMONA: The heavens forbid
But that our loves and comforts should increase
Even as our days do grow! . . .
OTHELLO: O my sweet,
I prattle out of fashion, and I dote
In mine own comforts.
                    Othello, Act ii, sc. 1, l. 194 [OTHELLO]

1430   Comfort's in heaven; and we are on the earth,
Where nothing lives but crosses, cares and grief.
                    Richard II, Act ii, sc. 2, l. 78 [YORK]

1431   Of comfort no man speak:
Let's talk of graves, of worms and epitaphs;
Make dust our paper and with rainy eyes
Write sorrow on the bosom of the earth.
Let's choose executors and talk of wills:
And yet not so, for what can we bequeath
Save our deposed bodies to the ground? . . .
And nothing can we call our own but death

And that small model of the barren earth
Which serves as paste and cover to our bones.
Richard II, Act iii, sc. 2, l. 144 [KING RICHARD]

1432   What comfort have we now?
By heaven, I'll hate him everlastingly
That bids me be of comfort any more.
Richard II, Act iii, sc. 2, l. 206 [KING RICHARD]

1433   As a decrepit father takes delight
To see his active child do deeds of youth,
So I, made lame by fortune's dearest spite,
Take all my comfort of thy worth and truth.
Sonnet xxxvii, l. 1

1434   He receives comfort like cold porridge.
The Tempest, Act ii, sc. 1, l. 10 [SEBASTIAN]

1435   Well, here's my comfort. [*Drinks*]
The Tempest, Act ii, sc. 2, l. 47 [STEPHANO]

Command

1436   We were not born to sue, but to command.
Richard II, Act i, sc. 1, l. 196 [KING RICHARD]

1437   I will be correspondent to command.
The Tempest, Act i, sc. 2, l. 297 [ARIEL]

1438   'I may command where I adore.' Why, she may command me:
I serve her; she is my lady.
Twelfth Night, Act ii, sc. 5, l. 126 [MALVOLIO]

Commendations

1439   You were ever good at sudden commendations,
Bishop of Winchester. But know, I come not
To hear such flattery now, and in my presence.
Henry VIII, Act v, sc. 3, l. 122 [KING HENRY]

1440   It pleaseth you, my royal father, to express
My commendations great, whose merit's less.
Pericles, Act ii, sc. 2, l. 8 [THAISA]

1441   TIMON: Sir, your jewel Hath suffer'd under praise.
JEWELER: What, my lord! dispraise?
TIMON: A mere satiety of commendations.
If I should pay you for 't as 'tis extoll'd,
It would unclew me quite.
Timon of Athens, Act i, sc. 1, l. 166 [TIMON]

Commodity

1442   'Tis a commodity will lose the gloss with lying; the longer kept,
the less worth.
All's Well that Ends Well, Act i, sc. 1, l. 166 [PAROLLES]

1443   That broker, that still breaks the pate of faith,
That daily break-vow, he that wins of all, . . .
That smooth-faced gentleman, tickling Commodity,
Commodity, the bias of the world. . . .
And why rail I on this Commodity?
But for because he hath not woo'd me yet.
King John, Act ii, sc. 1, l. 567 [BASTARD]

Companion

1444   CHIEF JUSTICE: God send the prince a better companion!
FALSTAFF: God send the companion a better prince.
II Henry IV, Act i, sc. 2, l. 223 [CHIEF JUSTICE]

1445   The prince but studies his companions
Like a strange tongue.
> *II Henry IV*, Act iv, sc. 4, l. 68 [WARWICK]

1446   I abhor such fanatical phantasimes, such insociable and point-devise companions.
> *Love's Labour's Lost,* Act v, sc. 1, l. 20 [HOLOFERNES]

1447   In companions
That do converse and waste the time together,
Whose souls do bear an equal yoke of love,
There must be needs a like proportion
Of lineaments, or manners and of spirit.
> *The Merchant of Venice*, Act iii, sc. 4, l. 11 [PORTIA]

Company

1448   We shall not then have his company to-night? . . . I would gladly have him see his company anatomized.
> *All's Well that Ends Well,* Act iv, sc. 3, l. 33 [LORD]

1449   Let us, Lepidus, not lack your company.
> *Antony and Cleopatra,* Act ii, sc. 2, l. 171 [ANTONY]

1450   Choose your own company, and command what cost
Your heart has mind to.
> *Antony and Cleopatra,* Act iii, sc. 4, l. 37 [ANTONY]

1451   Why, how now, monsieur! what a life is this
That your poor friends must woo your company?
> *As You Like It,* Act ii, sc. 7, l. 9 [DUKE]

1452   I thank you for your company; but, good faith, I had as lief have been myself alone.
> *As You Like It,* Act iii, sc. 2, l. 268 [JAQUES]

1453   Company, villanous company, hath been the spoil of me.
> *I Henry IV,* Act iii, sc. 3, l. 11 [FALSTAFF]

Keeping such vile company as thou art hath in reason taken from me all ostentation of sorrow.
> *II Henry IV,* Act ii, sc. 2, l. 52 [PRINCE OF WALES]

1454   It is certain that eitherwise bearing or ignorant carriage is caught as men take diseases, one of another: therefore let men take heed of their company.
> *II Henry IV,* Act v, sc. 1, l. 85 [FALSTAFF]

1455   Your company . . . hath very much beguiled
The tediousness and process of my travel.
> *Richard II,* Act ii, sc. 3, l. 10 [NORTHUMBERLAND]

[They] shall make their way seem short, . . .
By sight of what I have, your noble company.
> *Richard II,* Act ii, sc. 3, l. 17 [NORTHUMBERLAND]

(See also 2077.)

Comparisons

1456   PRINCE: I'll be no longer guilty of this sin; this sanguine coward, this bed-presser, this horseback-breaker, this huge hill of flesh,—
FALSTAFF: 'Sblood, you starveling, you elf-skin, you dried neat's tongue, you bull's pizzle, you stock-fish! O for breath to utter what is like thee! . . .
PRINCE: Well, breathe awhile, and when thou hast tired thyself in base comparisons, hear me speak.
> *I Henry IV,* Act ii, sc. 4, l. 268 [PRINCE]

1457   Comparisons are odorous.
> *Much Ado about Nothing,* Act iii, sc. 5, l. 18 [DOGBERRY]
> (An attempt at the proverbial phrase, "Comparisons are odious.")

Compassion

1458   It is no little thing to make
Mine eyes to sweat compassion.

Coriolanus, Act v, sc. 3, l. 195 [Coriolanus]

1459 O, if no harder than a stone thou art,
Melt at my tears, and be compassionate!

The Rape of Lucrece, l. 593 [Lucrece]

It boots thee not to be compassionate:
After our sentence plaining comes too late.

Richard II, Act i, sc. 3, l. 174 [King Richard]

1460   The senseless brands will sympathize
The heavy accent of thy moving tongue
And in compassion weep the fire out.

Richard II, Act v, sc. 1, l. 46 [King Richard]

1461 Although they were flesh'd villains, bloody dogs,
Melting with tenderness and kind compassion,
[They] Wept like two children.

Richard III, Act iv, sc. 3, l. 6 [Tyrrell]

Complexion

1462 Good my complexion! dost thou think, though I am caparisoned
like a man, I have a doublet and hose in my disposition?

As You Like It, Act iii, sc. 2, l. 204 [Rosalind]

1463 The best thing in him Is his complexion.

As You Like It, Act iii, sc. 5, l. 115 [Phebe]

1464 Antipholus S.: What complexion is she of?
Dromio S.: Swart, like my shoe.

The Comedy of Errors, Act iii, sc. 2, l. 103 [Antipholus of Syracuse]

Armado: Who was Samson's love, my dear Moth?
Moth: A woman, master.
Armado: Of what complexion? . . . Tell me precisely of what
complexion.
Moth: Of the sea-water green, sir.
Armado: Is that one of the four complexions?
Moth: As I have read, sir; and the best of them too.

Love's Labour's Lost, Act i, sc. 2, l. 80 [Armado]

1465 Of all complexions, the cull'd sovereignty
Do meet, as at a fair, in her fair cheek.

Love's Labour's Lost, Act iv, sc. 3, l. 234 [Biron]

1466 That excellent complexion, which did steal
The eyes of young and old.

Pericles, Act iv, sc. 1, l. 41 [Dionyza]

1467 Mislike me not for my complexion,
The shadow'd livery of the burnish'd sun,
To whom I am a neighbour and near bred.
Bring me the fairest creature northward born, . . .
And let us make incision for your love,
To prove whose blood is reddest, his or mine.

The Merchant of Venice, Act ii, sc. 1, l. 1 [Morocco]

Then will I swear beauty itself is black
And all they foul that thy complexion lack.

Sonnet cxxxii, l. 13

1468 Maria once told me . . . that, should she fancy, it should be one
of my complexion.

Twelfth Night, Act ii, sc. 5, l. 27 [Malvolio]

Compliment

1469   That they call compliment is like the encounter of two dog-apes,
and when a man thanks me heartily, methinks I have given him a
penny and he renders me the beggarly thanks.
As You Like It, Act ii, sc. 5, l. 26 [JAQUES]

1470   The time will not allow the compliment
Which very manners urges.
King Lear, Act v, sc. 3, l. 233 [ALBANY]

1471   Farewell compliment!
Romeo and Juliet, Act ii, sc. 2, l. 89 [JULIET]

1472   'Twas never merry world
Since lowly feigning was call'd compliment.
Twelfth Night, Act iii, sc. 1, l. 109 [OLIVIA]

Conceit

1473   Lay open to my earthly-gross conceit,
Smother'd in errors, feeble, shallow, weak,
The folded meaning of your words' deceit.
The Comedy of Errors, Act iii, sc. 2, l. 34 [ANTIPHOLUS OF SYRACUSE]

1474   Come, sister: I am press'd down with conceit—
Conceit, my comfort and my injury.
The Comedy of Errors, Act iv, sc. 2, l. 65 [ADRIANA]

1475   Conceit in weakest bodies strongest works.
Hamlet, Act iii, sc. 4, l. 114 [GHOST]

1476   There's no more conceit in him than is in a mallet.
II Henry IV, Act ii, sc. 4, l. 263 [FALSTAFF]

1477   I know not how conceit may rob
The treasury of life, when life itself
Yields to the theft.
King Lear, Act iv, sc. 6, l. 42 [EDGAR]

1478   Conceit, more rich in matter than in words,
Brags of his substance, not of ornament.
Romeo and Juliet, Act ii, sc. 6, l. 30 [JULIET]

1479   Think'st thou I am so shallow, so conceitless,
To be seduced by thy flattery?
The Two Gentlemen of Verona, Act iv, sc. 2, l. 96 [SILVIA]

Conceits

1480   Their conceits have wings
Fleeter than arrows, bullets, wind, thought, swifter things.
Love's Labour's Lost, Act v, sc. 2, l. 260 [BOYET]

1481   Dangerous conceits are, in their natures, poisons,
Which at the first are scarce found to distaste,
But with a little act upon the blood,
Burn like the mines of sulphur.
Othello, Act iii, sc. 3, l. 326 [IAGO]

Conclusion

1482   I knew 'twould be a bald conclusion.
The Comedy of Errors, Act ii, sc. 2, l. 110 [ANTIPHOLUS OF SYRACUSE]

1483   Most lame and impotent conclusion!
Othello, Act ii, sc. 1, l. 162 [DESDEMONA]

1484   This denoted a foregone conclusion.
Othello, Act iii, sc. 3, l. 428 [OTHELLO]

1485   A false conclusion: I hate it as an unfilled can.
Twelfth Night, Act ii, sc. 3, l. 6 [SIR TOBY]

Concord See also Discord

1486   Had I the power, I should
Pour the sweet milk of concord into hell,
Uproar the universal peace, confound
All unity on earth.
Macbeth, Act iv, sc. 3, l. 97 [MALCOLM]

1487   If the true concord of well-tuned sounds,
By unions married, do offend thine ear,
They do but sweetly chide thee, who confounds
In singleness the parts that thou shouldst bear.
Mark how one string, sweet husband to another,
Strikes each in each by mutual ordering,
Resembling sire and child and happy mother
Who all in one, one pleasing note do sing:
Whose speechless song, being many, seeming one,
Sings this to thee: 'thou single wilt prove none.'
Sonnet viii, l. 5

1488   You . . . mar the concord with too harsh a descant.
The Two Gentlemen of Verona, Act i, sc. 2, l. 94 [LUCETTA]

Confession

1489   I confess,
Here on my knee, before high heaven and you.
All's Well that Ends Well, Act i, sc. 3, l. 197 [HELENA]
Confess yourself to heaven;
Repent what's past; avoid what is to come.
Hamlet, Act iii, sc. 4, l. 149 [HAMLET]

1490   KING: Teach us, sweet madam, for our rude transgression
Some fair excuse.
PRINCESS: The fairest is confession.
Love's Labour's Lost, Act v, sc. 2, l. 431 [KING]

1491   BASSANIO: Promise me life, and I'll confess the truth.
PORTIA: Well, then, confess and live.
The Merchant of Venice, Act iii, sc. 2, l. 34 [BASSANIO]

1492   If it be confessed, it is not redressed.
The Merry Wives of Windsor, Act i, sc. 1, l. 107 [SHALLOW]

1493   To confess, and be hanged for his labour;—first, to be hanged,
and then to confess.
Othello, Act iv, sc. 1, l. 38 [OTHELLO]

1494   Be plain, good son, and homely in thy drift;
Riddling confession finds but riddling shrift.
Romeo and Juliet, Act ii, sc. 3, l. 55 [FRIAR LAURENCE]

Confusion

1495   Vast confusion waits,
As doth a raven on a sick-fall'n beast,
The imminent decay of wrested pomp.
King John, Act iv, sc. 3, l. 152 [BASTARD]

1496   Confusion now hath made his masterpiece!
Macbeth, Act ii, sc. 3, l. 71 [MACDUFF]

1497   Confusion's cure lives not in these confusions.
Romeo and Juliet, Act iv, sc. 5, l. 65 [FRIAR LAURENCE]

Conqueror

1498   Therefore, brave conquerors,—for so you are,
That war against your own affections
And the huge army of the world's desires, . . .
Your oaths are pass'd; and now subscribe your names,

That his own hand may strike his honour down
That violates the smallest branch herein.
Love's Labour's Lost, Act i, sc. 1, l. 8 [KING]

1499   And better conquest never canst thou make
Than arm thy constant and thy nobler parts
Against these giddy loose suggestions.
King John, Act iii, sc. 1, l. 290 [PANDULPH]

Conscience

1500   My conscience, thou art fetter'd
More than my shanks and wrists.
Cymbeline, Act v, sc. 4, l. 8 [POSTHUMUS]

1501   Conscience does make cowards of us all.
Hamlet, Act iii, sc. 1, l. 83 [HAMLET]
(For full quotation see 1847.)

1502   Now must your conscience my acquittance seal.
Hamlet, Act iv, sc. 7, l. 1 [KING]

1503   'Tis almost 'gainst my conscience.
Hamlet, Act v, sc. 2, l. 307 [LAERTES]

1504   PRINCE: Now, my masters, for a true face and good conscience.
FALSTAFF: Both which I have had: but their date is out.
I Henry IV, Act ii, sc. 4, l. 550 [PRINCE]
A good conscience will make any possible satisfaction.
II Henry IV, Epilogue, l. 22 [DANCER]
Done in the testimony of a good conscience.
Love's Labour's Lost, Act iv, sc. 2, l. 1 [SIR NATHANIEL]

1505   [He] Could not keep quiet in his conscience.
Henry V, Act i, sc. 2, l. 79 [CANTERBURY]

1506   O my Wolsey,
The quiet of my wounded conscience;
Thou art a cure fit for a king.
Henry VIII, Act ii, sc. 2, l. 74 [KING HENRY]

1507   Conscience, conscience! O, 'tis a tender place.
Henry VIII, Act ii, sc. 2, l. 143 [KING HENRY]

1508   My conscience first received a tenderness,
Scruple, and prick, on certain speeches utter'd
By the Bishop of Bayonne, then French ambassador; . . .
This . . . shook
The bosom of my conscience, enter'd me,
Yea, with a splitting power, and made to tremble
The region of my breast.
Henry VIII, Act ii, sc. 4, l. 170 [KING HENRY]

1509   I know myself now; and I feel within me
A peace above all earthly dignities,
A still and quiet conscience.
Henry VIII, Act iii, sc. 2, l. 378 [WOLSEY]

1510   Certainly my conscience will serve me to run from this Jew,
my master. The fiend is at mine elbow and tempts me saying to
me, . . . 'Good Launcelot, . . . use your legs, take the start, run
away.' . . . My conscience says 'Launcelot, budge not.' 'Budge,'
says the fiend . . . The fiend gives me more friendly counsel:
I will run.
The Merchant of Venice, Act ii, sc. 2, l. 1 [LAUNCELOT]

1511   Let not conscience,
Which is but cold, inflaming love i' thy bosom,
Inflame too nicely.
Pericles, Act iv, sc. 1, l. 4 [DIONYZA]

1512   The worm of Conscience shall begnaw thy soul!
                    Richard III, Act i, sc. 3, l. 222 [QUEEN MARGARET]
1513   Some certain dregs of conscience are yet within me. . . . It is a
        dangerous thing: it makes a man a coward: a man cannot steal,
        but it accuseth him; he cannot swear, but it checks him; he cannot
        lie with his neighbour's wife, but it detects him: 'tis a blushing
        shamefast spirit that mutinies in a man's bosom; it fills one full
        of obstacles: . . . it beggars any man that keeps it: . . . and
        every man that means to live well endeavours to trust to himself
        and to live without it.
                    Richard III, Act i, sc. 4, l. 124 [MURDERER]
1514   O coward conscience, how dost thou afflict me! . . .
        My conscience hath a thousand several tongues,
        And every tongue brings in a several tale,
        And every tale condemns me for a villain.
                    Richard III, Act v, sc. 3, l. 179 [KING RICHARD]
1515   Conscience is but a word that cowards use,
        Devised at first to keep the strong in awe.
                    Richard III, Act v, sc. 3, l. 309 [KING RICHARD]
1516   SEBASTIAN: But, for your conscience?
        ANTONIO: Ay, sir; where lies that? if 'twere a kibe,
        'Twould put me to my slipper: but I feel not
        This deity in my bosom.
                    The Tempest, Act ii, sc. 1, l. 275 [SEBASTIAN]
1517   I know thou art religious
        And hast a thing within thee called conscience.
                    Titus Andronicus, Act v, sc. 1, l. 74 [AARON]

Consideration

1518   Let's to supper, come, And drown consideration.
                    Antony and Cleopatra, Act iv, sc. 2, l. 44 [ANTONY]
1519   Consideration, like an angel, came
        And whipp'd the offending Adam out of him,
        Leaving his body as a paradise,
        To envelope and contain celestial spirits.
                    Henry V, Act i, sc. 1, l. 29 [CANTERBURY]

Conspiracy

1520   O conspiracy,
        Shamest thou to show thy dangerous brow by night,
        When evils are most free? O, then by day
        Where wilt thou find a cavern dark enough
        To mask thy monstrous visage? Seek none, conspiracy;
        Hide it in smiles and affability:
        For if thou put thy native semblance on,
        Not Erebus itself were dim enough
        To hide thee from prevention.
                    Julius Cæsar, Act ii, sc. 1, l. 77 [BRUTUS]
1521   O you pandarly rascals! there's a knot, a ging, a pack, a con-
        spiracy against me: now shall the devil be shamed.
                    The Merry Wives of Windsor, Act iv, sc. 2, l. 121 [FORD]
            ("Ging," gang.)
1522   While you here do snoring lie,
                        Open-eyed conspiracy
                        His time doth take.

If of life you keep a care,
Shake off slumber, and beware:
Awake! awake!
The Tempest, Act ii, sc. 1, l. 300 [ARIEL]

Constable

1523 DOGBERRY: Come hither, neighbour Seacole. . . . You are thought here to be the most senseless and fit man for constable of the watch: therefore bear you the lantern. This is your charge: you shall comprehend all vagrom men; you are to bid any man stand, in the prince's name.
WATCH: How if a' will not stand?
DOGBERRY: Why, then, take no note of him, but let him go; and presently call the rest of the watch together and thank God you are rid of a knave.
Much Ado about Nothing, Act iii, sc. 3, l. 13 [DOGBERRY]

1524 I am in case to justle a constable.
The Tempest, Act iii, sc. 2, l. 29 [TRINICULO]

Constancy

1525 While thou livest, dear Kate, take a fellow of plain and uncoined constancy; for he perforce must do thee right.
Henry V, Act v, sc. 2, l. 161 [KING HENRY]

1526 O constancy, be strong upon my side,
Set a huge mountain 'tween my heart and tongue.
Julius Cæsar, Act ii, sc. 4, l. 6 [PORTIA]

1527 I am constant as the northern star,
Of whose true-fix'd and resting quality
There is no fellow in the firmament.
Julius Cæsar, Act iii, sc. 1, l. 60 [CÆSAR]

Contemplation

1528 When holy and devout religious men
Are at their beads, 'tis hard to draw them thence,
So sweet is zealous contemplation.
Richard III, Act iii, sc. 7, l. 92 [BUCKINGHAM]
Contemplation makes a rare turkey-cock of him: how he jets under his advanced plumes!
Twelfth Night, Act ii, sc. 5, l. 35 [FABIAN]

Contempt

1529 What our contempt doth often hurl from us,
We wish it ours again.
Antony and Cleopatra, Act i, sc. 2, l. 127 [ANTONY]

1530 He did solicit you in free contempt
When he did need your loves, and do you think
That his contempt shall not be bruising to you,
When he hath power to crush?
Coriolanus, Act ii, sc. 3, l. 208 [BRUTUS]

1531   Forget not
With what contempt he wore the humble weed,
How in his suit he scorn'd you.
Coriolanus, Act ii, sc. 3, l. 228 [SICINIUS]

1532 Turn me away; and let the foul'st contempt
Shut door upon me.
Henry VIII, Act ii, sc. 4, l. 42 [QUEEN KATHARINE]
PRINCESS: Nor to their penn'd speech render we no grace,
But while 'tis spoke each turn away her face.

BOYET: Why, that contempt will kill the speaker's heart,
And quite divorce his memory from his part.
Love's Labour's Lost, Act v, sc. 2, l. 147 [PRINCESS]

Content

1533 Ere we have thy youthful wages spent,
We'll light upon some settled low content.
As You Like It, Act ii, sc. 3, l. 67 [ORLANDO]

1534 He that commends me to mine own content
Commends me to the thing I cannot get.
The Comedy of Errors, Act i, sc. 2, l. 33 [ANTIPHOLUS
OF SYRACUSE]

1535 I could be well content
To entertain the lag-end of my life
With quiet hours.
I Henry IV, Act v, sc. 1, l. 23 [WORCESTER]

I could be well content
To be mine own attorney in this case.
I Henry VI, Act v, sc. 3, l. 165 [SUFFOLK]

1536 Such is the fulness of my heart's content.
II Henry VI, Act i, sc. 1, l. 35 [KING HENRY]

1537 Our content is our best having.
Henry VIII, Act ii, sc. 3, l. 22 [OLD LADY]

1538 Nought's had, all's spent,
Where our desire is got without content:
'Tis safer•to be that which we destroy
Than by destruction dwell in doubtful joy.
Macbeth, Act iii, sc. 2, l. 5 [LADY MACBETH]

Convey

1539 'Convey,' the wise it call. 'Steal!' foh! a fico for the phrase!
The Merry Wives of Windsor, Act i, sc. 3, l. 32 [PISTOL]
("Fico," Italian for fig, a trifle.)

1540 BOLINGBROKE: Convey him to the Tower.
KING RICHARD: O, good! convey? conveyors are you all,
That rise thus nimbly by a true king's fall.
Richard II, Act iv, sc. 1, l. 316 [BOLINGBROKE]

Cooks and Cookery

1541 Epicurean cooks
Sharpen with cloyless sauce his appetite.
Antony and Cleopatra, Act ii, sc. 1, l. 24 [POMPEY]

1542 His neat cookery! he cut our roots
In characters,
And sauced our broths, as Juno had been sick
And he her dieter.
Cymbeline, Act iv, sc. 2, l. 48 [GUIDERIUS]

1543 The cook helps to make the gluttony.
II Henry IV, Act ii, sc. 4, l. 48 [FALSTAFF]

'Tis an ill cook that cannot lick his own fingers.
Romeo and Juliet, Act iv, sc. 2, l. 6 [SERVANT]
(Quoting an old proverb.)

Cophetua

1544 Let King Cophetua know the truth thereof.
II Henry IV, Act v, sc. 3, l. 107 [FALSTAFF]

1545 The magnanimous and most illustrate king Cophetua set eye upon
the pernicious and indubitate beggar Zenelophon.
Love's Labour's Lost, Act iv, sc. 1, l. 65 [BOYET]

1546   When King Cophetua loved the beggar maid.
                    Romeo and Juliet, Act ii, sc. 1, l. 14 [MERCUTIO]

Corinthian

1547   I am no proud Jack, like Falstaff, but a Corinthian, a lad of mettle,
        a good boy, by the Lord, so they call me, and when I am king of
        England, I shall command all the good lads in Eastcheap.
                    I Henry IV, Act ii, sc. 4, l. 13 [PRINCE]
        ("Corinthian," a sportsman, man about town, given to luxurious
        dissipation.)

Corn

1548   PUCELLE: Good morrow, gallants! want ye corn for bread? . . .
        BURGUNDY: [I'll] make thee curse the harvest of that corn.
                    I Henry VI, Act iii, sc. 2, l. 41 [PUCELLE]
                    These our ships . . .
        Are stored with corn to make your needy bread.
                    Pericles, Act i, sc. 4, l. 92 [PERICLES]
1549   Sow'd cockle reap'd no corn.
                    Love's Labour's Lost, Act iv, sc. 3, l. 383 [BIRON]
1550   Our corn's to reap, for yet our tithe's to sow.
                    Measure for Measure, Act iv, sc. 1, l. 76 [DUKE]
1551   First thresh the corn, then after burn the straw.
                    Titus Andronicus, Act ii, sc. 3, l. 123 [DEMETRIUS]

Corns

1552   The man that makes his toe
                What he his heart should make
                Shall of a corn cry woe,
                And turn his sleep to wake.
                    King Lear, Act iii, sc. 2, l. 31 [FOOL]
1553   Welcome, gentlemen! ladies that have their toes
        Unplagued with corns will have a bout with you.
        Ah ha, my mistress! which of you all
        Will now deny to dance? she that makes dainty,
        She, I'll swear, hath corns.
                    Romeo and Juliet, Act i, sc. 5, l. 19 [CAPULET]

Corruption

1554   Rank corruption, mining all within,
        Infects unseen.
                    Hamlet, Act iii, sc. 4, l. 148 [HAMLET]
1555   Corruption wins not more than honesty.
                    Henry VIII, Act iii, sc. 2, l. 444 [WOLSEY]
1556   What corruption in this life, that it will let this man live!
                    Measure for Measure, Act iii, sc. 1, l. 241 [ISABELLA]
1557   My business in this state
        Made me a looker on here in Vienna,
        Where I have seen corruption boil and bubble
        Till it o'er-run the stew.
                    Measure for Measure, Act v, sc. 1, l. 318 [DUKE]

Corse

1558   Let him be regarded
        As the most noble corse that ever herald
        Did follow to his urn.
                    Coriolanus, Act v, sc. 6, l. 144 [LORD]
1559   Villains, set down the corse; or, by Saint Paul,
        I'll make a corse of him that disobeys.
                    Richard III, Act i, sc. 2, l. 36 [GLOUCESTER]

Cost

1560   How little is the cost I have bestow'd
In purchasing the semblance of my soul
From out the state of hellish misery!
The Merchant of Venice, Act iii, sc. 4, l. 19 [PORTIA]

1561   The fashion of the world is to avoid cost, and you encounter it.
Much Ado about Nothing, Act i, sc. 1, l. 97 [DON PEDRO]

1562   It will cost thee dear.
Othello, Act v, sc. 2, l. 255 [GRATIANO]

Counsel

1563   Friendly counsel cuts off many foes.
I Henry VI, Act iii, sc. 1, l. 185 [KING HENRY]

1564   Bosom up my counsel, You'll find it wholesome.
Henry VIII, Act i, sc. 1, l. 112 [NORFOLK]

1565   Where you are liberal of your loves and counsels
Be sure you be not loose.
Henry VIII, Act ii, sc. 1, l. 126 [BUCKINGHAM]

1566   I can keep honest counsel, ride, run, mar a curious tale in telling
it, and deliver a plain message bluntly: . . . the best of me is
diligence.
King Lear, Act i, sc. 4, l. 34 [KENT]

1567   When a wise man gives thee better counsel, give me mine again:
I would have none but knaves follow it, since a fool gives it.
King Lear, Act ii, sc. 4, l. 75 [FOOL]

1568   Counsel may stop awhile what will not stay.
A Lover's Complaint, l. 159

1569   I pray thee, cease thy counsel,
Which falls into mine ears as profitless
As water in a sieve: give not me counsel,
Nor let no comforter delight mine ear
But such a one whose wrongs do suit with mine.
Much Ado about Nothing, Act v, sc. 1, l. 3 [LEONATO]

1570   All too late comes counsel to be heard,
Where will doth mutiny with wit's regard.
Richard II, Act ii, sc. 1, l. 27 [YORK]

1571   Did you ne'er hear say,
Two may keep counsel, putting one away?
Romeo and Juliet, Act ii, sc. 4, l. 208 [NURSE]
Two may keep counsel when the third's away.
Titus Andronicus, Act iv, sc. 2, l. 144 [AARON]

1572   When as thine eye hath chose the dame,
And stall'd the deer that thou shouldst strike, . . .
Take counsel of some wiser head,
Neither too young nor yet unwed.
Sonnets to Sundry Notes of Music, Pt. xix, l. 1

1573   They that thrive well take counsel of their friends.
Venus and Adonis, l. 640 [VENUS]

Counsellor

1574   Can he that speaks with the tongue of an enemy be a good
counsellor?
II Henry VI, Act iv, sc. 2, l. 181 [CADE]

1575   Good counsellors lack no clients.
Measure for Measure, Act i, sc. 2, l. 110 [POMPEY]

1576   Is he not a most profane and liberal counsellor?
Othello, Act ii, sc. 1, l. 165 [DESDEMONA]

1577   You are a counsellor,
And, by that virtue, no man dare accuse you.
> *Henry VIII*, Act v, sc. 3, l. 49 [SUFFOLK]

You are a counsellor; if you can command these elements to
silence, . . . use your authority: if you cannot, give thanks you
have lived so long.
> *The Tempest*, Act i, sc. 1, l. 23 [BOATSWAIN]

1578   Fit counsellor and servant for a prince,
Who by thy wisdom makest a prince thy servant.
> *Pericles*, Act i, sc. 2, l. 63 [PERICLES]

1579   Thou art a grave and noble counsellor.
> *Pericles*, Act v, sc. 1, l. 184 [PERICLES]

1580   He, his own affections' counsellor,
Is to himself—I will not say how true.
> *Romeo and Juliet*, Act i, sc. 1, l. 153 [MONTAGUE]

1581   He is . . . meet to be an emperor's counsellor.
> *The Two Gentlemen of Verona*, Act ii, sc. 4, l. 77 [DUKE]

Countenance

1582   Turn from me, then, that noble countenance,
Wherein the worship of the whole world lies.
> *Antony and Cleopatra*, Act iv, sc. 14, l. 85 [EROS]

1583   My grisly countenance made others fly;
None durst come near for fear of sudden death.
> *I Henry VI*, Act i, sc. 4, l. 47 [TALBOT]

1584   His countenance likes me not.
> *King Lear*, Act ii, sc. 2, l. 96 [KENT]

1585   This pert Biron was out of countenance quite.
> *Love's Labour's Lost*, Act v, sc. 2, l. 272 [PRINCESS]

I will not be put out of countenance.
> *Love's Labour's Lost*, Act v, sc. 2, l. 611 [HOLOFERNES]

BIRON: We have put thee in countenance.
HOLOFERNES: You have put me out of countenance.
> *Love's Labour's Lost*, Act v, sc. 2, l. 623 [BIRON]

Counterfeit

1586   Never call a true piece of gold a counterfeit: thou art essentially
mad, without seeming so.
> *I Henry IV*, Act ii, sc. 4, l. 539 [FALSTAFF]

1587   'Sblood, 'twas time to counterfeit, or that hot termagant Scot
had paid me scot and lot too. Counterfeit? I lie, I am no counterfeit: to die, is to be a counterfeit; for he is but the counterfeit
of a man who hath not the life of a man; but to counterfeit dying,
when a man thereby liveth, is to be no counterfeit, but the true
and perfect image of life indeed.
> *I Henry IV*, Act v, sc. 4, l. 114 [FALSTAFF]

Country

1588   When he did love his country, It honour'd him.
> *Coriolanus*, Act iii, sc. 1, l. 305 [BRUTUS]

1589   I do love
My country's good with a respect more tender,
More holy and profound, than mine own life.
> *Coriolanus*, Act iii, sc. 3, l. 110 [COMINIUS]

1590   Alas, how can we for our country pray,
Whereto we are bound? . . . Thou shalt no sooner
March to assault thy country, than to tread . . .
On thy mother's womb That brought thee to this world.
> *Coriolanus*, Act v, sc. 3, l. 107 [VOLUMNIA]

1591   MACDUFF: Bleed, bleed, poor country! . . .
      MALCOLM: I think our country sinks beneath the yoke;
      It weeps, it bleeds; and each new day a gash
      Is added to her wounds.
Macbeth, Act iv, sc. 3, l. 31 [MACDUFF]

1592   When I shall tread upon the tyrant's head,
      Or wear it on my sword, yet my poor country
      Shall have more vices than it had before.
Macbeth, Act iv, sc. 3, l. 45 [MALCOLM]

Courage

1593   I heard thee . . . Cry 'Courage! to the field!'
I Henry IV, Act ii, sc. 3, l. 53 [LADY PERCY]
      Three times did Richard make a lane to me,
      And thrice cried 'Courage, father! fight it out!'
III Henry VI, Act i, sc. 4, l. 9 [YORK]
      Courage, my masters! honour now or never!
III Henry VI, Act iv, sc. 3, l. 24 [WARWICK]
      Strike up the drum; cry 'Courage!' and away.
III King Henry VI, Act v, sc. 3, l. 24 [KING EDWARD]

1594   My courage try by combat, if thou darest,
      And thou shalt find that I exceed my sex.
I Henry VI, Act i, sc. 2, l. 89 [PUCELLE]

1595   My breast I'll burst with straining of my courage.
I Henry VI, Act i, sc. 5, l. 10 [TALBOT]

1596   My lord, cheer up your spirits: our foes are nigh,
      And this soft courage makes your followers faint.
III Henry VI, Act ii, sc. 2, l. 56 [QUEEN MARGARET]

1597   This may plant courage in their quailing breasts.
III Henry VI, Act ii, sc. 3, l. 54 [GEORGE]
      There is no quailing now.
I Henry IV, Act iv, sc. 1, l. 39 [HOTSPUR]

1598   Courage mounteth with occasion.
King John, Act ii, sc. 1, l. 82 [AUSTRIA]

1599   Screw your courage to the sticking-place,
      And we'll not fail.
Macbeth, Act i, sc. 7, l. 60 [LADY MACBETH]
      (Often misquoted "sticking-point.")

Court

1600   God send him well! The court's a learning place.
All's Well that Ends Well, Act i, sc. 1, l. 190 [HELENA]

1601   CLOWN: My business is but to the court.
      COUNTESS: To the court! . . .
      CLOWN: Truly, madam, if God have lent a man any manners, he may
easily put it off at court: he that cannot make a leg, put off 's cap,
kiss his hand and say nothing, has neither leg, hands, lip, nor cap;
and indeed such a fellow, to say precisely, were not for the court.
All's Well that Ends Well, Act ii, sc. 2, l. 4 [CLOWN]

1602   TOUCHSTONE: Wast ever in court, shepherd?
      CORIN: No, truly.
      TOUCHSTONE: Then, . . . Truly thou art damned, like an ill-
roasted egg all on one side.
      CORIN: For not being at court? Your reason.
      TOUCHSTONE: Why, if thou never wast at court, thou never sawest
good manners; if thou never sawest good manners, then thy
manners must be wicked; and wickedness is sin, and sin is damnation. Thou art in a parlous state, shepherd.

CORIN: Not a whit, Touchstone: those that are good manners at
the court are as ridiculous in the country as the behavior of the
country is most mockable at the court.
>   *As You Like It,* Act iii, sc. 2, l. 33 [TOUCHSTONE]

1603   The art o' the court, . . . whose top to climb
Is certain falling, or so slippery that
The fear 's as bad as falling.
>   *Cymbeline,* Act iii, sc. 3, l. 46 [BELARIUS]

1604   Gods, what lies I have heard!
Our courtiers say all 's savage but at court.
>   *Cymbeline,* Act iv, sc. 2, l. 33 [IMOGEN]

1605   This is the English, not the Turkish court;
Not Amurath an Amurath succeeds,
But Harry Harry.
>   *II Henry IV,* Act v, sc. 2, l. 47 [KING HENRY V]
(Amurath in 1596 succeeded his father to the Turkish throne,
and thereupon invited his brothers to a feast, where he had
them all strangled. The reference helps fix the date of the play
as 1597 or 1598.)

1606   Lord, who would live turmoiled in the court,
And may enjoy such quiet walks as these?
This small inheritance my father left me
Contenteth me, and worth a monarchy.
I seek not to wax great by others' waning,
Or gather wealth, I care not, with what envy:
Sufficeth that I have maintains my state
And sends the poor well pleased from my gate.
>   *II Henry VI,* Act iv, sc. 10, l. 18 [IDEN]

1607   KING RICHARD: What says King Bolingbroke? . . .
NORTHUMBERLAND: My lord, in the base court he doth attend
To speak with you; may it please you to come down?
KING RICHARD: Down, down I come, like glistering Phaethon,
Wanting the manage of unruly jades.
In the base court? Base court, where kings grow base,
To come at traitors' calls and do them grace.
In the base court? Come down? Down, court! down king!
For night-owls shriek where mounting larks should sing.
>   *Richard II,* Act iii, sc. 3, l. 173 [KING RICHARD]

1608   The emperor's court is like the house of Fame,
The palace full of tongues, of eyes, of ears.
>   *Titus Andronicus,* Act ii, sc. 1, l. 126 [AARON]

Courtesies

1609   He hath laid strange courtesies and great
Of late upon me.
>   *Antony and Cleopatra,* Act ii, sc. 2, l. 157 [ANTONY]

1610   I have been debtor to you for courtesies, which I will be ever
to pay and yet pay still.
>   *Cymbeline,* Act i, sc. 4, l. 38 [POSTHUMUS]

1611   Outward courtesies would fain proclaim
Favours that keep within.
>   *Measure for Measure,* Act v, sc. 1, l. 15 [DUKE]

Courtesy

1612   Dissembling courtesy! How fine this tyrant
Can tickle where she wounds!
>   *Cymbeline,* Act i, sc. 1, l. 84 [IMOGEN]

1613   Hopeless
To have the courtesy your cradle promised,
But to be still hot summer's tanlings and
The shrinking slaves of winter.
Cymbeline, Act iv, sc. 4, l. 27 [BELARIUS]

1614   Why, what a candy deal of courtesy
This fawning greyhound then did proffer me! . . .
And 'gentle Harry Percy,' and 'kind cousin;'
O, the devil take such cozeners!
I Henry IV, Act i, sc. 3, l. 251 [HOTSPUR]

1615   Though I be but Prince of Wales, yet I am the king of courtesy.
I Henry IV, Act ii, sc. 4, l. 12 [PRINCE]

1616   The mirror of all courtesy.
Henry VIII, Act ii, sc. 1, l. 53 [GENTLEMAN]

1617   A' can carve too, and lisp: why this is he
That kiss'd his hand away in courtesy.
Love's Labour's Lost, Act v, sc. 2, l. 323 [BIRON]
How courtesy would seem to cover sin,
When what is done is like an hypocrite,
The which is good in nothing but in sight!
Pericles, Act i, sc. 1, l. 121 [PERICLES]

1618   MERCUTIO: I am the very pink of courtesy.
ROMEO: Pink for flower.
MERCUTIO: Right.
Romeo and Juliet, Act ii, sc. 4, l. 61 [MERCUTIO]

1619   He is not the flower of courtesy, but I'll warrant him as gentle
as a lamb.
Romeo and Juliet, Act ii, sc. 5, l. 44 [NURSE]

Courtier

1620   TOUCHSTONE: Do not your courtier's hands sweat? . . .
CORIN: The courtier's hands are perfumed with civet.
As You Like It, Act iii, sc. 2, l. 56 [TOUCHSTONE]

1621   Not a courtier . . . hath a heart that is not
Glad at the thing they scowl at.
Cymbeline, Act i, sc. 1, l. 12 [GENTLEMAN]

1622   An English courtier may be wise,
And never see the Louvre.
Henry VIII, Act i, sc. 3, l. 22 [CHAMBERLAIN]

1623   I have been begging sixteen years in court,
And yet a courtier beggarly.
Henry VIII, Act ii, sc. 3, l. 82 [OLD LADY]

1624   Courtiers are free, as debonair, unarm'd,
As bending angels; that's their fame in peace:
But when they would seem soldiers, they have galls,
Good arms, strong joints, true swords; and, Jove's accord,
Nothing so full of heart.
Troilus and Cressida, Act i, sc. 3, l. 235 [ÆNEAS]

1625   I am a courtier. Seest thou not the air of the court in these en-
foldings? hath not my gait in it the measure of the court? receives
not thy nose court-odour from me? reflect I not on thy baseness
court-contempt?
The Winter's Tale, Act iv, sc. 4, l. 754 [AUTOLYCUS]

Covetousness

1626   When Marcus Brutus grows so covetous,
To lock such rascal counters from his friends,

Be ready, gods, with all your thunderbolts,
Dash him to pieces!
Julius Cæsar, Act iv, sc. 3, l. 79 [BRUTUS]

1627   I would not have you think that my desire of having is the sin
of covetousness: but, as you say, sir, let your bounty take a nap,
I will awake it anon.
Twelfth Night, Act v, sc. 1, l. 49 [CLOWN]

Cow

1628   I' the midst o' the fight, . . .
[She], like a cow in June, Hoists sail and flies.
Antony and Cleopatra, Act iii, sc. 10, l. 14 [SCARUS]

1629   It is said, 'God sends a curst cow short horns'; but to a cow too
curst he sends none.
Much Ado about Nothing, Act ii, sc. 1, l. 24 [BEATRICE]
(Quoting an old proverb.)

Coward

1630   He excels his brother for a coward, yet his brother is reputed one
of the best that is: in a retreat he outruns any lackey; marry, in
coming on he has the cramp.
All's Well that Ends Well, Act iv, sc. 3, l. 321 [PAROLLES]

1631   We'll have a swashing and a martial outside,
As many other mannish cowards have
That do outface it with their semblances.
As You Like It, Act i, sc. 3, l. 122 [ROSALIND]

1632   Thou mayst be valiant in a better cause;
But now thou seem'st a coward.
Cymbeline, Act iii, sc. 4, l. 74 [IMOGEN]

1633   Plenty and peace breeds cowards: hardness ever
Of hardiness is mother.
Cymbeline, Act iii, sc. 6, l. 21 [IMOGEN]

1634   Am I a coward?
Who calls me villain? breaks my pate across?
Plucks off my beard, and blows it in my face?
Tweaks me by the nose? gives me the lie i' the throat,
As deep as to the lungs? Who does me this? Ha!
'Swounds, I should take it: for it cannot be
But I am pigeon-liver'd and lack gall.
Hamlet, Act ii, sc. 2, l. 598 [HAMLET]

1635   I know them to be as true-bred cowards as ever turned back.
I Henry IV, Act i, sc. 2, l. 202 [POINS]
PRINCE: What, a coward, Sir John Paunch?
FALSTAFF: Indeed, I am not John of Gaunt, your grandfather;
but yet no coward, Hal.
I Henry IV, Act ii, sc. 2, l. 69 [PRINCE]

1636   An the Prince and Poins be not two arrant cowards, there's no
equity stirring: there's no more valour in that Poins than in a
wild-duck.
I Henry IV, Act ii, sc. 2, l. 105 [FALSTAFF]

1637   You are a shallow cowardly hind, and you lie. What a lack-
brain is this!
I Henry IV, Act ii, sc. 3, l. 17 [HOTSPUR]

1638   FALSTAFF: A plague of all cowards, I say, and a vengeance too!
marry and amen! . . . A plague of all cowards! . . . There is
nothing but roguery to be found in villanous man: yet a coward
is worse than a cup of sack with lime in it. A villanous coward
. . . A plague of all cowards, I say still.

PRINCE: How now, wool-sack! what mutter you? . . .
FALSTAFF: Are not you a coward? answer me that: and Poins there?
POINS: 'Zounds, ye fat paunch, and ye call me coward, by the Lord, I'll stab thee.
FALSTAFF: I call thee coward! I'll see thee damned ere I call thee coward: but I would give a thousand pound I could run as fast as thou canst. . . . You are straight enough in the shoulders, you care not who sees your back: call you that backing of your friends? A plague upon such backing! give me them that will face me. . . . A plague of all cowards, still say I.
I Henry IV, Act ii, sc. 4, l. 127 [FALSTAFF]

1639　Here had the conquest fully been seal'd up,
If Sir John Fastolfe had not play'd the coward: . . .
He . . . Cowardly fled, not having struck one stroke.
I Henry VI, Act i, sc. 1, l. 130 [MESSENGER]

1640　Sheep run not half so treacherous from the wolf,
Or horse or oxen from the leopard,
As you fly from your oft-subdued slaves.
I Henry VI, Act i, sc. 5, l. 30 [TALBOT]

1641　So cowards fight when they can fly no further;
So doves do peck the falcon's piercing talons;
So desperate thieves, all hopeless of their lives,
Breathe out invectives 'gainst the officers.
III Henry VI, Act i, sc. 4, l. 40 [CLIFFORD]

1642　Cowards die many times before their deaths;
The valiant never taste of death but once.
Julius Cæsar, Act ii, sc. 2, l. 32 [CÆSAR]

1643　I do find it cowardly and vile,
For fear of what might fall, so to prevent
The time of life: arming myself with patience
To stay the providence of some high powers
That govern us below.
Julius Cæsar, Act v, sc. 1, l. 104 [BRUTUS]

1644　O, coward that I am, to live so long,
To see my best friend ta'en before my face.
Julius Cæsar, Act v, sc. 3, l. 34 [CASSIUS]

1645　Thou slave, thou wretch, thou coward!
Thou little valiant, great in villany!
Thou ever strong upon the stronger side!
King John, Act iii, sc. 1, l. 115 [CONSTANCE]

LADY MACBETH: Wouldst thou have that
Which thou esteem'st the ornament of life,
And live a coward in thine own esteem,
Letting 'I dare not' wait upon 'I would,'
Like the poor cat i' the adage? . . .
MACBETH: I dare do all that may become a man;
Who dares do more is none.
Macbeth, Act i, sc. 7, l. 41 [LADY MACBETH]
(The adage is, "The cat loves fish, but is loath to wet her feet.")

1646　SIR TOBY: A very dishonest paltry boy, and more a coward than a hare. . . .
FABIAN: A coward, a most devout coward, religious in it.
Twelfth Night, Act iii, sc. 4, l. 420 [SIR TOBY]

1647　Not a more cowardly rogue in all Bohemia: if you had but looked big and spit at him he 'ld have run.
The Winter's Tale, Act iv, sc. 3, l. 112 [CLOWN]

Cowardice

1648   I hold it cowardice
To rest mistrustful where a noble heart
Hath pawn'd an open hand in sign of love.
III Henry VI, Act iv, sc. 2, l. 7 [WARWICK]

1649   That which in mean men we intitle patience
Is pale cold cowardice in noble breasts.
Richard II, Act i, sc. 2, l. 33 [DUCHESS OF GLOUCESTER]

Cozening

1650   I would all the world might be cozened; for I have been cozened
and beaten too. If it should come to the ear of the court, how I
have been transformed, and how my transformation hath been
washed and cudgelled, they would melt me out of my fat drop
by drop and liquor fishermen's boots with me: I warrant they
would whip me with their fine wits till I were as crestfallen as
a dried pear.
The Merry Wives of Windsor, Act iv, sc. 5, l. 95 [FALSTAFF]

Credit

1651   My credit now stands on such slippery ground,
That one of two bad ways you must conceit me,
Either a coward or a flatterer.
Julius Cæsar, Act iii, sc. 1, l. 191 [ANTONY]

1652   Neither have I money nor commodity
To raise a present sum: therefore go forth;
Try what my credit can in Venice do.
The Merchant of Venice, Act i, sc. 1, l. 178 [ANTONIO]

Crime

1653   If little faults, proceeding on distemper,
Shall not be wink'd at, how shall we stretch our eye
When capital crimes, chew'd, swallow'd and digested,
Appear before us?
Henry V, Act ii, sc. 2, l. 54 [KING HENRY]
My lord, these faults are easy, quickly answer'd;
But mightier crimes are laid unto your charge,
Whereof you cannot easily purge yourself.
II Henry VI, Act iii, sc. 1, l. 133 [SUFFOLK]

1654   By day and night he wrongs me; every hour
He flashes into one gross crime or other,
That sets us all at odds.
King Lear, Act i, sc. 3, l. 3 [GONERIL]

1655   Tremble, thou wretch,
That hast within thee undivulged crimes
Unwhipp'd of justice.
King Lear, Act iii, sc. 2, l. 51 [LEAR]

1656   Make me know
The nature of their crimes, that I may minister
To them accordingly.
Measure for Measure, Act ii, sc. 3, l. 6 [DUKE]

1657   If you bethink yourself of any crime
Unreconciled as yet to heaven and grace,
Solicit for it straight.
Othello, Act v, sc. 2, l. 27 [OTHELLO]

1658   Crimes, like lands, are not inherited.
Timon of Athens, Act v, sc. 4, l. 37 [SENATOR]

Cripple

1659   Would ye not think his cunning to be great, that could restore this cripple to his legs again?

II Henry VI, Act ii, sc. 1, l. 133 [GLOUCESTER]

1660   A cripple soon can find a halt.

Sonnets to Sundry Notes of Music, Pt. vi, l. 10

Critical

1661   That is some satire, keen and critical.

A Midsummer Night's Dream, Act v, sc. 1, l. 54 [THESEUS]

1662   I am nothing, if not critical.

Othello, Act ii, sc. 1, l. 120 [IAGO]

1663   Happy are they that hear their detractions and can put them to mending.

Much Ado about Nothing, Act ii, sc. 3, l. 238 [BENEDICK]

Crocodile

1664   LEPIDUS: Your serpent of Egypt is bred now of your mud by the operation of your sun: so is your crocodile. . . . What manner o' thing is your crocodile?
ANTONY: It is shaped, sir, like itself; and it is as broad as it hath breadth: it is just so high as it is. . . . And the tears of it are wet.

Antony and Cleopatra, Act ii, sc. 7, l. 29 [LEPIDUS]

1665   Gloucester's show
Beguiles him as the mournful crocodile
With sorrow snares relenting passengers,
Or as a snake roll'd in a flowering bank,
With shining checker'd slough, doth sting a child
That for the beauty thinks it excellent.

II Henry VI, Act iii, sc. 1, l. 225 [QUEEN]

Crotchets

1666   The duke had crotchets in him.

Measure for Measure, Act iii, sc. 2, l. 135 [LUCIO]

1667   Faith, thou hast some crotchets in thy head.

The Merry Wives of Windsor, Act ii, sc. 1, l. 158 [MRS. FORD]

1668   Why, these are very crotchets that he speaks.

Much Ado about Nothing, Act ii, sc. 3, l. 58 [DON PEDRO]

Crow

1669   A crow o' the same nest.

All's Well that Ends Well, Act iv, sc. 3, l. 319 [PAROLLES]

1670   ANTIPHOLUS E.: Well, I'll break in: go borrow me a crow.
DROMIO E.: A crow without feather? Master, mean you so?
For a fish without a fin, there's a fowl without a feather:
If a crow help us in, sirrah, we'll pluck a crow together.

The Comedy of Errors, Act iii, sc. 1, l. 80 [ANTIPHOLUS OF EPHESUS]

Get me an iron crow, and bring it straight
Unto my cell.

Romeo and Juliet, Act v, sc. 2, l. 21 [FRIAR LAURENCE]

1671   Break ope the locks o' the senate and bring in
The crows to peck the eagles.

Coriolanus, Act iii, sc. 1, l. 138 [CORIOLANUS]

1672   If you fall in the adventure, our crows shall fare the better for you; and there's an end.

Cymbeline, Act iii, sc. 1, l. 83 [CLOTEN]

He'll yield the crow a pudding one of these days.

Henry V, Act ii, sc. 1, l. 91 [HOSTESS]

Their executors, the knavish crows,
Fly o'er them, all impatient for their hour.
Henry V, Act iv, sc. 2, l. 51 [GRANDPRE]

1673   Hence will I drag thee headlong by the heels
Unto a dunghill which shall be thy grave, . . .
Leaving thy trunk for crows to feed upon.
II Henry VI, Act iv, sc. 10, l. 87 [IDEN]

1674   Crows are fatted with the murrion flock.
A Midsummer Night's Dream, Act ii, sc. 1, l. 97 [TITANIA]

1675   The crow doth sing as sweetly as the lark
When neither is attended.
The Merchant of Venice, Act v, sc. 1, l. 102 [PORTIA]

1676   The crow may bathe his coal-black wings in mire,
And unperceived fly with the filth away;
But if the like the snow-white swan desire,
The stain upon his silver down will stay.
The Rape of Lucrece, l. 1009 [LUCRECE]

Crown

1677   I will sit and watch here by the king.
Why doth the crown lie there upon his pillow,
Being so troublesome a bedfellow?
O polish'd perturbation! golden care!
That keep'st the ports of slumber open wide
To many a watchful night! sleep with it now!
Yet not so sound and half so deeply sweet
As he whose brow with homely biggen bound
Snores out the watch of night. O majesty!
When thou dost pinch thy bearer, thou dost sit
Like a rich armour worn in heat of day,
That scalds with safety.
II Henry IV, Act iv, sc. 5, l. 20 [PRINCE OF WALES]

1678   If you hide the crown
Even in your hearts, there will he rake for it.
Henry V, Act ii, sc. 4, l. 97 [EXETER]

1679   How sweet a thing it is to wear a crown;
Within whose circuit is Elysium
And all that poets feign of bliss and joy.
III Henry VI, Act i, sc. 2, l. 29 [RICHARD]

1680   A crown, or else a glorious tomb!
A sceptre, or an earthly sepulchre!
III Henry VI, Act i, sc. 4, l. 16 [YORK]

1681   Since this earth affords no joy to me, . . .
I'll make my heaven to dream upon the crown. . . .
And yet I know not how to get the crown,
For many lives stand between me and home:
And I—like one lost in a thorny wood,— . . .
Torment myself to catch the English crown:
And from that torment I will free myself,
Or hew my way out with a bloody axe.
Why, I can smile, and murder whiles I smile,
And cry 'Content' to that which grieves my heart,
And wet my cheeks with artificial tears,
And frame my face to all occasions.
I'll drown more sailors than the mermaid shall;
I'll slay more gazers than the basilisk;
I'll play the orator as well as Nestor,

Deceive more slily than Ulysses could,
And, like a Sinon, take another Troy.
I can add colours to the chameleon,
Change shapes with Proteus for advantages,
And set the murderous Machiavel to school.
Can I do this, and cannot get a crown?
Tut, were it farther off, I'll pluck it down.
III Henry VI, Act iii, sc. 2, 1. 165 [GLOUCESTER]

1682 Fearless minds climb soonest unto crowns.
III Henry VI, Act iv, sc. 7, 1. 62 [GLOUCESTER]

1683 Upon my head they placed a fruitless crown,
And put a barren sceptre in my gripe.
Macbeth, Act iii, sc. 1, 1. 61 [MACBETH]

1684 [He] wears upon his baby brow the round
And top of sovereignty.
Macbeth, Act iv, sc. 1, 1. 88 [MACBETH]

1685 A thousand flatterers sit within thy crown,
Whose compass is no bigger than thy head;
And yet, incaged in so small a verge,
The waste is no whit lesser than thy land.
Richard II, Act ii, sc. 1, 1. 100 [GAUNT]

1686 Give me the crown. Here, cousin, seize the crown; . . .
On this side my hand, and on that side yours.
Now is this golden crown like a deep well
That owes two buckets, filling one another,
The emptier ever dancing in the air,
The other down, unseen and full of water:
That bucket down and full of tears am I,
Drinking my griefs, whilst you mount up on high.
Richard II, Act iv, sc. 1, 1. 181 [KING RICHARD]

1687 Now mark me, how I will undo myself:
I give this heavy weight from off my head
And this unwieldy sceptre from my hand,
The pride of kingly sway from out my heart;
With mine own tears I wash away my balm,
With mine own hands I give away my crown.
Richard II, Act iv, sc. 1, 1. 203 [KING RICHARD]

1688 Our holy lives must win a new world's crown,
Which our profane hours here have stricken down.
Richard II, Act v, sc. 1, 1. 24 [KING RICHARD]

1689 HASTINGS: What news, what news, in this our tottering state?
CATESBY: It is a reeling world, indeed, my lord;
And I believe 'twill never stand upright
Till Richard wear the garland of the realm.
HASTINGS: How! wear the garland! dost thou mean the crown?
CATESBY: Ay, my good lord.
HASTINGS: I'll have this crown of mine cut from my shoulders.
Ere I will see the crown so foul misplaced.
Richard III, Act iii, sc. 2, 1. 37 [HASTINGS]

1690 The crown will find an heir: great Alexander
Left his to the worthiest; so his successor
Was like to be the best.
The Winter's Tale, Act v, sc. 1, 1. 47 [PAULINA]

Cruelty

1691 I must be cruel, only to be kind.
Hamlet, Act iii, sc. 4, 1. 178 [HAMLET]

1692   Come, you spirits,
That tend on mortal thoughts, unsex me here,
And fill me from the crown to the toe top-full
Of direst cruelty!
                Macbeth, Act i, sc. 5, l. 41 [LADY MACBETH]

1693 To fright you thus, methinks, I am too savage;
To do worse to you were fell cruelty,
Which is too nigh your person.
                Macbeth, Act iv, sc. 2, l. 70 [MESSENGER]

1694 Love make his heart of flint that you shall love;
And let your fervour, like my master's, be
Placed in contempt! Farewell, fair cruelty.
                Twelfth Night, Act i, sc. 5, l. 305 [VIOLA]
Get thee to yond same sovereign cruelty.
                Twelfth Night, Act ii, sc. 4, l. 83 [DUKE]

Crutch

1695 I'll lean upon one crutch and fight with t' other,
Ere stay behind this business.
                Coriolanus, Act i, sc. 1, l. 246 [TITUS]

1696 Ah! thus King Henry throws away his crutch
Before his legs be firm to bear his body.
                II Henry VI, Act iii, sc. 1, l. 189 [GLOUCESTER]

1697 Pluck the lined crutch from thy old limping sire,
With it beat out his brains!
                Timon of Athens, Act iv, sc. 1, l. 14 [TIMON]

1698 They that went on crutches ere he was born desire yet their life
to see him a man.
                The Winter's Tale, Act i, sc. 1, l. 44 [CAMILLO]

Cuckold See also **Horn**

1699 I hope to have friends for my wife's sake; . . . for the knaves
come to do that for me that I am aweary of. He that ears my land
spares my team and gives me leave to in the crop; if I be his
cuckold, he's my drudge; . . . ergo, he that kisses my wife is my
friend. . . .
            I the ballad will repeat,
                Which men full true shall find;
            Your marriage comes by destiny,
                Your cuckoo sings by kind.
                All's Well that Ends Well, Act i, sc. 3, l. 42 [CLOWN]

1700 I am not Samson, nor Sir Guy, nor Colbrand,
To mow 'em down before me; but if I spared any
That had a head to hit, either young or old,
He or she, cuckold or cuckold-maker,
Let me ne'er hope to see a chine again;
And that I would not for a cow, God save her.
                Henry VIII, Act v, sc. 4, l. 22 [MAN]
    (The last line, a proverbial phrase still current in southern
    England.)

1701 Your highness said even now I made you a duke: good my lord,
do not recompense me in making me a cuckold.
                Measure for Measure, Act v, sc. 1, l. 522 [LUCIO]
Why, this is like the mending of highways
In summer, where the ways are fair enough:
What, are we cuckolds ere we have deserved it?
                The Merchant of Venice, Act v, sc. 1, l. 263 [GRATIANO]

1702   Amaimon sounds well; Lucifer, well; Barbason, well; yet they are
        devils' additions, the names of fiends: but Cuckold! Wittol—
        Cuckold! the devil himself hath not such a name.
                    The Merry Wives of Windsor, Act ii, sc. 2, l. 311 [FORD]
        Fate, ordaining he should be a cuckold, held his hand.
                    The Merry Wives of Windsor, Act iii, sc. 5, l. 106 [FALSTAFF]
        The cuckold and the cuckold-maker are at it. Now, bull! now, dog!
                    Troilus and Cressida, Act v, sc. 7, l. 9 [THERSITES]
            (Referring to Menelaus and Paris.)
1703   There have been
        Or I am much deceived, cuckolds ere now;
        And many a man there is, even at this present,
        Now while I speak this, holds his wife by the arm,
        That little thinks she has been sluiced in 's absence
        And his pond fish'd by his next neighbour, by
        Sir Smile, his neighbour. . . . Should all despair
        That have revolted wives, the tenth of mankind
        Would hang themselves. Physic for 't there is none;
        It is a bawdy planet, that will strike
        Where 'tis predominant.
                    The Winter's Tale, Act i, sc. 2, l. 190 [LEONTES]

Cuckoo

1704   The cuckoo builds not for himself.
                    Antony and Cleopatra, Act ii, sc. 6, l. 28 [POMPEY]
            Being fed by us, you used us so
        As that ungentle gull, the cuckoo's bird,
        Useth the sparrow; did oppress our nest.
                    I Henry IV, Act v, sc. 1, l. 59 [WORCESTER]
        The hedge-sparrow fed the cuckoo so long,
        That it has its head bit off by its young.
                    King Lear, Act i, sc. 4, l. 235 [FOOL]
1705   When daisies pied and violets blue
            And lady-smocks all silver-white
            And cuckoo-buds of yellow hue
            Do paint the meadows with delight,
        The cuckoo then, on every tree,
        Mocks married men; for thus sings he,
                Cuckoo;
        Cuckoo, cuckoo: O Word of fear,
        Unpleasing to a married ear!
                    Love's Labour's Lost, Act v, sc. 2, l. 904 [SONG]
1706   The finch, the sparrow, and the lark,
            The plain-song cuckoo gray,
        Whose note full many a man doth mark,
            And dares not answer nay;—
        For, indeed, . . . who would give a bird the lie, though he cry
        'cuckoo' never so?
        A Midsummer Night's Dream, Act iii, sc. 1, l. 133 [BOTTOM, *singing*]

Cue

1707   The clock gives me my cue.
                    The Merry Wives of Windsor, Act iii, sc. 2, l. 46 [FORD]
        Remember you your cue.
                    The Merry Wives of Windsor, Act iii, sc. 3, l. 38 [MRS. FORD]
1708   Every one according to his cue.
                    A Midsummer Night's Dream, Act iii, sc. 1, l. 78 [QUINCE]

You speak all your part at once, cues and all.
>   *A Midsummer Night's Dream,* Act iii, sc. 1, l. 102 [QUINCE]

When my cue comes, call me, and I will answer.
>   *A Midsummer Night's Dream,* Act iv, sc. 1, l. 204 [BOTTOM]

1709   Speak, count, 'tis your cue.
>   *Much Ado about Nothing,* Act ii, sc. 1, l. 316 [BEATRICE]

You come upon your cue.
>   *Richard III,* Act iii, sc. 4, l. 27 [BUCKINGHAM]

Cup

1710   Why, what an intricate impeach is this!
I think you all have drunk of Circe's cup.
>   *The Comedy of Errors,* Act v, sc. 1, l. 269 [DUKE]

Fill the cup and let it come;
I'll pledge you a mile to the bottom.
>   *II Henry IV,* Act v, sc. 3, l. 56 [SILENCE]

Here, with a cup that's stored unto the brim.
>   *Pericles,* Act ii, sc. 3, l. 50 [SIMONIDES]

Cupid

1711   It may be said of him that Cupid hath clapp'd him o' the shoulder, but I'll warrant him heart-whole.
>   *As You Like It,* Act iv, sc. 1, l. 48 [ROSALIND]

1712   That same wicked bastard of Venus, that was begot of thought, conceived of spleen and born of madness, that blind rascally boy that abuses every one's eyes because his own are out, let him be judge how deep I am in love.
>   *As You Like It,* Act iv, sc. 1, l. 216 [ROSALIND]

1713   Cupid's butt-shaft is too hard for Hercules' club; and therefore too much odds for a Spaniard's rapier. . . . The passado he respects not, the duello he regards not: his disgrace is to be called boy; but his glory is to subdue men.
>   *Love's Labour's Lost,* Act i, sc. 2, l. 183 [ARMADO]

1714   And I, forsooth, in love! I, that have been love's whip;
A very beadle to a humorous sigh;
A critic, nay, a night-watch constable;
A domineering pedant o'er the boy;
Than whom no mortal so magnificent!
This whimpled, whining, purblind, wayward boy;
This senior-junior, giant-dwarf, Dan Cupid;
Regent of love-rhymes, lord of folded arms,
The anointed sovereign of sighs and groans,
Liege of all loiterers and malcontents,
Dread prince of plackets, king of codpieces,
Sole imperator and great general
Of trotting 'paritors.
>   *Love's Labour's Lost,* Act iii, sc. 1, l. 176 [BIRON]

1715   Sweet Cupid, thou hast thumped him with thy bird-bolt under the left pap.
>   *Love's Labour's Lost,* Act iv, sc. 3, l. 24 [BIRON]

1716   That very time I saw, . . .
Flying between the cold moon and the earth,
Cupid all arm'd: a certain aim he took
At a fair vestal throned by the west,
And loosed his love-shaft smartly from his bow,
As it should pierce a hundred thousand hearts;

But I might see young Cupid's fiery shaft
Quench'd in the chaste beams of the watery moon,
And the imperial votaress passed on,
In maiden meditation, fancy-free.
Yet mark'd I where the bolt of Cupid fell:
It fell upon a little western flower,
Before milk-white, now purple with love's wound,
And maidens call it love-in-idleness.
A Midsummer Night's Dream, Act ii, sc. 1, l. 155 [OBERON]

1717   Cupid is a knavish lad,
Thus to make poor females mad.
A Midsummer Night's Dream, Act iii, sc. 2, l. 440 [PUCK]

1718   If we can do this, Cupid is no longer an archer: his glory shall be
ours, for we are the only love-gods.
Much Ado about Nothing, Act ii, sc. 1, l. 401 [DON PEDRO]

1719   Of this matter
Is little Cupid's crafty arrow made,
That only wounds by hearsay.
Much Ado about Nothing, Act iii, sc. 1, l. 21 [HERO]

1720   Loving goes by haps:
Some Cupid kills with arrows, some with traps.
Much Ado about Nothing, Act iii, sc. 1, l. 105 [HERO]

1721   He hath twice or thrice cut Cupid's bow-string and the little hangman dare not shoot at him.
Much Ado about Nothing, Act iii, sc. 2, l. 11 [DON PEDRO]

1722   She'll not be hit
With Cupid's arrow; she hath Dian's wit;
And, in strong proof of chastity well arm'd,
From love's weak childish bow she lives unharm'd.
Romeo and Juliet, Act i, sc. 1, l. 214 [ROMEO]

1723   Speak to my gossip Venus one fair word,
One nick-name for her purblind son and heir,
Young Adam Cupid, he that shot so trim,
When King Cophetua loved the beggar-maid!
Romeo and Juliet, Act ii, sc. 1, l. 11 [MERCUTIO]

1724   Weak wanton Cupid
Shall from your neck unloose his amorous fold,
And, like a dew-drop from the lion's mane,
Be shook to air.
Troilus and Cressida, Act iii, sc. 3, l. 222 [PATROCLUS]

Cur

1725   This butcher's cur is venom-mouth'd, and I
Have not the power to muzzle him; therefore best
Not wake him in his slumber.
Henry VIII, Act i, sc. 1, l. 120 [BUCKINGHAM]

1726   SALARINO: It is the most impenetrable cur
That ever kept with men.
ANTONIO: Let him alone.
The Merchant of Venice, Act iii, sc. 3 l. 17 [SALARINO]

1727   O upright, just, and true-disposing God,
How do I thank thee that this carnal cur
Preys on the issue of his mother's body.
Richard III, Act iv, sc. 4, l. 55 [QUEEN MARGARET]

1728   Two curs shall tame each other: pride alone
Must tarre the mastiffs on, as 'twere their bone.
Troilus and Cressida, Act i, sc. 3, l. 391 [NESTOR]

Cure

1729   I know most sure
My art is not past power nor you past cure.
>   *All's Well that Ends Well,* Act ii, sc. 1, l. 160 [HELENA]
'Past cure is still past care.'
>   *Love's Labour's Lost,* Act v, sc. 2, l. 28 [ROSALINE]
(The line is in quotation marks, because Rosaline is repeating
an old proverb, referred to by Robert Greene.)

1730   Such a one were past cure, . . . unless they kept very good diet.
>   *Measure for Measure,* Act ii, sc. 1, l. 115 [POMPEY]
Past cure am I, now reason is past care.
>   *Sonnet* cxlvii, l. 9

Current

1731   His unjust unkindness . . . hath, like an impediment in the current, made it more violent and unruly.
>   *Measure for Measure,* Act iii, sc. 1, l. 251 [DUKE]

1732   The current that with gentle murmur glides,
Thou know'st, being stopp'd, impatiently doth rage;
But when his fair course is not hindered,
He makes sweet music with the enamell'd stones,
Giving a gentle kiss to every sedge
He overtaketh in his pilgrimage.
>   *The Two Gentlemen of Verona,* Act ii, sc. 7, l. 25 [JULIA]

Curse

1733   The most infectious pestilence upon thee! . . .
Hence, Horrible villain! or I'll spurn thine eyes
Like balls before me; I'll unhair thy head:
Thou shalt be whipp'd with wire, and stew'd in brine,
Smarting in lingering pickle.
>   *Antony and Cleopatra,* Act ii, sc. 5, l. 61 [CLEOPATRA]

1734   All the contagion of the south light on you,
You shames of Rome! you herd of—Boils and plagues
Plaster you o'er, that you may be abhorr'd
Further than seen and one infect another
Against the wind a mile! You souls of geese,
That bear the shapes of men, how have you run
From slaves that apes would beat! Pluto and hell!
All hurt behind; backs red, and faces pale
With fright and agued fear!
>   *Coriolanus,* Act i, sc. 4, l. 30 [CORIOLANUS]

1735   Now the red pestilence strike all trades in Rome,
And occupations perish!
>   *Coriolanus,* Act iv, sc. 1, l. 13 [VOLUMNIA]

1736   All curses madded Hecuba gave the Greeks,
And mine to boot, be darted on thee!
>   *Cymbeline,* Act iv, sc. 2, l. 313 [IMOGEN]

1737   QUEEN: Mischance and sorrow go along with you!
Heart's discontent and sour affliction
Be playfellows to keep you company! . . .
SUFFOLK: Cease, gentle queen, these execrations. . . .
QUEEN: Hast thou not spirit to curse thine enemy?
SUFFOLK: A plague upon them! wherefore should I curse them?
Would curses kill, as doth the mandrake's groan,
I would invent as bitter-searching terms,
As curst, as harsh and horrible to hear, . . .
As lean-faced Envy in her loathsome cave. . . .

Shall I not curse them! Poison be their drink!
Gall, worse than gall, the daintiest that they taste!
Their sweetest shade a grove of cypress trees!
Their chiefest prospect murdering basilisks!
Their softest touch as smart as lizards' stings!
Their music frightful as the serpent's hiss. . . .
QUEEN: Enough, sweet Suffolk; thou torment'st thyself;
And these dread curses, like the sun 'gainst glass,
Or like an overcharged gun, recoil,
And turn the force of them upon thyself. . . .
SUFFOLK: Now, by the ground that I am banish'd from,
Well could I curse away a winter's night,
Though standing naked on a mountain top,
Where biting cold would never let grass grow,
And think it but a minute spent in sport.
                    II Henry VI, Act iii, sc. 2, l. 300 [QUEEN]

1738   That's the curse of Rome.
                    King John, Act iii, sc. 1, l. 207 [BLANCH]

1739   Blasts and fogs upon thee!
The untented woundings of a father's curse
Pierce every sense about thee!
                    King Lear, Act i, sc. 4, l. 321 [LEAR]

1740   All the stored vengeances of heaven fall
On her ingrateful top! Strike her young bones,
You taking airs, with lameness! . . .
You nimble lightnings, dart your blinding flames
Into her scornful eyes! Infect her beauty,
You fen-suck'd fogs, drawn by the powerful sun,
To fall and blast her pride!
                    King Lear, Act ii, sc. 4, l. 164 [LEAR]

1741   Cursed be the hand that made these fatal holes!
Cursed be the heart that had the heart to do it!
Cursed the blood that let this blood from hence!
                    Richard III, Act i, sc. 2, l. 14 [ANNE]

1742   Can curses pierce the clouds and enter heaven?
Why then, give way, dull clouds, to my quick curses!
                    Richard III, Act i, sc. 3, l. 195 [QUEEN MARGARET]

1743   QUEEN ELIZABETH: O thou well skill'd in curses, stay awhile,
And teach me how to curse mine enemies!
QUEEN MARGARET: Forbear to sleep the nights, and fast the days;
Compare dead happiness with living woe;
Think that thy babes were fairer than they were,
And he that slew them fouler than he is:
Bettering thy loss makes the bad causer worse:
Revolving this will teach thee how to curse.
                    Richard III, Act iv, sc. 4, l. 116 [QUEEN ELIZABETH]

1744   I shall . . . never look upon thy face again.
Therefore take with thee my most heavy curse;
Which, in the day of battle, tire thee more
Than all the complete armour that thou wear'st! . . .
Bloody thou art, bloody will be thy end;
Shame serves thy life and doth thy death attend.
                    Richard III, Act iv, sc. 4, l. 185 [DUCHESS OF YORK]

1745   CALIBAN: As wicked dew as e'er my mother brush'd
With raven's feather from unwholesome fen
Drop on you both! a south-west blow on ye
And blister you all o'er!

PROSPERO: For this, be sure, to-night thou shalt have cramps,
Side-stitches that shall pen thy breath up. . . .
CALIBAN: All the charms
Of Sycorax, toads, beetles, bats, light on you! . . .
PROSPERO: I'll rack thee with old cramps,
Fill all thy bones with aches, make thee roar
That beasts shall tremble at thy din.
                        The Tempest, Act i, sc. 2, l. 321 [CALIBAN]
All the infections that the sun sucks up
From bogs, fens, flats, on Prosper fall and make him
By inch-meal a disease! His spirits hear me
And yet I needs must curse.
                        The Tempest, Act ii, sc. 2, l. 1 [CALIBAN]
1746 The common curse of mankind, folly and ignorance, be thine in
      great revenue!
                Troilus and Cressida, Act ii, sc. 3, l. 31 [THERSITES]
1747 THERSITES: Now, the rotten diseases of the south, the guts-griping,
      ruptures, catarrhs, loads o' gravel i' the back, lethargies, cold pal-
      sies, raw eyes, dirt-rotten livers, wheezing lungs, bladders full of
      imposthume, sciaticas, lime-kilns i' the palm, incurable bone-ache,
      and the rivelled fee-simple of the tetter, take and take again such
      preposterous discoveries!
      PATROCLUS: Why, thou damnable box of envy, thou, what meanest
      thou to curse thus?
                Troilus and Cressida, Act v, sc. 1, l. 19 [THERSITES]

Custom

1748 Why in this woolvish toge should I stand here,
      To beg of Hob and Dick? . . . Custom calls me to 't:
      What custom wills, in all things should we do 't,
      The dust on antique time would lie unswept,
      And mountainous error be too highly heapt
      For truth to o'er-peer.
                Coriolanus, Act ii, sc. 3, l. 122 [CORIOLANUS]
1749 HAMLET: The king doth wake to-night and takes his rouse,
      Keeps wassail, and the swaggering up-spring reels. . . .
      HORATIO: Is it a custom?
      HAMLET: Ay, marry, is 't:
      But to my mind, though I am native here
      And to the manner born, it is a custom
      More honour'd in the breach than the observance.
                        Hamlet, Act i, sc. 4, l. 8 [HAMLET]
1750 That monster, custom, who all sense doth eat,
      Of habits devil, is angel yet in this,
      That to the use of actions fair and good
      He likewise gives a frock or livery,
      That aptly is put on.
                        Hamlet, Act iii, sc. 4, l. 161 [HAMLET]
1751 HAMLET: Has this fellow no feeling of his business, that he sings
      at grave-making?
      HORATIO: Custom hath made it in him a property of easiness.
                        Hamlet, Act v, sc. 1, l. 73 [HAMLET]
      KING HENRY: I will kiss your lips, Kate.
      KATHARINE: Les dames et demoiselles pour être baisées devant
      leur noces, il n'est pas la coutume de France. . . .
      KING HENRY: It is not a fashion for the maids in France to kiss
      before they are married? . . . O Kate, nice customs curtsy to great

kings. . . . We are the makers of manners, Kate; and the liberty
that follows our places stops the mouth of all find-faults.
Henry V, Act v, sc. 2, l. 278 [KING HENRY]

1752   New customs,
Though they be never so ridiculous,
Nay, let 'em be unmanly, yet are follow'd.
Henry VIII, Act i, sc. 3, l. 2 [SANDS]

1753   Think of this, good peers,
But as a thing of custom: 'tis no other;
Only it spoils the pleasure of the time.
Macbeth, Act iii, sc. 4, l. 96 [LADY MACBETH]

1754   The tyrant custom, most grave senators,
Hath made the flinty and steel couch of war
My thrice-driven bed of down.
Othello, Act i, sc. 3, l. 230 [OTHELLO]

Cut-Purse

1755   A cut-purse of the empire and the rule,
That from a shelf the precious diadem stole,
And put it in his pocket!
Hamlet, Act iii, sc. 4, l. 99 [HAMLET]

1756   To have an open ear, a quick eye, and a nimble hand is necessary
for a cut-purse; a good nose is requisite also, to smell out work
for the other senses.
The Winter's Tale, Act iv, sc. 4, l. 684 [AUTOLYCUS]

D

Daffodils

1757   When daffodils begin to peer,
With heigh! the doxy over the dale,
Why, then comes in the sweet o' the year;
For the red blood reigns in the winter's pale.
The Winter's Tale, Act iv, sc. 3, l. 1 [AUTOLYCUS]

1758   Daffodils
That come before the swallow dares, and take
The winds of March with beauty.
The Winter's Tale, Act iv, sc. 4, l. 118 [PERDITA]

Dagger

1759   I will speak daggers to her, but use none.
Hamlet, Act iii, sc. 2, l. 414 [HAMLET]

1760   Thou hidest a thousand daggers in thy thoughts,
Which thou hast whetted on thy stony heart,
To stab at half an hour of my life.
II Henry IV, Act iv, sc. 5, l. 107 [KING HENRY]

1761   There is my dagger,
And here my naked breast; within, a heart
Dearer than Plutus mine, richer than gold: . . .
Strike, as thou didst at Cæsar.
Julius Cæsar, Act iv, sc. 3, l. 100 [CASSIUS]

1762   Is this a dagger which I see before me,
The handle toward my hand? Come, let me clutch thee.
I have thee not, and yet I see thee still, . . .
I see thee yet, in form as palpable
As this which now I draw.

Thou marshall'st me the way that I was going;
And such an instrument I was to use.
                              Macbeth, Act ii, sc. 1, l. 33 [MACBETH]
This is the air-drawn dagger which, you said,
Led you to Duncan.
                              Macbeth, Act iii, sc. 4, l. 63 [LADY MACBETH]

1763   There's daggers in men's smiles.
                              Macbeth, Act ii, sc. 3, l. 145 [DONALBAIN]

1764   Hath no man's dagger here a point for me?
                              Much Ado about Nothing, Act iv, sc. 1, l. 110 [LEONATO]

1765   O happy dagger!
This is thy sheath. [*Stabs herself*]; there rust, and let me die.
                              Romeo and Juliet, Act v, sc. 3, l. 169 [JULIET]
This dagger hath mista'en, . . .
And it mis-sheathed in my daughter's bosom!
                              Romeo and Juliet, Act v, sc. 3, l. 203 [CAPULET]

Damnation

1766   Truly, thou art damned. . . . Wilt thou rest damned? God help
thee, shallow man! God make incision in thee! thou art raw. . . .
if thou beest not damned for this, the devil himself will have no
shepherds.
                              As You Like It, Act iii, sc. 2, l. 38 [TOUCHSTONE]

1767   God damn me!
                              The Comedy of Errors, Act iv, sc. 3, l. 54 [DROMIO OF SYRACUSE]

1768   I'll not be juggled with:
To hell, allegiance! vows, to the blackest devil!
Conscience and grace, to the profoundest pit!
I dare damnation.
                              Hamlet, Act iv, sc. 5, l. 130 [LAERTES]

1769   I'll be damned for never a king's son in Christendom.
                              I Henry IV, Act i, sc. 2, l. 108 [FALSTAFF]

1770   I'll see her damned first; to Pluto's damned lake, by this hand,
to the infernal deep, with Erebus and tortures vile also. Hold
hook and line, say I. Down, down dogs! down faitors!
                              II Henry IV, Act ii, sc. 4, l. 171 [PISTOL]
("Faitor," a cheat, a vagrant.)

1771   Here's a good world! Knew you of this fair work?
Beyond the infinite and boundless reach
Of mercy, if thou didst this deed of death,
Art thou damn'd Hubert. . . . Thou 'rt damned as black . . .
Thou art more deep damn'd than Prince Lucifer:
There is not yet so ugly a fiend of hell
As thou shalt be, if thou didst kill this child. . . .
And if thou want'st a cord, the smallest thread
That ever spider twisted from her womb
Will serve to strangle thee; a rush will be a beam
To hang thee on; or, wouldst thou drown thyself,
Put but a little water in a spoon,
And it shall be as all the ocean,
Enough to stifle such a villain up.
                              KING JOHN, Act iv, sc. 3, l. 116 [BASTARD]

1772   'Twere damnation to think so base a thought.
                              The Merchant of Venice, Act ii, sc. 7, l. 49 [MOROCCO]

1773   Be of good cheer, for truly I think you are damned.
                              The Merchant of Venice, Act iii, sc. 5, l. 6 [LAUNCELOT]

1774   I am damned in hell for swearing . . . you were good soldiers
and tall fellows.
> *The Merry Wives of Windsor,* Act ii, sc. 2, l. 9 [FALSTAFF]

1775   Thou art damn'd to hell for this.
> *Richard II,* Act iv, sc. 1, l. 43 [AUMERLE]

Dancing

1776   Ha, my brave emperor,
Shall we dance now the Egyptian Bacchanals,
And celebrate our drink?
> *Antony and Cleopatra,* Act ii, sc. 7, l. 109 [ENOBARBUS]

1777   So, to your pleasures:
I am for other than for dancing measures.
> *As You Like It,* Act v, sc. 4, l. 198 [JAQUES]

1778   They bid us to the English dancing-schools,
And teach lavoltas high and swift corantos;
Saying our grace is only in our heels,
And that we are most lofty runaways.
> *Henry V,* Act iii, sc. 5, l. 32 [BOURBON]

1779   Let's have a dance ere we are married, that we may lighten our
own hearts and our wives' heels.
> *Much Ado about Nothing,* Act v, sc. 4, l. 119 [BENEDICK]

1780   LADY: Madam, we'll dance.
QUEEN: My legs can keep no measure in delight,
When my poor heart no measure keeps in grief:
Therefore, no dancing, girl.
> *Richard II,* Act iii, sc. 4, l. 6 [LADY]

1781   BENVOLIO: We'll measure them a measure and be gone. . . .
ROMEO: Not I, believe me: you have dancing shoes
With nimble soles: I have a soul of lead
So stakes me to the ground I cannot move.
> *Romeo and Juliet,* Act i, sc. 4, l. 10 [BENVOLIO]

1782   Let wantons light of heart
Tickle the senseless rushes with their heels.
> *Romeo and Juliet,* Act i, sc. 4, l. 35 [ROMEO]

1783   You and I are past our dancing days.
> *Romeo and Juliet,* Act i, sc. 5, l. 33 [CAPULET]

1784   When you do dance, I wish you
A wave o' the sea, that you might ever do
Nothing but that.
> *The Winter's Tale,* Act iv, sc. 4, l. 140 [FLORIZEL]

Danger

1785   Thou wretched, rash, intruding fool, farewell!
I took thee for thy better: take thy fortune;
Thou find'st to be too busy is some danger.
> *Hamlet,* Act iii, sc. 4, l. 31 [HAMLET]

1786   I prithee, take thy fingers from my throat;
For, though I am not splenitive and rash,
Yet have I something in me dangerous,
Which let thy wiseness fear.
> *Hamlet,* Act v, sc. 1, l. 283 [HAMLET]

1787   Send danger from the east unto the west,
So honour cross it from the north to south,
And let them grapple: O, the blood more stirs
To rouse a lion than to start a hare!
> *I Henry IV,* Act i, sc. 3, l. 195 [HOTSPUR]

1788   'The purpose you undertake is dangerous';—why, that's certain:
        'tis dangerous to take a cold, to sleep, to drink; but I tell you,
        my lord fool, out of this nettle, danger, we pluck this flower,
        safety.
                                I Henry IV, Act ii, sc. 3, l. 8 [HOTSPUR]

1789   I must go and meet with danger there,
        Or it will seek me in another place
        And find me worse provided.
                        II Henry IV, Act ii, sc. 3, l. 48 [NORTHUMBERLAND]

1790   The dangers of the days but newly gone,
        Whose memory is written on the earth
        With yet appearing blood.
                        II Henry IV, Act iv, sc. 1, l. 80 [ARCHBISHOP]

1791   'Tis true that we are in great danger;
        The greater therefore should our courage be.
                            Henry V, Act iv, sc. 1, l. 1 [KING HENRY]

1792   'Tis the more honour, because more dangerous.
                            III Henry VI, Act iv, sc. 3, l. 15 [WATCHMAN]

1793   Many men that stumble at the threshold
        Are well foretold that danger lurks within.
                        III Henry VI, Act iv, sc. 7, l. 11 [GLOUCESTER]

1794   Omission to do what is necessary
        Seals a commission to a blank of danger;
        And danger, like an ague, subtly taints
        Even then when we sit idly in the sun.
                    Troilus and Cressida, Act iii, sc. 3, l. 230 [PATROCLUS]

1795   In thy danger,
        If ever danger do environ thee,
        Commend thy grievance to my holy prayers,
        For I will be thy beadsman, Valentine.
                The Two Gentlemen of Verona, Act i, sc. 1, l. 15 [PROTEUS]

1796   Danger deviseth shifts; wit waits on fear.
                                Venus and Adonis, l. 689 [VENUS]

Daniel

1797   A Daniel come to judgement! yea, a Daniel!
        O wise young judge, how I do honour thee!
                        The Merchant of Venice, Act iv, sc. 1, l. 223 [SHYLOCK]

1798   A second Daniel, a Daniel, Jew!
        Now, infidel, I have you on the hip. . . .
        A Daniel, still say I, a second Daniel!
        I thank thee, Jew, for teaching me that word.
                        The Merchant of Venice, Act iv, sc. 1, l. 333 [GRATIANO]

Darkness

1799   It was so dark, Hal, that thou couldst not see thy hand.
                                I Henry IV, Act ii, sc. 4, l. 247 [FALSTAFF]

1800   If I must die
        I will encounter darkness as a bride,
        And hug it in mine arms.
                        Measure for Measure, Act iii, sc. 1, l. 84 [CLAUDIO]

1801   Following darkness like a dream.
                    A Midsummer Night's Dream, Act v, sc. 1, l. 393 [PUCK]

Darlings

1802   She shunn'd
        The wealthy curled darlings of our nation.
                                Othello, Act i, sc. 2, l. 67 [BRABANTIO]

1803   [They] are ready now
To eat those little darlings whom they loved.
        Pericles, Act i, sc. 4, l. 44 [CLEON]

Daughter

1804 HAMLET: Have you a daughter?
POLONIUS: I have, my lord.
HAMLET: Let her not walk i' the sun: conception is a blessing:
but not as your daughter may conceive. Friend, look to 't.
POLONIUS: Still harping on my daughter.
        Hamlet, Act ii, sc. 2, l. 182 [HAMLET]

1805 HAMLET: O Jephthah, judge of Israel, what a treasure hadst thou!
POLONIUS: What a treasure had he, my lord?
HAMLET: Why, 'One fair daughter and no more,
The which he loved passing well.'
POLONIUS: Still on my daughter.
        Hamlet, Act ii, sc. 2, l. 422 [HAMLET]

1806 Thou art my flesh, my blood, my daughter;
Or rather a disease that 's in my flesh,
Which I must needs call mine: thou art a boil,
A plague-sore, an embossed carbuncle,
In my corrupted blood.
        King Lear, Act ii, sc. 4, l. 224 [LEAR]

1807 Now, all the plagues that in the pendulous air
Hang fated o'er men's faults light on thy daughters. . . .
Death, traitor! nothing could have subdued nature
To such a lowness but his unkind daughters.
Is it the fashion, that discarded fathers
Should have thus little mercy on their flesh?
Judicious punishment! 'twas this flesh begot
Those pelican daughters.
        King Lear, Act iii, sc. 4, l. 69 [LEAR]

1808 Tigers, not daughters, what have you perform'd?
A father, and a gracious aged man,
Whose reverence even the head-lugg'd bear would lick,
Most barbarous, most degenerate! have you madded.
        King Lear, Act iv, sc. 2, l. 40 [ALBANY]

1809 Alack, what heinous sin is it in me
To be ashamed to be my father's child!
But though I am a daughter to his blood,
I am not to his manners.
     The Merchant of Venice, Act ii, sc. 3, l. 16 [JESSICA]

1810 [He] curses all Eve's daughters, of what complexion soever.
    The Merry Wives of Windsor, Act iv, sc. 2, l. 24 [MRS. PAGE]

1811 DON PEDRO: I think this is your daughter.
LEONATO: Her mother hath many times told me so.
   Much Ado about Nothing, Act i, sc. 1, l. 104 [DON PEDRO]
Thy mother was a piece of virtue, and
She said thou wast my daughter.
      The Tempest, Act i, sc. 2, l. 56 [PROSPERO]

1812 Your fair daughter . . . transported . . .
To the gross clasps of a lascivious Moor. . . .
Your daughter . . . hath made a gross revolt;
Tying her duty, beauty, wit and fortunes
To an extravagant and wheeling stranger
Of here and every where.
      Othello, Act i, sc. 1, l. 123 [RODERIGO]

1813   Fathers, from hence trust not your daughters' minds
        By what you see them act.
                        Othello, Act i, sc. 1, l. 171 [BRABANTIO]

1814   Call you me daughter? now, I promise you,
        You have show'd a tender fatherly regard,
        To wish me wed to one half lunatic;
        A mad-cap ruffian and a swearing Jack.
                The Taming of the Shrew, Act ii, sc. 1, l. 287 [KATHARINA]

Day

1815   We did sleep day out of countenance, and made the night light
        with drinking.
                Antony and Cleopatra, Act ii, sc. 2, l. 181 [ENOBARBUS]

1816   The bright day is done, And we are for the dark.
                Antony and Cleopatra, Act v, sc. 2, l. 193 [IRAS]

1817   You have look'd on better days.
                As You Like It, Act ii, sc. 7, l. 113 [ORLANDO]
        True it is that we have seen better days.
                As You Like It, Act ii, sc. 7, l. 120 [DUKE]
        Let's shake our heads and say, . . .
        'We have seen better days.'
                Timon of Athens, Act iv, sc. 2, l. 25 [FLAVIUS]

1818   A merrier day did never yet greet Rome.
                Coriolanus, Act v, sc. 4, l. 46 [MESSENGER]

1819   'Tis the breathing time of day with me.
                Hamlet, Act v, sc. 2, l. 181 [HAMLET]

1820   O, such a day,
        So fought, so follow'd and so fairly won,
        Came not till now to dignify the times,
        Since Cæsar's fortunes!
                II Henry IV, Act i, sc. 1, l. 20 [BARDOLPH]

1821   The day begins to break, and night is fled,
        Whose pitchy mantle over-veil'd the earth.
                I Henry VI, Act ii, sc. 2, l. 1 [BEDFORD]

1822   The gaudy, blabbing and remorseful day
        Is crept into the bosom of the sea.
                II Henry VI, Act iv, sc. 1, l. 1 [CAPTAIN]

1823   Here they have sat The live-long day.
                Julius Cæsar, Act i, sc. 1, l. 45 [MARULLUS]

1824   The day shall not be up so soon as I,
        To try the fair adventure of to-morrow.
                King John, Act v, sc. 5, l. 21 [LEWIS]

1825   In the posteriors of this day, which the rude multitude call the
        afternoon.
                Love's Labour's Lost, Act v, sc. 1, l. 94 [ARMADO]

1826   So foul and fair a day I have not seen.
                Macbeth, Act i, sc. 3, l. 38 [MACBETH]

1827   Thou seest the heavens, as troubled with man's act,
        Threaten his bloody stage: by the clock, 'tis day,
        And yet dark night strangles the travelling lamp:
        Is 't night's predominance, or the day's shame,
        That darkness does the face of earth entomb,
        When living light should kiss it?
                Macbeth, Act ii, sc. 4, l. 5 [ROSS]

1828   So great a day as this is cheaply bought.
                Macbeth, Act v, sc. 8, l. 37 [SIWARD]

1829   We burn daylight.
          The Merry Wives of Windsor, Act ii, sc. 1, l. 54 [MRS. FORD]
     Come, we burn daylight, ho!
               Romeo and Juliet, Act i, sc. 4, l. 43 [MERCUTIO]

1830   The wolves have prey'd; and look, the gentle day . . .
     Dapples the drowsy east with spots of grey.
         Much Ado about Nothing, Act v, sc. 3, l. 25 [DON PEDRO]

1831   So tedious is this day
     As is the night before some festival
     To an impatient child that hath new robes
     And may not wear them.
             Romeo and Juliet, Act iii, sc. 2, l. 28 [JULIET]

1832   Look, love, what envious streaks
     Do lace the severing clouds in yonder east:
     Night's candles are burnt out, and jocund day
     Stands tiptoe on the misty mountain tops.
              Romeo and Juliet, Act iii, sc. 5, l. 7 [ROMEO]

1833   The busy day,
     Waked by the lark, hath roused the ribald crows,
     And dreaming night will hide our joys no longer.
           Troilus and Cressida, Act iv, sc. 2, l. 8 [TROILUS]

1834   He makes a July's day short as December.
           The Winter's Tale, Act i, sc. 2, l. 169 [POLIXENES]

Death

1835   I have seen her die twenty times upon far poorer moment: I do
     think there is mettle in death, which commits some loving act
     upon her, she hath such a celerity in dying.
         Antony and Cleopatra, Act i, sc. 2, l. 146 [ENOBARBUS]

1836   She hath betrayed me and shall die the death.
          Antony and Cleopatra, Act iv, sc. 14, l. 26 [ANTONY]
          Die the death:
     When I have slain thee with my proper hand,
     I'll . . . on the gates of Lud's-town set your heads.
               Cymbeline, Act iv, sc. 2, l. 96 [CLOTEN]
          He must not only die the death,
     But thy unkindness shall his death draw out
     To lingering sufferance.
         Measure for Measure, Act ii, sc. 4, l. 165 [ANGELO]

1837   I will be
     A bridegroom in my death, and run into't
     As to a lover's bed.
         Antony and Cleopatra, Act iv, sc. 14, l. 100 [ANTONY]
     I will die bravely, like a bridegroom.
              King Lear, Act iv, sc. 6, l. 202 [LEAR]

1838   I am dying, Egypt, dying; only
     I here importune death awhile, until
     Of many thousand kisses the poor last
     I lay upon thy lips. . . . I am dying, Egypt, dying.
          Antony and Cleopatra, Act iv, sc. 15, l. 18 [ANTONY]

1839   Is it sin
     To rush into the secret house of death,
     Ere death dare come to us? . . .
     Our lamp is spent, it's out! . . . What's brave, what's noble,
     Let's do it after the high Roman fashion,
     And make death proud to take us.
          Antony and Cleopatra, Act iv, sc. 15, l. 80 [CLEOPATRA]

1840   Where art thou, death?
     Come hither, come! come, come, and take a queen
     Worth many babes and beggars! . . . This mortal house I'll ruin,
     Do Cæsar what he can. . . . Shall they hoist me up
     And show me to the shouting varletry
     Of censuring Rome? Rather a ditch in Egypt
     Be gentle grave unto me! rather on Nilus' mud
     Lay me stark naked, and let the water-flies
     Blow me into abhorring! rather make
     My country's high pyramids my gibbet,
     And hang me up in chains!
               Antony and Cleopatra, Act v, sc. 2, l. 46 [CLEOPATRA]
1841 If thou and nature can so gently part,
     The stroke of death is as a lover's pinch,
     Which hurts, and is desired.
               Antony and Cleopatra, Act v, sc. 2, l. 297 [CLEOPATRA]
     There cannot be a pinch in death
     More sharp than this is.
               Cymbeline, Act i, sc. 1, l. 130 [IMOGEN]
1842   So, fare thee well.
     Now boast thee, death, in thy possession lies
     A lass unparallel'd. Downy windows, close;
     And golden Phœbus never be beheld
     Of eyes again so royal!
               Antony and Cleopatra, Act v, sc. 2, l. 317 [CHARMIAN]
1843 He that hath a will to die by himself fears it not from another.
               Coriolanus, Act v, sc. 2, l. 110 [MENENIUS]
1844 They'll give him death by inches.
               Coriolanus, Act v, sc. 4, l. 43 [MESSENGER]
1845 Cured by the sure physician, death, who is the key
     To unbar these locks.
               Cymbeline, Act v, sc. 4, l. 5 [POSTHUMUS]
1846 Good Hamlet, cast thy nighted colour off,
     And let thine eye look like a friend on Denmark. . . .
     Thou know'st 'tis common; all that lives must die,
     Passing through nature to eternity.
               Hamlet, Act i, sc. 2, l. 68 [QUEEN]
     Death, as the Psalmist saith, is certain to all.
               II Henry IV, Act iii, sc. 2, l. 41 [SHALLOW]
     Well, death's the end of all.
               Romeo and Juliet, Act iii, sc. 3, l. 92 [NURSE]
     Well, we are born to die.
               Romeo and Juliet, Act iii, sc. 4, l. 4 [CAPULET]
1847 To be, or not to be: that is the question:
     Whether 'tis nobler in the mind to suffer
     The slings and arrows of outrageous fortune,
     Or to take arms against a sea of troubles,
     And by opposing end them? To die: to sleep;
     No more; and by a sleep to say we end
     The heart-ache and the thousand natural shocks
     That flesh is heir to, 'tis a consummation
     Devoutly to be wish'd. To die, to sleep;
     To sleep: perchance to dream: ay, there's the rub;
     For in that sleep of death what dreams may come
     When we have shuffled off this mortal coil,
     Must give us pause: there's the respect
     That makes calamity of so long life;

For who would bear the whips and scorns of time,
The oppressor's wrong, the proud man's contumely,
The pangs of despised love, the law's delay,
The insolence of office and the spurns
That patient merit of the unworthy takes,
When he himself might his quietus make
With a bare bodkin? who would fardels bear,
To grunt and sweat under a weary life,
But that the dread of something after death,
The undiscover'd country from whose bourn
No traveller returns, puzzles the will
And makes us rather bear those ills we have
Than fly to others that we know not of?
Thus conscience does make cowards of us all;
And thus the native hue of resolution
Is sicklied o'er with the pale cast of thought,
And enterprises of great pith and moment
With this regard their currents turn awry,
And lose the name of action.

> *Hamlet,* Act iii, sc. 1, l. 56 [HAMLET]

1848   How now? a rat? Dead, for a ducat, dead!

> *Hamlet,* Act iii, sc. 4, l. 23 [HAMLET]

1849   And will he not come again?
          No, no he is dead: Go to thy death-bed;
          He never will come again.

> *Hamlet,* Act iv, sc. 5, l. 191 [OPHELIA, *singing*]

1850   His means of death, his obscure funeral—
No trophy, sword, nor hatchment o'er his bones,
No noble rite nor funeral ostentation—
Cry to be heard, as 'twere from heaven to earth.

> *Hamlet,* Act iv, sc. 5, l. 213 [LAERTES]

1851   [She] Fell in the weeping brook. Her clothes spread wide;
And, mermaid-like, awhile they bore her up:
Which time she chanted snatches of old tunes; . . .
Till that her garments, heavy with their drink,
Pull'd the poor wretch from her melodious lay
To muddy death.

> *Hamlet,* Act iv, sc. 7, l. 176 [QUEEN]

1852   This fell sergeant, death,
Is strict in his arrest.

> *Hamlet,* Act v, sc. 2, l. 347 [HAMLET]

        That fell arrest
Without all bail shall carry me away.

> *Sonnet* lxxiv, l. 1

1853   O proud death,
What feast is toward in thine eternal cell,
That thou so many princes at a shot
So bloodily hast struck?

> *Hamlet,* Act v, sc. 2, l. 375 [FORTINBRAS]

1854   Doomsday is near; die all, die merrily.

> *I Henry IV,* Act iv, sc. 1, l. 134 [HOTSPUR]

1855   PRINCE: Thou owest God a death.
FALSTAFF: 'Tis not due yet; I would be loath to pay him before
his day. What need I be so forward with him that calls not
on me?

> *I Henry IV,* Act v, sc. 1, l. 126 [PRINCE]

A man can die but once: we owe God a death. . . . He that dies
this year is quit for the next.
                    II Henry IV, Act iii, sc. 2, l. 250 [FEEBLE]

1856   Death rock me asleep, abridge my doleful days!
                    II Henry IV, Act ii, sc. 4, l. 211 [PISTOL]

1857   FALSTAFF: What, is the old king dead?
        PISTOL: As nail in door.
                    II Henry IV, Act v, sc. 3, l. 126 [FALSTAFF]
        If I do not leave you all as dead as a doornail, I pray God I
        may never eat grass more.
                    II Henry VI, Act iv, sc. 10, l. 43 [CADE]

1858   The arbitrator of despairs,
        Just death, kind umpire of men's miseries,
        With sweet enlargement doth dismiss me hence.
                    I Henry VI, Act ii, sc. 5, l. 28 [MORTIMER]

1859   When I am dead and gone,
        May honourable peace attend thy throne!
                    II Henry VI, Act ii, sc. 3, l. 37 [GLOUCESTER]

1860   KING: Ah, what a sign it is of evil life,
        When death's approach is seen so terrible! . . .
        Lord cardinal, if thou think'st on heaven's bliss,
        Hold up thy hand, make signal of thy hope.
        He dies, and makes no sign. O God forgive him!
        WARWICK: So bad a death argues a monstrous life.
        KING: Forbear to judge, for we are sinners all.
                    II Henry VI, Act iii, sc. 3, l. 5 [KING]

1861   I am resolved for death or dignity.
                    II Henry VI, Act v, sc. 1, l. 194 [YORK]

1862   GRIFFITH: About the hour of eight, . . .
        He gave his honours to the world again,
        His blessed part to heaven, and slept in peace.
        KATHARINE: So may he rest; his faults lie gently on him!
                    Henry VIII, Act iv, sc. 2, l. 26 [GRIFFITH]

1863   CALPURNIA: When beggars die, there are no comets seen;
        The heavens themselves blaze forth the death of princes. . . .
        CÆSAR: Of all the wonders that I yet have heard,
        It seems to me most strange that men should fear;
        Seeing that death, a necessary end,
        Will come when it will come.
                    Julius Cæsar, Act ii, sc. 2, l. 30 [CALPURNIA]

1864   BRUTUS: Fates, we will know your pleasures:
        That we shall die, we know; 'tis but the time
        And drawing days out, that men stand upon.
        CASSIUS: Why, he that cuts off twenty years of life
        Cuts off so many years of fearing death.
        BRUTUS: Grant that, and then is death a benefit.
                    Julius Cæsar, Act iii, sc. 1, l. 98 [BRUTUS]

1865   MESSALA: Portia . . . is dead, and by strange manner.
        BRUTUS: Why, farewell, Portia. We must die, Messala;
        With meditating that she must die once,
        I have the patience to endure it now.
        MESSALA: Even so great men great losses should endure.
                    Julius Cæsar, Act iv, sc. 3, l. 189 [MESSALA]

1866   O, now doth Death line his dead chaps with steel;
        The swords of soldiers are his teeth, his fangs;

And now he feasts, mousing the flesh of men,
In undetermined differences of kings.
King John, Act ii, sc. 1, l. 352 [BASTARD]

1867   Here's a stay
That shakes the rotten carcass of old Death
Out of his rags!
King John, Act ii, sc. 1, l. 455 [BASTARD]

He's dead and rotten.
King Lear, Act v, sc. 3, l. 285 [LEAR]

1868   Death, death; O amiable lovely death!
Thou odoriferous stench! sound rottenness!
Arise forth from the couch of lasting night,
Thou hate and terror to prosperity,
And I will kiss thy detestable bones
And put my eyeballs in thy vaulty brows
And ring these fingers with thy household worms
And stop this gap of breath with fulsome dust
And be a carrion monster like thyself:
Come, grin on me, and I will think thou smilest
And buss thee as thy wife. Misery's love,
O, come to me!
King John, Act iii, sc. 4, l. 25 [CONSTANCE]

1869   O death, made proud with pure and princely beauty!
The earth had not a hole to hide this deed.
King John, Act iv, sc. 3, l. 35 [PEMBROKE]

1870   Have I not hideous death within my view,
Retaining but a quantity of life,
Which bleeds away, even as a form of wax
Resolveth from his figure 'gainst the fire?
King John, Act v, sc. 4, l. 22 [MELUN]

1871   Nothing in his life
Became him like the leaving it; he died
As one that had been studied in his death
To throw away the dearest thing he owed,
As 'twere a careless trifle.
Macbeth, Act i, sc. 4, l. 7 [MALCOLM]

1872   Better be with the dead,
Whom we, to gain our peace, have sent to peace,
Than on the torture of the mind to lie
In restless ecstasy. Duncan is in his grave;
After life's fitful fever he sleeps well;
Treason has done his worst: nor steel nor poison,
Malice domestic, foreign levy, nothing,
Can touch him further.
Macbeth, Act iii, sc. 2, l. 19 [MACBETH]

1873   Ring the alarum-bell! Blow, wind! come, wrack!
At least we'll die with harness on our back.
Macbeth, Act v, sc. 5, l. 51 [MACBETH]

1874   Be absolute for death; either death or life
Shall thereby be the sweeter. Reason thus with life:
If I do lose thee, I do lose a thing
That none but fools would keep; a breath thou art,
Servile to all the skyey influences,
That dost this habitation, where thou keep'st,
Hourly afflict: merely, thou art death's fool;
For him thou labour'st by thy flight to shun
And yet runn'st toward him still. . . . Thy best of rest is sleep,

And that thou oft provokest; yet grossly fear'st
Thy death, which is no more. . . . If thou art rich, thou'rt poor;
For, like an ass whose back with ingots bows,
Thou bear'st thy heavy riches but a journey,
And death unloads thee. . . . Thou hast nor youth nor age,
But, as it were, an after-dinner's sleep,
Dreaming on both. . . . What's yet in this
That bears the name of life? Yet in this life
Lie hid moe thousand deaths: yet death we fear,
That makes these odds all even.
Measure for Measure, Act iii, sc. 1, l. 5 [DUKE]

1875 The sense of death is most in apprehension.
Measure for Measure, Act iii, sc. 1, l. 78 [ISABELLA]

1876 Death is a fearful thing. . . . To die, and go we know not where;
To lie in cold obstruction and to rot;
This sensible warm motion to become
A kneaded clod; and the delighted spirit
To bathe in fiery floods, or to reside
In thrilling region of thick-ribbed ice; . . .
Imagine howling: 'tis too horrible!
The weariest and most loathed worldly life
That age, ache, penury and imprisonment
Can lay on nature is a paradise
To what we fear of death.
Measure for Measure, Act iii, sc. 1, l. 116 [CLAUDIO]

1877 A man that apprehends death no more dreadfully but as a drunken sleep.
•Measure for Measure, Act iv, sc. 2, l. 148 [PROVOST]

1878 Death's a great disguiser.
Measure for Measure, Act iv, sc. 2, l. 186 [DUKE]

1879 I am a tainted wether of the flock,
Meetest for death.
The Merchant of Venice, Act iv, sc. 1, l. 114 [ANTONIO]

1880 Speak me fair in death,
And, when the tale is told, bid her be judge
Whether Bassanio had not once a love.
The Merchant of Venice, Act iv, sc. 1, l. 275 [ANTONIO]

1881 If you find a man there, he shall die a flea's death.
The Merry Wives of Windsor, Act iv, sc. 2, l. 157 [MRS. FORD]

1882 Let Benedick, like cover'd fire,
Consume away in sighs, waste inwardly:
It were a better death than die with mocks,
Which is as bad as die with tickling.
Much Ado about Nothing, Act iii, sc. 1, l. 77 [HERO]

1883 If it were now to die,
'Twere now to be most happy.
Othello, Act ii, sc. 1, l. 191 [OTHELLO]

1884 A guiltless death I die. . . .
Commend me to my kind lord.
Othello, Act v, sc. 2, l. 122 [DESDEMONA]

1885 Death remember'd should be like a mirror,
Who tells us life's but breath, to trust it error.
Pericles, Act i, sc. 1, l. 45 [PERICLES]

1886 Ere six years, . . .
My oil-dried lamp and time-bewasted light
Shall be extinct with age and endless night;

My inch of taper will be burnt and done,
And blindfold death not let me see my son.
Richard II, Act i, sc. 3, l. 219 [GAUNT]

1887   Though death be poor, it ends a mortal woe.
Richard II, Act ii, sc. 1, l. 152 [YORK]

1888   Cry woe, destruction, ruin and decay;
The worst is death, and death will have his day.
Richard II, Act iii, sc. 2, l. 102 [KING RICHARD]

1889   Those whom you curse
Have felt the worst of death's destroying wound
And lie full low, graved in the hollow ground.
Richard II, Act iii, sc. 2, l. 138 [SCROOP]

1890   Nothing can we call our own but death
And that small model of the barren earth
Which serves as paste and cover to our bones.
Richard II, Act iii, sc. 2, l. 152 [RICHARD]

1891   Death and destruction dog thee at the heels.
Richard III, Act iv, sc. 1, l. 40 [QUEEN ELIZABETH]

1892   Alas, poor Romeo! he is already dead; stabbed with a white
wench's black eye; shot through the ear with a love-song; the very
pin of his heart cleft with the blind bow-boy's butt-shaft.
Romeo and Juliet, Act ii, sc. 4, l. 13 [MERCUTIO]

1893   How oft when men are at the point of death
Have they made merry! which their keepers call
A lightning before death.
Romeo and Juliet, Act v, sc. 3, l. 88 [ROMEO]

1894   O my love! my wife!
Death, that hath suck'd the honey of thy breath,
Hath had no power yet upon thy beauty:
Thou art not conquer'd; beauty's ensign yet
Is crimson in thy lips and in thy cheeks,
And death's pale flag is not advanced there. . . .
Why art thou yet so fair? shall I believe
That unsubstantial death is amorous,
And that the lean abhorred monster keeps
Thee here in dark to be his paramour?
Romeo and Juliet, Act v, sc. 3, l. 92 [ROMEO]

1895   Here will I set up my everlasting rest,
And shake the yoke of inauspicious stars
From this world-wearied flesh. Eyes, look your last!
Arms, take your last embrace! and lips, O you
The doors of breath, seal with a righteous kiss
A dateless bargain to engrossing death!
Romeo and Juliet, Act v, sc. 3, l. 110 [ROMEO]

1896   This sight of death is as a bell,
That warns my old age to a sepulchre.
Romeo and Juliet, Act v, sc. 3, l. 206 [LADY CAPULET]

1897   Death lies on her like an untimely frost
Upon the sweetest flower of all the field. . . .
O son! the night before thy wedding-day
Hath Death lain with thy wife. There she lies,
Flower that she was, deflowered by him.
Romeo and Juliet, Act iv, sc. 5, l. 28 [CAPULET]

1898   If thou survive my well-contented day,
When that churl Death with dust my bones shall cover
And shalt by fortune once more re-survey
These poor rude lines of thy deceased lover,

Compare them with the bettering of the time,
And though they be outstripp'd by every pen,
Reserve them for my love, not for their rhyme,
Exceeded by the height of happier men.

Sonnet xxxii, l. 1

1899   Death once dead, there's no more dying then.

Sonnet cxlvi, l. 14

1900   Now would I give a thousand furlongs of sea for an acre of barren
ground, long heath, brown furze, any thing. The wills above be
done! but I would fain die a dry death.

The Tempest, Act i, sc. 1, l. 69 [GONZAGO]

1901   He that dies pays all debts.

The Tempest, Act iii, sc. 2, l. 140 [STEPHANO]

1902   Come away, come away, death,
          And in sad cypress let me be laid;
        Fly away, fly away, breath;
          I am slain by a fair cruel maid.
        My shroud of white, stuck all with yew,
          O, prepare it!
        My part of death, no one so true
          Did share it!
        Not a flower, not a flower sweet,
          On my black coffin let there be strown;
        Not a friend, not a friend greet
          My poor corpse, where my bones shall be thrown:
        A thousand thousand sighs to save,
          Lay me, O, where
        Sad true lover never find my grave,
          To weep there!

Twelfth Night, Act ii, sc. 4, l. 52 [CLOWN]

1903   This youth that you see here
I snatch'd one half out of the jaws of death.

Twelfth Night, Act iii, sc. 4, l. 395 [ANTONIO]

1904   And I, most jocund, apt and willingly,
To do you rest, a thousand deaths would die.

Twelfth Night, Act v, sc. 1, l. 135 [VIOLA]

1905   'Hard-favour'd tyrant, ugly, meagre, lean,
Hateful divorce of love,'—thus chides she Death,—
'Grim-grinning ghost, earth's worm, what dost thou mean
To stifle beauty and to steal his breath? . . .
Thy mark is feeble age, but thy false dart
Mistakes that aim and cleaves an infant's heart.'

Venus and Adonis, l. 931 [VENUS]

Debate

1906   What's amiss,
May it be gently heard: when we debate
Our trivial difference loud, we do commit
Murder in healing wounds: then, noble partners, . . .
Touch you the sourest points with sweetest terms.

Antony and Cleopatra, Act ii, sc. 2, l. 19 [LEPIDUS]

1907   Two thousand souls and twenty thousand ducats
Will not debate the question of this straw.

Hamlet, Act iv, sc. 4, l. 26 [HAMLET]

1908   Hear him debate of commonwealth affairs,
You would say it hath been all in all his study.

Henry V, Act i, sc. 1, l. 41 [CANTERBURY]

Deceit

1909   I do not greatly care to be deceived.
That have no use for trusting.

Antony and Cleopatra, Act v, sc. 2, l. 14 [CLEOPATRA]

1910   KATHARINE: Les langages des hommes sont pleines de tromperies.
KING HENRY: What says she, fair one? that the tongues of men
are full of deceits?

Henry V, Act v, sc. 2, l. 118 [KATHARINE]

1911   That is good deceit
Which mates him first that first intends deceit.

II Henry VI, Act iii, sc. 1, l. 264 [SUFFOLK]

1912   Who cannot steal a shape that means deceit?

II Henry VI, Act iii, sc. 1, l. 79 [QUEEN]

1913   Look to her, Moor, if thou hast eyes to see:
She has deceived her father, and may thee.

Othello, Act i, sc. 3, l. 293 [BRABANTIO]

1914   She did deceive her father, marrying you;
And when she seem'd to shake and fear your looks,
She loved them most. . . . Why, go to, then;
She that, so young, could give out such a seeming,
To seel her father's eyes up close as oak—
He thought 'twas witchcraft.

Othello, Act iii, sc. 3, l. 206 [IAGO]

1915   Who makes the fairest show means most deceit.

Pericles, Act i, sc. 4, l. 75 [CLEON]

1916   Oh, that deceit should steal such gentle shapes,
And with a virtuous vizard hide foul guile!

Richard III, Act ii, sc. 2, l. 27 [DUCHESS OF YORK]

1917   O serpent heart, hid with a flowering face!
Did ever dragon keep so fair a cave? . . .
Was ever book containing such vile matter
So fairly bound? O that deceit should dwell
In such a gorgeous palace!

Romeo and Juliet, Act iii, sc. 2, l. 73 [JULIET]

Deed

1918   Better to leave undone, than by our deed
Acquire too high a fame when him we serve 's away.

Antony and Cleopatra, Act iii, sc. 1, l. 14 [VENTIDIUS]

1919   What poor an instrument May do a noble deed!

Antony and Cleopatra, Act v, sc. 2, l. 236 [CLEOPATRA]

1920   It is great
To do that thing that ends all other deeds;
Which shackles accidents and bolts up change;
Which sleeps, and never palates more the dug,
The beggar's nurse and Cæsar's.

Antony and Cleopatra, Act v, sc. 2, l. 4 [CLEOPATRA]

1921   Ill deeds are doubled with an evil word.

The Comedy of Errors, Act iii, sc. 2, l. 20 [LUCIANA]

How oft the sight of means to do ill deeds
Make deeds ill done!

King John, Act iv, sc. 2, l. 219 [KING JOHN]

1922   [He] rewards his deeds with doing them.

Coriolanus, Act ii, sc. 2, l. 131 [COMINIUS]

1923   Thou hast done a deed whereat valour will weep.

Coriolanus, Act v, sc. 6, l. 135 [LORD]

1924   Foul deeds will rise,
Though all the earth o'erwhelm them, to men's eyes.
Hamlet, Act i, sc. 2, l. 257 [HAMLET]

1925 QUEEN: O, what a rash and bloody deed is this!
HAMLET: A bloody deed! almost as bad, good mother,
As kill a king and marry with his brother.
Hamlet, Act iii, sc. 4, l. 27 [QUEEN]

1926   That we would do,
We should do when we would; for this 'would' changes
And hath abatements and delays as many
As there are tongues, are hands, are accidents;
And then this 'should' is like a spendthrift sigh,
That hurts by easing.
Hamlet, Act iv, sc. 7, l. 119 [KING]

1927 Doing is activity; and he will still be doing.
Henry V, Act iii, sc. 7, l. 108 [CONSTABLE]

1928 O graceless men! they know not what they do.
II Henry VI, Act iv, sc. 4, l. 38 [KING]
You know not what you do.
Romeo and Juliet, Act i, sc. 1, l. 72 [BENVOLIO]

1929   Things done well,
And with a care, exempt themselves from fear;
Things done without example, in their issue
Are to be fear'd.
Henry VIII, Act i, sc. 2, l. 88 [KING HENRY]

1930 [He] Hath given me some worthy cause to wish
Things done, undone.
Julius Cæsar, Act iv, sc. 2, l. 8 [BRUTUS]

1931 CASSIUS: Do not presume too much upon my love;
I may do that I shall be sorry for.
BRUTUS: You have done that you should be sorry for.
Julius Cæsar, Act iv, sc. 3, l. 64 [CASSIUS]

1932 If it were done when 'tis done, then 'twere well
It were done quickly: if the assassination
Could trammel up the consequence, and catch
With his surcease success; that but this blow
Might be the be-all and the end-all here,
But here, upon this bank and shoal of time,
We 'ld jump the life to come.
Macbeth, Act i, sc. 7, l. 1 [MACBETH]

1933 MACBETH: I have done the deed. Didst thou not hear a noise?
LADY MACBETH: I heard the owl scream and the crickets cry.
Macbeth, Act ii, sc. 2, l. 15 [MACBETH]

1934   These deeds must not be thought
After these ways; so, it will make us mad.
Macbeth, Act ii, sc. 2, l. 33 [LADY MACBETH]

1935   Things without all remedy
Should be without regard: what's done is done.
Macbeth, Act iii, sc. 2, l. 11 [LADY MACBETH]
What's done cannot be undone.
Macbeth, Act v, sc. 1, l. 75 [LADY MACBETH]
What is done cannot be now amended.
Richard III, Act iv, sc. 4, l. 291 [KING RICHARD]

1936 MACBETH: Ere the bat hath flown
His cloister'd flight, ere to black Hecate's summons
The shard-borne beetle with his drowsy hums
Hath rung night's yawning peal, there shall be done

A deed of dreadful note.
LADY MACBETH : What's to be done?
MACBETH : Be innocent of the knowledge, dearest chuck,
Till thou applaud the deed.
Macbeth, Act iii, sc. 2, l. 40 [MACBETH]

1937 Thou canst not say I did it : never shake
Thy gory locks at me.
Macbeth, Act iii, sc. 4, l. 50 [MACBETH]

1938 MACBETH : How now, you secret, black, and midnight hags !
What is 't you do?
WITCHES : A deed without a name.
Macbeth, Act iv, sc. 1, l. 48 [MACBETH]

1939 The flighty purpose never is o'ertook
Unless the deed go with it : from this moment
The very firstlings of my heart shall be
The firstlings of my hand. And even now,
To crown my thoughts with acts, be it thought and done. . . .
No boasting like a fool :
This deed I'll do before this purpose cool.
Macbeth, Act iv, sc. 1, l. 145 [MACBETH]

1940 Unnatural deeds Do breed unnatural troubles.
Macbeth, Act v, sc. 1, l. 79 [DOCTOR]

1941 O, what men dare do! what men may do! what men daily do, not
knowing what they do!
Much Ado about Nothing, Act iv, sc. 1, l. 19 [CLAUDIO]

1942 Do deeds to make heaven weep, all earth amazed.
Othello, Act iii, sc. 3, l. 371 [OTHELLO]

1943 Do the deed of darkness.
Pericles, Act iv, sc. 6, l. 31 [LYSIMACHUS]

1944 The tyrannous and bloody deed is done,
The most arch act of piteous massacre
That ever yet this land was guilty of.
Richard III, Act iv, sc. 3, l. 1 [TYRREL]

1945 'Tis deeds must win the prize.
The Taming of the Shrew, Act ii, sc. 1, l. 344 [BAPTISTA]

1946 Let my deeds be witness of my worth.
Titus Andronicus, Act v, sc. 1, l. 103 [AARON]

1947 Tut, I have done a thousand dreadful things
As willingly as one would kill a fly.
Titus Andronicus, Act v, sc. 1, l. 141 [AARON]

1948 If one good deed in all my life I did,
I do repent it from my very soul.
Titus Andronicus, Act v, sc. 3, l. 189 [AARON]

1949 Things won are done ; joy's soul lies in the doing.
Troilus and Cressida, Act i, sc. 2, l. 313 [CRESSIDA]

1950 One good deed dying tongueless
Slaughters a thousand waiting upon that.
The Winter's Tale, Act i, sc. 2, l. 92 [HERMIONE]

1951 What you do Still betters what is done.
The Winter's Tale, Act iv, sc. 4, l. 135 [FLORIZEL]

Deer

1952 My decayed fair
A sunny look of his would soon repair :
But, too unruly deer, he breaks the pale
And feeds from home : poor I am but his stale.
The Comedy of Errors, Act ii, sc. 1, l. 98 [ADRIANA]

1953   HOLOFERNES: The deer was, as you know, sanguis, in blood; ripe as
the pomewater, who now hangeth like a jewel in the ear of cælo, the
sky, the welkin, the heaven. . . .
SIR NATHANIEL: I assure ye it was a buck ot the first head.
HOLOFERNES: Sir Nathaniel, haud credo.
DULL: 'Twas not a haud credo; 'twas a pricket.
            Love's Labour's Lost, Act iv, sc. 2, l. 3 [HOLOFERNES]
("Pricket," a buck in his second year.)

1954   FALSTAFF: Who comes here? my doe?
MRS. FORD: Sir John! art thou there, my deer? my male deer?
FALSTAFF: My doe with the black scut! Let the sky rain potatoes;
let it thunder to the tune of Green Sleeves, hail kissing-comfits and
snow eringoes; let there come a tempest of provocation, I will
shelter me here.
MRS. FORD: Mistress Page is come with me, sweetheart.
FALSTAFF: Divide me like a bribe buck, each a haunch: I will keep
my sides to myself, my shoulders for the fellows of this walk, and
my horns I bequeath your husbands.
            The Merry Wives of Windsor, Act v, sc. 5, l. 17 [FALSTAFF]
("Eringoes," candied sea-holly root, formerly regarded as an
aphrodisiac.)

Defect

1955   Oft it chances in particular men,
That for some vicious mole of nature in them, . . .
Carrying, I say, the stamp of one defect, . . .
Shall in the general censure take corruption
From that particular fault.
            Hamlet, Act i, sc. 4, l. 23 [HAMLET]

1956   Full oft 'tis seen
Our means secure us, and our mere defects
Prove our commodities.
            King Lear, Act iv, sc. 1, l. 21 [GLOUCESTER]

Deformed

1957   BORACHIO: Seest thou not what a deformed thief this fashion is?
WATCHMAN (*Aside*): I know that Deformed; a' has been a vile
thief this seven year.
            Much Ado about Nothing, Act iii, sc. 3, l. 131 [BORACHIO]

1958   None can be call'd deformed but the unkind.
            Twelfth Night, Act iii, sc. 4, l. 401 [ANTONIO]

Degree

1959   Degree being vizarded,
The unworthiest shows as fairly in the mask.
The heavens themselves, the planets and this centre
Observe degree, priority and place.
            Troilus and Cressida, Act i, sc. 3, l. 83 [ULYSSES]

1960   O, when degree is shaked,
Which is the ladder of all high designs,
The enterprise is sick! . . .
Take but degree away, untune that string,
And, hark what discord follows! each string meets
In mere oppugnancy.
            Troilus and Cressida, Act i, sc. 3, l. 101 [ULYSSES]

Delay

1961   One inch of delay more is a South-sea of discovery.
            As You Like It, Act iii, sc. 2, l. 207 [ROSALIND]

1962   Delays have dangerous ends.
I Henry VI, Act iii, sc. 2, l. 33 [REIGNIER]

1963   The sun shines hot; and, if we use delay,
Cold biting winter mars our hoped-for hay.
III Henry VI, Act iv, sc. 8, l. 60 [KING EDWARD]

1964   Come, I have heard that fearful commenting
Is leaden servitor to dull delay;
Delay leads impotent and snail-paced beggary:
Then fiery expedition be my wing,
Jove's Mercury and herald for a king!
Come, muster men: my counsel is my shield;
We must be brief when traitors brave the field.
Richard III, Act iv, sc. 3, l. 49 [KING RICHARD]

1965   In delay
We waste our lights in vain, like lamps by day.
Romeo and Juliet, Act i, sc. 4, l. 44 [MERCUTIO]

Delights

1966   Why, all delights are vain; but that most vain,
Which with pain purchased doth inherit pain.
Love's Labour's Lost, Act i, sc. 1, l. 72 [BIRON]

1967   These violent delights have violent ends
And in their triumph die, like fire and powder,
Which as they kiss consume.
Romeo and Juliet, Act ii, sc. 6, l. 9 [FRIAR LAURENCE]

Demon

1968   Thy demon, that's thy spirit which keeps thee, is
Noble, courageous, high, unmatchable.
Antony and Cleopatra, Act ii, sc. 3, l. 19 [SOOTHSAYER]

1969   If that same demon that hath gull'd thee thus
Should with his iron gait walk the whole world,
He might return to vasty Tartar back,
And tell the legions 'I can never win
A soul so easy as that Englishman's.'
Henry V, Act ii, sc. 2, l. 121 [KING HENRY]

1970   GLOUCESTER: I am too childish-foolish for this world.
QUEEN MARGARET: Hie thee to hell for shame, and leave the world,
Thou cacodemon! there thy kingdom is.
Richard III, Act i, sc. 3, l. 142 [GLOUCESTER]
("Cacodemon," an evil spirit, a bad demon. From the Greek.)

Departure

1971   If every one knows us and we know none,
'Tis time, I think, to trudge, pack, and be gone.
The Comedy of Errors, Act iii, sc. 2, l. 157 [ANTIPHOLUS OF SYRACUSE]

1972   Whither do you follow your eyes so fast?
Coriolanus, Act ii, sc. 1, l. 109 [MENENIUS]
CAPTAIN: Whither away . . . in such haste?
FASTOLFE: Whither away! to save myself by flight.
I Henry VI, Act iii, sc. 3, l. 104 [CAPTAIN]
("Whither away" is frequently repeated.)

1973   POLONIUS: My honourable lord, I will most humbly take my leave
of you.
HAMLET: You cannot, sir, take from me any thing that I will more
willingly part withal: except my life, except my life, except my
life.
Hamlet, Act ii, sc. 2, l. 217 [POLONIUS]

1974   Will you shog off? I would have you solus.
                        Henry V, Act ii, sc. 1, l. 48 [NYM]
        Shall we shog?
                        Henry V, Act ii, sc. 3, l. 47 [NYM]
1975   Here, boys, here, here! shall we wag?
                The Merry Wives of Windsor, Act ii, sc. 1, l. 238 [HOST]
1976   You may be jogging whiles your boots are green.
                The Taming of the Shrew, Act iii, sc. 2, l. 213 [KATHARINA]

Description

1977   · For her own person,
        It beggar'd all description: she did lie
        In her pavilion—cloth-of-gold of tissue—
        O'er-picturing that Venus where we see
        The fancy outwork nature.
                Antony and Cleopatra, Act ii, sc. 2, l. 202 [ENOBARBUS]
1978   Description cannot suit itself in words
        To demonstrate the life of such a battle
        In life so lifeless as it shows itself.
                        Henry V, Act iv, sc. 2, l. 53 [GRANDPRÉ]
1979   Your wondrous rare description, noble earl,
        Of beauteous Margaret hath astonish'd me.
                        I Henry VI, Act v, sc. 5, l. 1 [KING HENRY]
1980   He hath achieved a maid
        That paragons description and wild fame;
        One that excels the quirks of blazoning pens,
        And in the essential vesture of creation
        Does tire the ingener. . . .
        Tempests themselves, high seas and howling winds, . . .
        As having sense of beauty, do omit
        Their mortal natures, letting go safely by
        The divine Desdemona.
                        Othello, Act ii, sc. 1, l. 61 [CASSIO]
1981   He went to bed to her very description.
                        Pericles, Act iv, sc. 2, l. 108 [BOULT]

Deserving

1982   Our slippery people,
        Whose love is never link'd to the deserver
        Till his deserts are past.
                Antony and Cleopatra, Act i, sc. 2, l. 192 [ANTONY]
1983   Use every man after his desert, and who should 'scape whipping?
                        Hamlet, Act ii, sc. 2, l. 555 [HAMLET]
1984   O, your desert speaks loud; and I should wrong it,
        To lock it in the wards of covert bosom,
        When it deserves, with characters of brass,
        A forted residence 'gainst the tooth of time
        And razure of oblivion.
                Measure for Measure, Act v, sc. 1, l. 9 [DUKE]
1985   Well you deserve: they well deserve to have
        That know the strong'st and surest way to get.
                Richard II, Act iii, sc. 3, l. 200 [KING RICHARD]

Desire

1986   Your heart's desires be with you!
                        As You Like It, Act i, sc. 2, l. 211 [CELIA]
1987   Most miserable Is the desire that's glorious.
                        Cymbeline, Act i, sc. 6, l. 6 [IMOGEN]

1988 Is it not strange that desire should so many years outlive per-
      formance?
                                    II Henry IV, Act ii, sc. 4, l. 286 [POINS]
1989 Desire my pilot is, beauty my prize;
      Then who fears sinking where such treasure lies?
                                    The Rape of Lucrece, l. 279 [TARQUIN]
1990 O, when mine eyes did see Olivia first,
      Methought she purged the air of pestilence!
      That instant was I turned into a hart;
      And my desires, like fell and cruel hounds,
      E'er since pursue me.
                                    Twelfth Night, Act i, sc. 1, l. 19 [DUKE]
1991   My desire,
      More sharp than filed steel, did spur me forth.
                                    Twelfth Night, Act iii, sc. 3, l. 4 [ANTONIO]
1992 The sea hath bounds, but deep desire hath none.
                                    Venus and Adonis, l. 389 [VENUS]

Desolation

1993 My desolation does begin to make
      A better life.
                                    Antony and Cleopatra, Act v, sc. 2, l. 1 [CLEOPATRA]
1994 O, you have lived in desolation here,
      Unseen, unvisited, much to our shame.
                                    Love's Labour's Lost, Act v, sc. 2, l. 357 [KING]

Despair

1995 O, beat away the busy meddling fiend
      That lays strong siege unto this wretch's soul
      And from his bosom purge this black despair!
                                    II Henry VI, Act iii, sc. 3, l. 21 [KING HENRY]
1996 KING LEWIS: Say, fair queen, whence springs this deep despair?
      QUEEN MARGARET: From such a cause as fills mine eyes with tears
      And stops my tongue, while heart is drown'd in cares.
                                    III Henry VI, Act iii, sc. 3, l. 12 [KING LEWIS]
1997 I'll join with black despair against my soul,
      And to myself become an enemy.
                                    Richard III, Act ii, sc. 2, l. 36 [QUEEN ELIZABETH]

Destinies

1998 As the Destinies decree.
                                    As You Like It, Act i, sc. 2, l. 111 [TOUCHSTONE]
1999 Mark'd by the Destinies to be avoided.
                                    III Henry VI, Act ii, sc. 2, l. 137 [QUEEN MARGARET]
2000 The Destinies do cut his thread of life.
                                    Pericles, Act i, sc. 2, l. 108 [HELICANUS]
2001 The Destinies will curse thee for this stroke;
      They bid thee crop a weed, thou pluck'st a flower.
                                    Venus and Adonis, l. 945 [VENUS]

Destiny

2002 Let determined things to destiny
      Hold unbewail'd their way.
                                    Antony and Cleopatra, Act iii, sc. 6, l. 84 [OCTAVIUS CÆSAR]
2003 'Tis fond to wail inevitable strokes,
      As 'tis to laugh at 'em.
                                    Coriolanus, Act iv, sc. 1, l. 26 [CORIOLANUS]

2004   Things must be as they may; and what a man cannot get, he may
lawfully deal for.
Pericles, Act ii, sc. 1, l. 119 [FISHERMAN]

2005   All unavoided is the doom of destiny.
Richard III, Act iv, sc. 4, l. 217 [KING RICHARD]

2006   Destiny, That hath to instrument this lower world
And what is in 't.
The Tempest, Act iii, sc. 3, l. 53 [ARIEL]

Destruction

2007   Bear him to the rock Tarpeian, and from thence
Into destruction cast him.
Coriolanus, Act iii, sc. 1, l. 213 [SICINIUS]

2008   Death doth front thee with apparent spoil
And pale destruction meets thee in the face.
I Henry VI, Act iv, sc. 2, l. 27 [GENERAL]

2009   [He] now is girdled with a waist of iron
And hemm'd about with grim destruction.
I Henry VI, Act iv, sc. 3, l. 20 [LUCY]

2010   She 's tickled now; her fume needs no spurs,
She'll gallop far enough to her destruction.
II Henry VI, Act i, sc. 3, l. 153 [BUCKINGHAM]

2011   You take a precipice for no leap of danger,
And woo your own destruction.
Henry VIII, Act v, sc. 1, l. 139 [KING HENRY]

2012   Destruction straight shall dog them at the heels.
Richard II, Act v, sc. 3, l. 139 [BOLINGBROKE]

2013   What is amiss in them, you gods, make suitable for destruction.
Timon of Athens, Act iii, sc. 6, l. 92 [TIMON]

2014   Destruction fang mankind!
Timon of Athens, Act iv, sc. 3, l. 23 [TIMON]

Device

2015   Dull not device by coldness and delay.
Othello, Act ii, sc. 3, l. 394 [IAGO]

2016   O excellent device! was there ever heard a better?
The Two Gentlemen of Verona, Act ii, sc. 1, l. 145 [SPEED]

Devil

2017   COUNTESS: Tell me thy reason why thou wilt marry.
CLOWN: My poor body, madam, requires it: I am driven on by the
flesh; and he must needs go that the devil drives.
All's Well that Ends Well, Act i, sc. 3, l. 29 [COUNTESS]
(Quoting an old proverb.)

2018   Why, sir, if I cannot serve you, I can serve as great a prince as
you are. . . . The black prince; alias, the prince of darkness;
alias, the devil. . . . I am a woodland fellow that always loved a
great fire; and the master I speak of ever keeps a good fire. But,
sure, he is the prince of the world.
All's Well that Ends Well, Act iv, sc. 5, l. 38 [CLOWN]

2019   He must have a long spoon that must needs eat with the devil.
The Comedy of Errors, Act iv, sc. 3, l. 64 [DROMIO OF SYRACUSE]
(Quoting an old proverb.)
This is a devil and no monster; I will leave him; I have no
long spoon.
The Tempest, Act ii, sc. 2, l. 102 [STEPHANO]

2020   Some devils ask but the parings of one's nail,
A rush, a hair, a drop of blood, a pin,

A nut, a cherry-stone;
But she, more covetous, would have a chain.
>   *The Comedy of Errors,* Act iv, sc. 3, l. 72 [DROMIO OF SYRACUSE]

2021   The devil hath power
To assume a pleasing shape; yes, and perhaps . . .
Abuses me to damn me.
>   *Hamlet,* Act ii, sc. 2, l. 628 [HAMLET]

2022   Let the devil wear black, for I'll have a suit of sables.
>   *Hamlet,* Act iii, sc. 2, l. 137 [HAMLET]

2023   POINS: Jack! how agrees the devil with thee about thy soul, that
thou soldest him on Good-Friday last for a cup of Madeira and
a cold capon's leg?
PRINCE: Sir John stands to his word, the devil shall have his
bargain; for he was never yet a breaker of proverbs: he will
give the devil his due.
>   *I Henry IV,* Act i, sc. 2, l. 126 [POINS]

Give the devil his due.
>   *Henry V,* Act iii, sc. 7, l. 26 [ORLEANS]
(Quoting an old proverb.)

2024   Heigh, heigh! the devil rides upon a fiddlestick.
>   *I Henry IV,* Act ii, sc. 4, l. 534 [PRINCE]

2025   Now I perceive the devil understands Welsh;
And 'tis no marvel he is so humorous.
>   *I Henry IV,* Act iii, sc. 1, l. 233 [HOTSPUR]

2026   GLENDOWER: Why, I can teach you, cousin, to command the devil.
HOTSPUR: And I can teach thee, coz, to shame the devil
By telling truth: tell truth and shame the devil.
If thou have power to raise him, bring him hither,
And I'll be sworn I have power to shame him hence.
O, while you live, tell truth and shame the devil.
>   *I Henry IV,* Act iii, sc. 1, l. 56 [GLENDOWER]
(Repeating an old proverb.)

2027   All other devils that suggest by treasons
Do botch and bungle up damnation
With patches, colours, and with forms being fetch'd
From glistering semblance of piety.
>   *Henry V,* Act ii, sc. 2, l. 114 [KING HENRY]

2028   Devil or devil's dam, I'll conjure thee:
Blood will I draw on thee, thou art a witch,
And straightway give thy soul to him thou servest.
>   *I Henry VI,* Act i, sc. 5, l. 5 [TALBOT]

2029   What, can the devil speak true? . . .
But . . . oftentimes to win us to our harm,
The instruments of darkness tell us truths,
Win us with honest trifles, to betray 's
In deeper consequence.
>   *Macbeth,* Act i, sc. 3, l. 107 [BANQUO]

2030   The devil damn thee black, thou cream-faced loon!
>   *Macbeth,* Act v, sc. 3, l. 11 [MACBETH]

2031   This outward-sainted deputy,
Whose settled visage and deliberate word
Nips youth i' the bud and follies doth enmew
As falcon doth the fowl, is yet a devil;
His filth within being cast, he would appear
A pond as deep as hell.
>   *Measure for Measure,* Act iii, sc. 1, l. 89 [ISABELLA]

2032   The devil can cite Scripture for his purpose.
                        The Merchant of Venice, Act i, sc. 3, l. 99 [ANTONIO]
       Then I sigh; and with a piece of scripture,
       Tell them that God bids us do good for evil:
       And thus I clothe my naked villany
       With old odd ends stolen out of holy writ;
       And seem a saint, when most I play the devil.
                          Richard III, Act i, sc. 3, l. 334 [GLOUCESTER]

2033   No man means evil but the devil, and we shall know him by his
       horns.
              The Merry Wives of Windsor, Act v, sc. 2, l. 15 [PAGE]

2034   I think the devil will not have me damned, lest the oil that's
       in me should set hell on fire.
          The Merry Wives of Windsor, Act v, sc. 5, l. 37 [FALSTAFF]

2035   Divinity of hell!
       When devils will the blackest sins put on,
       They do suggest at first with heavenly shows,
       As I do now.
                             Othello, Act ii, sc. 3, l. 356 [IAGO]

2036   CASSIO: What do you mean by this haunting of me?
       BIANCA: Let the devil and his dam haunt you!
                             Othello, Act iv, sc. 1, l. 152 [CASSIO]

2037   I look down towards his feet; but that's a fable.
       If that thou be'st a devil, I cannot kill thee.
                            Othello, Act v, sc. 2, l. 286 [OTHELLO]

2038   OTHELLO: Will you, I pray, demand that demi-devil
       Why he hath thus ensnared my soul and body?
       IAGO: Demand me nothing: what you know, you know;
       From this time forth I never will speak word.
                            Othello, Act v, sc. 2, l. 301 [OTHELLO]

2039   You are mortal,
       And mortal eyes cannot endure the devil.
       Avaunt, thou dreadful minister of hell! . . .
       For thou hast made the happy earth thy hell,
       Fill'd it with cursing cries and deep exclaims.
                             Richard III, Act i, sc. 2, l. 44 [ANNE]

2040   ANNE: O wonderful, when devils tell the truth!
       GLOUCESTER: More wonderful, when angels are so angry.
                             Richard III, Act i, sc. 2, l. 73 [ANNE]

2041   Take the devil in thy mind, and believe him not: he would insinu-
       ate with thee but to make thee sigh.
                        Richard III, Act i, sc. 4, l. 151 [MURDERER]

2042   A devil, a born devil, on whose nature
       Nurture can never stick; on whom my pains,
       Humanely taken, all, all lost, quite lost;
       And as with age his body uglier grows,
       So his mind cankers.
                         The Tempest, Act iv, sc. 1, l. 188 [PROSPERO]

2043   The devil knew not what he did when he made man politic;
       he crossed himself by 't.
                       Timon of Athens, Act iii, sc. 3, l. 28 [SERVANT]

2044   If there be devils, would I were a devil,
       To live and burn in everlasting fire,
       So I might have your company in hell,
       But to torment you with my bitter tongue!
                       Titus Andronicus, Act v, sc. 1, l. 147 [AARON]

2045   Sometimes we are devils to ourselves,
        When we will tempt the frailty of our powers,
        Presuming on their changeful potency.
                    Troilus and Cressida, Act iv, sc. 4, l. 96 [TROILUS]

2046   SIR TOBY: What, man! defy the devil: consider, he's an enemy
        to mankind. . . .
        MARIA: An you speak ill of the devil, how he takes it at heart! . . .
        FABIAN: Gently, gently! the fiend is rough, and will not be
        roughly used. . . .
        SIR TOBY: What, man! 'tis not for gravity to play at cherry-pit
        with Satan: bang him, foul collier!
                    Twelfth Night, Act iii, sc. 4, l. 108 [SIR TOBY]

2047   Why, man, he's a very devil; I have not seen such a firago.
                    Twelfth Night, Act iii, sc. 4, l. 310 [SIR TOBY]

2048   I am one of those gentle ones that will use the devil himself
        with courtesy.
                    Twelfth Night, Act iv, sc. 2, l. 36 [CLOWN]

2049   We took him for a coward, but he's the very devil incardinate.
                    Twelfth Night, Act v, sc. 1, l. 184 [SIR ANDREW]

Devotion

2050   'Tis too much proved—that with devotion's visage
        And pious action we do sugar o'er
        The devil himself.
                    Hamlet, Act iii, sc. 1, l. 47 [POLONIUS]

2051   I myself will lead a private life
        And in devotion spend my latter days.
                    III Henry VI, Act iv, sc. 6, l. 42 [KING HENRY]

Dice

2052   This is the ape of form, monsieur the nice,
        That, when he plays at tables, chides the dice
        In honourable terms.
                    Love's Labour's Lost, Act v, sc. 2, l. 325 [BIRON]

2053   I would outstare the sternest eyes that look,
        Outbrave the heart most daring on the earth,
        Pluck the young suckling cubs from the she-bear,
        Yea, mock the lion when he roars for prey,
        To win thee, lady. But, alas the while!
        If Hercules and Lichas play at dice
        Which is the better man, the greater throw
        May turn by fortune from the weaker hand.
                    The Merchant of Venice, Act ii, sc. 1, l. 27 [MOROCCO]

2054   Keep a gamester from the dice, and a good student from his
        book, and it is wonderful.
                    The Merry Wives of Windsor, Act iii, sc. 1, l. 38 [SHALLOW]

2055   By the hazard of the spotted die
        Let die the spotted.
                    Timon of Athens, Act v, sc. 4, l. 34 [SENATOR]

Difficulty

2056   All difficulties are but easy when they are known.
                    Measure for Measure, Act iv, sc. 2, l. 222 [DUKE]

Digestion

2057   A good digestion to you all.
                    Henry VIII, Act i, sc. 4, l. 62 [WOLSEY]

2058   Now, good digestion wait on appetite,
And health on both!
Macbeth, Act iii, sc. 4, l. 37 [MACBETH]

Din

2059   Think you a little din can daunt mine ears?
Have I not in my time heard lions roar?
The Taming of the Shrew, Act i, sc. 2, l. 200 [PETRUCHIO]

2060   O, 'twas a din to fright a monster's ear,
To make an earthquake.
The Tempest, Act ii, sc. 1, l. 314 [ANTONIO]

Dining

2061   MENENIUS: He had not dined:
The veins unfill'd, our blood is cold, and then
We pout upon the morning, are unapt
To give or to forgive; but when we have stuff'd
These pipes and these conveyances of our blood
With wine and feeding, we have suppler souls
Than in our priest-like fasts: therefore I'll watch him
Till he be dieted to my request,
And then I'll set upon him.
BRUTUS: You know the very road into his kindness,
And cannot lose your way.
Coriolanus, Act v, sc. 1, l. 50 [MENENIUS]

2062   Hath he dined, canst thou tell? for I would not speak with him
till after dinner.
Coriolanus, Act v, sc. 2, l. 36 [MENENIUS]

2063   But for your health, and your digestion's sake,
An after-dinner's breath.
Troilus and Cressida, Act ii, sc. 3, l. 120 [PATROCLUS]
(A reference to the proverb, "After dinner walk a mile.")

Discomfort

2064   As whence the sun 'gins his reflection
Shipwrecking storms and direful thunders break,
So from that spring whence comfort seem'd to come
Discomfort swells.
Macbeth, Act i, sc. 2, l. 25 [SERGEANT]

2065   Discomfort guides my tongue
And bids me speak of nothing but despair.
Richard II, Act iii, sc. 2, l. 65 [SALISBURY]

Discontent

2066   What's more miserable than discontent?
II Henry VI, Act iii, sc. 1, l. 201 [KING HENRY]

2067   'Tis wonderful
What may be wrought out of our discontent,
Now that their souls are topfull of offence.
King John, Act iii, sc. 4, l. 178 [PANDULPH]

2068   Here comes a man of comfort, whose advice
Hath often still'd my brawling discontent.
Measure for Measure, Act iv, sc. 1, l. 8 [MARIANA]

2069   I see your brows are full of discontent,
Your hearts of sorrow and your eyes of tears.
Richard II, Act iv, sc. 1, l. 331 [ABBOT]

2070   KATHARINA: A pretty peat! it is best
        Put finger in the eye, an she knew why.
        BIANCA: Sister, content you in my discontent.
                The Taming of the Shrew, Act i, sc. 1, l. 78 [KATHARINA]
2071   Best state, contentless,
        Hath a distracted and most wretched being,
        Worse than the worst, content.
                Timon of Athens, Act iv, sc. 3, l. 245 [APEMANTUS]

Discord

2072   'A tedious brief scene of young Pyramus
        And his love Thisbe; very tragical mirth.'
        Merry and tragical! tedious and brief!
        That is, hot ice and wondrous strange snow.
        How shall we find the concord of this discord?
                A Midsummer Night's Dream, Act v, sc. 1, l. 56 [THESEUS]
2073   Melodious discord, heavenly tune harsh-sounding,
        Ear's deep-sweet music, and heart's deep-sore wounding.
                Venus and Adonis, l. 431 [VENUS]

Discourse

2074   If voluble and sharp discourse be marr'd,
        Unkindness blunts it more than marble hard.
                The Comedy of Errors, Act ii, sc. 1, l. 92 [ADRIANA]
2075   Discourse is heavy, fasting; when we have supp'd
        We'll mannerly demand thee of thy story.
                Cymbeline, Act iii, sc. 6, l. 91 [BELARIUS]
2076   What means this passionate discourse,
        This peroration with such circumstance?
                II Henry VI, Act i, sc. 1, l. 104 [CARDINAL]
2077   These high wild hills and rough uneven ways
        Draws out our miles, and makes them wearisome;
        And yet your fair discourse hath been as sugar,
        Making the hard way sweet and delectable.
                Richard II, Act ii, sc. 3, l. 4 [NORTHUMBERLAND]
        Palmer's chat makes short their pilgrimage.
                The Rape of Lucrece, l. 791 [LUCRECE]
            (See also 1455.)
2078   I cannot too much muse
        Such shapes, such gestures and such sound, expressing,
        Although they want the use of tongue, a kind
        Of excellent dumb discourse.
                The Tempest, Act iii, sc. 3, l. 36 [ALONZO]
2079   Bid me discourse, I will enchant thine ear.
                Venus and Adonis, l. 145 [VENUS]

Discretion

2080   The better part of valour is discretion.
                I Henry IV, Act v, sc. 4, l. 122 [FALSTAFF]
2081   You should be ruled and led by some discretion.
                King Lear, Act ii, sc. 4, l. 150 [REGAN]
2082   I have seen the day of wrong through the little hole of discretion.
                Love's Labour's Lost, Act v, sc. 2, l. 733 [ARMADO]
2083   Let's teach ourselves that honourable stop,
        Not to outsport discretion.
                Othello, Act ii, sc. 3, l. 2 [OTHELLO]

Disdain

2084 BEATRICE: I wonder that you will still be talking, Signior Bene-
dick: nobody marks you.
BENEDICK: What, my dear Lady Disdain! are you yet living?
BEATRICE: Is it possible disdain should die while she has such
meet food to feed it as Signior Benedick?
Much Ado about Nothing, Act i, sc. 1, l. 117 [BEATRICE]

2085 Disdain and scorn ride sparkling in her eyes,
Misprising what they look on.
Much Ado about Nothing, Act iii, sc. 1, l. 51 [HERO]

2086 Do not press
My tongue-tied patience with too much disdain;
Lest sorrow lend me words and words express
The manner of my pity-wanting pain.
Sonnet cxl, l. 1

2087 In revenge of thy ingratitude,
I throw thy name against the bruising stones,
Trampling contemptuously on thy disdain.
The Two Gentlemen of Verona, Act i, sc. 2, l. 110 [JULIA]

Disease

2088 We do lance Diseases in our bodies.
Antony and Cleopatra, Act v, sc. 1, l. 36 [OCTAVIUS CÆSAR]

2089 SICINIUS: He's a disease that must be cut away.
MENENIUS: O, he's a limb that has but a disease;
Mortal, to cut it off; to cure it, easy.
Coriolanus, Act iii, sc. 1, l. 295 [SICINIUS]

2090 We, . . . like the owner of a foul disease,
To keep it from divulging, let it feed
Even on the pith of life.
Hamlet, Act iv, sc. 1, l. 21 [KING]

2091 Diseases desperate grown
By desperate appliance are relieved,
Or not at all.
Hamlet, Act iv, sc. 3, l. 9 [KING]

2092 It is the disease of not listening, the malady of not marking,
that I am troubled withal.
II Henry IV, Act i, sc. 2, l. 138 [FALSTAFF]

2093 We are all diseased,
And with our surfeiting and wanton hours
Have brought ourselves into a burning fever,
And we must bleed for it.
II Henry IV, Act iv, sc. 1, l. 54 [ARCHBISHOP]

2094 Before the curing of a strong disease,
Even in the instant of repair and health,
The fit is strongest.
King John, Act iii, sc. 4, l. 112 [PANDULPH]

2095 Where the greater malady is fix'd,
The lesser is scarce felt.
King Lear, Act iii, sc. 4, l. 8 [LEAR]

2096 Till then I'll sweat and seek about for eases,
And at that time bequeath you my diseases.
Troilus and Cressida, Act v, sc. 10, l. 56 [PANDARUS]

Dish

2097 Mark Antony . . . will to his Egyptian dish again.
Antony and Cleopatra, Act ii, sc. 6, l. 134 [ENOBARBUS]

2098   A dish for the gods.
                    Antony and Cleopatra, Act v, sc. 2, l. 275 [CLOWN]
2099   Let's kill him boldly, but not wrathfully;
        Let's carve him as a dish fit for the gods,
        Not hew him as a carcass fit for hounds.
                    Julius Cæsar, Act ii, sc. 1, l. 172 [BRUTUS]

Dishonour

2100   Since Cleopatra died,
        I have lived in such dishonour, that the gods
        Detest my baseness. I, that with my sword
        Quarter'd the world, and o'er green Neptune's back
        With ships made cities, condemn myself to lack
        The courage of a woman; less noble mind
        Than she which by her death our Cæsar tells
        'I am conqueror of myself.'
                    Antony and Cleopatra, Act iv, sc. 14, l. 56 [ANTONY]
2101   Ah, Humphrey, this dishonour in thine age
        Will bring thy head with sorrow to the ground!
                    II Henry VI, Act ii, sc. 3, l. 18 [GLOUCESTER]
2102   I rather would have lost my life betimes
        Than bring a burthen of dishonour home.
                    II Henry VI, Act iii, sc. 1, l. 297 [YORK]
2103   Never yet did base dishonour blur our name,
        But with our sword we wiped away the blot.
                    II Henry VI, Act iv, sc. 1, l. 39 [WHITMORE]

Dismissal

2104   Go thy ways, I begin to be aweary of thee. . . . Go thy ways.
                    All's Well that Ends Well, Act iv, sc. 5, l. 59 [LAFEU]
2105   Mistress, dispatch you with your safest haste,
        And get you from our court.
                    As You Like It, Act i, sc. 3, l. 43 [DUKE FREDERICK]
2106   Thou basest thing, avoid! hence, from my sight!
                    Cymbeline, Act i, sc. 1, l. 125 [CYMBELINE]
        O, get thee from my sight!
                    Cymbeline, Act v, sc. 5, l. 236 [IMOGEN]
        Hence, and avoid my sight!
                    King Lear, Act i, sc. 1, l. 126 [LEAR]
2107   Bestow this place on us a little while.
                    Hamlet, Act iv, sc. 1, l. 4 [QUEEN]
        Give us the place alone.
                    Twelfth Night, Act i, sc. 5, l. 235 [OLIVIA]
2108   You have good leave to leave us: when we need
        Your use and counsel, we shall send for you.
                    I Henry IV, Act i, sc. 3, l. 20 [KING HENRY]
2109   'Faith, and I'll send him packing.
                    I Henry IV, Act ii, sc. 4, l. 328 [FALSTAFF]
        Well, nobles, well, 'tis politicly done,
        To send me packing.
                    II Henry VI, Act iii, sc. 1, l. 341 [YORK]
        Trudge, plod away o' the hoof; seek shelter, pack!
                    The Merry Wives of Windsor, Act i, sc. 3, l. 91 [FALSTAFF]
                    Ere a fortnight make me elder,
        I'll send some packing that yet think not on it.
                    Richard III, Act iii, sc. 2, l. 62 [HASTINGS]

2110   No more, Pistol; I would not have you go off here: discharge
       yourself of our company, Pistol.
                        II Henry IV, Act ii, sc. 4, l. 146 [FALSTAFF]
2111   Stand not upon the order of your going,
       But go at once.
                        Macbeth, Act iii, sc. 4, l. 118 [LADY MACBETH]
2112   Leave procreants alone and shut the door.
                        Othello, Act iv, sc. 2, l. 28 [OTHELLO]
2113   KEEPER: Fellow, give place; here is no longer stay.
       KING: If thou love me, 'tis time thou wert away.
                        Richard II, Act v, sc. 5, l. 95 [KEEPER]
2114   Go, get thee hence, for I will not away.
                        Romeo and Juliet, Act v, sc. 3, l. 160 [JULIET]
2115   Will you hoist sail, sir? here lies your way.
                        Twelfth Night, Act i, sc. 5, l. 215 [MARIA]
2116   Go, sir, rub your chain with crums.
                        Twelfth Night, Act ii, sc. 3, l. 128 [SIR TOBY]
2117   Go off; I discard you: let me enjoy my private: go off.
                        Twelfth Night, Act iii, sc. 4, l. 99 [MALVOLIO]

Disorder

2118   Friends kill friends, and the disorder's such
       As war were hoodwink'd.
                        Cymbeline, Act v, sc. 2, l. 15 [LUCIUS]
2119   Shame and confusion! all is on the rout;
       Fear frames disorder, and disorder wounds
       Where it should guard.
                        II Henry VI, Act v, sc. 2, l. 31 [YOUNG CLIFFORD]
2120   You have displaced the mirth, broke the good meeting
       With most admired disorder.
                        Macbeth, Act iii, sc. 4, l. 109 [LADY MACBETH]

Displeasure

2121   PAROLLES: I know not how I have deserved to run into my lord's
       displeasure.
       LAFEU: You have made shift to run into 't, boots and spurs and
       all, like him that leaped into the custard.
                        All's Well that Ends Well, Act ii, sc. 5, l. 37 [PAROLLES]
2122   He hath incurred the everlasting displeasure of the king, who
       had even tuned his bounty to sing happiness to him.
                        All's Well that Ends Well, Act iv, sc. 3, l. 10 [LORD]
2123   Here is a purr of fortune's, sir, or of fortune's cat, . . . that has
       fallen into the unclean fishpond of her displeasure.
                        All's Well that Ends Well, Act v, sc. 2, l. 20 [CLOWN]
2124   Oft our displeasures, to ourselves unjust,
       Destroy our friends and after weep their dust:
       Our own love waking cries to see what's done,
       While shame full late sleeps out the afternoon.
                        All's Well that Ends Well, Act v, sc. 3, l. 63 [KING]
2125   That's a perilous shot out of an elder-gun, that a poor and a
       private displeasure can do against a monarch!
                        Henry V, Act iv, sc. 1, l. 210 [WILLIAMS]
2126   Run to meet displeasure farther from the doors,
       And grapple with him ere he come so nigh.
                        King John, Act v, sc. 1, l. 60 [BASTARD]

2127   Let us depart, I pray you,
Lest your displeasure should enlarge itself
To wrathful terms : this place is dangerous.
      Troilus and Cressida, Act v, sc. 2, l. 36 [ULYSSES]

Disposition

2128 I will be your Rosalind in a more coming-on disposition.
       As You Like It, Act iv, sc. 1, l. 112 [ROSALIND]

2129 I perchance hereafter shall think meet
To put an antic disposition on.
       Hamlet, Act i, sc. 5, l. 171 [HAMLET]

2130 Come, sir. I would you would . . . put away
These dispositions, that of late transform you
From what you really are.
       King Lear, Act i, sc. iv, l. 240 [GONERIL]

2131 Let this disposition have that scope
That dotage gives it.
       King Lear, Act i, sc. 4, l. 314 [GONERIL]

2132   I fear your disposition :
That nature which contemns its origin,
Cannot be border'd certain in itself.
       King Lear, Act iv, sc. 2, l. 31 [ALBANY]

2133 He is of a very melancholy disposition.
      Much Ado about Nothing, Act ii, sc. 1, l. 5 [HERO]

Her disposition, being addicted to a melancholy.
      Twelfth Night, Act ii, sc. 5, l. 222 [MARIA]

2134 She is of so free, so kind, so apt, so blessed a disposition, she
holds it a vice in her goodness not to do more than she is requested.
      Othello, Act ii, sc. 3, l. 326 [IAGO]

Dissembling

2135 I prithee, turn aside and weep for her [Fulvia] ;
Then bid adieu to me, and say the tears
Belong to Egypt : good now, play one scene
Of excellent dissembling ; and let it look
Like perfect honour.
      Antony and Cleopatra, Act i, sc. 3, l. 76 [CLEOPATRA]

2136 I would dissemble with my nature where
My fortunes and my friends at stake required
I should do so in honour.
      Coriolanus, Act iii, sc. 2, l. 62 [VOLUMNIA]

Dissension

2137 Civil dissension is a viperous worm
That gnaws the bowels of the commonwealth.
      I Henry VI, Act iii, sc. 1, l. 72 [KING HENRY]

2138 This late dissension grown betwixt the peers
Burns under feigned ashes of forged love
And will at last break out into a flame.
      I Henry VI, Act iii, sc. 1, l. 189 [EXETER]

2139 I feel such sharp dissension in my breast,
Such fierce alarums both of hope and fear,
As I am sick with working of my thoughts.
      I Henry VI, Act v, sc. 5, l. 84 [KING HENRY]

Distrust

2140 But, woe is me, you are so sick of late,
So far from cheer and from your former state,
That I distrust you. Yet, though I distrust,

Discomfort you, my lord, it nothing must.
                    Hamlet, Act iii, sc. 2, l. 174 [PLAYER QUEEN]
2141   One sudden foil should never breed distrust.
                    I Henry VI, Act iii, sc. 3, l. 11 [CHARLES]

Divinity

2142   There's a divinity that shapes our ends,
        Rough-hew them how we will.
                    Hamlet, Act v, sc. 2, l. 10 [HAMLET]
2143   Hear him but reason in divinity,
        And all-admiring with an inward wish
        You would desire the king were made a prelate.
                    Henry V, Act i, sc. 1, l. 38 [CANTERBURY]

Divorce

2144   If it appear not plain and prove untrue,
        Deadly divorce step between me and you!
                    All's Well that Ends Well, Act v, sc. 3, l. 318 [HELENA]
2145   Shouldst thou but hear I were licentious, . . .
        Wouldst thou not spit at me and spurn at me, . . .
        And from my false hand cut the wedding-ring
        And break it with a deep-divorcing vow?
                    The Comedy of Errors, Act ii, sc. 2, l. 133 [ADRIANA]
2146   I here divorce myself
        Both from thy table, Henry, and thy bed.
                    III Henry VI, Act i, sc. 1, l. 247 [QUEEN MARGARET]
2147   He counsels a divorce; a loss of her
        That, like a jewel, has hung twenty years
        About his neck, yet never lost her lustre;
        Of her that loves him with that excellence
        That angels love good men with.
                    Henry VIII, Act ii, sc. 2, l. 31 [NORFOLK]

Dog

2148   They have chose a consul that will from them take
        Their liberties: make them of no more voice
        Than dogs that are as often beat for barking
        As therefore kept to do so.
                    Coriolanus, Act ii, sc. 3, l. 222 [BRUTUS]
2149   Coward dogs
        Most spend their mouths when what they seem to threaten
        Runs far before them.
                    Henry V, Act ii, sc. 4, l. 69 [DAUPHIN]
2150   Le chien est retourné à sa propre vomissement, et la truie lavée
        au bourbier.
                    Henry V, Act iii, sc. 7, l. 68 [DAUPHIN]
            ("The dog is returned to his own vomit, and the sow washed
            in the muck.")
2151   Why, madam, if I were your father's dog,
        You should not use me so.
                    King Lear, Act ii, sc. 2, l. 143 [KENT]
2152   LEAR: The little dogs and all,
        Tray, Blanch, and Sweet-heart, see, they bark at me. . . .
        EDGAR: Avaunt, you curs!
            Be thy mouth or black or white,
            Tooth that poisons if it bite;

> Mastiff, greyhound, mongrel grim,
> Hound or spaniel, brach or lym,
> Or bobtail tyke or trundle-tail,
> Tom will make them weep and wail.
>
> *King Lear,* Act iii, sc. 6, l. 65 [LEAR]

2153 LEAR: Thou hast seen a farmer's dog bark at a beggar?
GLOUCESTER: Ay, sir.
LEAR: And the creature run from the cur? There thou mightst
behold the great image of authority: a dog's obeyed in office.

> *King Lear,* Act iv, sc. 6, l. 159 [LEAR]

2154 Mine enemy's dog,
Though he had bit me, should have stood that night
Against my fire.

> *King Lear,* Act iv, sc. 7, l. 36 [CORDELIA]

2155 Thou call'dst me dog before thou hadst a cause;
But, since I am a dog, beware my fangs.

> *The Merchant of Venice,* Act iii, sc. 3, l. 6 [SHYLOCK]

2156 In Aleppo once,
Where a malignant and a turban'd Turk
Beat a Venetian and traduced the state,
I took by the throat the circumcised dog
And smote him, thus.

> *Othello,* Act v, sc. 2, l. 352 [OTHELLO]

2157 Dogs bark at me as I halt by them.

> *Richard III,* Act i, sc. 1, l. 23 [GLOUCESTER]

2158 NURSE: Doth not rosemary and Romeo begin both with a letter?
ROMEO: Ay, nurse! what of that? both with an R.
NURSE: Ah, mocker? that's the dog's name.

> *Romeo and Juliet,* Act ii, sc. 4, l. 219 [NURSE]
> (A reference to the proverb, "R is the dog's letter," because
> it sounds like a snarl.)

2159 The watch-dogs bark: Bow-wow.

> *The Tempest,* Act i, sc. 2, l. 383 [BURTHEN]

2160 LORD: Away, unpeaceable dog, or I'll spurn thee hence.
APEMANTUS: I will fly, like a dog, the heels o' the ass.

> *Timon of Athens,* Act i, sc. 1, l. 281 [LORD]

2161 As true a dog as ever fought at head.

> *Titus Andronicus,* Act v, sc. 1, l. 102 [AARON]

2162 I think Crab my dog be the sourest-natured dog that lives: my
mother weeping, my father wailing, my sister crying, our maid
howling, our cat wringing her hands, and all our house in a great
perplexity, yet did not the cruel-hearted cur shed one tear.

> *The Two Gentlemen of Verona,* Act ii, sc. 3, l. 6 [LAUNCE]

Double-Dealer

2163 I might have cudgelled thee out of thy single life, to make thee
a double-dealer.

> *Much Ado about Nothing,* Act v, sc. 4, l. 116 [CLAUDIO]

2164 CLOWN: That would be double-dealing, sir. . . .
DUKE: Well, I will be so much a sinner, to be a double-dealer.

> *Twelfth Night,* Act v, sc. 1, l. 32 [CLOWN]

Doubt

2165 Doubting things go ill often hurts more
Than to be sure they do.

> *Cymbeline,* Act i, sc. 6, l. 95 [IMOGEN]

2166   To end one doubt by death
Revives two greater in the heirs of life.
II Henry IV, Act iv, sc. 1, l. 199 [ARCHBISHOP]

2167 Then comes my fit again: I had else been perfect,
Whole as the marble, founded as the rock,
As broad and general as the casing air:
But now I am cabin'd, cribb'd, confined, bound in
To saucy doubts and fears.
Macbeth, Act iii, sc. 4, l. 21 [MACBETH]

2168   Our doubts are traitors
And make us lose the good we oft might win
By fearing to attempt.
Measure for Measure, Act i, sc. 4, l. 77 [LUCIO]

2169   Modest doubt is call'd
The beacon of the wise, the tent that searches
To the bottom of the worst.
Troilus and Cressida, Act ii, sc. 2, l. 15 [HECTOR]

Douglas

2170 FALSTAFF: That sprightly Scot of Scots, Douglas, that runs
o' horseback up a hill perpendicular,—
PRINCE: He that rides at high speed and with his pistol kills a
sparrow flying.
FALSTAFF: You have hit it.
PRINCE: So he never did the sparrow.
I Henry IV, Act ii, sc. 4, l. 376 [FALSTAFF]

2171 DOUGLAS: My name is Douglas;
And I do haunt thee in the battle thus
Because some tell me that thou art a king. . . .
HOTSPUR: O Douglas, hadst thou fought at Holmedon thus,
I never had triumph'd upon a Scot.
I Henry IV, Act v, sc. 3, l. 3 [DOUGLAS]

Dower

2172 Virtue and she is her own dower.
All's Well that Ends Well, Act ii, sc. 3, l. 150 [KING]
Mine honesty shall be my dower.
III Henry VI, Act iii, sc. 2, l. 72 [LADY GREY]
Thy truth, then, be thy dower.
King Lear, Act i, sc. 1, l. 110 [LEAR]
Let her beauty be her wedding dower.
The Two Gentlemen of Verona, Act iii, sc. 1, l. 78 [DUKE]

2173 If thou be'st yet a fresh uncropped flower,
Choose thou thy husband, and I'll pay thy dower.
All's Well that Ends Well, Act v, sc. 3, l. 327 [KING]

2174   Love's not love
When it is mingled with regards that stand
Aloof from the entire point. . . . She is herself a dowry.
King Lear, Act i, sc. 1, l. 241 [FRANCE]

Dragon

2175 Swift, swift, you dragons of the night, that dawning
May bare the raven's eye!
Cymbeline, Act ii, sc. 2, l. 48 [IACHIMO]
Night's swift dragons cut the clouds full fast.
A Midsummer Night's Dream, Act iii, sc. 2, l. 379 [PUCK]

2176 Come not between the dragon and his wrath.
> *King Lear,* Act i, sc. 1, l. 124 [LEAR]

2177 Death-like dragons here affright thee hard.
> *Pericles,* Act i, sc. 1, l. 29 [ANTIOCHUS]

Dream

2178 'Tis still a dream, or else such stuff as madmen
Tongue and brain not.
> *Cymbeline,* Act v, sc. 4, l. 146 [POSTHUMUS]

2179 HAMLET: O God, I could be bounded in a nutshell and count
myself a king of infinite space, were it not that I had bad dreams.
GUILDENSTERN: Which dreams indeed are ambition, for the very
substance of the ambitious is merely the shadow of a dream.
HAMLET: A dream itself is but a shadow.
> *Hamlet,* Act ii, sc. 2, l. 260 [HAMLET]

2180 She dreamt to-night she saw my statua,
Which, like a fountain with an hundred spouts,
Did run pure blood ; and many lusty Romans
Came smiling, and did bathe their hands in it.
> *Julius Cæsar,* Act ii, sc. 2, l. 76 [CÆSAR]

2181 Wicked dreams abuse The curtain'd sleep.
> *Macbeth,* Act ii, sc. 1, l. 50 [MACBETH]

2182 There is some ill a-brewing towards my rest,
For I did dream of money-bags to-night.
> *The Merchant of Venice,* Act ii, sc. 5, l. 17 [SHYLOCK]

2183 I have had a dream, past the wit of man to say what dream it
was. . . . The eye of man hath not heard, the ear of man hath not
seen, man's hand is not able to taste, his tongue to conceive, nor
his heart to report, what my dream was.
> *A Midsummer Night's Dream,* Act iv, sc. 1, l. 211 [BOTTOM]

2184 Did you ever dream of such a thing?
> *Pericles,* Act iv, sc. 5, l. 5 [GENTLEMAN]

2185 This is the rarest dream that e'er dull sleep
Did mock sad fools withal.
> *Pericles,* Act v, sc. 1, l. 163 [PERICLES]

2186 My dream was lengthen'd after life ; . . .
A shadow like an angel . . . squeak'd out aloud,
'Clarence is come ; false, fleeting, perjured Clarence,
That stabb'd me in the field by Tewksbury.'
> *Richard III,* Act i, sc. 4, l. 43 [CLARENCE]

2187 I talk of dreams,
Which are the children of an idle brain,
Begot of nothing but vain fantasy.
> *Romeo and Juliet,* Act i, sc. 4, l. 96 [MERCUTIO]

2188 If I may trust the flattering truth of sleep,
My dreams presage some joyful news at hand.
> *Romeo and Juliet,* Act v, sc. 1, l. 1 [ROMEO]

2189 She . . . sits as one new-risen from a dream.
> *The Taming of the Shrew,* Act iv, sc. 1, l. 189 [CURTIS]

2190 The isle is full of noises,
Sounds and sweet airs, that give delight and hurt not, . . .
Voices that, if I then had waked after long sleep,
Will make me sleep again : and then, in dreaming,
The clouds methought would open and show riches
Ready to drop upon me, that, when I waked,
I cried to dream again.
> *The Tempest,* Act iii, sc. 2, l. 144 [CALIBAN]

2191   If I do dream, would all my wealth would wake me!
If I do wake, some planet strike me down,
That I may slumber in eternal sleep!
Titus Andronicus, Act ii, sc. 4, l. 13 [MARCUS]

2192   Let fancy still my sense in Lethe steep;
If it be thus to dream, still let me sleep!
Twelfth Night, Act iv, sc. 1, l. 66 [SEBASTIAN]

2193   This dream of mine,—
Being now awake, I'll queen it no inch farther,
But milk my ewes and weep.
The Winter's Tale, Act iv, sc. 4, l. 458 [PERDITA]

Drift

2194   What is the course and drift of your compact?
The Comedy of Errors, Act ii, sc. 2, l. 163 [ANTIPHOLUS OF SYRACUSE]

2195   We know your drift.
Coriolanus, Act iii, sc. 3, l. 116 [SICINIUS]

2196   O, understand my drift.
The Merry Wives of Windsor, Act ii, sc. 2, l. 251 [FORD]

2197   I will tell you my drift.
Much Ado about Nothing, Act ii, sc. 1, l. 404 [DON PEDRO]

Drinking

2198   I had rather heat my liver with drinking.
Antony and Cleopatra, Act i, sc. 2, l. 23 [CHARMIAN]

2199   They have made him drink alms-drink.
Antony and Cleopatra, Act ii, sc. 7, l. 5 [SERVANT]

2200   We'll teach you to drink deep ere you depart.
Hamlet, Act i, sc. 2, l. 175 [HAMLET]

2201   When . . . he calls for drink, I'll have prepared him
A chalice for the nonce.
Hamlet, Act iv, sc. 7, l. 160 [KING]

2202   They call drinking deep, dyeing scarlet; and when you breathe in
your watering, they cry 'hem!' and bid you play it off. . . . I am
so good a proficient in one quarter of an hour, that I can drink
with any tinker in his own language during my life.
I Henry IV, Act ii, sc. 4, l. 17 [PRINCE]

2203   Thin drink doth so over-cool their blood, . . . that they fall into a
kind of male green-sickness; and then, when they marry, they get
wenches.
II Henry IV, Act iv, sc. 3, l. 98 [FALSTAFF]

2204   Drink, sir, is a great provoker of three things, . . . nose-painting,
sleep, and urine. Lechery, sir, it provokes, and unprovokes; it provokes the desire, but it takes away the performance.
Macbeth, Act ii, sc. 3, l. 28 [PORTER]

2205   I have very poor and unhappy brains for drinking. I could well
wish courtesy would invent some other custom of entertainment.
Othello, Act ii, sc. 3, l. 34 [CASSIO]

2206   Is your Englishman so expert in his drinking?
Othello, Act ii, sc. 3, l. 82 [CASSIO]

2207   Drink that for me.
Richard III, Act iii, sc. 2, l. 108
[HASTINGS, *throwing his purse to a servant*]

2208   MARIA: He's drunk nightly in your company.
SIR TOBY: With drinking healths to my niece: I'll drink to her
as long as there is a passage in my throat and drink in Illyria:

he's a coward and a coystrill that will not drink to my niece till
his brains turn o' the toe like a parish-top.
Twelfth Night, Act i, sc. 3, l. 39 [MARIA]

Drones

2209   Drones hive not with me.
The Merchant of Venice, Act ii, sc. 5, l. 48 [SHYLOCK]

2210   Drones suck not eagles' blood but rob bee-hives.
II Henry VI, Act iv, sc. 1, l. 109 [SUFFOLK]

2211   Purge the land of these drones, that rob the bee of her honey.
Pericles, Act ii, sc. 1, l. 50 [FISHERMAN]

Drowning

2212   I have a kind of alacrity in sinking; if the bottom were as deep as
hell I should down.
The Merry Wives of Windsor, Act iii, sc. 5, l. 13 [FALSTAFF]

2213   Drowned, . . . a death that I abhor; for the water swells a man.
The Merry Wives of Windsor, Act iii, sc. 5, l. 16 [FALSTAFF]

2214   RODERIGO: I will incontinently drown myself. . . . It is silliness
to live when to live is torment; and then have we a prescription to
die when death is our physician.
IAGO: O villainous! . . . Ere I would say I would drown myself
for the love of a guinea-hen, I would change my humanity with a
baboon. . . . Come, be a man. Drown thyself! drown cats and
blind puppies. . . . If thou wilt needs damn thyself, do it a more
delicate way than drowning. . . . A pox of drowning thyself!
Othello, Act i, sc. 3, l. 306 [RODERIGO]

2215   'Tis double death to drown in ken of shore.
The Rape of Lucrece, l. 1114

2216   Lord, Lord! methought, what pain it was to drown!
What dreadful noise of waters in mine ears!
What ugly sights of death within mine eyes!
Methought I saw a thousand fearful wrecks;
Ten thousand men that fishes gnaw'd upon;
Wedges of gold, great anchors, heaps of pearl,
Inestimable stones, unvalued jewels,
All scatter'd in the bosom of the sea:
Some lay in dead men's skulls; and, in those holes
Where eyes did once inhabit, there were crept,
As 'twere in scorn of eyes, reflecting gems,
Which woo'd the slimy bottom of the deep,
And mock'd the dead bones that lay scatter'd by.
Richard III, Act i, sc. 4, l. 21 [CLARENCE]

2217   She is drowned already, sir, with salt water, though I seem to
drown her remembrance again with more.
Twelfth Night, Act ii, sc. 1, l. 31 [SEBASTIAN]

Drum

2218   I'll no more drumming; a plague of all drums!
All's Well that Ends Well, Act iv, sc. 4, l. 331 [PAROLLES]

2219   Hark! the drums Demurely wake the sleepers.
Antony and Cleopatra, Act iv, sc. 9, l. 31 [SOLDIER]

2220   Then strike up drums; God and Saint George for us!
III Henry VI, Act ii, sc. 1, l. 204 [EDWARD]
Drummer, strike up, and let us march away.
III Henry VI, Act iv, sc. 7, l. 50 [KING EDWARD]

Let the drum strike, and prove my title thine.
King Lear, Act v, sc. 3, l. 81 [Regan]

Strike up the drum towards Athens!
Timon of Athens, Act iv, sc. 3, l. 169 [Alcibiades]

2221   Indeed, your drums, being beaten, will cry out;
And so shall you, being beaten: do but start
An echo with the clamour of thy drum,
And even at hand a drum is ready braced
That shall reverberate all as loud as thine;
Sound but another, and another shall
As loud as thine rattle the welkin's ear
And mock the deep-mouth'd thunder.
King John, Act v, sc. 2, l. 166 [Bastard]

2222   At their chamber-door I'll beat the drum
Till it cry sleep to death.
King Lear, Act ii, sc. 4, l. 119 [Lear]

Drunkenness

2223   Mine, and most of our fortunes, to-night shall be—drunk to bed.
Antony and Cleopatra, Act i, sc. 2, l. 45 [Enobarbus]

2224   'Rivo!' says the drunkard. Call in ribs, call in tallow.
I Henry IV, Act ii, sc. 4, l. 124 [Prince]

2225   The gentleman has drunk himself out of his five sentences.
The Merry Wives of Windsor, Act i, sc. 1, l. 179 [Bardolph]

2226   Dogberry: You are to call at all the ale-houses, and bid those that
are drunk get them to bed.
Watch: How if they will not?
Dogberry: Why, then . . . you may say they are not the men you
took them for.
Much Ado about Nothing, Act iii, sc. 3, l. 44 [Dogberry]

2227   Do not think, gentlemen, I am drunk: this is my ancient; this is
my right hand, and this is my left: I am not drunk now; I can
stand well enough, and speak well enough. . . . You must not
think then that I am drunk.
Othello, Act ii, sc. 3, l. 117 [Cassio]

2228   I will ask him for my place again; he shall tell me I am a drunkard! Had I as many mouths as Hydra, such an answer would stop
them all.
Othello, Act ii, sc. 3, l. 306 [Cassio]

2229   Trinculo is reeling ripe: where should they
Find this grand liquor that hath gilded them?
How camest thou in this pickle?
The Tempest, Act v, sc. 1, l. 279 [Alonzo]

2230   Olivia: What's a drunken man like, fool?
Clown: Like a drowned man, a fool, and a mad man: one draught
above heat makes him a fool; the second mads him; and a third
drowns him.
Twelfth Night, Act i, sc. 5, l. 138 [Olivia]

2231   O, he's drunk, Sir Toby, an hour agone; his eyes were set at
eight i' the morning.
Twelfth Night, Act v, sc. 1, l. 204 [Clown]

Ducats

2232   I never heard a passion so confused,
So strange, outrageous, and so variable,
As the dog Jew did utter in the streets:
'My daughter! O my ducats! O my daughter!

Fled with a Christian! O my Christian ducats!
Justice! the law! my ducats, and my daughter!'
The Merchant of Venice, Act ii, sc. 8, 1. 12 [SALANIO]

Ducdame

2233   JAQUES: If it do come to pass
               That any man turn ass,
               Leaving his wealth and ease,
               A stubborn will to please,
           Ducdame, ducdame, ducdame:
               Here shall he see Gross fools as he,
           An if he will come to me.
           AMIENS: What's that 'ducdame'?
           JAQUES: 'Tis a Greek invocation, to call fools into a circle.
As You Like It, Act ii, sc. 5, 1. 52 [JAQUES]

Dumps

2234   Sing no more ditties, sing no moe,
               Of dumps so dull and heavy.
Much Ado about Nothing, Act ii, sc. 3, 1. 72 [BALTHASAR]
2235   Distress likes dumps when time is kept with tears.
The Rape of Lucrece, 1. 1127 [LUCRECE]
2236   When doleful dumps the mind oppress.
Romeo and Juliet, Act iv, sc. 5, 1. 129 [PETER]
2237   How now, daughter Katharine! in your dumps?
The Taming of the Shrew, Act ii, sc. 1, 1. 286 [BAPTISTA]
2238   Step out of these dreary dumps.
Titus Andronicus, Act i, sc. 1, 1. 390 [MARCUS]

Dust

2239   She whom all men praised . . . was in mine eye
           The dust that did offend it.
All's Well that Ends Well, Act v, sc. 3, 1. 53 [BERTRAM]
2240   Fear no more the heat o' the sun,
                        Nor the furious winter's rages;
                    Thou thy worldly task hast done,
                        Home art gone, and ta'en thy wages:
                    Golden lads and girls all must,
                    As chimney-sweepers, come to dust.

                    Fear no more the frown o' the great;
                        Thou art past the tyrant's stroke;
                    Care no more to clothe and eat;
                        To thee the reed is as the oak:
                    The sceptre, learning, physic, must
                    All follow this, and come to dust.

                    Fear no more the lightning-flash,
                        Nor the all-dreaded thunder-stone;
                    Fear not slander, censure rash;
                        Thou hast finish'd joy and moan:
                    All lovers young, all lovers must
                    Consign to thee, and come to dust.
Cymbeline, Act iv, sc. 2, 1. 258 [GUIDERIUS AND ARVIRAGUS]

Duty

2241   I hold my duty, as I hold my soul,
           Both to my God, and to my gracious king.
Hamlet, Act ii, sc. 2, 1. 44 [POLONIUS]

2242   I owe him little duty, and less love.
          I Henry VI, Act iv, sc. 4, l. 34 [SOMERSET]

2243   Think'st thou that duty shall have dread to speak,
    When power to flattery bows?
          King Lear, Act i, sc. 1, l. 149 [KENT]

2244   My ever-esteemed duty pricks me on.
          Love's Labour's Lost, Act i, sc. 1, l. 269 [ARMADO]
    My duty pricks me on.
          The Two Gentlemen of Verona, Act iii, sc. 1, l. 8 [PROTEUS]

2245   I do perceive here a divided duty.
          Othello, Act i, sc. 3, l. 181 [DESDEMONA]

2246   Fleet-wing'd duty with thought's feathers flies.
          The Rape of Lucrece, l. 1216

2247   Duty never yet did want his meed.
          The Two Gentlemen of Verona, Act ii, sc. 4, l. 112 [SILVIA]

Dwarf

2248   Alas, this is a child, a silly dwarf!
    It cannot be this weak and writhled shrimp
    Should strike such terror to his enemies.
          I Henry VI, Act ii, sc. 3, l. 22 [COUNTESS]

2249   I had rather, forsooth, go before you like a man than follow him
    like a dwarf.
          The Merry Wives of Windsor, Act iii, sc. 2, l. 5 [ROBIN]

2250   Get you gone, you dwarf;
    You minimus of hindering knot-grass made;
    You bead, you acorn!
          A Midsummer Night's Dream, Act iii, sc. 2, l. 328 [LYSANDER]

2251   A stirring dwarf we do allowance give
    Before a sleeping giant.
          Troilus and Cressida, Act ii, sc. 3, l. 146 [AGAMEMNON]

Dwelling

2252   ORLANDO: Where dwell you, pretty youth? . . .
    ROSALIND: Here in the skirts of the forest, like fringe upon a
    petticoat.
          As You Like It, Act iii, sc. 2, l. 352 [ORLANDO]

2253   FALSTAFF: 'Fore God, you have a goodly dwelling and a rich.
    SHALLOW: Barren, barren, barren; beggars all.
          II Henry IV, Act v, sc. 3, l. 6 [FALSTAFF]

E

Eagle

2254   CYMBELINE: [Thou] mightst have had the sole son of my queen!
    IMOGEN: O blest that I might not! I chose an eagle,
    And did avoid a puttock.
          Cymbeline, Act i, sc. 1, l. 138 [CYMBELINE]
    ("Puttock," a bird of prey, usually applied to the kite or buzzard,
    or to a person as having their attributes of ignobleness and
    greed.)

2255   If you have writ your annals true, 'tis there,
    That, like an eagle in a dove-cote, I
    Flutter'd your Volscians in Corioli.
          Coriolanus, Act v, sc. 6, l. 114 [CORIOLANUS]

2256   I saw Jove's bird, the Roman eagle, wing'd
      From the spongy south to this part of the west,
      There vanish'd in the sunbeams.
Cymbeline, Act iv, sc. 2, l. 348 [Soothsayer]

2257   Nay, if thou be that princely eagle's bird,
      Show thy descent by gazing 'gainst the sun.
III Henry VI, Act ii, sc. 1, l. 91 [Richard]

2258   Gnats are unnoted whereso'er they fly,
      But eagles gazed upon with every eye.
The Rape of Lucrece, l. 1014 [Lucrece]

2259   More pity that the eagle should be mew'd,
      While kites and buzzards prey at liberty.
Richard III, Act i, sc. 1, l. 132 [Hastings]

2260   The eagle suffers little birds to sing,
      And is not careful what they mean thereby,
      Knowing that with the shadow of his wings
      He can at pleasure stint their melody.
Titus Andronicus, Act iv, sc. 4, l. 83 [Tamora]

Ear

2261   Give every man thine ear, but few thy voice.
Hamlet, Act i, sc. 3, l. 68 [Polonius]

2262   The box of the ear that the prince gave you, . . . you took it
like a sensible lord.
II Henry IV, Act i, sc. 2, l. 219 [Falstaff]
      Give him a box o' the ear and that will make 'em red again.
II Henry VI, Act iv, sc. 7, l. 91 [Cade]
      If he took you a box o' the ear, you might have your action of
slander.
Measure for Measure, Act ii, sc. 1, l. 189 [Escalus]

2263   His ear . . . is stopp'd with other flattering sounds,
      As praises, of whose taste the wise are fond,
      Lascivious metres, to whose venom sound
      The open ear of youth doth always listen.
Richard II, Act ii, sc. 1, l. 17 [York]

Ears

2264   The Florentines and Senoys are by the ears.
All's Well that Ends Well, Act i, sc. 2, l. 1 [King]

2265   Were half to half the world by the ears and he
      Upon my party, I 'ld revolt to make
      Only my wars with him.
Coriolanus, Act i, sc. 1, l. 237 [Marcius]

2266   Friar Laurence: I see that mad men have no ears.
      Romeo: How should they, when that wise man have no eyes?
Romeo and Juliet, Act iii, sc. 3, l. 51 [Friar Laurence]
      Falstaff: Pistol!
      Pistol: He hears with ears.
      Evans: The tevil and his tam! what phrase is this, 'he hears with
ears'? why, it is affectations.
The Merry Wives of Windsor, Act i, sc. 1, l. 149 [Falstaff]

2267   [His] warlike ears could never brook retreat.
III Henry VI, Act i, sc. 1, l. 5 [York]

Earth

2268   This goodly frame, the earth, seems to me a sterile promontory,
this most excellent canopy, the air, look you, this brave o'erhanging firmament, this majestical roof fretted with golden fire, why it

appears no other thing to me than a foul and pestilent congregation of vapours.
Hamlet, Act ii, sc. 2, l. 309 [HAMLET]

2269   Earth, gape open wide and eat him quick,
As thou dost swallow up this good king's blood.
Richard III, Act i, sc. 2, l. 65 [ANNE]

2270   What are these
So wither'd and so wild in their attire,
That look not like the inhabitants o' the earth,
And yet are on it? . . .
The earth hath bubbles as the water has,
And these are of them.
Macbeth, Act i, sc. 3, l. 39 [BANQUO]

2271   Thou sure and firm-set earth,
Hear not my steps which way they walk, for fear
The very stones prate of my whereabout.
Macbeth, Act ii, sc. 1, l. 56 [MACBETH]

2272   We'll mingle our bloods together in the earth,
From whence we had our being and our birth.
Pericles, Act i, sc. 2, l. 113 [HELICANUS]

2273   The earth hath swallow'd all my hopes but she,
She is the hopeful lady of my earth.
Romeo and Juliet, Act i, sc. 2, l. 14 [CAPULET]

2274   The earth can have but earth, which is his due;
My spirit is thine, the better part of me.
Sonnet lxxiv, l. 7

Ease

2275   Shall I not take mine ease in mine inn but I shall have my pocket
picked?
I Henry IV, Act iii, sc. 3, l. 92 [FALSTAFF]

Easy

2276   That's as easy As to set dogs on sheep.
Coriolanus, Act ii, sc. 1, l. 272 [SICINIUS]

2277   'Tis as easy as lying.
Hamlet, Act iii, sc. 2, l. 372 [HAMLET]

2278   As easy as a cannon will shoot point-blank twelve score.
The Merry Wives of Windsor, Act iii, sc. 2, l. 33 [FORD]

2279   Any pains that I take for you is as easy as thanks.
Much Ado about Nothing, Act ii, sc. 3, l. 271 [BENEDICK]

Eating

2280   He hath eaten me out of house and home; he hath put all my
substance into that fat belly of his.
II Henry IV, Act ii, sc. 1, l. 81 [HOSTESS]

2281   We shall do nothing but eat and make good cheer,
And praise God for the merry year;
When flesh is cheap and females dear,
And lusty lads roam here and there
     So merrily.
II Henry IV, Act v, sc. 3, l. 18 [SILENCE]

2282   BASSANIO: Please you to dine with us.
SHYLOCK: Yes, to smell pork; to eat of the habitation which your
prophet the Nazarite conjured the devil into. I will buy with you,
sell with you, talk with you, walk with you, and so following,
but I will not eat with you, drink with you, nor pray with you.
The Merchant of Venice, Act i, sc. 3, l. 33 [BASSANIO]

Echo

2283   By heaven, he echoes me,
As if there were some monster in his thought
Too hideous to be shown.
Othello, Act iii, sc. 3, l. 106 [OTHELLO]

2284   Bondage is hoarse, and may not speak aloud;
Else would I tear the cave where Echo lies,
And make her airy tongue more hoarse than mine,
With repetition of my Romeo's name.
Romeo and Juliet, Act ii, sc. 2, l. 161 [JULIET]

2285   Then do they spend their mouths, Echo replies,
As if another chase were in the skies.
Venus and Adonis, l. 695 [VENUS]

Ecstasy

2286   This is the very coinage of your brain:
This bodiless creation ecstasy
Is very cunning in.
Hamlet, Act iii, sc. 4, l. 137 [QUEEN]

2287   The ecstasy hath so much overborne her that my daughter is
sometime afeard she will do a desperate outrage to herself.
Much Ado about Nothing, Act ii, sc. 3, l. 157 [LEONATO]

Egg

2288   PANDARUS: He esteems her no more than I esteem an addle egg.
CRESSIDA: If you love an addle egg as well as you love an idle
head, you would eat chickens i' the shell.
Troilus and Cressida, Act i, sc. 2, l. 144 [PANDARUS]

2289   LEONTES: Mine honest friend,
Will you take eggs for money?
MAMILLIUS: No, my lord, I'll fight.
LEONTES: You will! why happy man be 's dole!
The Winter's Tale, Act i, sc. 2, l. 160 [LEONTES]

Elbow

2290   Go, pluck him by the elbow; I must speak with him.
II Henry IV, Act i, sc. 2, l. 81 [CHIEF JUSTICE]

2291   ANGELO: Elbow is your name? why dost thou not speak, Elbow?
POMPEY: He cannot, sir; he 's out at elbow.
Measure for Measure, Act ii, sc. 1, l. 59 [ANGELO]

2292   Here, man; I am at thy elbow.
Much Ado about Nothing, Act iii, sc. 3, l. 106 [CONRADE]
Fear nothing; I'll be at thy elbow.
Othello, Act v, sc. 1, l. 3 [IAGO]

Election

2293   He that hath kill'd my king and whored my mother,
Popp'd in between the election and my hopes.
Hamlet, Act v, sc. 2, l. 64 [HAMLET]
(Explaining why Hamlet did not succeed his father as king.)

2294   I do prophesy the election lights
On Fortinbras: he has my dying voice.
Hamlet, Act v, sc. 2, l. 366 [HAMLET]

2295   Before we make election, give me leave
To show some reason, of no little force,
That York is most unmeet of any man.
II Henry VI, Act i, sc. 3, l. 165 [SUFFOLK]

Elephant

2296 The elephant hath joints, but none for courtesy, his legs are legs
for necessity, not for flexure.
Troilus and Cressida, Act ii, sc. 3, l. 113 [ULYSSES]

Elizabeth

2297 GARTER: Heaven, from thy endless goodness, send prosperous life,
long, and ever happy, to the high and mighty princess of England,
Elizabeth! . . .
KING: What is her name?
CRANMER: Elizabeth. . . . Let me speak, sir. . . .
This royal infant—heaven shall move about her!—
Though in her cradle, yet now promises
Upon this land a thousand thousand blessings,
Which time shall bring to ripeness: she shall be . . .
A pattern to all princes living with her,
And all that shall succeed: . . . all princely graces
That mould up such a mighty piece as this is,
With all the virtues that attend the good,
Shall still be doubled on her: truth shall nurse her,
Holy and heavenly thoughts still counsel her: . . .
In her days every man shall eat in safety,
Under his own vine, what he plants; and sing
The merry songs of peace to all his neighbours. . . .
She shall be, to the happiness of England,
An aged princess; many days shall see her
And yet no day without a deed to crown it.
Would I had known no more! but she must die,
She must, the saints must have her; yet a virgin,
A most unspotted lily shall she pass
To the ground, and all the world shall mourn her.
Henry VIII, Act v, sc. 5, l. 1 [GARTER]

Emulation

2298   The general's disdain'd
By him one step below, he by the next,
The next by him beneath; so every step,
Exampled by the first pace that is sick
Of his superior, grows to an envious fever
Of pale and bloodless emulation.
Troilus and Cressida, Act i, sc. 3, l. 129 [ULYSSES]

2299 Emulation hath a thousand sons
That one by one pursue: if you give way,
Or hedge aside from the direct forthright,
Like to an enter'd tide, they all rush by
And leave you hindmost.
Troilus and Cressida, Act iii, sc. 3, l. 156 [ULYSSES]

2300 The obligation of our blood forbids
A gory emulation 'twixt us twain.
Troilus and Cressida, Act iv, sc. 5, l. 122 [HECTOR]

End See also Beginning and End

2301 All's well that ends well: still the fine's the crown;
Whate'er the course, the end is the renown.
All's Well that Ends Well, Act iv, sc. 4, l. 35 [HELENA]
All's well that ends well yet,
Though time seem so adverse and means unfit.
All's Well that Ends Well, Act v, sc. 1, l. 25 [HELENA]

2302   Mistress, 'respice finem,' respect your end.
        The Comedy of Errors, Act iv, sc. 4, l. 43 [DROMIO OF EPHESUS]
        (Henderson translates it, "Keep your eye upon the goal.")
2303   They say he made a good end.
                                    Hamlet, Act iv, sc. 5, l. 186 [OPHELIA]
2304   Let the end try the man.
                                II Henry IV, Act ii, sc. 2, l. 50 [PRINCE]
2305   La fin couronne les œuvres.
                                II Henry VI, Act v, sc. 2, l. 28 [CLIFFORD]
        (The end crowns the work.)
                        The end crowns all,
        And that old common arbitrator, Time,
        Will one day end it.
                        Troilus and Cressida, Act iv, sc. 5, l. 224 [HECTOR]
2306   Let all the ends thou aim'st at be thy country's,
        Thy God's, and truth's.
                                Henry VIII, Act iii, sc. 2, l. 447 [WOLSEY]
2307   O, that a man might know
        The end of this day's business ere it come!
        But it sufficeth that the day will end,
        And then the end is known.
                                Julius Cæsar, Act v, sc. 1, l. 123 [BRUTUS]
2308   A little harm done to a great good end
        For lawful policy remains enacted.
                                The Rape of Lucrece, l. 528 [TARQUIN]
2309   Lo, as at English feasts, so I regreet
        The daintiest last, to make the end most sweet.
                                Richard II, Act i, sc. 3, l. 68 [BOLINGBROKE]
2310   There be some sports are painful, and their labour
        Delight in them sets off: some kinds of baseness
        Are nobly undergone and most poor matters
        Point to rich ends.
                                The Tempest, Act iii, sc. 1, l. 1 [FERDINAND]
2311   My ending is despair,
        Unless I be relieved by prayer,
        Which pierces so that it assaults
        Mercy itself and frees all faults.
                                The Tempest, Epilogue, l. 15 [PROSPERO]
2312   I will leave all as I found it, and there an end.
                                Troilus and Cressida, Act i, sc. 1, l. 90 [PANDARUS]

Endurance

2313   What cannot be avoided
        'Twere childish weakness to lament or fear.
                                III Henry VI, Act v, sc. 4, l. 37 [QUEEN MARGARET]
        What cannot be eschew'd must be embraced.
                                The Merry Wives of Windsor, Act v, sc. 5, l. 251 [PAGE]
2314   Out of a fortitude of soul I feel,
        To endure more miseries and greater far
        Than my weak-hearted enemies dare offer.
                                Henry VIII, Act iii, sc. 2, l. 387 [WOLSEY]

Enemy

2315   Be able for thine enemy Rather in power than use.
                                All's Well that Ends Well, Act i, sc. 1, l. 74 [COUNTESS]

2316   I know thou hadst rather
       Follow thine enemy in a fiery gulf
       Than flatter him in a bower.
                      Coriolanus, Act iii, sc. 2, l. 90 [VOLUMNIA]

2317   Why, Harry, do I tell thee of my foes,
       Which art my near'st and dearest enemy?
                      I Henry IV, Act iii, sc. 2, l. 122 [KING HENRY]

2318   Those that were your father's enemies
       Have steep'd their galls in honey and do serve you
       With hearts create of duty and of zeal.
                      Henry V, Act ii, sc. 2, l. 29 [GREY]

2319   In cases of defence 'tis best to weigh
       The enemy more mighty than he seems.
                      Henry V, Act ii, sc. 4, l. 43 [DAUPHIN]

2320   What valiant foemen, like to autumn's corn,
       Have we mow'd down in tops of all their pride!
                      III Henry VI, Act v, sc. 7, l. 3 [KING EDWARD]

2321   You have many enemies, that know not
       Why they are so, but, like to village curs,
       Bark when their fellows do.
                      Henry VIII, Act ii, sc. 4, l. 158 [KING HENRY]

2322   Thou art come to answer
       A stony adversary, an inhuman wretch
       Uncapable of pity, void and empty
       From any dram of mercy.
                      The Merchant of Venice, Act iv, sc. 1, l. 3 [DUKE]

2323   'Jockey of Norfolk, be not too bold,
       For Dickon thy master is bought and sold.'
       A thing devised by the enemy.
                      Richard III, Act v, sc. 3, l. 304 [KING RICHARD]

England See also Britain

2324   This royal throne of kings, this scepter'd isle,
       This earth of majesty, this seat of Mars,
       This other Eden, demi-paradise,
       This fortress built by Nature for herself
       Against infection and the hand of war,
       This happy breed of men, this little world,
       This precious stone set in the silver sea,
       Which serves it in the office of a wall
       Or as a moat defensive to a house,
       Against the envy of less happier lands,
       This blessed plot, this earth, this realm, this England,
       This nurse, this teeming womb of royal kings,
       Fear'd by their breed and famous by their birth,
       Renowned for their deeds as far from home,
       For Christian service and true chivalry,
       As is the sepulchre in stubborn Jewry
       Of the world's ransom, blessed Mary's Son,
       This land of such dear souls, this dear, dear land,
       Dear for her reputation through the world,
       Is now leased out, I die pronouncing it,
       Like to a tenement or pelting farm:
       England, bound in with the triumphant sea,
       Whose rocky shore beats back the envious siege
       Of watery Neptune, is now bound in with shame,
       With inky blots and rotten parchment bonds:

That England, that was wont to conquer others,
Hath made a shameful conquest of itself.
Ah, would the scandal vanish with my life,
How happy then were my ensuing death!

Richard II, Act ii, sc. 1, l. 40 [GAUNT]

2325 England's ground, farewell; sweet soil, adieu!
My mother, and my nurse, that bears me yet!
Where'er I wander, boast of this I can,
Though banish'd, yet a trueborn Englishman.

Richard II, Act i, sc. 3, l. 306 [BOLINGBROKE]

2326 CLOWN: Young Hamlet, . . . he that is mad and sent into England.
HAMLET: Ay, marry, why was he sent into England?
CLOWN: Why, because he was mad. . . . 'Twill not be seen in him there; there the men are as mad as he.

Hamlet, Act v, sc. 1, l. 161 [CLOWN]

2327 It was always yet the trick of our English nation, if they have a good thing, to make it too common.

II Henry IV, Act i, sc. 2, l. 241 [FALSTAFF]

2328 O England! model to thy inward greatness,
Like little body with a mighty heart,
What mightst thou do, that honour would thee do,
Were all thy children kind and natural!

Henry V, Act ii, Prologue, l. 16 [CHORUS]

2329 My people are with sickness much enfeebled, . . .
Who when they were in health, I tell thee, herald,
I thought upon one pair of English legs
Did march three Frenchmen.

Henry V, Act iii, sc. 6, l. 154 [KING HENRY]

2330 That island of England breeds very valiant creatures; their mastiffs are of unmatchable courage.

Henry V, Act iii, sc. 7, l. 150 [RAMBURES]

2331 CHARLES: At pleasure here we lie near Orleans;
Otherwhiles the famish'd English, like pale ghosts,
Faintly besiege us one hour in a month.
ALENÇON: They want their porridge and their fat bull-beeves:
Either they must be dieted like mules
And have their provender tied to their mouths
Or piteous they will look, like drowned mice.

I Henry VI, Act i, sc. 2, l. 6 [CHARLES]

2332 Froissart, a countryman of ours, records
England all Olivers and Rowlands bred
During the time Edward the Third did reign.

I Henry VI, Act i, sc. 2, l. 29 [ALENÇON]

2333 England is safe, if true within itself. . . .
Let us be back'd with God and with the seas
Which He hath given for fence impregnable,
And with their helps only defend ourselves;
In them and in ourselves our safety lies.

III Henry VI, Act iv, sc. 1, l. 40 [HASTINGS]

2334   That pale, that white-faced shore,
Whose foot spurns back the ocean's roaring tides
And coops from other lands her islanders, . . .
That England, hedged in with the main,
That water-walled bulwark, still secure
And confident from foreign purposes.

King John, Act ii, sc. 1, l. 23 [AUSTRIA]

2335   From the mouth of England
Add thus much more, that no Italian priest
Shall tithe or toll in our dominions.
King John, Act iii, sc. 1, 1. 152 [KING JOHN]

2336 You degenerate, you ingrate revolts,
You bloody Neroes, ripping up the womb
Of your dear mother England, blush for shame;
For your own ladies and pale-visaged maids
Like Amazons come tripping after drums,
Their thimbles into armed gauntlets change,
Their needles to lances, and their gentle hearts
To fierce and bloody inclination.
King John, Act v, sc. 2, 1. 151 [BASTARD]

2337 This England never did, and never shall,
Lie at the proud foot of a conqueror,
But when it first did help to wound itself.
Now these her princes are come home again,
Come the three corners of the world in arms,
And we shall shock them. Nought shall make us rue,
If England to itself do rest but true.
King John, Act v, sc. 7, 1. 112 [BASTARD]

2338 England, where, indeed, they are most potent in potting: your
Dane, your German, and your swag-bellied Hollander are nothing
to your English.
Othello, Act ii, sc. 3, 1. 78 [IAGO]

2339 Were I in England now, as once I was, and had this fish painted,
not a holiday fool there but would give a piece of silver: there
would this monster make a man; any strange beast there makes
a man: when they will not give a doit to relieve a lame beggar,
they will lay out ten to see a dead Indian.
The Tempest, Act ii, sc. 2, 1. 30 [TRINCULO]

English

2340 Here will be an old abusing of God's patience and the king's
English.
The Merry Wives of Windsor, Act i, sc. 4, 1. 5 [QUICKLY]

2341 Have I lived to stand at the taunt of one that makes fritters of
English? This is enough to be the decay of lust and late-walking
through the realm.
The Merry Wives of Windsor, Act v, sc. 5, 1. 150 [FALSTAFF]

Enough

2342 Enough, with over-measure.
Coriolanus, Act iii, sc. 1, 1. 140 [BRUTUS]
Pauca, there's enough.
Henry V, Act ii, sc. 1, 1. 83 [PISTOL]

2343   Before my body
I throw my warlike shield. Lay on, Macduff,
And damn'd be he that first cries 'Hold, enough!'
Macbeth, Act v, sc. 8, 1. 32 [MACBETH]

Entertainment

2344 I prithee, shepherd, if that love or gold
Can in this desert place buy entertainment,
Bring us where we may rest ourselves and feed.
As You Like It, Act ii, sc. 4, 1. 72 [ROSALIND]

2345 Let us devise Some entertainment for them.
Love's Labour's Lost, Act iv, sc. 3, 1. 372 [KING]

Some entertainment of time, some show in the posterior of the day.
Love's Labour's Lost, Act v, sc. 1, l. 124 [HOLOFERNES]

2346   Note if your lady strain his entertainment
With any strong or vehement importunity;
Much will be seen in that.
Othello, Act iii, sc. 3, l. 250 [IAGO]

Envy

2347   When envy breeds unkind division,
There comes the ruin, there begins confusion.
I Henry VI, Act iv, sc. 1, l. 193 [EXETER]

2348   Now I feel
Of what coarse metal ye are moulded, envy:
How eagerly ye follow my disgraces,
As if it fed ye! and how sleek and wanton
Ye appear in every thing may bring my ruin!
Henry VIII, Act iii, sc. 2, l. 238 [WOLSEY]

         Men that make
Envy and crooked malice nourishment
Dare bite the best.
Henry VIII, Act v, sc. 3, l. 43 [CRANMER]

2349   Now climbeth Tamora Olympus' top, . . .
Advanced beyond pale envy's threatening reach,
As when the golden sun salutes the morn.
Titus Andronicus, Act ii, sc. 1, l. 1 [AARON]

Errand

2350   Diomed has got that . . . young knave's sleeve . . . in his helm:
I would fain see them meet; that that same young Trojan ass
. . . might send that Greekish whore-masterly villain, with the
sleeve, back . . . of a sleeveless errand.
Troilus and Cressida, Act v, sc. 4, l. 3 [THERSITES]

(The origin of the phrase "sleeveless errand" was this: "Now
this is the guise in which the messengers journeyed: one sleeve
was on the cap of each of them in front, as a sign that they
were messengers, in order that through what hostile land
soever they might pass, no harm might be done them."—The
Mabinogian: Dream of Mayen Wledig. (c. 1450) Without
the sleeve, they would be unable to perform their errand, thus
it would be sleeveless, bootless, futile.)

Error

2351   O hateful error, melancholy's child,
Why dost thou show to the apt thoughts of men
The things that are not? O error, soon conceived,
Thou never comest unto a happy birth,
But kill'st the mother that engender'd thee!
Julius Cæsar, Act v, sc. 3, l. 67 [MESSALA]

Eternity

2352   Eternity was in our lips and eyes,
Bliss in our brows' bent; none our parts so poor,
But was a race of heaven: they are so still,
Or thou, the greatest soldier of the world,
Art turned the greatest liar.
Antony and Cleopatra, Act i, sc. 3, l. 35 [CLEOPATRA]

2353   ROSALIND: Tell me how long you would have her after you had
possessed her.

ORLANDO: For ever and a day.
                    As You Like It, Act iv, sc. 1, l. 143 [ROSALIND]
Bid Bianca farewell for ever and a day.
                    The Taming of the Shrew, Act iv, sc. 4, l. 98 [BIONDELLO]
2354   He wants nothing of a god but eternity and a heaven to throne in.
                    Coriolanus, Act v, sc. 4, l. 25 [MENENIUS]

Eunuch

2355   An they were sons of mine, I'd have them whipped; or I would
send them to the Turk to make eunuchs of.
                    All's Well that Ends Well, Act ii, sc. 3, l. 92 [LAFEU]
2356   CLEOPATRA: Thou, eunuch Mardian! . . . I take no pleasure
In aught an eunuch has. . . . Hast thou affections?
MARDIAN: Yes, gracious madam. . . . Fierce affections, and think
What Venus did with Mars.
                    Antony and Cleopatra, Act i, sc. 5, l. 8 [CLEOPATRA]
2357   As well a woman with an eunuch play'd
As with a woman.
                    Antony and Cleopatra, Act ii, sc. 5, l. 5 [CLEOPATRA]
2358   The voice of unpaved eunuch can never amend.
                    Cymbeline, Act ii, sc. 3, l. 34 [CLOTEN]

Evening

2359   Now Phaëthon hath tumbled from his car,
And made an evening at the noontide prick.
                    III Henry VI, Act i, sc. 4, l. 33 [CLIFFORD]
2360   How still the evening is,
As hush'd on purpose to grace harmony.
                    Much Ado about Nothing, Act ii, sc. 3, l. 40 [CLAUDIO]

Events

2361   High events as these
Strike those that make them; and their story is
No less in pity than his glory which
Brought them to be lamented.
                    Antony and Cleopatra, Act v, sc. 2, l. 363 [OCTAVIUS CÆSAR]
2362   By bad courses may be understood
That their events can never fall out good.
                    Richard II, Act ii, sc. 1, l. 213 [YORK]

Evidence

2363   My precious queen, forbear;
And give true evidence to his love, which stands
An honourable trial.
                    Antony and Cleopatra, Act i, sc. 3, l. 73 [ANTONY]
2364   Who finds the heifer dead and bleeding fresh
And sees fast by a butcher with an axe,
But will suspect 'twas he that made the slaughter?
Who finds the partridge in the puttock's nest,
But may imagine how the bird was dead,
Although the kite soar with unbloodied beak?
                    II Henry VI, Act iii, sc. 2, l. 188 [WARWICK]
2365   What is my offence?
Where are the evidence that do accuse me?
What lawful quest have given their verdict up
Unto the frowning judge? or who pronounced
The bitter sentence of poor Clarence' death?
                    Richard III, Act i, sc. 4, l. 187 [CLARENCE]

Evil

2366   Oppress'd with two weak evils, age and hunger.
As You Like It, Act ii, sc. 7, l. 132 [ORLANDO]

2367   No evil lost is wail'd when it is gone.
The Comedy of Errors, Act iv, sc. 2, l. 24 [LUCIANA]

2368   Evils that take leave,
On their departure most of all show evil.
King John, Act iii, sc. 4, l. 114 [PANDULPH]

2369   The evil that thou causest to be done,
That is thy means to live. Do thou but think
What 'tis to cram a maw or clothe a back
From such a filthy vice: say to thyself,
From their abominable and beastly touches
I drink, I eat, array myself, and live.
Canst thou believe thy living is a life,
So stinkingly depending?
Measure for Measure, Act iii, sc. 2, l. 21 [DUKE]

2370   O you blessed ministers above,
Keep me in patience, and with ripen'd time
Unfold the evil which is here wrap't up
In countenance!
Measure for Measure, Act v, sc. 1, l. 115 [ISABELLA]

2371   And 'Honi soit qui mal y pense' write
In emerald tufts, flowers purple, blue, and white.
The Merry Wives of Windsor, Act v, sc. 5, l. 73 [QUICKLY]
(Evil to him who thinks evil.)

Example

2372   He stopp'd the fliers;
And by his rare example made the coward
Turn terror into sport.
Coriolanus, Act ii, sc. 2, l. 107 [COMINIUS]

2373   [He] lived in court, . . . most praised, most loved,
A sample to the youngest, to the more mature
A glass that feated them, and to the graver,
A child that guided dotards.
Cymbeline, Act i, sc. 1, l. 45 [GENTLEMAN]

2374   So hot a speed with such advice disposed,
Such temperate order in so fierce a cause,
Doth want example.
King John, Act iii, sc. 4, l. 11 [LEWIS]

Excess

2375   To guard a title that was rich before,
To gild refined gold, to paint the lily,
To throw a perfume on the violet,
To smooth the ice, or add another hue
Unto the rainbow, or with taper-light
To seek the beauteous eye of heaven to garnish,
Is wasteful and ridiculous excess.
King John, Act iv, sc. 2, l. 10 [SALISBURY]
Distribution should undo excess,
And each man have enough.
King Lear, Act iv, sc. 1, l. 73 [GLOUCESTER]
(The lines which Huey Long took for his motto.)

2376   The profit of excess Is but to surfeit.
The Rape of Lucrece, l. 138

Exchequer

2377   Rob me the exchequer the first thing thou doest, and do it with
unwashed hands too.
I Henry IV, Act iii, sc. 3, l. 206 [FALSTAFF]

2378   I will be cheater to them both, and they shall be exchequers to me.
The Merry Wives of Windsor, Act i, sc. 3, l. 78 [FALSTAFF]

2379   You have an exchequer of words, and, I think, no other treasure
to give your followers.
The Two Gentlemen of Verona, Act ii, sc. 4, l. 43 [VALENTINE]

Excuse

2380   I must excuse what cannot be amended.
Coriolanus, Act iv, sc. 7, l. 11 [AUFIDIUS]

2381   Your play needs no excuse. Never excuse.
A Midsummer Night's Dream, Act v, sc. 1, l. 361 [THESEUS]

2382   Why seek'st thou then to cover with excuse
That which appears in proper nakedness?
Much Ado about Nothing, Act iv, sc. 1, l. 176 [LEONATO]

2383   The excuse that thou dost make in this delay
Is longer than the tale thou dost excuse.
Romeo and Juliet, Act ii, sc. 5, l. 33 [JULIET]

Executioner

2384   The common executioner,
Whose heart the accustom'd sight of death makes hard,
Falls not the axe upon the humbled neck
But first begs pardon.
As You Like It, Act iii, sc. 5, l. 3 [SILVIUS]

2385   GLOUCESTER: Think'st thou I am an executioner?
KING HENRY: A persecutor, I am sure, thou art:
If murdering innocents be executing,
Why, then thou art an executioner.
III Henry VI, Act v, sc. 6, l. 30 [GLOUCESTER]

2386   Arise, dissembler: though I wish thy death,
I will not be the executioner.
Richard III, Act i, sc. 2, l. 185 [ANNE]

Expectation

2387   Oft expectation fails and most oft there
Where most it promises, and oft it hits
Where hope is coldest and despair most fits.
All's Well that Ends Well, Act ii, sc. 1, l. 145 [HELENA]

2388   Expectation fainted, Longing for what it had not.
Antony and Cleopatra, Act iii, sc. 6, l. 47 [OCTAVIUS CÆSAR]

2389   Sadly I survive,
To mock the expectation of the world,
To frustrate prophecies and to raze out
Rotten opinion, who hath writ me down
After my seeming.
II Henry IV, Act v, sc. 2, l. 125 [HENRY V.]

2390   He hath borne himself beyond the promise of his age, doing, in
the figure of a lamb, the feats of a lion; he hath indeed better
bettered expectation.
Much Ado about Nothing, Act i, sc. 1, l. 13 [MESSENGER]

2391   I am giddy; expectation whirls me round.
The imaginary relish is so sweet
That it enchants my sense.
Troilus and Cressida, Act iii, sc. 2, l. 19 [TROILUS]

Experience

2392   ROSALIND: To have seen much and to have nothing, is to have
rich eyes and poor hands.
JAQUES: Yes, I have gained my experience.
ROSALIND: And your experience makes you sad. I had rather
have a fool to make me merry than experience to make me sad;
and to travel for it too!
As You Like It, Act iv, sc. 1, l. 23 [ROSALIND]

2393   Our courtiers say all's savage but at court:
Experience, O, thou disprovest report.
Cymbeline, Act iv, sc. 2, l. 34 [IMOGEN]

2394   ARMADO: How hast thou purchased this experience?
MOTH: By my penny of observation.
Love's Labour's Lost, Act iii, sc. 1, l. 27 [ARMADO]

2395   Experience be a jewel that I have purchased at an infinite rate.
The Merry Wives of Windsor, Act ii, sc. 2, l. 213 [FORD]

2396   Experience is by industry achieved
And perfected by the swift course of time.
The Two Gentlemen of Verona, Act i, sc. 3, l. 22 [ANTONIO]

2397   His years but young, but his experience old;
His head unmellow'd, but his judgement ripe.
The Two Gentlemen of Verona, Act ii, sc. 4, l. 69 [VALENTINE]

Extremes

2398   Fierce extremes
In their continuance will not feed themselves.
King John, Act v, sc. 7, l. 13 [PRINCE HENRY]

2399   Haply my presence
May well abate the over-merry spleen
Which otherwise would grow into extremes.
The Taming of the Shrew, Induction, sc. 1, l. 136 [LORD]

2400   O brother, speak with possibilities,
And do not break into these deep extremes.
Titus Andronicus, Act iii, sc. 1, l. 215 [MARCUS]

Extremity

2401   Where is your ancient courage? you were used
To say extremity was the trier of spirits;
That common chances common men could bear.
Coriolanus, Act iv, sc. 1, l. 3 [CORIOLANUS]

2402   The middle of humanity thou never knewest, but the extremity
of both ends: when thou wast in thy gilt and thy perfume, they
mocked thee for too much curiosity; in thy rags thou knowest
none, but art despised for the contrary.
Timon of Athens, Act iv, sc. 3, l. 300 [APEMANTUS]

Eye

2403   Faster than his tongue
Did make offence his eye did heal it up.
As You Like It, Act iii, sc. 5, l. 116 [PHEBE]

2404   Thou tell'st me there is murder in mine eye:
'Tis pretty, sure, and very probable,
That eyes, that are the frail'st and softest things,
Who shut their coward gates on atomies,
Should be call'd tyrants, butchers, murderers! . . .
Lie not, to say mine eyes are murderers!
Now show the wound mine eye hath made in thee:
Scratch thee but with a pin, and there remains

Some scar of it; lean but upon a rush,
The cicatrice and capable impressure
Thy palm some moment keeps; but now mine eyes,
Which I have darted at thee, hurt thee not,
Nor, I am sure, there is no force in eyes
That can do hurt.
                    As You Like It, Act iii, sc. 5, l. 10 [PHEBE]

2405   He is able to pierce a corslet with his eye.
                    Coriolanus, Act v, sc. 4, l. 21 [MENENIUS]

2406   Her lids, . . . white and azure laced
With blue of heaven's own tinct.
                    Cymbeline, Act ii, sc. 2, l. 20 [IACHIMO]

2407   Our very eyes
Are sometimes like our judgements, blind.
                    Cymbeline, Act iv, sc. 2, l. 301 [IMOGEN]

2408   What an infinite mock is this, that a man should have the best
use of eyes to see the way of blindness!
                    Cymbeline, Act v, sc. 4, l. 195 [GAOLER]

2409   O Hamlet, speak no more:
Thou turn'st mine eyes into my very soul.
                    Hamlet, Act iii, sc. 4, l. 88 [QUEEN]

2410   How is 't with you,
That you do bend your eye on vacancy
And with the incorporal air do hold discourse?
                    Hamlet, Act iii, sc. 4, l. 116 [QUEEN]

2411   Go, clear thy crystals.
                    Henry V, Act ii, sc. 3, l. 56 [PISTOL]
To what, my love, shall I compare thine eye?
Crystal is muddy.
            A Midsummer Night's Dream, Act iii, sc. 2, l. 138 [DEMETRIUS]

2412   There is none of you so mean and base,
That hath not noble lustre in your eyes.
                    Henry V, Act iii, sc. 1, l. 29 [KING HENRY]

2413   A largess universal like the sun
His liberal eye doth give to every one.
                    Henry V, Act iv, Prologue, l. 43 [CHORUS]

2414   One eye thou hast, to look to heaven for grace:
The sun with one eye vieweth all the world.
                    I Henry VI, Act i, sc. 4, l. 83 [TALBOT]

2415   These eyes, like lamps whose wasting oil is spent,
Wax dim, as drawing to their exigent.
                    I Henry VI, Act ii, sc. 5, l. 8 [MORTIMER]

2416   Thou baleful messenger, out of my sight!
Upon thy eye-balls murderous tyranny
Sits in grim majesty, to fright the world.
Look not upon me, for thine eyes are wounding.
                    II Henry VI, Act iii, sc. 2, l. 48 [KING]

2417   My eye's too quick, my heart o'erweens too much,
Unless my hand and strength could equal them.
                    III Henry VI, Act iii, sc. 2, l. 144 [RICHARD]

2418   These eyes, that now are dimm'd with death's black veil,
Have been as piercing as the mid-day sun,
To search the secret treason of the world.
                    III Henry VI, Act v, sc. 2, l. 16 [WARWICK]

2419   The eye sees not itself,
But by reflection, by some other things.
                    Julius Cæsar, Act i, sc. 2, l. 52 [BRUTUS]

2420 KING PHILIP: What say'st thou, boy? look in the lady's face.
LEWIS: I do, my lord; and in her eye I find
A wonder, or a wondrous miracle,
The shadow of myself form'd in her eye; . . .
I do protest I never loved myself
Till now infixed I beheld myself
Drawn in the flattering table of her eye.
BASTARD: Drawn in the flattering table of her eye!
    Hang'd in the frowning wrinkle of her brow!
And quarter'd in her heart! he doth espy
    Himself love's traitor: this is pity now,
That, hang'd and drawn and quarter'd, there should be
In such a love so vile a lout as he.
                    King John, Act ii, sc. 1, l. 495 [KING PHILIP]

2421 A still-soliciting eye, and such a tongue
As I am glad I have not.
                    King Lear, Act i, sc. 1, l. 234 [CORDELIA]

2422 Out, vile jelly! Where is thy lustre now?
                    King Lear, Act iii, sc. 7, l. 83 [CORNWALL]

2423 LEAR: O, ho, are you there with me? No eyes in your head, nor
no money in your purse? Your eyes are in a heavy case, your purse
in a light: yet you see how this world goes.
GLOUCESTER: I see it feelingly.
LEAR: What, art mad? A man may see how this world goes with
no eyes. Look with thine ears. . . .
        Get thee glass eyes;
And, like a scurvy politician, seem
To see the things thou dost not.
                    King Lear, Act iv, sc. 6, l. 147 [LEAR]

2424 Why, this would make a man a man of salt
To use his eyes for garden water-pots,
Ay, and laying autumn's dust.
                    King Lear, Act iv, sc. 6, l. 199 [LEAR]

2425 Methought all his senses were lock'd in his eye,
As jewels in crystal for some prince to buy.
                    Love's Labour's Lost, Act ii, sc. 1, l. 242 [BOYET]

2426 So sweet a kiss the golden sun gives not
    To those fresh morning drops upon the rose,
As thy eye-beams, when their fresh rays have smote
    The night of dew that on my cheeks down flows.
                    Love's Labour's Lost, Act iv, sc. 3, l. 25 [KING]

2427 By heaven, the wonder in a mortal eye!
                    Love's Labour's Lost, Act iv, sc. 3, l. 85 [DUMAIN]

2428 Where is any author in the world
Teaches such beauty as a woman's eye? . . .
From women's eyes this doctrine I derive:
They sparkle still the right Promethean fire;
They are the books, the arts, the academes,
That show, contain and nourish all the world.
                    Love's Labour's Lost, Act iv, sc. 3, l. 312 [BIRON]

2429   Sometimes from her eyes
I did receive fair speechless messages.
                    The Merchant of Venice, Act i, sc. 1, l. 163 [BASSANIO]

2430 I'll take my leave of the Jew in the twinkling of an eye.
                    The Merchant of Venice, Act ii, sc. 2, l. 177 [LAUNCELOT]
Ay, with a twink.—Before you can say 'come' and 'go.'
                    The Tempest, Act iv, sc. 1, l. 43 [PROSPERO]

2431   Your eyes are lode-stars.
> *A Midsummer Night's Dream,* Act i, sc. 1, l. 183 [HELENA]

Stars, stars, And all eyes else dead coals.
> *The Winter's Tale,* Act v, sc. 1, l. 67 [LEONTES]

2432   His eyes were green as leeks.
> *A Midsummer Night's Dream,* Act v, sc. 1, l. 342 [THISBE]

Her eyes are grey as glass.
> *The Two Gentlemen of Verona,* Act iv, sc. 4, l. 197 [JULIA]

Mine eyes are gray and bright and quick in turning.
> *Venus and Adonis,* l. 140 [VENUS]

2433   I have a good eye, uncle; I can see a church by daylight.
> *Much Ado about Nothing,* Act ii, sc. 1, l. 87 [BEATRICE]

2434   IAGO: What an eye she has! methinks it sounds a parley of provocation.

CASSIO: An inviting eye; and yet methinks right modest.
> *Othello,* Act ii, sc. 3, l. 22 [IAGO]

2435   Mine eyes do itch; Doth that bode weeping?
> *Othello,* Act iv, sc. 3, 1 58 [DESDEMONA]

2436   ANNE: Out of my sight! thou dost infect my eyes.

GLOUCESTER: Thine eyes, sweet lady, have infected mine.

ANNE: Would they were basilisks, to strike thee dead!

GLOUCESTER: I would they were, that I might die at once;

For now they kill me with a living death.

Those eyes of thine from mine have drawn salt tears,

Shamed their aspect with store of childish drops.
> *Richard III,* Act 1, sc. 2, l. 149 [ANNE]

2437   She speaks, yet she says nothing: what of that?

Her eye discourses; . . . her eyes in heaven

Would through the airy region stream so bright

The birds would sing and think it were not night.
> *Romeo and Juliet,* Act ii, sc. 2, l. 12 [ROMEO]

2438   Alack, there lies more peril in thine eye

Than twenty of their swords.
> *Romeo and Juliet,* Act ii, sc. 2, l. 71 [ROMEO]

2439   Men's eyes were made to look, and let them gaze.
> *Romeo and Juliet,* Act iii, sc. 1, l. 58 [MERCUTIO]

2440   If I could write the beauty of your eyes

And in fresh numbers number all your graces,

The age to come would say 'This poet lies;

Such heavenly touches ne'er touch'd earthly faces.'
> *Sonnet xvii,* l. 5

2441   Mine eye hath play'd the painter and hath stell'd

Thy beauty's form in table of my heart.
> *Sonnet xxiv,* l. 1

2442   Thine eyes that taught the dumb on high to sing

And heavy ignorance aloft to fly,

Have added feathers to the learned's wing,

And given grace a double majesty.
> *Sonnet lxxviii,* l. 5

2443   There lives more life in one of your fair eyes

Than both your poets can in praise devise.
> *Sonnet lxxxiii,* l. 13

2444   O me, what eyes hath Love put in my head,

Which have no correspondence with true sight!

Or, if they have, where is my judgement fled,

That censures falsely what they see aright? . . .

> O, how can Love's eye be true,
> That is so vex'd with watching and with tears? . . .
> O cunning Love! with tears thou keep'st me blind,
> Lest eyes well-seeing thy foul faults should find.
>
> *Sonnet* cxlviii, l. 1

2445 What stars do spangle heaven with such beauty,
As those two eyes become that heavenly face?
The Taming of the Shrew, Act iv, sc. 5, l. 31 [PETRUCHIO]

2446 PROSPERO: The fringed curtains of thine eye advance
And say what thou seest yond. . . .
MIRANDA: A thing divine, for nothing natural
I ever saw so noble. . . .
FERDINAND: Most sure, the goddess
On whom these airs attend! . . . My prime request,
Which I do last pronounce, is, O you wonder!
If you be maid or no?
MIRANDA: No wonder, sir; But certainly a maid. . . .
PROSPERO: At the first sight, They have changed eyes.
The Tempest, Act i, sc. 2, l. 407 [PROSPERO]

2447 Things in motion sooner catch the eye
Than what not stirs.
Troilus and Cressida, Act iii, sc. 3, l. 183 [ULYSSES]

2448 The lustre in your eye, heaven in your cheek,
Pleads your fair usage.
Troilus and Cressida, Act iv, sc. 4, l. 120 [DIOMEDES]

2449 Her two blue windows faintly she up-heaveth,
Like the fair sun, when in his fresh array
He cheers the morn and all the earth relieveth.
Venus and Adonis, l. 482

Eye-Sore

2450 Yea, though I die, the scandal will survive,
And be an eye-sore in my golden coat.
The Rape of Lucrece, l. 204 [LUCRECE]

2451 Fie, doff this habit, shame to your estate,
An eye-sore to our solemn festival!
The Taming of the Shrew, Act iii, sc. 2, l. 101 [BAPTISTA]

F

Face

2452 Hadst thou Narcissus in thy face, to me
Thou wouldst appear most ugly.
Antony and Cleopatra, Act ii, sc. 5, l. 95 [CLEOPATRA]

2453 MENAS: All men's faces are true, whatso'er their hands are.
ENOBARBUS: But there is never a fair woman has a true face.
MENAS: No slander; they steal hearts.
Antony and Cleopatra, Act ii, sc. 6, l. 102 [MENAS]

2454 The tartness of his face sours ripe grapes.
Coriolanus, Act v, sc. 4, l. 18 [MENENIUS]

2455 Do thou amend thy face, and I'll amend my life; thou art our
admiral, thou bearest the lantern in the poop, but 'tis in the nose of
thee; thou art the Knight of the Burning Lamp. . . . I have maintained that salamander of yours with fire any time this two and
thirty years; God reward me for it!
I Henry IV, Act iii, sc. 3, l. 26 [FALSTAFF]
(He is speaking to Bardolph.)

2456   Good Bardolph, put thy face between his sheets, and do the office
        of a warming-pan.
                              Henry V, Act ii, sc. 1, l. 87 [Boy]
2457   His face is all bubukles, and whelks, and knobs, and flames o' fire:
        and his lips blows at his nose, and it is like a coal of fire, some-
        times plue and sometimes red.
                              Henry V, Act iii, sc. 6, l. 109 [Fluellen]
2458   A fellow . . . whose face is not worth sunburning, that never looks
        in his glass for love of any thing he sees there. . . . My comfort
        is, that old age, that ill layer up of beauty, can do no more spoil
        upon my face.
                              Henry V, Act v, sc. 2, l. 155 [King Henry]
2459   In thy face I see
        The map of honour, truth and loyalty.
                              II Henry VI, Act iii, sc. 1, l. 202 [King Henry]
2460   Ye have angels' faces, but heaven knows your hearts.
                              Henry VIII, Act iii, sc. 1, l. 145 [Queen Katharine]
2461   If my legs were two such riding-rods,
        My arms such eel-skins stuff'd, my face so thin
        That in mine ear I durst not stick a rose
        Lest men should say 'Look, where three-farthings goes!'
        And, to his shape, were heir to all this land,
        Would I might never stir from off this place,
        I would give it every foot to have this face;
        I would not be sir Nob in any case. . . .
        Your face hath got five hundred pound a year,
        Yet sell your face for five pence and 'tis dear.
                              King John, Act i, sc. 1, l. 140 [Bastard]
2462   I have seen better faces in my time
        Than stands on any shoulder that I see
        Before me at this instance.
                              King Lear, Act ii, sc. 2, l. 99 [Kent]
2463   Was this a face
        To be opposed against the warring winds?
        To stand against the deep dread-bolted thunder?
        In the most terrible and nimble stroke
        Of quick, cross lightning?
                              King Lear, Act iv, sc. 7, l. 31 [Cordelia]
2464   There's no art
        To find the mind's construction in the face.
                              Macbeth, Act i, sc. 4, l. 11 [Duncan]
2465   Your face, my thane, is as a book where men
        May read strange matters.
                              Macbeth, Act i, sc. 5, l. 63 [Lady Macbeth]
2466   Make our faces vizards to our hearts,
        Disguising what they are.
                              Macbeth, Act iii, sc. 2, l. 34 [Macbeth]
2467   His face is the worst thing about him.
                              Measure for Measure, Act ii, sc. 1, l. 163 [Pompey]
2468   If my word be sterling yet in England,
        Let it command a mirror hither straight,
        That it may show me what a face I have,
        Since it is bankrupt of his majesty. . . .
        Give me the glass, and therein will I read.
        No deeper wrinkles yet? hath sorrow struck
        So many blows upon this face of mine,
        And made no deeper wounds? O flattering glass,

Like to my followers in prosperity,
Thou dost beguile me! Was this face the face
That every day under his household roof
Did keep a thousand men? was this the face
That, like the sun, did make beholders wink?
Was this the face that faced so many follies,
And was at last out-faced by Bolingbroke?
A brittle glory shineth in this face:
As brittle as the glory is the face.
Richard II, Act iv, sc. 1, 1. 264 [KING RICHARD]

2469 Read o'er the volume of young Paris' face
And find delight writ there with beauty's pen;
Examine every married lineament
And see how one another lends content,
And what obscured in this fair volume lies
Find written in the margent of his eyes.
Romeo and Juliet, Act i, sc. 3, 1. 81 [LADY CAPULET]

2470 A woman's face with Nature's own hand painted
Hast thou, the master-mistress of my passion.
Sonnet xx, 1. 1

2471 Believe me, sister, of all the men alive
I never yet beheld that special face
Which I could fancy more than any other.
The Taming of the Shrew, Act ii, sc. 1, 1. 10 [BIANCA]

2472 Thou hast faced many things; . . . face not me: thou hast braved
many men; brave not me. I will neither be faced nor braved.
The Taming of the Shrew, Act iv, sc. 3, 1. 123 [GRUMIO]

2473 VIOLA: Good madam, let me see your face. . . .
OLIVIA: We will draw the curtain and show you the picture.
[*Unveiling*] . . . 'Tis in grain, sir; 'twill endure wind and
weather.
VIOLA: 'Tis beauty truly blent, whose red and white
Nature's own sweet and cunning hand laid on:
Lady, you are the cruell'st she alive,
If you will lead these graces to the grave
And leave the world no copy.
Twelfth Night, Act i, sc. 5, 1. 248 [VIOLA]

2474 That face of his I do remember well;
Yet, when I saw it last, it was besmear'd
As black as Vulcan in the smoke of war.
Twelfth Night, Act v, sc. 1, 1. 54 [DUKE]

Fairy

2475 QUICKLY: Fairies, black, grey, green, and white,
You moonshine revellers, and shades of night,
You orphan heirs of fixed destiny,
Attend your office and your quality.
Crier Hobgoblin, make the fairy oyes.
PISTOL: Elves, list your names; silence, you airy toys.
Cricket, to Windsor chimneys shalt thou leap,
Where fires thou find'st unraked and hearths unswept,
There pinch the maids as blue as bilberry:
Our radiant queen hates sluts and sluttery.
The Merry Wives of Windsor, Act v, sc. 5, 1. 41 [QUICKLY]

2476 Over hill, over dale,
Through brush, through brier,

Over park, over pale,
　　Through flood, through fire,
I do wander every where,
Swifter than thè moon's sphere;
And I serve the fairy queen,
To dew her orbs upon the green.
The cowslips tall her pensioners be:
In their gold coats spots you see;
Those be rubies, fairy favours,
In those freckles live their savours:
I must go seek some dew-drops here
And hang a pearl in every cowslip's ear.
　　　A Midsummer Night's Dream, Act ii, sc. 1, l. 2 [FAIRY]

2477　Either I mistake your shape and making quite,
Or else you are that shrewd and knavish sprite
Call'd Robin Goodfellow: are not you he
That frights the maidens of the villagery;
Skim milk, and sometimes labour in the quern
And bootless make the breathless housewife churn? . . .
Those that Hobgoblin call you and sweet Puck,
You do their work, and they shall have good luck.
　　　A Midsummer Night's Dream, Act ii, sc. 1, l. 32 [FAIRY]

2478　　　You spotted snakes with double tongue,
　　　　Thorny hedgehogs, be not seen;
　　　Newts and blind-worms, do no wrong,
　　　　Come not near our fairy queen.
　　　A Midsummer Night's Dream, Act ii, sc. 2, l. 9 [SONG]

Faith

2479　O, where is faith? O, where is loyalty?
If it be banish'd from the frosty head,
Where shall it find a harbour in the earth?
　　　II Henry VI, Act v, sc. 1, l. 166 [KING HENRY]

2480　There are no tricks in plain and simple faith;
But hollow men, like horses hot at hand,
Make gallant show and promise of their mettle;
But when they should endure the bloody spur,
They fall their crests, and, like deceitful jades,
Sink in the trial.
　　　Julius Cæsar, Act iv, sc. 2, l. 22 [BRUTUS]

2481　He wears his faith but as the fashion of his hat; it ever changes
with the next block.
　　　Much Ado about Nothing, Act i, sc. 1, l. 76 [BEATRICE]

2482　　　　Better have none
Than plural faith which is too much by one.
　　　The Two Gentlemen of Verona, Act v, sc. 4, l. 51 [SILVIA]

Falchion

2483　[His] purple falchion painted to the hilt
In blood of those that had encounter'd him.
　　　III Henry VI, Act i, sc. 4, l. 12 [YORK]

2484　I have seen the day, with my good biting falchion
I would have made them skip.
　　　King Lear, Act v, sc. 3, l. 276 [LEAR]

2485　　　　Queen Margaret saw
The murderous falchion smoking in his blood;
The which thou once didst bend against her breast.
　　　Richard III, Act i, sc. 2, l. 94 [ANNE]

Falcon

2486   On Tuesday last,
A falcon, towering in her pride of place,
Was by a mousing owl hawk'd at and kill'd.
Macbeth, Act ii, sc. 4, l. 11 [OLD MAN]

2487 My falcon now is sharp and passing empty;
And till she stoop she must not be full-gorged,
For then she never looks upon her lure.
The Taming of the Shrew, Act iv, sc. 1, l. 193 [PETRUCHIO]

2488 Ay, you shall fight your hearts out ere I part you. The falcon as the
tercel, for all the ducks i' the river.
Troilus and Cressida, Act iii, sc. 2, l. 55 [PANDARUS]

Fall

2489   Be cheerful; wipe thine eyes;
Some falls are means the happier to arise.
Cymbeline, Act iv, sc. 2, l. 402 [LUCIUS]

2490 I have touch'd the highest point of all my greatness;
And, from that full meridian of my glory,
I haste now to my setting: I shall fall
Like a bright exhalation in the evening,
And no man see me more.
Henry VIII, Act iii, sc. 2, l. 223 [WOLSEY]

2491 Press not a falling man too far! 'tis virtue:
His faults lie open to the laws; let them,
Not you, correct him.
Henry VIII, Act iii, sc. 2, l. 333 [CHAMBERLAIN]
'Tis a cruelty To load a falling man.
Henry VIII, Act v, sc. 3, l. 76 [CRANMER]

2492 Farewell! a long farewell, to all my greatness!
This is the state of man: to-day he puts forth
The tender leaves of hopes; to-morrow blossoms,
And bears his blushing honours thick upon him;
The third day come a frost, a killing frost,
And, when he thinks, good easy man, full surely
His greatness is a-ripening, nips his root,
And then he falls as I do. I have ventured,
Like little wanton boys that swim on bladders,
This many summers in a sea of glory,
But far beyond my depth: my high-blown pride
At length broke under me and now has left me,
Weary and old with service, to the mercy
Of a rude stream, that must for ever hide me.
Henry VIII, Act iii, sc. 2, l. 351 [WOLSEY]

2493 We will fall for it.
Julius Cæsar, Act ii, sc. 1, l. 128 [BRUTUS]

2494 Let us be keen, and rather cut a little,
Than fall, and bruise to death.
Measure for Measure, Act ii, sc. 1, l. 5 [ESCALUS]

2495 And then my husband—God be with his soul!
A' was a merry man—took up the child:
'Yea,' quoth he, 'dost thou fall upon thy face?
Thou wilt fall backward when thou hast more wit;
Wilt thou not, Jule?' and, by my holidame,
The pretty wretch left crying and said, 'Ay.'
Romeo and Juliet, Act i, sc. 3, l. 39 [NURSE]

Falsehood See also Lying

2496   Your bait of falsehood takes this carp of truth.
                              Hamlet, Act ii, sc. 1, l. 63 [POLONIUS]
2497   O what a goodly outside falsehood hath!
                    The Merchant of Venice, Act i, sc. 3, l. 103 [ANTONIO]

Falseness

2498   I am falser than vows made in wine.
                              As You Like It, Act iii, sc. 5, l. 73 [ROSALIND]
2499   As false as dicers' oaths.
                              Hamlet, Act iii, sc. 4, l. 45 [HAMLET]
2500   Away, and mock the time with fairest show:
        False face must hide what the false heart doth know.
                              Macbeth, Act i, sc. 7, l. 81 [MACBETH]
2501   If she be false, O, then heaven mocks itself!
                              Othello, Act iii, sc. 3, l. 278 [OTHELLO]
2502   Heaven truly knows that thou art false as hell.
                              Othello, Act iv, sc. 2, l. 39 [OTHELLO]
2503   OTHELLO: She was false as water.
        EMILIA: Thou art as rash as fire to say
        That she was false: O, she was heavenly true!
                              Othello, Act v, sc. 2, l. 134 [OTHELLO]
2504   Falseness cannot come from thee; for thou look'st
        Modest as Justice, and thou seem'st a palace
        For the crown'd Truth to dwell in.
                              Pericles, Act v, sc. i, l. 121 [PERICLES]
2505   O, never say that I was false of heart,
        Though absence seem'd my flame to qualify.
                                          Sonnet cix, l. 1
2506   If I be false, or swerve a hair from truth,
        When time is old and hath forgot itself,
        When waterdrops have worn the stones of Troy,
        And blind oblivion swallow'd cities up,
        And mighty states characterless are grated
        To dusty nothing, yet let memory,
        From false to false, among false maids in love,
        Upbraid my falsehood! when they've said 'as false
        As air, as water, wind, or sandy earth,
        As fox to lamb, as wolf to heifer's calf,
        Pard to the hind, or stepdame to her son,
        'Yea,' let them say, to stick the heart of falsehood,
        'As false as Cressid.'
                    Troilus and Cressida, Act iii, sc. 2, l. 191 [CRESSIDA]
2507   False
        As o'er-dyed blacks, as wind, as waters, false
        As dice are to be wish'd by one that fixes
        No bourn 'twixt his and mine.
                    The Winter's Tale, Act i, sc. 2, l. 131 [LEONTES]

Falstaff

2508   What, old acquaintance! could not all this flesh
        Keep in a little life? Poor Jack, farewell!
        I could have better spared a better man:
        O, I should have a heavy miss of thee,
        If I were much in love with vanity!
        Death hath not struck so fat a deer to-day,
        Though many dearer, in this bloody fray.
                              I Henry IV, Act v, sc. 4, l. 102 [PRINCE]

2509   I am not a double man: but if I be not Jack Falstaff, then am I
        a Jack.

                                I Henry IV, Act v, sc. 4, l. 141 [FALSTAFF]

2510   Ah, you whoreson little valiant villain, you! . . . Ah, you sweet
        little rogue, you! . . . Thou art as valorous as Hector of Troy,
        worth five of Agamemnon, and ten times better than the Nine.
        . . . I'll canvass thee between a pair of sheets. . . . Thou whore-
        son little tidy Bartholomew boar-pig, when wilt thou leave fight-
        ing o' days and foining o' nights, and begin to patch up thine old
        body for heaven?

                            II Henry IV, Act ii, sc. 4, l. 225 [DOLL TEARSHEET]

2511   FALSTAFF: Harry, now I do not speak to thee in drink but in tears,
        not in pleasure but in passion, not in words only, but in woes also:
        and yet there is a virtuous man whom I have often noted in thy
        company, but I know not his name.
        PRINCE: What manner of man, an it like your majesty?
        FALSTAFF: A goodly portly man, i' faith, and a corpulent; of a
        cheerful look, a pleasing eye and a most noble carriage; and, as I
        think, his age some fifty, or, by 'r lady, inclining to three score;
        and now I remember me, his name is Falstaff: if that man should
        be lewdly given, he deceiveth me; for, Harry, I see virtue in his
        looks. If then the tree may be known by the fruit, as the fruit by
        the tree, then, peremptorily I speak it, there is virtue in that
        Falstaff: him keep with, the rest banish.

                                I Henry IV, Act ii, sc. 4, l. 456 [FALSTAFF]

2512   PRINCE: There is a devil haunts thee in the likeness of an old fat
        man; a tun of man is thy companion. Why dost thou converse with
        that trunk of humours, that bolting-hatch of beastliness, . . . that
        villanous abominable misleader of youth, Falstaff, that old white-
        bearded Satan?
        FALSTAFF: My lord, the man I know. . . . That he is old, the more
        the pity, his white hairs do witness it; but that he is, saving your
        grace, a whoremaster, that I utterly deny. If sack and sugar be a
        fault, God help the wicked! if to be old and merry be a sin, then
        many an old host that I know is damned: if to be fat be to be
        hated, then Pharaoh's lean kine are to be loved. No, my good lord,
        banish Peto, banish Bardolph, banish Poins, but for sweet Jack
        Falstaff, . . . banish him not thy Harry's company: banish plump
        Jack, and banish all the world.

                                I Henry IV, Act ii, sc. 4, l. 492 [PRINCE]

2513   FALSTAFF: My king! my Jove! I speak to thee, my heart!
        KING: I know thee not, old man: fall to thy prayers;
        How ill white hairs become a fool and jester!
        I have long dream'd of such a kind of man,
        So surfeit-swell'd, so old and so profane;
        But, being awaked, I do despise my dream:
        Make less thy body hence, and more thy grace;
        Leave gormandizing; know the grave doth gape
        For thee thrice wider than for other men.
        Reply not to me with a fool-born jest.
        Presume not that I am the thing I was;
        For God doth know, so shall the world perceive,
        That I have turn'd away my former self;
        So will I those that kept me company.
        When thou dost hear I am as I have been,
        Approach me, and thou shalt be as thou wast,
        The tutor and the feeder of my riots:

Till then, I banish thee on pain of death, . . .
Not to come near our person by ten mile. . . .
FALSTAFF: Master Shallow, I owe you a thousand pound.
II Henry IV, Act v, sc. 5, l. 50 [FALSTAFF]

2514   HOSTESS: Come in quickly to Sir John. Ah, poor heart! he is so
shaked of a burning quotidian tertian, that it most lamentable
to behold. Sweet men, come to him.
NYM: The king hath run bad humours on the knight; that's the
even of it.
PISTOL: Nym, thou hast spoke the right;
His heart is fracted and corroborate.
Henry V, Act ii, sc. 1, l. 122 [HOSTESS]

2515   PISTOL: Falstaff he is dead,
And we must yearn therefore.
BARDOLPH: Would I were with him, wheresome'er he is, either in
heaven or in hell!
HOSTESS: Nay, sure, he's not in hell: he's in Arthur's bosom, if
ever man went to Arthur's bosom. A' made a finer end and went
away an it had been any christom child; a' parted even just between
twelve and one, even at the turning o' the tide: for after I saw him
fumble with the sheets and play with flowers and smile upon his
fingers' ends, I knew there was but one way; for his nose was as
sharp as a pen, and a' babbled of green fields. . . .A' bade me lay
more clothes on his feet: I put my hand into the bed and felt them,
and they were as cold as any stone; then I felt to his knees, and
they were as cold as any stone, and so upward and upward, and
all was as cold as any stone.
Henry V, Act ii, sc. 3, l. 5 [PISTOL]

Fame

2516   Fame . . . can not
Better be held nor more attain'd than by
A place below the first: for what miscarries
Shall be the general's fault, though he perform
To the utmost of a man.
Coriolanus, Act i, sc. 1, l. 267 [BRUTUS]

2517   The man is noble and his fame folds in
This orb o' the earth.
Coriolanus, Act v, sc. 6, l. 126 [LORD]

2518   Let Fame, that all hunt after in their lives,
Live register'd upon our brazen tombs
And then grace us in the disgrace of death;
When, spite of cormorant devouring Time,
The endeavour of this present breath may buy
That honour that shall bate his scythe's keen edge
And make us heirs of all eternity.
Love's Labour's Lost, Act i, sc. 1, l. 1 [KING]

2519   He lives in fame, though not in life.
Richard III, Act iii, sc. 1, l. 88 [PRINCE]
(Referring to Julius Cæsar, qv.)

2520   He lives in fame that died in virtue's cause.
Titus Andronicus, Act i, sc. 1, l. 389 [SONS]

Familiarity

2521   Be thou familiar, but by no means vulgar.
Hamlet, Act i, sc. 3, l. 61 [POLONIUS]

2522   Upon familiarity will grow more contempt.
The Merry Wives of Windsor, Act i, sc. 1, l. 258 [SLENDER]

Famine

2523   Famine,
Ere clean it o'erthrow nature, makes it valiant.
                              Cymbeline, Act iii, sc. 6, l. 19 [IMOGEN]
2524   Famine is in thy cheeks,
Need and oppression starveth in thine eyes,
Contempt and beggary hangs upon thy back.
                          Romeo and Juliet, Act v, sc. 1, l. 69 [ROMEO]

Fancy

2525   Pacing through the forest,
Chewing the food of sweet and bitter fancy.
                          As You Like It, Act iv, sc. 3, l. 102 [OLIVER]
2526   Tell me where is fancy bred,
                          Or in the heart, or in the head?
                          How begot, how nourished?
                              Reply, reply.
                          It is engender'd in the eyes,
                          With gazing fed; and fancy dies
                          In the cradle where it lies.
                              Let us all ring fancy's knell:
                              I'll begin it—Ding, dong, bell.
                      The Merchant of Venice, Act iii, sc. 2, l. 63 [SONG]

Fantasticoes

2527   The pox of such antic, lisping, affecting fantasticoes; these new
tuners of accents! 'By Jesu, a very good blade! a very tall man!
a very good whore!' Why, is not this a lamentable thing, grandsire, that we should be thus afflicted with these strange flies, these
fashion-mongers, these perdona-mi's, who stand so much on the
new form, that they cannot sit at ease on the old bench?
                          Romeo and Juliet, Act ii, sc. 3, l. 31 [MERCUTIO]

Farewell

2528   Farewell, my dearest sister, fare thee well:
The elements be kind to thee, and make
Thy spirits all of comfort! fare thee well.
                  Antony and Cleopatra, Act iii, sc. 2, l. 39 [OCTAVIUS CÆSAR]
2529   FALSTAFF: Farewell: you shall find me in Eastcheap.
PRINCE: Farewell, thou latter spring! farewell, All-hallown
summer!
                              I Henry IV, Act i, sc. 2, l. 175 [FALSTAFF]
2530   BRUTUS: Whether we shall meet again I know not.
Therefore our everlasting farewell take:
For ever, and for ever, farewell, Cassius!
If we do meet again, why, we shall smile;
If not, why then, this parting was well made.
CASSIUS: For ever, and for ever, farewell, Brutus!
If we do meet again, we'll smile indeed;
If not, 'tis true this parting was well made.
                              Julius Cæsar, Act v, sc. 1, l. 115 [BRUTUS]
2531   PORTIA: And so farewell, till we shall meet again.
LORENZO: Fair thoughts and happy hours attend on you!
                      The Merchant of Venice, Act iii, sc. 4, l. 40 [PORTIA]
2532   O Hero, what a Hero hadst thou been,
If half thy outward graces had been placed
About thy thoughts and counsels of thy heart!

But fare thee well, most foul, most fair, farewell,
Thou pure impiety and impious purity!
For thee I'll lock up all the gates of love,
And on my eyelids shall conjecture hang,
To turn all beauty into thoughts of harm,
And never shall it more be gracious.
> *Much Ado about Nothing,* Act iv, sc. 1, l. 101 [CLAUDIO]

2533 O, now, for ever
Farewell the tranquil mind! farewell content!
Farewell the plumed troop, and the big wars,
That make ambition virtue! O, farewell!
Farewell the neighing steed, and the shrill trump,
The spirit-stirring drum, the ear-piercing fife,
The royal banner, and all quality,
Pride, pomp and circumstance of glorious war!
And, O you mortal engines, whose rude throats
The immortal Jove's dread clamours counterfeit,
Farewell! Othello's occupation 's gone!
> *Othello,* Act iii, sc. 3, l. 347 [OTHELLO]

2534 BAGOT: Farewell: if heart's presages be not vain,
We three here part that ne'er shall meet again. . . .
GREEN: Farewell at once, for once, for all and ever.
BUSHY: Well, we may meet again.
BAGOT: I fear me, never.
> *Richard II,* Act ii, sc. 2, l. 142 [BAGOT]

2535 Farewell till soon.
> *Richard III,* Act iv, sc. 3, l. 35 [KING RICHARD]

2536 Farewell! thou art too dear for my possessing.
> *Sonnet* lxxxvii, l. 1

Farm

2537 Let me be no assistant for a state,
But keep a farm and carters.
> *Hamlet,* Act ii, sc. 2, l. 166 [POLONIUS]

2538 Here's a farmer, that hanged himself on the expectation of plenty.
> *Macbeth,* Act ii, sc. 3, l. 4 [PORTER]

Fashion

2539 I do not like the fashion of your garments: you will say they are
Persian attire; but let them be changed.
> *King Lear,* Act iii, sc. 6, l. 84 [LEAR]

2540 Now will he lie ten nights awake, carving the fashion of a new
doublet.
> *Much Ado about Nothing,* Act ii, sc. 3, l. 18 [BENEDICK]

2541 BORACHIO: The fashion of a doublet, or a hat, or a cloak, is nothing to a man. . . .
CONRADE: Yes, the fashion is the fashion.
BORACHIO: Tush! I may as well say the fool's the fool. . . .
Seest thou not what a deformed thief this fashion is? . . . how gid-
dily a' turns about all the hot-bloods between fourteen and five-
and-thirty? . . .
CONRADE: All this I see: and I see that the fashion wears out
more apparel than the man.
> *Much Ado about Nothing,* Act iii, sc. 3, l. 125 [BORACHIO]

2542 Old fashions please me best; I am not so nice,
To change true rules for old inventions.
> *The Taming of the Shrew,* Act iii, sc. 1, l. 80 [BIANCA]

Fast and Loose

2543   Shall these hands . . . play fast and loose with faith?
King John, Act iii, sc. 1, l. 239 [KING PHILIP]

2544   COSTARD: Let me not be pent up, sir; I will fast, being loose.
MOTH: No, sir; that were fast and loose: thou shalt to prison.
Love's Labour's Lost, Act i, sc. 2, l. 160 [COSTARD]

Fasting

2545   A thousand men have broke their fasts to-day
That ne'er shall dine unless thou yield the crown.
III Henry VI, Act ii, sc. 2, l. 127 [EDWARD]

2546   'Tis but a three years' fast:
The mind shall banquet, though the body pine:
Fat paunches have lean pates, and dainty bits
Make rich the ribs, but bankrupt quite the wits.
Love's Labour's Lost, Act i, sc. 1, l. 24 [LONGAVILLE]

2547   ARMADO: Villain, thou shalt fast for thy offences ere thou be
pardoned.
COSTARD: Well, sir, I hope, when I do it, I shall do it on a full
stomach.
Love's Labour's Lost, Act i, sc. 2, l. 151 [ARMADO]

Fate

2548   Do not please sharp fate
To grace it with your sorrows: bid that welcome
Which comes to punish us, and we punish it
Seeming to bear it lightly.
Antony and Cleopatra, Act iv, sc. 14, l. 135 [ANTONY]

2549   My fate cries out,
And makes each petty artery in this body
As hardy as the Nemean lion's nerve.
Hamlet, Act i, sc. 4, l. 81 [HAMLET]

2550   O God! that one might read the book of fate,
And see the revolution of the times
Make mountains level, and the continent,
Weary of solid firmness, melt itself
Into the sea! and, other times, to see
The beachy girdle of the ocean
Too wide for Nature's hips.
II Henry IV, Act iii, sc. 1, l. 45 [KING HENRY]

2551   What fates impose, that men must needs abide;
It boots not to resist both wind and tide.
III Henry VI, Act iv, sc. 3, l. 58 [KING EDWARD]

2552   Men at some time are masters of their fates.
Julius Cæsar, Act i, sc. 2, l. 139 [CASSIUS]

2553   What can be avoided
Whose end is purposed by the mighty gods?
Julius Cæsar, Act ii, sc. 2, l. 26 [CÆSAR]

2554   What should be spoken here, where our fate,
Hid in an auger-hole, may rush, and seize us?
Macbeth, Act ii, sc. 3, l. 127 [DONALBIN]

2555   O Fate! take not away thy heavy hand.
Death is the fairest cover for her shame
That may be wished for.
Much Ado about Nothing, Act iv, sc. 1, l. 116 [LEONATO]

2556   Who can control his fate?
Othello, Act v, sc. 2, l. 265 [OTHELLO]

2557   For me, I am the mistress of my fate.
                              The Rape of Lucrece, l. 1069 [LUCRECE]

Father

2558   Ere I could
       Give him that parting kiss which I had set
       Betwixt two charming words, comes in my father,
       And like the tyrannous breathing of the north,
       Shakes all our buds from growing.
                              Cymbeline, Act i, sc. 3, l. 33 [IMOGEN]

2559   Do not for ever with thy vailed lids
       Seek for thy noble father in the dust.
                              Hamlet, Act i, sc. 2, l. 70 [QUEEN]

2560   A figure like your father,
       Arm'd at point exactly, cap-a-pe.
                              Hamlet, Act i, sc. 2, l. 199 [HORATIO]

2561   'Tis sweet and commendable in your nature, Hamlet,
       To give these mourning duties to your father :
       But, you must know, your father lost a father ;
       That father lost, lost his, and the survivor bound
       In filial obligation for some term
       To do obsequious sorrow : but to persever
       In obstinate condolement is a course
       Of impious stubbornness. . . . Fie ! 'tis a fault to heaven,
       A fault against the dead, a fault to nature,
       To reason most absurd ; whose common theme
       Is death of fathers.
                              Hamlet, Act i, sc. 2, l. 87 [KING]

2562   He took my father grossly, full of bread ;
       With all his crimes broad blown, as flush as May ;
       And how his audit stands who knows save heaven?
                              Hamlet, Act iii, sc. 3, l. 81 [HAMLET]

2563   QUEEN : Hamlet, thou hast thy father much offended.
       HAMLET : Mother, you have my father much offended.
       QUEEN : Come come, you answer with an idle tongue.
       HAMLET : Go, go, you question with a wicked tongue.
                              Hamlet, Act iii, sc. 4, l. 9 [QUEEN]

2564   Laertes, was your father dear to you?
       Or are you like the painting of a sorrow,
       A face without a heart?
                              Hamlet, Act iv, sc. 7, l. 108 [KING]

2565   I bid you be assured,
       I'll be your father and your brother too ;
       Let me but bear your love, I'll bear your cares.
                              II Henry IV, Act v, sc. 2, l. 57 [KING HENRY V]

2566   Now beshrew my father's ambition ! he was thinking of civil wars
       when he got me : therefore was I created with a stubborn outside,
       with an aspect of iron, that, when I come to woo ladies, I fright
       them.
                              Henry V, Act v, sc. 2, l. 242 [KING HENRY]

2567   I cannot joy, until I be resolved
       Where our right valiant father is become.
       I saw him in the battle range about ;
       And watch'd him how he singled Clifford forth.
       Methought he bore him in the thickest troop
       As doth a lion in a herd of neat ;

Or as a bear, encompass'd round with dogs,
Who having pinch'd a few and made them cry,
The rest stand all aloof and bark at him.
So fared our father with his enemies;
So fled his enemies my warlike father:
Methinks, 'tis prize enough to be his son.
III Henry VI, Act ii, sc. 1, 1. 9 [RICHARD]

2568   'Tis a happy thing
To be the father unto many sons.
III Henry VI, Act iii, sc. 2, 1. 104 [KING EDWARD]

2569   Fathers that wear rags
                    Do make their children blind;
                But fathers that bear bags
                    Shall see their children kind.
King Lear, Act ii, sc. 4, 1. 48 [FOOL]

2570   O heavens, this is my true-begotten father!
The Merchant of Venice, Act ii, sc. 2, 1. 36 [LAUNCELOT]

2571   It is a wise father that knows his own child.
The Merchant of Venice, Act ii, sc. 2, 1. 80 [LAUNCELOT]

2572   Be advised, fair maid:
To you your father should be as a god;
One that composed your beauties, yea, and one
To whom you are but as a form in wax
By him imprinted and within his power
To leave the figure or disfigure it.
A Midsummer Night's Dream, Act i, sc. 1, 1. 46 [THESEUS]

2573   Who would be a father!
Othello, Act i, sc. 1, 1. 165 [BRABANTIO]

2574   BOLINGBROKE: O loyal father of a treacherous son!
Thou sheer, immaculate and silver fountain,
From whence this stream through muddy passages
Hath held his current and defiled himself!
Thy overflow of good converts to bad,
And thy abundant goodness shall excuse
This deadly blot in thy digressing son.
YORK: So shall my virtue be his vice's bawd; . . .
Mine honour lives when his dishonour dies,
Or my shamed life in his dishonour lies:
Thou kill'st me in his life; giving him breath,
The traitor lives, the true man 's put to death.
Richard II, Act v, sc. 3, 1. 60 [BOLINGBROKE]

2575   VINCENTIO: Art thou his father?
PEDANT: Ay, sir; so his mother says, if I may believe her.
The Taming of the Shrew, Act v, sc. 1, 1. 33 [VINCENTIO]

2576   Full fathom five thy father lies;
                    Of his bones are coral made;
                Those are pearls that were his eyes:
                    Nothing of him that doth fade
                But doth suffer a sea-change
                Into something rich and strange.
                Sea-nymphs hourly ring his knell: . . .
                    Ding-dong, bell.
The Tempest, Act i, sc. 2, 1. 396 [ARIEL]

2577   Methinks a father
Is at the nuptial of his son a guest
That best becomes the table.
The Winter's Tale, Act iv, sc. 4, 1. 404 [POLIXENES]

Fatness

2578   He's fat, and scant of breath.
                        Hamlet, Act v, sc. 2, l. 299 [QUEEN]
2579   A gross fat man, as fat as butter.
                        I Henry IV, Act ii, sc. 4, l. 560 [CARRIER]
2580   O, give me the spare men, and spare me the great ones. . . . O,
         give me always a little lean, old, chapt, bald shot.
                        II Henry IV, Act iii, sc. 2, l. 288 [FALSTAFF]
2581   Let me have men about me that are fat;
         Sleek-headed men and such as sleep o' nights:
         Yond Cassius has a lean and hungry look;
         He thinks too much: such men are dangerous. . . .
         Such men as he be never at heart's ease
         Whiles they behold a greater than themselves,
         And therefore are they very dangerous.
                        Julius Cæsar, Act i, sc. 2, l. 192 [CÆSAR]

Fault

2582   Our rash faults
         Make trivial price of serious things we have,
         Not knowing them until we know their grave.
                        All's Well that Ends Well, Act v, sc. 3, l. 60 [KING]
2583   Taunt my faults
         With such full licence as both truth and malice
         Have power to utter.
                        Antony and Cleopatra, Act i, sc. 2, l. 111 [ANTONY]
2584   OCTAVIUS CÆSAR: He fishes, drinks, and wastes
         The lamps of night in revel; . . . you shall find there
         A man who is the abstract of all faults
         That all men follow.
         LEPIDUS: I must not think there are
         Evils enow to darken all his goodness:
         His faults in him seem as the spots of heaven,
         More fiery by night's blackness; hereditary,
         Rather than purchased; what he cannot change,
         Than what he chooses.
                        Antony and Cleopatra, Act i, sc. 4, l. 4 [OCTAVIUS CÆSAR]
2585   A rarer spirit never
         Did steer humanity: but you, gods, will give us
         Some faults to make us men.
                        Antony and Cleopatra, Act v, sc. 1, l. 32 [AGRIPPA]
2586   Tut, these are petty faults to faults unknown,
         Which time will bring to light.
                        II Henry VI, Act iii, sc. 1, l. 64 [BUCKINGHAM]
         The fault unknown is as a thought unacted.
                        The Rape of Lucrece, l. 527 [TARQUIN]
2587   The fault, dear Brutus, is not in our stars,
         But in ourselves, that we are underlings.
                        Julius Cæsar, Act i, sc. 2, l. 140 [CASSIUS]
2588   Oftentimes excusing of a fault
         Doth make the fault the worse by the excuse,
         As patches set upon a little breach
         Discredit more in hiding of the fault
         Than did the fault before it was so patch'd.
                        King John, Act iv, sc. 2, l. 30 [PEMBROKE]
2589   Who cover faults, at last shame them derides.
                        King Lear, Act i, sc. 1, l. 284 [CORDELIA]

2590   If she be made of white and red,
                       Her faults will ne'er be known,
                       For blushing cheeks by faults are bred
                       And fears by pale white shown.
                              Love's Labour's Lost, Act i, sc. 2, l. 104 [MOTH]

2591   Condemn the fault, and not the actor of it?
        Why, every fault's condemn'd ere it be done:
        Mine were the very cipher of a function,
        To fine the faults whose fine stands in record,
        And let go by the actor.
                              Measure for Measure, Act ii, sc. 2, l. 37 [ANGELO]

2592   That we were all, as some would seem to be,
        From our faults, or faults from seeming, free!
                              Measure for Measure, Act iii, sc. 2, l. 40 [DUKE]

2593   Shame to him whose cruel striking
        Kills for faults of his own liking.
                              Measure for Measure, Act iii, sc. 2, l. 281 [DUKE]
        Wilt thou whip thine own faults in other men?
                              Timon of Athens, Act v, sc. 1, l. 42 [TIMON]

2594   They say, best men are moulded out of faults;
        And, for the most, become much more the better
        For being a little bad.
                              Measure for Measure, Act v, sc. 1, l. 444 [MARIANA]

2595   His worst fault is that he is given to prayer; he is something
        peevish that way: but nobody but has his fault.
        The Merry Wives of Windsor, Act i, sc. 4, l. 13 [MISTRESS QUICKLY]
        Every man has his fault, and honesty is his.
                              Timon of Athens, Act iii, sc. 1, l. 29 [LUCULLUS]

2596   O, what a world of vile ill-favour'd faults
        Looks handsome in three hundred pounds a year!
                The Merry Wives of Windsor, Act iii, sc. 4, l. 32 [ANNE PAGE]
        Faults that are rich are fair.
                              Timon of Athens, Act i, sc. 2, l. 13 [TIMON]

2597   Men's faults do seldom to themselves appear;
        Their own transgressions partially they smother.
                              The Rape of Lucrece, l. 633 [LUCRECE]

2598   All men make faults.
                                                       Sonnet xxxv, l. 5

2599   Some say thy fault is youth, some wantonness;
        Some say thy grace is youth and gentle sport;
        Both grace and faults are loved of more and less;
        Thou makest faults graces that to thee resort.
                                                       Sonnet xcvi, l. 1

2600   There's something in me that reproves my fault;
        But such a headstrong potent fault it is,
        That it but mocks reproof.
                              Twelfth Night, Act iii, sc. 4, l. 223 [OLIVIA]

Fear

2601   Distill'd Almost to jelly with the act of fear.
                              Hamlet, Act i, sc. 2, l. 204 [HORATIO]

2602   There is not such a word
        Spoke of in Scotland as this term of fear.
                              I Henry IV, Act iv, sc. 1, l. 84 [DOUGLAS]

2603   Feel, masters, how I shake; . . . an 'twere an aspen leaf.
                              II Henry IV, Act ii, sc. 4, l. 115 [HOSTESS]

2604 Of all base passions, fear is most accursed.
I Henry VI, Act v, sc. 2, l. 18 [PUCELLE]

2605 Let pale-faced fear keep with the mean-born man,
And find no harbour in a royal heart.
II Henry VI, Act iii, sc. 1, l. 335 [YORK]

2606 Gelidus timor occupat artus, it is thee I fear.
II Henry VI, Act iv, sc. 1, l. 117 [SUFFOLK]
("Chill fear seizes my limbs," a variation of VERGIL, Æneid,
bk. vii, l. 446, Subitus tremor occupat artus.)

2607 [They are] beside themselves with fear.
Julius Cæsar, Act iii, sc. 1, l. 180 [BRUTUS]

2608   I am sick and capable of fears,
Oppress'd with wrongs and therefore full of fears,
A widow, husbandless, subject to fears,
A woman, naturally born to fears.
King John, Act iii, sc. 1, l. 12 [CONSTANCE]

2609   Present fears
Are less than horrible imaginings.
Macbeth, Act i, sc. 3, l. 137 [MACBETH]

2610 I may tell pale-hearted fear it lies,
And sleep in spite of thunder.
Macbeth, Act iv, sc. 1, l. 85 [MACBETH]

2611   When our actions do not,
Our fears do make us traitors.
Macbeth, Act iv, sc. 2, l. 3 [LADY MACDUFF]

2612 Go, prick thy face, and over-red thy fear,
Thou lily-liver'd boy. . . . Those linen cheeks of thine
Are counsellors to fear.
Macbeth, Act v, sc. 3, l. 14 [MACBETH]

2613 I have almost forgot the taste of fears:
The time has been, my senses would have cool'd
To hear a night-shriek; and my fell of hair
Would at a dismal treatise rouse and stir
As life were in 't: I have supp'd full with horrors;
Direness, familiar to my slaughterous thoughts,
Cannot once start me.
Macbeth, Act v, sc. 5, l. 9 [MACBETH]

2614 Extreme fear can neither fight nor fly,
But coward-like with trembling terror die.
The Rape of Lucrece, l. 230 [TARQUIN]

2615 To fear the foe, since fear oppresseth strength,
Gives in your weakness strength unto your foe,
And so your follies fight against yourself.
Fear, and be slain; no worse can come to fight:
And fight and die is death destroying death;
Where fearing dying pays death servile breath.
Richard II, Act iii, sc. 2, l. 180 [CARLISLE]

2616 I am surprised with an uncouth fear;
A chilling sweat o'er-runs my trembling joints
Titus Andronicus, Act ii, sc. 3, l. 211 [QUINTUS]

2617 TROILUS: Fears make devils of cherubins; they never see truly.
CRESSIDA: Blind fear, that seeing reason leads, finds safer footing
than blind reason stumbling without fear: to fear the worst oft
cures the worst.
Troilus and Cressida, Act iii, sc. 2, l. 73 [TROILUS]

2618 Fear doth teach [the heart] divination.
Venus and Adonis, l. 670 [VENUS]

Feast

2619   To the latter end of a fray and the beginning of a feast
Fits a dull fighter and a keen guest.
I Henry IV, Act iv, sc. 2, l. 86 [FALSTAFF]
(An old proverb derived from the Greek.)

2620   This night I hold an old accustom'd feast,
Whereto I have invited many a guest,
Such as I love; and you, among the store,
One more, most welcome, makes my number more.
At my poor house look to behold this night
Earth-treading stars that make dark heaven light.
Romeo and Juliet, Act i, sc. 2, l. 20 [CAPULET]

2621   We have a trifling foolish banquet towards.
Romeo and Juliet, Act i, sc. 5, l. 124 [CAPULET]

2622   Therefore are feasts so solemn and so rare,
Since, seldom coming, in the long year set,
Like stones of worth they thinly placed are,
Or captain jewels in the carcanet.
Sonnet lii, l. 6

2623   Feasts are too proud to give thanks to the gods.
Timon of Athens, Act i, sc. 2, l. 62 [APEMANTUS]

Feather

2624   You boggle shrewdly, every feather starts you.
All's Well that Ends Well, Act v, sc. 3, l. 232 [BERTRAM]

2625   The best feather of our wing.
Cymbeline, Act i, sc. 6, l. 186 [IACHIMO]

2626   With seasonable swiftness add
More feathers to our wings.
Henry V, Act i, sc. 2, l. 306 [KING HENRY]

2627   There's not a piece of feather in our host—
Good argument, I hope, we will not fly.
Henry V, Act iv, sc. 3, l. 112 [KING HENRY]

2628   Seems he a dove? his feathers are but borrowed,
For he's disposed as the hateful raven.
II Henry VI, Act iii, sc. 1, l. 75 [QUEEN]

2629   Look, as I blow this feather from my face,
And as the air blows it to me again, . . .
Commanded always by the greater gust;
Such is the lightness of you common men.
III Henry VI, Act iii, sc. 1, l. 84 [KING HENRY]

2630   What plume of feathers is he that indited this letter?
What vane? what weathercock? did you ever hear better?
Love's Labour's Lost, Act iv, sc. 1, l. 96 [PRINCESS]

2631   You weigh equally; a feather will turn the scale.
Measure for Measure, Act iv, sc. 2, l. 31 [PROVOST]

2632   I do fear,
When every feather sticks in his own wing,
Lord Timon will be left a naked gull.
Timon of Athens, Act ii, sc. 1, l. 29 [SENATOR]

2633   I am a feather for each wind that blows.
The Winter's Tale Act ii, sc. 3, l. 154 [LEONTES]

Fellow

2634   All the learned and authentic fellows.
All's Well that Ends Well, Act ii, sc. 3, l. 14 [LAFEU]

2635   A snipt-taffeta fellow, whose villanous saffron would have made
      all the unbaked and doughy youth of a nation in his colour.
All's Well that Ends Well, Act iv, sc. 5, l. 2 [LAFEU]

2636   A fellow of no mark nor likelihood.
I Henry IV, Act iii, sc. 2, l. 46 [KING HENRY]

2637   BARDOLPH: Well said; thou 'rt a good fellow.
      FEEBLE: Faith, I'll bear no base mind.
II Henry IV, Act iii, sc. 2, l. 256 [BARDOLPH]

2638   If he be not fellow with the best king, thou shalt find the best king
      of good fellows.
Henry V, Act v, sc. 2, l. 261 [KING HENRY]

2639   A barren-spirited fellow; one that feeds
      On abjects, orts and imitations,
      Which, out of use and staled by other men,
      Begin his fashion.
Julius Cæsar, Act iv, sc. 1, l. 36 [ANTONY]

2640   A very superficial, ignorant, unweighing fellow.
Measure for Measure, Act iii, sc. 2, l. 147 [LUCIO]

2641   A paltry fellow, . . .
      A milk-sop, one that never in his life
      Felt so much cold as over shoes in snow.
Richard III, Act v, sc. 3, l. 323 [KING RICHARD]

2642   There be good fellows in the world, an a man could light on them.
The Taming of the Shrew, Act i, sc. 1, l. 132 [HORTENSIO]

2643   Thou 'rt a tall fellow: hold thee that to drink.
The Taming of the Shrew, Act iv, sc. 4, l. 17 [TRANIO]

2644   Thou art a tall fellow of thy hands.
The Winter's Tale, Act v, sc. 2, l. 177 [CLOWN]

Fellowship

2645   This it is to have a name in great men's fellowship: I had as
      lief have a reed that will do me no service as a partisan I could
      not heave.
Antony and Cleopatra, Act ii, sc. 7, l. 12 [SERVANT]

2646   Out upon such half-faced fellowship!
I Henry IV, Act i, sc. 3, l. 208 [HOTSPUR]

2647   Gallants, lads, boys, hearts of gold, all the titles of good-fellow-
      ship come to you! What, shall we be merry?
I Henry IV, Act ii, sc. 4, l. 309 [FALSTAFF]

2648   Tell me true,
      Even in the soul of sound good-fellowship.
Troilus and Cressida, Act iv, sc. 1, l. 51 [PARIS]

Fetters

2649   These strong Egyptian fetters I must break,
      Or lose myself in dotage.
Antony and Cleopatra, Act i, sc. 2, l. 120 [ANTONY]

2650   We will fetters put upon this fear,
      Which now goes too free-footed.
Hamlet, Act iii, sc. 3, l. 25 [KING]

Fever

2651   What 's fever but a fit of madness?
The Comedy of Errors, Act v, sc. 1, l. 76 [ABBESS]

2652   Think'st thou the fiery fever will go out
      With titles blown from adulation?
Henry V, Act iv, sc. 1, l. 270 [KING HENRY]

2653   This fever, that hath troubled me so long,
       Lies heavy on me; O, my heart is sick! . . .
       Ay me! this tyrant fever burns me up.
                    King John, Act v, sc. 3, l. 3 [KING JOHN]

2654   I would forget her; but a fever she
       Reigns in my blood, and will remember'd be.
              Love's Labour's Lost, Act iv, sc. 3, l. 95 [DUMAIN]

Fiction

2655   For thy fiction,
       Why, thy verse swells with stuff so fine and smooth
       That thou art even natural in thine art.
                  Timon of Athens, Act v, sc. 1, l. 86 [TIMON]

2656   If this were played upon a stage now, I should condemn it as an
       improbable fiction.
              Twelfth Night, Act iii, sc. 4, l. 140 [FABIAN]

Fidelity

2657   LUCIUS: Thy name?
       IMOGEN: Fidele, sir.
       LUCIUS: Thou dost approve thyself the very same:
       Thy name well fits thy faith, thy faith thy name.
                  Cymbeline, Act iv, sc. 2, l. 379 [LUCIUS]

2658   Like a bold champion, I assume the lists,
       Nor ask advice of any other thought
       But faithfulness and courage.
                  Pericles, Act i, sc. 1, l. 61 [PERICLES]

2659   Day serves not light more faithful than I'll be.
                  Pericles, Act i, sc. 2, l. 110 [HELICANUS]

Fiend

2660   Take heed o'the foul fiend; obey thy parents; keep thy word
       justly; swear not; commit not with man's sworn spouse; set not
       thy sweet heart on proud array. . . . Let not the creaking of
       shoes nor the rustling of silks betray thy poor heart to woman:
       keep thy foot out of brothels, thy hand out of plackets, thy pen
       from lenders' books, and defy the foul fiend.
                  King Lear, Act iii, sc. 4, l. 81 [EDGAR]

2661   This is the foul fiend Flibbertigibbet: he begins at curfew, and
       walks till the first cock; he gives the web and the pin, squints the
       eye, and makes the harelip; mildews the white wheat, and hurts
       the poor creature of earth.
                  King Lear, Act iii, sc. 4, l. 120 [EDGAR]

2662   Be these juggling fiends no more believed,
       That palter with us in a double sense;
       That keep the word of promise to our ear,
       And break it to our hope.
                  Macbeth, Act v, sc. 8, l. 19 [MACBETH]

2663   Fare thee well:
       A fiend like thee might bear my soul to hell.
              Twelfth Night, Act iii, sc. 4, l. 236 [OLIVIA]

2664   Out, hyperbolical fiend! how vexest thou this man!
              Twelfth Night, Act iv, sc. 2, l. 28 [CLOWN]

Fife

2665   Hear you me, Jessica:
       Lock up my doors; and when you hear the drum
       And the vile squealing of the wry-neck'd fife.
       Clamber not you up to the casements then,

Nor thrust your head into the public street
To gaze on Christian fools with varnish'd faces.
The Merchant of Venice, Act ii, sc. 5, 1. 29 [SHYLOCK]

2666   Farewell . . . The ear-piercing fife.
Othello, Act iii, sc. 3, 1. 352 [OTHELLO]

Fig

2667   Figo for thy friendship! . . . The fig of Spain!
Henry V, Act iii, sc. 6, 1. 60 [PISTOL]
("The fig of Spain," a contemptuous gesture made by thrusting
the thumb between two of the closed fingers.)

2668   A fig for Peter!
II Henry VI, Act ii, sc. 3, 1. 68 [HORNER]

Fighting

2669   I'll fight maliciously: . . . I'll set my teeth
And send to darkness all that stop me. . . .
There's sap in 't yet. The next time I do fight,
I'll make death love me; for I will contend
Even with his pestilent scythe.
Antony and Cleopatra, Act iii, sc. 13, 1. 177 [ANTONY]

2670   I would they 'ld fight i' the fire or i' the air;
We 'ld fight there too.
Antony and Cleopatra, Act iv, sc. 10, 1. 3 [ANTONY]

2671   Now put your shields before your hearts, and fight
With hearts more proof than shields.
Coriolanus, Act i, sc. 4, 1. 24 [CORIOLANUS]

2672   A' shall not tread on me;
I'll run away till I am bigger, but then I'll fight.
Coriolanus, Act v, sc. 3, 1. 127 [SON OF CORIOLANUS]

2673   Why, I will fight with him upon this theme
Until my eyelids will no longer wag.
Hamlet, Act v, sc. 1, 1. 289 [HAMLET]

2674   FALSTAFF: If I fought not with fifty of them, I am a bunch of
radish. . . .
PRINCE: Pray God you have not murdered some of them.
FALSTAFF: Nay, that's past praying for: I have peppered two of
them; two I am sure I have paid, two rogues in buckram suits.
I Henry IV, Act ii, sc. 4, 1. 205 [FALSTAFF]

2675   We . . . fought a long hour by Shrewsbury clock.
I Henry IV, Act v, sc. 4, 1. 153 [FALSTAFF]

2676   PUCELLE: Fight till the last gasp; I will be your guard.
CHARLES: What she says I'll confirm. We'll fight it out.
I Henry VI, Act i, sc. 2, 1. 127 [PUCELLE]
Will ye, like soldiers, come and fight it out?
I Henry VI, Act iii, sc. 2, 1. 66 [TALBOT]
Let's fight it out and not stand cavilling thus.
III Henry VI, Act i, sc. 1, 1. 117 [MONTAGUE]

2677   As gentle and as jocund as to jest
Go I to fight.
Richard II, Act i, sc. 3, 1. 95 [MOWBRAY]

2678   Now they are clapper-clawing one another.
Troilus and Cressida, Act v, sc. 4, 1. 1 [THERSITES]

Fighting: Duelling

2679   [We have come] to see thee fight, to see thee foin, to see thee
traverse; . . . to see thee pass thy punto, thy stock, thy reverse,
thy distance, thy montant.
The Merry Wives of Windsor, Act ii, sc. 3, 1. 24 [HOST]

2680 LEONATO: Villainy . . . I'll prove it on his body, if he dare,
Despite his nice fence and his active practice. . . .
ANTONIO: Sir boy, I'll whip you from your foining fence.
Much Ado about Nothing, Act v, sc. 1, l. 75 [LEONATO]

2681 He fights as you sing prick-song, keeps time, distance, and proportion; rests me his minim rest, one, two, and the third in your
bosom: the very butcher of a silk button, a duellist, a duellist;
a gentleman of the very first house, of the first and second cause:
ah, the immortal passado! the punto reverso! the hai!
Romeo and Juliet, Act ii, sc. 4, l. 22 [MERCUTIO]

Finger

2682 In faith, I'll break thy little finger, Harry,
An if thou wilt not tell me all things true.
I Henry IV, Act ii, sc. 3, l. 90 [LADY PERCY]

2683 I have him . . . between my finger and my thumb.
II Henry IV, Act iv, sc. 3, l. 142 [FALSTAFF]

2684 No man's pie is freed From his ambitious finger.
Henry VIII, Act i, sc. 1, l. 52 [BUCKINGHAM]

2685 Good man, sit down. Now let me see the proudest
He, that dares most, but wag a finger at thee:
By all that 's holy, he had better starve
Than but once think this place becomes thee not.
Henry VIII, Act v, sc. 3, l. 130 [KING HENRY]

2686 I'll ne'er put my finger in the fire, and need not.
The Merry Wives of Windsor, Act i, sc. 4, l. 90 [MISTRESS
QUICKLY]

2687 Yet again your fingers to your lips? would they were clyster-
pipes for your sake!
Othello, Act ii, sc. 1, l. 177 [IAGO]
Peace, Trojan; lay thy finger on thy lips!
Troilus and Cressida, Act i, sc. 3, l. 240 [ÆNEAS]

2688 Men's natures wrangle with inferior things,
Though great ones are their object. 'Tis even so;
For let our finger ache, and it indues
Our other healthful members even to that sense
Of pain.
Othello, Act iii, sc. 4, l. 144 [DESDEMONA]

2689 I love and honour him,
But must not break my back to heal his finger.
Timon of Athens, Act ii, sc. 1, l. 23 [SENATOR]

Fire

2690 One fire drives out one fire; one nail, one nail;
Rights by rights falter, strengths by strengths do fail.
Coriolanus, Act iv, sc. 7, l. 54 [AUFIDIUS]
As fire drives out fire, so pity pity.
Julius Cæsar, Act iii, sc. 1, l. 171 [BRUTUS]

2691 What, frighted with false fire!
Hamlet, Act iii, sc. 2, l. 277 [HAMLET]

2692 A little fire is quickly trodden out,
Which, being suffer'd, rivers cannot quench.
III Henry VI, Act iv, sc. 8, l. 7 [CLARENCE]

2693 I need not add more fuel to your fire,
For well I wot ye blaze to burn them out.
III Henry VI, Act v, sc. 4, l. 70 [KING EDWARD]

2694   Know you not,
That fire that mounts the liquor till 't run o'er,
In seeming to augment it wastes it?
> *Henry VIII,* Act i, sc. 1, l. 143 [NORFOLK]

2695   Those that with haste will make a mighty fire
Begin it with weak straws.
> *Julius Cæsar,* Act i, sc. 3, l. 107 [CASSIUS]

2696   A little fire in a wild field were like an old lecher's heart; a small
spark, all the rest on 's body cold.
> *King Lear,* Act iii, sc. 4, l. 116 [FOOL]

2697   Fire and brimstone!
> *Othello,* Act iv, sc. 1, l. 245 [OTHELLO]; *Twelfth Night,*
> Act ii, sc. 5, l. 55 [SIR TOBY]

2698   Small lights are soon blown out, huge fires abide,
And with the wind in greater fury fret.
> *The Rape of Lucrece,* l. 647 [TARQUIN]

2699   Violent fires soon burn out themselves.
> *Richard II,* Act ii, sc. 1, l. 34 [GAUNT]
One fire burns out another's burning.
> *Romeo and Juliet,* Act i, sc. 2, l. 46 [BENVOLIO]

2700   Methinks King Richard and myself should meet
With no less terror than the elements
Of fire and water, when their slumbering shock
At meeting tears the cloudy cheeks of heaven.
Be he the fire, I'll be the yielding water:
The rage be his, whilst on earth I rain
My waters; on the earth, and not on him.
> *Richard II,* Act iii, sc. 3, l. 54 [BOLINGBROKE]

2701   Where two raging fires meet together
They do consume the thing that feeds their fury:
Though little fires grow great with little wind,
Yet extreme gusts will blow out fire and all.
> *The Taming of the Shrew,* Act ii, sc. 1, l. 133 [PETRUCHIO]

2702   The fire i' the flint
Shows not till it be struck.
> *Timon of Athens,* Act i, sc. 1, l. 22 [POET]

2703   JULIA: His little speaking shows his love but small.
LUCETTA: Fire that 's closest kept burns most of all.
> *The Two Gentlemen of Verona,* Act i, sc. 2, l. 29 [JULIA]

2704   Thus have I shunn'd the fire for fear of burning,
And drench'd me in the sea, where I am drown'd.
> *The Two Gentlemen of Verona,* Act i, sc. 3, l. 78 [PROTEAS]

Fish

2705   'Twas merry when
You wager'd on your angling; when your diver
Did hang a salt-fish on his hook, which he
With fervency drew up.
> *Antony and Cleopatra,* Act ii, sc. 5, l. 15 [CHARMIAN]

2706   The imperious seas breed monsters, for the dish
Poor tributory rivers as sweet fish.
> *Cymbeline,* Act iv, sc. 2, l. 35 [IMOGEN]

2707   POLONIUS: Do you know me, my lord?
HAMLET: Excellent well; you are a fishmonger.
> *Hamlet,* Act ii, sc. 2, l. 173 [POLONIUS]

2708   Bait the hook well; this fish will bite.
> *Much Ado about Nothing,* Act ii, sc. 3, l. 113 [CLAUDIO]

2709 The pleasant'st angling is to see the fish
   Cut with her golden oars the silver stream,
   And greedily devour the treacherous bait.
         Much Ado about Nothing, Act iii, sc. 1, l. 26 [URSULA]

2710 THIRD FISHERMAN: Master, I marvel how the fishes live in
   the sea.
   FIRST FISHERMAN: Why, as men do a-land; the great ones eat
   up the little ones.
         Pericles, Act ii, sc. 1, l. 30 [FIRST FISHERMAN]

2711 Here's a fish hangs in the net, like a poor man's right in the law;
   'twill hardly come out.
         Pericles, Act ii, sc. 1, l. 122 [FISHERMAN]

2712 The fish lives in the sea, and 'tis much pride
   For fair without the fair within to hide.
         Romeo and Juliet, Act i, sc. 3, l. 89 [LADY CAPULET]

Flat

2713 WORCESTER: Those prisoners you shall keep.
   HOTSPUR: Nay, I will; that's flat.
         I Henry IV, Act i, sc. 3, l. 218 [WORCESTER]

2714 I'll not march through Coventry with them, that's flat.
         I Henry IV, Act iv, sc. 2, l. 43 [FALSTAFF]

2715 The boy hath sold him . . . a goose, that's flat.
         Love's Labour's Lost, Act iii, sc. 1, l. 102 [COSTARD]

Flattery

2716 That was laid on with a trowel.
         As You Like It, Act i, sc. 2, l. 112 [CELIA]

2717 'Tis holy sport to be a little vain,
   When the sweet breath of flattery conquers strife.
         The Comedy of Errors, Act iii, sc. 2, l. 27 [LUCIANA]

2718 He water'd his new plants with dews of flattery.
         Coriolanus, Act v, sc. 6, l. 23 [AUFIDIUS]

2719   Nay, do not think I flatter;
   For what advancement may I hope from thee
   That no revenue hast but thy good spirits,
   To feed and clothe thee? Why should the poor be flatter'd?
   No, let the candied tongue lick absurd pomp,
   And crook the pregnant hinges of the knee
   Where thrift may follow fawning.
         Hamlet, Act iii, sc. 2, l. 61 [HAMLET]

2720 By God, I cannot flatter; I do defy
   The tongues of soothers; but a braver place
   In my heart's love hath no man than yourself.
         I Henry IV, Act iv, sc. 1, l. 6 [HOTSPUR]

2721 'Tis sin to flatter.
         III Henry VI, Act v, sc. 6, l. 3 [KING HENRY]
   Flattery is the bellows blows up sin.
         Pericles, Act i, sc. 2, l. 39 [HELICANUS]

2722   The words I utter
   Let none think flattery, for they'll find 'em truth.
         Henry VIII, Act v, sc. 5, l. 16 [CRANMER]

2723   He loves to hear
   That unicorns may be betray'd with trees,
   And bears with glasses, elephants with holes,
   Lions with toils and men with flatterers.

But when I tell him he hates flatterers,
He says he does, being then most flattered.
>   *Julius Cæsar,* Act ii, sc. 1, l. 203 [DECIUS]

2724   They flattered me like a dog: and told me I had white hairs in my
beard ere the black ones were there.
>   *King Lear,* Act iv, sc. 6, l. 97 [LEAR]

2725   No visor doth become black villany
So well as soft and tender flattery.
>   *Pericles,* Act iv, sc. 4, l. 44 [GOWER]

2726   Because I cannot flatter and speak fair,
Smile in men's faces, smooth, deceive, and cog,
Duck with French nods and apish courtesy,
I must be held a rancorous enemy.
Cannot a plain man live and think no harm,
But thus his simple truth must be abused
By silken, sly, insinuating Jacks?
>   *Richard III,* Act i, sc. 3, l. 47 [GLOUCESTER]

2727   Drink up the monarch's plague, this flattery.
>   *Sonnet* cxiv, l. 2

2728   He that loves to be flattered is worthy of the flatterer.
>   *Timon of Athens,* Act i, sc. 1, l. 232 [APEMANTUS]

2729   O, that men's ears should be
To counsel deaf, but not to flattery!
>   *Timon of Athens,* Act i, sc. 2, l. 255 [APEMANTUS]

2730   Who dares,
In purity of manhood stand upright,
And say 'This man's a flatterer'?
>   *Timon of Athens,* Act iv, sc. 3, l. 13 [TIMON]

2731   Take no repulse, whatever she doth say;
For 'get you gone,' she doth not mean 'away!'
Flatter and praise, commend, extol their graces;
Though ne'er so black, say they have angels' faces.
>   *The Two Gentlemen of Verona,* Act iii, sc. 1, l. 100 [VALENTINE]

Flea

2732   A' saw a flea stick upon Bardolph's nose, and a' said it was a black
soul burning in hell-fire.
>   *Henry V,* Act ii, sc. 3, l. 42 [BOY]

2733   That's a valiant flea that dare eat his breakfast on the lip of a
lion.
>   *Henry V,* Act iii, sc. 7, l. 156 [ORLEANS]

Flesh

2734   On the Alps
It is reported thou didst eat strange flesh,
Which some did die to look on.
>   *Antony and Cleopatra,* Act i, sc. 4, l. 66 [OCTAVIUS CÆSAR]

2735   If you buy ladies' flesh at a million a dram, you cannot preserve it
from tainting.
>   *Cymbeline,* Act i, sc. 4, l. 146 [IACHIMO]

2736   O, that this too too solid flesh would melt,
Thaw and resolve itself into a dew!
>   *Hamlet,* Act i, sc. 2, l. 129 [HAMLET]

2737   Lay her i' the earth:
And from her fair and unpolluted flesh
May violets spring!
>   *Hamlet.* Act v, sc. 1, l. 261 [LAERTES]

2738   I have more flesh than another man, and therefore more frailty.
                        I Henry IV, Act iii, sc. 3, l. 87 [FALSTAFF]

2739   God knows thou art a collop of my flesh;
        And for thy sake have I shed many a tear. . . .
        Kneel down and take my blessing, good my girl.
        Wilt thou not stoop? Now cursed be the time
        Of thy nativity! I would the milk
        Thy mother gave thee when thou suck'dst her breast,
        Had been a little ratsbane for thy sake!
                        I Henry VI, Act v, sc. 4, l. 18 [SHEPHERD]

2740   Such is the simplicity of man to hearken after the flesh.
                        Love's Labour's Lost, Act i, sc. 1, l. 220 [COSTARD]

2741   You'll ask me why I rather choose to have
        A weight of carrion flesh than to receive
        Three thousand ducats: I'll not answer that:
        But, say, it is my humour: is it answer'd?
        What if my house be troubled with a rat
        And I be pleased to give ten thousand ducats
        To have it baned? What, are you answer'd yet?
                        The Merchant of Venice, Act iv, sc. 1, l. 40 [SHYLOCK]

2742   Why, this bond is forfeit;
        And lawfully by this the Jew may claim
        A pound of flesh, to be by him cut off
        Nearest the merchant's heart.
                        The Merchant of Venice, Act iv, sc. 1, l. 230 [PORTIA]

2743   This bond doth give thee here no jot of blood;
        The words expressly are 'a pound of flesh':
        Take then thy bond, take thou thy pound of flesh;
        But, in the cutting it, if thou dost shed
        One drop of Christian blood, thy lands and goods
        Are, by the laws of Venice, confiscate
        Unto the state of Venice.
                        The Merchant of Venice, Act iv, sc. 1, l. 306 [PORTIA]

2744   As pretty piece of flesh as any in Messina.
                        Much Ado about Nothing, Act iv, sc. 2, l. 84 [DOGBERRY]

2745   SAMPSON : 'Tis known I am a pretty piece of flesh.
        GREGORY : 'Tis well thou art not fish.
                        Romeo and Juliet, Act i, sc. 1, l. 34 [SAMPSON]
        (A reference to the proverb, "Neither fish, flesh, nor good red
        herring.")

2746   BENVOLIO : Here comes Romeo.
        MERCUTIO : Without his roe, like a dried herring : O flesh, flesh,
        how art thou fishified!
                        Romeo and Juliet, Act ii, sc. 4, l. 38 [BENVOLIO]

2747   My flesh is soft and plump, my marrow burning.
                        Venus and Adonis, l. 142 [VENUS]

Flesh and Blood

2748   I have been, madam, a wicked creature, as you and all flesh and
        blood are.
                        All's Well that Ends Well, Act i, sc. 3, l. 38 [CLOWN]

2749   Our flesh and blood is grown so vile, my lord,
        That it doth hate what gets it.
                        King Lear, Act iii, sc. 4, l. 150 [GLOUCESTER]

2750   As true we are as flesh and blood can be.
                        Love's Labour's Lost, Act iv, sc. 3, l. 215 [BIRON]

2751   I would see his own person in flesh and blood.
                            Love's Labour's Lost, Act i, sc. 1, l. 185 [DULL]
2752   SHYLOCK: My daughter is my flesh and blood.
        SALARINO: There is more difference between thy flesh and hers
        than between jet and ivory.
                    The Merchant of Venice, Act iii, sc. 1, l. 40 [SHYLOCK]
2753   Let no man but I
        Do execution on my flesh and blood.
                            Titus Andronicus, Act iv, sc. 2, l. 83 [AARON]
2754   She's a changeling, and none of your flesh and blood. . . . She
        being none of your flesh and blood, your flesh and blood has not
        offended the king; and so your flesh and blood is not to be pun-
        ished by him.
                            The Winter's Tale, Act iv, sc. 4, l. 703 [CLOWN]

Flood

2755   Great floods have flown From simple sources.
                    All's Well that Ends Well, Act ii, sc. 1, l. 142 [HELENA]
2756   No flood by raining slaketh.
                            The Rape of Lucrece, l. 1677 [LUCRECE]
2757   [I] pass'd, methought, the melancholy flood,
        With that grim ferryman which poets write of,
        Unto the kingdom of perpetual night.
                            Richard III, Act i, sc. 4, l. 46 [CLARENCE]

Flowers

2758   Thou shalt not lack
        The flower that's like thy face, pale primrose, nor
        The azured harebell, like thy veins, no, nor
        The leaf of eglantine, whom not to slander
        Out-sweeten'd not thy breath.
                            Cymbeline, Act iv, sc. 2, l. 220 [GUIDERIUS]
2759   These flowers are like the pleasures of the world.
                            Cymbeline, Act iv, sc. 2, l. 296 [IMOGEN]
2760   ARMADO: I am that flower,—
        DUMAIN: That mint.
        LONGAVILLE: That columbine.
                    Love's Labour's Lost, Act v, sc. 2, l. 661 [ARMADO]
2761   I know a bank where the wild thyme blows,
        Where oxlips and the nodding violet grows,
        Quite over-canopied with lusty woodbine,
        With sweet musk-roses and with eglantine.
                    A Midsummer Night's Dream, Act ii, sc. 1, l. 249 [OBERON]
2762   I will rob Tellus of her weed
        To strew thy green with flowers: the yellows, blues,
        The purple violets, and marigolds,
        Shall as a carpet hang upon thy grave,
        While summer-days do last.
                            Pericles, Act iv, sc. 1, l. 13 [MARINA]
2763   No man inveigh against the wither'd flower,
        But chide rough winter that the flower hath kill'd:
        Not that devour'd, but that which doth devour,
        Is worthy blame.
                            The Rape of Lucrece, l. 1254
2764   Flowers distill'd, though they with winter meet,
        Leese but their show; their substance still lives sweet.
                            Sonnet v, l. 13

2765   The summer's flower is to the summer sweet,
Though to itself it only live and die,
But if that flower with base infection meet,
The basest weed outbraves his dignity:
For sweetest things turn sourest by their deeds;
Lilies that fester small far worse than weeds.
Sonnet xciv, l. 9

2766   Fair flowers that are not gather'd in their prime
Rot and consume themselves in little time.
Venus and Adonis, l. 131 [VENUS]

2767   Reverend sirs,
For you there 's rosemary and rue; these keep
Seeming and savour all the winter long: . . .
The year growing ancient, . . . the fairest flowers o' the season
Are our carnations and streak'd gillyvors,
Which some call nature's bastards. . . . Here 's flowers for you:
Hot lavender, mints, savory, marjoram:
The marigold, that goes to bed wi' the sun
And with him rises weeping: these are flowers
Of middle summer, and I think they are given
To men of middle age. . . .
I would I had some flowers o' the spring that might
Become your time of day; and yours, and yours,
That wear upon your virgin branches yet
Your maidenheads growing: . . . violets dim,
But sweeter than the lids of Juno's eyes
Or Cytherea's breath; pale primroses,
That die unmarried; . . . bold oxlips and
The crown imperial; lilies of all kinds
The flower-de-luce being one.
The Winter's Tale, Act iv, sc. 4, l. 73 [PERDITA]

Fly

2768   This was but as a fly by an eagle.
Antony and Cleopatra, Act ii, sc. 2, l. 186 [ENOBARBUS]

2769   As flies to wanton boys, are we to the gods,
They kill us for their sport.
King Lear, Act iv, sc. 1, l. 38 [GLOUCESTER]

2770   You are like one that superstitiously
Doth swear to the gods that winter kills the flies.
Pericles, Act iv, sc. 3, l. 50 [DIONYZA]

2771   TITUS: What dost thou strike at, Marcus, with thy knife?
MARCUS: At that that I have kill'd, my lord; a fly.
TITUS: Out on thee, murderer! thou kill'st my heart. . . .
MARCUS: Alas, my lord, I have but kill'd a fly.
TITUS: But how if that fly had a father and mother?
How would he hang his slender gilded wings,
And buzz lamenting doings in the air!
Poor harmless fly,
That, with his pretty buzzing melody,
Came here to make us merry! and thou hast kill'd him.
MARCUS: Pardon me, sir; it was a black ill-favour'd fly.
Like to the empress' Moor; therefore I kill'd him.
Titus Andronicus, Act iii, sc. 2, l. 53 [TITUS]

Follower

2772   Thou canst not, in the course of gratitude, but be a diligent follower of mine.
Cymbeline, Act iii, sc. 5, l. 121 [CLOTEN]

2773   He will never follow any thing
That other men begin.
                    Julius Cæsar, Act ii, sc. 1, l. 151 [BRUTUS]

2774   You were wont to be a follower, but now you are a leader.
          The Merry Wives of Windsor, Act iii, sc. 2, l. 2 [MRS. PAGE]

Folly

2775   He uses his folly like a stalking-horse and under the presentation
of that he shoots his wit.
                    As You Like It, Act v, sc. 4, 111 [DUKE]

2776   We call a nettle but a nettle and
The faults of fools but folly.
                    Coriolanus, Act ii, sc. 1, l. 207 [MENENIUS]

2777   O, too much folly is it, well I wot,
To hazard all our lives in one small boat.
                    I Henry VI, Act iv, sc. 6, l. 32 [TALBOT]

2778   Beat at this gate that let thy folly in,
And thy dear judgement out!
                    King Lear, Act i, sc. 4, l. 293 [LEAR]

2779   As you have one eye upon my follies, as you hear them unfolded,
turn another into the register of your own.
          The Merry Wives of Windsor, Act ii, sc. 2, l. 192 [FORD]

2780   Why should . . . tyrant folly lurk in gentle breasts?
                    The Rape of Lucrece, l. 851 [LUCRECE]

2781   CLOWN: Beshrew me, the knight's in admirable fooling. . . .
SIR ANDREW: He does it with a better grace, but I do't more
natural.
                    Twelfth Night, Act ii, sc. 3, 85 [CLOWN]

2782   Foolery, sir, does walk about the orb like the sun, it shines every
where.
                    Twelfth Night, Act iii, sc. 1, l. 44 [CLOWN]

Food

2783   Fair ladies, you drop manna in the way
Of starved people.
                    The Merchant of Venice, Act v, sc. 1, l. 294 [LORENZO]

2784   The food that to him now is as luscious as locusts, shall be to him
shortly as bitter as colonquintida.
                    Othello, Act i, sc. 3, l. 354 [IAGO]

2785   Who wanteth food, and will not say he wants it,
Or can conceal his hunger till he famish?
                    Pericles, Act i, sc. 4, l. 11 [CLEON]

2786   He ten times pines that pines beholding food.
                    The Rape of Lucrece, l. 1115

2787   With eager feeding food doth choke the feeder.
                    Richard II, Act ii, sc. 1, l. 37 [GAUNT]

2788   So are you to my thoughts as food to life,
Or as sweet-seasoned showers are to the ground.
                    Sonnet lxxv, l. 1

2789   GRUMIO: What say you to a piece of beef and mustard?
KATHARINA: A dish that I do love to feed upon.
GRUMIO: Ay, but the mustard is too hot a little.
KATHARINA: Why then, the beef, and let the mustard rest.
GRUMIO: Nay then, I will not: you shall have the mustard,
Or else you get no beef of Grumio.
                    The Taming of the Shrew, Act iv, sc. 3, l. 23 [GRUMIO]

2790 O, knowst thou not his looks are my soul's food?
Pity the dearth that I have pined in,
By longing for that food so long a time.
The Two Gentlemen of Verona, Act i, sc. 7, l. 15 [JULIA]

Fool

2791 Take but good note, and you shall see in him
The triple pillar of the world transform'd
Into a strumpet's fool.
Antony and Cleopatra, Act i, sc. 1, l. 11 [PHILO]

2792 The dulness of the fool is the whetstone of the wits.
As You like It, Act i, sc. 2, l. 57 [CELIA]

2793 A fool, a fool! I met a fool i' the forest, . . .
Who laid him down and bask'd him in the sun,
And rail'd on Lady Fortune in good terms,
In good set terms, and yet a motley fool.
'Good morrow, fool,' quoth I. 'No, sir,' quoth he,
'Call me not fool till heaven hath sent me fortune.'
And then he drew a dial from his poke,
And, looking on it with lack-lustre eye,
Says very wisely, 'It is ten o'clock:
Thus we may see,' quoth he, 'how the world wags:
'Tis but an hour ago since it was nine,
And after one hour more 'twill be eleven:
And so, from hour to hour, we ripe and ripe,
And then, from hour to hour, we rot and rot;
And thereby hangs a tale.' . . . O noble fool!
A worthy fool! Motley 's the only wear.
As You Like It, Act ii, sc. 7, l. 12 [JAQUES]

2794 He that a fool doth very wisely hit
Doth very foolishly, although he smart,
Not to seem senseless of the bob.
As You Like It, Act ii, sc. 7, l. 53 [JAQUES]

2795 JAQUES: I was seeking for a fool when I found you.
ORLANDO: He is drowned in the brook; look but in, and you shall
see him.
As You Like It, Act iii, sc. 2, l. 303 [JAQUES]

2796 There is, sure, another flood toward, and these couples are coming
to the ark. Here comes a pair of very strange beasts, which in all
tongues are called fools.
As You Like It, Act v, sc. 4, l. 35 [JAQUES]

2797 DUKE: By my faith, he is very swift and sententious.
TOUCHSTONE: According to the fool's bolt, sir, and such dulcet
diseases.
As You Like It, Act v, sc. 4, l. 65 [DUKE]
A fool's bolt is soon shot.
Henry V, Act iii, sc. 7, l. 132 [ORLEANS]
(A proverb dating back to 1250.)

2798 Come, come, no longer will I be a fool,
To put the finger in the eye and weep.
The Comedy of Errors, Act ii, sc. 2, l. 205 [ADRIANA]

2799 Fools are not mad folks.
Cymbeline, Act ii, sc. 3, l. 105 [IMOGEN]

2800 This Cloten was a fool, an empty purse;
There was no money in 't: not Hercules
Could have knock'd out his brains, for he had none.
Cymbeline, Act iv, sc. 2, l. 113 [GUIDERIUS]

2801   Ay, me, most credulous fool,
Egregious murderer, thief, any thing
That's due to all the villains past, in being,
To come! O give me cord, or knife, or poison,
Some upright justicer! . . . It is I
That all the abhorred things o' the earth amend
By being worse than they.
                        Cymbeline, Act v, sc. 5, l. 210 [POSTHUMUS]

2802   These tedious old fools.
                            Hamlet, Act ii, sc. 2, l. 224 [HAMLET]

2803   Let the doors be shut upon him, that he may play the fool no
where but in 's own house.
                            Hamlet, Act iii, sc. 1, l. 135 [HAMLET]

2804   Cannot you tell that? every fool can tell that.
                            Hamlet, Act v, sc. 1, l. 159 [CLOWN]

2805   Why, what a wasp-stung and impatient fool
Art thou to break into this woman's mood,
Tying thine ear to no tongue but thine own!
                    I Henry IV, Act i, sc. 3, l. 236 [NORTHUMBERLAND]

2806   GLOUCESTER: Why, what a peevish fool was that of Crete,
That taught his son the office of a fowl!
And yet, for all his wings, the fool was drown'd.
KING HENRY: I, Dædalus; my poor boy, Icarus;
Thy father, Minos, that denied our course.
                    III Henry VI, Act v, sc. 6, l. 18 [GLOUCESTER]

2807   Now, by my life,
Old fools are babes again; and must be used
With checks as flatteries.
                        King Lear, Act i, sc. 3, l. 18 [GONERIL]

2808   LEAR: Dost thou call me fool, boy?
FOOL: All thy other titles thou hast given away; that thou wast
born with.
                        King Lear, Act i, sc. 4, l. 162 [LEAR]

2809   I am even The natural fool of fortune.
                        King Lear, Act iv, sc. 6, l. 193 [LEAR]
O, I am fortune's fool.
                        Romeo and Juliet, Act iii, sc. 1, l. 141 [ROMEO]

2810   And my poor fool is hang'd! No, no, no life!
Why should a dog, a horse, a rat, have life,
And thou no breath at all?
                        King Lear, Act v, sc. 3, l. 305 [LEAR]

2811   I dare not call them fools; but this I think,
When they are thirsty, fools would fain have drink.
                    Love's Labour's Lost, Act v, sc. 2, l. 371 [ROSALINE]

2812   Lord, what fools these mortals be!
                    A Midsummer Night's Dream, Act iii, sc. 2, l. 115 [PUCK]

2813   Every grise of fortune
Is smooth'd by that below: the learned pate
Ducks to the golden fool.
                        Timon of Athens, Act iv, sc. 3, l. 16 [TIMON]

2814   Farewell, my lord: I as your lover speak;
The fool slides o'er the ice that you should break.
                    Troilus and Cressida, Act iii, sc. 3, l. 214 [ULYSSES]

2815   There is no slander in an allowed fool, though he do nothing but
rail.
                        Twelfth Night, Act i, sc. 5, l. 108 [OLIVIA]

2816   Fools are as like husbands as pilchards are to herrings; the husband's the bigger.
Twelfth Night, Act iii, sc. 1, l. 39 [CLOWN]

Fools and Wise Men

2817   TOUCHSTONE: The more pity, that fools may not speak wisely
what wise men do foolishly.
CELIA: By my troth, thou sayest true; for since the little wit that
fools have was silenced, the little foolery that wise men have makes
a great show.
As You Like It, Act i, sc. 2, l. 92 [TOUCHSTONE]

2818   I do now remember a saying, 'The fool doth think he is wise, but
the wise man knows himself to be a fool.'
As You Like It, Act v, sc. 1, l. 33 [TOUCHSTONE]

2819   Those that I reverence those I fear, the wise:
At fools I laugh, not fear them.
Cymbeline, Act iv, sc. 2, l. 95 [GUIDERIUS]

2820   Thus we play the fools with the time, and the spirits of the wise
sit in the clouds and mock us.
II Henry IV, Act ii, sc. 2, l. 154 [PRINCE]

2821   God give them wisdom that have it; and those that are fools,
let them use their talents.
Twelfth Night, Act i, sc. 5, l. 14 [CLOWN]

2822   This fellow is wise enough to play the fool;
And to do that well craves a kind of wit: . . .
For folly that he wisely shows is fit;
But wise men, folly-fall'n, quite taint their wit.
Twelfth Night, Act iii, sc. 1, l. 67 [VIOLA]

2823   These wise men that give fools money get themselves a good
report—after fourteen years' purchase.
Twelfth Night, Act iv, sc. 1, l. 23 [CLOWN]

Foot

2824   I will set this foot of mine as far
As who goes farthest.
Julius Cæsar, Act i, sc. 3, l. 119 [CASSIUS]

2825   Nay, but make haste; the better foot before.
King John, Act iv, sc. 2, l. 170 [KING JOHN]
Come on, my lords, the better foot before.
Titus Andronicus, Act ii, sc. 3, l. 192 [AARON]

2826   O, so light a foot
Will ne'er wear out the everlasting flint.
Romeo and Juliet, Act ii, sc. 6, l. 16 [FRIAR LAURENCE]

2827   I will kiss thy foot: I prithee, be my god. . . . I'll kiss thy foot:
I'll swear myself thy subject.
The Tempest, Act ii, sc. 2, l. 153 [CALIBAN]

2828   I, thy Caliban, For aye thy foot-licker.
The Tempest, Act iv, sc. 1, l. 218 [CALIBAN]

Football

2829   Am I so round with you as you with me,
That like a football you do spurn me thus?
The Comedy of Errors, Act ii, sc. 1, l. 82 [DROMIO OF EPHESUS]

2830   You base foot-ball player.
King Lear, Act i, sc. 4, l. 95 [KENT]

Foppery

2831   I had as lief have the foppery of freedom as the morality of
imprisonment.
Measure for Measure, Act i, sc. 2, l. 138 [LUCIO]

2832   Let not the sound of shallow foppery enter
My sober house.
The Merchant of Venice, Act ii, sc. 5, l. 36 [SHYLOCK]

Forgetfulness

2833   That we have been familiar,
Ingrate forgetfulness shall poison, rather
Than pity note how much.
Coriolanus, Act v, sc. 2, l. 91 [CORIOLANUS]

2834   How might a prince of my great hopes forget
So great indignities you laid upon me? . . .
May this be wash'd in Lethe, and forgotten?
II Henry IV, Act v, sc. 2, l. 68 [HENRY V]

2835   GLOUCESTER: Be patient, gentle Nell; forget this grief.
DUCHESS: Ah, Gloucester, teach me to forget myself.
II Henry VI, Act ii, sc. 4, l. 26 [GLOUCESTER]

2836   I'll not endure it: you forget yourself. . . .
Urge me no more, I shall forget myself.
Julius Cæsar, Act iv, sc. 3, l. 29 [CASSIUS]

2837   I would not have you, lord, forget yourself.
King John, Act iv, sc. 3, l. 83 [HUBERT]
Shall I forget myself to be myself?
Richard III, Act iv, sc. 4, l. 420 [QUEEN ELIZABETH]

2838   But men are men; the best sometimes forget.
Othello, Act ii, sc. 3, l. 241 [IAGO]

2839   That is not forgot Which ne'er I did remember.
Richard II, Act ii, sc. 3, l. 37 [PERCY]

2840   O . . . that I could forget what I have been,
Or not remember what I must be now!
Richard II, Act iii, sc. 3, l. 138 [KING RICHARD]

2841   Almost shoulder'd in the swallowing gulf
Of blind forgetfulness and dark oblivion.
Richard III, Act iii, sc. 7, l. 129 [BUCKINGHAM]

Forgiveness

2842   I have forgiven and forgotten all.
All's Well that Ends Well, Act v, sc. 3, l. 9 [COUNTESS]

2843   Pray you now, forget and forgive.
King Lear, Act iv, sc. 7, l. 84 [LEAR]
Forget, forgive; conclude and be agreed.
Richard II, Act i, sc. 1, l. 156 [KING RICHARD]

2844   If thy revengeful heart cannot forgive,
Lo, here I lend thee this sharp-pointed sword;
Which if thou please to hide in this true bosom,
And let the soul forth that adoreth thee,
I lay it naked to the deadly stroke,
And humbly beg the death upon my knee.
Richard III, Act i, sc. 2, l. 174 [GLOUCESTER]

2845   Do as the heavens have done, forget your evil;
With them forgive yourself.
The Winter's Tale, Act v, sc. 1, l. 5 [CLEOMENES]

Fortune

2846   I am now, sir, muddied in fortune's mood, and smell somewhat
strong of her strong displeasure. . . . I am a man whom fortune
hath cruelly scratched.

          All's Well that Ends Well, Act v, sc. 2, l. 4 [PAROLLES]

2847   I know not
What counts harsh fortune cast upon my face,
But in my bosom shall she never come
To make my heart her vassal.

          Antony and Cleopatra, Act ii, sc. 6, l. 54 [POMPEY]

2848   MENAS: Pompey doth this day laugh away his fortune.
ENOBARBUS: If he do, sure, he cannot weep 't back again.

          Antony and Cleopatra, Act ii, sc. 6, l. 110 [MENAS]

2849   Our fortune on the sea is out of breath,
And sinks most lamentably.

          Antony and Cleopatra, Act iii, sc. 10, l. 25 [CANIDIUS]

2850   Fortune knows
We scorn her most when most she offers blows.

          Antony and Cleopatra, Act iii, sc. 11, l. 74 [ANTONY]

2851   O sun, thy uprise shall I see no more:
Fortune and Antony part here; even here
Do we shake hands.

          Antony and Cleopatra, Act iv, sc. 12, l. 18 [ANTONY]

2852   Let me rail so high,
That the false housewife Fortune break her wheel,
Provok'd by my offence.

          Antony and Cleopatra, Act iv, sc. 15, l. 43 [CLEOPATRA]

2853   Let me sit and mock the good housewife Fortune from her wheel,
that her gifts may henceforth be bestowed equally.

          As You Like It, Act i, sc. 2, l. 35 [CELIA]

2854   Wear this for me, one out of suits with fortune,
That could give more but that her hand lacks means.

          As You Like It, Act i, sc. 2, l. 257 [ROSALIND]

2855   Now the fair goddess, Fortune,
Fall deep in love with thee.

          Coriolanus, Act i, sc. 5, l. 21 [LARTIUS]

2856   Fortune's blows,
When most struck home, being gentle wounded, craves
A noble cunning.

          Coriolanus, Act iv, sc. 1, l. 7 [CORIOLANUS]

2857   O giglot fortune!

          Cymbeline, Act iii, sc. 1, l. 31 [QUEEN]

2858   All other doubts, by time let them be clear'd.
Fortune brings in some boats that are not steer'd.

          Cymbeline, Act iv, sc. 3, l. 45 [PISANIO]

2859   On fortune's cap we are not the very button.

          Hamlet, Act ii, sc. 2, l. 233 [GUILDERNSTERN]

2860   Out, out, thou strumpet, Fortune! All you gods
In general synod, take away her power;
Break all the spokes and fellies from her wheel,
And bowl the round nave down the hill of heaven,
As low as to the fiends!

          Hamlet, Act ii, sc. 2, l. 514 [PLAYER]

2861   Thou hast been . . .
A man that fortune's buffets and rewards
Has ta'en with equal thanks: and blest are those
Whose blood and judgement are so well commingled,

That they are not a pipe for fortune's finger
To sound what stop she please.
Hamlet, Act iii, sc. 2, l. 70 [HAMLET]

2862   Si fortune me tormente, sperato me contento.
II Henry IV, Act ii, sc. 4, l. 196 [PISTOL]
(Repeated in v, 5, 102, as "Si fortuna me tormenta, spero contenta." The correct reading is, "Si fortuna me tormenta, il sperare me contenta," i.e. "If fortune torments me, hope contents me.")

2863   Will Fortune never come with both hands full,
But write her fair words still in foulest letters?
She either gives a stomach and no food;
Such are the poor, in health; or else a feast
And takes away the stomach; such are the rich,
That have abundance and enjoy it not.
II Henry IV, Act iv, sc. 4, l. 103 [KING]

2864   PISTOL: Giddy Fortune's furious fickle wheel,
That goddess blind,
That stands upon the rolling restless stone— . . .
FLUELLEN: Fortune is painted blind, with a muffler afore her eyes,
to signify to you that Fortune is blind: and she is painted also
with a wheel, to signify to you . . . that she is turning, and inconstant, and mutability, and variation.
Henry V, Act iii, sc. 6, l. 26 [PISTOL]

2865   Though fortune's malice overthrow my state,
My mind exceeds the compass of her wheel.
III Henry VI, Act iv, sc. 3, l. 46 [KING EDWARD]

2866   Fortune is merry,
And in this mood will give us any thing.
Julius Cæsar, Act iii, sc. 2, l. 271 [ANTONY]

2867   When Fortune means to men most good,
She looks upon them with a threatening eye.
King John, Act iii, sc. 4, l. 119 [PANDULPH]

2868   A good man's fortune may grow out at heels.
King Lear, Act ii, sc. 2, l. 164 [KENT]

2869   Fortune, good night; smile once more; turn thy wheel!
King Lear, Act ii, sc. 2, l. 180 [KENT]

2870   Fortune, that arrant whore,
Ne'er turns the key to the poor.
King Lear, Act ii, sc. 4, l. 52 [FOOL]

2871   For thee, oppressed king, am I cast down;
Myself could else out-frown false fortune's frown.
King Lear, Act v, sc. 3, l. 5 [CORDELIA]

2872   If Fortune be a woman, she's a good wench for this gear.
The Merchant of Venice, Act ii, sc. 2, l. 173 [LAUNCELOT]

2873   Since this fortune falls to you,
Be content and seek no new.
If you be well pleased with this
And hold your fortune for your bliss,
Turn you where your lady is
And claim her with a loving kiss.
The Merchant of Venice, Act iii, sc. 2, l. 134 [BASSANIO, *reading*]

2874   Give me your hand Bassanio: fare you well!
Grieve not that I am fallen to this for you;
For herein Fortune shows herself more kind
Than is her custom: it is still her use
To let the wretched man outlive his wealth,

To view with hollow eye and wrinkled brow
An age of poverty; from which lingering penance
Of such misery doth she cut me off.
The Merchant of Venice, Act iv, sc. 1, l. 265 [ANTONIO]

2875   O fortune, fortune! all men call thee fickle:
If thou art fickle, what does thou with him
That is renown'd for faith? Be fickle, fortune;
For then, I hope, thou wilt not keep him long.
Romeo and Juliet, Act iii, sc. 5, l. 60 [JULIET]

2876   My father dead, my fortune lives for me;
And I do hope good days and long to see.
The Taming of the Shrew, Act i, sc. 2, l. 192 [PETRUCHIO]

Fortunes

2877   From seventeen years till now almost fourscore
Here lived I, but now live here no more.
At seventeen years many their fortunes seek;
But at fourscore it is too late a week:
Yet fortune cannot recompense me better
Than to die well and not my master's debtor.
As You Like It, Act ii, sc. 3, l. 71 [ADAM]

2878   All the unsettled humours of the land,
Rash, inconsiderate, fiery voluntaries,
With ladies' faces and fierce dragons' spleens,
Have sold their fortunes at their native homes,
Bearing their birthrights proudly on their backs,
To make a hazard of new fortunes here:
In brief, a braver choice of dauntless spirits
Than now the English bottoms have waft o'er
Did never float upon the swelling tide,
To do offence and scath in Christendom.
King John, Act ii, sc. 1, l. 66 [CHATILLON]

Foundation

2879   There is no sure foundation set on blood,
No certain life achieved by others' death.
King John, Act iv, sc. 2, l. 104 [KING JOHN]

2880   God save the foundation!
Much Ado about Nothing, Act v, sc. 1, l. 327 [DOGBERRY]

2881   In those foundations which I build upon,
The centre is not big enough to bear
A school-boy's top.
The Winter's Tale, Act ii, sc. 1, l. 101 [LEONTES]

Fountain

2882   You are the fount that makes small brooks to flow:
Now stops thy spring; my sea shall suck thee dry,
And swell so much the higher by their ebb.
III Henry VI, Act iv, sc. 8, l. 55 [KING EDWARD]

2883   Mud not the fountain that gave drink to thee.
The Rape of Lucrece, l. 577 [LUCRECE]

Fox

2884   The fox barks not when he would steal the lamb.
II Henry VI, Act iii, sc. 1, l. 55 [SUFFOLK]

2885   Were 't not madness, then,
To make the fox surveyor of the fold?
II Henry VI, Act iii, sc. 1, l. 252 [SUFFOLK]

2886   When the fox hath once got in his nose,
        He'll soon find means to make the body follow.
                        III Henry VI, Act iv, sc. 7, l. 25 [GLOUCESTER]
2887   Alas, poor Proteus! thou hast entertain'd
        A fox to be the shepherd of thy lambs.
                The Two Gentlemen of Verona, Act iv, sc. 4, l. 96 [JULIA]

Frailty

2888   Frailty, Thy name is woman!
                        Hamlet, Act i, sc. 2, l. 146 [HAMLET]
2889   We all are men,
        In our own natures frail, and capable
        Of our flesh; few are angels: out of which frailty
        And want of wisdom, you, that best should teach us,
        Have misdemean'd yourself.
                        Henry VIII, Act v, sc. 3, l. 11 [CHANCELLOR]
2890   How easy is it for the proper-false
        In women's waxen hearts to set their forms!
        Alas, our frailty is the cause, not we!
        For such as we are made of, such we be.
                        Twelfth Night, Act ii, sc. 2, l. 30 [VIOLA]

France

2891   France is a dog-hole, and it no more merits
        The tread of a man's foot. . . .
        France is a stable; we that dwell in 't jades.
                All's Well that Ends Well, Act ii, sc. 3, l. 291 [PAROLLES]
2892   My thoughts and wishes bend again toward France.
                        Hamlet, Act i, sc. 2, l. 55 [LAERTES]
2893   France and England, whose very shores look pale
        With envy of each other's happiness.
                        Henry V, Act v, sc. 2, l. 378 [FRENCH KING]
2894   We are
        In France, amongst a fickle wavering nation.
                        I Henry VI, Act iv, sc. 1, l. 138 [KING HENRY]

France: The French

2895   Proud of their numbers and secure in soul,
        The confident and over-lusty French
        Do the low-rated English play at dice.
                        Henry V, Act iv, Prologue, l. 17 [CHORUS]
2896   Done like a Frenchman: turn, and turn again!
                        I Henry VI, Act iii, sc. 3, l. 85 [PUCELLE]

Friar

2897   A Chartreux friar, . . . who fed him every minute
        With words of sovereignty.
                        Henry VIII, Act i, sc. 2, l. 148 [SURVEYOR]
2898   It was a friar of orders grey,
        As he forth walked on his way.
                The Taming of the Shrew, Act iv, sc. 1, l. 148 [PETRUCHIO, *singing*]

Friend

2899   Keep thy friend Under thy own life's key.
                        All's Well that Ends Well, Act i, sc. 1, l. 75 [COUNTESS]
2900   O Lord, Lord! it is a hard matter for friends to meet; but
        mountains may be removed with earthquakes and so encounter.
                        As You Like It, Act iii, sc. 2, l. 194 [CELIA]

2901   A back-friend, a shoulder-clapper.
      The Comedy of Errors, Act iv, sc. 2, l. 37 [DROMIO OF SYRACUSE]

2902   Those friends thou hast, and their adoption tried,
    Grapple them to thy soul with hoops of steel;
    But do not dull thy palm with entertainment
    Of each new-hatch'd, unfledged comrade.
      Hamlet, Act i, sc. 3, l. 62 [POLONIUS]

2903   You do, surely, bar the door upon your own liberty, if you deny
    your griefs to your friend.
      Hamlet, Act iii, sc. 2, l. 351 [ROSENCRANTZ]

2904   To his good friends thus wide I'll ope my arms;
    And like the kind life-rendering pelican,
    Repast them with my blood.
      Hamlet, Act iv, sc. 5, l. 145 [LAERTES]

2905   A friend i' the court is better than a penny in purse.
      II Henry IV, Act v, sc. 1, l. 34 [SHALLOW]

2906   We are advertised by our loving friends.
      III Henry VI, Act v, sc. 3, l. 18 [KING EDWARD]
    I by friends am well advertised.
      Richard III, Act iv, sc. 4, l. 501 [MESSENGER]
    ("Advertised" in the sense of advised.)

2907   Those you make friends
    And give your hearts to, when they once perceive
    The least rub in your fortunes, fall away
    Like water from ye, never found again
    But where they mean to sink ye.
      Henry VIII, Act ii, sc. 1, l. 127 [BUCKINGHAM]

2908   CASSIUS: A friend should bear a friend's infirmities,
    But Brutus makes mine greater than they are. . . .
    You love me not.
    BRUTUS: I do not like your faults.
    CASSIUS: A friendly eye could never see such faults.
    BRUTUS: A flatterer's would not, though they seem
    As high as huge Olympus.
    CASSIUS: Come, Antony, and young Octavius, come,
    Revenge yourselves alone on Cassius,
    For Cassius is aweary of the world;
    Hated by one he loves; braved by his brother;
    Check'd like a bondman; all his faults observed,
    Set in a note-book, learn'd, and conn'd by rote,
    To cast into my teeth. O, I could weep
    My spirit from mine eyes!
      Julius Cæsar, Act iv, sc. 3, l. 86 [CASSIUS]

2909   Alas, I then have chid away my friend!
    He hath a stern look, but a gentle heart.
      King John, Act iv, sc. 1, l. 87 [ARTHUR]

2910   To wail friends lost
    Is not by much so wholesome-profitable
    As to rejoice at friends but newly found.
      Love's Labour's Lost, Act v, sc. 2, l. 759 [KING]

2911   PORTIA: Is it your dear friend that is thus in trouble?
    BASSANIO: The dearest friend to me, the kindest man,
    The best-condition'd and unwearied spirit
    In doing courtesies, and one in whom
    The ancient Roman honour more appears
    Than any that draws breath in Italy.
      The Merchant of Venice, Act iii, sc. 2, l. 294 [PORTIA]

2912   I will never love that which my friend hates.
                     Much Ado about Nothing, Act v, sc. 2, l. 71 [BEATRICE]

2913   I have professed me thy friend and I confess me knit to thy
       deserving with cables of perdurable toughness.
                              Othello, Act i, sc. 3, l. 342 [IAGO]

2914   Thou dost conspire against thy friend, Iago,
       If thou but think'st him wrong'd and makest his ear
       A stranger to thy thoughts.
                           Othello, Act iii, sc. 3, l. 142 [OTHELLO]

2915   I count myself in nothing else so happy
       As in a soul remembering my good friends.
                     Richard II, Act ii, sc. 3, l. 46 [BOLINGBROKE]

2916   I am not of that feather to shake off
       My friend when he must need me.
                   Timon of Athens, Act i, sc. 1, l. 100 [TIMON]

2917   O you gods, think I, what need we have any friends, if we should
       ne'er have need of 'em? . . . We are born to do benefits: and
       what better or properer can we call our own than the riches of
       our friends?
                     Timon of Athens, Act i, sc. 2, l. 98 [TIMON]

2918   I am wealthy in my friends.
                    Timon of Athens, Act ii, sc. 2, l. 193 [TIMON]

2919   Who can call him
       His friend that dips in the same dish?
               Timon of Athens, Act iii, sc. 2, l. 72 [STRANGER]

2920   I to myself am dearer than a friend.
           The Two Gentlemen of Verona, Act ii, sc. 6, l. 23 [PROTEUS]

Friend and Enemy

2921   O world, thy slippery turns! Friends now fast sworn,
       Whose double bosoms seem to wear one heart, . . .
       Unseparable, shall within this hour,
       On a dissension of a doit, break out
       To bitterest enmity; so, fellest foes,
       Whose passions and whose plots have broke their sleep,
       To take the one the other, by some chance, . . .
       Shall grow dear friends And interjoin their issues.
                  Coriolanus, Act iv, sc. 4, l. 12 [CORIOLANUS]

2922   The great man down, you mark his favourite flies;
       The poor advanced makes friends of enemies. . . .
       For who not needs shall never lack a friend,
       And who in want a hollow friend doth try,
       Directly seasons him his enemy.
                  Hamlet, Act iii, sc. 2, l. 214 [PLAYER KING]

2923   You had rather be at a breakfast of enemies than a dinner of
       friends.
                     Timon of Athens, Act i, sc. 2, l. 78 [TIMON]

2924   Happier is he that has no friend to feed
       Than such that do e'en enemies exceed.
                  Timon of Athens, Act i, sc. 2, l. 209 [FLAVIUS]

2925   What viler thing upon the earth than friends
       Who can bring noblest minds to basest ends!
       How rarely does it meet with this time's guise,
       When man was wish'd to love his enemies!
       Grant I may ever love, and rather woo
       Those that would mischief me than those that do!
                  Timon of Athens, Act iv, sc. 3, l. 470 [FLAVIUS]

2926 DUKE: How dost thou, my good fellow?
CLOWN: Truly, sir, the better for my foes and the worse for
my friends.
Twelfth Night, Act v, sc. 1, l. 11 [DUKE]

2927 O time most accurst,
'Mongst all foes that a friend should be the worst!
The Two Gentlemen of Verona, Act v, sc. 4, l. 71 [VALENTINE]

Friendship

2928 Heigh-ho! sing heigh-ho! unto the green holly:
Most friendship is feigning, most loving mere folly.
As You Like It, Act ii, sc. 7, l. 180 [AMIENS]

2929 There is flattery in friendship.
Henry V, Act iii, sc. 7, l. 124 [CONSTABLE]

2930 When did friendship take
A breed for barren metal of his friend?
The Merchant of Venice, Act i, sc. 3, l. 134 [ANTONIO]

2931 Friendship is constant in all other things
Save in the office and affairs of love:
Therefore all hearts in love use their own tongues;
Let every eye negotiate for itself
And trust no agent; for beauty is a witch
Against whose charms faith melteth into blood.
Much Ado about Nothing, Act ii, sc. 1, l. 183 [CLAUDIO]

2932 Friendship's full of dregs:
Methinks false hearts should never have sound legs.
Timon of Athens, Act i, sc. 2, l. 239 [APEMANTUS]

Frost

2933 KING: Biron is like an envious sneaping frost
That bites the first-born infants of the spring.
BIRON: Well, say I am; why should proud summer boast
Before the birds have any cause to sing?
Why should I joy in any abortive birth?
At Christmas I no more desire a rose
Than wish a snow in May's new-fangled mirth;
But like of each thing that in season grows.
Love's Labour's Lost, Act i, sc. 1, l. 100 [KING]

Frown

2934 So frown'd he once, when, in an angry parle,
He smote the sledded Polacks on the ice.
Hamlet, Act i, sc. 1, l. 62 [HORATIO]

2935 HERMIA: I frown upon him, yet he loves me still.
HELENA: O that your frowns would teach my smiles such skill!
A Midsummer Night's Dream, Act i, sc. 1, l. 194 [HERMIA]

2936 Show a fair presence and put off these frowns,
An ill-beseeming semblance for a feast.
Romeo and Juliet, Act i, sc. 5, l. 75 [CAPULET]

2937 Take up this good old man, and cheer the heart
That dies in tempest of thy angry frown.
Titus Andronicus, Act i, sc. 1, l. 457 [TAMORA]

Fruit

2938 TOUCHSTONE: This is a very false gallop of verses: why do
you infect yourself with them?
ROSALIND: Peace, you dull fool! I found them on a tree.
TOUCHSTONE: Truly, the tree yields bad fruit.
ROSALIND: I'll graff it with you, and then I shall graff it with a

medlar : then it will be the earliest fruit i' the country : for you'll
be rotten ere you be half ripe, and that 's the right virtue of the
medlar.

> *As You Like It,* Act iii, sc. 2, l. 119 [TOUCHSTONE]

2939   The weakest kind of fruit
Drops earliest to the ground.

> *The Merchant of Venice,* Act iv, sc. 1, l. 115 [ANTONIO]

The ripest fruit first falls.

> *Richard II,* Act ii, sc. 1, l. 153 [KING RICHARD]

2940   Though other things grow fair against the sun,
Yet fruits that blossom first will first be ripe.

> *Othello,* Act ii, sc. 3, l. 382 [IAGO]

2941   The mellow plum doth fall, the green sticks fast,
Or being early pluck'd is sour to taste.

> *Venus and Adonis,* l. 527 [ADONIS]

Fury

2942   Thou shouldst come like a Fury crown'd with snakes,
Not like a formal man.

> *Antony and Cleopatra,* Act ii, sc. 5, l. 40 [CLEOPATRA]

2943   To be furious
Is to be frighted out of fear : and in that mood
The dove will peck the estridge.

> *Antony and Cleopatra,* Act iii, sc. 15, l. 195 [ENOBARBUS]

2944   Dizzy-eyed fury and great rage of heart
Suddenly made him from my side to start.

> *I Henry VI,* Act iv, sc. 7, l. 11 [TALBOT]

2945   Men ne'er spend their fury on a child.

> *III Henry VI,* Act v. sc. 5, l. 57 [QUEEN]

2946   Make pale our cheek, chasing the royal blood
With fury from his native residence.

> *Richard II,* Act ii, sc. 1, l. 118 [KING RICHARD]

G

Gain See also Loss and Gain

2947   Since kings break faith upon commodity,
Gain, be my lord, for I will worship thee.

> *King John,* Act ii, sc. 1, l. 597 [BASTARD]

2948   That which serves and seeks for gain,
    And follows but for form,
Will pack when it begins to rain,
    And leave thee in the storm.

> *King Lear,* Act ii, sc. 4, l. 79 [FOOL]

2949   Despair to gain doth traffic oft for gaining ;
And when great treasure is the meed proposed,
Though death be adjunct, there 's no death supposed.
Those that much covet are with gain so fond,
For what they have not, that which they possess
They scatter and unloose it from their bond,
And so, by hoping more, they have but less.

> *The Rape of Lucrece,* l. 131

Gall

2950   Come to my woman's breasts,
And take my milk for gall, you murdering ministers.

> *Macbeth,* Act. i, sc. 5, l. 48 [LADY MACBETH]

2951   This intrusion shall
Now seeming sweet convert to bitter gall.
Romeo and Juliet, Act i, sc. 5, l. 93 [TYBALT]

2952   O deadly gall, and theme of all our scorns!
For which we lose our heads to gild his horns.
Troilus and Cressida, Act iv, sc. 5, l. 30 [ULYSSES]

2953   Write it in a martial hand; be curst and brief; it is no matter
how witty, so it be eloquent and full of invention: taunt him with
the license of ink. . . . Let there be gall enough in thy ink, though
thou write with a goose-pen, no matter.
Twelfth Night, Act iii, sc. 2, l. 45 [SIR TOBY]

Game

2954   SOOTHSAYER: If thou dost play with him at any game,
Thou art sure to lose; and, of that natural luck,
He beats thee 'gainst the odds. . . .
ANTONY: True: the very dice obey him;
And in our sports my better cunning faints
Under his chance: if we draw lots, he speeds;
His cocks do win the battle still of mine.
Antony and Cleopatra, Act ii, sc. 3, l. 25 [SOOTHSAYER]

2955   The game is up.
Cymbeline, Act iii, sc. 3, l. 107 [BELARIUS]

2956   He knows the game: how true he keeps the wind!
III Henry VI, Act iii, sc. 2, l. 14 [CLARENCE]

Garland

2957   Be it known . . . to all the world, that Caius Marcius
Wears this war's garland.
Coriolanus, Act i, sc. 9, l. 59 [COMINIUS]

2958   He comes the third time home with the oaken garland.
Coriolanus, Act ii, sc. 1, l. 137 [VOLUMNIA]

2959   There is a willow grows aslant a brook,
That shows his hoar leaves in the glassy stream;
There with fantastic garlands did she come
Of crow-flowers, nettles, daisies, and long purples
That liberal shepherds give a grosser name,
But our cold maids do dead men's fingers call them.
Hamlet, Act iv, sc. 7, l. 169 [QUEEN]

2960   They promised me eternal happiness;
And brought me garlands, Griffith, which I feel
I am not worthy yet to wear.
Henry VIII, Act iv, sc. 2, l. 90 [KATHARINE]

2961   What fashion will you wear the garland of? about your neck,
like an usurer's chain? or under your arm, like a lieutenant's scarf?
Much Ado about Nothing, Act ii, sc. 1, l. 195 [BENEDICK]

Gate

2962   I am for the house with the narrow gate, which I take to be too
little for pomp to enter: some that humble themselves may; but
the many will be too chill and tender, and they'll be for the flowery
way that leads to the broad gate and the great fire.
All's Well that Ends Well, Act iv, sc. 5, l. 54 [CLOWN]

2963   Stoop, boys; this gate
Instructs you how to adore the heavens and bows you
To a morning's holy office: the gates of monarchs
Are arch'd so high that giants may jet through.
Cymbeline, Act iii, sc. 3, l. 2 [BELARIUS]

Gaunt

2964   Old John of Gaunt, time-honour'd Lancaster,
Hast thou, according to thy oath and band,
Brought hither Henry Hereford, thy bold son?
Richard II, Act i, sc. 1, l. 1 [KING RICHARD]

2965   KING RICHARD: How is 't with aged Gaunt?
GAUNT: O, how that name befits my composition!
Old Gaunt indeed, and gaunt in being old:
Within me grief hath kept a tedious fast;
And who abstains from meat that is not gaunt?
For sleeping England long time have I watch'd;
Watching breeds leanness, leanness is all gaunt. . . .
Gaunt am I for the grave, gaunt as a grave,
Whose hollow womb inherits naught but bones.
Richard II, Act ii, sc. 1, l. 72 [KING RICHARD]

Gentleman

2966   My master hath been an honourable gentleman: tricks he hath
had in him, which gentlemen have.
All's Well that Ends Well, Act v, sc. 3, l. 238 [PAROLLES]

2967   Call you that keeping for a gentleman of my birth, that differs not
from the stalling of an ox?
As You Like It, Act i, sc. 1, l. 10 [ORLANDO]

2968   There is no ancient gentlemen but gardeners, ditchers, and grave-
makers: they hold up Adam's profession.
Hamlet, Act v, sc. 1, l. 34 [CLOWN]

2969   An absolute gentleman, full of most excellent differences, of very
soft society and great showing: indeed, to speak feelingly of him,
he is the card or calendar of gentry, for you shall find in him the
continent of what part a gentleman would see.
Hamlet, Act v, sc. 2, l. 111 [OSRIC]

2970   He is a worthy gentleman,
Exceedingly well read, and profited
In strange concealments, valiant as a lion
And wondrous affable and as bountiful
As mines of India.
I Henry IV, Act iii, sc. 1, l. 165 [MORTIMER]

2971   It was never merry world in England since gentlemen came up.
II Henry VI, Act iv, sc. 2, l. 9 [HOLLAND]

2972   MOTH: You are a gentleman and a gamester, sir.
ARMADO: I confess both: they are both the varnish of a complete
man.
Love's Labour's Lost, Act i, sc. 2, l. 43 [MOTH]

2973   All the wealth I had
Ran in my veins, I was a gentleman.
The Merchant of Venice, Act iii, sc. 2, l. 257 [BASSANIO]

2974   FORD: You are a gentleman of excellent breeding, admirable discourse, of great admittance, authentic in your place and person,
generally allowed for your many war-like, court-like, and learned
preparations.
FALSTAFF: O, sir!
FORD: Believe it, for you know it.
The Merry Wives of Windsor, Act ii, sc. 2, l. 233 [FORD]

2975   We are gentlemen
That neither in our hearts nor outward eyes
Envy the great nor do the low despise.
Pericles, Act ii, sc. 3, l. 24 [KNIGHT]

2976   A sweeter and a lovelier gentleman,
Framed in the prodigality of nature,
Young, valiant, wise, and, no doubt, right royal,
The spacious world cannot again afford.
Richard III, Act i, sc. 2, l. 243 [GLOUCESTER]

2977   Since every Jack became a gentleman,
There's many a gentle person made a Jack.
Richard III, Act i, sc. 3, l. 72 [GLOUCESTER]

2978   He bears him like a portly gentleman :
And, to say truth, Verona brags of him
To be a virtuous and well govern'd youth.
Romeo and Juliet, Act i, sc. 5, l. 68 [CAPULET]

2979   O, he's a lovely gentleman !
Romeo's a dishclout to him : an eagle, madam,
Hath not so green, so quick, so fair an eye
As Paris hath.
Romeo and Juliet, Act iii, sc. 5, l. 220 [NURSE]

2980   'Tis a gentleman here—a plague o' these pickle-herring !
Twelfth Night, Act i, sc. 5, l. 128 [SIR TOBY]

2981   O Eglamour, thou art a gentleman—
Think not I flatter, for I swear I do not—
Valiant, wise, remorseful, well accomplish'd.
The Two Gentlemen of Verona, Act iv, sc. 3, l. 11 [SILVIA]

2982   CLOWN : You denied to fight with me the other day, because I
was no gentleman born. . . . Give me the lie, do, and try whether
I am not now a gentleman born.
AUTOLYCUS : I know you now, sir, a gentleman born. . . .
CLOWN : I was a gentleman born before my father. . . .
SHEPHERD : We must be gentle, now we are gentlemen.
The Winter's Tale, Act v, sc. 2, l. 140 [CLOWN]

2983   If it be ne'er so false, a true gentleman may swear it in the behalf
of his friend.
The Winter's Tale, Act v, sc. 2, l. 175 [CLOWN]

Gentleness

2984   DUKE :   Your gentleness shall force
More than your force move us to gentleness. . . .
ORLANDO : If ever you have look'd on better days, . . .
Let gentleness my strong enforcement be.
As You Like It, Act ii, sc. 7, l. 102 [DUKE]

2985   I have not from your eyes that gentleness
And show of love as I was wont to have.
Julius Cæsar, Act i, sc. 2, l. 33 [CASSIUS]

2986   I find you passing gentle.
'Twas told me you were rough and coy and sullen,
And now I find report a very liar ;
For thou art pleasant, gamesome, passing courteous,
But slow in speech, yet sweet as spring-time flowers.
The Taming of the Shrew, Act ii, sc. 1, l. 244 [PETRUCHIO]

Germans

2987   Germans are honest men.
The Merry Wives of Windsor, Act iv, sc. 5, l. 73 [HOST]

2988   German from the waist downward, all slops.
Much Ado about Nothing, Act iii, sc. 2, l. 35 [DON PEDRO]

Ghost

2989   Unhand me, gentlemen.
By heaven, I'll make a ghost of him that lets me!
                            Hamlet, Act i, sc. 4, l. 84 [HAMLET]

2990   If Henry were recall'd to life again,
These news would cause him once more yield the ghost.
                        I Henry VI, Act i, sc. 1, l. 66 [GLOUCESTER]

2991   Oft have I seen a timely-parted ghost,
Of ashy semblance, meagre, pale and bloodless,
Being all descended to the labouring heart.
                    II Henry VI, Act iii, sc. 2, l. 161 [WARWICK]

2992   So, underneath the belly of their steeds, . . .
The noble gentleman gave up the ghost.
                    III Henry VI, Act ii, sc. 3, l. 20 [RICHARD]
Our army, . . . ready to give up the ghost.
                        Julius Cæsar, Act v, sc. 1, l. 89 [CASSIUS]

2993   The ghost of Cæsar hath appear'd to me
Two several times by night; at Sardis once,
And, this last night, here in Philippi fields:
I know my hour is come.
                        Julius Cæsar, Act v, sc. 5, l. 17 [BRUTUS]

2994   Vex not his ghost: O, let him pass! he hates him much
That would upon the rack of this tough world
Stretch him out longer.
                        King Lear, Act v, sc. 3, l. 313 [KENT]

2995   Blind sight, dead life, poor mortal living ghost,
Woe's scene, world's shame, grave's due by life usurp'd,
Brief abstract and record of tedious days,
Rest thy unrest on England's lawful earth.
                Richard III, Act iv, sc. 4, l. 26 [DUCHESS OF YORK]

Gibbet

2996   Unless a man should marry a gallows and beget young gibbets,
I never saw one so prone.
                    Cymbeline, Act v, sc. 4, l. 207 [GAOLER]

2997   Hang no more about me, I am no gibbet for you. Go. A short
knife and a thong! To your manor of Pickt-hatch, go!
        The Merry Wives of Windsor, Act ii, sc. 2, l. 19 [FALSTAFF]

Gift

2998   The gift doth stretch itself as 'tis received.
            All's Well that Ends Well, Act ii, sc. 1, l. 4 [KING]

2999   I see a man here needs not live by shifts,
When in the streets he meets such golden gifts.
            The Comedy of Errors, Act iii, sc. 2, l. 188 [ANTIPHOLUS
                                                OF SYRACUSE]

3000   To the noble mind
Rich gifts wax poor when givers prove unkind.
                        Hamlet, Act iii, sc. 1, l. 100 [OPHELIA]

3001   SLENDER: I know the young gentlewoman; she has good gifts.
EVANS: Seven hundred pounds and possibilities is goot gifts.
        The Merry Wives of Windsor, Act i, sc. 1, l. 62 [SLENDER]

3002   Men take women's gifts for impudence.
                        Pericles, Act ii, sc. 3, l. 69 [THAISA]

Girdle

3003   OBERON: Be thou here again
Ere the leviathan can swim a league.

PUCK: I'll put a girdle round about the earth
In forty minutes.
> *A Midsummer Night's Dream,* Act ii, sc. 1, l. 173 [OBERON]

3004 DON PEDRO: I think he be angry indeed.
CLAUDIO: If he be, he knows how to turn his girdle.
> *Much Ado about Nothing,* Act v, sc. 1, l. 141 [DON PEDRO]
> (A reference to the old proverb, "If you be angry, turn the
> buckle of your girdle behind you," as a harmless outlet for
> your anger.)

Girl

3005
> The full sum of me . . .
> Is an unlesson'd girl, unschool'd, unpractised;
> Happy in this, she is not yet so old
> But she may learn; happier than this,
> She is not bred so dull but she can learn;
> Happiest of all is that her gentle spirit
> Commits itself to yours to be directed,
> As from her lord, her governor, her king.
>> *The Merchant of Venice,* Act iii, sc. 2, l. 159 [PORTIA]

3006 Why, this it is to be a peevish girl,
That flies her fortune when it follows her.
> *The Two Gentlemen of Verona,* Act v, sc. 2, l. 49 [THURIO]

3007 I hold him but a fool that will endanger
His body for a girl that loves him not.
> *The Two Gentlemen of Verona,* Act v, sc. 4, l. 133 [THURIO]

Glass

3008 You go not till I set you up a glass
Where you may see the inmost part of you.
> *Hamlet,* Act iii, sc. 4, l. 19 [HAMLET]

3009 Broken glass no cement can redress.
> *The Passionate Pilgrim,* Sonnet xiii, l. 12

3010 I'll be at charges for a looking-glass,
And entertain some score or two of tailors,
To study fashions to adorn my body: . . .
Shine out, fair sun, till I have bought a glass,
That I may see my shadow as I pass.
> *Richard III,* Act i, sc. 2, l. 256 [GLOUCESTER]

Glendower

3011
> The noble Mortimer,
> Leading the men of Herefordshire to fight
> Against the irregular and wild Glendower,
> Was by the rude hands of that Welshman taken.
>> *I Henry IV,* Act i, sc. 1, l. 39 [WESTMORELAND]

3012 He durst as well have met the devil alone
As Owen Glendower for an enemy.
> *I Henry IV,* Act i, sc. 3, l. 116 [KING HENRY]

3013 FALSTAFF: He of Wales, that gave Amamon the bastinado and
made Lucifer cuckold and swore the devil his true liegeman upon
the cross of a Wales hook—what a plague call you him?
POINS: O, Glendower.
FALSTAFF: Owen, Owen, the same.
> *I Henry IV,* Act ii, sc. 4, l. 370 [FALSTAFF]

Glory

3014   Glory is like a circle in the water,
Which never ceaseth to enlarge itself
Till by broad spreading it disperse to nought.
I Henry VI, Act i, sc. 2, l. 133 [PUCELLE]

3015   I see thy glory like a shooting star
Fall to the base earth from the firmament.
Richard II, Act ii, sc. 4, l. 19 [SALISBURY]

3016   Like madness is the glory of this life.
Timon of Athens, Act i, sc. 2, l. 139 [APEMANTUS]

3017   O, the fierce wretchedness that glory brings us!
Timon of Athens, Act iv, sc. 2, l. 30 [FLAVIUS]

Glow-Worm

3018   The glow-worm shows the matin to be near,
And 'gins to pale his uneffectual fire.
Hamlet, Act i, sc. 5, l. 89 [GHOST]

3019   And twenty glow-worms shall our lanterns be,
To guide our measure round about the tree.
The Merry Wives of Windsor, Act v, sc. 5, l. 82 [EVANS]

Gnat

3020   When the sun shines let foolish gnats make sport,
But creep in crannies when he hides his beams.
The Comedy of Errors, Act ii, sc. 2, l. 30 [ANTIPHOLUS OF SYRACUSE]

3021   The common people swarm like summer flies;
And whither fly the gnats but to the sun?
III Henry VI, Act ii, sc. 6, l. 8 [CLIFFORD]

Goat

3022   Thou damned and luxurious mountain goat!
Henry V, Act iv, sc. 4, l. 20 [PISTOL]

3023   Am I ridden with a Welsh goat too? shall I have a coxcomb of
frize? 'Tis time I were choked with a piece of toasted cheese.
The Merry Wives of Windsor, Act v, sc. 5, l. 145 [FALSTAFF]

God

3024   Art thou god to shepherd turn'd,
That a maiden's heart hath burn'd? . . .
Why, thy godhead laid apart,
Warr'st thou with a woman's heart?
As You Like It, Act iv, sc. 3, l. 40 [ROSALIND, *reading*]

3025   God be at your table!
Hamlet, Act iv, sc. 5, l. 44 [OPHELIA]

3026   From a God to a bull? a heavy declension! it was Jove's case.
From a prince to a prentice? a low transformation! that shall be
mine.
II Henry IV, Act ii, sc. 2, l. 192 [PRINCE]

3027   God and his angels guard your sacred throne
And make you long become it!
Henry V, Act i, sc. 2, l. 7 [CANTERBURY]

3028   We are in God's hand, brother.
Henry V, Act iii, sc. 6, l. 178 [KING HENRY]
In the great hand of God I stand.
Macbeth, Act ii, sc. 3, l. 136 [BANQUO]

3029   Though they can outstrip men, they have no wings to fly from
God: war is his beadle, war is his vengeance.
Henry V, Act iv, sc. 1, l. 181 [KING HENRY]

3030 O God of battles! steel my soldiers' hearts;
Possess them not with fear; take from them now
The sense of reckoning, if the opposed numbers
Pluck their hearts from them.
Henry V, Act iv, sc. 1, l. 306 [KING HENRY]

3031 O God, thy arm was here;
And not to us, but to thy arm alone,
Ascribe we all! . . . God fought for us.
Henry V, Act iv, sc. 8, l. 111 [KING HENRY]

3032 God, the best maker of all marriages,
Combine your hearts in one.
Henry V, Act v, sc. 2, l. 387 [QUEEN ISABEL]

3033 Now, God be praised, that to believing souls
Gives light in darkness, comfort in despair!
II Henry VI, Act ii, sc. 1, l. 66 [KING HENRY]

3034 Poor soul, God's goodness hath been great to thee;
Let never day nor night unhallow'd pass,
But still remember what the Lord hath done.
II Henry VI, Act ii, sc. 1, l. 85 [KING HENRY]

3035 God shall be my hope,
My stay, my guide, and lantern to my feet.
II Henry VI, Act ii, sc. 3, l. 24 [KING HENRY]

3036 If my suspect be false, forgive me, God,
For judgement only doth belong to Thee.
II Henry VI, Act iii, sc. 2, l. 139 [KING HENRY]

3037 Had I but served my God with half the zeal
I served my king, he would not in mine age
Have left me naked to mine enemies.
Henry VIII, Act iii, sc. 2, l. 455 [WOLSEY]

3038 God's a good man. . . . God is to be worshipped.
Much Ado about Nothing, Act iii, sc. 4, l. 40 [DOGBERRY]

3039 Write down, that they hope they serve God: and write God first;
for God defend but God should go before such villains!
Much Ado about Nothing, Act iv, sc. 2, l. 20 [DOGBERRY]

3040 'Zounds, sir, you are one of those that will not serve God, if the
devil bid you.
Othello, Act i, sc. 1, l. 107 [IAGO]

3041 God's above all; and there be souls must be saved, and there be
souls must not be saved.
Othello, Act ii, sc. 3, l. 106 [CASSIO]

3042 God, the widow's champion and defence.
Richard II, Act i, sc. 2, l. 43 [GAUNT]

3043 But He, that hath the steerage of my course,
Direct my sail!
Romeo and Juliet, Act i, sc. 4, l. 112 [ROMEO]

3044 Thy gracious self,
Which is the god of my idolatry.
Romeo and Juliet, Act ii, sc. 2, l. 113 [JULIET]

3045 God have mercy upon one of our souls! He may have mercy upon
mine; but my hope is better, and so look to thyself.
Twelfth Night, Act iii, sc. 4, l. 184 [SIR TOBY]

Gods

3046 If the great gods be just, they shall assist
The deeds of justest men.
Antony and Cleopatra, Act ii, sc. 1, l. 1 [POMPEY]

3047 The gods look down, and this unnatural scene
  They laugh at.
         Coriolanus, Act v, sc. 3, l. 184 [CORIOLANUS]

3048 To your protection I commend me, gods.
  From fairies and the tempters of the night
  Guard me, beseech ye.
         Cymbeline, Act ii, sc. 2, l. 8 [IMOGEN]

3049 It is the part of men to fear and tremble,
  When the most mighty gods by tokens send
  Such dreadful heralds to astonish us.
         Julius Cæsar, Act i, sc. 3, l. 54 [CASCA]

3050 The gods to-day stand friendly, that we may,
  Lovers in peace, lead on our days to age!
         Julius Cæsar, Act v, sc. 1, l. 94 [CASSIUS]

3051 I told him, the revenging gods
  'Gainst parricides did all their thunders blend.
         King Lear, Act ii, sc. 1, l. 48 [EDMUND]

3052 The gods are just, and of our pleasant vices
  Make instruments to plague us.
         King Lear, Act v, sc. 3, l. 170 [EDGAR]

3053 Now the hot-blooded gods assist me. . . . When gods have hot
  backs, what shall poor men do?
      The Merry Wives of Windsor, Act v, sc. 5, l. 2 [FALSTAFF]

3054   O you gods!
  Why do you make us love your goodly gifts,
  And snatch them straight away?
         Pericles, Act iii, sc. 1, l. 22 [PERICLES]

3055   The gods themselves,
  Humbling their deities to love, have taken
  The shapes of beasts upon them: Jupiter
  Became a bull, and bellow'd; the green Neptune
  A ram, and bleated; and the fire-robed god,
  Golden Apollo, a poor humble swain.
       The Winter's Tale, Act iv, sc. 4, l. 25 [FLORIZEL]

Gold

3056   Though gold bides still
  The tester's touch, yet often-touching will
  Wear gold.
      The Comedy of Errors, Act ii, sc. 1, l. 110 [ADRIANA]

3057 'Tis gold
  Which buys admittance; oft it doth; yea, and makes
  Diana's rangers false themselves, yield up
  Their deer to the stand o' the stealer; and 'tis gold
  Which makes the true man kill'd and saves the thief. . . .
  What can it not do and undo?
         Cymbeline, Act ii, sc. 3, l. 72 [CLOTEN]

3058 Gold cannot come amiss.
         II Henry VI, Act i, sc. 2, l. 92 [HUME]

3059   All that glisters is not gold;
     Often have you heard that told: . . .
     Gilded tombs do worms enfold.
   The Merchant of Venice, Act ii, sc. 7, l. 65 [MOROCCO, *reading*]

3060   Thou gaudy gold,
  Hard food for Midas, I will none of thee.
    The Merchant of Venice, Act iii, sc. 2, l. 101 [BASSANIO]

3061   O Buckingham, now do I play the touch,
      To try if thou be current gold indeed.
                       Richard III, Act iv, sc. 2, l. 8 [KING RICHARD]

3062   Gold were as good as twenty orators.
                       Richard III, Act iv, sc. 2, l. 38 [PAGE]

3063   She will not . . .
      Ope her lap to saint-seducing gold.
                   Romeo and Juliet, Act i, sc. 1, l. 220 [ROMEO]

3064   There's thy gold, worse poison to men's souls,
      Doing more murders in this loathsome world,
      Than these poor compounds that thou mayst not sell.
                   Romeo and Juliet, Act v, sc. 1, l. 80 [ROMEO]

3065   The strongest castle, tower, and town,
      The golden bullet beats it down.
                   Sonnets to Sundry Notes of Music, Pt. xix, l. 29

3066   What is here?
      Gold? yellow, glittering, precious gold? . . .
      Thus much of this will make black white, foul fair,
      Wrong right, base noble, old young, coward valiant. . . .
      This yellow slave, will knit and break religions, . . .
      Make the hoar leprosy adored, . . . this is it
      That makes the wappen'd widow wed again. . . .
      Thou common whore of mankind.
                   Timon of Athens, Act iv, sc. 3, l. 25 [TIMON]

3067   [Gold] thou sweet king-killer, and dear divorce
      'Twixt natural son and sire! thou bright defiler
      Of Hymen's purest bed! thou valiant Mars!
      Thou ever young, fresh, loved and delicate wooer,
      Whose blush doth thaw the consecrated snow
      That lies on Dian's lap! thou visible god
      That solder'st close impossibilities,
      And makest them kiss! that speak'st with every tongue
      To every purpose!
                   Timon of Athens, Act iv, sc. 3, l. 383 [TIMON]

3068   What a god's gold,
      That he is worshipp'd in a baser temple
      Than where swine feed!
      'Tis thou that rigg'st the bark and plough'st the foam,
      Settlest admired reverence in a slave:
      To thee be worship! and thy saints for aye
      Be crown'd with plagues that thee alone obey!
                   Timon of Athens, Act v, sc. 1, l. 50 [TIMON]

3069   This is fairy gold.
                   The Winter's Tale, Act iii, sc. 3, l. 127 [SHEPHERD]

Goodness

3070   Good alone
      Is good without a name. Vileness is so:
      The property by what it is should go,
      Not by the title.
                   All's Well that Ends Well, Act ii, sc. 3, l. 135 [KING]

3071   We must do good against evil.
                   All's Well that Ends Well, Act ii, sc. 5, l. 55 [LAFEU]

3072   Can one desire too much of a good thing?
                   As You Like It, Act iv, sc. 1, l. 123 [ROSALIND]

3073   Goodness, growing to a plurisy,
      Dies in his own too much.
                   Hamlet, Act iv, sc. 7, l. 117 [KING]

3074   There is some soul of goodness in things evil,
Would men observingly distil it out. . . .
Thus we may gather honey from the weed,
And make a moral of the devil himself.
Henry V, Act iv, sc. 1, l. 4 [KING HENRY]
Captive good attending captain ill.
Sonnet lxvi, l. 12

3075   Thou art as opposite to every good
As the Antipodes are unto us,
Or as the south to the septentrion.
III Henry VI, Act i, sc. 4, l. 134 [YORK]

3076   The hand that hath made you fair hath made you good: the goodness that is cheap in beauty makes beauty brief in goodness; but
grace, being the soul of your complexion, shall keep the body of it
ever fair.
Measure for Measure, Act iii, sc. 1, l. 183 [DUKE]

3077   I never did repent for doing good.
The Merchant of Venice, Act iii, sc. 4, l. 10 [PORTIA]

3078   O, mickle is the powerful grace that lies
In herbs, plant, stones, and their true qualities:
For nought so vile that on the earth doth live
But to the earth some special good doth give,
Nor aught so good but strain'd from that fair use
Revolts from true birth, stumbling on abuse: . . .
Within the infant rind of this small flower
Poison hath residence and medicine power:
For this, being smelt, with that part cheers each **part**;
Being tasted, slays all senses with the heart.
Two such opposed kings encamp them still
In man as well as herbs, grace and rude will;
And where the worser is predominant,
Full soon the canker death eats up that plant.
Romeo and Juliet, Act ii, sc. 3, l. 15 [FRIAR LAURENCE]

3079   Undone by goodness! Strange, unusual blood,
When man's worst sin is, he does too much good!
Timon of Athens, Act iv, sc. 2, l. 38 [FLAVIUS]

3080   Good things should be praised.
The Two Gentlemen of Verona, Act iii, sc. 1, l. 353 [LAUNCE]

Gossip

3081   SALARINA: As they say, if my gossip Report be an honest woman
of her word.
SALANIO: I would she were as lying a gossip in that as ever
knapped ginger or made her neighbours believe she wept for the
death of a third husband.
The Merchant of Venice, Act iii, sc. 1, l. 7 [SALARINA]

3082   Hold your tongue,
Good prudence; smatter with your gossips, go. . . .
Utter your gravity o'er a gossip's bowl;
For here we need it not.
Romeo and Juliet, Act iii, sc. 5, l. 171 [CAPULET]

3083   Shall she live to betray this guilt of ours,
A long-tongued babbling gossip?
Titus Andronicus, Act iv, sc. 2, l. 149 [AARON]

Government

3084   Government, though high and low and lower,
Put into parts, doth keep in one consent,

Congreeing in a full and natural close,
Like music.
Henry V, Act i, sc. 2, l. 180 [EXETER]

3085 'Tis government makes [women] seem divine;
The want thereof makes thee abominable.
III Henry VI, Act i, sc. 4, l. 132 [YORK]

Grace

3086 [He] is so full of grace, that it flows over
Of all that need.
Antony and Cleopatra, Act v, sc. 2, l. 24 [PROCULEIUS]

3087 FALSTAFF: Grace thou wilt have none.
PRINCE: What, none?
FALSTAFF: No, by my troth, not so much as will serve as a prologue to an egg and butter.
I Henry IV, Act i, sc. 2, l. 20 [FALSTAFF]

3088 You men of Harfleur,
Take pity of your town and of your people, . . .
Whiles yet the cool and temperate wind of grace
O'erblows the filthy and contagious clouds
Of heady murder, spoil and villany.
Henry V, Act iii, sc. 3, l. 27 [KING HENRY]

3089 The king-becoming graces,
As justice, verity, temperance, stableness,
Bounty, perseverance, mercy, lowliness,
Devotion, patience, courage, fortitude,
I have no relish of them.
Macbeth, Act iv, sc. 3, l. 91 [MALCOLM]

3090 LUCIO: Grace is grace, despite of all controversy: as, for example,
thou thyself art a wicked villain, despite of all grace.
GENTLEMAN: Well, there went but a pair of shears between us.
Measure for Measure, Act i, sc. 2, l. 25 [LUCIO]

3091 Alack, when once our grace we have forgot,
Nothing goes right: we would, and we would not.
Measure for Measure, Act iv, sc. 4, l. 36 [ANGELO]

3092 Hail to thee, lady! and the grace of heaven,
Before, behind thee and on every hand,
Enwheel thee round!
Othello, Act ii, sc. 1, l. 85 [CASSIO]

3093 Grace me no grace, nor uncle me no uncle:
I am no traitor's uncle; and the word 'grace'
In an ungracious mouth is but profane.
Richard II, Act ii, sc. 3, l. 86 [YORK]

3094 O momentary grace of mortal men,
Which we more hunt for than the grace of God!
Who builds his hopes in air of your good looks,
Lives like a drunken sailor on a mast,
Ready, with every nod, to tumble down
Into the fatal bowels of the deep.
Richard III, Act iii, sc. 4, l. 98 [HASTINGS]

3095 Immortal gods, I crave no pelf;
I pray for no man but myself:
Grant I may never prove so fond,
To trust a man on his oath or bond;
Or a harlot, for her weeping;
Or a dog that seems a-sleeping;
Or my friends, if I should need 'em.

Amen. So 1all to 't ;
Rich men sin, and I eat root.
Timon of Athens, Act i, sc. 2, l. 63 [APEMANTUS, *his Grace*]

Grandam

3096 Had she been light, like you,
Of such a merry, nimble, stirring spirit,
She might ha' been a grandam ere she died.
Love's Labour 's Lost, Act v, sc. 2, l. 15 [KATHARINE]

3097 A grandam's name is little less in love
Than is the doting title of a mother ;
They are as children but one step below,
Even of your mettle, of your very blood.
Richard III, Act iv, sc. 4, l. 299 [KING RICHARD]

Grapes

3098 O, you will eat no grapes, my royal fox?
Yes, but you will my noble grapes, an if
My royal fox could reach them.
All's Well that Ends Well, Act ii, sc. 1, l. 73 [LAFEU]
(A reference to Æsop's fable of the fox and the grapes.)

3099 The heathen philosopher, when he had a desire to eat a grape,
would open his lips when he put it into his mouth ; meaning thereby that grapes were made to eat and lips to open.
As You Like It, Act v, sc. 1, l. 36 [TOUCHSTONE]

Grass

3100 I am no great Nebuchadnezzar, sir ; I have not much skill in grass.
All's Well that Ends Well, Act iv, sc. 5, l. 21 [CLOWN]

3101 'While the grass grows,'—the proverb is something musty.
Hamlet, Act iii, sc. 2, l. 358 [HAMLET]
(The proverb is, "While the grass grows, the horse starves,"
after the Latin, "Dum herba crescit equus moritur.")

3102 How lush and lusty the grass looks ! how green !
The Tempest, Act ii, sc. 1, l. 52 [GONZALO]

3103 The grass stoops not, she treads on it so light.
Venus and Adonis, l. 1028

Grave

3104 Here lie I down, and measure out my grave.
As You Like It, Act ii, sc. 6, l. 2 [ADAM]

3105 Renowned be thy grave !
Cymbeline, Act iv, sc. 2, l. 281 [GUIDERIUS and ARVIRAGUS]

3106 They bore him barefaced on the bier ;
Hey non nonny, nonny, hey nonny ;
And in his grave rained many a tear :—
Fare you well, my dove !
Hamlet, Act iv, sc. 5, l. 164 [OPHELIA]

3107 FIRST CLOWN : What is he that builds stronger than either the
mason, the shipwright, or the carpenter ?
SECOND CLOWN : The gallows-maker ; for that frame outlives a
thousand tenants. . . .
FIRST CLOWN : Say 'a grave-maker' : the houses that he makes last
till doomsday.
Hamlet, Act v, sc. 1, l. 47 [FIRST CLOWN]

3108 A pick-axe, and a spade, a spade,
For and a winding sheet :
O, a pit of clay for to be made
For such a guest is meet.
Hamlet, Act v, sc. 1, l. 102 [CLOWN]

3109 Get thee gone and dig my grave thyself,
And bid the merry bells ring to thine ear
That thou art crowned, not that I am dead. . . .
Only compound me with forgotten dust;
Give that which gave thee life unto the worms.
II Henry IV, Act iv, sc. 5, l. 111 [KING HENRY]

3110 The grave doth gape, and doting death is near.
Henry V, Act ii, sc. 1, l. 65 [PISTOL]

3111 Look, who comes here! a grave unto a soul;
Holding the eternal spirit, against her will,
In the vile prison of afflicted breath.
King John, Act iii, sc. 4, l. 17 [KING JOHN]

3112 So be my grave my peace, as here I give
Her father's heart from her!
King Lear, Act i, sc. 1, l. 127 [LEAR]

3113 If he be married,
My grave is like to be my wedding bed.
Romeo and Juliet, Act i, sc. 5, l. 136 [JULIET]

3114 Graves at my command
Have waked their sleepers, oped, and let 'em forth
By my so potent art.
The Tempest, Act v, sc. 1, l. 48 [PROSPERO]

3115 Timon hath made his everlasting mansion
Upon the beached verge of the salt flood;
Who once a day with his embossed froth
The turbulent surge shall cover: thither come,
And let my grave-stone be your oracle.
Timon of Athens, Act v, sc. 1, l. 218 [TIMON]

Gravity

3116 How ill agrees it with your gravity
To counterfeit thus grossly with your slave.
The Comedy of Errors, Act ii, sc. 2, l. 170 [ADRIANA]

3117 What doth gravity out of his bed at midnight?
I Henry IV, Act ii, sc. 4, l. 325 [FALSTAFF]

3118 Our youths and wildness shall no whit appear,
But all be buried in his gravity.
Julius Cæsar, Act ii, sc. 1, l. 148 [METELLUS]

3119 Yea, my gravity,
Wherein—let no man hear me—I take pride,
Could I with boot change for an idle plume,
Which the air beats for vain.
Measure for Measure, Act ii, sc. 4, l. 9 [ANGELO]

Greatness

3120 The soul and body rive not more in parting
Than greatness going off.
Antony and Cleopatra, Act iv, sc. 13, l. 5 [CHARMIAN]

3121 Rightly to be great
Is not to stir without great argument,
But greatly to find quarrel in a straw
When honour 's at the stake.
Hamlet, Act iv, sc. 4, l. 53 [HAMLET]

3122 Greatness knows itself.
I Henry IV, Act iv, sc. 3, l. 74 [HOTSPUR]

3123 Great men have reaching hands: oft have I struck
Those that I never saw and struck them dead.
II Henry VI, Act iv, sc. 7, l. 85 [LORD SAY]

3124 The abuse of greatness is, when it disjoins
       Remorse from power.
                         Julius Cæsar, Act ii, sc. 1, l. 18 [BRUTUS]
3125 Great men may jest with saints; 'tis wit in them,
       But in the less foul profanation.
                    Measure for Measure, Act ii, sc. 2, l. 128 [ISABELLA]
3126 He's so great can make his will his act.
                              Pericles, Act i, sc. 2, l. 18 [PERICLES]
3127 The mightier man, the mightier is the thing
       That makes him honour'd, or begets him hate.
                         The Rape of Lucrece, l. 1004 [LUCRECE]
3128 They that stand high have many blasts to shake them;
       And if they fall, they dash themselves to pieces.
                    Richard III, Act i, sc. 3, l. 259 [QUEEN MARGARET]
3129 Great men should drink with harness on their throats.
                    Timon of Athens, Act i, sc. 2, l. 53 [APEMANTUS]
3130 'Tis certain, greatness, once fall'n out with fortune,
       Must fall out with men too: . . . for men, like butterflies,
       Show not their mealy wings but to the summer.
                 Troilus and Cressida, Act iii, sc. 3, l. 75 [ACHILLES]
3131 What great ones do the less will prattle of.
                         Twelfth Night, Act i, sc. 2, l. 33 [CAPTAIN]
3132 Be not afraid of greatness: some are born great, some achieve
       greatness and some have greatness thrust upon 'em.
                 Twelfth Night, Act ii, sc. 5, l. 158 [MALVOLIO, *reading*]
       (Quoted by Clown in v, 1, 378.)
3133 A great man, I'll warrant; I know by the picking on's teeth.
                    The Winter's Tale, Act iv, sc. 4, l. 778 [CLOWN]

Greek

3134 CASSIUS: Did Cicero say any thing?
       CASCA: Ay, he spoke Greek.
       CASSIUS: To what effect?
       CASCA: Nay, an I tell you that, I'll ne'er look you i' the face again:
       but those that understood him smiled at one another and shook
       their heads; but, for mine own part, it was Greek to me.
                         Julius Cæsar, Act i, sc. 2, l. 281 [CASSIUS]

Green

3135 Your mind is all as youthful as your blood. . . .
       How green you are and fresh in this old world.
                         King John, Act iii, sc. 4, l. 125 [PANDULPH]
3136   We have done but greenly,
       In hugger-mugger to inter him.
                              Hamlet, Act iv, sc. 5, l. 83 [KING]
3137 Green indeed is the colour of lovers.
                    Love's Labour's Lost, Act i, sc. 2, l. 90 [ARMADO]

Greyhound

3138 Holding Corioli in the name of Rome,
       Even like a fawning greyhound in the leash,
       To let him slip at will.
                         Coriolanus, Act i, sc. 6, l. 38 [MARCIUS]
3139 I see you stand like greyhounds in the slips,
       Straining upon the start. The game's afoot:
       Follow your spirit, and upon this charge
       Cry 'God for Harry, England, and Saint George!'
                         Henry V. Act iii, sc. 1, l. 31 [KING HENRY]

3140   Edward and Richard, like a brace of greyhounds
        Having the fearful flying hare in sight, . . .
        Are at our backs.
                III Henry VI, Act ii, sc. 5, l. 129 [QUEEN MARGARET]
3141   O, sir, Lucentio slipp'd me like his greyhound,
        Which runs himself and catches for his master.
                The Taming of the Shrew, Act v, sc. 2, l. 52 [TRANIO]

Grief

3142   My heart is heavy and mine age is weak;
        Grief would have tears, and sorrow bids me speak.
            All's Well that Ends Well, Act iii, sc. 4, l. 41 [COUNTESS]
3143   Would I might never
        O'ertake pursued success, but I do feel,
        By the rebound of yours, a grief that smites
        My very heart at root.
            Antony and Cleopatra, Act v, sc. 2, l. 102 [DOLABELLA]
3144   O, grief hath changed me since you saw me last,
        And careful hours with time's deformed hand
        Have written strange defeatures in my face.
            The Comedy of Errors, Act v, sc. 1, l. 297 [ÆGEON]
3145   Some griefs are med'cinable; that is one of them,
        For it doth physic love.
            Cymbeline, Act iii, sc. 2, l. 33 [IMOGEN]
3146   Great griefs, I see medicine the less.
            Cymbeline, Act iv, sc. 2, l. 243 [BELARIUS]
3147   What is he whose grief
        Bears such an emphasis? whose phrase of sorrow
        Conjures the wandering stars, and makes them stand
        Like wonder-wounded hearers?
            Hamlet, Act v, sc. 1, l. 277 [HAMLET]
3148   My heart is drowned with grief,
        Whose flood begins to flow within mine eyes.
            II Henry VI, Act iii, sc. 1, l. 198 [KING HENRY]
3149   Oft have I heard that grief softens the mind
        And makes it fearful and degenerate;
        Think therefore on revenge and cease to weep.
            II Henry VI, Act iv, sc. 4, l. 1 [QUEEN]
3150   O Cassius, I am sick of many griefs.
            Julius Cæsar, Act iv, sc. 3, l. 144 [BRUTUS]
3151   Now is that noble vessel full of grief,
        That it runs over even at his eyes.
            Julius Cæsar, Act v, sc. 5, l. 13 [CLITUS]
3152   I will instruct my sorrows to be proud;
        For grief is proud and makes his owner stoop.
        To me and to the state of my great grief
        Let kings assemble; for my grief's so great
        That no supporter but the huge firm earth
        Can hold it up: here I and sorrows sit;
        Here is my throne, bid kings come bow to it.
            King John, Act iii, sc. 1, l. 68 [CONSTANCE]
3153   PANDULPH: You hold too heinous a respect of grief.
        CONSTANCE: He talks to me that never had a son.
        KING PHILIP: You are as fond of grief as of your child.
        CONSTANCE: Grief fills the room up of my absent child,
        Lies in his bed, walks up and down with me,
        Puts on his pretty looks, repeats his words,

Remembers me of all his gracious parts,
Stuffs out his vacant garments with his form;
Then, have I reason to be fond of grief?
Fare you well: had you such a loss as I,
I could give better comfort than you do.
                      King John, Act iii, sc. 4, l. 90 [PANDULPH]

3154 Every one can master a grief but he that has it.
                 Much Ado about Nothing, Act iii, sc. 2, l. 28 [BENEDICK]

3155 Bid sorrow wag, cry 'hem!' when he should groan,
Patch grief with proverbs, make misfortunes drunk
With candle-wasters.
                  Much Ado about Nothing, Act v, sc. 1, l. 16 [LEONATO]

3156 Men can counsel and speak comfort to that grief
Which they themselves not feel; but, tasting it,
Their counsel turns to passion, which before
Would give preceptial medicine to rage,
Fetter strong madness in a silken thread,
Charm ache with air and agony with words.
                  Much Ado about Nothing, Act v, sc. 1, l. 20 [LEONATO]

3157   My particular grief
Is of so flood-gate and o'erbearing nature
That it englutts and swallows other sorrows.
                          Othello, Act i, sc. 3, l. 55 [BRABANTIO]

3158 CLEON: My Dionyza, shall we rest us here,
And by relating tales of others' griefs,
See if 'twill teach us to forget our own?
DIONYZA: That were to blow at fire in hope to quench it.
                             Pericles, Act i, sc. 4, l. 1 [CLEON]

3159 True grief is fond and testy as a child.
                                 The Rape of Lucrece, l. 1094

3160 Sad souls are slain in merry company;
Grief best is pleased with grief's society.
                                 The Rape of Lucrece, l. 1110

3161 Great grief grieves most at that would do it good;
Deep woes roll forward like a gentle flood,
Who, being stopp'd, the bounding banks o'erflows;
Grief, dallied with, nor law nor limit knows.
                        The Rape of Lucrece, l. 1117 [LUCRECE]

3162   Grief boundeth where it falls,
Not with the empty hollowness, but weight.
                        Richard II, Act i, sc. 2, l. 58 [DUCHESS]

3163 GAUNT: What is six winters? they are quickly gone.
BOLINGBROKE: To men in joy; but grief makes one hour ten.
                        Richard II, Act i, sc. 3, l. 260 [GAUNT]

3164 Must I . . . boast of nothing else
But that I was a journeyman to grief?
                     Richard II, Act i, sc. 3, l. 273 [BOLINGBROKE]

3165 Each substance of a grief hath twenty shadows,
Which shows like grief itself, but is not so;
For sorrow's eye, glazed with blinding tears,
Divides one thing entire to many objects.
                          Richard II, Act ii, sc. 2, l. 14 [BUSHY]

3166 BOLINGBROKE: I thought you had been willing to resign.
KING RICHARD: My crown I am; but still my griefs are mine:
You my glories and my state depose,
But not my griefs; still am I king of those.
                     Richard II, Act iv, sc. 1, l. 190 [BOLINGBROKE]

3167   My grief lies all within;
And these external manners of laments
Are merely shadows to the unseen grief
That swells with silence in the tortured soul.
Richard II, Act iv, sc. 1, 1. 295 [KING RICHARD]

3168 One desperate grief cures with another's languish.
Romeo and Juliet, Act i, sc. 2, 1. 49 [BENVOLIO]

3169 Evermore weeping for your cousin's death?
What, wilt thou wash him from his grave with tears?
An if thou couldst, thou couldst not make him live;
Therefore have done: some grief shows much of love:
But much of grief shows still some want of wit.
Romeo and Juliet, Act iii, sc. 5, 1. 70 [LADY CAPULET]

3170 He's something stained With grief that's beauty's canker.
The Tempest, Act i, sc. 2, 1. 413 [PROSPERO]

3171   Grief has so wrought on him,
He takes false shadows for true substances.
Titus Andronicus, Act iii, sc. 2, 1. 79 [MARCUS]

3172 I have heard my grandsire say full oft
Extremity of griefs would make men mad.
Titus Andronicus, Act iv, sc. 1, 1. 18 [LUCIUS]

3173 What grief hath set the jaundice on your cheeks?
Troilus and Cressida, Act i, sc. 3, 1. 1 [AGAMEMNON]

3174 The grief is fine, full, perfect, that I taste.
Troilus and Cressida, Act iv, sc. 4, 1. 3 [CRESSIDA]

3175 Grief hath two tongues, and never woman yet
Could rule them both without ten women's wit.
Venus and Adonis, 1. 1007 [VENUS]

3176   What's gone and what's past help
Should be past grief.
The Winter's Tale, Act iii, sc. 2, 1. 223 [PAULINA]

Ground

3177 We go to gain a little patch of ground
That hath in it no profit but the name.
To pay five ducats, five, I would not farm it.
Hamlet, Act iv, sc. 4, 1. 18 [CAPTAIN]

3178 I do affect the very ground, which is base, when her shoe, which
is baser, guided by her foot, which is basest, doth tread.
Love's Labour's Lost, Act i, sc. 2, 1. 173 [ARMADO]

Guest

3179 Make yourself my guest Whilst you abide here.
Antony and Cleopatra, Act ii, sc. 2, 1. 249 [AGRIPPA]

3180 To-night in Harfleur will we be your guest;
To-morrow for the march are we addrest.
Henry V, Act iii, sc. 3, 1. 57 [KING HENRY]

3181   I have heard it said, unbidden guests
Are often welcomest when they are gone.
I Henry VI, Act ii, sc. 2, 1. 55 [BEDFORD]

Guilt

3182   It started like a guilty thing
Upon a fearful summons.
Hamlet, Act i, sc. 1, 1. 148 [HORATIO]

3183 To my sick soul, as sin's true nature is,
Each toy seems prologue to some great amiss:

So full of artless jealousy is guilt,
It spills itself in fearing to be spilt.
>   *Hamlet,* Act iv, sc. 5, l. 17 [QUEEN]

3184   Guiltiness will speak,
Though tongues were out of use.
>   *Othello,* Act v, sc. 1, l. 109 [IAGO]

3185   They whose guilt within their bosoms lie
Imagine every eye beholds their blame.
>   *The Rape of Lucrece,* l. 1342

3186   Their great guilt,
Like poison given to work a great time after,
Now 'gins to bite the spirits.
>   *The Tempest,* Act iii, sc. 3, l. 105 [GONZALO]

Guts See also Bowels

3187   Let vultures gripe thy guts! for gourd and fullam holds,
And high and low beguiles the rich and poor.
>   *The Merry Wives of Windsor,* Act i, sc. 3, l. 94 [PISTOL]

3188   Is it not strange that sheeps' guts should hale souls out of men's
bodies?
>   *Much Ado about Nothing,* Act ii, sc. 3, l. 61 [BENEDICK]

H

Habit

3189   Costly thy habit as thy purse can buy,
But not express'd in fancy; rich, not gaudy;
For the apparel oft proclaims the man.
>   *Hamlet,* Act i, sc. 3, l. 70 [POLONIUS]

3190   If thou didst put this sour-cold habit on
To castigate thy pride, 'twere well: but thou
Dost it enforcedly.
>   *Timon of Athens,* Act iv, sc. 3, l. 239 [APEMANTUS]

3191   LUCETTA: But in what habit will you go along?
JULIA: Not like a woman; for I would prevent
The loose encounters of lascivious men.
Gentle Lucetta, fit me with such weeds
As may beseem some well-reputed page. . . .
LUCETTA: What fashion, madam, shall I make your breeches? . . .
You must needs have them with a codpiece, madam.
JULIA: Out, out, Lucetta! that will be ill-favour'd.
>   *The Two Gentlemen of Verona,* Act ii, sc. 7, l. 39 [LUCETTA]

Hair

3192   ROSALIND: His very hair is of a dissembling colour.
CELIA: Something browner than Judas's. . . .
ROSALIND: I' faith, his hair is of a good colour.
CELIA: An excellent colour: your chestnut was ever the only
colour.
>   *As You Like It,* Act iii, sc. 4, l. 7 [ROSALIND]

3193   DROMIO S.: What [Time] hath scanted men in hair he hath given
them in wit.
ANTIPHOLUS S.: But there's many a man hath more hair than wit.
DROMIO S.: Not a man of those but he hath the wit to lose his hair.
>   *The Comedy of Errors,* Act ii, sc. 2, l. 82 [DROMIO OF SYRACUSE]

3194   How is it that . . .
Your bedded hair, like life in excrements,
Start up and stand on end.
                              Hamlet, Act iii, sc. 4, l. 121 [QUEEN]
3195   The weight of a hair will turn the scales between their avoirdupois.
                              II Henry IV, Act ii, sc. 4, l. 279 [FALSTAFF]
3196   These gray locks, the pursuivants of death,
Nestor-like aged in an age of care,
Argue the end of Edmund Mortimer.
                              I Henry VI, Act ii, sc. 5, l. 5 [MORTIMER]
3197   His silver hairs
Will purchase us a good opinion
And buy men's voices to commend our deeds.
                              Julius Cæsar, Act ii, sc. 1, l. 144 [METULLUS]
3198   Her sunny locks
Hang on her temples like a golden fleece.
                              The Merchant of Venice, Act i, sc. 1, l. 169 [BASSANIO]
3199   Here in her hairs
The painter plays the spider and hath woven
A golden mesh to entrap the hearts of men
Faster than gnats in cobwebs.
                              The Merchant of Venice, Act iii, sc. 2, l. 121 [BASSANIO]
3200   I profess requital to a hair's breadth.
                              The Merry Wives of Windsor, Act iv, sc. 2, l. 3 [FALSTAFF]
3201   PANDARUS: Quoth she, 'Here's but two and fifty hairs on your
chin, and one of them is white.' . . . 'Two and fifty hairs,' quoth
he, 'and one white: that white hair is my father, and all the rest
are his sons.' 'Jupiter,' quoth she, 'which of these hairs is Paris,
my husband?' 'The forked one,' quoth he, 'pluck 't out, and give
it him.' But there was such laughing! and Helen so blushed, and
Paris so chafed, and all the rest so laughed, that it passed.
CRESSIDA: So let it now; for it has been a great while going by.
                              Troilus and Cressida, Act i, sc. 2, l. 171 [PANDARUS]
3202   SPEED: 'Item: She hath more hair than wit.' . . .
LAUNCE: More hair than wit? It may be: I'll prove it. The cover
of the salt hides the salt, and therefore it is more than the salt;
the hair that covers the wit is more than the wit, for the greater
hides the less.
                              The Two Gentlemen of Verona, Act iii, sc. 1, l. 361 [SPEED]

Hand

3203   There is gold, and here
My bluest veins to kiss; a hand that kings
Have lipp'd, and trembled kissing.
                              Antony and Cleopatra, Act ii, sc. 5, l. 27 [CLEOPATRA]
3204   These hands do lack nobility, that they strike
A meaner than myself; since I myself
Have given myself the cause.
                              Antony and Cleopatra, Act ii, sc. 5, l. 82 [CLEOPATRA]
3205   THYREUS: Give me grace to lay My duty on your hand.
CLEOPATRA: Your Cæsar's father oft,
When he hath mused of taking kingdoms in,
Bestow'd his lips on that unworthy place,
As it rain'd kisses.
                              Antony and Cleopatra, Act iii, sc. 13, l. 81 [THYREUS]
3206   To let a fellow that will take rewards
And say 'God quit you!' be familiar with

My playfellow, your hand, this kingly seal
And plighter of high hearts!

Antony and Cleopatra, Act iii, sc. 13, l. 123 [Antony]

3207   Henceforth
The white hand of a lady fever thee,
Shake thou to look on 't.

Antony and Cleopatra, Act iii, sc. 13, l. 137 [Antony]

3208   That self hand,
Which writ his honour in the acts it did,
Hath, with the courage which the heart did lend it,
Splitted the heart.

Antony and Cleopatra, Act v, sc. 1, l. 21 [Dercetas]

3209   Pinch: Give me your hand and let me feel your pulse.
Antipholus E.: There is my hand, and let it feel your ear.

The Comedy of Errors, Act iv, sc. 4, l. 55 [Pinch]

3210   What if this cursed hand
Were thicker than itself with brother's blood,
Is there not rain enough in the sweet heavens
To wash it white as snow?

Hamlet, Act iii, sc. 3, l. 43 [King]

3211   The hand of little employment hath the daintier sense.

Hamlet, Act v, sc. 1, l. 77 [Hamlet]

3212   Give me thy fist, thy fore-foot to me give:
Thy spirits are most tall.

Henry V, Act ii, sc. 1, l. 71 [Pistol]

3213   Lay not thy hands on me; forbear, I say;
Their touch affrights me as a serpent's sting.

II Henry VI, Act iii, sc. 2, l. 46 [King Henry]

3214   There's no better sign of a brave mind than a hard hand.

II Henry VI, Act iv, sc. 2, l. 21 [Bevis]

3215   I had rather chop this hand off at a blow,
And with the other fling it at thy face,
Than bear so low a sail, to strike to thee.

III Henry VI, Act v, sc. 1, l. 50 [Warwick]

3216   The fairest hand I ever touch'd! O beauty,
Till now I never knew thee!

Henry VIII, Act i, sc. 4, l. 75 [King Henry]

(Referring to Anne Bullen.)

3217   Let each man render me his bloody hand;
First, Marcus Brutus, will I shake with you.

Julius Cæsar, Act iii, sc. 1, l. 184 [Antony]

3218   This hand of mine
Is yet a maiden and an innocent hand,
Not painted with the crimson spots of blood.

King John, Act iv, sc. 2, l. 251 [Hubert]

3219   Gloucester: O, let me kiss that hand!
Lear: Let me wipe it first; it smells of mortality.

King Lear, Act iv, sc. 6, l. 135 [Gloucester]

3220   To her white hand see thou commend This seal'd-up counsel.

Love's Labour's Lost, Act iii, sc. 1, l. 169 [Biron]

3221   A giving hand, though foul, shall have fair praise.

Love's Labour's Lost, Act iv, sc. 1, l. 23 [Princess]

3222   Maria: Wide o' the bow hand! i' faith, your hand is out. . . .
Boyet: An if my hand be out, then belike your hand is in.

Love's Labour's Lost, Act iv, sc. 1, l. 135 [Maria]

3223   That phraseless hand,
Whose white weights down the airy scale of praise.
A Lover's Complaint, l. 225

3224   MACBETH : Will all great Neptune's ocean wash this blood
Clean from my hand? No, this my hand will rather
The multitudinous seas incarnadine,
Making the green one red.
LADY MACBETH : My hands are of your colour; but I shame
To wear a heart so white.
Macbeth, Act ii, sc. 2, l. 60 [MACBETH]

3225   Out, damned spot! out, I say! . . . What, will these hands ne'er
be clean? . . . Here's the smell of the blood still: all the perfumes
of Arabia will not sweeten this little hand.
Macbeth, Act v, sc. 1, l. 39 [LADY MACBETH]

3226   I know the hand: in faith, 'tis a fair hand;
And whiter than the paper it writ on
Is the fair hand that writ.
The Merchant of Venice, Act ii, sc. 4, l. 12 [LORENZO]
I think we do know the sweet Roman hand.
Twelfth Night, Act iii, sc. 4, l. 30 [MALVOLIO]

3227   Her lily hand her rosy cheek lies under,
Cozening the pillow of a lawful kiss.
The Rape of Lucrece, l. 386

3228   O, had the monster seen those lily hands
Tremble, like aspen leaves, upon a lute,
And make the silken strings delight to kiss them,
He would not then have touch'd them for his life.
Titus Andronicus, Act ii, sc. 4, l. 44 [MARCUS]

3229   Her hand,
In whose comparison all whites are ink,
Writing their own reproach, to whose soft seizure
The cygnet's down is harsh and spirit of sense
Hard as the palm of plowman.
Troilus and Cressida, Act i, sc. 1, l. 55 [TROILUS]

3230   By my troth, thou hast an open hand.
Twelfth Night, Act iv, sc. 1, l. 22 [CLOWN]

Hand and Heart

3231   Now join your hands, and with your hands your hearts.
III Henry VI, Act iv, sc. 6, l. 39 [KING HENRY]

3232   CASSIUS : Give me your hand.
BRUTUS : And my heart too.
Julius Cæsar, Act iv, sc. 3, l. 117 [CASSIUS]

3233   OTHELLO : Give me your hand: this hand is moist, my lady.
DESDEMONA : It yet hath felt no age nor known no sorrow.
OTHELLO : This argues fruitfulness and liberal heart. . . .
'Tis a good hand, A frank one.
DESDEMONA : You may, indeed, say so;
For 'twas that hand that gave away my heart.
OTHELLO : A liberal hand: the hearts of old gave hands;
But now our heraldry is hands, not hearts.
Othello, Act iii, sc. 4, l. 36 [OTHELLO]

3234   My heart is not confederate with my hand.
Richard II, Act v, sc. 3, l. 53 [AUMERLE]

3235   By heaven, my heart is purged from grudging hate;
And with my hand, I seal my true heart's love.
Richard III, Act ii, sc. 1, l. 9 [RIVERS]

3236   FERDINAND: Here's my hand.
        MIRANDA: And mine, with my heart in't.
                        The Tempest, Act iii, sc. 1, l. 89 [FERDINAND]

Hanging

3237   Hanging is the word, sir. . . . O, the charity of a penny cord!
        it sums up thousands in a trice: you have no true debtor and
        creditor but it.
                        Cymbeline, Act v, sc. 4, l. 154 [GAOLER]

3238   Marry, I'll see thee hanged first.
                        I Henry IV, Act ii, sc. 1, l. 44 [CARRIER]
        I'll see thee hanged on Sunday first.
                The Taming of the Shrew, Act ii, sc. 1, l. 301 [KATHARINA]

3239   Go hang thyself in thine own heir-apparent garters.
                        I Henry IV, Act ii, sc. 2, l. 47 [FALSTAFF]

3240   If I become not a cart as well as another man, a plague on my
        bringing up! I hope I shall as soon be strangled with a halter as
        another.
                        I Henry IV, Act ii, sc. 4, l. 545 [FALSTAFF]

3241   O, burn her, burn her! hanging is too good.
                        I Henry VI, Act v, sc. 4, l. 33 [SHEPHERD]

3242   I do find your hangman is a more penitent trade than your bawd;
        he doth oftener ask forgiveness.
                        Measure for Measure, Act iv, sc. 2, l. 52 [POMPEY]

3243   He that drinks all night, and is hanged betimes in the morning,
        may sleep the sounder all the next day.
                        Measure for Measure, Act iv, sc. 3, l. 48 [POMPEY]

3244   The ancient saying is no heresy,
        Hanging and wiving goes by destiny.
                The Merchant of Venice, Act ii, sc. 9, l. 82 [NERISSA]

3245   I have great comfort from this fellow: methinks he hath no
        drowning mark upon him; his complexion is perfect gallows.
        Stand fast, good Fate, to his hanging. . . . If he be not born to
        be hanged, our case is miserable.
                        The Tempest, Act i, sc. 1, l. 31 [GONZALO]
        Go, go, be gone, to save your ship from wreck,
        Which cannot perish having thee aboard,
        Being destined to a drier death on shore.
                The Two Gentlemen of Verona, Act i, sc. 1, l. 156 [PROTEUS]

3246   Let them hang themselves in their own straps.
                        Twelfth Night, Act i, sc. 3, l. 13 [SIR TOBY]

3247   Go hang yourselves all! you are idle shallow things:
        I am not of your element.
                        Twelfth Night, Act iii, sc. 4, l. 136 [MALVOLIO]

3248   He that is well hanged in this world needs to fear no colours.
                        Twelfth Night, Act i, sc. 5, l. 5 [CLOWN]

3249   Many a good hanging prevents a bad marriage.
                        Twelfth Night, Act i, sc. 5, l. 20 [CLOWN]

3250   A man is never undone until he be hanged.
                The Two Gentlemen of Verona, Act ii, sc. 5, l. 5 [LAUNCE]

Hap

3251   More blessed hap did ne'er befall our state.
                        I Henry VI, Act i, sc. 6, l. 10 [CHARLES]

3252   WARWICK: How now, my lord? what hap? what hope of good?
        GEORGE: Our hap is loss, our hope but sad despair;
        Our ranks are broke, and ruin follows us.
                        III Henry VI, Act ii, sc. 3, l. 8 [WARWICK]

3253   More direful hap betide that hated wretch . . .
Than I can wish to adders, spiders, toads.
Richard III, Act i, sc. 2, l. 17 [ANNE]

3254   Hap what hap may, I'll roundly go about her.
The Taming of the Shrew, Act iv, sc. 4, l. 109 [LUCENTIO]

Happiness

3255   How bitter a thing it is to look into happiness through another
man's eyes!
As You Like It, Act v, sc. ii, l. 48 [ORLANDO]

3256   Now, my masters, happy man be his dole, say I.
I Henry IV, Act ii, sc. 2, l. 81 [FALSTAFF]
("Dole," lot in life, destiny. A proverbial phrase repeated in
The Merry Wives of Windsor, iii, 4, 68; *The Taming of the
Shrew,* i, 1, 144; *The Winter's Tale,* i, 2, 163.)

3257   Happy thou art not;
For what thou hast not, still thou strivest to get,
And what thou hast, forget'st.
Measure for Measure, Act iii, sc. 1, l. 21 [DUKE]

3258   It is no mean happiness to be seated in the mean. Superfluity comes
sooner by white hairs, but competency lives longer.
The Merchant of Venice, Act i, sc. 2, l. 8 [NERISSA]

3259   O happiness enjoy'd but of a few!
And, if possess'd, as soon decay'd and done
As is the morning's silver-melting dew
Against the golden splendour of the sun!
The Rape of Lucrece, l. 22

3260   Wish me partaker of thy happiness
When thou dost meet good hap.
The Two Gentlemen of Verona, Act i, sc. 1, l. 14 [PROTEUS]

Hard

3261   He was ever too hard for him; I have heard him say so himself.
Coriolanus, Act iv, sc. 5, l. 195 [SERVANT]
Charles, I will play no more to-night;
My mind's not on 't; you are too hard for me.
Henry VIII, Act v, sc. 1, l. 56 [KING HENRY]

3262   They use to write it on the top of letters: 'twill go hard with you.
II Henry VI, Act iv, sc. 2, l. 108 [DICK]
If law, authority and power deny not,
It will go hard with poor Antonio.
The Merchant of Venice, Act iii, sc. 2, l. 292 [JESSICA]

3263   Thy heart as hard as steel.
III Henry VI, Act ii, sc. 1, l. 201 [RICHARD]
Give her no token but stones; for she's as hard as steel.
The Two Gentlemen of Verona, Act i, sc. 1, l. 148 [SPEED]
Art thou obdurate, flinty, hard as steel?
Venus and Adonis, l. 199 [VENUS]
More hard than stones.
Titus Andronicus, Act iii, sc. 1, l. 45 [TITUS]

Hare

3264   BASTARD: You are the hare of whom the proverb goes,
Whose valour plucks dead lions by the beard. . . .
AUSTRIA: What cracker is this same that deafs our ears
With this abundance of superfluous breath?
King John, Act ii, sc. 1, l. 137 [BASTARD]
(The proverb is, "Hares may pluck dead lions by the beard.")

3265   ROMEO: What hast thou found?
        MERCUTIO: No hare, sir; unless a hare, sir, in a lenten pie, that
        is something stale and hoar ere it be spent. [*Sings*]
                        An old hare hoar,
                        And an old hare hoar,
                    Is very good meat in Lent:
                        But a hare that is hoar
                        Is too much for a score,
                    When it hoars ere it be spent.
                        Romeo and Juliet, Act ii, sc. 4, l. 137 [ROMEO]

Harm

3266   Ten thousand harms, more than the ills I know,
        My idleness doth hatch.
                    Antony and Cleopatra, Act i, sc. 2, l. 133 [ANTONY]
3267   Let me still take away the harms I fear,
        Not fear still to be taken.
                        King Lear, Act i, sc. 4, l. 352 [GONERIL]
3268   I have done no harm. But I remember now
        I am in this earthly world; where to do harm
        Is often laudable, to do good sometime
        Accounted dangerous folly.
                        Macbeth, Act iv, sc. 2, l. 74 [LADY MACDUFF]
3269   Thou hast not half that power to do me harm
        As I have to be hurt.
                        Othello, Act v, sc. 2, l. 162 [EMILIA]
3270   None can cure their harms by wailing them.
                        Richard III, Act ii, sc. 2, l. 103 [GLOUCESTER]

Harmony

3271   How irksome is this music to my heart!
        When such strings jar, what hope of harmony?
                        II Henry VI, Act ii, sc. 1, l. 56 [KING HENRY]
3272   Cause the musicians play me that sad note
        I named my knell, whilst I sit meditating
        On that celestial harmony I go to.
                        Henry VIII, Act iv, sc. 2, l. 78 [KATHARINE]
3273   How sweet the moonlight sleeps upon this bank!
        Here will we sit and let the sounds of music
        Creep in our ears: soft stillness and the night
        Become the touches of sweet harmony.
        Sit, Jessica. Look how the floor of heaven
        Is thick inlaid with patines of bright gold:
        There's not the smallest orb which thou behold'st
        But in his motion like an angel sings,
        Still quiring to the young-eyed cherubins;
        Such harmony is in immortal souls;
        But whilst this muddy vesture of decay
        Doth grossly close it in, we cannot hear it.
                    The Merchant of Venice, Act v, sc. 1, l. 56 [LORENZO]
3274   The harmony of their tongues hath into bondage
        Brought my too diligent ear.
                        The Tempest, Act iii, sc. 1, l. 41 [FERDINAND]
3275   Had he heard the heavenly harmony
        Which that sweet tongue hath made,
        He would have dropp'd his knife, and fell asleep
        As Cerberus at the Thracian poet's feet.
                        Titus Andronicus, Act ii, sc. 4, l. 48 [MARCUS]

Harping

3276   He seems
Proud and disdainful, harping on what I am,
Not what he knew I was.
Antony and Cleopatra, Act iii, sc. 13, l. 142 [ANTONY]

3277   Still harping on my daughter.
Hamlet, Act ii, sc. 2, l. 180 [POLONIUS]

3278   Harp not on that, nor do not banish reason
For inequality.
Measure for Measure, Act v, sc. 1, l. 64 [ISABELLA]

3279   KING RICHARD: Harp not on that string, madam; that is past.
QUEEN ELIZABETH: Harp on it still shall I till heart-strings break.
Richard III, Act iv, sc. 4, l. 364 [KING RICHARD]

Harpy

3280   Thou art like the harpy,
Which, to betray, dost, with thine angel's face,
Seize with thine eagle's talons.
Pericles, Act iv, sc. 3, l. 46 [CLEON]

Haste

3281   This sweaty haste
Doth make the night joint-labourer with the day.
Hamlet, Act i, sc. 1, l. 77 [MARCELLUS]

3282   This, I take it, Is the main motive . . .
Of this post-haste and romage in the land.
Hamlet, Act i, sc. 1, l. 104 [HORATIO]

3283   Let your haste commend your duty.
Hamlet, Act i, sc. 2, l. 39 [KING]

3284   [We] In haste, post-haste, are come to join with you.
III Henry VI, Act ii, sc. 1, l. 139 [WARWICK]
He requires your haste-post-haste appearance.
Othello, Act i, sc. 2, l. 37 [CASSIO]

3285   KING JOHN: Nay, but make haste; the better foot before; . . .
Be Mercury, set feathers to thy heels,
And fly like thought from them to me again.
BASTARD: The spirit of the time shall teach me speed.
King John, Act iv, sc. 2, l. 170 [KING JOHN]

3286   Haste still pays haste, and leisure answers leisure;
Like doth quit like, and MEASURE still FOR MEASURE.
Measure for Measure, Act v, sc. 1, l. 415 [DUKE]

3287   The affair cries haste, And speed must answer it.
Othello, Act i, sc. 3, l. 277 [DUKE]

3288   Let your breath cool yourself, telling your haste.
Pericles, Act i, sc. 1, l. 161 [ANTIOCHUS]

3289   He tires betimes that spurs too fast betimes.
Richard II, Act ii, sc. 1, l. 36 [GAUNT]

3290   Bloody with spurring, fiery-red with haste.
Richard II, Act ii, sc. 3, l. 58 [NORTHUMBERLAND]

3291   ROMEO: O, let us hence; I stand on sudden haste.
FRIAR LAURENCE: Wisely and slow; they stumble that run fast.
Romeo and Juliet, Act ii, sc. 3, l. 93 [ROMEO]

Hate

3292   In time we hate that which we often fear.
Antony and Cleopatra, Act i, sc. 3, l. 12 [CHARMIAN]

3293   My soul, yet I know not why, hates nothing more than he.
As You Like It, Act i, sc. 1, l. 174 [OLIVER]

3294   There is the man of my soul's hate.
                              Coriolanus, Act i, sc. 5, l. 11 [MARCIUS]

3295   CORIOLANUS: I do hate thee worse than a promise-breaker.
       AUFIDIUS: We hate alike:
       Not Afric owns a serpent I abhor
       More than thy fame and envy.
                              Coriolanus, Act i, sc. 8, l. 1 [CORIOLANUS]

3296   The prayers of priests nor time of sacrifice,
       Embarquements all of fury, shall lift up
       Their rotten privilege and customs 'gainst
       My hate to Marcius.
                              Coriolanus, Act i, sc. 10, l. 21 [AUFIDIUS]

3297   What! I, that kill'd her husband and his father,
       To take her in her heart's extremest hate,
       With curses in her mouth, tears in her eyes,
       The bleeding witness of her hatred by.
                              Richard III, Act i, sc. 2, l. 231 [GLOUCESTER]

3298   Romeo, the hate I bear thee can afford
       No better term than this,—thou art a villain.
                              Romeo and Juliet, Act iii, sc. 1, l. 63 [TYBALT]

3299   'I hate' from hate away she threw,
       And saved my life, saying 'not you.'
                                                Sonnet, cxlv, l. 13

Havoc

3300   Do not cry havoc, where you should but hunt
       With modest warrant.
                              Coriolanus, Act iii, sc. 1, l. 273 [MENENIUS]
       (To cry "havoc," i.e. to give no quarter.)

3301   Cry 'Havoc' and let slip the dogs of war.
                              Julius Cæsar, Act iii, sc. 1, l. 273 [ANTONY]
       Cry 'Havoc!' kings; back to the stained field.
                              King John, Act ii, sc. 1, l. 257 [BASTARD]

Hawthorn

3302   Gives not the hawthorn-bush a sweeter shade
       To shepherds looking on their silly sheep,
       Than doth a rich embroider'd canopy
       To kings that fear their subjects' treachery?
                              III Henry VI, Act ii, sc. 5, l. 42 [KING HENRY]

3303   Through the sharp hawthorn blows the cold wind.
                              King Lear, Act iii, sc. 4, l. 47 [EDGAR]

       (Repeated in l. 102.)

Hay

3304   'Twas her brother that, in pure kindness to his horse, buttered
       his hay.
                              King Lear, Act ii, sc. 4, l. 128 [FOOL]

3305   TITANIA: Or say, sweet love, what thou desirest to eat.
       BOTTOM: Truly, a peck of provender: I could munch your good
       dry oats. Methinks I have a great desire to a bottle of hay: good
       hay, sweet hay, hath no fellow.
                A Midsummer Night's Dream, Act iv, sc. 1, l. 32 [TITANIA]

Hazard

3306   It is
       A charge too heavy for my strength, but yet
       We'll strive to bear it for your worthy sake
       To the extreme edge of hazard.
                  All's Well that Ends Well, Act iii, sc. 3, l. 3 [BERTRAM]

3307   Were it good
To set the exact wealth of all our states
All at one cast? to set so rich a main
On the nice hazard of one doubtful hour?
I Henry IV, Act iv, sc. 1, l. 45 [HOTSPUR]

3308   Why, now, blow wind, swell billow, and swim bark!
The storm is up, and all is on the hazard.
Julius Cæsar, Act v, sc. 1, l. 67 [CASSIUS]

3309   Slave, I have set my life upon a cast,
And I will stand the hazard of the die.
Richard III, Act v, sc. 4, l. 9 [KING RICHARD]

Head

3310   A' never broke any man's head but his own, and that was against
a post when he was drunk.
Henry V, Act iii, sc. 2, l. 43 [BOY]

3311   Foolish curs, that run winking into the mouth of a Russian bear,
and have their heads crushed like rotten apples!
Henry V, Act iii, sc. 7, l. 153 [ORLEANS]

3312   The sale of offices and towns in France . . .
Would make thee quickly hop without thy head.
II Henry VI, Act i, sc. 3, l. 138 [QUEEN]

3313   Rather let my head
Stoop to the block than these knees bow to any
Save to the God of heaven and to my king.
II Henry VI, Act iv, sc. 1, l. 124 [SUFFOLK]

3314   Off with the traitor's head!
III Henry VI, Act ii, sc. 8, l. 85 [WARWICK]
Off with his guilty head!
III Henry VI, Act v, sc. 5, l. 3 [KING EDWARD]
(A phrase frequently repeated.)

3315   Thy head stands so tickle on thy shoulders that a milkmaid, if
she be in love, may sigh it off.
Measure for Measure, Act i, sc. 2, l. 176 [LUCIO]

3316   Inch-thick, knee-deep, o'er head and ears a fork'd one!
The Winter's Tale, Act i, sc. 2, l. 186 [LEONTES]

Health

3317   What is infirm from your sound parts shall fly,
Health shall live free and sickness freely die.
All's Well that Ends Well, Act ii, sc. 1, l. 170 [HELENA]

3318   Health, alack, with youthful wings is flown
From this bare wither'd trunk.
II Henry IV, Act iv, sc. 5, l. 229 [KING HENRY]

3319   CASSIUS: Have mind upon your health, tempt me no farther.
BRUTUS: Away, slight man!
Julius Cæsar, Act iv, sc. 3, l. 36 [CASSIUS]

3320   GENTLEMAN: I am sound.
LUCIO: Nay, not as one would say, healthy; but so sound as
things that are hollow: thy bones are hollow; impiety has made a
feast of thee.
Measure for Measure, Act i, sc. 2, l. 54 [GENTLEMAN]

3321   Testy sick men, when their deaths be near,
No news but health from their physicians know.
Sonnet, cxl, l. 7

Hearing

3322   No more . . . offend our sense of hearing; hush!
Cymbeline, Act v, sc. 4, l. 93 [JUPITER]

3323　　Warble, child; make passionate my sense of hearing.
　　　　　　　　　Love's Labour's Lost, Act iii, sc. 1, l. 1 [ARMADO]
3324　　Sweet royalty, bestow on me the sense of hearing.
　　　　　　　　　Love's Labour's Lost, Act v, sc. 2, l. 670 [ARMADO]
3325　　MRS. FORD: Did you ever hear the like?
　　　　MRS. PAGE: Letter for letter.
　　　　　　　The Merry Wives of Windsor, Act ii, sc. 1, l. 70 [MRS. FORD]
3326　　FIRST GENTLEMAN: Did you ever hear the like?
　　　　SECOND GENTLEMAN: No, nor never shall do in such a place as
　　　　this.
　　　　　　　　　　Pericles, Act iv, sc. 5, l. 1 [FIRST GENTLEMAN]

Heart See also Hand and Heart

3327　　　　　　　　Cheer your heart:
　　　　Be you not troubled with the time, which drives
　　　　O'er your content these strong necessities.
　　　　　　　Antony and Cleopatra, Act iii, sc. 6, l. 81 [OCTAVIUS CÆSAR]
3328　　ANTONY: Cold-hearted toward me?
　　　　CLEOPATRA: Ah, dear, if I be so,
　　　　From my cold heart let heaven engender hail,
　　　　And poison it in the source; and the first stone
　　　　Drop in my neck: as it determines, so
　　　　Dissolve my life!
　　　　　　　　Antony and Cleopatra, Act iii, sc. 13, l. 158 [ANTONY]
3329　　Measureless liar, thou hast made my heart
　　　　Too great for what contains it.
　　　　　　　　　Coriolanus, Act v, sc. 6, l. 102 [CORIOLANUS]
3330　　　　　　Hold, hold, my heart;
　　　　And you, my sinews, grow not instant old,
　　　　But bear me stiffly up.
　　　　　　　　　　Hamlet, Act i, sc. 5, l. 93 [HAMLET]
3331　　Bow, stubborn knees; and heart with strings of steel,
　　　　Be soft as sinews of the new-born babe!
　　　　　　　　　Hamlet, Act iii, sc. 3, l. 70 [KING]
3332　　Leave wringing of your hands: peace! sit you down,
　　　　And let me wring your heart; for so I shall,
　　　　If it be made of penetrable stuff,
　　　　If damned custom have not brass'd it so
　　　　That it be proof and bulwark against sense.
　　　　　　　　　Hamlet, Act iii, sc. 4, l. 34 [HAMLET]
3333　　QUEEN: O Hamlet, thou hast cleft my heart in twain.
　　　　HAMLET: O, throw away the worser part of it,
　　　　And live the purer with the other half.
　　　　　　　　　Hamlet, Act iii, sc. 4, l. 156 [QUEEN]
3334　　It warms the very sickness in my heart,
　　　　That I shall live and tell him to his teeth,
　　　　'Thus didest thou.'
　　　　　　　　　Hamlet, Act iv, sc. 7, l. 56 [LAERTES]
3335　　Thou wouldst not think how ill all's here about my heart: but
　　　　it is no matter.
　　　　　　　　　Hamlet, Act v, sc. 2, l. 222 [HAMLET]
3336　　　　　　I will ease my heart,
　　　　Albeit I make a hazard of my head.
　　　　　　　　　I Henry IV, Act i, sc. 3, l. 127 [HOTSPUR]
3337　　A good heart's worth gold.
　　　　　　　　　II Henry IV, Act ii, sc. 4, l. 34 [HOSTESS]
3338　　A good leg will fall; a straight back will stoop; a black beard will
　　　　turn white; a curled pate will grow bald; a fair face will wither;

a full eye will wax hollow; but a good heart, Kate, is the sun and
the moon; or rather the sun and not the moon; for it shines bright
and never changes, but keeps his course truly.

Henry V, Act v, sc. 2, l. 168 [KING HENRY]

3339   A pure unspotted heart,
Never yet taint with love, I send the king.

I Henry VI, Act v, sc. 3, l. 182 [MARGARET]

3340   O, Lord, that lends me life,
Lend me a heart replete with thankfulness!
For thou hast given me in this beauteous face
A world of earthly blessings to my soul.

II Henry VI, Act i, sc. 1, l. 19 [KING HENRY]

3341   A heart unspotted is not easily daunted.

II Henry VI, Act iii, sc. 1, l. 100 [GLOUCESTER]

3342   SUFFOLK: I go.
QUEEN: And take my heart with thee.
SUFFOLK: A jewel lock'd into the wofull'st cask
That ever did contain a thing of worth.
Even as a splitted bark, so sunder we:
This way I fall to death.
QUEEN: This way for me.

II Henry VI, Act iii, sc. 2, l. 407 [SUFFOLK]

3343   Unhappy that I am, I cannot heave
My heart into my mouth.

King Lear, Act i, sc. 1, l. 93 [CORDELIA]

3344   Nor are those empty-hearted whose low sound
Reverbs no hollowness.

King Lear, Act i, sc. 1, l. 155 [KENT]

3345   A heavy heart bears not a nimble tongue.

Love's Labour's Lost, Act v, sc. 2, l. 748 [PRINCESS]

3346   I . . . Kept hearts in liveries, but mine own was free,
And reign'd, commanding, in his monarchy.

A Lover's Complaint, l. 195

3347   I am pale at mine heart to see thine eyes so red.

Measure for Measure, Act iv, sc. 3, l. 157 [LUCIO]

3348   A kind heart he hath; a woman would run through fire and water
for such a kind heart.

The Merry Wives of Windsor, Act iii, sc. 4, l. 106
[MISTRESS QUICKLY]

3349   My heart Is true as steel.

A Midsummer Night's Dream, Act ii, sc. 1, l. 197 [HELENA]

3350   Nature never framed a woman's heart
Of prouder stuff than that of Béatrice.

Much Ado about Nothing, Act iii, sc. 1, l. 49 [HERO]

3351   He hath a heart as sound as a bell and his tongue is the clapper,
for what his heart thinks his tongue speaks.

Much Ado about Nothing, Act iii, sc. 2, l. 13 [DON PEDRO]

3352   O God, that I were a man! I would eat his heart in the market-
place. . . . I cannot be a man with wishing, therefore I will die a
woman with grieving.

Much Ado about Nothing, Act iv, sc. 1, l. 308 [BEATRICE]

3353   I will live in thy heart, die in thy lap, and be buried in thy eyes.

Much Ado about Nothing, Act v, sc. 2, l. 104 [BENEDICK]

3354   I will wear my heart upon my sleeve
For daws to peck at.

Othello, Act i, sc. 1, l. 64 [IAGO]

3355   This did I fear, . . . For he was great of heart.
                         Othello, Act v, sc. 2, l. 360 [CASSIO]

3356   By our ears our hearts oft tainted be.
                              The Rape of Lucrece, l. 38

3357   Faint not, faint heart, but stoutly say 'So be it.'
                         The Rape of Lucrece, l. 1209 [LUCRECE]

3358   Show me thy humble heart, and not thy knee,
       Whose duty is deceivable and false.
                         Richard II, Act ii, sc. 3, l. 83 [YORK]

3359   O, cut my lace in sunder, that my pent heart
       May have some scope to beat!
                         Richard III, Act iv, sc. 1, l. 34 [QUEEN ELIZABETH]

3360   My bosom's lord sits lightly in his throne;
       And all this day an unaccustom'd spirit
       Lifts me above the ground with cheerful thoughts.
                         Romeo and Juliet, Act v, sc. 1, l. 3 [ROMEO]

3361   My heart suspects more than mine eye can see.
                         Titus Andronicus, Act ii, sc. 3, l. 213 [QUINTUS]

3362   By innocence I swear, and by my youth,
       I have one heart, one bosom, and one truth,
       And that no woman has; nor never none
       Shall mistress be of it, save I alone.
                         Twelfth Night, Act iii, sc. 1, l. 169 [VIOLA]

3363   A heart
       As full of sorrows as the sea of sands.
                         The Two Gentlemen of Verona, Act iv, sc. 3, l. 32 [SILVIA]

3364   Remove your siege from my unyielding heart;
       To love's alarms it will not ope the gate.
                         Venus and Adonis, l. 423 [ADONIS]

3365   My heart stands armed in mine ear,
       And will not let a false sound enter there;
       Lest the deceiving harmony should run
       Into the quiet closure of my breast;
       And then my little heart were quite undone,
       In his bedchamber to be barr'd of rest.
       No, lady, no; my heart longs not to groan,
       But soundly sleeps, while now it sleeps alone.
                         Venus and Adonis, l. 779 [ADONIS]

3366   I have a tremor cordis on me: my heart dances;
       But not for joy; not joy.
                         The Winter's Tale, Act i, sc. 2, l. 110 [LEONTES]

3367   I saw his heart in 's face.
                         The Winter's Tale, Act i, sc. 2, l. 447 [POLIXENES]

Heart: The Breaking Heart

3368   If my heart were great, 'Twould burst at this.
                         All's Well that Ends Well, Act iv, sc. 3, l. 366 [PAROLLES]

3369   This blows my heart:
       If swift thought break it not, a swifter mean
       Shall outstrike thought: but thought will do 't, I feel.
                         Antony and Cleopatra, Act iv, sc. 6, l. 34 [ENOBARBUS]

3370   The seven-fold shield of Ajax cannot keep
       The battery from my heart. O, cleave my sides!
       Heart, once be stronger than thy continent,
       Crack thy frail case!
                         Antony and Cleopatra, Act iv, sc. 14, l. 38 [ANTONY]

3371 Now cracks a noble heart. Good night, sweet prince;
      And flights of angels sing thee to thy rest!
                    Hamlet, Act v, sc. 2, l. 370 [HORATIO]
3372 Fret till your proud heart break; . . .
      You shall digest the venom of your spleen,
      Though it do split you; for, from this day forth,
      I'll use you for my mirth, yea, for my laughter,
      When you are waspish.
                    Julius Cæsar, Act iv, sc. 3, l. 42 [BRUTUS]
3373 The tackle of my heart is crack'd and burn'd,
      And all the shrouds wherewith my life should sail
      Are turned to one thread, one little hair:
      My heart hath one poor string to stay it by,
      Which holds but till thy news be uttered;
      And then all this thou seest is but a clod
      And module of confounded royalty.
                    King John, Act v, sc. 7, l. 52 [KING JOHN]
3374 My old heart is crack'd, is crack'd!
                    King Lear, Act ii, sc. 1, l. 92 [GLOUCESTER]
3375   His flaw'd heart,
      Alack, too weak the conflict to support!
      'Twixt two extremes of passion, joy and grief,
      Burst smilingly.
                    King Lear, Act v, sc. 3, l. 196 [EDGAR]
3376 Break, heart; I prithee, break!
                    King Lear, Act v, sc. 3, l. 312 [KENT]
3377 Your heart is burst, you have lost half your soul;
      Even now, now, very now, an old black ram
      Is tupping your white ewe.
                    Othello, Act i, sc. 1, l. 87 [IAGO]
3378 My heart is great; but it must break with silence,
      Ere 't be disburden'd with a liberal tongue.
                    Richard II, Act ii, sc. 1, l. 228 [ROSS]
3379   O heart, heavy heart,
      Why sigh'st thou without breaking?
                    Troilus and Cressida, Act iv, sc. 4, l. 17 [PANDARUS]

Heart: The Hard Heart

3380 The splitting rocks cower'd in the sinking sands
      And would not dash me with their ragged sides,
      Because thy flinty heart, more hard than they,
      Might in thy palace perish Margaret.
                    II Henry VI, Act iii, sc. 2, l. 97 [QUEEN]
3381 My heart is turn'd to stone: and while 'tis mine,
      It shall be stony.
                    II Henry VI, Act v, sc. 2, l. 50 [YOUNG CLIFFORD]
      My heart is turned to stone; I strike it, and it hurts my hand.
                    Othello, Act iv, sc. 1, l. 193 [OTHELLO]
3382   Were thy heart as hard as steel,
      As thou hast shown it flinty by thy deeds,
      I come to pierce it, or to give thee mine.
                    III Henry VI, Act ii, sc. 1, l. 201 [RICHARD]
3383 You blocks, you stones, you worse than senseless things!
      O you hard hearts, you cruel men of Rome,
      Knew you not Pompey?
                    Julius Cæsar, Act i, sc. 1, l. 40 [MARULLUS]

3384   Is there any cause in nature that makes these hard hearts?
                              King Lear, Act iii, sc. 6, l. 81 [LEAR]

3385   Stone him with harden'd hearts, harder than stones.
                              The Rape of Lucrece, l. 978 [LUCRECE]

3386   I have said too much unto a heart of stone
        And laid mine honour too unchary out.
                              Twelfth Night, Act iii, sc. 4, l. 221 [OLIVIA]

Heart: The Merry Heart

3387   A cup of wine that's brisk and fine,
                And drink unto the leman mine;
                And a merry heart lives long-a.
                              II Henry IV, Act v, sc. 3, l. 48 [SILENCE]

3388   A light heart lives long.
                              Love's Labour's Lost, Act v, sc. 2, l. 18 [KATHARINE]

3389   DON PEDRO: In faith, lady, you have a merry heart.
        BEATRICE: Yes, my lord; I thank it, poor fool, it keeps on the
        windy side of care.
                              Much Ado about Nothing, Act ii, sc. 1, l. 324 [DON PEDRO]

3390   Jog on, jog on, the foot-path way,
                And merrily hent the stile-a:
                A merry heart goes all the day,
                Your sad tires in a mile-a.
                              The Winter's Tale, Act iv, sc. 3, l. 132 [AUTOLYCUS]

Heat

3391   Pray . . . that our armies join not in a hot day; . . . if it be a hot
        day, and I brandish any thing but a bottle, I would I might never
        spit white again.
                              II Henry IV, Act i, sc. 2, l. 232 [FALSTAFF]

3392   Be not so hot.
                              Measure for Measure, Act v, sc. 1, l. 315 [DUKE]
        Not so hot, good sir.
                              The Winter's Tale, Act ii, sc. 3, l. 32 [PAULINA]
        (Frequently repeated.)

3393   O rash false heat, wrapp'd in repentant cold,
        Thy hasty spring still blasts, and ne'er grows old!
                              The Rape of Lucrece, l. 48

Heaven

3394   Let heaven kiss earth! now let not Nature's hand
        Keep the wild flood confined! let order die!
                              II Henry IV, Act i, sc. 1, l. 153 [NORTHUMBERLAND]

3395   GLOUCESTER: Were it not good your grace could fly to heaven?
        KING: The treasury of everlasting joy.
        CARDINAL: Thy heaven is on earth; thine eyes and thoughts
        Beat on a crown, the treasure of thy heart.
                              II Henry VI, Act ii, sc. 1, l. 17 [GLOUCESTER]

3396   I'll make my heaven in a lady's lap,
        And deck my body in gay ornaments,
        And witch sweet ladies with my words and looks.
                              III Henry VI, Act iii, sc. 2, l. 148 [RICHARD]

3397   The will of heaven Be done in this and all things!
                              Henry VIII, Act i, sc. 1, l. 209 [BUCKINGHAM]
        The will of heaven be done, and the king's pleasure.
                              Henry VIII, Act i, sc. 1, l. 215 [ABERGAVENNY]

3398   Heaven has an end in all.
                              Henry VIII, Act ii, sc. 1, l. 124 [BUCKINGHAM]

3399   Heaven is above all yet; there sits a judge
That no king can corrupt.
Henry VIII, Act iii, sc. 1, 1. 99 [QUEEN KATHARINE]

3400   Father cardinal, I have heard you say
That we shall see and know our friends in heaven:
If that be true, I shall see my boy again;
For since the birth of Cain, the first male child,
To him that did but yesterday suspire,
There was not such a gracious creature born.
King John, Act iii, sc. 4, 1. 76 [CONSTANCE]

3401   O me! my uncle's spirit is in these stones:
Heaven take my soul, and England keep my bones!
King John, Act iv, sc. 3, 1. 9 [ARTHUR]

3402   Heaven doth with us as we with torches do,
Not light them for themselves; for if our virtues
Did not go forth of us, 'twere all alike
As if we had them not.
Measure for Measure, Act i, sc. 1, 1. 33 [DUKE]

3403   The young gentleman, according to Fates and Destinies and such
odd sayings, the Sisters Three and such branches of learning, is
indeed deceased, or, as you would say in plain terms, gone to
heaven.
The Merchant of Venice, Act ii, sc. 2, 1. 64 [LAUNCELOT]

3404   The means that heaven yields must be embraced,
And not neglected; else, if heaven would,
And we will not, heaven's offer we refuse,
The proffer'd means of succour and redress.
Richard II, Act iii, sc. 2, 1. 29 [CARLISLE]

3405   The selfsame heaven
That frowns on me looks sadly upon him.
Richard III, Act v, sc. 3, 1. 285 [KING RICHARD]

3406   Heaven and yourself
Had part in this fair maid; now heaven hath all,
And all the better is it for the maid:
Your part in her you could not keep from death,
But heaven keeps his part in eternal life.
Romeo and Juliet, Act iv, sc. 5, 1. 66 [FRIAR LAURENCE]

Heaven and Hell

3407   Trip him, that his heels may kick at heaven,
And that his soul may be as damn'd and black
As hell, whereto it goes.
Hamlet, Act iii, sc. 3, 1. 93 [HAMLET]

3408   I'll make my heaven to dream upon the crown,
And, whiles I live, to account this world but hell.
III Henry VI, Act iii, sc. 2, 1. 168 [GLOUCESTER]

3409   My comfort is that heaven will take our souls,
And plague injustice with the pains of hell.
Richard II, Act iii, sc. 1, 1. 33 [GREEN]

3410   March on, join bravely, let us to 't pell-mell;
If not to heaven, then hand in hand to hell.
Richard III, Act v, sc. 3, 1. 312 [KING RICHARD]

Heavens

3411   Though usurpers sway the rule awhile,
Yet heavens are just, and time suppresseth wrongs.
III Henry VI, Act iii, sc. 3, 1. 77 [MARGARET]

3412   O, let the heavens
Give him defence against the elements,
For I have lost him on a dangerous sea.
                    Othello, Act ii, sc. 1, l. 44 [CASSIO]
3413   The heavens do lour upon you for some ill;
Move them no more by crossing their high will.
          Romeo and Juliet, Act iv, sc. 5, l. 94 [FRIAR LAURENCE]
3414   Do as the heavens have done, forget your evil;
With them forgive yourself.
          The Winter's Tale, Act v, sc. 1, l. 5 [CLEOMENES]

Heaviness

3415   Here's sport indeed! How heavy weighs my lord!
Our strength is all gone into heaviness,
That makes the weight.
          Antony and Cleopatra, Act iv, sc. 15, l. 33 [CLEOPATRA]
3416   The heaviness and guilt within my bosom
Takes off my manhood.
                    Cymbeline, Act v, sc. 2, l. 1 [IACHIMO]
3417   Rest your gentle head upon her lap,
And she will sing the song that pleaseth you
And on your eyelids crown the god of sleep,
Charming your blood with pleasing heaviness,
Making the difference 'twixt wake and sleep
As is the difference betwixt day and night
The hour before the heavenly-harness'd team
Begins his golden progress in the east.
          I Henry IV, Act iii, sc. 1, l. 218 [GLENDOWER]
3418   You promised . . . To lay aside life-harming heaviness
And entertain a cheerful disposition.
                    Richard II, Act ii, sc. 2, l. 2 [BUSHY]

Hector

3419   BIRON: Hide thy head, Achilles: here comes Hector. . . .
BOYET: But is this Hector?
KING: I think Hector was not so clean-timbered.
LONGAVILLE: His leg is too big for Hector's.
DUMAIN: More calf, certain.
          Love's Labour's Lost, Act v, sc. 2, l. 636 [BIRON]
3420   Hector, whose patience
Is, as a virtue, fix'd, to-day was moved:
He chid Andromache and struck his armourer,
And, like as there was husbandry in war,
Before the sun rose he was harness'd light,
And to the field goes he; where every flower
Did as a prophet, weep what it foresaw
In Hector's wrath.
          Troilus and Cressida, Act i, sc. 2, l. 4 [ALEXANDER]
3421   PANDARUS: That's Hector. . . . There's a fellow! . . .
There's a brave man, niece. O brave Hector. Look how he looks!
there's a countenance! Is't not a brave man? . . . It does a man's
heart good. Look you what hacks are on his helmet. . . .
CRESSIDA: Be those with swords?
PANDARUS: Swords, any thing, he cares not; an the devil come
to him, it's all one; by God's lid, it does one's heart good.
          Troilus and Cressida, Act i, sc. 2, l. 215 [PANDARUS]
3422   In the extremity of great and little,
Valour and pride excell themselves in Hector;

The one almost as infinite as all,
The other blank as nothing.
Troilus and Cressida, Act iv, sc. 5, l. 79 [ÆNEAS]

3423 HECTOR: Now is my day's work done; I'll take good breath:
Rest, sword; thou hast thy fill of blood and death.
[*He puts off his helmet and hangs his shield behind him. Enter
Achilles and Myrmidons.*]
ACHILLES: Look, Hector, how the sun begins to set;
How ugly night comes breathing at his heels:
Even with the vail and darkling of the sun,
To close the day up, Hector's life is done.
HECTOR: I am unarm'd; forego this vantage, Greek.
ACHILLES: Strike, fellows, strike; this is the man I seek. [*Hector
falls.*]
Troilus and Cressida, Act v, sc. 8, l. 3 [HECTOR]

3424 Go in to Troy, and say there, Hector's dead:
There is a word will Priam turn to stone;
Make wells and Niobes of the maids and wives,
Cold statues of the youth, and, in a word,
Scare Troy out of itself. But, march away:
Hector is dead: there is no more to say.
Troilus and Cressida, Act v, sc. 10, l. 17 [TROILUS]

Hedge

3425 The king in this perceives him, how he coasts
And hedges his own way.
Henry VIII, Act iii, sc. 2, l. 38 [CHAMBERLAIN]

3426 I myself sometimes, leaving the fear of God on the left hand and
hiding mine honour in my necessity, am fain to shuffle, to hedge
and to lurch.
The Merry Wives of Windsor, Act ii, sc. 2, l. 26 [FALSTAFF]

3427 Walk before toward the sea-side; . . . I will but look upon the
hedge and follow you.
The Winter's Tale, Act iv, sc. 4, l. 855 [AUTOLYCUS]
(A famous euphemism.)

Heels

3428 Darest thou be so valiant as to play the coward with thy indenture,
and show it a fair pair of heels and run from it?
I Henry IV, Act ii, sc. 4, l. 52 [PRINCE]

3429 Hang me up by the heels for a rabbit-sucker or a poulter's hare.
I Henry IV, Act ii, sc. 4, l. 481 [FALSTAFF]

3430 To punish you by the heels would amend the attention of your
ears; and I care not if I do become your physician.
II Henry IV, Act i, sc. 2, l. 141 [CHIEF JUSTICE]

3431 Heavens and honour be witness that no want of resolution in me,
but only my followers' base and ignominious treasons, makes me
betake me to my heels.
II Henry VI, Act iv, sc. 8, l. 64 [CADE]

3432 I'll lay ye all By the heels.
Henry VIII, Act v, sc. 4, l. 82 [CHAMBERLAIN]

3433 FALSTAFF: Well, sirs, I am almost out at heels.
PISTOL: Why, then, let kibes ensue.
The Merry Wives of Windsor, Act i, sc. 3, l. 34 [FALSTAFF]

Helen

3434 In Troy, there lies the scene. . . .
Troy, within whose strong immures

The ravish'd Helen, Menelaus' queen,
With wanton Paris sleeps.
Troilus and Cressida, Prologue, l. 1

3435   Helen must needs be fair,
When with your blood you daily paint her thus.
Troilus and Cressida, Act i, sc. 1, l. 93 [TROILUS]

3436   A Grecian queen, whose youth and freshness
Wrinkles Apollo's, and makes stale the morning. . . .
Is she worth keeping? why, she is a pearl,
Whose price hath launch'd above a thousand ships,
And turn'd crown'd kings to merchants.
Troilus and Cressida, Act ii, sc. 2, l. 78 [TROILUS]

3437   Well may we fight for her whom, we know well,
The world's large spaces cannot parallel.
Troilus and Cressida, Act ii, sc. 2, l. 161 [PARIS]

3438   She is a theme of honour and renown,
A spur to valiant and magnanimous deeds,
Whose present courage may beat down our foes,
And fame in time to come canonize us.
Troilus and Cressida, Act ii, sc. 2, l. 199 [TROILUS]

Hell See also Heaven and Hell

3439   All hell shall stir for this.
Henry V, Act v, sc. 1, l. 72 [PISTOL]

3440   Till I root out their accursed line
And leave not one alive, I live in hell.
III Henry VI, Act i, sc. 3, l. 32 [CLIFFORD]

3441   Down, down to hell; and say I sent thee thither.
III Henry VI, Act v, sc. 6, l. 67 [GLOUCESTER]

3442   Hell is murky!
Macbeth, Act v, sc. 1, l. 40 [LADY MACBETH]

3443   You . . . have the office opposite to Saint Peter,
And keep the gate of hell!
Othello, Act iv, sc. 2, l. 91 [OTHELLO]

3444   The king's son, Ferdinand,
With hair up-staring,—then like reeds, not hair,—
Was the first man that leap'd; cried, 'Hell is empty,
And all the devils are here.'
The Tempest, Act i, sc. 2, l. 212 [ARIEL]

Help

3445   'Tis not enough to help the feeble up,
But to support him after.
Timon of Athens, Act i, sc. 1, l. 107 [TIMON]

3446   Cease to lament for that thou canst not help,
And study help for that which thou lament'st.
The Two Gentlemen of Verona, Act iii, sc. 1, l. 241 [PROTEUS]

Hem

3447   I would try, if I could cry 'hem' and have him.
As You Like It, Act i, sc. 3, l. 18 [ROSALIND]

3448   She . . . hems, and beats her heart ;
Spurns enviously at straws.
Hamlet, Act iv, sc. 5, l. 5 [GENTLEMAN]

3449   Bid sorrow wag, cry 'hem' when he could groan.
Much Ado about Nothing, Act v, sc. 1, l. 16 [LEONATO]

3450   Cough, or cry 'hem,' if any body comes.
Othello, Act iv, sc. 2, l. 30 [OTHELLO]

3451   Now play me Nestor; hem, and stroke thy beard.
                    Troilus and Cressida, Act i, sc. 3, l. 165 [ULYSSES]

Hercules

3452   FIRST SOLDIER: What should this mean?
        SECOND SOLDIER: 'Tis the god Hercules, whom Antony loved,
        Now leaves him.
                    Antony and Cleopatra, Act iv, sc. 3, l. 16 [FIRST SOLDIER]
3453   Resume that spirit, when you were wont to say,
        If you had been the wife of Hercules,
        Six of his labours you 'ld have done, and saved
        Your husband so much sweat.
                    Coriolanus, Act iv, sc. 1, l. 16 [CORIOLANUS]
3454   COMINIUS: He will shake Your Rome about your ears.
        MENENIUS: As Hercules Did shake down mellow fruit.
                    Coriolanus, Act iv, sc. 6, l. 98 [COMINIUS]
3455   Hercules himself must yield to odds.
                    III Henry VI, Act ii, sc. 1, l. 53 [MESSENGER]
3456   HOLOFERNES: The page [shall present] Hercules.
        ARMADO: Pardon, sir; error: he is not quantity enough for that
        Worthy's thumb: he is not so big as the end of his club.
        HOLOFERNES: Shall I have audience? he shall present Hercules in
        minority: his enter and exit shall be strangling a snake; and I
        will have an apology for that purpose.
        MOTH: An excellent device! so, if any of the audience hiss, you
        may cry 'Well done, Hercules! now thou crushest the snake!' that
        is the way to make an offence gracious, though few have the grace
        to do it.
                    Love's Labour's Lost, Act v, sc. 1, l. 136 [HOLOFERNES]
3457   Go, Hercules!
        Live thou, I live: with much much more dismay
        I view the fight than thou that makest the fray.
                    The Merchant of Venice, Act iii, sc. 2, l. 60 [PORTIA]
3458   She would have made Hercules have turned spit, yea, and have
        cleft his club to make the fire too.
                    Much Ado about Nothing, Act ii, sc. 1, l. 261 [BENEDICK]

Here and There

3459   Here, there, and everywhere enraged he flew.
                    I Henry VI, Act i, sc. 1, l. 124 [MESSENGER]
3460   That's neither here nor there.
                    The Merry Wives of Windsor, Act i, sc. 4, l. 112 [QUICKLY]
        'Tis neither here nor there.
                    Othello, Act iv, sc. 3, l. 59 [EMILIA]
3461   We cannot be here and there too.
                    Romeo and Juliet, Act i, sc. 5, l. 15 [SERVANT]

Heresy

3462   What is here?
        The scriptures of the loyal Leonatus
        All turn'd to heresy? Away, away,
        Corrupters of my faith! you shall no more
        Be stomachers to my heart.
                    Cymbeline, Act iii, sc. 4, l. 82 [IMOGEN]
3463   The heresies that men do leave
        Are hated most of those they did deceive.
                    A Midsummer Night's Dream, Act ii, sc. 2, l. 139 [LYSANDER]

Heretic

3464 Again, there is sprung up An heretic, an arch one.
     Henry VIII, Act iii, sc. 2, l. 103 [WOLSEY]
3465   They know he is
A most arch heretic, a pestilence
That does infect the land.
     Henry VIII, Act v, sc. 1, l. 45 [GARDINER]
3466 Blessed shall he be that doth revolt
From his allegiance to an heretic.
     King John, Act iii, sc. 1, l. 174 [PANDULPH]
3467 Thou wast ever an obstinate heretic in the despite of beauty.
     Much Ado about Nothing, Act i, sc. 1, l. 236 [DON PEDRO]
3468 It is an heretic that makes the fire,
Not she which burns in 't.
     The Winter's Tale, Act ii, sc. 3, l. 115 [PAULINA]

Herod

3469 Let me have a child at fifty, to whom Herod of Jewry may do homage.
     Antony and Cleopatra, Act i, sc. 2, l. 27 [CHARMIAN]
3470 ALEXAS : Herod of Jewry dare not look upon you
But when you are well pleased.
CLEOPATRA : That Herod's head I'll have.
     Antony and Cleopatra, Act iii, sc. 3, l. 3 [ALEXAS]
3471 It out-herods Herod.
     Hamlet, Act iii, sc. 2, l. 16 [HAMLET]
3472 What a Herod of Jewry is this !
     The Merry Wives of Windsor, Act ii, sc. 1, l. 20 [MRS. PAGE]

Hesperides

3473 Still climbing trees in the Hesperides.
     Love's Labour's Lost, Act iv, sc. 3, l. 341 [BIRON]
3474 Before thee stands this fair Hesperides,
With golden fruit, but dangerous to be touch'd.
     Pericles, Act i, sc. 1, l. 27 [ANTIOCHUS]

Hill

3475 To climb steep hills Requires slow pace at first.
     Henry VIII, Act i, sc. 1, l. 131 [NORFOLK]
3476 GLOUCESTER : When shall we come to the top of that same hill ? . . .
EDGAR : Come on, sir ; here 's the place : stand still. How fearful
And dizzy 'tis, to cast one's eyes so low !
The crows and choughs that wing the midway air
Show scarce so gross as beetles : half way down
Hangs one that gathers samphire, dreadful trade !
Methinks he seems no bigger than his head :
The fishermen, that walk upon the beach,
Appear like mice.
     King Lear, Act iv, sc. 6, l. 1 [GLOUCESTER]
3477 Who digs hills because they do aspire,
Throws down one mountain to cast up a higher.
     Pericles, Act i, sc. 4, l. 5 [DIONYZA]

Hip

3478 If I can catch him once upon the hip,
I will feed fat the ancient grudge I bear him.
     The Merchant of Venice, Act i, sc. 3, l. 47 [SHYLOCK]
3479 Now, infidel, I have you on the hip.
     The Merchant of Venice, Act iv, sc. 1, l. 334 [GRATIANO]

3480 I'll have our Michael Cassio on the hip.
Othello, Act ii, sc. 1, l. 314 [IAGO]
(The phrase is derived from wrestling. To have the adversary
on the hip is to be able to throw him.)

Hiren

3481 PISTOL: Have we not Hiren here? . . . Die men like dogs! give
crowns like pins! Have we not Hiren here?
HOSTESS: O' my word, captain, there's none such here. What the
good-year! do you think I would deny her?
II Henry IV, Act ii, sc. 4, l. 175 [PISTOL]
(Hiren is a corruption of Irene. Pistol is referring to his
sword, but Mistress Quickly supposes he is asking for some
woman. The line is probably from a lost play by George Peele,
entitled, *The Turkish Mahomet and Hyren the Fair Greek.*)

History

3482 There is a history in all men's lives,
Figuring the nature of the times deceased;
The which observed, a man may prophesy,
With a near aim, of the main chance of things
As yet not come to life, which in their seeds
And weak beginnings lie intreasured.
II Henry IV, Act iii, sc. 1, l. 80 [WARWICK]

3483 Either our history shall with full mouth
Speak freely of our acts, or else our grave,
Like Turkish mute, shall have a tongueless mouth,
Not worshipp'd with a waxen epitaph.
Henry V, Act i, sc. 2, l. 230 [KING HENRY]

3484 If I should tell my history, it would seem
Like lies disdain'd in the reporting.
Pericles, Act v, sc. 1, l. 119 [MARINA]

Hit

3485 A hit, a very palpable hit.
Hamlet, Act v, sc. 2, l. 293 [OSRIC]

3486 You have hit it.
I Henry IV, Act ii, sc. 4, l. 381 [FALSTAFF]
(Frequently repeated.)

3487 MARIA: You still wrangle with her, Boyet, and she strikes at
the brow.
BOYET: But she herself is hit lower: have I hit her now? . . .
ROSALINE: Thou canst not hit it, hit it, hit it,
Thou canst not hit it, my good man.
Love's Labour's Lost, Act iv, sc. 1, l. 127 [MARIA]

3488 But, hit or miss,
Our project's life this shape of sense assumes:
Ajax employ'd plucks down Achilles' plumes.
Troilus and Cressida, Act i, sc. 3, l. 385 [ULYSSES]

Hoarding

3489 Didst thou never hear
That things ill-got had ever bad success?
And happy always for it was that son
Whose father for his hoarding went to hell?
III Henry VI, Act ii, sc. 2, l. 45 [KING]

Hobby-Horse

3490 The hobby-horse, whose epitaph is 'For O, for O, the hobby-horse
is forgot.'
Hamlet, Act iii, sc. 2, l. 144 [HAMLET]

3491 ARMADO: But O,—but O,—
MOTH: The hobby-horse is forgot.
ARMADO: Callest thou my love 'hobby-horse'?
MOTH: No, master; the hobby-horse is but a colt, and your love
perhaps a hackney.
Love's Labour's Lost, Act iii, sc. 1, l. 29 [ARMADO]
(The reference is said to be to a popular ballad of the day deal-
ing with the omission of the hobby-horse in May-day games.)

Holiday

3492 If all the year were playing holidays,
To sport would be as tedious as to work;
But when they seldom come, they wish'd for come.
I Henry IV, Act i, sc. 2, l. 227 [PRINCE]

3493 This day, no man think
Has business at his house; for all shall stay:
This little one shall make it holiday.
Henry VIII, Act v, sc. 5, l. 75 [KING HENRY]

3494 KING PHILIP: This blessed day
Ever in France shall be kept festival. . . .
The yearly course that brings this day about
Shall never see it but a holiday. . . .
CONSTANCE: What hath this day deserved? what hath it done,
That it in golden letters should be set
Among the high tides in the calendar?
King John, Act iii, sc. 1, l. 75 [KING PHILIP]

3495 Awhile to work, and after holiday.
Richard II, Act iii, sc. 1, l. 44 [BOLINGBROKE]

Holiness

3496 All his mind is bent to holiness,
To number Ave-Maries on his beads;
His champions are the prophets and apostles,
His weapons holy saws of sacred writ,
His study is his tilt-yard, and his loves
Are brazen images of canonized saints.
II Henry VI, Act i, sc. 3, l. 58 [QUEEN]

3497 I know him for a man divine and holy;
Not scurvy, nor a temporary meddler,
As he's reported by this gentleman.
Measure for Measure, Act v, sc. 1, l. 144 [FRIAR PETER]

Home

3498 Go thou toward home; where I will never come
Whilst I can shake my sword or hear the drum.
All's Well that Ends Well, Act ii, sc. 5, l. 95 [BERTRAM]

3499 What hempen home-spuns have we swaggering here?
A Midsummer Night's Dream, Act iii, sc. 1, l. 79 [PUCK]

3500 Home-keeping youth have ever homely wits.
The Two Gentlemen of Verona, Act i, sc. 1, l. 2 [VALENTINE]

3501 ANTONIO: Tell me, Panthino, what sad talk was that
Wherewith my brother held you in the cloister?
PANTHINO: 'Twas of his nephew Proteus, your son.
ANTONIO: Why, what of him?

PANTHINO: He wonder'd that your lordship
Would suffer him to spend his youth at home,
While other men, of slender reputation,
Put forth their sons to seek preferment out:
Some to the wars, to try their fortune there;
Some to discover islands far away;
Some to the studious universities.
The Two Gentlemen of Verona, Act i, sc. 3, l. 1 [ANTONIO]

Honesty

3502 Though honesty be no puritan, yet it will do no hurt; it will
wear the surplice of humility over the black gown of a big heart.
All's Well that Ends Well, Act i, sc. 3, l. 98 [CLOWN]

3503 The honour of a maid is her name; and no legacy is so rich
as honesty.
All's Well that Ends Well, Act iii, sc. 5, l. 12 [MARIANA]

Mine honesty shall be my dower.
III Henry VI, Act iii, sc. 2, l. 72 [LADY GREY]

3504 AUDREY: Would you not have me honest?
TOUCHSTONE: No, truly, unless thou wert hard-favoured; for
honesty coupled to beauty is to have honey a sauce to sugar. . . .
AUDREY: Well, I am not fair; and therefore I pray the gods
make me honest.
As You Like It, Act iii, sc. 3, l. 28 [AUDREY]

3505 Rich honesty dwells like a miser, sir, in a poor house; as your
pearl in your foul oyster.
As You Like It, Act v, sc. 4, l. 62 [TOUCHSTONE]

3506 To be honest, as this world goes, is to be one man picked out
of ten thousand.
Hamlet, Act ii, sc. 2, l. 178 [HAMLET]

3507 There's neither honesty, manhood, nor good fellowship in thee.
I Henry IV, Act i, sc. 2, l. 155 [FALSTAFF]

3508 An honest man, sir, is able to speak for himself, when a knave
is not.
II Henry IV, Act v, sc. 1, l. 50 [DAVY]

3509 Where I could not be honest,
I never yet was valiant.
King Lear, Act v, sc. 1, l. 23 [ALBANY]

3510 If she be less than an honest woman, she is indeed more than I
took her for.
The Merchant of Venice, Act iii, sc. 5, l. 45 [LAUNCELOT]

3511 DOGBERRY: Goodman Verges, sir, . . . an old man, sir, and his wits
are not so blunt as, God help, I would desire they were; but, in
faith, honest as the skin between his brows.
VERGES: Yes, I thank God I am as honest as any man living that
is an old man and no honester than I. . . .
DOGBERRY: An honest soul, i' faith, sir; by my troth he is, as
ever broke bread.
Much Ado about Nothing, Act iii, sc. 4, l. 12 [DOGBERRY]

3512 I durst, my lord, to wager she is honest,
Lay down my soul at stake: if you think other,
Remove your thought; it doth abuse your bosom.
If any wretch have put this in your head,
Let heaven requite it with the serpent's curse!
For, if she be not honest, chaste, and true,
There's no man happy.
Othello, Act iv, sc. 2, l. 12 [EMILIA]

3513   DESDEMONA: I hope my noble lord esteems me honest.
        OTHELLO: O, ay; as summer flies are in the shambles,
        That quicken even with blowing.
                                Othello, Act iv, sc. 2, l. 65 [DESDEMONA]
3514   An honest man he is, and hates the slime
        That sticks on filthy deeds.
                                Othello, Act v, sc. 2, l. 148 [OTHELLO]
3515   O wretched fool,
        That livest to make thine honesty a vice!
        O monstrous world! Take note, take note, O world,
        To be direct and honest is not safe. . . .
        1 should be wise, for honesty's a fool
        And loses that it works for.
                                Othello, Act iii, sc. 3, l. 375 [IAGO]
3516   If it be so,
        We need no grave to bury honesty:
        There's not a grain of it the face to sweeten
        Of the whole dungy earth.
                    The Winter's Tale, Act ii, sc. 1, l. 154 [ANTIGONUS]
3517   What a fool Honesty is! and Trust, his sworn brother, a very
        simple gentleman!
                    The Winter's Tale, Act iv, sc. 4, l. 605 [AUTOLYCUS]
3518   Though I am not naturally honest, I am so sometimes by chance.
                    The Winter's Tale, Act iv, sc. 4, l. 731 [AUTOLYCUS]
3519   If I had a mind to be honest, I see Fortune would not suffer me:
        she drops booties in my mouth.
                    The Winter's Tale, Act iv, sc. 4, l. 862 [AUTOLYCUS]

Honey

3520   They surfeited with honey and began
        To loathe the taste of sweetness, whereof a little
        More than a little is by much too much.
                    I Henry IV, Act iii, sc. 2, l. 71 [KING HENRY]
3521   The sweetest honey
        Is loathsome in its own deliciousness
        And in the taste confounds the appetite.
                    Romeo and Juliet, Act ii, sc. 6, l. 11 [FRIAR LAURENCE]
3522   I think the honey guarded with a sting.
                    The Rape of Lucrece, l. 493 [TARQUIN]
3523   When ye have the honey ye desire,
        Let not the wasp outlive, us both to sting.
                    Titus Andronicus, Act ii, sc. 3, l. 131 [TAMORA]

Honeysuckle

3524   Say that thou overheard'st us;
        And bid her steal into the pleached bower,
        Where honeysuckles, ripen'd by the sun,
        Forbid the sun to enter, like favorites,
        Made proud by princes, that advance their pride
        Against that power that bred it.
                    Much Ado about Nothing, Act iii, sc. 1, l. 6 [HERO]

Honour

3525   Aged honour cites a virtuous youth.
                    All's Well that Ends Well, Act i, sc. 3, l. 220 [HELENA]

3526   See that you come
Not to woo honour, but to wed it; when
The bravest questant shrinks, find what you seek,
That fame may cry you loud.
                    All's Well that Ends Well, Act ii, sc. 1, l. 14 [KING]
3527   That is honour's scorn,
Which challenges itself as honour's born
And is not like the sire: honours thrive,
When rather from our acts we them derive
Than our foregoers: the mere word's a slave
Debosh'd on every tomb; on every grave
A lying trophy, and as oft is dumb
Where dust and damn'd oblivion is the tomb
Of honour'd bones indeed.
                    All's Well that Ends Well, Act ii, sc. 3, l. 140 [KING]
3528   'Tis not my profit that does lead mine honour;
Mine honour, it.
                    Antony and Cleopatra, Act ii, sc. 7, l. 82 [POMPEY]
3529   If I lose mine honour,
I lose myself; better I were not yours
Than yours so branchless.
                    Antony and Cleopatra, Act iii, sc. 4, l. 22 [ANTONY]
3530   Never, O never, do his ghost the wrong
To hold your honour more precise and nice
With others than with him!
                    II Henry IV, Act ii, sc. 3, l. 39 [LADY PERCY]
3531   Honour and policy, like unsever'd friends,
I' the war do grow together.
                    Coriolanus, Act iii, sc. 2, l. 42 [VOLUMNIA]
3532   Thou hast affected the fine strains of honour,
To imitate the graces of the gods.
                    Coriolanus, Act v, sc. 3, l. 149 [VOLUMNIA]
3533   He sits 'mongst men like a descended god:
He hath a kind of honour sets him off,
More than a mortal seeming.
                    Cymbeline, Act i, sc. 6, l. 169 [IACHIMO]
3534   The heavens hold firm
The walls of thy dear honour, keep unshak'd
That temple, thy fair mind, that thou mayst stand
To enjoy thy banish'd lord and this great land!
                    Cymbeline, Act ii, sc. 1, l. 67 [LORD]
3535   I have pick'd the lock and ta'en
The treasure of her honour.
                    Cymbeline, Act ii, sc. 2, l. 41 [IACHIMO]
3536   Let there be no honour
Where there is beauty; truth, where semblance; love,
Where there's another man.
                    Cymbeline, Act ii, sc. 4, l. 108 [POSTHUMUS]
3537   By heaven, methinks it were an easy leap
To pluck bright honour from the pale-faced moon,
Or dive into the bottom of the deep,
Where fathom-line could never touch the ground,
And pluck up drowned honour by the locks;
So he that doth redeem her thence might wear
Without corrival all her dignities.
                    I Henry IV, Act i, sc. 3, l. 201 [HOTSPUR]

3538   If well-respected honour bid me on,
        I hold as little counsel with weak fear
        As you, my lord, or any Scot that this day lives.
                              I Henry IV, Act iv, sc. 3, l. 10 [VERNON]
3539   Honour pricks me on. Yea, but how if honour prick me off when
        I come on? how then? Can honour set to a leg? no: or an arm?
        no: or take away the grief of a wound? no. Honour hath no skill
        in surgery, then? no. What is honour? a word. . . . What is that
        honour? air. A trim reckoning. Who hath it? he that died
        o' Wednesday. Doth he feel it? no. Doth he hear it? no. . . .
        Will it not live with the living? no. . . . Therefore I'll none of it.
        Honour is a mere scutcheon: and so ends my catechism.
                              I Henry IV, Act v, sc. 1, l. 130 [FALSTAFF]
3540   WESTMORELAND: O that we now had here
        But one ten thousand of those men in England
        That do no work to-day!
        KING HENRY: What's he that wishes so?
        My cousin Westmoreland? No, my fair cousin:
        If we are mark'd to die, we are enow
        To do our country loss; and if to live,
        The fewer men, the greater share of honour.
        God's will! I pray thee, wish not one man more.
        By Jove, I am not covetous for gold,
        Nor care I who doth feed upon my cost;
        It yearns me not if men my garments wear;
        Such outward things dwell not in my desires:
        But if it be a sin to covet honour,
        I am the most offending soul alive.
        No, faith, my coz, wish not a man from England:
        God's peace! I would not lose so great an honour
        As one man more, methinks, would share from me
        For the best hope I have. O, do not wish one more!
        Rather proclaim it, Westmoreland, through my host,
        That he which hath no stomach to this fight,
        Let him depart; his passport shall be made
        And crowns for convoy put into his purse:
        We would not die in that man's company
        That fears his fellowship to die with us.
        This day is call'd the feast of Crispian:
        He that outlives this day, and comes safe home,
        Will stand a tip-toe when this day is named,
        And rouse him at the name of Crispian.
        He that shall live this day, and see old age,
        Will yearly on the vigil feast his neighbours,
        And say 'To-morrow is Saint Crispian':
        Then will he strip his sleeve and show his scars,
        And say, 'These wounds I had on Crispin's day'.
        Old men forget; yet all shall be forgot,
        But he'll remember with advantages
        What feats he did that day: then shall our names,
        Familiar in his mouth as household words,
        Harry the king, Bedford and Exeter,
        Warwick and Talbot, Salisbury and Gloucester,
        Be in their flowing cups freshly remember'd.
        This story shall the good man teach his son;
        And Crispin Crispian shall ne'er go by,
        From this day to the ending of the world,

But we in it shall be remembered;
We few, we happy few, we band of brothers:
For he to-day that sheds his blood with me
Shall be my brother; be he ne'er so vile,
This day shall gentle his condition:
And gentlemen in England now a-bed
Shall think themselves accursed they were not here,
And hold their manhoods cheap whiles any speaks
That fought with us upon Saint Crispin's day.
Henry V, Act iv, sc. 3, l. 16 [WESTMORELAND]

3541 And those that leave their valiant bones in France,
Dying like men, though buried in your dunghills,
They shall be famed; for there the sun shall greet them,
And draw their honours reeking up to heaven;
Leaving their earthly parts to choke your clime.
Henry V, Act iv, sc. 3, l. 98 [KING HENRY]

3542 Honour's train Is longer than her foreskirt.
Henry VIII, Act ii, sc. 3, l. 97 [OLD LADY]

3543 [He has] from these shoulders,
These ruin'd pillars, out of pity, taken
A load would sink a navy, too much honour:
O, 'tis a burden, Cromwell, 'tis a burden
Too heavy for a man that hopes for heaven!
Henry VIII, Act iii, sc. 2, l. 381 [WOLSEY]

3544 Set honour in one eye and death i' the other,
And I will look on both indifferently:
For let the gods so speed me as I love
The name of honour more than I fear death.
Julius Cæsar, Act i, sc. 2, l. 86 [BRUTUS]

3545 Thou art a fellow of a good respect;
Thy life hath had some smatch of honour in it.
Julius Cæsar, Act v, sc. 5, l. 45 [BRUTUS]

3546 If his name be George, I'll call him Peter;
For new-made honour doth forget men's names;
'Tis too respective and too sociable
For your conversion.
King John, Act i, sc. 1, l. 186 [BASTARD]

3547 To plainness honour 's bound,
When majesty stoops to folly.
King Lear, Act i, sc. 1, l. 150 [KENT]

3548 You stand upon your honour! Why, thou unconfinable baseness,
it is as much as I can do to keep the terms of my honour precise:
I, I, I myself sometimes, leaving the fear of God on the left hand
and hiding mine honour in my necessity, am fain to shuffle, to
hedge and to lurch; and yet you, you rogue, will ensconce your
rages, your cat-a-mountain looks, your red-lattice phrases, and
your bold-beating oaths, under the shelter of your honour!
The Merry Wives of Windsor, Act ii, sc. 2, l. 23 [FALSTAFF]

3549 Honour is an essence that 's not seen;
They have it very oft that have it not.
Othello, Act iv, sc. 1, l. 16 [IAGO]

3550 Why should honour outlive honesty?
Let it go all.
Othello, Act v, sc. 2, l. 245 [OTHELLO]

3551 Honour we love;
For who hates honour hates the gods above.
Pericles, Act ii, sc. 3, l. 21 [SIMONIDES]

3552 Honour and beauty, in the owner's arms,
Are weakly fortress'd from a world of harms.
The Rape of Lucrece, l. 27
3553 Mine honour is my life; both grow in one;
Take honour from me, and my life is done.
Richard II, Act i, sc. 1, l. 182 [MOWBRAY]
3554 As the sun breaks through the darkest clouds,
So honour peereth in the meanest habit.
The Taming of the Shrew, Act iv, sc. 3, l. 174 [PETRUCHIO]
3555 Who bates mine honour shall not know my coin.
Timon of Athens, Act iii, sc. 3, l. 26 [SEMPRONIUS]
3556 Give me a staff of honour for mine age,
But not a sceptre to control the world.
Titus Andronicus, Act i, sc. 1, l. 198 [TITUS]
3557   Take then the instant way;
For honour travels in a strait so narrow,
Where one but goes abreast: keep then the path.
Troilus and Cressida, Act iii, sc. 3, l. 153 [ULYSSES]
3558 Mine honour keeps the weather of my fate:
Life every man holds dear: but the brave man
Holds honour far more precious-dear than life.
Troilus and Cressida, Act v, sc. 3, l. 26 [HECTOR]
3559 Have you not set mine honour at the stake
And baited it with all the unmuzzled thoughts
That tyrannous heart can think?
Twelfth Night, Act iii, sc. 1, l. 129 [OLIVIA]

Honours

3560   Knighthoods and honours, borne
As I wear mine, are titles but of scorn.
Cymbeline, Act v, sc. 2, l. 6 [IACHIMO]
3561 All the budding honours on thy crest
I'll crop, to make a garland for my head.
I Henry IV, Act v, sc. 4, l. 72 [PRINCE]
3562 Though we lay these honours on this man,
To ease ourselves of divers slanderous loads,
He shall but bear them as the ass bears gold,
To groan and sweat under the business,
Either led or driven, as we point the way;
And having brought our treasure where we will,
Then take we down his load, and turn him off,
Like to the empty ass, to shake his ears,
And graze in commons.
Julius Cæsar, Act iv, sc. 1, l. 19 [ANTONY]
3563   New honours come upon him,
Like our strange garments, cleave not to their mould
But with the aid of use.
Macbeth, Act i, sc. 3, l. 145 [BANQUO]
3564   Not a man, for being simply man,
Hath any honour, but honour for those honours
That are without him, as place, riches, favour,
Prizes of accident as oft as merit.
Troilus and Cressida, Act iii, sc. 3, l. 80 [ACHILLES]

Hope

3565   [He] lined himself with hope,
Eating the air on promise of supply, . . .
And so, with great imagination

Proper to madmen, led his powers to death,
And winking leap'd into destruction.
II Henry IV, Act i, sc. 3, l. 27 [BARDOLPH]

3566 HASTINGS: It never yet did hurt
To lay down likelihoods and forms of hope. . . .
BARDOLPH: A cause on foot
Lives so in hope as in early spring
We see the appearing buds; which to prove fruit,
Hope gives not so much warrant as despair
That frosts will bite them.
II Henry IV, Act i, sc. 3, l. 34 [HASTINGS]

3567 Thus do the hopes we have in him touch ground
And dash themselves to pieces.
II Henry IV, Act iv, sc. 1, l. 17 [MOWBRAY]

3568 He that will not fight for such a hope,
Go home to bed, and like the owl by day,
If he arise, be mock'd and wonder'd at.
III Henry VI, Act v, sc. 4, l. 55 [SOMERSET]

3569 BIRON: How low soever the matter, I hope to God for high words.
LONGAVILLE: A high hope for a low heaven: God grant us
patience.
Love's Labour's Lost, Act i, sc. 1, l. 193 [BIRON]

3570   Was the hope drunk
Wherein you dress'd yourself? hath it slept since?
And wakes it now, to look so green and pale
At what it did so freely?
Macbeth, Act i, sc. 7, l. 35 [LADY MACBETH]

3571 Hope is a curtal dog in some affairs.
The Merry Wives of Windsor, Act ii, sc. 1, l. 114 [PISTOL]

3572 I will despair, and be at enmity
With cozening hope: he is a flatterer,
A parasite, a keeper back of death,
Who gently would dissolve the bands of life,
Which false hope lingers in extremity.
Richard II, Act ii, sc. 2, l. 68 [QUEEN]

3573 Hope to joy is little less in joy
Than hope enjoy'd.
Richard II, Act ii, sc. 3, l. 15 [NORTHUMBERLAND]

3574 True hope is swift, and flies with swallow's wings;
Kings it makes gods, and meaner creatures kings.
Richard III, Act v, sc. 2, l. 23 [RICHMOND]

3575   Sit down, and rest;
Even here I will put off my hope and keep it
No longer for my flatterer.
The Tempest, Act iii, sc. 3, l. 6 [ALONSO]

3576 When I do tell thee, there my hopes lie drown'd,
Reply not in how many fathoms deep
They lie indrench'd.
Troilus and Cressida, Act i, sc. 1, l. 49 [TROILUS]

3577 The ample proposition that hope makes
In all designs begun on earth below
Fails in the promised largess.
Troilus and Cressida, Act i, sc. 3, l. 2 [AGAMEMNON]

3578 Hope is a lover's staff; walk hence with that
And manage it against despairing thoughts.
The Two Gentlemen of Verona, Act iii, sc. 1, l. 246 [PROTEUS]

Horns See also Cuckold

3579   Here we have no temple but the wood, no assembly but horn-
        beasts. But what though? As horns are odious, they are necessary.
                        As You Like It, Act iii, sc. 3, l. 50 [TOUCHSTONE]

3580   What shall he have that kill'd the deer?
        His leather skin and horns to wear. . . .
        Take thou no scorn to wear the horn;
        It was a crest ere thou wast born:
            Thy father's father wore it,
            And thy father bore it:
        The horn, the horn, the lusty horn
        Is not a thing to laugh to scorn.
                        As You Like It, Act iv, sc. 2, l. 11 [FORESTERS]

3581   If I have horns to make one mad, let the proverb go with me:
        I'll be horn-mad.
                        The Merry Wives of Windsor, Act iii, sc. 5, l. 157 [FORD]

3582   Under your patience, gentle empress,
        'Tis thought you have a goodly gift in horning. . . .
        Jove shield your husband from his hounds to-day!
        'Tis pity they should take him for a stag.
                        Titus Andronicus, Act ii, sc. 3, l. 66 [LAVINIA]

Horror

3583   O horror, horror, horror! Tongue nor heart
        Cannot conceive nor name thee!
                        Macbeth, Act ii, sc. 3, l. 69 [MACDUFF]

3584   On horror's head horrors accumulate.
                        Othello, Act iii, sc. 3, l. 370 [OTHELLO]

Horse

3585   Ere twice the horses of the sun shall bring
        Their fiery torcher his diurnal ring.
                        All's Well that Ends Well, Act ii, sc. 1, l. 164 [HELENA]

3586   Is he on his horse?
        O happy horse, to bear the weight of Antony!
        Do bravely, horse! for wot'st thou whom thou movest?
        The demi-Atlas of this earth, the arm
        And burgonet of men.
                        Antony and Cleopatra, Act i, sc. 5, l. 20 [CLEOPATRA]

3587   O, for a horse with wings!
                        Cymbeline, Act iii, sc. 2, l. 49 [IMOGEN]

3588   The French . . . can well on horseback: but this gallant
        Had witchcraft in't; he grew unto his seat;
        And to such wondrous doing brought his horse,
        As had he been incorpsed and demi-natured
        With the brave beast.
                        Hamlet, Act iv, sc. 7, l. 84 [KING]

3589   What horse? a roan? . . . That roan shall be my throne.
        Well, I will back him straight: O esperance!
                        I Henry IV, Act ii, sc. 3, l. 72 [HOTSPUR]

3590   DAUPHIN: I will not change my horse with any that treads but
        on four pasterns. Ça, ha! he bounds from the earth, as if his
        entrails were hairs; le cheval volant, the Pegasus, chez les narines
        de feu! When I bestride him, I soar, I am a hawk: he trots the
        air; the earth sings when he touches it; the basest horn of his hoof
        is more musical than the pipe of Hermes.
        ORLEANS: He's of the colour of the nutmeg.

DAUPHIN: And of the heat of the ginger. . . . He is pure air
and fire. . . . It is the prince of palfreys; his neigh is like the
bidding of a monarch and h's countenance enforces homage.
Henry V, Act iii, sc. 7, l. 11 [DAUPHIN]

3591   Those that tame wild horses
Pace 'em not in their hands to make 'em gentle,
But stop their mouths with stubborn bits, and spur 'em,
Till they obey the manage.
Henry VIII, Act v, sc. 3, l. 21 [GARDINER]

3592 [The Neapolitan prince] that 's a colt indeed, for he doth nothing but talk of his horse; and he makes it a great appropriation
to his own good parts, that he can shoe him himself. I am much
afeard my lady his mother played false with a smith.
The Merchant of Venice, Act i, sc. 2, l. 43 [PORTIA]

3593 Where is the horse that doth untread again
His tedious measures with the unbated fire
That he did pace them first?
The Merchant of Venice, Act ii, sc. 6, l. 10 [SALARINO]

3594 How fondly dost thou spur a forward horse!
Richard II, Act iv, sc. 1, l. 72 [FITZWATER]

3595 GROOM: Roan Barbary,
That horse that thou so often hast bestrid,
That horse that I so carefully have dress'd! . . .
KING RICHARD: That jade hath eat bread from my royal hand;
This hand hath made him proud with clapping him.
Would he not stumble? would he not fall down,
Since pride must have a fall, and break the neck
Of that proud man that did usurp his back?
Forgiveness, horse! why do I rail on thee,
Since thou, created to be awed by man,
Wast born to bear? I was not made a horse;
And yet I bear a burthen like an ass,
Spur-gall'd and tired by jauncing Bolingbroke.
Richard II, Act v, sc. 5, l. 78 [GROOM]

3596 Give me another horse: bind up my wounds.
Richard III, Act v, sc. 3, l. 177 [KING RICHARD]

3597 A horse! a horse! my kingdom for a horse!
Richard III, Act v, sc. 4, l. 7 [KING RICHARD]

3598 Round hoof'd, short-jointed, fetlocks shag and long,
Broad breast, full eye, small head and nostril wide,
High crest, short ears, straight legs, and passing strong,
Thin mane, thick tail, broad buttock, tender hide:
Look, what a horse should have he did not lack,
Save a proud rider on so proud a back.
Venus and Adonis, l. 295

Host

3599 BARDOLPH: How now, mine host Pistol!
PISTOL: Base tike, call'st thou me host?
Now, by this hand, I swear, I scorn the term;
Nor shall my Nell keep lodgers.
Henry V, Act ii, sc. 1, l. 30 [BARDOLPH]

3600 You know your own degrees; sit down; at first
And last the hearty welcome. . . .
Ourself will mingle with society,
And play the humble host.
Macbeth, Act iii, sc. 4, l. 1 [MACBETH]

3601   FALSTAFF: Mine host of the Garter!
      HOST: What says my bully-rook? speak scholarly and wisely.
            The Merry Wives of Windsor, Act i, sc. 3, l. 1 [FALSTAFF]

3602   Look where my ranting host of the Garter comes: there is either
      liquor in his pate or money in his purse when he looks so merrily.
            The Merry Wives of Windsor, Act ii, sc. 1, l. 196 [PAGE]

3603   Let us knog our prains together to be revenge on this same scall,
      scurvy, cogging companion, the host of the Garter.
            The Merry Wives of Windsor, Act iii, sc. 1, l. 122 [EVANS]

3604   Bully knight! bully Sir John! speak from thy lungs military: art
      thou there? it is thine host, thine Ephesian, calls.
            The Merry Wives of Windsor, Act iv, sc. 5, l. 17 [HOST]
      ("Ephesian," a boon companion.)

Hostess

3605   FALSTAFF: Is not my hostess of the tavern a most sweet wench?
      PRINCE: As the honey of Hybla, my old lad of the castle. And is
      not a buff jerkin a most sweet robe of durance?
      FALSTAFF: How now, how now, mad wag! what, in thy quips and
      thy quiddities? What a plague have I to do with a buff jerkin?
      PRINCE: Why, what a pox have I to do with my hostess of the
      tavern?
      FALSTAFF: Well, thou hast called her to a reckoning many a time
      and oft.
            I Henry IV, Act i, sc. 2, l. 45 [FALSTAFF]

3606   A woeful hostess brooks not merry guests.
            The Rape of Lucrece, l. 1125 [LUCRECE]

Hotspur

3607   On Holy-rood day, the gallant Hotspur there,
      Young Harry Percy and brave Archibald,
      That ever-valiant and approved Scot,
      At Holmedon met.
            I Henry IV, Act i, sc. 1, l. 52 [WESTMORELAND]

3608   I am not yet of Percy's mind, the Hotspur of the north; he that
      kills me some six or seven dozen of Scots at a breakfast, washes his
      hands, and says to his wife, 'Fie upon this quiet life! I want work!'
      'O my sweet Harry,' says she, 'how many hast thou killed to-day?'
      'Give my roan horse a drench,' says he; and answers 'Some four-
      teen,' an hour after; 'a trifle, a trifle.'
            I Henry IV, Act ii, sc. 4, l. 113 [PRINCE]

3609   That same mad fellow of the north, Percy.
            I Henry IV, Act ii, sc. 4, l. 369 [FALSTAFF]

3610   GLENDOWER: Sit, cousin Percy; sit, good cousin Hotspur,
      For by that name as oft as Lancaster
      Doth speak of you, his cheek looks pale and with
      A rising sigh he wisheth you in heaven.
      HOTSPUR: And you in hell, as oft as he hears Owen Glendower
      spoke of.
            I Henry IV, Act iii, sc. 1, l. 7 [GLENDOWER]

3611   This Hotspur, Mars in swathling clothes,
      This infant warrior.
            I Henry IV, Act iii, sc. 2, l. 112 [KING HENRY]

3612   The land is burning; Percy stands on high;
      And either we or they must lower lie.
            I Henry IV, Act iii, sc. 3, l. 227 [PRINCE]

3613   HOTSPUR: Where is . . .
        The nimble-footed madcap Prince of Wales,
        And his comrades, that daff'd the world aside,
        And bid it pass?
        VERNON: All furnish'd, all in arms;
        All plumed like estridges that wing the wind;
        Bated like eagles having lately bathed;
        Glittering in golden coats like images;
        As full of spirit as the month of May,
        And gorgeous as the sun at midsummer;
        Wanton as youthful goats, wild as young bulls.
        I saw young Harry, with his beaver on,
        His cuisses on his thighs, gallantly arm'd,
        Rise from the ground like feather'd Mercury,
        And vaulted with such ease into his seat,
        As if an angel dropp'd down from the clouds,
        To turn and wind a fiery Pegasus
        And witch the world with noble horsemanship. . . .
        HOTSPUR: Come, let me taste my horse,
        Who is to bear me like a thunderbolt
        Against the bosom of the Prince of Wales:
        Harry to Harry shall, hot horse to horse,
        Meet and ne'er part till one drop down a corse.
                            I Henry IV, Act iv, sc. I, l. 94 [HOTSPUR]
3614   Tell your nephew
        The Prince of Wales doth join with all the world
        In praise of Henry Percy. . . .
        I do not think a braver gentleman,
        More active-valiant or more valiant-young,
        More daring or more bold, is now alive
        To grace this latter age with noble deeds.
        For my part, I may speak it to my shame,—
        I have a truant been to chivalry;
        And so I hear he doth account me too;
        Yet this before my father's majesty—
        I am content that he shall take the odds
        Of his great name and estimation,
        And will, to save the blood on either side,
        Try fortune with him in a single fight.
                            I Henry IV, Act v, sc. I, l. 85 [PRINCE]
3615   The Douglas and the Hotspur both together
        Are confident against a world in arms.
                            I Henry IV, Act v, sc. I, l. 115 [PRINCE]
3616   A hare-brain'd Hotspur, govern'd by a spleen.
                            I Henry IV, Act v, sc. 2, l. 19 [WORCESTER]
3617   HOTSPUR: O, Harry, thou hast robb'd me of my youth!
        I better brook the loss of brittle life
        Than those proud titles thou hast won of me;
        They wound my thoughts worse than thy sword my flesh:
        But thought 's the slave of life, and life time's fool;
        And time, that takes survey of all the world,
        Must have a stop. O, I could prophesy,
        But that the earthy and cold hand of death
        Lies on my tongue: no, Percy, thou art dust,
        And food for—   (*Dies*)
        PRINCE: For worms, brave Percy: fare thee well, great heart!
        Ill-weaved ambition, how much art thou shrunk!

When that this body did contain a spirit,
A kingdom for it was too small a bound;
But now two paces of the vilest earth
Is room enough: this earth that bears thee dead
Bears not alive so stout a gentleman. . . .
Adieu! and take thy praise with thee to heaven!
Thy ignominy sleep with thee in the grave,
But not remember'd in thy epitaph!
I Henry IV, Act v, sc. 4, l. 77 [HOTSPUR]

3618   He was indeed the glass
Wherein the noble youth did dress themselves. . . .
He was the mark, the glass, copy and book
That fashion'd others. And him, O wondrous him!
O miracle of men! . . . So came I a widow;
And never shall have length of life enough
To rain upon remembrance with mine eyes,
That it may grow and sprout as high as heaven,
For recordation to my noble husband.
II Henry IV, Act ii, sc. 3, l. 21 [LADY PERCY]

Hour

3619   You come most carefully upon your hour.
Hamlet, Act i, sc. 1, l. 6 [FRANCISCO]

3620   My hour is almost come,
When I to sulphurous and tormenting flame
Must render up myself.
Hamlet, Act i, sc. 5, l. 3 [GHOST]

3621   Uncle, adieu: O, let the hours be short
Till fields and blows and groans applaud our sport!
I Henry IV, Act i, sc. 3, l. 301 [HOTSPUR]

3622   Now bind my brows with iron; and approach
The ragged'st hour that time and spite dare bring.
II Henry IV, Act i, sc. 1, l. 150 [NORTHUMBERLAND]

3623   Talbot, farewell; thy hour is not yet come.
I Henry VI, Act i, sc. 5, l. 13 [PUCELLE]

3624   So many hours must I tend my flock;
So many hours must I take my rest;
So many hours must I contemplate;
So many hours must I sport myself.
III Henry VI, Act ii, sc. 5, l. 31 [KING]

3625   There should be hours for necessities,
Not for delights; times to repair our nature
With comforting repose, and not for us
To waste these times.
Henry VIII, Act v, sc. 1, l. 2 [GARDINER]

3626   Let this pernicious hour
Stand aye accursed in the calendar!
Macbeth, Act iv, sc. 1, l. 133 [MACBETH]

3627   O, insupportable! O heavy hour!
Methinks it should be now a huge eclipse
Of sun and moon, and that the affrighted globe
Should yawn at alteration.
Othello, Act v, sc. 2, l. 98 [OTHELLO]

3628   Ay me! sad hours seem long.
Romeo and Juliet, Act i, sc. 1, l. 167 [ROMEO]

House

3629   I will not ruinate my father's house,
    Who gave his blood to lime the stones together.
III Henry VI, Act v, sc. 1, l. 83 [CLARENCE]

3630   He that has a house to put 's head in has a good head-piece.
King Lear, Act iii, sc. 2, l. 25 [FOOL]
    Who can speak broader than he that has no house to put his head
    in? such may rail against great buildings.
Timon of Athens, Act iii, sc. 4, l. 63 [SERVANT]

3631   Our house is hell, and thou, a merry devil,
    Didst rob it of some taste of tediousness.
The Merchant of Venice, Act ii, sc. 3, l. 2 [JESSICA]

3632   Who lets so fair a house fall to decay,
    Which husbandry in honour must uphold
    Against the stormy gusts of winter's day
    And barren rage of death's eternal cold?
    O, none but unthrifts!
Sonnet xiii, l. 9

Howling

3633   Pray you, no more of this; 'tis like the howling of Irish wolves
    against the moon.
As You Like It, Act v, sc. 2, l. 115 [ROSALIND]

3634   Imagine howling: 'tis too horrible!
Measure for Measure, Act iii, sc. 1, l. 128 [CLAUDIO]

3635   O friar, the damned use that word in hell;
    Howlings attend it.
Romeo and Juliet, Act iii, sc. 3, l. 48 [ROMEO]

3636   A plague upon this howling! they are louder than the weather or
    our office.
The Tempest, Act i, sc. 1, l. 39 [BOATSWAIN]

3637   If it be aught to the old tune, my lord,
    It is as fat and fulsome to mine ear
    As howling after music.
Twelfth Night, Act v, sc. 1, l. 111 [OLIVIA]

Humanity

3638   How look I,
    That I should seem to lack humanity?
Cymbeline, Act iii, sc. 2, l. 15 [PISANIO]

3639   Humanity must perforce prey on itself,
    Like monsters of the deep.
King Lear, Act iv, sc. 2, l. 49 [ALBANY]

Humility

3640   Who were below him
    He used as creatures of another place
    And bow'd his eminent top to their low ranks,
    Making them proud of his humility.
All's Well that Ends Well, Act i, sc. 2, l. 41 [KING]

3641   On him put
    The napless vesture of humility.
Coriolanus, Act ii, sc. 1, l. 249 [BRUTUS]

3642   Humble as the ripest mulberry
    That will not hold the handling.
Coriolanus, Act iii, sc. 2, l. 79 [VOLUMNIA]

3643   I have sounded the very base-string of humility. Sirrah, I am
        sworn brother to a leash of drawers; and can call them all by
        their Christian names, as Tom, Dick, and Francis.
                            I Henry IV, Act ii, sc. 4, l. 6 [PRINCE]

3644   I . . . dress'd myself in such humility
        That I did pluck allegiance from men's hearts,
        Loud shouts and salutations from their mouths,
        Even in the presence of the crowned king.
                        I Henry IV, Act iii, sc. 2, l. 50 [KING HENRY]

Humour

3645   Now I am in a holiday humour.
                        As You Like It, Act iv, sc. 1, l. 68 [ROSALIND]

3646   I am now of all humours that have showed themselves humours
        since the old days of goodman Adam to the pupil age of this present
        twelve o'clock at midnight.
                        I Henry IV, Act ii, sc. 4, l. 104 [PRINCE]

3647   That's the humour of it.
                            Henry V, Act ii, sc. 1, l. 63 [NYM]
        (The phrase appears frequently.)

3648   The humour of it is too hot, that is the very plain-song of it.
                            Henry V, Act iii, sc. 2, l. 5 [NYM]

3649   NYM: I like not the humour of lying. . . . I love not the humour
        of bread and cheese, and there's the humour of it. Adieu.
        [*Exits*]
        PAGE: 'The humour of it,' quoth a'! here's a fellow frights
        humour out of his wits.
                The Merry Wives of Windsor, Act ii, sc. 1, l. 132 [NYM]

3650   Shall quips and sentences and these paper bullets of the brain awe
        a man from the career of his humour?
                Much Ado about Nothing, Act ii, sc. 3, l. 250 [BENEDICK]

3651   Every humour hath his adjunct pleasure,
        Wherein it finds a joy above the rest.
                                            Sonnet xci, l. 5

Hunting

3652   Hold, Warwick, seek thee out some other chase,
        For I myself must hunt this deer to death.
                        II Henry VI, Act v, sc. 2, l. 14 [YORK]
        Nay, Warwick, single out some other chase:
        For I myself will hunt this wolf to death.
                        III Henry VI, Act ii, sc. 4, l. 12 [RICHARD]

3653   The hunt is up, the morn is bright and grey,
        The fields are fragrant and the woods are green:
        Uncouple here, . . . and ring a hunter's peal,
        That all the court may echo with the noise.
                        Titus Andronicus, Act ii, sc. 2, l. 1 [TITUS]

Hurt

3654   I never did her hurt in all my life:
        I never spake bad word, nor did ill turn
        To any living creature: believe me, la,
        I never kill'd a mouse, nor hurt a fly:
        I trod upon a worm against my will,
        But I wept for it.
                        Pericles, Act iv, sc. 1, l. 75 [MARINA]

3655   BENVOLIO: What, art thou hurt?
        MERCUTIO: Ay, ay, a scratch, a scratch; marry, 'tis enough. . . .

'Tis not so deep as a well, nor so wide as a church-door; but 'tis enough, 'twill serve: ask for me to-morrow, and you shall find me a grave man. I am peppered, I warrant, for this world. . . . They have made worms' meat of me.

Romeo and Juliet, Act iii, sc. 1, 1. 95 [BENVOLIO]

3656 VIOLA: Why do you speak to me? I never hurt you. . . .
SIR ANDREW: If a bloody coxcomb be a hurt, you have hurt me: I think you set nothing by a bloody coxcomb.

Twelfth Night, Act v, sc. 1, 1. 190 [VIOLA]

Husband

3657 Get thee a good husband, and use him as he uses thee.

All's Well that Ends Well, Act i, sc. 1, 1. 227 [PAROLLES]

3658 When thou canst get the ring upon my finger which never shall come off, and show me a child begotten of thy body that I am father to, then call me husband.

All's Well that Ends Well, Act iii, sc. 2, 1. 59 [HELENA, *reading*]

3659 O, that I knew this husband, which, you say, must charge his horns with garlands.

Antony and Cleopatra, Act i, sc. 2, 1. 3 [CHARMIAN]

3660 [Her] beauty claims
No worse a husband than the best of men.

Antony and Cleopatra, Act ii, sc. 2, 1. 131 [AGRIPPA]

3661 In second husband let me be accurst!
None wed the second but who kill'd the first. . . .
The instances that second marriage move
Are base respects of thrift, but none of love:
A second time I kill my husband dead,
When second husband kisses me in bed.

Hamlet, Act iii, sc. 2, 1. 189 [PLAYER QUEEN]

3662 Why have my sisters husbands, if they say
They loved you all? Haply, when I shall wed,
That lord whose hand must take my plight shall carry
Half my love with him, half my care and duty:
Sure, I shall never marry like my sisters,
To love my father all.

King Lear, Act i, sc. 1, 1. 101 [CORDELIA]

3663 Her husband will be from home. Alas! the sweet woman leads an ill life with him: he's a very jealousy man: she leads a very frampold life with him, good heart.

The Merry Wives of Windsor, Act ii, sc. 2, 1. 92
[MISTRESS QUICKLY]

3664 By my troth, niece, thou wilt never get thee a husband, if thou be so shrewd of thy tongue.

Much Ado about Nothing, Act ii, sc. 1, 1. 19 [LEONATO]

3665 LEONATO: Well, niece, I hope to see you one day fitted with a husband.
BEATRICE: Not till God makes men of some other metal than earth. Would it not grieve a woman to be overmastered with a piece of valiant dust? to make an account of her life to a clod of wayward marl? No, uncle, I'll none. Adam's sons are my brethren; and, truly, I hold it a sin to match in my kindred.

Much Ado about Nothing, Act ii, sc. 1, 1. 60 [LEONATO]

3666 BEATRICE: I may sit in a corner and cry heigh-ho for a husband!
DON PEDRO: Lady Beatrice, I will get you one.
BEATRICE: I would rather have one of your father's getting. Hath

your grace ne'er a brother like you? Your father got excellent
husbands, if a maid could come by them.
Much Ado about Nothing, Act ii, sc. 1, l. 334 [BEATRICE]

3667　HERO: My heart is exceedingly heavy.
MARGARET: 'Twill be heavier soon by the weight of a man.
HERO: Fie upon thee! art not ashamed?
MARGARET: Of what, lady? . . . Is not marriage honourable? . . .
Is there any harm in 'the heavier for a husband'?
Much Ado about Nothing, Act iii, sc. 4, l. 26 [HERO]

3668　Who would not make her husband a cuckold to make him a monarch? I should venture purgatory for 't.
Othello, Act iv, sc. 3, l. 75 [EMILIA]

3669　While I play the good husband at home, my son and my servant
spend all at the university.
The Taming of the Shrew, Act v, sc. 1, l. 71 [VINCENTIO]

3670　Thy husband is thy lord, thy life, thy keeper,
Thy head, thy sovereign; one that cares for thee,
And for thy maintenance commits his body
To painful labour both by sea and land,
To watch the night in storms, the day in cold,
Whilst thou liest warm at home, secure and safe;
And craves no other tribute at thy hands
But love, fair looks, and true obedience;
Too little payment for so great a debt.
Such duty as the subject owes the prince
Even such a woman oweth to her husband;
And when she is froward, peevish, sullen, sour,
And not obedient to his honest will,
What is she but a foul contending rebel
And graceless traitor to her loving lord?
I am ashamed that women are so simple
To offer war where they should kneel for peace,
Or seek for rule, supremacy and sway,
When they are bound to serve, love and obey.
Why are our bodies soft and weak and smooth,
Unapt to toil and trouble in the world,
But that our soft conditions and our hearts
Should well agree with our external parts?
Come, come, you froward and unable worms!
My mind hath been as big as one of yours,
My heart as great, my reason haply more,
To bandy word for word and frown for frown;
But now I see our lances are but straws,
Our strength as weak, our weakness past compare,
That seeming to be most which we indeed least are.
Then vail your stomachs, for it is no boot,
And place your hands below your husband's foot;
In token of which duty, if he please,
My hand is ready; may it do him ease.
The Taming of the Shrew, Act v, sc. 2, l. 146 [KATHARINA]

Husband and Wife

3671　I do think it is their husbands' faults
If wives do fall: say that they slack their duties,
And pour our treasures into foreign laps, . . .
Why, we have galls, and though we have some grace,
Yet have we some revenge. Let husbands know

Their wives have sense like them: they see and smell,
And have their palates both for sweet and sour
As husbands have. . . . And have not we affections,
Desires for sport, and frailty, as men have?
Then let them use us well: else let them know
The ills we do, their ills instruct us so.
Othello, Act iv, sc. 3, l. 87 [EMILIA]

3672 MIRANDA: Hence bashful cunning!
And prompt me, plain and holy innocence!
I am your wife, if you will marry me,
If not, I'll die your maid: to be your fellow
You may deny me; but I'll be your servant,
Whether you will or no. . . . My husband, then?
FERDINAND: Ay, with a heart as willing
As bondage e'er of freedom: here's my hand.
MIRANDA: And mine, with my heart in't.
The Tempest, Act iii, sc. 1, l. 81 [MIRANDA]

3673   Let still the woman take
An elder than herself; so wears she to him,
So sways she level in her husband's heart:
For, boy, however we do praise ourselves,
Our fancies are more giddy and unfirm,
More longing, wavering, sooner lost and worn,
Than women's are. . . .
Then let thy love be younger than thyself,
Or thy affection cannot hold the bent;
For women are as roses, whose fair flower
Being once display'd, doth fall that very hour.
Twelfth Night, Act ii, sc. 4, l. 30 [DUKE]

Hymen

3674   Wedding is great Juno's crown:
O blessed bond of board and bed!
'Tis Hymen peoples every town;
High wedlock then be honoured:
Honour, high honour and renown,
To Hymen, god of every town!
As You Like It, Act v, sc. 4, l. 147 [HYMEN]

3675 Full thirty times hath Phoebus' cart gone round . . .
Since love our hearts and Hymen did our hands
Unite commutual in most sacred bands.
Hamlet, Act iii, sc. 2, l. 165 [PLAYER KING]

3676   Hymen hath brought the bride to bed,
Where, by the loss of maidenhead,
A babe is moulded.
Pericles, Act iii, Introduction, l. 9 [GOWER]

I

Ice

3677 Tut, tut, thou art all ice, thy kindness freezeth.
Richard III, Act iv, sc. 2, l. 22 [KING RICHARD]

3678 Break the ice and do this feat.
The Taming of the Shrew, Act i, sc. 2, l. 267 [TRANIO]

3679 CURTIS: Who is that calls so coldly?
GRUMIO: A piece of ice: if thou shouldst doubt it, thou mayst

slide from my shoulder to my heel with no greater a run but my
head and my neck.
The Taming of the Shrew, Act iv, sc. 1, l. 13 [CURTIS]

Ides

3680   SOOTHSAYER: Beware the ides of March.
CÆSAR: What man is that?
BRUTUS: A soothsayer bids you beware the ides of March. . . .
CÆSAR: He is a dreamer; let us leave him.
Julius Cæsar, Act i, sc. 2, l. 18 [SOOTHSAYER]

3681   CÆSAR: [To the Soothsayer] The ides of March are come.
SOOTHSAYER: Ay, Cæsar; but not gone.
Julius Cæsar, Act iii, sc. 1, l. 1 [CÆSAR]

3682   Remember March, the ides of March remember.
Julius Cæsar, Act iv, sc. 3, l. 17 [BRUTUS]

Idleness

3683   ANTONY: I should take you for idleness itself.
CLEOPATRA: 'Tis sweating labour
To bear such idleness so near the heart.
Antony and Cleopatra, Act i, sc. 3, l. 92 [ANTONY]

3684   I know you all, and will awhile uphold
The unyoked humour of your idleness.
I Henry IV, Act i, sc. 2, l. 218 [PRINCE]

Idolatry

3685   This is the liver-vein, which makes flesh a deity,
A green goose a goddess: pure, pure idolatry.
Love's Labour's Lost, Act iv, sc. 3, l. 74 [BIRON]

3686   Demetrius, I'll avouch it to his head,
Made love to Nedar's daughter, Helena,
And won her soul; and she, sweet lady, dotes,
Devoutly dotes, dotes in idolatry,
Upon this spotted and inconstant man.
A Midsummer Night's Dream, Act i, sc. 1, l. 106 [LYSANDER]

3687   'Tis mad idolatry
To make the service greater than the god.
Troilus and Cressida, Act ii, sc. 2, l. 56 [HECTOR]

If

3688   I knew when seven justices could not take up a quarrel, but when
the parties were met themselves, one of them thought but of an If,
as, 'If you said so, then I said so;' and they shook hands and swore
brothers. Your If is the only peacemaker; much virtue in If.
As You Like It, Act v, sc. 4, l. 102 [TOUCHSTONE]

3689   Tellest thou me of 'ifs'?
Richard III, Act iii, sc. 4, l. 77 [GLOUCESTER]

Ignorance

3690   Let me not burst in ignorance.
Hamlet, Act i, sc. 4, l. 46 [HAMLET]

3691   Ignorance is the curse of God,
Knowledge the wing wherewith we fly to heaven.
II Henry VI, Act iv, sc. 7, l. 78 [LORD SAY]

3692   His ignorance were wise,
Where now his knowledge must prove ignorance.
Love's Labour's Lost, Act ii, sc. 1, l. 102 [PRINCESS]

3693   HOLOFERNES: Twice-sod simplicity, *bis coctus!*
O thou monster Ignorance, how deformed dost thou look!

NATHANIEL: Sir, he hath never fed of the dainties that are bred
in a book: he hath not eat paper, as it were; he hath not drunk
ink: his intellect is not replenished; he is only an animal, only
sensible in the duller parts.

Love's Labour's Lost, Act iv, sc. 2, l. 22 [HOLOFERNES]

3694 ANGELO: Either you are ignorant,
Or seem so craftily; and that's not good.
ISABELLA: Let me be ignorant, and in nothing good
But graciously to know I am no better.

Measure for Measure, Act ii, sc. 4, l. 74 [ANGELO]

3695 Dull unfeeling barren ignorance
Is made my gaoler to attend on me.

Richard II, Act i, sc. 3, l. 168 [MOWBRAY]

3696 I had rather be a tick in a sheep than such a valiant ignorance.

Troilus and Cressida, Act iii, sc. 3, l. 315 [THERSITES]

3697 There is no darkness but ignorance.

Twelfth Night, Act iv, sc. 2, l. 46 [CLOWN]

Ill

3698 Many times
Doth ill deserve by doing well; what's worse,
Must court'sy at the censure.

Cymbeline, Act iii, sc. 3, l. 53 [BELARIUS]

3699 Ill, to example ill,
Would from my forehead wipe a perjured note;
For none offend when all alike do dote.

Love's Labour's Lost, Act iv, sc. 3, l. 124 [DUMAIN]

3700 In venturing ill we leave to be
The things we are for that which we expect.

The Rape of Lucrece, l. 148

3701 O benefit of ill! now I find true
That better is by evil still made better.

Sonnet cxix, l. 9

3702 There's nothing ill can dwell in such a temple:
If the ill spirit have so fair a house,
Good things will strive to dwell with 't.

The Tempest, Act i, sc. 2, l. 457 [MIRANDA]

Imagination

3703 My imaginations are as foul
As Vulcan's stithy.

Hamlet, Act iii, sc. 2, l. 88 [HAMLET]

3704 Give me an ounce of civet, good apothecary, to sweeten my
imagination.

King Lear, Act iv, sc. 6, l. 132 [LEAR]

3705 The lunatic, the lover, and the poet
Are of imagination all compact:
One sees more devils than vast hell can hold,
That is, the madman: the lover, all as frantic,
Sees Helen's beauty in a brow of Egypt:
The poet's eye, in a fine frenzy rolling,
Doth glance from heaven to earth, from earth to heaven;
And as imagination bodies forth
The forms of things unknown, the poet's pen
Turns them to shapes and gives to airy nothing
A local habitation and a name.
Such tricks hath strong imagination,

That, if it would but apprehend some joy,
It comprehends some bringer of that joy;
Or in the night, imagining some fear,
How easy is a bush supposed a bear!
        A Midsummer Night's Dream, Act v, sc. 1, l. 7 [THESEUS]
3706 HIPPOLYTA: This is the silliest stuff that ever I heard.
THESEUS: The best in this kind are but shadows; and the worst
are no worse, if imagination amend them.
        A Midsummer Night's Dream, Act v, sc. 1, l. 212 [HIPPOLYTA]

Immortality

3707 I have Immortal longings in me. . . .
I am fire and air; my other elements
I give to baser life.
        Antony and Cleopatra, Act v, sc. 2, l. 282 [CLEOPATRA]
3708 Look, here's the warrant, Claudio, for thy death:
'Tis now dead midnight, and by eight to-morrow
Thou must be made immortal.
        Measure for Measure, Act iv, sc. 2, l. 66 [PROVOST]

Imperfection

3709   Sleeping within my orchard,
My custom always of the afternoon, . . .
Thus was I, sleeping, by a brother's hand
Of life, of crown, of queen, at once dispatch'd:
Cut off even in the blossoms of my sin,
Unhousel'd, disappointed, unaneled,
No reckoning made, but sent to my account
With all my imperfections on my head.
        Hamlet, Act i, sc. 5, l. 59 [GHOST]

Impossibility

3710   What impossibility would slay
In common sense, sense saves another way.
        All's Well that Ends Well, Act ii, sc. 1, l. 180 [KING]
3711 Murdering impossibility, to make
What cannot be, slight work.
        Coriolanus, Act v, sc. 3, l. 61 [CORIOLANUS]
3712   Bid me run,
And I will strive with things impossible;
Yea, get the better of them.
        Julius Cæsar, Act ii, sc. 1, l. 324 [LIGARIUS]
3713 Make not impossible That which but seems unlike.
        Measure for Measure, Act v, sc. 1, l. 51 [ISABELLA]
3714 Nothing is impossible.
        The Two Gentlemen of Verona, Act iii, sc. 1, l. 379 [LAUNCE]

Indirection

3715 Thus do we of wisdom and of reach,
With windlasses and with assays of bias,
By indirections find directions out.
        Hamlet, Act ii, sc. 1, l. 64 [POLONIUS]
3716 The better act of purposes mistook
Is to mistake again; though indirect,
Yet indirection thereby grows direct,
And falsehood falsehood cures, as fire cools fire
Within the scorched veins of one new-burn'd.
        King John, Act iii, sc. 1, l. 274 [PANDULPH]

Indiscretion

3717   Our indiscretion sometimes serves us well,
       When our deep plots do pall.
                              Hamlet, Act v, sc. 2, l. 8 [HAMLET]

3718   All's not offence that indiscretion finds
       And dotage terms so.
                      King Lear, Act ii, sc. 4, l. 199 [GONERIL]

Infirmity

3719   Infirmity doth still neglect all office
       Whereto our health is bound; we are not ourselves
       When nature, being oppress'd, commands the mind
       To suffer with the body.
                       King Lear, Act ii, sc. 4, l. 107 [LEAR]

3720   MALVOLIO: Infirmity, that decays the wise, doth ever make the
       better fool.
       CLOWN: God send you, sir, a speedy infirmity, for the better in-
       creasing your folly.
                  Twelfth Night, Act i, sc. 5, l. 81 [MALVOLIO]

3721   Infirmity
       Which waits upon worn times hath something seized
       His wish'd ability.
                  The Winter's Tale, Act v, sc. 1, l. 141 [FLORIZEL]

Ingratitude

3722   Blow, blow, thou winter wind,
           Thou art not so unkind
               As man's ingratitude;
           Thy tooth is not so keen,
           Because thou art not seen,
               Although thy breath be rude.
                  As You Like It, Act ii, sc. 7, l. 174 [AMIENS]

3723   Ingratitude, thou marble-hearted fiend,
       More hideous when thou show'st thee in a child
       Than the sea-monster!
                       King Lear, Act i, sc. 4, l. 281 [LEAR]

3724   Filial ingratitude!
       Is it not as this mouth should tear this hand
       For lifting food to't? But I will punish home.
                       King Lear, Act iii, sc. 4, l. 14 [LEAR]

3725   O worthiest cousin!
       The sin of my ingratitude even now
       Was heavy on me: thou art so far before
       That swiftest wing of recompense is slow
       To overtake thee.
                       Macbeth, Act i, sc. 4, l. 14 [DUNCAN]

3726   I hate ingratitude more in a man
       Than lying, vainness, babbling, drunkenness,
       Or any taint of vice whose strong corruption
       Inhabits our frail blood.
                  Twelfth Night, Act iii, sc. 4, l. 387 [VIOLA]

Inheritance

3727   'In terram Salicam mulieres ne succedant':
       'No woman shall succeed in Salique land':
       Which Salique land the French unjustly glose
       To be the realm of France. . . .
       Yet their own authors faithfully affirm

That the land Salique is in Germany,
Between the floods of Sala and of Elbe.
Henry V, Act i, sc. **2,** l. 38 [CANTERBURY]

3728   In the book of Numbers is it writ,
When the man dies, let the inheritance
Descend unto the daughter.
Henry V, Act i, sc. **2,** l. 98 [CANTERBURY]

3729   Stay yet, Lord Salisbury; I'll go with thee,
And find the inheritance of this poor child,
His little kingdom of a forced grave.
That blood which owed the breath of all this isle,
Three foot of it doth hold: bad world the while!
King John, Act iv, sc. **2,** l. 96 [PEMBROKE]

Iniquity

3730   Why dost thou converse with . . . that grey iniquity, that father
ruffian, that vanity in years?
I Henry IV, Act ii, sc. **4,** l. 494 [PRINCE]

3731   I lack iniquity
Sometimes to do me service: nine or ten times
I had thought to have yerk'd him here under the ribs.
Othello, Act i, sc. **2,** l. 3 [IAGO]

3732   How now! wholesome iniquity have you that a man may deal
withal, and defy the surgeon?
Pericles, Act iv, sc. **6,** l. 28 [LYSIMACHUS]

Injury

3733   The record of what injuries you did us,
Though written in our flesh, we shall remember
As things but done by chance.
Antony and Cleopatra, Act v, sc. **2,** l. 118 [CÆSAR]

3734   He hath so planted his honours in their eyes, and his actions in
their hearts, that for their tongues to be silent, and not confess
so much, were a kind of ingrateful injury.
Coriolanus, Act ii, sc. **2,** l. 32 [OFFICER]

3735   To wilful men,
The injuries that they themselves procure
Must be their schoolmasters.
King Lear, Act ii, sc. **4,** l. 305 [REGAN]

Innocence

3736   CHARMIAN: The man is innocent.
CLEOPATRA: Some innocents 'scape not the thunderbolt.
Antony and Cleopatra, Act ii, sc. **5,** l. 76 [CHARMIAN]

3737   As innocent . . .
As is the sucking lamb or harmless dove.
II Henry VI, Act iii, sc. **1,** l. 69 [KING HENRY]

3738   The trust I have is in mine innocence,
And therefore am I bold and resolute.
II Henry VI, Act iv, sc. **4,** l. 59 [LORD SAY]

3739   It will help me nothing
To plead mine innocence; for that dye is on me
Which makes my whitest part black.
Henry VIII, Act i, sc. **1,** l. 207 [BUCKINGHAM]

3740   By noting of the lady I have mark'd
A thousand blushing apparitions
To start into her face, a thousand innocent shames
In angel whiteness beat away those blushes. . . .

Call me a fool; . . . trust not my age,
My reference, calling, nor divinity,
If this sweet lady lie not guiltless here
Under some biting error.
>> *Much Ado about Nothing,* Act iv, sc. 1, l. 160 [FRIAR]

3741 Play the pious innocent.
>> *Pericles,* Act iv, sc. 3, l. 17 [DIONYZA]

3742 Innocence shall make
False accusation blush and tyranny
Tremble at patience.
>> *The Winter's Tale,* Act iii, sc. 2, l. 31 [HERMIONE]

Inspiration

3743 Was Mahomet inspired with a dove?
Thou with an eagle art inspired then.
Helen, the mother of great Constantine,
Nor yet Saint Philip's daughters were like thee.
>> *I Henry VI,* Act i, sc. 2, l. 140 [CHARLES]

3744 Every man
After the hideous storm that follow'd, was
A thing inspired.
>> *Henry VIII,* Act i, sc. 1, l. 89 [BUCKINGHAM]

3745 Holy men at their death have good inspirations.
>> *The Merchant of Venice,* Act i, sc. 2, l. 31 [NERISSA]

Instant

3746 Let's take the instant by the forward top.
>> *All's Well that Ends Well,* Act v, sc. 3, l. 39 [KING]

3747 Upon that instant.
>> *Henry V,* Act i, sc. 1, l. 91 [CANTERBURY]
(Frequently repeated.)

3748 At any unseasonable instant of the night.
>> *Much Ado about Nothing,* Act ii, sc. 2, l. 16 [BORACHIO]

Instinct

3749 I'll never
Be such a gosling to obey instinct, but stand
As if a man were author of himself
And knew no other kin.
>> *Coriolanus,* Act v, sc. 3, l. 34 [CORIOLANUS]

3750 'Tis wonder
That an invisible instinct should frame them
To royalty unlearn'd, honour untaught,
Civility not seen from other, valour
That wildly grows in them, but yields a crop
As if it had been sow'd.
>> *Cymbeline,* Act iv, sc. 2, l. 176 [BELARIUS]

3751 Beware instinct. . . . Instinct is a great matter. I was now a
coward on instinct.
>> *I Henry IV,* Act ii, sc. 4, l. 301 [FALSTAFF]

3752 Before the times of change, . . .
By a divine instinct men's minds mistrust
Ensuing dangers.
>> *Richard III,* Act ii, sc. 3, l. 41 [CITIZEN]

Intent

3753 My project may deceive me.
But my intents are fix'd and will not leave me.
>> *All's Well that Ends Well,* Act i, sc. 1, l. 243 [HELENA]

3754   His act did not o'ertake his bad intent,
And must be buried but as an intent
That perish'd by the way: thoughts are no subjects;
Intents but merely thoughts.
                    Measure for Measure, Act v, sc. 1, l. 456 [ISABELLA]
3755   My intents are savage-wild,
More fierce and more inexorable far
Than empty tigers or the roaring sea.
                    Romeo and Juliet, Act v, sc. 3, l. 37 [ROMEO]

Iron

3756   I dare not fight; but I will wink and hold out mine iron: . . .
it will toast cheese, and it will endure cold as another man's
sword will.
                    Henry V, Act ii, sc. 1, l. 7 [NYM]
3757   I'll make thee eat iron like an ostrich, and swallow my sword like
a great pin.
                    II Henry VI, Act iv, sc. 10, l. 31 [SADE]
3758   Strike now, or else the iron cools.
                    III Henry VI, Act v, sc. 1, l. 49 [GLOUCESTER]
3759   ARTHUR: Will you put out mine eyes? . . .
HUBERT: I have sworn to do it;
And with hot irons must I burn them out.
ARTHUR: Ah, none but in this iron age would do it! . . .
Are you more stubborn-hard than hammer'd iron?
                    King John, Act iv, sc. 1, l. 56 [ARTHUR]
3760   Iron may hold with her, but never lutes.
                    The Taming of the Shrew, Act ii, sc. 1, l. 147 [HORTENSIO]

Itch

3761   She loved not the savour of tar nor of pitch,
Yet a tailor might scratch her where'er she did itch.
                    The Tempest, Act ii, sc. 2, l. 54 [STEPHANO]
3762   I would thou didst itch from head to foot and I had the scratching
of thee; I would make thee the loathsomest scab in Greece.
                    Troilus and Cressida, Act ii, sc. 1, l. 29 [THERSITES]

Ivy

3763   I will wind thee in my arms; . . . the female ivy so
Enrings the barky fingers of the elm.
                    A Midsummer Night's Dream, Act iv, sc. 1, l. 43 [TITANIA]
3764   He was
The ivy which had hid my princely trunk,
And suck'd my verdure out on 't.
                    The Tempest, Act i, sc. 2, l. 85 [PROSPERO]

J

Jack

3765   But long I will not be Jack out of office.
                    I Henry VI, Act i, sc. 1, l. 175 [WINCHESTER]
3766   You little Jack-a-Lent, have you been true to us?
                    The Merry Wives of Windsor, Act iii, sc. 3, l. 27 [MRS. PAGE]
(See also v, 5, 134. A Jack-a-Lent was a puppet thrown at
during Lenten fairs.)

I stand fooling here, his Jack o' the clock.

> *Richard II*, Act v, sc. 5, l. 60 [King Richard]
> (A Jack o' the clock was the mechanical figure which struck
> the bell with a hammer, to indicate the hours and quarters.)

3767 Do you play the flouting Jack, to tell us Cupid is a good hare-
finder and Vulcan a rare carpenter?

> *Much Ado about Nothing*, Act i, sc. 1, l. 186 [Benedick]

3768 Jack shall have Jill; Nought shall go ill.

> *A Midsummer Night's Dream*, Act iii, sc. 2, l. 461 [Puck]

3769 Be the jacks fair within, and the jills fair without?

> *The Taming of the Shrew*, Act iv, sc. 1, l. 52 [Grumio]

Jade

3770 Let the galled jade wince, our withers are unwrung.

> *Hamlet*, Act iii, sc. 2, l. 252 [Hamlet]

First Carrier: Poor jade, is wrung in the withers out of all cess.
Second Carrier: Peas and beans are as dank here as a dog, and
that is the next way to give poor jades the bots.

> *1 Henry IV*, Act ii, sc. 1, l. 8 [First Carrier]

3771 The horsemen sit like fixed candlesticks,
With torch-staves in their hand; and their poor jades
Lob down their heads, dropping the hides and hips,
The gum down-roping from their pale-dead eyes,
And in their pale dull mouths the gimmal bit
Lies foul with chew'd grass, still and motionless.

> *Henry V*, Act iv, sc. 2, l. 45 [Grandpré]

3772 How like a jade he stood, tied to the tree,
Servilely master'd with a leathern rein!

> *Venus and Adonis*, l. 391 [Venus]

Jay

3773   Some jay of Italy . . . hath betray'd him:
Poor I am stale, a garment out of fashion.

> *Cymbeline*, Act iii, sc. 4, l. 51 [Imogen]

3774 What is the jay more precious than the lark,
Because his feathers are more beautiful?

> *The Taming of the Shrew*, Act iv, sc. 3, l. 176 [Petruchio]

Jealousy

3775 I will be more jealous of thee than a Barbary cock-pigeon over his
hen.

> *As You Like It*, Act iv, sc. 1, l. 150 [Rosalind]

3776 Self-harming jealousy! fie, beat it hence! . . .
How many fond fools serve mad jealousy!

> *The Comedy of Errors*, Act ii, sc. 1, l. 102 [Luciana]

3777 Each jealous of the other, as the stung
Are of the adder.

> *King Lear*, Act v, sc. 1, l. 56 [Edmund]

3778 Let them say of me, 'As jealous as Ford, that searched a hollow
walnut for his wife's leman.'

> *The Merry Wives of Windsor*, Act iv, sc. 2, l. 170 [Ford]

3779 Iago: Beware, my lord, of jealousy;
It is the green-eyed monster which doth mock
The meat it feeds on: that cuckold lives in bliss
Who, certain of his fate, loves not his wronger;
But, O, what damned minutes tells he o'er
Who dotes, yet doubts, suspects, yet strongly loves. . . .

OTHELLO: Why, why is this?
Think'st thou I 'ld make a life of jealousy
To follow still the changes of the moon
With fresh suspicions? No; to be once in doubt
Is once to be resolved: exchange me for a goat,
When I shall turn the business of my soul
To such exsufflicate and blown surprises,
Matching thy inference. . . . No, Iago;
I'll see before I doubt; when I doubt, prove;
And on the proof, there is no more than this,—
Away at once with love or jealousy.
Othello, Act iii, sc. 3, l. 165 [IAGO]

3780   EMILIA: Is not this man jealous? . . .
DESDEMONA: Alas the day! I never gave him cause,
EMILIA: But jealous souls will not be answer'd so;
They are not ever jealous for the cause,
But jealous for they are jealous: 'tis a monster
Begot upon itself, born on itself.
Othello, Act iii, sc. 4, l. 99 [EMILIA]

3781   Love, thou know'st, is full of jealousy.
The Two Gentlemen of Verona, Act ii, sc. 4, l. 177 [VALENTINE]

3782   Bid Suspicion double-lock the door,
Lest Jealousy, that sour unwelcome guest,
Should, by his stealing in, disturb the feast.
Venus and Adonis, l. 448 [VENUS]

3783   Where Love reigns, disturbing Jealousy
Doth call himself Affection's sentinel;
Gives false alarms, suggesteth mutiny,
And in a peaceful hour doth cry 'Kill, kill!'
Distempering gentle Love in his desire,
As air and water do abate the fire.
Venus and Adonis, l. 649 [VENUS]

Jerusalem

3784   KING: Doth any name particular belong
Unto the lodging where I first did swoon?
WARWICK: 'Tis call'd Jerusalem, my noble lord.
KING: Laud be to God! even there my life must end.
It hath been prophesied to me many years,
I should not die but in Jerusalem;
Which vainly I supposed the Holy Land:
But bear me to that chamber; there I'll lie;
In that Jerusalem shall Harry die.
II Henry IV, Act iv, sc. 5, l. 233 [KING]

3785   So part we sadly in this troublous world,
To meet with joy in sweet Jerusalem.
III Henry VI, Act v, sc. 5, l. 7 [QUEEN MARGARET]

Jest

3786   Hold, sir, for God's sake! now your jest is earnest.
The Comedy of Errors, Act ii, sc. 2, l. 24 [DROMIO OF SYRACUSE]

3787   Jesters do oft prove prophets.
King Lear, Act v, sc. 3, l. 71 [REGAN]

3788   A jest's prosperity lies in the ear
Of him that hears it, never in the tongue
Of him that makes it.
Love's Labour's Lost, Act v, sc. 2, l. 871 [ROSALINE]

3789   You break jests as braggards do their blades, which, God be
        thanked, hurt not.
                        Much Ado about Nothing, Act v, sc. 1, l. 189 [BENEDICK]
3790   Is it else your pleasure,
        Like pleasant travellers, to break a jest
        Upon the company you overtake?
                        The Taming of the Shrew, Act iv, sc. 5, l. 71 [VINCENTIO]
3791   SIR ANDREW: What's your jest?
        MARIA: A dry jest, sir.
        SIR ANDREW: Are you full of them?
        MARIA: Ay, sir, I have them at my fingers' ends.
                        Twelfth Night, Act i, sc. 3, l. 80 [SIR ANDREW]
3792   He must observe their mood on whom he jests,
        The quality of persons, and the time.
                        Twelfth Night, Act iii, sc. 1, l. 69 [VIOLA]
3793   With some excellent jests, fire-new from the mint, you should
        have banged the youth into dumbness.
                        Twelfth Night, Act iii, sc. 2, l. 24 [FABIAN]
3794   O jest unseen, inscrutable, invisible,
        As a nose on a man's face, or a weathercock on a steeple!
                        The Two Gentlemen of Verona, Act ii, sc. 1, l. 141 [SPEED]

Jew

3795   They were bound, every man of them; or I am a Jew else, an
        Ebrew Jew.
                        I Henry IV, Act ii, sc. 4, l. 197 [FALSTAFF]
3796   My sweet ounce of man's flesh! my incony Jew!
                        Love's Labour's Lost, Act iii, sc. 1, l. 137 [COSTARD]
        ("Incony," perhaps from the French *inconnu,* unknown; rare,
        fine, delicate.)
3797   I am a Jew. Hath not a Jew eyes? hath not a Jew hands, organs,
        dimensions, senses, affections, passions? fed with the same food,
        hurt with the same weapons, subject to the same diseases, healed
        by the same means, warmed and cooled by the same winter and
        summer, as a Christian is? If you prick us, do we not bleed? if
        you tickle us, do we not laugh? if you poison us, do we not die?
        and if you wrong us, shall we not revenge?
                        The Merchant of Venice, Act iii, sc. 1, l. 64 [SHYLOCK]
3798   I pray you, think you question with the Jew:
        You may as well go stand upon the beach
        And bid the main flood bate his usual height;
        You may as well use question with the wolf
        Why he hath made the ewe bleat for the lamb;
        You may as well forbid the mountain pines
        To wag their high tops and to make no noise,
        When they are fretten with the gusts of heaven;
        You may as well do anything most hard,
        As seek to soften that—than which what's harder?—
        His Jewish heart.
                        The Merchant of Venice, Act iv, sc. 1, l. 70 [ANTONIO]

Jewel

3799   From the east to western Ind,
        No jewel is like Rosalind.
                        As You Like it, Act iii, sc. 2, l. 93 [ROSALIND, *reading*]

3800   The jewel that we find, we stoop and take 't
        Because we see it; but what we do not see
        We tread upon, and never think of it.
                    Measure for Measure, Act ii, sc. 1, l. 24 [ANGELO]

3801   On the finger of a throned queen
        The basest jewel will be well esteem'd.
                                            Sonnet, xcvi, l. 5

3802   Why, man, she is mine own,
        And I as rich in having such a jewel
        As twenty seas, if all their sands were pearl,
        The water nectar, and the rocks pure gold.
            The Two Gentlemen of Verona, Act ii, sc. 4, l. 168 [VALENTINE]

3803   Win her with gifts, if she respect not words:
        Dumb jewels often in their silent kind
        More than quick words do move a woman's mind.
            The Two Gentlemen of Verona, Act iii, sc. 1, l. 89 [VALENTINE]

Joan of Arc

3804   A holy maid hither with me I bring,
        Which by a vision sent to her from heaven
        Ordained is to raise this tedious siege
        And drive the English forth the bounds of France.
        The spirit of deep prophecy she hath,
        Exceeding the nine sibyls of old Rome:
        What 's past and what 's to come she can descry.
                    I Henry VI, Act i, sc. 2, l. 51 [BASTARD OF ORLEANS]

3805   'Tis Joan, not we, by whom the day is won;
        For which I will divide my crown with her,
        And all the priests and friars in my realm
        Shall in procession sing her endless praise.
        A statlier pyramis to her I'll rear
        Than Rhodope's or Memphis' ever was:
        In memory of her when she is dead,
        Her ashes, in an urn more precious
        Than the rich-jewel'd coffer of Darius,
        Transported shall be at high festivals
        Before the kings and queens of France.
        No longer on Saint Denis shall we cry,
        But Joan la Pucelle shall be France's saint.
                        I Henry VI, Act i, sc. 6, l. 17 [CHARLES]

3806   BURGUNDY: What 's that Pucelle whom they term so pure?
        TALBOT: A maid, they say.
        BEDFORD: A maid! and be so martial!
        BURGANDY: Pray God she prove not masculine ere long,
        If underneath the standard of the French
        She carry armour as she hath begun.
                    I Henry VI, Act ii, sc. 1, l. 20 [BURGUNDY]

3807   YORK: Take her away; for she hath lived too long,
        To fill the world with vicious qualities.
        PUCELLE: First, let me tell you whom you have condemn'd:
        Not me begotten of a shepherd swain,
        But issued from the progeny of kings;
        Virtuous and holy; chosen from above,
        By inspiration of celestial grace
        To work exceeding miracles on earth. . . .
        Joan of Arc hath been
        A virgin from her tender infancy,

Chaste and immaculate in very thought;
Whose maiden blood, thus rigorously effused,
Will cry for vengeance at the gates of heaven.
I Henry VI, Act v, sc. 4, l. 34 [YORK]

Journey

3808   I have a journey, sir, shortly to go;
My master calls me, I must not say no.
King Lear, Act v, sc. 3, l. 321 [KENT]

3809   Here is my journey's end, here is my butt,
And very sea-mark of my utmost sail.
Othello, Act v, sc. 2, l. 267 [OTHELLO]

Jove

3810   Jove sometimes went disguised, and why not I?
II Henry VI, Act iv, sc. 1, l. 49 [SUFFOLK]

3811   Remember, Jove, thou wast a bull for thy Europa. . . . You were
also, Jupiter, a swan for the love of Leda. . . . A fault done first
in the form of a beast. . . . And then another fault in the semblance of a fowl.
The Merry Wives of Windsor, Act v, sc. 5, l. 3 [FALSTAFF]

3812   O thou great thunder-darter of Olympus, forget that thou art
Jove, the king of gods, . . . if ye take not that little little less
than little wit from them that they have!
Troilus and Cressida, Act ii, sc. 3, l. 12 [THERSITES]

Joy

3813   Make the coming hour o'erflow with joy
And pleasure drown the brim.
All's Well that Ends Well, Act ii, sc. 4, l. 47 [PAROLLES]

3814   Briefly die their joys
That place them on the truth of girls and boys.
Cymbeline, Act v, sc. 5, l. 106 [LUCIUS]

3815   The gods do mean to strike me To death with mortal joy.
Cymbeline, Act v, sc. 5, l. 234 [CYMBELINE]

3816   With a defeated joy,—
With an auspicious and a dropping eye,
With mirth in funeral and with dirge in marriage,
In equal scale weighing delight and dole.
Hamlet, Act i, sc. 2, l. 10 [KING]

3817   My lord and lady, it is now our time . . .
To cry good joy: good joy, my lord and lady!
The Merchant of Venice, Act iii, sc. 2, l. 188 [NERISSA]

3818   He finds the joys of heaven here on earth.
The Merchant of Venice, Act iii, sc. 5, l. 81 [JESSICA]

3819   Joy, gentle friends! joy and fresh days of love
Accompany your hearts!
A Midsummer Night's Dream, Act v, sc. 1, l. 29 [THESEUS]

3820   O Helicanus, strike me, honour'd sir;
Give me a gash, put me to present pain;
Lest this great sea of joys rushing upon me
O'erbear the shores of my mortality,
And drown me with their sweetness.
Pericles, Act v, sc. 1, l. 192 [PERICLES]

3821   Ah, Juliet, if the measure of thy joy
Be heap'd like mine and that thy skill be more

To blazon it, then sweeten with thy breath
This neighbour air.
Romeo and Juliet, Act ii, sc. 6, l. 24 [ROMEO]

3822 Sweets with sweets war not, joy delights in joy.
Sonnet viii, l. 2

3823 Swooning destruction, or some joy too fine,
Too subtle-potent, tuned too sharp in sweetness,
For the capacity of my ruder powers:
I fear it much; and I do fear besides
That I shall lose distinction in my joys.
Troilus and Cressida, Act iii, sc. 2, l. 24 [TROILUS]

3824 There might you have beheld one joy crown another, so and in
such manner that it seemed sorrow wept to take leave of them,
for their joy waded in tears.
The Winter's Tale, Act v, sc. 2, l. 49 [GENTLEMAN]

Judas

3825 To say the truth, so Judas kiss'd his master,
And cried 'all hail!' when as he meant all harm.
III Henry VI, Act v, sc. 7, l. 33 [GLOUCESTER]

3826 BIRON: A kissing traitor. How art thou proved Judas? . . .
HOLOFERNES: Begin, sir; you are my elder.
BIRON: Well followed: Judas was hanged on an elder.
Love's Labour's Lost, Act v, sc. 2, l. 605 [BIRON]

Judge

3827 Forbear to judge, for we are sinners all.
II Henry VI, Act iii, sc. 3, l. 31 [KING HENRY]

3828 KING JOHN: From whom has thou this great commission, France,
To draw my answer from thy articles?
KING PHILIP: From that supernal judge, that stirs good thoughts
In any breast of strong authority,
To look into the blots and stains of right.
King John, Act ii, sc. 1, l. 110 [KING JOHN]

3829   How would you be,
If He, which is the top of judgement, should
But judge you as you are?
Measure for Measure, Act ii, sc. 2, l. 75 [ISABELLA]

3830 It doth appear you are a worthy judge;
You know the law, your exposition
Hath been most sound: I charge you by the law,
Whereof you are a well-deserving pillar,
Proceed to judgement.
The Merchant of Venice, Act iv, sc. 1, l. 236 [PORTIA]

3831 O noble judge! O excellent young man! . . .
O wise and upright judge!
How much more elder art thou than thy looks!
The Merchant of Venice, Act iv, sc. 1, l. 246 [SHYLOCK]

3832 When the judge is robb'd the prisoner dies.
The Rape of Lucrece, l. 1652 [LUCRECE]

Judgement

3833   Men's judgements are
A parcel of their fortunes; and things outward
Do draw the inward quality after them,
To suffer all alike.
Antony and Cleopatra, Act iii, sc. 13, l. 31 [ENOBARBUS]

3834   The effect of judgement Is oft the cause of fear.
                  Cymbeline, Act iv, sc. 2, l. 111 [BELARIUS]

3835   In choosing for yourself, you show'd your judgement,
     Which being shallow, you shall give me leave
     To play the broker in mine own behalf.
              III Henry VI, Act iv, sc. 1, l. 61 [CLARENCE]

3836   O judgement! thou art fled to brutish beasts,
     And men have lost their reason.
              Julius Cæsar, Act iii, sc. 2, l. 109 [ANTONY]

3837   The judgement of the heavens, that makes us tremble,
     Touches us not with pity.
              King Lear, Act v, sc. 3, l. 231 [ALBANY]

3838   I have seen,
     When, after execution, judgement hath
     Repented o'er his doom.
           Measure for Measure, Act ii, sc. 2, l. 10 [PROVOST]

Jury

3839   The jury, passing on the prisoner's life,
     May in the sworn twelve have a thief or two
     Guiltier than him they try.
           Measure for Measure, Act ii, sc. 1, l. 19 [ANGELO]

3840   In christening shalt thou have two godfathers:
     Had I been judge, thou shouldst have had ten more
     To bring thee to the gallows, not the font.
         The Merchant of Venice, Act iv, sc. 1, l. 398 [GRATIANO]

3841   FABIAN: I will prove it legitimate, sir, upon the oaths of judge-
     ment and reason.
     SIR TOBY: And they have been grand-jury-men since before
     Noah was a sailor.
           Twelfth Night, Act iii, sc. 2, l. 16 [FABIAN]

Just

3842   Horatio, thou art e'en as just a man
     As e'er my conversation coped withal.
            Hamlet, Act iii, sc. 2, l. 59 [HAMLET]

3843   Now, for our consciences, the arms are fair,
     When the intent of bearing them is just.
           I Henry IV, Act v, sc. 2, l. 88 [HOTSPUR]

3844   Be just, and fear not.
           Henry VIII, Act iii, sc. 2, l. 446 [WOLSEY]

Justice

3845   Tremble, thou wretch,
     That hast within thee undivulged crimes
     Unwhipp'd of justice.
           King Lear, Act iii, sc. 2, l. 51 [LEAR]

3846   This even-handed justice
     Commends the ingredients of our poison'd chalice
     To our own lips.
           Macbeth, Act i, sc. 7, l. 10 [MACBETH]

3847   O worthy prince, dishonour not your eye
     By throwing it on any other object
     Till you have heard me in my true complaint
     And given me justice, justice, justice, justice!
         Measure for Measure, Act v, sc. 1, l. 22 [ISABELLA]

3848   As thou urgest justice, be assured
        Thou shalt have justice, more than thou desirest.
                    The Merchant of Venice, Act iv, sc. 1, l. 315 [PORTIA]
3849   Justice is feasting while the widow weeps.
                    The Rape of Lucrece, l. 905 [LUCRECE]
3850   Sith there's no justice in earth nor hell,
        We will solicit heaven and move the gods
        To send down Justice for to wreak our wrongs.
                    Titus Andronicus, Act iv, sc. 3, l. 49 [TITUS]

K

Kerns

3851   The uncivil kerns of Ireland are in arms
        And temper clay with blood of Englishmen.
                    II Henry VI, Act iii, sc. 1, l. 310 [CARDINAL]
3852   The western isles of kerns and gallowglasses.
                    Macbeth, Act i, sc. 2, l. 15 [SERGEANT]
3853   Now for our Irish wars:
        We must supplant those rough rug-headed kerns,
        Who live like venom where no venom else
        But only they have privilege to live.
                    Richard II, Act ii, sc. 1, l. 155 [KING RICHARD]

Kickshaw

3854   Some pigeons, Davy, a couple of short-legged hens, a joint of
        mutton, and any pretty little tiny kickshaws, tell William cook.
                    II Henry IV, Act v, sc. 1, l. 27 [SHALLOW]
        ("Kickshaw", from *quelque chose,* a fancy dish in cookery, a
        "something" French.)
3855   SIR ANDREW: I delight in masques and revels. . . .
        SIR TOBY: Art thou good at these kickshawses, knight?
                    Twelfth Night, Act i, sc. 3, l. 122
        (In this sense, something dainty or elegant.)

Killing

3856   I kill thee, make thee away, translate thy life into death, thy
        liberty into bondage: I will deal in poison with thee, or in
        bastinado, or in steel. . . . I will kill thee a hundred and fifty
        ways: therefore tremble, and depart.
                    As You Like It, Act v, sc. 1, l. 58 [TOUCHSTONE]
3857   BASSANIO: Do all men kill the things they do not love?
        SHYLOCK: Hates any man the thing he would not kill?
        BASSANIO: Every offence is not a hate at first.
        SHYLOCK: What, wouldst thou have a serpent sting thee twice?
                    The Merchant of Venice, Act iv, sc. 1, l. 66 [BASSANIO]
3858   I would have him nine years a-killing.
                    Othello, Act iv, sc. 1, l. 187 [OTHELLO]
3859   Thou hast kill'd the sweetest innocent
        That e'er did lift up eye.
                    Othello, Act v, sc. 2, l. 200 [EMILIA]
3860   To kill, I grant, is sin's extremest gust;
        But, in defence, by mercy, 'tis most just.
                    Timon of Athens, Act iii, sc. 5, l. 54 [ALCIBIADES]
3861   Henceforth guard thee well;
        For I'll not kill thee there, nor there, nor there;

But, by the forge that stithied Mars his helm,
I'll kill thee every where, yea, o'er and o'er.
Troilus and Cressida, Act iv, sc. 5, l. 254 [HECTOR]

Kin

3862 CYMBELINE: What wouldst thou, boy? Is he thy kin? . . .
IMOGEN: He is a Roman; no more kin to me
Than I to your highness; who, being born your vassal,
Am something nearer.
Cymbeline, Act v, sc. 5, l. 108 [CYMBELINE]

3863 A little more than kin, and less than kind.
Hamlet, Act i, sc. 2, l. 65 [HAMLET]

3864 PAGE: [She is] a proper gentlewoman, sir, and a kinswoman of my master's.
PRINCE: Even such kin as the parish heifers are to the town bull.
. . . This Doll Tearsheet should be some road.
POINS: I warrant you; as common as the way between Saint Alban's and London.
II Henry IV, Act ii, sc. 2, l. 169 [PAGE]

Kindness

3865 Kindness, nobler ever than revenge.
As You Like It, Act iv, sc. 3, l. 129 [OLIVER]

3866   When a world of men
Could not prevail with all their oratory,
Yet hath a woman's kindness over-ruled.
I Henry VI, Act ii, sc. 2, l. 48 [TALBOT]

3867 Be kind and courteous to this gentleman;
Hop in his walks and gambol in his eyes;
Feed him with apricocks and dewberries,
With purple grapes, green figs and mulberries.
A Midsummer Night's Dream, Act iii, sc. 1, l. 167 [TITANIA]

3868   To ease them of their griefs,
Their fears of hostile strokes, their aches, losses,
Their pangs of love, and other incident throes
That nature's fragile vessel doth sustain
In life's uncertain voyage, I will some kindness do them.
Timon of Athens, Act v, sc. 1, l. 201 [TIMON]

King

3869 The king's a beggar, now the play is done.
All's Well that Ends Well, Epilogue, l. 1 [KING]

3870 [He] had superfluous kings for messengers
Not many moons gone by.
Antony and Cleopatra, Act iii, sc. 12, l. 5 [DOLABELLA]

3871   That it should come to this!
But two months dead: nay, not so much, not two:
So excellent a king; that was, to this,
Hyperion to a satyr; so loving to my mother
That he might not beteem the winds of heaven
Visit her face too roughly.
Hamlet, Act i, sc. 2, l. 137 [HAMLET]

3872 A king of shreds and patches.
Hamlet, Act iii, sc. 4, l. 102 [HAMLET]

3873 Let the bloat king tempt you again to bed;
Pinch wanton on your cheek; call you his mouse;
And let him, for a pair of reechy kisses,

Or paddling in your neck with his damn'd fingers,
Make you to ravel all this matter out.
Hamlet, Act iii, sc. 4, l. 182 [HAMLET]

3874   There's such divinity doth hedge a king,
That treason can but peep to what it would,
Acts little of his will.
Hamlet, Act iv, sc. 5, l. 123 [KING]

3875   A king's son. If I do not beat thee out of thy kingdom with a
dagger of lath, and drive all thy subjects afore thee like a flock of
wild-geese, I'll never wear hair on my face more. You Prince
of Wales!
I Henry IV, Act ii, sc. 4, l. 153 [FALSTAFF]

3876   The skipping king, he ambled up and down
With shallow jesters and rash bavin wits, . . .
Mingled his royalty with capering fools, . . .
Grew a companion to the common streets,
Enfeoff'd himself to popularity; . . .
So when he had occasion to be seen,
He was but as the cuckoo is in June,
Heard, not regarded.
I Henry IV, Act iii, sc. 2, l. 60 [KING HENRY]

3877   The king's a bawcock, and a heart of gold,
A lad of life, an imp of flame;
Of parents good, of fist most valiant:
I kiss his dirty shoe, and from heart-string
I love the lovely bully.
Henry V, Act iv, sc. 1, l. 44 [PISTOL]
("Bawcock," from the French *beau coq,* fine cock, fine fellow.)

3878   The king is but a man, as I am: the violet smells to him as it doth
to me; the element shows to him as it doth to me; all his senses
have but human conditions: his ceremonies laid by, in his nakedness he appears but a man; and though his affections are higher
mounted than ours, yet, when they stoop, they stoop with the like
wing.
Henry V, Act iv, sc. 1, l. 105 [KING HENRY]

3879   That's a perilous shot out of an elder-gun, that a poor and a
private displeasure can do against a monarch!
Henry V, Act iv, sc. 1, l. 210 [WILLIAMS]

3880   Upon the king! let our lives, our souls,
Our debts, our careful wives,
Our children and our debts lay on the king!
We must bear all. O hard condition,
Twin-born with greatness! . . . what infinite heart's ease
Must kings neglect, that private men enjoy!
Henry V, Act iv, sc. 1, l. 247 [KING HENRY]

3881   The presence of a king engenders love
Amongst his subjects and his loyal friends,
As it disanimates his enemies.
I Henry VI, Act iii, sc. 1, l. 181 [GLOUCESTER]

3882   Was never subject long'd to be a king
As I do long and wish to be a subject.
II Henry VI, Act iv, sc. 9, l. 5 [KING HENRY]

3883   Thou setter up and plucker down of kings.
III Henry VI, Act ii, sc. 3, l. 37 [EDWARD]
Proud setter up and puller down of kings.
III Henry VI, Act iii, sc. 3, l. 157 [MARGARET]

3884 KING HENRY: Men may talk of kings, and why not I?
      KEEPER: Ay, but thou talk'st as if thou wert a king.
      KING HENRY: Why, so I am, in mind; and that's enough.
      KEEPER: But, if thou be a king, where is thy crown?
      KING HENRY: My crown is in my heart, not on my head;
      Not deck'd with diamonds and Indian stones,
      Nor to be seen: my crown is called content:
      A crown it is that seldom kings enjoy.
                          III Henry VI, Act iii, sc. 1, l. 58 [KING HENRY]

3885 Whiles he thought to steal the single ten,
      The king was slily finger'd from the deck.
                          III Henry VI, Act v, sc. 1, l. 43 [GLOUCESTER]

3886 Who lived king, but I could dig his grave?
      And who durst smile when Warwick bent his brow?
                          III Henry VI, Act v, sc. 2, l. 21 [WARWICK]

3887 What earthly name to interrogatories
      Can task the free breath of a sacred king?
                          King John, Act iii, sc. 1, l. 147 [KING JOHN]

3888 It is the curse of kings to be attended
      By slaves that take their humours for a warrant
      To break within the bloody house of life,
      And on the winking of authority
      To understand a law, to know the meaning
      Of dangerous majesty, when perchance it frowns
      More upon humour than advised respect.
                          King John, Act iv, sc. 2, l. 208 [KING JOHN]

3889 What surety of the world, what hope, what stay,
      When this was now a king, and now is clay?
                          King John, Act v, sc. 7, l. 68 [PRINCE HENRY]

3890 GLOUCESTER: The trick of that voice I do well remember:
      Is 't not the king?
      LEAR: Ay, every inch a king.
                          King Lear, Act iv, sc. 6, l. 108 [GLOUCESTER]

3891 O me, with what strict patience have I sat,
      To see a king transformed to a gnat!
      To see great Hercules whipping a gig,
      And profound Solomon to tune a jig,
      And Nestor play at push-pin with the boys,
      And critic Timon laugh at idle toys!
                          Love's Labour's Lost, Act iv, sc. 3, l. 165 [BIRON]

3892 A substitute shines brightly as a king
      Until a king be by, and then his state
      Empties itself, as doth an inland brook
      Into the main of waters.
                          The Merchant of Venice, Act v, sc. 1, l. 94 [PORTIA]

3893 Kings are earth's gods; in vice their law's their will;
      And if Jove stray, who dares say Jove doth ill?
                          Pericles, Act i, sc. 1, l. 103 [PERICLES]

3894 Kings like gods should govern every thing.
                          The Rape of Lucrece, l. 602 [LUCRECE]

3895 He was a wise fellow, and had good discretion, that, being bid to
      ask what he would of the king, desired he might know none of his
      secrets.
                          Pericles, Act i, sc. 3, l. 4 [THALIARD]

3896 He is a happy king, since he gains from his subjects the name of
      good by his government.
                          Pericles, Act ii, sc. 1, l. 108 [PERICLES]

3897   Though This king was great, his greatness was no guard
       To bar heaven's shaft, but sin had his reward.
                        Pericles, Act ii, sc. 4, l. 14 [HELICANUS]
3898   O, be remember'd, no outrageous thing
       From vassal actors can be wiped away;
       Then kings' misdeeds cannot be hid in clay.
                        The Rape of Lucrece, l. 607 [LUCRECE]
3899   Not all the water in the rough rude sea
       Can wash the balm off from an anointed king;
       The breath of worldly men cannot depose
       The deputy elected by the Lord.
                        Richard II, Act iii, sc. 2, l. 54 [KING RICHARD]
3900   I had forgot myself: am I not king?
       Awake, thou coward majesty! thou sleepest.
       Is not the king's name twenty thousand names?
       Arm, arm, my name! a puny subject strikes
       At thy great glory.
                        Richard II, Act iii, sc. 2, l. 83 [KING RICHARD]
       The king's name is a tower of strength.
                        Richard III, Act v, sc. 3, l. 12 [KING RICHARD]
3901   For God's sake, let us sit upon the ground
       And tell sad stories of the death of kings:
       How some have been deposed; some slain in war;
       Some haunted by the ghosts they have deposed;
       Some poison'd by their wives; some sleeping kill'd;
       All murder'd: for within the hollow crown
       That rounds the mortal temples of a king
       Keeps Death his court and there the antic sits,
       Scoffing his state and grinning at his pomp, . . .
       Infusing him with self and vain conceit,
       As if this flesh which walls about our life
       Were brass impregnable, and humour'd thus
       Comes at the last and with a little pin
       Bores through his castle wall, and farewell king!
                        Richard II, Act iii, sc. 2, l. 155 [KING RICHARD]
3902   What must the king do now? must he submit? . . .
       I'll give my jewels for a set of beads,
       My gorgeous palace for a hermitage, . . .
       My sceptre for a palmer's walking-staff, . . .
       And my large kingdom for a little grave,
       A little, little grave, an obscure grave;
       Or I'll be buried in the king's highway,
       Some way of common trade, where subjects' feet
       May hourly trample on their sovereign's head;
       For on my heart they tread now whilst I live;
       And buried once, why not upon my head?
                        Richard II, Act iii, sc. 3, l. 143 [KING RICHARD]
3903   What subject can give sentence on his king?
       And who sits here that is not Richard's subject?
       Thieves are not judged but they are by to hear,
       Although apparent guilt be seen in them;
       And shall the figure of God's majesty,
       His captain, steward, deputy-elect,
       Anointed, crowned, planted many years,
       Be judged by subject and inferior breath,
       And he himself not present? O, forfend it, God,
       That in a Christian climate souls refined

Should show so heinous, black, obscene a deed!
I speak to subjects, and a subject speaks,
Stirr'd up by God, thus boldly for his king.
Richard II, Act iv, sc. 1, l. 121 [CARLISLE]

3904   These men, . . .
Did they not sometime cry, 'all hail!' to me?
So Judas did to Christ: but he, in twelve,
Found truth in all but one; I, in twelve thousand, none.
God save the king! Will no man say amen?
Richard II, Act iv, sc. 1, l. 167 [KING RICHARD]

3905   Alack the heavy day,
That I have worn so many winters out,
And know not now what name to call myself!
O that I were a mockery king of snow,
Standing before the sun of Bolingbroke,
To melt myself away in water-drops!
Richard II, Act iv, sc. 1, l. 257 [KING RICHARD]

3906 Thus play I in one person many people,
And none contented: sometimes am I king;
Then treasons make me wish myself a beggar,
And so I am: then crushing penury
Persuades me I was better when a king.
Richard II, Act v, sc. 5, l. 31 [KING RICHARD]

3907 Poor key-cold figure of a holy king!
Richard III, Act i, sc. 2, l. 5 [ANNE]

3908 Thus have I had thee, as a dream doth flatter,
In sleep a king, but waking no such matter.
Sonnet lxxxvii, l. 13

3909 By the bare scalp of Robin Hood's fat friar,
This fellow were a king for our wild faction!
The Two Gentlemen of Verona, Act iv, sc. 1, l. 36 [OUTLAW]

Kingdom

3910 Kingdoms are clay: our dungy earth alike ·
Feeds beast as man.
Antony and Cleopatra, Act i, sc. 1, l. 35 [ANTONY]

3911 KING: You perceive the body of our kingdom,
How foul it is; what rank diseases grow,
And with what danger, near the heart of it.
WARWICK: It is but as a body yet distemper'd;
Which to his former strength may be restored
With good advice and little medicine.
II Henry IV, Act iii, sc. 1, l. 38 [KING]

3912 O my poor kingdom, sick with civil blows!
When that my care could not withhold thy riots,
What wilt thou do when riot is thy care?
O, thou wilt be a wilderness again,
Peopled with wolves, thy old inhabitants!
II Henry IV, Act iv, sc. 5, l. 134 [KING HENRY]

3913 I weep for joy
To stand upon my kingdom once again.
Dear earth, I do salute thee with my hand,
Though rebels wound thee with their horses' hoofs.
Richard II, Act iii, sc. 2, l. 4 [KING RICHARD]

3914 Mine ear is open and my heart prepared:
The worst is worldly loss thou canst unfold.

Say, is my kingdom lost? why, 'twas my care;
And what loss is it to be rid of care?
> *Richard II,* Act iii, sc. 2, l. 93 [KING RICHARD]

Kiss

3915 The greater cantle of the world is lost
With very ignorance; we have kiss'd away
Kingdoms and provinces.
> *Antony and Cleopatra,* Act iii, sc. 10, l. 6 [SCARUS]

3916 CELIA: Marry, his kisses are Judas's own children. . . .
ROSALIND: His kissing is as full of sanctity as the touch of holy
bread. . . .
CELIA: A nun of winter's sisterhood kisses not more religiously;
the very ice of chastity is in them.
> *As You Like It,* Act iii, sc. 4, l. 10 [CELIA]

3917 If I were a woman I would kiss as many of you as had beards
that pleased me, complexions that liked me and breaths that I defied
not.
> *As You Like It,* Epilogue, l. 19 [ROSALIND]

3918   O, a kiss
Long as my exile, sweet as my revenge!
Now, by the jealous queen of heaven, that kiss
I carried from thee, dear; and my true lip
Hath virgin'd it e'er since.
> *Coriolanus,* Act v, sc. 3, l. 44 [CORIOLANUS]

3919 I understand thy kisses and thou mine,
And that's a feeling disputation:
But I will never be a truant, love,
Till I have learned thy language; for thy tongue
Makes Welsh as sweet as ditties highly penn'd,
Sung by a fair queen in a summer's bower,
With ravishing division, to her lute.
> *I Henry IV,* Act iii, sc. 1, l. 205 [MORTIMER]

3920   Take, O, take those lips away,
        That so sweetly were forsworn;
      And those eyes, the break of day,
        Lights that do mislead the morn:
      But my kisses bring again, bring again;
      Seals of love, but seal'd in vain, seal'd in vain.
> *Measure for Measure,* Act iv, sc. 1, l. 1 [BOY]

3921 Speak, cousin; or, if you cannot, stop his mouth with a kiss.
> *Much Ado about Nothing,* Act ii, sc. 1, l. 321 [BEATRICE]

3922   Then would he . . . kiss me hard,
As if he pluck'd up kisses by the roots
That grew upon my lips.
> *Othello,* Act iii, sc. 3, l. 421 [IAGO]

3923 IAGO: What, to kiss in private?
OTHELLO: An unauthorized kiss.
> *Othello,* Act iv, sc. 1, l. 2 [IAGO]

3924 I kiss'd thee ere I kill'd thee: no way but this;
Killing myself, to die upon a kiss.
> *Othello,* Act v, sc. 2, l. 358 [OTHELLO]

3925 ROMEO: If I profane with my unworthiest hand
    This holy shrine, the gentle fine is this:
My lips, two blushing pilgrims, ready stand
    To smooth that rough touch with a tender kiss.
JULIET: Good pilgrim, you do wrong your hand too much,
    Which mannerly devotion shows in this;

> For saints have hands that pilgrims' hands do touch,
>> And palm to palm is holy palmers' kiss.
> ROMEO: Have not saints lips, and holy palmers too?
> JULIET: Ay, pilgrim, lips that they must use in prayer.
> ROMEO: O, then, dear saint, let lips do what hands do;
> They pray, grant thou, lest faith turn to despair.
> JULIET: Saints do not move, though grant for prayers' sake.
> ROMEO: Then move not while my prayer's effect I take.
> Thus from my lips, by yours, my sin is purged.
> JULIET: Then have my lips the sin that they have took.
> ROMEO: Sin from my lips? O trespass sweetly urged!
> Give me my sin again.
> JULIET: You kiss by the book.
>> *Romeo and Juliet,* Act i, sc. 5, l. 95 [ROMEO]

3926 Were kisses all the joys in bed,
One woman would another wed.
Sonnets to Sundry Notes of Music, Pt. xix, l. 47

3927   He took the bride about the neck
And kiss'd her lips with such a clamorous smack
That at the parting all the church did echo.
The Taming of the Shrew, Act iii, sc. 2, l. 179 [GREMIO]

3928 Alas, poor heart, that kiss is comfortless
As frozen water to a starved snake.
Titus Andronicus, Act iii, sc. 1, l. 251 [MARCUS]

3929 Let's kiss and part, for we have much to do.
Titus Andronicus, Act iii, sc. 1, l. 288 [TITUS]

3930 CRESSIDA: In kissing do you render or receive?
PATROCLUS: Both take and give.
CRESSIDA: I'll make my match to live,
The kiss you take is better than you give;
Therefore no kiss.
Troilus and Cressida, Act iv, sc. 5, l. 36 [CRESSIDA]

3931   I'll smother thee with kisses; . . .
Ten kisses short as one, one long as twenty.
Venus and Adonis, l. 18 [VENUS]

3932   You may ride's
With one soft kiss a thousand furlongs ere
With spur we heat an acre.
The Winter's Tale, Act i, sc. 2, l. 94 [HERMIONE]

Kite

3933 I should have fatted all the region kites
With this slave's offal.
Hamlet, Act ii, sc. 2, l. 607 [HAMLET]

3934 I . . . made a prey for carrion kites and crows
Even of the bonny beast he loved so well.
II Henry VI, Act v, sc. 2, l. 11 [YORK]

3935 My traffic is sheets; when the kite builds, look to lesser linen.
The Winter's Tale, Act iv, sc. 3, l. 23 [AUTOLYCUS]

Knave

3936 Use the carp as you may; for he looks like a poor, decayed, ingenious, foolish, rascally knave.
All's Well that Ends Well, Act v, sc. 2, l. 24 [CLOWN]

3937 We are arrant knaves all.
Hamlet, Act iii, sc. 1, l. 131 [HAMLET]

3938   Three misbegotten knaves in Kendal green came at my back and
let drive at me.
I Henry IV, Act ii, sc. 4, l. 245 [FALSTAFF]

3939   A crafty knave does need no broker.
II Henry VI, Act i, sc. 2, l. 100 [HUME]

3940   You, sir, more knave than fool, after your master.
King Lear, Act i, sc. 4, l. 337 [GONERIL]

3941   I know thee for . . . a knave; a rascal; an eater of broken meats;
a base, proud, shallow, beggarly, three-suited, hundred-pound,
filthy, worsted-stocking knave; a lily-livered, action-taking knave.
. . . one that wouldst be a bawd, . . . and art nothing but the
composition of a knave, beggar, coward, pandar, and the son and
heir of a mongrel bitch.
King Lear, Act ii, sc. 2, l. 13 [KENT]

3942   Masters, it is proved already that you are little better than false
knaves; and it will go near to be thought so shortly.
Much Ado about Nothing, Act iv, sc. 2, l. 22 [DOGBERRY]

3943   You shall mark
Many a duteous and knee-crooking knave,
That, doting on his own obsequious bondage,
Wears out his time, much like his master's ass,
For nought but provender, and when he's old, cashier'd:
Whip me such honest knaves. Others there are
Who, trimm'd in forms and visages of duty,
Keep yet their hearts attending on themselves,
And, throwing but shews of service on their lords,
Do well thrive by them and when they have lined their coats
Do themselves homage: these fellows have some soul;
And such a one do I profess myself.
Othello, Act i, sc. 1, l. 44 [IAGO]

3944   A slipper and subtle knave, a finder of occasions; . . . a devilish
knave . . . a pestilent complete knave.
Othello, Act ii, sc. 1, l. 247 [IAGO]

3945   Scurvy knave! I am none of his flirt-gills; I am none of his skains-
mates.
Romeo and Juliet, Act ii, sc. 4, l. 161 [NURSE]

3946   HORTENSIO: Madam, my instrument's in tune.
BIANCA: Let's hear. O fie! the treble jars.
LUCENTIO: Spit in the hole, man, and tune again. . . .
HORTENSIO: Madam, 'tis now in tune.
LUCENTIO: All but the base.
HORTENSIO: The base is right; 'tis the base knave that jars.
The Taming of the Shrew, Act iii, sc. 1, l. 40 [HORTENSIO]

3947   A whoreson, beetle-headed, flap-ear'd knave.
The Taming of the Shrew, Act iv, sc. 1, l. 160 [PETRUCHIO]

3948   An ass-head and a coxcomb and a knave, a thin-faced knave, a gull.
Twelfth Night, Act v, sc. 1, l. 212 [SIR TOBY]

Knavery

3949   'Tis as arrant a piece of knavery, mark you now, as can be offer't;
in your conscience, now, is it not?
Henry V, Act iv, sc. 7, l. 2 [FLUELLEN]

3950   I should think this a gull, but that the white-bearded fellow
speaks it: knavery cannot, sure, hide himself in such reverence.
Much Ado about Nothing, Act ii, sc. 3, l. 124 [BENEDICK]

3951   Knavery's plain face is never seen till used.
Othello, Act ii, sc. 1, l. 321 [IAGO]

3952   Here such patchery, such juggling and such knavery. . . . The
         dry serpigo on the subject! and war and lechery confound all!
                         Troilus and Cressida, Act ii, sc. 3, l. 77 [THERSITES]

Knee

3953   Down, ladies; let us shame him with our knees.
                                   Coriolanus, Act v, sc. 3, l. 169 [VOLUMNIA]
3954   I am too blunt and saucy: here's my knee.
                                  Cymbeline, Act v, sc. 5, l. 325 [BELARIUS]
3955   PRINCE: Here comes lean Jack, here comes bare-bone. How now,
         my sweet creature of bombast! How long is't ago, Jack, since
         thou sawest thine own knee?
         FALSTAFF: My own knee! when I was about thy years, Hal, I was
         not an eagle's talon in the waist; I could have crept into any
         alderman's thumb-ring.
                             I Henry IV, Act ii, sc. 4, l. 358 [PRINCE]
3956   Why, Warwick, hath thy knee forgot to bow?
         Old Salisbury, shame to thy silver hair,
         Thou mad misleader of thy brain-sick son!
         What, wilt thou on thy deathbed play the ruffian,
         And seek for sorrow with thy spectacles?
                         II Henry VI, Act v, sc. 1, l. 161 [KING HENRY]
3957   I cannot be much lower than my knees.
                                   Pericles, Act i, sc. 2, l. 47 [HELICANUS]
3958   Fair cousin, you debase your princely knee
         To make the base earth proud with kissing it.
                         Richard II, Act iii, sc. 3, l. 190 [KING RICHARD]
3959   Supple knees
         Feed arrogance and are the proud man's fees.
                         Troilus and Cressida, Act iii, sc. 3, l. 48 [ULYSSES]

Knife

3960   EDGAR: What means that bloody knife?
         GENTLEMAN: 'Tis hot, it smokes:
         It came even from the heart of . . . Your lady, sir.
                             King Lear, Act v, sc. 3, l. 223 [EDGAR]
3961   Even her she sheathed in her harmless breast
         A harmful knife, that thence her soul unsheathed.
                                   The Rape of Lucrece, l. 1723
3962   No doubt the murderous knife was dull and blunt
         Till it was whetted on thy stone-hard heart.
                         Richard III, Act iv, sc. 4, l. 226 [QUEEN ELIZABETH]
3963   Give me some present counsel, or, behold,
         'Twixt my extremes and me this bloody knife
         Shall play the umpire.
                         Romeo and Juliet, Act iv, sc. 1, l. 61 [JULIET]
3964   The hardest knife ill-used doth lose his edge.
                                         Sonnet xcv, l. 14

Knight

3965   Do me right, And dub me knight: Samingo.
                         II Henry IV, Act v, sc. 3, l. 77 [SILENCE]
3966   Knights of the garter were of noble birth,
         Valiant and virtuous, full of haughty courage.
                         I Henry VI, Act iv, sc. 1, l. 34 [TALBOT]
3967   Edward Plantagenet, arise a knight;
         And learn this lesson, draw thy sword in right.
                         III Henry VI, Act ii, sc. 2, l. 61 [KING HENRY]

3968   He is knight, dubbed with unhatched rapier and on carpet consideration.
Twelfth Night, Act iii, sc. 4, l. 257 [SIR TOBY]

Knot

3969   Come, thou mortal wretch,
With thy sharp teeth this knot intrinsicate
Of life at once untie.
Antony and Cleopatra, Act v, sc. 2, l. 306 [CLEOPATRA]

3970   I would he had continued to his country
As he began, and not unknit himself
The noble knot he made.
Coriolanus, Act iv, sc. 2, l. 30 [SICINIUS]

3971   As slippery as the Gordian knot was hard.
Cymbeline, Act ii, sc. 2, l. 34 [IACHIMO]

3972   Turn him to any cause of policy,
The Gordian knot of it he will unloose,
Familiar as his garter.
Henry V, Act i, sc. 1, l. 45 [CANTERBURY]

3973   Blunt wedges rive hard knots.
Troilus and Cressida, Act i, sc. 3, l. 316 [ULYSSES]
O time! thou must untangle this, not I;
It is too hard a knot for me to untie!
Twelfth Night, Act ii, sc. 2, l. 41 [VIOLA]

Knowledge

3974   He was excellent indeed, madam: . . . he was skillful enough to
have lived still, if knowledge could be set up against mortality.
All's Well that Ends Well, Act i, sc. 1, l. 32 [LAFEU]

3975   He is very great in knowledge and accordingly valiant.
All's Well that Ends Well, Act ii, sc. 5, l. 8 [BERTRAM]

3976   I know what I know.
The Comedy of Errors, Act iii, sc. 1, l. 11 [DROMIO OF EPHESUS]
(Repeated in *Measure for Measure,* iii, 2, 16.)

3977   We know what we are, but know not what we may be.
Hamlet, Act iv, sc. 5, l. 42 [OPHELIA]

L

Labour

3978   Now all labour
Mars what it does; yea, very force entangles
Itself with strength.
Antony and Cleopatra, Act iv, sc. 14, l. 47 [ANTONY]

3979   Sir, I am a true labourer: I earn that I eat, get that I wear, owe no
man hate, envy no man's happiness, glad of other men's good, content with my harm, and the greatest of my pride is to see my
ewes graze and my lambs suck.
As You Like It, Act iii, sc. 2, l. 77 [CORIN]

3980   This fool's speed
Be cross'd with slowness; labour be his meed!
Cymbeline, Act iii, sc. 5, l. 168 [PISANIO]

3981   While these do labour for their own preferment,
Behoves it us to labour for the realm.
II Henry VI, Act i, sc. 1, l. 181 [SALISBURY]

3982   Your labour is but lost.
                              III Henry VI, Act iii, sc. 1, l. 32 [KING]
        You do but lose your labour.
                       Measure for Measure, Act v, sc. 1, l. 433 [DUKE]
        I have had my labour for my travail.
                    Troilus and Cressida, Act i, sc. 1, l. 70 [PANDARUS]
3983   The labour we delight in physics pain.
                              Macbeth, Act ii, sc. 3, l. 55 [MACBETH]
3984   Leave that labour to great Hercules;
        And let it be more than Alcides' twelve.
                The Taming of the Shrew, Act i, sc. 2, l. 257 [GREMIO]

Lady

3985   If ladies be but young and fair,
        They have the gift to know it.
                       As You Like It, Act ii, sc. 7, l. 37 [JAQUES]
3986   A lady
        So fair, and fasten'd to an empery,
        Would make the great'st king double,—to be partner'd
        With tomboys hired with that self exhibition
        Which your own coffers yield!
                    Cymbeline, Act i, sc. 6, l. 119 [IACHIMO]
3987   She's a lady
        So tender of rebukes that words are strokes
        And strokes death to her.
                    Cymbeline, Act iii, sc. 5, l. 40 [QUEEN]
3988   The lady doth protest too much, methinks.
                       Hamlet, Act iii, sc. 2, l. 240 [QUEEN]
3989   I see the lady hath a thing to grant,
        Before the king will grant her humble suit.
                III Henry VI, Act iii, sc. 2, l. 12 [GLOUCESTER]
3990   Fair ladies mask'd are roses in their bud;
        Dismask'd, their damask sweet commixture shown,
        Are angels vailing clouds, or roses blown.
                Love's Labour's Lost, Act v, sc. 2, l. 295 [BOYET]

Lamb See also Wolf and Lamb

3991   The lamb entreats the butcher: where's thy knife?
        Thou art too slow to do thy master's bidding,
        When I desire it too.
                    Cymbeline, Act iii, sc. 4, l. 99 [IMOGEN]
3992   Come you to seek the lamb here of the fox?
        Good night to your redress!
                Measure for Measure, Act v, sc. 1, l. 300 [DUKE]
3993   I'll sacrifice the lamb that I do love,
        To spite a raven's heart within a dove.
                Twelfth Night, Act v, sc. 1, l. 133 [DUKE]

Lamentation

3994   Moderate lamentation is the right of the dead, excessive grief
        the enemy to the living.
                All's Well that Ends Well, Act i, sc. 1, l. 64 [LAFEU]
3995   Give me no help in lamentation;
        I am not barren to bring forth complaints:
        All springs reduce their currents to mine eyes,
        That I, being govern'd by the watery moon,
        May send forth plenteous tears to drown the world.
                Richard III, Act ii, sc. 2, l. 66 [QUEEN ELIZABETH]

Language

3996   He has been bred i' the wars
Since he could draw a sword, and is ill school'd
In bolted language; meal and bran together
He throws without distinction.
Coriolanus, Act iii, sc. 1, l. 320 [MENENIUS]

3997   There is not chastity enough in language
Without offence to utter them.
Much Ado about Nothing, Act iv, sc. 1, l. 98 [DON JOHN]

3998   The language I have learn'd these forty years,
My native English, now must I forego.
Richard II, Act i, sc. 3, l. 159 [MOWBRAY]

3999   You taught me language; and my profit on 't
Is, I know how to curse.
The Tempest, Act i, sc. 2, l. 363 [CALIBAN]

4000   There 's language in her eye, her cheek, her lip,
Nay, her foot speaks; her wanton spirits look out
At every joint and motive of her body.
Troilus and Cressida, Act iv, sc. 5, l. 55 [ULYSSES]

Lapwing

4001   Far from her nest the lapwing cries away.
The Comedy of Errors, Act iv, sc. 2, l. 26 [ADRIANA]

4002   This lapwing runs away with the shell on his head.
Hamlet, Act v, sc. 2, l. 193 [HORATIO]

4003   Look where Beatrice, like a lapwing, runs
Close by the ground, to hear our conference.
Much Ado about Nothing, Act iii, sc. 1, l. 24 [HERO]

Lark

4004   My dial goes not true: I took this lark for a bunting.
All's Well that Ends Well, Act ii, sc. 5, l. 7 [LAFEU]

4005   Hark, hark! the lark at heaven's gate sings,
And Phœbus 'gins arise,
His steeds to water at those springs
On chaliced flowers that lies;
The winking Mary-buds begin
To ope their golden eyes:
With every thing that pretty is,
My lady sweet, arise.
Cymbeline, Act ii, sc. 3, l. 21 [SONG]

4006   PUCK: Fairy king, attend, and mark:
I do hear the morning lark.
OBERON: Then, my queen, in silence sad,
Trip we after night's shade.
A Midsummer Night's Dream, Act iv, sc. 1, l. 97 [PUCK]

4007   Stir with the lark to-morrow, gentle Norfolk.
Richard III, Act v, sc. 3, l. 56 [KING RICHARD]

4008   JULIET: Wilt thou be gone? It is not yet near day:
It was the nightingale, and not the lark,
That pierced the fearful hollow of thine ear;
Nightly she sings on yond pomegranate-tree:
Believe me, love, it was the nightingale.
ROMEO: It was the lark, the herald of the morn,
No nightingale. . . .
JULIET: It is, it is: hie hence, be gone, away!
It is the lark that sings so out of tune,
Straining harsh discords and unpleasing sharps.

Some say the lark makes sweet division;
This doth not so, for she divideth us:
Some say the lark and loathed toad change eyes;
O, now I would they had changed voices too!
Since arm in arm that voice doth us affray,
Hunting thee hence with hunt's-up to the day.
Romeo and Juliet, Act iii, sc. 5, l. 1 [JULIET]

4009 Lo, here the gentle lark, weary of rest,
From his moist cabinet mounts up on high,
And wakes the morning, from whose silver breast
The sun ariseth in his majesty.
Venus and Adonis, l. 853

4010 The lark, that tirra-lyra chants,
With heigh! with heigh! the thrush and the jay,
Are summer songs for me and my aunts,
While we lie tumbling in the hay.
The Winter's Tale, Act iv, sc. 3, l. 9 [AUTOLYCUS]

Lateness

4011 I am glad I was up so late; for that's the reason I was up so early.
Cymbeline, Act ii, sc. 3, l. 37 [CLOTEN]
To be up late is to be up late.
Twelfth Night, Act ii, sc. 3, l. 5 [SIR ANDREW]

4012 Better three hours too soon than a minute too late.
The Merry Wives of Windsor, Act ii, sc. 2, l. 332 [FORD]

4013 Better once than never, for never too late.
The Taming of the Shrew, Act v, sc. 1, l. 155 [PETRUCHIO]

Latin

4014 LORD SAY: Kent, . . . 'tis 'bona terra, mala gens.'
CADE: Away with him; he speaks Latin.
II Henry VI, Act iv, sc. 7, l. 61 [LORD SAY]

4015 NATHANIEL: Laus Deo, bene intelligo.
HOLOFERNES: Bon, bon, fort bon. Priscian a little scratched, 'twill serve.
Love's Labour's Lost, Act v, sc. 1, l. 30 [NATHANIEL]

4016 COSTARD: Go to; thou hast it at dunghill, at the fingers' ends, as they say.
HOLOFERNES: O, I smell false Latin; dunghill for unguem.
Love's Labour's Lost, Act v, sc. 1, l. 81 [COSTARD]

4017 HORTENSIO: 'Alla nostra casa ben venuto.' . . .
GRUMIO: Nay, 'tis no matter, sir, what he 'leges in Latin.
The Taming of the Shrew, Act i, sc. 2, l. 25 [HORTENSIO]
(Strangely enough, Grumio, although a native of Italy, mistakes Italian for Latin.)

Laughter

4018 I will laugh like a hyen, and that when thou art inclined to sleep.
As You Like It, Act iv, sc. 1, l. 156 [ROSALIND]

4019 The jolly Briton . . . laughs from 's free lungs,
Cries 'O, Can my sides hold?'
Cymbeline, Act i, sc. 6, l. 67 [IACHIMO]

4020 O, I am stabb'd with laughter!
Love's Labour's Lost, Act v, sc. 2, l. 80 [BOYET]

4021 To move wild laughter in the throat of death?
It cannot be; it is impossible:
Mirth cannot move a soul in agony.
Love's Labour's Lost, Act v, sc. 2, l. 865 [BIRON]

4022   Let us not be laughing-stocks to other men's humours.
                    The Merry Wives of Windsor, Act iii, sc. 1, l. 88 [EVANS]
4023   Now will I question Cassio of Bianca,
        A housewife that by selling her desires
        Buys herself bread and clothes. . . .
        He, when he hears of her, cannot refrain
        From the excess of laughter.
                            Othello, Act iv, sc. 1, l. 94 [IAGO]
4024   They laugh that win.
                            Othello, Act iv, sc. 1, l. 125 [OTHELLO]
4025   I shall laugh myself to death at this puppy-headed monster.
                        The Tempest, Act ii, sc. 2, l. 158 [TRINCULO]
4026   If you . . . will laugh yourself into stitches, follow me.
                        Twelfth Night, Act iii, sc. 2, l. 72 [MARIA]

Law

4027   FIRST CLOWN: He that is not guilty of his own death shortens
        not his own life.
        SECOND CLOWN: But is this law?
        FIRST CLOWN: Ay, marry, is 't; crowner's quest law.
                        Hamlet, Act v, sc. 1, l. 22 [FIRST CLOWN]
4028   I prithee, sweet wag, shall there be a gallows standing in England
        when thou art king? and resolution thus fobbed as it is with the
        rusty curb of old father antic, the law?
                        I Henry IV, Act i, sc. 2, l. 66 [FALSTAFF]
4029   Faith, I have been a truant in the law,
        And never yet could frame my will to it;
        And therefore frame the law unto my will.
                        I Henry VI, Act ii, sc. 4, l. 7 [SUFFOLK]
4030   Between two hawks, which flies the higher pitch;
        Between two dogs, which hath the deeper mouth;
        Between two blades, which bears the better temper;
        Between two horses, which doth bear him best;
        Between two girls, which hath the merriest eye;
        I have perhaps some shallow spirit of judgement;
        But in these nice sharp quillets of the law,
        Good faith, I am no wiser than a daw.
                        I Henry VI, Act ii, sc. 4, l. 11 [WARWICK]
4031   Base dunghill villain and mechanical,
        I'll have thy head for this thy traitor's speech. . . .
        Let him have all the rigour of the law.
                        II Henry VI, Act i, sc. 3, l. 197 [YORK]
4032   When law can do no right,
        Let it be lawful that law bar no wrong.
                        King John, Act iii, sc. 1, l. 185 [CONSTANCE]
4033   We must not make a scarecrow of the law,
        Setting it up to fear the birds of prey,
        And let it keep one shape, till custom make it
        Their perch and not their terror.
                        Measure for Measure, Act ii, sc. 1, l. 1 [ANGELO]
4034   The law hath not been dead, though it hath slept.
                        Measure for Measure, Act ii, sc. 2, l. 90 [ANGELO]
4035   Has he affections in him,
        That thus can make him bite the law by the nose?
                        Measure for Measure, Act iii, sc. 1, l. 108 [CLAUDIO]
4036   Laws for all faults,
        But faults so countenanced, that the strong statutes

Stand like the forfeits in a barber's shop,
As much in mock as mark.
Measure for Measure, Act v, sc. 1, l. 321 [DUKE]

4037   In law, what plea so tainted and corrupt
But, being season'd with a gracious voice,
Obscures the show of evil?
The Merchant of Venice, Act iii, sc. 2, l. 75 [BASSANIO]

4038   Wrest once the law to your authority:
To do a great right, do a little wrong,
And curb this cruel devil of his will.
The Merchant of Venice, Act iv, sc. 1, l. 215 [BASSANIO]

4039   The bloody book of law
You shall yourself read in the bitter letter.
Othello, Act i, sc. 3, l. 67 [DUKE]

4040   I am loath to break our country's laws.
Nor friends nor foes, to me welcome you are:
Things past redress are now with me past care.
Richard II, Act ii, sc. 3, l. 170 [YORK]

4041   Let us take the law of our sides. . . . Is the law of our side?
Romeo and Juliet, Act i, sc. 1, l. 44 [SAMPSON]

4042   Do as adversaries do in law,
Strive mightily, but eat and drink as friends.
The Taming of the Shrew, Act i, sc. 2, l. 278 [TRANIO]

4043   The law, which is past depth
To those who, without heed, do plunge into 't.
Timon of Athens, Act iii, sc. 5, l. 12 [ALCIBIADES]

4044   That keeps you from the blow of the law. . . . Keep o' the windy
side of the law.
Twelfth Night, Act iii, sc. 4, l. 168 [FABIAN]

4045   Let the law go whistle.
The Winter's Tale, Act iv, sc. 4, l. 713 [CLOWN]

Lawyer

4046   May not that be the skull of a lawyer? Where be his quiddities
now, his quillets, his cases, his tenures, and his tricks?
Hamlet, Act v, sc. 1, l. 106 [HAMLET]

4047   The first thing we do, let's kill all the lawyers.
II Henry VI, Act iv, sc. 2, l. 84 [DICK]

4048   Like the breath of an unfee'd lawyer; you gave me nothing for it.
King Lear, Act i, sc. 4, l. 142 [FOOL]

Lead

4049   Love, I am full of lead.
Antony and Cleopatra, Act iii, sc. 11, l. 72 [ANTONY]

4050   I am as hot as molten lead, and as heavy too: God keep lead out
of me! I need no more weight than mine own bowels.
I Henry IV, Act v, sc. 3, l. 34 [FALSTAFF]

4051   What say'st thou, man, before dead Henry's corse?
Speak softly, or the loss of these great towns
Will make him burst his lead and rise from death.
I Henry VI, Act i, sc. 1, l. 62 [BEDFORD]

4052   ARMADO: The way is but short: away!
MOTH: As swift as lead, sir.
ARMADO: The meaning, pretty ingenious?
Is not lead a metal, heavy, dull, and slow?
MOTH: Minime, honest master; or rather, master, no.
ARMADO: I say lead is slow.

Moth : You are too swift, sir, to say so :
Is that lead slow which is fired from a gun?
Love's Labour's Lost, Act iii, sc. 1, 1. 57 [ARMADO]

4053   Let us be lead within thy bosom, Richard,
And weigh thee down to ruin, shame, and death !
Richard III, Act v, sc. 3, 1. 152 [GHOSTS]

4054   Mine eyes are turn'd to fire, my heart to lead:
Heavy heart's lead, melt at mine eyes' red fire !
So shall I die by drops of hot desire.
Venus and Adonis, 1. 1072 [VENUS]

Learning

4055   Learning [is] a mere hoard of gold kept by a devil, till sack com-
mences it and sets it in act and use.
II Henry IV, Act iv, sc. 3, 1. 125 [FALSTAFF]

4056   Learning is but an adjunct to ourself,
And where we are our learning likewise is.
Love's Labour's Lost, Act iv, sc. 3, 1. 314 [BIRON]

4057   O Lord, I could have stay'd here all the night
To hear good counsel : O, what learning is !
Romeo and Juliet, Act iii, sc. 3, 1. 160 [NURSE]

4058   GREMIO : O this learning, what a thing it is !
GRUMIO : O this woodcock, what an ass it is !
The Taming of the Shrew, Act i, sc. 2, 1. 160 [GREMIO]

Leg

4059   Now for our mountain sport : up to yond hill ;
Your legs are young.
Cymbeline, Act iii, sc. 3, 1. 10 [BELARIUS]

4060   When you and I met at Saint Alban's last,
Your legs did better service than your hands.
III Henry VI, Act ii, sc. 2, 1. 103 [QUEEN MARGARET]

4061   Ha, ha! he wears cruel garters. Horses are tied by the heads,
dogs and bears by the neck, monkeys by the loins, and men by
the legs : when a man's over-lusty at legs, then he wears wooden
nether-stocks.
King Lear, Act ii, sc. 4, 1. 7 [FOOL]

4062   You make a leg.
Richard II, Act iii, sc. 3, 1. 175 [KING RICHARD]

4063   SIR TOBY : Taste your legs, sir ; put them in motion.
VIOLA : My legs do better understand me, sir, than I understand
what you mean by bidding me taste my legs.
SIR TOBY : I mean, to go, sir, to enter.
Twelfth Night, Act iii, sc. 1, 1. 87 [SIR TOBY]

Leisure

4064   When thou hast leisure, say thy prayers ; when thou hast none,
remember thy friends.
All's Well that Ends Well, Act i, sc. 1, 1. 227 [PAROLLES]

4065   I hope I shall have leisure to make good.
The Comedy of Errors, Act v, sc. 1, 1. 375
[ANTIPHOLUS OF SYRACUSE]

4066   DUKE : Might you dispense with your leisure, I would by and by
have some speech with you.
ISABELLA : I have no superfluous leisure.
Measure for Measure, Act iii, sc. 1, 1. 154 [DUKE]

Lending See also Borrowing and Lending

4067 FALSTAFF: Will your lordship lend me a thousand pound to furnish me forth?
CHIEF JUSTICE: Not a penny, not a penny; you are too impatient to bear crosses.
II Henry IV, Act i, sc. 2, l. 250 [FALSTAFF]

4068 BASSANIO: This is Signior Antonio.
SHYLOCK [*Aside*]: How like a fawning publican he looks!
I hate him for he is a Christian,
But more for that in low simplicity
He lends out money gratis and brings down
The rate of usance here with us in Venice.
The Merchant of Venice, Act i, sc. 3, l. 41 [BASSANIO]

4069 If thou wilt lend this money, lend it not
As to thy friends; . . . but rather to thine enemy,
Who, if he break, thou mayst with better face
Exact the penalty.
The Merchant of Venice, Act i, sc. 3, l. 133 [ANTONIO]

4070 Out of my lean and low ability
I'll lend you something.
Twelfth Night, Act iii, sc. 4, l. 377 [VIOLA]

Lenity

4071   If he have power,
Then vail your ignorance; if none, awake
Your dangerous lenity.
Coriolanus, Act iii, sc. 1, l. 97 [CORIOLANUS]

4072 When lenity and cruelty play for a kingdom, the gentler gamester is the soonest winner.
Henry V, Act iii, sc. 6, l. 118 [KING]

4073 My gracious liege, this too much lenity
And harmful pity must be laid aside.
III Henry VI, Act ii, sc. 2, l. 9 [CLIFFORD]

4074 What makes robbers bold but too much lenity?
III Henry VI, Act ii, sc. 6, l. 22 [CLIFFORD]

4075 A little more lenity to lechery would do no harm in him: something too crabbed that way, friar.
Measure for Measure, Act iii, sc. 2, l. 103 [LUCIO]

4076 Away to heaven, respective lenity,
And fire-eyed fury be my conduct now!
Romeo and Juliet, Act iii, sc. 1, l. 128 [ROMEO]

Leopard

4077 KING RICHARD: Lions make leopards tame.
MOWBRAY: Yes, but not change his spots.
Richard II, Act i, sc. 1, l. 175 [KING RICHARD]

4078 Wert thou a horse, thou wouldst be seized by the leopard; wert thou a leopard, thou wert german to the lion and the spots of thy kindred were jurors on thy life.
Timon of Athens, Act iv, sc. 3, l. 343 [TIMON]

Lesson

4079 I shall the effect of this good lesson keep,
As watchman to my heart.
Hamlet, Act i, sc. 3, l. 45 [OPHELIA]

4080 Thou shalt see how apt it is to learn
Any hard lesson that may do thee good.
Much Ado about Nothing, Act i, sc. 1, l. 294 [DON PEDRO]

4081   I am no breeching scholar in the schools;
      I'll not be tied to hours nor 'pointed times,
      But learn my lessons as I please myself.
The Taming of the Shrew, Act iii, sc. 1, l. 18 [BIANCA]

Letter

4082   The letter is too long by half a mile.
Love's Labour's Lost, Act v, sc. 2, l.· 54 [MARGARET]

4083   What, have I scaped love-letters in the holiday-time of my beauty,
      and am I now a subject for them?
The Merry Wives of Windsor, Act ii, sc. 1, l. 1 [MRS. PAGE]

4084   Thou whoreson zed! thou unnecessary letter!
King Lear, Act ii, sc. 2, l. 69 [KENT]

Liberty

4085   I must have liberty
      Withal, as large a charter as the wind,
      To blow on whom I please; for so fools have;
      And they that are most galled with my folly,
      They most must laugh.
As You Like It, Act ii, sc. 7, l. 47 [JAQUES]

4086   CINNA: Liberty! Freedom! Tyranny is dead!
      Run hence, proclaim, cry it about the streets.
      CASSIUS: Some to the common pulpits, and cry out
      'Liberty, freedom and enfranchisement!'
Julius Cæsar, Act iii, sc. 1, l. 78 [CINNA]

4087   Liberty plucks justice by the nose;
      The baby beats the nurse, and quite athwart
      Goes all decorum.
Measure for Measure, Act i, sc. 3, l. 29 [DUKE]

Library

4088   My library was dukedom large enough.
The Tempest, Act i, sc. 2, l. 109 [PROSPERO]

4089   Come, and take choice of all my library,
      And so beguile thy sorrow.
Titus Andronicus, Act iv, sc. 1, l. 34 [TITUS]

Lie and Lying

4090   You lie, up to the hearing of the gods.
Antony and Cleopatra, Act v, sc. 2, l. 95 [CLEOPATRA]

4091   JAQUES: How did you find the quarrel on the seventh cause?
      TOUCHSTONE: Upon a lie seven times removed: . . . as thus, sir.
      I did dislike the cut of a certain courtier's beard: he sent me word,
      if I said his beard was not cut well, he was in the mind it was:
      this is called the Retort Courteous. If I sent him word again, 'it
      is not well cut,' he would send me word, he cut it to please him-
      self: this is called the Quip Modest. If again 'it was not well cut,'
      he disabled my judgement: this is called the Reply Churlish.
      If again 'it was not well cut,' he would answer I spake not true:
      this is called the Reproof Valiant. If again 'it was not well cut,'
      he would say I lied: this is called the Countercheck Quarrelsome:
      and so to the Lie Circumstantial and the Lie Direct.
      JAQUES: And how oft did you say his beard was not well cut?
      TOUCHSTONE: I durst go no further than the Lie Circumstantial,
      nor he durst not give me the Lie Direct; and so we measured
      swords and parted.
As You Like It, Act v, sc. 4, l. 70 [JAQUES]

4092   To lapse in fulness
Is sorer than to lie for need, and falsehood
Is worse in kings than beggars.
Cymbeline, Act iii, sc. 6, l. 12 [IMOGEN]

4093   If I do lie and do
No harm by it, though the gods hear, I hope
They'll pardon it.
Cymbeline, Act iv, sc. 2, l. 377 [IMOGEN]

4094   FALSTAFF: I tell thee what, Hal, if I tell thee a lie, spit in my face, call me horse. . . .
PRINCE: These lies are like their father that begets them; gross as a mountain, open, palpable.
I Henry IV, Act ii, sc. 4, l. 213 [FALSTAFF]

4095   Lord, Lord, how this world is given to lying.
I Henry IV, Act v, sc. 4, l. 150 [FALSTAFF]

4096   If a lie may do thee grace,
I'll gild it with the happiest terms I have.
I Henry IV, Act v, sc. 4, l. 161 [PRINCE]

4097   O, it is much that a lie with a light oath and a jest with a sad brow will do with a fellow that never had the ache in his shoulders!
II Henry IV, Act v, sc. 1, l. 94 [FALSTAFF]

4098   If he say so, may his pernicious soul
Rot half a grain a day! he lies to the heart. . . .
You told a lie; an odious, damned lie;
Upon my soul, a lie, a wicked lie.
Othello, Act v, sc. 2, l. 155 [EMILIA]

4099   SURREY: Dishonourable boy!
That lie shall lie so heavy on my sword,
That it shall render vengeance and revenge
Till thou the lie-giver and that lie do lie
In earth as quiet as thy father's skull. . . .
FITZWATER: If I dare eat, or drink, or breathe, or live,
I dare meet Surrey in a wilderness,
And spit upon him, whilst I say he lies,
And lies, and lies.
Richard II, Act iv, sc. 1, l. 65 [SURREY]

4100   Lies well steel'd with weighty arguments.
Richard III, Act i, sc. 1, l. 148 [GLOUCESTER]

4101   He . . . having into truth, by telling of it,
Made such a sinner of his memory,
To credit his own lie.
The Tempest, Act i, sc. 2, l. 100 [PROSPERO]

4102   As many lies as will lie in thy sheet of paper, though the sheet were big enough for the bed of Ware in England, set 'em down.
Twelfth Night, Act iii, sc. 2, l. 50 [SIR TOBY]

4103   Let me have no lying: it becomes nothing but tradesmen.
The Winter's Tale, Act iv, sc. 4, l. 743 [AUTOLYCUS]

Lie in One's Throat

4104   FALSTAFF: Why, sir, did I say you were an honest man? . . .
I had lied in my throat, if I had said so. . . .
SERVANT: You lie in your throat, if you say I am any other than an honest man.
II Henry IV, Act i, sc. 2, l. 92 [FALSTAFF]
("To lie in your throat" is a proverbial phrase, meaning to lie outrageously and knowingly.)

4105   That's a lie in thy throat.
                        Henry V, Act iv, sc. 8, l. 17 [FLUELLEN]
4106   Well, I do nothing in the world but lie, and lie in my throat.
                        Love's Labour's Lost, Act iv, sc. 3, l. 12 [BIRON]
4107   SIMONIDES: Traitor, thou liest. . . .
        PERICLES: Even in his throat—unless it be the king—
        That calls me traitor, I return the lie.
                        Pericles, Act ii, sc. 5, l. 55 [SIMONIDES]
4108   As low as to thy heart,
        Through the false passage of thy throat, thou liest.
                        Richard II, Act i, sc. 1, l. 124 [MOWBRAY]

Lie: The Liar

4109   I know him a notorious liar,
        Think him a great way fool, solely a coward.
                        All's Well that Ends Well, Act i, sc. 1, l. 111 [HELENA]
4110   I am full sorry
        That he approves the common liar, who
        Thus speaks of him at Rome.
                        Antony and Cleopatra, Act i, sc. 1, l. 59 [DEMETRIUS]
4111   Faith, here's an equivocator, that could swear in both the scales
        against either scale.
                        Macbeth, Act ii, sc. 3, l. 10 [PORTER]
4112   Shall I tell you a lie? I do despise a liar as I do despise one that
        is false, or as I despise one that is not true.
                        The Merry Wives of Windsor, Act i, sc. 1, l. 68 [EVANS]
4113   God and good men hate so foul a liar.
                        Richard II, Act i, sc. 1, l. 114 [MOWBRAY]

Life

4114   'Let me not live,' quoth he,
        'After my flame lacks oil, to be the snuff
        Of younger spirits, whose apprehensive senses
        All but new things disdain; whose judgements are
        Mere fathers of their garments; whose constancies
        Expire before their fashions.' This he wish'd:
        I after him do after him wish too,
        Since I nor wax nor honey can bring home,
        I quickly were dissolved from my hive,
        To give some labourers room.
                        All's Well that Ends Well, Act i, sc. 2, l. 58 [KING]
4115   The web of our life is of a mingled yarn, good and ill together:
        our virtues would be proud, if our faults whipped them not; and
        our crimes would despair, if they were not cherished by our
        virtues.
                        All's Well that Ends Well, Act iv, sc. 3, l. 83 [LORD]
4116   I love long life better than figs.
                        Antony and Cleopatra, Act i, sc. 2, l. 32 [CHARMIAN]
4117   Now, my co-mates and brothers in exile,
        Hath not old custom made this life more sweet
        Than that of painted pomp? Are not these woods
        More free from peril than the envious court?
        Here feel we but the penalty of Adam,
        The seasons' difference, as the icy fang
        And churlish chiding of the winter's wind; . . .
        And this our life, exempt from public haunt

Finds tongues in trees, books in the running brooks,
Sermons in stones and good in every thing.
As You Like It, Act ii, sc. 1, l. 1 [DUKE]

4118 CORIN: And how like you this shepherd's life, Master Touchstone?
TOUCHSTONE: Truly, shepherd, in respect of itself, it is a good
life; but in respect that it is a shepherd's life, it is naught. In
respect that it is solitary, I like it very well; but in respect that
it is private, it is a very vile life. . . .
As You Like It, Act iii, sc. 2, l. 11 [CORIN]

4119 This carol they began that hour, . . .
How that life was but a flower; . . .
And therefore take the present time, . . .
For love is crowned with the prime
In spring time.
As You Like It, Act v, sc. 3, l. 27 [PAGES]

4120 Prefer a noble life before a long.
Coriolanus, Act iii, sc. 1, l. 152 [CORIOLANUS]

4121 O, this life
Is nobler than attending for a check,
Richer than doing nothing for a bauble,
Prouder than rustling in unpaid-for silk:
Such gain the cap of him that makes 'em fine,
Yet keeps his books uncross'd: no life to ours.
Cymbeline, Act iii, sc. 3, l. 21 [BELARIUS]

4122 What pleasure, sir, find we in life, to lock it
From action and adventure?
Cymbeline, Act iv, sc. 4, l. 2 [ARVIRAGUS]

4123 I do not set my life at a pin's fee;
And for my soul, what can it do to that,
Being a thing immortal as itself?
Hamlet, Act i, sc. 4, l. 65 [HAMLET]

4124 A man's life's no more than to say 'One.'
Hamlet, Act v, sc. 2, l. 74 [HAMLET]

4125 The end of life cancels all bands.
I Henry IV, Act iii, sc. 2, l. 157 [PRINCE]

4126 For mine own part, I could be well content
To entertain the lag-end of my life
With quiet hours.
I Henry IV, Act v, sc. 1, l. 23 [WORCESTER]

4127 O gentlemen, the time of life is short!
To spend that shortness basely were too long,
If life did ride upon a dial's point,
Still ending at the arrival of an hour.
And if we live, we live to tread on kings;
If die, brave death, when princes die with us!
I Henry IV, Act v, sc. 2, l. 82 [HOTSPUR]

4128 'Where is the life that late I led?' they say:
Why, here it is; welcome these pleasant days!
II Henry IV, Act v, sc. 3, l. 149 [PISTOL]

4129 The art and practic part of life
Must be the mistress to this theoric.
Henry V, Act i, sc. 1, l. 51 [CANTERBURY]

4130 Of all my lands
Is nothing left me but my body's length.
Why, what is pomp, rule, reign, but earth and dust?
And, live we how we can, yet die we must.
III Henry VI, Act v, sc. 2, l. 25 [WARWICK]

4131   I cannot tell what you and other men
Think of this life; but, for my single self,
I had as lief not be as live to be
In awe of such a thing as I myself.
Julius Cæsar, Act i, sc. 2, l. 93 [CASSIUS]

4132   CASSIUS: Life, being weary of these worldly bars,
Never lacks power to dismiss itself.
If I know this, know all the world besides,
That part of tyranny that I do bear
I can shake off at pleasure.
CASCA: So can I:
So every bondman in his own hand bears
The power to cancel his captivity.
Julius Cæsar, Act i, sc. 3, l. 96 [CASSIUS]

4133   Life is as tedious as a twice-told tale
Vexing the dull ear of a drowsy man.
King John, Act iii, sc. 4, l. 108 [LEWIS]

4134   My life I never held but as a pawn
To wage against my enemies.
King Lear, Act i, sc. 1, l. 157 [KENT]

4135   O, our lives' sweetness!
That we the pain of death would hourly die
Rather than die at once!
King Lear, Act v, sc. 3, l. 184 [EDGAR]

4136   I have lived long enough: my way of life
Is fall'n into the sere, the yellow leaf;
And that which should accompany old age,
As honour, love, obedience, troops of friends,
I must not look to have; but in their stead,
Curses, not loud but deep, mouth-honour, breath,
Which the poor heart would fain deny, and dare not.
Macbeth, Act v, sc. 3, l. 23 [MACBETH]

4137   To-morrow, and to-morrow, and to-morrow,
Creeps in this petty pace from day to day
To the last syllable of recorded time,
And all our yesterdays have lighted fools
The way to dusty death. Out, out, brief candle!
Life's but a walking shadow, a poor player
That struts and frets his hour upon the stage
And then is heard no more: it is a tale
Told by an idiot, full of sound and fury,
Signifying nothing.
Macbeth, Act v, sc. 5, l. 19 [MACBETH]

4138   I am so out of love with life that I will sue to be rid of it.
Measure for Measure, Act iii, sc. 1, l. 173 [CLAUDIO]

4139   That life is better life, past fearing death,
Than that which lives to fear.
Measure for Measure, Act v, sc. 1, l. 402 [DUKE]

4140   Nay, take my life and all: pardon not that:
You take my house when you do take the prop
That doth sustain my house; you take my life
When you do take the means whereby I live.
The Merchant of Venice, Act iv, sc. 1, l. 374 [SHYLOCK]

4141   Because I know also life is a shuttle, I am in haste.
The Merry Wives of Windsor, Act v, sc. 1, l. 26 [FALSTAFF]

4142   I fetch my life and being
From men of royal siege, and my demerits

May speak unbonneted to as proud a fortune
As this that I have reach'd.
                              Othello, Act i, sc. 2, l. 21 [OTHELLO]

4143   KING RICHARD: Why, uncle, thou hast many years to live.
GAUNT: But not a minute, king, that thou canst give:
Shorten my days thou canst with sullen sorrow,
And pluck nights from me, but not lend a morrow;
Thou canst help time to furrow me with age,
But stop no wrinkle in his pilgrimage.
                    Richard II, Act i, sc. 3, l. 225 [KING RICHARD]

4144   Even through the hollow eyes of death I spy life peering.
                Richard II, Act ii, sc. 1, l. 270 [NORTHUMBERLAND]

4145   Where is the life that late I led?
        The Taming of the Shrew, Act iv, sc. 1, l. 143 [PETRUCHIO, *singing*]

4146   ADRIAN: This island . . . must needs be of a subtle, tender and
delicate temperance. . . .
GONZALO: Here is every thing advantageous to life.
ANTONIO: True; save means to live.
                        The Tempest, Act ii, sc. 1, l. 41 [ADRIAN]

4147   We are such stuff
As dreams are made on, and our little life
Is rounded with a sleep.
                    The Tempest, Act iv, sc. 1, l. 156 [PROSPERO]

4148   Life's uncertain voyage.
                    Timon of Athens, Act v, sc. 1, l. 205 [TIMON]

4149   SIR TOBY: Does not our life consist of the four elements?
SIR ANDREW: Faith, so they say; but I think it rather consists of
eating and drinking.
                    Twelfth Night, Act ii, sc. 3, l. 10 [SIR TOBY]

4150   Life, I prize it not a straw.
            The Winter's Tale, Act iii, sc. 2, l. 110 [HERMIONE]

4151   For the life to come, I sleep out the thought of it.
            The Winter's Tale, Act iv, sc. 3, l. 30 [AUTOLYCUS]

Light

4152   Light is an effect of fire, and fire will burn; ergo, light wenches
will burn.
        The Comedy of Errors, Act iv, sc. 3, l. 57 [DROMIO OF SYRACUSE]

4153   Light seeking light doth light of light beguile:
So, ere you find where light in darkness lies,
Your light grows dark by losing of your eyes.
Study me how to please the eye indeed
    By fixing it upon a fairer eye,
Who dazzling so, that eye shall be his heed
    And give him light that it was blinded by.
                Love's Labour's Lost, Act i, sc. 1, l. 77 [BIRON]

4154   Put out the light, and then put out the light;
If I quench thee, thou flaming minister,
I can again thy former light restore,
Should I repent me: but once put out thy light,
Thou cunning'st pattern of excelling nature,
I know not where is that Promethean heat
That can thy light relume.
                        Othello, Act v, sc. 2, l. 7 [OTHELLO]

Lightning

4155   Now he'll outstare the lightning.
            Antony and Cleopatra, Act iii, sc. 13, l. 195 [ENOBARBUS]

4156   I . . . Have bared my bosom to the thunder-stone;
       And when the cross blue lightning seem'd to open
       The breast of heaven, I did present myself
       Even in the aim and very flash of it.
                       Julius Cæsar, Act i, sc. 3, l. 49 [CASSIUS]
4157   Brief as the lightning in the collied night,
       That, in a spleen, unfolds both heaven and earth,
       And ere a man hath power to say 'Behold!'
       The jaws of darkness do devour it up:
       So quick bright things come to confusion.
             A Midsummer Night's Dream, Act i, sc. 1, l. 145 [LYSANDER]
4158   I have no joy of this contract to-night:
       It is too rash, too unadvised, too sudden;
       Too like the lightning, which doth cease to be
       Ere one can say 'It lightens.'
                     Romeo and Juliet, Act ii, sc. 2, l. 117 [JULIET]
4159   Jove's lightnings, the precursors
       O' the dreadful thunder-claps, more momentary
       And sight-outrunning were not.
                       The Tempest, Act i, sc. 2, l. 201 [ARIEL]

Likeness

4160   These hands are not more like.
                       Hamlet, Act i, sc. 2, l. 212 [HORATIO]
4161   'Tis alike as my fingers is to my fingers.
                       Henry V, Act iv, sc. 7, l. 32 [FLUELLEN]
4162   'Tis as like you as cherry is to cherry.
                     Henry VIII, Act v, sc. 1, l. 168 [OLD LADY]
4163   As like
       As rain to water, or devil to his dam.
                     King John, Act ii, sc. 1, l. 127 [CONSTANCE]
4164   She's as like this as a crab's like an apple.
                       King Lear, Act i, sc. 5, l. 15 [FOOL]
4165   An apple, cleft in two, is not more twin
       Than these two creatures.
                     Twelfth Night, Act v, sc. 1, l. 230 [ANTONIO]
4166   They say we are almost as like as eggs.
                   The Winter's Tale, Act i, sc. 2, l. 129 [LEONTES]
4167   TRANIO: He . . . somewhat doth resemble you.
       BIONDELLO: As much as an apple doth an oyster.
                 The Taming of the Shrew, Act iv, sc. 2, l. 100 [TRANIO]

Lily

4168   How bravely thou becomest thy bed, fresh lily,
       And whiter than the sheets.
                     Cymbeline, Act ii, sc. 2, l. 15 [IACHIMO]
4169   O sweetest, fairest lily!
       My brother wears thee not the one half so well
       As when thou grew'st thyself.
                   Cymbeline, Act iv, sc. 2, l. 201 [GUIDERIUS]

Line

4170   What, will the line stretch out to the crack of doom?
                     Macbeth, Act iv, sc. 1, l. 117 [MACBETH]

Lion

4171   The hind that would be mated by the lion
       Must die for love.
             All's Well that Ends Well, Act i, sc. 1, l. 102 [HELENA]

4172   'Tis better playing with a lion's whelp
      Than with an old one dying.
           Antony and Cleopatra, Act iii, sc. 13, l. 94 [ENOBARBUS]

4173   He is a lion That I am proud to hunt.
           Coriolanus, Act i, sc. 1, l. 239 [CORIOLANUS]

4174   The lion will not touch the true prince.
           I Henry IV, Act ii, sc. 4, l. 302 [FALSTAFF]

4175   The man that once did sell the lion's skin,
      While the beast lived, was killed with hunting him.
           Henry V, Act iv, sc. 3, l. 93 [KING HENRY]

4176   Small curs are not regarded when they grin;
      But great men tremble when the lion roars.
           II Henry VI, Act iii, sc. 1, l. 18 [QUEEN]

4177   Of Salisbury, who can report of him,
      That winter lion, who in rage forgets
      Aged contusions and all brush of time,
      And, like a gallant in the brow of youth,
      Repairs him with occasion?
           II Henry VI, Act v, sc. 3, l. 1 [YORK]

4178   To whom do lions cast their gentle looks?
      Not to the beast that would usurp their den.
      Whose hand is that the forest bear doth lick?
      Not his that spoils her young before her face.
      Who 'scapes the lucking serpent's mortal sting?
      Not he that sets his foot upon her back.
           III Henry VI, Act ii, sc. 2, l. 11 [CLIFFORD]

4179   When the lion fawns upon the lamb,
      The lamb will never cease to follow him.
           III Henry VI, Act iv, sc. 8, l. 49 [KING HENRY]

4180   He parted frowning from me, as if ruin
      Leap'd from his eyes: so looks the chafed lion
      Upon the daring huntsman that has gall'd him;
      Then makes him nothing.
           Henry VIII, Act iii, sc. 2, l. 205 [WOLSEY]

4181   Against the Capitol I met a lion,
      Who glared upon me, and went surly by,
      Without annoying me.
           Julius Cæsar, Act i, sc. 3, l. 20 [CASCA]

4182   He that perforce robs lions of their hearts
      May easily win a woman's.
           King John, Act i, sc. 1, l. 268 [BASTARD]

4183   Sirrah, were I at home,
      At your den, sirrah, with your lioness,
      I would set an ox-head to your lion's hide,
      And make a monster of you. . . .
      O, tremble, for you hear the lion roar.
           King John, Act ii, sc. 1, l. 290 [BASTARD]

4184   Thou wear a lion's hide! doff it for shame,
      And hang a calf's-skin on those recreant limbs.
           King John, Act iii, sc. 1, l. 128 [CONSTANCE]

4185   What, shall they seek the lion in his den,
      And fright him there? and make him tremble there?
      O, let it not be said.
           King John, Act v, sc. 1, l. 57 [BASTARD]

4186   Thus dost thou hear the Nemean lion roar
      'Gainst thee, thou lamb, that standest as his prey.

Submissive fall his princely feet before,
  And he from forage will incline to play:
But if thou strive, poor soul what art thou then?
Food for his rage, repasture for his den.
                    Love's Labour 's Lost, Act iv, sc. 1, l. 90 [BOYET]

4187   QUINCE: Snug, the joiner; you the lion's part. . . .
SNUG: Have you the lion's part written? Pray you, if it be, give it
me, for I am slow of study.
QUINCE: You may do it extempore, for it is nothing but roaring.
BOTTOM: Let me play the lion too: I will roar, that I will do any
man's heart good to hear me. . . .
QUINCE: An you should do it too terribly, you would fright the
duchess and the ladies. . . .
BOTTOM: I will roar you as gently as any sucking dove; I will
roar you as 'twere any nightingale.
                    A Midsummer Night's Dream, Act i, sc. 2, l. 66 [QUINCE]

4188   A lion among ladies is a most dreadful thing; for there is not a
more fearful wild-fowl than your lion living.
                    A Midsummer Night's Dream, Act iii, sc. 1, l. 32 [BOTTOM]

4189   LYSANDER: This lion is a very fox for his valour.
THESEUS: True; and a goose for his discretion.
DEMETRIUS: Not so, my lord; for his valour cannot carry his
discretion; and the fox carries the goose.
THESEUS: His discretion, I am sure, cannot carry his valour; for
the goose carries not the fox.
                    A Midsummer Night's Dream, Act v, sc. 1, l. 233 [LYSANDER]

4190   Well roared, Lion.
                    A Midsummer Night's Dream, Act v, sc. 1, l. 270 [DEMETRIUS]

4191   In war was never lion raged more fierce,
In peace was never gentle lamb more mild,
Than was that young and princely gentleman.
                    Richard II, Act ii, sc. 1, l. 173 [YORK]

4192   The lion dying thrusteth forth his paw,
And wounds the earth, if nothing else, with rage
To be o'erpower'd; and wilt thou, pupil-like,
Take thy correction mildly, kiss the rod,
And fawn on rage with base humility,
Which art a lion and a king of beasts?
                    Richard II, Act v, sc. 1, l. 29 [QUEEN]

4193   The lion moved with pity did endure
To have his princely paws pared all away.
                    Titus Andronicus, Act ii, sc. 3, l. 151 [LAVINIA]

Lip

4194   There was a pretty redness in his lip,
A little riper and more lusty red
Than that mix'd in his cheek; 'twas just the difference
Betwixt the constant red and mingled damask.
                    As You Like It, Act iii, sc. 5, l. 120 [PHEBE]

4195   You have witchcraft in your lips, Kate: there is more eloquence
in a sugar touch of them than in the tongues of the French council.
                    Henry V, Act v, sc. 2, l. 300 [KING HENRY]

4196   His coward lips did from their colour fly,
And that same eye whose bend doth awe the world
Did lose his lustre.
                    Julius Cæsar, Act i, sc. 2, l. 122 [CASSIUS]

4197   Here are sever'd lips,
Parted with sugar breath: so sweet a bar
Should sunder such sweet friends.
        The Merchant of Venice, Act iii, sc. 2, l. 119 [BASSANIO]

4198   Divers philosophers hold that the lips is parcel of the mouth.
        The Merry Wives of Windsor, Act i, sc. 1, l. 236 [EVANS]

4199   Thy lips, those kissing cherries, tempting grow!
        A Midsummer Night's Dream, Act iii, sc. 2, l. 140 [DEMETRIUS]

4200   Teach not thy lips such scorn, for they were made
For kissing, lady, not for such contempt.
        Richard III, Act i, sc. 2, l. 172 [GLOUCESTER]

4201   Their lips were four red roses on a stalk,
Which in their summer beauty kiss'd each other.
        Richard III, Act iv, sc. 3, l. 12 [TYRREL]

4202   They may
Steal immortal blessing from her lips
Who, even in pure and vestal modesty,
Still blush, as thinking their own kisses sin.
        Romeo and Juliet, Act iii, sc. 3, l. 35 [ROMEO]

4203   I'll take that winter from your lips, fair lady.
        Troilus and Cressida, Act iii, sc. 5, l. 23 [ACHILLES]

4204   Diana's lip is not more smooth and rubious.
        Twelfth Night, Act i, sc. 4, l. 31 [DUKE]

4205   Graze on my lips; and if those hills be dry,
Stray lower, where the pleasant fountains lie.
        Venus and Adonis, l. 233 [VENUS]

Liver

4206   This way will I take upon me to wash your liver as clean as a
sound sheep's heart, that there shall not be one spot of love in 't.
        As You Like It, Act iii, sc. 2, l. 443 [ROSALIND]

4207   The liver white and pale, which is the badge of pusillanimity and
cowardice.
        II Henry IV, Act iv, sc. 3, l. 113 [FALSTAFF]

4208   He is white-livered and red faced; by the means where of a' faces
it out, but fights not.
        Henry V, Act iii, sc. 2, l. 34 [BOY]

4209   Milk-liver'd man!
That bear'st a cheek for blows, a head for wrongs.
        King Lear, Act iv, sc. 2, l. 50 [GONERIL]

4210   How many cowards, whose hearts are all as false
As stairs of sand, wear yet upon their chins
The beards of Hercules and frowning Mars,
Who, inward searched, have livers white as milk.
        The Merchant of Venice, Act iii, sc. 2, l. 83 [BASSANIO]

4211   STANLEY: Richmond is on the seas.
KING RICHARD: There let him sink, and be the seas on him!
White-liver'd runagate, what does he there?
        Richard III, Act iv, sc. 4, l. 463 [STANLEY]

4212   If he were opened, and you find so much blood in his liver as will
clog the foot of a flea, I'll eat the rest of the anatomy.
        Twelfth Night, Act iii, sc. 2, l. 65 [SIR TOBY]

4213   Were my wife's liver
Infected as her life, she would not live
The running of one glass.
        The Winter's Tale, Act i, sc. 2, l. 304 [LEONTES]

Livery

4214 The silver livery of advised age.
> *II Henry VI,* Act v, sc. 2, l. 47 [YOUNG CLIFFORD]

A maid-child call'd Marina; who, O goddess,
Wears yet thy silver livery.
> *Pericles,* Act v, sc. 3, l. 6 [PERICLES]

4215 O, 'tis the cunning livery of hell,
The damned'st body to invest and cover
In priestly guards!
> *Measure for Measure,* Act iii, sc. 1, l. 95 [ISABELLA]

4216 One twelve moons more she'll wear Diana's livery:
This by the eye of Cynthia hath she vow'd,
And on her virgin honour will not break it.
> *Pericles,* Act ii, sc. 5, l. 10 [SIMONIDES]

4217 Since . . . My wedded lord I ne'er shall see again,
A vestal livery will I take me to,
And never more have joy.
> *Pericles,* Act iii, sc. 4, l. 9 [THAISA]

4218 Her vestal livery is but sick and green
And none but fools do wear it; cast it off.
> *Romeo and Juliet,* Act ii, sc. 2, l. 8 [ROMEO]

London

4219   The famed Cassibelan . . .
Made Lud's town with rejoicing fires bright
And Britons strut with courage.
> *Cymbeline,* Act iii, sc. 1, l. 30 [CLOTEN]

4220 When I have slain thee with my proper hand,
I'll follow those that even now fled hence,
And on the gates of Lud's-town set your heads.
> *Cymbeline,* Act iv, sc. 2, l. 97 [CLOTEN]

4221 I hope to see London once ere I die.
> *II Henry IV,* Act v, sc. 3, l. 61 [DAVY]

4222   But now behold,
In the quick forge and working-house of thought,
How London doth pour out her citizens!
> *Henry V,* Act v, Prologue, l. 22 [CHORUS]

4223 Why, Via! to London will we march amain,
And once again bestride our foaming steeds,
And once again cry 'Charge upon our foes!'
But never once again turn back and fly.
> *III Henry VI,* Act ii, sc. 1, l. 182 [WARWICK]

Lord

4224 Scurvy, old, filthy, scurvy lord! . . . I'll beat him, by my life, if
. . . he were double and double a lord.
> *All's Well that Ends Well,* Act ii, sc. 3, l. 250 [PAROLLES]

You scurvy lord!
> *Troilus and Cressida,* Act ii, sc. 1, l. 56 [THERSITES]

4225 I remember, when the fight was done,
When I was dry with rage and extreme toil,
Breathless and faint, leaning upon my sword,
Came there a certain lord, neat, and trimly dress'd,
Fresh as a bridegroom; and his chin new reap'd
Show'd like a stubble-land at harvest-home;
He was perfumed like a milliner;
And 'twixt his finger and his thumb he held

A pouncet-box, which ever and anon
He gave his nose and took 't away again;
Who therewith angry, when it next came there,
Took it in snuff; and still he smil'd and talk'd,
And as the soldiers bore dead bodies by,
He call'd them untaught knaves, unmannerly,
To bring a slovenly unhandsome corse
Betwixt the wind and his nobility,
With many holiday and lady terms
He question'd me. . . . He made me mad
To see him shine so brisk and smell so sweet
And talk so like a waiting-gentlewoman
Of guns and drums and wounds,—God save the mark!—
And telling me the sovereign'st thing on earth
Was parmaceti for an inward bruise;
And that it was great pity, so it was,
This villanous salt-petre should be digg'd
Out of the bowels of the harmless earth,
Which many a good tall fellow had destroy'd
So cowardly; and but for these vile guns,
He would himself have been a soldier.
I Henry IV, Act i, sc. 3, l. 30 [HOTSPUR]

4226   Here's the lord of the soil come to seize me for a stray, for entering his fee-simple without leave.
II Henry VI, Act iv, sc. 10, l. 26 [CADE]

4227   Lord of thy presence and no land beside.
King John, Act i, sc. 1, l. 137 [ELINOR]
Lord of our presence, Angiers, and of you.
King John, Act ii, sc. 1, l. 367 [KING JOHN]

4228   APEMANTUS: Heavens, that I were a lord!
TIMON: What wouldst do then, Apemantus?
APEMANTUS: E'en as Apemantus does now; hate a lord with my
heart.
Timon of Athens, Act i, sc. 1, l. 233 [APEMANTUS]

4229   Blunt-witted lord, ignoble in demeanour!
II Henry VI, Act iii, sc. 2, l. 210 [SUFFOLK]

4230   Thou mongrel beef-witted lord! . . . Thou sodden-witted lord!
Troilus and Cressida, Act ii, sc. 1, l. 14 [THERSITES]

4231   No man is the lord of any thing . . .
Till he communicate his parts to others;
Nor doth he of himself know them for aught
Till he behold them form'd in the applause
Where they 're extended.
Troilus and Cressida, Act iii, sc. 3, l. 115 [ULYSSES]

Loss

4232   FIRST LORD: How mightily sometimes we make us comforts of
our losses!
SECOND LORD: And how mightily some other times we drown our
gain in tears!
All's Well that Ends Well, Act iv, sc. 3, l. 76 [FIRST LORD]

4233   Your loss is great, so your regard should be;
My worth unknown, no loss is known in me.
Upon my death the French can little boast;
In yours they will, in you all hopes are lost.
I Henry VI, Act iv, sc. 5, l. 22 [JOHN TALBOT]

4234   QUEEN: I can give the loser leave to chide.
        GLOUCESTER: Far truer spoke than meant: I lose, indeed;
        Beshrew the winners, for they play'd me false!
        And well such losers may have leave to speak.
                              II Henry VI, Act iii, sc. 1, l. 182 [QUEEN]
                    Losers will have leave
        To ease their stomachs with their bitter tongues.
                              Titus Andronicus, Act iii, sc. 1, l. 233 [TITUS]

4235   His losses,
        That have of late so huddled on his back,
        Enow to press a royal merchant down
        And pluck commiseration of his state
        From brassy bosoms and rough hearts of flint.
                              The Merchant of Venice, Act iv, sc. 1, l. 27 [DUKE]

4236   A fellow that hath had losses, and one that hath two gowns and
        everything handsome about him.
                              Much Ado about Nothing, Act iv, sc. 2, l. 90 [DOGBERRY]

4237   They that lose half with greater patience bear it
        Than they whose whole is swallowed in confusion.
                              The Rape of Lucrece, l. 1158 [LUCRECE]

4238   QUEEN ELIZABETH: Was never widow had so dear a loss!
        CHILDREN: Were never orphans had so dear a loss!
        DUCHESS OF YORK: Was never mother had so dear a loss!
                              Richard III, Act ii, sc. 2, l. 77 [QUEEN ELIZABETH]

Love

4239   Now, Dian, from thy altar do I fly,
        And to imperial Love, that god most high,
        Do my sighs stream.
                              All's Well that Ends Well, Act ii, sc. 3, l. 80 [HELENA]

4240   Love make your fortunes twenty times above
        Her that so wishes and her humble love!
                              All's Well that Ends Well, Act ii, sc. 3, l. 88 [HELENA]

4241   Love that comes too late,
        Like a remorseful pardon slowly carried,
        To the great sender turns a sour offence,
        Crying, 'That's good that's gone.'
                              All's Well that Ends Well, Act v, sc. 3, l. 57 [KING]

4242   CLEOPATRA: If it be love indeed, tell me how much.
        ANTONY: There's beggary in the love that can be reckon'd.
        CLEOPATRA: I'll set a bourn how far to be beloved.
        ANTONY: Then must thou needs find out new heaven, new earth.
                              Antony and Cleopatra, Act i, sc. 1, l. 14 [CLEOPATRA]

4243   You shall be more beloving than beloved.
                              Antony and Cleopatra, Act i, sc. 2, l. 22 [SOOTHSAYER]

4244   O most false love!
        Where be the sacred vials thou shouldst fill
        With sorrowful water?
                              Antony and Cleopatra, Act i, sc. 3, l. 61 [CLEOPATRA]

4245   You . . . have prevented
        The ostentation of our love, which, left unshown,
        Is often left unloved.
                              Antony and Cleopatra, Act iii, sc. 6, l. 51 [OCTAVIUS CÆSAR]

4246   Love no man in good earnest; nor no further in sport neither than
        with safety of a pure blush thou mayst in honour come off again.
                              As You Like It, Act i, sc. 2, l. 30 [CELIA]

4247 If thou remember'st not the slightest folly
That ever love did make thee run into,
Thou hast not loved.
As You Like It, Act ii, sc. 4, l. 34 [SILVIUS]

4248 When I was in love I broke my sword upon a stone and bid him
take that for coming a-night to Jane Smile; and I remember the
kissing of her batlet and the cow's dugs that her pretty chopt
hands had milked. . . . We that are true lovers run into strange
capers; but as all is mortal in nature, so is all nature in love
mortal in folly.
As You Like It, Act ii, sc. 4, l. 46 [TOUCHSTONE]

4249 ROSALIND: There is a man haunts the forest, that abuses our young
plants with carving 'Rosalind' on their barks; . . . if I could
meet that fancy-monger, I would give him some good counsel,
for he seems to have the quotidian of love upon him.
ORLANDO: I am he that is so love-shaked: I pray you, tell me
your remedy.
ROSALIND: There is none of my uncle's marks upon you: he
taught me how to know a man in love; in which cage of rushes
I am sure you are not prisoner.
ORLANDO: What were his marks?
ROSALIND: A lean cheek, which you have not, a blue eye and
sunken, which you have not, . . . a beard neglected, which you
have not: . . . then your hose should be ungartered, your bonnet
unbanded, your sleeve unbuttoned, your shoe untied and everything
about you demonstrating a careless desolation; but you are no such
man; you are rather point-device in your accoutrements as loving
yourself than seeming the lover of any other. . . . In good sooth,
are you he that hangs the verses on the trees, wherein Rosalind is
so admired?
ORLANDO: I swear to thee, youth, by the white hand of Rosalind,
I am that he, that unfortunate he.
ROSALIND: But are you so much in love as your rhymes speak?
ORLANDO: Neither rhyme nor reason can express how much.
As You Like It, Act iii, sc. 2, l. 377 [ROSALIND]

4250 Love is merely a madness, and, I tell you, deserves as well a dark
house and a whip as madmen do: and the reason why they are not
so punished and cured is, that the lunacy is so ordinary that the
whippers are in love too.
As You Like It, Act iii, sc. 2, l. 420 [ROSALIND]

4251 Mistress, know thyself: down on your knees,
And thank heaven, fasting, for a good man's love. . . .
Cry the man mercy; love him; take his offer:
Foul is most foul, being foul to be a scoffer.
As You Like It, Act iii, sc. 5, l. 57 [ROSALIND]

4252 So holy and so perfect is my love,
And I in such a poverty of grace,
That I shall think it a most plenteous crop
To glean the broken ears after the man
That the main harvest reaps: loose now and then
A scatter'd smile, and that I'll live upon.
As You Like It, Act iii, sc. 5, l. 99 [SILVIUS]

4253 The poor world is almost six thousand years old, and in all this
time there was not any man died in his own person, videlicet, in a
love cause. . . . Men have died from time to time and worms have
eaten them, but not for love.
As You Like It, Act iv, sc. 1, l. 95 [ROSALIND]

4254   PHEBE: Good shepherd, tell this youth what 'tis to love.
       SILVIUS: It is to be all made of sighs and tears; . . .
       It is to be all made of faith and service. . . .
       It is to be all made of fantasy,
       All made of passion and all made of wishes,
       All adoration, duty, and observance,
       All humbleness, all patience and impatience,
       All purity, all trial, all deservings.
                         As You Like It, Act v, sc. 2, l. 89 [PHEBE]
4255   I shall be loved when I am lack'd.
                         Coriolanus, Act iv, sc. 1, l. 15 [CORIOLANUS]
4256   Whom best I love I cross; to make my gift
       The more delay'd, delighted.
                         Cymbeline, Act v, sc. 4, l. 101 [JUPITER]
4257   This is the very ecstasy of love,
       Whose violent property fordoes itself
       And leads the will to desperate undertakings
       As oft as any passion under heaven
       That does afflict our natures.
                         Hamlet, Act ii, sc. 1, l. 102 [POLONIUS]
4258   Doubt that the stars are fire;
             Doubt that the sun doth move;
           Doubt truth to be a liar;
             But never doubt I love.
                         Hamlet, Act ii, sc. 2, l. 116 [POLONIUS, *reading*]
4259   Where love is great, the littlest doubts are fear;
       Where little fears grow great, great love grows there.
                         Hamlet, Act iii, sc. 2, l. 181 [PLAYER QUEEN]
4260   This world is not for aye, nor 'tis not strange
       That even our loves should with our fortunes change;
       For 'tis a question left us yet to prove,
       Whether love lead fortune, or else fortune love.
                         Hamlet, Act iii, sc. 2, l. 210 [PLAYER KING]
4261   ROSENCRANTZ: My lord, you once did love me.
       HAMLET: So I do still, by these pickers and stealers.
                         Hamlet, Act iii, sc. 2, l. 347 [ROSENCRANTZ]
4262   How should I your true love know
             From another one?
           By his cockle hat and staff,
             And his sandal shoon.
           He is dead and gone, lady,
             He is dead and gone;
           At his head a grass-green turf,
             At his heels a stone.
                         Hamlet, Act iv, sc. 5, l. 23 [OPHELIA, *singing*]
4263   Love is begun by time; . . .
       Time qualifies the spark and fire of it;
       There lives within the very flame of love
       A kind of wick or snuff that will abate it.
                         Hamlet, Act iv, sc. 7, l. 112 [KING]
4264   I loved Ophelia: forty thousand brothers
       Could not, with all their quantity of love,
       Make up my sum.
                         Hamlet, Act v, sc. 1, l. 292 [HAMLET]
4265   HOTSPUR: Away, you trifler! Love! I love thee not,
       I care not for thee, Kate: this is no world
       To play with mammets and to tilt with lips:

We must have bloody noses and crack'd crowns,
And pass them current too. . . .
LADY PERCY : Do you not love me? do you not, indeed?
Well, do not then ; for since you love me not,
I will not love myself.
I Henry IV, Act ii, sc. 3, l. 93 [HOTSPUR]

4266 Why, love forswore me in my mother's womb :
And, for I should not deal in her soft laws,
She did corrupt frail nature with some bribe,
To shrink mine arm up like a wither'd shrub ;
To make an envious mountain on my back,
Where sits deformity to mock my body ;
To shape my legs of an unequal size ;
To disproportion me in every part,
Like to a chaos, or an unlick'd bear-whelp
That carries no impression like the dam.
III Henry VI, Act iii, sc. 2, l. 153 [KING RICHARD]

4267 Myself have often heard him say and swear
That this his love was an eternal plant,
Whereof the root was fix'd in virtue's ground,
The leaves and fruit maintain'd with beauty's sun.
III Henry VI, Act iii, sc. 3, l. 123 [WARWICK]

4268 This word 'love,' which greybeards call divine,
Be resident in men like one another
And not in me.
III Henry VI, Act v, sc. 6, l. 81 [GLOUCESTER]

4269 When love begins to sicken and decay,
It useth an enforced ceremony.
Julius Cæsar, Act iv, sc. 2, l. 20 [BRUTUS]

4270 If lusty love should go in quest of beauty,
Where should he find it fairer than in Blanch?
If zealous love should go in search of virtue,
Where should he find it purer than in Blanch?
If love ambitious sought a match of birth,
Whose veins bound richer blood than Lady Blanch?
King John, Act ii, sc. 1, l. 426 [CITIZEN]

4271 I love you more than words can wield the matter ;
Dearer than eye-sight, space, and liberty ;
Beyond what can be valued, rich or rare ;
No less than life, with grace, health, beauty, honour,
As much as child e'er loved, or father found ;
A love that makes breath poor, and speech unable ;
Beyond all manner of so much I love you.
King Lear, Act i, sc. 1, l. 56 [GONERIL]

4272 I am sure my love 's More richer than my tongue.
King Lear, Act i, sc. 1, l. 79 [CORDELIA]

4273 My love is most immaculate white and red.
Love's Labour's Lost, Act i, sc. 2, l. 97 [ARMADO]

4274 I do love that country girl that I took in the park with the
rational hind Costard.
Love's Labour's Lost, Act i, sc. 2, l. 122 [ARMADO]

4275 Love is a familiar ; Love is a devil : there is no evil angel but Love.
Yet was Samson so tempted, and he had an excellent strength ; yet
was Solomon so seduced, and he had a very good wit. . . . Adieu,
valour ! rust rapier ! be still, drum ! for your manager is in love.
Love's Labour's Lost, Act i, sc. 2, l. 178 [ARMADO]

4276   Well, I will love, write, sigh, pray, sue and groan:
Some men must love my lady and some Joan.
Love's Labour's Lost, Act iii, sc. 1, l. 206 [BIRON]

4277   By heaven, I do love: and it hath taught me to rhyme and to be
melancholy.
Love's Labour's Lost, Act iv, sc. 3, l. 14 [BIRON]

4278   On a day—alack the day!—
Love, whose month is ever May,
Spied a blossom passing fair
Playing in the wanton air.
Love's Labour's Lost, Act iv, sc. 3, l. 101 [DUMAIN]

4279   BIRON: When shall you hear that I
Will praise a hand, a foot, a face, an eye,
A gait, a state, a brow, a breast, a waist,
A leg, a limb?
KING: Soft! whither away so fast?
A true man or a thief that gallops so?
BIRON: I post from love: good lover, let me go.
Love's Labour's Lost, Act iv, sc. 3, l. 183 [BIRON]

4280   Love, first learned in a lady's eyes,
Lives not alone immured in the brain; . . .
It adds a precious seeing to the eye.
Love's Labour's Lost, Act iv, sc. 3, l. 327 [BIRON]

4281   Love's feeling is more soft and sensible
Than are the tender horns of cockled snails;
Love's tongue proves dainty Bacchus gross in taste:
For valour, is not Love a Hercules,
Still climbing trees in the Hesperides?
Subtle as Sphinx; as sweet and musical
As bright Apollo's lute, strung with his hair;
And when Love speaks, the voice of all the gods
Make heaven drowsy with the harmony.
Never durst poet touch a pen to write
Until his ink were temper'd with Love's sighs;
O, then his lines would ravish savage ears
And plant in tyrants mild humility.
Love's Labour's Lost, Act iv, sc. 3, l. 337 [BIRON]

4282   Love doth approach disguised,
Armed in arguments; you'll be surprised:
Muster your wits; stand in your own defence;
Or hide your heads like cowards, and fly hence.
Love's Labour's Lost, Act v, sc. 2, l. 83 [BOYET]

4283   Love is full of unbefitting strains,
All wanton as a child, skipping and vain,
Form'd by the eye and therefore, like the eye,
Full of strange shapes, of habits and of forms,
Varying in subjects as the eye doth roll
To every varied object in his glance.
Love's Labour's Lost, Act v, sc. 2, l. 770 [BIRON]

4284   O most potential love! vow, bond, nor space,
In thee hath neither sting, knot, nor confine,
For thou art all, and all things else are thine.
When thou impressest, what are precepts worth
Of stale example? When thou wilt inflame,
How coldly those impediments stand forth
Of wealth, of filial fear, law, kindred, fame!
Love's arms are peace, 'gainst rule, 'gainst sense, 'gainst shame,

And sweetens, in the suffering pangs it bears,
The aloes of all forces, shocks, and fears.
A Lover's Complaint, l. 264

4285   Love talks with better knowledge, and knowledge with dearer love.
Measure for Measure, Act iii, sc. 2, l. 159 [DUKE]

4286   GRATIANO: Now, by my hood, a Gentile and no Jew.
LORENZO: Beshrew me but I love her heartily;
For she is wise, if I can judge of her,
And fair she is, if that mine eyes be true,
And true she is as she hath proved herself,
And therefore, like herself, wise, fair and true,
Shall she be placed in my constant soul.
The Merchant of Venice, Act ii, sc. 6, l. 51 [GRATIANO]

4287   How all the other passions fleet to air,
As doubtful thoughts, and rash-embraced despair,
And shuddering fear, and green-eyed jealousy!
O love, Be moderate; allay thy exstasy;
In measure rein thy joy; scant this excess.
I feel too much thy blessing: make it less,
For fear I surfeit.
The Merchant of Venice, Act iii, sc. 2, l. 109 [PORTIA]
Love moderately; long love doth so.
Romeo and Juliet, Act ii, sc. 6, l. 14 [FRIAR LAURENCE]

4288   SHALLOW: Can you love the maid?
SLENDER: I will marry her, sir, at your request: but if there be
no great love in the beginning, yet heaven may decrease it upon
better acquaintance, when we are married and have more occasion to know one another.
The Merry Wives of Windsor, Act i, sc. 1, l. 252 [SHALLOW]

4289   I do mean to make love to Ford's wife: I spy entertainment in
her; she discourses, she carves, she gives the leer of invitation.
. . . I have writ me here a letter to her: and here another to
Page's wife, who even now gave me good eyes too, examined my
parts with most judicious œillades. . . . O, she did so course over
my exteriors with such a greedy intention, that the appetite of her
eye did seem to scorch me up like a burning glass. . . . She bears
the purse, too; she is a region in Guiana, all gold and bounty. . . .
They shall be my East and West Indies, and I will trade to
them both.
The Merry Wives of Windsor, Act i, sc. 3, l. 48 [FALSTAFF]

4290   Love like a shadow flies when substance love pursues;
Pursuing that that flies, and flying what pursues.
The Merry Wives of Windsor, Act ii, sc. 2, l. 215 [FORD]

4291   [My love was] like a fair house built on another man's ground;
so that I have lost my edifice by mistaking the place where I
erected it.
The Merry Wives of Windsor, Act ii, sc. 2, l. 224 [FORD]

4292   Remember, Jove, thou wast a bull for thy Europa; love set on
thy horns. O powerful love! that in some respects makes a beast
a man, in some other, a man a beast. You were also, Jupiter, a
swan for the love of Leda. O omnipotent love! how near the
god drew to the complexion of a goose!
The Merry Wives of Windsor, Act v, sc. 5, l. 3 [FALSTAFF]

4293   In love the heavens themselves do guide the state;
Money buys lands, and wives are sold by fate.
The Merry Wives of Windsor, Act v, sc. 5, l. 245 [FORD]

4294   Ay me! for aught that I could ever read,
        Could ever hear by tale or history,
        The course of true love never did run smooth.
            A Midsummer Night's Dream, Act i, sc. 1, l. 132 [LYSANDER]
4295   O hell! to choose love by another's eyes.
            A Midsummer Night's Dream, Act i, sc. 1, l. 140 [HERMIA]
4296   I had rather hear my dog bark at a crow than a man swear he
        loves me.
            Much Ado about Nothing, Act i, sc. 1, l. 132 [BEATRICE]
4297   Speak low, if you speak love.
            Much Ado about Nothing, Act ii, sc. 1, l. 103 [DON PEDRO]
4298   Time goes on crutches till love have all his rites.
            Much Ado about Nothing, Act ii, sc. 1, l. 372 [CLAUDIO]
4299   I do much wonder that one man, seeing how much another man
        is a fool when he dedicates his behaviours to love, will, after he
        hath laughed at such shallow follies in others, become the argu-
        ment of his own scorn by falling in love.
            Much Ado about Nothing, Act ii, sc. 3, l. 7 [BENEDICK]
4300   I will not be sworn but love may transform me to an oyster; but
        I'll take my oath on it, till he have made an oyster of me, he shall
        never make me such a fool.
            Much Ado about Nothing, Act ii, sc. 3, l. 24 [BENEDICK]
4301   Ah, Benedick, love on; I will requite thee,
        Taming my wild heart to thy loving hand:
        If thou dost love, my kindness shall incite thee
        To bind our loves up in a holy band.
            Much Ado about Nothing, Act iii, sc. 1, l. 111 [BEATRICE]
4302   If he be not in love with some woman, there is no believing old
        signs: a' brushes his hat o' mornings; what should that bode?
            Much Ado about Nothing, Act iii, sc. 2, l. 41 [CLAUDIO]
4303   In loving, Leander the good swimmer, Troilus the first employer
        of pandars, and a whole bookful of these quondam carpet-mongers,
        . . . they were never so truly turned over and over as my poor
        self in love.
            Much Ado about Nothing, Act v, sc. 2, l. 30 [BENEDICK]
4304   BEATRICE: For which of my good parts did you first suffer love
        for me?
        BENEDICK: Suffer love! a good epithet! I do suffer love indeed,
        for I love thee against my will.
            Much Ado about Nothing, Act v, sc. 2, l. 65 [BEATRICE]
4305   So justly to your grave ears I'll present
        How I did thrive in this fair lady's love. . . .
        Her father loved me; oft invited me;
        Still question'd me the story of my life, . . .
        Wherein I spake of most disastrous chances,
        Of moving accidents by flood and field,
        Of hair-breadth scapes i' the imminent deadly breach,
        Of being taken by the insolent foe
        And sold to slavery, of my redemption thence
        And portance in my travels' history:
        Wherein of antres vast and deserts idle,
        Rough quarries, rocks, and hills whose heads touch heaven,
        It was my hint to speak,—such was the process;
        And of the Cannibals that each other eat,
        The Anthropophagi and men whose heads
        Do grow beneath their shoulders. This to hear
        Would Desdemona seriously incline: . . .

She gave me for my pains a world of sighs:
She swore, in faith, 'twas strange, 'twas passing strange,
'Twas pitiful, 'twas wondrous pitiful: . . .
She loved me for the dangers I had pass'd,
And I loved her that she did pity them.
This only is the witchcraft I have used.

Othello, Act i, sc. 3, l. 124 [OTHELLO]

4306 That I did love the Moor to live with him,
My downright violence and storm of fortunes
May trumpet to the world: my heart's subdued
Even to the very quality of my lord:
I saw Othello's visage in his mind,
And to his honours and his valiant parts
Did I my soul and fortunes consecrate.

Othello, Act i, sc. 3, l. 249 [DESDEMONA]

4307 They say, base men being in love have then a nobility in their
natures more than is native to them.

Othello, Act ii, sc. 1, l. 217 [IAGO]

4308 Excellent wretch! Perdition catch my soul,
But I do love thee! and when I love thee not,
Chaos is come again.

Othello, Act iii, sc. 3, l. 90 [OTHELLO]

4309 O, love's best habit is a soothing tongue.

The Passionate Pilgrim, Pt. i, l. 11

4310 She burn'd with love, as straw with fire flameth;
She burn'd out love, as soon as straw out-burneth.

The Passionate Pilgrim, Pt. vii, l. 13

4311 Fair is my love, but not so fair as fickle;
Mild as a dove, but neither true nor trusty;
Brighter than glass, and yet, as glass is, brittle;
Softer than wax, and yet, as iron, rusty.

The Passionate Pilgrim, Pt. vii, l. 1

4312 Love thrives not in the heart that shadows dreadeth.

The Rape of Lucrece, l. 270 [TARQUIN]

4313 Against love's fire fear's frost hath dissolution.

The Rape of Lucrece, l. 355 [TARQUIN]

4314   There is no creature loves me;
And if I die, no soul shall pity me.

Richard III, Act v, sc. 3, l. 200 [KING RICHARD]

4315 Love is a smoke raised with the fume of sighs;
Being purged, a fire sparkling in lovers' eyes;
Being vex'd, a sea nourish'd with lovers' tears:
What is it else? a madness most discreet,
A choking gall, and a preserving sweet.

Romeo and Juliet, Act i, sc. 1, l. 196 [ROMEO]

4316 BENVOLIO: Alas, that love, so gentle in his view,
Should be so tyrannous and rough in proof!
ROMEO: Alas, that love, whose view is muffled still,
Should, without eyes, see pathways to his will!

Romeo and Juliet, Act i, sc. 1, l. 175 [BENVOLIO]

4317 ROMEO: Is love a tender thing? it is too rough,
Too rude, too boisterous, and it pricks like thorn.
MERCUTIO: If love be rough with you, be rough with love;
Prick love for pricking, and you beat love down.

Romeo and Juliet, Act i, sc. 4, l. 25 [ROMEO]

4318   With love's light wings did I o'erperch these walls;
For stony limits cannot hold love out,
And what love can do that dares love attempt.
Romeo and Juliet, Act ii, sc. 2, l. 66 [ROMEO]

4319   JULIET: I would not for the world they saw thee here.
ROMEO: I have night's cloak to hide me from their sight;
An thou but love me, let them find me here:
My life were better ended by their hate,
Than death prorogued, wanting of thy love.
JULIET: By whose direction found'st thou out this place?
ROMEO: By love, who first did prompt me to inquire;
He lent me counsel, and I lent him eyes.
Romeo and Juliet, Act ii, sc. 2, l. 74 [JULIET]

4320   If that thy bent of love be honourable,
Thy purpose marriage, send me word to-morrow,
By one that I'll procure to come to thee,
Where and what time thou wilt perform the rite;
And all my fortunes at thy foot I'll lay,
And follow thee, my lord, throughout the world.
Romeo and Juliet, Act ii, sc. 2, l. 143 [JULIET]

4321   Love goes toward love, as schoolboys from their books,
But love from love, toward school with heavy looks.
Romeo and Juliet, Act ii, sc. 2, l. 156 [ROMEO]

4322   Young men's love then lies
Not truly in their hearts, but in their eyes.
Romeo and Juliet, Act ii, sc. 3, l. 67 [FRIAR LAURENCE]

4323   Love's heralds should be thoughts,
Which ten times faster glide than the sun's beams,
Driving back shadows over louring hills:
Therefore do nimble-pinion'd doves draw love,
And therefore hath the wind-swift Cupid wings.
Romeo and Juliet, Act ii, sc. 5, l. 4 [JULIET]

4324   My true love is grown to such excess
I cannot sum up sum of half my wealth.
Romeo and Juliet, Act ii, sc. 6, l. 33 [JULIET]

4325   O, I have bought the mansion of a love,
But not possess'd it, and, though I am sold,
Not yet enjoy'd.
Romeo and Juliet, Act iii, sc. 2, l. 26 [JULIET]

4326   Ah me! how sweet is love itself possess'd,.
When but love's shadows are so rich in joy!
Romeo and Juliet, Act v, sc. 1, l. 10 [ROMEO]

4327   As an unperfect actor on the stage
Who with his fear is put besides his part,
Or some fierce thing replete with too much rage,
Whose strength's abundance weakens his own heart,
So I, for fear of trust, forget to say
The perfect ceremony of love's rite,
And in mine own love's strength seem to decay,
O'er charged with burden of mine own love's might,
O, let my books be then the eloquence
And dumb presagers of my speaking breast,
Who plead for love and look for recompense
More than that tongue that more hath more express'd,
O, learn to read what silent love hath writ:
To hear with eyes belongs to love's fine wit.
Sonnet xxiii, l. 1

4328 When in disgrace with fortune and men's eyes,
I all alone beweep my outcast state
And trouble deaf heaven with my bootless cries,
And look upon myself and curse my fate, . . .
Haply I think on thee, and then my state,
Like to the lark at break of day arising
From sullen earth, sings hymns at heaven's gate;
For thy sweet love remember'd such wealth brings
That then I scorn to change my state with kings.

Sonnet **xxix**, l. 1

4329 Some glory in their birth, some in their skill,
Some in their wealth, some in their bodies' force,
Some in their garments, though new-fangled ill,
Some in their hawks and hounds, some in their horse . . .
Thy love is better than high birth to me,
Richer than wealth, prouder than garments' cost,
Of more delight than hawks or horses be;
And having thee, of all men's pride I boast:
Wretched in this alone, that thou mayst take
All this away and me most wretched make.

Sonnet **xci**, l. 1

4330 That love is merchandized whose rich esteeming
The owner's tongue doth publish every where.

Sonnet **cii**, l. 3

JULIA: They do not love that do not show their love.
LUCETTA: O, they love least that let men know their love.
The Two Gentlemen of Verona, Act i, sc. 2, l. 31 [JULIA]

4331 Let not my love be call'd idolatry,
Nor my beloved as an idol show,
Since all alike my songs and praises be,
To one, of one, still such, and ever so.
Kind is my love to-day, to-morrow kind,
Still constant in a wondrous excellence.

Sonnet **cv**, l. 1

4332   Eternal love in love's fresh case
Weighs not the dust and injury of age.

Sonnet **cviii**, l. 9

4333 Let me not to the marriage of true minds
Admit impediments. Love is not love
Which alters when it alteration finds,
Or bends with the remover to remove:
O, no! it is an ever-fixed mark
That looks on tempests and is never shaken;
It is the star to every wandering bark,
Whose worth's unknown, although his height be taken.
Love's not time's fool, though rosy lips and cheeks
Within his bending sickle's compass come;
Love alters not with his brief hours and weeks,
But bears it out even to the edge of doom.
If this be error and upon me proved,
I never writ, nor no man ever loved.

Sonnet **cxvi**, l. 1

4334 And ruin'd love, when it is built anew,
Grows fairer than at first, more strong, far greater.

Sonnet **cxix**, l. 11

4335 When my love swears that she is made of truth,
I do believe her, though I know she lies,

That she might think me some untutor'd youth,
Unlearned in the world's false subtleties.
Thus vainly thinking that she thinks me young,
Although she knows my days are past the best,
Simply I credit her false-speaking tongue:
On both sides thus is simple truth suppress'd. . . .
Therefore I lie with her and she with me,
And in our faults by lies we flatter'd be.

Sonnet cxxxviii, l. 1

(Repeated in *The Passionate Pilgrim*, Pt. i.)

4336 Love is my sin and thy dear virtue hate,
Hate of my sin, grounded on sinful loving.

Sonnet cxlii, l. 1

4337 Love is too young to know what conscience is;
Yet who knows not conscience is born of love?

Sonnet cli, l. 1

4338 Love's fire heats water, water cools not love.

Sonnet cliv, l. 14

4339   On a day, alack the day!
Love, whose month is ever May,
Spied a blossom passing fair,
Playing in the wanton air.

Sonnets to Sundry Notes of Music, Pt. xvii, l. 1

4340 Love, love, nothing but love, still more:
For, O love's bow Shoots buck and doe:
The shaft confounds, Not that it wounds,
But tickles still the sore.

Troilus and Cressida, Act iii, sc. 1, l. 123 [PANDARUS]

4341 My love admits no qualifying dross.

Troilus and Cressida, Act iv, sc. 4, l. 9 [CRESSIDA]

4342 Still sweet love is food for fortune's tooth.

Troilus and Cressida, Act iv, sc. 5, l. 293 [TROILUS]

4343 O spirit of love! how quick and fresh art thou,
That, notwithstanding thy capacity
Receiveth as the sea, nought enters there,
Of what validity and pitch soe'er,
But falls into abatement and low price,
Even in a minute: so full of shapes in fancy
That it alone is high fantastical.

Twelfth Night, Act i, sc. 1, l. 9 [DUKE]

VALENTINE: Like a cloistress, she will veiled walk
And water once a day her chamber round
With eye-offending brine: all this to season
A brother's dead love, which she would keep fresh
And lasting in her sad remembrance.
DUKE: O, she that hath a heart of that fine frame
To pay this debt of love but to a brother,
How will she love, when the rich golden shaft
Hath kill'd the flock of all affections else! . . .
Away before me to sweet beds of flowers:
Love-thoughts lie rich when canopied with bowers.

Twelfth Night, Act i, sc. 1, l. 28 [VALENTINE]

4344 If I did love you in my master's flame,
With such a suffering, such a deadly life, . . .
[I'd] make me a willow cabin at your gate,
And call upon my soul within the house;
Write loyal cantons of contemned love

And sing them loud even in the dead of night;
Halloo your name to the reverberate hills
And make the babbling gossip of the air
Cry out 'Olivia!' O, you should not rest
Between the elements of air and earth,
But you should pity me!

                   Twelfth Night, Act i, sc. 5, l. 283 [VIOLA]

4345
      My love, more noble than the world,
Prizes not quantity of dirty lands: . . .
But 'tis that miracle and queen of gems
That nature pranks her in attracts my soul.

                   Twelfth Night, Act ii, sc. 4, l. 84 [DUKE]

4346
      Him I love
More than I love these eyes, more than my life,
More, by all mores, than e'er I shall love wife.
If I do feign, you witnesses above,
Punish my life for tainting of my love!

                 Twelfth Night, Act v, sc. 1, l. 137 [VIOLA]

4347
PROTEUS: Upon some book I love I'll pray for thee.
VALENTINE: That's on some shallow story of deep love:
How young Leander cross'd the Hellespont.
PROTEUS: That's a deep story of a deeper love;
For he was more than over shoes in love.
VALENTINE: 'Tis true; for you are over boots in love,
And yet you never swum the Hellespont.

       The Two Gentlemen of Verona, Act i, sc. 1, l. 20 [PROTEUS]

4348
To be in love, where scorn is bought with groans;
Coy looks with heart-sore sighs; one fading moment's mirth
With twenty watchful, weary, tedious nights. . . .
Love is your master, for he masters you:
And he that is so yoked by a fool,
Methinks, should not be chronicled for wise.

      The Two Gentlemen of Verona, Act i, sc. 1, l. 29 [VALENTINE]

4349
Fie, fie, how wayward is this foolish love
That, like a testy babe, will scratch the nurse
And presently all humble kiss the rod.

        The Two Gentlemen of Verona, Act i, sc. 2, l. 57 [JULIA]

4350
O how this spring of love resembleth
   The uncertain glory of an April day,
Which now shows all the beauty of the sun,
   And by and by a cloud takes all away!

       The Two Gentlemen of Verona, Act i, sc. 3, l. 84 [PROTEUS]

4351
SPEED: He, being in love, could not see to garter his hose, and
you, being in love, cannot see to put on your hose.
VALENTINE: Belike, boy, then, you are in love; for last morning
you could not see to wipe my shoes.
SPEED: True, sir; I was in love with my bed.

       The Two Gentlemen of Verona, Act ii, sc. 1, l. 82 [SPEED]

4352
The chameleon Love can feed on the air.

      The Two Gentlemen of Verona, Act ii, sc. 1, l. 179 [SPEED]

4353
I have done penance for contemning Love,
Whose high imperious thoughts have punish'd me
With bitter fasts, with penitential groans,
With nightly tears and daily heart-sore sighs;
For in revenge of my contempt of love,
Love hath chased sleep from my enthralled eyes
And made them watchers of mine own heart's sorrow.

O gentle Proteus, Love's a mighty lord
And hath so humbled me, as, I confess,
There is no woe to his correction
Nor to his service no such joy on earth.
Now no discourse, except it be of love;
Now can I break my fast, dine, sup and sleep,
Upon the very naked name of love.
            The Two Gentlemen of Verona, Act ii, sc. 4, l. 129 [VALENTINE]

4354   VALENTINE: Call her divine.
PROTEUS: I will not flatter her.
VALENTINE: O, flatter me; for love delights in praises.
            The Two Gentlemen of Verona, Act ii, sc. 4, l. 147 [VALENTINE]

4355   Even as one heat another heat expels,
Or as one nail by strength drives out another,
So the remembrance of my former love
Is by a newer object quite forgotten. . . .
Now my love is thaw'd;
Which, like a waxen image 'gainst a fire,
Bears no impression of the thing it was.
            The Two Gentlemen of Verona, Act ii, sc. 4, l. 191 [PROTEUS]

4356   Didst thou but know the inly touch of love,
Thou wouldst as soon go kindle fire with snow
As seek to quench the fire of love with words.
            The Two Gentlemen of Verona, Act ii, sc. 7, l. 18 [JULIA]

4357   Love is like a child,
That longs for everything that he can come by.
            The Two Gentlemen of Verona, Act iii, sc. 1, l. 124 [DUKE]

4358   Spaniel-like, the more she spurns my love,
The more it grows and fawneth on her still. . . .
For you know that love
Will creep in service where it cannot go.
            The Two Gentlemen of Verona, Act iv, sc. 2, l. 14 [PROTEUS]

4359   O, 'tis a curse in love, and still approved,
When women cannot love where they're beloved!
            The Two Gentlemen of Verona, Act v, sc. 4, l. 43 [PROTEUS]

4360   Art thou a woman's son, and canst not feel
What 'tis to love? how want of love tormenteth?
            Venus and Adonis, l. 201 [VENUS]

4361   'I know not love,' quoth he, 'nor will not know it; . . .
'Tis much to borrow, and I will not owe it;
For I have heard it is a life in death,
That laughs and weeps, and all but with a breath.'
            Venus and Adonis, l. 409 [ADONIS]

4362   Love keeps his revels where there are but twain.
            Venus and Adonis, l. 123 [VENUS]

4363   Love is a spirit all compact of fire,
Not gross to sink, but light, and will aspire.
            Venus and Adonis, l. 149 [VENUS]

4364   Love makes young men thrall and old men dote; . . .
Love is wise in folly, foolish-witty.
            Venus and Adonis, l. 837

4365   Here I prophesy:
Sorrow on love hereafter shall attend:
It shall be waited on with jealousy,
Find sweet beginning, but unsavoury end. . . .
It shall suspect where is no cause of fear;
It shall not fear where it should most mistrust;

It shall be merciful and too severe,
And most deceiving when it seems most just.
Venus and Adonis, l. 1135 [VENUS]

4366 Three crabbed months had sour'd themselves to death,
Ere I could make thee open thy white hand
And clap thyself my love: then didst thou utter
'I am yours forever.'
The Winter's Tale, Act i, sc. 2, l. 102 [LEONTES]

4367 He says he loves my daughter:
I think so too; for never gazed the moon
Upon the water as he'll stand and read
As 'twere my daughter's eyes: and, to be plain,
I think there is not half a kiss to choose
Who loves another best.
The Winter's Tale, Act iv, sc. 4, l. 171 [SHEPHERD]

Love and Hate

4368 Let not your hate encounter with my love
For loving where you do.
All's Well that Ends Well, Act i, sc. 3, l. 214 [HELENA]

4369 Great Mars, I put myself into thy file:
Make me but like my thoughts, and I shall prove
A lover of thy drum, hater of love.
All's Well that Ends Well, Act iii, sc. 3, l. 9 [BERTRAM]

4370 The hated, grown to strength,
Are newly grown to love.
Antony and Cleopatra, Act i, sc. 3, l. 48 [ANTONY]

4371 There be some women . . . would have gone near
To fall in love with him; but, for my part,
I love him not nor hate him not; and yet
I have more cause to hate him than to love him.
As You Like It, Act iii, sc. 5, l. 124 [PHEBE]

4372 Though I do hate him as I do hell-pains,
Yet, for necessity of present life,
I must show out a flag and sign of love,
Which is indeed but sign.
Othello, Act i, sc. 1, l. 155 [IAGO]

4373 Yield up, O love, thy crown and hearted throne
To tyrannous hate!
Othello, Act iii, sc. 3, l. 448 [OTHELLO]

4374 Sweet love, I see, changing his property,
Turns to the sourest and most deadly hate.
Richard II, Act iii, sc. 2, l. 135 [SCROOP]

4375 The love of wicked men converts to fear;
That fear to hate, and hate turns one or both
To worthy danger and deserved death.
Richard II, Act v, sc. 1, l. 66 [KING RICHARD]

4376 Here's much to do with hate, but more with love.
Why, then, O brawling love! O loving hate!
O any thing, of nothing first create!
O heavy lightness! serious vanity!
Mis-shapen chaos of well-seeming forms!
Feather of lead, bright smoke, cold fire, sick health!
Still-waking sleep, that is not what it is!
This love feel I, that feel no love in this.
Romeo and Juliet, Act i, sc. 1, l. 181 [ROMEO]

4377   My only love sprung from my only hate!
Too early seen unknown, and known too late!
Prodigious birth of love it is to me,
That I must love a loathed enemy.
Romeo and Juliet, Act i, sc. 5, l. 140 [JULIET]

4378   Love will not be spurr'd to what it loathes.
The Two Gentlemen of Verona, Act v, sc. 2, l. 7 [JULIA]

Love and Reason

4379   Love's counsellor should fill the bores of hearing
To the smothering of the sense.
Cymbeline, Act iii, sc. 2, l. 58 [IMOGEN]

4380   Love's reason's without reason.
Cymbeline, Act iv, sc. 2, l. 22 [ARVIRAGUS]

4381   Who can be wise, amazed, temperate and furious,
Loyal and neutral, in a moment? No man:
The expedition of my violent love
Outrun the pauser, reason.
Macbeth, Act ii, sc. 3, l. 114 [MACBETH]

4382   Ask me no reason why I love you; for though Love use Reason
for his physician, he admits him not for his counsellor.
The Merry Wives of Windsor, Act ii, sc. 1, l. 4
[MRS. PAGE, reading Falstaff's letter]

4383   Reason and love keep little company together now-a-days; the
more the pity that some honest neighbours will not make them
friends. Nay, I can gleek upon occasion.
A Midsummer Night's Dream, Act iii, sc. 1, l. 147 [BOTTOM]
("Gleek," sneer, scoff.)

4384   To be wise and love
Exceeds man's might; that dwells with gods above.
Troilus and Cressida, Act iii, sc. 2, l. 163 [CRESSIDA]

4385   A murderous guilt shows not itself more soon
Than love that would be hid: love's night is noon.
Cesario, by the roses of the spring,
By maidhood, honour, truth and every thing,
I love thee so, that, maugre all thy pride,
Nor wit nor reason can my passion hide.
Do not extort thy reasons from this clause,
For that I woo, thou therefore hast no cause;
But, rather, reason thus with reason fetter,—
Love sought is good, but given unsought is better.
Twelfth Night, Act iii, sc. 1, l. 159 [OLIVIA]

Love at First Sight

4386   Dead shepherd, now I find thy saw of might,
'Who ever loved that loved not at first sight?'
As You Like It, Act iii, sc. 5, l. 81 [PHEBE]
(The shepherd was Christopher Marlowe who died in 1593, six
years before As You Like It was written, and from whose Hero
and Leander [Sestiad i, l. 176] the quoted line is taken.)

4387   Your brother and my sister no sooner met but they looked, no
sooner looked but they loved, no sooner loved but they sighed,
no sooner sighed but they asked one another the reason, no sooner
knew the reason but they sought the remedy; and in these degrees
have they made a pair of stairs to marriage which they will climb
incontinent, or else be incontinent before marriage: they are in the
very wrath of love and they will together; clubs cannot part them.
As You Like It, Act v, sc. 2, l. 35 [ROSALIND]

4388   TRANIO: I pray, sir, tell me, is it possible
That love should of a sudden take such hold?
LUCENTIO: O Tranio, till I found it to be true,
I never thought it possible or likely;
But see, while idly I stood looking on,
I found the effect of love in idleness.
> *The Taming of the Shrew,* Act i, sc. 1, l. 151 [TRANIO]

4389   Hear my soul speak:
The very instant that I saw you, did
My heart fly to your service: there resides,
To make me slave to it. . . . I
Beyond all limit of what else i' the world
Do love, prize, honour you.
> *The Tempest,* Act iii, sc. 1, l. 63 [FERDINAND]

4390   Even so quickly may one catch the plague?
> *Twelfth Night,* Act i, sc. 5, l. 314 [OLIVIA]

Love Is Blind

4391   BURGUNDY: Can you blame her . . . if she deny the appearance of
a naked blind boy in her naked seeing self? It were, my lord, a hard
condition for a maid to consign to.
KING HENRY: Yet they do wink and yield, as love is blind and
enforces.
> *Henry V,* Act v, sc. 2, l. 316 [BURGUNDY]

4392   Love is blind and lovers cannot see
The pretty follies that themselves commit.
> *The Merchant of Venice,* Act ii, sc. 6, l. 36 [JESSICA]

4393   Things base and vile, holding no quantity,
Love can transpose to form and dignity:
Love looks not with the eyes, but with the mind;
And therefore is wing'd Cupid painted blind.
> *A Midsummer Night's Dream,* Act i, sc. 1, l. 232 [HELENA]

4394   BENVOLIO: Blind is his love and best befits the dark.
MERCUTIO: If love be blind, love cannot hit the mark.
Now will he sit under a medlar tree,
And wish his mistress were that kind of fruit
As maids call medlars, when they laugh alone.
> *Romeo and Juliet,* Act ii, sc. 1, l. 33 [BENVOLIO]

4395   Lovers can see to do their amorous rites
By their own beauties; or, if love be blind,
It best agrees with night.
> *Romeo and Juliet,* Act iii, sc. 2, l. 8 [JULIET]

4396   If you love her you cannot see her. Because Love is blind.
> *The Two Gentlemen of Verona,* Act ii, sc. 1, l. 75 [SPEED]

Love: The Lover

4397   In thy youth thou wast as true a lover
As ever sigh'd upon a midnight pillow.
> *As You Like It,* Act ii, sc. 4, l. 26 [SILVIUS]

4398   It is as easy to count atomies as to resolve the propositions of a
lover.
> *As You Like It,* Act iii, sc. 2, l. 245 [CELIA]

4399   The oath of a lover is no stronger than the word of a tapster;
they are both the confirmer of false reckonings.
> *As You Like It,* Act iii, sc. 4, l. 33 [CELIA]

At lovers' perjuries, They say, Jove laughs.
> *Romeo and Juliet,* Act ii, sc. 2, l. 92 [JULIET]

4400　　The sight of lovers feedeth those in love.
　　　　　　　　　　As You Like It, Act iii, sc. 4, l. 60 [ROSALIND]
4401　　It was a lover and his lass,
　　　　　　With a hey, and a ho, and a hey nonino,
　　　　That o'er the green corn-field did pass
　　　　　　In the spring time, the only pretty ring time,
　　　　When birds do sing, hey ding a ding ding:
　　　　Sweet lovers love the spring.
　　　　　　　　　　As You Like It, Act v, sc. 3, l. 17 [PAGES]
4402　　A lover's eyes will gaze an eagle blind;
　　　　A lover's ear will hear the lowest sound.
　　　　　　　　　　Love's Labour's Lost, Act iv, sc. 3, l. 334 [BIRON]
4403　　Lovers ever run before the clock.
　　　　　　　　　The Merchant of Venice, Act ii, sc. 6, l. 4 [GRATIANO]
　　　　　　Lovers break not hours,
　　　　Unless it be to come before their time.
　　　　　　　The Two Gentlemen of Verona, Act v, sc. 1, l. 4 [EGLAMOUR]
4404　　Thou wilt be like a lover presently
　　　　And tire the hearer with a book of words.
　　　　　　　　Much Ado about Nothing, Act i, sc. 1, l. 308 [DON PEDRO]
4405　　A pair of star-cross'd lovers take their life.
　　　　　　　　　　　Romeo and Juliet, Prologue, l. 6
4406　　How silver-sweet sound lovers' tongues by night,
　　　　Like softest music to attending ears!
　　　　　　　　　Romeo and Juliet, Act ii, sc. 2, l. 166 [ROMEO]
4407　　A lover may bestride the gossamer
　　　　That idles in the wanton summer air,
　　　　And yet not fall; so light is vanity.
　　　　　　　Romeo and Juliet, Act ii, sc. 6, l. 18 [FRIAR LAURENCE]
4408　　They say all lovers swear more performance than they are able and
　　　　yet reserve an ability that they never perform.
　　　　　　　　Troilus and Cressida, Act iii, sc. 2, l. 91 [CRESSIDA]
4409　　Come hither, boy: if ever thou shalt love,
　　　　In the sweet pangs of it remember me;
　　　　For such as I am all true lovers are,
　　　　Unstaid and skittish in all motions else,
　　　　Save in the constant image of the creature
　　　　That is beloved.
　　　　　　　　　　Twelfth Night, Act ii, sc. 4, l. 15 [DUKE]
4410　　Lovers say, the heart hath treble wrong
　　　　When it is barr'd the aidance of the tongue.
　　　　　　　　　　　　Venus and Adonis, l. 329
4411　　Foul words and frowns must not repel a lover.
　　　　　　　　　　　　Venus and Adonis, l. 573
4412　　Lovers' hours are long, though seeming short.
　　　　　　　　　　　　Venus and Adonis, l. 842

Loyalty

4413　　The loyalty well held to fools does make
　　　　Our faith mere folly: yet he that can endure
　　　　To follow with allegiance a fall'n lord
　　　　Does conquer him that did his master conquer,
　　　　And earns a place i' the story.
　　　　　　　Antony and Cleopatra, Act iii, sc. 13, l. 42 [ENOBARBUS]
4414　　Master, go on, and I will follow thee
　　　　To the last gasp, with truth and loyalty.
　　　　　　　　　　As You Like It, Act ii, sc. 3, l. 69 [ADAM]

4415   I Can nothing render but . . . my loyalty,
Which ever has and ever shall be growing,
Till death, that winter, kill it.
                              Henry VIII, Act iii, sc. 2, l. 177 [WOLSEY]

4416   I will persevere in my course of loyalty, though the conflict be
sore between that and my blood.
                              King Lear, Act iii, sc. 5, l. 23 [EDMUND]

4417   End life when I end loyalty!
        A Midsummer Night's Dream, Act ii, sc. 2, l. 63 [LYSANDER]

Luck

4418   I hear him mock
The luck of Cæsar, which the gods give men
To excuse their after wrath.
                Antony and Cleopatra, Act v, sc. 2, l. 289 [CLEOPATRA]

4419   Was there ever man had such luck! when I kissed the jack, upon
an up-cast to be hit away!
                              Cymbeline, Act ii, sc. 1, l. 1 [CLOTEN]

4420   No ill luck stirring but what lights on my shoulders; no sighs
but of my breathing; no tears but of my shedding.
                The Merchant of Venice, Act iii, sc. 1, l. 99 [SHYLOCK]

4421   If it be my luck, so; if not, happy man be his dole!
                The Merry Wives of Windsor, Act iii, sc. 4, l. 67 [SLENDER]

4422   As good luck would have it.
                The Merry Wives of Windsor, Act iii, sc. 5, l. 84 [FALSTAFF]

4423   This is the third time; I hope good luck lies in odd numbers. . . .
They say there is divinity in odd numbers, either in nativity, chance,
or death.
                The Merry Wives of Windsor, Act v, sc. 1, l. 2 [FALSTAFF]

4424   'Twere hard luck, being in so preposterous estate as we are.
                The Winter's Tale, Act v, sc. 2, l. 158 [CLOTEN]

Lust

4425   But, O strange men!
That can such sweet use make of what they hate,
When saucy trusting of the cozen'd thoughts
Defiles the pitchy night: so lust doth play
With what it loathes for that which is away.
                All's Well that Ends Well, Act iv, sc. 4, l. 21 [HELENA]

4426   His captain's heart,
Which in the scuffles of great fights hath burst
The buckles on his breast, reneges all temper,
And is become the bellows and the fan
To cool a gipsy's lust.
                Antony and Cleopatra, Act i, sc. 1, l. 6 [PHILO]

4427   How dearly would it touch thee to the quick
Shouldst thou but hear I were licentious
And that this body, consecrate to thee,
By ruffian lust should be contaminate!
                The Comedy of Errors, Act ii, sc. 2, l. 132 [ADRIANA]

4428   Fie on sinful fantasy!
                  Fie on lust and luxury!
                  Lust is but a bloody fire,
                  Kindled with unchaste desire,
                  Fed in heart, whose flames aspire
                  As thoughts do blow them higher and higher.
The Merry Wives of Windsor, Act v, sc. 5, l. 97 [MISTRESS QUICKLY]

4429   Tears harden lust, though marble wear with raining.
                                            The Rape of Lucrece, l. 560

4430   Light and lust are deadly enemies.
                                            The Rape of Lucrece, l. 674

4431   The expense of spirit in a waste of shame
        Is lust in action; and till action, lust
        Is perjured, murderous, bloody, full of blame,
        Savage, extreme, rude, cruel, not to trust;
        Enjoy'd no sooner, but despised straight,
        Past reason hunted, and no sooner had
        Past reason hated, as a swallow'd bait
        On purpose laid to make the taker mad. . . .
        All this the world well knows; yet none knows well
        To shun the heaven that leads men to this hell.
                                            Sonnet cxxix, l. 1

4432   As I hope
        For quiet days, fair issue and long life,
        With such love as 'tis now, the murkiest den,
        The most opportune place, the strong'st suggestion
        Our worser genius can, shall never melt
        Mine honour into lust, to take away
        The edge of that day's celebration
        When I shall think, or Phœbus' steeds are founder'd,
        Or Night kept chain'd below.
                            The Tempest, Act iv, sc. 1, l. 23 [FERDINAND]

4433   Love comforteth like sunshine after rain,
        But Lust's effect is tempest after sun;
        Love's gentle spring doth always fresh remain,
        Lust's winter comes ere summer half be done:
        Love surfeits not. Lust like a glutton dies;
        Love is all truth, Lust full of forged lies.
                                Venus and Adonis, l. 799 [ADONIS]

M

Mab

4434   I see Queen Mab hath been with you.
        She is the fairies' midwife, and she comes
        In shape no bigger than an agate-stone
        On the fore-finger of an alderman,
        Drawn with a team of little atomies
        Athwart men's noses as they lie asleep;
        Her waggon-spokes made of long spinners' legs; . . .
        Her waggoner a small grey-coated gnat; . . .
        Her chariot is an empty hazel-nut, . . .
        And in this state she gallops night by night
        Through lovers' brains, and then they dream of love.
                        Romeo and Juliet, Act i, sc. 4, l. 53 [MERCUTIO]

4435   This is that very Mab
        That plats the manes of horses in the night,
        And bakes the elf-locks in foul sluttish hairs,
        Which once untangled much misfortune bodes:
        This is the hag, when maids lie on their backs,
        That presses them and learns them first to bear.
                        Romeo and Juliet, Act i, sc. 4, l. 88 [MERCUTIO]

Madness

4436   Though I am mad, I will not bite him.
            Antony and Cleopatra, Act ii, sc. 5, 1. 80 [CLEOPATRA]

4437   DROMIO E.: Sure my master is horn-mad.
        ADRIANA: Horn-mad, thou villain?
        DROMIO E.: I mean not cuckold-mad;
        But, sure, he is stark mad.
            The Comedy of Errors, Act ii, sc. 1, 1. 57 [DROMIO OF EPHESUS]
        If he had found the young man, he would have been horn-mad.
        The Merry Wives of Windsor, Act i, sc. 4, 1. 51 [MISTRESS QUICKLY]
            (Also iii, 5, 155. See also 3581.)
        If this should ever happen, thou wouldst be horn-mad.
                Much Ado about Nothing, Act i, sc. 1, 1. 271 [CLAUDIO]

4438   It would make a man mad as a buck to be so bought and sold.
            The Comedy of Errors, Act iii, sc. 1, 1. 72 [DROMIO OF EPHESUS]

4439   Your noble son is mad:
        Mad call I it; for, to define true madness,
        What is 't but to be nothing else but mad? . . .
        That he is mad, 'tis true: 'tis true, 'tis pity;
        And pity 'tis 'tis true.
                    Hamlet, Act ii, sc. 2, 1. 92 [POLONIUS]

4440   Though this be madness, yet there is method in 't.
                Hamlet, Act ii, sc. 2, 1. 207 [POLONIUS]

4441   How pregnant sometimes his replies are! a happiness that often
        madness hits on, which reason and sanity could not so prosperously
        be delivered of.
                    Hamlet, Act ii, sc. 2, 1. 213 [POLONIUS]

4442   I am but mad north-north-west: when the wind is southerly I know
        a hawk from a handsaw.
                    Hamlet, Act ii, sc. 2, 1. 398 [HAMLET]

4443   Madness in great ones must not unwatch'd go.
                Hamlet, Act iii, sc. 1, 1. 196 [KING]

4444   Madness would not err,
        Nor sense to ecstasy was ne'er so thrall'd,
        But it reserved some quantity of choice.
                Hamlet, Act iii, sc. 4, 1. 73 [HAMLET]

4445   It is not madness
        That I have utter'd. . . . Mother, for love of grace,
        Lay not that flattering unction to your soul,
        That not your trespass, but my madness speaks.
                    Hamlet, Act iii, sc. 4, 1. 141 [HAMLET]

4446   KING: How does Hamlet?
        QUEEN: Mad as the sea and wind, when both contend
        Which is the mightier.
                    Hamlet, Act iv, sc. 1, 1. 6 [KING]

4447   Good Lord, what madness rules in brainsick men!
                I Henry VI, Act iv, sc. 1, 1. 111 [KING HENRY]

4448   To Bedlam with him; has the man grown mad? . . .
        He is a traitor; let him to the Tower,
        And chop away that factious pate of his.
                II Henry VI, Act v, sc. 1, 1. 131 [CLIFFORD]

4449   I am not mad: this hair I tear is mine;
        My name is Constance; I was Geffrey's wife;
        Young Arthur is my son, and he is lost:
        I am not mad: I would to heaven I were!
        For then, 'tis like I should forget myself:
        O, if I could, what grief I should forget!

Preach some philosophy to make me mad,
And thou shalt be canonized, cardinal;
For being not mad, but sensible of grief,
My reasonable part produces reason
How I may be delivered of these woes,
And teaches me to kill or hang myself:
If I were mad, I should forget my son,
Or madly think a babe of clouts were he:
I am not mad; too well, too well I feel
The different plague of each calamity.
>>*King John,* Act iii, sc. 4, l. 45 [CONSTANCE]

4450 O, that way madness lies; let me shun that.
>>*King Lear,* Act iii, sc. 4, l. 21 [LEAR]

4451 He's mad that trusts in the tameness of a wolf, a horse's health,
a boy's love, or a whore's oath.
>>*King Lear,* Act iii, sc. 6, l. 19 [FOOL]

4452 'Tis the times' plague, when madmen lead the blind.
>>*King Lear,* Act iv, sc. 1, l. 48 [GLOUCESTER]

4453 He was met even now
As mad as the vex'd sea; singing aloud;
Crown'd with rank fumiter and furrow-weeds,
With bur-docks, hemlock, nettles, cuckoo-flowers,
Darnel, and all the idle weeds that grow
In our sustaining corn.
>>*King Lear,* Act iv, sc. 4, l. 1 [CORDELIA]

4454 If she be mad,—as I believe no other,—
Her madness hath the oddest frame of sense,
Such a dependency of thing on thing,
As e'er I heard in madness.
>>*Measure for Measure,* Act v, sc. 1, l. 60 [DUKE]

4455 Any madness I ever yet beheld seemed but tameness, civility and
patience, to this his distemper.
>>*The Merry Wives of Windsor,* Act iv, sc. 2, l. 27 [MRS. PAGE]

4456 LEONATO: You will never run mad, niece.
BEATRICE: No, not till a hot January.
>>*Much Ado about Nothing,* Act i, sc. 1, l. 93 [LEONATO]

4457 BENVOLIO: Why, Romeo, art thou mad?
ROMEO: Not mad, but bound more than a madman is:
Shut up in prison, kept without my food,
Whipp'd and tormented.
>>*Romeo and Juliet,* Act i, sc. 2, l. 55 [BENVOLIO]

4458 Why, this is very midsummer madness.
>>*Twelfth Night,* Act iii, sc. 4, l. 61 [OLIVIA]

Maid

4459 I am a simple maid, and therein wealthiest,
That I protest I simply am a maid.
>>*All's Well that Ends Well,* Act ii, sc. 3, l. 72 [HELENA]

4460 Maids are May when they are maids, but the sky changes when
they are wives.
>>*As You Like It,* Act iv, sc. 1, l. 148 [ROSALIND]

4461 The chariest maid is prodigal enough
If she unmask her beauty to the moon.
>>*Hamlet,* Act i, sc. 3, l. 36 [LAERTES]

4462 Be somewhat scanter of your maiden presence;
Set your entreatments at a higher rate
Than a command to parley.
>>*Hamlet,* Act i, sc. 3, l. 121 [POLONIUS]

4463   What is 't to me, when you yourselves are cause,
        If your pure maidens fall into the hand
        Of hot and forcing violation?
                        Henry V, Act iii, sc. 3, l. 19 [KING HENRY]

4464   A maid, yet rosed over with the virgin crimson of modesty.
                        Henry V, Act v, sc. 2, l. 322 [BURGUNDY]

4465   She that 's a maid now, and laughs at my departure,
        Shall not be a maid long, unless things be cut shorter.
                        King Lear, Act i, sc. 5, l. 55 [FOOL]

4466   POMPEY: Yonder man is carried to prison. . . .
        MRS. OVERDONE: What 's his offence?
        POMPEY: Groping for trout in a peculiar river.
        MRS. OVERDONE: What, is there a maid with child by him?
        POMPEY: No, but there 's a woman with maid by him.
                Measure for Measure, Act i, sc. 2, l. 87 [POMPEY]

4467   When maidens sue,
        Men give like gods; but when they weep and kneel,
        All their petitions are as freely theirs
        As they themselves would owe them.
                Measure for Measure, Act i, sc. 4, l. 80 [LUCIO]

4468   DUKE: What, are you married?
        MARIANA: No, my lord.
        DUKE: Are you a maid?
        MARIANA: No, my lord.
        DUKE: A widow, then?
        MARIANA: Neither, my lord.
        DUKE: Why, you are nothing then: neither maid, widow, nor
        wife?
                Measure for Measure, Act v, sc. 1, l. 171 [DUKE]

4469   A maiden hath no tongue but thought.
                The Merchant of Venice, Act iii, sc. 2, l. 8 [PORTIA]

4470   Whether a maid so tender . . . Would ever have . . .
        Run from her guardage to the sooty bosom
        Of such a thing as thou.
                   Othello, Act i, sc. 2, l. 66 [BRABANTIO]

4471   A maiden never bold;
        Of spirit so still and quiet, that her motion
        Blush'd at herself.
                 Othello, Act i, sc. 3, l. 94 [BRABANTIO]

4472   An honest maid as ever broke bread.
      The Merry Wives of Windsor, Act i, sc. 4, l. 161 [MISTRESS QUICKLY]

4473   Katherine the curst!
        A title for a maid of all titles the worst.
             The Taming of the Shrew, Act i, sc. 2, l. 129 [GRUMIO]

Majesty

4474   The cease of majesty
        Dies not alone; but, like a gulf, doth draw
        What 's near it with it: it is a massy wheel,
        Fix'd on the summit of the highest mount,
        To whose huge spokes ten thousand lesser things
        Are mortised and adjoin'd; which, when it falls,
        Each small annexment, petty consequence,
        Attends the boisterous ruin. Never alone
        Did the king sigh, but with a general groan.
                Hamlet, Act iii, sc. 3, l. 15 [ROSENCRANTZ]

4475   Majesty might never yet endure
       The moody frontier of a servant brow.
                           I Henry IV, Act i, sc. 3, l. 18 [KING HENRY]
4476   Ha, majesty! how high thy glory towers,
       When the rich blood of kings is set on fire!
                           King John, Act ii, sc. 1, l. 350 [BASTARD]

Make and Mar

4477   OLIVER: Now, sir: what make you here?
       ORLANDO: Nothing: I am not taught to make any thing.
       OLIVER: What mar you then, sir?
       ORLANDO: Marry, sir, I am helping you to mar that which God
       made, a poor unworthy brother of yours, with idleness.
                           As You Like It, Act i, sc. 1, l. 31 [OLIVER]
4478   It makes him, and it mars him.
                           Macbeth, Act ii, sc. 3, l. 36 [PORTER]
4479   Make and mar The foolish Fates.
                           A Midsummer Night's Dream, Act i, sc. 2, l. 39 [BOTTOM]
4480   It makes us, or it mars us; think on that.
                           Othello, Act v, sc. 1, l. 4 [IAGO]
4481   PARIS: Younger than she are happy mothers made.
       CAPULET: And too soon marr'd are those so early made.
                           Romeo and Juliet, Act i, sc. 2, l. 12 [PARIS]

Man

4482   And say a soldier, Dian, told thee this,
       Men are to mell with, boys are not to kiss.
                           All's Well that Ends Well, Act iv, sc. 3, l. 257 [SOLDIER, *reading*]
4483   A man is master of his liberty:
       Time is their master, and when they see time
       They'll go or come. . . .
       There's nothing situate under heaven's eye
       But hath his bound, in earth, in sea, in sky:
       The beasts, the fishes and the winged fowls
       Are their males' subjects and at their controls:
       Men, more divine, the masters of all these,
       Lords of the wide world and wild watery seas,
       Indued with intellectual sense and souls,
       Of more pre-eminence than fish and fowls,
       Are masters to their females, and their lords:
       Then let your will attend on their accords.
                           The Comedy of Errors, Act ii, sc. 1, l. 7 [LUCIANA]
4484   What, are men mad? Hath nature given them eyes
       To see this vaulted arch, and the rich crop
       Of sea and land, which can distinguish 'twixt
       The fiery orbs above and the twinn'd stones
       Upon the number's beach? and can we not
       Partition make with spectacles so precious
       'Twixt fair and foul?
                           Cymbeline, Act i, sc. 6, l. 32 [IACHIMO]
4485   A headless man! The garments of Posthumus!
       I know the shape of's leg; this is his hand;
       His foot Mercurial; his Martial thigh;
       The brawns of Hercules: but his Jovial face—
       Murder in heaven?—Hoy!—'Tis gone. Pisanio hath . . .

From this most bravest vessel of the world
Struck the main-top!
                                   Cymbeline, Act iv, sc. 2, l. 308 [IMOGEN]

4486   HAMLET: My father!—methinks I see my father. . . .
In my mind's eye, Horatio.
HORATIO: I saw him once; he was a goodly king.
HAMLET: He was a man, take him for all in all,
I shall not look upon his like again.
                                        Hamlet, Act i, sc. 2, l. 184 [HAMLET]

4487   What a piece of work is a man! how noble in reason! how infinite
in faculty! in form and moving how express and admirable! in
action how like an angel! in apprehension how like a god! the
beauty of the world! the paragon of animals! And yet, to me, what
is this quintessence of dust? man delights not me: no, nor woman
neither.
                                       Hamlet, Act ii, sc. 2, l. 317 [HAMLET]

4488   What is a man,
If his chief good and market of his time
Be but to sleep and feed? a beast, no more.
Sure, he that made us with such large discourse,
Looking before and after, gave us not
That capability and god-like reason
To fust in us unused.
                                      Hamlet, Act iv, sc. 4, l. 33 [HAMLET]

4489   I do remember him at Clement's Inn like a man made after supper
of a cheese-paring: when a' was naked, he was, for all the world,
like a forked radish, with a head fantastically carved upon it with
a knife; . . . a' was the very genius of famine, . . . for you might
have thrust him and all his apparel into an eel-skin.
                                   II Henry IV, Act iii, sc. 2, l. 331 [FALSTAFF]

4490   This bold bad man.
                                   Henry VIII, Act ii, sc. 2, l. 44 [CHAMBERLAIN]

4491   As proper men as ever trod upon neat's leather have gone upon
my handiwork.
                                   Julius Cæsar, Act i, sc. 1, l. 29 [COBBLER]
A proper man, as one shall see in a summer's day.
                          A Midsummer Night's Dream, Act i, sc. 2, l. 88 [QUINCE]
As proper a man as ever went on four legs cannot make him
give ground.
                                   The Tempest, Act ii, sc. 2, l. 63 [STEPHANO]

4492   So in the world; 'tis furnished well with men,
And men are flesh and blood, and apprehensive.
                                   Julius Cæsar, Act iii, sc. 1, l. 66 [CÆSAR]

4493   This is a slight unmeritable man,
Meet to be sent on errands.
                                   Julius Cæsar, Act iv, sc. 1, l. 12 [ANTONY]

4494   Is man no more than this? Consider him well. Thou owest the
worm no silk, the beast no hide, the sheep no wool, the cat no
perfume. . . . Thou art the thing itself: unaccommodated man is
no more but such a poor, bare, forked animal as thou art.
                                   King Lear, Act iii, sc. 4, l. 107 [LEAR]

4495   O, the difference of man and man!
To thee a woman's services are due:
My fool usurps my body.
                                   King Lear, Act iv, sc. 2, l. 26 [GONERIL]

4496   FIRST MURDERER: We are men, my liege.
MACBETH: Ay, in the catalogue ye go for men;
As hounds and greyhounds, mongrels, spaniels, curs,

Shoughs, water-rugs and demi-wolves are clept
All by the name of dogs.

> *Macbeth,* Act iii, sc. 1, l. 91 [FIRST MURDERER]

4497　LADY MACBETH: Are you a man?
MACBETH: Ay, and a bold one, that dare look on that
Which might appal the devil.
LADY MACBETH: O proper stuff! . . . O, these flaws and starts,
Imposters to true fear, would well become
A woman's story at a winter's fire,
Authorized by her grandam.

> *Macbeth,* Act iii, sc. 4, l. 58 [LADY MACBETH]

4498　　　　　　Man, proud man,
Drest in a little brief authority,
Most ignorant of what he's most assured,
His glassy essence, like an angry ape,
Plays such fantastic tricks before high heaven
As make the angels weep.

> *Measure for Measure,* Act ii, sc. 2, l. 117 [ISABELLA]

4499　O, what may man within him hide,
Though angel on the outward side!

> *Measure for Measure,* Act iii, sc. 2, l. 285 [DUKE]

4500　NERISSA: How say you by the French lord, Monsieur Le Bon?
PORTIA: God made him, and therefore let him pass for a man.
. . . He is every man in no man; if a throstle sing, he falls straight
a capering: he will fence with his own shadow. . . .
NERISSA: How like you the young German? . . .
PORTIA: When he is best, he is a little worse than a man, and
when he is worst, he is little better than a beast.

> *The Merchant of Venice,* Act i, sc. 2, l. 58 [NERISSA]

4501　　　　　Never did I know
A creature, that did bear the shape of man,
So keen and greedy to confound a man.

> *The Merchant of Venice,* Act iii, sc. 2, l. 277 [SALERIO]

4502　A man of my kidney, . . . that am as subject to heat as butter.

> *The Merry Wives of Windsor,* Act iii, sc. 5, l. 119 [FALSTAFF]

Belike this is a man of that quirk.

> *Twelfth Night,* Act iii, sc. 4, l. 269 [VIOLA]

4503　In the shape of man, . . . I fear not Goliath with a weaver's beam.

> *The Merry Wives of Windsor,* Act v, sc. 1, l. 24 [FALSTAFF]

4504　Hard-handed men that work in Athens here,
And never labour'd in their minds till now.

> *A Midsummer Night's Dream,* Act v, sc. 1, l. 72 [PHILOSTRATE]

4505　He is no less than a stuffed man.

> *Much Ado about Nothing,* Act i, sc. 1, l. 58 [BEATRICE]

4506　　　　Sigh no more, ladies, sigh no more,
　　　　　Men were deceivers ever,
　　　　One foot in sea and one on shore,
　　　　　To one thing constant never:
　　　　Then sigh not so, but let them go,
　　　　　And be you blithe and bonny,
　　　　Converting all your sounds of woe
　　　　　Into Hey nonny, nonny.

> *Much Ado about Nothing,* Act ii, sc. 3, l. 64 [BALTHASAR]

4507　Are you good men and true?

> *Much Ado about Nothing,* Act iii, sc. 3, l. 1 [DOGBERRY]

4508　An two men ride of a horse, one must ride behind.

> *Much Ado about Nothing,* Act iii, sc. 5, l. 40 [DOGBERRY]

4509   If I know more of any man alive
   Than that which maiden modesty doth warrant,
   Let all my sins lack mercy!
             Much Ado about Nothing, Act iv, sc. 1, l. 180 [HERO]

4510   'Tis not a year or two shows us a man:
   They are all but stomachs, and we all but food;
   They eat us hungerly, and when they are full,
   They belch us.
             Othello, Act iii, sc. 4, l. 103 [EMILIA]

4511   Men are not gods,
   Nor of them look for such observances
   As fit the bridal.
             Othello, Act iii, sc. 4, l. 148 [DESDEMONA]

4512   IAGO: Would you would bear your fortune like a man!
   OTHELLO: A horned man's a monster and a beast.
   IAGO: There's many a beast then in a populous city,
   And many a civil monster . . . Good sir, be a man.
             Othello, Act iv, sc. 1, l. 62 [IAGO]

4513   A man whom both the waters and the wind,
   In that vast tennis-court, have made the ball
   For them to play upon, entreats you pity him.
             Pericles, Act ii, sc. 1, l. 63 [PERICLES]

4514   There's no trust,
   No faith, no honesty in men; all perjured,
   All forsworn, all naught, all dissemblers.
             Romeo and Juliet, Act iii, sc. 2, l. 85 [NURSE]

4515   You know . . . no such men as you have reckon'd up,
   As Stephen Sly and old John Naps of Greece,
   And Peter Turph and Henry Pimpernell,
   And twenty more such names and men as these,
   Which never were nor no man ever saw.
             The Taming of the Shrew, Induction, sc. 2, l. 94 [SERVANT]

4516   How beauteous mankind is! O brave new world,
   That has such creatures in't!
             The Tempest, Act v, sc. 1, l. 183 [MIRANDA]

4517   Every man shift for all the rest, and let no man take care for himself; for all is but fortune.
             The Tempest, Act v, sc. 1, l. 256 [STEPHANO]

4518   The strain of man's bred out into baboon and monkey.
             Timon of Athens, Act i, sc. 1, l. 259 [APEMANTUS]

4519   I wonder men dare trust themselves with men.
             Timon of Athens, Act i, sc. 2, l. 45 [APEMANTUS]

4520   I am Misanthropos, and hate mankind.
   For my part, I do wish thou wert a dog,
   That I might love thee something.
             Timon of Athens, Act iv, sc. 3, l. 53 [TIMON]

4521   Do you know what a man is? Is not birth, beauty, good shape, discourse, manhood, learning, gentleness, virtue, youth, liberality, and such like, the spice and salt that season a man?
             Troilus and Cressida, Act i, sc. 2, l. 274 [PANDARUS]

4522   O heavens, what some men do,
   While some men leave to do!
   How some men creep in skittish fortune's hall,
   While others play the idiot in her eyes!
             Troilus and Cressida, Act iii, sc. 3, l. 132 [ULYSSES]

4523   OLIVIA: What kind o' man is he?
   MALVOLIO: Why, of mankind.

OLIVIA: What manner of man?
MALVOLIO: Of very ill manner.
                              Twelfth Night, Act i, sc. 5, l. 159 [OLIVIA]

4524   I will be point-devise the very man.
                              Twelfth Night, Act ii, sc. 5, l. 178 [MALVOLIO]

4525   JULIA: It is a lesser blot, modesty finds,
       Women to change their shapes than men their minds.
       PROTEUS: Than men their minds! 'tis true. O heaven, were man
       But constant, he were perfect! that one error
       Fills him with faults; makes him run through all the sins:
       Inconstancy falls off ere it begins.
                              The Two Gentlemen of Verona, Act v, sc. 4, l. 108 [JULIA]

4526   Thou art no man, though of a man's complexion,
       For men will kiss even by their own direction.
                              Venus and Adonis, l. 215 [VENUS]

Man and Woman

4527   He is A man worth any woman.
                              Cymbeline, Act i, sc. 1, l. 145 [IMOGEN]

4528   Is there no way for men to be but women
       Must be half-workers?
                              Cymbeline, Act ii, sc. 5, l. 1 [POSTHUMUS]

4529   Father and mother is man and wife; man and wife is one flesh.
                              Hamlet, Act iv, sc. 3, l. 53 [HAMLET]

4530   He is the half part of a blessed man,
       Left to be finished by such as she;
       And she a fair divided excellence,
       Whose fulness of perfection lies in him.
                              King John, Act ii, sc. 1, l. 437 [CITIZEN]

4531   I never yet saw man,
       How wise, how noble, young, how rarely featured,
       But she would spell him backward. . . .
       So turns she every man the wrong side out
       And never gives to truth and virtue that
       Which simpleness and merit purchaseth.
                              Much Ado about Nothing, Act iii, sc. 1, l. 59 [HERO]

4532   Though men can cover crimes with bold stern looks,
       Poor women's faces are their own faults' books.
                              The Rape of Lucrece, l. 1252

4533   Women may fall, when there's no strength in men.
                              Romeo and Juliet, Act ii, sc. 3, l. 80 [FRIAR LAURENCE]

4534   Art thou a man? thy form cries out thou art:
       Thy tears are womanish; thy wild acts denote
       The unreasonable fury of a beast:
       Unseemly woman in a seeming man!
       Or ill-beseeming beast in seeming both!
                              Romeo and Juliet, Act iii, sc. 3, l. 109 [FRIAR LAURENCE]

4535   A woman impudent and mannish grown
       Is not more loathed than an effeminate man
       In time of action.
                              Troilus and Cressida, Act iii, sc. 3, l. 217 [PATROCLUS]

Manhood

4536   Manhood is call'd foolery, when it stands
       Against a falling fabric.
                              Coriolanus, Act iii, sc. 1, l. 246 [COMINIUS]

4537   Go thy ways, old Jack; die when thou wilt, if manhood, good
       manhood, be not forgot upon the face of the earth, then am I

a shotten herring. There live not three good men unhanged in
England; and one of them is fat and grows old: God help the
while!
I Henry IV, Act ii, sc. 4, l. 142 [FALSTAFF]

4538   Manhood is melted into courtesies, valour into compliment, and
men are only turned into tongue, and trim ones too: he is now as
valiant as Hercules that only tells a lie and swears it.
Much Ado about Nothing, Act iv, sc. 1, l. 322 [BEATRICE]

Manners

4539   Goaded with most sharp occasions,
Which lay nice manners by.
All's Well that Ends Well, Act v, sc. 1, l. 14 [HELENA]

4540   TOUCHSTONE: Wast ever in court, shepherd?
CORIN: No, truly.
TOUCHSTONE: Then thou art damned. . . . If thou never wast at
court, thou never sawest good manners; if thou never sawest
good manners, then thy manners must be wicked; and wickedness is sin, and sin is damnation. Thou art in a parlous state,
shepherd.
CORIN: Not a whit, Touchstone: those that are good manners
at the court are as ridiculous in the country as the behaviour of
the country is most mockable at the court.
As You Like It, Act iii, sc. 2, l. 35 [TOUCHSTONE]

4541   I am much sorry, sir,
You put me to forget a lady's manners,
By being so verbal.
Cymbeline, Act ii, sc. 3, l. 109 [IMOGEN]

4542   WORCESTER: In faith, my lord, you are too wilful-blame; . . .
You must needs learn, lord, to amend this fault:
Though sometimes it show greatness, courage, blood,—
And that's the dearest grace it renders you,—
Yet oftentimes it doth present harsh rage,
Defect of manners, want of government,
Price, haughtiness, opinion and disdain. . . .
HOTSPUR: Well, I am school'd: good manners be your speed!
I Henry IV, Act iii, sc. 1, l. 177 [WORCESTER]

4543   Men's evil manners live in brass; their virtues
We write in water.
Henry VIII, Act iv, sc. 2, l. 45 [GRIFFITH]

4544   Frame your manners to the time.
The Taming of the Shrew, Act i, sc. 1, l. 232 [LUCENTIO]

4545   Here's a million of manners.
The Two Gentlemen of Verona, Act ii, sc. 1, l. 104 [SPEED]

Mantuan

4546   Ah, good old Mantuan! I may speak of thee as the traveller doth
of Venice:
Venetia, Venetia,
Chi non ti vede non ti pretia.
Old Mantuan, old Mantuan! who understandeth thee not, loves
thee not.
Love's Labour's Lost, Act iv, sc. 2, l. 97 [HOLOFERNES]
(The old Mantuan of course was Vergil, who was born at
Mantua. The Italian proverb is from Florio's *Second Frutes*
[1591], whence Shakespeare probably took it.)

Mark

4547   I think you have hit the mark.
                    Henry VIII, Act ii, sc. 1, l. 165 [GENTLEMAN]
4548   MARIA: A mark marvellous well shot, for they both did hit it.
       BOYET: A mark! O, mark but that mark! A mark, says my lady!
       Let the mark have a prick in 't, to mete at, if it may be.
                    Love's Labour's Lost, Act iv, sc. 1, l. 132 [MARIA]
4549   God bless the mark!
                    Othello, Act i, sc. 1, l. 33 [IAGO]
4550   BENVOLIO: I aim'd so near, when I supposed you loved.
       ROMEO: A right good mark-man! And she 's fair I love.
       BENVOLIO: A right fair mark, fair coz, is soonest hit.
                    Romeo and Juliet, Act i, sc. 1, l. 211 [BENVOLIO]

Marriage

4551   A young man married is a man that 's marred.
                    All's Well that Ends Well, Act ii, sc. 3, l. 315 [PAROLLES]
4552   If you shall marry,
       You give away this hand, and that is mine;
       You give away heaven's vows, and those are mine;
       You give away yourself, which is known mine.
                    All's Well that Ends Well, Act v, sc. 3, l. 169 [DIANA]
4553   JAQUES: Will you be married, motley?
       TOUCHSTONE: As the ox hath his bow, sir, the horse his curb and
       the falcon her bells, so man hath his desires; and as pigeons bill,
       so wedlock would be nibbling.
                    As You Like It, Act iii, sc. 3, l. 79 [JAQUES]
4554   CELIA: Will you, Orlando, have to wife this Rosalind?
       ORLANDO: I will. . . .
       ROSALIND: Now tell me how long you would have her after you
       have possessed her.
       ORLANDO: For ever and a day.
       ROSALIND: Say 'a day' without the 'ever.'
                    As You Like It, Act iv, sc. 1, l. 130 [CELIA]
4555   I press in here, sir, amongst the rest of the country copulatives,
       to swear and to forswear; according as marriage binds and blood
       breaks: a poor virgin, sir, an ill-favoured thing, sir, but mine
       own; a poor humour of mine, sir, to take that that no man else will.
                    As You Like It, Act v, sc. 4, l. 57 [TOUCHSTONE]
4556   She, even she, . . . married with my uncle,
       My father's brother, but no more like my father
       Than I to Hercules: within a month:
       Ere yet the salt of most unrighteous tears
       Had left the flushing in her galled eyes,
       She married. O, most wicked speed, to post
       With such dexterity to incestuous sheets!
       It is not nor it cannot come to good:
       But break, my heart; for I must hold my tongue.
                    Hamlet, Act i, sc. 2, l. 151 [HAMLET]
4557   If thou wilt needs marry, marry a fool; for wise men know well
       enough what monsters you make of them. . . . I say, we will
       have no more marriages.
                    Hamlet, Act iii, sc. 1, l. 143 [HAMLET]
4558   Thou didst swear to me upon a parcel-gilt goblet, sitting in my
       Dolphin-chamber, at the round table, by a sea-coal fire, upon
       Wednesday in Wheeson week, when the prince broke thy head
       for liking his father to a singing-man of Windsor, thou didst

swear to me then, as I was washing thy wound, to marry me
and make me my lady thy wife.
II Henry IV, Act ii, sc. 1, l. 93 [HOSTESS]

4559 Marriage is a matter of more worth
Than to be dealt in by attorneyship; . . .
For what is wedlock forced but a hell,
An age of discord and continual strife?
Whereas the contrary bringeth bliss,
And is a pattern of celestial peace.
I Henry VI, Act v, sc. 5, l. 55 [SUFFOLK]

4560 Hasty marriage seldom proveth well. . . .
God forbid that I should wish them sever'd
Whom God hath join'd together.
III Henry VI, Act iv, sc. 1, l. 18 [GLOUCESTER]

4561 CHAMBERLAIN: It seems the marriage with his brother's wife
Has crept too near his conscience.
SUFFOLK: No, his conscience Has crept too near another lady.
Henry VIII, Act ii, sc. 2, l. 17 [CHAMBERLAIN]

4562 O curse of marriage,
That we can call these delicate creatures ours,
And not their appetites! I had rather be a toad,
And live upon the vapour of a dungeon,
Than keep a corner in the thing I love
For others' uses. Yet 'tis the plague of great ones;
Prerogatived are they less than the base;
'Tis destiny unshunnable, like death.
Othello, Act iii, sc. 3, l. 268 [OTHELLO]

4563 She's not well married that lives married long;
But she's best married that dies married young.
Romeo and Juliet, Act iv, sc. 5, l. 77 [FRIAR LAURENCE]

4564 I come to wive it wealthily in Padua;
If wealthily, then happily in Padua.
The Taming of the Shrew, Act i, sc. 2, l. 75 [PETRUCHIO]

4565 Will you, nill you, I will marry you.
Now, Kate, I am a husband for your turn;
For, by this light, whereby I see thy beauty, . . .
Thou must be married to no man but me. . . .
We will have rings and things and fine array;
And kiss me, Kate, we will be married o' Sunday.
The Taming of the Shrew, Act ii, sc. 1, l. 273 [PETRUCHIO]

4566 I knew a wench married in an afternoon as she went to the
garden for parsley to stuff a rabbit; and so may you.
The Taming of the Shrew, Act iv, sc. 4, l. 100 [BIONDELLO]

Master

4567 There is no more such masters: I may wander
From east to occident, cry out for service,
Try many, all good, serve truly, never
Find such another master.
Cymbeline, Act iv, sc. 2, l. 371 [IMOGEN]

4568 In this place most master wear no breeches.
II Henry VI, Act i, sc. 3, l. 149 [DUCHESS]

4569 We cannot all be masters, nor all masters
Cannot be truly follow'd.
Othello, Act i, sc. 1, l. 43 [IAGO]

4570 I will be master of what is mine own:
She is my goods, my chattels; she is my house,

My household stuff, my field, my barn,
My horse, my ox, my ass, my any thing;
And here she stands, touch her whoever dare.
            The Taming of the Shrew, Act iii, sc. 2, l. 231 [PETRUCHIO]

Matter

4571   What's the matter?
                        Antony and Cleopatra, Act i, sc. 3, l. 18 [ANTONY]
        How now! what's the matter?
                        Hamlet, Act ii, sc. 1, l. 75 [POLONIUS]
        How now! whose mare's dead, what's the matter?
                        II Henry IV, Act ii, sc. 1, l. 46 [FALSTAFF]
        (Phrases repeated *ad nauseam* throughout the plays, some-
        times three or four times in a single scene [*King Lear,* ii, 2],
        a dozen times in a single play [*Othello*].)
4572   I could have given less matter A better ear.
                        Antony and Cleopatra, Act ii, sc. 1, l. 31 [POMPEY]
4573   Small to greater matters must give way.
                        Antony and Cleopatra, Act ii, sc. 2, l. 11 [LEPIDUS]
4574   I love to cope him in these sullen fits,
        For then he's full of matter.
                        As You Like It, Act ii, sc. 1, l. 67 [DUKE]
4575   When you are gravelled for lack of matter, you might take
        occasion to kiss.
                        As You Like It, Act iv, sc. 1, l. 74 [ROSALIND]
4576   More matter, with less art.
                        Hamlet, Act ii, sc. 2, l. 95 [QUEEN]
4577   We'll put the matter to the present push.
                        Hamlet, Act v, sc. 1, l. 318 [KING]
4578   Thy honesty and love doth mince this matter.
                        Othello, Act ii, sc. 3, l. 247 [OTHELLO]
4579   More matter for a May morning.
                        Twelfth Night, Act iii, sc. 4, l. 156 [FABIAN]

May

4580   I did meet thee once with Helena,
        To do observance to a morn of May.
        A Midsummer Night's Dream, Act i, sc. 1, l. 166 [LYSANDER]
4581   No doubt they rose up early to observe
        The rite of May.
        A Midsummer Night's Dream, Act iv, sc. 1, l. 136 [THESEUS]
4582   Impossible . . . to make 'em sleep
        On May-day morning.
                        Henry VIII, Act v, sc. 4, l. 12 [MAN]

Mazzard

4583   Chapless, and knocked about the mazzard with a sexton's spade:
        here's fine revolution, an we had the trick to see't.
                        Hamlet, Act v, sc. 1, l. 97 [HAMLET]
4584   Let me go, sir, Or I'll knock you o'er the mazzard.
                        Othello, Act ii, sc. 3, l. 154 [CASSIO]

Mead

4585   The even mead, that erst brought sweetly forth
        The freckled cowslip, burnet and green clover,
        Wanting the scythe, all uncorrected, rank,
        Conceives by idleness and nothing teems

But hateful docks, rough thistles, kecksies, burs,
Losing both beauty and utility.
Henry V, Act v, sc. 2, l. 48 [BURGUNDY]

4586   Champains rich'd
With plenteous rivers and wide-skirted meads.
King Lear, Act i, sc. 1, l. 64 [LEAR]

4587   Meet we . . . in dale, forest, or mead,
By paved fountain or by rushy brook.
A Midsummer Night's Dream, Act ii, sc. 1, l. 83 [TITANIA]

Meals

4588   Unquiet meals make ill digestions. . . .
In food, in sport, and life's preserving rest
To be disturb'd would mad or man or beast.
The Comedy of Errors, Act v, sc. 1, l. 73 [ABBESS]

4589   Give them great meals of beef and iron and steel, they will
eat like wolves and fight like devils.
Henry V, Act iii, sc. 7, l. 161 [CONSTABLE]

Meaning

4590   POMPEY: I have fair meanings, sir.
ANTONY: And fair words to them.
Antony and Cleopatra, Act ii, sc. 6, l. 67 [POMPEY]

4591   What's your dark meaning, mouse, of this light word? . . .
We need more light to find your meaning out.
Love's Labour's Lost, Act v, sc. 2, l. 19 [ROSALINE]

4592   Take our good meaning, for our judgement sits
Five times in that ere once in our five wits.
Romeo and Juliet, Act i, sc. 4, l. 46 [MERCUTIO]

4593   Without characters, fame lives long.
Thus, like the formal vice, Iniquity,
I moralize two meanings in one word.
Richard III, Act iii, sc. 1, l. 81 [GLOUCESTER]

Measure

4594   Measure for measure must be answered.
III Henry VI, Act ii, sc. 6, l. 55 [WARWICK]

4595   There is measure in every thing, and so dance out the answer.
Much Ado about Nothing, Act ii, sc. 1, l. 74 [BEATRICE]

Meat

4596   It is meat and drink to me to see a clown.
As You Like It, Act v, sc. 1, l. 11 [TOUCHSTONE]

SLENDER: You are afraid if you see the bear loose, are you not?
ANNE: Ay, indeed, sir.
SLENDER: That's meat and drink to me, now.
The Merry Wives of Windsor, Act i, sc. 1, l. 304 [SLENDER]

4597   The capon burns, the pig falls from the spit,
The clock hath strucken twelve upon the bell;
My mistress made it one upon my cheek:
She is so hot because the meat is cold;
The meat is cold because you come not home;
You come not home because you have no stomach;
You have no stomach having broke your fast;
But we that know what 'tis to fast and pray
Are penitent for your default to-day. . . .
Methinks your maw, like mine, should be your clock
And strike you home without a messenger.
The Comedy of Errors, Act i, sc. 2, l. 44 [DROMIO OF EPHESUS]

4598   Thou say'st his meat was sauced with thy upbraidings.
                    The Comedy of Errors, Act v, sc. 1, l. 73 [ABBESS]
4599   What! you poor, base, rascally, cheating, lack-linen mate!
        Away, you mouldy rogue, away! I am meat for your master.
                    II Henry IV, Act ii, sc. 4, l. 133 [DOLL TEARSHEET]
4600   KATHARINA: I pray you, husband, be not so disquiet:
        The meat was well, if you were so contented.
        PETRUCHIO: I tell thee, Kate, 'twas burnt and dried away;
        And I expressly am forbid to touch it,
        For it engenders choler, planteth anger.
                    The Taming of the Shrew, Act iv, sc. 1, l. 171 [KATHARINA]

Medicine

4601   I have seen a medicine
        That's able to breathe life into a stone,
        Quicken a rock, and make you dance canary.
                    All's Well that Ends Well, Act ii, sc. 1, l. 75 [LAFEU]
4602   By medicine life may be prolong'd, yet death
        Will seize the doctor too.
                    Cymbeline, Act v, sc. 5, l. 29 [CYMBELINE]
4603   If the rascal have not given me medicines to make me love him,
        I'll be hanged; it could not be else; I have drunk medicines.
                    I Henry IV, Act ii, sc. 2, l. 19 [FALSTAFF]
4604   Work on, my medicine, work! Thus credulous fools are caught;
        And many worthy and chaste dames even thus,
        All guiltless, meet reproach.
                    Othello, Act iv, sc. 1, l. 45 [IAGO]

Meditation

4605   Close up his eyes and draw the curtain close;
        And let us all to meditation.
                    II Henry VI, Act iii, sc. 3, l. 32 [KING HENRY]
4606   We'll leave you to your meditations
        How to live better.
                    Henry VIII, Act iii, sc. 2, l. 345 [NORFOLK]
4607   In maiden meditation fancy-free.
                    A Midsummer Night's Dream, Act ii, sc. 1, l. 164 [OBERON]

Meekness

4608   They can be meek that have no other cause.
                    The Comedy of Errors, Act ii, sc. 1, l. 33 [ADRIANA]
4609   You're meek and humble-mouth'd; . . . but your heart
        Is cramm'd with arrogancy, spleen, and pride.
                    Henry VIII, Act ii, sc. 4, l. 107 [QUEEN KATHARINE]
4610   DUCHESS: God bless thee; and put meekness in thy mind,
        Love, charity, obedience, and true duty!
        GLOUCESTER: Amen: and make me die a good old man!
                    Richard III, Act ii, sc. 2, l. 106 [DUCHESS]

Melancholy

4611   I take my young lord to be a very melancholy man. . . . He
        will look upon his boot and sing; mend the ruff and sing; pick
        his teeth and sing. I know a man that had this trick of
        melancholy sold a goodly manor for a song.
                    All's Well that Ends Well, Act iii, sc. 2, l. 4 [CLOWN]
4612   I can suck melancholy out of a song, as a weasel sucks eggs.
                    As You Like It, Act ii, sc. 5, l. 12 [JAQUES]
4613   I have neither the scholar's melancholy, which is emulation,
        nor the musician's, which is fantastical, nor the courtier's, which

is proud, nor the soldier's, which is ambitious, nor the lawyer's,
which is politic, nor the lady's, which is nice, nor the lover's,
which is all these: but it is a melancholy of mine own, compounded of many simples, extracted from many objects, and
indeed the sundry contemplation of my travels, in which my
often rumination wraps me in a most humorous sadness.

As You Like It, Act iv, sc. 1, l. 10 [JAQUES]

4614   Sweet recreation barr'd, what doth ensue
But moody and dull melancholy,
Kinsman to grim and comfortless despair,
And at her heels a huge infectious troop
Of pale distemperatures and foes to life?

The Comedy of Errors, Act v, sc. 1, l. 78 [ABBESS]

4615   O melancholy!
Who ever yet could sound thy bottom? find
The ooze, to show what coast thy sluggish crare
Might easiliest harbor in?

Cymbeline, Act iv, sc. 2, l. 203 [BELARIUS]

("Crare," a small trading vessel.)

4616   There's something in his soul,
O'er which his melancholy sits on brood;
And I do doubt the hatch and the disclose
Will be some danger.

Hamlet, Act iii, sc. 1, l. 172 [KING]

4617   'Sblood, I am as melancholy as a gib cat or a lugged bear.

I Henry IV, Act i, sc. 2, l. 82 [FALSTAFF]

4618   If that surly spirit, melancholy,
Had baked thy blood and made it heavy-thick,
Which else runs tickling up and down the veins,
Making that idiot, laughter, keep men's eyes
And strain their cheeks to idle merriment.

King John, Act iii, sc. 3, l. 42 [KING JOHN]

4619   My cue is villanous melancholy, with a sigh like
Tom o' Bedlam.

King Lear, Act i, sc. 2, l. 147 [EDMUND]

4620   Why should . . .
The sad companion, dull-eyed melancholy,
Be my so used a guest?

Pericles, Act i, sc. 2, l. 2 [PERICLES]

4621   Melancholy is the nurse of frenzy.

The Taming of the Shrew, Induction, sc. 2, l. 135
[MESSENGER]

Memory

4622   Why should I write this down, that's riveted,
Screw'd to my memory?

Cymbeline, Act ii, sc. 2, l. 43 [IACHIMO]

4623   Of our dear brother's death,
The memory be green.

Hamlet, Act i, sc. 2, l. 1 [KING]

4624   LAERTES: Farewell, Ophelia; and remember well
What I have said to you.
OPHELIA: 'Tis in my memory lock'd,
And you yourself shall keep the key of it.

Hamlet, Act i, sc. 3, l. 84 [LAERTES]

4625   GHOST: Adieu, adieu! Hamlet, remember me. . . .
HAMLET: Remember thee!

Ay, thou poor ghost, while memory holds a seat
In this distracted globe. Remember thee!
Yea, from the table of my memory
I'll wipe away all trivial fond records,
All saws of books, all forms, all pressures past,
That youth and observation copied there;
And thy commandment all alone shall live
Within the book and volume of my brain,
Unmix'd with baser matter.
Hamlet, Act i, sc. 5, l. 91 [GHOST]

4626 O heavens! die two months ago, and not forgotten yet! Then
there's hope a great man's memory may outlive his life half
a year: but, by'r lady, he must build churches, then.
Hamlet, Act iii, sc. 2, l. 140 [HAMLET]

4627 I'll note you in my book of memory.
I Henry VI, Act ii, sc. 4, l. 101 [PLANTAGENET]

4628 Begot in the ventrical of memory, nourished in the womb of
pia mater, and delivered upon the mellowing of occasion.
Love's Labour's Lost, Act iv, sc. 2, l. 71 [HOLOFERNES]

4629 Memory, the warder of the brain,
Shall be a fume, and the receipt of reason
A limbeck only.
Macbeth, Act i, sc. 7, l. 65 [LADY MACBETH]

4630   It comes o'er my memory,
As doth the raven o'er the infected house,
Boding to all.
Othello, Act iv, sc. 1, l. 20 [OTHELLO]

Merchant

4631 NURSE: I pray you, sir, what saucy merchant was this, that
was so full of his ropery?
ROMEO: A gentleman, nurse, that loves to hear himself talk,
and will speak more in a minute than he will stand to in a
month.
Romeo and Juliet, Act ii, sc. 4, l. 152 [NURSE]

4632 A merchant of great traffic through the world.
The Taming of the Shrew, Act i, sc. 1, l. 12 [LUCENTIO]

4633 Faith, gentlemen, now I play a merchant's part,
And venture madly on a desperate mart.
The Taming of the Shrew, Act ii, sc. 1, l. 328 [BAPTISTA]

4634 Let us, like merchants, show our foulest wares,
And think, perchance, they'll sell.
Troilus and Cressida, Act i, sc. 3, l. 359 [ULYSSES]

Mercy

4635 There is no more mercy in him than there is milk in a male
tiger.
Coriolanus, Act v, sc. 4, l. 30 [MENENIUS]

4636   Whereto serves mercy
But to confront the visage of offence?
Hamlet, Act iii, sc. 3, l. 46 [KING]

4637 I cry you, mercy, 'tis but Quid for Quo.
I Henry VI, Act v, sc. 3, l. 109 [MARGARET]

4638 Mercy is not itself, that oft looks so;
Pardon is still the nurse of second woe.
Measure for Measure, Act ii, sc. 1, l. 297 [ESCALUS]

4639   No ceremony that to great ones 'longs,
Not the king's crown, nor the 'deputed sword,
The marshal's truncheon, nor the judge's robe,
Become them with one half so good a grace
As mercy does.
Measure for Measure, Act ii, sc. 2, l. 59 [ISABELLA]

4640   Lawful mercy Is nothing kin to foul redemption.
Measure for Measure, Act ii, sc. 4, l. 112 [ISABELLA]

4641   DUKE: How shalt thou hope for mercy, rendering none?
SHYLOCK: What judgement should I dread, doing no wrong?
The Merchant of Venice, Act iv, sc. 1, l. 88 [DUKE]

4642   The quality of mercy is not strain'd,
It droppeth as the gentle rain from heaven
Upon the place beneath: it is twice blest;
It blesseth him that gives and him that takes:
'Tis mightiest in the mightiest: it becomes
The throned monarch better than his crown;
His sceptre shows the force of temporal power,
The attribute to awe and majesty,
Wherein doth sit the dread and fear of kings;
But mercy is above this sceptred sway;
It is enthroned in the hearts of kings,
It is an attribute to God himself;
And earthly power doth then show likest God's
When mercy seasons justice. Therefore, Jew,
Though justice be thy plea, consider this,
That, in the course of justice, none of us
Should see salvation: we do pray for mercy;
And that same prayer doth teach us all to render
The deeds of mercy.
The Merchant of Venice, Act iv, sc. 1, l. 184 [PORTIA]

4643   Mercy but murders, pardoning those that kill.
Romeo and Juliet, Act iii, sc. 1, l. 202 [PRINCE]

4644   I'll turn my mercy out o' doors and make a stockfish of thee.
The Tempest, Act iii, sc. 2, l. 78 [STEPHANO]

4645   Nothing emboldens sin so much as mercy.
Timon of Athens, Act iii, sc. 5, l. 3 [SENATOR]

4646   Wilt thou draw near the nature of the gods?
Draw near them then in being merciful:
Sweet mercy is nobility's true badge.
Titus Andronicus, Act i, sc. 1. 117 [TAMORA]

4647   Brother, you have a vice of mercy in you,
Which better fits a lion than a man.
Troilus and Cressida, Act v, sc. 3, l. 37 [TROILUS]

Merit

4648   If men were to be saved by merit, what hole in hell were hot enough for him?
I Henry IV, Act i, sc. 2, l. 120 [FALSTAFF]

4649   You see, my good wenches, how men of merit are sought after:
the undeserver may sleep, when the man of action is called on.
II Henry IV, Act ii, sc. 4, l. 405 [FALSTAFF]

4650   The force of his own merit makes his way;
A gift that heaven gives for him, which buys
A place next to the king.
Henry VIII, Act i, sc. 1, l. 64 [NORFOLK]

4651   Who shall go about
To cozen fortune and be honourable
Without the stamp of merit? Let none presume
To wear an undeserved dignity.
The Merchant of Venice, Act ii, sc. 9, l. 37 [ARAGON]

4652   Our head shall go bare till merit crown it.
Troilus and Cressida, Act iii, sc. 2, l. 100 [TROILUS]

Mermaid

4653   O, train me not, sweet mermaid, with thy note
To drown me in thy sister's flood of tears:
Sing, siren, for thyself and I will dote;
Spread o'er the silver waves thy golden hairs. . . .
But, lest myself be guilty to self-wrong,
I'll stop mine ears against the mermaid's song.
The Comedy of Errors, Act iii, sc. 2, l. 45
[ANTIPHOLUS OF SYRACUSE]

4654   Once I sat upon a promontory,
And heard a mermaid on a dolphin's back
Uttering such dulcet and harmonious breath
That the rude sea grew civil at her song
And certain stars shot madly from their spheres,
To hear the sea-maid's music.
A Midsummer Night's Dream, Act ii, sc. 1, l. 149 [OBERON]

Merry

4655   OPHELIA: You are merry, my lord.
HAMLET: Who, I? . . . O God, your only jig-maker. What should
a man do but be merry?
Hamlet, Act iii, sc. 2, l. 129 [OPHELIA]

4656   PRINCE: Shall we be merry?
POINS: As merry as crickets, my lad.
I Henry IV, Act ii, sc. 4, l. 99 [PRINCE]

4657   Be merry, be merry, my wife has all;
For women are shrews, both short and tall:
'Tis merry in hall when beards wag all,
And welcome merry Shrove-tide.
II Henry IV, Act v, sc. 3, l. 35 [SILENCE]

4658   'Tis ever common
That men are merriest when they are from home.
Henry V, Act i, sc. 2, l. 271 [KING HENRY]

4659   As merry
As, first, good company, good wine, good welcome,
Can make good people.
Henry VIII, Act i, sc. 4, l. 5 [GUILDFORD]

4660   By my christendom,
So I were out of prison and kept sheep,
I should be as merry as the day is long.
King John, Act iv, sc. 1, l. 16 [ARTHUR]
Saint Peter . . . shows me where the bachelors sit, and there
live we as merry as the day is long.
Much Ado about Nothing, Act ii, sc. 1, l. 50 [BEATRICE]

4661   Be merry, and employ your chiefest thoughts
To courtship and such fair ostents of love.
The Merchant of Venice, Act ii, sc. 8, l. 43 [ANTONIO]

4662   I am not merry; but I do beguile
The thing I am, by seeming otherwise.
Othello, Act ii, sc. 1, l. 123 [DESDEMONA]

Metal

4663 Here's metal more attractive.
Hamlet, Act iii, sc. 2, l. 117 [HAMLET]

4664   I am made
Of the self-same metal that my sister is.
King Lear, Act i, sc. 1, l. 70 [REGAN]

4665 Let there be some more test made of my metal,
Before so noble and so great a figure
Be stamp'd upon it.
Measure for Measure, Act i, sc. 1, l. 49 [ANGELO]

4666 They have all been touch'd and found base metal.
Timon of Athens, Act iii, sc. 3, l. 6 [SERVANT]

Mettle

4667 Of unimproved mettle hot and full.
Hamlet, Act i, sc. 1, l. 96 [HORATIO]

4668 I did not think Master Silence had been a man of this mettle.
II Henry IV, Act v, sc. 3, l. 40 [FALSTAFF]

4669   You, good yeomen,
Whose limbs were made in England, show us here
The mettle of your pasture.
Henry V, Act iii, sc. 1, l. 25 [KING HENRY]

4670 By this day and this light, the fellow has mettle enough in his
belly. . . . I pray you to serve God, and keep you out of prawls, and
prabbles.
Henry V, Act iv, sc. 8, l. 66 [FLUELLEN]

4671 Why, now I see there's mettle in thee.
Othello, Act iv, sc. 2, l. 206 [IAGO]

Midnight

4672 In the dead vast and middle of the night.
Hamlet, Act i, sc. 2, l. 198 [HORATIO]
Upon the heavy middle of the night.
Measure for Measure, Act iv, sc. 1, l. 35 [ISABELLA]

4673 'Tis now the very witching time of night,
When churchyards yawn and hell itself breathes out
Contagion to this world: now could I drink hot blood,
And do such bitter business as the day
Would quake to look on.
Hamlet, Act iii, sc. 2, l. 406 [HAMLET]

4674   Now the hungry lion roars,
   And the wolf behowls the moon;
  Whilst the heavy ploughman snores,
   All with weary task foredone. . . .
  Now it is the time of night
   That the graves all gaping wide,
  Every one lets forth his sprite,
   In the church-way paths to glide.
A Midsummer Night's Dream, Act v, sc. 1, l. 378 [PUCK]

4675 We have heard the chimes at midnight, Master Shallow.
II Henry IV, Act iii, sc. 2, l. 229 [FALSTAFF]

4676 The iron tongue of midnight hath told twelve:
Lovers, to bed; 'tis almost fairy time.
A Midsummer Night's Dream, Act v, sc. 1, l. 370 [THESEUS]

Millstones

4677 Your eyes drop millstones, when fools' eyes drop tears.
Richard III, Act i, sc. 3, l. 354 [GLOUCESTER]

4678   He will weep . . . millstones; as he lesson'd us to weep.
                            Richard III, Act i, sc. 4, l. 245 [MURDERER]
4679   PANDARUS: Hecuba laughed until that her eyes ran o'er.
        CRESSIDA: With mill-stones.
                            Troilus and Cressida, Act i, sc. 2, l. 156 [PANDARUS]

Mind

4680   Give me leave
        To speak my mind, and I will through and through
        Cleanse the foul body of the infected world,
        If they will patiently receive my medicine.
                            As You Like It, Act ii, sc. 7, l. 58 [JAQUES]
4681   O, what a noble mind is here o'erthrown!
        The courtier's, soldier's, scholar's, eye, tongue, sword;
        The expectancy and rose of the fair state,
        The glass of fashion and the mould of form,
        The observed of all observers, quite, quite down!
        And I, of ladies most deject and wretched,
        That suck'd the honey of his music vows,
        Now see that noble and most sovereign reason,
        Like sweet bells jangled, out of tune and harsh;
        That unmatch'd form and feature of blown youth
        Blasted with ecstasy: O, woe is me,
        To have seen what I have seen, see what I see!
                            Hamlet, Act iii, sc. 1, l. 158 [OPHELIA]
4682   'Tis with my mind
        As with the tide swell'd up unto his height,
        That makes a still-stand, running neither way.
                            II Henry IV, Act ii, sc. 3, l. 62 [NORTHUMBERLAND]
4683   The incessant care and labour of his mind
        Hath wrought the mure that should confine it in
        So thin that life looks through and will break out.
                            II Henry IV, Act iv, sc. 4, l. 118 [CLARENCE]
4684   You bear a gentle mind, and heavenly blessings
        Follow such creatures.
                            Henry VIII, Act ii, sc. 3, l. 57 [CHAMBERLAIN]
        (Referring to Anne Bullen.)
4685   It is meet
        That noble minds keep ever with their likes;
        For who so firm that cannot be seduced?
                            Julius Cæsar, Act i, sc. 2, l. 313 [CASSIUS]
4686   When the mind's free,
        The body's delicate: the tempest in my mind
        Doth from my senses take all feeling else
        Save what beats there.
                            King Lear, Act iii, sc. 4, l. 11 [LEAR]
4687   Infected minds
        To their deaf pillows will discharge their secrets:
        More needs she the divine than the physician.
                            Macbeth, Act v, sc. 1, l. 80 [DOCTOR]
4688   The mind I sway by and the heart I bear
        Shall never sag with doubt nor shake with fear.
                            Macbeth, Act v, sc. 3, l. 9 [MACBETH]
4689   MACBETH: How does your patient, doctor?
        DOCTOR: Not so sick, my lord,
        As she is troubled with thick-coming fancies,
        That keep her from her rest.

MACBETH: Cure her of that.
Canst thou not minister to a mind diseased,
Pluck from the memory a rooted sorrow,
Raze out the written troubles of the brain
And with some sweet oblivious antidote
Cleanse the stuff'd bosom of that perilous stuff
Which weighs upon the heart?
DOCTOR: Therein the patient Must minister to himself.
Macbeth, Act v, sc. 3, l. 37 [MACBETH]

4690 Your mind is tossing on the ocean;
There, where your argosies with portly sail, . . .
Do overpeer the petty traffickers,
That curtsy to them, do them reverence,
As they fly by them with their woven wings.
The Merchant of Venice, Act i, sc. 1, l. 8 [SALARINO]

4691 Men that hazard all
Do it in hope of fair advantages:
A golden mind stoops not to shows of dross.
The Merchant of Venice, Act ii, sc. 7, l. 18 [MOROCCO]

4692 IAGO: Patience, I say, your mind perhaps may change.
OTHELLO: Never, Iago. Like to the Pontic sea,
Whose icy current and compulsive course
Ne'er feels retiring ebb, but keeps due on
To the Propontic and the Hellespont,
Even so my bloody thoughts, with violent pace,
Shall ne'er look back, ne'er ebb to humble love,
Till that a capable and wide revenge
Swallow them up.
Othello, Act iii, sc. 3, l. 452 [IAGO]

4693 Men have marble, women waxen, minds.
The Rape of Lucrece, l. 1240

4694 Our purses shall be proud, our garments poor;
For 'tis the mind that makes the body rich.
The Taming of the Shrew, Act iv, sc. 3, l. 172 [PETRUCHIO]

4695 Neglecting worldly ends, all dedicate
To closeness and the bettering of my mind.
The Tempest, Act i, sc. 2, l. 89 [PROSPERO]

4696 My mind is troubled, like a fountain stirr'd;
And I myself see not the bottom of it.
Troilus and Cressida, Act iii, sc. 3, l. 311 [ACHILLES]

4697 She bore a mind that envy could not but call fair.
Twelfth Night, Act ii, sc. 1, l. 31 [SEBASTIAN]

4698 [May] the tailor make thy doublet of changeable taffeta, for thy
mind is a very opal.
Twelfth Night, Act ii, sc. 4, l. 76 [CLOWN]

Mine

4699 Mine will now be yours;
And, should we shift estates, yours would be mine.
Antony and Cleopatra, Act v, sc. 2, l. 150 [CLEOPATRA]
What's mine is yours and what is yours is mine.
Measure for Measure, Act v, sc. 1, l. 543 [DUKE]

4700 This title honours me and mine.
III Henry VI, Act iv, sc. 1, l. 72 [QUEEN ELIZABETH]
She shall have me and mine.
The Taming of the Shrew, Act ii, sc. 1, l. 385 [GREMIO]

4701   Mine own, and not mine own.
                A Midsummer Night's Dream, Act iv, sc. 1, l. 196 [HELENA]

4702   Mine and mine I loved and mine I praised
        And mine that I was proud on, mine so much
        That I myself was to myself not mine.
                Much Ado about Nothing, Act iv, sc. 1, l. 138 [LEONATO]

4703   Then love-devouring death do what he dare;
        It is enough I may but call her mine.
                Romeo and Juliet, Act ii, sc. 6, l. 8 [ROMEO]

4704   And if I die to-morrow, this is hers,
        If whilst I live she will be only mine.
                The Taming of the Shrew, Act ii, sc. 1, l. 363 [GREMIO]

Minister

4705   He that of greatest works is finisher
        Oft does them by the weakest minister.
                All's Well that Ends Well, Act ii, sc. 1, l. 139 [HELENA]

4706   Break thou in pieces and consume to ashes,
        Thou foul accursed minister of hell!
                I Henry VI, Act v, sc. 4, l. 92 [YORK]

4707   Avaunt, thou dreadful minister of hell!
                Richard III, Act i, sc. 2, l. 46 [ANNE]

4708   TAMORA: These are my ministers, and come with me.
        TITUS: Are these thy ministers? what are they call'd?
        TAMORA: Rapine and Murder; therefore called so,
        Cause they take vengeance of such kind of men.
        TITUS: Good Lord, how like the empress' sons they are!
                Titus Andronicus, Act v, sc. 2, l. 60 [TAMORA]

Minutes

4709   The pilot's glass
        Hath told the thievish minutes how they pass.
                All's Well that Ends Well, Act ii, sc. 1, l. 168 [HELENA]

4710   O God! methinks it were a happy life,
        To be no better than a homely swain; . . .
        To carve out dials quaintly, point by point,
        Thereby to see the minutes how they run.
                III Henry VI, Act ii, sc. 5, l. 21 [KING]

4711   Like as the waves make toward the pebbled shore,
        So do our minutes hasten to their end.
                Sonnet lx, l. 1

4712   The dial [will show] how thy precious minutes waste.
                Sonnet lxxvii, l. 2

Miracles

4713   Great seas have dried
        When miracles have by the greatest been denied.
                All's Well that Ends Well, Act ii, sc. 1, l. 143 [HELENA]

4714   They say miracles are past; and we have our philosophical persons,
        to make modern and familiar, things supernatural and causeless.
        Hence it is that we make trifles of terrors, ensconsing ourselves
        into seeming knowledge, when we should submit ourselves to an
        unknown fear.
                All's Well that Ends Well, Act ii, sc. 3, l. 1 [LAFEU]

4715   Miracles are ceased;
        And therefore we must needs admit the means
        How things are perfected.
                Henry V, Act i, sc. 1, l. 67 [CANTERBURY]

4716   CARDINAL: Duke Humphrey has done a miracle to-day.
SUFFOLK: True; made the lame to leap and fly away.
GLOUCESTER: But you have done more miracles than I;
You made in a day, my lord, whole towns to fly.

II Henry VI, Act ii, sc. 1, l. 161 [CARDINAL]

Mirth

4717   Then is there mirth in heaven
When earthly things made even
Atone together.

As You Like It, Act v, sc. 4, l. 114 [HYMEN]

4718   IMOGEN: Continues well my lord? . . .
Is he disposed to mirth? I hope he is.
IACHIMO: Exceeding pleasant; none a stranger there
So merry and so gamesome: he is call'd
The Briton reveller.

Cymbeline, Act i, sc. 6, l. 56 [IMOGEN]

4719   I have of late—but wherefore I know not—lost all my mirth.

Hamlet, Act ii, sc. 2, l. 307 [HAMLET]

4720   Be large in mirth.

Macbeth, Act iii, sc. 4, l. 11 [MACBETH]

4721   With mirth and laughter let old wrinkles come,
And let my liver rather heat with wine
Than my heart cool with mortifying groans.
Why should a man, whose blood is warm within,
Sit like his grandsire cut in alabaster?
Sleep when he wakes and creep into the jaundice
By being peevish?

The Merchant of Venice, Act i, sc. 1, l. 80 [GRATIANO]

4722   I would entreat you rather to put on
Your boldest suit of mirth, for we have friends
That purpose merriment.

The Merchant of Venice, Act ii, sc. 2, l. 210 [BASSANIO]

4723   Awake the pert and nimble spirit of mirth:
Turn melancholy forth to funerals.

A Midsummer Night's Dream, Act i, sc. 1, l. 13 [THESEUS]

4724   From the crown of his head to the sole of his foot, he is all mirth.

Much Ado about Nothing, Act iii, sc. 2, l. 9 [DON PEDRO]

4725   How well this honest mirth becomes their labour!

Pericles, Act ii, sc. 1, l. 99 [PERICLES]

4726   Prepare for mirth, for mirth becomes a feast.

Pericles, Act ii, sc. 3, l. 7 [SIMONIDES]

4727   Who buys a minute's mirth to wail a week?
Or sells eternity to get a toy?
For one sweet grape who will the vine destroy?

The Rape of Lucrece, l. 213 [TARQUIN]

4728   Let's be red with mirth.

The Winter's Tale, Act iv, sc. 4, l. 54 [FLORIZEL]

Mischief

4729   OPHELIA: What means this, my lord?
HAMLET: Marry, this is miching mallecho; it means mischief.

Hamlet, Act iii, sc. 2, l. 147 [OPHELIA]

("Miching mallecho," sneaking villainy.)

4730   He cares not what mischief he does, if his weapon be out: he will
foin like any devil; he will spare neither man, woman, nor child.

II Henry IV, Act ii, sc. 1, l. 16 [HOSTESS]

("Foin," to thrust with a sword.)

4731 You see what mischief and what murder too
   Hath been enacted through your enmity;
   Then be at peace, except ye thirst for blood.
        I Henry VI, Act iii, sc. 1, l. 115 [WARWICK]

4732 O God, what mischiefs work the wicked ones,
   Heaping confusion on their own heads thereby!
        II Henry VI, Act ii, sc. 1, l. 186 [KING HENRY]

4733   Mischief, thou art afoot,
   Take thou what course thou wilt!
        Julius Cæsar, Act iii, sc. 2, l. 265 [ANTONY]

4734 To mourn a mischief that is past and gone
   Is the next way to draw new mischief on.
        Othello, Act i, sc. 3, l. 204 [DUKE]

4735   O mischief, thou art swift
   To enter in the thoughts of desperate men!
        Romeo and Juliet, Act v, sc. 1, l. 35 [ROMEO]

Miser

4736 I can compare our rich misers to nothing so fitly as to a whale;
   a' plays and tumbles, driving the poor fry before him, and at last
   devours them all at a mouthful.
        Pericles, Act ii, sc. 1, l. 32 [FISHERMAN]

4737 The aged man that coffers-up his gold
   Is plagued with cramps and gouts and painful fits;
   And scarce hath eyes his treasure to behold,
   But like still-pining Tantalus he sits,
   And useless barns the harvest of his wits;
   Having no other pleasure of his gain
   But torment that it cannot cure his pain.
        The Rape of Lucrece, l. 855 [LUCRECE]

Misery

4738 Thus misery doth part The flux of company.
        As You Like It, Act ii, sc. 1, l. 51 [JAQUES]
   (A variation of the proverb, "Poverty parts good company.")

4739 Nothing almost sees miracles But misery.
        King Lear, Act ii, sc. 2, l. 172 [KENT]

4740 The miserable have no other medicine
   But only hope.
        Measure for Measure, Act iii, sc. 1, l. 2 [CLAUDIO]

4741 Misery makes sport to mock itself.
        Richard II, Act ii, sc. 1, l. 85 [GAUNT]

4742 Misery acquaints a man with strange bed-fellows.
        The Tempest, Act ii, sc. 2, l. 44 [TRINCULO]

4743   Willing misery
   Outlives incertain pomp, is crown'd before:
   The one is filling still, never complete;
   The other, at high wish.
        Timon of Athens, Act iv, sc. 3, l. 242 [APEMANTUS]

4744 It easeth some, though none it ever cured,
   To think their dolour others have endured.
        The Rape of Lucrece, l. 1581
   (A variation of the proverb, "Misery loves company.")

Misfortune

4745 The cheapest of us is ten groats too dear.
   What art thou? and how comest thou hither,

Where no man never comes but that sad dog
That brings me food to make misfortune live?
Richard II, Act v, sc. 5, l. 68 [KING RICHARD]

4746 One writ with me in sour misfortune's book!
Romeo and Juliet, Act v, sc. 3, l. 82 [ROMEO]

Mistress

4747 To each of you a fair and virtuous mistress
Fall, when Love please! marry, to each, but one!
All's Well that Ends Well, Act ii, sc. 3, l. 63 [HELENA]

4748 My eyes, my lord, can look as swift as yours:
You saw the mistress, I beheld the maid.
The Merchant of Venice, Act iii, sc. 2, l. 199 [GRATIANO]

4749 My mistress' eyes are nothing like the sun;
Coral is far more red than her lips' red;
If snow be white, why then her breasts are dun;
If hairs be wires, black wires grow on her head.
I have seen roses damask'd red and white,
But no such roses see I in her cheeks;
And in some perfumes is there more delight
Than in the breath that from my mistress reeks.
I love to hear her speak, yet well I know
That music hath a far more pleasing sound;
I grant I never saw a goddess go;
My mistress, when she walks, treads on the ground:
And yet, by heaven, I think my love as rare
As any she belied with false compare.
Sonnet cxxx, l. 1

4750 The mistress which I serve quickens what's dead
And makes my labours pleasures: O she is
Ten times more gentle than her father's crabb'd,
And he's composed of harshness.
The Tempest, Act iii, sc. 1, l. 6 [FERDINAND]

4751 O mistress mine, where are you roaming?
O, stay and hear; your true love's coming,
That can sing both high and low:
Trip no further, pretty sweeting;
Journeys end in lovers meeting,
Every wise man's son doth know.

What is love? 'tis not hereafter;
Present mirth hath present laughter;
What's to come is still unsure:
In delay there lies no plenty;
Then come kiss me, sweet and twenty,
Youth's a stuff will not endure.
Twelfth Night, Act ii, sc. 3, l. 40 [CLOWN]

Mocking

4752 Nay, but the devil take mocking: speak, sad brow and true maid.
As You Like It, Act iii, sc. 2, l. 226 [ROSALIND]

4753 Afflict me with thy mocks, pity me not;
As till that time I shall not pity thee.
As You Like It, Act iii, sc. 5, l. 33 [PHEBE]

4754 FRENCH AMBASSADOR: [The Dauphin] sends you
This tun of treasure. . . .
KING HENRY: What treasure, uncle?

EXETER: Tennis-balls, my liege.
KING HENRY: We are glad the Dauphin is so pleasant with us;
His present and your pains we thank you for:
When we have match'd our rackets to these balls,
We will, in France, by God's grace, play a set
Shall strike his father's crown into the hazard. . . .
And tell the pleasant prince this mock of his
Hath turn'd his balls to gun-stones; and his soul
Shall stand sore charged for the wasteful vengeance
That shall fly with them: for many a thousand widows
Shall this his mock mock out of their dear husbands;
Mock mothers from their sons, mock castles down;
And some are yet ungotten and unborn
That shall have cause to curse the Dauphin's scorn. . . .
His jest will savour but of shallow wit
When thousands weep more than did laugh at it.
                    Henry V, Act i, sc. 2, l. 254 [FRENCH AMBASSADOR]

Modesty

4755   Her looks do argue her replete with modesty;
Her words do show her wit incomparable;
All her perfections challenge sovereignty:
One way or other, she is for a king,
And she shall be my love, or else my queen.
                    III Henry VI, Act iii, sc. 2, l. 84 [KING EDWARD]

4756   Can it be
That modesty may more betray our sense
Than woman's lightness?
                    Measure for Measure, Act ii, sc. 2, l. 168 [ANGELO]

4757   Pray thee, take pain
To allay with some cold drops of modesty
Thy skipping spirit.
                    The Merchant of Venice, Act ii, sc. 2, l. 194 [BASSANIO]

4758   Do not impeach your modesty too much, . . .
To trust the opportunity of night
And the ill counsel of a desert place
With the rich worth of your virginity.
                    A Midsummer Night's Dream, Act ii, sc. 1, l. 214 [DEMETRIUS]

4759   My modesty, The jewel in my dower.
                    The Tempest, Act iii, sc. 1, l. 53 [MIRANDA]

Money

4760   He that wants money, means and content is without three good
friends.
                    As You Like It, Act iii, sc. 2, l. 26 [CORIN]

4761   IMOGEN: Here's money for my meat:
I would have left it on the board so soon
As I had made my meal, and parted
With prayers for the provider.
GUIDERIUS: Money, youth?
ARVIRAGUS: All gold and silver rather turn to dirt!
As 'tis no better reckon'd, but of those
Who worship dirty gods.
                    Cymbeline, Act iii, sc. 6, l. 50 [IMOGEN]

4762   I can raise no money by vile means:
By heaven, I had rather coin my heart,
And drop my blood for drachmas, than to wring

From the hard hands of peasants their vile trash
By any indirection.
> *Julius Cæsar,* Act iv, sc. **3**, l. **71** [BRUTUS]

4763   Tester I'll have in pouch when thou shalt lack,
Base Phrygian Turk!
> *The Merry Wives of Windsor,* Act i, sc. **3**, l. **96** [PISTOL]

4764   FORD: They say, if money go before, all ways do lie open.
FALSTAFF: Money is a good soldier, sir, and will on.
> *The Merry Wives of Windsor,* Act ii, sc. **2**, l. **175** [FORD]

4765   Put money in thy purse. . . . I say, put money in thy purse; . . .
put money in thy purse, . . . put but money in thy purse, . . . fill
thy purse with money: . . . put money in thy purse. . . . Make
all the money thou canst. . . . Go, make money. . . . Traverse!
go, provide thy money.
> *Othello,* Act i, sc. **3**, l. **345** [IAGO]

4766   I tell you, he that can lay hold of her
Shall have the chinks.
> *Romeo and Juliet,* Act i, sc. **5**, l. **118** [NURSE]

4767   Nothing comes amiss, so money comes withal.
> *The Taming of the Shrew,* Act i, sc. **2**, l. **82** [GRUMIO]

Monk

4768   All hoods make not monks.
> *Henry VIII,* Act iii, sc. **1**, l. **23** [QUEEN KATHARINE]
("Habit maketh no monk" was the earliest form of this
proverb.)

4769   Cucullus non facit monachum.
> *Measure for Measure,* Act v, sc. **1**, l. **263** [LUCIO]
(Quoting the Latin form of the proverb, "The cowl doesn't
make the monk.")

4770   Cucullus non facit monachum; that's as much to say as I wear
not motley in my brain.
> *Twelfth Night,* Act i, sc. **5**, l. **62** [CLOWN]

Monument

4771   If the quick fire of youth light not your mind,
You are no maiden, but a monument.
> *All's Well that Ends Well,* Act iv, sc. **2**, l. **5** [BERTRAM]

4772   Sore-shaming
Those rich-left heirs that let their fathers lie
Without a monument!
> *Cymbeline,* Act iv, sc. **2**, l. **225** [ARVIRAGUS]

4773   This grave shall have a living monument.
> *Hamlet,* Act v, sc. **1**, l. **320** [KING]

4774   If a man do not erect in this age his own tomb ere he dies, he
shall live no longer in monument than the bell rings and the
widow weeps.
> *Much Ado about Nothing,* Act v, sc. **2**, l. **80** [BENEDICK]

4775   Make my bridal bed
In that dim monument where Tybalt lies.
> *Romeo and Juliet,* Act iii, sc. **5**, l. **202** [JULIET]

4776   Your monument shall be my gentle verse,
Which eyes not yet created shall o'er-read,
And tongues to be your being shall rehearse
When all the breathers of this world are dead.
> *Sonnet* lxxxi, l. **9**

4777   This monument five hundred years hath stood,
Which I have sumptuously re-edified:
Here none but soldiers and Rome's servitors
Repose in fame.
Titus Andronicus, Act i, sc. 1, l. 350 [TITUS]

Moon

4778   Alack, our terrene moon
Is now eclipsed; and it portends alone
The fall of Antony!
Antony and Cleopatra, Act iii, sc. 13, l. 153 [ANTONY]

4779   Be witness to me, O thou blessed moon,
When men revolted shall upon record
Bear hateful memory, poor Enobarbus did
Before thy face repent. . . .
O sovereign mistress of true melancholy,
The poisonous damp of night disponge upon me,
That life, a very rebel to my will,
May hang no longer on me. Throw my heart
Against the flint and hardness of my fault;
Which, being dried with grief, will break to powder; . . .
But let the world rank me in register
A master-leaver and a fugitive.
Antony and Cleopatra, Act iv, sc. 9, l. 7 [ENOBARBUS]

4780   What may this mean,
That thou, dead corse, again in complete steel,
Revisit'st thus the glimpses of the moon,
Making night hideous.
Hamlet, Act i, sc. 4, l. 51 [HAMLET]

4781   FALSTAFF: When thou art king, let not us that are squires of the
night's body be called thieves of the day's beauty: let us be Diana's
foresters, gentlemen of the shade, minions of the moon; and let
men say we be men of good government, being governed, as the
sea is, by our noble and chaste mistress the moon. . . .
PRINCE: Thou sayest well, and it holds well too; for the fortune
of us that are the moon's men doth ebb and flow like the sea, . . .
now in as low an ebb as the foot of the ladder and by and by in
as high a flow as the ridge of the gallows.
I Henry IV, Act i, sc. 2, l. 26 [FALSTAFF]

4782   My lord, they say five moons were seen to-night;
Four fixed, and the fifth did whirl about
The other four in wondrous motion.
Old men and beldams in the streets
Do prophesy upon it dangerously.
King John, Act iv, sc. 2, l. 182 [HUBERT]

4783   Though it be night, yet the moon shines; I'll make a sop o' the
moonshine of you.
King Lear, Act ii, sc. 2, l. 34 [KENT]

A calendar, a calendar! look in the almanac: find out moonshine.
A Midsummer Night's Dream, Act iii, sc. 1, l. 54 [BOTTOM]

4784   DULL: What was a month old at Cain's birth, that's not five
weeks old as yet.
HOLOFERNES: Dictynna, goodman Dull; Dictynna.
DULL: What is Dictynna?
NATHANIEL: A title to Phoebe, to Luna, to the moon.

HOLOFERNES : The moon was a month old when Adam was no more,
And raught not to five weeks when he came to five-score.
>   *Love's Labour's Lost,* Act iv, sc. 2, l. 36 [DULL]
4785   The moon sleeps with Endymion
And would not be awaked.
>   *The Merchant of Venice,* Act v, sc. 1, l. 109 [PORTIA]
4786   By yonder moon I swear you do me wrong.
>   *The Merchant of Venice,* Act v, sc. 1, l. 142 [GRATIANO]
ROMEO : Lady, by yonder blessed moon I swear
That tips with silver all these fruit-tree tops—
JULIET : O, swear not by the moon, the inconstant moon,
That monthly changes in her circled orb,
Lest that thy love prove likewise variable.
>   *Romeo and Juliet,* Act ii, sc. 2, l. 107 [ROMEO]
4787   THESEUS : Now, fair Hippolyta, our nuptial hour
Draws on apace ; four happy days bring in
Another moon : but, O, methinks how slow
This old moon wanes ! she lingers my desires,
Like to a step-dame or a dowager
Long withering out a young man's revenue.
HIPPOLYTA : Four days will quickly steep themselves in night ;
Four nights will quickly dream away the time ;
And then the moon, like to a silver bow
New-bent in heaven, shall behold the night
Of our solemnities.
>   *A Midsummer Night's Dream,* Act i, sc. 1, l. 1 [THESEUS]
4788   The moon, the governess of floods,
Pale in her anger, washes all the air,
That rheumatic diseases do abound.
>   *A Midsummer Night's Dream,* Act ii, sc. 1, l. 103 [TITANIA]
4789   The moon methinks looks with a watery eye ;
And when she weeps, weeps every little flower,
Lamenting some enforced chastity.
>   *A Midsummer Night's Dream,* Act iii, sc. 1, l. 203 [TITANIA]
4790   It is the very error of the moon ;
She comes more nearer earth than she was wont,
And makes men mad.
>   *Othello,* Act v, sc. 2, l. 109 [OTHELLO]
4791   The moon being clouded presently is miss'd,
But little stars may hide them when they list.
>   *The Rape of Lucrece,* l. 1007 [LUCRECE]
4792   CALIBAN : Hast thou not dropp'd from heaven?
STEPHANO : Out o' the moon, I do assure thee : I was the man i' the
moon when time was.
CALIBAN : I have seen thee in her and I do adore thee :
My mistress showed me thee and thy dog and thy bush.
>   *The Tempest,* Act ii, sc. 2, l. 141 [CALIBAN]
(A reference to the fable of the man who was banished to the
moon for burning brush on Sunday.)
4793   Moon-calf, speak once in thy life, if thou beest a good moon-calf.
>   *The Tempest,* Act iii, sc. 2, l. 24 [STEPHANO]
4794   So pale did shine the moon on Pyramus
When he by night lay bathed in maiden blood.
>   *Titus Andronicus,* Act ii, sc. 3, l. 231 [MARTIUS]
4795   'Tis not that time of moon with me to make one in so skipping
a dialogue.
>   *Twelfth Night,* Act i, sc. 5, l. 215 [OLIVIA]

Morning

4796   This morning, like the spirit of a youth
      That means to be of note, begins betimes.
             Antony and Cleopatra, Act iv, sc. 4, l. 26 [Antony]

4797   But, look, the morn, in russet mantle clad,
      Walks o'er the dew of yon high eastward hill.
             Hamlet, Act i, sc. 1, l. 166 [Horatio]

4798   See how the morning opes her golden gates,
      And takes her farewell of the glorious sun!
      How well remembers it the prime of youth,
      Trimm'd like a younker prancing to his love!
             III Henry VI, Act ii, sc. 1, l. 21 [Richard]

4799   The grey-eyed morn smiles on the frowning night,
      Chequering the eastern clouds with streaks of light,
      And flecked darkness like a drunkard reels
      From forth day's path and Titan's fiery wheels.
            Romeo and Juliet, Act ii, sc. 3, l. 1 [Friar Laurence]

4800   Full many a glorious morning have I seen
      Flatter the mountain-tops with sovereign eye,
      Kissing with golden face the meadows green,
      Gilding pale streams with heavenly alchemy.
                    Sonnet xxxiii, l. 1

Morsel

4801   I was A morsel for a monarch.
            Antony and Cleopatra, Act i, sc. 5, l. 31 [Cleopatra]

4802   I found you as a morsel cold upon
      Dead Cæsar's trencher.
            Antony and Cleopatra, Act iii, sc. 13, l. 116 [Antony]

4803   Now comes in the sweetest morsel of the night, and we must hence
      and leave it unpicked.
            II Henry IV, Act ii, sc. 4, l. 396 [Falstaff]

4804   How doth my dear morsel, thy mistress? Procures she still, ha?
            Measure for Measure, Act iii, sc. 2, l. 56 [Lucio]

4805   You To the perpetual wink for aye might put
      This ancient morsel, this Sir Prudence, who
      Should not upbraid our course.
            The Tempest, Act ii, sc. 1, l. 285 [Antonio]

Mortality

4806   Here on my knee I beg mortality,
      Rather than life preserved with infamy.
            I Henry VI, Act iv, sc. 5, l. 32 [John Talbot]

4807   We cannot hold mortality's strong hand: . . .
      Think you I bear the shears of destiny?
      Have I commandment on the pulse of life?
            King John, Act iv, sc. 2, l. 82 [King John]

4808   Had I but died an hour before this chance,
      I had lived a blessed time; for, from this instant,
      There's nothing serious in mortality:
      All is but toys: renown and grace is dead.
            Macbeth, Act ii, sc. 3, l. 97 [Macbeth]

Mortimer

4809   King Henry: I shall never hold that man my friend
      Whose tongue shall ask me for one penny cost
      To ransom home revolted Mortimer.
      Hotspur: Revolted Mortimer!

He never did fall off, my sovereign liege,
But by the chance of war: to prove that true
Needs no more but one tongue for all those wounds,
Those mouthed wounds, which valiantly he took
When on the gentle Severn's sedgy bank,
In single opposition, hand to hand,
He did confound the best part of an hour
In changing hardiment with great Glendower:
Three times they breathed and three times did they drink,
Upon agreement, of swift Severn's flood;
Who then, affrighted with their bloody looks,
Ran fearfully among the trembling reeds,
And hid his crisp head in the hollow bank
Bloodstained with these valiant combatants.
                    I Henry IV, Act i, sc. 3, l. 90 [KING HENRY]

Mote

4810   A mote it is to trouble the mind's eye.
                    Hamlet, Act i, sc. 1, l. 112 [HORATIO]
4811   ARTHUR: Is there no remedy?
        HUBERT: None, but to lose your eyes.
        ARTHUR: O heaven, that there were but a mote in yours,
        A grain, a dust, a gnat, a wandering hair,
        Any annoyance in that precious sense!
                    King John, Act iv, sc. 1, l. 91 [ARTHUR]
4812   You found his mote; the king your mote did see;
        But I a beam do find in each of three.
                    Love's Labour's Lost, Act iv, sc. 3, l. 161 [BIRON]
4813   A mote will turn the balance.
                    A Midsummer Night's Dream, Act v, sc. 1, l. 325 [DEMETRIUS]

Mother

4814   Taint not thy mind, nor let thy soul contrive
        Against thy mother aught: leave her to heaven
        And to those thorns that in her bosom lodge,
        To prick and sting her.
                    Hamlet, Act i, sc. 5, l. 85 [GHOST]
4815   Heaven shield my mother play'd my father fair!
                    Measure for Measure, Act iii, sc. 1, l. 141 [ISABELLA]
4816   Thou art a widow; yet thou art a mother,
        And hast the comfort of thy children left thee.
                    Richard III, Act ii, sc. 2, l. 55 [DUCHESS]
4817   Thou art thy mother's glass, and she in thee
        Calls back the lovely April of her prime.
                    Sonnet iii, l. 10
4818   Your mother was most true to wedlock, prince;
        For she did print your royal father off,
        Conceiving you.
                    The Winter's Tale, Act v, sc. 1, l. 124 [LEONTES]

Mourning

4819   We mourn in black: why mourn we not in blood?
        Henry is dead and never shall revive:
        Upon a wooden coffin we attend,
        And death's dishonourable victory
        We with our stately presence glorify,
        Like captives bound to a triumphant car.
                    I Henry VI, Act i, sc. 1, l. 17 [EXETER]

4820 Some will mourn in ashes, some coal-black,
     For the deposing of a rightful king.
                         Richard II, Act v, sc. 1, l. 49 [KING RICHARD]

4821 Come, mourn with me for that I do lament,
     And put on sullen black incontinent.
                         Richard II, Act v, sc. 6, l. 49 [BOLINGBROKE]

4822 No longer mourn for me when I am dead
     Than you shall hear the surly sullen bell
     Give warning to the world that I am fled
     From this vile world, with vilest worms to dwell: . . .
     O if, I say, you look upon this verse
     When I perhaps compounded am with clay,
     Do not so much as my poor name rehearse,
     But let your love even with my life decay.
                                        Sonnet lxxi, l. 1

Mouse

4823 BERNARDO: Have you had a quiet guard?
     FRANCISCO: Not a mouse stirring.
                         Hamlet, Act i, sc. 1, l. 10 [BERNARDO]

4824 You, ladies, you, whose gentle hearts do fear
     The smallest monstrous mouse that creeps on floor,
     May now perchance both quake and tremble here,
     When lion rough in wildest rage doth roar.
              A Midsummer Night's Dream, Act v, sc. 1, l. 222 [LION]

Mouth

4825   Here's a large mouth, indeed,
     That spits forth death and mountains, rocks and seas,
     Talks as familiarly of roaring lions
     As maids of thirteen do of puppy-dogs!
     What cannoneer begot this lusty blood?
     He speaks plain cannon fire, and smoke and bounce.
                         King John, Act ii, sc. 1, l. 457 [BASTARD]

4826   O perilous mouths,
     That bear in them one and the self-same tongue,
     Either of condemnation or approof;
     Bidding the law make curt'sy to their will;
     Hooking both right and wrong to the appetite,
     To follow as it draws!
                    Measure for Measure, Act ii, sc. 4, l. 172 [ISABELLA]

4827 These mouths, who but of late, earth, sea, and air
     Were all too little to content and please, . . .
     They are now starved for want of exercise.
                         Pericles, Act i, sc. 4, l. 34 [CLEON]

Multitude

4828 What would you have, you curs? . . .
     He that trusts to you,
     Where he should find you lions, finds you hares;
     Where foxes, geese; you are no surer, no,
     Than is the coal of fire upon the ice,
     Or hailstone in the sun. . . . He that depends
     Upon your favours swims with fins of lead
     And hews down oaks with rushes. Hang ye! Trust ye?
     With every minute you do change a mind
     And call him noble that was now your hate,
     Him vile that was your garland.
                    Coriolanus, Act i, sc. 1, l. 174 [CORIOLANUS]

4829   Ingratitude is monstrous, and for the multitude to be ingrateful,
were to make a monster of the multitude.
Coriolanus, Act ii, sc. 3, l. 10 [CITIZEN]

4830   He himself stuck not to call us the many-headed multitude.
Coriolanus, Act ii, sc. 3, l. 17 [CITIZEN]

4831   The beast with many heads butts me away.
Coriolanus, Act iv, sc. 1, l. 1 [CORIOLANUS]

4832   The mutable, rank-scented many.
Coriolanus, Act iii, sc. 1, l. 66 [CORIOLANUS]

4833   Will you hence, Before the tag return?
Coriolanus, Act iii, sc. 1, l. 247 [COMINIUS]

4834   You common cry of curs! whose breath I hate
As reek o' the rotten fens, whose loves I prize
As the dead carcasses of unburied men
That do corrupt my air, I banish you!
Coriolanus, Act iii, sc. 3, l. 120 [CORIOLANUS]

4835   An habitation giddy and unsure
Hath he that buildeth on the vulgar heart.
II Henry IV, Act i, sc. 3, l. 89 [ARCHBISHOP]

4836   See how the giddy multitude do point,
And nod their heads!
II Henry VI, Act ii, sc. 4, l. 21 [DUCHESS]

4837   Was ever feather so lightly blown to and fro as this multitude?
II Henry VI, Act iv, sc. 8, l. 57 [CADE]

4838   Another lean unwash'd artificer
Cuts off his tale and talks of Arthur's death.
King John, Act iv, sc. 2, l. 201 [HUBERT]

4839   The fool multitude, that choose by show,
Not learning more than the fond eye doth teach;
Which pries not to the interior, but, like the martlet,
Builds in the weather on the outward wall,
Even in the force and road of casualty.
The Merchant of Venice, Act ii, sc. 9, l. 26 [ARRAGON]

4840   I will not choose what many men desire,
Because I will not jump with common spirits
And rank me with the barbarous multitudes.
The Merchant of Venice, Act ii, sc. 9, l. 31 [ARRAGON]

Mum

4841   Seal up your lips, and give no words but mum:
The business asketh silent secrecy.
II Henry VI, Act i, sc. 2, l. 89 [HUME]

4842   Yes, forsooth, I will hold my tongue. . . . Mum, mum.
King Lear, Act i, sc. 4, l. 213 [FOOL]

4843   Well said, master; mum! and gaze your fill.
The Taming of the Shrew, Act i, sc. 1, l. 73 [TRANIO]

4844   TRINCULO: Why, I said nothing.
STEPHANO: Mum, then, and no more. Proceed.
The Tempest, Act iii, sc. 2, l. 58 [TRINCULO]

Murder

4845   Murder most foul, as in the best it is;
But this most foul, strange and unnatural.
Hamlet, Act i, sc. 5, l. 27 [GHOST]

4846   Murder, though it hath no tongue, will speak
With most miraculous organ.
Hamlet, Act ii, sc. 2, l. 622 [HAMLET]

4847   Murder, as hating what himself hath done,
Doth lay it open to urge on revenge. . . .
Sir Richard, what think you? . . . This is the very top,
The height, the crest, or crest unto the crest,
Of murder's arms: this is the bloodiest shame,
The wildest savagery, the vilest stroke,
That ever wall-eyed wrath or staring rage
Presented to the tears of soft remorse.
King John, Act iv, sc. 3, l. 37 [SALISBURY]

4848   Wither'd murder,
Alarum'd by his sentinel, the wolf,
Whose howl's his watch, thus with his stealthy pace,
With Tarquin's ravishing strides, towards his design
Moves like a ghost.
Macbeth, Act ii, sc. 1, l. 52 [MACBETH]

4849   Most sacrilegious murder hath broke ope
The Lord's anointed temple, and stole thence
The life o' the building.
Macbeth, Act ii, sc. 3, l. 72 [MACDUFF]

4850   Truth will come to light; murder cannot be hid long.
The Merchant of Venice, Act ii, sc. 2, l. 84 [LAUNCELOT]
O wondrous thing! How easily murder is discovered!
Titus Andronicus, Act ii, sc. 3, l. 287 [TAMORA]

4851   Though in the trade of war I have slain men,
Yet do I hold it very stuff o' the conscience
To do no contrived murder.
Othello, Act i, sc. 2, l. 1 [IAGO]

4852   Murder's out of tune,
And sweet revenge grows harsh.
Othello, Act v, sc. 2, l. 115 [OTHELLO]

4853   An honourable murderer, if you will;
For nought I did in hate, but all in honour.
Othello, Act v, sc. 2, l. 294 [OTHELLO]

4854   The great King of kings
Hath in the tables of his law commanded
That thou shalt do no murder.
Richard III, Act i, sc. 4, l. 200 [CLARENCE]

4855   I must talk of murders, rapes, and massacres,
Acts of black night, abominable deeds,
Complots of mischief, treason, villanies
Ruthful to hear, yet piteously performed.
Titus Andronicus, Act v, sc. 1, l. 63 [AARON]

Muse

4856   O for a Muse of fire, that would ascend
The brightest heaven of invention,
A kingdom for a stage, princes to act
And monarchs to behold the swelling scene!
Henry V, Prologue, l. 1 [CHORUS]

4857   The thrice three Muses mourning for the death
Of Learning, late deceased in beggary.
A Midsummer Night's Dream, Act v, sc. 1, l. 52 [THESEUS, reading]

Music

4858   Give me some music; music, moody food
Of us that trade in love.
Antony and Cleopatra, Act ii, sc. 5, l. 1 [CLEOPATRA]

4859   Those musicians that shall play to you
        Hang in the air a thousand leagues from hence,
        And straight they shall be here.
                        I Henry IV, Act iii, sc. 1, l. 226 [GLENDOWER]

4860   Music oft hath such a charm
        To make bad good, and good provoke to harm.
                        Measure for Measure, Act iv, sc. 1, l. 14 [DUKE]

4861   Let music sound while he doth make his choice;
        Then, if he lose, he makes a swan-like end,
        Fading in music. . . . He may win;
        And what is music then? Then music is
        Even as the flourish when true subjects bow
        To a new-crowned monarch; such it is
        As are those dulcet sounds in break of day
        That creep into the dreaming bridegroom's ear
        And summon him to marriage.
                        The Merchant of Venice, Act iii, sc. 2, l. 43 [PORTIA]

4862   JESSICA: I am never merry when I hear sweet music.
        LORENZO: The reason is, your spirits are attentive.
        For do but note a wild and wanton herd, . . .
        Their savage eyes turn'd to a modest gaze
        By the sweet power of music; therefore the poet
        Did feign that Orpheus drew trees, stones and floods;
        Since nought so stockish, hard and full of rage,
        But music for the time doth change his nature.
        The man that hath no music in himself,
        Nor is not moved with concord of sweet sounds,
        Is fit for treasons, stratagems and spoils,
        The motions of his spirit are dull as night
        And his affections dark as Erebus.
        Let no such man be trusted.
                        The Merchant of Venice, Act v, sc. 1, l. 69 [JESSICA]

4863   I have a reasonable good ear in music. Let's have the tongs and
        the bones.
                        A Midsummer Night's Dream, Act iv, sc. 1, l. 30 [BOTTOM]

4864   HIPPOLYTA: I was with Hercules and Cadmus once,
        When in a wood of Crete they bay'd the bear
        With hounds of Sparta: never did I hear
        Such gallant chiding; for, besides the groves,
        The skies, the fountains, every region near
        Seem'd all one musical cry: I never heard
        So musical a discord, such sweet thunder.
        THESEUS: My hounds are bred out of the Spartan kind, . . .
        Slow in pursuit, but match'd in mouth like bells.
                        A Midsummer Night's Dream, Act iv, sc. 1, l. 116 [HIPPOLYTUS]

4865   I have known when there was no music with him but the drum
        and the fife; and now had he rather hear the tabor and the pipe.
                        Much Ado about Nothing, Act ii, sc. 3, l. 11 [BENEDICK]

4866   Loud music is too harsh for ladies' heads,
        Since they love men in arms as well as beds.
                        Pericles, Act ii, sc. 3, l. 97 [SIMONIDES]

4867   SIMONIDES: I am beholding to you
        For your sweet music this last night . . .
        Sir, you are music's master.
        PERICLES: The worst of all her scholars, my good lord.
                        Pericles, Act ii, sc. 5, l. 25 [SIMONIDES]

4868 But, hark, what music? . . . The music of the spheres! . . .
Do you not hear? . . . Most heavenly music!
It nips me unto listening, and thick slumber
Hangs upon mine eyes: let me rest.
    Pericles, Act v, sc. 1, l. 225 [PERICLES]
I had rather hear you to solicit that
Than music from the spheres.
    Twelfth Night, Act iii, sc. 1, l. 120 [OLIVIA]

4869   Let rich music's tongue
Unfold the imagined happiness that both
Receive in either by this dear encounter.
    Romeo and Juliet, Act ii, sc. 6, l. 27 [ROMEO]

4870 When griping grief the heart doth wound,
   And doleful dumps the mind oppress,
  Then music with her silver sound,
   With speedy help doth lend redress.
    Romeo and Juliet, Act iv, sc. 5, l. 128 [PETER]

4871 Wilt thou have music? hark! Apollo plays
And twenty caged nightingales do sing.
    The Taming of the Shrew, Induction, sc. 2, l. 37 [LORD]

4872 Preposterous ass, that never read so far
To know the cause why music was ordain'd!
Was it not to refresh the mind of man
After his studies or his unusual pain?
    The Taming of the Shrew, Act iii, sc. 1, l. 9 [HORTENSIO]

4873 Where should this music be? i' the air or the earth? . . .
This music crept by me upon the waters,
Allaying both their fury and my passion
With its sweet air.
    The Tempest, Act i, sc. 2, l. 387 [FERDINAND]

4874 If music be the food of love, play on;
Give me excess of it, that, surfeiting,
The appetite may sicken, and so die.
That strain again! it had a dying fall:
O, it came o'er my ear like the sweet sound
That breathes upon a bank of violets,
Stealing and giving odour!
    Twelfth Night, Act i, sc. 1, l. 1 [DUKE]

Must

4875 Thither I must, although against my will.
    The Comedy of Errors, Act iv, sc. 1, l. 112 [DROMIO OF SYRACUSE]
Whither I must, I must.
    I Henry IV, Act ii, sc. 3, l. 108 [HOTSPUR]

4876 COMINIUS: 'Twill serve, if he Can there to frame his spirit.
VOLUMNIA: He must, and will. . . .
CORIOLANUS: Must I go show them my unbarbed sconce?
Must I with base tongue give my noble heart
A lie that it must bear? Well, I will do 't.
    Coriolanus, Act iii, sc. 2, l. 96 [COMINIUS]

4877 Needs must I like it well.
    Richard II, Act iii, sc. 2, l. 4 [KING RICHARD]
 ("Needs must" is repeated frequently throughout the plays.)

4878 PARIS: That may be must be, love. . . .
JULIET: What must be shall be.
FRIAR LAURENCE: That's a certain text.
    Romeo and Juliet, Act iv, sc. 1, l. 20 [PARIS]

4879   What you cannot as you would achieve,
You must perforce accomplish as you may.
Titus Andronicus, Act ii, sc. 1, l. 105 [AARON]

Mustardseed

4880   BOTTOM : Your name, I beseech you, sir?
MUSTARDSEED : Mustardseed.
BOTTOM : Good Master Mustardseed, I know your patience well;
that same cowardly giant-like ox-beef hath devoured many a gen-
tleman of your house : I promise you your kindred hath made my
eyes water ere now. I desire your more acquaintance, good Master
Mustardseed.
A Midsummer Night's Dream, Act iii, sc. 1, l. 194 [BOTTOM]

N

Nails

4881   'Tis too late to pare her nails now.
All's Well that Ends Well, Act v, sc. 2, l. 31 [LAFEU]
Every one may pare his nails with a wooden dagger.
Henry V, Act iv, sc. 4, l. 76 [BOY]
Like a mad lad, Pare thy nails, dad; Adieu, goodman devil.
Twelfth Night, Act iv, sc. 2, l. 139 [CLOWN]
(A reference to the old jingle, "Cut your nails on Sunday, your
safety seek; The devil will have you the rest of the week.")

4882   Let Patient Octavia plough thy visage up
With her prepared nails.
Antony and Cleopatra, Act iv, sc. 12, l. 38 [ANTONY]
I am sure my nails Are stronger than mine eyes.
Antony and Cleopatra, Act v, sc. 2. l. 223 [IRAS]

4883   Could I come near your beauty with my nails,
I 'ld leave my ten commandments in your face.
II Henry VI, Act i, sc. 3, l. 144 [DUCHESS]
("Ten commandments," a proverbial phrase indicating the
finger-nails.)

4884   With her nails
She'll flay thy wolvish visage.
King Lear, Act i, sc. 4, l. 329 [LEAR]

4885   But that still use of grief makes wild grief tame,
My tongue should to thy ears not name my boys
Till that my nails were anchor'd in thine eyes.
Richard III, Act iv, sc. 4, l. 229 [QUEEN ELIZABETH]

Name

4886   O villain! thou hast stolen both mine office and my name,
The one ne'er got me credit, the other mickle blame.
The Comedy of Errors, Act iii, sc. 1, l. 44 [DROMIO OF EPHESUS]

4887   CORIOLANUS : Necessity Commands me name myself.
AUFIDIUS : What is thy name?
CORIOLANUS : A name unmusical to the Volscians' ears,
And harsh in sound to thine. . . .
My name is Caius Marcius, who hath done
To thee particularly and to all the Volsces
Great hurt and mischief; thereto witness may
My surname, Coriolanus : . . . only that name remains.
Coriolanus, Act iv, sc. 5, l. 62 [CORIOLANUS]

4888　O good Horatio, what a wounded name,
　　　Things standing thus unknown, shall live behind me!
　　　　　　　　　　　　　Hamlet, Act v, sc. 2, l. 355 [HAMLET]
4889　I would to God thou and I knew where a commodity of good
　　　names were to be bought.
　　　　　　　　　　　　　I Henry IV, Act i, sc. 2, l. 92 [FALSTAFF]
4890　Go to; 'homo' is a common name to all men.
　　　　　　　　　　　　　I Henry IV, Act ii, sc. 1, l. 107 [GADSHILL]
4891　　　　　　　My name is lost;
　　　By treason's tooth bare-gnawn and canker-bit.
　　　　　　　　　　　　　King Lear, Act v, sc. 3, l. 121 [EDGAR]
4892　I cannot tell what the dickens his name is.
　　　　　　The Merry Wives of Windsor, Act iii, sc. 2, l. 19 [MRS. PAGE]
4893　Your name is great In mouths of wisest censure.
　　　　　　　　　　　　　Othello, Act ii, sc. 3, l. 192 [OTHELLO]
4894　Good name in man and woman, dear my lord,
　　　Is the immediate jewel of their souls:
　　　Who steals my purse steals trash; 'tis something, nothing;
　　　'Twas mine, 'tis his, and has been slave to thousands;
　　　But he that filches from me my good name
　　　Robs me of that which not enriches him
　　　And makes me poor indeed.
　　　　　　　　　　　　　Othello, Act iii, sc. 3, l. 155 [IAGO]
4895　O Romeo, Romeo! wherefore art thou Romeo?
　　　Deny thy father and refuse thy name. . . .
　　　'Tis but thy name that is my enemy; . . .
　　　What's in a name? that which we call a rose
　　　By any other name would smell as sweet.
　　　　　　　　　　　　　Romeo and Juliet, Act ii, sc. 2, l. 33 [JULIET]

Nature

4896　　　　　　　'Tis often seen
　　　Adoption strives with nature and choice breeds
　　　A native slip to us from foreign seeds.
　　　　　　　　All's Well that Ends Well, Act i, sc. 3, l. 150 [COUNTESS]
4897　He bow'd his nature, never known before
　　　But to be rough, unswayable and free.
　　　　　　　　　　　　　Coriolanus, Act v, sc. 6, l. 25 [AUFIDIUS]
4898　How hard it is to hide the sparks of nature!
　　　　　　　　　　　　　Cymbeline, Act iii, sc. 3, l. 79 [BELARIUS]
4899　O worthiness of nature! breed of greatness!
　　　Cowards father cowards, and base things sire base:
　　　Nature hath meal and bran, contempt and grace.
　　　　　　　　　　　　　Cymbeline, Act iv, sc. 2, l. 25 [BELARIUS]
4900　　　　　　　O thou goddess,
　　　Thou divine Nature, how thyself thou blazon'st
　　　In these two princely boys! They are as gentle
　　　As zephyrs blowing below the violet,
　　　Now wagging his sweet head; and yet as rough,
　　　Their royal blood enchafed, as the rudest wind
　　　That by the top doth take the mountain pine,
　　　And make him stoop to the vale.
　　　　　　　　　　　　　Cymbeline, Act iv, sc. 2, l. 169 [BELARIUS]
4901　Nature doth abhor to make his bed
　　　With the defunct, or sleep upon the dead.
　　　　　　　　　　　　　Cymbeline, Act iv, sc. 2, l. 357 [LUCIUS]

4902   Nature, crescent, does not grow alone
        In thews and bulk, but, as this temple waxes,
        The inward service of the mind and soul
        Grows wide withal.
                                        Hamlet, Act i, sc. 3, l. 11 [LAERTES]

4903   Nature is fine in love, and where 'tis fine,
        It sends some precious instance of itself
        After the thing it loves.
                                        Hamlet, Act iv, sc. 5, l. 161 [LAERTES]

4904   Nature her custom holds,
        Let shame say what it will.
                                        Hamlet, Act iv, sc. 7, l. 188 [LAERTES]

4905   'Tis dangerous when the baser nature comes
        Between the pass and fell incensed points
        Of mighty opposites.
                                        Hamlet, Act v, sc. 2, l. 60 [HAMLET]

4906   Diseased nature oftentimes breaks forth
        In strange eruptions; oft the teeming earth
        Is with a kind of colic pinch'd and vex'd
        By the imprisoning of unruly wind
        Within her womb; which, for enlargement striving,
        Shakes the old beldame earth and topples down
        Steeples and moss-grown towers.
                                        I Henry IV, Act iii, sc. 1, l. 27 [HOTSPUR]

4907   If the young dace be a bait for the old pike, I see no reason in
        the law of nature but I may snap at him.
                                        II Henry IV, Act iii, sc. 2, l. 357 [FALSTAFF]

4908   The deep of night is crept upon our talk,
        And nature must obey necessity.
                                        Julius Cæsar, Act iv, sc. 3, l. 226 [BRUTUS]

4909   Thou, nature, art my goddess: to thy law
        My services are bound.
                                        King Lear, Act i, sc. 2, l. 1 [EDMUND]

4910   Nature's above art in that respect.
                                        King Lear, Act iv, sc. 6, l. 86 [LEAR]

4911   Yet do I fear thy nature;
        It is too full o' the milk of human kindness
        To catch the nearest way: thou wouldst be great,
        Art not without ambition, but without
        The illness should attend it: what thou wouldst highly
        That wouldst thou holily; wouldst not play false,
        And yet wouldst wrongly win.
                                        Macbeth, Act i, sc. 5, l. 17 [LADY MACBETH]

4912   Now o'er the one half-world Nature seems dead.
                                        Macbeth, Act ii, sc. 1, l. 49 [MACBETH]

4913   In his royalty of nature
        Reigns that which would be fear'd: 'tis much he dares;
        And, to that dauntless temper of his mind,
        He hath a wisdom that doth guide his valour
        To act in safety.
                                        Macbeth, Act iii, sc. 1, l. 50 [MACBETH]

4914   Nature never lends
        The smallest scruple of her excellence
        But, like a thrifty goddess, she determines
        Herself the glory of a creditor,
        Both thanks and use.
                                        Measure for Measure, Act i, sc. 1, l. 37 [DUKE]

4915   Our natures do pursue,
      Like rats that ravin down their proper bane,
      A thirsty evil; and when we drink we die.
                    Measure for Measure, Act i, sc. 2, l. 132 [CLAUDIO]

4916   Nature hath framed strange fellows in her time:
      Some that will evermore peep through their eyes
      And laugh like parrots at a bag-piper,
      And other of such vinegar aspect
      That they'll not show their teeth in way of smile,
      Though Nestor swear the jest be laughable.
                    The Merchant of Venice, Act i, sc. 1, l. 52 [SALARINO]

4917   Is this the nature
      Whom passion could not shake? whose solid virtue
      The shot of accident, nor dart of chance,
      Could neither graze, nor pierce?
                    Othello, Act iv, sc. 1, l. 276 [LODOVICO]

4918   Though fond nature bids us all lament,
      Yet nature's tears are reason's merriment.
                    Romeo and Juliet, Act iv, sc. 5, l. 82 [FRIAR LAURENCE]

4919   Nature's bequest gives nothing but doth lend,
      And being frank she lends to those are free.
                                              Sonnet iv, l. 3

4920   My nature is subdued
      To that it works in, like the dyer's hand.
                                              Sonnet cxi, l. 6

4921   Nature, as it grows again toward earth,
      Is fashion'd for the journey, dull and heavy.
                    Timon of Athens, Act ii, sc. 2, l. 227 [TIMON]

4922   Not nature,
      To whom all sores lay siege, can bear great fortunes;
      But thy contempt of nature.
                    Timon of Athens, Act iv, sc. 3, l. 6 [TIMON]

4923   One touch of nature makes the whole world kin.
                    Troilus and Cressida, Act iii, sc. 3, l. 175 [ULYSSES]

4924   How sometimes nature will betray its folly
      Its tenderness and make itself a pastime
      To harder bosoms!
                    The Winter's Tale, Act i, sc. 2, l. 151 [LEONTES]

Neat

4925   Wherein is he . . . neat and cleanly, but to carve a capon and
      eat it?
                    I Henry IV, Act ii, sc. 4, l. 502 [PRINCE]

4926   We must be neat; not neat, but cleanly, captain:
      And yet the steer, the heifer and the calf
      Are all call'd neat.
                    The Winter's Tale, Act i, sc. 2, l. 123 [LEONTES]

4927   He's a present for any emperor that ever trod on neat's leather.
                    The Tempest, Act ii, sc. 2, l. 74 [STEPHANO]

Necessity

4928   The strong necessity of time commands
      Our services awhile.
                    Antony and Cleopatra, Act i, sc. 3, l. 42 [ANTONY]

4929   I abjure all roofs, and choose
      To wage against the enmity o' the air;

To be a comrade with the wolf and owl,—
Necessity's sharp pinch!
King Lear, Act ii, sc. 4, l. 211 [LEAR]

4930 The art of our necessities is strange,
That can make vile things precious.
King Lear, Act iii, sc. 2, l. 70 [LEAR]

4931 If I break faith, this word shall speak for me:
I am forsworn on 'mere necessity.'
Love's Labour's Lost, Act i, sc. 1, l. 154 [BIRON]

4932 Teach thy necessity to reason thus;
There is no virtue like necessity.
Richard II, Act i, sc. 3, l. 277 [GAUNT]

4933 Are you content . . . To make a virtue of necessity
And live, as we do, in this wilderness?
The Two Gentlemen of Verona, Act iv, sc. 1, l. 61 [OUTLAW]

4934 I am sworn brother, sweet,
To grim Necessity, and he and I
Will keep a league till death.
Richard II, Act v, sc. 1, l. 20 [KING RICHARD]

Neck

4935 I had as lief thou didst break his neck as his finger.
As You Like It, Act i, sc. 1, l. 153 [OLIVER]

4936 He hath left undone
That which shall break his neck or hazard mine,
Whene'er we come to our account.
Coriolanus, Act iv, sc. 7, l. 24 [AUFIDIUS]

4937 Mischief and despair
Drive you to break your necks or hang yourselves.
I Henry VI, Act v, sc. 4, l. 90 [PUCELLE]

4938 Yield not thy neck
To fortune's yoke, but let thy dauntless mind
Still ride in triumph over all mischance.
III Henry VI, Act iii, sc. 3, l. 16 [KING LEWIS]
An thou wilt needs thrust thy neck into a yoke, wear the print of it
and sigh away Sundays.
Much Ado about Nothing, Act i, sc. 1, l. 203 [BENEDICK]

4939 Now thy proud neck bears half my burthen'd yoke;
From which even here I slip my weary neck,
And leave the burthen of it all on thee.
Richard III, Act iv, sc. 4, l. 111 [QUEEN MARGARET]

4940 She hung about my neck; and kiss on kiss
She vied so fast, protesting oath on oath,
That in a twink she won me to her love.
The Taming of the Shrew, Act ii, sc. 1, l. 310 [PETRUCHIO]

Need

4941 O, reason not with need: our basest beggars
Are in the poorest things superfluous:
Allow not nature more than nature needs,
Man's life's as cheap as beast's.
King Lear, Act ii, sc. 4, l. 267 [LEAR]

4942 You envy my advancement and my friends:
God grant we never may have need of you!
Richard III, Act i, sc. 3, l. 75 [QUEEN ELIZABETH]

4943 God be thanked, there's no need of me,
And much I need to help you, if need were.
Richard III, Act iii, sc. 7, l. 165 [GLOUCESTER]

4944   Thou art like one of those fellows that when he enters the confines
       of a tavern claps me his sword upon the table and says 'God send
       me no need of thee!'
                              Romeo and Juliet, Act iii, sc. 1, l. 5 [MERCUTIO]

4945   Immediate are my needs, and my relief
       Must not be toss'd and turn'd to me in words,
       But find supply immediate.
                              Timon of Athens, Act ii, sc. 1, l. 25 [SENATOR]

Nero

4946   O heart, lose not thy nature; let not ever
       The soul of Nero enter this firm bosom:
       Let me be cruel, not unnatural.
                              Hamlet, Act iii, sc. 2, l. 411 [HAMLET]

4947   I will . . . like thee, Nero,
       Play on the lute, beholding the towns burn.
                              I Henry VI, Act i, sc. 4, l. 95 [TALBOT]

4948   You bloody Neroes, ripping up the womb
       Of your dear mother England, blush for shame.
                              King John, Act v, sc. 2, l. 151 [BASTARD]

4949   Nero is an angler in the lake of darkness.
                              King Lear, Act iii, sc. 6, l. 8 [EDGAR]

News

4950   The nature of bad news infects the teller.
                              Antony and Cleopatra, Act i, sc. 2, l. 99 [MESSENGER]

4951   Though it be honest, it is never good
       To bring bad news: give to a gracious message
       An host or tongues; but let ill tidings tell
       Themselves when they be felt.
                              Antony and Cleopatra, Act ii, sc. 5, l. 85 [CLEOPATRA]

4952   If 't be summer news,
       Smile to 't before; if winterly, thou need'st
       But keep that countenance still.
                              Cymbeline, Act iii, sc. 4, l. 12 [IMOGEN]

4953   There's villanous news abroad.
                              I Henry IV, Act ii, sc. 4, l. 366 [FALSTAFF]

4954   The first bringer of unwelcome news
       Hath but a losing office, and his tongue
       Sounds ever after as a sullen bell,
       Remember'd tolling a departed friend.
                              II Henry IV, Act i, sc. 1, l. 100 [NORTHUMBERLAND]

4955   PISTOL: Sir John, I am thy Pistol and thy friend,
       And helter-skelter have I rode to thee,
       And tidings do I bring and lucky joys
       And golden times and happy news of price. . . .
       FALSTAFF: O base Assyrian knight, what is thy news?
       Let King Cophetua know the truth thereof.
       SILENCE: And Robin Hood, Scarlet, and John.
       PISTOL: Shall dung-hill curs confront the Helicons?
       And shall good news be baffled?
       Then, Pistol, lay thy head in Furies' lap.
                              II Henry IV, Act v, sc. 3, l. 97 [PISTOL]

4956   These news, I must confess, are full of grief.
                              III Henry VI, Act iv, sc. 4, l. 13 [RIVERS]

4957   Do not seek to stuff
       My head with more ill news, for it is full.
                              King John, Act iv, sc. 2, l. 133 [KING JOHN]

4958   I saw a smith stand with his hammer, thus,
The whilst his iron did on the anvil cool,
With open mouth swallowing a tailor's news.
King John, Act iv, sc. 2, l. 193 [HUBERT]

4959   The news is not so tart.
King Lear, Act iv, sc. 2, l. 87 [GONERIL]

4960   There is no composition in these news
That gives them credit.
Othello, Act i, sc. 3, l. 1 [DUKE]

4961   Though the news be sad, yet tell them merrily;
If good, thou shamest the music of sweet news
By playing it to me with so sour a face.
Romeo and Juliet, Act ii, sc. 5, l. 22 [JULIET]

4962   News, old news, and such news as you never heard of!
The Taming of the Shrew, Act iii, sc. 2, l. 30 [BIONDELLO]

4963   My ears are stopt and cannot hear good news,
So much of bad already hath possess'd them.
The Two Gentlemen of Verona, Act iii, sc. 1, l. 205 [VALENTINE]

News: What News?

4964   HAMLET: What's the news?
ROSENCRANTZ: None, my lord, but that the world's grown honest.
HAMLET: Then is doomsday near.
Hamlet, Act ii, sc. 2, l. 240 [HAMLET]

4965   BASTARD: Sans compliment, what news abroad? . . .
HUBERT: O, my sweet sir, news fitting to the night,
Black, fearful, comfortless and horrible.
BASTARD: Show me the very wound of this ill news:
I am no woman, I'll not swoon at it.
King John, Act v, sc. 6, l. 16 [BASTARD]

4966   ESCALUS: What news abroad i' the world?
DUKE: None, but that there is so great a fever on goodness, that
the dissolution of it must cure it. . . . This news is old enough, yet
it is every day's news.
Measure for Measure, Act iii, sc. 2, l. 234 [ESCALUS]

4967   What news on the Rialto?
The Merchant of Venice, Act i, sc. 3, l. 39 [SHYLOCK]
(Repeated in iii, 1, 1.)
What's the news with thee?
A Midsummer Night's Dream, Act i, sc. 1, l. 21 [THESEUS]

4968   SPEED: What news, then, in your paper?
LAUNCE: The blackest news that ever thou heard'st.
SPEED: Why, man, how black?
LAUNCE: Why, as black as ink.
The Two Gentlemen of Verona, Act iii, sc. 1, l. 283 [SPEED]

4969   FIRST GENTLEMAN: The news, Rogero?
ROGERO: Nothing but bonfires: the oracle is fulfilled; the king's
daughter is found: such a deal of wonder is broken out within
this hour that ballad-makers cannot be able to express it. . . .
This news which is called true is so like an old tale, that the
verity of it is in strong suspicion.
The Winter's Tale, Act v, sc. 2, l. 24 [FIRST GENTLEMAN]

Night

4970   Let's have one other gaudy night; call to me
All my sad captains; fill our bowls once more.
Antony and Cleopatra, Act iii, sc. 13, l. 182 [ANTONY]

4971   A great cause of the night is lack of the sun.
As You Like It, Act iii, sc. 2, l. 28 [CORIN]
When the sun sets, who doth not look for night?
Richard III, Act ii, sc. 3, l. 34 [CITIZEN]

4972   Come, my coach! Good night, ladies; good night, sweet ladies;
good night, good night.
Hamlet, Act iv, sc. 5, l. 72 [OPHELIA]

4973   GADSHILL: We have the receipt of fern-seed, we walk invisible.
CHAMBERLAIN: Nay, by my faith, I think you are more behold-
ing to the night than to fern-seed for your walking invisible.
I Henry IV, Act ii, sc. 1, l. 98 [GADSHILL]

4974   Now comes in the sweet o' the night.
II Henry IV, Act v, sc. 3, l. 52 [SILENCE]

4975   This night, wherein the cub-drawn bear would couch,
The lion and the belly-pinched wolf
Keep their fur dry.
King Lear, Act iii, sc. 1, l. 12 [GENTLEMAN]

4976   Things that love night
Love not such nights as these; the wrathful skies
Gallow the very wanderers of the dark,
And make them keep their caves.
King Lear, Act iii, sc. 2, l. 42 [KENT]

4977   Here's a night pities neither wise man nor fool.
King Lear, Act iii, sc. 2, l. 14 [FOOL]

4978   This is a brave night to cool a courtesan.
King Lear, Act iii, sc. 2, l. 79 [FOOL]

4979   'Tis a naughty night to swim in.
King Lear, Act iii, sc. 4, l. 116 [FOOL]

4980   Come, thick night,
And pall thee in the dunnest smoke of hell,
That my keen knife sees not the wound it makes,
Nor heaven peep through the blanket of the dark,
To cry 'Hold, hold!'
Macbeth, Act i, sc. 5, l. 51 [LADY MACBETH]

4981   Come, seeling night,
Scarf up the tender eye of pitiful day;
And with thy bloody and invisible hand
Cancel and tear to pieces that great bond
Which keeps me pale! Light thickens; and the crow
Makes wing to the rocky wood:
Good things of day begin to droop and drowse;
Whiles night's black agents to their preys do rouse.
Macbeth, Act iii, sc. 2, l. 46 [MACBETH]

4982   The night has been unruly: where we lay,
Our chimneys were blown down; . . . the obscure bird
Clamour'd the livelong night: some say, the earth
Was feverous and did shake.
Macbeth, Act ii, sc. 3, l. 59 [LENNOX]

4983   I must become a borrower of the night
For a dark hour or twain.
Macbeth, Act iii, sc. 1, l. 27 [BANQUO]

4984   MACBETH: What is the night?
LADY MACBETH: Almost at odds with morning, which is which.
Macbeth, Act iii, sc. 4, l. 126 [MACBETH]

4985   Receive what cheer you may:
The night is long that never finds the day.
Macbeth, Act iv, sc. 3, l. 239 [MALCOLM]

4986   This will last out a night in Russia,
When nights are longest there.

Measure for Measure, Act ii, sc. 1, l. 139 [ANGELO]

4987   LORENZO: The moon shines bright: in such a night as this,
When the sweet wind did gently kiss the trees
And they did make no noise, in such a night
Troilus methinks mounted the Trojan walls
And sigh'd his soul toward the Grecian tents,
Where Cressid lay that night.
JESSICA: In such a night
Did Thisbe fearfully o'ertrip the dew
And saw the lion's shadow ere himself
And ran dismay'd away.
LORENZO: In such a night
Stood Dido with a willow in her hand
Upon the wild sea banks and waft her love
To come again to Carthage.
JESSICA: In such a night
Medea gather'd the enchanted herbs
That did renew old Æson.
LORENZO: In such a night
Did Jessica steal from the wealthy Jew
And with an unthrift love did run from Venice
As far as Belmont.
JESSICA: In·such a night
Did young Lorenzo swear he loved her well,
Stealing her soul with many vows of faith
And ne'er a true one.
LORENZO: In such a night
Did pretty Jessica, like a little shrew,
Slander her love, and he forgave it her.

The Merchant of Venice, Act v, sc. 1, l. 1 [LORENZO]

4988   PORTIA: This night methinks is but the daylight sick;
It looks a little paler: 'tis a day,
Such as the day is when the sun is hid.
BASSANIO: We should hold day with the Antipodes,
If you would walk in absence of the sun.

The Merchant of Venice, Act v, sc. 1, l. 124 [PORTIA]

4989   It is not night when I do see your face,
Therefore I think I am not in the night.

A Midsummer Night's Dream, Act ii, sc. 1, l. 221 [HELENA]

4990   Dark night, that from the eye his function takes,
The ear more quick of apprehension makes;
Wherein it doth impair the seeing sense,
It pays the hearing double recompense.

A Midsummer Night's Dream, Act iii, sc. 2, l. 177 [HERMIA]

4991   This is the night
That either makes me or foredoes me quite.

Othello, Act v, sc. 1, l. 128 [IAGO]

4992   Good night, good rest. Ah, neither be my share:
She bade good night that kept my rest away;
And daff'd me to a cabin hanged with care,
To descant on the doubts of my decay.

The Passionate Pilgrim, Pt. xiv, l. 1

4993   Sable night, mother of dread and fear.

The Rape of Lucrece, l. 117

4994   The eye of heaven is out, and misty night
      Covers the shame that follows sweet delight.
                  The Rape of Lucrece, l. 356 [Tarquin]

4995   O comfort-killing Night, image of hell!
      Dim register and notary of shame!
      Black stage for tragedies and murders fell!
      Vast sin-concealing chaos! nurse of blame!
      Blind muffled bawd! dark harbour for defame!
                  The Rape of Lucrece, l. 764 [Lucrece]

4996   O, I have pass'd a miserable night,
      So full of ugly sights, of ghastly dreams,
      That, as I am a Christian faithful man,
      I would not spend another such a night,
      Though 'twere to buy a world of happy days,
      So full of dismal terror was the time!
            Richard III, Act i, sc. 4, l. 2 [Clarence]

4997   Gallop apace, you fiery-footed steeds,
      Towards Phœbus' lodging: such a waggoner
      As Phæthon would whip you to the west,
      And bring in cloudy night immediately.
      Spread thy close curtain, love-performing night.
          Romeo and Juliet, Act iii, sc. 2, l. 1 [Juliet]

4998   Come, civil night,
      Thou sober-suited matron, all in black
      And learn me how to lose a winning match,
      Play'd for a pair of stainless maidenhoods:
      Hood my unmann'd blood, bating in my cheeks,
      With thy black mantle. . . .
      Come, gentle night, come, loving, black-brow'd night,
      Give me my Romeo; and, when he shall die,
      Take him and cut him out in little stars,
      And he will make the face of heaven so fine
      That all the world will be in love with night,
      And pay no worship to the garish sun.
         Romeo and Juliet, Act iii, sc. 2, l. 10 [Juliet]

4999   Give not a windy night a rainy morrow.
                        Sonnet xc, l. 7

5000   Night, . . . with venomous wights she stays
      As tediously as hell, but flies the grasps of love
      With wings more momentary-swift than thought.
         Troilus and Cressida, Act iv, sc. 2, l. 12 [Troilus]

5001   The dragon-wing of night o'erspreads the earth.
         Troilus and Cressida, Act v, sc. 8, l. 17 [Achilles]

Nightingale

5002   My nightingale,
      We have beat them to their beds.
        Antony and Cleopatra, Act iv, sc. 8, l. 18 [Antony]

5003   The nightingale, if she should sing by day,
      When every goose is cackling, would be thought
      No better a musician than the wren.
        The Merchant of Venice, Act v, sc. 1, l. 104 [Portia]

Nile

5004   Thus do they, sir, they take the flow o' the Nile
      By certain scales i' the pyramid; they know,
      By the height, the lowness, or the mean, if dearth

> Or foison follow: the higher Nilus swells,
> The more it promises: as it ebbs, the seedsman
> Upon the slime and ooze scatters his grain,
> And shortly comes to harvest.
> > *Antony and Cleopatra*, Act ii, sc. 7, l. 20 [ANTONY]

Nobility

5005   Thrice-nobler than myself!
Thou teachest me, O valiant Eros, what
I should, and thou couldst not. My queen and Eros
Have by their brave instruction got upon me
A nobleness in record.
> *Antony and Cleopatra*, Act iv, sc. 14, l. 96 [ANTONY]

5006   I sin in envying his nobility,
And were I any thing but what I am,
I would wish me only he.
> *Coriolanus*, Act i, sc. 1, l. 234 [MARCIUS]

5007   A nobler sir ne'er lived 'Twixt sky and ground.
> *Cymbeline*, Act v, sc. 5, l. 145 [IACHIMO]

5008   True nobility is exempt from fear:
More can I bear than you dare execute.
> *II Henry VI*, Act iv, sc. 1, l. 129 [SUFFOLK]

5009   BEVIS: O miserable age! Virtue is not regarded in handicrafts-men.
HOLLAND: The nobility think scorn to go in leather aprons.
> *II Henry VI*, Act iv, sc. 2, l. 11 [BEVIS]

5010   Can ye endure to hear this arrogance?
And from this fellow? If we live thus tamely,
To be thus jaded by a piece of scarlet,
Farewell nobility!
> *Henry VIII*, Act iii, sc. 2, l. 278 [SURREY]

5011   Would God that any in this noble presence
Were enough noble to be upright judge
Of noble Richard! then true noblesse would
Learn him forbearance from so foul a wrong.
> *Richard II*, Act iv, sc. 1, l. 117 [CARLISLE]

5012   Many fair promotions
Are daily given to ennoble those
That scarce, some two days since, were worth a noble.
> *Richard III*, Act i, sc. 3, l. 80 [GLOUCESTER]

Nod

5013   I will practice the insinuating nod and be off to them most counterfeitly.
> *Coriolanus*, Act ii, sc. 3, l. 107 [CORIOLANUS]

5014   PANDARUS: I'll show you Troilus anon: if he sees me, you shall see him nod at me.
CRESSIDA: Will he give you the nod? . . . If he do the rich shall have more.
> *Troilus and Cressida*, Act i, sc. 2, l. 210 [PANDARUS]

Noddle

5015   Well, I will smite his noddles.
> *The Merry Wives of Windsor*, Act iii, sc. 1, l. 128 [EVANS]

5016   Doubt not her care should be
To comb your noddle with a three-legg'd stool
And paint your face and use you like a fool.
> *The Taming of the Shrew*, Act i, sc. 1, l. 63 [KATHARINA]

Nonpareil

5017   Spake you of Cæsar? How! the nonpareil!
          Antony and Cleopatra, Act iii, sc. 2, l. 11 [ENOBARBUS]

5018   My wife [seem'd] the nonpareil of this [time].
          Cymbeline, Act ii, sc. 5, l. 7 [POSTHUMUS]

5019   Thou art the best o' the cut-throats, . . .
    The nonpareil.
          Macbeth, Act iii, sc. 4, l. 18 [MACBETH]

5020   His daughter; he himself Calls her a nonpareil.
          The Tempest, Act iii, sc. 2, l. 107 [CALIBAN]

5021   If you were the devil, you are fair, . . .
    The nonpareil of beauty.
          Twelfth Night, Act i, sc. 5, l. 270 [VIOLA]

Nose

5022   We will nothing pay For wearing our own noses.
          Cymbeline, Act iii, sc. 1, l. 13 [CLOTEN]

5023   Thou canst tell why one's nose stands in the middle on 's face?
    . . . Why, to keep one's eyes of either side 's nose; that what a
    man cannot smell out, he may spy into.
          King Lear, Act i, sc. 5, l. 19 [FOOL]

5024   All that follow their noses are led by their eyes, but blind men;
    and there 's not a nose among twenty but can smell him that 's
    stinking.
          King Lear, Act ii, sc. 4, l. 70 [FOOL]

5025   It was not for nothing that my nose fell a-bleeding on Black-
    Monday last at six o'clock i' the morning.
          The Merchant of Venice, Act ii, sc. 5, l. 24 [LAUNCELOT]

5026   [He] will as tenderly be led by the nose
    As asses are.
          Othello, Act i, sc. 3, l. 407 [IAGO]

Nothing

5027   To say nothing, to do nothing, to know nothing, and to have noth-
    ing, is to be a great part of your title; which is within a very little
    of nothing.
          All's Well that Ends Well, Act ii, sc. 4, l. 25 [CLOWN]

5028   'Twas but a bolt of nothing, shot at nothing,
    Which the brain makes of fumes.
          Cymbeline, Act iv, sc. 2, l. 300 [IMOGEN]

5029   I am nothing: or if not,
    Nothing to be were better.
          Cymbeline, Act iv, sc. 2, l. 367 [IMOGEN]

5030   An a' do nothing but speak nothing, a' shall be nothing here.
          II Henry IV, Act ii, sc. 4, l. 207 [FALSTAFF]

5031   Having nothing, nothing can he lose.
          III Henry VI, Act iii, sc. 3, l. 152 [WARWICK]

5032   Nothing will come of nothing.
          King Lear, Act i, sc. 1, l. 92 [LEAR]

5033   FOOL: Can you make no use of nothing, nuncle?
    LEAR: Why, no, boy; nothing can be made out of nothing.
          King Lear, Act i, sc. 4, l. 144 [FOOL]

5034   Is whispering nothing?
    Is leaning cheek to cheek? is meeting noses?
    Kissing with inside lip? stopping the career
    Of laughter with a sigh? . . . horsing foot on foot?
    Skulking in corners? wishing clocks more swift?
    Hours, minutes? noon, midnight? and all eyes

> Blind with the pin and web but theirs, theirs only,
> That would unseen be wicked? is this nothing?
> Why, then the world and all that's in't is nothing;
> The covering sky is nothing; Bohemia nothing;
> My wife is nothing; nor nothing have these nothings,
> If this be nothing.
>
> *The Winter's Tale,* Act i, sc. 2, l. 284 [LEONTES]

Novelty

5035   Novelty is only in request; and it is as dangerous to be aged in
any kind of course, as it is virtuous to be constant in any under-
taking.
Measure for Measure, Act iii, sc. 2, l. 237 [DUKE]

5036   All with one consent praise new-born gawds,
Though they are made and moulded of things past,
And give to dust that is a little gilt
More laud than gilt o'er-dusted.
The present eye praises the present object.
Troilus and Cressida, Act iii, sc. 3, l. 176 [ULYSSES]

Nunnery

5037   Get thee to a nunnery: why wouldst thou be a breeder of sinners?
. . . Go thy ways to a nunnery. . . . Get thee to a nunnery, go:
farewell. . . . To a nunnery, go, and quickly too. . . . To a
nunnery, go.
Hamlet, Act iii, sc. 1, l. 122 [HAMLET]

Nymphs

5038   You nymphs, call'd Naiads, of the wandring brooks,
With your sedged crowns and ever-harmless looks,
Leave your crisp channels and on this green land
Answer your summons; Juno does command:
Come, temperate nymphs, and help to celebrate
A contract of true love; be not too late.
The Tempest, Act iv, sc. 1, l. 128 [IRIS]

O

5039   The little O, the earth.
Antony and Cleopatra, Act v, sc. 2, l. 81 [CLEOPATRA]
(For full quotation see 256.)

5040   May we cram
Within this wooden O the very casques
That did affright the air at Agincourt?
Henry V, Act i, Prologue, l. 13 [CHORUS]

5041   Thou art an O without a figure; . . . thou art nothing.
King Lear, Act i, sc. 4, l. 212 [FOOL]

5042   O that your face were not so full of O's!
Love's Labour's Lost, Act v, sc. 2, l. 45 [ROSALINE]

5043   Why should you fall into so deep an O?
Romeo and Juliet, Act iii, sc. 3, l. 90 [NURSE]

Oak

5044   An oak, whose boughs were moss'd with age
And high top bald with dry antiquity.
As You Like It, Act iv, sc. 3, l. 105 [OLIVER]

5045   To a cruel war I sent him; from whence he returned, his brows
bound with oak.
>> *Coriolanus,* Act i, sc. 3, l. 15 [VOLUMNIA]

5046   He proved best man i' the field, and for his meed
Was brow-bound with the oak.
>> *Coriolanus,* Act ii, sc. 2, l. 101 [COMINIUS]

5047   Many strokes, though with a little axe,
Hew down and fell the hardest-timber'd oak.
>> *III Henry VI,* Act ii, sc. 1, l. 54 [MESSENGER]

Oath

5048   All men
Have the like oaths: he had sworn to marry me
When his wife's dead; therefore I'll lie with him
When I am buried. Since Frenchmen are so braid,
Marry that will, I live and die a maid.
>> *All's Well that Ends Well,* Act iv, sc. 2, l. 70 [DIANA]
("Braid," deceitful.)

5049   TOUCHSTONE: No, by mine honour, but I was bid to come for you.
ROSALIND: Where learned you that oath, fool?
TOUCHSTONE: Of a certain knight that swore by his honour they
were good pancakes and swore by his honour the mustard was
naught.
>> *As You Like It,* Act i, sc. 2, l. 63 [TOUCHSTONE]

5050   Sword is an oath, and oaths must have their course.
>> *Henry V,* Act ii, sc. 1, l. 106 [PISTOL]

5051   The word is 'Pitch and Pay': Trust none;
For oaths are straws, men's faiths are wafer-cakes,
And hold-fast is the only dog, my duck.
Therefore, Caveto be thy counsellor.
>> *Henry V,* Act ii, sc. 3, l. 51 [PISTOL]

5052   It is great sin to swear unto a sin,
But greater sin to keep a sinful oath.
Who can be bound by any solemn vow
To do a murderous deed, to rob a man,
To force a spotless virgin's chastity,
To reave the orphan of his patrimony,
To wring the widow from her custom'd right,
And have no other reason for this wrong
But that he was bound by a solemn oath?
>> *II Henry VI,* Act v, sc. 1, l. 182 [SALISBURY]

5053   For a kingdom any oath may be broken.
>> *III Henry VI,* Act i, sc. 2, l. 16 [EDWARD]

5054   Having sworn too hard a keeping oath,
Study to break it and not break my troth.
>> *Love's Labour's Lost,* Act i, sc. 1, l. 65 [BIRON]

5055   I'll lay my head to any good man's hat,
These oaths and laws will prove an idle scorn.
>> *Love's Labour's Lost,* Act i, sc. 1, l. 310 [BIRON]

5056   Swearing till my very roof was dry
With oaths of love.
>> *The Merchant of Venice,* Act iii, sc. 2, l. 206 [GRATIANO]

5057   An oath, an oath, I have an oath in heaven:
Shall I lay perjury upon my soul?
>> *The Merchant of Venice,* Act iv, sc. 1, l. 228 [SHYLOCK]

5058   Then fate o'er-rules, that, one man holding troth,
A million fail, confounding oath on oath.
>> *A Midsummer Night's Dream,* Act iii, sc. 2, l. 92 [PUCK]

5059   I'll take thy word for faith, not ask thine oath:
        Who shuns not to break one will sure crack both.
                        Pericles, Act i, sc. 2, l. 120 [PERICLES]

5060   Cracking the strong warrant of an oath,
        Mark'd with a blot, damn'd in the book of heaven.
                  Richard II, Act iv, sc. 1, l. 235 [KING RICHARD]

5061   God pardon all oaths that are broke to me!
        God keep all vows unbroke that swear to thee!
                  Richard II, Act iv, sc. 1, l. 214 [KING RICHARD]

5062   Look thou be true; do not give dalliance
        Too much the rein; the strongest oaths are straw
        To the fire i' the blood.
                The Tempest, Act iv, sc. 1, l. 51 [PROSPERO]

5063   An idiot holds his bauble for a god
        And keeps the oath which by that god he swears.
              Titus Andronicus, Act v, sc. 1, l. 79 [AARON]

5064   It comes to pass oft that a terrible oath, with a swaggering accent
        sharply twanged off, gives manhood more approbation than ever
        proof itself would have earned him.
              Twelfth Night, Act iii, sc. 4, l. 197 [SIR TOBY]

5065   JULIA: A thousand oaths, an ocean of his tears
        And instances of infinite of love
        Warrant me welcome to my Proteus.
        LUCETTA: All these are servants to deceitful men.
          The Two Gentlemen of Verona, Act ii, sc. 7, l. 70 [JULIA]

Obedience

5066   I am his fortune's vassal. . . . I hourly learn
        A doctrine of obedience; and would gladly
        Look him i' the face.
          Antony and Cleopatra, Act v, sc. 2, l. 29 [CLEOPATRA]

5067   What he bids be done is finished with his bidding.
              Coriolanus, Act v, sc. 4, l. 24 [MENENIUS]

5068   Therefore doth heaven divide
        The state of man in divers functions,
        Setting endeavour in continual motion;
        To which is fixed, as an aim or butt,
        Obedience.
              Henry V, Act i, sc. 2, l. 183 [CANTERBURY]

5069   Let them obey that know not how to rule.
              II Henry VI, Act v, sc. 1, l. 6 [YORK]

5070   You have obedience scanted,
        And well are worth the want that you have wanted.
            King Lear, Act i, sc. 1, l. 281 [GONERIL]

Occasion

5071   A very little thief of occasion will rob you of a great deal of
        patience.
           Coriolanus, Act ii, sc. 1, l. 31 [MENENIUS]

5072   Occasion smiles upon a second leave.
             Hamlet, Act i, sc. 3, l. 54 [LAERTES]

5073   How all occasions do inform against me,
        And spur my dull revenge.
           Hamlet, Act iv, sc. 4, l. 32 [HAMLET]

5074   [I] am right glad to catch this good occasion
        Most thoroughly to be winnow'd, where my chaff
        And corn shall fly asunder.
          Henry VIII, Act v, sc. 1, l. 109 [CRANMER]

5075 Withhold thy speed, dreadful occasion!
O, make a league with me!
King John, Act iv, sc. 2, l. 125 [KING JOHN]

5076   Beshrew my soul
But I do love the favour and the form
Of this most fair occasion, by the which
We will untread the steps of damned flight.
King John, Act v, sc. 4, l. 49 [SALISBURY]

Odd and Even

5077 NURSE: How long is it now To Lammas-tide?
LADY CAPULET: A fortnight and odd days.
NURSE: Even or odd, of all days in the year,
Come Lammas-tide at night shall she be fourteen.
Romeo and Juliet, Act i, sc. 3, l. 14 [NURSE]

5078 MENELAUS: I'll give you boot, I'll give you three for one.
CRESSIDA: You're an odd man; give even, or give none.
MENELAUS: An odd man, lady! every man is odd.
CRESSIDA: No, Paris is not; for you know 'tis true,
That you are odd, and he is even with you.
Troilus and Cressida, Act iv, sc. 5, l. 40 [MENELAUS]

Odds

5079 'Tis odds beyond arithmetic.
Coriolanus, Act iii, sc. 1, l. 245 [COMINIUS]

5080 Your grace hath laid the odds o' the weaker side.
Hamlet, Act v, sc. 2, l. 272 [HAMLET]

5081 I will lay odds that, ere this year expire,
We bear our civil swords and native fire
As far as France.
II Henry IV, Act v, sc. 5, l. 111 [LANCASTER]

5082 EXETER: There's five to one. . . .
SALISBURY: God's arm strike with us! 'tis a fearful odds.
Henry V, Act iv, sc. 3, l. 4 [EXETER]

5083 LEONTES: You are married?
FLORIZEL: We are not, sir, nor are we like to be;
The stars, I see, will kiss the valleys first:
The odds for high and low's alike.
The Winter's Tale, Act v, sc. 1, l. 203 [LEONTES]

Offence

5084 O, my offence is rank, it smells to heaven;
It hath the primal eldest curse upon 't,
A brother's murder. . . .
May one be pardon'd and retain the offence?
In the corrupted currents of this world
Offence's gilded hand may shove by justice,
And oft 'tis seen the wicked prize itself
Buys out the law: but 'tis not so above;
There is no shuffling, there the action lies,
In his true nature; and we ourselves compell'd,
Even to the teeth and forehead of our faults,
To give in evidence.
Hamlet, Act iii, sc. 3, l. 36 [KING]

5085 Where the offence is let the great axe fall.
Hamlet, Act iv, sc. 5, l. 218 [KING]

5086   I'll so offend, to make offence a skill;
        Redeeming time when men think least I will.
                I Henry IV, Act i, sc. 2, 1. 239 [PRINCE HENRY]

5087   All offences, my lord, come from the heart.
                Henry V, Act iv, sc. 8, 1. 49 [WILLIAMS]

5088   O, he sits high in all the people's hearts:
        And that which would appear offence in us,
        His countenance, like richest alchemy,
        Will change to virtue and to worthiness.
            Julius Cæsar, Act i, sc. 3, 1. 157 [CASCA]

5089   In such a time as this it is not meet
        That every nice offence should bear his comment.
            Julius Cæsar, Act iv, sc. 3, 1. 7 [CASSIUS]

5090   All my offences that abroad you see
        Are errors of the blood, none of the mind.
                  A Lover's Complaint, 1. 183

5091   Hence hath offence his quick celerity
        When it is borne in high authority.
           Measure for Measure, Act iv, sc. 2, 1. 113 [DUKE]

5092   The offender's sorrow lends but weak relief
        To him that bears the strong offence's cross.
                    Sonnet xxxiv, 1. 11

Officer

5093   Art thou officer? Or art thou base, common and popular?
               Henry V, Act iv, sc. 1, 1. 37 [PISTOL]

5094   Cassio, I love thee;
        But never more be officer of mine.
            Othello, Act ii, sc. 3, 1. 248 [OTHELLO]

Omen

5095   In the most high and palmy state of Rome,
        A little ere the mightiest Julius fell,
        The graves stood tenantless and the sheeted dead
        Did squeak and gibber in the Roman streets: . . .
        And prologue to the omen coming on.
           Hamlet, Act i, sc. 1, 1. 113 [HORATIO]

5096   I have seen tempests, when the scolding winds
        Have rived the knotty oaks, and I have seen
        The ambitious ocean swell and rage and foam,
        To be exalted with the threatening clouds;
        But never till to-night, never till now,
        Did I go through tempest dropping fire.
        Either there is a civil strife in heaven,
        Or else the world, too saucy with the gods,
        Incenses them to send destruction.
           Julius Cæsar, Act i, sc. 3, 1. 5 [CASCA]

5097   A lioness hath whelped in the streets;
        And graves have yawn'd, and yielded up their dead;
        Fierce fiery warriors fought upon the clouds,
        In ranks and squadrons and right form of war,
        Which drizzled blood upon the Capitol;
        The noise of battle hurtled in the air,
        Horses did neigh, and dying men did groan,
        And ghosts did shriek and squeal about the streets.
        O Cæsar! these things are beyond all use,
        And I do fear them.
           Julius Cæsar, Act ii, sc. 2, 1. 17 [CALPURNIA]

One

5098   One is one too many.
       The Comedy of Errors, Act iii, sc. 1, l. 35 [DROMIO OF SYRACUSE]

5099   All's one to me.
       II Henry VI, Act i, sc. 3, l. 105 [KING]
       'Tis all one to me.
       Troilus and Cressida, Act i, sc. 1, l. 80 [PANDARUS]
       The Winter's Tale, Act v, sc. 2, l. 131 [AUTOLYCUS]

5100   One for all, or all for one we gage.
       The Rape of Lucrece, l. 144

Opinion

5101   What's the matter, you dissentious rogues,
       That, rubbing the poor itch of your opinion,
       Make yourselves scabs?
       Coriolanus, Act i, sc. 1, l. 168 [CORIOLANUS]

5102   In the gross and scope of my opinion,
       This bodes some strange eruption to our state.
       Hamlet, Act i, sc. 1, l. 68 [HORATIO]

5103   The most fond and winnowed opinions.
       Hamlet, Act v, sc. 2, l. 201 [HAMLET]

5104   Had I so lavish of my presence been,
       So common-hackney'd in the eyes of men,
       So stale and cheap to vulgar company,
       Opinion, that did help me to the crown,
       Had still kept loyal to possession
       And left me in reputeless banishment.
       I Henry IV, Act iii, sc. 2, l. 39 [KING HENRY]

5105   I have bought
       Golden opinions from all sorts of people,
       Which would be worn now in their newest gloss,
       Not cast aside so soon.
       Macbeth, Act i, sc. 7, l. 32 [MACBETH]

5106   There are a sort of men whose visages
       Do cream and mantle like a standing pond,
       And do a wilful stillness entertain,
       With purpose to be dress'd in an opinion
       Of wisdom, gravity, profound conceit. . . .
       But fish not, with this melancholy bait,
       For this fool gudgeon, this opinion.
       The Merchant of Venice, Act i, sc. 1, l. 88 [GRATIANO]

5107   Opinion, a sovereign mistress of effects.
       Othello, Act i, sc. 3, l. 225 [DUKE]

5108   Opinion's but a fool, that makes us scan
       The outward habit by the inward man.
       Pericles, Act ii, sc. 2, l. 56 [SIMONIDES]

5109   A plague of opinion: a man may wear it on both sides, like a
       leather jerkin.
       Troilus and Cressida, Act iii, sc. 3, l. 266 [THERSITES]

Opportunity

5110   O Opportunity, thy guilt is great!
       'Tis thou that executest the traitor's treason:
       Thou set'st the wolf where he the lamb may get:
       Whoever plots the sin, thou 'point'st the season. . . .
       How comes it then, vile Opportunity,
       Being so bad, such numbers seek for thee?
       The Rape of Lucrece, l. 876 [LUCRECE]

Oracle

5111   Oracles are hardly attain'd, And hardly understood.
                            II Henry VI, Act i, sc. 4, l. 74 [YORK]

5112   I am Sir Oracle,
        And when I ope my lips let no dog bark!
                    The Merchant of Venice, Act i, sc. 1, l. 93 [GRATIANO]

Orator

5113   Very good orators, when they are out, they will spit.
                        As You Like It, Act iv, sc. 1, l. 75 [ROSALIND]

5114   I'll play the orator as well as Nestor,
        Deceive more slily than Ulysses could,
        And, like a Sinon, take another Troy.
        I can add colours to the chameleon,
        Change shapes with Proteus for advantages,
        And set the murderous Machiavel to school.
                        III Henry VI, Act iii, sc. 2, l. 188 [RICHARD]

5115   Full well hath Clifford play'd the orator,
        Inferring arguments of mighty force.
                        III Henry VI, Act ii, sc. 2, l. 43 [KING HENRY]

5116   Her modest eloquence with sighs is mixed,
        Which to her oratory adds more grace.
        She puts the period often from his place.
                                The Rape of Lucrece, l. 563

5117   More I could tell, but more I dare not say;
        The text is old, the orator too green.
                            Venus and Adonis, l. 805 [ADONIS]

Ornament

5118   The world is still deceived with ornament. . . .
        Thus ornament is but the guiled shore
        To a most dangerous sea; the beauteous scarf
        Veiling an Indian beauty; in a word,
        The seeming truth which cunning time puts on
        To entrap the wisest.
                    The Merchant of Venice, Act iii, sc. 2, l. 74 [BASSANIO]

Orpheus

5119   Orpheus with his lute made trees,
                As the mountain tops that freeze,
                    Bow themselves when he did sing:
                To his music plants and flowers
                Ever sprung; as sun and showers
                    There had made a lasting spring.

                Every thing that heard him play,
                Even the billows of the sea,
                    Hung their heads, and then lay by.
                In sweet music is such art,
                Killing care and grief of heart
                    Fall asleep, or hearing, die.
                            Henry VIII, Act iii, sc. 1, l. 3 [SONG]

5120   Moody Pluto winks while Orpheus plays.
                                The Rape of Lucrece, l. 553

5121   Orpheus' lute was strung with poets' sinews,
        Whose golden touch could soften steel and stones,
        Make tigers tame and huge leviathans
        Forsake unsounded deeps to dance on sands.
                    The Two Gentlemen of Verona, Act iii, sc. 2, l. 78 [PROTEUS]

Owl

5122   They say the owl was a baker's daughter.
Hamlet, Act iv, sc. 5, l. 41 [OPHELIA]

5123   Yesterday the bird of night did sit
Even at noon-day upon the market-place,
Hooting and shrieking.
Julius Cæsar, Act i, sc. 3, l. 26 [CASCA]

5124   When icicles hang by the wall
       And Dick the shepherd blows his nail
   And Tom bears logs into the hall
       And milk comes frozen home in pail,
When blood is nipp'd and ways be foul,
Then nightly sings the staring owl,
       Tu-whit;
Tu-who, a merry note,
While greasy Joan doth keel the pot.
Love's Labour's Lost, Act v, sc. 2, l. 922 [SONG]

5125   It was the owl that shriek'd, the fatal bellman,
Which gives the stern'st good-night.
Macbeth, Act ii, sc. 2, l. 4 [LADY MACBETH]

5126   The clamorous owl that nightly hoots and wonders
At our quaint spirits.
A Midsummer Night's Dream, Act ii, sc. 2, l. 6 [TITANIA]

5127   The owl, night's herald, shrieks, ''Tis very late';
The sheep are gone to fold, birds to their nest.
Venus and Adonis, l. 531 [ADONIS]

P

Pack-Horse

5128   Shall pack-horses
And hollow pamper'd jades of Asia,
Which cannot go but thirty mile a day,
Compare with Cæsars?
II Henry IV, Act ii, sc. 4, l. 176 [PISTOL]

5129   Ere you were queen, yea, or your husband king,
I was a pack-horse in his great affairs;
A weeder-out of his proud adversaries,
A liberal rewarder of his friends.
Richard III, Act i, sc. 3, l. 122 [GLOUCESTER]

Pain

5130   How light and portable my pain seems now,
When that which makes me bend makes the king bow.
King Lear, Act iii, sc. 6, l. 115 [EDGAR]

5131   One pain is lessen'd by another's anguish.
Romeo and Juliet, Act i, sc. 2, l. 47 [BENVOLIO]
(A variation of the proverb, "Misery loves company.")

Pains

5132   Lord, how we lose our pains!
All's Well that Ends Well, Act v, sc. 1, l. 24 [WIDOW]

5133   You lay out too much pains
For purchasing but trouble.
Cymbeline, Act ii, sc. 3, l. 92 [IMOGEN]

5134   'Tis good for men to love their present pains
Upon example; so the spirit is eased:
And when the mind is quicken'd, out of doubt,
The organs, though defunct and dead before,
Break up their drowsy grave and newly move,
With casted slough and fresh legerity.
Henry V, Act iv, sc. 1, l. 18 [KING HENRY]

Painting

5135   I have heard of your paintings too, well enough; God has given
you one face, and you make yourselves another: you jig, you
amble, and you lisp, and nickname God's creatures, and make your
wantonness your ignorance.
Hamlet, Act iii, sc. 1, l. 148 [HAMLET]

5136   Why should false painting imitate his cheek
And steal dead seeing of his living hue?
Why should poor beauty indirectly seek
Roses of shadow, since his rose is true?
Sonnet lxvii, l. 6

Palm

5138   IRAS: There's a palm presages chastity, if nothing else. . . .
CHARMIAN: Nay, if an oily palm be not a fruitful prognostication,
I cannot scratch mine ear.
Antony and Cleopatra, Act i, sc. 2, l. 49 [IRAS]

5139   Let me tell you, Cassius, you yourself
Are much condemn'd to have an itching palm.
Julius Cæsar, Act iv, sc. 3, l. 9 [BRUTUS]

5140   He takes her by the palm. . . . Didst thou not see her paddle
with the palm of his hand?
Othello, Act ii, sc. 1, l. 168 [IAGO]

5141   You shall see him a palm in Athens again, and flourish with the
highest.
Timon of Athens, Act v, sc. 1, l. 12 [PAINTER]

5142   To be paddling palms and pinching fingers,
As now they are, and making practised smiles,
As in a looking-glass, and then to sigh, as 'twere
The mort o' the deer; O, that is entertainment
My bosom likes not, nor my brows! . . . Still virginalling
Upon his palm!
The Winter's Tale, Act i, sc. 2, l. 115 [LEONTES]

Pandar

5143   Shall I Sir Pandarus of Troy become,
And by my side wear steel? then, Lucifer take all!
The Merry Wives of Windsor, Act i, sc. 3, l. 81 [PISTOL]

5144   I cannot come to Cressid but by Pandar.
Troilus and Cressida, Act i, sc. 1, l. 98 [TROILUS]

5145   Let all pitiful goers-between be called to the world's end after my
name; call them all Pandars; let all constant men be Troiluses,
all false women Cressids, and all brokers-between Pandars!
Troilus and Cressida, Act iii, sc. 2, l. 208 [PANDARUS]

Paradise

5146   You would for paradise break faith and troth;
And Jove, for your love, would infringe an oath.
Love's Labour's Lost, Act iv, sc. 3, l. 143 [KING]

5147   If ye should lead her into a fool's paradise, as they say, it were
        a very gross kind of behaviour.
                            Romeo and Juliet, Act ii, sc. 4, l. 175 [NURSE]
5148   Let me live here ever;
        So rare a wonder'd father and a wife
        Makes this place Paradise.
                            The Tempest, Act iv, sc. 1, l. 122 [FERDINAND]

Paradox

5149   These are old fond paradoxes to make fools laugh i' the alehouse.
                            Othello, Act ii, sc. 1, l. 139 [DESDEMONA]
5150   You undergo too strict a paradox,
        Striving to make an ugly deed look fair.
                            Timon of Athens, Act iii, sc. 5, l. 24 [SENATOR]
5151   Success or loss, what is or is not, serves
        As stuff for these two to make paradoxes.
                            Troilus and Cressida, Act i, sc. 3, l. 183 [ULYSSES]

Paramour

5152   Fitter is my study and my books
        Than wanton dalliance with a paramour.
                            I Henry VI, Act v, sc. 1, l. 22 [KING]
5153   Fond man, remember that thou hast a wife;
        Then how can Margaret be thy paramour?
                            I Henry VI, Act v, sc. 3, l. 81 [SUFFOLK]
5154   QUINCE: He is a very paramour for a sweet voice.
        FLUTE: You must say 'paragon': a paramour is, God bless us, a
        thing of naught.
                            A Midsummer Night's Dream, Act iv, sc. 2, l. 12 [QUINCE]

Parasite

5155   Live loathed and long,
        Most smiling, smooth, detested parasites,
        Courteous destroyers, affable wolves, meek bears,
        You fools of fortune, trencher-friends, time's flies,
        Cap and knee slaves, vapours, and minute-jacks!
                            Timon of Athens, Act iii, sc. 6, l. 103 [TIMON]

Pardon

5156   I minded him how royal 'twas to pardon
        When it was less expected.
                            Coriolanus, Act v, sc. 1, l. 18 [COMINIUS]
5157   Pardon's the word to all.
                            Cymbeline, Act v, sc. 5, l. 422 [CYMBELINE]
5158   Give me your pardon, sir: I've done you wrong;
        But pardon 't, as you are a gentleman.
                            Hamlet, Act v, sc. 2, l. 238 [HAMLET]
5159   I humbly do beseech you of your pardon
        For too much loving you.
                            Othello, Act iii, sc. 3, l. 212 [IAGO]
5160   For ever may my knees grow to the earth,
        My tongue cleave to my roof within my mouth,
        Unless a pardon ere I rise or speak.
                            Richard II, Act v, sc. 3, l. 30 [AUMERLE]
5161   An if I were thy nurse, thy tongue to teach,
        'Pardon' should be the first word of thy speech. . . .
        The word is short, but not so short as sweet;
        No word like 'pardon' for kings' mouths so meet.
                            Richard II, Act v, sc. 3, l. 113 [DUCHESS]

Paris

5162   ÆNEAS : Paris returned home and hurt.
        TROILUS : By whom, Æneas?
        ÆNEAS :   By Menelaus.
        TROILUS : Let Paris bleed: 'tis but a scar to scorn;
        Paris is gored with Menelaus' horn.
                        Troilus and Cressida, Act i, sc. 1, l. 112 [ÆNEAS]

5163   Troy must not be, nor goodly Ilion stand;
        Our firebrand brother, Paris, burns us all.
                        Troilus and Cressida, Act ii, sc. 2, l. 109 [CASSANDRA]

5164   Paris, you speak
        Like one besotted on your sweet delights:
        You have the honey still, but these the gall;
        So to be valiant is no praise at all.
                        Troilus and Cressida, Act ii, sc. 2, l. 142 [PRIAM]

Parting

5165   POSTHUMUS : Should we be taking leave
        As long a term as yet we have to live,
        The loathness to depart would grow. Adieu!
        IMOGEN :   Nay, stay a little.
        Were you but riding forth to air yourself,
        Such parting were too petty.
                        Cymbeline, Act i, sc. 1, l. 107 [POSTHUMUS]

5166   Without more circumstance at all,
        I hold it fit that we shake hands and part;
        You as your business and desire shall point you; . . .
        And for mine own poor part, Look you, I'll go pray.
                        Hamlet, Act i, sc. 5, l. 127 [HAMLET]

5167   And even there, his eye being big with tears,
        Turning his face, he put his hand behind him,
        And with affection wondrous sensible
        He wrung Bassanio's hand; and so they parted.
                        The Merchant of Venice, Act ii, sc. 8, l. 46 [SALARINO]

5168   QUEEN : And must we be divided? must we part?
        KING RICHARD : Ay, hand from hand, my love, and heart from
        heart.
                        Richard II, Act v, sc. 1, l. 81 [QUEEN]

5169   'Tis almost morning; I would have thee gone:
        And yet no further than a wanton's bird;
        Who lets it hop a little from her hand,
        Like a poor prisoner in his twisted gyves,
        And with a silk thread plucks it back again. . . .
        Good night, good night! parting is such sweet sorrow,
        That I shall say good night till it be to-morrow.
                        Romeo and Juliet, Act ii, sc. 2, l. 177 [JULIET]

Passion

5170   ROSALIND : Jove, Jove! this shepherd's passion
        Is much upon my fashion.
        TOUCHSTONE : And mine; but it grows somewhat stale with me.
                        As You Like It, Act ii, sc. 4, l. 61 [ROSALIND]

5171   Give me that man
        That is not passion's slave, and I will wear him
        In my heart's core, ay, in my heart of heart.
                        Hamlet, Act iii, sc. 2, l. 76 [HAMLET]

5172   The bravery of his grief did put me
       Into a towering passion.
                              Hamlet, Act v, sc. 2, l. 79 [HAMLET]
5173   Passion, I see, is catching.
                              Julius Cæsar, Act iii, sc. 1, l. 283 [ANTONY]
5174   This passion, and the death of a dear friend, would go near to
       make a man look sad.
                              A Midsummer Night's Dream, Act v, sc. 1, l. 293 [THESEUS]
5175   Passion, having my best judgment collied,
       Assays to lead the way.
                              Othello, Act ii, sc. 3, l. 206 [OTHELLO]
5176   O well-painted passion!
                              Othello, Act iv, sc. 1, l. 268 [OTHELLO]
5177   Alas, why gnaw you so your nether lip?
       Some bloody passion shakes your very frame:
       These are portents: but yet I hope, I hope,
       They do not point on me.
                              Othello, Act v, sc. 2, l. 43 [DESDEMONA]
5178   The passions of the mind,
       That have their first conceptions by mis-dread,
       Have after-nourishment and life by care;
       And what was first but fear what might be done,
       Grows elder now and cares it be not done.
                              Pericles, Act i, sc. 2, l. 11 [PERICLES]

Past

5179   Things that are past are done with me.
                              Antony and Cleopatra, Act i, sc. 2, l. 101 [ANTONY]
5180   O thoughts of men accursed!
       Past and to come seems best; things present worst.
                              II Henry IV, Act i, sc. 3, l. 107 [ARCHBISHOP]
5181   What's past and what's to come is strew'd with husks
       And formless ruin of oblivion.
                              Troilus and Cressida, Act iv, sc. 5, l. 166 [AGAMEMNON]

Pasture

5182   Good pasture makes fat sheep.
                              As You Like It, Act iii, sc. 2, l. 28 [CORIN]
5183   It is the pasture lards the rother's sides,
       The want that makes him lean.
                              Timon of Athens, Act iv, sc. 3, l. 12 [TIMON]

Pat

5184   Now might I do it pat.
                              Hamlet, Act iii, sc. 3, l. 73 [HAMLET]
5185   Pat he comes like the catastrophe of the old comedy.
                              King Lear, Act i, sc. 2, l. 146 [EDMUND]
5186   It will fall pat as I told you.
                              A Midsummer Night's Dream, Act v, sc. 1, l. 188 [PYRAMUS]

Path

5187   Do not, as some ungracious pastors do,
       Show me the steep and thorny way to heaven;
       Whiles, like a puff'd and reckless libertine,
       Himself the primrose path of dalliance treads,
       And recks not his own rede.
                              Hamlet, Act i, sc. 3, l. 47 [OPHELIA]

5188   Go, tread the path that thou shalt ne'er return.
> *Richard III,* Act i, sc. 1, l. 117 [GLOUCESTER]

5189   The path is smooth that leadeth on to danger.
> *Venus and Adonis,* l. 788 [ADONIS]

Patience

5190   Patience is sottish, and impatience does
Become a dog that's mad.
> *Antony and Cleopatra,* Act iv, sc. 15, l. 79 [CLEOPATRA]

5191   Upon the heat and flame of thy distemper
Sprinkle cool patience.
> *Hamlet,* Act iii, sc. 4, l. 123 [QUEEN]

5192   As patient as the female dove.
> *Hamlet,* Act v, sc. 1, l. 309 [QUEEN]

5193   You tread upon my patience.
> *I Henry IV,* Act i, sc. 3, l. 4 [KING HENRY]

5194   Though patience be a tired mare, yet she will plod.
> *Henry V,* Act ii, sc. 1, l. 26 [NYM]

5195   I will be the pattern of all patience.
> *King Lear,* Act iii, sc. 2, l. 37 [LEAR]

5196   I thank God I have as little patience as another man; and therefore I can be quiet.
> *Love's Labour's Lost,* Act i, sc. 2, l. 170 [COSTARD]

5197   I do oppose
My patience to his fury, and am arm'd
To suffer, with a quietness of spirit,
The very tyranny and rage of his.
> *The Merchant of Venice,* Act iv, sc. 1, l. 10 [ANTONIO]

5198   'Tis all men's office to speak patience
To those that wring under the load of sorrow,
But no man's virtue nor sufficiency
To be so moral when he shall endure
The like himself.
> *Much Ado about Nothing,* Act v, sc. 1, l. 27 [LEONATO]

5199   What cannot be preserved when fortune takes,
Patience her injury a mockery makes.
> *Othello,* Act i, sc. 3, l. 206 [DUKE]

5200   How poor are they that have not patience!
> *Othello,* Act ii, sc. 3, l. 376 [IAGO]

5201   Thou dost look
Like Patience gazing on kings' graves, and smiling
Extremity out of act.
> *Pericles,* Act v, sc. 1, l. 138 [PERICLES]

5202   Patience is stale, and I am weary of it.
> *Richard II,* Act v, sc. 5, l. 105 [KING RICHARD]

5203   For patience she will prove a second Grissel.
> *The Taming of the Shrew,* Act ii, sc. 1, l. 297 [PETRUCHIO]

5204   Patience herself, what goddess e'er she be,
Doth lesser blench at sufferance than I.
> *Troilus and Cressida,* Act i, sc. 1, l. 27 [TROILUS]

Payment

5206   Base is the slave that pays.
> *Henry V,* Act ii, sc. 1, l. 99 [PISTOL]

5207   He is well paid that is well satisfied.
> *The Merchant of Venice,* Act iv, sc. 1, l. 415 [PORTIA]

5208   You pay a great deal too dear for what's given freely.
> *The Winter's Tale,* Act i, sc. 1, l. 18 [CAMILLO]

Peace

5209 The time of universal peace is near:
Prove this a prosperous day, the three-nook'd world
Shall bear the olive freely.
Antony and Cleopatra, Act iv, sc. 6, l. 5 [OCTAVIUS CÆSAR]
Peace puts forth her olive every where.
II Henry IV, Act iv, sc. 4, l. 86 [WESTMORELAND]

5210 Blessed are the peacemakers on earth.
II Henry VI, Act ii, sc. 1, l. 35 [KING]

5211 Our peace will, like a broken limb united,
Grow stronger for the breaking.
II Henry IV, Act iv, sc. 1, l. 222 [ARCHBISHOP]

5212 A peace is of the nature of a conquest;
For then both parties nobly are subdued,
And neither party loser.
II Henry IV, Act iv, sc. 2, l. 89 [ARCHBISHOP]

5213 I demand, before this royal view,
What rub or what impediment there is,
Why that the naked, poor and mangled Peace,
Dear nurse of arts, plenties and joyful births,
Should not in this best garden of the world,
Our fertile France, put up her lovely visage?
Henry V, Act v, sc. 2, l. 32 [BURGUNDY]

5214 Still in thy right hand carry gentle peace,
To silence envious tongues.
Henry VIII, Act iii, sc. 2, l. 445 [WOLSEY]

5215 The peace of heaven is theirs that lift their swords
In such a just and charitable war.
King John, Act ii, sc. 1, l. 35 [AUSTRIA]

5216 This weak piping time of peace.
Richard III, Act i, sc. 1, l. 24 [GLOUCESTER]

5217 TYBALT: What, art thou drawn among these heartless hinds?
Turn thee, Benvolio, look upon thy death.
BENVOLIO: I do but keep the peace. . . .
TYBALT: What, drawn, and talk of peace! I hate the word
As I hate hell.
Romeo and Juliet, Act i, sc. 1, l. 73 [TYBALT]

5218 'Tis not so hard, I think,
For men so old as we to keep the peace.
Romeo and Juliet, Act i, sc. 2, l. 2 [CAPULET]

Peacock

5219 Let frantic Talbot triumph for a while
And like a peacock sweep along his tail;
We'll pull his plumes and take away his train.
I Henry VI, Act iii, sc. 3, l. 5 [PUCELLE]

5220 He stalks up and down like a peacock,—a stride and a stand.
Troilus and Cressida, Act iii, sc. 3, l. 251 [THERSITES]

Pearl

5221 The firm Roman to great Egypt sends
This treasure of an oyster.
Antony and Cleopatra, Act i, sc. 5, l. 43 [ALEXAS]

5222 Bright orient pearl, alack, too timely shaded!
Fair creature, kill'd too soon by death's sharp sting!
Like a green plum that hangs upon a tree,
And falls, through wind, before the fall should be.
The Passionate Pilgrim, l. 133

5223 Pearls are fair; and the old saying is
      Black men are pearls in beauteous ladies' eyes.
                    The Two Gentlemen of Verona, Act v, sc. 2, 1. 11 [PROTEUS]

Penny

5224   Take an inventory of all I have,
      To the last penny; 'tis the king's.
                                    Henry VIII, Act iii, sc. 2, 1. 451 [WOLSEY]

5225 An I had but one penny in the world, thou shouldst have it to buy
      gingerbread, . . . thou halfpenny purse of wit, thou pigeon-egg of
      discretion.
                        Love's Labour's Lost, Act v, sc. 1, 1. 74 [COSTARD]

Perfection

5226 The chief perfections of that lovely dame,
      Had I sufficient skill to utter them,
      Would make a volume of enticing lines,
      Able to ravish any dull conceit.
                              I Henry VI, Act v, sc. 5, 1. 12 [SUFFOLK]

5227 She's a most exquisite lady. . . . She is indeed perfection.
                              Othello, Act ii, sc. 3, 1. 18 [CASSIO]

5228 No perfection is so absolute,
      That some impurity doth not pollute.
                        The Rape of Lucrece, 1. 853 [LUCRECE]

Perjury

5229 Thus pour the stars down plagues for perjury.
      Can any face of brass hold longer out?
                        Love's Labour's Lost, Act v, sc. 2, 1. 394 [BIRON]

5230 Now, to our perjury we add more terror,
      We are again forsworn, in will and error.
                        Love's Labour's Lost, Act v, sc. 2, 1. 470 [BIRON]

5231 Why, this is flat perjury, to call a prince's brother villain.
                    Much Ado about Nothing, Act iv, sc. 2, 1. 44 [DOGBERRY]

5232   Sweet soul, take heed,
      Take heed of perjury; thou art on thy death-bed. . . .
      O perjured woman, thou dost stone my heart!
                              Othello, Act v, sc. 2, 1. 50 [OTHELLO]

Perseverance

5233   Perseverance, dear my lord,
      Keeps honour bright: to have done is to hang
      Quite out of fashion, like a rusty mail
      In monumental mockery.
                        Troilus and Cressida, Act iii, sc. 3, 1. 150 [ULYSSES]

Persuasion

5234 God give thee the spirit of persuasion and him the ears of profiting,
      that what thou speakest may move and what he hears may be
      believed.
                              I Henry IV, Act i, sc. 2, 1. 170 [FALSTAFF]

5235 Better consider what you have to do
      Than I, that have not well the gift of tongue,
      Can lift your blood up with persuasion.
                              I Henry IV, Act v, sc. 2, 1. 77 [HOTSPUR]

5236   She hath prosperous art
      When she will play with reason and discourse,
      And well she can persuade.
                        Measure for Measure, Act i, sc. 2, 1. 189 [CLAUDIO]

Petticoat

5237   When old robes are worn out, there are members to make new.
        . . . Your old smock brings forth a new petticoat.
            Antony and Cleopatra, Act i, sc. 2, l. 170 [ENOBARBUS]
5238   Methought he had made two holes in the ale-wife's new petticoat
        and so peeped through.
            II Henry IV, Act ii, sc. 2, l. 88 [PAGE]
5239   You might still have worn the petticoat,
        And ne'er have stol'n the breech from Lancaster.
            III Henry VI, Act v, sc. 5, l. 23 [GLOUCESTER]

Phaethon

5240   Why, Phaethon,—for thou art Merops' son,—
        Wilt thou aspire to guide the heavenly car
        And with thy daring folly burn the world?
        Wilt thou reach stars, because they shine on thee?
            The Two Gentlemen of Verona, Act iii, sc. 1, l. 153 [DUKE]

Philippi

5241   BRUTUS: How ill this taper burns! Ha! who comes here?
        I think it is the weakness of mine eyes
        That shapes this monstrous apparition.
        It comes upon me. Art thou any thing?
        Art thou some god, some angel, or some devil,
        That makest my blood cold and my hair to stare?
        Speak to me what thou art.
        GHOST OF CÆSAR: Thy evil spirit, Brutus.
        BRUTUS: Why comest thou?
        GHOST: To tell thee thou shalt see me at Philippi.
        BRUTUS: Well; then I shall see thee again?
        GHOST: Ay, at Philippi.
        BRUTUS: Why, I will see thee at Philippi, then.
            Julius Cæsar, Act iv, sc. 3, l. 275 [BRUTUS]

Philomela

5242   While Philomela sits and sings, I sit and mark,
        And wish her lays were tuned like the lark;
        For she doth welcome daylight with her ditty,
        And drives away dark dismal-dreaming night.
            The Passionate Pilgrim, l. 197
5243   Philomel in summer's front doth sing
        And stops her pipe in growth of riper days.
            Sonnet cii, l. 7
5244   His Philomel must lose her tongue to-day,
        Thy sons make pillage of her chastity.
            Titus Andronicus, Act ii, sc. 3, l. 43 [AARON]

Philosophy

5245   Hast any philosophy in thee, shepherd? . . . Such a one is a
        natural philosopher.
            As You Like It, Act iii, sc. 2, l. 23 [TOUCHSTONE]
5246   There are more things in heaven and earth, Horatio,
        Than are dreamt of in your philosophy.
            Hamlet, Act i, sc. 5, l. 166 [HAMLET]
5247   There is something in this more than natural, if philosophy could
        find it out.
            Hamlet, Act ii, sc. 2, l. 385 [HAMLET]

5248   Of your philosophy you make no use,
If you give place to accidental evils.
Julius Cæsar, Act iv, sc. 3, l. 145 [CASSIUS]

5249   I fear he will prove the weeping philosopher when he grows old,
being so full of unmannerly sadness in his youth.
The Merchant of Venice, Act i, sc. 2, l. 52 [PORTIA]

5250   I pray thee, peace. I will be flesh and blood;
For there was never yet philosopher
That could endure the toothache patiently,
However they have writ the style of gods
And made a push at chance and sufferance.
Much Ado about Nothing, Act v, sc. 1, l. 34 [LEONATO]

5251   FRIAR LAURENCE: I'll give thee armour; . . .
Adversity's sweet milk, philosophy,
To comfort thee, though thou art banished.
ROMEO: . . . Hang up philosophy!
Unless philosophy can make a Juliet
Displant a town, reverse a prince's doom,
It helps not, it prevails not: talk no more.
Romeo and Juliet, Act iii, sc. 3, l. 54 [FRIAR LAURENCE]

5252   Continue your resolve
To suck the sweets of sweet philosophy.
The Taming of the Shrew, Act i, sc. 1, l. 27 [TRANIO]

Phœnix

5253   From their ashes shall be rear'd
A phœnix that shall make all France afeard.
I Henry VI, Act iv, sc. 7, l. 92 [LUCY]

5254   When The bird of wonder dies, the maiden phœnix,
Her ashes new create another heir,
As great in admiration as herself.
Henry VIII, Act v, sc. 5, l. 41 [CRANMER]

Phrase

5255   The gallant militarist—that was his own phrase.
All's Well that Ends Well, Act iv, sc. 3, l. 162 [LORD]

5256   That's an ill phrase, a vile phrase; 'beautified' is a vile phrase.
Hamlet, Act ii, sc. 2, l. 111 [POLONIUS]

5257   The phrase would be more german to the matter, if we could carry
cannon by our sides.
Hamlet, Act v, sc. 2, l. 166 [HAMLET]

5258   The phrase is to the matter.
Measure for Measure, Act v, sc. 1, l. 90 [ISABELLA]

5259   Sodden business! there's a stewed phrase indeed!
Troilus and Cressida, Act iii, sc. 1, l. 45 [SERVANT]

Physic

5260   I will not cast away my physic but on those that are sick.
As You Like It, Act iii, sc. 2, l. 376 [ROSALIND]

5261   He brings his physic After his patient's death.
Henry VIII, Act iii, sc. 2, l. 40 [CHAMBERLAIN]

5262   Throw physic to the dogs; I'll none of it.
Macbeth, Act v, sc. 3, l. 47 [MACBETH]

5263   'Tis a physic that's bitter to sweet end.
Measure for Measure, Act iv, sc. 6, l. 7 [ISABELLA]

Physician

5264   Medice, teipsum—
        Protector, see to 't well, protect yourself.
                        II Henry VI, Act ii, sc. 1, l. 52 [CARDINAL]
        (Physician, heal thyself.)
5265   Kill thy physician, and the fee bestow
        Upon thy foul disease.
                        King Lear, Act i, sc. 1, l. 166 [KENT]
5266   Trust not the physician;
        His antidotes are poison, and he slays
        Moe than you rob.
                        Timon of Athens, Act iv, sc. 3, l. 434 [TIMON]
5267   He will be the physician that should be the patient.
                        Troilus and Cressida, Act ii, sc. 3, l. 223 [AGAMEMNON]
5268   The patient dies while the physician sleeps.
                        The Rape of Lucrece, l. 904 [LUCRECE]

Pickpurse

5269   I think he is not a pick-purse nor a horse-stealer, but for his
        verity in love I do think him as concave as a covered goblet or
        a worm-eaten nut.
                        As You Like It, Act iii, sc. 4, l. 24 [CELIA]
5270   GADSHILL: What ho! chamberlain.
        CHAMBERLAIN: At hand, quoth pick-purse.
                        1 Henry IV, Act ii, sc. 1, l. 53 [GADSHILL]
5271   He, he, and you, and you, my liege, and I,
        Are pick-purses in love, and we deserve to die.
                        Love's Labour's Lost, Act iv, sc. 3, l. 208 [BIRON]

Picture

5272   Look here, upon this picture, and on this,
        The counterfeit presentment of two brothers.
        See, what a grace was seated on this brow;
        Hyperion's curls; the front of Jove himself;
        An eye like Mars, to threaten and command;
        A station like the herald Mercury
        New-lighted on a heaven-kissing hill;
        A combination and a form indeed,
        Where every god did seem to set his seal,
        To give the world assurance of a man:
        This was your husband. Look you now, what follows:
        Here is your husband; like a mildew'd ear,
        Blasting his wholesome brother. Have you eyes?
        Could you on this fair mountain leave to feed,
        And batten on this moor?
                        Hamlet, Act iii, sc. 4, l. 53 [HAMLET]
5273   Dost thou love pictures? we will fetch thee straight
        Adonis painted by the running brook,
        And Cytherea all in sedges hid,
        Which seem to move and wanton with her breath,
        Even as the waving sedges play with wind.
                        The Taming of the Shrew, Induction, sc. 2, l. 51 [SERVANT]
5274   TITUS: How likest thou this picture, Apemantus? . . . Wrought
        he not well that painted it?
        APEMANTUS: He wrought better that made the painter; and yet
        he 's but a filthy piece of work.
                        Timon of Athens, Act i, sc. 1, l. 198 [TITUS]

Pike

5275 Let us revenge this with our pikes, ere we become rakes.
Coriolanus, Act i, sc. 1, l. 23 [CITIZEN]

5276 Beat thou the drum, that it speak mournfully:
Trail your steel pikes.
Coriolanus, Act v, sc. 6, l. 151 [AUFIDIUS]

5277 Trail'st thou the puissant pike?
Henry V, Act iv, sc. 1, l. 40 [PISTOL]

Pilate

5278 Though some of you with Pilate wash your hands,
Showing an outward pity; yet you Pilates
Have here deliver'd me to my sour cross,
And water cannot wash away your sin.
Richard II, Act iv, sc. 1, l. 239 [KING RICHARD]

5279 How fain, like Pilate, would I wash my hands
Of this most grievous guilty murder done!
Richard III, Act i, sc. 4, l. 279 [MURDERER]

Pilgrim

5280 There are pilgrims going to Canterbury with rich offerings, and
traders riding to London with fat purses.
I Henry IV, Act i, sc. 2, l. 140 [POINS]

5281 A true-devoted pilgrim is not weary
To measure kingdoms with his feeble steps.
The Two Gentlemen of Verona, Act ii, sc. 7, l. 9 [JULIA]

Pilot

5282 What though the mast be now blown over-board,
The cable broke, the holding anchor lost,
And half our sailors swallow'd in the flood?
Yet lives our pilot still.
III Henry VI, Act v, sc. 4, l. 3 [QUEEN MARGARET]

5283 I am no pilot; yet, wert thou as far
As that vast shore wash'd with the farthest sea,
I would adventure for such merchandise.
Romeo and Juliet, Act ii, sc. 2, l. 82 [ROMEO]

Pin

5284 By the world, I would not care a pin, if the other three were in.
Love's Labour's Lost, Act iv, sc. 3, l. 20 [BIRON]

5285 Not worth a pin.
The Two Gentlemen of Verona, Act ii, sc. 7, l. 55 [LUCETTA]

Pinch

5286   Think on me,
That am with Phœbus' amorous pinches black,
And wrinkled deep in time.
Antony and Cleopatra, Act i, sc. 5, l. 27 [CLEOPATRA]

5287 They'll . . . pinch us black and blue.
The Comedy of Errors, Act ii, sc. 2, l. 194 [DROMIO OF SYRACUSE]

5288 Pinch the maids as blue as bilberry.
The Merry Wives of Windsor, Act v, sc. 5, l. 49 [PISTOL]

5289 Those [maids] as sleep and think not on their sins,
Pinch them, arms, legs, backs, shoulders, sides and shins.
The Merry Wives of Windsor, Act v, sc. 5, l. 57 [EVANS]

5290   Thou shalt be pinch'd
      As thick as honeycomb, each pinch more stinging
      Than bees that made 'em.
                         The Tempest, Act i, sc. 2, l. 328 [PROSPERO]
5291 From toe to crown he'll fill our skins with pinches.
                         The Tempest, Act iv, sc. 1, l. 233 [CALIBAN]

Pine

5292 This pine is bark'd That overtopp'd them all.
                   Antony and Cleopatra, Act iv, sc. 12, l. 23 [ANTONY]
5293 Ay me! the bark peel'd from the lofty pine,
      His leaves will wither and his sap decay;
      So must my soul, her bark being peel'd away.
                         The Rape of Lucrece, l. 1167 [LUCRECE]

Pirates

5294 Pirates may make cheap pennyworths of their pillage,
      And purchase friends and give to courtesans,
      Still revelling like lords till all be gone;
      While as the silly owner of the goods
      Weeps over them and wrings his hapless hands, . . .
      Ready to starve and dare not touch his own.
                         II Henry VI, Act i, sc. 1, l. 221 [YORK]
5295 Ships are but boards, sailors but men: there be land-rats and
      water-rats, water-thieves and land-thieves, I mean pirates.
                   The Merchant of Venice, Act i, sc. 3, l. 23 [SHYLOCK]

Pitch

5296 There is a thing, Harry, which thou hast often heard of and it
      is known to many in our land by the name of pitch: this pitch, as
      ancient writers do report, doth defile; so doth the company thou
      keepest.
                         I Henry IV, Act ii, sc. 4, l. 457 [FALSTAFF]
5297 I am toiling in a pitch,—pitch that defiles.
                   Love's Labour's Lost, Act iv, sc. 3, l. 3 [BIRON]
5298 They that touch pitch will be defiled.
                   Much Ado about Nothing, Act iii, sc. 3, l. 61 [DOGBERRY]

Pitchers

5299 ARCHBISHOP: Good madam, be not angry with the child.
      QUEEN ELIZABETH: Pitchers have ears.
                         Richard III, Act ii, sc. 4, l. 36 [ARCHBISHOP]
      (Referring to the proverb, "Small pitchers have wide ears," or
      "Little pitchers have big ears.")
5300 Pitchers have ears, and I have many servants.
                   The Taming of the Shrew, Act iv, sc. 4, l. 52 [BAPTISTA]

Pity

5301   O, then, give pity
      To her, whose state is such that cannot choose
      But lend and give where she is sure to lose.
                   All's Well that Ends Well, Act i, sc. 3, l. 223 [HELENA]
5302   If there be
      Yet left in heaven as small a drop of pity
      As a wren's eye, fear'd gods, a part of it!
                         Cymbeline, Act iv, sc. 2, l. 303 [IMOGEN]
5303 My pity hath been balm to heal their wounds, . . .
      My mercy dried their water-flowing tears.
                         III Henry VI, Act iv, sc. 8, l. 41 [KING HENRY]

5304   Pity, like a naked new-born babe,
    Striding the blast, or heaven's cherubim, horsed
    Upon the sightless couriers of the air,
    Shall blow the horrid deed in every eye,
    That tears shall drown the wind.
                 Macbeth, Act i, sc. 7, l. 21 [MACBETH]

5305   ISABELLA: Yet show some pity.
    ANGELO: I show it most of all when I show justice;
    For then I pity those I do not know,
    Which a dismiss'd offence would after gall.
            Measure for Measure, Act ii, sc. 2, l. 99 [ISABELLA]

5306   The pity of it, Iago! O Iago, the pity of it, Iago!
              Othello, Act iv, sc. 1, l. 206 [OTHELLO]

5307   Soft pity enters at an iron gate.
             The Rape of Lucrece, l. 595 [LUCRECE]

5308   Tear-falling pity dwells not in this eye.
           Richard III, Act iv, sc. 2, l. 65 [KING RICHARD]

5309   Is there no pity sitting in the clouds,
    That sees into the bottom of my grief?
           Romeo and Juliet, Act iii, sc. 5, l. 198 [JULIET]

5310   Pity is the virtue of the law,
    And none but tyrants use it cruelly.
           Timon of Athens, Act iii, sc. 5, l. 8 [ALCIBIADES]

5311   For the love of all the gods,
    Let's leave the hermit pity with our mothers,
    And when we have our armours buckled on,
    The venom'd vengeance ride upon our swords,
    Spur them to ruthful work, rein them from ruth.
           Troilus and Cressida, Act v, sc. 3, l. 44 [TROILUS]

5312   VIOLA: I pity you.
    OLIVIA: That's a degree to love.
    VIOLA: No, not a grize; for 'tis a vulgar proof,
    That very oft we pity enemies.
           Twelfth Night, Act iii, sc. 1, l. 134 [VIOLA]
     (A reference to the proverbial saying, "Pity is near akin to
    love." "Grize," step, stair.)

Place

5313   Captain I'll be no more;
    But I will eat and drink, and sleep as soft
    As captain shall: simply the thing I am
    Shall make me live. Who knows himself a braggart,
    Let him fear this, for it will come to pass
    That every braggart shall be found an ass.
    Rust sword! cool, blushes! and, Parolles, live
    Safest in shame! being fool'd, by foolery thrive!
    There's place and means for every man alive.
           All's Well that Ends Well, Act iv, sc. 3, l. 367 [PAROLLES]

5314   In the world I fill up a place, which may be better supplied when
    I have made it empty.
           As You Like It, Act i, sc. 2, l. 205 [ORLANDO]

5315   If I am
    Traduced by ignorant tongues, . . . let me say
    'Tis but the fate of place, and the rough brake
    That virtue must go through.
           Henry VIII, Act i, sc. 2, l. 71 [WOLSEY]

5316   O place, O form,
How often dost thou with thy case, thy habit,
Wrench awe from fools and tie the wiser souls
To thy false seeming!
                    Measure for Measure, Act ii, sc. 4, l. 12 [ANGELO]

5317   O place and greatness! millions of false eyes
Are stuck upon thee: volumes of report
Run with these false and most contrarious quests
Upon thy doings: thousand escapes of wit
Make thee the father of their idle dreams
And rack thee in their fancies.
                    Measure for Measure, Act iv, sc. 1, l. 60 [DUKE]

5318   I know my place as I would they should do theirs.
                    Twelfth Night, Act ii, sc. 5, l. 59 [MALVOLIO]

Plague

5319   A plague upon you both! . . . A plague upon you all!
                    I Henry IV, Act ii, sc. 2, l. 22 [FALSTAFF]
          (Frequently repeated.)

5320   A plague o' both your houses!
                    Romeo and Juliet, Act iii, sc. 1, l. 94, 99, 103, 111 [MERCUTIO]

Plainness

5321   As plain as the plain bald head of father Time himself.
                    The Comedy of Errors, Act ii, sc. 2, l. 70
                    [DROMIO OF SYRACUSE]

5322   KENT: 'Tis my occupation to be plain. . . .
CORNWALL: This is some fellow,
Who, having been praised for bluntness, doth affect
A saucy roughness; . . . he cannot flatter, he,
An honest mind and plain, he must speak truth!
An they will take it, so; if not, he's plain:
These kind of knaves I know, which in this plainness
Harbour more craft and more corrupter ends
Than twenty silly ducking observants
That stretch their duties nicely.
                    King Lear, Act ii, sc. 2, l. 98 [KENT]

5323   I was always plain with you, and so now I speak my agitation
of the matter.
                    The Merchant of Venice, Act iii, sc. 5, l. 4 [LAUNCELOT]

5324   You were to blame, I must be plain with you.
                    The Merchant of Venice, Act v, sc. 1, l. 166 [PORTIA]

5325   I pray thee, understand a plain man in his plain meaning.
                    The Merchant of Venice, Act iii, sc. 5, l. 62 [LORENZO]

Planet

5326   What! shall we curse the planets of mishap
That plotted thus our glory's overthrow?
Or shall we think the subtle-witted French
Conjurers and sorcerers?
                    I Henry VI, Act i, sc. 1, l. 23 [EXETER]
          Be opposite all planets of good luck
To my proceedings.
                    Richard III, Act iv, sc. 4, l. 402 [KING RICHARD]

5327   There's some ill planet reigns:
I must be patient till the heavens look
With an aspect more favourable.
                    The Winter's Tale, Act ii, sc. 1, l. 104 [HERMIONE]

Play

5328   If it be true that good wine needs no bush, 'tis true that a good
       play needs no epilogue.
                                As You Like It, Epilogue, l. 3 [ROSALIND]

5329   The play, I remember, pleased not the million; it was caviare to
       the general.
                                Hamlet, Act ii, sc. 2, l. 457 [HAMLET]
       ("The general" was the crowd that stood in front of the stage
       in the cheapest places.)

5330   I have heard
       That guilty creatures, sitting at a play
       Have by the very cunning of the scene
       Been struck so to the soul that presently
       They have proclaim'd their malefactions;
       For murder, though it have no tongue, will speak
       With most miraculous organ. . . . The play 's the thing
       Wherein I'll catch the conscience of the king.
                                Hamlet, Act ii, sc. 2, l. 617 [HAMLET]

5331   HAMLET: Will you play upon this pipe? . . .
       GUILDENSTERN : I know no touch of it, my lord.
       HAMLET: 'Tis as easy as lying. . . . Why, look you now, how
       unworthy a thing you make of me! You would play upon me; you
       would seem to know my stops; you would pluck out the heart of
       my mystery; you would sound me from my lowest note to the top
       of my compass: and there is much music, excellent voice, in this
       little organ; yet cannot you make it speak. 'Sblood, do you think
       I am easier to be played on than a pipe? Call me what instru-
       ment you will, though you can fret me, yet you cannot play
       upon me.
                                Hamlet, Act iii, sc. 2, l. 366 [HAMLET]

5332   Play out the play.
                                I Henry IV, Act ii, sc. 4, l. 533 [FALSTAFF]

5333   You shall find no boy's play here.
                                I Henry IV, Act v, sc. 4, l. 76 [FALSTAFF]

5334   'Tis ten to one this play can never please
       All that are here: some come to take their ease,
       And sleep an act or two; . . . others, to hear the city
       Abused extremely, and to cry 'That 's witty!'
                                Henry VIII, Epilogue, l. 1

5335   Our play is, The most lamentable comedy, and most cruel death
       of Pyramus and Thisby.
                                A Midsummer Night's Dream, Act i, sc. 2, l. 11 [QUINCE]

5336   Come now; what masques, what dances shall we have,
       To wear away this long age of three hours
       Between our after-supper and bed-time? . . .
       What revels are at hand? Is there no play,
       To ease the anguish of a torturing hour?
                                A Midsummer Night's Dream, Act v, sc. 1, l. 32 [THESEUS]

5337   TROILUS: When many times the captive Grecian falls,
       Even in the fan and wind of your fair sword,
       You bid them rise, and live.
       HECTOR: O, 'tis fair play.
       TROILUS: Fool's play, by heaven, Hector.
                                Troilus and Cressida, Act v, sc. 3, l. 40 [TROILUS]

5338   Go, play, boy, play; thy mother plays, and I
       Play too, but so disgraced a part, whose issue

Will hiss me to my grave: contempt and clamour
Will be my knell.
> *The Winter's Tale,* Act i, sc. 2, l. 187 [LEONTES]

Pleasure

5339   There's not a minute of our lives should stretch
Without some pleasure now.
> *Antony and Cleopatra,* Act i, sc. 1, l. 46 [ANTONY]

5340   The present pleasure,
By revolution lowering, does become
The opposite of itself.
> *Antony and Cleopatra,* Act i, sc. 2, l. 128 [ANTONY]

5341   Pleasure and action make the hours seem short.
> *Othello,* Act ii, sc. 3, l. 385 [IAGO]

5342   Why should the private pleasure of some one
Become the public plague of many moe?
> *The Rape of Lucrece,* l. 1478 [LUCRECE]

5343   Pleasure and revenge
Have ears more deaf than adders to the voice
Of any true decision.
> *Troilus and Cressida,* Act ii, sc. 2, l. 171 [HECTOR]

Plot

5344   Let us assay our plot; which, if it speed,
Is wicked meaning in a lawful deed
And lawful meaning in a lawful act,
Where both not sin, and yet a sinful fact.
> *All's Well that Ends Well,* Act iii, sc. 7, l. 44 [HELENA]

5345   By the Lord, our plot is a good plot as ever was laid; our friends
true and constant: a good plot, good friends, and full of expectation; an excellent plot, very good friends.
> *I Henry IV,* Act ii, sc. 3, l. 19 [HOTSPUR]

5346   There is a plot against my life, my crown;
All's true that is mistrusted.
> *The Winter's Tale,* Act ii, sc. 1, l. 47 [LEONTES]

Poetry

5347   TOUCHSTONE: Truly, I would the gods had made thee poetical.
AUDREY: I do not know what 'poetical' is: is it honest in deed
and word? is it a true thing?
TOUCHSTONE: No, truly; for the truest poetry is the most feigning; and lovers are given to poetry, and what they swear in
poetry may be said as lovers they do feign.
> *As You Like It,* Act iii, sc. 3, l. 16 [TOUCHSTONE]

5348   GLENDOWER: I can speak English, lord, as well as you;
For I was train'd up in the English court;
Where, being but young, I framed to the harp
Many an English ditty lovely well
And gave the tongue a helpful ornament,
A virtue that was never seen in you.
HOTSPUR: And I am glad of it with all my heart:
I had rather be a kitten and cry mew
Than one of these same metre ballad-mongers;
I had rather hear a brazen canstick turn'd,
Or a dry wheel grate on the axle-tree;
And that would set my teeth nothing on edge,
Nothing so much as mincing poetry.
> *I Henry IV,* Act iii, sc. 1, l. 121 [GLENDOWER]

5349   The elegancy, facility, and golden cadence of poesy.
                 Love's Labour's Lost, Act iv, sc. 2, l. 126 [HOLOFERNES]
5350   Much is the force of heaven-bred poesy.
                 The Two Gentlemen of Verona, Act iii, sc. 2, l. 71 [DUKE]

Poison

5351   I feed myself with most delicious poison.
                 Antony and Cleopatra, Act i, sc. 5, l. 26 [CLEOPATRA]
5352   O, get thee from my sight;
       Thou gavest me poison: dangerous fellow, hence!
       Breathe not where princes are.
                 Cymbeline, Act v, sc. 5, l. 237 [IMOGEN]
5353   O, I die, Horatio;
       The potent poison quite o'er-crows my spirit.
                 Hamlet, Act v, sc. 2, l. 363 [HAMLET]
5354   That same sword-and-buckler Prince of Wales,
       But that I think his father loves him not, . . .
       I would have him poison'd with a pot of ale.
                 I Henry IV, Act i, sc. 3, l. 230 [HOTSPUR]
5355   In poison there is physic.
                 II Henry IV, Act i, sc. 1, l. 137 [NORTHUMBERLAND]
5356   Hide not thy poison with such sugar'd words.
                 II Henry VI, Act iii, sc. 2, l. 45 [KING]
5357   Sweet, sweet, sweet poison for the age's tooth.
                 King John, Act i, sc. 1, l. 213 [BASTARD]
5358   OTHELLO: Give me some poison, Iago; this night: I'll not expostu-
       late with her, lest her body and beauty unprovide my mind again:
       this night, Iago.
       IAGO: Do it not with poison, strangle her in her bed, even the
       bed she hath contaminated.
       OTHELLO: Good, good: the justice of it pleases.
                 Othello, Act iv, sc. 1, l. 215 [OTHELLO]
5359   They love not poison that do poison need.
                 Richard II, Act v, sc. 6, l. 38 [BOLINGBROKE]
5360   GLOUCESTER: Why dost thou spit at me?
       ANNE: Would it were mortal poison, for thy sake!
       GLOUCESTER: Never came poison from so sweet a place.
       ANNE: Never hung poison on a fouler toad.
                 Richard III, Act i, sc. 2, l. 144 [GLOUCESTER]
5361   Hold, here is forty ducats: let me have
       A dram of poison, such soon-speeding gear
       As will disperse itself through all the veins
       That the life-weary taker may fall dead
       And that the trunk may be discharged of breath
       As violently as hasty powder fired
       Doth hurry from the fatal cannon's womb.
                 Romeo and Juliet, Act v, sc. 1, l. 59 [ROMEO]

Policy

5362   Never did base and rotten policy
       Colour her working with such deadly wounds.
                 I Henry IV, Act i, sc. 3, l. 108 [HOTSPUR]
5363   Turn him to any cause of policy,
       The Gordian knot of it he will unloose,
       Familiar as his garter.
                 Henry V, Act i, sc. 1, l. 45 [CANTERBURY]

Politician

5364 It might be the pate of a politician, . . . one that would circumvent God.
Hamlet, Act v, sc. 1, l. 86 [HAMLET]

5365   Get thee glass eyes;
And, like a scurvy politician seem
To see the things thou dost not.
King Lear, Act iv, sc. 6, l. 174 [LEAR]

5366 I had as lief be a Brownist as a politician.
Twelfth Night, Act iii, sc. 2, l. 33 [SIR ANDREW]

Pomp

5367   The tide of pomp
That beats upon the high shore of the world.
Henry V, Act iv, sc. 1, l. 281 [KING HENRY]

5368 Vain pomp and glory of this world, I hate ye:
I feel my heart new open'd.
Henry VIII, Act iii, sc. 2, l. 365 [WOLSEY]

5369   Take physic, pomp;
Expose thyself to feel what wretches feel.
King Lear, Act iii, sc. 4, l. 33 [LEAR]

Pot

5370 Were not I a little pot and soon hot, my very lips might freeze
to my teeth, . . . ere I should come by a fire to thaw me.
The Taming of the Shrew, Act iv, sc. 1, l. 6 [GRUMIO]
(A reference to the proverb, "A little pot is soon hot.")

Potations

5371 Forswear thin potations.
II Henry IV, Act iv, sc. 3, l. 135 [FALSTAFF]

5372   Now, my sick fool Roderigo,
Whom love hath turn'd almost the wrong side out,
To Desdemona hath to-night caroused
Potations pottle-deep.
Othello, Act ii, sc. 3, l. 53 [IAGO]

Poverty

5373 My friends were poor but honest.
All's Well that Ends Well, Act i, sc. 3, l. 201 [HELENA]

5374 I am as poor as Job, my lord, but not so patient.
II Henry IV, Act i, sc. 2, l. 144 [FALSTAFF]

5375 She bears a duke's revenues on her back,
And in her heart she scorns our poverty.
II Henry VI, Act i, sc. 3, l. 83 [QUEEN]

5376 GLOUCESTER: Now, good sir, what are you?
EDGAR: A most poor man, made tame to fortune's blows;
Who, by the art of known and feeling sorrows,
Am pregnant to good pity.
King Lear, Act iv, sc. 6, l. 224 [GLOUCESTER]

5377 His father . . . is an honest exceeding poor man.
The Merchant of Venice, Act ii, sc. 2, l. 54 [GOBBO]

5378 FORD: One that is as slanderous as Satan?
PAGE: And as poor as Job?
FORD: And as wicked as his wife?
EVANS: And given to fornications?
The Merry Wives of Windsor, Act v, sc. 5, l. 159 [FORD]

5379 Poor and content is rich and rich enough,
But riches fineless is as poor as winter
To him that ever fears he shall be poor.
Othello, Act iii, sc. 3, l. 172 [IAGO]

5380 APOTHECARY: My poverty, but not my will, consents.
ROMEO: I pay thy poverty, and not thy will.
Romeo and Juliet, Act v, sc. 1, l. 75 [APOTHECARY]

5381 O world, how apt the poor are to be proud!
If one should be a prey, how much the better
To fall before the lion than the wolf!
Twelfth Night, Act iii, sc. 1, l. 138 [OLIVIA]

Powder

5382 PRINCE: I did never see such pitiful rascals.
FALSTAFF: Tut, tut; good enough to toss; food for powder, food
for powder; they'll fill a pit as well as better: tush, man, mortal
men, mortal men.
I Henry IV, Act iv, sc. 2, l. 70 [PRINCE]

Power

5383 Power, unto itself most commendable,
Hath not a tomb so evident as a chair
To extol what it hath done.
Coriolanus, Act iv, sc. 7, l. 51 [AUFIDIUS]

5384 That Power that made you king
Hath power to keep you king in spite of all.
Richard II, Act iii, sc. 2, l. 27 [CARLISLE]

Praise

5385 I will praise any man that will praise me.
Antony and Cleopatra, Act ii, sc. 6, l. 91 [ENOBARBUS]

5386 Worse than the sun in March,
This praise doth nourish agues.
I Henry IV, Act iv, sc. 1, l. 111 [HOTSPUR]

5387 Make her chronicle As rich with praise
As is the ooze and bottom of the sea
With sunken wreck and sumless treasuries.
Henry V, Act i, sc. 2, l. 163 [CANTERBURY]

5388 Praise we may afford To any lady that subdues a lord.
Love's Labour's Lost, Act iv, sc. 1, l. 39 [PRINCESS]

5389 She's too low for a high praise, too brown for a fair praise, and
too little for a great praise.
Much Ado about Nothing, Act i, sc. 1, l. 173 [BENEDICK]

5390 Thou shalt find she will outstrip all praise
And make it half behind her.
The Tempest, Act iv, sc. 1, l. 10 [PROSPERO]

5391 Ah, when the means are gone to buy this praise,
The breath is gone whereof this praise is made:
Feast-won, fast-lost; one cloud of winter showers,
These flies are couch'd.
Timon of Athens, Act ii, sc. 2, l. 178 [FLAVIUS]

5392 Praise us as we are tasted, allow us as we prove.
Troilus and Cressida, Act iii, sc. 2, l. 99 [TROILUS]

5393 Cram's with praise and Make's As fat as tame things: . . .
Our praises are our wages.
The Winter's Tale, Act i, sc. 2, l. 91 [HERMIONE]

Praise: Self-Praise

5394 This comes too near the praising of myself.
The Merchant of Venice, Act iii, sc. 4, l. 22 [PORTIA]

5395 There's not one wise man among twenty that will praise himself.
Much Ado about Nothing, Act v, sc. 2, l. 75 [BEATRICE]

5396 When no friends are by, men praise themselves.
Titus Andronicus, Act v, sc. 3, l. 118 [LUCIUS]

5397 The worthiness of praise distains his worth,
If that the praised himself bring the praise forth:
But what the repining enemy commends,
That breath fame blows; that praise, sole pure, transcends.
Troilus and Cressida, Act i, sc. 3, l. 241 [ÆNEAS]

5398 Whatever praises itself but in the deed, devours the deed in the
praise.
Troilus and Cressida, Act ii, sc. 3, l. 167 [AGAMEMNON]

Prayer

5399 We, ignorant of ourselves,
Beg often our own harms, which the wise powers
Deny us for our good; so find we profit
By losing of our prayers.
Antony and Cleopatra, Act ii, sc. 1, l. 5 [MENECRATES]

5400 The fair Ophelia! Nymph, in thy orisons
Be all my sins remember'd.
Hamlet, Act iii, sc. 1, l. 89 [HAMLET]

5401 Pray can I not,
Though inclination be as sharp as will:
My stronger guilt defeats my strong intent;
And, like a man to double business bound,
I stand in pause where I shall first begin,
And both neglect. . . .
And what's in prayer but this two-fold force,
To be forestalled ere we come to fall,
Or pardon'd being down? . . . But, O, what form of prayer
Can serve my term? 'Forgive me my foul murder'?
That cannot be; since I am still possess'd
Of those effects for which I did the murder.
Hamlet, Act iii, sc. 3, l. 38 [KING]

5402 I'll bribe you, . . .
Not with fond shekels of the tested gold,
Or stones whose rates are either rich or poor
As fancy values them; but with true prayers
That shall rise up at heaven and enter there
Ere sun-rise, prayers from preserved souls,
From fasting maids whose minds are dedicate
To nothing temporal.
Measure for Measure, Act ii, sc. 2, l. 145 [ISABELLA]

5403 When I would pray and think, I think and pray
To several subjects. Heaven hath my empty words; . . .
Heaven in my mouth, . . .
And in my heart the strong and swelling evil
Of my conception.
Measure for Measure, Act ii, sc. 4, l. 1 [ANGELO]

5404 If you require a little space for prayer,
I grant it: pray; but be not tedious,
For the gods are quick of ear.
Pericles, Act iv, sc. 1, l. 68 [LEONINE]

5405   He prays but faintly and would be denied.
                          Richard II, Act v, sc. 3, l. 103 [DUCHESS]
5406   She prayed, that never prayed before.
                The Taming of the Shrew, Act iv, sc. 1, l. 82 [GRUMIO]

Precedent

5407   But, ah, who ever shunn'd by precedent
        The destined ill she must herself assay?
                                    A Lover's Complaint, l. 155
5408   There is no power in Venice
        Can alter a decree established:
        'Twill be recorded for a precedent,
        And many an error by the same example
        Will rush into the state.
                The Merchant of Venice, Act iv, sc. 1, l. 218 [PORTIA]

Precept

5409   You were used to load me
        With precepts that would make invincible
        The heart that conn'd them.
                Coriolanus, Act iv, sc. 1, l. 9 [CORIOLANUS]
5410   These few precepts in thy memory
        See thou character.
                        Hamlet, Act i, sc. 3, l. 58 [POLONIUS]

Pribbles

5411   It were a goot motion if we leave our pribbles and prabbles.
                The Merry Wives of Windsor, Act i, sc. 1, l. 56 [EVANS]
5412   Given to . . . pribbles and prabbles.
                The Merry Wives of Windsor, Act v, sc. 5, l. 169 [EVANS]

Pride

5413   My pride fell with my fortunes.
                    As You Like It, Act i, sc. 2, l. 264 [ROSALIND]
5414   Why, who cries out on pride,
        That can therein tax any private party?
        Doth it not flow as hugely as the sea,
        Till that the weary very means do ebb?
                    As You Like It, Act ii, sc. 7, l. 70 [JAQUES]
5415   'Fly pride,' says the peacock.
            The Comedy of Errors, Act iv, sc. 3, l. 81 [DROMIO OF SYRACUSE]
        (Quoting an old proverb.)
5416   You blame Marcius for being proud? . . . You talk of pride; O
        that you could turn your eyes toward the napes of your necks,
        and make but an interior survey of your good selves! O that you
        could!
                        Coriolanus, Act ii, sc. 1, l. 36 [MENENIUS]
5417   Pride, which out of daily fortune ever taints
        The happy man.
                    Coriolanus, Act iv, sc. 7, l. 37 [AUFIDIUS]
5418   Pride went before, ambition follows him.
                    II Henry VI, Act i, sc. 1, l. 180 [SALISBURY]
5419   Stand I condemn'd for pride and scorn so much?
        Contempt, farewell! and maiden pride, adieu!
        No glory lives behind the back of such.
                Much Ado about Nothing, Act iii, sc. 1, l. 108 [BEATRICE]
5420   King Stephen was a worthy peer,
                His breeches cost him but a crown;

> He held them sixpence all too dear,
>   With that he call'd the tailor lown.
> He was a wight of high renown,
>   And thou art but of low degree:
> 'Tis pride that pulls the country down;
>   Then take thine auld cloak about thee.
> > *Othello*, Act ii, sc. 3, l. 92 [IAGO]

5421 Pride must have a fall.
> > *Richard II*, Act v, sc. 5, l. 88 [KING RICHARD]

5422 AJAX: Why should a man be proud? How doth pride grow? . . .
AGAMEMNON: He that is proud eats up himself: pride is his own
glass, his own trumpet, his own chronicle. . . .
AJAX: I do hate a proud man, as I hate the engendering of toads.
> > *Troilus and Cressida*, Act ii, sc. 3, l. 161 [AJAX]

5423   Pride hath no other glass
> To show itself but pride.
> > *Troilus and Cressida*, Act iii, sc. 3, l. 47 [ULYSSES]

5424 How one man eats into another's pride,
> While pride is fasting in his wantonness!
> > *Troilus and Cressida*, Act iii, sc. 3, l. 136 [ULYSSES]

Prince

5425 The hearts of princes kiss obedience,
> So much they love it; but to stubborn spirits
> They swell, and grow as terrible as storms.
> > *Henry VIII*, Act iii, sc. 1, l. 162 [WOLSEY]

5426   O, how wretch'd
> Is that poor man that hangs on princes' favours!
> There is, betwixt that smile he would aspire to,
> That sweet aspect of princes, and their ruin,
> More pangs and fears than wars or women have:
> And when he falls, he falls like Lucifer,
> Never to hope again.
> > *Henry VIII*, Act iii, sc. 2, l. 366 [WOLSEY]

5427 The prince of darkness is a gentleman:
> Modo he's call'd, and Mahu.
> > *King Lear*, Act iii, sc. 4, l. 148 [EDGAR]

5428 Princes in this should live like gods above,
> Who freely give to every one that comes
> To honour them:
> And princes not doing so are like to gnats,
> Which make a sound, but kill'd are wondered at.
> > *Pericles*, Act ii, sc. 3, l. 59 [SIMONIDES]

5429 Princes are the glass, the school, the book,
> Where subjects' eyes do learn, do read, do look.
> > *The Rape of Lucrece*, l. 615 [LUCRECE]

5430 Princes have but their titles for their glories,
> An outward honour for an inward toil.
> > *Richard III*, Act i, sc. 4, l. 78 [BRAKENBURY]

5431 A begging prince what beggar pities not?
> > *Richard III*, Act i, sc. 4, l. 274 [CLARENCE]

5432 Ah, ha, my lord, this prince is not an Edward!
> He is not lolling on a lewd day-bed,
> But on his knees at meditation;
> Not dallying with a brace of courtezans,
> But meditating with two deep divines;
> Not sleeping, to engross his idle body,

But praying, to enrich his watchful soul:
Happy were England, would this gracious prince
Take on himself the sovereignty thereof.

Richard III, Act iii, sc. 7, l. 71 [BUCKINGHAM]

Princess

5433   The preyful princess pierced and prick'd a pretty pleasing pricket.

Love's Labour's Lost, Act iv, sc. 2, l. 58 [HOLOFERNES]

5434   LEONTES: His princess, say you, with him?
GENTLEMAN: Ay, the most peerless piece of earth, I think,
That e'er the sun shone bright on. . .
Women will love her, that she is a woman
More worth than any man; men, that she is
The rarest of all women.

The Winter's Tale, Act v, sc. 1, l. 93 [LEONTES]

Printing

5435   Thou hast most traitorously corrupted the youth of the realm in
erecting a grammar school: and whereas, before, our forefathers
had no other books but the score and the tally, thou hast caused
printing to be used, and, contrary to the king, his crown and
dignity, thou hast built a paper-mill.

II Henry VI, Act iv, sc. 7, l. 35 [CADE]

5436   All this I speak in print, for in print I found it.

The Two Gentlemen of Verona, Act ii, sc. 1, l. 175 [SPEED]

Prison

5437   HAMLET: What have you, my good friends, deserved at the hands
of fortune, that she sends you to prison thither?
GUILDENSTERN: Prison, my lord!
HAMLET: Denmark's a prison.
ROSENCRANTZ: Then is the world one.
HAMLET: A goodly one; in which there are many confines, wards,
and dungeons.

Hamlet, Act ii, sc. 2, l. 245 [HAMLET]

5438   Come, let's away to prison:
We two alone will sing like birds i' the cage:
When thou dost ask me blessing, I'll kneel down,
And ask of thee forgiveness: so we'll live,
And pray, and sing, and tell old tales, and laugh
At gilded butterflies, and hear poor rogues
Talk of court news; and we'll talk with them too,
Who loses and who wins; who's in, who's out;
And take upon's the mystery of things,
As if we were God's spies: and we'll wear out,
In a wall'd prison, packs and sects of great ones,
That ebb and flow by the moon.

King Lear, Act v, sc. 3, l. 8 [LEAR]

5439   I have been studying how I may compare
This prison where I live unto the world:
And for because the world is populous
And here is not a creature but myself,
I cannot do it; yet I'll hammer it out.

Richard II, Act v, sc. 5, l. 1 [KING RICHARD]

5440   Might I but through my prison once a day
Behold this maid: all corners else o' the earth
Let liberty make use of; space enough
Have I in such a prison.

The Tempest, Act i, sc. 2, l. 490 [FERDINAND]

Prize

5441   KING: And is not this an honourable spoil?
A gallant prize? ha, cousin, is it not?
WESTMORELAND: It is a conquest for a prince to boast of.
I Henry IV, Act i, sc. 1, l. 74 [KING]

5442   A goodly prize, fit for the devil's grace!
I Henry VI, Act v, sc. 3, l. 33 [YORK]

5443   This swift business
I must uneasy make, lest too light winning
Make the prize light.
The Tempest, Act i, sc. 2, l. 450 [PROSPERO]

Prodigal

5444   Shall I keep your hogs and eat husks with them? What prodigal
portion have I spent, that I should come to such penury?
As You Like It, Act i, sc. 1, l. 40 [ORLANDO]

5445   He that goes in the calf's skin that was killed for the Prodigal.
The Comedy of Errors, Act iv, sc. 3, l. 16
[DROMIO OF SYRACUSE]

5446   You would think that I had a hundred and fifty tattered prodigals
lately come from swine-keeping, from eating draff and husks.
I Henry IV, Act iv, sc. 2, l. 37 [FALSTAFF]

5447   How like a younker or a prodigal
The scarfed bark puts from her native bay,
Hugg'd and embraced by the strumpet wind!
How like the prodigal doth she return,
With over-weather'd ribs and ragged sails,
Lean, rent and beggar'd by the strumpet wind!
The Merchant of Venice, Act ii, sc. 6, l. 14 [GRATIANO]

5448   A prodigal course
Is like the sun's; but not, like his, recoverable.
Timon of Athens, Act iii, sc. 4, l. 12 [LUCIUS]

5449   I have received my proportion, like the prodigious son.
The Two Gentlemen of Verona, Act ii, sc. 3, l. 3 [LAUNCE]

Promise

5450   Thy promises are like Adonis' gardens
That one day bloom'd and fruitful were the next.
I Henry VI, Act i, sc. 6, l. 6 [CHARLES]

5451   He was ever precise in promise-keeping.
Measure for Measure, Act i, sc. 2, l. 76 [LUCIO]

5452   His promises fly so beyond his state
That what he speaks is all in debt; he owes
For every word.
Timon of Athens, Act i, sc. 2, l. 203 [FLAVIUS]

Promise and Performance

5453   His promises were, as he then was, mighty;
But his performance, as he is now, nothing.
Henry VIII, Act iv, sc. 2, l. 41 [KATHARINE]

5454   Promising is the very air of the time: it opens the eyes of expectation: performance is ever the duller for the act. . . . To promise
is most courtly and fashionable: performance is a kind of will or
testament which argues a great sickness in his judgement that
makes it.
Timon of Athens, Act v, sc. 1, l. 24 [PAINTER]

5455 He will spend his mouth and promise, like Brabbler the hound;
but when he performs, astronomers foretell it.
Troilus and Cressida, Act v, sc. 1, l. 98 [THERSITES]

Prosperity

5456 Thou shalt thrust thy hand as deep
Into the purse of rich prosperity
As Lewis himself: so, nobles, shall you all,
That knit your sinews to the strength of mine.
King John, Act v, sc. 2, l. 60 [LEWIS]

5457 Welcome the sour cup of prosperity! Affliction may one day smile
again; and till then, sit thee down, sorrow.
Love's Labour s Lost, Act i, sc. 1, l. 315 [COSTARD]

5458 CAMILLO: Prosperity's the very bond of love,
Whose fresh complexion and whose heart together
Affliction alters. . . .
PERDITA: Affliction may subdue the cheek,
But not take in the mind.
The Winter's Tale, Act iv, sc. 4, l. 583 [CAMILLO]

Proverb

5459 They said they were an-hungry; sigh'd forth proverbs
That hunger broke stone walls, that dogs must eat,
That meat was made for mouths, that the gods sent not
Corn for the rich men only.
Coriolanus, Act i, sc. 1, l. 209 [CORIOLANUS]

5460 The ancient proverb will be well effected:
'A staff is quickly found to beat a dog.'
II Henry VI, Act iii, sc. 1, l. 170 [GLOUCESTER]

5461 The old proverb is very well parted between my master Shylock
and you, sir; you have the grace of God, sir, and he hath
enough.
The Merchant of Venice, Act ii, sc. 2, l. 157 [LAUNCELOT]

5462 Fast bind, fast find;
A proverb never stale in thrifty mind.
The Merchant of Venice, Act ii, sc. 5, l. 54 [SHYLOCK]

5463 The country proverb known,
That every man should take his own,
In your waking shall be shown:
Jack shall have Jill;
Nought shall go ill;
The man shall have his mare again, and all shall be well.
A Midsummer Night's Dream, Act iii, sc. 2, l. 458 [PUCK]

5464 I am proverb'd with a grandsire phrase;
I'll be a candle-holder and look on.
Romeo and Juliet, Act i, sc. 4, l. 38 [ROMEO]

Providence

5465 We defy augury: there's a special providence in the fall of a
sparrow.
Hamlet, Act v, sc. 2, l. 230 [HAMLET]

5466 The providence that's in a watchful state
Knows almost every grain of Plutus' gold,
Finds bottom in the uncomprehensive deeps,
Keeps place with thought and almost, like the gods,
Does thoughts unveil in their dumb cradles.
Troilus and Cressida, Act iii, sc. 3, l. 196 [ULYSSES]

Pulse

5467   My pulse, as yours, doth temperately keep time,
       And makes as healthful music.
                               Hamlet, Act iii, sc. 4, l. 140 [HAMLET]

5468   Presently through all thy veins shall run
       A cold and drowsy humour, for no pulse
       Shall keep his native progress, but surcease.
                     Romeo and Juliet, Act iv, sc. 1, l. 95 [FRIAR LAURENCE]

Puritan

5469   She would make a puritan of the devil, if he should cheapen a
       kiss of her.
                               Pericles, Act iv, sc. 6, l. 10 [BAWD]

5470   MARIA: Go shake your ears. . . . For Monsieur Malvolio, let
       me alone with him: if I do not gull him into a nayword, and make
       him a common recreation, do not think I have wit enough to lie
       straight in my bed. . . .
       SIR TOBY: Tell us something of him.
       MARIA: Marry, sir, sometimes he is a kind of puritan.
       SIR ANDREW: O, if I thought that, I 'ld beat him like a dog.
                               Twelfth Night, Act ii, sc. 3, l. 135 [MARIA]

5471   But one puritan amongst them, and he sings psalms to hornpipes.
                               The Winter's Tale, Act iv, sc. 3, l. 47 [CLOWN]

Purpose

5472   What we do determine oft we break.
       Purpose is but the slave to memory,
       Of violent birth, but poor validity:
       Which now, like fruit unripe, sticks on the tree;
       But fall, unshaken, when they mellow be. . . .
       What to ourselves in passion we propose,
       The passion ending, doth the purpose lose.
                               Hamlet, Act iii, sc. 2, l. 197 [PLAYER KING]

5473   Do not forget: this visitation
       Is but to whet thy almost blunted purpose.
                               Hamlet, Act iii, sc. 4, l. 110 [GHOST]

5474   Infirm of purpose! Give me the daggers.
                               Macbeth, Act ii, sc. 2, l. 52 [LADY MACBETH]

5475   My purpose is, indeed, a horse of that colour.
                               Twelfth Night, Act ii, sc. 3, l. 181 [MARIA]

Purse

5476   We that take purses go by the moon and the seven stars, and not
       by Phœbus, he, 'that wandering knight so fair.'
                               I Henry IV, Act i, sc. 2, l. 15 [FALSTAFF]

5477   I can get no remedy against this consumption of the purse: borrow-
       ing only lingers and lingers it out, but the disease is incurable.
                               II Henry IV, Act i, sc. 2, l. 264 [FALSTAFF]

5478   My purse, my person, my extremest means,
       Lie all unlock'd to your occasions.
                       The Merchant of Venice, Act i, sc. 1, l. 138 [ANTONIO]

5479   Their love
       Lies in their purses, and whoso empties them
       By so much fills their hearts with deadly hate.
                               Richard II, Act ii, sc. 2, l. 129 [BAGOT]

5480   OLIVIA: I thank you for your pains: spend this for me.
       VIOLA: I am no fee'd post, lady; keep your purse.
                               Twelfth Night, Act i, sc. 5, l. 302 [OLIVIA]

Pursuit

5481   All things that are
Are with more spirit chased than enjoy'd.
The Merchant of Venice, Act ii, sc. 6, l. 12 [SALARINO]

5482   That she beloved knows nought that knows not this:
Men prize the thing ungain'd more than it is:
That she was never yet that ever knew
Love got so sweet as when desire did sue.
Therefore this maxim out of love I teach:
Achievement is command; ungain'd, beseech.
Troilus and Cressida, Act i, sc. 2, l. 314 [CRESSIDA]

Pythagoras

5483   O, be thou damn'd, inexecrable dog!
And for thy life let justice be accused.
Thou almost makest me waver in my faith
To hold opinion with Pythagoras,
That souls of animals infuse themselves
Into the trunks of men: thy currish spirit
Govern'd a wolf, who, hang'd for human slaughter,
Even from the gallows did his fell soul fleet,
And, whilst thou lay'st in thy unhallow'd dam,
Infus'd itself in thee; for thy desires
Are wolvish, bloody, starved and ravenous.
The Merchant of Venice, Act iv, sc. 1, l. 128 [GRATIANO]

5484   CLOWN: What is the opinion of Pythagoras concerning wild fowl?
MALVOLIO: That the soul of our grandam might happily inhabit
a bird.
Twelfth Night, Act iv, sc. 2, l. 54 [CLOWN]

Q

Quality

5485   Come, give us a taste of your quality.
Hamlet, Act ii, sc. 2, l. 452 [HAMLET]

5486   You are not of our quality.
I Henry IV, Act iv, sc. 3, l. 36 [HOTSPUR]

5487   BAWD: Boult, has she any qualities?
BOULT: She has a good face, speaks well, and has excellent good
clothes: there's no further necessity of qualities can make her
be refused.
Pericles, Act iv, sc. 2, l. 50 [BAWD]

Quarrel

5488   Holy seems the quarrel
Upon your grace's part; black and fearful
On the opposer.
All's Well that Ends Well, Act iii, sc. 1, l. 4 [LORD]

5489   ANTONY: If you'll patch a quarrel, . . . It must not be with
this. . . .
CÆSAR: You patch'd up your excuses.
Antony and Cleopatra, Act ii, sc. 2, l. 52 [ANTONY]

5490   As quarrelous as the weasel.
Cymbeline, Act iii, sc. 4, l. 162 [PISANIO]

He'll be as full of quarrel and offence
As my young mistress' dog.
Othello, Act ii, sc. 3, l. 52 [IAGO]

5491   Beware Of entrance to a quarrel, but being in,
Bear 't that the opposed may beware of thee.
Hamlet, Act i, sc. 3, l. 66 [POLONIUS]

5492   Be it thy course to busy giddy minds
With foreign quarrels.
II Henry IV, Act iv, sc. 5, l. 214 [KING HENRY]

5493   Thrice is he arm'd that hath his quarrel just,
And he but naked, though lock'd up in steel,
Whose conscience with injustice is corrupted.
II Henry VI, Act iii, sc. 2, l. 233 [KING]

5494   YORK: What is your quarrel? how began it first?
EDWARD: No quarrel, but a slight contention.
III Henry VI, Act i, sc. 2, l. 5 [YORK]

5495   The best quarrels, in the heat are cursed
By those that feel their sharpness.
King Lear, Act v, sc. 3, l. 56 [EDMUND]

5496   Launcelot and I are out.
The Merchant of Venice, Act iii, sc. 5, l. 34 [JESSICA]

5497   In a false quarrel there is no true valour.
Much Ado about Nothing, Act v, sc. 1, l. 120 [BENEDICK]

5498   I can draw as soon as another man, if I see occasion in a good
quarrel, and the law on my side.
Romeo and Juliet, Act ii, sc. 4, l. 167 [PETER]

5499   Thou art as hot a Jack in thy mood as any in Italy. . . . Why,
thou wilt quarrel with a man that hath a hair more, or a hair
less, in his beard than thou hast: thou wilt quarrel with a man
for cracking nuts, having no other reason but because thou hast
hazel eyes. . . . Thy head is as full of quarrels as an egg is full
of meat, and yet thy head hath been beaten as addle as an egg for
quarrelling: thou hast quarrelled with a man for coughing in the
street, because he hath wakened thy dog that hath lain asleep in
the sun: didst thou not fall out with a tailor for wearing his new
doublet before Easter? with another for tying his new shoes with
old riband? and yet thou wilt tutor me from quarrelling!
Romeo and Juliet, Act iii, sc. 1, l. 12 [MERCUTIO]

5500   Quarrelling . . .
Is valour misbegot and came into the world
When sects and factions were newly born.
Timon of Athens, Act iii, sc. 5, l. 27 [SENATOR]

5501   This petty brabble will undo us all.
Titus Andronicus, Act ii, sc. 1, l. 62 [AARON]

Queen

5502   Fie, wrangling queen!
Whom every thing becomes, to chide, to laugh,
To weep; whose every passion fully strives
To make itself, in thee, fair and admired!
Antony and Cleopatra, Act i, sc. 1, l. 48 [ANTONY]

5503   I come, my queen: . . . Stay for me:
Where souls do couch on flowers, we'll hand in hand,
And with our sprightly port make the ghosts gaze:
Dido and her Æneas shall want troops,
And all the haunt be ours.
Antony and Cleopatra, Act iv, sc. 14, l. 50 [ANTONY]

5504   PLAYER: 'But who, O, who had seen the mobled queen'—
        HAMLET: 'The mobled queen'?
        POLONIUS: That's good; 'mobled queen' is good.
            ("Mobled," having the face or head muffled.)
                            Hamlet, Act ii, sc. 2, l. 525 [PLAYER]

⌐05   FALSTAFF:Weep not, sweet queen; for trickling tears are vain. . . .
        For God's sake, lords, convey my tristful queen;
        For tears do stop the floodgates of her eyes.
        HOSTESS: O Jesu, he doth it as like one of these harlotry players
        as ever I see!
        FALSTAFF: Peace, good pint-pot; peace, good tickle-brain.
                            I Henry IV, Act ii, sc. 4, l. 432 [FALSTAFF]

5506   To be a queen in bondage is more vile
        Than is a slave in base servility;
        For princes should be free.
                            I Henry VI, Act v, sc. 3, l. 112 [MARGARET]

5507   The fairest queen that ever king received.
                            II Henry VI, Act i, sc. 1, l. 16 [SUFFOLK]

5508   Ay me, unhappy!
        To be a queen, and crown'd with infamy!
                            II Henry VI, Act iii, sc. 2, l. 70 [QUEEN]

5509   I know I am too mean to be your queen,
        And yet too good to be your concubine.
                            III Henry VI, Act iii, sc. 2, l. 97 [LADY GREY]

5510   ANNE BULLEN: By my troth and maidenhead,
        I would not be a queen.
        OLD LADY: Beshrew me, I would,
        And venture maidenhead for 't.
                            Henry VIII, Act ii, sc. 3, l. 23 [ANNE BULLEN]

5511   I had rather be a country servant-maid
        Than a great queen, with this condition,
        To be thus taunted, scorn'd, and baited at.
                            Richard III, Act i, sc. 3, l. 107 [QUEEN ELIZABETH]

5512   I call'd thee then poor shadow, painted queen;
        The presentation of but what I was;
        The flattering index of a direful pageant; . . .
        A dream of what thou wert, a breath, a bubble, . . .
        A queen in jest, only to fill the scene.
                            Richard III, Act iv, sc. 4, l. 83 [QUEEN MARGARET]

5513   The queen your mother rounds apace: we shall
        Present our services to a fine new prince
        One of these days.
                            The Winter's Tale, Act ii, sc. 1, l. 17 [LADY]

Quick

5514   How dearly would it touch thee to the quick.
                            The Comedy of Errors, Act ii, sc. 2, l. 132 [ADRIANA]

5515   I'll tent him to the quick.
                            Hamlet, Act ii, sc. 2, l. 626 [HAMLET]

5516   I am struck to the quick.
                            The Tempest, Act v, sc. 1, l. 25 [PROSPERO]

5517   But, Titus, I have touch'd thee to the quick.
                            Titus Andronicus, Act iv, sc. 4, l. 36 [TAMORA]

Quietness

5518   Quietness, grown sick of rest, would purge
        By any desperate change.
                            Antony and Cleopatra, Act i, sc. 3, l. 53 [ANTONY]

5519   I will sit as quiet as a lamb.
                    King John, Act iv, sc. 1, l. 80 [ARTHUR]
5520   Lie . . . as quiet as thy father's skull.
                    Richard II, Act iv, sc. 1, l. 69 [SURREY]

Quittance

5521   Omittance is no quittance.
                    As You Like It, Act iii, sc. 5, l. 133 [PHEBE]
5522   We . . . shall forget the office of our hand
        Sooner than quittance of desert and merit.
                    Henry V, Act ii, sc. 2, l. 34 [KING HENRY]
5523   No gift to him
        But breeds the giver a return exceeding
        All use of quittance.
                    Timon of Athens, Act i, sc. 1, l. 289 [LORD]

R

Rabble

5524   'Sdeath!
        The rabble should have first unroof'd the city,
        Ere so prevail'd with me.
                    Coriolanus, Act i, sc. 1, l. 222 [MARCIUS]
5525   'Twas you incensed the rabble:
        Cats, that can judge as fitly of his worth
        As I can of those mysteries which heaven
        Will not have earth to know.
                    Coriolanus, Act iv, sc. 2, l. 33 [VOLUMNIA]
5526   Methinks I should not thus be led along,
        Mail'd up in shame, with papers on my back,
        And follow'd with a rabble that rejoice
        To see my tears and hear my deep-fet groans.
                    II Henry VI, Act ii, sc. 4, l. 30 [DUCHESS]
5527   The rabblement hooted and clapped their chopped hands and threw
        up their sweaty night-caps and uttered such a deal of stinking
        breath because Cæsar refused the crown that it had almost choked
        Cæsar.
                    Julius Cæsar, Act i, sc. 2, l. 246 [CASCA]

Rack

5528   To the rack with him! We'll touse you
        Joint by joint, but we will know his purpose.
                    Measure for Measure, Act v, sc. 1, l. 313 [ESCALUS]
5529   BASSANIO: I live upon the rack.
        PORTIA: Upon the rack, Bassanio! then confess
        What treason there is mingled with your love.
        BASSANIO: None but that ugly treason of mistrust,
        Which makes me fear the enjoying of my love:
        There may as well be amity and life
        'Tween snow and fire, as treason and my love.
        PORTIA: Ay, but I fear you speak upon the rack,
        Where men enforced do speak any thing.
                    The Merchant of Venice, Act iii, sc. 2, l. 25 [BASSANIO]
5530   Avaunt! be gone! thou hast set me on the rack:
        I swear 'tis better to be much abused
        Than but to know 't a little.
                    Othello, Act iii, sc. 3, l. 335 [OTHELLO]

Raiment

5531 Ne'er ask me what raiment I'll wear; for I have no more doublets than backs, no more stockings than legs, nor no more shoes than feet; nay, sometime more feet than shoes, or such shoes as my toes look through the over-leather.

The Taming of the Shrew, Induction, sc. 2, l. 11 [SLY]

5532 Be thou ashamed that I have took upon me
Such an immodest raiment, if shame live
In a disguise of love.

The Two Gentlemen of Verona, Act v, sc. 4, l. 105 [JULIA]

Rain

5533 The property of rain is to wet and fire to burn.

As You Like It, Act iii, sc. 2, l. 27 [CORIN]

5534 Much rain wears the marble.

III Henry VI, Act iii, sc. 2, l. 50 [GLOUCESTER]

5535 When the rain came to wet me once, and the wind to make me chatter, . . . there I smelt 'em out. . . . I am not ague-proof.

King Lear, Act iv, sc. 6, l. 101 [LEAR]

5536 When that I was and a little tiny boy,
With hey, ho, the wind and the rain,
A foolish thing was but a toy,
For the rain it raineth every day.

Twelfth Night, Act v, sc. 1, l. 398 [CLOWN]

5537 Rain added to a river that is rank
Perforce will force it overflow the bank.

Venus and Adonis, l. 71

Ram

5538 My flocks feed not, My ewes breed not,
My rams speed not, All is amiss.

Sonnets to Sundry Notes of Music, Pt. xviii, l. 1

5539 They call this bed-work, mappery, closet-war;
So that the ram that batters down the wall,
For the great swing and rudeness of his poise,
They place before his hand that made the engine.

Troilus and Cressida, Act i, sc. 3, l. 205 [ULYSSES]

Rancour

5540 Rancour will out.

II Henry VI, Act i, sc. 1, l. 142 [GLOUCESTER]

5541 The broken rancour of your high-swoln hearts,
But lately splinter'd, knit, and join'd together,
Must gently be preserved, cherish'd, and kept.

Richard III, Act ii, sc. 2, l. 117 [BUCKINGHAM]

Rapier

5542 Many wearing rapiers are afraid of goose-quills.

Hamlet, Act ii, sc. 2, l. 359 [ROSENCRANTZ]

5543 If you grow foul with me, Pistol, I will scour you with my rapier, as I may, in fair terms.

Henry V, Act ii, sc. 1, l. 60 [NYM]

5544 Master Starve-lackey, the rapier and dagger man.

Measure for Measure, Act iv, sc. 3, l. 16 [POMPEY]

5545 Wear thy good rapier bare, and put it home.

Othello, Act v, sc. 1, l. 2 [IAGO]

Rascal

5546 I, A dull and muddy-mettled rascal.

Hamlet, Act ii, sc. 2, l. 594 [HAMLET]

5547 Peace, ye fat-kidneyed rascal! what a brawling dost thou keep!
I Henry IV, Act ii, sc. 2, l. 5 [PRINCE]

5548 What a pagan rascal is this! an infidel!
I Henry IV, Act ii, sc. 3, l. 32 [HOTSPUR]

5549 Away, you cut-purse rascal! you filthy bung, away! . . . Away,
you bottle-ale rascal! you basket-hilt stale juggler, you! . . .
I cannot endure such a fustian rascal.
II Henry IV, Act ii, sc. 4, l. 137 [DOLL TEARSHEET]

5550 Why, this is an arrant counterfeit rascal; I remember him now;
a bawd, a cutpurse.
Henry V, Act iii, sc. 6, l. 64 [GOWER]

5551 What a damned Epicurean rascal is this!
The Merry Wives of Windsor, Act ii, sc. 2, l. 300 [FORD]

5552 HECTOR: What art thou, Greek? art thou for Hector's match?
Art thou of blood and honour?
THERSITES: No, no, I am a rascal; a scurvy railing knave; a very
filthy rogue.
Troilus and Cressida, Act v, sc. 4, l. 28 [HECTOR]

5553 I marvel your ladyship takes delight in such a barren rascal: I
saw him put down the other day with an ordinary fool that has
no more brain than a stone.
Twelfth Night, Act i, sc. 5, l. 90 [MALVOLIO]

Rashness

5554 Who cannot condemn rashness in cold blood?
Timon of Athens, Act iii, sc. 5, l. 53 [ALCIBIADES]

5555 Forgive my general and exceptless rashness,
You perpetual-sober gods!
Timon of Athens, Act iv, sc. 3, l. 502 [TIMON]

Raven

5556 'The croaking raven doth bellow for revenge.'
Hamlet, Act iii, sc. 2, l. 264 [HAMLET]
(Quoted from *The True Tragedie of Richard III.*)
I would croak like a raven; I would bode, I would bode.
Troilus and Cressida, Act v, sc. 2, l. 191 [THERSITES]

5557   The raven himself is hoarse
That croaks the fatal entrance of Duncan
Under my battlements.
Macbeth, Act i, sc. 5, l. 39 [LADY MACBETH]

5558 Who will not change a raven for a dove?
A Midsummer Night's Dream, Act ii, sc. 2, l. 114 [LYSANDER]

5559 The raven doth not hatch a lark.
Titus Andronicus, Act ii, sc. 3, l. 149 [LAVINIA]

5560 Did ever raven sing so like a lark,
That gives sweet tidings of the sun's uprise?
Titus Andronicus, Act iii, sc. 1, l. 158 [TITUS]

5561 The raven chides blackness.
Troilus and Cressida, Act ii, sc. 3, l. 221 [ULYSSES]
(A proverb which, in various forms, dates back to Alcæus,
c. 595 B.C.)

Readiness

5562 If it be now, 'tis not to come; if it be not to come, it will be now;
if it be not now, yet it will come: the readiness is all: since no
man has aught of what he leaves, what is 't to leave betimes?
Hamlet, Act v, sc. 2, l. 232 [HAMLET]

5563   Let's briefly put on manly readiness,
And meet i' the hall together.
Macbeth, Act ii, sc. 3, l. 140 [MACBETH]

Reading

5564   Because they could not read, thou hast hanged them; when, indeed,
only for that cause they have been most worthy to live.
II Henry VI, Act iv, sc. 7, l. 49 [CADE]

5565   He reads much;
He is a great observer and he looks
Quite through the deeds of men.
Julius Cæsar, Act i, sc. 2, l. 201 [CÆSAR]

5566   He is. . . . Exceedingly well read.
I Henry IV, Act iii, sc. 1, l. 166 [MORTIMER]

5567   [He is] well read in poetry
And other books, good ones, I warrant ye.
The Taming of the Shrew, Act i, sc. 2, l. 170 [GREMIO]

5568   To be a well-favoured man is the gift of fortune: but to write and
read comes by nature.
Much Ado about Nothing, Act iii, sc. 3, l. 14 [DOGBERRY]

Reaping

5569   They that reap must sheaf and bind.
As You Like It, Act iii, sc. 2, l. 113 [TOUCHSTONE]

5570   When wit and youth come to harvest,
Your wife is like to reap a proper man.
Twelfth Night, Act iii, sc. 2, l. 143 [OLIVIA]

Reason

5571   POINS: Come, your reason, Jack, your reason.
FALSTAFF: What, upon compulsion? 'Zounds, an I were at the
strappado, or all the racks in the world, I would not tell you on
compulsion. Give you a reason on compulsion! if reasons were as
plentiful as blackberries, I would give no man a reason upon compulsion, I.
I Henry IV, Act ii, sc. 4, l. 260 [POINS]

5572   There is no English soul
More stronger to direct you than yourself,
If with the sap of reason you would quench,
Or but allay, the fire of passion.
Henry VIII, Act i, sc. 1, l. 146 [NORFOLK]

5573   Have we eaten on the insane root
That takes the reason prisoner?
Macbeth, Act i, sc. 3, l. 84 [BANQUO]

5574   Let your reason serve
To make the truth appear where it seems hid,
And hide the false seems true.
Measure for Measure, Act v, sc. 1, l. 65 [ISABELLA]

5575   The will of man is by his reason sway'd;
And reason says you are the worthier maid.
Things growing are not ripe until their season:
So I, being young, till now ripe not to reason;
And touching now the point of human skill,
Reason becomes the marshal to my will
And leads me to your eyes, where I o'erlook
Love's stories written in love's richest book.
A Midsummer Night's Dream, Act ii, sc. 2, l. 115 [LYSANDER]

5576   If the balance of our lives had not one scale of reason to poise
another of sensuality, the blood and baseness of our natures would
conduct us to most preposterous conclusions: but we have reason
to cool our raging motions, our carnal stings, our unbitted lusts.
Othello, Act i, sc. 3, l. 331 [IAGO]

5577   It fits thee not to ask the reason why.
Pericles, Act i, sc. 1, l. 158 [ANTIOCHUS]

5578   Reason and respect
Make livers pale and lustihood deject.
Troilus and Cressida, Act ii, sc. 2, l. 49 [TROILUS]

5579   JULIA: Your reason?
LUCETTA: I have no other but a woman's reason;
I think him so because I think him so.
The Two Gentlemen of Verona, Act i, sc. 2, l. 22 [JULIA]

Reasons

5580   Good reasons must, of force, give place to better.
Julius Cæsar, Act iv, sc. 3, l. 203 [BRUTUS]

5581   Strong reasons make strong actions.
King John, Act iii, sc. 4, l. 182 [LEWIS]

5582   Your reasons at dinner have been sharp and sententious: pleasant
without scurrility, witty without affection, audacious without
impudency, learned without opinion, and strange without heresy.
Love's Labour's Lost, Act v, sc. 1, l. 2 [NATHANIEL]
(Referring to Holofernes.)

5583   Gratiano speaks an infinite deal of nothing, more than any man
in all Venice. His reasons are two grains of wheat hid in two
bushels of chaff: you shall seek all day ere you find them, and
when you have them, they are not worth the search.
The Merchant of Venice, Act i, sc. 1, l. 114 [BASSANIO]

Rebellion

5584   We nourish 'gainst our senate
The cockle of rebellion, insolence, sedition,
Which we ourselves have plough'd for, sow'd and scatter'd.
Coriolanus, Act iii, sc. 1, l. 69 [CORIOLANUS]

5585   Thus ever did rebellion find rebuke. . . .
Rebellion in this land shall lose his sway,
Meeting the check of such another day.
I Henry IV, Act v, sc. 5, l. 1 [KING]

5586   My lord your son had only but the corpse,
But shadows and the shows of men, to fight;
For that same word, rebellion, did divide
The action of their bodies from their souls. . . .
This word, rebellion, it had froze them up
As fish are in a pond.
II Henry IV, Act i, sc. 1, l. 192 [MORTON]

5587   Fly, noble English, you are bought and sold;
Unthread the rude eye of rebellion
And welcome home again discarded faith.
King John, Act v, sc. 4, l. 10 [MELUN]

Red

5588   Your colour, I warrant you, is as red as any rose, in good truth, la!
II Henry IV, Act ii, sc. 4, l. 27 [HOSTESS]

5589   GLOUCESTER: What colour is this cloak of?
SIMPCOX: Red, master; red as blood.
II Henry VI, Act ii, sc. 1, l. 109 [GLOUCESTER]

5590 As red as fire! nay, then her wax must melt.
III Henry VI, Act iii, sc. 2, l. 51 [CLARENCE]

5591 Like a red morn, that ever yet betoken'd
Wrack to the seaman, tempest to the field,
Sorrow to shepherds, woe unto the birds,
Gusts and foul flaws to herdmen and to herds.
Venus and Adonis, l. 453
(A reference to various proverbial jingles derived from
Matthew xvi, 2-3: "When it is evening, ye say, It will be fair
weather: for the sky is red. And in the morning, It will be foul
weather today: for the sky is red and lowring.")

Redemption

5592 O worthy duke,
You bid me seek redemption of the devil.
Measure for Measure, Act v, sc. 1, l. 29 [ISABELLA]

5593 O villain! thou wilt be condemned into everlasting redemption for
this.
Much Ado about Nothing, Act iv, sc. 2, l. 58 [DOGBERRY]

5594 I charge you, as you hope to have redemption
By Christ's dear blood shed for our grievous sins,
That you depart and lay no hands on me:
The deed you undertake is damnable.
Richard III, Act i, sc. 4, l. 194 [CLARENCE]

Reformation

5595 When this loose behaviour I throw off, . . .
—Like bright metal on a sullen ground,
My reformation, glittering o'er my fault,
Shall show more goodly and attract more eyes
Than that which hath no foil to set it off.
I Henry IV, Act i, sc. 2, l. 231 [PRINCE HENRY]

5596 Never came reformation in a flood,
With such a heady currance, scouring faults.
Henry V, Act i, sc. 1, l. 33 [CANTERBURY]

Relief

5597 Wherever sorrow is, relief would be.
As You Like It, Act iii, sc. 5, l. 86 [SILVIUS]

5598 For this relief much thanks.
Hamlet, Act i, sc. 1, l. 8 [FRANCISCO]

Religion

5599 I see you have some religion in you, that you fear.
Cymbeline, Act i, sc. 4, l. 148 [IACHIMO]

5600 Sweet religion makes a rhapsody of words.
Hamlet, Act iii, sc. 4, l. 47 [HAMLET]

5601 I know her for A spleeny Lutheran.
Henry VIII, Act iii, sc. 2, l. 98 [WOLSEY]

5602 It is religion that doth make vows kept;
But thou hast sworn against religion.
King John, Act iii, sc. 1, l. 279 [PANDULPH]

5603 In religion,
What damned error, but some sober brow
Will bless it and approve it with a text?
The Merchant of Venice, Act iii, sc. 2, l. 77 [BASSANIO]

Remedies

5604　Our remedies oft in ourselves do lie,
Which we ascribe to heaven.
All's Well that Ends Well, Act i, sc. 1, l. 231 [HELENA]

5605　When remedies are past, the griefs are ended
By seeing the worst, which late on hopes depended.
Othello, Act i, sc. 3, l. 202 [DUKE]

Remembrance

5606　Praising what is lost Makes the remembrance dear.
All's Well that Ends Well, Act v, sc. 3, l. 19 [KING]

5607　There's rosemary; that's for remembrance; pray, love, remember;
and there is pansies, that's for thoughts.
Hamlet, Act iv, sc. 5, l. 175 [OPHELIA]

5608　When to the sessions of sweet silent thought
I summon up remembrance of things past,
I sigh the lack of many a thing I sought,
And with old woes new wail my dear time's waste; . . .
But if the while I think on thee, dear friend,
All losses are restored and sorrows end.
Sonnet xxx, l. 1

5609　Let us not burthen our remembrances
With a heaviness that's gone.
The Tempest, Act v, sc. 1, l. 199 [PROSPERO]

Remorse

5610　Never did the Cyclops' hammers fall
On Mars's armour forged for proof eterne
With less remorse than Pyrrhus' bleeding sword
Now falls on Priam.
Hamlet, Act ii, sc. 2, l. 510 [PLAYER]

5611　What says Monsieur Remorse? what says Sir John Sack and
Sugar?
I Henry IV, Act i, sc. 2, l. 124 [POINS]

5612　Stop up the access and passage to remorse,
That no compunctious visitings of nature
Shake my fell purpose!
Macbeth, Act i, sc. 5, l. 45 [LADY MACBETH]

Remuneration

5613　ARMADO: There is remuneration; for the best ward of mine honour
is rewarding my dependents. . . .
COSTARD: Remuneration! O, that's the Latin word for three
farthings: three farthings—remuneration.—'What's the price of
this inkle?'—'One penny.'—'No, I'll give you a remuneration': why,
it carries it. Remuneration! why, it is a fairer name than French
crown. I will never buy and sell out of this word.
BIRON: O, my good knave Costard! exceedingly well met.
COSTARD: Pray you, sir, how much carnation ribbon may a man
buy for a remuneration?
BIRON: What is a remuneration?
COSTARD: Marry, sir, halfpenny farthing.
BIRON: Why, then, three-farthing worth of silk.
Love's Labour's Lost, Act iii, sc. 1, l. 132 [ARMADO]

Renown

5614　Honour . . . no better than picture-like to hang by the wall,
if renown made it not stir.
Coriolanus, Act i, sc. 3, l. 11 [VOLUMNIA]

5615   TALBOT: Thou never hadst renown, nor canst not lose it.
       JOHN: Yes, your renowned name: shall flight abuse it?
                                   I Henry VI, Act iv, sc. 5, l. 40 [TALBOT]
5616   And cull'd these fiery spirits from the world,
       To outlook conquest and to win renown.
                                   King John, Act v, sc. 2, l. 114 [DAUPHIN]

Repentance

5617   Try what repentance can: what can it not?
       Yet what can it when one cannot repent?
                                   Hamlet, Act iii, sc. 3, l. 65 [KING]
5618   I'll repent, and that suddenly, while I am in some liking; I shall
       be out of heart shortly, and then I shall have no strength to repent.
                                   I Henry IV, Act iii, sc. 3, l. 5 [FALSTAFF]
5619   Who by repentance is not satisfied
       Is nor of heaven nor earth, for these are pleased,
       By penitence the Eternal's wrath's appeased.
                                   The Two Gentlemen of Verona, Act v, sc. 4, l. 79 [VALENTINE]

Repose

5620   Our foster-nurse of nature is repose.
                                   King Lear, Act iv, sc. 4, l. 12 [DOCTOR]
5621   Good night, good night! as sweet repose and rest
       Come to thy heart as that within my breast.
                                   Romeo and Juliet, Act ii, sc. 2, l. 123 [JULIET]
5622   This is a strange repose, to be asleep
       With eyes wide open; standing, speaking, moving,
       And yet so fast asleep.
                                   The Tempest, Act ii, sc. 1, l. 213 [SEBASTIAN]

Reputation

5623   Though my estate be fallen, I was well born, . . .
       And would not put my reputation now
       In any staining act.
                                   All's Well that Ends Well, Act iii, sc. 7, l. 4 [WIDOW]
5624   I have offended reputation,
       A most unnoble swerving.
                                   Antony and Cleopatra, Act iii, sc. 11, l. 49 [ANTONY]
5625   His reputation is as arrant a villain and a Jacksauce as ever his
       black shoe trod upon God's ground.
                                   Henry V, Act iv, sc. 7, l. 147 [FLUELLEN]
5626   IAGO: What, are you hurt, lieutenant?
       CASSIO: Ay, past all surgery. . . . Reputation, reputation, reputa-
       tion! O, I have lost my reputation! I have lost the immortal part
       of myself, and what remains is bestial. . . .
       IAGO: Reputation is an idle and most false imposition; oft got
       without merit, and lost without deserving.
                                   Othello, Act ii, sc. 3, l. 259 [IAGO]
5627   The purest treasure mortal times afford
       Is spotless reputation: that away,
       Men are but gilded loam or painted clay.
                                   Richard II, Act i, sc. 1, l. 177 [MOWBRAY]
5628   I see my reputation is at stake.
       My fame is shrewdly gored.
                                   Troilus and Cressida, Act iii, sc. 3, l. 227 [ACHILLES]

Respect

5629   Men so noble,
However faulty, yet should find respect
For what they have been.
                    Henry VIII, Act v, sc. 3, l. 74 [CROMWELL]

5630   Nothing is good, I see, without respect.
                    The Merchant of Venice, Act v, sc. 1, l. 99 [PORTIA]

5631   Is there no respect of place, persons, nor time in you?
                    Twelfth Night, Act ii, sc. 3, l. 98 [MALVOLIO]

Rest

5632   The crickets sing, and man's o'erlabour'd sense
Repairs itself by rest.
                    Cymbeline, Act ii, sc. 2, l. 11 [IACHIMO]

5633   Night hangs upon mine eyes; my bones would rest,
That have but labour'd to attain this hour.
                    Julius Cæsar, Act v, sc. 5, l. 41 [BRUTUS]

Retribution

5634   'Tis the sport to have the enginer
Hoist with his own petar.
                    Hamlet, Act iii, sc. 4, l. 206 [HAMLET]

5635   Heat not a furnace for your foe so hot
That it do singe yourself.
                    Henry VIII, Act i, sc. 1, l. 140 [NORFOLK]

5636   SUFFOLK: I told ye all,
When we first set this dangerous stone a-rolling,
'Twould fall upon ourselves. . . .
CROMWELL: Ye blew the fire that burns ye: now have at ye!
                    Henry VIII, Act v, sc. 3, l. 104 [SUFFOLK]

5637   We but teach
Bloody instructions, which, being taught, return
To plague the inventor.
                    Macbeth, Act i, sc. 7, l. 8 [MACBETH]

Revel

5638   Now, my honey love,
We will return unto thy father's house
And revel it as bravely as the best,
With silken coats and caps and golden rings,
With ruffs and cuffs and fardingales and things;
With scarfs and fans and double change of bravery,
With amber bracelets, beads and all this knavery.
                    The Taming of the Shrew, Act iv, sc. 3, l. 52 [PETRUCHIO]

5639   Our revels now are ended. These our actors,
As I foretold you, were all spirits and
Are melted into air, into thin air:
And, like the baseless fabric of this vision,
The cloud-capp'd towers, the gorgeous palaces,
The solemn temples, the great globe itself,
Yea, all which it inherit, shall dissolve
And, like this insubstantial pageant faded,
Leave not a rack behind.
                    The Tempest, Act iv, sc. 1, l. 148 [PROSPERO]

Revenge

5640   I, with wings as swift
As meditation or the thoughts of love,
May sweep to my revenge.
                              Hamlet, Act i, sc. 5, l. 29 [HAMLET]

5641   Now might I do it pat, now he is praying;
And now I'll do 't. And so he goes to heaven;
And so am I revenged. That would be scann'd:
A villain kills my father; and for that,
I, his sole son, do this same villain send
To heaven. O, this is hire and salary, not revenge.
                              Hamlet, Act iii, sc. 3, l. 73 [HAMLET]

5642   Revenge should have no bounds.
                              Hamlet, Act iv, sc. 7, l. 129 [KING]

5643   Rouse up revenge from ebon den with fell Alecto's snake.
                              II Henry IV, Act v, sc. 5, l. 39 [PISTOL]

5644   Let's make us medicines of our great revenge,
To cure this deadly grief.
                              Macbeth, Act iv, sc. 3, l. 214 [MALCOLM]

5645   PISTOL: Wilt thou revenge?
NYM: By welkin and her star!
PISTOL: With wit or steel?
NYM: With both the humours I. . . .
PISTOL: Thou art the Mars of malcontents: I second thee; troop
on.
                              The Merry Wives of Windsor, Act i, sc. 3, l. 100 [PISTOL]

5646   How shall I be revenged on him? for revenged I will be, as sure
as his guts are made of puddings.
                              The Merry Wives of Windsor, Act ii, sc. 1, l. 31 [MRS. PAGE.]

5647   How shall I be revenged on him? I think the best way were to
entertain him with hope, till the wicked fire of lust have melted
him in his own grease.
                              The Merry Wives of Windsor, Act ii, sc. 1, l. 67 [MRS. FORD]

5648   Time hath not yet so dried this blood of mine,
Nor age so eat up my invention,
Nor fortune made such havoc of my means,
Nor my bad life reft me so much of friends,
But they shall find, awaked in such a kind,
Both strength of limb and policy of mind,
Ability in means and choice of friends,
To quit me of them throughly.
                              Much Ado about Nothing, Act iv, sc. 1, l. 195 [LEONATO]

5649   Now, I do love her too,
Not out of absolute lust, . . .
But partly led to diet my revenge,
For that I do suspect the lusty Moor
Hath leap'd into my seat; the thought whereof
Doth, like a poisonous mineral, gnaw my inwards;
And nothing can or shall content my soul
Till I am even'd with him, wife for wife.
                              Othello, Act ii, sc. 1, l. 299 [IAGO]

5650   O, that the slave had forty thousand lives!
One is too poor, too weak for my revenge. . . .
Arise, black vengeance, from thy hollow cell!
                              Othello, Act iii, sc. 3, l. 442 [OTHELLO]

5651   Had all his hairs been lives, my great revenge
        Had stomach for them all.
                        Othello, Act v, sc. 2, l. 74 [OTHELLO]
5652   Can vengeance be pursued further than death?
                        Romeo and Juliet, Act v, sc. 3, l. 55 [PARIS]
5653   A vengeance on your crafty wither'd hide!
        Yet I have faced it with a card of ten.
                        The Taming of the Shrew, Act ii, sc. 1, l. 406 [TRANIO]
5654   To revenge is no valour, but to bear.
                        Timon of Athens, Act iii, sc. 5, l. 39 [SENATOR]
5655   Vengeance is in my heart, death in my hand,
        Blood and revenge are hammering in my head.
                        Titus Andronicus, Act ii, sc. 3, l. 38 [AARON]

Reverence

5656   BELARIUS: Though mean and mighty, rotting
        Together, have one dust, yet reverence,
        That angel of the world, doth make distinction
        Of place 'tween high and low. . . .
        GUIDERIUS: Thersites' body is as good as Ajax',
        When neither are alive.
                        Cymbeline, Act iv, sc. 2, l. 246 [BELARIUS]

Reward

5657   He that rewards me, God reward him! If I do grow great, I'll
        grow less, for I'll purge, and leave sack, and live cleanly as a
        nobleman should do.
                        I Henry IV, Act v, sc. 4, l. 167 [FALSTAFF]
5658   Long since we were resolved of your truth,
        Your faithful service and your toil in war,
        Yet never have you tasted our reward,
        Or been reguerdon'd with so much as thanks,
        Because till now we never saw your face.
                        I Henry VI, Act iii, sc. 4, l. 20 [KING HENRY]

Rhetoric

5659   To have is to have; for it is a figure in rhetoric that drink, being
        poured out of a cup into a glass, by filling the one doth empty the
        other.
                        As You Like It, Act v, sc. 1, l. 45 [TOUCHSTONE]
5660   Sweet smoke of rhetoric!
                        Love's Labour's Lost, Act iii, sc. 1, l. 65 [ARMADO]
5661   Fie, painted rhetoric! O, she needs it not.
                        Love's Labour's Lost, Act iv, sc. 3, l. 239 [BIRON]
5662   Did not the heavenly rhetoric of thine eye,
        'Gainst whom the world cannot hold argument,
        Persuade my heart to this false perjury?
                        Love's Labour's Lost, Act iv, sc. 3, l. 60 [LONGAVILLE]
                        (Repeated in *The Passionate Pilgrim,* Sonnet iii, l. 1.)
5663   Practise rhetoric in your common talk.
                        The Taming of the Shrew, Act i, sc. 1, l. 35 [TRANIO]

Rheumatic

5664   You are both, i' good truth, as rheumatic as two dry toasts.
                        II Henry IV, Act ii, sc. 4, l. 62 [HOSTESS]
5665   He was rheumatic, and talked of the whore of Babylon.
                        Henry V, Act ii, sc. 3, l. 40 [HOSTESS]

Rhyme

5666 I'll rhyme you so eight years together, dinners and suppers and sleeping-hours excepted: it is the right butter-women's rank to market.
As You Like It, Act iii, sc. 2, l. 101 [TOUCHSTONE]

5667 Oh, rhymes are guards on wanton Cupid's hose:
Disfigure not his shop.
Love's Labour's Lost, Act iv, sc. 3, l. 58 [BIRON]

5668 I cannot show it [my love] in rhyme; I have tried: I can find out no rhyme to 'lady' but 'baby,' an innocent rhyme; for 'scorn,' 'horn,' a hard rhyme; for 'school,' 'fool,' a babbling rhyme; very ominous endings: no, I was not born under a rhyming planet.
Much Ado about Nothing, Act v, sc. 2, l. 35 [BENEDICK]

5669 Not marble, nor the gilded monuments
Of princes, shall outlive this powerful rhyme.
Sonnet lv, l. 1

Rhyme and Reason

5670 Neither rhyme nor reason can express how much.
As You Like It, Act iii, sc. 2, l. 418 [ORLANDO]

5671 In the why and the wherefore is neither rhyme nor reason.
The Comedy of Errors, Act ii, sc. 2, l. 48
[DROMIO OF SYRACUSE]

5672 These fellows of infinite tongue, that can rhyme themselves into ladies' favours, they do always reason themselves out again. What! a speaker is but a prater; a rhyme is but a ballad.
Henry V, Act v, sc. 2, l. 164 [KING HENRY]

5673 BIRON: Fit in his time and place.
DUMAIN: In reason nothing.
BIRON: Something then in rhyme.
Love's Labour's Lost, Act i, sc. 1, l. 98 [BIRON]

5674 VALENTINE: How now, sir? what are you reasoning with yourself?
SPEED: Nay, I was rhyming: 'tis you that have the reason.
The Two Gentlemen of Verona, Act ii, sc. 1, l. 148 [VALENTINE]

Richard

5675 ELINOR: He hath a trick of Cœur-de-lion's face. . . .
KING: Mine eye hath well examined his parts
And finds them perfect Richard.
King John, Act i, sc. 1, l. 85 [ELINOR]

5676 Kneel thou down, Philip, but rise more great,
Arise sir Richard and Plantagenet.
King John, Act i, sc. 1, l. 161 [KING]

5677 Richard, that robb'd the lion of his heart
And fought the holy wars in Palestine.
King John, Act ii, sc. 1, l. 3 [LEWIS]

5678 Richard yet lives, hell's black intelligencer, . . .
Earth gapes, hell burns, fiends roar, saints pray,
To have him suddenly convey'd away.
Cancel his bond of life, dear God, I pray,
That I may live to say, The dog is dead.
Richard III, Act iv, sc. 4, l. 71 [QUEEN MARGARET]

Riches

5679 TOUCHSTONE: Art thou rich?
WILLIAM: Faith, sir, so so.

TOUCHSTONE: 'So so' is good, very good, very excellent good;
and yet it is not; it is but so so.
                    As You Like It, Act v, sc. 1, l. 27 [TOUCHSTONE]
5680 Fairest Cordelia, thou art most rich, being poor;
Most choice, forsaken; and most loved, despised!
                    King Lear, Act i, sc. 1, l. 253 [FRANCE]
5681 Poorly rich, so wanteth in his store,
That, cloy'd with much, he pineth still for more.
                    The Rape of Lucrece, l. 97

Richmond

5682 Sleep, Richmond, sleep in peace, and wake in joy;
Good angels guard thee from the boar's annoy.
                    Richard III, Act v, sc. 3, l. 155 [GHOSTS]
5683 The king enacts more wonders than a man,
Daring an opposite to every danger:
His horse is slain, and all on foot he fights,
Seeking for Richmond in the throat of death.
                    Richard III, Act v, sc. 4, l. 5 [CATESBY]
5684 I think there be six Richmonds in the field;
Five have I slain to-day instead of him.
                    Richard III, Act v, sc. 4, l. 11 [KING RICHARD]

Riddance

5685 MOROCCO: Portia, adieu. I have too grieved a heart
To take a tedious leave: thus losers part. [*Exit*]
PORTIA: A gentle riddance. Draw the curtains, go.
Let all of his complexion choose me so.
                    The Merchant of Venice, Act ii, sc. 7, l. 76 [MOROCCO]
5686 THERSITES: I will see you hanged like clotpoles, ere I come any
more to your tents: I will keep where there is wit stirring and
leave the faction of fools. [*Exit*]
PATROCLUS: A good riddance.
                    Troilus and Cressida, Act ii, sc. 1, l. 128 [THERSITES]
("Clotpoles," thick or wooden heads.)

Right

5687 Do you two know how you are censured . . . of us of the right-
hand file?
                    Coriolanus, Act ii, sc. 1, l. 24 [MENENIUS]
(The "Right", the aristocracy, against the "Left", the people.)
5688 O God, that right should thus overcome might!
                    II Henry IV, Act v, sc. 4, l. 27 [HOSTESS]
5689 God defend the right!
                    II Henry VI, Act ii, sc. 3, l. 55 [KING]
(Repeated in *Richard II,* i, 3, 101, and *Love's Labour's Lost,*
i, 1, 213.)
Pray that the right may thrive.
                    King Lear, Act v, sc. 2, l. 2 [EDGAR]
Heaven prosper the right!
                    The Merry Wives of Windsor, Act iii, sc. 1, l. 30 [EVANS]
5690 With blood and sword and fire to win your right.
                    Henry V, Act i, sc. 2, l. 131 [CANTERBURY]
5691 I'll win our ancient right in France again,
Or die a soldier, as I lived a king.
                    Richard III, Act iii, sc. 1, l. 92 [PRINCE]
5692 When right with right wars who shall be most right!
                    Troilus and Cressida, Act iii, sc. 2, l. 179 [TROILUS]

Right and Wrong

5693   King Henry, be thy title right or wrong,
Lord Clifford vows to fight in thy defence.
> *III Henry VI,* Act i, sc. 1, l. 159 [CLIFFORD]

5694   I . . . do him right that, answering one foul wrong,
Lives not to act another.
> *Measure for Measure,* Act ii, sc. 2, l. 103 [ANGELO]

5695   To do a great right, do a little wrong.
> *The Merchant of Venice,* Act iv, sc. 1, l. 216 [BASSANIO]

5696   I have had feeling of my cousin's wrongs,
And labour'd all I could to do him right,
But in this kind to come, in braving arms,
Be his own carver and cut out his way,
To find out right with wrong, it may not be.
> *Richard II,* Act ii, sc. 3, l. 141 [YORK]

5697   Give me thy poigniard: you shall know, my boys,
Your mother's hand shall right your mother's wrong.
> *Titus Andronicus,* Act ii, sc. 3, l. 120 [TAMORA]

5698   You heavy people, circle me about,
That I may turn me to each one of you,
And swear unto my soul to right your wrongs.
> *Titus Andronicus,* Act iii, sc. 1, l. 278 [TITUS]

5699   Right and wrong,
Between whose endless jar justice resides,
Should lose their names, and so should justice too.
> *Troilus and Cressida,* Act i, sc. 3, l. 116 [ULYSSES]

Ring

5700   PORTIA: But now I was the lord
Of this fair mansion, master of my servants,
Queen o'er myself; and even now, but now,
This house, these servants and this same myself
Are yours, my lord: I give them with this ring;
Which, when you part from, lose, or give away,
Let it presage the ruin of your love
And be my vantage to exclaim on you. . . .
BASSANIO: When this ring
Parts from this finger, then parts life from hence:
O, then be bold to say Bassanio's dead!
> *The Merchant of Venice,* Act iii, sc. 2, l. 169 [PORTIA]

5701   PORTIA: A quarrel, ho, already! what's the matter?
GRATIANO: About a hoop of gold, a paltry ring
That she did give me, whose posy was
For all the world like cutler's poetry
Upon a knife, 'Love me, and leave me not.'
> *The Merchant of Venice,* Act v, sc. 1, l. 146 [PORTIA]

5702   Look, how this ring encompasseth thy finger,
Even so thy breast encloseth my poor heart;
Wear both of them, for both of them are thine.
> *Richard III,* Act i, sc. 2, l. 204 [GLOUCESTER]

5703   He that runs fastest gets the ring.
> *The Taming of the Shrew,* Act i, sc. 1, l. 145 [HORTENSIO]

Ripeness

5704   EDGAR: Give me thy hand; come on.
GLOUCESTER: No farther, sir; a man may rot even here.
EDGAR: What, in ill thoughts again? Men must endure

Their going hence, even as their coming hither:
Ripeness is all.

King Lear, Act v, sc. 2, l. 7 [EDGAR]

River

5705   There is a river in Macedon, and there is also moreover a river at
Monmouth, . . . and there is salmons in both.

Henry V, Act iv, sc. 7, l. 28 [FLUELLEN]

5706   To shallow rivers, to whose falls
Melodious birds sing madrigals;
There will we make our peds of roses,
And a thousand fragrant posies.

The Merry Wives of Windsor, Act iii, sc. 1, l. 17 [EVANS]

Robbery

5707   He that is robb'd, not wanting what is stol'n,
Let him not know 't, and he 's not robb'd at all.

Othello, Act iii, sc. 3, l. 342 [OTHELLO]

5708   The robb'd that smiles steals something from the thief;
He robs himself that spends a bootless grief.

Othello, Act i, sc. 3, l. 208 [DUKE]

Robin

5709   Bonny sweet Robin is all my joy.

Hamlet, Act iv, sc. 5, l. 187 [OPHELIA]

5710   MRS. PAGE: Here comes little Robin.
MRS. FORD: How now, my eyas-musket! What news with you?

The Merry Wives of Windsor, Act iii, sc. 3, l. 21 [MRS. PAGE]

("Eyas-musket," a fledgling sparrow-hawk.)

Rogue

5711   O, what a rogue and peasant slave am I!

Hamlet, Act ii, sc. 2, l. 577 [HAMLET]

5712   What a frosty-spirited rogue is this! . . . 'Zounds, an I were
now by this rascal, I could brain him with his lady's fan. . . .
What a pagan rascal is this! an infidel! . . . O, I could divide
myself and go to buffets, for moving such a dish of skim milk with
so honourable an action!

I Henry IV, Act ii, sc. 3, l. 23 [HOTSPUR]

5713   Ah, thou honey-seed rogue! thou art a honey-seed, a man-queller,
and a woman-queller. . . . thou rogue! do, thou hempseed!

II Henry IV, Act ii, sc. 1, l. 57 [HOSTESS]

5714   You blue-bottle rogue, you filthy famished correctioner, if you be
not swinged, I'll forswear half-kirtles.

II Henry IV, Act v, sc. 4, l. 22 [DOLL]

5715   A whoreson, glass-gazing, super-serviceable, finical rogue.

King Lear, Act ii, sc. 2, l. 19 [KENT]

5716   Such smelling rogues as these,
Like rats, oft bite the holy cords atwain
Which are too intrinse t' unloose; smooth every passion
That in the natures of their lords rebel;
Bring oil to fire, snow to their colder moods;
Renege, affirm, and turn their halcyon beaks
With every gale and vary of their masters,
Knowing nought, like dogs, but following.

King Lear, Act ii, sc. 2, l. 79 [KENT]

5717   SLY: I'll pheeze you, in faith.
        HOSTESS: A pair of stocks, you rogue!
        SLY: Ye are a baggage: the Slys are no rogues; look in the
        chronicles; we came in with Richard Conqueror.
                    The Taming of the Shrew, Induction, sc. 1, l. 1 [SLY]

Roman

5718   A Roman by a Roman Valiantly vanquish'd.
                    Antony and Cleopatra, Act iv, sc. 15, l. 57 [ANTONY]
5719   A Roman with a Roman's heart can suffer.
                    Cymbeline, Act v, sc. 5, l. 81 [LUCIUS]
5720   I am more an antique Roman than a Dane.
                    Hamlet, Act v, sc. 2, l. 352 [HORATIO]
5721   Romans now
        Have thews and limbs like to their ancestors.
                    Julius Cæsar, Act i, sc. 3, l. 80 [CASSIUS]
5722   Who is here so rude that would not be a Roman?
                    Julius Cæsar, Act iii, sc. 2, l. 33 [BRUTUS]
5723   BRUTUS: Now, as you are a Roman, tell me true.
        MESSALA: Then like a Roman bear the truth I tell.
                    Julius Cæsar, Act iv, sc. 3, l. 187 [BRUTUS]
5724   Are yet two Romans living such as these?
        The last of all the Romans, fare thee well!
        It is impossible that ever Rome
        Should breed thy fellow.
                    Julius Cæsar, Act v, sc. 3, l. 98 [BRUTUS]
5725   This was the noblest Roman of them all: . . .
        His life was gentle, and the elements
        So mix'd in him that Nature might stand up
        And say to all the world 'This was a man.'
                    Julius Cæsar, Act v, sc. 5, l. 68 [ANTONY]

Rome

5726   Let Rome in Tiber melt, and the wide arch
        Of the ranged empire fall! Here is my space.
                    Antony and Cleopatra, Act i, sc. 1, l. 33 [ANTONY]
5727   You may as well
        Strike at the heaven with your staves as lift them
        Against the Roman state.
                    Coriolanus, Act i, sc. 1, l. 69 [MENENIUS]
5728   Now the good gods forbid
        That our renowned Rome, whose gratitude
        Towards her deserved children is enroll'd
        In Jove's own book, like an unnatural dam
        Should now eat up her own!
                    Coriolanus, Act iii, sc. 1, l. 290 [MENENIUS]
5729   GLOUCESTER: Am I not protector, saucy priest?
        WINCHESTER: And am I not a prelate of the church?
        GLOUCESTER: Yes, as an outlaw in a castle keeps
        And useth it to patronize his theft. . . .
        WINCHESTER: Rome shall remedy this.
        WARWICK: Roam thither, then.
                    I Henry VI, Act iii, sc. 1, l. 45 [GLOUCESTER]
5730   When could they say till now, that talk'd of Rome
        That her wide walls encompass'd but one man?
        Now is it Rome indeed and room enough
        When there is in it but one only man.
                    Julius Cæsar, Act i, sc. 2, l. 154 [CASSIUS]

Rose

5731 Against the blown rose may they stop their nose
That kneel'd unto the buds.
Antony and Cleopatra, Act iii, sc. 13, l. 39 [CLEOPATRA]

5732 PLANTAGENET: Let him that is a true-born gentleman,
And stands upon the honour of his birth,
If he suppose that I have pleaded truth,
From off this brier pluck a white rose with me.
SOMERSET: Let him that is no coward nor no flatterer,
But dare maintain the party of the truth,
Pluck a red rose from off this thorn with me. . . .
PLANTAGENET: Hath not thy rose a canker, Somerset?
SOMERSET: Hath not thy rose a thorn, Plantagenet? . . .
WARWICK: Here I prophesy, this brawl to-day, . . .
Shall send between the red rose and the white
A thousand souls to death and deadly night.
I Henry VI, Act ii, sc. 4, l. 27 [PLANTAGENET]

5733 When I have pluck'd the rose,
I cannot give it vital growth again,
It needs must wither.
Othello, Act v, sc. 2, l. 13 [OTHELLO]

5734 Sweet rose, fair flower, untimely pluck'd, soon vaded,
Pluck'd in the bud, and vaded in the spring!
The Passionate Pilgrim, Pt. x, l. 1

5735 The rose looks fair, but fairer we it deem
For that sweet odour which doth in it live.
Sonnet liv, l. 3

Rose and Thorn

5736 This thorn
Doth to our rose of youth rightly belong;
Our blood to us, this to our blood is born.
All's Well that Ends Well, Act i, sc. 3, l. 135 [COUNTESS]

5737 When you have our roses,
You barely leave our thorns to prick ourselves
And mock us with our bareness.
All's Well that Ends Well, Act iv, sc. 2, l. 17 [DIANA]

5738 I know what thorns the growing rose defends.
The Rape of Lucrece, l. 492 [LUCRECE]

5739 Roses have thorns, and silver fountains mud.
Sonnet xxxv, l. 2

5740 What though the rose have prickles, yet 'tis pluck'd.
Venus and Adonis, l. 574

Rotten

5741 You'll be rotten ere you be half ripe.
As You Like It, Act iii, sc. 2, l. 125 [ROSALIND]
(For full quotation see 2938.)

5742 Something is rotten in the state of Denmark.
Hamlet, Act i, sc. 4, l. 90 [HAMLET]

Rowland

5743 Child Rowland to the dark tower came,
His word was still,—Fie, foh, and fum,
I smell the blood of a British man.
King Lear, Act iii, sc. 4, l. 188 [EDGAR]
(Quoting an old Scottish ballad.)

Rub

5744 Ay, there's the rub.
                                    Hamlet, Act iii, sc. 1, l. 65 [HAMLET]
5745   We doubt not now
But every rub is smoothed on our way.
                                    Henry V, Act ii, sc. 2, l. 187 [KING HENRY]
5746 Leave no rubs nor botches in the work.
                                    Macbeth, Act iii, sc. 1, l. 134 [MACBETH]
5747 LADY: Madam, we'll play at bowls.
QUEEN: 'Twill make me think the world is full of rubs,
And that my fortune runs against the bias.
                                    Richard II, Act iii, sc. 4, l. 3 [LADY]

Rudeness

5748 BRUTUS: What a blunt fellow is this grown to be! . . .
CASSIUS: This rudeness is a sauce to his good wit,
Which gives men stomach to digest his words
With better appetite.
                                    Julius Cæsar, Act i, sc. 2, l. 299 [BRUTUS]
5749   Hear thee, Gratiano,
Thou art too wild, too rude and bold of voice;
Parts that become thee happily enough
And in such eyes as ours appear not faults;
But where thou art not known, why, there they show
Something too liberal.
                                    The Merchant of Venice, Act ii, sc. 2, l. 189 [BASSANIO]

Rue

5750 There's rue for you; and here's some for me: we may call it
herb-grace o' Sundays: O, you must wear your rue with a difference.
                                    Hamlet, Act iv, sc. 5, l. 181 [OPHELIA]
5751 Here did she fall a tear; here in this place
I'll set a bank of rue, sour herb of grace:
Rue, even for ruth, here shortly shall be seen,
In the remembrance of a weeping queen.
                                    Richard II, Act iii, sc. 4, l. 104 [GARDENER]

Rule

5752 Suffolk, the new-made duke that rules the roast.
                                    II Henry VI, Act i, sc. 1, l. 109 [GLOUCESTER]
5753 Give place: by heaven, thou shalt rule no more
O'er him whom heaven created for thy ruler.
                                    II Henry VI, Act v, sc. 1, l. 104 [YORK]
5754 Were they to be ruled, and not to rule,
This sickly land might solace as before.
                                    Richard III, Act ii, sc. 3, l. 29 [CITIZEN]

Rumour

5755 Open your ears; for which of you will stop
The vent of hearing when loud Rumour speaks?
I, from the orient to the drooping west,
Making the wind my post-horse, still unfold
The acts commenced on this ball of earth:
Upon my tongues continual slanders ride,
The which in every language I pronounce,
Stuffing the ears of men with false reports.
I speak of peace while covert enmity
Under the smile of safety wounds the world:

And who but Rumor, who but only I,
Make fearful musters and prepared defence,
Whiles the big year, swoln with some other grief,
Is thought with child by the stern tyrant war,
And no such matter? Rumour is a pipe
Blown by surmises, jealousies, conjectures,
And of so easy and so plain a stop
That the blunt monster with uncounted heads,
The still-discordant wavering multitude,
Can play upon it. . . . From Rumour's tongues
They bring smooth comforts false, worse than true wrongs.
II Henry IV, Induction, l. 2 [RUMOUR]

5756   Rumour doth double, like the voice and echo,
The numbers of the fear'd.
II Henry IV, Act iii, sc. 1, l. 97 [WARWICK]

5757   This from rumour's tongue
I idly heard; if true or false I know not.
King John, Act iv, sc. 2, l. 123 [MESSENGER]

5758   Cruel are the times, . . . when we hold rumour
From what we fear, yet know not what we fear,
But float upon a wild and violent sea
Each way and move.
Macbeth, Act iv, sc. 2, l. 18 [ROSS]

Running

5759   I would give a thousand pound I could run as fast as thou canst.
I Henry IV, Act ii, sc. 4, l. 162 [FALSTAFF]
PRINCE: You are lions too, you ran away upon instinct. . . .
BARDOLPH: 'Faith, I ran when I saw others run.
I Henry IV, Act ii, sc. 4, l. 331 [PRINCE]

5760   We may outrun,
By violent swiftness, that which we run at,
And lose by over-running.
Henry VIII, Act i, sc. 1, l. 141 [NORFOLK]

Rust

5761   I were better to be eaten to death with a rust than to be scoured
to nothing with perpetual motion.
II Henry IV, Act i, sc. 2, l. 245 [FALSTAFF]

5762   Foul-cankering rust the hidden treasure frets,
But gold that's put to use more gold begets.
Venus and Adonis, l. 767 [VENUS]

S

Sack

5763   O monstrous! but one half-pennyworth of bread to this intolerable
deal of sack!
I Henry IV, Act ii, sc. 4, l. 591 [PRINCE]

5764   A good sherris-sack . . . ascends me into the brain; dries me there
all the foolish and dull and crudy vapours which environ it; makes
it apprehensive, quick, forgetive, full of nimble fiery and delectable
shapes; which, delivered o'er to the voice, the tongue, which is
the birth, becomes excellent wit. . . . If I had a thousand sons,
the first humane principle I would teach them should be, to forswear thin potations and to addict themselves to sack.
II Henry IV, Act iv, sc. 3, l. 103 [FALSTAFF]

5765   More sacks to the mill!
                        Love's Labour's Lost, Act iv, sc. 3, l. 81 [BIRON]
5766   Your hearts are mighty, your skins are whole, and let burnt sack
       be the issue.
                        The Merry Wives of Windsor, Act iii, sc. 1, l. 111 [HOST]
5767   Thy eyes are almost set in thy head. . . . My man-monster hath
       drown'd his tongue in sack.
                        The Tempest, Act iii, sc. 2, l. 10 [STEPHANO]
5768   Was there ever man a coward that hath drunk so much sack as
       I today?
                        The Tempest, Act iii, sc. 2, l. 31 [TRINCULO]

Sacrifice

5769   Let us be sacrificers, but not butchers, Caius.
                        Julius Cæsar, Act ii, sc. 1, l. 166 [BRUTUS]
5770   Upon such sacrifices, my Cordelia,
       The gods themselves throw incense.
                        King Lear, Act v, sc. 3, l. 20 [LEAR]

Sadness

5771   See where he is: . . . if you find him sad,
       Say I am dancing; if in mirth, report
       That I am sudden sick.
                        Antony and Cleopatra, Act i, sc. 3, l. 3 [CLEOPATRA]
5772   CLEOPATRA: Was he sad or merry?
       ALEXAS: Like to the time o' the year between the extremes
       Of hot and cold, he was not sad nor merry.
       CLEOPATRA: O well-divided disposition! Note him,
       Note him, good Charmian, 'tis the man; but note him: . . .
       O heavenly mingle! Be'st thou sad or merry,
       The violence of either thee becomes,
       So does it no man else.
                        Antony and Cleopatra, Act i, sc. 5, l. 50 [CLEOPATRA]
5773   ARTHUR: You are sad.
       HUBERT: Indeed, I have been merrier.
       ARTHUR: Mercy on me!
       Methinks nobody should be sad but I:
       Yet, I remember, when I was in France,
       Young gentlemen would be as sad as night,
       Only for wantonness.
                        King John, Act iv, sc. 1, l. 11 [ARTHUR]
5774   In sooth, I know not why I am so sad:
       It wearies me; you say it wearies you;
       But how I caught it, found it, or came by it,
       What stuff 'tis made of, whereof it is born,
       I am to learn;
       And such a want-wit sadness makes of me,
       That I have much ado to know myself.
                        The Merchant of Venice, Act i, sc. 1, l. 1 [ANTONIO]
5775   You are sad
       Because you are not merry: and 'twere as easy
       For you to laugh and leap and say you are merry
       Because you are not sad.
                        The Merchant of Venice, Act i, sc. 1, l. 47 [SALARINO]

Safety

5776   I long that we were safe and sound aboard.
                        The Comedy of Errors, Act iv, sc. 4, l. 154
                                    [ANTIPHOLUS OF SYRACUSE]

5777   Be wary then; best safety lies in fear.
                            Hamlet, Act i, sc. 3, l. 43 [LAERTES]

5778   And yet thou shalt be safe? such safety finds
        The trembling lamb environed with wolves.
                            III Henry VI, Act i, sc. 1, l. 241 [QUEEN MARGARET]

5779   He that steeps his safety in true blood
        Shall find but bloody safety and untrue.
                            King John, Act iii, sc. 4, l. 147 [PANDULPH]

Sail

5780   Behold the threaden sails,
        Borne with the invisible and creeping wind,
        Draw the huge bottoms through the furrow'd sea,
        Breasting the lofty surge.
                            Henry V, Act iii, Prologue, l. 10 [CHORUS]

5781   Now Margaret
        Must strike her sail and learn awhile to serve
        Where kings command.
                            III Henry VI, Act iii, sc. 3, l. 4 [QUEEN MARGARET]

5782   In a sieve I'll thither sail,
        And, like a rat without a tail,
        I'll do, I'll do, and I'll do.
                            Macbeth, Act i, sc. 3, l. 8 [WITCH]

5783   We have laugh'd to see the sails conceive
        And grow big-bellied with the wanton wind.
                            A Midsummer Night's Dream, Act ii, sc. 1, l. 128 [TITANIA]

Saint

5784   O, thou hast damnable iteration and are indeed able to corrupt
        a saint.
                            I Henry IV, Act i, sc. 2, l. 101 [FALSTAFF]

5785   I know thou worshippest Saint Nicholas as truly as a man of
        falsehood may.
                            I Henry IV, Act ii, sc. 1, l. 71 [CHAMBERLAIN]

5786   Saint George, that swinged the dragon, and ere since
        Sits on his horse back at mine hostess' door.
                            King John, Act ii, sc. 1, l. 288 [BASTARD]

5787   O cunning enemy, that, to catch a saint,
        With saints dost bait thy hook!
                            Measure for Measure, Act ii, sc. 2, l. 180 [ANGELO]

Salad

5788   LAFEU: 'Twas a good lady: we may pick a thousand salads ere we
        light on such another herb.
        CLOWN: Indeed, sir, she was the sweet-marjoram of the salad, or
        rather, the herb of grace.
                            All's Well that Ends Well, Act iv, sc. 5, l. 13 [LAFEU]

5789   My salad days,
        When I was green in judgement: cold in blood.
                            Antony and Cleopatra, Act i, sc. 5, l. 73 [CLEOPATRA]

5790   There were no sallets in the lines to make the matter savoury, nor
        no matter in the phrase that might indict the author of affectation.
                            Hamlet, Act ii, sc. 2, l. 463 [HAMLET]

Salve

5791   Let us hence, my sovereign, to provide
        A salve for any sore that may betide.
                            III Henry VI, Act iv, sc. 6, l. 87 [WARWICK]

5792   ARMADO: Doth the inconsiderate take salve for l'envoy, and the
       word l'envoy for a salve?
       MOTH: Do the wise think them other? is not l'envoy a salve?
       ARMADO: No, page: it is an epilogue or discourse, to make plain
       Some obscure precedence that hath before been sain.
                         Love's Labour's Lost, Act iii, sc. 1, l. 78 [ARMADO]

Sands

5793   The sands are number'd that make up my life;
       Here must I stay, and here my life must end.
                               III Henry VI, Act i, sc. 4, l. 25 [YORK]
5794   Now our sands are almost run;
           More a little, and then dumb.
                               Pericles, Act v, sc. 2, l. 1 [GOWER]
5795   Come unto these yellow sands,
               And there take hands:
           Courtsied when you have and kiss'd
               The wild waves whist,
           Foot it featly here and there;
               And, sweet sprites, the burthen bear.
                               The Tempest, Act i, sc. 2, l. 376 [ARIEL]

Sap

5796   We will yet do well. . . . There's sap in't yet.
                         Antony and Cleopatra, Act iii, sc. 13, l. 188 [ANTONY]
5797   FLORIZEL: There's some sap in this.
       CAMILLO: A course more promising
       Than a wild dedication of yourselves
       To unpath'd waters, undream'd shores.
                         The Winter's Tale, Act iv, sc. 4, l. 575 [FLORIZEL]

Satan

5798   He talked of Satan and of Limbo and of Furies and I know not
       what.
                   All's Well that Ends Well, Act v, sc. 3, l. 261 [PAROLLES]
5799   ANTIPHOLUS S.: Satan, avoid! I charge thee, tempt me not!
       DROMIO S.: Master, is this Mistress Satan?
       ANTIPHOLUS S.: It is the devil.
       DROMIO S.: Nay, she is worse, she is the devil's dam.
                               The Comedy of Errors, Act iv, sc. 3, l. 48
                                        [ANTIPHOLUS OF SYRACUSE]
5800   I charge thee, Satan, housed within this man,
       To yield possession to my holy prayers
       And to thy state of darkness hie thee straight:
       I conjure thee by all the saints in heaven.
                         The Comedy of Errors, Act iv, sc. 4, l. 57 [PINCH]

Satisfaction

5801   Nor gives it satisfaction to our blood,
       That we must curb it upon others' proof;
       To be forbid the sweets that seem so good,
       For fear of harms that preach in our behoof.
                                   A Lover's Complaint, l. 162
5802   Where's satisfaction?
       It is impossible you should see this,
       Were they as prime as goats, as hot as monkeys,
       As salt as wolves in pride, and fools as gross
       As ignorance made drunk.
                               Othello, Act iii, sc. 3, l. 401 [IAGO]

5803 ROMEO: O, wilt thou leave me so unsatisfied?
JULIET: What satisfaction canst thou have to-night?
Romeo and Juliet, Act ii, sc. 2, l. 125 [ROMEO]

Saying

5804   The common saw,
That out of heaven's benediction comest
To the warm sun!
King Lear, Act ii, sc. 2, l. 167 [KENT]

5805 ROSALINE: Shall I come upon thee with an old saying, that was a
man when King Pepin of France was a little boy? . . .
BOYET: So I may answer thee with one as old, that was a woman
when Queen Guinover of Britain was a little wench.
Love's Labour's Lost, Act iv, sc. 1, l. 121 [ROSALINE]

5806 Who fears a sentence or an old man's saw
Shall by a painted cloth be kept in awe.
The Rape of Lucrece, l. 244 [TARQUIN]

5807 I can tell thee where that saying was born.
Twelfth Night, Act i, sc. 5, l. 8 [MARIA]

Scandal

5808   We in the world's wide mouth
Live scandalized and foully spoken of.
I Henry IV, Act i, sc. 3, l. 153 [WORCESTER]

5809 Greatest scandal waits on greatest state.
The Rape of Lucrece, l. 1006 [LUCRECE]

5810 Your love and pity doth the impression fill
Which vulgar scandal stamp'd upon my brow;
For what care I who calls me well or ill,
So you o'er-green my bad, my good allow?
Sonnet cxii, l. 1

Scar

5811 A scar nobly got, or a noble scar, is a good livery of honour.
All's Well that Ends Well, Act iv, sc. 5, l. 108 [LAFEU]

5812 Show me one scar character'd on thy skin:
Men's flesh preserved so whole do seldom win.
II Henry VI, Act iii, sc. 1, l. 300 [YORK]

5813 He jests at scars that never felt a wound.
Romeo and Juliet, Act ii, sc. 2, l. 1 [ROMEO]

5814 O, sir, to such as boasting show their scars
A mock is due.
Troilus and Cressida, Act iv, sc. 5, l. 290 [TROILUS]

Sceptre

5815   It were for me
To throw my sceptre at the injurious gods;
To tell them that this world did equal theirs
Till they had stol'n our jewel.
Antony and Cleopatra, Act iv, sc. 15, l. 74 [CLEOPATRA]

5816 'Tis much when sceptres are in children's hands.
I Henry VI, Act iv, sc. 1, l. 192 [EXETER]

5817 A sceptre snatch'd with an unruly hand
Must be as boisterously maintain'd as gain'd.
King John, Act iii, sc. 4, l. 135 [PANDULPH]

Scorn

5818 We were better parch in Afric sun
Than in the pride and salt scorn of his eyes.
Troilus and Cressida, Act i, sc. 3, l. 370 [ULYSSES]

5819   O, what a deal of scorn looks beautiful
In the contempt and anger of his lip.
Twelfth Night, Act iii, sc. 1, l. 157 [OLIVIA]

Scorpion

5820   Seek not a scorpion's nest,
Nor set no footing on this unkind shore.
II Henry VI, Act iii, sc. 2, l. 86 [QUEEN]

5821   MACBETH : O, full of scorpions is my mind, dear wife!
Thou know'st that Banquo, and his Fleance, lives.
LADY MACBETH : But in them nature's copy's not eterne.
Macbeth, Act iii, sc. 2, l. 36 [MACBETH]

Scotland

5822   There's a saying very old and true,
    'If that you will France win,
    Then with Scotland first begin':
For once the eagle England being in prey,
To her unguarded nest the weasel Scot
Comes sneaking and so sucks her princely eggs,
Playing the mouse in absence of the cat,
To tear and havoc more than she can eat.
Henry V, Act i, sc. 2, l. 166 [WESTMORELAND]

5823   MACDUFF: Stands Scotland where it did?
ROSS: Alas, poor country!
Almost afraid to know itself. It cannot
Be call'd our mother, but our grave.
Macbeth, Act iv, sc. 3, l. 164 [MACDUFF]

Scruple

5824   I will not bate thee a scruple.
All's Well that Ends Well, Act ii, sc. 3, l. 234 [LAFEU]

5825   Every thing adheres together, that no dram of a scruple, no scruple
of a scruple, no obstacle . . . can come between me and the full
prospect of my hopes.
Twelfth Night, Act iii, sc. 4, l. 87 [MALVOLIO]

Sea

5826   You were used to say . . .
That when the sea was calm, all boats alike
Show'd mastership in floating.
Coriolanus, Act iv, sc. 1, l. 6 [CORIOLANUS]

5827   The sea, all water, yet receives rain still
And in abundance addeth to his store.
Sonnet cxxxv, l. 9

5828   If the winds rage, doth not the sea wax mad,
Threatening the welkin with his big-swoln face?
Titus Andronicus, Act iii, sc. 1, l. 223 [TITUS]

5829   The sea being smooth,
How many shallow bauble boats dare sail
Upon her patient breast, making their way
With those of nobler bulk!
Troilus and Cressida, Act i, sc. 3, l. 34 [NESTOR]

5830   You may as well
Forbid the sea for to obey the moon
As or by oath remove or counsel shake
The fabric of his folly.
The Winter's Tale, Act i, sc. 2, l. 426 [CAMILLO]

Season

5831   How many things by season seasoned are
     To their right praise and true perfection!
            The Merchant of Venice, Act v, sc. 1, l. 107 [PORTIA]
5832   The seasons alter: hoary-headed frosts
     Fall in the fresh lap of the crimson rose,
     And on old Hiems' thin and icy crown
     An odorous chaplet of sweet summer buds
     Is, as in mackery, set; the spring, the summer,
     The chiding autumn, angry winter, change
     Their wonted liveries, and the mazed world,
     By their increase, now knows not which is which.
         A Midsummer Night's Dream, Act ii, sc. 1, l. 107 [TITANIA]

Secrecy

5833   In nature's infinite book of secrecy
     A little I can read.
          Antony and Cleopatra, Act i, sc. 2, l. 9 [SOOTHSAYER]
5834   This to me
     In dreadful secrecy impart they did.
              Hamlet, Act i, sc. 2, l. 206 [HORATIO]
5835   'Tis a secret must be locked within the teeth and the lips.
          Measure for Measure, Act iii, sc. 2, l. 142 [LUCIO]
5836   I will make a Star-chamber matter of it.
        The Merry Wives of Windsor, Act i, sc. 1, l. 1 [SHALLOW]
5837   What I am, and what I would, are as secret as maidenhead.
            Twelfth Night, Act i, sc. 5, l. 231 [VIOLA]

Security

5838   A whoreson Achitophel! a rascally yea-forsooth knave! to bear a
     gentleman in hand, and then stand upon security! The whoreson
     smooth-pates, . . . if a man is through with them in honest taking
     up, then they must stand upon security. I had as lief they would
     put ratsbane in my mouth as offer to stop it with security. . . .
     Well, he may sleep in security; for he hath the horn of abundance,
     and the lightness of his wife shines through it.
            II Henry IV, Act i, sc. 2, l. 42 [FALSTAFF]
5839   Thus have we swept suspicion from our seat
     And made our footstool of security.
         III Henry VI, Act v, sc. 7, l. 13 [KING EDWARD]
5840   Security Is mortals' chiefest enemy.
             Macbeth, Act iii, sc. 5, l. 32 [HECATE]
5841   Secure of thunder's crack or lightning flash.
          Titus Andronicus, Act ii, sc. 1, l. 3 [AARON]

Seeming

5842   All good seeming,
     By thy revolt, O husband, shall be thought
     Put on for villany; not born where 't grows,
     But worn a bait for ladies.
           Cymbeline, Act iii, sc. 4, l. 56 [IMOGEN]
5843   QUEEN: Why seems it so particular with thee?
     HAMLET: Seems, madam! nay, it is; I know not 'seems.'
     'Tis not alone my inky cloak, good mother,
     Nor customary suits of solemn black, . . .
     That can denote me truly: these indeed seem, . . .

But I have that within which passeth show;
These but the trappings and the suits of woe.
Hamlet, Act i, sc. 2, l. 76 [QUEEN]

5844   I do profess to be no less than I seem; to serve him truly that will
put me in trust; to love him that is honest; to converse with him
that is wise, and says little; to fear judgement; to fight when I
cannot choose; and to eat no fish.
King Lear, Act i, sc. 4, l. 14 [KENT]

5845   Seeming! I will write against it:
You seem to me as Dian in her orb,
As chaste as is the bud ere it be blown;
But you are more intemperate in your blood
Than Venus, or those pamper'd animals
That rage in savage sensuality.
Much Ado about Nothing, Act iv, sc. 1, l. 57 [CLAUDIO]

5846   Thou art not what thou seem'st; and if the same,
Thou seem'st not what thou art, a god, a king.
The Rape of Lucrece, l. 600 [LUCRECE]

5847   Men should be what they seem;
Or those that be not, would they might seem none!
Othello, Act iii, sc. 3, l. 126 [IAGO]

Self

5848   I will from henceforth rather be myself,
Mighty and to be fear'd, than my condition;
Which hath been smooth as oil, soft as young down,
And therefore lost that title of respect
Which the proud soul ne'er pays but to the proud.
I Henry IV, Act i, sc. 3, l. 5 [KING HENRY]

5849   'Tis in ourselves that we are thus or thus.
Othello, Act i, sc. 3, l. 322 [IAGO]

Self-Love

5850   Self-love, my liege, is not so vile a sin
As self-neglecting.
Henry V, Act ii, sc. 4, l. 74 [DAUPHIN]

5851   Love thyself last: cherish those hearts that hate thee.
Henry VIII, Act iii, sc. 2, l. 443 [WOLSEY]

5852   Sin of self-love possesseth all mine eye
And all my soul and all my every part.
Sonnet lxii, l. 1

5853   You are sick of self-love, Malvolio, and taste with a distempered
appetite.
Twelfth Night, Act i, sc. 5, l. 98 [OLIVIA]

Self-Slaughter

5854   Against self-slaughter
There is a prohibition so divine
That cravens my weak hand.
Cymbeline, Act iii, sc. 4, l. 78 [IMOGEN]

5855   O, . . . that the Everlasting had not fix'd
His canon 'gainst self-slaughter!
Hamlet, Act i, sc. 2, l. 131 [HAMLET]

Selling

5856   Sell when you can: you are not for all markets.
As You Like It, Act iii, sc. 5, l. 60 [ROSALIND]

5857   To things of sale a seller's praise belongs.
                        Love's Labour's Lost, Act iv, sc. 3, l. 240 [BIRON]

Sepulchre

5858   The sepulchre,
        Wherein we saw thee quietly inurn'd,
        Hath oped his ponderous and marble jaws.
                        Hamlet, Act i, sc. 4, l. 48 [HAMLET]
5859   To entail him and his heirs unto the crown,
        What is it, but to make thy sepulchre
        And creep into it far before thy time?
                        III Henry VI, Act i, sc. 1, l. 235 [QUEEN MARGARET]

Serpent

5860   He's . . . murmuring 'Where's my serpent of old Nile?'
        For so he calls me.
                        Antony and Cleopatra, Act i, sc. 5, l. 25 [CLEOPATRA]
5861   GHOST: The serpent that did sting thy father's life
        Now wears his crown.
        HAMLET: O my prophetic soul! My uncle!
        GHOST: Ay, that incestuous, that adulterate beast,
        With witchcraft of his wit, . . . won to his shameful lust
        The will of my most seeming-virtuous queen:
        O Hamlet, what a falling-off was there!
                        Hamlet, Act i, sc. 5, l. 39 [GHOST]
5862   Think him as a serpent's egg
        Which, hatch'd, would, as his kind, grow mischievous,
        And kill him in the shell.
                        Julius Cæsar, Act ii, sc. 1, l. 32 [BRUTUS]
5863   France, thou mayst hold a serpent by the tongue,
        A chafed lion by the mortal paw,
        A fasting tiger safer by the tooth,
        Than keep in peace that hand which thou dost hold.
                        King John, Act iii, sc. 1, l. 259 [PANDULPH]
5864   Look like the innocent flower,
        But be the serpent under 't.
                        Macbeth, Act i, sc. 5, l. 66 [LADY MACBETH]
5865   There the grown serpent lies; the worm that's fled
        Hath nature that in time will venom breed,
        No teeth for the present.
                        Macbeth, Act iii, sc. 4, l. 29 [MACBETH]
5866   Both like serpents are, who, though they feed
        On sweetest flowers, yet they poison breed.
                        Pericles, Act i, sc. 1, l. 132 [PERICLES]
5867   Who sees the lurking serpent steps aside.
                        The Rape of Lucrece, l. 362

Servant

5868   I had rather be their servant in my way
        Than sway with them in theirs.
                        Coriolanus, Act ii, sc. 1, l. 219 [CORIOLANUS]
5869   Every good servant does not all commands:
        No bond but to do just ones.
                        Cymbeline, Act v, sc. 1, l. 5 [POSTHUMUS]
5870   I will not sort you with the rest of my servants, for, to speak to you
        like an honest man, I am most dreadfully attended.
                        Hamlet, Act ii, sc. 2, l. 274 [HAMLET]

Service

5871   Service is no heritage.
            All's Well that Ends Well, Act i, sc. 3, l. 25 [CLOWN]
    (Quoting an old proverb.)
         'Tis the curse of service,
Preferment goes by letter and affection,
And not by old gradation, where each second
Stood heir to the first.
                  Othello, Act i, sc. 1, l. 35 [IAGO]

5872   O good old man, how well in thee appears
The constant service of the antique world,
When service sweat for duty, not for mead!
Thou art not for the fashion of these times,
When none will sweat but for promotion,
And having that, do choke their service up
Even with the having: it is not so with thee,
But, poor old man, thou prunest a rotten tree,
That cannot so much as a blossom yield
In lieu of all thy pains and husbandry.
         As You Like It, Act ii, sc. 3, l. 56 [ORLANDO]

5873   To serve bravely is to come halting off.
           II Henry IV, Act ii, sc. 4, l. 54 [FALSTAFF]

5874   So service shall with steeled sinews toil,
And labour shall refresh itself with hope.
           Henry V, Act ii, sc. 2, l. 36 [SCROOP]

5875   Will your grace command me any service to the world's end? I will
go on the slightest errand now to the Antipodes that you can
devise to send me on; I will fetch you a toothpicker now from the
furthest inch of Asia, bring you the length of Prester John's foot,
fetch you a hair off the great Cham's beard, do you any embassage to the Pigmies, rather than hold three words' conference with
this harpy.
        Much Ado about Nothing, Act ii, sc. 1, l. 271 [BENEDICK]

5876   Remember I have done thee worthy service;
Told thee no lies, made thee no mistakings.
           The Tempest, Act i, sc. 2, l. 247 [ARIEL]

Shadow

5877   I am but shadow of myself:
You are deceived, my substance is not here.
           I Henry VI, Act ii, sc. 3, l. 50 [TALBOT]

5878   Must he be then as shadow of himself?
Adorn his temples with a coronet,
And yet, in substance and authority,
Retain but privilege of a private man?
         I Henry VI, Act v, sc. 4, l. 133 [ALENÇON]

5879   Avaunt! and quit my sight! let the earth hide thee!
Thy bones are marrowless, thy blood is cold;
Thou hast no speculation in those eyes
Which thou dost glare with. . . . What man dare, I dare:
Approach thou like the rugged Russian bear,
The arm'd rhinoceras, or the Hyrcan tiger;
Take any shape but that, and my firm nerves
Shall never tremble: . . . Hence, horrible shadow!
Unreal mockery, hence!
           Macbeth, Act iii, sc. 4, l. 93 [MACBETH]

5880   Come like shadows, so depart.
                                Macbeth, Act iv, sc. 1, l. 111 [WITCHES]
5881   Some there be that shadows kiss;
        Such have but a shadow's bliss.
                        The Merchant of Venice, Act ii, sc. 9, l. 66 [ARAGON]
5882   At his own shadow let the thief run mad,
        Himself himself seek every hour to kill!
                                The Rape of Lucrece, l. 997 [LUCRECE]
5883   RATCLIFF: Nay, good my lord, be not afraid of shadows.
        KING RICHARD: By the apostle Paul, shadows to-night
        Have struck more terror to the soul of Richard
        Than can the substance of ten thousand soldiers
        Armed in proof, and led by shallow Richmond.
                            Richard III, Act v, sc. 3, l. 215 [RATCLIFF]

Shall

5884   Hear you this Triton of the minnows? mark you
        His absolute 'shall'? . . . His peremptory "shall."
                        Coriolanus, Act iii, sc. 1, l. 89 [CORIOLANUS]
5885   'And shall!' what villain was it spake that word?
                        Titus Andronicus, Act i, sc. 1, l. 359 [TITUS]

Shame

5886   Wouldst thou be window'd in great Rome and see
        Thy master thus with pleach'd arms, bending down
        His corrigible neck, his face subdued
        To penetrative shame?
                        Antony and Cleopatra, Act iv, sc. 14, l. 72 [ANTONY]
        ("Pleach'd," folded together.)
5887   Shame hath a bastard fame, well managed.
                        The Comedy of Errors, Act iii, sc. 2, l. 19 [LUCIANA]
5888   O shame! where is thy blush? . . . proclaim no shame
        When the compulsive ardour gives the charge,
        Since frost itself as actively doth burn
        And reason panders will.
                                Hamlet, Act iii, sc. 4, l. 82 [HAMLET]
5889   DAUPHIN: Reproach and everlasting shame
        Sits mocking on our plumes. . . .
        BOURBON: Shame and eternal shame, nothing but shame!
        Let us die in honour. . . . I'll to the throng:
        Let life be short; else shame will be too long.
                                Henry V, Act iv, sc. 5, l. 4 [DAUPHIN]
5890   Bitter shame hath spoil'd the sweet world's taste,
        That it yields nought but shame and bitterness.
                                King John, Act iii, sc. 4, l. 110 [LEWIS]
5891   Let shame come when it will, I do not call it:
        I do not bid the thunder-bearer shoot,
        Nor tell tales of thee to high-judging Jove;
        Mend when thou canst; be better at thy leisure.
                                King Lear, Act ii, sc. 4, l. 229 [LEAR]
5892   KING: In love, I hope: sweet fellowship in shame.
        BIRON: One drunkard loves another of the name.
                        Love's Labour's Lost, Act iv, sc. 3, l. 49 [KING]
5893   Shame folded up in blind concealing night,
        When most unseen, then most doth tyrannize.
                                The Rape of Lucrece, l. 675

5894   Live in thy shame, but die not shame with thee!
        These words hereafter my tormentors be!
        Convey me to my bed, then to my grave:
        Love they to live that love and honour have.
                                Richard II, Act ii, sc. 1, l. 135 [GAUNT]

5895   He was not born to shame:
        Upon his brow shame is ashamed to sit;
        For 'tis a throne where honour may be crown'd
        Sole monarch of the universal earth.
                                Romeo and Juliet, Act iii, sc. 2, l. 91 [JULIET]

5896   Hence, broker-lackey! ignomy and shame
        Pursue thy life, and live aye with thy name!
                                Troilus and Cressida, Act v, sc. 10, l. 33 [TROILUS]
        (Referring to Pandarus.)

Shepherd

5897   I am shepherd to another man
        And do not shear the fleeces that I graze:
        My master is of churlish disposition
        And little recks to find the way to heaven
        By doing deeds of hospitality.
                                As You Like It, Act ii, sc. 4, l. 78 [CORIN]

5898   You foolish shepherd, wherefore do you follow her,
        Like foggy south puffing with wind and rain?
        You are a thousand times a properer man
        Than she a woman: 'tis such fools as you
        That makes the world full of ill-favour'd children:
        'Tis not her glass, but you, that flatters her.
                                As You Like It, Act iii, sc. 5, l. 49 [ROSALIND]

5899   The shepherd's homely curds,
        His cold thin drink out of his leather bottle,
        His wonted sleep under a fresh tree's shade,
        All which secure and sweetly he enjoys,
        Is far beyond a prince's delicates,
        His viands sparkling in a golden cup,
        His body couched in a curious bed,
        When care, mistrust, and treason waits on him.
                                III Henry VI, Act ii, sc. 5, l. 47 [KING]

5900   Sleepest or wakest thou, jolly shepherd?
            Thy sheep be in the corn;
        And for one blast of thy minikin mouth,
            Thy sheep shall take no harm.
                                King Lear, Act iii, sc. 6, l. 43 [EDGAR]

5901   PROTEUS: Indeed, a sheep doth very often stray,
        An if the shepherd be a while away. . . .
        SPEED: The shepherd seeks the sheep, and not the sheep the
        shepherd.
                                The Two Gentlemen of Verona, Act i, sc. 1, l. 74 [PROTEUS]

Ship

5902   O noble emperor, do not fight by sea;
        Trust not to rotten planks.
                                Antony and Cleopatra, Act iii, sc. 7, l. 62 [SOLDIER]

5903   These our ships, you happily may think
        Are like the Trojan horse was stuff'd within
        With bloody veins, expecting overthrow,
        Are stored with corn to make your needy bread.
                                Pericles, Act i, sc. 4, l. 92 [PERICLES]

Shirt

5904   The shirt of Nessus is upon me.
                    Antony and Cleopatra, Act iv, sc. 12, l. 43 [ANTONY]
          ("Shirt of Nessus," a poisoned shirt, a source of misfortune
          from which there is no escape; a fatal present.)

5905   Sir, I would advise you to shift a shirt: the violence of action
          hath made you reek as a sacrifice.
                    Cymbeline, Act i, sc. 2, l. 1 [LORD]

5906   HOSTESS: You owe me money, Sir John; and now you pick a
          quarrel to beguile me of it: I bought you a dozen shirts to your
          back.
          FALSTAFF: Dowlas, filthy dowlas: I have given them away to
          bakers' wives, and they have made bolters of them.
          HOSTESS: Now, as I am a true woman, holland of eight shillings
          an ell.
                    I Henry IV, Act iii, sc. 3, l. 76 [HOSTESS]
          ("Dowlas," a coarse kind of linen.)

5907   There's but a shirt and a half in all my company. . . . But that's
          all one; they'll find linen enough on every hedge.
                    I Henry IV, Act iv, sc. 2, l. 46 [FALSTAFF]

5908   The inventory of thy shirts, as, one for superfluity, and another
          for use!
                    II Henry IV, Act ii, sc. 2, l. 21 [PRINCE]

Shoe

5909   The whoreson smooth-pates do now wear nothing but high shoes,
          and bunches of keys at their girdles.
                    II Henry IV, Act i, sc. 2, l. 44 [FALSTAFF]

5910   I kiss his dirty shoe.
                    Henry V, Act iv, sc. 1, l. 47 [PISTOL]
          How does thy honour? Let me lick thy shoe.
                    The Tempest, Act iii, sc. 2, l. 26 [CALIBAN]

5911   Spare none but such as go in clouted shoon;
          For they are thrifty honest men.
                    II Henry VI, Act iv, sc. 2, l. 195 [CADE]
          ("Clouted," patched.)

5912   MARULLUS: What trade are you? . . .
          COMMONER: I am but, as you would say, a cobbler. . . . A mender
          of bad soles. . . . A surgeon to old shoes.
                    Julius Cæsar, Act i, sc. 1, l. 9 [MARULLUS]

5913   It is written, that the shoemaker should meddle with his yard, the
          tailor with his last, the fisher with his pencil, and the painter with
          his nets.
                    Romeo and Juliet, Act i, sc. 2, l. 39 [SERVANT]
          (A reference to the proverb, "Shoemaker, stick to your last.")

Short and Long

5914   'Tis very strange, that is the brief and the tedious of it.
                    All's Well that Ends Well, Act ii, sc. 3, l. 33 [PAROLLES]

5915   The short and the long is, I serve the Jew.
                    The Merchant of Venice, Act ii, sc. 2, l. 135 [LAUNCELOT]

5916   He loves your wife; that's the short and the long.
                    The Merry Wives of Windsor, Act ii, sc. 1, l. 136 [NYM]

5917   This is the short and the long of it.
                    The Merry Wives of Windsor, Act ii, sc. 2, l. 60 [MISTRESS QUICKLY]

5918   The short and the long is, our play is preferred.
                    A Midsummer Night's Dream, Act iv, sc. 2, l. 37 [BOTTOM]

Shower

5919 Throw up thine eye! see, see what showers arise,
Blown with the windy tempest of my heart.
III Henry VI, Act ii, sc. 5, l. 85 [FATHER]

5920 Small showers last long, but sudden storms are short.
Richard II, Act ii, sc. 1, l. 35 [GAUNT]

Sicklemen

5921 You sunburnt sicklemen, of August weary,
Come hither from the furrow and be merry;
Make holiday, your rye-straw hats put on
And these fresh nymphs encounter every one
In country footing.
The Tempest, Act iv, sc. 1, l. 134 [IRIS]

Sickness

5922 [He] is troubled with the green sickness.
Antony and Cleopatra, Act iii, sc. 2, l. 5 [ENOBARBUS]

5923 The more one sickens the worse at ease he is.
As You Like It, Act iii, sc. 2, l. 24 [CORIN]

5924 I am not very sick, Since I can reason of it.
Cymbeline, Act iv, sc. 2, l. 13 [IMOGEN]

5925 MESSENGER: He is grievous sick.
HOTSPUR: 'Zounds! how has he the leisure to be sick
In such a justling time? . . .
Sick now! droop now! this sickness doth infect
The very life-blood of our enterprise. . . .
WORCESTER: Your father's sickness is a maim to us.
HOTSPUR: A perilous gash, a very limb lopp'd off.
I Henry IV, Act iv, sc. 1, l. 16 [MESSENGER]

5926 Is Brutus sick? and is it physical
To walk unbraced and suck up the humours
Of the dank morning? What, is Brutus sick,
And will he steal out of his wholesome bed,
To dare the vile contagion of the night
And tempt the rheumy and unpurged air
To add unto his sickness?
Julius Cæsar, Act ii, sc. 1, l. 261 [PORTIA]

5927 Sickness is catching: O were favour so.
A Midsummer Night's Dream, Act i, sc. 1, l. 186 [HELENA]

5928 Many do keep their chambers are not sick.
Timon of Athens, Act iii, sc. 4, l. 75 [SERVILIUS]

5929 ULYSSES: He is not sick.
AJAX: Yes, lion-sick, sick of proud heart: you may call it melancholy, if you will favour the man; but, by my head, 'tis pride.
Troilus and Cressida, Act ii, sc. 3, l. 92 [ULYSSES]
(Referring to Achilles.)

Sigh

5930 He raised a sigh so piteous and profound
As it did seem to shatter all his bulk.
Hamlet, Act ii, sc. 1, l. 94 [OPHELIA]

5931 A plague of sighing and grief! it blows a man up like a bladder.
I Henry IV, Act ii, sc. 4, l. 365 [FALSTAFF]

5932 If the wind were down, I could drive the boat with my sighs.
The Two Gentlemen of Verona, Act ii, sc. 3, l. 60 [LAUNCE]

Sight

5933   GENTLEMAN: You saw the ceremony? . . . How was it?
        GENTLEMAN: Well worth seeing.
                            Henry VIII, Act iv, sc. 1, l. 59 [GENTLEMAN]
5934   MACBETH: This is a sorry sight.
        LADY MACBETH: A foolish thought, to say a sorry sight.
                            Macbeth, Act ii, sc. 2, l. 21 [MACBETH]
5935   You make me strange . . .
        When now I think you can behold such sights,
        And keep the natural ruby of your cheeks,
        When mine is blanch'd with fear.
                            Macbeth, Act iii, sc. 4, l. 112 [MACBETH]
5936   I can see yet without spectacles and I see no such matter.
                            Much Ado about Nothing, Act i, sc. 1, l. 191 [BENEDICK]
5937   If you dare not trust that you see, confess not that you know.
                            Much Ado about Nothing, Act iii, sc. 2, l. 122 [DON JOHN]
5938   To see sad sights moves more than hear them told,
        For then the eye interprets to the ear.
                            The Rape of Lucrece, l. 1324
5939   He that is strucken blind cannot forget
        The precious treasure of his eyesight lost.
                            Romeo and Juliet, Act i, sc. 1, l. 238 [ROMEO]

Sign

5940   ARMADO: Boy, what sign is it when a man of great spirit grows
        melancholy?
        MOTH: A great sign, sir, that he will look sad.
                            Love's Labour's Lost, Act i, sc. 2, l. 1 [ARMADO]
5941   The bay-trees in our country are all wither'd
        And meteors fright the fixed stars of heaven;
        The pale-faced moon looks bloody on the earth
        And lean-look'd prophets whisper fearful change; . . .
        These signs forerun the death or fall of kings.
                            Richard II, Act ii, sc. 4, l. 8 [CAPTAIN]

Silence

5942   Be check'd for silence, But never tax'd for speech.
                            All's Well that Ends Well, Act i, sc. 1, l. 76 [COUNTESS]
5943   I pray you all,
        If you have hitherto conceal'd this sight,
        Let it be tenable to your silence still;
        And what soever else shall hap to-night,
        Give it an understanding, but no tongue.
                            Hamlet, Act i, sc. 2, l. 246 [HAMLET]
5944   The rest is silence.
                            Hamlet, Act v, sc. 2, l. 369 [HAMLET]
5945   Silence is only commendable
        In a neat's tongue dried and a maid not vendible.
                            The Merchant of Venice, Act i, sc. 1, l. 111 [GRATIANO]
5946   Silence is the perfectest herald of joy: I were but little happy, if
        I could say how much.
                            Much Ado about Nothing, Act ii, sc. 1, l. 316 [CLAUDIO]
5947   With certain half-caps and cold-moving nods
        They froze me into silence.
                            Timon of Athens, Act ii, sc. 2, l. 221 [FLAVIUS]
5948   I may command where I adore:
        But silence, like a Lucrece knife,

With bloodless stroke my heart doth gore:
M.O.A.I. doth sway my life.
Twelfth Night, Act ii, sc. 5, l. 115 [MALVOLIO, *reading*]

5949　The silence often of pure innocence
Persuades when speaking fails.
The Winter's Tale, Act ii, sc. 2, l. 41 [PAULINA]

Silver

5950　Thou pale and common drudge 'Tween man and man.
The Merchant of Venice, Act iii, sc. 2, l. 103 [BASSANIO]
(Referring to silver.)

5951　FIRST MUSICIAN : Silver hath a sweet sound. . . .
SECOND MUSICIAN : I say 'silver sound,' because musicians sound
for silver.
Romeo and Juliet, Act iv, sc. 5, l. 133 [FIRST MUSICIAN]

Silvia

5952　What light is light, if Silvia be not seen?
What joy is joy if Silvia be not by? . . .
Except I be by Silvia in the night,
There is no music in the nightingale;
Unless I look on Silvia in the day,
There is no day for me to look upon.
The Two Gentlemen of Verona, Act iii, sc. 1, l. 174 [VALENTINE]

5953　Who is Silvia? what is she
That all our swains commend her?
Holy, fair and wise is she;
The heaven such grace doth lend her,
That she might admired be.

Is she kind as she is fair?
For beauty lives with kindness.
Love doth to her eyes repair,
To help him of his blindness,
And, being help'd, inhabits there.
The Two Gentlemen of Verona, Act iv, sc. 2, l. 39 [SONG]

Simplicity

5954　Twice-sod simplicity, bis coctus!
Love's Labour's Lost, Act iv, sc. 2, l. 22 [HOLOFERNES]
("Twice-sod," twice-boiled.)

5955　Never anything can be amiss,
When simpleness and duty tender it. . . .
Where I have come, great clerks have purposed
To greet me with premeditated welcomes;
Where I have seen them shiver and look pale,
Make periods in the midst of sentences,
Throttle their practised accent in their fears
And in conclusion dumbly have broke off,
Not paying me a welcome. Trust me, sweet,
Out of this silence yet I pick'd a welcome;
And in the modesty of fearful duty
I read as much as from the rattling tongue
Of saucy and audacious eloquence.
Love, therefore, and tongue-tied simplicity
In least speak most, to my capacity.
A Midsummer Night's Dream, Act v, sc. 1, l. 82 [THESEUS]

Sin

5956   I think 't no sin
To cozen him that would unjustly win.
                    All's Well that Ends Well, Act iv, sc. 2, l. 75 [DIANA]

5957   Most mischievous foul sin, in chiding sin:
For thou thyself hast been a libertine,
As sensual as the brutish sting itself.
                              As You Like It, Act ii, sc. 7, l. 64 [DUKE]

5958   That is another simple sin in you, to bring the ewes and rams
together and to offer to get your living by the copulation of cattle.
                    As You Like It, Act iii, sc. 2, l. 83 [TOUCHSTONE]

5959   Have you a ruffian that will swear, drink, dance,
Revel the night, rob, murder, and commit
The oldest sins the newest kind of ways?
                         II Henry IV, Act iv, sc. 5, l. 125 [KING]

5960   Then is sin struck down like an ox, and iniquity's throat cut like
a calf.
                         II Henry VI, Act iv, sc. 2, l. 28 [BEVIS]

5961   God forgive the sin of all those souls
That to their everlasting residence,
Before the dew of evening fall, shall fleet,
In dreadful trial of our kingdom's king!
                    King John, Act ii, sc. 1, l. 283 [KING JOHN]

5962   I am a man
More sinn'd against than sinning.
                         King Lear, Act iii, sc. 2, l. 59 [LEAR]

5963   Plate sin with gold,
And the strong lance of justice hurtless breaks;
Arm it in rags, a pigmy's straw doth pierce it.
                         King Lear, Act iv, sc. 6, l. 169 [LEAR]

5964   Do not call it sin in me,
That I am forsworn for thee;
Thou whom for Jove would swear
Juno but an Ethiope were;
And deny himself for Jove,
Turning mortal for thy love.
                    Love's Labour's Lost, Act iv, sc. 3, l. 115 [DUMAIN]

5965   Some rise by sin, and some by virtue fall:
Some run from brakes of vice, and answer none:
And some condemned for a fault alone.
                    Measure for Measure, Act ii, sc. 1, l. 38 [ESCALUS]

5966   Our compell'd sins
Stand more for number than accompt.
                    Measure for Measure, Act ii, sc. 4, l. 57 [ANGELO]

5967   Thy sin's not accidental, but a trade.
                    Measure for Measure, Act iii, sc. 1, l. 149 [ISABELLA]

5968   LAUNCELOT: The sins of the father are to be laid upon the chil-
dren. . . .
JESSICA: So the sins of my mother should be visited upon me. . . .
LAUNCELOT: When I shun Scylla, your father, I fall in Charybdis,
your mother: well, you are gone both ways.
JESSICA: I shall be saved by my husband: he hath made me a
Christian.
                    The Merchant of Venice, Act iii, sc. 5, l. 1 [LAUNCELOT]

5969   O, what authority and show of truth
Can cunning sin cover itself withal!
                    Much Ado about Nothing, Act iv, sc. 1, l. 37 [CLAUDIO]

5970 Few love to hear the sins they love to act.
Pericles, Act i, sc. 1, l. 92 [PERICLES]

5971 One sin, I know, another doth provoke:
Murder's as near to lust as flame to smoke:
Poison and treason are the hands of sin,
Ay, and the targets to put off the shame.
Pericles, Act i, sc. 1, l. 137 [PERICLES]

5972 The blackest sin is clear'd with absolution.
The Rape of Lucrece, l. 354 [TARQUIN]

5973 Thy princely office how canst thou fulfill,
When, pattern'd by thy fault, foul sin may say,
He learn'd to sin, and thou didst teach the way?
The Rape of Lucrece, l. 628 [LUCRECE]

5974 The time shall not be many hours of age
More than it is ere foul sin gathering head
Shall break into corruption.
Richard II, Act v, sc. 1, l. 57 [KING RICHARD]
(Quoted by King Henry in *II Henry IV,* iii, 1, 76.)

5975 Now, by the stock and honour of my kin,
To strike him dead I hold it not a sin.
Romeo and Juliet, Act i, sc. 5, l. 60 [TYBALT]

5976 I beseech thee, youth,
Put not another sin upon my head,
By urging me to fury: O, be gone!
By heaven, I love thee better than myself;
For I come hither arm'd against myself:
Stay not, be gone; live, and hereafter say,
A madman's mercy bade thee run away.
Romeo and Juliet, Act v, sc. 3, l. 61 [ROMEO]

5977 I have done sin;
For which the heavens, taking angry note,
Have left me issueless.
The Winter's Tale, Act v, sc. 1, l. 171 [LEONTES]

Singing

5978 O! she will sing the savageness out of a bear.
Othello, Act iv, sc. 1, l. 199 [OTHELLO]

5979 She sings like one immortal, and she dances
As goddess-like to her admired lays.
Pericles, Act v, Induction, l. 3 [GOWER]

5980 I cannot sing,
Nor heel the high lavolt, nor sweeten talk,
Nor play at subtle games; fair virtues all,
To which the Grecians are most prompt and pregnant.
Troilus and Cressida, Act iv, sc. 4, l. 87 [TROILUS]

5981 When you sing
I 'ld have you buy and sell so, so give alms,
Pray so; and for the ordering of your affairs,
To sing them too.
The Winter's Tale, Act iv, sc. 4, l. 137 [FLORIZEL]

Singularity

5982 Let's hear . . . in what fashion,
More than his singularity, he goes
Upon this present action.
Coriolanus Act i, sc. 1, l. 280 [SICINIUS]

5983   Put thyself into the trick of singularity: . . . a sad face, a reverend
       carriage, a slow tongue.
                                 Twelfth Night, Act iii, sc. 4, l. 79 [MALVOLIO]

Sister

5984   A sister I bequeath you, whom no brother
       Did ever love so dearly: let her live
       To join our kingdoms and our hearts.
                          Antony and Cleopatra, Act ii, sc. 2, l. 152 [CÆSAR]

5985   If you did wed my sister for her wealth,
           Then for her wealth's sake, use her with more kindness:
       Or if you like elsewhere, do it by stealth,
           Muffle your false love with some show of blindness.
       Let not my sister read it in your eye. . . .
       'Tis double wrong, to truant with your bed
           And let her read it in thy looks at board.
                        The Comedy of Errors, Act iii, sc. 2, l. 5 [LUCIANA]

5986   [I have lost]
       A sister driven into desperate terms,
       Whose worth, if praises may go back again,
       Stood challenger on mount of all the age
       For her perfections.
                                  Hamlet, Act iv, sc. 7, l. 26 [LAERTES]

5987   The weird sisters, hand in hand,
       Posters of the sea and land,
       Thus do go about, about.
                                 Macbeth, Act i, sc. 3, l. 32 [WITCHES]

5988   Betimes I will to the weird sisters:
       More shall they speak; for now I am bent to know,
       By the worst means, the worst.
                             Macbeth, Act iii, sc. 4, l. 133 [MACBETH]

5989   The Sisters Three.
                   The Merchant of Venice, Act ii, sc. 2, l. 66 [LAUNCELOT]

Six and Seven

5990   All is uneven,
       And every thing is left at six and seven.
                              Richard II, Act ii, sc. 2, l. 121 [YORK]

Skin

5991   My skin hangs about me like an old lady's loose gown; I am with-
       ered like an old apple-john.
                            I Henry IV, Act iii, sc. 3, l. 3 [FALSTAFF]

5992   He shall have the skins of our enemies, to make dog's-leather of.
                             II Henry VI, Act iv, sc. 2, l. 25 [BEVIS]

5993   Yet I'll not shed her blood,
       Nor scar that whiter skin of her than snow,
       And smooth as monumental alabaster.
                                Othello, Act v, sc. 2, l. 3 [OTHELLO]

Sky

5994   So foul a sky clears not without a storm.
                            King John, Act iv, sc. 2, l. 108 [KING JOHN]

5995   Men judge by the complexion of the sky
           The state and inclination of the day:
       So may you by my dull and heavy eye,
           My tongue hath but a heavier tale to say.
                           Richard II, Act iii, sc. 2, l. 194 [SCROOP]

5996   The skies look grimly
And threaten present blusters. In my conscience,
The heavens with that we have in hand are angry
And frown upon's.
The Winter's Tale, Act iii, sc. 3, l. 3 [MARINER]

Slander

5997   Slander lives upon succession,
For ever housed where it gets possession.
The Comedy of Errors, Act iii, sc. 1, l. 105 [BALTHAZAR]

5998   No, be assured, you shall not find me, daughter,
After the slander of most stepmothers,
Evil-eyed unto you.
Cymbeline, Act i, sc. 1, l. 70 [QUEEN]

5999   'Tis slander,
Whose edge is sharper than the sword, whose tongue
Outvenoms all the worms of Nile.
Cymbeline, Act iii, sc. 4, l. 35 [PISANIO]
          Slander,
Whose sting is sharper than the sword's.
The Winter's Tale, Act ii, sc. 3, l. 86 [PAULINA]

6000   Done to death by slanderous tongues
               Was the Hero that here lies:
          Death, in guerdon of her wrongs,
               Gives her fame which never dies.
          So the life that died with shame
          Lives in death with glorious fame.
Much Ado about Nothing, Act v, sc. 3, l. 3 [CLAUDIO]

6001   If thou dost slander her and torture me,
Never pray more; abandon all remorse.
Othello, Act iii, sc. 3, l. 368 [OTHELLO]

6002   I will be hang'd if some eternal villain,
Some busy and insinuating rogue, . . .
Have not devised this slander; I'll be hang'd else. . . .
O heaven, . . . put in every honest hand a whip
To lash the rascals naked through the world
Even from the east to the west!
Othello, Act iv, sc. 2, l. 130 [EMILIA]

6003   I am disgraced, impeach'd and baffled here,
Pierced to the soul with slander's venomed spear,
The which no balm can cure but his heart-blood
Which breathed this poison.
Richard II, Act i, sc. 1, l. 170 [MOWBRAY]

6004   That is no slander, sir, which is a truth.
Romeo and Juliet, Act iv, sc. 1, l. 33 [JULIET]

6005   Slander's mark was ever yet the fair.
Sonnet lxx, l. 2

Slave

6006   A most perfidious slave,
With all the spots o' the world tax'd and debosh'd;
Whose nature sickens but to speak a truth.
All's Well that Ends Well, Act v, sc. 3, l. 206 [BERTRAM]

6007   Thou, an Egyptian puppet, shalt be shown
In Rome, as well as I: mechanic slaves
With greasy aprons, rules, and hammers, shall

Uplift us to the view; in their thick breaths,
Rank of gross diet, shall we be enclouded.
Antony and Cleopatra, Act v, sc. 2, l. 209 [CLEOPATRA]

6008   A base slave,
A hilding for a livery, a squire's cloth,
A pantler, not so eminent.
Cymbeline, Act ii, sc. 3, l. 127 [CLOTEN]

6009   One-trunk-inheriting slave.
King Lear, Act ii, sc. 2, l. 20 [KENT]

6010   You have among you many a purchased slave,
Which, like your asses and your dogs and mules,
You use in abject and in slavish parts,
Because you bought them: shall I say to you,
Let them be free, marry them to your heirs?
Why sweat they under burthens? let their beds
Be made as soft as yours and let their palates
Be season'd with such viands? You will answer
'The slaves are ours.'
The Merchant of Venice, Act iv, sc. 1, l. 90 [SHYLOCK]

6011   Being your slave, what should I do but tend
Upon the hours and times of your desire?
I have no precious time at all to spend,
Nor services to do, till you require.
Sonnet lvii, l. 1

6012   Thou poisonous slave, got by the devil himself
Upon thy wicked dam, come forth!
The Tempest, Act i, sc. 2, l. 319 [PROSPERO]

6013   Say, wall-eyed slave, whither wouldst thou convey
This growing image of thy fiend-like face?
Titus Andronicus, Act v, sc. 1, l. 44 [LUCIUS]

6014   A slave whose gall coins slanders like a mint.
Troilus and Cressida, Act i, sc. 3, l. 193 [NESTOR]

Sleep

6015   Give me to drink mandragora. . . .
That I might sleep out this great gap of time
My Antony is away.
Antony and Cleopatra, Act i, sc. 5, l. 4 [CLEOPATRA]

6016   I'll go sleep, if I can; if I cannot, I'll rail against all the first-
born of Egypt.
As You Like It, Act ii, sc. 5, l. 62 [JAQUES]

6017   Sleep rock thy brain;
And never come mischance between us twain!
Hamlet, Act iii, sc. 2, l. 237 [PLAYER QUEEN]

6018   Fast asleep behind the arras, and snorting like a horse.
I Henry IV, Act ii, sc. 4, l. 577 [PETO]

6019   How many thousand of my poorest subjects
Are at this hour asleep! O sleep, O gentle sleep,
Nature's soft nurse, how have I frighted thee,
That thou no more wilt weigh my eyelids down
And steep my senses in forgetfulness? . . .
O thou dull god, why liest thou with the vile
In loathsome beds, and leavest the kingly couch
A watch-case or a common 'larum bell?
Wilt thou upon the high and giddy mast
Seal up the ship-boy's eyes, and rock his brains
In cradle of the rude imperious surge? . . .

Canst thou, O partial sleep, give thy repose
To the wet sea-boy in an hour so rude
And in the calmest and most stillest night,
With all appliances and means to boot,
Deny it to a king? Then happy low, lie down!
Uneasy lies the head that wears a crown.

II Henry IV, Act iii, sc. 1, l. 4 [KING HENRY]

6020 This sleep is sound indeed; this is a sleep
That from this golden rigol hath divorced
So many English kings.

II Henry IV, Act iv, sc. 5, l. 35 [PRINCE]

6021 'Tis not the balm, the sceptre and the ball,
The sword, the mace, the crown imperial,
The intertissued robe of gold and pearl,
The farced title running 'fore the king,
The throne he sits on, nor the tide of pomp
The beats upon the high shore of the world, . . .
Not all these, laid in bed majestical,
Can sleep so soundly as the wretched slave,
Who with a body fill'd and vacant mind
Gets him to rest, cramm'd with distressful bread; . . .
Winding up days with toil and nights with sleep.

Henry V, Act iv, sc. 1, l. 277 [KING HENRY]

6022 Boy! Lucius! Fast asleep? It is no matter;
Enjoy the honey-heavy dew of slumber:
Thou hast no figures nor no fantasies,
Which busy care draws in the brains of men;
Therefore thou sleep'st so sound.

Julius Cæsar, Act ii, sc. 1, l. 229 [BRUTUS]

6023 Sleep shall neither night nor day
Hang upon his pent-house lid;
He shall live a man forbid:
Weary se'nnights nine times nine
Shall he dwindle, peak and pine.

Macbeth, Act i, sc. 3, l. 19 [WITCH]

6024 Methought I heard a voice cry 'Sleep no more!
Macbeth does murder sleep,' the innocent sleep,
Sleep that knits up the ravell'd sleave of care,
The death of each day's life, sore labour's bath,
Balm of hurt minds, great nature's second course,
Chief nourisher in life's feast. . . .
'Glamis hath murder'd sleep, and therefore Cawdor
Shall sleep no more; Macbeth shall sleep no more.'

Macbeth, Act ii, sc. 2, l. 35 [MACBETH]

6025   The sleeping and the dead
Are but as pictures.

Macbeth, Act ii, sc. 2, l. 53 [LADY MACBETH]

6026 Shake off this downy sleep, death's counterfeit,
And look on death itself!

Macbeth, Act ii, sc. 3, l. 81 [MACDUFF]

6027 You lack the season of all natures, sleep.

Macbeth, Act iii, sc. 4, l. 141 [LADY MACBETH]

6028   Thy best of rest is sleep,
And that thou oft provokest; yet grossly fear'st
Thy death, which is no more.

Measure for Measure, Act iii, sc. 1, l. 17 [DUKE]

6029   O'er their brows death-counterfeiting sleep
       With leaden legs and batty wings doth creep.
                 A Midsummer Night's Dream, Act iii, sc. **2**, l. 364 [OBERON]
6030   Sleep, that sometimes shuts up sorrow's eye,
       Steal me awhile from mine own company.
                 A Midsummer Night's Dream, Act iii, sc. **2**, l. 435 [HELENA]
6031   I have an exposition of sleep come upon me.
                 A Midsummer Night's Dream, Act iv, sc. **1**, l. 41 [BOTTOM]
6032   Not poppy, nor mandragora,
       Nor all the drowsy syrups of the world,
       Shall ever medicine thee to that sweet sleep
       Which thou owedst yesterday.
                 Othello, Act iii, sc. **3**, l. 330 [IAGO]
6033   Sleep dwell upon thine eyes, peace in thy breast!
       Would I were sleep and peace, so sweet to rest!
                 Romeo and Juliet, Act ii, sc. **2**, l. 187 [ROMEO]
6034   Grim death, how foul and loathsome is thine image!
                 The Taming of the Shrew, Induction, sc. **1**, l. 35 [LORD]
6035   Sleep . . . seldom visits sorrow; when it 'doth,
       It is a comforter.
                 The Tempest, Act ii, sc. **1**, l. 195 [SEBASTIAN]
6036   Endeavour thyself to sleep, and leave thy vain bibble babble.
                 Twelfth Night, Act iv, sc. **2**, l. 104 [CLOWN]

Slippery

6037   He that stands upon a slippery place
       Makes nice of no vile hold to stay him up.
                 King John, Act iii, sc. **4**, l. 137 [PANDULPH]
6038   Slippery standers,
       To love that lean'd on them as slippery too,
       Do one pluck down another and together
       Die in the fall.
                 Troilus and Cressida, Act iii, sc. **3**, l. 84 [ACHILLES]

Smell

6039   What say you to young master Fenton? he capers, he dances, he
       has eyes of youth, he writes verses, he speaks holiday, he smells
       April and May.
                 The Merry Wives of Windsor, Act iii, sc. **2**, l. 66 [HOST]
6040   [They] smell like Bucklersbury in simple time.
                 The Merry Wives of Windsor, Act iii, sc. **3**, l. 79 [FALSTAFF]
6041   There was the rankest compound of villanous smell that ever
       offended nostril.
                 The Merry Wives of Windsor, Act iii, sc. **5**, l. 85 [FALSTAFF]
6042   What have we here? a man or a fish? dead or alive? A fish: he
       smells like a fish; a very ancient and fish-like smell.
                 The Tempest, Act ii, sc. **2**, l. 26 [TRINCULO]
6043   You smell this business with a sense as cold
       As is a dead man's nose.
                 The Winter's Tale, Act ii, sc. **1**, l. 151 [LEONTES]

Smile

6044   O villain, villain, smiling, damned villain!
       My tables,—meet it is I set it down,
       That one may smile, and smile, and be a villain;
       At least I'm sure it may be so in Denmark.
                 Hamlet, Act i, sc. **5**, l. 106 [HAMLET]

6045 Why, I can smile, and murder whiles I smile,
And cry 'Content' to that which grieves my heart,
And wet my cheeks with artificial tears,
And frame my face to all occasions.
III Henry VI, Act iii, sc. 2, l. 182 [RICHARD]

6046 Seldom he smiles, and smiles in such a sort
As if he mock'd himself and scorn'd his spirit
That could be moved to smile at anything.
Julius Cæsar, Act i, sc. 2, l. 205 [CÆSAR]

6047 He does smile his face into more lines than is in the new map
with the augmentation of the Indies.
Twelfth Night, Act iii, sc. 2, l. 84 [MARIA]

6048 A smile recures the wounding of a frown.
Venus and Adonis, l. 465

Smoke

6049 Thus must I from the smoke into the smother;
From tyrant duke unto a tyrant brother.
As You Like It, Act i, sc. 2, l. 299 [ORLANDO]

6050 The helpless smoke of words doth me no right.
The remedy indeed to do me good
Is to let forth my foul-defiled blood.
The Rape of Lucrece, l. 1027 [LUCRECE]

Snail

6051 ROSALIND: Nay, an you be so tardy, come no more in my sight: I
had as lief be wooed of a snail. . . . For though he comes slowly,
he carries his house on his head; a better jointure, I think, than
you make a woman: besides, he brings his destiny with him.
ORLANDO: What's that?
ROSALIND: Why, horns, which such as you are fain to be beholding to your wives for.
As You Like It, Act iv, sc. 1, l. 51 [ROSALIND]

6052 I can tell why a snail has a house. . . . To put his head in; not
to give it away to his daughters, and leave his horns without
a case.
King Lear, Act i, sc. 5, l. 29 [FOOL]

Snake

6053 I fear me you but warm the starved snake,
Who, cherish'd in your breasts, will sting your hearts.
II Henry VI, Act iii, sc. 1, l. 343 [YORK]
(A reference to the fable of Æsop, of the peasant who warmed
a snake in his bosom.)

6054 We have scotch'd the snake, not kill'd it:
She'll close and be herself, whilst our poor malice
Remains in danger of her former tooth.
Macbeth, Act iii, sc. 2, l. 13 [MACBETH]

Snow

6055 Cold snow melts with the sun's hot beams.
II Henry VI, Act iii, sc. 1, l. 223 [QUEEN]

6056 A little snow, tumbled about,
Anon becomes a mountain.
King John, Act iii, sc. 4, l. 176 [PANDULPH]

6057 Right, as snow in harvest.
Richard III, Act i, sc. 4, l. 248 [MURDERER]

Society

6058 Society is no comfort to one not sociable.
                          Cymbeline, Act iv, sc. 2, l. 12 [IMOGEN]

6059 This is worshipful society
      And fits the mounting spirit like myself.
                          King John, Act i, sc. 1, l. 205 [BASTARD]

6060 Society, saith the text, is the happiness of life.
                          Love's Labour's Lost, Act iv, sc. 2, l. 168 [NATHANIEL]

Soldier

6061 O, wither'd is the garland of the war,
      The soldier's pole is fall'n : . . . the odds is gone,
      And there is nothing left remarkable
      Beneath the visiting moon.
                          Antony and Cleopatra, Act iv, sc. 15, l. 63 [CLEOPATRA]

6062   Thou wast a soldier
      Even to Cato's wish, not fierce and terrible
      Only in strokes ; but with thy grim looks . . .
      Thou madest thine enemies shake, as if the world
      Were feverous and did tremble.
                          Coriolanus, Act i, sc. 4, l. 55 [LARTIUS]

6063 O, farewell, honest soldier.
                          Hamlet, Act i, sc. 1, l. 16 [MARCELLUS]

6064 If I be not ashamed of my soldiers, I am a soused gurnet. . . .
      My whole charge consists of ancients, corporals, lieutenants, gentle-
      men of companies, slaves as ragged as Lazarus in the painted cloth,
      where the glutton's dogs licked his sores ; and such as indeed were
      never soldiers, . . . the cankers of a calm world and a long
      peace ; . . . you would think that I had a hundred and fifty tattered
      prodigals, lately come from swine-keeping, from eating draff and
      husks. . . . No eye hath seen such scarecrows. I'll not march
      through Coventry with them, that's flat.
                          I Henry IV, Act iv, sc. 2, l. 13 [FALSTAFF]

6065   Fair Katherine, and most fair,
      Will you vouchsafe to teach a soldier terms
      Such as will enter to a lady's ear
      And plead his love-suit to her gentle heart?
                          Henry V, Act v, sc. 2, l. 98 [KING HENRY]

6066 Soldiers' stomachs always serve them well.
                          I Henry VI, Act ii, sc. 3, l. 80 [TALBOT]

6067 A braver soldier never couched lance,
      A gentler heart did never sway in court.
                          I Henry VI, Act iii, sc. 2, l. 134 [TALBOT]

6068 I am a soldier and unapt to weep
      Or to exclaim on fortune's fickleness.
                          I Henry VI, Act v, sc. 3, l. 133 [REIGNIER]

6069   They are soldiers,
      Witty, courteous, liberal, full of spirit.
                          III Henry VI, Act i, sc. 2, l. 42 [YORK]

6070 CASSIUS :   I am a soldier, I,
      Older in practice, abler than yourself
      To make conditions. . . .
      BRUTUS : You say you are a better soldier :
      Let it appear so ; make your vaunting true,
      And it shall please me well : for mine own part,
      I shall be glad to learn of noble men.

CASSIUS: You wrong me every way; you wrong me, Brutus;
I said an elder soldier, not a better:
Did I say 'better'?
                                    Julius Cæsar, Act iv, sc. 3, l. 30 [CASSIUS]

6071   Fie, my lord, fie! a soldier, and afeard?
                                    Macbeth, Act v, sc. 1, l. 41 [LADY MACBETH]

6072   ROSS: Your son, my lord, has paid a soldier's debt:
He only lived but till he was a man; . . .
But like a man he died. . . .
SIWARD: Had he his hurts before?
ROSS: Ay, on the front.
SIWARD: Why, then, God's soldier be he!
Had I as many sons as I have hairs,
I would not wish them to a fairer death:
And so, his knell is knoll'd.
                                    Macbeth, Act v, sc. 8, l. 38 [ROSS]

6073   There's not a soldier of us all, that, in the thanksgiving before
meat, do relish the petition well that prays for peace.
                                    Measure for Measure, Act i, sc. 2, l. 15 [GENTLEMAN]

6074   Some wine, Ho!
And let me the canakin clink, clink;
And let me the canakin clink:
A soldier's but a man;—
A life's but a span;
Why, then, let a soldier drink.
                                    Othello, Act ii, sc. 3, l. 70 [IAGO]

6075   He is a soldier fit to stand by Cæsar.
                                    Othello, Act ii, sc. 3, l. 127 [IAGO]

6076   'Tis the soldier's life
To have their balmy slumbers waked with strife.
                                    Othello, Act ii, sc. 3, l. 257 [OTHELLO]

6077   For one to say a soldier lies, is stabbing.
                                    Othello, Act iii, sc. 4, l. 5 [CLOWN]

6078   Soldiers should brook as little wrongs as gods.
                                    Timon of Athens, Act iii, sc. 5, l. 117 [ALCIBIADES]

6079   We are soldiers;
And may that soldier a mere recreant prove,
That means not, hath not, or is not in love!
                                    Troilus and Cressida, Act i, sc. 3, l. 286 [AGAMEMNON]

Son

6080   O wonderful son, that can so astonish a mother!
                                    Hamlet, Act iii, sc. 2, l. 340 [HAMLET]

6081   Thou makest me sad and makest me sin
In envy that my Lord Northumberland
Should be the father to so blest a son,
A son who is the theme of honour's tongue;
Amongst a grove, the very straightest plant;
Who is sweet Fortune's minion and her pride:
Whilst I, by looking on the praise of him,
See riot and dishonour stain the brow
Of my young Harry. O that it could be proved
That some night-tripping fairy had exchanged
In cradle-clothes our children where they lay,
And call'd mine Percy, his Plantagenet!
Then would I have his Harry, and he mine.
                                    I Henry IV, Act i, sc. 1, l. 78 [KING HENRY]

6082   That thou art my son, I have partly thy mother's word, partly my own opinion, but chiefly a villanous trick of thine eye and a foolish hanging of thy nether lip, that doth warrant me.
I Henry IV, Act ii, sc. 4, 1. 447 [FALSTAFF]

6083   SHALLOW: Shadow, whose son art thou?
SHADOW: My mother's son, sir.
FALSTAFF: Thy mother's son! like enough, and thy father's shadow: so the son of the female is the shadow of the male: it is often so, indeed.
II Henry IV, Act iii, sc. 2, 1. 137 [SHALLOW]

6084   See, sons, what things you are!
How quickly nature falls into revolt
When gold becomes her object!
For this the foolish over-careful fathers
Have broke their sleep with thoughts, their brains with care,
Their bones with industry; . . .
When, like the bee, culling from every flower
The virtuous sweets,
Our thighs pack'd with wax, our mouths with honey,
We bring it to the hive, and, like the bees,
Are murdered for our pains.
II Henry IV, Act iv, sc. 5, 1. 65 [KING HENRY]

6085   Who should succeed the father but the son?
III Henry VI, Act ii, sc. 2, 1. 94 [CLIFFORD]

6086   O Lord! my boy, my Arthur, my fair son!
My life, my joy, my food, my all the world!
My widow-comfort, and my sorrows' cure!
King John, Act iii, sc. 4, 1. 103 [CONSTANCE]

6087   KENT: Is not this your son, my lord?
GLOUCESTER: His breeding, sir, hath been at my charge. . . . This young fellow's mother . . . had a son for her cradle ere she had a husband for her bed. . . . Though this knave came something saucily into the world before he was sent for, yet was his mother fair; there was good sport at his making.
King Lear, Act i, sc. 1, 1. 8 [KENT]

6088   Good wombs have borne bad sons.
The Tempest, Act i, sc. 2, 1. 120 [MIRANDA]

6089   My son i' the ooze is bedded, and
I'll seek him deeper than e'er plummet sounded
And with him there lie mudded.
The Tempest, Act iii, sc. 3, 1. 100 [ALONZO]

Song

6090   Have you no song, forester, for this purpose? . . . Sing it: 'Tis no matter how it be in tune, so it make noise enough.
As You Like It, Act iv, sc. 2, 1. 6 [JAQUES]

6091   TOUCHSTONE: By my troth, well met. Come, sit, sit, and a song.
SECOND PAGE: We are for you: sit i' the middle.
FIRST PAGE: Shall we clap to 't roundly, without hawking or spitting or saying we are hoarse, which are the only prologues to a bad voice?
SECOND PAGE: I' faith, i' faith; and both in a tune, like two gipsies on a horse.
As You Like It, Act v, sc. 3, 1. 8 [TOUCHSTONE]

6092   Come sing me a bawdy song, make me merry.
I Henry IV, Act iii, sc. 3, 1. 15 [FALSTAFF]

6093   The sly whoresons
Have got a speeding trick to lay down ladies;
A French song and a fiddle has no fellow.
                              Henry VIII, Act i, sc. 3, l. 39 [LOVELL]

6094   In what key shall a man take you to go in the song?
                    Much Ado about Nothing, Act i, sc. 1, l. 187 [BENEDICK]

6095   Sing a song that old was sung. . . .
It hath been sung at festivals,
On ember-eves and holy-ales;
And lords and ladies in their lives
Have read it for restoratives:
The purchase is to make men glorious;
Et bonum quo antiquius, eo melius.
                              Pericles, Act i, Prelude, l. 1 [GOWER]

6096   Stretched metre of an antique song.
                                                    Sonnet xvii, l. 12

6097   Give me some music. Now, good morrow, friends.
Now, good Cesario, but that piece of song,
That old and antique song we heard last night:
Methought it did relieve my passion much,
More than light airs and recollected terms
Of these most brisk and giddy-paced times. . . .
Mark it, Cesario, it is old and plain;
The spinsters and the knitters in the sun
And the free maids that weave their thread with bones
Do use to chant it: it is silly sooth,
And dallies with the innocence of love,
Like the old age.
                              Twelfth Night, Act ii, sc. 4, l. 1 [DUKE]

Sore

6098   To strange sores strangely they strain the cure.
                    Much Ado about Nothing, Act iv, sc. 1, l. 254 [FRIAR]

6099   My lord Sebastian,
The truth you speak doth lack some gentleness
And time to speak it in: you rub the sore,
When you should bring the plaster.
                              The Tempest, Act ii, sc. 1, l. 136 [GONZALO]

Sorrow

6100   Notes of sorrow out of tune are worse
Than priests and fanes that lie.
                              Cymbeline, Act iv, sc. 2, l. 241 [GUIDERIUS]

6101   More in sorrow than in anger.
                              Hamlet, Act i, sc. 2, l. 232 [HORATIO]

6102   When sorrows come, they come not single spies,
But in battalions.
                              Hamlet, Act iv, sc. 5, l. 78 [KING]

6103   Sorrow so royally in you appears
That I will deeply put the fashion on
And wear it in my heart.
                              II Henry IV, Act v, sc. 2, l. 51 [HENRY V]

6104   O, how this mother swells up toward my heart!
Hysterica passio, down, thou climbing sorrow,
Thy element's below.
                              King Lear, Act ii, sc. 4, l. 56 [LEAR]

6105 Bad is the trade that must play fool to sorrow,
      Angering itself and others.
                        King Lear, Act iv, sc. 1, l. 40 [EDGAR]

6106 Well, set thee down, sorrow! for so they say the fool said, and
      so say I.
                Love's Labour's Lost, Act iv, sc. 3, l. 4 [BIRON]

6107 To show an unfelt sorrow is an office
      Which the false man does easy.
                        Macbeth, Act ii, sc. 3, l. 142 [MALCOLM]

6108   Each new morn
      New widows howl, new orphans cry, new sorrows
      Strike heaven on the face.
                        Macbeth, Act iv, sc. 3, l. 4 [MACDUFF]

6109 What man! ne'er pull your hat upon your brows;
      Give sorrow words: the grief that does not speak
      Whispers the o'er-fraught heart and bids it break.
                        Macbeth, Act iv, sc. 3, l. 208 [MALCOLM]

6110 Sorrow's heaviness doth heavier grow
      For debt that bankrupt sleep doth sorrow owe.
          A Midsummer Night's Dream, Act iii, sc. 2, l. 84 [DEMETRIUS]

6111 One sorrow never comes but brings an heir,
      That may succeed as his inheritor.
                        Pericles, Act i, sc. 4, l. 63 [CLEON]

6112 Deep sounds make lesser noise than shallow fords,
      And sorrow ebbs, being blown with wind of words.
                        The Rape of Lucrece, l. 1329

6113 Short time seems long in sorrow's sharp sustaining.
                        The Rape of Lucrece, l. 1573

6114 Sorrow ends not when it seemeth done.
                        Richard II, Act i, sc. 2, l. 61 [DUCHESS]

6115 GAUNT: Gnarling sorrow hath less power to bite
      The man that mocks at it and sets it light.
      BOLINGBROKE: O, who can hold a fire in his hand
      By thinking on the frosty Caucasus?
      Or cloy the hungry edge of appetite
      By bare imagination of a feast?
      Or wallow naked in December snow
      By thinking on fantastic summer's heat?
      O, no! the apprehension of the good
      Gives but the greater feeling to the worse:
      Fell sorrow's tooth doth never rankle more
      Than when it bites, but lanceth not the sore.
                        Richard II, Act i, sc. 3, l. 292 [GAUNT]

6116 Sorrow breaks seasons and reposing hours,
      Makes the night morning, and the noontide night.
                        Richard III, Act i, sc. 4, l. 76 [BRAKENBURY]

6117 It were lost sorrow to wail one that's lost.
                        Richard III, Act ii, sc. 2, l. 11 [DUCHESS OF YORK]

6118 Eighty odd years of sorrow have I seen,
      And each hour's joy wreck'd with a week of teen.
                        Richard III, Act iv, sc. 1, l. 96 [DUCHESS OF GLOUCESTER]

6119 Sorrow concealed, like an oven stopp'd,
      Doth burn the heart to cinders where it is.
                        Titus Andronicus, Act ii, sc. 4, l. 36 [MARCUS]

6120 Sorrow flouted at is double death.
                        Titus Andronicus, Act iii, sc. 1, l. 246 [MARCUS]

6121   Sorrow is an enemy,
And would usurp upon my watery eyes,
And make them blind with tributary tears.
> *Titus Andronicus,* Act iii, sc. 1, l. 268 [TITUS]

6122 Sorrow, that is couch'd in seeming gladness,
Is like that mirth fate turns to sudden sadness.
> *Troilus and Cressida,* Act i, sc. 1, l. 39 [TROILUS]

6123 An oven that is stopp'd, or river stay'd,
Burneth more hotly, swelleth with more rage:
So of concealed sorrow may be said.
> *Venus and Adonis,* l. 331

6124 My lord, your sorrow was too sore laid on,
Which sixteen winters cannot blow away,
So many summers dry: scarce any joy
Did ever so long live; no sorrow
But kill'd itself much sooner.
> *The Winter's Tale,* Act v, sc. 3, l. 49 [CAMILLO]

Soul

6125 Believe this of me, there can be no kernel in this light nut; the
soul of this man is his clothes.
> *All's Well that Ends Well,* Act ii, sc. 5, l. 46 [LAFEU]

6126 To darkness fleet souls that fly backwards.
> *Cymbeline,* Act v, sc. 3, l. 25 [POSTHUMUS]

6127 O wretched state! O bosom black as death!
O limed soul, that, struggling to be free,
Art more engaged! Help, angels! Make assay!
> *Hamlet,* Act iii, sc. 3, l. 67 [KING]

6128 But, look, amazement on thy mother sits:
O, step between her and her fighting soul.
> *Hamlet,* Act iii, sc. 4, l. 112 [GHOST]

6129 Open Thy gate of mercy, gracious God!
My soul flies through these wounds to seek out Thee.
> *III Henry VI,* Act i, sc. 4, l. 177 [YORK]

6130 Now my soul's palace is become a prison.
> *III Henry VI,* Act ii, sc. 1, l. 74 [EDWARD]

6131   Within this wall of flesh
There is a soul counts thee her creditor
And with advantage means to pay thy love.
> *King John,* Act iii, sc. 3, l. 19 [KING JOHN]

6132 Ay, marry, now my soul hath elbow-room;
It would not out at windows nor at doors.
> *King John,* Act v, sc. 7, l. 28 [KING JOHN]

6133 I have a kind soul that would give you thanks
And knows not how to do it but with tears.
> *King John,* Act v, sc. 7, l. 108 [PRINCE HENRY]

6134 That unlettered small-knowing soul.
> *Love's Labour's Lost,* Act i, sc. 1, l. 256 [ARMADO]

6135 Why, all the souls that were were forfeit once;
And He that might the vantage best have took
Found out the remedy.
> *Measure for Measure,* Act ii, sc. 2, l. 73 [ISABELLA]

6136 An evil soul producing holy witness
Is like a villain with a smiling cheek,
A goodly apple rotten at the heart.
> *The Merchant of Venice,* Act i, sc. 3, l. 100 [ANTONIO]

6137 Not on thy sole, but on thy soul, harsh Jew,
Thou makest thy knife keen; but no metal can,
No, not the hangman's axe, bear half the keenness
Of thy sharp envy.
The Merchant of Venice, Act iv, sc. 1, l. 123 [GRATIANO]

6138 Thinkest thou I'll endanger my soul gratis?
The Merry Wives of Windsor, Act ii, sc. 2, l. 17 [FALSTAFF]

6139 My parts, my title and my perfect soul
Shall manifest me rightly.
Othello, Act i, sc. 2, l. 31 [OTHELLO]

6140   O ill-starr'd wench,
Pale as thy smock! When we shall meet at compt,
This look of thine will hurl my soul from heaven,
And fiends will snatch at it. . . . Whip me, ye devils! . . .
Blow me about in winds! roast me in sulphur!
Wash me in steepdown gulfs of liquid fire!
O Desdemona! Desdemona! dead!
Othello, Act v, sc. 2, l. 272 [OTHELLO]

6141   I will not vex your souls—
Since presently your souls must part your bodies.
Richard II, Act iii, sc. 1, l. 2 [BOLINGBROKE]

6142 Mount, mount, my soul! thy seat is up on high;
Whilst my gross flesh sinks downward, here to die.
Richard II, Act v, sc. 5, l. 112 [KING RICHARD]

6143 Truly, the souls of men are full of dread.
Richard III, Act ii, sc. 3, l. 38 [CITIZEN]

6144   Mercutio's soul
Is but a little way above our heads,
Staying for thine to keep him company:
Either thou, or I, or both, must go with him.
Romeo and Juliet, Act iii, sc. 1, l. 131 [ROMEO]

6145 Poor soul, the centre of my sinful earth—
My sinful earth these rebel powers array—
Why dost thou pine within and suffer dearth,
Painting thy outward walls so costly gay?
Sonnet cxlvi, l. 1

6146 Let fools do good, and fair men call for grace,
Aaron will have his soul black like his face.
Titus Andronicus, Act iii, sc. 1, l. 205 [AARON]

6147   I stalk about her door
Like a strange soul upon the Stygian banks
Staying for waftage. O, be thou my Charon,
And give me quick transportance to those fields
Where I may wallow in the lily-beds
Proposed for the deserver! O gentle Pandarus,
From Cupid's shoulder pluck his painted wings,
And fly with me to Cressid!
Troilus and Cressida, Act iii, sc. 2, l. 8 [TROILUS]

Sovereignty

6148   I do but dream on sovereignty;
Like one that stands upon a promontory,
And spies a far-off shore where he would tread,
Wishing his foot were equal with his eye,
And chides the sea that sunders him from thence
Saying, he'll lade it dry to have his way.
III Henry VI, Act iii, sc. 2, l. 134 [GLOUCESTER]

6149   Put in her tender heart the aspiring flame
        Of golden sovereignty.
                    Richard III, Act iv, sc. 4, l. 328 [KING RICHARD]

Spaniel

6150   You play the spaniel,
        And think with wagging of your tongue to win me.
                    Henry VIII, Act v, sc. 3, l. 126 [KING HENRY]
6151   I am your spaniel; and, Demetrius,
        The more you beat me, I will fawn on you.
                    A Midsummer Night's Dream, Act ii, sc. 1, l. 203 [HELENA]

Spark

6152   'Tis not his fault, the spark. . . . Good sparks and lustrous, a
        word, good metals.
                    All's Well that Ends Well, Act ii, sc. 1, l. 25 [PAROLLES]
6153   Nay, then, this spark will prove a raging fire,
        If wind and fuel be brought to feed it with.
                    II Henry VI, Act iii, sc. 1, l. 302 [QUEEN]
6154   He doth indeed show some sparks that are like wit.
                    Much Ado about Nothing, Act ii, sc. 3, l. 193 [DON PEDRO]
6155   I see some sparks of better hope, which elder years
        May happily bring forth.
                    Richard II, Act v, sc. 3, l. 21 [BOLINGBROKE]

Sparrow

6156   GURNEY: Good leave, good Philip.
        BASTARD: Philip! sparrow: James,
        There's toys abroad: anon I'll tell thee more.
                    King John, Act i, sc. 1, l. 231 [GURNEY]
6157   Sparrows must not build in his house-eaves, because they are
        lecherous.
                    Measure for Measure, Act iii, sc. 2, l. 185 [LUCIO]

Speech

6158   I do not much dislike the matter, but
        The manner of his speech.
                    Antony and Cleopatra, Act ii, sc. 2, l. 113 [OCTAVIUS CÆSAR]
6159   Thou speakest wiser than thou art ware of.
                    As You Like It, Act ii, sc. 4, l. 58 [ROSALIND]
6160   What should we speak of
        When we are old as you? when we shall hear
        The rain and wind beat dark December, how
        In this our pinching cave, shall we discourse
        The freezing hours away?
                    Cymbeline, Act iii, sc. 3, l. 35 [ARVIRAGUS]
6161   Marry, well said; very well said.
                    Hamlet, Act ii, sc. 1, l. 6 [POLONIUS]
        That's well said.
                    Measure for Measure, Act ii, sc. 2, l. 110 [LUCIO]
        (A phrase used twenty-eight times in the plays.)
6162   How smart a lash that speech doth give my conscience.
                    Hamlet, Act iii, sc. 1, l. 50 [KING]
6163   A knavish speech sleeps in a foolish ear.
                    Hamlet, Act iv, sc. 2, l. 25 [HAMLET]
6164   We must speak by the card, or equivocation will undo us.
                    Hamlet, Act v, sc. 1, l. 148 [HAMLET]
6165   Let me speak to the yet unknowing world
        How these things came about: so shall you hear

Of carnal, bloody, and unnatural acts,
Of accidental judgements, casual slaughters,
Of deaths put on by cunning and forced cause.
Hamlet, Act v, sc. 2, l. 390 [HORATIO]

6166   When he speaks,
The air, a charter'd libertine, is still,
And the mute wonder lurketh in men's ears,
To steal his sweet and honey'd sentences.
Henry V, Act i, sc. 1, l. 47 [CANTERBURY]

6167   We will . . . believe in heart
That what you speak is in your conscience wash'd
As pure as sin with baptism.
Henry V, Act i, sc. 2, l. 30 [KING HENRY]

6168   Things are often spoke and seldom meant:
But that my heart accordeth with my tongue.
II Henry VI, Act iii, sc. 1, l. 268 [SUFFOLK]

6169   'Tis better said than done.
III Henry VI, Act iii, sc. 2, l. 90 [LADY GREY]

6170   I had a thing to say,
But I will fit it with some better time. . . .
I had a thing to say, but let it go.
King John, Act iii, sc. 3, l. 25 [KING JOHN]

6171   Mend your speech a little,
Lest it may mar your fortunes.
King Lear, Act i, sc. 1, l. 96 [LEAR]

6172   The weight of this sad time we must obey;
Speak what we feel, not what we ought to say.
King Lear, Act v, sc. 3, l. 323 [ALBANY]

6173   Vir sapit qui pauca loquitur.
Love's Labour's Lost, Act iv, sc. 2, l. 82 [HOLOFERNES]
          (Repeating a Latin proverb, "It's a wise man who speaks little.")

6174   One rubbed his elbow thus, and fleer'd and swore
A better speech was never spoke before.
Love's Labour's Lost, Act v, sc. 2, l. 109 [BOYET]

6175   It oft falls out
To have what we would have, we speak not what we mean.
Measure for Measure, Act ii, sc. 4, l. 116 [ISABELLA]

6176   Mistress Anne Page? She has brown hair, and speaks small like a woman.
The Merry Wives of Windsor, Act i, sc. 1, l. 48 [SLENDER]

6177   It is spoke as a Christian ought to speak.
The Merry Wives of Windsor, Act i, sc. 1, l. 103 [EVANS]

6178   She speaks poniards, and every word stabs.
Much Ado about Nothing, Act ii, sc. 1, l. 255 [BENEDICK]

6179   He was wont to speak plain and to the purpose, like an honest man and a soldier; and now is he turned orthography.
Much Ado about Nothing, Act ii, sc. 3, l. 18 [BENEDICK]

6180   DON PEDRO: Runs not this speech like iron through your blood?
CLAUDIO: I have drunk poison whiles he utter'd it.
Much Ado about Nothing, Act v, sc. 1, l. 252 [DON PEDRO]

6181   Rude am I in my speech,
And little bless'd with the soft phrase of peace;
For since these arms of mine had seven years' pith,
Till now some nine moons wasted, they have used
Their dearest action in the tented field,

And little of this great world can I speak,
More than pertains to feats of broil and battle,
And therefore little shall I grace my cause
In speaking for myself.
Othello, Act i, sc. 3, l. 81 [OTHELLO]

6182 He speaks home, madam: you may relish him more in the soldier
than in the scholar.
Othello, Act ii, sc. 1, l. 166 [CASSIO]

6183 I will speak as liberal as the north:
Let heaven and men and devils, let them all,
All, all, cry shame against me, yet I'll speak.
Othello, Act v, sc. 2, l. 220 [EMILIA]

6184 Free speech and fearless I to thee allow.
Richard II, Act i, sc. 1, l. 123 [KING RICHARD]

6185 ROMEO: Shall this speech be spoke for our excuse?
Or shall we on without apology?
BENVOLIO: The date is out of such prolixity:
We'll have no Cupid hoodwink'd with a scarf,
Bearing a Tartar's painted bow of lath,
Scaring the ladies like a crow-keeper;
Nor no without-book prologue, faintly spoke
After the prompter, for our entrance.
Romeo and Juliet, Act i, sc. 4, l. 1 [ROMEO]

6186 Speaking is for beggars; he wears his tongue in 's arms.
Troilus and Cressida, Act iii, sc. 3, l. 271 [THERSITES]

6187 He speaks nothing but madman: fie on him!
Twelfth Night, Act i, sc. 5, l. 114 [OLIVIA]

6188 I would be loath to cast away my speech, for besides that it is
excellently well penned, I have taken great pains to con it.
Twelfth Night, Act i, sc. 5, l. 183 [VIOLA]

Speed

6189 Repair thou to me with as much speed as thou wouldst fly death.
I have words to speak in thine ear will make thee dumb.
Hamlet, Act iv, sc. 6, l. 23 [HORATIO, *reading*]
Bend you with your dearest speed.
I Henry IV, Act v, sc. 5, l. 36 [KING HENRY]

6190 The dove pursues the griffin; the mild hind
Makes speed to catch the tiger; bootless speed,
When cowardice pursues and valour flies.
A Midsummer Night's Dream, Act ii, sc. 1, l. 232 [HELENA]

6191 BAPTISTA: How speed you with my daughter?
PETRUCHIO: How but well, sir? how but well? It were impossible
I should speed amiss.
The Taming of the Shrew, Act ii, sc. 1, l. 283 [BAPTISTA]

Spider

6192   Spider-like,
Out of his self-drawing web, he gives us note.
Henry VIII, Act i, sc. 1, l. 62 [NORFOLK]

6193   There may be in the cup
A spider steep'd, and one may drink, depart,
And yet partake no venom, for his knowledge
Is not infected: but if one present
The abhorr'd ingredient to his eye, make known
How he hath drunk, he cracks his gorge, his sides,
With violent hefts.
The Winter's Tale, Act ii, sc. 1, l. 39 [LEONTES]

Spirit

6194   Methinks in thee some blessed spirit doth speak
His powerful sound within an organ weak.
All's Well that Ends Well, Act ii, sc. 1, l. 178 [KING]

6195   Be thou a spirit of health or goblin damn'd,
Bring with thee airs from heaven or blasts from hell,
Be thy intents wicked or charitable,
Thou comest in such a questionable shape
That I will speak to thee.
Hamlet, Act i, sc. 4, l. 40 [HAMLET]

6196   I am thy father's spirit,
Doom'd for a certain term to walk the night,
And for the day confined to fast in fires,
Till the foul crimes done in my days of nature
Are burnt and purged away.
Hamlet, Act i, sc. 5, l. 8 [GHOST]

6197   Rest, rest, perturbed spirit!
Hamlet, Act i, sc. 5, l. 182 [HAMLET]

6198   The spirit within thee hath been so at war
And thus hast so bestirr'd thee in thy sleep,
That beads of sweat have stood upon thy brow,
Like bubbles in a late-disturbed stream.
I Henry IV, Act ii, sc. 3, l. 59 [LADY PERCY]

6199   I am not gamesome: I do lack some part
Of that quick spirit that is in Antony.
Julius Cæsar, Act i, sc. 2, l. 28 [BRUTUS]

6200   Nor stony tower, nor walls of beaten brass,
Nor airless dungeon, nor strong links of iron,
Can be retentive to the strength of spirit.
Julius Cæsar, Act i, sc. 3, l. 93 [CASSIUS]

6201   This is a gift that I have, simple, simple; a foolish extravagant
spirit, full of forms, figures, shapes, objects, ideas, apprehensions,
motions, revolutions.
Love's Labour's Lost, Act iv, sc. 2, l. 67 [HOLOFERNES]

6202   A jewel in a ten-times-barr'd-up chest
Is a bold spirit in a loyal breast.
Richard II, Act i, sc. 1, l. 180 [MOWBRAY]

6203   That gallant spirit hath aspired the clouds,
Which too untimely here did scorn the earth.
Romeo and Juliet, Act iii, sc. 1, l. 122 [BENVOLIO]

6204   Bring a corollary, rather than want a spirit.
The Tempest, Act iv, sc. 1, l. 57 [PROSPERO]

Spirits

6205   Prithee, go hence;
Or I shall show the cinders of my spirits
Through the ashes of my chance.
Antony and Cleopatra, Act v, sc. 2, l. 172 [CLEOPATRA]

6206   GLENDOWER: I can call spirits from the vasty deep.
HOTSPUR: Why, so can I, or so can any man,
But will they come when you do call for them?
I Henry IV, Act iii, sc. 1, l. 53 [GLENDOWER]

6207   With my vex'd spirits I cannot take a truce,
But they will quake and tremble all this day.
King John, Act iii, sc. 1, l. 17 [CONSTANCE]

6208   Hie thee hither,
That I may pour my spirits in thine ear;

And chastise with the valour of my tongue
All that impedes thee from the golden round.
Macbeth, Act i, sc. 5, l. 26 [LADY MACBETH]

6209   Your spirits shine through you.
Macbeth, Act iii, sc. 1, l. 128 [MACBETH]

6210   Spirits are not finely touch'd
But to fine issues.
Measure for Measure, Act i, sc. 1, l. 36 [DUKE]

6211   I know her spirits are as coy and wild
As haggerds of the rock.
Much Ado about Nothing, Act iii, sc. 1, l. 35 [HERO]

6212   I see this hath a little dash'd your spirits.
Othello, Act iii, sc. 3, l. 214 [IAGO]

6213   I have a thousand spirits in one breast,
To answer twenty thousand such as you.
Richard II, Act iv, sc. 1, l. 58 [AUMERLE]

6214   I have heard, but not believed, the spirits o' the dead
May walk again.
The Winter's Tale, Act iii, sc. 3, l. 16 [ANTIGONOUS]

Sponge

6215   HAMLET: To be demanded of a sponge! what replication should
be made by the son of a king?
ROSENCRANTZ: Take you me for a sponge, my lord?
HAMLET: Ay, sir, that soaks up the king's countenance, his re-
wards, his authorities.
Hamlet, Act iv, sc. 2, l. 12 [HAMLET]

6216   I will do any thing, Nerissa, ere I'll be married to a sponge.
The Merchant of Venice, Act i, sc. 2, l. 107 [PORTIA]

Sport

6217   That sport best pleases that doth least know how.
Love's Labour's Lost, Act v, sc. 2, l. 517 [PRINCESS]

6218   She is sport for Jove. . . . And, I'll warrant her, full of game.
Othello, Act ii, sc. 3, l. 17 [IAGO]

6219   What sport shall we devise here in this garden,
To drive away the heavy thought of care?
Richard II, Act iii, sc. 4, l. 1 [QUEEN]

6220   Sport royal, I warrant you.
Twelfth Night, Act ii, sc. 3, l. 187 [MARIA]

Spring

6221   The spring is near when green geese are a-breeding.
Love's Labour's Lost, Act i, sc. 1, l. 97 [BIRON]

6222   See where she comes, apparell'd like the spring.
Pericles, Act i, sc. 1, l. 12 [PERICLES]

6223   Unruly blasts wait on the tender spring.
The Rape of Lucrece, l. 869 [LUCRECE]

Springe

6224   Ay, springes to catch woodcocks.
Hamlet, Act i, sc. 3, l. 115 [POLONIUS]

6225   OSRIC: How is 't, Laertes?
LAERTES: Why, as a woodcock to mine own springe, Osric;
I am justly kill'd with mine own treachery.
Hamlet, Act v, sc. 2, l. 315 [OSRIC]

6226   If the springe hold, the cock's mine.
The Winter's Tale, Act iv, sc. 3, l. 36 [AUTOLYCUS]

Sprite

6227   These be fine things, an if they be not sprites,
        That's a brave god and bears celestial liquor.
                            The Tempest, Act ii, sc. 2, l. 121 [CALIBAN]

Stag

6228   A poor sequester'd stag,
        That from the hunter's aim had ta'en a hurt,
        Did come to languish, and . . . heaved forth such groans
        That their discharge did stretch his leathern coat
        Almost to bursting, and the big round tears
        Coursed one another down his innocent nose
        In piteous chase.
                            As You Like It, Act ii, sc. 1, l. 33 [LORD]

6229   I am here a Windsor stag; and the fattest, I think, i' the forest.
                            The Merry Wives of Windsor, Act v, sc. 5, l. 14 [FALSTAFF]

Stake

6230   We are at the stake,
        And bay'd about with many enemies;
        And some that smile have in their hearts, I fear,
        Millions of mischiefs.
                            Julius Cæsar, Act iv, sc. 1, l. 48 [OCTAVIUS]

6231   I am tied to the stake, and I must stand the course.
                            King Lear, Act iii, sc. 7, l. 54 [GLOUCESTER]

6232   They have tied me to a stake; I cannot fly,
        But, bear-like, I must fight the course.
                            Macbeth, Act v, sc. 7, l. 1 [MACBETH]

Star

6233   'Twere all one
        That I should love a bright particular star
        And think to wed it.
                            All's Well that Ends Well, Act i, sc. 1, l. 96 [HELENA]

6234   The star is fall'n. And time is at his period.
                            Antony and Cleopatra, Act iv, sc. 14, l. 106 [GUARD]

6235   The moist star
        Upon whose influence Neptune's empire stands
        Was sick almost to doomsday with eclipse.
                            Hamlet, Act i, sc. 1, l. 118 [HORATIO]

6236   Look, the unfolding star calls up the shepherd.
                            Measure for Measure, Act iv, sc. 2, l. 219 [DUKE]

6237   Night's swift dragons cut the clouds full fast,
        And yonder shines Aurora's harbinger:
        At whose approach, ghosts, wandering here and there,
        Troop home to churchyards.
                            A Midsummer Night's Dream, Act iii, sc. 2, l. 379 [PUCK]

6238   That full star that ushers in the even.
                            Sonnet cxxxii, l. 7

6239   I find my zenith doth depend upon
        A most auspicious star, whose influence
        If now I court not but omit, my fortunes
        Will ever after droop.
                            The Tempest, Act i, sc. 2, l. 181 [PROSPERO]

Stars

6240   My good stars, that were my former guides,
        Have empty left their orbs, and shot their fires
        Into the abysm of hell.
                            Antony and Cleopatra, Act iii, sc. 13, l. 145 [ANTONY]

6241   We could not stall together in the whole world:
       But yet let me lament . . . that our stars,
       Unreconciliable, should divide
       Our equalness to this.
Antony and Cleopatra, Act v, sc. 1, l. 39 [CÆSAR]

6242   Two stars keep not their motion in one sphere,
       Nor can one England brook a double reign.
I Henry IV, Act v, sc. 4, l. 65 [PRINCE]

6243   What! we have seen the seven stars.
II Henry IV, Act ii, sc. 4, l. 201 [PISTOL]
       ("Seven stars," used formerly of the planets; also of the
       Pleiades and the Great Bear.)
       FOOL: The reason why the seven stars are no more than seven
       is a pretty reason.
       LEAR: Because they are not eight?
King Lear, Act i, sc. 5, l. 38 [FOOL]

6244   Now, now, you stars that move in your right spheres,
       Where be your powers? show now your mended faiths.
       And instantly return with me again.
       To push destruction and perpetual shame
       Out of the weak door of our fainting land.
King John, Act v, sc. 7, l. 74 [BASTARD]

6245   GLOUCESTER: These late eclipses in the sun and moon portend no
       good to us. . . .
       EDMUND: This is the excellent foppery of the world, that, when
       we are sick in fortune, . . . we make guilty of our disasters the
       sun, the moon, and the stars: as if we were villains by necessity;
       fools by heavenly compulsion; . . . an admirable evasion of
       whore-master man, to lay his goatish disposition to the charge of
       a star.
King Lear, Act i, sc. 2, l. 112 [GLOUCESTER]

6246   The stars above us govern our conditions.
King Lear, Act iv, sc. 3, l. 35 [KENT]

6247   We'll feast here awhile,
       Until our stars that frown lend us a smile.
Pericles, Act i, sc. 4, l. 107 [PERICLES]

6248   My stars shine darkly over me: the malignancy of my fate might
       perhaps distemper yours.
Twelfth Night, Act ii, sc. 1, l. 3 [SEBASTIAN]

6249   But truer stars did govern Proteus' birth;
       His words are bonds, his oaths are oracles,
       His love sincere, his thoughts immaculate,
       His tears pure messengers sent from his heart,
       His heart as far from fraud as heaven from earth.
The Two Gentlemen of Verona, Act ii, sc. 7, l. 74 [JULIA]

Stature

6250   I would I had thy inches.
Antony and Cleopatra, Act i, sc. 3, l. 40 [CLEOPATRA]

6251   JAQUES: What stature is she of?
       ORLANDO: Just as high as my heart.
       JAQUES: You are full of pretty answers.
As You Like It, Act iii, sc. 2, l. 285 [JAQUES]

6252   He is as tall a man of his hands as any is between this and his
       head; he hath fought with a warrener.
The Merry Wives of Windsor, Act i, sc. 4, l. 26 [SIMPLE]

6253 Now I perceive that she hath made compare
Between our statures; she hath urged her height;
And with her personage, her tall personage,
Her height, forsooth, she hath prevail'd with him . . .
How low am I? I am not yet so low
But that my nails can reach unto thine eyes.
A Midsummer Night's Dream, Act iii, sc. 2, l. 290 [HERMIA]

Statute

6254 CADE: Away, burn all the records of the realm: my mouth shall
be the parliament of England.
HOLLAND, *aside:* Then we are like to have biting statutes, unless
his teeth be pulled out.
II Henry VI, Act iv, sc. 7, l. 16 [CADE]

6255 We have strict statutes and most biting laws,
The needful bits and curbs to headstrong wills,
Which for this fourteen years we have let slip;
Even like an o'ergrown lion in a cave,
That goes not out to prey.
Measure for Measure, Act i, sc. 3, l. 19 [DUKE]

6256 He . . . follows close the rigour of the statute.
Measure for Measure, Act i, sc. 4, l. 67 [LUCIO]

Stealing

6257 LUCIO: Thou concludest like the sanctimonious pirate, that went
to sea with the Ten Commandments, but scraped one out of the
table.
GENTLEMAN: 'Thou shalt not steal'?
LUCIO: Ay, that he razed.
Measure for Measure, Act i, sc. 2, l. 7 [LUCIO]

6258 TRINCULO: We steal by line and level, an 't like your grace.
STEPHANO: I thank thee for that jest; here's a garment for 't:
wit shall not go unrewarded while I am king of this country.
'Steal by line and level' is an excellent pass of pate; there's an-
other garment for 't.
The Tempest, Act iv, sc. 1, l. 239 [TRINCULO]

6259   Easy it is
Of a cut loaf to steal a shive, we know.
Titus Andronicus, Act ii, sc. 1, l. 86 [DEMETRIUS]
(Quoting an old proverb. "Shive," slice.)

Stomach

6260 It goes much against my stomach.
As You Like It, Act iii, sc. 2, l. 22 [TOUCHSTONE]

6261 Our stomachs will make what's homely savoury.
Cymbeline, Act iii, sc. 6, l. 32 [BELARIUS]

6262 [He hath] Shark'd up a list of lawless resolutes,
For food and diet, to some enterprise
That hath a stomach in 't.
Hamlet, Act i, sc. 1, l. 97 [HORATIO]

6263 The winds grow high; so do your stomachs, lords.
How irksome is this music to my heart!
When such strings jar, what hope of harmony?
II Henry VI, Act ii, sc. 1, l. 54 [KING HENRY]

6264 He is a very valiant trencher-man; he hath an excellent stomach.
Much Ado about Nothing, Act i, sc. 1, l. 51 [BEATRICE]

6265 High-stomach'd are they both, and full of ire,
In rage deaf as the sea, hasty as fire.
Richard II, Act i, sc. 1, l. 18 [RICHARD]

Stones

6266 Spit, and throw stones, cast mire upon me, set
The dogs o' the street to bay me.
Cymbeline, Act v, sc. 5, l. 222 [POSTHUMUS]

6267 The gods throw stones of sulphur on me!
Cymbeline, Act v, sc. 5, l. 240 [PISANIO]

6268 By gar, I will cut all his two stones; by gar, he shall not have a
stone to throw at his dog.
The Merry Wives of Windsor, Act i, sc. 4, l. 117 [CAIUS]

6269 Are there no stones in heaven
But what serve for the thunder?
Othello, Act v, sc. 2, l. 234 [OTHELLO]

6270 Stones dissolved in water do convert.
O, if no harder than a stone thou art,
Melt at my tears, and be compassionate.
The Rape of Lucrece, l. 592 [LUCRECE]

6271 He is a stone, a very pebble-stone, and has no more pity in him
than a dog.
The Two Gentlemen of Verona, Act ii, sc. 3, l. 11 [LAUNCE]

6272 Stone at rain relenteth.
Venus and Adonis, l. 199 [VENUS]

Storm

6273 I will stir up in England some black storm
Shall blow ten thousand souls to heaven or hell;
And this fell tempest shall not cease to rage
Until the golden circuit on my head,
Like to the glorious sun's transparent beams,
Do calm the fury of this mad-bred flaw.
II Henry VI, Act iii, sc. 1, l. 349 [YORK]

6274 I am resolved to bear a greater storm
Than any thou canst conjure up to-day.
II Henry VI, Act v, sc. 1, l. 198 [CLIFFORD]

6275 Ay, now begins a second storm to rise;
For this is he that moves both wind and tide.
III Henry VI, Act iii, sc. 3, l. 47 [QUEEN MARGARET]

6276 Untimely storms make men expect a dearth.
Richard III, Act ii, sc. 3, l. 35 [CITIZEN]

Story

6277 Let us from point to point this story know,
To make the even truth in pleasure flow.
All's Well that Ends Well, Act v, sc. 3, l. 325 [KING]

6278 The story is extant, and writ in choice Italian.
Hamlet, Act iii, sc. 2, l. 273 [HAMLET]

6279 I'll to my closet; and go read with thee
Sad stories chanced in the times of old.
Titus Andronicus, Act iii, sc. 2, l. 82 [TITUS]

6280 Their copious stories oftentimes begun
End without audience and are never done.
Venus and Adonis, l. 845

Stranger

6281 Strangers and foes do sunder, and not kiss.
All's Well that Ends Well, Act ii, sc. 5, l. 91 [HELENA]

6282 JAQUES: God be wi' you: let's meet as little as we can.
ORLANDO: I do desire we may be better strangers.
As You Like It, Act iii, sc. 2, l. 273 [JAQUES]

6283   HORATIO: O day and night, but this is wondrous strange!
HAMLET: And therefore as a stranger give it welcome.
Hamlet, Act i, sc. 5, l. 164 [HORATIO]

6284   Good God, betimes remove
The means that make us strangers!
Macbeth, Act iv, sc. 3, l. 162 [MALCOLM]

Strawberry

6285   The strawberry grows underneath the nettle
And wholesome berries thrive and ripen best
Neighbour'd by fruit of baser quality.
Henry V, Act i, sc. 1, l. 60 [ELY]

Stream

6286   The petty streams that pay a daily debt
To their salt sovereign, with their fresh falls' haste
Add to his flow, but alter not his taste.
The Rape of Lucrece, l. 649 [TARQUIN]

6287   All in vain you strive against the stream.
Venus and Adonis, l. 773 [ADONIS]

Strength

6288   I have no strength in measure, yet a reasonable measure in
strength.
Henry V, Act v, sc. 2, l. 140 [KING HENRY]

6289   O, it is excellent
To have a giant's strength; but it is tyrannous
To use it like a giant.
Measure for Measure, Act ii, sc. 2, l. 107 [ISABELLA]

6290   Strength should be lord of imbecility,
And the rude son should strike his father dead.
Troilus and Cressida, Act i, sc. 3, l. 114 [ULYSSES]

Study

6291   BIRON: What is the end of study? let me know.
KING: Why, that to know, which else we should not know.
BIRON: Things hid and barr'd, you mean, from common sense?
KING: Ay, that is study's god-like recompense. . . .
BIRON: Study is like the heaven's glorious sun,
That will not be deep-search'd with saucy looks:
Small have continual plodders ever won
Save base authority from others' books.
These earthly godfathers of heaven's lights
That give a name to every fixed star
Have no more profit of their shining nights
Than those that walk and wot not what they are.
Too much to know is to know nought but fame;
And every godfather can give a name.
Love's Labour's Lost, Act i, sc. 1, l. 55 [BIRON]

6292   You, to study now it is too late,
Climb o'er the house to unlock the little gate. . . .
So study evermore is overshot:
While it doth study to have what it would
It doth forget to do the thing it should,
And when it hath the thing it hunteth most,
'Tis won as towns with fire, so won, so lost.
Love's Labour's Lost, Act i, sc. 1, l. 108 [BIRON]

6293 When would you, my lord, or you, or you,
Have found the ground of study's excellence
Without the beauty of a woman's face?
Love's Labour's Lost, Act iv, sc. 3, l. 299 [BIRON]

6294 LUCENTIO: For the time I study,
Virtue and that part of philosophy
Will I apply that treats of happiness. . . .
TRANIO: Music and poesy use to quicken you;
The mathematics and the metaphysics,
Fall to them as you find your stomach serves you;
No profit grows where is no pleasure ta'en:
In brief, sir, study what you most affect.
The Taming of the Shrew, Act i, sc. 1, l. 17 [LUCENTIO]

Style

6295 Why, 'tis a boisterous and cruel style,
A style for challengers; why, she defies me,
Like Turk to Christian.
As You Like It, Act iv, sc. 3, l. 31 [ROSALIND]

6296 What means his grace, that he hath changed his style?
No more but, plain and bluntly, 'To the king!'
Hath he forgot he is his sovereign?
Or doth this churlish superscription
Pretend some alteration in good will?
I Henry VI, Act iv, sc. 1, l. 50 [GLOUCESTER]

6297 Here is a silly-stately style indeed!
The Turk, that two and fifty kingdoms hath,
Writes not so tedious a style as this.
I Henry VI, Act iv, sc. 7, l. 72 [PUCELLE]

6298 [His] large style
Agrees not with the leanness of his purse.
II Henry VI, Act i, sc. 1, l. 112 [GLOUCESTER]

6299 KING RICHARD: Then in plain terms tell her my loving tale.
QUEEN ELIZABETH: Plain and not honest is too harsh a style.
Richard III, Act iv, sc. 4, l. 359 [KING RICHARD]

Subject

6300 Every subject's duty is the king's; but every subject's soul is his own.
Henry V, Act iv, sc. 1, l. 192 [KING]

6301 VERGES: If he will not stand when he is bidden, he is none of the prince's subjects.
DOGBERRY: True, and they are to meddle with none but the prince's subjects.
Much Ado about Nothing, Act iii, sc. 3, l. 32 [VERGES]

Submission

6302 Submission, Dauphin! 'tis a mere French word;
We English warriors wot not what it means.
I Henry VI, Act iv, sc. 7, l. 54 [LUCY]

6303 O calm, dishonourable, vile submission!
Alla stoccata carries it away.
Romeo and Juliet, Act iii, sc. 1, l. 76 [MERCUTIO]
("Alla stoccata," a thrust with a rapier.)

Success

6304 I know he will be glad of our success;
We are the Jasons, we have won the fleece.
The Merchant of Venice, Act iii, sc. 2, l. 243 [GRATIANO]

6305   Doubt not but success
        Will fashion the event in better shape
        Than I can lay it down in likelihood.
                        Much Ado about Nothing, Act iv, sc. 1, l. 236 [FRIAR]

Sufferance

6306   Of sufferance comes ease.
                        II Henry IV, Act v, sc. 4, l. 28 [HOSTESS]
6307   Thy nature did commence in sufferance, time
        Hath made thee hard in 't.
                        Timon of Athens, Act iv, sc. 3, l. 268 [TIMON]

Suffering

6308   Thou hast been
        As one, in suffering all, that suffers nothing.
                        Hamlet, Act iii, sc. 2, l. 70 [HAMLET]
6309   Who alone suffers suffers most i' the mind,
        Leaving free things and happy shows behind:
        But then the mind much sufferance doth o'erskip,
        When grief hath mates, and bearing fellowship.
                        King Lear, Act iii, sc. 6, l. 111 [EDGAR]

Suggestion

6310   Why do I yield to that suggestion
        Whose horrid image doth unfix my hair
        And make my seated heart knock at my ribs,
        Against the use of nature?
                        Macbeth, Act i, sc. 3, l. 134 [MACBETH]
6311   They'll take suggestion as a cat laps milk;
        They'll tell the clock to any business that
        We say befits the hour.
                        The Tempest, Act ii, sc. 1, l. 288 [ANTONIO]

Summer

6312   With the word the time will bring on summer,
        When briers shall have leaves as well as thorns,
        And be as sweet as sharp.
                        All's Well that Ends Well, Act iv, sc. 4, l. 31 [HELENA]
6313   Expect Saint Martin's summer, halcyon days.
                        I Henry VI, Act i, sc. 2, l. 131 [PUCELLE]
6314   There is so hot a summer in my bosom,
        That all my bowels crumble up to dust:
        I am a scribbled form, drawn with a pen
        Upon a parchment, and against this fire
        Do I shrink up. . . . Poison'd, . . . forsook, cast off.
                        King John, Act v, sc. 7, l. 30 [KING JOHN]
6315   Short summers lightly have a forward spring.
                        Richard III, Act iii, sc. 1, l. 94 [GLOUCESTER]
6316   Shall I compare thee to a summer's day?
        Thou art more lovely and more temperate:
        Rough winds do shake the darling buds of May,
        And summer's lease hath all too short a date:
        Sometime too hot the eye of heaven shines,
        And often is his gold complexion dimm'd;
        And every fair from fair sometime declines,
        By chance or nature's changing course untrimm'd;
        But thy eternal summer shall not fade.
                        Sonnet xviii, l. 1

Sun

6317   Herein will I imitate the sun,
Who doth permit the base contagious clouds
To smother up his beauty from the world,
That, when he please again to be himself,
Being wanted, he may be more wonder'd at,
By breaking through the foul and ugly mists
Of vapours that did seem to strangle him.
I Henry IV, Act i, sc. 2, l. 220 [PRINCE]

6318   Shall the blessed sun of heaven prove a micher and eat blackberries? a question not to be asked. Shall the son of England prove
a thief and take purses? a question to be asked.
I Henry IV, Act ii, sc. 4, l. 453 [FALSTAFF]

6319   O Phœbus, hadst thou never given consent
That Phaëthon should check thy fiery steeds,
Thy burning car never had scorch'd the earth!
III Henry VI, Act ii, sc. 6, l. 11 [CLIFFORD]

6320   No sun shall ever usher forth mine honours,
Or gild again the noble troops that waited
Upon my smiles. . . . Seek the king;
That sun, I pray, may never set.
Henry VIII, Act iii, sc. 2, l. 410 [WOLSEY]

6321   O setting sun,
As in thy red rays thou dost sink to night,
So in his red blood Cassius' day is set;
The sun of Rome is set! Our day is gone;
Clouds, dews, and dangers come; our deeds are done!
Julius Cæsar, Act v, sc. 3, l. 60 [TITINIUS]

6322   The sun is in the heaven, and the proud day,
Attended with the pleasures of the world,
Is all too wanton and too full of gawds
To give me audience.
King John, Act iii, sc. 3, l. 34 [KING JOHN]

6323   I 'gin to be a-weary of the sun,
And wish the estate o' the world were now undone.
Macbeth, Act v, sc. 5, l. 49 [MACBETH]

6324   The setting sun, and music at the close,
As the last taste of sweets, is sweetest last,
Writ in remembrance more than things long past.
Richard II, Act ii, sc. 1, l. 12 [GAUNT]

6325   When the searching eye of heaven is hid
Behind the globe, that lights the lower world,
Then thieves and robbers range abroad unseen
In murders and in outrage, boldly here;
But when from under this terrestrial ball
He fires the proud tops of the eastern pines
And darts his light through every guilty hole,
Then murders, treasons, and detected sins,
The cloak of night being pluck'd from off their backs,
Stand bare and naked, trembling at themselves.
Richard II, Act iii, sc. 2, l. 37 [KING RICHARD]

6326   The weary sun hath made a golden set,
And, by the bright track of his fiery car,
Gives signal of a bloody day to-morrow.
Richard III, Act v, sc. 3, l. 19 [RICHMOND]

6327   The worshipp'd sun
Peer'd forth the golden window of the east.
                              Romeo and Juliet, Act i, sc. 1, l. 125 [BENVOLIO]

6328   But, soft: what light through yonder window breaks?
It is the east, and Juliet is the sun.
Arise, fair sun, and kill the envious moon,
Who is already sick and pale with grief,
That thou her maid art far more fair than she.
                              Romeo and Juliet, Act ii, sc. 2, l. 2 [ROMEO]

6329   The sun itself sees not till heaven clears.
                              Sonnet cxlviii, l. 12

6330   PETRUCHIO: Let's see; I think 'tis now some seven o'clock. . . .
KATHARINA: I dare assure you, sir, 'tis almost two. . . .
PETRUCHIO: It shall be what o'clock I say it is.
HORTENSIO: Why, so this gallant will command the sun.
                              The Taming of the Shrew, Act iv, sc. 3, l. 189 [PETRUCHIO]

6331   I have bedimm'd
The noontide sun, call'd forth the mutinous winds,
And 'twixt the green sea and the azured vault
Set roaring war.
                              The Tempest, Act v, sc. 1, l. 41 [PROSPERO]

6332   Men shut their doors against a setting sun.
                              Timon of Athens, Act i, sc. 2, l. 150 [APEMANTUS]

6333   O blessed breeding sun, draw from the earth
Rotten humidity.
                              Timon of Athens, Act iv, sc. 3, l. 1 [TIMON]

6334   Is the sun dimm'd, that gnats do fly at it?
                              Titus Andronicus, Act iv, sc. 4, l. 82 [TAMORA]

6335   The selfsame sun that shines upon his court
Hides not his visage from cur cottage but
Looks on alike.
                              The Winter's Tale, Act iv, sc. 4, l. 454 [PERDITA]

Sunshine

6336   Ne'er may he live to see a sunshine day,
That cries 'Retire,' if Warwick bid him stay.
                              III Henry VI, Act ii, sc. 1, l. 187 [RICHARD]

6337   That sunshine brew'd a shower for him,
That wash'd his father's fortune forth of France.
                              III Henry VI, Act ii, sc. 2, l. 156 [EDWARD]

6338   You have seen
Sunshine and rain at once: her smiles and tears
Were like a better way: those happy smilets,
That play'd on her ripe lip, seem'd not to know
What guests were in her eyes: which parted thence,
As pearls from diamonds dropp'd.
                              King Lear, Act iv, sc. 3, l. 19 [GENTLEMAN]

6339   Vouchsafe to show the sunshine of your face,
That we, like savages, may worship it.
                              Love's Labour's Lost, Act v, sc. 2, l. 201 [BIRON]

Superstition

6340   He is superstitious grown of late,
Quite from the main opinion he held once
Of fantasy, of dreams and ceremonies.
                              Julius Cæsar, Act ii, sc. 1, l. 195 [CASSIUS]

6341   SAILOR: The sea works high, the wind is loud, and will not lie
till the ship be cleared of the dead.
PERICLES: That's your superstition.
SAILOR: Pardon us, sir; with us at sea it hath been still observed;
and we are strong in custom.

Pericles, Act iii, sc. 1, l. 48 [SAILOR]

Supper

6342   About the sixth hour; when beasts most graze, birds best peck,
and men sit down to that nourishment which is called supper.

Love's Labour's Lost, Act i, sc. 1, l. 238 [KING]

6343   An you'll come to supper to-night, you may; an you will not,
come when you are next prepared for.

Othello, Act iv, sc. 1, l. 167 [BIANCA]

Sureness

6344   As sure as day.

I Henry IV, Act iii, sc. 1, l. 255 [HOTSPUR]

6345   As sure as bark on tree.

Love's Labour's Lost, Act v, sc. 2, l. 285 [MARIA]

6346   Sure as death.

Titus Andronicus, Act i, sc. 1, l. 487 [SATURNINUS]

6347   Sure as I live.

The Two Gentlemen of Verona, Act iv, sc. 4, l. 17 [LAUNCE]

6348   I'll make assurance double sure,
And take a bond of fate.

Macbeth, Act iv, sc. 1, l. 83 [MACBETH]

Surety

6349   One of the greatest in the Christian world
Shall be my surety; 'fore whose throne 'tis needful,
Ere I can perfect mine intents, to kneel.

All's Well that Ends Well, Act iv, sc. 4, l. 2 [HELENA]

6350   She call'd the saints to surety.

All's Well that Ends Well, Act v, sc. 3, l. 108 [KING]

6351   [You] givest such sarcenet surety for thy oaths,
As if thou never walk'st further than Finsbury.

I Henry IV, Act iii, sc. 1, l. 257 [HOTSPUR]

6352   The wound of peace is surety, Surety secure.

Troilus and Cressida, Act ii, sc. 2, l. 14 [HECTOR]

Surfeit

6353   As surfeit is the father of much fast,
So every scope by the immoderate use
Turns to restraint.

Measure for Measure, Act i, sc. 2, l. 130 [CLAUDIO]

6354   They are as sick that surfeit with too much as they that starve
with nothing.

The Merchant of Venice, Act i, sc. 2, l. 6 [NERISSA]

6355   A surfeit of the sweetest things
The deepest loathing to the stomach brings.

A Midsummer Night's Dream, Act ii, sc. 2, l. 137 [LYSANDER]

6356   Will the cold brook,
Candied with ice, caudle thy morning taste,
To cure thy o'er-night's surfeit?

Timon of Athens, Act iv, sc. 3, l. 225 [APEMANTUS]

Suspicion

6357   See what a ready tongue suspicion hath!
        He that but fears the thing he would not know
        Hath by instinct knowledge from others' eyes
        That what he fear'd is chanced.
                        II Henry IV, Act i, sc. 1, l. 84 [NORTHUMBERLAND]

6358   Suspicion always haunts the guilty mind.
                        III Henry VI, Act v, sc. 6, l. 11 [GLOUCESTER]

Swallow

6359   Swallows have built
        In Cleopatra's sails their nests: the augurers
        Say they know not, they cannot tell; look grimly.
                        Antony and Cleopatra, Act iv, sc. 12, l. 3 [SCARUS]

6360   The swallow follows not summer more willingly than we your
        lordship.
                        Timon of Athens, Act iii, sc. 6, l. 31 [LORD]

6361   I have horse will follow where the game
        Makes way, and run like swallows o'er the plain.
                        Titus Andronicus, Act ii, sc. 2, l. 23 [TITUS]

Swan

6362   Be not offended, nature's miracle,
        Thou art allotted to be ta'en by me:
        So doth the swan her downy cygnets save,
        Keeping them prisoner underneath her wings.
                        I Henry VI, Act v, sc. 3, l. 54 [SUFFOLK]

6363   With this, we charged again: but, out, alas!
        We bodged again; as I have seen a swan
        With bootless labour swim against the tide
        And spend her strength with over-matching waves.
                        III Henry VI, Act i, sc. 4, l. 18 [YORK]
        ("Bodged," bungled.)

6364   'Tis strange that death should sing.
        I am the cygnet to this pale faint swan,
        Who chants a doleful hymn to his own death,
        And from the organ-pipe of frailty sings
        His soul and body to their lasting rest.
                        King John, Act v, sc. 7, l. 20 [PRINCE HENRY]

6365   I will play the swan, And die in music.
                        Othello, Act v, sc. 2, l. 247 [EMILIA]

6366   And now this pale swan in her watery nest
        Begins the sad dirge of her certain ending.
                        The Rape of Lucrece, l. 1611

6367   With unattainted eye,
        Compare her face with some that I shall show,
        And I will make thee think thy swan a crow.
                        Romeo and Juliet, Act i, sc. 2, l. 90 [BENVOLIO]

Swearing

6368   A whoreson jackanapes must take me up for swearing; as if I
        borrowed mine oaths of him and might not spend them at my
        pleasure. . . . When a gentleman is disposed to swear, it is not
        for any standers-by to curtail his oaths, ha?
                        Cymbeline, Act ii, sc. 1, l. 4 [CLOTEN]

6369   HAMLET: Swear 't . . . upon my sword.
        GHOST [*Beneath*]: Swear.

HAMLET: Ah, ha, boy! say'st thou so? art thou there, truepenny?
Come on—you hear this fellow in the cellarage—
Consent to swear. . . . Swear by my sword.
GHOST [*Beneath*]: Swear.
HAMLET: Hic et ubique? then we'll shift our ground. . . .
Swear by my sword.
GHOST [*Beneath*]: Swear.
HAMLET: Well said, old mole! canst work i' the earth so fast?
A worthy pioneer! . . . Rest, rest, perturbed spirit!
Hamlet, Act i, sc. 5, l. 145 [HAMLET]

6370   HOTSPUR: Come, Kate, I'll have your song too.
LADY PERCY: Not mine, in good sooth.
HOTSPUR: Not yours; in good sooth! Heart! you swear like a
comfit-maker's wife. 'Not you, in good sooth,' and 'as true as I
live,' and 'as God shall mend me,' and 'as sure as day.' . . .
Swear me, Kate, like a lady as thou art,
A good mouth-filling oath, and leave 'in sooth,'
And such protest of pepper-gingerbread,
To velvet-guards and Sunday-citizens.
I Henry IV, Act iii, sc. 1, l. 250 [HOTSPUR]

6371   All those swearings [will I] keep as true in soul
As doth that orbed continent the fire
That severs day from night.
Twelfth Night, Act v, sc. 1, l. 277 [VIOLA]

Sweat

6372   The sweat of industry would dry and die,
But for the end it works to.
Cymbeline, Act iii, sc. 6, l. 31 [BELARIUS]

6373   Falstaff sweats to death,
And lards the lean earth as he walks along:
Were 't not for laughing, I should pity him.
I Henry IV, Act ii, sc. 2, l. 115 [PRINCE]

6374   The honourable captain there
Drops bloody sweat from his war-wearied limbs.
I Henry VI, Act iv, sc. 4, l. 17 [LUCY]

Sweet

6375   Sweets to the sweet, farewell! . . .
I thought thy bride-bed to have deck'd, sweet maid,
And not have strew'd thy grave.
Hamlet, Act v, sc. 1, l. 266 [QUEEN]

6376   The ladies call him sweet;
The stairs, as he treads on them, kiss his feet.
Love's Labour's Lost, Act v, sc. 2, l. 329 [BIRON]

6377   Ah, sweet Anne Page!
The Merry Wives of Windsor, Act iii, sc. 1, l. 40 [SLENDER]

6378   Sweets grown common lose their dear delight.
Sonnet cii, l. 12

Sweet and Sour

6379   All yet seems well; and if it end so meet,
The bitter past, more welcome is the sweet.
All's Well that Ends Well, Act v, sc. 3, l. 333 [KING]

6380   Sweetest nut hath sourest rind.
As You Like It, Act iii, sc. 2, l. 115 [TOUCHSTONE]

6381   The sweets we wish for turn to loathed sours,
Even in the moment that we call them ours.
The Rape of Lucrece, l. 867 [LUCRECE]

6382   Things sweet to taste prove in digestion sour.
                    Richard II, Act i, sc. 3, l. 236 [GAUNT]
6383   Speak sweetly, man, although thy looks be sour.
                    Richard II, Act iii, sc. 2, l. 193 [KING RICHARD]

Swiftness

6384   Momentany as a sound,
       Swift as a shadow, short as any dream.
                    A Midsummer Night's Dream, Act i, sc. 1, l. 143 [LYSANDER]
6385   Look how I go,
       Swifter than arrow from the Tartar's bow.
                    A Midsummer Night's Dream, Act iii, sc. 2, l. 100 [PUCK]
6386   Too swift arrives as tardy as too slow.
                    Romeo and Juliet, Act ii, sc. 6, l. 15 [FRIAR LAURENCE]

Swimming

6387   Like an unpractised swimmer, plunging still,
       With too much labour drowns for want of skill.
                    The Rape of Lucrece, l. 1098
6388   I can swim like a duck. I'll be sworn.
                    The Tempest, Act ii, sc. 2, l. 132 [TRINCULO]

Swine

6389   'Tis old, but true; Still swine eats all the draff.
                    The Merry Wives of Windsor, Act iv, sc. 2, l. 108 [MRS. PAGE]
6390   A churlish swine, . . .
       Whose tushes never sheathed he whetteth still,
       Like to a mortal butcher bent to kill.
                    Venus and Adonis, l. 616 [VENUS]

Sword

6391   FALSTAFF: I have 'scaped by miracle; . . . my sword hacked like
       a hand-saw—ecce signum! I never dealt better since I was a
       man. . . .
       PRINCE: What a slave art thou, to hack thy sword as thou hast
       done, and then say it was in fight! What trick, what device, what
       starting-hole, canst thou now find out to hide thee from this open
       and apparent shame? . . .
       PETO: He hacked it with his dagger, and said he would swear
       truth out of England but he would make you believe it was done
       in fight.
                    I Henry IV, Act ii, sc. 4, l. 185 [FALSTAFF]
6392   Come, brother John; full bravely hast thou flesh'd
       Thy maiden sword.
                    I Henry IV, Act v, sc. 4, l. 133 [PRINCE]
6393   Take heed . . .
       How you awake our sleeping sword of war.
                    Henry V, Act i, sc. 2, l. 21 [KING]
6394   Sword and shield In bloody field
       Doth win immortal fame.
                    Henry V, Act iii, sc. 2, l. 9 [PISTOL]
6395   Sword, hold thy temper; heart, be wrathful still:
       Priests pray for enemies, but princes kill.
                    II Henry VI, Act v, sc. 2, l. 70 [RICHARD]
6396   Get thee a sword, though made of lath.
                    II Henry VI, Act iv, sc. 2, l. 1 [BEVIS]
       Go to; have your lath glued within your sheath
       Till you know better how to handle it.
                    Titus Andronicus, Act ii, sc. 1, l. 41 [DEMETRIUS]

6397   That such a slave as this should wear a sword,
Who wears no honesty.
King Lear, Act ii, sc. 2, l. 78 [KENT]

6398   Know thou this, that men
Are as the time is : to be tender-minded
Does not become a sword.
King Lear, Act v, sc. 3, l. 30 [EDMUND]

6399   Swords I smile at, weapons laugh to scorn,
Brandish'd by man that 's of a woman born.
Macbeth, Act v, sc. 7, l. 12 [MACBETH]

6400   Why should I play the Roman fool, and die
On mine own sword?
Macbeth, Act v, sc. 8, l. 1 [MACBETH]

6401   He who the sword of heaven will bear
Should be as holy as severe.
Measure for Measure, Act iii, sc. 2, l. 275 [DUKE]

6402   With blade, with bloody blameful blade,
He bravely broach'd his boiling bloody breast.
A Midsummer Night's Dream, Act v, sc. 1, l. 147 [QUINCE]

6403   Keep up your bright swords, for the dew will rust them.
Othello, Act i, sc. 2, l. 59 [OTHELLO]

6404   Every puny whipster gets my sword.
Othello, Act v, sc. 2, l. 244 [OTHELLO]

6405   Draw not thy sword to guard iniquity,
For it was lent thee all that brood to kill.
The Rape of Lucrece, l. 626 [LUCRECE]

6406   What my tongue speaks my right drawn sword may prove.
Richard II, Act i, sc. 1, l. 46 [BOLINGBROKE]

6407   Will you pluck your sword out of his pilcher by the ears? make
haste, lest mine be about your ears ere it be out.
Romeo and Juliet, Act iii, sc. 1, l. 83 [MERCUTIO]

6408   Strip your sword stark naked; for meddle you must, that's
certain, or forswear to wear iron about you.
Twelfth Night, Act iii, sc. 4, l. 275 [SIR TOBY]

T

Tail

6409   We do fear this body hath a tail
More perilous than the head.
Cymbeline, Act iv, sc. 2, l. 144 [BELARIUS]

6410   It should seem, then, that Dobbin's tail grows backward.
The Merchant of Venice, Act ii, sc. 2, l. 102 [LAUNCELOT]

6411   Come cut and long-tail.
The Merry Wives of Windsor, Act iii, sc. 4, l. 47 [SLENDER]

Tailor

6412   CLOTEN : Know'st me not by my clothes?
GUIDERIUS : No, nor thy tailor, rascal.
Who is thy grandfather ; he made those clothes,
Which, as it seems, make thee.
Cymbeline, Act iv, sc. 2, l. 81 [CLOTEN]

6413   KENT : You cowardly rascal, . . . a tailor made thee. . . .
CORNWALL : A tailor make a man?
KENT : Ay, a tailor, sir : a stone-cutter or a painter could not
have made him so ill.
King Lear, Act ii, sc. 2, l. 59 [KENT]

Taking

6414   Who seeks, and will not take when once 'tis offer'd,
Shall never find it more.
Antony and Cleopatra, Act ii, sc. 7, l. 89 [MENAS]

6415   What a taking was he in when your husband asked who was in
the basket!
The Merry Wives of Windsor, Act iii, sc. 3, l. 190 [MRS. PAGE]

Tale

6416   Thereby hangs a tale.
As You Like It, Act ii, sc. 7, l. 28 [JAQUES]
(The phrase is repeated in *The Merry Wives of Windsor,*
i, 4, 159; *The Taming of the Shrew,* iv, 1, 60.)
CLOWN: Are these, I pray you, wind-instruments?
MUSICIAN: Ay, marry, are they, sir.
CLOWN: O, thereby hangs a tail.
MUSICIAN: Whereby hangs a tale, sir?
CLOWN: Marry, sir, by many a wind-instrument that I know.
Othello, Act iii, sc. 1, l. 7 [CLOWN]

6417   But that I am forbid
To tell the secrets of my prison-house,
I could a tale unfold whose lightest word
Would harrow up thy soul, freeze thy young blood,
Make thy two eyes, like stars, start from their spheres,
Thy knotted and combined locks to part
And each particular hair to stand on end,
Like quills upon the fretful porpentine.
Hamlet, Act i, sc. 5, l. 13 [GHOST]

6418   Mark now, how a plain tale shall put you down.
I Henry IV, Act ii, sc. 4, l. 282 [PRINCE]

6419   This is the strangest tale that ever I heard.
I Henry IV, Act v, sc. 4, l. 158 [LANCASTER]

6420   List a brief tale;
And when 'tis told, O, that my heart would burst!
King Lear, Act v, sc. 3, l. 181 [EDGAR]

6421   I will a round unvarnish'd tale deliver.
Othello, Act i, sc. 3, l. 90 [OTHELLO]

6422   In winter's tedious nights sit by the fire
With good old folks and let them tell thee tales
Of woeful ages long ago betid;
And ere thou bid good night, to quit their griefs,
Tell thou the lamentable tale of me.
Richard II, Act v, sc. 1, l. 40 [KING RICHARD]

6423   KING RICHARD: Be eloquent in my behalf to her.
QUEEN ELIZABETH: An honest tale speeds best being plainly told.
Richard III, Act iv, sc. 4, l. 357 [KING RICHARD]

6424   I have seen the day
That I have worn a visor and could tell
A whispering tale in a fair lady's ear,
Such as would please.
Romeo and Juliet, Act i, sc. 5, l. 23 [CAPULET]

6425   Your tale, sir, would cure deafness.
The Tempest, Act i, sc. 2, l. 106 [MIRANDA]

6426   I will tell no tales.
The Tempest, Act v, sc. 1, l. 129 [PROSPERO]

6427   A sad tale's best for winter.
The Winter's Tale, Act ii, sc. 1, l. 25 [MAMILLIUS]

6428   Like an old tale still, which will have metter to rehearse, though
        credit be asleep and not an ear open.
                            The Winter's Tale, Act v, sc. 2, l. 67 [GENTLEMAN]

Talk

6429   [He] talks like a knell, and his hum is a battery.
                            Coriolanus, Act v, sc. 4, l. 22 [MENENIUS]
6430   Talk thy tongue weary; speak:
        I have heard I am a strumpet; and mine ear,
        Therein false struck, can take no greater wound,
        Nor tent to bottom that.
                            Cymbeline, Act iii, sc. 4, l. 116 [IMOGEN]
6431   He angers me
        With telling me of the moldwarp and the ant,
        Of the dreamer Merlin and his prophecies,
        And of a dragon and a finless fish,
        A clip-wing'd griffin and a moulten raven,
        A couching lion and a ramping cat,
        And such a deal of skimble-skamble stuff
        As puts me from my faith. . . . He is as tedious
        As a tired horse, a railing wife;
        Worse than a smoky house: I had rather live
        With cheese and garlic in a windmill, far,
        Than feed on cates and have him talk to me
        In any summer-house in Christendom.
                            I Henry IV, Act iii, sc. 1, l. 148 [HOTSPUR]
6432   [He] talks as familiarly of John a Gaunt as if he had been sworn
        brother to him; and I'll be sworn a' ne'er saw him but once in
        the Tilt-yard.
                            II Henry IV, Act iii, sc. 2, l. 346 [FALSTAFF]
6433   There is no tiddle taddle nor pibble pabble in Pompey's camp.
                            Henry V, Act iv, sc. 1, l. 71 [FLUELLEN]
6434   'Tis no time to talk.
                            III Henry VI, Act iv, sc. 5, l. 24 [GLOUCESTER]
6435   If I chance to talk a little wild, forgive me;
        I had it from my father.
                            Henry VIII, Act i, sc. 4, l. 26 [SANDS]
6436   How you do talk!
                            Henry VIII, Act ii, sc. 3, l. 44 [ANNE BULLEN]
6437   Let it serve for table-talk.
                            The Merchant of Venice, Act iii, sc. 5, l. 93 [LORENZO]
6438   The bookist theoric, . . . mere prattle, without practice.
                            Othello, Act i, sc. 1, l. 24 [IAGO]
6439   GREMIO: What! this gentleman will out-talk us all.
        LUCENTIO: Sir, give him head: I know he'll prove a jade.
                            The Taming of the Shrew, Act i, sc. 2, l. 248 [GREMIO]
6440   SPEED: She doth talk in her sleep.
        LAUNCE: It's no matter for that, so she sleep not in her talk.
                            The Two Gentlemen of Verona, Act iii, sc. 1, l. 333 [SPEED]

Tapster

6441   MOTH: How many is one thrice told?
        ARMADO: I am ill at reckoning; it fitteth the spirit of a tapster.
                            Love's Labour's Lost, Act i, sc. 2, l. 41 [MOTH]
6442   Though you change your place, you need not change your trade;
        I'll be your tapster still.
                            Measure for Measure, Act i, sc. 2, l. 111 [POMPEY]

6443   ESCALUS: What trade are you of, sir?
        POMPEY: A tapster; a poor widow's tapster. . . .
        ESCALUS: Come hither to me, Master Froth. Master Froth, I
        would not have you acquainted with tapsters: they will draw
        you, Master Froth, and you will hang them.
                    Measure for Measure, Act ii, sc. 1, l. 206 [ESCALUS]

6444   FALSTAFF: A tapster is a good trade: an old cloak makes a new
        jerkin; a withered serving-man a fresh tapster. . . .
        BARDOLPH: It is a life that I have desired: I will thrive.
        PISTOL: O base Hungarian wight! wilt thou the spigot wield?
                    The Merry Wives of Windsor, Act i, sc. 3, l. 18 [FALSTAFF]

Task

6445   The long day's task is done, And we must sleep.
                    Antony and Cleopatra, Act iv, sc. 14, l. 35 [ANTONY]

6446   [Their] sore task
        Does not divide the Sunday from the week.
                    Hamlet, Act i, sc. 1, l. 75 [MARCELLUS]

6447   Alas, poor duke! the task he undertakes
        Is numbering sands and drinking oceans dry;
        Where one on his side fights, thousands will fly.
                    Richard II, Act ii, sc. 2, l. 145 [GREEN]

Teaching

6448   It hath been taught us from the primal state,
        That he which is was wish'd until he were;
        And the ebb'd man, ne'er loved till ne'er worth love,
        Comes dear by being lack'd.
                    Antony and Cleopatra, Act i, sc. 4, l. 41 [OCTAVIUS CÆSAR]

6449   Teach me, dear creature, how to think and speak.
                    The Comedy of Errors, Act iii, sc. 2, l. 33
                    [ANTIPHOLUS OF SYRACUSE]

6450   Say, I taught thee,
        Say, Wolsey, that once trod the ways of glory,
        And sounded all the depths and shoals of honour,
        Found thee a way, out of his wreck, to rise in;
        A sure and safe one, though thy master miss'd it.
                    Henry VIII, Act iii, sc. 2, l. 435 [WOLSEY]

6451   I have taught him, even as one would say precisely, 'thus I
        would teach a dog.'
                    The Two Gentlemen of Verona, Act iv, sc. 4, l. 5 [LAUNCE]

Tear

6452   We cannot call her winds and waters sighs and tears; they are
        greater storms and tempests than almanacs can report: . . .
        she makes a shower of rain as well as Jove.
                    Antony and Cleopatra, Act i, sc. 2, l. 154 [ENOBARBUS]

6453   The tears live in an onion that should water this sorrow.
                    Antony and Cleopatra, Act i, sc. 2, l. 176 [ENOBARBUS]

6454   Thou old and true Menenius,
        Thy tears are salter than a younger man's,
        And venomous to thine eyes.
                    Coriolanus, Act iv, sc. 1, l. 21 [CORIOLANUS]

6455   At a few drops of women's rheum, which are
        As cheap as lies, he sold the blood and labour
        Of our great action.
                    Coriolanus, Act v, sc. 6, l. 46 [AUFIDIUS]

6456   My tears that fall Prove holy water on thee.
                              Cymbeline, Act v, sc. 5, l. 268 [CYMBELINE]
6457   She follow'd my poor father's body,
       Like Niobe, all tears.
                              Hamlet, Act i, sc. 2, l. 148 [HAMLET]
6458   Too much of water hast thou, poor Ophelia,
       And therefore I forbid my tears: but yet . . .
       The woman will be out.
                              Hamlet, Act iv, sc. 7, l. 186 [LAERTES]
6459   The pretty and sweet manner of it forced
       Those waters from me which I would have stopp'd;
       But I had not so much of man in me,
       And all my mother came into mine eyes
       And gave me up to tears.
                              Henry V, Act iv, sc. 6, l. 28 [EXETER]
6460   Tears virginal
       Shall be to me even as the dew to fire.
                              II Henry VI, Act v, sc. 2, l. 52 [YOUNG CLIFFORD]
6461   Cromwell, I did not think to shed a tear
       In all my miseries; but thou hast forced me,
       Out of thy honest truth, to play the woman.
                              Henry VIII, Act iii, sc. 2, l. 428 [WOLSEY]
6462   How now, foolish rheum!
       Turning dispiteous torture out of door!
       I must be brief, lest resolution drop
       Out at mine eyes in tender womanish tears.
                              King John, Act iv, sc. 1, l. 33 [HUBERT]
6463   Trust not those cunning waters of his eyes,
       For villany is not without such rheum;
       And he, long traded in it, makes it seem
       Like rivers of remorse and innocency.
                              King John, Act iv, sc. 3, l. 107 [SALISBURY]
6464   Let not women's weapons, water-drops,
       Stain my man's cheeks!
                              King Lear, Act ii, sc. 4, l. 279 [LEAR]
6465   O father, what a hell of witchcraft lies
       In the small orb of one particular tear!
       But with the inundation of the eyes
       What rocky heart to water will not wear?
                              A Lover's Complaint, l. 288
6466   More merry tears
       The passion of loud laughter never shed.
             A Midsummer Night's Dream, Act v, sc. 1, l. 69 [PHILOSTRATE]
6467   Did he break into tears? . . . A kind overflow of kindness: there
       are no faces truer than those that are so washed.
                   Much Ado about Nothing, Act i, sc. 1, l. 24 [LEONATO]
6468   If that the earth could team with woman's tears,
       Each drop she falls would prove a crocodile.
                              Othello, Act iv, sc. 1, l. 256 [OTHELLO]
6469   We'll make foul weather with despised tears;
       Our sighs and they shall lodge the summer corn,
       And make a dearth in this revolting land.
       Or shall we play the wanton with our woes,
       And make some pretty match with shedding tears?
       As thus, to drop them still upon one place,
       Till they have fretted us a pair of graves

Within the earth; and, therein laid,—there lies
Two kinsmen digg'd their graves with weeping eyes.
Richard II, Act iii, sc. 3, l. 161 [KING RICHARD]

6470   Tears show their love, but want their remedies.
Richard II, Act iii, sc. 3, l. 203 [KING RICHARD]

6471   Mine eyes are full of tears, I cannot see:
And yet salt water blinds them not so much
But they can see a sort of traitors here.
Nay, if I turn mine eyes upon myself,
I find myself a traitor with the rest;
For I have given here my soul's consent
To undeck the pompous body of a king;
Made glory base, and sovereignty a slave,
Proud majesty a subject, state a peasant.
Richard II, Act iv, sc. 1, l. 244 [KING RICHARD]

6472   The liquid drops of tears that you have shed
Shall come again, transform'd to orient pearl,
Advantaging their loan with interest
Of ten times double gain of happiness.
Richard III, Act iv, sc. 4, l. 321 [KING RICHARD]

6473   Many a morning hath he there been seen,
With tears augmenting the fresh morning's dew.
Romeo and Juliet, Act i, sc. 1, l. 137 [MONTAGUE]

6474   What potions have I drunk of Siren tears,
Distill'd from hemlocks foul as hell within.
Sonnet cxix, l. 1

6475   And if the boy have not a woman's gift
To rain a shower of commanded tears,
An onion will do well for such a shift,
Which in a napkin being close convey'd
Shall in despite enforce a watery eye.
The Taming of the Shrew, Induction, sc. 1, l. 124 [LORD]

6476   Let it be your glory
To see her tears; but be your heart to them
As unrelenting flint to drops of rain.
Titus Andronicus, Act ii, sc. 3, l. 139 [DEMETRIUS]

6477   Cry, Trojans, cry! lend me ten thousand eyes,
And I will fill them with prophetic tears.
Troilus and Cressida, Act ii, sc. 2, l. 101 [CASSANDRA]

6478   I am yet so near the manners of my mother, that upon the least
occasion more mine eyes will tell tales of me.
Twelfth Night, Act ii, sc. 1, l. 43 [SEBASTIAN]

6479   Why, man, if the river were dry, I am able to fill it with my tears.
The Two Gentlemen of Verona, Act ii, sc. 3, l. 59 [LAUNCE]

Teeth See also **Tooth**

6480   By Isis, I will give thee bloody teeth,
If thou with Cæsar paragon again
My man of men.
Antony and Cleopatra, Act i, sc. 5, l. 70 [CLEOPATRA]

6481   It warms the very sickness in my heart,
That I shall live and tell him to his teeth,
'Thus didest thou.'
Hamlet, Act iv, sc. 7, l. 56 [LAERTES]

6482   When my knightly stomach is sufficed,
Why then I suck my teeth.
King John, Act i, sc. 1, l. 191 [BASTARD]

6483   This is the flower that smiles on every one,
To show his teeth, as white as whale's bone.
Love's Labour's Lost, Act v, sc. 2, l. 331 [BIRON]

Tell-Tale

6484   Therefore will he wipe his tables clean,
And keep no tell-tale to his memory.
II Henry IV, Act iv, sc. 1, l. 201 [ARCHBISHOP]

6485   You speak to Casca, and to such a man
That is no fleering tell-tale.
Julius Cæsar, Act i, sc. 3, l. 116 [CASCA]

6486   We are no tell-tales, madam; fear you not.
The Merchant of Venice, Act v, sc. 1, l. 123 [LORENZO]

6487   An honest, willing, kind fellow, . . . and I warrant you no tell-tale nor no breed-bate.
The Merry Wives of Windsor, Act i, sc. 4, l. 11
[MISTRESS QUICKLY]

Temper

6488   You keep a constant temper.
Coriolanus, Act v, sc. 2, l. 100 [AUFIDIUS]

6489   I know you have a gentle, noble temper,
A soul as even as a calm.
Henry VIII, Act iii, sc. 1, l. 165 [WOLSEY]

6490   The brain may devise laws for the blood, but a hot temper
leaps o'er a cold decree.
The Merchant of Venice, Act i, sc. 2, l. 19 [PORTIA]

Temperance

6491   What hotter hours,
Unregister'd in vulgar fame, you have
Luxuriously pick'd out: for, I am sure,
Though you can guess what temperance should be,
You know not what it is.
Antony and Cleopatra, Act iii, sc. 13, l. 118 [ANTONY]

6492   What, are you chafed?
Ask God for temperance; that 's the appliance only
Which your disease requires.
Henry VIII, Act i, sc. 1, l. 124 [NORFOLK]

Tempest

6493   I have seen tempests, when the scolding winds
Have rived the knotty oaks, and I have seen
The ambitious ocean swell and rage and foam,
To be exalted with the threatening clouds:
But never till to-night, never till now,
Did I go through a tempest dropping fire.
Either there is a civil strife in heaven,
Or else the world, too saucy with the gods,
Incenses them to send destruction.
Julius Cæsar, Act i, sc. 3, l. 5 [CASCA]

6494   If after every tempest come such calms,
May the winds blow till they have waken'd death!
And let the labouring bark climb hills of seas
Olympus-high and duck again as low
As hell's from heaven!
Othello, Act ii, sc. 1, l. 187 [OTHELLO]

6495   But, lords, we hear this fearful tempest sing,

Yet seek no shelter to avoid the storm;
We see the wind sit sore upon our sails,
And yet we strike not, but securely perish.
>> *Richard II,* Act ii, sc. 1, l. 263 [NORTHUMBERLAND]

Temptation

6496 'Tis one thing to be tempted, Escalus,
Another thing to fall.
>> *Measure for Measure,* Act ii, sc. 1, l. 17 [ANGELO]

6497 I am that way going to temptation,
Where prayers cross.
>> *Measure for Measure,* Act ii, sc. 2, l. 158 [ANGELO]

6498 The tempter or the tempted, who sins most?
>> *Measure for Measure,* Act ii, sc. 2, l. 164 [ANGELO]

6499 Most dangerous
Is that temptation that doth goad us on
To sin in loving virtue.
>> *Measure for Measure,* Act ii, sc. 2, l. 181 [ANGELO]

6500 I never tempted her with word too large;
But, as a brother to his sister, show'd
Bashful sincerity and comely love.
>> *Much Ado about Nothing,* Act iv, sc. 1, l. 53 [CLAUDIO]

6501 Good gentle youth, tempt not a desperate man.
>> *Romeo and Juliet,* Act v, sc. 3, l. 59 [ROMEO]

Testament See also **Will**

6502 'Poor deer,' quoth he, 'thou makest a testament
As worldings do, giving thy sum of more
To that which had too much.'
>> *As You Like It,* Act ii, sc. 1, l. 47 [FIRST LORD]

6503 Here 's a parchment with the seal of Cæsar; . . .
Let but the commons hear this testament . . .
And they would go and kiss dead Cæsar's wounds
And dip their napkins in his sacred blood,
Yea, beg a hair of him for memory,
And, dying, mention it within their wills,
Bequeathing it as a rich legacy
Unto their issue.
>> *Julius Cæsar,* Act iii, sc. 2, l. 133 [ANTONY]

Thanks

6504 Proffers not took reap thanks for their reward.
>> *All's Well that Ends Well,* Act ii, sc. 1, l. 150 [KING]

6505 The thanks I give
Is telling you that I am poor of thanks
And scarce can spare them.
>> *Cymbeline,* Act ii, sc. 3, l. 93 [IMOGEN]

6506 Receive such thanks As fits a king's remembrance.
>> *Hamlet,* Act ii, sc. 2, l. 25 [QUEEN]

6507 Beggar that I am, I am even poor in thanks; but I thank you:
and sure, dear friends, my thanks are too dear a halfpenny.
>> *Hamlet,* Act ii, sc. 2, l. 280 [HAMLET]

6508 Take his thanks that yet hath nothing else.
>> *III Henry VI,* Act v, sc. 4, l. 59 [PRINCE EDWARD]

6509 For your great graces
Heap'd upon me, poor undeserver, I
Can nothing render but allegiant thanks.
>> *Henry VIII,* Act iii, sc. 2, l. 174 [WOLSEY]

6510 My recompense is thanks, that's all;
Yet my good will is great, though the gift small.
Pericles, Act iii, sc. 4, l. 17 [THAISA]

6511 All my treasury Is yet but unfelt thanks. . . .
Evermore thanks, the exchequer of the poor.
Richard II, Act ii, sc. 3, l. 60 [BOLINGBROKE]

6512 CAPULET: Doth she not give us thanks? Is she not proud? . . .
JULIET: Proud can I never be of what I hate;
But thankful even for hate, that it meant love.
CAPULET: How now, now now, chop-logic! What is this? . . .
Thank me no thankings, nor proud me no prouds.
Romeo and Juliet, Act iii, sc. 5, l. 143 [CAPULET]

6513 This kindness merits thanks. . . .
The poorest service is repaid with thanks.
The Taming of the Shrew, Act iv, sc. 3, l. 41 [PETRUCHIO]

6514 Thanks to men
Of noble minds is honourable meed.
Titus Andronicus, Act i, sc. 1, l. 215 [BASSIANUS]

6515 I give thee thanks in part of thy deserts,
And will with deeds requite thy gentleness.
Titus Andronicus, Act i, sc. 1, l. 236 [SATURNINUS]

6516 I can no other answer make but thanks,
And thanks, and ever; oft good turns
Are shuffled off with such uncurrent pay.
Twelfth Night, Act iii, sc. 3, l. 14 [SEBASTIAN]

Theft

6517 Nym and Bardolph are sworn brothers in filching, and in Calais
they stole a fire-shovel: I knew by that piece of service the men
would carry coals.
Henry V, Act iii, sc. 2, l. 48 [BOY]

6518 His thefts were too open; his filching was like an unskilful
singer; he kept not time.
The Merry Wives of Windsor, Act i, sc. 3, l. 28 [FALSTAFF]

6519 Let us not be dainty of leave-taking,
But shift away: there's warrant in that theft
Which steals away, when there's no mercy left.
Macbeth, Act ii, sc. 3, l. 150 [MALCOLM]

6520 I'll example you with thievery:
The sun's a thief, and with his great attraction
Robs the vast sea: the moon's an arrant thief,
And her pale fire she snatches from the sun:
The sea's a thief, whose liquid surge resolves
The moon into salt tears: the earth's a thief,
That feeds and breathes by a composture stolen
From general excrement: each thing's a thief.
Timon of Athens, Act iv, sc. 3, l. 438 [TIMON]

6521 O, theft most base,
That we have stol'n what we do fear to keep!
Troilus and Cressida, Act ii, sc. 2, l. 92 [TROILUS]

6522 We would give much, to use violent thefts,
And rob in the behalf of charity.
Troilus and Cressida, Act v, sc. 3, l. 21 [ANDROMACHE]

Theft: The Thief

6523 If our eyes had authority, here they might take two thieves kissing.
Antony and Cleopatra, Act ii, sc. 6, l. 99 [ENOBARBUS]

6524   What simple thief brags of his own attaint?
                    The Comedy of Errors, Act iii, sc. 2, l. 16 [LUCIANA]
6525   A plague upon it when thieves cannot be true to one another!
                    I Henry IV, Act ii, sc. 2, l. 30 [FALSTAFF]
6526   The thieves are all scatter'd and possess'd with fear
        So strongly that they dare not meet each other;
        Each takes his fellow for an officer.
                    I Henry IV, Act ii, sc. 2, l. 112 [PRINCE]
6527   See how yond justice rails upon yond simple thief. Hark, in thine
        ear: change places; and, handy-dandy, which is the justice, which
        is the thief?
                    King Lear, Act iv, sc. 6, l. 155 [LEAR]
6528   Thieves for their robbery have authority
        When judges steal themselves.
                    Measure for Measure, Act ii, sc. 2, l. 176 [ANGELO]
6529   Every true man's apparel fits your thief: if it be too little for
        your thief, your true man thinks it big enough; if it be too big
        for your thief, your thief thinks it is little enough: so every true
        man's apparel fits your thief.
                    Measure for Measure, Act iv, sc. 2, l. 46 [ABHORSON]
6530   If you meet a thief, you may suspect him, by virtue of your office,
        to be no true man: and, for such kind of men, the less you meddle
        or make with them, why, the more is for your honesty.
                    Much Ado about Nothing, Act iii, sc. 3, l. 53 [DOGBERRY]
6531   BORACHIO: What a deformed thief this fashion is.
        WATCH: I know that Deformed; a' has been a vile thief this
        seven year; a' goes up and down like a gentleman: I remember
        his name. . . . I know him; a' wears a lock.
                    Much Ado about Nothing, Act iii, sc. 3, l. 131 [BORACHIO]
6532   Rich preys make true men thieves.
                    Venus and Adonis, l. 724 [VENUS]

Thing

6533   If things go well.
                    Coriolanus, Act i, sc. 1, l. 274 [SICINIUS]
        They can tell you how things go.
                    The Merry Wives of Windsor, Act iii, sc. 4, l. 69 [SLENDER]
        You shall hear how things go.
                    The Merry Wives of Windsor, Act iv, sc. 5, l. 126
                                    [MISTRESS QUICKLY]
6534   Presume not that I am the thing I was.
                    II Henry IV, Act v, sc. 5, l. 60 [KING HENRY]
6535   I see a thing Bitter to me as death.
                    Cymbeline, Act v, sc. 5, l. 103 [IMOGEN]
6536   Men may construe things after their fashion,
        Clean from the purpose of the things themselves.
                    Julius Cæsar, Act i, sc. 3, l. 34 [CICERO]
6537   Can such things be?
                    Macbeth, Act iii, sc. 4, l. 110 [MACBETH]
6538   In such indexes, although small pricks
        To their subsequent volumes, there is seen
        The baby figure of the giant mass
        Of things to come at large.
                    Troilus and Cressida, Act i, sc. 3, l. 343 [NESTOR]
6539   What one thing, what another.
                    Troilus and Cressida, Act v, sc. 3, l. 103 [PANDARUS]

Thorn See also Rose and Thorn

6540   The care you have of us,
To mow down thorns that would annoy our foot,
Is worthy praise.
                    II Henry VI, Act iii, sc. 1, l. 66 [KING HENRY]

6541   What! can so young a thorn begin to prick?
                    III Henry VI, Act v, sc. 5, l. 13 [KING EDWARD]

6542   I know what thorns the growing rose defends.
                    The Rape of Lucrece, l. 492 [TARQUIN]

Thought

6543   He was disposed to mirth; but on the sudden
A Roman thought hath struck him.
                    Anthony and Cleopatra, Act i, sc. 2, l. 86 [CLEOPATRA]

6544   ROSALIND: Certainly a woman's thought runs before her actions.
ORLANDO: So do all thoughts; they are winged.
                    As You Like It, Act iv, sc. 1, l. 140 [ROSALIND]

6545   There is nothing either good or bad, but thinking makes it so.
                    Hamlet, Act ii, sc. 2, l. 256 [HAMLET]

6546   Thou art a blessed fellow to think as every man thinks: never
a man's thought in the world keeps the road-way better than
thine.
                    II Henry IV, Act ii, sc. 2, l. 61 [PRINCE]

6547   Do you think me a swallow, an arrow or a bullet? have I, in
my poor and old motion, the expedition of thought?
                    II Henry IV, Act iv, sc. 3, l. 37 [FALSTAFF]

6548   Faster than spring-time showers comes thought on thought,
And not a thought but thinks on dignity.
                    II Henry VI, Act iii, sc. 1, l. 337 [YORK]

6549   Chew upon this.
                    Julius Cæsar, Act i, sc. 2, l. 171 [BRUTUS]

6550   You do unbend your noble strength to think
So brainsickly of things.
                    Macbeth, Act ii, sc. 2, l. 45 [LADY MACBETH]

6551   BENVOLIO: Be ruled by me, forget to think of her.
ROMEO: O, teach me how I can forget to think.
BENVOLIO: By giving liberty unto thine eyes;
Examine other beauties.
                    Romeo and Juliet, Act i, sc. 1, l. 231 [BENVOLIO]

6552   Nimble thought can jump both sea and land
As soon as think the place where he would be.
                    Sonnet xliv, l. 7

6553   Flout 'em and scout 'em
And scout 'em and flout 'em;
    Thought is free.
                    The Tempest, Act iii, sc. 2, l. 130 [STEPHANO]

Thought is free.
                    Twelfth Night, Act i, sc. 3, l. 73 [MARIA]

Thoughts

6554   Our worser thoughts heavens mend!
                    Antony and Cleopatra, Act i, sc. 2, l. 64 [CHARMIAN]

6555   Make not your thoughts your prisons.
                    Antony and Cleopatra, Act v, sc. 2, l. 185 [CÆSAR]

6556   Give thy thoughts no tongue,
Nor any unproportion'd thought his act.
                    Hamlet, Act i, sc. 3, l. 59 [POLONIUS]

6557 Our thoughts are ours, their ends none of our own.
                    Hamlet, Act iii, sc. 2, l. 223 [PLAYER KING]
6558   O, from this time forth,
      My thoughts be bloody, or be nothing worth.
                    Hamlet, Act iv, sc. 4, l. 65 [HAMLET]
      I do begin to have bloody thoughts.
                    The Tempest, Act iv, sc. 1, l. 220 [STEPHANO]
6559 My thoughts are whirled like a potter's wheel;
      I know not where I am, nor what I do.
                    I Henry VI, Act i, sc. 5, l. 19 [TALBOT]
6560 Now, York, or never steel thy fearful thoughts,
      And change misdoubt to resolution.
                    II Henry VI, Act iii, sc. 1, l. 331 [YORK]
6561   I am afraid
      His thinkings are below the moon, not worth
      His serious considering.
                    Henry VIII, Act iii, sc. 2, l. 133 [KING HENRY]
6562   Merciful powers,
      Restrain in me the cursed thoughts that nature
      Gives way to in repose!
                    Macbeth, Act ii, sc. 1, l. 7 [BANQUO]
6563 Give thy worst of thoughts The worst of words.
                    Othello, Act iii, sc. 3, l. 132 [OTHELLO]
6564 Unstain'd thoughts do seldom dream on evil.
                    The Rape of Lucrece, l. 87
6565 Thoughts are but dreams till their effects be tried.
                    The Rape of Lucrece, l. 353 [TARQUIN]
6566 Thoughts tending to ambition, they do plot
      Unlikely wonders; how these vain weak nails
      May tear a passage through the flinty ribs
      Of this hard world, my ragged prison walls,
      And, for they cannot, die in their own pride.
      Thoughts tending to content flatter themselves
      That they are not the first of fortune's slaves,
      Nor shall not be the last; like silly beggars
      Who sitting in the stocks refuge their shame,
      That many have and others must sit there;
      And in this thought they find a kind of ease,
      Bearing their own misfortunes on the back
      Of such as have before endured the like.
                    Richard II, Act v, sc. 5, l. 18 [KING RICHARD]
6567 Fair thoughts be your fair pillow!
                    Troilus and Cressida, Act iii, sc. 1, l. 49 [PANDARUS]
6568 My thoughts were like unbridled children grown
      Too headstrong for their mother.
                    Troilus and Cressida, Act iii, sc. 2, l. 130 [CRESSIDA]
6569   He cures in me
      Thoughts that would thick my blood.
                    The Winter's Tale, Act i, sc. 2, l. 170 [POLIXENES]

Threat

6570 There is no terror, Cassius, in your threats,
      For I am arm'd so strong in honesty
      That they pass by me as the idle wind,
      Which I respect not.
                    Julius Cæsar, Act iv, sc. 3, l. 67 [BRUTUS]

6571   Why, boy, although our mother, unadvised,
        Gave you a dancing rapier by your side,
        Are you so desperate grown, to threat your friends.
                        Titus Andronicus, Act ii, sc. 1, l. 38 [DEMETRIUS]

Three

6572   ARMADO: The fox, the ape, the humble-bee,
        Were still at odds, being but three.
        MOTH: Until the goose came out of door,
        And stay'd the odds by adding four.
                        Love's Labour's Lost, Act iii, sc. 1, l. 90 [ARMADO]
6573   FIRST WITCH: When shall we three meet again
        In thunder, lightning, or in rain?
        SECOND WITCH: When the hurlyburly's done,
        When the battle's lost and won.
        THIRD WITCH: That will be ere the set of sun. . . .
        ALL: Fair is foul, and foul is fair:
        Hover through the fog and filthy air.
                        Macbeth, Act i, sc. 1, l. 1 [FIRST WITCH]

Thrift

6574   HAMLET: But what is your affair in Elsinore? . . .
        HORATIO: My lord, I came to see your father's funeral.
        HAMLET: I pray thee, do not mock me, fellow student;
        I think it was to see my mother's wedding.
        HORATIO: Indeed, my lord, it follow'd hard upon.
        HAMLET: Thrift, thrift Horatio! the funeral baked meats
        Did coldly furnish forth the marriage tables.
        Would I had met my dearest foe in heaven
        Or ever I had seen that day, Horatio!
                        Hamlet, Act i, sc. 2, l. 174 [HAMLET]
6575   How, i' the name of thrift, Did he rake this together?
                        Henry VIII, Act iii, sc. 2, l. 109 [KING HENRY]
6576   Thrift is blessing, if men steal it not.
                        The Merchant of Venice, Act i, sc. 3, l. 91 [SHYLOCK]
6577   Hold, sirrah, bear you these letters tightly:
        Sail like my pinnace to these golden shores.
        Rogues, hence, avaunt! vanish like hail-stones go:
        Trudge, plod away o' the hoof; seek shelter, pack!
        Falstaff will learn the humour of the age,
        French thrift, you rogues; myself and skirted page.
                        The Merry Wives of Windsor, Act i, sc. 3, l. 88 [FALSTAFF]

Throne

6578   The head is not more native to the heart,
        The hand more instrumental to the mouth,
        Than is the throne of Denmark to thy father.
                        Hamlet, Act i, sc. 2, l. 47 [KING]
6579   Let the world take note,
        You are the most immediate to our throne.
                        Hamlet, Act i, sc. 2, l. 108 [KING]
6580   God and his angels guard your sacred throne
        And make you long become it.
                        Henry V, Act i, sc. 2, l. 7 [CANTERBURY]

Thumb

6581 By the pricking of my thumbs,
Something wicked this way comes.
Open, locks, whoever knocks!
Macbeth, Act iv, sc. 1, l. 44 [WITCH]

6582 SAMPSON: I will bite my thumb at them; which is a disgrace to
them, if they bear it. . . .
ABRAHAM: Do you bite your thumb at us, sir? . . .
SAMPSON: No, sir, I do not bite my thumb at you, sir, but I bite
my thumb, sir.
Romeo and Juliet, Act i, sc. 1, l. 48 [SAMPSON]

Thunder

6583   Thou hast affected . . .
To tear with thunder the wide cheeks o' the air,
And yet to charge thy sulphur with a bolt
That should but rive an oak.
Coriolanus, Act v, sc. 3, l. 151 [VOLUMNIA]

6584   Are ye so hot, sir? . . .
If Talbot do but thunder, rain will follow.
I Henry VI, Act iii, sc. 2, l. 58 [PUCELLE]

6585 You sulphurous and thought-executing fires,
Vaunt-couriers to oak-cleaving thunderbolts,
Singe my white head! And thou, all-shaking thunder,
Smite flat the thick rotundity o' the world!
Crack nature's moulds, all germans spill at once,
That make ungrateful man!
King Lear, Act iii, sc. 2, l. 4 [LEAR]

6586 What is the cause of thunder?
King Lear, Act iii, sc. 4, l. 160 [LEAR]

6587   Could great men thunder
As Jove himself does, Jove would ne'er be quiet,
For every pelting, petty officer
Would use his heaven for thunder;
Nothing but thunder! Merciful Heaven,
Thou rather with thy sharp and sulphurous bolt
Split'st the unwedgeable and gnarled oak
Than the soft myrtle.
Measure for Measure, Act ii, sc. 2, l. 110 [ISABELLA]

6588   Have I not heard . . .
Heaven's artillery thunder in the skies?
The Taming of the Shrew, Act i, sc. 2, l. 205 [PETRUCHIO]

6589   Methought . . . the thunder,
That deep and dreadful organ-pipe, pronounced
The name of Prosper.
The Tempest, Act iii, sc. 3, l. 98 [ALONZO]

6590   To the dread rattling thunder
Have I given fire and rifted Jove's stout oak
With his own bolt.
The Tempest, Act v, sc. 1, l. 44 [PROSPERO]

Tide

6591 There is a tide in the affairs of men,
Which, taken at the flood, leads on to fortune;
Omitted, all the voyage of their life
Is bound in shallows and in miseries.
On such a full sea are we now afloat;

And we must take the current when it serves,
Or lose our ventures.

Julius Cæsar, Act iv, sc. 3, l. 218 [BRUTUS]

6592   My uncontrolled tide
Turns not, but swells the higher by this let.

The Rape of Lucrece, l. 645 [TARQUIN]

6593   The approaching tide
Will shortly fill the reasonable shore
That now lies foul and muddy.

The Tempest, Act v, sc. 1, l. 80 [PROSPERO]

Tidings

6594   Ram thou thy fruitful tidings in mine ears,
That long time have been barren. . . .
Pour out the pack of matter to mine ear,
The good and bad together.

Antony and Cleopatra, Act ii, sc. 5, l. 24 [CLEOPATRA]

6595   I prithee, take the cork out of thy mouth that I may drink thy tidings.

As You Like It, Act iii, sc. 2, l. 209 [ROSALIND]

6596   DOUGLAS: That's the worst tidings that I hear of yet.
WORCESTER: Ay, by my faith, that bears a frosty sound.

I Henry IV, Act iv, sc. 1, l. 127 [DOUGLAS]

6597   NORTHUMBERLAND: What good tidings comes with you? . . .
TRAVERS: Joyful tidings.

II Henry IV, Act i, sc. 1, l. 33 [NORTHUMBERLAND]

6598   Good tidings, my Lord Hastings.

II Henry IV, Act iv, sc. 2, l. 106 [WESTMORELAND]

6599   Sad tidings I bring to you out of France,
Of loss, of slaughter and discomfiture.

I Henry VI, Act i, sc. 1, l. 58 [MESSENGER]

6600   These tidings nip me, and I hang the head
As flowers with frost or grass beat down with storms.

Titus Andronicus, Act iv, sc. 4, l. 70 [SATURNINUS]

Tiger

6601   The tiger now hath seized the gentle hind.

Richard III, Act ii, sc. 4, l. 50 [QUEEN ELIZABETH]

6602   When did the tiger's young ones teach the dam?

Titus Andronicus, Act ii, sc. 3, l. 142 [LAVINIA]

Time

6603   I play the noble housewife with the time
To entertain 't so merrily with a fool.

All's Well that Ends Well, Act ii, sc. 2, l. 62 [COUNTESS]

6604   We are old, and on our quick'st decrees
The inaudible and noiseless foot of Time
Steals ere we can effect them.

All's Well that Ends Well, Act v, sc. 3, l. 40 [KING]

6605   Every time
Serves for the matter that is then born in 't.

Antony and Cleopatra, Act ii, sc. 2, l. 9 [ENOBARBUS]

6606   They live like the old Robin Hood of England, . . . and fleet the time carelessly, as they did in the golden world.

As You Like It, Act i, sc. 1, l. 122 [CHARLES]

6607   I like this place,
And willingly could waste my time in it.
                As You Like It, Act ii, sc. 4, l. 94 [CELIA]

6608   Under the shade of melancholy boughs,
Lose and neglect the creeping hours of time.
                As You Like It, Act ii, sc. 7, l. 111 [ORLANDO]

6609   Time travels in divers paces with divers persons. . . . He trots
hard with a young maid between the contract of her marriage and
the day it is solemnized. . . . [He] ambles with a priest that lacks
Latin and a rich man that hath not the gout. . . . [He gallops]
with a thief to the gallows. . . . [He stands still] with lawyers
in the vacation.
                As You Like It, Act iii, sc. 2, l. 325 [ROSALIND]

6610   Time is the old justice that examines all such offenders, and let
Time try.
                As You Like It, Act iv, sc. 1, l. 203 [ROSALIND]

6611   ANTIPHOLUS S.: There's a time for all things. . . .
DROMIO S.: There's no time for a man to recover his hair that
grows bald by nature. . . . Time himself is bald and therefore to
the world's end will have bald followers.
The Comedy of Errors, Act ii, sc. 2, l. 66 [ANTIPHOLUS OF SYRACUSE]

6612   'Tis high time that I were hence.
                The Comedy of Errors, Act iii, sc. 2, l. 162
                                [ANTIPHOLUS OF SYRACUSE]

6613   Have you not heard men say
That Time comes stealing on by night and day?
        The Comedy of Errors, Act iv, sc. 2, l. 59 [DROMIO OF SYRACUSE]

6614   The time is out of joint: O cursed spite,
That ever I was born to set it right!
                Hamlet, Act i, sc. 5, l. 189 [HAMLET]

6615   FALSTAFF: Now, Hal, what time of day is it, lad? . . .
PRINCE: What a devil hast thou to do with the time of the day?
Unless hours were cups of sack and minutes capons and clocks the
tongues of bawds and dials the signs of leaping-houses and the
blessed sun himself a fair hot wench in flame-coloured taffeta, I
see no reason why thou shouldst be so superfluous to demand
the time of the day.
                I Henry IV, Act i, sc. 2, l. 1 [FALSTAFF]

6616   We see which way the stream of time doth run,
And are enforced from our most quiet there
By the rough torrent of occasion.
                II Henry IV, Act iv, sc. 1, l. 70 [ARCHBISHOP]

6617   For holy offices I have a time; a time
To think upon the part of business which
I bear i' the state; and nature does require
Her times of preservation, which perforce
I, her frail son, amongst my brethren mortal,
Must give my tendance to.
                Henry VIII, Act iii, sc. 2, l. 144 [WOLSEY]

6618   Many a time and oft
Have you climb'd up to walls and battlements.
                Julius Cæsar, Act i, sc. 1, l. 42 [MARULLUS]
        Many a time and oft
In the Rialto you have rated me.
                The Merchant of Venice, Act i, sc. 3, l. 108 [SHYLOCK]
Many a time and often I ha' dined with him.
                Timon of Athens, Act iii, sc. 1, l. 25 [LUCULLUS]

6619   This day I breathed first: time is come round,
        And where I did begin, there shall I end;
        My life is run his compass.
                        Julius Cæsar, Act v, sc. 3, l. 23 [CASSIUS]

6620   Old Time, the clock-setter, that bald sexton Time,
        Is it as he will?
                        King John, Act iii, sc. 1, l. 324 [BASTARD]

6621   Time shall unfold what plaited cunning hides.
                        King Lear, Act i, sc. 1, l. 283 [CORDELIA]

6622   If you can look into the seeds of time,
        And say which grain will grow and which will not,
        Speak then to me, who neither beg nor fear
        Your favours nor your hate.
                        Macbeth, Act i, sc. 3, l. 58 [BANQUO]

6623   Come what come may,
        Time and the hour runs through the roughest day.
                        Macbeth, Act i, sc. 3, l. 147 [MACBETH]

6624   To beguile the time, Look like the time.
                        Macbeth, Act i, sc. 5, l. 64 [LADY MACBETH]

6625   Nor time nor place Did then adhere.
                        Macbeth, Act i, sc. 7, l. 51 [LADY MACBETH]

6626   There are many events in the womb of time which will be
        delivered.
                        Othello, Act i, sc. 3, l. 377 [IAGO]

6627   Time's the king of men,
        For he's their parent, and he is their grave,
        And gives them what he will, not what they crave.
                        Pericles, Act ii, sc. 3, l. 45 [PERICLES]

6628   Time's office is to fine the hate of foes;
        To eat up errors by opinion bred; . . .
        Time's glory is to calm contending kings,
        To unmask falsehood and bring truth to light; . . .
        To cheer the ploughman with increaseful crops,
        And waste huge stones with little water-drops.
                        The Rape of Lucrece, l. 936 [LUCRECE]

6629   Let him have time to mark how slow time goes
        In time of sorrow, and how swift and short
        His time of folly and his time of sport.
                        The Rape of Lucrece, l. 990 [LUCRECE]

6630   O Time, thou tutor both to good and bad,
        Teach me to curse him that thou taught'st this ill.
                        The Rape of Lucrece, l. 995 [LUCRECE]

6631   O, call back yesterday, bid time return! . . .
        To-day, to-day, unhappy day, too late,
        O'erthrows thy joys, friends, fortune and thy state.
                        Richard II, Act iii, sc. 2, l. 69 [SALISBURY]

6632   Music do I hear?
        Ha, ha! keep time: how sour sweet music is,
        When time is broke, and no proportion kept!
        So is it in the music of men's lives. . . .
        I wasted time, and now doth time waste me;
        For now hath time made me his numbering clock:
        My thoughts are minutes; and with sighs they jar
        Their watches on unto mine eyes, the outward watch,
        Whereto my finger, like a dial's point
        Is pointing still, in cleansing them from tears.
                        Richard II, Act v, sc. 5, l. 41 [KING RICHARD]

6633   Never-resting time leads summer on
        To hideous winter and confounds him there.

Sonnet v, l. 5

6634   Devouring Time, blunt thou the lion's paws,
        And make the earth devour her own sweet brood;
        Pluck the keen teeth from the fierce tiger's jaws,
        And burn the long-lived phœnix in her blood;
        Make glad the sorry seasons as thou fleets,
        And do whate'er thou wilt, swift-footed Time,
        To the wide world and all her fading sweets;
        But I forbid thee one more heinous crime:
        O, carve not with thy hours my love's fair brow,
        Nor draw no lines there with thine antique pen.
        Him in thy course untainted do allow
        For beauty's pattern to succeeding men.
        Yet, do thy worst, old Time: despite thy wrong,
        My love shall in my verse ever live young.

Sonnet xix, l. 1

6635   Time doth transfix the flourish set on youth
        And delves the parallels in beauty's brow,
        Feeds on the rarities of nature's truth,
        And nothing stands but for his scythe to mow.

Sonnet lx, l. 9

6636   When I have seen by Time's fell hand defaced
        The rich proud cost of outworn buried age;
        When sometime lofty towers I see down-razed
        And brass eternal slave to mortal rage; . . .
        Ruin hath taught me thus to ruminate,
        That Time will come and take my love away.

Sonnet lxiv, l. 1

6637   Rocks impregnable are not so stout,
        Nor gates of steel so strong, but Time decays.

Sonnet lxv, l. 8

6638   That time of year thou mayst in me behold
        When yellow leaves, or none, or few, do hang
        Upon those boughs which shake against the cold,
        Bare ruin'd choirs, where late the sweet birds sang.

Sonnet lxxiii, l. 1

6639   Thou by the dial's shady stealth mayst know
        Time's thievish progress to eternity.

Sonnet lxxvii, l. 7

6640   What seest thou else
        In the dark backward and abysm of time?

The Tempest, Act i, sc. 2, l. 49 [PROSPERO]

6641   The gods are above; time must friend or end.

Troilus and Cressida, Act i, sc. 2, l. 83 [PANDARUS]

6642   Time hath, my lord, a wallet at his back,
        Wherein he puts alms for oblivion,
        A great-sized monster of ingratitudes:
        Those scraps are good deeds past; which are devour'd
        As fast as they are made, forgot as soon
        As done. . . . For time is like a fashionable host
        That slightly shakes his parting guest by the hand,
        And with his arms outstretch'd, as he would fly,
        Grasps in the comer.

Troilus and Cressida, Act iii, sc. 3, l. 145 [ULYSSES]

6643 Injurious time now with a robber's haste
Crams his rich thievery up, he knows not how:
As many farewells as be stars in heaven, . . .
He fumbles up into a loose adieu,
And scants us with a single famish'd kiss,
Distasted with the salt of broken tears.
Troilus and Cressida, Act iv, sc. 4, l. 44 [TROILUS]

6644 Thus the whirligig of time brings in his revenges.
Twelfth Night, Act v, sc. 1, l. 385 [CLOWN]

6645 Time is the nurse and breeder of all good.
The Two Gentlemen of Verona, Act iii, sc. 1, l. 243 [PROTEUS]

Times

6646 The times are wild; contention, like a horse
Full of high feeding, madly hath broke loose
And bears down all before him.
II Henry IV, Act i, sc. 1, l. 9 [NORTHUMBERLAND]

6647 Construe the times to their necessities,
And you will say indeed, it is the time
And not the king, that doth you injuries.
II Henry IV, Act iv, sc. 1, l. 105 [WESTMORELAND]

6648 O, these naughty times
Put bars between the owners and their rights!
The Merchant of Venice, Act iii, sc. 2, l. 18 [PORTIA]

Title

6649 Him that thou magnifiest with all these titles
Stinking and fly-blown lies here at our feet.
I Henry VI, Act iv, sc. 7, l. 75 [PUCELLE]

6650 Now does he feel his title
Hang loose about him, like a giant's robe
Upon a dwarfish thief.
Macbeth, Act v, sc. 2, l. 20 [ANGUS]

Tom

6651 Who gives any thing to poor Tom? whom the foul fiend hath
led through fire and through flame, through ford and whirlpool,
o'er bog and quagmire? . . . Bless thy five wits! Tom's a-cold.
. . . Do poor Tom some charity, whom the foul fiend vexes. . . .
Tom's a-cold.
King Lear, Act iii, sc. 4, l. 51 [EDGAR]

6652 Poor Tom; that eats the swimming frog, the toad, the tadpole,
the wall-newt and the water; drinks the green mantle of the
standing pool; . . .
  But mice and rats, and such small deer,
  Have been Tom's food for seven long year.
King Lear, Act iii, sc. 4, l. 134 [EDGAR]

Tongue

6653 Many a man's tongue shakes out his master's undoing.
All's Well that Ends Well, Act ii, sc. 4, l. 24 [CLOWN]

6654 Tongue, I must put you into a butterwoman's mouth and buy
myself another of Bajazet's mule, if you prattle me into these
perils.
All's Well that Ends Well, Act iv, sc. 1, l. 43 [PAROLLES]

6655 Speak to me home, mince not the general tongue.
Antony and Cleopatra, Act i, sc. 2, l. 109 [ANTONY]

6656   Her tongue will not obey her heart, nor can
Her heart inform her tongue,—the swan's down-feather,
That stands upon the swell at full of tide,
And neither way inclines.
                    Antony and Cleopatra, Act iii, sc. 2, 1. 47 [ANTONY]

6657   Cry 'holla' to thy tongue, I prithee; it curvets unseasonably.
                    As You Like It, Act iii, sc. 2, 1. 257 [CELIA]

6658   Be not thy tongue thy own shame's orator.
                    The Comedy of Errors, Act iii, sc. 2, 1. 10 [LUCIANA]

6659   He hath a killing tongue and a quiet sword.
                    Henry V, Act iii, sc. 2, 1. 36 [BOY]

6660   This knave's tongue begins to double.
                    II Henry VI, Act ii, sc. 3, 1. 93 [YORK]

6661   Let thy tongue be equal with thy heart.
                    II Henry VI, Act v, sc. 1, 1. 89 [YORK]

6662   She-wolf of France, . . .
Whose tongue more poisons than the adder's tooth.
                    III Henry VI, Act i, sc. 4, 1. 111 [YORK]

6663   O, that my tongue were in the thunder's mouth!
Then with a passion I would shake the world.
                    King John, Act iii, sc. 4, 1. 38 [CONSTANCE]

6664   She hath . . . struck me with her tongue,
Most serpent-like, upon the very heart.
                    King Lear, Act ii, sc. 4, 1. 161 [LEAR]

6665   So on the tip of his subduing tongue
All kind of arguments and question deep,
All replication prompt, and reason strong,
For his advantage still did wake and sleep:
To make the weeper laugh, the laugher weep,
He had the dialect and different skill,
Catching all passions in his craft of will.
                    A Lover's Complaint, 1. 120

6666   Maiden-tongued he was, and thereof free.
                    A Lover's Complaint, 1. 100

6667   The tongues of mocking wenches are as keen
    As is the razor's edge invisible,
Cutting a smaller hair than may be seen,
    Above the sense of sense; so sensible
Seemeth their conference; their conceits have wings
Fleeter than arrows, bullets, wind, thought, swifter things.
                    Love's Labour's Lost, Act v, sc. 2, 1. 256 [BOYET]

6668   The world's large tongue
Proclaims you for a man replete with mocks,
Full of comparisons and wounding flouts,
Which you on all estates will execute
That lie within the mercy of your wit.
                    Love's Labour's Lost, Act v, sc. 2, 1. 852 [ROSALINE]

6669   Your tongue's sweet air
More tunable than lark to shepherd's ear,
When wheat is green, when hawthorn buds appear.
                    A Midsummer Night's Dream, Act i, sc. 1, 1. 183 [HELENA]

6670   BENEDICK: Well, you are a rare parrot-teacher.
BEATRICE: A bird of my tongue is better than a beast of yours.
BENEDICK: I would my horse had the speed of your tongue, and
so good a continuer.
                    Much Ado about Nothing, Act i, sc. 1, 1. 139 [BENEDICK]

6671 O God, sir, here's a dish I love not: I cannot endure my Lady
Tongue.
> *Much Ado about Nothing,* Act ii, sc. 1, l. 283 [BENEDICK]

6672 Now my tongue's use is to me no more
Than an unstringed viol or a harp. . . .
Within my mouth you have engaol'd my tongue,
Doubly portcullis'd with my teeth and lips.
> *Richard II,* Act i, sc. 3, l. 161 [MOWBRAY]

6673   They say the tongues of dying men
Enforce attention like deep harmony. . . .
He that no more must say is listen'd more
Than they whom youth and ease have taught to glose.
More are men's ends mark'd than their lives before.
> *Richard II,* Act ii, sc. 1, l. 5 [GAUNT]

6674 His tongue is now a stringless instrument.
> *Richard II,* Act ii, sc. 1, l. 149 [NORTHUMBERLAND]

6675 I never sued to friend nor enemy;
My tongue could never learn sweet smoothing words;
But, now thy beauty is proposed my fee,
My proud heart sues, and prompts my tongue to speak.
> *Richard III,* Act i, sc. 2, l. 168 [GLOUCESTER]

6676 Smooth not thy tongue with filed talk, . . .
But plainly say thou lovest her well,
And set thy person forth to sell.
> *Sonnets to Sundry Notes of Music,* Pt. xix, l. 8

6677 My tongue shall tell the anger of my heart,
Or else my heart concealing it will break.
> *The Taming of the Shrew,* Act iv, sc. 3, l. 77 [KATHARINA]

6678 ANTONIO: Fie, what a spendthrift is he of his tongue! . . .
SEBASTIAN: He will be talking.
> *The Tempest,* Act ii, sc. 1, l. 24 [ANTONIO]

6679   None of us cared for Kate;
For she had a tongue with a tang.
> *The Tempest,* Act ii, sc. 2, l. 51 [STEPHANO]

6680 Keep a good tongue in your head. . . . While thou livest, keep
a good tongue in thy head.
> *The Tempest,* Act iii, sc. 2, l. 37 [STEPHANO]

6681 Let thy tongue tang arguments of state.
> *Twelfth Night,* Act ii, sc. 5, l. 165 [MALVOLIO, *reading*]

6682 That man that hath a tongue, I say, is no man,
If with his tongue he cannot win a woman.
> *The Two Gentlemen of Verona,* Act iii, sc. 1, l. 104 [VALENTINE]

6683 If I prove honey-mouth'd, let my tongue blister
And never to my red-look'd anger be
The trumpet any more.
> *The Winter's Tale,* Act ii, sc. 2, l. 33 [PAULINA]

Tongues

6684   Why should this a desert be?
   For it is unpeopled? No;
   Tongues I'll hang on every tree,
   That shall civil sayings show.
> *As You Like It,* Act iii, sc. 2, l. 133 [CELIA, *reading*]

6685 SIR ANDREW: I would I had bestowed that time in the tongues that
I have in fencing, dancing and bear-baiting: O, had I but followed
the arts!
SIR TOBY: Then hadst thou had an excellent head of hair.
> *Twelfth Night,* Act i, sc. 3, l. 97 [SIR ANDREW]

Tongue-Tied

6686   Since you are tongue-tied and so loath to speak,
       In dumb significants proclaim your thoughts.
                           I Henry VI, Act ii, sc. 4, l. 25 [PLANTAGENET]

6687   These gracious words revive my drooping thoughts
       And give my tongue-tied sorrows leave to speak.
                        III Henry VI, Act iii, sc. 3, l. 21 [QUEEN MARGARET]

6688   Be not tongue-tied: go with me
       And in the breath of bitter words let's smother
       My damned son, which thy two sweet sons smother'd.
                           Richard III, Act iv, sc. 4, l. 132 [DUCHESS]

6689   Tongue-tied our queen? speak you.
                           The Winter's Tale, Act i, sc. 2, l. 26 [LEONTES]

Tooth See also Teeth

6690   As the Dutchman says, I'll like a maid the better, whilst I have
       a tooth in my head.
                     All's Well that Ends Well, Act ii, sc. 3, l. 47 [LAFEU]
       An old trot with ne'er a tooth in her head.
                        The Taming of the Shrew, Act i, sc. 2, l. 80 [GRUMIO]

6691   CHAMBERLAIN: Your colt's tooth is not cast yet.
       SANDS: No, my lord;
       Nor shall not, while I have a stump.
                           Henry VIII, Act i, sc. 3, l. 48 [CHAMBERLAIN]

6692   Tooth that poisons if it bite.
                           King Lear, Act iii, sc. 6, l. 70 [EDGAR]

6693   When he bites,
       His venom tooth will rankle to the death.
                        Richard III, Act i, sc. 3, l. 290 [QUEEN MARGARET]

Tooth-Ache

6694   He that sleeps feels not the tooth-ache.
                           Cymbeline, Act v, sc. 4, l. 177 [GAOLER]

6695   BENEDICK: I have the tooth-ache.
       DON PEDRO: Draw it.
       BENEDICK: Hang it!
       CLAUDIO: You must hang it first, and draw it afterwards.
       DON PEDRO: What! sigh for the tooth-ache?. . .
       BENEDICK: Yet is this no charm for the tooth-ache.
                     Much Ado about Nothing, Act iii, sc. 2, l. 21 [BENEDICK]

6696   There was never yet philosopher
       That could endure the tooth-ache patiently.
                     Much Ado about Nothing, Act v, sc. 1, l. 35 [LEONATO]

Torture

6697   With vilest torture let my life be ended.
                     All's Well that Ends Well, Act ii, sc. 1, l. 177 [HELENA]

6698   Thou 'lt torture me to leave unspoken that
       Which, to be spoke, would torture thee.
                           Cymbeline, Act v, sc. 5, l. 139 [IACHIMO]

6699   That deep torture may be call'd a hell
       When more is felt than one hath power to tell.
                           The Rape of Lucrece, l. 1287 [LUCRECE]

6700   What studied torments, tyrant, hast for me?
       What wheels? racks? fires? what flaying? boiling?
       In leads or oils? what old or newer torture

Must I receive, whose every word deserves
To taste of thy most worst?
The Winter's Tale, Act iii, sc. 2, l. 175 [PAULINA]

Towers

6701 Tarsus, . . . Whose towers bore heads so high they kiss'd the clouds.
Pericles, Act i, sc. 4, l. 24 [CLEON]
6702 Yond towers, whose wanton tops do buss the clouds,
Must kiss their own feet.
Troilus and Cressida, Act iv, sc. 5, l. 219 [ULYSSES]

Toy

6703 Triumphs for nothing and lamenting toys
Is jollity for apes and grief for boys.
Cymbeline, Act iv, sc. 2, l. 193 [GUIDERIUS]
6704   What infamy will there arise,
When foreign princes shall be certified
That for a toy, a thing of no regard,
King Henry's peers and chief nobility
Destroy'd themselves, and lost the realm of France!
I Henry VI, Act iv, sc. 1, l. 143 [KING HENRY]

Traveller

6705 ROSALIND: Well, this is the forest of Arden.
TOUCHSTONE: Ay, now am I in Arden; the more fool I; when I
was at home, I was in a better place: but travellers must be
content.
As You Like It, Act ii, sc. 4, l. 15 [ROSALIND]
6706 Farewell, Monsieur Traveller: look you lisp and wear strange
suits, disable all the benefits of your own country, be out of love
with your nativity and almost chide God for making you that
countenance you are, or I will scarce think you have swam in a
gondola.
As You Like It, Act iv, sc. 1, l. 32 [ROSALIND]
6707   Our court, you know, is haunted
With a refined traveller of Spain;
A man in all the world's new fashion planted,
That hath a mint of phrases in his brain;
One whom the music of his own vain tongue
Doth ravish like enchanting harmony; . . .
How you delight, my lords, I know not, I;
But, I protest, I love to hear him lie.
Love's Labour's Lost, Act i, sc. 1, l. 163 [KING]
6708 The west yet glimmers with some streaks of day:
Now spurs the lated traveller apace
To gain the timely inn.
Macbeth, Act iii, sc. 3, l. 5 [MURDERER]
6709   Travellers ne'er did lie,
Though fools at home condemn 'em.
The Tempest, Act iii, sc. 3, l. 26 [ANTONIO]

Treachery

6710 Nay, but the man that was his bedfellow,
Whom he hath dull'd and cloy'd with gracious favours,
That he should, for a foreign purse, so sell
His sovereign's life to death and treachery.
Henry V, Act ii, sc. 2, l. 8 [EXETER]

6711　And for thy treachery, what's more manifest?
　　　　In that thou laid'st a trap to take my life,
　　　　　　　　　　I Henry VI, Act iii, sc. 1, l. 21 [GLOUCESTER]

6712　O monstrous treachery! can this be so,
　　　　That in alliance, amity and oaths,
　　　　There should be found such false dissembling guile?
　　　　　　　　　　I Henry VI, Act iv, sc. 1, l. 61 [GLOUCESTER]

6713　Against such lewdsters and their lechery
　　　　Those that betray them do no treachery.
　　　　　　　The Merry Wives of Windsor, Act v, sc. 3, l. 23 [MRS. PAGE]

6714　He is composed and framed of treachery.
　　　　　　Much Ado about Nothing, Act v, sc. 1, l. 256 [DON PEDRO]

Treason

6715　　　　　　　Shall our coffers, then,
　　　　Be emptied to redeem a traitor home?
　　　　Shall we buy treason? and indent with fears,
　　　　When they have lost and forfeited themselves?
　　　　No, on the barren mountains let him starve.
　　　　　　　　　　I Henry IV, Act i, sc. 3, l. 86 [KING HENRY]

6716　Suspicion all our lives shall be stuck full of eyes;
　　　　For treason is but trusted like the fox,
　　　　Who, ne'er so tame, so cherish'd and lock'd up,
　　　　Will have a wild trick of his ancestors.
　　　　Look how we can, or sad or merrily,
　　　　Interpretation will misquote our looks,
　　　　And we shall feed like oxen at a stall,
　　　　The better cherish'd, still the nearer death.
　　　　　　　　　　I Henry IV, Act v, sc. 2, l. 8 [WORCESTER]

6717　Some guard these traitors to the block of death,
　　　　Treason's true bed and yielder up of breath.
　　　　　　　　　　II Henry IV, Act iv, sc. 2, l. 122 [LANCASTER]

6718　Treason and murder ever kept together,
　　　　As two yoke-devils sworn to either's purpose,
　　　　Working so grossly in a natural cause,
　　　　That admiration did not hoop at them.
　　　　　　　　　　Henry V, Act ii, sc. 2, l. 105 [KING]

6719　The purest spring is not so free from mud
　　　　As I am clear from treason to my sovereign.
　　　　　　　　　　II Henry VI, Act iii, sc. 1, l. 101 [GLOUCESTER]

6720　O treason of the blood!
　　　　　　　　　　Othello, Act i, sc. 1, l. 170 [BRABANTIO]

Treason: The Traitor

6721　DUKE FREDERICK:　　Thus do all traitors:
　　　　If their purgation did consist in words,
　　　　They are as innocent as grace itself. . . .
　　　　ROSALIND: Treason is not inherited, my lord; . . .
　　　　My father was no traitor.
　　　　　　　As You Like It, Act i, sc. 3, l. 54 [DUKE FREDERICK]

6722　　　　　　　Though those that are betray'd
　　　　Do feel the treason sharply, yet the traitor
　　　　Stands in worse case of woe.
　　　　　　　　　　Cymbeline, Act iii, sc. 4, l. 87 [IMOGEN]

6723　An arrant traitor as any is in the universal world.
　　　　　　　　　　Henry V, Act iv, sc. 8, l. 9 [FLUELLEN]

6724　A subtle traitor needs no sophister.
　　　　　　　　　　II Henry VI, Act v, sc. 1, l. 191 [QUEEN]

6725   I protest,
         Maugre thy strength, youth, place, and eminence,
         Despite thy victor sword and fire-new fortune,
         Thy valour and thy heart, thou art a traitor:
         False to thy gods, thy brother, and thy father;
         Conspirant 'gainst this high-illustrious prince;
         And, from the extremest upward of thy head
         To the descent and dust below thy foot,
         A most toad-spotted traitor.
                        King Lear, Act v, sc. 3, l. 130 [EDGAR]

6726   SON: Was my father a traitor, mother?
         LADY MACDUFF: Ay, that he was.
         SON: What is a traitor?
         LADY MACDUFF: Why, one that swears and lies.
         SON: And be all traitors that do so?
         LADY MACDUFF: Every one that does so is a traitor, and must be
         hanged.
         SON: And must they all be hanged that swear and lie?
         LADY MACDUFF: Every one.
         SON: Who must hang them?
         LADY MACDUFF: Why, the honest men.
         SON: Then the liars and swearers are fools, for there are liars
         and swearers enow to beat the honest men and hang up them.
                        Macbeth, Act iv, sc. 2, l. 45 [SON]

6727   If ever I were traitor,
         My name be blotted from the book of life,
         And I from heaven banish'd as from hence!
                        Richard II, Act i, sc. 3, l. 201 [MOWBRAY]

6728   LOVEL: Here is the head of that ignoble traitor,
         The dangerous and unsuspected Hastings.
         GLOUCESTER: So dear I loved the man, that I must weep.
         I took him for the plainest harmless creature
         That breathed upon this earth a Christian; . . .
         So smooth he daub'd his vice with show of virtue, . . .
         He lived from all attainder of suspect.
                        Richard III, Act iii, sc. 5, l. 22 [LOVEL]

Tree

6729   Under the greenwood tree
         Who loves to lie with me,
         And turn his merry note
         Unto the sweet bird's throat,
         Come hither, come hither, come hither:
         Here shall he see No enemy
         But winter and rough weather.
                        As You Like It, Act ii, sc. 5, l. 1 [AMIENS]

6730   O Rosalind! these trees shall be my books
         And in their barks my thoughts I'll character;
         That every eye which in this forest looks
         Shall see thy virtue witness'd every where.
         Run, run, Orlando; carve on every tree
         The fair, the chaste and unexpressive she.
                        As You Like It, Act iii, sc. 2, l. 5 [ORLANDO]

6731   Then was I as a tree
         Whose boughs did bend with fruit; but in one night
         A storm of robbery, call it what you will,

Shook down my mellow hangings, nay, my leaves,
And left me bare to weather.
> *Cymbeline*, Act iii, sc. 3, l. 60 [BELARIUS]

6732   The tree may be known by the fruit, as the fruit by the tree.
> *I Henry IV*, Act ii, sc. 4, l. 471 [FALSTAFF]

6733   Superfluous branches
We lop away, that bearing boughs may live.
> *Richard II*, Act iii, sc. 4, l. 63 [GARDENER]

6734   I have a tree, which grows here in my close,
That mine own use invites me to cut down,
And shortly must I fell it: tell my friends,
Tell Athens, in the sequence of degree
From high to low throughout, that whoso please
To stop affliction, let him take his haste,
Come hither, ere my tree hath felt the axe,
And hang himself.
> *Timon of Athens*, Act v, sc. 1, l. 208 [TIMON]

Trick

6735   Some trick not worth an egg.
> *Coriolanus*, Act iv, sc. 4, l. 21 [CORIOLANUS]

Some tricks, some quillets, how to cheat the devil.
> *Love's Labour's Lost*, Act iv, sc. 3, l. 288 [LONGAVILLE]

6736   I know a trick worth two of that.
> *I Henry IV*, Act ii, sc. 1, l. 40 [CARRIER]

6737   I see the trick on 't: here was a consent
Knowing aforehand of our merriment,
To dash it like a Christmas comedy:
Some carry-tale, some please-man, some slight zany,
Some mumble-news, some trencher-knight, some Dick, . . .
Told our intents before.
> *Love's Labour's Lost*, Act v, sc. 2, l. 460 [BIRON]

6738   You always end with a jade's trick: I know you of old.
> *Much Ado about Nothing*, Act i, sc. 1, l. 145 [BEATRICE]

6739   An he begin once, he'll rail in his rope-tricks.
> *The Taming of the Shrew*, Act i, sc. 2, l. 112 [GRUMIO]

6740   Put thyself into the trick of singularity.
> *Twelfth Night*, Act ii, sc. 5, l. 166 [MALVOLIO, *reading*]

Trifle

6741   Small things make base men proud.
> *II Henry VI*, Act iv, sc. 1, l. 106 [SUFFOLK]

6742   MRS. FORD: O woman, if it were not for one trifling respect, I could
come to such honour!
MRS. PAGE: Hang the trifle, woman! take the honour. . . . Dispense with trifles.
> *The Merry Wives of Windsor*, Act ii, sc. 1, l. 43 [MRS. FORD]

6743   Trifles light as air
Are to the jealous confirmations strong
As proofs of holy writ.
> *Othello*, Act iii, sc. 3, l. 322 [IAGO]

6744   My father named me Autolycus; who being, as I am, littered under
Mercury, was likewise a snapper-up of unconsidered trifles.
> *The Winter's Tale*, Act iv, sc. 3, l. 24 [AUTOLYCUS]

Triumph

6745   Set thee on triumphant chariots and
Put garlands on thy head.
> *Antony and Cleopatra*, Act iii, sc. 1, l. 10 [SILIUS]

6746   Thou most beauteous inn,
Why should hard-favour'd grief be lodged in thee,
When triumph is become an alehouse guest?
Richard II, Act v, sc. 1, l. 13 [QUEEN]

Trouble

6747   Be not deceiv'd: if I have veil'd my look,
I turn the trouble of my countenance
Merely upon myself.
Julius Cæsar, Act i, sc. 2, l. 37 [BRUTUS]

6748   Double, double toil and trouble;
Fire burn, and cauldron bubble.
Macbeth, Act iv, sc. 1, l. 10, 20, 35 [WITCHES]

6749   DON PEDRO: Good Signior Leonato, you are come to meet your
trouble. . . .
LEONATO: Never came trouble to my house in the likeness of your
grace: for trouble being gone, comfort should remain; but when
you depart from me, sorrow abides and happiness takes his leave.
Much Ado about Nothing, Act i, sc. 1, l. 96 [DON PEDRO]

6750   I have been in such a pickle since I saw you last.
The Tempest, Act v, sc. 1, l. 282 [TRINCULO]

Trout

6751   Groping for trouts in a peculiar river.
Measure for Measure, Act i, sc. 2, l. 91 [POMPEY]

6752   Here comes the trout that must be caught with tickling.
Twelfth Night, Act ii, sc. 5, l. 25 [MARIA]

Troy

6753   Cloud-kissing Ilion.
The Rape of Lucrece, l. 1370

6754   Had doting Priam check'd his son's desire,
Troy had been bright with fame and not with fire.
The Rape of Lucrece, l. 1490 [LUCRECE]

6755   AGAMEMNON: After seven years' siege yet Troy walls stand. . . .
ULYSSES: Troy in our weakness stands, not in her strength.
Troilus and Cressida, Act i, sc. 3, l. 12 [AGAMEMNON]

Troy: The Trojans

6756   Tut! there are other Trojans that thou dreamest not of, the
which for sport sake are content to do the profession some grace.
. . . I am joined with no foot land-rakers, no long-staff sixpenny
strikers, none of these mad mustachio purple-hued malt-worms;
but with nobility and tranquillity, burgomasters and great oneyers,
such as can hold in, such as will strike sooner than speak, and
speak sooner than drink, and drink sooner than pray.
I Henry IV, Act ii, sc. 1, l. 78 [GADSHILL]

6757   Each Trojan that is master of his heart,
Let him to field.
Troilus and Cressida, Act i, sc. 1, l. 4 [TROILUS]

True

6758   This above all: to thine own self to be true,
And it must follow, as the night the day,
Thou canst not then be false to any man.
Hamlet, Act i, sc. 3, l. 78 [POLONIUS]

6759   My man's as true as steel.
Romeo and Juliet, Act ii, sc. 4, l. 210 [ROMEO]
("As true as steel" is repeated in *A Midsummer Night's Dream*,
ii, 1, 197; *Troilus and Cressida*, iii, 2, 184.)

6760   There is no time so miserable but a man may be true.
                    Timon of Athens, Act iv, sc. 3, l. 462 [BANDIT]

6761   True swains in love shall in the world to come
       Approve their truths by Troilus: when their rhymes,
       Full of protest, or oath and big compare,
       Want similes, truth tired with iteration,
       As true as steel, as plantage to the moon,
       As sun to day, as turtle to her mate,
       As iron to adamant, as earth to the centre, . . .
       'As true as Troilus' shall crown up the verse,
       And sanctify the numbers.
                    Troilus and Cressida, Act iii, sc. 2, l. 180 [TROILUS]

Trumpet

6762   Make all our trumpets speak; give them all breath,
       Those clamorous harbingers of blood and death.
                    Macbeth, Act v, sc. 6, l. 9 [MACDUFF]

6763   It is most expedient for the wise, if Don Worm, his conscience,
       find no impediment to the contrary, to be the trumpet of his own
       virtues.
                    Much Ado about Nothing, Act v, sc. 2, l. 85 [BENEDICK]

Trust

6764   Trust not him that hath once broken faith.
                    III Henry VI, Act iv, sc. 4, l. 30 [QUEEN ELIZABETH]

6765   He was a gentleman on whom I built
       An absolute trust.
                    Macbeth, Act i, sc. 4, l. 13 [DUNCAN]

6766   I will no more trust him when he leers than I will a serpent when
       he hisses.
                    Troilus and Cressida, Act v, sc. 1, l. 96 [THERSITES]

6767   Who should be trusted, now, when one's right hand
       Is perjured to the bosom? Proteus,
       I am sorry I must never trust thee more,
       But count the world a stranger for thy sake.
                    The Two Gentlemen of Verona, Act v, sc. 4, l. 67 [VALENTINE]

Truth

6768   Who tells me true, though in his tale lie death,
       I hear him as he flatter'd.
                    Antony and Cleopatra, Act i, sc. 2, l. 102 [ANTONY]

6769   That truth should be silent I had almost forgot.
                    Antony and Cleopatra, Act ii, sc. 2, l. 110 [ENOBARBUS]

6770   If circumstances lead me, I will find
       Where truth is hid, though it were hid indeed
       Within the centre.
                    Hamlet, Act ii, sc. 2, l. 157 [POLONIUS]

6771   What, art thou mad? is not the truth the truth?
                    I Henry IV, Act ii, sc. 4, l. 254 [FALSTAFF]
       Truth is truth.
                    King John, Act i, sc. 1, l. 105 [ROBERT]
       Truth is truth To the end of reckoning.
                    Measure for Measure, Act v, sc. 1, l. 46 [ISABELLA]

6772   The truth of it stands off as gross
       As black and white.
                    Henry V, Act ii, sc. 2, l. 103 [KING]

6773   Truth loves open dealing.
                    Henry VIII, Act iii, sc. 1, l. 40 [QUEEN KATHARINE]

6774 Truth's a dog must to kennel; he must be whipped out, when
Lady the brach may stand by the fire and stink.
King Lear, Act i, sc. 4, l. 124 [FOOL]

6775 Painfully to pore upon a book
To seek the light of truth; while truth the while
Doth falsely blind the eyesight of his look.
Love's Labour's Lost, Act i, sc. 1, l. 74 [BIRON]

6776 There is scarce truth enough alive to make societies secure; but
security enough to make fellowships accurst: much upon this
riddle runs the wisdom of the world.
Measure for Measure, Act iii, sc. 2, l. 240 [DUKE]

6777 Truth can never be confirm'd enough,
Though doubts did ever sleep.
Pericles, Act v, sc. 1, l. 203 [PERICLES]

6778 Truth hath a quiet breast.
Richard II, Act i, sc. 3, l. 96 [MOWBRAY]

6779 O, how much more doth beauty beauteous seem
By that sweet ornament which truth doth give!
Sonnet liv, l. 1

6780 Simple truth miscall'd simplicity.
Sonnet lxvi, l. 11

6781 Whiles others fish with craft for great opinion,
I with great truth catch mere simplicity;
Whiles some with cunning gild their copper crowns,
With truth and plainness I do wear mine bare.
Fear not my truth: the moral of my wit
Is 'plain and true'; that's all the reach of it.
Troilus and Cressida, Act iv, sc. 4, l. 106 [TROILUS]

6782 What, gone without a word?
Ay, so true love should do: it cannot speak;
For truth hath better deeds than words to grace it.
The Two Gentlemen of Verona, Act ii, sc. 2, l. 16 [PROTEUS]

Turkey-Cock

6783 GOWER: Here he comes, swelling like a turkey-cock.
FLUELLEN: 'Tis no matter for his swellings nor his turkey-cocks.
Henry V, Act v, sc. 1, l. 14 [GOWER]

6784 A rare turkey-cock: . . . see how he jets under his advanced
plumes!
Twelfth Night, Act ii, sc. 5, l. 36 [FABIAN]

Turn

6785 This young maid might do her
A shrewd turn, if she pleased.
All's Well that Ends Well, Act iii, sc. 5, l. 70 [WIDOW]

6786 Do my Lord of Canterbury
A shrewd turn, and he is your friend for ever.
Henry VIII, Act v, sc. 3, l. 177 [KING HENRY]

6787 Come, you and I must walk a turn together.
Henry VIII, Act v, sc. 1, l. 93 [KING HENRY]

6788 You did wish that I would make her turn:
Sir, she can turn, and turn, and yet go on,
And turn again; and she can weep, sir, weep.
Othello, Act iv, sc. 1, l. 263 [OTHELLO]

6789 AARON: Why, then, it seems, some certain snatch or so
Would serve your turns.
CHIRON: Ay, so the turn was served.
Titus Andronicus, Act ii, sc. 1, l. 95 [AARON]

Turn: Good Turn

6790 MESSENGER: He's bound unto Octavia.
CLEOPATRA: For what good turn?
MESSENGER: For the best turn i' the bed.
Antony and Cleopatra, Act ii, sc. 5, l. 58 [MESSENGER]

6791 They knew what they did; I am to do a good turn for them.
Hamlet, Act iv, sc. 6, l. 22 [HORATIO, *reading*]

6792 Truly, sir, for your kindness, I owe you a good turn.
Measure for Measure, Act iv, sc. 2, l. 61 [POMPEY]

6793 When nature framed this piece, she meant thee a good turn.
Pericles, Act iv, sc. 2, l. 150 [BAWD]

6794 Never did passenger in summer's heat
More thirst for drink than she for this good turn.
Venus and Adonis, l. 91

Turtle-Dove

6795 They both came swiftly running,
Like to a pair of loving turtle-doves
That could not live asunder day or night.
I Henry VI, Act ii, sc. 2, l. 29 [BURGUNDY]

6796 I had rather be a giantess and lie under Mount Pelion. Well, I
will find you twenty lascivious turtles ere one chaste man.
The Merry Wives of Windsor, Act ii, sc. 1, l. 81 [MRS. PAGE]

6797 PETRUCHIO: O slow-wing'd turtle! shall a buzzard take thee?
KATHARINA: Ay, for a turtle, as he takes a buzzard.
The Taming of the Shrew, Act ii, sc. 1, l. 208 [PETRUCHIO]

6798 I, an old turtle
Will wing me to some wither'd bough.
The Winter's Tale, Act v, sc. 3, l. 132 [PAULINA]

Tyranny

6799 Tyranny, which never quaff'd but blood,
Would, by beholding him, have wash'd his knife
With gentle eye-drops.
II Henry IV, Act iv, sc. 5, l. 86 [WARWICK]

6800 Thou hast by tyranny these many years
Wasted our country, slain our citizens,
And sent our sons and husbands captivate.
I Henry VI, Act ii, sc. 3, l. 40 [COUNTESS]

6801 So let high-handed tyranny range on,
Till each man drop by lottery.
Julius Cæsar, Act ii, sc. 1, l. 118 [BRUTUS]

6802 The tyranny of the open night's too rough
For nature to endure.
King Lear, Act iii, sc. 4, l. 2 [KENT]

6803 Great tyranny! lay thou thy basis sure,
For goodness dare not check thee.
Macbeth, Act iv, sc. 3, l. 32 [MACDUFF]

6804 Insulting tyranny begins to jet
Upon the innocent and aweless throne.
Richard III, Act ii, sc. 4, l. 51 [QUEEN ELIZABETH]

Tyranny: The Tyrant

6805 She Phebes me: mark how the tyrant writes.
As You Like It, Act iv, sc. 3, l. 39 [ROSALIND]

6806   We are no tyrant, but a Christian king;
        Unto whose grace our passion is as subject
        As are our wretches fetter'd in our prisons.
                    Henry V, Act i, sc. 2, l. 241 [KING HENRY]

6807   How can tyrants safely govern home,
        Unless abroad they purchase great alliance?
                    III Henry VI, Act iii, sc. 3, l. 69 [MARGARET]

6808   Live to be the show and gaze o' the time:
        We'll have thee, as our rarer monsters are,
        Painted upon a pole, and underwrit,
        'Here you may see the tyrant.'
                    Macbeth, Act v, sc. 8, l. 24 [MACDUFF]

6809   My chief humour is for a tyrant: I could play Ercles rarely,
        or a part to tear a cat in, to make all split. . . . This is Ercles'
        vein, a tyrant's vein.
                    A Midsummer Night's Dream, Act i, sc. 2, l. 30 [BOTTOM]

6810   'Tis time to fear when tyrants seem to kiss.
                    Pericles, Act i, sc. 2, l. 79 [PERICLES]

U

Ugliness

6811   Fellow, be gone: I cannot brook thy sight:
        This news hath made thee a most ugly man. . . .
        Ugly and slanderous to thy mother's womb,
        Full of unpleasing blots and sightless stains.
                    King John, Act iii, sc. 1, l. 36 [CONSTANCE]

6812   I am as ugly as a bear;
        For beasts that meet me run away for fear.
                    A Midsummer Night's Dream, Act ii, sc. 2, l. 94 [HELENA]

Unction

6813   Lay not that flattering unction to your soul.
                    Hamlet, Act iii, sc. 4, l. 145 [HAMLET]

6814   I bought an unction of a mountebank,
        So mortal that, but dip a knife in it,
        Where it draws blood no cataplasm so rare,
        Collected from all simples that have virtue
        Under the moon, can save the thing from death
        That is but scratch'd withal.
                    Hamlet, Act iv, sc. 7, l. 142 [LAERTES]

Unhappiness

6815   I am the most unhappy woman living. . . .
        Almost no grave allow'd me; like the lily,
        That once was mistress of the field and flourished,
        I'll hang my head and perish.
                    Henry VIII, Act iii, sc. 1, l. 147 [QUEEN KATHARINE]

6816   I have heard my daughter say, she hath often dreamed of un-
        happiness and waked herself with laughing.
                    Much Ado about Nothing, Act ii, sc. 1, l. 360 [LEONATO]

6817   SILVIA: O miserable, unhappy that I am!
        PROTEUS: Unhappy were you, madame, ere I came;
        But by my coming I have made you happy.
        SILVIA: By thy approach thou makest me most unhappy.
                    The Two Gentlemen of Verona, Act v, sc. 4, l. 28 [SILVIA]

Unity

6818   We still have slept together,
Rose at an instant, learn'd, play'd, eat together,
And wheresoe'er we went, like Juno's swans,
Still we went coupled and inseparable.
As You Like It, Act i, sc. 3, l. 75 [CELIA]

6819   We grew together
Like to a double cherry, seeming parted,
But yet an union in partition;
Two lovely berries moulded on one stem.
A Midsummer Night's Dream, Act iii, sc. 2, l. 208 [HELENA]

6820 You peers, continue this united league. . . .
Now, princely Buckingham, seal thou this league
With thy embracements to my wife's allies,
And make me happy in your unity.
Richard III, Act ii, sc. 1, l. 2 [KING EDWARD]

Unkindness

6821   Give me a bowl of wine,
In this I bury all unkindness, Cassius.
Julius Cæsar, Act iv, sc. 3, l. 158 [BRUTUS]

6822 Come, we have a hot venison pasty to dinner: come, gentlemen, I
hope we shall drink down all unkindness.
The Merry Wives of Windsor, Act i, sc. 1, l. 202 [PAGE]

6823 Comfort forswear me! Unkindness may do much;
And his unkindness may defeat my life,
But never taint my love.
Othello, Act iv, sc. 2, l. 159 [DESDEMONA]

6824 If you were by my unkindness shaken,
As I by yours, you've pass'd a hell of time.
Sonnet cxx, l. 5

Use

6825 Use almost can change the stamp of nature,
And either master the devil, or throw him out
With wondrous potency.
Hamlet, Act iii, sc. 4, l. 168 [HAMLET]

6826 She that herself will sliver and disbranch
From her material sap, perforce must wither
And come to deadly use.
King Lear, Act iv, sc. 2, l. 34 [ALBANY]

6827 How use doth breed a habit in a man!
The Two Gentlemen of Verona, Act v, sc. 4, l. 1 [VALENTINE]

6828 Torches are made to light, jewels to wear,
Dainties to taste, fresh beauty for the use,
Herbs for their smell, and sappy plants to bear;
Things growing to themselves are growth's abuse.
Venus and Adonis, l. 163 [VENUS]

Usury

6829 Thou art a most pernicious usurer,
Froward by nature, enemy to peace,
Lascivious, wanton, more than well beseems
A man of thy profession and degree.
I Henry VI, Act iii, sc. 1, l. 17 [GLOUCESTER]

6830 Signior Antonio, many a time and oft
In the Rialto you have rated me

About my moneys and my usances:
Still have I borne it with a patient shrug,
For sufferance is the badge of all our tribe.
You call me misbeliever, cut-throat dog,
And spit upon my Jewish gaberdine,
And all for use of that which is mine own.
>> *The Merchant of Venice,* Act i, sc. 3, l. 107 [SHYLOCK]

6831 That use is not forbidden usury
Which happies those that pay the willing loan.
>> *Sonnet* vi, l. 5

V

Valentine

6832 To-morrow is Saint Valentine's day,
　　All in the morning betime,
And I a maid at your window,
　　To be your Valentine.
Then up he rose, and donn'd his clothes,
　　And dupp'd the chamber door;
Let in the maid, that out a maid
　　Never departed more.

By Gis and by Saint Charity,
　　Alack, and fie for shame!
Young men will do't, if they come to't;
　　By cock, they are to blame.
Quoth she, before you tumbled me,
　　You promised me to wed.
So would I ha' done, by yonder sun,
　　An thou hadst not come to my bed.
>> *Hamlet,* Act iv, sc. 5, l. 48 [OPHELIA, *singing*]

6833 　　Saint Valentine is past:
Begin these wood-birds but to couple now?
>> *A Midsummer Night's Dream,* Act iv, sc. 1, l. 143 [THESEUS]

Valour

6834 　　When valour preys on reason,
It eats the sword it fights with.
>> *Antony and Cleopatra,* Act iii, sc. 13, l. 199 [ENOBARBUS]

6835 　　The deeds of Coriolanus
Should not be utter'd feebly. It is held
That valour is the chiefest virtue, and
Most dignifies the haver: if it be,
The man I speak of cannot in the world
Be singly counterpoised.
>> *Coriolanus,* Act ii, sc. 2, l. 86 [COMINIUS]

6836 　　Let me make men know
More valour in me than my habits show.
>> *Cymbeline,* Act v, sc. 1, l. 29 [POSTHUMUS]

6837 Thou knowest I am as valiant as Hercules.
>> *I Henry IV,* Act ii, sc. 4, l. 300 [FALSTAFF]
I take him to be as valiant as Hector.
>> *Much Ado about Nothing,* Act ii, sc. 3, l. 195 [DON PEDRO]

6838 His valour shown upon our crests to-day
Hath taught us how to cherish such high deeds
Even in the bosom of our adversaries.
I Henry IV, Act v, sc. 5, l. 29 [PRINCE]

6839 Courageous Feeble! thou wilt be as valiant as the wrathful dove
or most magnanimous mouse. . . . Most forcible Feeble.
II Henry IV, Act iii, sc. 2, l. 170 [FALSTAFF]

6840 Awake remembrance of these valiant dead
And with your puissant arm renew their feats.
Henry V, Act i, sc. 2, l. 115 [ELY]

6841 He is as full of valour as of kindness;
Princely in both.
Henry V, Act iv, sc. 3, l. 15 [BEDFORD]

6842 What valour were it, when a cur doth grin,
For one to thrust his hand between his teeth,
When he might spurn him with his foot away?
III Henry VI, Act i, sc. 4, l. 56 [NORTHUMBERLAND]

6843 True valour still a true respect should have.
The Rape of Lucrece, l. 201 [TARQUIN]

6844   They were red-hot with drinking;
So full of valour that they smote the air
For breathing in their faces; beat the ground
For kissing of their feet.
The Tempest, Act iv, sc. 1, l. 171 [ARIEL]

6845 She did show favour to the youth in your sight only to exasperate
you, to awake your dormouse valour, to put fire in your heart,
and brimstone in your liver.
Twelfth Night, Act iii, sc. 2, l. 20 [FABIAN]

6846 There is no love-broker in the world can more prevail in man's
commendation with woman than report of valour.
Twelfth Night, Act iii, sc. 2, l. 39 [SIR TOBY]

Value

6847 Things of like value differing in the owners
Are prized by their masters: believe 't, dear lord,
You mend the jewel by the wearing it.
Timon of Athens, Act i, sc. 1, l. 170 [JEWELLER]

6848 TROILUS: What is aught, but as 'tis valued?
HECTOR: But value dwells not in particular will;
It holds his estimate and dignity
As well wherein 'tis precious of itself
As in the prizer.
Troilus and Cressida, Act ii, sc. 2, l. 52 [TROILUS]

Vanity

6849 You shall find his vanities forespent
Were but the outside of the Roman Brutus,
Covering discretion with a coat of folly;
As gardeners do with ordure hide those roots
That shall first appear and be most delicate.
Henry V, Act ii, sc. 4, l. 36 [CONSTABLE]

6850 Light vanity, insatiate cormorant,
Consuming means, soon preys upon itself.
Richard II, Act ii, sc. 1, l. 38 [GAUNT]

Vein

6851 ADRIANA: Is 't good to soothe him in these contraries?
PINCH: It is no shame: the fellow finds his vein
And, yielding to him, humours well his frenzy.
                    The Comedy of Errors, Act iv, sc. 4, l. 82 [ADRIANA]

6852 I am not in the giving vein to-day.
                    Richard III, Act iv, sc. 2, l. 119 [KING RICHARD]

Venom

6853 LAERTES: No medicine in the world can do thee good; . . .
The treacherous instrument is in thy hand,
Unbated and envenom'd. . . .
HAMLET: The point envenom'd too! Then, venom, do thy work.
[*Stabs the king*]
                    Hamlet, Act v, sc. 2, l. 325 [LAERTES]

6854 Envenom him with words, or get thee gone
And leave those woes alone which I alone
Am bound to under-bear.
                    King John, Act iii, sc. 1, l. 63 [CONSTANCE]

Ventures

6855   Diseased ventures
That play with all infirmities for gold
Which rottenness can lend nature! such boil'd stuff
As well might poison poison.
                    Cymbeline, Act i, sc. 6, l. 123 [IACHIMO]

6856 My ventures are not in one bottom trusted,
Nor to one place; nor is my whole estate
Upon the fortune of this present year.
                    The Merchant of Venice, Act i, sc. 1, l. 42 [ANTONIO]

6857 Have all his ventures fail'd? What, not one hit?
                    The Merchant of Venice, Act iii, sc. 2, l. 270 [BASSANIO]

6858 Things out of hope are compass'd oft with venturing,
Chiefly in love, whose leave exceeds commission.
                    Venus and Adonis, l. 567 [VENUS]

Venus

6859 Venus smiles not in a house of tears.
                    Romeo and Juliet, Act iv, sc. 1, l. 8 [PARIS]

6860 Venus, the heart-blood of beauty, love's invisible soul.
                    Troilus and Cressida, Act iii, sc. 1, l. 35 [SERVANT]

Verily

6861 HERMIONE: You'll stay?
POLIXENES: No, madam. . . . I may not, verily.
HERMIONE: Verily! . . . Verily
You shall not go: a lady's "Verily" 's
As potent as a lord's. . . . How say you?
My prisoner or my guest? by your dread 'Verily,'
One of them you shall be.
                    The Winter's Tale, Act i, sc. 2, l. 44 [HERMIONE]

Verse

6862 CELIA: Didst thou hear these verses?
ROSALIND: O, yes, I heard them all, and more too; for some of
them had in them more feet than the verses would bear.
                    As You Like It, Act iii, sc. 2, l. 172 [CELIA]

6863   ORLANDO: Good day and happiness, dear Rosalind.
       JAQUES: Nay, then, God be wi' you an you talk in blank verse.
                              As You Like It, Act iv, sc. 1, l. 30 [ORLANDO]
6864   The lady shall say her mind freely, or the blank verse shall halt
       for 't.
                              Hamlet, Act ii, sc. 2, l. 339 [HAMLET]
6865   CINNA: I am Cinna the poet.
       CITIZEN: Tear him for his bad verses, tear him for his bad
       verses.
                              Julius Cæsar, Act iii, sc. 3, l. 32 [CINNA]
6866   Was it the proud full sail of his great verse,
       Bound for the prize of all too precious you,
       That did my ripe thoughts in my brain inhearse,
       Making their tomb the womb wherein they grew?
                              Sonnet lxxxvi, l. 1
6867   When we for recompense have praised the vile,
       It stains the glory in that happy verse
       Which aptly sings the good.
                              Timon of Athens, Act i, sc. 1, l. 15 [POET]

Vessel

6868   I must comfort the weaker vessel.
                              As You Like It, Act ii, sc. 4, l. 6 [ROSALIND]
6869   HOSTESS: One must bear, and that must be you: you are the
       weaker vessel, as they say, the emptier vessel.
       DOLL: Can a weak empty vessel bear such a huge full hogshead?
                              II Henry IV, Act ii, sc. 4, l. 65 [HOSTESS]
6870   The saying is true, 'The empty vessel makes the greatest sound.'
                              Henry V, Act iv, sc. 4, l. 73 [BOY]

Vice

6871   Through tatter'd clothes small vices do appear;
       Robes and furr'd gowns hide all.
                              King Lear, Act iv, sc. 6, l. 168 [LEAR]
6872   There is a vice that most I do abhor,
       And most desire should meet the blow of justice;
       For which I would not plead, but that I must;
       For which I must not plead, but that I am
       At war 'twixt will and will not.
                              Measure for Measure, Act ii, sc. 2, l. 29 [ISABELLA]
6873   Twice treble shame on Angelo,
       To weed my vice and let his grow!
                              Measure for Measure, Act iii, sc. 2, l. 283 [DUKE]
6874   Vice repeated is like the wandering wind,
       Blows dust in others' eyes, to spread itself.
                              Pericles, Act i, sc. 1, l. 96 [PERICLES]
6875   Canker vice the sweetest buds doth love.
                              Sonnet lxx, l. 7
6876   O, what a mansion have those vices got
       Which for their habitation chose out thee,
       Where beauty's veil doth cover every blot,
       And all things turn to fair that eyes can see!
                              Sonnet xcv, l. 9
6877   I ne'er heard yet
       That any of these bolder vices wanted
       Less impudence to gainsay what they did
       Than to perform it first.
                              The Winter's Tale, Act iii, sc. 2, l. 55 [LEONTES]

Vice and Virtue

6878 Apparel vice like virtue's harbinger; . . .
Teach sin the carriage of a holy saint.
The Comedy of Errors, Act iii, sc. 2, 1. 12 [LUCIANA]

6879 Forgive me this my virtue;
For in the fatness of these pursy times
Virtue itself of vice must pardon beg,
Yea, curb and woo for leave to do him good.
Hamlet, Act iii, sc. 4, 1. 152 [HAMLET]

6880 There is no vice so simple but assumes
Some mark of virtue on his outward parts.
The Merchant of Venice, Act iii, sc. 2, 1. 81 [BASSANIO]

6881 Do but see his vice;
'Tis to his virtue a just equinox,
The one as long as the other.
Othello, Act ii, sc. 3, 1. 128 [IAGO]

6882 Virtue itself turns vice, being misapplied;
And vice sometimes by action dignified.
Romeo and Juliet, Act ii, sc. 3, 1. 21 [FRIAR LAURENCE]

6883 Virtue that transgresses is but patched with sin; and sin that
amends is but patched with virtue.
Twelfth Night, Act i, sc. 5, 1. 52 [CLOWN]

Victory

6884 Upon your sword
Sit laurel victory! and smooth success
Be strew'd before your feet!
Antony and Cleopatra, Act i, sc. 3, 1. 99 [CLEOPATRA]

6885 Either victory, or else a grave.
III Henry VI, Act ii, sc. 2, 1. 174 [EDWARD]

6886 To whom God will, there be the victory!
III Henry VI, Act ii, sc. 5, 1. 15 [KING HENRY]

6887 The harder match'd, the greater victory.
III Henry VI, Act v, sc. 1, 1. 70 [KING EDWARD]

6888 A victory is twice itself when the achiever brings home full
numbers.
Much Ado about Nothing, Act i, sc. 1, 1. 8 [LEONATO]

Vileness

6889 Wisdom and goodness to the vile seem vile:
Filths savour but themselves.
King Lear, Act iv, sc. 2, 1. 38 [ALBANY]

6890 'Tis better to be vile than vile esteem'd,
When not to be receives reproach of being.
Sonnet cxxi, 1. 1

Villain

6891 I am alone the villain of the earth,
And feel I am so most.
Antony and Cleopatra, Act iv, sc. 6, 1. 30 [ENOBARBUS]

6892 OLIVER: Wilt thou lay hands on me, villain?
ORLANDO: I am no villain: I am the youngest son of Sir Rowland de Boys; he was my father, and he is thrice a villain that
says such a father begot villains.
As You Like It, Act i, sc. 1, 1. 63 [OLIVER]

6893 One Pinch, a hungry, lean-faced villain,
A mere anatomy, a mountebank,
A threadbare juggler and a fortune-teller,

A needy, hollow-eyed, sharp-looking wretch,
A living-dead man.
The Comedy of Errors, Act v, sc. 1, l. 238
[ANTIPHOLUS OF EPHESUS]

6894   Sirrah, if thou wouldst not be a villain, but do me true service,
. . . what villany soe'er I bid thee do, to perform it directly
and truly, I would think thee an honest man.
Cymbeline, Act iii, sc. 5, l. 109 [CLOTEN]

6895   HAMLET: There's ne'er a villain dwelling in all Denmark
But he's an arrant knave.
HORATIO: There needs no ghost, my lord, come from the grave
To tell us this.
Hamlet, Act i, sc. 5, l. 123 [HAMLET]

6896   Bloody, bawdy villain!
Remorseless, treacherous, lecherous, kindless villain!
Hamlet, Act ii, sc. 2, l. 608 [HAMLET]

6897   O villain, villain! . . . Abhorred villain! Unnatural, detested,
brutish villain!
King Lear, Act i, sc. 2, l. 81 [GLOUCESTER]

6898   I know thee well: a serviceable villain;
As duteous to the vices of thy mistress
As badness would desire.
King Lear, Act iv, sc. 6, l. 257 [EDGAR]

6899   I would not be the villain that thou think'st
For the whole space that's in the tyrant's grasp,
And the rich East to boot.
Macbeth, Act iv, sc. 3, l. 35 [MACDUFF]

6900   When rich villains have need of poor ones, poor ones may make
what price they will.
Much Ado about Nothing, Act iii, sc. 3, l. 121 [BORACHIO]

6901   O villain! thou wilt be condemned into everlasting redemption
for this.
Much Ado about Nothing, Act iv, sc. 2, l. 58 [DOGBERRY]

6902   God knows I loved my niece;
And she is dead, slander'd to death by villains,
That dare as well answer a man indeed
As I dare take a serpent by the tongue:
Boys, apes, braggarts, Jacks, milksops!
Much Ado about Nothing, Act v, sc. 1, l. 87 [ANTONIO]

6903   Which is the villain? let me see his eyes,
That, when I note another man like him,
I may avoid him.
Much Ado about Nothing, Act v, sc. 1, l. 269 [LEONATO]

6904   And what's he then that says I play the villain?
Othello, Act ii, sc. 3, l. 342 [IAGO]

6905   O villains, vipers, damn'd without redemption!
Dogs, easily won to fawn on any man!
Snakes in my heart-blood warm'd, that sting my heart!
Three Judases, each one thrice worse than Judas!
Richard II, Act iii, sc. 2, l. 129 [KING RICHARD]

6906   Since I cannot be a lover,
To entertain these fair well-spoken days,
I am determined to prove a villain
And hate the idle pleasures of these days.
Richard III, Act i, sc. 1, l. 28 [GLOUCESTER]

6907   Villain and he be many miles asunder.
Romeo and Juliet, Act iii, sc. 5, l. 82 [JULIET]

Villany

6908   O villany! Ho, let the door be lock'd:
Treachery! Seek it out.
Hamlet, Act v, sc. 2, l. 322 [HAMLET]

6909   Their villany goes against my weak stomach, and therefore I must
cast it up.
Henry V, Act iii, sc. 2, l. 58 [BOY]

6910   There 's villany abroad.
Love's Labour's Lost, Act i, sc. 1, l. 190 [DULL]

6911   The villany you teach me, I will execute, and it shall go hard
but I will better the instruction.
The Merchant of Venice, Act iii, sc. 1, l. 79 [SHYLOCK]

6912   There 's nothing level in our cursed natures
But direct villany.
Timon of Athens, Act iv, sc. 3, l. 19 [TIMON]

Vine

6913   Come, I will fasten on this sleeve of thine:
Thou art an elm, my husband, I a vine,
Whose weakness married to thy stronger state
Makes me with thy strength to communicate.
The Comedy of Errors, Act ii, sc. 2, l. 175 [ADRIANA]

6914   Her vine, the merry cheerer of the heart,
Unpruned dies.
Henry V, Act v, sc. 2, l. 41 [BURGUNDY]

6915   The vines of France and milk of Burgundy.
King Lear, Act i, sc. 1, l. 86 [LEAR]

Vinegar

6916   Did not goodwife Keech, the butcher's wife, come in then . . .
to borrow a mess of vinegar; telling us she had a good dish of
prawns?
II Henry IV, Act ii, sc. 1, l. 101 [HOSTESS]

6917   I warrant there 's vinegar and pepper in it.
Twelfth Night, Act iii, sc. 4, l. 158 [SIR ANDREW]

Violet

6918   A violet in the youth of primy nature,
Forward, not permanent, sweet, not lasting,
The perfume and suppliance of a minute.
Hamlet, Act i, sc. 3, l. 7 [LAERTES]

6919   Who are the violets now
That strew the green lap of the new come spring?
Richard II, Act v, sc. 2, l. 46 [DUCHESS]

6920   The forward violet thus did I chide:
Sweet thief, whence didst thou steal thy sweet that smells,
If not from my love's breath?
Sonnet xcix, l. 1

Virgin

6921   I would not—though 'tis my familiar sin
With maids to seem the lapwing and to jest,
Tongue far from heart—play with all virgins so:
I hold you as a thing ensky'd and sainted,
By your renouncement an immortal spirit,
And to be talk'd with in sincerity.
Measure for Measure, Act i, sc. 4, l. 31 [LUCIO]

6922   HERMIA: I beseech your grace that I may know
The worst that may befall me in this case,

If I refuse to wed Demetrius.
THESEUS: Either to die the death or to abjure
For ever the society of men.
Therefore, fair Hermia, question your desires;
Know of your youth, examine well your blood,
Whether. . . . You can endure the livery of a nun,
For aye to be in shady cloister mew'd,
To live a barren sister all your life,
Chanting faint hymns to the cold fruitless moon.
Thrice-blessed they that master so their blood,
To undergo such maiden pilgrimage;
But earthlier happy is the rose distill'd,
Than that which withering on the virgin thorn
Grows, lives and dies in single blessedness.
HERMIA: So will I grow, so live, so die, my lord,
Ere I will yield my virgin patent up
Unto his lordship, whose unwished yoke
My soul consents not to give sovereignty.
A Midsummer Night's Dream, Act i, sc. 1, l. 62 [HERMIA]

6923   If fires be hot, knives sharp, or waters deep,
Untied I still my virgin knot shall keep.
Pericles, Act iv, sc. 2, l. 159 [MARINA]

6924   Take my daughter: but
If thou dost break her virgin-knot before
All sanctimonious ceremonies may
With full and holy rite be minister'd,
No sweet aspersion shall the heavens let fall
To make this contract grow; but barren hate,
Sour-eyed disdain and discord shall bestrew
The union of your bed with weeds so loathly
That you shall hate it both: therefore take heed,
As Hymen's lamps shall light you. . . .
Look thou be true; do not give dalliance
Too much the rein: the strongest oaths are straw
To the fire i' the blood.
The Tempest, Act iv, sc. 1, l. 13 [PROSPERO]

Virginity

6925   PAROLLES: Are you meditating on virginity?
HELENA: Ay. You have some stain of soldier in you: let me
ask you a question. Man is enemy to virginity; how may we
barricado it against him?
PAROLLES: Keep him out. . . . Loss of virginity is rational increase and there was never virgin got till virginity was first lost.
. . . Virginity is peevish, proud, idle, made of self-love, which
is the most inhibited sin in the canon.
All's Well that Ends Well, Act i, sc. 1, l. 121 [PAROLLES]

6926   Good my lord,
Ask him upon his oath, if he does think
He had not my virginity.
All's Well that Ends Well, Act v, sc. 3, l. 184 [DIANA]

6927   BAWD: Boult, take her away; use her at thy pleasure: crack the
glass of her virginity, and make the rest malleable.
BOULT: An if she were a thornier piece of ground than she is,
she shall be ploughed.
Pericles, Act iv, sc. 6, l. 150 [BAWD]

Virtue

6928 From lowest place when virtuous things proceed,
The place is dignified by the doer's deed:
Where great additions swell's and virtue none,
It is a dropsied honour.
> *All's Well that Ends Well,* Act ii, sc. 3, l. 132 [KING]

6929 O infinite virtue, comest thou smiling from
The world's great snare uncaught?
> *Antony and Cleopatra,* Act iv, sc. 8, l. 17 [CLEOPATRA]

6930 Why are you virtuous? why do people love you?
And wherefore are you gentle, strong, and valiant? . . .
Know you not, master, to some kind of men
Their graces serve them but as enemies?
> *As You Like It,* Act ii, sc. 3, l. 5 [ADAM]

6931 But virtue, as it never will be moved,
Though lewdness court it in a shape of heaven,
So lust, though to a radiant angel link'd,
Will sate itself in a celestial bed,
And prey on garbage.
> *Hamlet,* Act i, sc. 5, l. 53 [GHOST]

6932 Virtue cannot so inoculate our old stock but we shall relish of it.
> *Hamlet,* Act iii, sc. 1, l. 119 [HAMLET]

6933 Assume a virtue, if you have it not.
> *Hamlet,* Act iii, sc. 4, l. 160 [HAMLET]

6934 Virtue is of so little regard in these coster-monger times that true
valour is turned bear-herd: all the other gifts appertinent to man,
as the malice of this age shapes them, are not worth a gooseberry.
> *II Henry IV,* Act i, sc. 2, l. 191 [FALSTAFF]

6935 These days are dangerous:
Virtue is choked with foul ambition
And charity chased hence by rancour's hand;
Foul subornation is predominant
And equity exiled.
> *II Henry VI,* Act iii, sc. 1, l. 142 [GLOUCESTER]

6936 'Tis virtue that doth make [women] most admired;
The contrary doth make thee wonder'd at.
> *III Henry VI,* Act i, sc. 4, l. 130 [YORK]

6937 Holy men I thought ye,
Upon my soul, two reverend cardinal virtues;
But cardinal sins and hollow hearts I fear ye.
> *Henry VIII,* Act iii, sc. 1, l. 102 [QUEEN KATHARINE]

6938 My heart laments that virtue cannot live
Out of the teeth of emulation.
> *Julius Cæsar,* Act ii, sc. 3, l. 13 [ARTEMIDORUS]

6939 His virtues
Will plead like angels, trumpet-tongued, against
The deep damnation of his taking-off.
> *Macbeth,* Act i, sc. 7, l. 18 [MACBETH]

6940 Virtue is bold, and goodness never fearful.
> *Measure for Measure,* Act iii, sc. 1, l. 215 [DUKE]

6941 Can virtue hide itself? Go to, mum; . . . graces will appear, and
there's an end.
> *Much Ado about Nothing,* Act ii, sc. 1, l. 126 [URSULA]

6942 I hold it ever,
Virtue and cunning were endowments greater
Than nobleness and riches: careless heirs

May the two latter darken and expend;
But immortality attends the former,
Making a man a god.
                                    Pericles, Act iii, sc. 2, l. 26 [CERIMON]
6943   O unlook'd-for evil,
When virtue is profaned in such a devil!
                                    The Rape of Lucrece, l. 846 [LUCRECE]
6944   What virtue breeds iniquity devours.
                                    The Rape of Lucrece, l. 872 [LUCRECE]
6945   O, let not virtue seek
Remuneration for the thing it was;
For beauty, wit,
High birth, vigour of bone, desert in service,
Love, friendship, charity, are subjects all
To envious and calumniating time.
                         Troilus and Cressida, Act iii, sc. 3, l. 169 [ULYSSES]
6946   Virtue is beauty, but the beauteous evil
Are empty trunks o'erflourish'd by the devil.
                              Twelfth Night, Act iii, sc. 4, l. 402 [ANTONIO]

Vocation

6947   PRINCE: I see a good amendment of life in thee; from praying to
purse-taking.
FALSTAFF: Why, Hal, 'tis my vocation, Hal; 'tis no sin for a man
to labour in his vocation.
                                    I Henry IV, Act i, sc. 2, l. 115 [PRINCE]
6948   Yet it is said, labour in thy vocation.
                              II Henry VI, Act iv, sc. 2, l. 17 [HOLLAND]

Voice

6949   I thank you for your voices: thank you:
Your most sweet voices: now you have left your voices,
I have no further with you.
                                    Coriolanus, Act ii, sc. 3, l. 179 [CITIZEN]
6950   Her voice was ever soft,
Gentle, and low, an excellent thing in woman.
                                    King Lear, Act v, sc. 3, l. 272 [LEAR]
6951   LORENZO: That is the voice,
Or I am much deceived, of Portia.
PORTIA: He knows me as the blind man knows the cuckoo,
By the bad voice.
                         The Merchant of Venice, Act v, sc. 1, l. 110 [LORENZO]
6952   I'll speak in a monstrous little voice.
                    A Midsummer Night's Dream, Act i, sc. 2, l. 55 [BOTTOM]
6953   O, good my lord, tax not so bad a voice
To slander music any more than once.
                         Much Ado about Nothing, Act ii, sc. 3, l. 46 [BALTHASAR]
6954   An he had been a dog that should have howled thus, they would
have hanged him: and I pray God his bad voice bode no mischief.
I had as lief have heard the night-raven, come what plague could
have come after it.
                         Much Ado about Nothing, Act ii, sc. 3, l. 81 [BENEDICK]
6955   Thy voice is thunder, but thy looks are humble.
                                    Richard III, Act i, sc. 4, l. 173 [CLARENCE]
6956   O, for a falconer's voice,
To lure this tassel-gentle back again!
                              Romeo and Juliet, Act ii, sc. 2, l. 159 [JULIET]

6957   Thy small pipe
Is as the maiden's organ, shrill and sound.
Twelfth Night, Act i, sc. 4, l. 32 [DUKE]

6958 A mellifluous voice, as I am true knight.
Twelfth Night, Act ii, sc. 3, l. 54 [SIR ANDREW]

Vow

6959 'Tis not the many oaths that makes the truth,
But the plain single vow that is vow'd true.
All 's Well that Ends Well, Act iv, sc. 2, l. 21 [DIANA]

6960   Riotous madness
To be entangled with those mouth-made vows,
Which break themselves in swearing!
Antony and Cleopatra, Act i, sc. 3, l. 27 [CLEOPATRA]

6961 Men's vows are women's traitors.
Cymbeline, Act iii, sc. 4, l. 56 [IMOGEN]

6962 Do not believe his vows; for they are brokers,
Not of that dye which their investments show,
But mere implorators of unholy suits,
Breathing like sanctified and pious bawds,
The better to beguile.
Hamlet, Act i, sc. 3, l. 127 [POLONIUS]

6963 Vows were ever brokers to defiling.
A Lover's Complaint, l. 173

6964 Vows for thee broke deserve not punishment.
A woman I forswore; but I will prove,
Thou being a goddess, I forswore not thee:
My vow was earthly, thou a heavenly love;
Thy grace being gain'd cures all disgrace in me.
Vows are but breath, and breath a vapour is: . . .
If by me broke, what fool is not so wise
To lose an oath to win a paradise?
Love's Labour 's Lost, Act iv, sc. 3, l. 63 [LONGAVILLE]
(Repeated with some slight variations in *The Passionate Pilgrim,* Sonnet iii, l. 4.)

6965 PRINCESS: Hold your vow:
Nor God, nor I, delights in perjured men.
KING: Rebuke me not for that which you provoke:
The virtue of your eye must break my oath.
PRINCESS: You nickname virtue: vice you should have spoke;
For virtue's office never breaks men's troth.
Love's Labour 's Lost, Act v, sc. 2, l. 345 [PRINCESS]

6966   My good Lysander!
I swear to thee by Cupid's strongest bow,
By his best arrow with the golden head,
By the simplicity of Venus' doves,
By that which knitteth souls and prospers loves,
And by that fire which burn'd the Carthage queen,
When the false Troyan under sail was seen,
By all the vows that ever men have broke,
In number more than ever women spoke,
In that same place thou hast appointed me,
To-morrow truly will I meet with thee.
A Midsummer Night's Dream, Act i, sc. 1, l. 168 [HERMIA]

6967 Look, when I vow, I weep; and vows so born,
In their nativity all truth appears.
A Midsummer Night's Dream, Act iii, sc. 2, l. 124 [LYSANDER]

6968   The gods are deaf to hot and peevish vows:
        They are polluted offerings, more abhorr'd
        Than spotted livers in the sacrifice. . . .
        It is the purpose that makes strong the vow;
        But vows to every purpose must not hold.
                    Troilus and Cressida, Act v, sc. 3, l. 16 [CASSANDRA]

6969   Unheedful vows may heedfully be broken,
        And he wants wit that wants resolved will
        To learn his wit to exchange the bad for better.
                    The Two Gentlemen of Verona, Act ii, sc. 6, l. 11 [PROTEUS]

Vulgar

6970   So do our vulgar drench their peasant limbs
        In blood of princes.
                    Henry V, Act iv, sc. 7, l. 80 [MONTJOY]

6971   I'll about
        And drive away the vulgar from the streets.
                    Julius Cæsar, Act i, sc. 1, l. 75 [FLAVIUS]

6972   O base and obscure vulgar!
                    Love's Labour's Lost, Act iv, sc. 1, l. 70 [BOYET, *reading*]

W

Walking

6973   When he walks, he moves like an engine, and the ground shrinks
        before his treading.
                    Coriolanus, Act v, sc. 4, l. 19 [MENENIUS]

6974   Here walk I in the black brow of night
        To find you out.
                    King John, Act v, sc. 6, l. 17 [HUBERT]

6975   The right-valiant Banquo walk'd too late; . . .
        Men must not walk too late.
                    Macbeth, Act iii, sc. 6, l. 5 [LENNOX]

6976   I have known those which have walked in their sleep who have
        died holily in their beds.
                    Macbeth, Act v, sc. 1, l. 66 [DOCTOR]

6977   DON PEDRO: Lady, will you walk about with your friend?
        HERO: So you walk softly and look sweetly and say nothing, I
        am yours for the walk; and especially when I walk away.
                    Much Ado about Nothing, Act ii, sc. 1, l. 90 [DON PEDRO]

6978   Why does the world report that Kate doth limp?
        O slanderous world! Kate like the hazel-twig
        Is straight and slender and as brown in hue
        As hazel nuts and sweeter than the kernels.
        O, let me see thee walk: thou dost not halt.
                    The Taming of the Shrew, Act ii, sc. 1, l. 254 [PETRUCHIO]

6979   Pray you, tread softly, that the blind mole may not
        Hear a foot fall.
                    The Tempest, Act iv, sc. 1, l. 193 [CALIBAN]

Want

6980   Women are not
        In their best fortunes strong; but want will perjure
        The ne'er touch'd vestal.
                    Antony and Cleopatra, Act iii, sc. 12, l. 29 [OCTAVIUS CÆSAR]

6981   She again wants nothing to name want,
        If want it be not that she is not he.
                              King John, Act ii, sc. 1, l. 435 [CITIZEN]
6982   He that keeps nor crust nor crum,
        Weary of all, shall want some.
                              King Lear, Act i, sc. 4, l. 217 [FOOL]
6983   For what I have I need not to repeat;
        And what I want it boots not to complain.
                              Richard II, Act iii, sc. 4, l. 16 [QUEEN]
6984   BANDITTI: We are not thieves, but men that much do want.
        TIMON: Your greatest want is, you want much of meat.
        Why should you want? Behold, the earth hath roots;
        Within this mile break forth a hundred springs;
        The oaks bear mast, the briers scarlet hips;
        The bounteous housewife, nature, on each bush
        Lays her full mess before you. Want! why want?
                              Timon of Athens, Act iv, sc. 3, l. 418 [BANDITTI]

Wantonness

6985   A wightly wanton with a velvet brow,
        With two pitch-balls stuck in her face for eyes;
        Ay, and by heaven, one that will do the deed
        Though Argus were her eunuch and her guard:
        And I to sigh for her! to watch for her!
                              Love's Labour's Lost, Act iii, sc. 1, l. 198 [BIRON]
6986   Lord, Lord! your worship's a wanton. Well, heaven forgive you
        and all of us, I pray!
                              The Merry Wives of Windsor, Act ii, sc. 2, l. 57 [MISTRESS QUICKLY]
6987   The spirit of wantonness is, sure, scared out of him: if the devil
        have him not in fee-simple, with fine and recovery, he will never,
        I think, in the way of waste, attempt us again.
                              The Merry Wives of Windsor, Act iv, sc. 2, l. 223 [MRS. PAGE]
6988   Pardon me, wife. Henceforth do what thou wilt;
        I rather will suspect the sun with cold
        Than thee with wantonness.
                              The Merry Wives of Windsor, Act iv, sc. 4, l. 6 [FORD]
6989   O, 'tis the spite of hell, the field's arch-mock,
        To lip a wanton in a secure couch,
        And to suppose her chaste!
                              Othello, Act iv, sc. 1, l. 71 [IAGO]

War

6990   To the wars, my boy, to the wars!
        He wears his honour in a box unseen,
        That hugs his kicky-wicky here at home,
        Spending his manly marrow in her arms,
        Which should sustain the bound and high curvet
        Of Mars's fiery steed.
                              All's Well that Ends Well, Act ii, sc. 3, l. 295 [PAROLLES]
6991   [He] had the whole theoric of war in the knot of his scarf, and
        the practice in the chape of his dagger.
                              All's Well that Ends Well, Act iv, sc. 3, l. 163 [LORD]
                    ("Chape," the metal mounting of a sheath.)
6992   The end of war's uncertain.
                              Coriolanus, Act v, sc. 3, l. 141 [VOLUMNIA]
6993   Consider, sir, the chance of war.
                              Cymbeline, Act v, sc. 5, l. 75 [LUCIUS]

6994   No more the thirsty entrance of this soil
Shall daub her lips with her own children's blood;
No more shall trenching war channel her fields,
Nor bruise her flowers with the armed hoofs
Of hostile paces. . . .
The edge of war, like an ill-sheathed knife,
No more shall cut his master.
I Henry IV, Act i, sc. 1, l. 5 [KING HENRY]

6995   They come like sacrifices in their trim,
And to the fire-eyed maid of smoky war
All hot and bleeding will we offer them:
The mailed Mars shall on his altar sit
Up to the ears in blood.
I Henry IV, Act iv, sc. 1, l. 113 [HOTSPUR]

6996   Will you again unknit
The churlish knot of all-abhorred war?
I Henry IV, Act v, sc. 1, l. 15 [KING HENRY]

6997   List his discourse of war, and you shall hear
A fearful battle render'd you in music.
Henry V, Act i, sc. 1, l. 43 [CANTERBURY]

6998   Impious war,
Array'd in flames like to the prince of fiends,
Do, with his smirch'd complexion, all fell feats
Enlink'd to waste and desolation.
Henry V, Act iii, sc. 3, l. 15 [KING HENRY]

6999   O war, thou son of hell,
Whom angry heavens do make their minister,
Throw in the frozen bosoms of our part
Hot coals of vengeance! Let no soldier fly.
He that is truly dedicate to war
Hath no self-love, nor he that loves himself
Hath not essentially but by circumstance
The name of valour.
II Henry VI, Act v, sc. 2, l. 33 [YOUNG CLIFFORD]

7000   It is war's prize to take all vantages;
And ten to one is no impeach of valour.
III Henry VI, Act i, sc. 4, l. 59 [NORTHUMBERLAND]

7001   Now for the bare-pick'd bones of majesty
Doth dogged war bristle his angry crest
And snarleth in the gentle eyes of peace.
King John, Act iv, sc. 3, l. 148 [BASTARD]

7002   Your breath first kindled the dead coal of wars
Between this chastised kingdom and myself,
And brought in matter that should feed this fire;
And now 'tis far too huge to be blown out
With that same weak wind which enkindled it.
King John, Act v, sc. 2, l. 83 [LEWIS]

7003   I drew this gallant head of war,
And cull'd these fiery spirits from the world,
To outlook conquest and to win renown
Even in the jaws of danger and of death.
King John, Act v, sc. 2, l. 113 [LEWIS]

7004   He is come to open
The purple testament of bleeding war.
Richard II, Act iii, sc. 3, l. 93 [KING RICHARD]

7005   Grim-visaged war hath smooth'd his wrinkled front;
And now, instead of mounting barbed steeds

To fright the souls of fearful adversaries,
He capers nimbly in a lady's chamber
To the lascivious pleasing of a lute.
Richard III, Act i, sc. 1, l. 9 [GLOUCESTER]

7006   At last, though long, our jarring notes agree:
And time it is, when raging war is done,
To smile at scapes and perils overblown.
The Taming of the Shrew, Act v, sc. 2, l. 1 [LUCENTIO]

7007   Follow thy drum;
With man's blood paint the ground, gules, gules;
Religious canons, civil laws are cruel;
Then what should war be?
Timon of Athens, Act iv, sc. 3, l. 58 [TIMON]

War and Peace

7008   What would you have, you curs,
That like nor peace nor war? the one affrights you,
The other makes you proud.
Coriolanus, Act i, sc. 1, l. 172 [MARCIUS]

7009   SECOND SERVANT: This peace is nothing, but to rust iron, increase
tailors, and breed ballad-makers.
FIRST SERVANT: Let me have war, say I; it exceeds peace as far
as day does night; it's spritely, waking, audible, and full of vent.
Peace is a very apoplexy, lethargy; mulled, deaf, sleepy, insensi-
ble; a getter of more bastard children than war's a destroyer of
men.
SECOND SERVANT: 'Tis so: and as war, in some sort, may be said
to be a ravisher, so it cannot be denied but peace is a great
maker of cuckolds.
Coriolanus, Act iv, sc. 5, l. 233 [SECOND SERVANT]

7010   Never was a war did cease,
Ere bloody hands were wash'd, with such a peace.
Cymbeline, Act v, sc. 5, l. 484 [CYMBELINE]

7011   War, or peace, or both at once may be
As things acquainted and familiar to us.
II Henry IV, Act v, sc. 2, l. 138 [KING HENRY]

7012   My most redoubted father,
It is most meet we arm us 'gainst the foe;
For peace itself should not so dull a kingdom,
Though war nor no known quarrel were in question,
But that defences, musters, preparations,
Should be maintain'd, assembled, and collected,
As were a war in expectation.
Henry V, Act ii, sc. 4, l. 14 [DAUPHIN]

7013   In peace there's nothing so becomes a man
As modest stillness and humility:
But when the blast of war blows in our ears,
Then imitate the action of the tiger;
Stiffen the sinews, summon up the blood,
Disguise fair nature with hard-favour'd rage; . . .
Now set the teeth and stretch the nostril wide,
Hold hard the breath and bend up every spirit
To his full height.
Henry V, Act iii, sc. 1, l. 3 [KING HENRY]

War: The Warrior

7014   Thou art my warrior; I holp to frame thee.
Coriolanus, Act v, sc. 3, l. 62 [VOLUMNIA]

7015   The painful warrior famoused for fight,
       After a thousand victories once foil'd,
       Is from the book of honour razed quite,
       And all the rest forgot for which he toil'd.
                                        Sonnet xxv. l. 9

Wasp

7016   In thy weak hive a wandering wasp hath crept,
       And suck'd the honey which thy chaste bee kept.
                        The Rape of Lucrece, l. 839 [LUCRECE]
7017   Injurious wasps, to feed on such sweet honey
       And kill the bees that yield it with your stings!
                The Two Gentlemen of Verona, Act i, sc. 2, l. 106 [JULIA]

Waste

7018   CHIEF JUSTICE: Your means are very slender and your waste is
       great.
       FALSTAFF: I would it were otherwise; I would my means were
       greater, and my waist slenderer.
                        II Henry IV, Act i, sc. 2, l. 160 [CHIEF JUSTICE]

Watching

7019   Hostess, clap to the doors: watch to-night, pray to-morrow.
                        I Henry IV, Act ii, sc. 4, l. 307 [FALSTAFF]
7020   Watch thou and wake when others be asleep.
                        II Henry VI, Act i, sc. 1, l. 249 [YORK]
7021   PORTIA: Lie not a night from home; watch me like Argus:
       If you do not, if I be left alone,
       Now, by mine honour, which is yet mine own,
       I'll have that doctor for my bedfellow.
       NERISSA: And I his clerk. . . .
       GRATIANO: Well, do you so: let me not take him, then;
       For if I do, I'll mar the young clerk's pen.
                        The Merchant of Venice, Act v, sc. 1, l. 230 [PORTIA]

Water

7022   Smooth runs the water where the brook is deep.
                        II Henry VI, Act iii, sc. 1, l. 53 [SUFFOLK]
       Deep sounds make lesser noise than shallow fords.
                        The Rape of Lucrece, l. 1329
7023   Court holy-water in a dry house is better than this rain-water
       out o' door.
                        King Lear, Act iii, sc. 2, l. 11 [FOOL]
7024   Here's that which is too weak to be a sinner, honest water, which
       ne'er left man i' the mire.
                        Timon of Athens, Act i, sc. 2, l. 58 [APEMANTUS]
7025   What, man! more water glideth by the mill
       Than wots the miller of.
                        Titus Andronicus, Act ii, sc. 1, l. 85 [DEMETRIUS]

Wave

7026   We will not from the helm to sit and weep,
       But keep our course, though the rough wind say no. . . .
       As good to chide the waves as speak them fair.
                        III Henry VI, Act v, sc. 4, l. 21 [QUEEN MARGARET]
7027   The yesty waves
       Confound and swallow navigation up.
                        Macbeth, Act iv, sc. 1, l. 53 [MACBETH]

7028   What care these roarers for the name of king?
> *The Tempest,* Act i, sc. 1, l. 18 [BOATSWAIN]

7029   If by your art, my dearest father, you have
Put the wild waters in this roar, allay them.
The sky, it seems, would pour down stinking pitch,
But that the sea, mounting to the welkin's cheek,
Dashes the fire out.
> *The Tempest,* Act i, sc. 2, l. 1 [MIRANDA]

7030   The wild waves, . . .
Whose ridges with the meeting clouds contend.
> *Venus and Adonis,* l. 819

Wax

7031   Thy noble shape is but a form of wax,
Digressing from the valour of a man.
> *Romeo and Juliet,* Act iii, sc. 3, l. 126 [FRIAR LAURENCE]

7032   What wax so frozen but dissolves with tempering,
And yields at last to very light impression?
> *Venus and Adonis,* l. 565 [VENUS]

Way

7033   They'll be for the flowery way that leads to the broad gate and
the great fire.
> *All's Well that Ends Well,* Act iv, sc. 5, l. 57 [CLOWN]
(For full quotation see 2962.)
Go the primrose way to the everlasting bonfire.·
> *Macbeth,* Act ii, sc. 3, l. 23 [PORTER]

7034   I am so lated in the world, that I
Have lost my way for ever.
> *Antony and Cleopatra,* Act iii, sc. 11, l. 3 [ANTONY]

7035   I am amazed, methinks, and lost my way
Among the thorns and dangers of this world.
> *King John,* Act iv, sc. 3, l. 140 [BASTARD]

7036   Yea, marry, that's the eftest way.
> *Much Ado about Nothing,* Act iv, sc. 2, l. 38 [DOGBERRY]

7037   KING RICHARD: Go, count thy way with sighs; I mine with
groans.
QUEEN: So longest way shall have the longest moans.
KING: Twice for one step I'll groan, the way being short,
And piece the way out with a heavy heart.
> *Richard II,* Act v, sc. 1, l. 89 [KING RICHARD]

Weakness

7038   The weakest goes to the wall.
> *Romeo and Juliet,* Act i, sc. 1, l. 18 [GREGORY]

7039   I am weaker than a woman's tear,
Tamer than sleep, fonder than ignorance,
Less valiant than the virgin in the night.
> *Troilus and Cressida,* Act i, sc. 1, l. 9 [TROILUS]

Wealth

7040   Who cannot keep his wealth must keep his house.
> *Timon of Athens,* Act iii, sc. 3, l. 42 [SERVANT]

7041   Who would not wish to be from wealth exempt,
Since riches point to misery and contempt?
> *Timon of Athens,* Act iv, sc. 2, l. 31 [FLAVIUS]

Weapon

7042   Be well assured
You put sharp weapons in a madman's hands.
II Henry VI, Act iii, sc. 1, l. 346 [YORK]

7043   Men do their broken weapons rather use
Than their bare hands.
Othello, Act i, sc. 3, l. 174 [DUKE]

7044   Behold, I have a weapon;
A better never did itself sustain
Upon a soldier's thigh: I have seen the day
That, with this little arm and this good sword,
I have made my way through more impediments
Than twenty times your stop.
Othello, Act v, sc. 2, l. 259 [OTHELLO]

Weariness

7045   ROSALIND: O Jupiter, how weary are my spirits!
TOUCHSTONE: I care not for my spirits, if my legs were not weary.
As You Like It, Act ii, sc. 4, l. 1 [ROSALIND]

7046   Weariness
Can snore upon the flint, when resty sloth
Finds the down pillow hard.
Cymbeline, Act iii, sc. 6, l. 33 [BELARIUS]

7047   PRINCE: Before God, I am exceeding weary.
POINS: Is 't come to that? I had thought weariness durst not have
attached one of so high blood.
PRINCE: Faith, it does me; though it discolours the complexion
of my greatness to acknowledge it.
II Henry IV, Act ii, sc. 2, l. 1 [PRINCE]

7048   Was ever man so beaten? was ever man so raved? was ever man
so weary?
The Taming of the Shrew, Act iv, sc. 1, l. 2 [GRUMIO]

7049   O master, master, I have watch'd so long
That I am dog-weary.
The Taming of the Shrew, Act iv, sc. 2, l. 59 [BIONDELLO]

Weather

7050   I must make fair weather yet a while.
II Henry VI, Act v, sc. 1, l. 30 [YORK]

7051   Many can brook the weather that love not the wind.
Love's Labour's Lost, Act iv, sc. 2, l. 34 [NATHANIEL]

7052   It is impossible you should take true root but by the fair weather
that you make yourself.
Much Ado about Nothing, Act i, sc. 3, l. 24 [CONRADE]

7053   It is foul weather in us all, good sir,
When you are cloudy.
The Tempest, Act ii, sc. 1, l. 141 [GONZALO]

Weed

7054   We bring forth weeds,
When our quick minds lie still; and our ills told us
Is as our earing.
Antony and Cleopatra, Act i, sc. 2, l. 113 [ANTONY]

7055   Duller shouldst thou be than the fat weed
That roots itself in ease on Lethe wharf,
Wouldst thou not stir in this.
Hamlet, Act i, sc. 5, l. 32 [GHOST]

7056 Do not spread the compost on the weeds,
To make them ranker.
Hamlet, Act iii, sc. 4, l. 151 [HAMLET]

7057 Most subject is the fattest soil to weeds.
II Henry IV, Act iv, sc. 4, l. 54 [KING HENRY]

7058 Now 'tis the spring, and weeds are shallow-rooted;
Suffer them now, and they'll o'ergrow the garden
And choke the herbs for want of husbandry.
II Henry VI, Act iii, sc. 1, l. 31 [QUEEN]

7059 What doth cherish weeds but gentle air?
III Henry VI, Act ii, sc. 6, l. 21 [CLIFFORD]

7060 He weeds the corn and still lets grow the weeding.
Love's Labour's Lost, Act i, sc. 1, l. 96 [LONGAVILLE]

7061 O thou weed,
Who art so lovely fair and smell'st so sweet
That the sense aches at thee, would thou hadst ne'er been born!
Othello, Act iv, sc. 2, l. 67 [OTHELLO]

7062 Unwholesome weeds take root with precious flowers.
The Rape of Lucrece, l. 870 [LUCRECE]

7063 I will go root away
The noisome weeds, which without profit suck
The soil's fertility from wholesome flowers.
Richard II, Act iii, sc. 4, l. 37 [GARDENER]

7064 Small herbs have grace, great weeds do grow apace:
And since, methinks, I would not grow so fast,
Because sweet flowers are slow and weeds make haste.
Richard III, Act ii, sc. 4, l. 13 [YORK]

7065 You said that idle weeds are fast in growth:
The prince my brother hath outgrown me far.
Richard III, Act iii, sc. 1, l. 103 [YORK]

Weeping

7066 Look, they weep;
And I, an ass, am onion-eyed: for shame,
Transform us not to women.
Antony and Cleopatra, Act iv, sc. 2, l. 34 [ENOBARBUS]

7067 I will weep for nothing, like Diana in the fountain, and I will do
that when you are disposed to be merry.
As You Like It, Act iv, sc. 1, l. 155 [ROSALIND]

7068 O lady, weep no more, lest I give cause
To be suspected of more tenderness
Than doth become a man.
Cymbeline, Act i, sc. 1, l. 93 [POSTHUMUS]

7069 To weep is to make less the depth of grief:
Tears then for babes; blows and revenge for me!
III Henry VI, Act ii, sc. 1, l. 85 [RICHARD]

7070 You think I'll weep; No, I'll not weep:
I have full cause of weeping; but this heart
Shall break into a hundred thousand flaws,
Or ere I'll weep.
King Lear, Act ii, sc. 4, l. 285 [LEAR]

7071 Wipe thine eyes;
The good-years shall devour them, flesh and fell,
Ere they shall make us weep: we'll see 'em starve first.
King Lear, Act v, sc. 3, l. 23 [LEAR]

7072 How much better it is to weep at joy than to joy at weeping!
Much Ado about Nothing, Act i, sc. 1, l. 28 [LEONATO]

7073   Come weep with me; past hope, past cure, past help!
                    Romeo and Juliet, Act iv, sc. 1, l. 45 [JULIET]
7074   PANDARUS: Well, cousin, I told you a thing yesterday. . . . I'll
       be sworn 'tis true; he will weep you as 'twere a man born in
       April.
       CRESSIDA: And I'll spring up in his tears, an 'twere a nettle
       against May.
                Troilus and Cressida, Act i, sc. 2, l. 185 [PANDARUS]
7075   I am not prone to weeping, as our sex
       Commonly are; the want of which vain dew
       Perchance shall dry your pities: but I have
       That honourable grief lodged here which burns
       Worse than tears drown.
                The Winter's Tale, Act ii, sc. 1, l. 108 [HERMIONE]

Welcome

7076   ANTIPHOLUS E.: You're sad, Signior Balthazar: pray God our
       cheer
       May answer my good will and your good welcome here.
       BALTHAZAR: I hold your dainties cheap, sir, and your welcome
       dear. . . .
       Small cheer and great welcome makes a merry feast.
                        The Comedy of Errors, Act iii, sc. 1, l. 19
                                        [ANTIPHOLUS OF EPHESUS]
7077   The night to the owl and morn to the lark less welcome.
                        Cymbeline, Act iii, sc. 6, l. 94 [ARVIRAGUS]
7078   The appurtenance of welcome is fashion and ceremony.
                        Hamlet, Act ii, sc. 2, l. 389 [HAMLET]
7079   You're welcome, my fair guests: that noble lady,
       Or gentleman, that is not freely merry,
       Is not my friend: this, to confirm my welcome;
       And to you all, good health.
                        Henry VIII, Act i, sc. 4, l. 34 [WOLSEY]
7080   Bear welcome in your eye, Your hand, your tongue.
                        Macbeth, Act i, sc. 5, l. 65 [LADY MACBETH]
7081   Sir, you are very welcome to our house:
       It must appear in other ways than words,
       Therefore I scant this breathing courtesy.
                The Merchant of Venice, Act v, sc. 1, l. 139 [PORTIA]
7082   Welcome ever smiles, and farewell goes out sighing.
                Troilus and Cressida, Act iii, sc. 3, l. 168 [ULYSSES]
7083   A man is . . . never welcome to a place till some certain shot
       be paid and the hostess say 'Welcome!'
                The Two Gentlemen of Verona, Act ii, sc. 5, l. 6 [LAUNCE]
7084   Welcome hither, As is the spring to the earth.
                The Winter's Tale, Act v, sc. 1, l. 151 [LEONTES]

Welkin

7085   Let the welkin roar.
       Shall we fall foul for toys?
                        II Henry IV, Act ii, sc. 4, l. 182 [PISTOL]
7086   Amaze the welkin with your broken staves!
                Richard III, Act v, sc. 3, l. 341 [KING RICHARD]
7087   SIR TOBY: Shall we make the welkin dance indeed? shall we
       rouse the night-owl in a catch that will draw three souls out of
       one weaver? shall we do that?
       SIR ANDREW: An you love me, let's do it: I am dog at a catch.
                Twelfth Night, Act ii, sc. 3, l. 59 [SIR TOBY]

Wench

7088   I know a wench of excellent discourse,
Pretty and witty, wild and yet, too, gentle.
The Comedy of Errors, Act iii, sc. 1, l. 109
[ANTIPHOLUS OF EPHESUS]

7089   She's the kitchen wench and all grease. . . . I warrant, her rags
and the tallow in them will burn a Poland winter: if she lives till
doomsday, she'll burn a week longer than the whole world.
The Comedy of Errors, Act iii, sc. 2, l. 97
[DROMIO OF SYRACUSE]

7090   Here she comes in the habit of a light wench, and thereof comes
that the wenches say 'God damn me'; that's as much as to say
'God make me a light wench.'
The Comedy of Errors, Act iv, sc. 3, l. 52
[DROMIO OF SYRACUSE]

7091   Light wenches may prove plagues to men forsworn.
Love's Labour's Lost, Act iv, sc. 3, l. 385 [BIRON]

Westward-Ho

7092   OLIVIA: There lies your way, due west.
VIOLA: Then westward-ho!
Twelfth Night, Act iii, sc. 1, l. 145 [OLIVIA]

Wheel

7093   Let go thy hold when a great wheel runs down a hill, lest it
break thy neck with following it; but the great one that goes
up the hill, let him draw thee after.
King Lear, Act ii, sc. 4, l. 72 [FOOL]

7094   Thou art a soul in bliss; but I am bound
Upon a wheel of fire, that mine own tears
Do scald like molten lead.
King Lear, Act iv, sc. 7, l. 47 [LEAR]

7095   The wheel is come full circle.
King Lear, Act v, sc. 3, l. 174 [EDMUND]

Whisper

7096   You have . . . never admitted
A private whisper, no, not with such friends
That thought them sure of you.
Coriolanus, Act v, sc. 3, l. 6 [AUFIDIUS]

7097   They shake their heads
And whisper one another in the ear;
And he that speaks doth gripe the hearer's wrist,
Whilst he that hears makes fearful action,
With wrinkled brows, with nods, and rolling eyes.
King John, Act iv, sc. 2, l. 188 [HUBERT]

7098   Foul whisperings are abroad.
Macbeth, Act v, sc. 1, l. 79 [DOCTOR]

Whiteness

7099   White his shroud as the mountain snow.
Hamlet, Act iv, sc. 5, l. 27 [OPHELIA]
("White as snow:" see *Hamlet*, iii, 6, 46; iv, 5, 195.)
Whiter than snow.
Othello, Act v, sc. 2, l. 4 [OTHELLO]
White as driven snow.
The Winter's Tale, Act iv, sc. 4, l. 220 [AUTOLYCUS]

7100 Thou tremblest; and the whiteness in thy cheek
Is apter than thy tongue to tell thy errand.
Even such a man, so faint, so spiritless,
So dull, so dead in look, so woe-begone,
Drew Priam's curtain in the dead of night,
And would have told him half his Troy was burnt;
But Priam found the fire ere he his tongue,
And I my Percy's death ere thou report'st it.
II Henry IV, Act i, sc. 1, l. 69 [NORTHUMBERLAND]

Whore

7101 Thou rascal beadle, hold thy bloody hand:
Why dost thou lash that whore? Strip thine own back;
Thou hotly lust'st to use her in that kind
For which thou whipp'st her.
King Lear, Act iv, sc. 6, l. 164 [LEAR]

7102 Ever your fresh whore and your powdered bawd.
Measure for Measure, Act iii, sc. 2, l. 61 [LUCIO]

7103 EVANS: What is your genitive case plural, William? . . .
WILLIAM: Genitive,—horum, harum, horum.
QUICKLY: Vengeance of Jenny's case! fie on her! never name
her, child, if she be a whore. . . . You do ill to teach the child
such words.
The Merry Wives of Windsor, Act iv, sc. 1, l. 60 [EVANS]

7104 'Tis the strumpet's plague
To beguile many and be beguiled by one.
Othello, Act iv, sc. 1, l. 97 [IAGO]

7105 This is a subtle whore,
A closet lock and key of villanous secrets:
And yet she'll kneel and pray; I have seen her do 't.
Othello, Act iv, sc. 2, l. 21 [OTHELLO]

7106 OTHELLO: Was this fair paper, this most goodly book
Made to write 'whore' upon? . . . Are you not a strumpet?
DESDEMONA: No, as I am a Christian.
If to preserve this vessel for my lord
From any other foul unlawful touch
Be not to be a strumpet, I am none.
OTHELLO: What, not a whore? . . . I cry you mercy, then:
I took you for that cunning whore of Venice
That married with Othello.
Othello, Act iv, sc. 2, l. 70 [OTHELLO]

7107 He call'd her whore: a beggar in his drink
Could not have laid such terms upon his callet. . . .
Hath she forsook so many noble matches,
Her father, and her country, and her friends,
To be call'd whore? would it not make one weep? . . .
Why should he call her whore? who keeps her company?
What place? what time? what form? what likelihood?
Othello, Act iv, sc. 2, l. 120 [EMILIA]

7108 I cannot say 'whore':
It doth abhor me now I speak the word;
To do the act that might the addition earn
Not the world's mass of vanity could make me.
Othello, Act iv, sc. 2, l. 161 [DESDEMONA]

7109 This fell whore of thine
Hath in her more destruction than thy sword,
For all her cherubin look.
Timon of Athens, Act iv, sc. 3, l. 63 [TIMON]

7110   Be a whore still: . . . Give them diseases: . . .
Make use of thy salt hours; bring down rose-cheeked youth
To the tub-fast and the diet. . . . Consumptions sow
In hollow bones of man.
Timon of Athens, Act iv, sc. 3, l. 83 [TIMON]

Why

7111   The 'why' is plain as way to parish church.
As You Like It, Act ii, sc. 7, l. 52 [JAQUES]

7112   ANTIPHOLUS S.: Dost thou not know? . . . Shall I tell you why?
DROMIO S.: Ay, sir, wherefore; for they say every why has a
wherefore. . . .
Was there ever any man thus beaten out of season,
When in the why and the wherefore is neither rhyme nor reason?
The Comedy of Errors, Act ii, sc. 2, l. 41
[ANTIPHOLUS OF SYRACUSE]

7113   Say, why is this? wherefore? what should we do?
Hamlet, Act i, sc. 4, l. 56 [HAMLET]

7114   There is occasions and causes why and wherefore in all things.
Henry V, Act v, sc. 1, l. 3 [FLUELLEN]

Wickedness

7115   What rein can hold licentious wickedness
When down the hill he holds his fierce career?
Henry V, Act iii, sc. 3, l. 22 [KING HENRY]

7116   Such is thy audacious wickedness,
Thy lewd, pestiferous and dissentious pranks,
As very infants prattle of thy pride.
I Henry VI, Act iii, sc. 1, l. 14 [GLOUCESTER]

Widow

7117   HOSTESS: I am a poor widow of Eastcheap. . . .
CHIEF JUSTICE: Are you not ashamed to enforce a poor widow to
so rough a course to come by her own?
II Henry IV, Act ii, sc. 1, l. 76 [HOSTESS]

7118   How may we content This widow lady?
King John, Act ii, sc. 1, l. 547 [KING PHILIP]
The lady widow of Vitruvio.
Romeo and Juliet, Act i, sc. 2, l. 69 [ROMEO, *reading*]

7119   O, it grieves my soul,
That I must draw this metal from my side
To be a widow-maker!
King John, Act v, sc. 2, l. 15 [SALISBURY]

7120   A beauty-waning and distressed widow,
Even in the afternoon of her best days,
Made pride and purchase of his lustful eye.
Richard III, Act iii, sc. 7, l. 185 [BUCKINGHAM]

7121   I' faith, he'll have a lusty widow now,
That shall be woo'd and wedded in a day.
The Taming of the Shrew, Act iv, sc. 2, l. 50 [TRANIO]

Wife

7122   War is no strife
To the dark house and the detested wife.
All's Well that Ends Well, Act ii, sc. 3, l. 308 [BERTRAM]

7123   Here comes my clog.
             All's Well that Ends Well, Act ii, sc. 5, 1. 58 [BERTRAM]
          (Referring to his wife.)
          Stealing away from his father with his clog at his heels.
             The Winter's Tale, Act iv, sc. 4, 1. 693 [AUTOLYCUS]
7124   My wife is shrewish when I keep not hours.
                        The Comedy of Errors, Act iii, sc. 1, 1. 2
                                      [ANTIPHOLUS OF EPHESUS]
7125   VOLUMNIA: O, thy wife!
          CORIOLANUS: My gracious silence, hail!
                        Coriolanus, Act ii, sc. 1, 1. 192 [VOLUMNIA]
7126   I have heard it said, the fittest time to corrupt a man's wife is
          when she's fallen out with her husband.
                        Coriolanus, Act iv, sc. 3, 1. 33 [ROMAN]
7127   IMOGEN: Why did you throw your wedded lady from you?
          Think that you are upon a rock; and now
          Throw me again. [*Embracing him.*]
          POSTHUMUS: Hang there like fruit, my soul,
          Till the tree die!
                        Cymbeline, Act v, sc. 5, 1. 261 [IMOGEN]
7128   The piece of tender air, thy virtuous daughter,
          Which we call 'mollis aer'; and 'mollis aer'
          We term it 'mulier': which 'mulier' I divine
          Is this most constant wife.
                        Cymbeline, Act v, sc. 5, 1. 446 [SOOTHSAYER]
7129   There will be a world of water shed
          Upon the parting of your wives and you. . . .
          I am afraid my daughter will run mad,
          So much she doteth on her Mortimer.
                        I Henry IV, Act iii, sc. 1, 1. 94 [GLENDOWER]
7130   Thy wife is proud; she holdeth thee in awe,
          More than God or religious churchmen may.
                        I Henry VI, Act i, sc. 1, 1. 39 [WINCHESTER]
7131   Go thy ways, Kate:
          That man i' the world who shall report he has
          A better wife, let him in nought be trusted,
          For speaking false in that: thou art, alone,
          If thy rare qualities, sweet gentleness,
          Thy meekness saint-like, . . . could speak thee out
          The queen of earthly queens.
                        Henry VIII, Act ii, sc. 4, 1. 133 [KING HENRY]
7132   PORTIA: Dwell I but in the suburbs
          Of your great pleasure? If it be no more,
          Portia is Brutus' harlot, not his wife.
          BRUTUS: You are my true and honourable wife,
          As dear to me as are the ruddy drops
          That visit my sad heart.
                        Julius Cæsar, Act ii, sc. 1, 1. 285 [PORTIA]
7133   Sirrah, your brother is legitimate;
          Your father's wife did after wedlock bear him.
          And if she did play false, the fault was hers;
          Which fault lies on the hazards of all husbands
          That marry wives.
                        King John, Act i, sc. 1, 1. 116 [KING]
7134   What, I! I love! I sue! I seek a wife!
          A woman, that is like a German clock,
          Still a-repairing, ever out of frame,

And never going aright, being a watch,
But being watch'd that it may still go right!
> *Love's Labour's Lost,* Act iii, sc. 1, l. 191 [BIRON]

7135   Antonio, I am married to a wife
Which is as dear to me as life itself;
But life itself, my wife, and all the world,
Are not to be esteem'd above thy life:
I would lose all, ay, sacrifice them all
Here to this devil to deliver you.
> *The Merchant of Venice,* Act iv, sc. 1, l. 282 [BASSANIO]

7136   Let me give light, but let me not be light;
For a light wife doth make a heavy husband.
> *The Merchant of Venice,* Act v, sc. 1, l. 129 [PORTIA]

7137   [Mistress Page] is as fartuous a civil modest wife, . . . as any
is in Windsor.
> *The Merry Wives of Windsor,* Act ii, sc. 2, l. 102
> [MISTRESS QUICKLY]

(Mistress Quickly means to say "virtuous.")

7138   We'll leave a proof, by that which we will do,
Wives may be merry, and yet honest too.
> *The Merry Wives of Windsor,* Act iv, sc. 2, l. 105 [MRS. PAGE]

7139   Prince, thou art sad; get thee a wife, get thee a wife: there is
no staff more reverend than one tipped with horn.
> *Much Ado about Nothing,* Act v, sc. 4, l. 126 [BENEDICK]

7140   A fellow almost damn'd in a fair wife.
> *Othello,* Act i, sc. 1, l. 21 [IAGO]

7141   Look to your wife; observe her well with Cassio; . . .
I know our country disposition well;
In Venice they do let heaven see the pranks
They dare not show their husbands; their best conscience
Is not to leave 't undone, but keep 't unknown.
> *Othello,* Act iii, sc. 3, l. 197 [IAGO]

7142   My dearest wife was like this maid, and such a one
My daughter might have been: my queen's square brows;
Her stature to an inch; as wand-like straight;
As silver-voiced; her eyes as jewel-like
And cased as richly; in pace another Juno;
Who starves the ears she feeds, and makes them hungry,
The more she gives them speech.
> *Pericles,* Act v, sc. 1, l. 108 [PERICLES]

7143   This is a way to kill a wife with kindness.
> *The Taming of the Shrew,* Act iv, sc. 1, l. 211 [PETRUCHIO]

7144   Nature craves
All dues be render'd to their owners: now,
What nearer debt in all humanity
Than wife is to the husband?
> *Troilus and Cressida,* Act ii, sc. 2, l. 173 [HECTOR]

7145   My wife's a hobby-horse, deserves a name
As rank as any flax-wench that puts to
Before her troth-plight.
> *The Winter's Tale,* Act i, sc. 2, l. 276 [LEONTES]

Wilderness

7146   A wilderness is populous enough,
So Suffolk had thy heavenly company:
For where thou art, there is the world itself,

With every several pleasure in the world,
And where thou art not, desolation.
                    II Henry VI, Act iii, sc. 2, l. 360 [SUFFOLK]

7147   Such a warped slip of wilderness
        Ne'er issued from his blood.
                    Measure for Measure, Act iii, sc. 1, l. 142 [ISABELLA]

Will

7148   To come thus was I not constrain'd, but did it
        On my free will.
                    Antony and Cleopatra, Act iii, sc. 6, l. 56 [OCTAVIA]

7149   [He] would make his will Lord of his reason.
                    Antony and Cleopatra, Act iii, sc. 13, l. 3 [ENOBARBUS]

7150   Blest be those,
        How mean soe'er, that have their honest wills.
                    Cymbeline, Act i, sc. 6, l. 8 [IMOGEN]

7151   The cloyed will,
        That satiate yet unsatisfied desire, that tub
        Both fill'd and running, ravening first the lamb,
        Longs after for the garbage.
                    Cymbeline, Act i, sc. 6, l. 47 [IACHIMO]

7152   Our wills and fates do so contrary run
        That our devices still are overthrown.
                    Hamlet, Act iii, sc. 2, l. 221 [PLAYER KING]

7153   Nor never Hydra-headed wilfulness
        So soon did lose his seat and all at once.
                    Henry V, Act i, sc. 1, l. 35 [CANTERBURY]

7154   Ill will never said well.
                    Henry V, Act iii, sc. 7, l. 123 [ORLEANS]

7155   Like rich hangings in a homely house,
        So was his will in his old feeble body.
                    II Henry VI, Act v, sc. 3, l. 12 [RICHARD]

7156   Will is deaf and hears no heedful friends.
                    The Rape of Lucrece, l. 495 [TARQUIN]

7157   Whoever hath her wish, thou hast thy 'Will,'
        And 'Will' to boot, and 'Will' in overplus.
                    Sonnet cxxxv, l. 1

7158   What I will, I will, and there an end.
                    The Two Gentlemen of Verona, Act i, sc. 3, l. 65 [ANTONIO]

Will: Testament See also Testament

7159   He hath . . . made his will and read it
        To public ear.
                    Antony and Cleopatra, Act iii, sc. 4, l. 4 [ANTONY]

7160   SLENDER: Now, good mistress Anne,—
        ANNE: What is your will?
        SLENDER: My will! 'od's heartlings, that's a pretty jest indeed!
        I ne'er made my will yet, I thank heaven; I am not such a sickly
        creature, I give heaven praise.
                    The Merry Wives of Windsor, Act iii, sc. 4, l. 58 [SLENDER]

7161   I'll make my will then, and, as sick men do, . . .
        So I bequeath a happy peace to you, . . .
        My riches to the earth, from whence they came.
                    Pericles, Act i, sc. 1, l. 47 [PERICLES]

7162   Bid a sick man in sadness make his will:
        Ah, word ill-urged to one that is so ill!
                    Romeo and Juliet, Act i, sc. 1, l. 208 [ROMEO]

Willow

7163   In hope he'll prove a widower shortly,
       I'll wear a willow garland for his sake.
                     III Henry VI, Act iii, sc. 3, l. 227 [BONA]
           (Quoted in iv, 1, 100.)

7164   I offered him my company to a willow-tree, either to make him
       a garland, as being forsaken, or to bind him up a rod, as
       being worthy to be whipped.
                     Much Ado about Nothing, Act ii, sc. 1, l. 225 [BENEDICK]

7165   My mother had a maid called Barbara :
       She was in love, and he she loved proved mad
       And did forsake her : she had a song of 'willow';
       An old thing 'twas, but it express'd her fortune. . . .
               The poor soul sat sighing by a sycamore tree,
                   Sing all a green willow;
               Her hand on her bosom, her head on her knee,
                   Sing willow, willow, willow.
                     Othello, Act iv, sc. 3, l. 26 [DESDEMONA]

7166   Sing all a green willow must be my garland.
                     Othello, Act iv, sc. 3, l. 51 [DESDEMONA]

Wind

7167   There is something in the wind.
                     The Comedy of Errors, Act iii, sc. 1, l. 69
                                       [ANTIPHOLUS OF EPHESUS]

7168   The wind sits in the shoulder of your sail.
                     Hamlet, Act i, sc. 3, l. 56 [POLONIUS]

7169   If I travel but four foot by the squier further afoot, I shall break
       my wind. . . . Eight yards of uneven ground is threescore and
       ten miles a foot with me; and the stony-hearted villains know it
       well enough.
                     I Henry IV, Act ii, sc. 2, l. 12 [FALSTAFF]

7170   How now, lad! is the wind in that door, i' faith?
                     I Henry IV, Act iii, sc. 3, l. 102 [FALSTAFF]
       Is it possible? Sits the wind in that corner?
                     Much Ado about Nothing, Act ii, sc. 3, l. 102 [BENEDICK]

7171   We shall be winnow'd with so rough a wind
       That even our corn shall seem as light as chaff.
                     II Henry IV, Act iv, sc. 1, l. 194 [MOWBRAY]

7172   FALSTAFF: What wind blew you hither, Pistol?
       PISTOL: Not the ill wind which blows no man to good.
                     II Henry IV, Act v, sc. 3, l. 89 [FALSTAFF]

7173   Ill blows the wind that profits nobody.
                     III Henry VI, Act ii, sc. 5, l. 55 [SON]

7174   Blow, winds, and crack your cheeks! rage! blow!
       You cataracts and hurricanes, spout
       Till you have drench'd our steeples, drown'd the cocks!
                     King Lear, Act iii, sc. 2, l. 1 [LEAR]

7175   My wind cooling my broth
       Would blow me to an ague, when I thought
       What harm a wind too great at sea might do.
                     The Merchant of Venice, Act i, sc. 1, l. 22 [SALARINO]

7176   HORTENSIO: Tell me now, sweet friend, what happy gale
       Blows you from Padua here to old Verona?
       PETRUCHIO: Such wind as scatters young men through the world

To seek their fortunes further than at home,
Where small experience grows.
                The Taming of the Shrew, Act i, sc. 2, l. 48 [HORTENSIO]
7177   The splitting wind
Makes flexible the knees of knotted oaks.
                Troilus and Cressida, Act i, sc. 3, l. 49 [NESTOR]

Wine

7178   Let's all take hands,
Till that the conquering wine hath steep'd our sense
In soft and delicate Lethe.
                Antony and Cleopatra, Act ii, sc. 7, l. 112 [ANTONY]
7179   I am . . . one that loves a cup of hot wine with not a drop of
allaying Tiber in 't.
                Coriolanus, Act ii, sc. 1, l. 51 [MENENIUS]
7180   You have drunk too much canaries; and that's a marvellous
searching wine, and it perfumes the blood before one can say
'What's this?'
                II Henry IV, Act ii, sc. 4, l. 29 [HOSTESS]
7181   A man cannot make him laugh; but that's no marvel, he drinks
no wine.
                II Henry IV, Act iv, sc. 3, l. 95 [FALSTAFF]
7182   The wine of life is drawn, and the mere lees
Is left this vault to brag of.
                Macbeth, Act ii, sc. 3, l. 100 [MACBETH]
7183   Give me some wine; fill full.
I drink to the general joy o' the whole table.
                Macbeth, Act iii, sc. 4, l. 88 [MACBETH]
7184   CASSIO: O thou invisible spirit of wine, if thou hast no name
to be known by, let us call thee devil! . . . O God, that men
should put an enemy in their mouths to steal away their brains!
. . . Every inordinate cup is unblessed and the ingredient is a
devil.
IAGO: Come, come, good wine is a good familiar creature, if it
be well used: exclaim no more against it.
                Othello, Act ii, sc. 3, l. 283 [CASSIO]
7185   Come and crush a cup of wine.
                Romeo and Juliet, Act i, sc. 2, l. 86 [SERVANT]
7186   Go, suck the subtle blood o' the grape,
Till the high fever seethe your blood to froth,
And so 'scape hanging.
                Timon of Athens, Act iv, sc. 3, l. 432 [TIMON]

Wing

7187   As for you, that love to be protected
Under the wings of our protector's grace,
Bring your suits anew.
                II Henry VI, Act i, sc. 3, l. 40 [QUEEN]
7188   I have pursued her as love hath pursued me; which hath been
on the wing of all occasions.
                The Merry Wives of Windsor, Act ii, sc. 2, l. 208 [FORD]

Winking

7189   KING HENRY: Teach your cousin to consent winking.
BURGUNDY: I will wink on her to consent, my lord, if you will
teach her to know my meaning: for maids, well summered and
warm kept, are like flies at Bartholomew-tide, blind, though they
have their eyes.
                Henry V, Act v, sc. 2, l. 331 [KING HENRY]

7190   When most I wink, then do mine eyes best see.
Sonnet xliii, l. 1

7191   Here's three solidares for thee: good boy, wink at me, and say
thou sawest me not.
Timon of Athens, Act iii, sc. 1, l. 46 [LUCULLUS]

Winning

7192   I shall win at the odds.
Hamlet, Act v, sc. 2, l. 222 [HAMLET]

7193   Nothing can seem foul to those that win.
I Henry IV, Act v, sc. 1, l. 8 [KING]

7194   Near or far off, well won is still well shot,
And I am I, howe'er I was begot.
King John, Act i, sc. 1, l. 174 [BASTARD]

7195   Win me and wear me.
Much Ado about Nothing, Act v, sc. 1, l. 82 [ANTONIO]

7196   They laugh that win.
Othello, Act iv, sc. 1, l. 125 [OTHELLO]

7197   TROILUS: Why was my Cressid then so hard to win?
CRESSIDA: Hard to seem won: but I was won, my lord,
With the first glance.
Troilus and Cressida, Act iii, sc. 2, l. 124 [TROILUS]

Winning and Losing

7198   As I my poor self did exchange for you,
To your so infinite loss, so in our trifles
I shall win of you.
Cymbeline, Act i, sc. 1, l. 119 [POSTHUMUS]

7199   LORD: Your lordship is the most patient man in loss, the most
coldest that ever turned up ace.
CLOTEN: It would make any man cold to lose. . . .
LORD: You are most hot and furious when you win.
CLOTEN: Winning will put any man into courage.
Cymbeline, Act ii, sc. 3, l. 1 [LORD]

7200   What shall I do to win my lord again?
Good friend, go to him; for, by this light of heaven,
I know not how I lost him.
Othello, Act iv, sc. 2, l. 149 [DESDEMONA]

Winter

7201   Winter's not gone yet, if the wild-geese fly that way.
King Lear, Act ii, sc. 4, l. 46 [FOOL]

7202   This side is Hiems, Winter, this Ver, the Spring; the one maintained by the owl, the other by the cuckoo.
Love's Labour's Lost, Act v, sc. 2, l. 901 [ARMADO]

7203   Now is the winter of our discontent
Made glorious summer by this sun of York;
And all the clouds that lour'd upon our house
In the deep bosom of the ocean buried.
Richard III, Act i, sc. 1, l. 1 [GLOUCESTER]

7204   When great leaves fall, the winter is at hand.
Richard III, Act ii, sc. 3, l. 33 [CITIZEN]

7205   Winter tames man, woman and beast.
The Taming of the Shrew, Act iv, sc. 1, l. 25 [GRUMIO]

Wisdom

7206   Wisdom and fortune combating together,
If that the former dare but what it can,
No chance may shake it.
Antony and Cleopatra, Act iii, sc. 13, l. 79 [THYREUS]

7207   Learn of the wise, and perpend.
                    As You Like It, Act iii, sc. 2, l. 68 [TOUCHSTONE]

7208   Wisdom cries out in the streets, and no man regards it.
                    I Henry IV, Act i, sc. 2, l. 99 [PRINCE]

7209   Great lords, wise men ne'er sit and wail their loss,
       But cheerly seek how to redeem their harms.
                    III Henry VI, Act v, sc. 4, l. 1 [QUEEN MARGARET]

7210   Thus wisdom wishes to appear most bright
       When it doth tax itself.
                    Measure for Measure, Act ii, sc. 4, l. 78 [ANGELO]

7211   There are a sort of men . . . reputed wise
       For saying nothing, when, I am very sure,
       If they should speak, would almost damn those ears
       Which, hearing them, would call their brothers fools.
                    The Merchant of Venice, Act i, sc. 1, l. 96 [GRATIANO]

7212   She that in wisdom never was so frail
       To change the cod's head for the salmon's tail.
                    Othello, Act ii, sc. 1, l. 155 [IAGO]

7213   Sad pause and deep regard beseem the sage.
                    The Rape of Lucrece, l. 277 [TARQUIN]

7214   All places that the eye of heaven visits
       Are to a wise man ports and happy havens.
                    Richard II, Act i, sc. 3, l. 275 [GAUNT]

Wisdom and Folly
See also Fools and Wise Men

7215   Full oft we see
       Cold wisdom waiting on superfluous folly.
                    All's Well that Ends Well, Act i, sc. 1, l. 115 [HELENA]

7216   PRINCESS: None are so surely caught, when they are catch'd,
       As wit turn'd fool: folly, in wisdom hatch'd,
       Hath wisdom's warrant and the help of school
       And wit's own grace to grace a learned fool.
       ROSALINE: The blood of youth burns not with such excess
       As gravity's revolt to wantonness.
       MARGARET: Folly in fools bears not so strong a note
       As foolery in the wise, when wit doth dote;
       Since all the power thereof it doth apply
       To prove, by wit, worth in simplicity.
                    Love's Labour's Lost, Act v, sc. 2, l. 69 [PRINCESS]

Wish

7217   You think none but your sheets are privy to your wishes.
                    Antony and Cleopatra, Act i, sc. 2, l. 41 [ALEXAS]

7218   Wishers were ever fools.
                    Antony and Cleopatra, Act iv, sc. 15, l. 37 [CLEOPATRA]

7219   PRINCE: I never thought to hear you speak again.
       KING: Thy wish was father, Harry, to that thought.
                    II Henry IV, Act iv, sc. 5, l. 92 [PRINCE]

7220   If wishes would prevail with me,
       My purpose would not fail with me,
       But thither would I hie.
                    Henry V, Act iii, sc. 2, l. 16 [PISTOL]

7221   PRINCESS: Sweet health and fair desires consort your grace!
       KING: Thy own wish wish I thee in every place!
                    Love's Labour's Lost, Act ii, sc. 1, l. 178 [PRINCESS]

7222   Most mighty liege, and my companion peers,
Take from my mouth the wish of happy years.
Richard II, Act i, sc. 3, l. 93 [MOWBRAY]

7223   Look, what is best, that best I wish in thee:
This wish I have; then ten times happy me!
Sonnet xxxvii, l. 13

Wit

7224   I shall ne'er be ware of mine own wit till I break my shins against it.
As You Like It, Act ii, sc. 4, l. 59 [TOUCHSTONE]

7225   You have a nimble wit: I think 'twas made of Atalanta's heels.
As You Like It, Act iii, sc. 2, l. 292 [JAQUES]

7226   ROSALIND: The wiser, the waywarder: make the doors upon a woman's wit and it will out at the casement; shut that and 'twill out at the key-hole; stop that, 'twill fly with the smoke out at the chimney.
ORLANDO: A man that had a wife with such a wit, he might say, 'Wit, whither wilt?'
ROSALIND: Nay, you might keep that check for it till you met your wife's wit going to your neighbour's bed.
ORLANDO: And what wit could wit have to excuse that?
ROSALIND: Marry, to say she came to seek you there. You will never take her without her answer, unless you take her without her tongue.
As You Like It, Act iv, sc. 1, l. 162 [ROSALIND]

7227   Your wit, . . . 'tis strongly wedged up in a block-head.
Coriolanus, Act ii, sc. 3, l. 29 [CITIZEN]

7228   The brain of this foolish-compounded clay, man, is not able to invent any thing that tends to laughter, more than I invent or is invented on me: I am not only witty in myself, but the cause that wit is in other men.
II Henry IV, Act i, sc. 2, l. 8 [FALSTAFF]

7229   His wit's as thick as Tewkesbury mustard.
II Henry IV, Act ii, sc. 4, l. 262 [FALSTAFF]

7230   Thou hast pared thy wit o' both sides, and left nothing i' the middle.
King Lear, Act i, sc. 4, l. 204 [FOOL]

7231   He that has and a little tiny wit,—
   With hey, ho, the wind and the rain,—
Must make content with his fortunes fit,
   For the rain it raineth every day.
King Lear, Act iii, sc. 2, l. 74 [FOOL]

7232   ARMADO: He surely affected her for her wit.
MOTH: It was so, sir; for she had a green wit.
Love's Labour's Lost, Act i, sc. 2, l. 92 [ARMADO]

7233   Biron they call him; but a merrier man,
Within the limit of becoming mirth,
I never spent an hour's talk withal:
His eye begets occasion for his wit;
For every object that the one doth catch
The other turns to a mirth-moving jest,
Which his fair tongue, conceit's expositor,
Delivers in such apt and gracious words
That aged ears play truant at his tales
And younger hearings are quite ravished;
So sweet and voluble is his discourse.
Love's Labour's Lost, Act ii, sc. 1, l. 66 [ROSALINE]

7234   Your wit's too hot; it speeds too fast, 'twill tire.
Love's Labour's Lost, Act ii, sc. 1, l. 120 [BIRON]

7235   O' my troth, most sweet jests! most incony vulgar wit!
Love's Labour's Lost, Act iv, sc. 1, l. 144 [COSTARD]

7236   Now, by the salt wave of the Mediterranean, a sweet touch, a
quick venue of wit! snip, snap, quick and home! it rejoiceth my
intellect: true wit!
Love's Labour's Lost, Act v, sc. 1, l. 61 [ARMADO]

7237   This fellow pecks up wit as pigeons pease,
And utters it again when God doth please:
He is wit's pedler, and retails his wares
At wakes and wassails, meetings, markets, fairs;
And we that sell by gross, the Lord doth know,
Have not the grace to grace it with such show.
Love's Labour's Lost, Act v, sc. 2, l. 315 [BIRON]

7238   Wilt thou show the whole wealth of thy wit in an instant?
The Merchant of Venice, Act iii, sc. 5, l. 61 [LORENZO]

7239   Repair thy wit, good youth, or it will fall
To cureless ruin.
The Merchant of Venice, Act iv, sc. 1, l. 141 [SHYLOCK]

7240   See now how wit may be made a Jack-a-Lent, when 'tis upon ill
employment!
The Merry Wives of Windsor, Act v, sc. 5, l. 134 [FALSTAFF]

7241   They never meet but there's a skirmish of wit between them,
Much Ado about Nothing, Act i, sc. 1, l. 63 [LEONATO]

7242   If he have wit enough to keep himself warm, let him bear it for
a difference between himself and his horse.
Much Ado about Nothing, Act i, sc. 1, l. 68 [BEATRICE]

7243   Your wit ambles well; it goes easily.
Much Ado about Nothing, Act v, sc. 1, l. 159 [BENEDICK]

7244   BENEDICK: Thy wit is as quick as the greyhound's mouth; it catches.
MARGARET: And yours as blunt as the fencer's foils, which hit,
but hurt not.
BENEDICK: A most manly wit, Margaret: it will not hurt a woman.
Much Ado about Nothing, Act v, sc. 2, l. 11 [BENEDICK]

7245   If she be fair and wise, fairness and wit,
The one's for use, the other useth it. . . .
If she be black, and thereto have a wit,
She'll find a white that shall her blackness fit.
Othello, Act ii, sc. 1, l. 130 [IAGO]

7246   Thou know'st we work by wit, and not by witchcraft;
And wit depends on dilatory time.
Othello, Act ii, sc. 3, l. 378 [IAGO]

7247   To do this is within the compass of man's wit.
Othello, Act iii, sc. 4, l. 21 [CLOWN]

7248   Some such squire he was
That turn'd your wit the seamy side without,
And made you to suspect me with the Moor.
Othello, Act iv, sc. 2, l. 145 [EMILIA]

7249   Thy wit, that ornament to shape and love, . . .
Like powder in a skilless soldier's flask,
Is set a-fire by thine own ignorance.
Romeo and Juliet, Act iii, sc. 3, l. 130 [FRIAR LAURENCE]

7250   KATHARINA: Where did you study all this goodly speech?
PETRUCHIO: It is extempore, from my mother-wit.
KATHARINA: A witty mother! witless else her son.
The Taming of the Shrew, Act ii, sc. 1, l. 264 [KATHARINA]

7251   He's winding up the watch of his wit; by and by it will strike.
                    The Tempest, Act ii, sc. 1, l. 12 [SEBASTIAN]

7252   Ajax, who wears his wit in his belly and his guts in his head,
. . . Has not so much wit . . . as will stop the eye of Helen's
needle. . . . A great deal of your wit, too, lies in your sinews, or
else there be liars. Hector shall have a great catch, if he knock
out either of your brains: a' were as good crack a fusty nut with
no kernel.
             Troilus and Cressida, Act ii, sc. 1, l. 79 [THERSITES]

7253   AJAX: An all men were o' my mind—
ULYSSES: Wit would be out of fashion.
             Troilus and Cressida, Act ii, sc. 3, l. 224 [AJAX]

7254   Methinks sometimes I have no more wit than a Christian or an
ordinary man has: but I am a great eater of beef and I believe that
does harm to my wit.
           Twelfth Night, Act i, sc. 3, l. 89 [SIR ANDREW]

7255   Thou wert as witty a piece of Eve's flesh as any in Illyria.
             Twelfth Night, Act i, sc. 5, l. 30 [CLOWN]

7256   As the old hermit of Prague, that never saw pen and ink, very
wittily said to a niece of King Gorboduc, 'That that is is.'
           Twelfth Night, Act iv, sc. 2, l. 14 [CLOWN]

Wit: Wits

7257   Leave this keen encounter of our wits,
And fall somewhat into a slower method.
             Richard III, Act i, sc. 2, l. 115 [GLOUCESTER]

7258   Nay, if thy wits run the wild-goose chase, I have done, for thou
hast more of the wild-goose in one of thy wits than, I am sure,
I have in my whole five. . . . Thy wit is a very bitter sweeting;
it is a most sharp sauce. . . . A wit of cheveril, that stretches
from an inch narrow to an ell broad!
           Romeo and Juliet, Act ii, sc. 4, l. 75 [MERCUTIO]

7259   Wit, an't be thy will, put me into good fooling! Those wits that
think they have thee, do very often prove fools; and I, that am
sure I lack thee, may pass for a wise man: for what says
Quinapalus? 'Better a witty fool than a foolish wit.'
             Twelfth Night, Act i, sc. 5, l. 35 [CLOWN]

7260   By my troth, we that have good wits have much to answer for;
we shall be flouting; we cannot hold.
            As You Like It, Act v, sc. 1, l. 12 [TOUCHSTONE]

Wit: Wits: Mental Faculty

7261   I knew he was not in his perfect wits.
           The Comedy of Errors, Act v, sc. 1, l. 42 [ANGELO]

7262   My wits begin to turn.
             King Lear, Act iii, sc. 2, l. 67 [LEAR]

7263   His wits begin to unsettle.
            King Lear, Act iii, sc. 4, l. 167 [KENT]

7264   Trouble him not, his wits are gone.
            King Lear, Act iii, sc. 6, l. 94 [KENT]

7265   His wits
Are drown'd and lost in his calamities.
           Timon of Athens, Act iv, sc. 3, l. 88 [ALCIBIADES]

7266   And what an if
His sorrows have so overwhelm'd his wits,
Shall we be thus afflicted in his wreaks,
His fits, his frenzy, and his bitterness?
          Titus Andronicus, Act iv, sc. 4, l. 9 [SATURNINUS]

Witch

7267   They say this town is full of cozenage,
As, nimble jugglers that deceive the eye,
Dark-working sorcerers that change the mind,
Soul-killing witches that deform the body, . . .
And many such-like liberties of sin.
The Comedy of Errors, Act i, sc. 2, l. 97 [ANTIPHOLUS OF SYRACUSE]

7268   See how the ugly witch doth bend her brows,
As if with Circe she would change my shape.
I Henry VI, Act v, sc. 3, l. 34 [YORK]

7269   Wizards know their times:
Deep night, dark night, the silent of the night,
The time of night when Troy was set on fire;
The time when screech-owls cry and bandogs howl,
And spirits walk and ghosts break up their graves.
II Henry VI, Act i, sc. 4, l. 19 [BOLINGBROKE]

7270   Aroint thee, witch, aroint thee!
King Lear, Act iii, sc. 4, l. 129 [EDGAR]
'Aroint thee, witch!' the rump-fed ronyon cries.
Macbeth, Act i, sc. 3, l. 6 [WITCH]
("Ronyon," a mangy or scabby creature. "Aroint," begone.)

7271   Out of my door, you witch, you rag, you baggage, you polecat,
you ronyon! out, out! I'll conjure you, I'll fortune-tell you.
The Merry Wives of Windsor, Act iv, sc. 2, l. 193 [FORD]

7272   Hast thou forgot
The foul witch Sycorax, who with age and envy
Was grown into a hoop?
The Tempest, Act i, sc. 2, l. 258 [PROSPERO]

Woe

7273   One woe doth tread upon another's heel,
So fast they follow.
Hamlet, Act iv, sc. 7, l. 164 [QUEEN]

7274   Would I were dead! if God's good will were so;
For what is in this world but grief and woe?
III Henry VI, Act ii, sc. 5, l. 19 [KING HENRY]

7275   Fellowship in woe doth woe assuage.
The Rape of Lucrece, l. 790 [LUCRECE]
Sour woe delights in fellowship
And needly will be rank'd with other griefs.
Romeo and Juliet, Act iii, sc. 2, l. 116 [JULIET]

7276   Woe doth the heavier sit
When it perceives it is but faintly borne.
Richard II, Act i, sc. 3, l. 280 [GAUNT]

7277   So, Green, thou art the midwife to my woe; . . .
Now hath my soul brought forth her prodigy,
And I, a gasping new-deliver'd mother,
Have woe to woe, sorrow to sorrow join'd.
Richard II, Act ii, sc. 2, l. 62 [QUEEN]

7278   God for his mercy! what a tide of woes
Comes rushing on this woeful land at once!
Richard II, Act ii, sc. 2, l. 98 [YORK]

7279   Wise men ne'er sit and wail their woes,
But presently prevent the ways to wail.
Richard II, Act iii, sc. 2, l. 178 [CARLISLE]

7280   All these woes shall serve
For sweet discourses in our time to come.
Romeo and Juliet, Act iii, sc. 5, l. 51 [ROMEO]

Wolf

7281 MENENIUS: Pray you, who does the wolf love?
SICINIUS: The lamb.
MENENIUS: Ay, to devour him; as the hungry plebeians would the
noble Marcius.
BRUTUS: He 's a lamb indeed, that baes like a bear.
MENENIUS: He 's a bear indeed, that lives like a lamb.
Coriolanus, Act ii, sc. 1, l. 8 [MENENIUS]

7282 CHIEF JUSTICE: Since all is well, keep it so: wake not a sleeping
wolf.
FALSTAFF: To wake a wolf is as bad as to smell a fox.
II Henry IV, Act i, sc. 2, l. 173 [CHIEF JUSTICE]

7283 Thee I'll chase hence, thou wolf in sheep's array.
I Henry VI, Act i, sc. 3, l. 55 [GLOUCESTER]

7284 Is he a lamb? his skin is surely lent him,
For he 's inclined as is the ravenous wolf.
II Henry VI, Act iii, sc. 1, l. 77 [QUEEN]

7285 Poor man! I know he would not be a wolf,
But that he sees the Romans are but sheep;
He were no lion, were not Romans hinds.
Julius Cæsar, Act i, sc. 3, l. 104 [CASSIUS]

7286 How many lambs might the stern wolf betray,
If like a lamb he could his looks translate!
Sonnet xcvi, l. 9

Woman

7287 Was this fair face the cause, quoth she,
Why the Grecians sacked Troy?
Fond done, done fond,
Was this King Priam's joy?
With that she sighed as she stood,
And gave this sentence then;
Among nine bad if one be good,
There 's yet one good in ten. . . .
One good woman in ten! . . . An we might have a good woman
born but one every blazing star, or at an earthquake, 'twould
mend the lottery well. A man may draw his heart out ere a' pluck
one.
All's Well that Ends Well, Act i, sc. 3, l. 74 [CLOWN]

7288 No more, but e'en a woman, and commanded
By such poor passion as the maid that milks
And does the meanest chares.
Antony and Cleopatra, Act iv, sc. 15, l. 72 [CLEOPATRA]

7289 I have nothing
Of woman in me: now from head to foot
I am marble-constant; now the fleeting moon
No planet is of mine.
Antony and Cleopatra, Act v, sc. 2, l. 238 [CLEOPATRA]

7290 A very honest woman, but something given to lie; as a woman
should not do, but in the way of honesty.
Antony and Cleopatra, Act v, sc. 2, l. 252 [CLOWN]

7291 The devil himself will not eat a woman: I know that a woman
is a dish for the gods, if the devil dress her not. But, truly, these
same whoreson devils do the gods great harm in their women; for
in every ten that they make, the devils mar five.
Antony and Cleopatra, Act v, sc. 2, l. 274 [CLOWN]

7292   I could find in my heart to disgrace my man's apparel and to cry
       like a woman; but I must comfort the weaker vessel, as doublet
       and hose ought to show itself courageous to petticoat.
                          As You Like It, Act ii, sc. 4, l. 4 [ROSALIND]
       Women, being the weaker vessels, are ever thrust to the wall.
                          Romeo and Juliet, Act i, sc. 1, l. 20 [SAMPSON]
       (That is, thrust to the inner side of the pavement to protect
       them.)

7293   Do you not know I am a woman? when I think, I must speak.
                          As You Like It, Act iii, sc. 2, l. 263 [ROSALIND]

7294   ORLANDO: Can you remember any of the principal evils that he
       laid to the charge of women?
       ROSALIND: There were none principal; they were all like one an-
       other as half-pence are, every one fault seeming monstrous till his
       fellow-fault came to match it.
                          As You Like It, Act iii, sc. 2, l. 369 [ORLANDO]

7295   That woman that cannot make her fault her husband's occasion,
       let her never nurse her child herself, for she will breed it like
       a fool!
                          As You Like It, Act iv, sc. 1, l. 177 [ROSALIND]

7296   Women's gentle brain
       Could not drop forth such giant-rude invention,
       Such Ethiope words, blacker in their effect
       Than in their countenance.
                          As You Like It, Act iv, sc. 3, l. 33 [ROSALIND]

7297   The pleasing punishment that women bear.
                          The Comedy of Errors, Act i, sc. 1, l. 47 [ÆGEON]

7298   Alas, poor women! make us but believe,
       Being compact of credit, that you love us;
       Though others have the arm, show us the sleeve;
       We in your motion turn and you may move us.
                          The Comedy of Errors, Act iii, sc. 2, l. 21 [LUCIANA]

7299   The venom clamours of a jealous woman
       Poisons more deadly than a mad dog's tooth.
                          The Comedy of Errors, Act v, sc. 1, l. 69 [ABBESS]

7300   The vows of women
       Of no more bondage be, to where they are made,
       Than they are to their virtues; which is nothing.
                          Cymbeline, Act ii, sc. 4, l. 110 [POSTHUMUS]

7301   There's no motion
       That tends to vice in man, but I affirm
       It is the woman's part: be it lying, note it,
       The woman's; flattering, hers; deceiving, hers;
       Lust and rank thoughts, hers; revenges, hers; . . .
       All faults that may be named, nay that hell knows,
       Why, hers.
                          Cymbeline, Act ii, sc. 5, l. 20 [POSTHUMUS]

7302   'Tis said a woman's fitness comes by fits.
                          Cymbeline, Act iv, sc. 1, l. 6 [CLOTEN]

7303   Who is 't can read a woman?
                          Cymbeline, Act v, sc. 5, l. 48 [CYMBELINE]

7304   One that was a woman, sir; but, rest her soul, she's dead.
                          Hamlet, Act v, sc. 1, l. 145 [CLOWN]

7305   Whither I must, I must; and, to conclude,
       This evening must I leave you, gentle Kate.
       I know you wise, but yet no farther wise
       Than Harry Percy's wife: constant you are,

But yet a woman: and for secrecy,
No lady closer; for I well believe
Thou wilt not utter what thou dost not know;
And so far will I trust thee, gentle Kate. . . .
Not an inch further.
I Henry IV, Act ii, sc. 3, l. 108 [HOTSPUR]

7306 A poor lone woman.
II Henry IV, Act ii, sc. 1, l. 37 [HOSTESS]

7307 BOY: A' said they [women] were devils incarnate. . . . A' said
once, the devil would have him about women.
HOSTESS: A' did in some sort, indeed, handle women.
Henry V, Act ii, sc. 3, l. 33 [BOY]

7308 O tiger's heart wrapt in a woman's hide! . . .
Women are soft, mild, pitiful and flexible;
Thou stern, obdurate, flinty, rough, remorseless. . . .
You are more inhuman, more inexorable,
O, ten times more, than tigers of Hyrcania.
III Henry VI, Act i, sc. 4, l. 137 [YORK]

7309 She's a woman to be pitied much:
Her sighs will make a battery in his breast;
Her tears will pierce into a marble heart;
The tiger will be mild whiles she doth mourn.
III Henry VI, Act iii, sc. 1, l. 36 [KING HENRY]

7310 Two women placed together makes cold weather.
Henry VIII, Act i, sc. 4, l. 22 [CHAMBERLAIN]

7311 Sir, as I have a soul, she is an angel;
Our king has all the Indies in his arms,
And more and richer, when he strains that lady: . . .
Believe me, sir, she is the goodliest woman
That ever lay by man.
Henry VIII, Act iv, sc. 1, l. 44 [GENTLEMAN]

7312 I grant I am a woman; but withal
A woman that Lord Brutus took to wife:
I grant I am a woman; but withal
A woman well-reputed, Cato's daughter.
Think you I am no stronger than my sex,
Being so father'd and so husbanded?
Julius Cæsar, Act ii, sc. 1, l. 292 [PORTIA]

7313 How hard it is for women to keep counsel!
Julius Cæsar, Act ii, sc. 4, l. 9 [PORTIA]

7314 Ay me, how weak a thing
The heart of woman is!
Julius Cæsar, Act ii, sc. 4, l. 41 [PORTIA]

7315 There was never yet fair woman but she made mouths in a glass.
King Lear, Act iii, sc. 2, l. 35 [FOOL]

7316 See thyself, devil!
Proper deformity seems not in the fiend
So horrid as in woman. . . . Howe'er thou art a fiend,
A woman's shape doth shield thee.
King Lear, Act iv, sc. 2, l. 59 [ALBANY]

7317 Down from the waist they are Centaurs,
Though women all above:
But to the girdle do the gods inherit,
Beneath is all the fiends';
There's hell, there's darkness, there's the sulphurous pit,
Burning, scalding, stench, consumption; fie!
King Lear, Act iv, sc. 6, l. 126 [LEAR]

7318   A child of our grandmother Eve, a female; or, for thy more
sweet understanding, a woman.
Love's Labour's Lost, Act i, sc. 1, l. 266 [ARMADO]

7319   You should be women,
And yet your beards forbid me to interpret
That you are so.
Macbeth, Act i, sc. 3, l. 45 [BANQUO]

7320   O, I could play the woman with mine eyes
And braggart with my tongue!
Macbeth, Act iv, sc. 3, l. 230 [MACDUFF]

7321   ANGELO: Women are frail too.
ISABELLA: Ay, as the glasses where they view themselves; . . .
Women! Help Heaven! men their creation mar
In profiting by them. Nay, call us ten times frail;
For we are soft as our complexions are,
And credulous to false prints. . . .
ANGELO: Be that you are,
That is, a woman; if you be more, you're none.
Measure for Measure, Act ii, sc. 4, l. 125 [ANGELO]

7322   What, is there none of Pygmalion's images, newly made woman,
to be had now?
Measure for Measure, Act iii, sc. 2, l. 47 [LUCIO]

7323   One woman is fair, yet I am well; another is wise, yet I am well;
another virtuous, yet I am well; but till all graces be in one
woman, one woman shall not come in my grace.
Much Ado about Nothing, Act ii, sc. 3, l. 27 [BENEDICK]

7324   He hath a person and a smooth dispose
To be suspected, framed to make women false.
Othello, Act i, sc. 3, l. 403 [IAGO]

7325   You are pictures out of doors,
Bells in your parlours, wild-cats in your kitchens,
Saints in your injuries, devils being offended,
Players in your housewifery, and housewives in your beds. . . .
Nay, it is true, or else I am a Turk:
You rise to play and go to bed to work.
Othello, Act ii, sc. 1, l. 110 [IAGO]

7326   I do attend here on the general;
And think it no addition, nor my wish,
To have him see me woman'd.
Othello, Act iii, sc. 4, l. 193 [CASSIO]

7327   A fine woman! a fair woman! a sweet woman! . . . O, the world
hath not a sweeter creature: she might lie by an emperor's side
and command him tasks.
Othello, Act iv, sc. 1, l. 189 [OTHELLO]

7328   Play the maid's part, still answer nay, and take it.
Richard III, Act iii, sc. 7, l. 51 [BUCKINGHAM]
Have you not heard it said full oft,
A woman's nay doth stand for nought?
Sonnets to Sundry Notes of Music, Pt. xix, l. 41
Maids in modesty say 'no' to that
Which they would have the profferer construe 'ay.'
The Two Gentlemen of Verona, Act i, sc. 2, l. 55 [JULIA]

7329   Let not the heavens hear these tell-tale women
Rail on the Lord's anointed.
Richard III, Act iv, sc. 4, l. 149 [KING RICHARD]

7330   The wiles and guiles that women work,
Dissembled with an outward show,

The tricks and toys that in them lurk,
The cock that treads them shall not know.
>> *Sonnets to Sundry Notes of Music,* Pt. xix, l. 37

7331 KATHARINA: Asses are made to bear, and so are you.
PETRUCHIO: Women are made to bear, and so are you.
>> *The Taming of the Shrew,* Act ii, sc. 1, l. 200 [KATHARINA]

7332 Kindness in women, not their beauteous looks,
Shall win my love.
>> *The Taming of the Shrew,* Act iv, sc. 2, l. 41 [HORTENSIO]

7333 A woman moved is like a fountain troubled,
Muddy, ill-seeming, thick, bereft of beauty;
And while it is so, none so dry or thirsty
Will deign to sip or touch one drop of it.
>> *The Taming of the Shrew,* Act v, sc. 2, l. 142 [KATHARINA]

7334 VINCENTIO: 'Tis a good hearing when children are toward.
LUCENTIO: But a harsh hearing when women are froward.
>> *The Taming of the Shrew,* Act v, sc. 2, l. 182 [VINCENTIO]

7335 For several virtues
Have I liked several women; never any
With so full soul, but some defect in her
Did quarrel with the noblest grace she owed
And put it to the foil: but you, O you,
So perfect and so peerless, are created
Of every creature's best.
>> *The Tempest,* Act iii, sc. 1, l. 42 [FERDINAND]

7336 PANDARUS: You are such a woman! one knows not at what ward
you lie.
CRESSIDA: Upon my back, to defend my belly; upon my wit, to
defend my wiles.
>> *Troilus and Cressida,* Act i, sc. 2, l. 282 [PANDARUS]

7337 O that I thought it could be in a woman . . .
To feed for aye her lamp and flames of love;
To keep her constancy in plight and youth,
Outliving beauty's outward, with a mind
That doth renew swifter than blood decays!
>> *Troilus and Cressida,* Act iii, sc. 2, l. 165 [TROILUS]

7338 Ah, poor our sex! this fault in us I find,
The error of our eye directs our mind:
What error leads must err; O, then conclude
Minds sway'd by eyes are full of turpitude.
>> *Troilus and Cressida,* Act v, sc. 2, l. 109 [CRESSIDA]

7339 DUKE: There is no woman's sides
Can bide the beating of so strong a passion
As love doth give my heart; no woman's heart
So big, to hold so much; they lack retention.
Alas, their love may be call'd appetite,
No motion of the liver, but the palate,
That suffer surfeit, cloyment and revolt;
But mine is all as hungry as the sea,
And can digest so much. . . .
VIOLA: Ay, but I know . . .
Too well what love women to men may owe:
In faith, they are as true of heart as we.
My father had a daughter loved a man. . . .
DUKE: And what's her history?
VIOLA: A blank, my lord. She never told her love,
But let concealment, like a worm i' the bud,

Feed on her damask cheek: she pined in thought,
And with a green and yellow melancholy
She sat like patience on a monument,
Smiling at grief. Was not this love indeed?
We men may say more, swear more; but indeed
Our shows are more than will; for still we prove
Much in our vows, but little in our love.
DUKE: But died thy sister of her love, my boy?
VIOLA: I am all the daughters of my father's house,
And all the brothers too: and yet I know not.
Twelfth Night, Act ii, sc. 4, 1. 96 [DUKE]

7340   A woman sometimes scorns what best contents her, . . .
For scorn at first makes after-love the more.
The Two Gentlemen of Verona, Act iii, sc. 1, 1. 92 [VALENTINE]

7341   SPEED: 'Item: She is slow in words.'
LAUNCE: O villain, that set this down among her vices! To be
slow in words is a woman's only virtue.
The Two Gentlemen of Verona, Act iii, sc. 1, 1. 336 [SPEED]

7342   Women say so, That will say any thing.
The Winter's Tale, Act i, sc. 2, 1. 130 [LEONTES]

7343   She was a woman and was turned into a cold fish for she would
not exchange flesh with one that loved her.
The Winter's Tale, Act iv, sc. 4, 1. 283 [AUTOLYCUS]

Womb

7344   Hear, nature, hear; dear goddess, hear!
Suspend thy purpose, if thou didst intend
To make this creature fruitful!
Into her womb convey sterility!
Dry up in her the organs of increase;
And from her derogate body never spring
A babe to honour her!
King Lear, Act i, sc. 4, 1. 297 [LEAR]

7345   Your brother and his lover have embraced:
As those that feed grow full; as blossoming time,
That from the seedness the bare fallow brings
To teeming foison, even so her plenteous womb
Expresseth his full tilth and husbandry.
Measure for Measure, Act i, sc. 4, 1. 40 [LUCIO]

7346   O my accursed womb, the bed of death!
A cockatrice hast thou hatch'd to the world,
Whose unavoided eye is murderous.
Richard III, Act iv, sc. 1, 1. 54 [QUEEN ELIZABETH]

7347   From forth the kennel of thy womb hath crept
A hell-hound that doth hunt us all to death:
That dog, that had his teeth before his eyes,
To worry lambs and lap their gentle blood,
That foul defacer of God's handiwork,
That excellent grand tyrant of the earth,
That reigns in galled eyes of weeping souls,
Thy womb let loose to chase us to our graves.
Richard III, Act iv, sc. 4, 1. 47 [QUEEN MARGARET]

7348   Where is she so fair whose unear'd womb
Disdains the tillage of thy husbandry?
Sonnet iii, 1. 5

7349   Ensear thy fertile and conceptious womb,
Let it no more bring out ingrateful man!

Go great with tigers, dragons, wolves, and bears;
Teem with new monsters, whom thy upward face
Hath to the marbled mansion all above
Never presented!

Timon of Athens, Act iv, sc. 3, l. 187 [TIMON]

Wonder

7350 O wonderful, wonderful and most wonderful wonderful! and yet
again wonderful, and after that, out of all hooping!

As You Like It, Act iii, sc. 2, l. 201 [CELIA]

7351 I . . . Was made a wonder and a pointing-stock.

II Henry VI, Act ii, sc. 4, l. 46 [DUCHESS]

7352 GLOUCESTER: That would be ten days' wonder at the least.
CLARENCE: That's a day longer than a wonder lasts.
GLOUCESTER: By so much is the wonder in extremes.

III Henry VI, Act iii, sc. 2, l. 113 [GLOUCESTER]

7353 Navarre shall be the wonder of the world;
Our court shall be a little Academe,
Still and contemplative in living art.

Love's Labour's Lost, Act i, sc. 1, l. 12 [KING]

7354 LUCENTIO: Here is a wonder, if you talk of a wonder.
HORTENSIO: And so it is; I wonder what it bodes.
PETRUCHIO: Marry, peace it bodes, and love and quiet life, . . .
And, to be short, what not that's sweet and happy?

The Taming of the Shrew, Act v, sc. 2, l. 106 [LUCENTIO]

Wood

7355 SUFFOLK: I'll win this Lady Margaret. For whom?
Why, for my king: tush, that's a wooden thing.
MARGARET: He talks of wood: it is some carpenter.

I Henry VI, Act v, sc. 3, l. 88 [SUFFOLK]

7356 Brave followers, yonder stands the thorny wood,
Which, by the heavens' assistance and your strength,
Must by the roots be hewn up yet ere night.

III Henry VI, Act v, sc. 4, l. 67 [KING EDWARD]

7357 In the wood, where often you and I
Upon faint primrose-beds were wont to lie,
Emptying our bosoms of their counsel sweet,
There my Lysander and myself shall meet.

A Midsummer Night's Dream, Act i, sc. 1, l. 214 [HERMIA]

Woodcock

7358 CLIFFORD: Ay, ay, so strives the woodcock with the gin.
NORTHUMBERLAND: So doth the cony struggle in the net.
YORK: So triumph thieves upon their conquer'd booty;
So true men yield, with robbers so o'ermatch'd.

III Henry VI, Act i, sc. 4, l. 61 [CLIFFORD]

7359 Now is the woodcock near the gin.

Twelfth Night, Act ii, sc. 5, l. 92 [FABIAN]

Wooing

7360 Men are April when they woo, December when they wed.

As You Like It, Act iv, sc. 1, l. 147 [ROSALIND]

Women are angels, wooing.

Troilus and Cressida, Act i, sc. 2, l. 312 [CRESSIDA]

7361 I' faith, Kate, my wooing is fit for thy understanding. I am glad
thou canst speak no better English; for, if thou couldst, thou

wouldst find me such a plain king that thou wouldst think I had
sold my farm to buy my crown. I know no ways to mince it in
love, but directly to say 'I love you'. . . . If you would put me
to verses or to dance for your sake, Kate, why you undid me. . . .
I speak to thee plain soldier: if thou canst love me for this, take
me; if not, to say to thee that I shall die, is true; but for thy
love, by the Lord, no; yet I love thee too. And while thou livest,
dear Kate, take a fellow of plain and uncoined constancy; for he
perforce must do thee right, because he hath not the gift to woo
in other places: for these fellows of infinite tongue, that can
rhyme themselves into ladies' favours, they do always reason themselves out again. What! a speaker is but a prater; a rhyme is
but a ballad. A good leg will fall: a straight back will stoop; a
black beard will turn white; a curled pate will grow bald; a fair
face will wither; a full eye will wax hollow: but a good heart,
Kate, is the sun and the moon; or rather the sun and not the
moon: for it shines bright and never changes, but keeps his course
truly. If thou would have such a one, take me; and take me,
take a soldier; take a soldier, take a king. . . . Shalt not thou
and I, between Saint Denis and Saint George, compound a boy,
half French, half English, that shall go to Constantinople and
take the Turk by the beard? shall we not? what sayest thou, my
fair flower-de-luce? . . . Tell me, most fair Katherine, will you
have me? Put off your maiden blushes; avouch the thoughts of
your heart with the looks of an empress; take me by the hand,
and say 'Harry of England, I am thine.'
>   *Henry V*, Act v, sc. 2, l. 125 [KING HENRY]
7362 She's beautiful and therefore to be woo'd;
She is a woman, therefore to be won.
>   *I Henry VI*, Act v, sc. 3, l. 78 [SUFFOLK]
She is a woman, therefore may be woo'd;
She is a woman, therefore may be won.
>   *Titus Andronicus*, Act ii, sc. 1, l. 82 [DEMETRIUS]
Was ever woman in this humour woo'd?
Was ever woman in this humour won?
>   *Richard III*, Act i, sc. 2, l. 228 [GLOUCESTER]
7363 O, never will I trust to speeches penn'd,
>   Nor to the motion of a schoolboy's tongue,
Nor never come in vizard to my friend,
>   Nor woo in rhyme, like a blind harper's song!
Taffeta phrases, silken terms precise,
>   Three-piled hyperboles, spruce affectation,
Figures pedantical; these summer-flies
>   Have blown me full of maggot ostentation:
I do forswear them; and I here protest,
>   By this white glove,—how white the hand, God knows!—
Henceforth my wooing mind shall be express'd
>   In russet yeas, and honest kersey noes.
>   *Love's Labour's Lost*, Act v, sc. 2, l. 402 [BIRON]
7364 Our wooing doth not end like an old play;
Jack hath not Jill.
>   *Love's Labour's Lost*, Act v, sc. 2, l. 884 [BIRON]
7365 PISTOL: Sir John affects thy wife. . . .
He wooes both high and low, both rich and poor,
Both young and old, one with another, Ford;
He loves the gallimaufry: Ford, perpend. . . .
O, odious is the name!

FORD: What name, sir?
PISTOL: The Horn, I say, Farewell.
Take heed, have open eyes, for thieves do foot by night:
Take heed, ere summer comes or cuckoo-birds do sing.
    The Merry Wives of Windsor, Act ii, sc. 1, l. 115 [PISTOL]

7366   Albeit, I will confess, thy father's wealth
Was the first motive when I woo'd thee, Anne:
Yet, wooing thee, I found thee of more value
Than stamps in gold or sums in sealed bags;
And 'tis the very riches of thyself
That now I aim at.
    The Merry Wives of Windsor, Act iii, sc. 4, l. 13 [FENTON]

7367   Your wrongs do set a scandal on my sex.
We cannot fight for love, as men may do;
We should be woo'd and were not made to woo.
    A Midsummer Night's Dream, Act ii, sc. 1, l. 240 [HELENA]
Though I loved you well, I woo'd you not:
And yet, good faith, I wish'd myself a man,
O that we women had men's privilege
Of speaking first.
    Troilus and Cressida, Act iii, sc. 2, l. 134 [CRESSIDA]

7368   With a good leg and a good foot, uncle, and money enough in
his purse, such a man would win any woman in the world, if
a' could get her good-will.
    Much Ado about Nothing, Act ii, sc. 1, l. 15 [BEATRICE]

7369   Wooing, wedding, and repenting, is as a Scotch jig, a measure,
and a cinque pace: the first suit is hot and hasty, like a Scotch
jig, and full as fantastical; the wedding, mannerly-modest, as a
measure, full of state and ancientry; and then comes repentance
and, with his bad legs, falls into the cinque pace faster and
faster, till he sink into his grave.
    Much Ado about Nothing, Act ii, sc. 1, l. 76 [BEATRICE]

7370   I cannot woo in festival terms.
    Much Ado about Nothing, Act v, sc. 2, l. 39 [BENEDICK]

7371   When a woman woos, what woman's son
Will sourly leave her till she have prevailed?
    Sonnet xli, l. 7

7372   Woo her, wed her and bed her.
    The Taming of the Shrew, Act i, sc. 1, l. 149 [GREMIO]

7373   PETRUCHIO: I am rough and woo not like a babe.
BAPTISTA: Well mayst thou woo, and happy be thy speed!
    The Taming of the Shrew, Act ii, sc. 1, l. 138 [PETRUCHIO]

7374   I'll . . . woo her with some spirit when she comes.
Say that she rail; why then I'll tell her plain
She sings as sweetly as a nightingale:
Say that she frown; I'll say she looks as clear
As morning roses newly wash'd in dew: . . .
If she deny to wed, I'll crave the day
When I shall ask the banns and when be married.
    The Taming of the Shrew, Act ii, sc. 1, l. 170 [PETRUCHIO]

7375   I must, forsooth, be forced
To give my hand opposed against my heart
Unto a mad-brain rudesby full of spleen;
Who woo'd in haste and means to wed at leisure.
    The Taming of the Shrew, Act iii, sc. 2, l. 8 [KATHARINA]

7376   Why should he despair that knows to court it
       With words, fair looks and liberality?
                    Titus Andronicus, Act ii, sc. 1, l. 91 [DEMETRIUS]
7377   Our kindred, though they be long ere they are wooed, they are
       constant being won; they are burs, I can tell you; they 'll stick
       where they are thrown.
                    Troilus and Cressida, Act iii, sc. 2, l. 117 [PANDARUS]

Word

7378   CELIA: Why, cousin! why, Rosalind! Cupid have mercy! Not a
       word?
       ROSALIND: Not one to throw at a dog.
       CELIA: No, thy words are too precious to be cast away upon
       curs; throw some of them at me.
                    As You Like It, Act i, sc. 3, l. 1 [CELIA]
7379   ROSALIND: Answer me in one word.
       CELIA: You must borrow me Gargantua's mouth first: 'tis a word
       too great for any mouth of this age's size.
                    As You Like It, Act iii, sc. 2, l. 237 [ROSALIND]
7380   I will not eat my word.
                    As You Like It, Act v, sc. 4, l. 155 [PHEBE]
       BEATRICE: Will you not eat your word?
       BENEDICK: With no sauce that can be devised to it.
                    Much Ado about Nothing, Act iv, sc. 1, l. 280 [BEATRICE]
7381   BARDOLPH: A soldier is better accommodated than with a wife.
       SHALLOW: Better accommodated! it is good, yea, indeed, is it.
       . . . It comes of 'accomodo': very good; a good phrase.
       BARDOLPH: Pardon me, sir; I have heard the word. Phrase, call
       you it? by this good day, I know not the phrase; but I will main-
       tain the word with my sword to be a soldier-like word, and a
       word of exceeding good command, by heaven. Accommodated;
       that is, when a man is, as they say, accommodated.
                    II Henry IV, Act iii, sc. 2, l. 72 [BARDOLPH]
7382   'Tis needful that the most immodest word
       Be look'd upon and learn'd; which once attain'd,
       Your highness knows, comes to no further use
       But to be known and hated.
                    II Henry IV, Act iv, sc. 4, l. 70 [WARWICK]
7383   I have been as good as my word.
                    Henry V, Act iv, sc. 8, l. 35 [WILLIAMS]
       I'll be as good as my word.
                    The Merry Wives of Windsor, Act iii, sc. 4, l. 115
                                              [MISTRESS QUICKLY]
7384   Had I but said, I would have kept my word,
       But when I swear, it is irrevocable.
                    II Henry VI, Act iii, sc. 2, l. 293 [KING HENRY]
7385   BRUTUS: Words before blows: is it so, countrymen?
       OCTAVIUS: Not that we love words better, as you do.
       BRUTUS: Good words are better than bad blows, Octavius.
       ANTONY: In your bad strokes, Brutus, you give good words. . . .
       CASSIUS: Antony, The posture of your blows are yet unknown;
       But for your words, they rob the Hybla bees,
       And leave them honeyless.
       ANTONY: Not stingless too.
       BRUTUS: O, yes, and soundless too;

For you have stol'n their buzzing, Antony,
And very wisely threat before you sting.
>> *Julius Cæsar,* Act v, sc. 1, l. 27 [BRUTUS]

7386 I'll talk a word with this same learned Theban.
>> *King Lear,* Act iii, sc. 4, l. 162 [LEAR]

7387 The word is well culled, chose, sweet and apt.
>> *Love's Labour's Lost,* Act v, sc. 1, l. 97 [HOLOFERNES]

7388 BIRON: White-handed mistress, one sweet word with thee.
PRINCESS: Honey, and milk, and sugar; there is three.
>> *Love's Labour's Lost,* Act v, sc. 2, l. 230 [BIRON]

7389 I that do speak a word, May call it back again.
>> *Measure for Measure,* Act ii, sc. 2, l. 57 [ISABELLA]

7390 How every fool can play upon the word!
>> *The Merchant of Venice,* Act iii, sc. 5, l. 48 [LORENZO]

7391 One does not know
How much an ill word may empoison liking.
>> *Much Ado about Nothing,* Act iii, sc. 1, l. 85 [HERO]

7392 How long a time lies in one little word!
Four lagging winters and four wanton springs
End in a word: such is the breath of kings.
>> *Richard II,* Act i, sc. 3, l. 213 [BOLINGBROKE]

7393 Make it a word and a blow.
>> *Romeo and Juliet,* Act iii, sc. 1, l. 43 [MERCUTIO]

7394 Hob, nob, is his word; give 't or take 't.
>> *Twelfth Night,* Act iii, sc. 4, l. 262 [SIR TOBY]

Word and Deed

7395 KING HENRY: You have said well.
WOLSEY: And ever may your highness yoke together . . .
My doing well With my well saying!
KING HENRY: 'Tis well said again;
And 'tis a kind of good deed to say well:
And yet words are no deeds.
>> *Henry VIII,* Act iii, sc. 2, l. 149 [KING HENRY]

7396 Let deeds express what's like to be their words.
>> *Coriolanus,* Act iii, sc. 1, l. 132 [CORIOLANUS]

7397 The harlot's cheek, beautied with plastering art,
Is not more ugly to the thing that helps it
Than is my deed to my most painted word.
>> *Hamlet,* Act iii, sc. 1, l. 51 [KING]

7398 Your large speeches may your deeds approve,
That good effects may spring from words of love.
>> *King Lear,* Act i, sc. 1, l. 187 [KENT]

7399 I want that glib and oily art
To speak and purpose not.
>> *King Lear,* Act i, sc. 1, l. 227 [CORDELIA]

7400 Words to the heat of deeds too cold breath gives.
>> *Macbeth,* Act ii, sc. 1, l. 61 [MACBETH]

7401 If to do were as easy as to know what were good to do, chapels
had been churches and poor men's cottages princes' palaces. It is
a good divine that follows his own instructions: I can easier
teach twenty what were good to be done, than be one of the twenty
to follow mine own teaching.
>> *The Merchant of Venice,* Act i, sc. 2, l. 14 [PORTIA]

7402 Your words and performances are no kin together.
>> *Othello,* Act iv, sc. 2, l. 184 [RODERIGO]

7403   Talkers are no good doers.
                        Richard III, Act i, sc. 3, 1. 352 [MURDERER]
7404   So said, so done, is well.
                The Taming of the Shrew, Act i, sc. 2, 1. 186 [GREMIO]
7405   Foul-spoken coward, that thunder'st with thy tongue,
        And with thy weapon nothing darest perform!
                    Titus Andronicus, Act ii, sc. 1, 1. 58 [CHIRON]
7406   Words pay no debts, give her deeds.
                Troilus and Cressida, Act iii, sc. 2, 1. 59 [PANDARUS]
7407   They that have the voice of lions and the act of hares, are they
        not monsters?
                Troilus and Cressida, Act iii, sc. 2, 1. 95 [CRESSIDA]
7408   I'll endeavour deeds to match these words.
                Troilus and Cressida, Act iv, sc. 5, 1. 259 [HECTOR]

Words

7409   Methinks I hear him now; his plausive words
        He scatter'd not in ears, but grafted them,
        To grow there and to bear.
                All's Well that Ends Well, Act i, sc. 2, 1. 53 [KING]
7410   PAROLLES: I love not many words.
        LORD: No more than a fish loves water.
                All's Well that Ends Well, Act iii, sc. 6, 1. 91 [PAROLLES]
7411   [Her] words all ears took captive.
                All's Well that Ends Well, Act v, sc. 3, 1. 17 [LAFEU]
7412   He words me, girls, he words me, that I should not
        Be noble to myself.
                Antony and Cleopatra, Act v, sc. 2, 1. 191 [CLEOPATRA]
7413   As fast as she answers thee with frowning looks, I'll sauce her
        with bitter words.
                As You Like It, Act iii, sc. 5, 1. 68 [ROSALIND]
7414   What care I for words? yet words do well
        When he that speaks them pleases those that hear.
                As You Like It, Act iii, sc. 5, 1. 111 [PHEBE]
7415   Words are but wind.
                The Comedy of Errors, Act iii, sc. 1, 1. 75 [DROMIO OF EPHESUS]
7416   [He hopes] to purge himself with words.
                Coriolanus, Act v, sc. 6, 1. 8 [AUFIDIUS]
7417   Have not I
        An arm as big as thine? a heart as big?
        Thy words, I grant, are bigger, for I wear not
        My dagger in my mouth.
                Cymbeline, Act iv, sc. 2, 1. 76 [GUIDERIUS]
7418   POLONIUS: What do you read, my lord?
        HAMLET: Words, words, words.
                Hamlet, Act ii, sc. 2, 1. 193 [POLONIUS]
        Words, words, mere words, no matter from the heart.
                Troilus and Cressida, Act v, sc. 3, 1. 108 [TROILUS]
7419   My words fly up, my thoughts remain below:
        Words without thoughts never to heaven go.
                Hamlet, Act iii, sc. 3, 1. 97 [KING]
7420   These words, like daggers, enter in mine ears.
                Hamlet, Act iii, sc. 4, 1. 95 [QUEEN]
7421   That ever this fellow should have fewer words than a parrot,
        and yet the son of a woman! His industry is up-stairs and
        down-stairs; his eloquence the parcel of reckoning.
                I Henry IV, Act ii, sc. 4, 1. 109 [PRINCE]

7422 By my troth, captain, these are very bitter words.
                          II Henry IV, Act ii, sc. 4, l. 184 [HOSTESS]

7423 He hath heard that men of few words are the best men; and therefore he scorns to say his prayers, lest a' should be thought a coward.
                          Henry V, Act iii, sc. 2, l. 39 [BOY]

7424   Believe my words,
For they are certain and unfallible.
                          I Henry VI, Act i, sc. 2, l. 58 [BASTARD OF ORLEANS]

7425   These haughty words of hers
Have batter'd me like roaring cannon-shot.
                          I Henry VI, Act iii, sc. 3, l. 78 [BURGUNDY]

7426 These words of yours draw life-blood from my heart.
                          I Henry VI, Act iv, sc. 6, l. 43 [JOHN TALBOT]

7427 Her words y-clad with wisdom's majesty,
Makes me from wondering fall to weeping joys.
                          II Henry VI, Act i, sc. 1, l. 33 [KING HENRY]

7428 Look to it, lords; let not his smoothing words
Bewitch your hearts; be wise and circumspect.
                          II Henry VI, Act i, sc. 1, l. 156 [CARDINAL]

7429 Ah, kill me with thy weapon, not with words!
My breast can better brook thy dagger's point
Than can my ears that tragic history.
                          III Henry VI, Act v, sc. 6, l. 26 [KING HENRY]

7430 Zounds! I was never so bethump'd with words
Since I first call'd my brother's father dad.
                          King John, Act ii, sc. 1, l. 466 [BASTARD]

7431 MOTH: They have been at a great feast of languages, and stolen
the scraps.
COSTARD: O, they have lived long on the alms-basket of words.
I marvel thy master hath not eaten thee for a word; for thou art
not so long by the head as honorificabilitudinitatibus: thou art
easier swallowed than a flap-dragon.
                          Love's Labour's Lost, Act v, sc. 1, l. 38 [MOTH]
            ("Honorificabilitudinitatibus," a made-up word on the Latin
            honorificabilitudo, honorableness, has often been called the longest
            word in the English language; "antidisestablishmentarianism"
            beats it by one letter.)

7432 Honest plain words best pierce the ear of grief.
                          Love's Labour's Lost, Act v, sc. 2, l. 763 [BIRON]

7433 The words of Mercury are harsh after the songs of Apollo.
                          Love's Labour's Lost, Act v, sc. 2, l. 940 [ARMADO]

7434 So well thy words become thee as thy wounds;
They smack of honour both.
                          Macbeth, Act i, sc. 2, l. 43 [DUNCAN]

7435   I have words
That would be howl'd out in the desert air,
Where hearing should not latch them.
                          Macbeth, Act iv, sc. 3, l. 193 [ROSS]

7436 You but waste your words.
                          Measure for Measure, Act ii, sc. 2, l. 72 [ANGELO]

7437 Here are a few of the unpleasant'st words
That ever blotted paper.
                          The Merchant of Venice, Act iii, sc. 2, l. 254 [BASSANIO]

7438 I would have sworn his disposition would have gone to the truth
of his words; but they do no more adhere and keep place together
than the Hundredth Psalm to the tune of 'Green Sleeves.'
                          The Merry Wives of Windsor, Act ii, sc. 1, l. 60 [MRS. FORD]

7439   His words are a very fantastical banquet, just so many strange
       dishes.
                    Much Ado about Nothing, Act ii, sc. 3, l. 20 [BENEDICK]
7440   Foul words is but foul wind, and foul wind is but foul breath,
       and foul breath is noisome.
                    Much Ado about Nothing, Act v, sc. 2, l. 52 [BEATRICE]
7441   But words are words; I never yet did hear
       That the bruised heart was pierced through the ear.
                    Othello, Act i, sc. 3, l. 218 [BRABANTIO]
7442   [Thou] weigh'st thy words before thou givest them breath.
                    Othello, Act iii, sc. 3, l. 119 [OTHELLO]
7443   I understand a fury in your words,
       But not the words.
                    Othello, Act iv, sc. 2, l. 33 [DESDEMONA]
7444   Out, idle words, servants to shallow fools!
       Unprofitable sounds, weak arbitrators!
                    The Rape of Lucrece, l. 1016 [LUCRECE]
7445   Let not my cold words here accuse my zeal:
       'Tis not the trial of a woman's war,
       The bitter clamour of two eager tongues,
       Can arbitrate this cause betwixt us twain;
       The blood is hot that must be cool'd for this.
                    Richard II, Act i, sc. 1, l. 47 [MOWBRAY]
7446   Where words are scarce, they are seldom spent in vain,
       For they breathe truth that breathe their words in pain.
                    Richard II, Act ii, sc. 1, l. 7 [GAUNT]
7447   Let's fight with gentle words
       Till time lend friends and friends their helpful swords.
                    Richard II, Act iii, sc. 3, l. 131 [AUMERLE]
7448   DUCHESS OF YORK: Why should calamity be full of words?
       QUEEN ELIZABETH: Windy attorneys to their client woes; . . .
       Let them have scope: though what they do impart
       Help not at all, yet do they ease the heart.
                    Richard III, Act iv, sc. 4, l. 126 [DUCHESS OF YORK]
7449   All my best is dressing old words new.
                    Sonnet lxxvi, l. 11
7450   'Twixt such friends as we Few words suffice.
                    The Taming of the Shrew, Act i, sc. 2, l. 65 [PETRUCHIO]
       Few words to fair faith.
                    Troilus and Cressida, Act iii, sc. 2, l. 105 [TROILUS]
7451   You cram these words into mine ears against
       The stomach of my sense.
                    The Tempest, Act ii, sc. 1, l. 106 [ALONSO]
7452   These words are razors to my wounded heart.
                    Titus Andronicus, Act i, sc. 1, l. 314 [TITUS]
7453   I will enchant the old Andronicus
       With words more sweet, and yet more dangerous
       Than baits to fish, or honey-stalks to sheep.
                    Titus Andronicus, Act iv, sc. 4, l. 89 [TAMORA]
7454   CLOWN: To see this age! A sentence is but a cheveril glove to
       a good wit: how quickly the wrong side may be turned outward!
       VIOLA: Nay, that's certain; they that dally nicely with words may
       quickly make them wanton.
                    Twelfth Night, Act iii, sc. 1, l. 12 [CLOWN]
7455   Words are very rascals since bonds disgraced them. . . . Words
       are grown so false, I am loath to prove reason with them.
                    Twelfth Night, Act iii, sc. 1, l. 24 [CLOWN]

7456   Methinks his words do from such passion fly
That he believes himself.
> *Twelfth Night,* Act iii, sc. 4, l. 407 [VIOLA]

7457   A fine volley of words, gentlemen, and quickly shot off.
> *The Two Gentlemen of Verona,* Act ii, sc. 4, l. 32 [SILVIA]

Work

7458   There's other work in hand.
> *Cymbeline,* Act v, sc. 5, l. 103 [IMOGEN]

7459   I cannot draw a cart, nor eat dried oats;
If it be man's work, I'll do it.
> *King Lear,* Act v, sc. 3, l. 38 [CAPTAIN]

7460   Now I have done a good day's work.
> *Richard III,* Act ii, sc. 1, l. 1 [KING EDWARD]

7461   MARIA: Does it work upon him?
SIR TOBY: Like aqua-vitae with a midwife.
> *Twelfth Night,* Act ii, sc. 5, l. 214 [MARIA]

7462   This has been some stair-work, some trunk-work, some behind-door-work.
> *The Winter's Tale,* Act iii, sc. 3, l. 75 [SHEPHERD]

7463   Every lane's end, every shop, church, session, hanging, yields a careful man work.
> *The Winter's Tale,* Act iv, sc. 4, l. 699 [AUTOLYCUS]

World

7464   Sir, fare you well:
Hereafter in a better world than this,
I shall desire more love and knowledge of you.
> *As You Like It,* Act i, sc. 2, l. 295 [LEBEAU]

7465   O, what a world is this, when what is comely
Envenoms him that bears it!
> *As You Like It,* Act ii, sc. 3, l. 14 [ADAM]

7466   DUKE: Thou seest we are not all alone unhappy:
This wide and universal theatre
Presents more woeful pageants than the scene
Wherein we play in.
JAQUES: All the world's a stage,
And all the men and women merely players:
They have their exits and their entrances;
And one man in his time plays many parts,
His acts being seven ages. At first the infant,
Mewling and puking in the nurse's arms,
And then the whining school-boy, with his satchel
And shining morning face, creeping like snail
Unwilling to school. And then the lover,
Sighing like furnace, with a woeful ballad
Made to his mistress' eyebrow. Then a soldier,
Full of strange oaths and bearded like the pard,
Jealous in honour, sudden and quick in quarrel,
Seeking the bubble reputation
Even in the cannon's mouth. And then the justice,
In fair round belly with good capon lined,
With eyes severe and beard of formal cut,
Full of wise saws and modern instances;
And so he plays his part. The sixth age shifts
Into the lean and slipper'd pantaloon,
With spectacles on nose and pouch on side,
His youthful hose, well saved, a world too wide

For his shrunk shank, and his big manly voice
Turning again toward childish treble, pipes
And whistles in his sound. Last scene of all,
That ends this strange eventful history
Is second childishness and mere oblivion,
Sans teeth, sans eyes, sans taste, sans every thing.
                    As You Like It, Act ii, sc. 7, l. 136 [DUKE]

7467   I to the world am like a drop of water
        That in the ocean seeks another drop.
                    The Comedy of Errors, Act i, sc. 2, l. 35
                                    [ANTIPHOLUS OF SYRACUSE]

7468   How weary, stale, flat and unprofitable,
        Seem to me all the uses of this world!
        Fie on 't! ah fie! 'tis an unweeded garden,
        That grows to seed; things rank and gross in nature
        Possess it merely.
                    Hamlet, Act i, sc. 2, l. 133 [HAMLET]

7469   Why, let the stricken deer go weep,
            The hart ungalled play;
        For some must watch, while some must sleep:
            So runs the world away.
                    Hamlet, Act iii, sc. 2, l. 282 [HAMLET]

7470   A bad world, I say, I would I were a weaver; I could sing psalms
        or any thing.
                    I Henry IV, Act ii, sc. 4, l. 148 [FALSTAFF]

7471   Let me tell the world.
                    I Henry IV, Act v, sc. 2, l. 66 [VERNON]
        I'll tell the world.
                    Measure for Measure, Act ii, sc. 4, l. 153 [ISABELLA]

7472   Let this world no longer be a stage
        To feed contention in a lingering act;
        But let one spirit of the first-born Cain
        Reign in all bosoms, that, each heart being set
        On bloody courses, the rude scene may end,
        And darkness be the burier of the dead!
                    II Henry IV, Act i, sc. 1, l. 155 [NORTHUMBERLAND]

7473   A foutre for the world and worldlings base!
        I speak of Africa and golden joys.
                    II Henry IV, Act v, sc. 3, l. 103 [PISTOL]

7474   O, let the vile world end,
        And the premised flames of the last day
        Knit earth and heaven together!
        Now let the general trumpet blow his blast!
                    II Henry VI, Act v, sc. 2, l. 40 [YOUNG CLIFFORD]

7475   Thou seest the world, Volumnius, how it goes;
        Our enemies have beat us to the pit:
        It is more worthy to leap in ourselves,
        Than tarry till they push us.
                    Julius Cæsar, Act v, sc. 5, l. 22 [BRUTUS]

7476   Mad world, mad kings! mad composition!
                    King John, Act ii, sc. 1, l. 561 [BASTARD]

7477   World, world, O world!
        But that thy strange mutations make us hate thee,
        Life would not yield to age.
                    King Lear, Act iv, sc. 1, l. 10 [EDGAR]

7478   Nay, had she been true,
        If heaven would make me such another world

Of one entire and perfect chrysolite,
I 'ld not have sold her for it.
Othello, Act v, sc. 2, l. 143 [OTHELLO]

7479 SECOND MURDERER: I am one, my liege,
Whom the vile blows and buffets of the world
Have so incensed that I am reckless what
I do to spite the world.
FIRST MURDERER: And I another
So weary with disasters, tugg'd with fortune,
That I would set my life on any chance,
To mend it, or be rid on 't.
Macbeth, Act iii, sc. 1, l. 108 [SECOND MURDERER]

7480 GRATIANO: You look not well, Signior Antonio;
You have too much respect upon the world:
They lose it that do buy it with much care. . . .
ANTONIO: I hold the world but as the world, Gratiano;
A stage where every man must play a part,
And mine a sad one.
The Merchant of Venice, Act i, sc. 1, l. 73 [GRATIANO]

7481 O wicked, wicked world! One that is well-nigh worn to pieces
with age to show himself a young gallant!
The Merry Wives of Windsor, Act ii, sc. 1, l. 20 [MRS. PAGE]

7482 FALSTAFF: I will not lend thee a penny.
PISTOL: Why, then the world's mine oyster,
Which I with sword will open.
The Merry Wives of Windsor, Act ii, sc. 2, l. 1 [FALSTAFF]

7483 The mazed world . . . now knows not which is which.
A Midsummer Night's Dream, Act ii, sc. 1, l. 113 [TITANIA]

7484 The world must be peopled.
Much Ado about Nothing, Act ii, sc. 3, l. 252 [BENEDICK]

7485 God help us, it is a world to see.
Much Ado about Nothing, Act iii, sc. 5, l. 38 [DOGBERRY]

7486 God take King Edward to his mercy,
And leave the world for me to bustle in!
Richard III, Act i, sc. 1, l. 151 [GLOUCESTER]

7487 The world is not thy friend nor the world's law:
The world affords no law to make thee rich;
Then be not poor, but break it and take this.
Romeo and Juliet, Act v, sc. 1, l. 72 [ROMEO]

7488 Paucas pallabris: let the world slide.
The Taming of the Shrew, Induction, sc. 1, l. 5 [SLY]

7489 Let the world slip: we shall ne'er be younger.
The Taming of the Shrew, Induction, sc. 2, l. 143 [SLY]

7490 Crowns in my purse I have and goods at home,
And so am come abroad to see the world.
The Taming of the Shrew, Act i, sc. 2, l. 57 [PETRUCHIO]

7491 CURTIS: I prithee, good Grumio, tell me, how goes the world?
GRUMIO: A cold world, Curtis.
The Taming of the Shrew, Act iv, sc. 1, l. 35 [CURTIS]
POET: How goes the world?
PAINTER: It wears, sir, as it grows.
Timon of Athens, Act i, sc. 1, l. 2 [POET]

7492 He that is giddy thinks the world turns round.
The Taming of the Shrew, Act v, sc. 2, l. 20 [WIDOW]

7493 TIMON: What wouldst thou do with the world, Apemantus, if
it lay in thy power?

APEMANTUS: Give it to the beasts, to be rid of the men.
Timon of Athens, Act iv, sc. 3, l. 321 [TIMON]

7494 Is it a world to hide virtues in?
Twelfth Night, Act i, sc. 3, l. 140 [SIR TOBY]

7495 I am afraid this great lubber, the world, will prove a cockney.
Twelfth Night, Act iv, sc. 1, l. 14 [CLOWN]

Worm

7496 CLEOPATRA: Hast thou the pretty worm of Nilus there, that kills and pains not?
CLOWN: Truly, I have him: but I would not be the party that should desire you to touch him, for his biting is immortal; those that do die of it do seldom or never recover. . . . The worm is not to be trusted but in the keeping of wise people, for, indeed, there is no goodness in the worm.
Antony and Cleopatra, Act v, sc. 2, l. 243 [CLEOPATRA]

7497 KING: Now, Hamlet, where's Polonius?
HAMLET: At supper.
KING: At supper! where?
HAMLET: Not where he eats, but where he is eaten: a certain convocation of politic worms are e'en at him. Your worm is your only emperor for diet. . . . A man may fish with the worm that hath eat of a king, and eat of the fish that hath fed of that worm.
Hamlet, Act iv, sc. 3, l. 17 [KING]

7498 The smallest worm will turn being trodden on,
And doves will peck in safeguard of their brood. . . .
In protection of their tender ones,
Who hath not seen them, even with those wings
Which sometime they have used with fearful flight,
Make war with him that climb'd unto their nest,
Offering their own lives in their young's defence?
III Henry VI, Act ii, sc. 2, l. 17 [CLIFFORD]

7499 　　　　The blind mole casts
Copp'd hills towards heaven, to tell the earth is throng'd
By man's oppression: and the poor worm doth die for 't.
Pericles, Act i, sc. 1, l. 100 [PERICLES]

7500 She quickly pooped him; she made him roast-meat for worms.
Pericles, Act iv, sc. 2, l. 25 [BOULT]

7501 Why should the worm intrude the maiden bud?
Or hateful cuckoos hatch in sparrows' nests?
The Rape of Lucrece, l. 848 [LUCRECE]

Worst

7502 Since the affairs of men rest still incertain,
Let's reason with the worst that may befall.
Julius Cæsar, Act v, sc. 1, l. 96 [CASSIUS]

7503 　　　　　To be worst,
The lowest and most dejected thing of fortune,
Stands still in esperance, lives not in fear:
The lamentable change is from the best;
The worst returns to laughter. . . . The worst is not
So long as we can say 'This is the worst.'
King Lear, Act iv, sc. 1, l. 2 [EDGAR]

7504 　　　　We are not the first
Who, with best meaning, have incurr'd the worst.
King Lear, Act v, sc. 3, l. 3 [CORDELIA]

7505   Things at the worst will cease, or else climb upward
         To what they were before.
                              Macbeth, Act iv, sc. 2, l. 24 [Ross]

Worth

7506   Yet art thou good for nothing but taking up; and that thou art
         scarce worth.
                    All's Well that Ends Well, Act ii, sc. 3, l. 219 [Lafeu]
7507   Goneril: I have been worth the whistle. . . .
         Albany: You are not worth the dust which the rude wind
         Blows in your face.
                              King Lear, Act iv, sc. 2, l. 29 [Goneril]
7508   It so falls out
         That what we have we prize not to the worth
         Whiles we enjoy it, but being lack'd and lost,
         Why, then we rack the value, then we find
         The virtue that possession would not show us
         While it was ours. So will it fare with Claudio:
         When he shall hear she died upon his words,
         The idea of her life shall sweetly creep
         Into his study of imagination,
         And every lovely organ of her life
         Shall come apparell'd in more precious habits,
         More moving-delicate and full of life,
         Into the eye and prospect of his soul,
         Than when she lived indeed.
                    Much Ado about Nothing, Act iv, sc. 1, l. 219 [Friar]
7509   They are but beggars that can count their worth.
                              Romeo and Juliet, Act ii, sc. 6, l. 32 [Juliet]
7510   [Our child] was blurted at and held a malkin,
         Not worth the time of day.
                              Pericles, Act iv, sc. 3, l. 34 [Dionyza]

Wound

7511   With a wound I must be cured.
                    Antony and Cleopatra, Act iv, sc. 14, l. 78 [Antony]
7512   Alas, poor shepherd! searching of thy wound,
         I have by hard adventure found mine own.
                    As You Like It, Act ii, sc. 4, l. 44 [Rosalind]
7513   Then shall you know the wounds invisible
         That love's keen arrows make.
                    As You Like It, Act iii, sc. 5, l. 30 [Silvius]
7514   I am loath to gall a new-healed wound.
                    II Henry IV, Act i, sc. 2, l. 166 [Chief Justice]
7515   Let grievous, ghastly, gaping wounds
         Untwine the Sisters Three!
                    II Henry IV, Act ii, sc. 4, l. 212 [Pistol]
7516   Stop the rage betime,
         Before the wound do grow uncurable;
         For, being green, there is great hope of help.
                    II Henry VI, Act iii, sc. 1, l. 285 [Post]
7517   What wound did ever heal but by degrees?
                              Othello, Act ii, sc. 3, l. 377 [Iago]
7518   To see the salve doth make the wound ache more.
                              The Rape of Lucrece, l. 1116
7519   O, gentlemen, see, see! dead Henry's wounds
         Open their congeal'd mouths and bleed afresh.
                              Richard III, Act i, sc. 2, l. 55 [Anne]

7520　　Now to the bottom dost thou search my wound.
                    Titus Andronicus, Act ii, sc. 3, l. 262 [SATURNINUS]
7521　　Those wounds heal ill that men do give themselves.
                    Troilus and Cressida, Act iii, sc. 3, l. 229 [PATROCLU]
7522　　　　　　My bosom as a bed
　　　　Shall lodge thee till thy wound be thoroughly heal'd;
　　　　And thus I search it with a sovereign kiss.
                    The Two Gentlemen of Verona, Act i, sc. 2, l. 114 [JULIA]
7523　　The private wound is deepest.
                    The Two Gentlemen of Verona, Act v, sc. 4, l. 71 [VALENTINE]
7524　　She finds a hound . . . licking of his wound,
　　　　'Gainst venom'd sores the only sovereign plaster.
                    Venus and Adonis, l. 913

Wrath

7525　　The good gods assuage thy wrath, and turn the dregs of it upon
　　　　this varlet here.
                    Coriolanus, Act v, sc. 2, l. 82 [MENENIUS]
7526　　KING JOHN: France, I am burn'd up with inflaming wrath;
　　　　A rage whose heat hath this condition,
　　　　That nothing can allay, nothing but blood,
　　　　The blood, the dearest-valued blood, of France.
　　　　KING PHILIP: Thy rage shall burn thee up, and thou shalt turn
　　　　To ashes, ere our blood shall quench that fire:
　　　　Look to thyself, thou art in jeopardy.
                    King John, Act iii, sc. 1, l. 340 [KING JOHN]
7527　　Come not within the measure of my wrath.
                    The Two Gentlemen of Verona, Act v, sc. 4, l. 127 [VALENTINE]

Wren

7528　　　　　　The poor wren,
　　　　The most diminutive of birds, will fight,
　　　　Her young ones in her nest, against the owl.
                    Macbeth, Act iv, sc. 2, l. 9 [LADY MACDUFF]
7529　　The throstle with his note so true,
　　　　The wren with little quill.
                    A Midsummer Night's Dream, Act iii, sc. 1, l. 130
                                                    [BOTTOM, *singing*]
7530　　　　　　The world is grown so bad,
　　　　That wrens make prey where eagles dare not perch.
                    Richard III, Act i, sc. 3, l. 70 [GLOUCESTER]

Wretch

7531　　Poor naked wretches, whereso'er you are,
　　　　That bide the pelting of this pitiless storm,
　　　　How shall your houseless heads and unfed sides,
　　　　Your loop'd and window'd raggedness, defend you
　　　　From seasons such as these?
                    King Lear, Act iii, sc. 4, l. 28 [LEAR]
7532　　Is wretchedness deprived that benefit,
　　　　To end itself by death? 'Twas yet some comfort,
　　　　When misery could beguile the tyrant's rage,
　　　　And frustrate his proud will.
                    King Lear, Act iv, sc. 6, l. 61 [GLOUCESTER]
7533　　Out, you green-sickness carrion! out, you baggage!
　　　　You tallow-face! . . . Disobedient wretch! . . .
　　　　My fingers itch.
                    Romeo and Juliet, Act iii, sc. 5, l. 157 [CAPULET]

7534 Sly frantic wretch, that hop'st to make me great,
In hope thyself should govern Rome and me.
Titus Andronicus, Act iv, sc. 4, l. 59 [SATURNINUS]

Writing

7535 I once did hold it, as our statists do,
A baseness to write fair and labour'd much
How to forget that learning, but sir, now
It did me yeoman's service.
Hamlet, Act v, sc. 2, l. 33 [HAMLET]

7536 CADE: Dost thou use to write thy name? or hast thou a mark
to thyself, like an honest plain-dealing man?
CLERK: Sir, I thank God, I have been so well brought up that I
can write my name.
ALL: He hath confessed: away with him! he's a villain and a
traitor.
CADE: Away with him, I say! hang him with his pen and ink-
horn about his neck.
II Henry VI, Act iv, sc. 2, l. 109 [CADE]

Wrong

7537 Be it my wrong you are from me exempt,
But wrong not that wrong with a more contempt.
The Comedy of Errors, Act ii, sc. 2, l. 173 [ADRIANA]

7538 Beyond imagination is the wrong
That she this day hath shameless thrown on me.
The Comedy of Errors, Act v, sc. 1, l. 201
[ANTIPHOLUS OF EPHESUS]

7539 We do it wrong, being so majestical,
To offer it the show of violence;
For it is, as the air, invulnerable,
And our vain blows malicious mockery.
Hamlet, Act i, sc. 1, l. 144 [MARCELLUS]

7540 Tell him from me that he hath done me wrong.
III Henry VI, Act iii, sc. 3, l. 231 [WARWICK]
You do me wrong to take me out o' the grave.
King Lear, Act iv, sc. 7, l. 45 [LEAR]

7541 O masters, if I were disposed to stir
Your hearts and minds to mutiny and rage,
I should do Brutus wrong, and Cassius wrong,
Who, you all know, are honourable men:
I will not do them wrong; I rather choose
To wrong the dead, to wrong myself and you,
Than I will wrong such honourable men.
Julius Cæsar, Act iii, sc. 2, l. 126 [ANTONY]

7542   Thus to persist
In doing wrong extenuates not wrong,
But makes it much more heavy.
Troilus and Cressida, Act ii, sc. 2, l. 186 [HECTOR]

Wrongs

7543   Why dost not speak?
Think'st thou it honourable for a noble man
Still to remember wrongs?
Coriolanus, Act v, sc. 3, l. 154 [VOLUMNIA]

7544 You will not pocket up wrong: art thou not ashamed?
I Henry IV, Act iii, sc. 3, l. 184 [PRINCE]

7545   It is plain pocketing up of wrongs.
                          Henry V, Act iii, sc. 2, l. 54 [BOY]
7546   AUSTRIA: Well, ruffian, I must pocket up these wrongs, Because . . .
        BASTARD: Your breeches best may carry them.
                          King John, Act iii, sc. 1, l. 200 [AUSTRIA]
7547   He's truly valiant that can wisely suffer
        The worst that man can breathe, and make his wrongs
        His outsides, to wear them like his raiment, carelessly. . . .
        If wrongs be evils and enforce us kill,
        What folly 'tis to hazard life for ill!
                          Timon of Athens, Act iii, sc. 5, l. 31 [SENATOR]
7548   Steel to the very back,
        Yet wrung with wrongs more than our backs can bear.
                          Titus Andronicus, Act iv, sc. 3, l. 47 [TITUS]

Y

Yorick

7549   CLOWN: This same skull, sir, was Yorick's skull, the king's
        jester. . . .
        HAMLET: Let me see. Alas, poor Yorick! I knew him, Horatio:
        a fellow of infinite jest, of most excellent fancy. . . . Where be
        your gibes now? your gambols? your songs? your flashes of
        merriment, that were wont to set the table on a roar? Not one
        now, to mock your own grinning? quite chap-fallen? Now get
        you to my lady's chamber, and tell her, let her paint an inch thick,
        to this favour she must come; make her laugh at that.
                          Hamlet, Act v, sc. 1, l. 198 [CLOWN]

Youth

7550   Natural rebellion, done i' the blaze of youth;
        When oil and fire, too strong for reason's force,
        O'erbears it and burns on.
                          All's Well that Ends Well, Act v, sc. 3, l. 6 [COUNTESS]
7551   He wears the rose
        Of youth upon him; from which the world should note
        Something particular.
                          Antony and Cleopatra, Act iii, sc. 13, l. 20 [ANTONY]
7552   All's brave that youth mounts and folly guides.
                          As You Like It, Act iii, sc. 4, l. 48 [CELIA]
7553   It is a pretty youth: not very pretty:
        But, sure, he's proud, and yet his pride becomes him.
                          As You Like It, Act iii, sc. 5, l. 113 [PHEBE]
7554   Methinks you are my glass, and not my brother.
        I see by you I am a sweet-faced youth.
                          The Comedy of Errors, Act v, sc. 1, l. 418
                          [DROMIO OF EPHESUS]
7555   Youth and comeliness plucked all gaze his way.
                          Coriolanus, Act i, sc. 3, l. 8 [VOLUMNIA]
        The fairest youth that ever made eye swerve.
                          The Winter's Tale, Act iv, sc. 4, l. 383 [FLORIZEL]
7556   Rebellious hell,
        If thou canst mutine in a matron's bones,
        To flaming youth let virtue be as wax.
                          Hamlet, Act iii, sc. 4, l. 82 [HAMLET]

7557   By Gis and by Saint Charity,
           Alack, and fie for shame!
        Young men will do 't, if they come to 't;
           By cock, they are to blame.
                  Hamlet, Act iv, sc. 5, l. 59 [OPHELIA, *singing*]

7558   Strike; down with them; cut the villains' throats: ah! whoreson
caterpillars! bacon-fed knaves! they hate us youth. . . . What,
ye knaves! young men must live. You are grand-jurors, are ye?
we'll jure ye, 'faith.
                  I Henry IV, Act ii, sc. 2, l. 87 [FALSTAFF]

7559   Though the camomile, the more it is trodden on the faster it
grows, yet youth, the more it is wasted the sooner it wears.
               I Henry IV, Act ii, sc. 4, l. 444 [FALSTAFF]

7560   In the very May-morn of his youth,
Ripe for exploits and mighty enterprises.
                 Henry V, Act i, sc. 2, l. 120 [ELY]
His May of youth and bloom of lustihood.
       Much Ado About Nothing, Act v, sc. 1, l. 76 [LEONATO]

7561   Now all the youth of England are on fire,
And silken dalliance in the wardrobe lies.
          Henry V, Act ii, Prologue, l. 1 [CHORUS]

7562   These are the youths that thunder at a playhouse, and fight for
bitten apples; that no audience, but the tribulation of Tower-
hill, or the limbs of Limehouse, their dear brothers, are able
to endure.
              Henry VIII, Act v, sc. 4, l. 63 [PORTER]

7563   LEAR: But goes thy heart with this? . . . So young, and so
untender?
CORDELIA: So young, my lord, and true.
              King Lear, Act i, sc. 1, l. 107 [LEAR]

7564   Youth so apt to pluck a sweet!
         Love's Labour's Lost, Act iv, sc. 3, l. 114 [DUMAIN]
    (Repeated in *Sonnets to Sundry Notes of Music,* Pt. xvii, l. 13.)

7565   In her youth
There is a prone and speechless dialect
Such as move men.
          Measure for Measure, Act i, sc. 2, l. 187 [CLAUDIO]

7566   A hare is madness the youth, to skip o'er the meshes of good
counsel the cripple.
         The Merchant of Venice, Act i, sc. 2, l. 20 [PORTIA]

7567   Though we be justices and doctors and churchmen, Master
Page, we have some salt of our youth in us; we be the sons
of women.
      The Merry Wives of Windsor, Act ii, sc. 3, l. 47 [SHALLOW]

7568   So wise so young, they say, do never live long.
           Richard III, Act iii, sc. 1, l. 79 [GLOUCESTER]

7569   So cunning and so young is wonderful.
         Richard III, Act iii, sc. 1, l. 135 [BUCKINGHAM]

7570   A proper stripling and an amorous!
         The Taming of the Shrew, Act i, sc. 2, l. 144 [GRUMIO]

7571   Lust and liberty
Creep in the minds and marrows of our youth,
That 'gainst the stream of virtue they may strive,
And drown themselves in riot!
          Timon of Athens, Act iv, sc. 1, l. 25 [TIMON]

7572   Young men, whom Aristotle thought
Unfit to hear moral philosophy.   .
Troilus and Cressida, Act ii, sc. 2, 1. 166 [HECTOR]
(To quote Aristotle, Hector is looking forward nearly a
thousand years.)

7573   Youth is bought more oft than begg'd or borrow'd.
Twelfth Night, Act iii, sc. 4, 1. 3 [OLIVIA]

7574   Home-keeping youth have ever homely wits.
Were 't not affection chains thy tender days
To the sweet glances of thy honour'd love,
I rather would entreat thy company
To see the wonders of the world abroad
Than, living dully sluggardized at home,
Wear out thy youth with shapeless idleness.
But since thou lovest, love still and thrive therein,
Even as I would when I to love begin.
The Two Gentlemen of Verona, Act i, sc. 1, 1. 2 [VALENTINE]

Youth and Age

7575   By heaven, it is as proper to our age
To cast beyond ourselves in our opinions
As it is common for the younger sort
To lack discretion.
Hamlet, Act ii, sc. 1, 1. 114 [POLONIUS]

7576   A very riband in the cap of youth,
Yet needful too; for youth no less becomes
The light and careless livery that it wears
Than settled age his sables and his weeds,
Importing health and graveness.
Hamlet, Act iv, sc. 7, 1. 78 [KING]

7577   Your lordship, though not clean past your youth, hath yet some
smack of age in you, some relish of the saltness of time; and I
most humbly beseech your lordship to have a reverent care of
your health.
II Henry IV, Act i, sc. 2, 1. 112 [FALSTAFF]

7578   FALSTAFF: You that are old consider not the capacities of us
that are young; you do measure the heat of our livers with the
bitterness of your galls: and we that are in the vaward of our
youth, I must confess, are wags too.
CHIEF JUSTICE: Do you set down your name in the scroll of
youth, that are written down old with all the characters of age?
Have you not a moist eye? a dry hand? a yellow cheek? a white
beard? a decreasing leg? an increasing belly? is not your voice
broken? your wind short? your chin double? your wit single?
and every part about you blasted with antiquity? and will you
yet call yourself young? . . .
FALSTAFF: I am old only in judgement and understanding; and
he that will caper with me for a thousand marks, let him lend
me the money, and have at him!
II Henry IV, Act i, sc. 2, 1. 195 [FALSTAFF]

7579   A man can no more separate age and covetousness than a' can
part young limbs and lechery: but the gout galls the one, and the
pox pinches the other.
II Henry IV, Act i, sc. 2, 1. 256 [FALSTAFF]

7580   LEAR: How old art thou?
KENT: Not so young, sir, to love a woman for singing, nor so

old to dote on her for any thing: I have years on my back
forty eight.
King Lear, Act i, sc. 4, l. 39 [LEAR]

7581 The oldest hath borne most: we that are young
Shall never see so much, nor live so long.
King Lear, Act v, sc. 3, l. 325 [ALBANY]

7582 Thou hast nor youth nor age,
But, as it were, an after-dinner's sleep,
Dreaming on both; for all thy blessed youth
Becomes as aged, and doth beg the alms
Of palsied eld; and when thou art old and rich,
Thou hast neither heat, affection, limb, nor beauty
To make thy riches pleasant.
Measure for Measure, Act iii, sc. 1, l. 32 [DUKE]

7583 Young in limbs, in judgement old.
The Merchant of Venice, Act ii, sc. 7, l. 71 [MOROCCO, *reading*]

7584 I never knew so young a body with so old a head.
The Merchant of Venice, Act iv, sc. 1, l. 164 [BELLARIO]

7585 Crabbed age and youth cannot live together;
Youth is full of pleasance, age is full of care;
Youth like summer morn, age like winter weather;
Youth like summer brave, age like winter bare.
Youth is full of sport, age's breath is short;
    Youth is nimble, age is lame;
Youth is hot and bold, age is weak and cold;
    Youth is wild and age is tame.
Age, I do abhor thee; youth, I do adore thee.
The Passionate Pilgrim, Pt. xii, l. 1

7586 When forty winters shall besiege thy brow,
And dig deep trenches in thy beauty's field,
Thy youth's proud livery, so gazed on now,
Will be a tatter'd weed, of small worth held.
Sonnet ii, l. 1

7587 See, to beguile the old folks, how the young folks lay their
heads together!
The Taming of the Shrew, Act i, sc. 2, l. 138 [GRUMIO]

7588 GREMIO: Skipper, stand back: 'tis age that nourisheth.
TRANIO: But youth in ladies' eyes that flourisheth.
The Taming of the Shrew, Act ii, sc. 1, l. 341 [GREMIO]

7589 O thou dissembling cub! what wilt thou be
When time hath sow'd a grizzle on thy case?
Twelfth Night, Act v, sc. 1, l. 167 [DUKE]

INDEX AND CONCORDANCE

SUGGESTIONS
FOR THE USE OF THE INDEX

This is really a word index to all the quotations in the book, with the entries grouped alphabetically by leading words, and followed by the number of the quotation in the text, so that it may be turned to instantly.

The principal word of the quotation is always used as the key word in the index, and where there is more than one such word, both are given. The key word is, of course, usually a noun, but sometimes a saying is remembered by some peculiar adjective or verb, and in such cases these also are given, in order that a quotation which is not exactly remembered, or of which only one word is remembered, may be traced through any one of a number of channels. For example the phrase "honey-heavy dew of slumber" will be found indexed under "honey-heavy", "dew", and "slumber". Unusual or unique words are also indexed, such as "one-trunk-inheriting slave", or "intertissued robe", which are indexed not only under "slave" and "robe" but also under the unusual modifying adjectives.

Where no phrase or key word is remembered by the reader, but only the general tenor of the quotation, he should turn to the text and look through the entries under the appropriate subject-heading. In such cases the cross-references should not be overlooked.

All entries are necessarily very brief, but an effort has been made to give sufficient context to enable the reader to identify the quotations readily. It should be pointed out, however, that the mind of the reader will not always run exactly in accord with the mind of the indexer, and so the phrase which springs to the reader's memory may not be the exact one which the indexer chose for his entry, in which case a little perseverance may be required to turn up the quotation desired.

No one can get the full benefit of this book without understanding thoroughly the use of the index. If the reader will take time to familiarize himself with the suggestions given above, he will find the book far more useful and satisfactory than it could otherwise be.

A

Abatement : falls into a., 4343
Abed after midnight, 554
Ability in means, 5648
  a. they never perform, 4408
  out of my lean a., 4070
Abjects : feeds on a., 2639
Able rather in power, 2315
Abraham : bosom of good old A., 1
  sleep in A.'s bosom, 1
Absence, 3-10
  a. flame to qualify, 2505
  a. makes us unthrifty, 10
  I dote on his very a., 6
  like winter hath a. been, 8
  O a., what a torment, 7
Absent : I have been a., 298
Absolute, 11-13
  how a. she's in 't, 13
  how a. the knave is, 12
  you are too a., 11
Absolution : clear'd with a., 5972
Abstemious : be more a., 18
Abstinence, 14-18
  a. engenders maladies, 15
  easiness to next a., 14
  he doth with a. subdue, 17
  man of stricture and a., 16
Abstract of tedious days, 2995
Abundance : have a., enjoy it not, 2863
  he hath horn of a., 5838
  in a. addeth to her store, 5827
Abuse, 19-23
  a. of greatness is remorse, 5124
  no a., Hal, no a., 21
Abused : better be much a., 5530
Abuses : cries out upon a., 20
  level at my a., reckon own, 23
  poor a. of the time, 19
Abysm : dark a. of time, 6640
Academe : our court an A., 7353
Academes : books, arts, a., 2428
Accent, 24-28
  a. did they teach him, 28
  any a. from thy tongue, 26
  throttle a. in fears, 5955
  you miss the a., 27
  your a. is something finer, 24
Accents for malicious sounds, 25
Access to remorse, 5612
Accident, 29-35
  a. brought me to her eye, 32
  day was yours by a., 31
  'tis an a. heaven provides, 33
  virtue a. could not pierce, 4917
Accidents : be not with a. opprest, 30
  moving a. by flood, field, 4305
  solemn things answer a., 29
  think no more of night's a., 34

Accommodated : better a. good, 7381
Accost, Sir Andrew, a., 780
Account : come to our a., 4936
Ace : coldest ever turned a., 7199
Ache : charm a. with air, 3156
  never had a. in shoulders, 4097
Acheron : as black as A., 680
Achievement is command, 5482
Achiever brings home full numbers, 6888
Achilles : hide thy head, A., 3419
Achitophel : whoreson A., 5838
Acquaintance : I desire your a., 4880
  what, old a., 2508
Act, 36-67
  a. has three branches, 39
  a. of shame committed, 44
  be great in a., 43
  be same in a. as desire, 45
  did a. of darkness with her, 44
  future ages groan for this foul a., 49
  he finished his mortal a., 52
  his a. did not overtake intent, 3754
  if I do not a. it, hiss, 56
  loathsome a. of lust, 44
  no a. of common passage, 36
  smile heavens upon this a., 50
  some a. that hath no relish, 37
  such an a. blurs grace, 38
  this a. is as ancient tale, 42
  this a. shows horrible, 46
  this a. so evilly born, 41
  this a. will be my fame, 48
  what a. that roars so loud, 38
Acting : between a. of thing, 40
Action, 68-77
  a. is eloquence, 68
  dearest a. in tented field, 6181
  graceless a. of heavy hand, 74
  he sold labour of our a., 6455
  her pretty a. did outsell, 70
  I'll bring mine a., 69
  imitate a. of tiger, 7013
  in a. how like angel, 4487
  make 't an a., 69
  man of a. called on, 4649
  pleasure and a. make hours short, 5341
  rarer a. is in virtue, 77
  suit the a. to the word, 54
  till a., lust is perjured, 4431
Actions blacker than the night, 76
  many a. in one purpose, 71
  planted a. in hearts, 3734
  strong reasons make strong a., 5581
  we must not stint a., 72
Active-valiant, valiant-young, 3614
Actor, 60-67
  after well-graced a. leaves, 66
  as unperfect a. on stage, 4327

good-will showed, a. may plead, 60
Actors are at hand, 65
best a. in the world, 61
these a. were spirits, 5639
Acts of black night, 4855
all your a. are queens, 53
carnal, unnatural a., 6165
his a. being seven ages, 7466
thy a. denote fury of beast, 4534
Adam, 78-82
A. was a gardener, 80
A.'s sons are my brethren, 3665
feel but penalty of A., 4117
had he been A., tempter Eve, 81
in innocency A. fell, 79
moon month old when A. was no more,
4784
Scripture says "A. digged", 78
since days of goodman A., 3646
they hold up A.'s profession, 2968
Adder, 83-90
a. hisses where birds sing, 86
art thou like a. waxen deaf, 83
bright day brings forth a., 84
guard it with lurking a., 87
is the a. better than eel, 88
jealous as stung are of a., 3777
starts like one that spies a., 90
Adders : more deaf than a., 5343
Additions swell us, 6928
Addle as an egg, 5499
Adhere : they no more a., 7438
Adheres : every thing a., 5825
Admiral : thou art our a., 2455
Admiration, 91-94
a. did not hoop at them, 6718
great in a. as herself, 5254
indeed the top of a., 94
season your a. for a while, 91
with more than a. he admired, 93
Adonis painted by running brook, 5273
promises like A. gardens, 5459
Adoption strives with nature, 4896
Adoration : all a., 4254
Adulation : titles blown from a., 2652
Adulterers by obedience, 96
Adultery : die for a., no, 95
Adultress : she's an a., 99
they call'd me foul a., 98
Advancement : what a. hope, 2719
you envy my a., 4942
Advantage, 100-103
a. better soldier than rashness, 102
a. feeds him fat, 101
a. which doth ever cool, 100
for his a. still wake, 6665
let not a. slip, 103
with a. means to pay, 6131
Advantageous to life, 4146
Adversaries : as a. do in law, 4042
Adversary : stony a., 2322
Adversity, 104-107
a.'s milk, philosophy, 5251
let me embrace thee, sour a., 106
man cross'd with a., 107
sweet are uses of a., 104
wretched soul, bruised with a., 105
Advertised by friends, 2906
Advice, 108-113
a. makes wits more keen, 108
dote on her with a., 113

restored with good a., 3911
take homely man's a., 110
this a. is free, 112
we desired your good a., 109
Advisings : fasten on my a., 111
Aery in cedar's top, 671
Affair cries haste, 3287
what is your a., 6574
Affairs of men incertain, 7502
tide in a. of men, 6591
Affectation : author of a., 5790
spruce a., 7363
Affection, 114-128
a. chains my tender days, 7574
a. faints not like coward, 127
a. is a coal, 126
a. is my captain, 122
a., mistress of passion, 120
a., thy intention stabs, 128
keep in rear of a., 117
my a. hath unknown bottom, 115
nothing can a.'s course control, 123
out, a., all bond break, 116
with a. wondrous sensible, 5167
Affections dark as Erebus, 4862
a. most busied alone, 124
had she a., 125
has he a. in him, 4035
his a. higher mounted, 3878
salt and hidden loose a., 121
thy a. do hold a wing, 118
with what wings shall a. fly, 119
wrestle with thy a., 114
Affliction, 129-136
a. is enamour'd of thy parts, 134
a. may one day smile, 5457
a. may subdue cheek, 5458
fresh complexion a. alters, 5458
henceforth I'll bear a., 132
shake patiently a. off, 131
this a. has a taste, 136
try me with a., 133
whoso please to stop a., 6734
Afric owns a serpent, 3295
Africa : I speak of A., 7473
After-supper : between a. and bedtime
5336
Afternoon : in a. of best days, 7120
Agate-stone : no bigger than a., 4434
Age, 137-168
a. cannot wither her, 140
a. from folly give freedom, 139
a. I do abhor thee, 7585
a., ill layer of beauty, 2458
a. is unnecessary, 153
a. is weak and cold, 7585
a. like winter weather, 7585
a. so eat up my invention, 5648
a. with stealing steps, 145
crabbed a. and youth, 7585
faint defects of a., 164
furrow me with a., 4143
lead our days to a., 3050
let me embrace thine a., 162
mine a. is weak, 3142
my a. is as lusty winter, 141
on us did a. steal on, 137
policy and reverence of a., 151
proper to a. to cast beyond, 7575
respect waits on wrinkled a., 159
separate a. and covetousness, 7579

settled a. becomes sables, 7576
silver livery of advised a., 4214
some smack of a. in you, 7577
'tis a. that nourisheth, 7588
trust not my a., 3740
two evils, a., hunger, 2366
when a. in, wit out, 157
with a. grown into a hoop, 7272
worn to pieces with a., 7481
Age: the Age, 166-168
a. is grown so picked, 166
drossy a. dotes on, 167
grace a. with noble deeds, 3614
I would excel golden a., 168
Nestor-like aged in a., 3196
Aged that coffers up gold, 4737
as dangerous a. as virtuous, 5035
Agenor : daughter of A., 533
Agent : trust no a., 2931
Agents : night's a. rouse, 4981
Agincourt, 169-171
affright air at A., 169
call we this field of A., 171
casques affright at A., 5040
disgrace name of A., 170
Agitation : speak my a., 5323
Agony : charm a. with words, 2156
Ague-proof : I am not a., 5535
Air, 172-181
a. and water abate fire, 3783
a. bites shrewdly, 174
a. breathes on us sweetly, 180
a. charter'd libertine, 6166
a. is quick there, 174
a. of paradise fan house, 172
a. recommends itself, 179
do not saw a. with hand, 54
eating a. on promise, 3565
empty, vast, wandering a., 178
give him a., 177
he is pure a., fire, 3590
I pray you, give her a., 177
melted into a., thin a., 5639
methinks I scent morning a., 175
nipping and eager a., 174
piece of tender a., 7128
tempt rheumy unpurged a., 5926
thou unsubstantial a., 178
walk out of the a., 176
where a. comes out, a. comes in, 173
with incorporal a. discourse, 2410
Airs from heaven, 6195
Ajax wears wit in belly, 7251
seven-fold shield of A., 3370
Thersites' body good as A., 5656
Alabaster : cut in a., 4721
smooth as monumental a., 5993
Alarum of hope and fear, 2139
Alchemy : gilding streams with a., 4800
his countenance, like a., 5088
Ale, 182-186
give my fame for pot of a., 182
poisoned with pot of a., 5354
pot of smallest a., 184
quart of a. is dish for king, 186
she brews good a., 185
were he not warm'd with a., 183
Alecto : fell A.'s snake, 5643
Alehouse : fools laugh in a., 5149
Ale-wife's new petticoat, 5238

Alexander, 187-191
A. killed his best friend, 198
A. was born in Macedon, 188
dust of A. stopping bunghole, 187
Alisander the conqueror, 191
scutcheon declares I am A., 190
All : one for a., a. for one, 5100
Alla stoccata carries it, 6303
Allegiance : follow with a., 4413
pluck a. from hearts, 3644
revolt from a. to heretic, 3466
Alliance in a. guile, 6712
purchase great a., 6807
Almanacs : greater tempests than a., 6452
Alms, 192-195
a. for oblivion, 6642
beg a. of palsied eld, 7582
fortune's a., 193, 194
one bred of a., 192
one that by a. doth live, 195
Alms-basket of words, 7431
Alone, 196-199
a. I did it, 196
how can it be said I am a., 197
let her a., 199
Alteration : alters when a. finds, 4333
Amazement on thy mother sits, 6128
Amazons : like A. come tripping, 2336
Ambition, 200-208
a.'s debt is paid, 205
a. of so airy a quality, 202
a., soldier's virtue, 200
beshrew my father's a., 2566
fling away a., 203
ill-weaved a., 3617
lowliness is young a.'s ladder, 204
pride went before, a. follows, 5418
thou art not without a., 4911
thoughts tending to a., 6566
thriftless a. will ravin up, 207
tongue-tied a., 208
vaulting a., o'erleaps itself, 206
virtue choked with foul a., 6935
Amen, a. to that fair prayer, 210
a. stuck in my throat, 209
will no man say a., 3904
Amendment : good a. in thee, 6947
Amiss : all is a., 5538
Amity, 211-214
a. and life 'tween snow, 5529
a. that wisdom knits not, 214
bind this knot of a., 212
hold you in perpetual a., 211
I come to crave a., 213
Anatomize : my body to a., 788
Anatomy : eat his a., 4212
mere a., a mountebank, 6893
Ancestors that come after him, 217
a. who stood equivalent to kings, 219
burial amongst their a., 218
have wild trick of a., 6716
my a. did Tarquin drive, 216
she lies buried with a., 218
when I am sleeping with a., 215
Anchor : holding a. lost, 5282
Ancient, fish-like smell, 6042
Ancients : my charge consists of a., 6064
Andromache : he chid A., 3420
Andronicus : enchant old A., 7453
Angel, 220-236
an a., earthly paragon, 220

an a. is not evil, 224
a. dropp'd from clouds, 3613
a. is like you, Kate, 223
better a. is a man, 236
curse his better a., 232
guess one a. in another's hell, 236
in action like an a., 4487
ministering a. shall sister be, 222
no evil a. but love, 4275
speak again, bright a., 228
that a. of the world, 5656
the more a. she, 226
they have a. faces, 2731
though a. on outward side, 4499
till my bad a. fire good one out, 236
write good a. on devil's horn, 231
Angels and ministers of grace, 221
a. are bright still, 225
a. officed all, 172
a. vailing clouds, 3990
flights of a. sing thee, 3371
good a. fly o'er head, 230
good a. guard thee, 233
good a. guard thee from boar, 5682
good a. guard thy battle, 233
go with me, my good a., 229
help, a., make assay, 6127
if a. fight, men must fall, 227
plead like a., 6939
tricks as make a. weep, 4498
women are a., wooing, 7360

Anger, 237-245
a. has a privilege, 242
a. is like full-hot horse, 240
a. is my meat, 238
carries a. as flint bears fire, 241
more in sorrow than a., 6101
my tongue tell a. of heart, 6677
never a. made good guard, 237
never to red-look'd a. be trumpet, 6683
to be in a. is impiety, 245
touch me with noble a., 243
Angler in lake of darkness, 4948
Angling : pleasant'st a., 2709
wager'd on your a., 2705
Anguish of torturing hour, 5336
pain lessen'd by another's a., 5131
Animal : he is only an a., 3693
man a forked a., 4494
Animals rage in sensuality, 5845
souls of a. infuse, 5483
Anointed : rail on Lord's a., 7329

Answer, 246-254
a. made it none, 249
a. me in one word, 7379
good lenten a., 253
I can no a. make, 6516
I have a. will serve all, 246
is that an a., 251
never take her without a., 7226
silly a. befitting sheep, 254
we cannot take this for a., 252
you a. with idle tongue, 2563
your a. is enigmatical, 250
Answers : full of pretty a., 6251
Anthropophagi, whose heads, 4305
Antic : father a., the law, 4028
there the a. sits, 3901
Antidote : oblivious a., 4689
Antidotes : his a. poison, 5266

Antipodes : hold day with A., 4988
I will go to A., 5875
opposite as A., 3075
Antiquity : blasted with a., 7578
Antiquius : bonum quo a., 6095
Antony, 255-257
A. that revels long, 257
fortune and A. part, 2851
I dreamed there was an Emperor A., 256
none but A. should conquer A., 255
portends fall of A., 4778
Antres vast, 4305
Anvil : iron on a. cool, 4958
Ape, 258-265
a. is dead, 264
keeps them, like an a., 261
like the famous a., 260
more new-fangled than a., 258
out you mad-headed a., 262
Apes and monkeys would chatter, 259
a., braggarts, Jacks, 6902
jollity for a., 6703
lead a. in hell, 263
we shall be turned to a., 265
Apollo humble swain, 3055
hark, A. plays, 4871
musical as A.'s lute, 4281
words harsh after songs of A., 7433
Apology : on without a., 6185
Apostraphas : you find not a., 27
Apothecary, 266-268
bid a. bring the poison, 266
I do remember an a., 267
O true a., thy drugs are quick, 268
Apparel oft proclaims man, 3189
disgrace my man's a., 7292
every man's a. fits thief, 6529
Apparitions : thousand a., 3740
Appearance, 269-280
deny a. of blind boy, 4391
thou hast a grim a., 269
what a ragged a., 270
Appetite, 281-288
a. an universal wolf, 287
a. of her eye scorched me, 4289
cloy the edge of a., 6115
digest words with better a., 5748
doth not the a. alter, 285
hooking right and wrong to a., 4826
I am strong in a., 281
increase of a. had grown, 282
leaden a., unapt to toy, 288
O a., stand aloof, 283
surfeiting, a. may sicken, 4874
taste with distempered a., 5853
who riseth from feast with a., 284
Appetites : make a. more keen, 286
Applaud thee to the echo, 289
Applause, 289-294
a. where they're extended, 4231
broils in loud a., 293
hearing a. and shout, 290
his silence drinks up a., 294
laughs out a loud a., 292
this general a. and shout, 291
Apple, cleft, not more twin, 4165
as a. doth an oyster, 4167
as like as crab to a., 4164
goodly a. rotten at heart, 6136
like Eve's a., thy beauty, 530

Apple-john : withered like a., 5991
Apples : fight for bitten a., 7562
Appliance disease requires, 6492
Apprehension of the good, 6115
  ear more quick of a., 4990
  in a. how like a god, 4487
Apprehensions : full of a., 6201
Approach makest me unhappy, 6817
Appurtenance of welcome, 7078
Apricocks : feed him with a., 3867
April, 295-299
  A. is in her eyes, 295
  A. never came so sweet, 296
  he smells A. and May, 6039
  man born in A., 7074
  men are A. when they woo, 7360
  proud-pied A., 298
  she calls back A., 4817
  spongy A., 299
  uncertain glory of A. day, 4350
  well-apparell'd A., 297
Aprons : go in leather a., 5009
Aqua-vitae with midwife, 7461
Arbitrator : common a., Time, 2305
Arbitrators : weak a., 7444
Arbitrement, 300-303
  a. is like to be bloody, 302
  a. of swords, 300
  incensed to mortal a., 303
  keep aloof from strict a., 301
Arch : let a. of empire fall, 5726
Arch-mock : the fiend's a., 6989
Archibald, valiant Scot, 3607
Arden : forest of A., 6705
Argosies with portly sail, 4690
Arguing make us sweat, 309
Argument, 304-319
  a. all bare of worth, 316
  a. is cuckold and whore, 318
  a. that fell out last night, 305
  finer than staple of a., 312
  given us bloody a., 319
  good a. we will not fly, 2627
  he will maintain his a., 308
  hold longer a. in notes, 313
  how did this a. begin, 311
  I cannot fight upon a., 317
  I force not a. a straw, 314
  it would be a. for a week, 306
  nor stir without great a., 3121
  prove a. of laughter, 306
  rarest a. of wonder, 304
  sheathed swords for lack of a., 307
  you are still my a., 315
Arguments : all kind of a., 6665
  a. of mighty force, 5115
  ear-kissing a., 310
  tang a. of state, 6681
Argus were her eunuch, 6985
  watch me like A., 7021
Arithmetic, 320-325
  dizzy the a. of memory, 322
  no a. but her brain, 325
  spare your a., 321
  'tis odds beyond a., 5079
Arithmetician : a great a., 323
Arm like wither'd shrub, 4266
  God's a. strike with us, 5082
  have not I an a., 7417
  meet we a. us, 7012

under a., like scarf, 2961
  with your a. renew feats, 6840
Armed : thrice a. that hath quarrel just
  5493
Armour : I'll give thee a., 5251
  Mars' a. forged for proof, 5610
Armourers accomplishing knights, 328
Armours : have a. buckled on, 5311
Arms fair when bearing just, 3843
  love's a. are peace, 4284
  my a. eel-skins stuff'd, 2461
  since a. had seven years pith, 6181
  twine a. about that body, 787
  wind thee in my a., 3763
Army, 326-330
  his a. a ragged multitude, 329
  hum of either a. sounds, 328
  our a. dispersed already, 327
  within ken our a. lies, 326
Arras : asleep behind a., 6018
Array : proud a., 2660
Arrogance : can ye endure this a., 5010
  supple knees feed a., 3959
Arrow, 331-334
  a. shot from archer, 334
  a. with golden head, 6066
  shot mine a. o'er house, 332
  swifter than a., 6385
Arrows too slightly timber'd, 331
  as many a. come to one mark, 71
  fleeter than a., 6667
Art, 335-337
  a. and practice of life, 4129
  a. made tongue-tied, 367
  a. of our necessities, 4930
  beautified with plastering a., 7397
  his a. is of such power, 337
  I want that oily a., 7399
  more matter with less a., 4576
  natural in thine a., 2655
  nature's above a., 4910
  no a. to find mind in face, 2464
  thou art all my a., 336
Arthur : he's in A.'s bosom, 2515
  my A., my fair son, 6086
  young A. is my son, 4449
Artificer : unwash'd a., 4838
Artillery : heaven's a., 6588
Artist : some good, others exceed, 335
Arts, academes, 2428
  had I but followed a., 6685
Ashes of my chance, 6205
  consume to a., 4706
  feigned a. of love, 2138
  her a. create an heir, 5254
  her a. more precious, 3805
  my a. may bring forth, 648
  some will mourn in a., 4820
Asleep with eyes open, 5622
  fast a., behind arras, 6018
  fast a., no matter, 6022
  standing, yet fast a., 5622
Aspect : of vinegar a., 4916
  sweet a. of princes, 5426
Aspen : shake as a. leaf, 2603
Aspersion : no sweet a., 6924
Ass, 338-349
  a. knows when cart draws horse, 343
  bear them as a. bears gold, 3562
  come, you virtuous a., 756
  egregiously an a., 348

he is both ox and a., 344
I am an a., long ears, 340
I am such a tender a., 345
I perceive I am made an a., 344
I think thou art an a., 339
like to a., shake ears, 3562
methought I was enamour'd of an a., 346
preposterous a., 4872
'tis so, I am an a., 338
what a thrice-double a. was I, 349
what an a. am I, 341
write me down an a., 347
your a. will not mend his pace, 342
Ass-head of a coxcomb, 3948
Assay : angels, make a., 6127
Asses are made to bear, 7331
led by nose, as a., 5026
like your a., dogs, 6010
Assurance of a man, 5272
make a. double sure, 6348
Assyrian : base A. knight, 4955
Astronomers foretell it, 5455
Atomies : easy to count a., 4398
shut gates on a., 2404
team of little a., 4434
Attainder of suspect, 6728
Attaint : what thief brags of a., 6524
Attempt, 350-355
a. not deed confounds us, 355
give over this a., 351
man may stagger in this a., 352
quality and hair of our a., 354
this a. I am soldier to, 353
Attempts : impossible be strange a., **350**
Attendance : dance a., 357
I dance a. here, 358
I danced a. on his will, 356
Attire : wild in a., 2270
Attention : enforce a. like deep harmony, 6673
Attorneys : windy a., 7448
Attorneyship : dealt with by a., 4559
Attribute to awe and majesty, 4642
a. to God himself, 4642
Audacious without impudency, 5582
Audacity : arm me, a., 803
Audience : end without a., 6280
no a. able to endure, 7562
too wanton to give a., 6322

Audit : how his a. stands, 2562
Auger-hole : hid in a., 2554
Augmentation of Indies, 6047
Augurers say they know not, 6359
Augurs have brought forth, 725
Augury : we defy a., 5465
Authentic in your place, 2974
learned and a. fellows, 2634
Author : as if man were a., 3749
where is any a. in world, 2428
Authorities : two a. are up, 362
Authority, 359-368
art made tongue-tied by a., 367
a. led by golden gold, 368
a. melts from me, 360
a. skins vice o' the top, 366
a. though it err, 366
base a. from others' books, 6291
drest in a little brief a., 4498
it is borne in high a., 5091
no fettering of a., 359
on the winking of a., 3888
they prank them in a., 361
thieves have a. when judges steal, 6528
thus can demigod A. make us pay, 364
what a. and show of truth, 5969
wrest law to your a., 4038
Authorized by her grandam, 4497
Autolycus : father named me A., 6744
Avaunt, and quit my sight, 5879
Ave-Maries : number A., 3496
Avoirdupois : turn scales between a., 3195
Avouch it to his head, 3686
Away : whither a. so fast, 4279
Awe : creating a. in others, 1158
live in a. of myself, 4131
wrench a. from fools, 5316
Axe, 369-373
absolved him with an a., 372
a. of death, 370
cutt'st with golden a., 416
falls not a. upon neck, 2384
stay grinding of the a., 369
we set a. to thy root, 371
where offence is let great a. fall, 5085
Axle-tree : wheel grate on a., 5348
Ay and No was no good divinity, 375
dismiss me with ay or no, 374

B

Babbled of green fields, 2515
Babe, 377-385
come on, poor b., 385
love b. that milks me, 381
prettiest b. ere I nursed, 384
testy b., scratch nurse, 4349
Babes : ah, my tender b., 383
pity these tender b., 382
think thy b. fairer, 1743
Baboon : bred into b., 4518
change humanity with b., 2214
Baby beats the nurse, 4087
b. not out of clouts, 380
my b. sucks nurse asleep, 378
Babylon : the whore of B., 5665
Bacchanals : Egyptian B., 1776
Bacchus with pink eyne, 386

Bachelor, 387-391
I am a b., 388
I will live a b., 390
I would die a b., 391
never see b. of three score, 389
Bachelors : where b. sit, 4660
Back : lie on b. to defend belly, 7336
straight b. will stoop, 7361
Back-friend, 2901
Backs red, faces pale, 1734
Backward : spell him b., 4531
Bacon : hang-dog Latin for b., 393
Bacon-fed knaves, 1124
Bacons : on, b., on, 392
Bad is the world, 399
creating b. perfect best, 396
I count myself but b., 395

make b. good, 4860
pick b. from b., 398
things b. begun, 397
too b. for b. report, 394
too b. to curse, 394
you o'er-green my b., 5810
Badge of all our tribe, 6830
white liver b. of cowardice, 4207
Bag : with b. and baggage, 400, 401
Bag-pipe sings i' the nose, 120
Bag-piper : laugh at b., 4916
Baggage : out of my door, you b., 7271
out, you b., 7533
ye are a b., 5717
Bail : arrest without b., 1852
Bait of falsehood, 2496
devour treacherous b., 2709
fish not with melancholy b., 5106
swallow'd b., 4431
young dace b. for pike, 4907
Bajazet : B.'s mule, 6654
Baker : owl was b.'s daughter, 5122
Balance : mote will turn b., 4813
Bald with antiquity, 5044
time himself is b., 6611
Ball to play upon, 4513
swift as a b., 125
Ballad, 402-408
b. made to eyebrow, 7466
b. of king and beggar, 406
in a particular b., 405
love b. even too well, 407
love b. in print of life, 408
rhyme is but a b., 5672
rhymers b. out of tune, 403
Ballad-makers, 4969
Ballad-mongers : metre b., 5348
Ballads : have b. made, 404
traduced by odious b., 402
Balm of hurt minds, 6024
no b. can cure, 6003
'tis not b., sceptre, 6021
wash b. from anointed king, 389
Banbury : you B. cheese, 1269
Bandogs howl, 7269
Bands : dissolve b. of life, 3572
end of life cancels b., 4125
Bang : you'll bear a b., 388
Banish plump Jack, b. world, 2512
I b. thee on pain of death, 2513
we b. him our city, 409
we b. you our territories, 412
Banished : hence-b. is b. from world, 416
Banishment, 409-417
bitter bread of b., 413
everlasting doom of b., 417
left in reputeless b., 5104
more pain in b. than death, 414
tread the paths of b., 412
Bank and shoal of time, 1932
b. where wild thyme blows, 2761
Severn's sedgy b., 4809
Banners of the French, 419
France spreads his b., 419
hang b. on outward walls, 420
Norweyan b. flout the sky, 419
see their b. wave again, 418
Banns : say the b., 7374
Banquet : foolish b., 2621
his words are fantastical b., 7439

Banquo walk'd too late, 6975
Baptism : pure with b., 6167
Barbara : maid B., 7165
Barbarous, degenerate, 1808
Barbary cock-pigeon, 3775
roan B., 3595
Barbason sounds well, 1702
Barber : I must to the b., 345
Bare-bone : here comes b., 3955
Bare-gnawn, canker-bit, 4891
Bareness : mock us with b., 5737
Bargain, 421-428
clap hands and a b., 423
clap this royal b. up, 424
dateless b. to death, 1895
in way of b. I'll cavil, 421
lest the b. catch cold, 422
seal b. with holy kiss, 428
to sell b. well is cunning, 425
world-without-end b., 426
Barge she sat in, 429
see the b. be ready, 430
Bark peel'd from pine, 5293
b. when their fellows do, 2321
even as splitted b., 3342
let labouring b. climb, 6492
scarfed b. puts from bay, 5447
Barne : a very pretty b., 1284
Barnes are blessings, 696
Barns and garners never empty, 696
b. harvest of his wits, 4737
Barricado it against him, 6925
no b. for a belly, 621
Bartholomew boar-pig, 2510
Bartholomew-tide : at B., 7189
Basan : hill of B., 431
Base : art thou b., common, 5093
b. things sire b., 4899
Base-string of humility, 3643
Baseness nobly undergone, 2310
b. of our natures, 5576
b. to write fair, 7535
thou unconfinable b., 3548
why brand us with b., 438
Basilisk : slay more than b., 1681
Basilisks : would they were b., 2436
Basket on house's top, 260
Bassanio : say B. is dead, 5700
Bastard, 432-439
blood proclaims me b., 432
he is b. to the time, 437
I am a b. begot, 439
my boy a b., 436
that same b. of Venus, 1712
why b. ? wherefore base, 438
Bastards : nature's b., 2767
we are all b., 432
Bastardy : slandered with b., 434
Bath : sore labour's b., 6024
Batlet : kissing of her b., 4248
Battalions : sorrows come in b., 6102
Batten on this moor, 5272
Battery : her sighs make b., 7309
his hum is a b., 6429
Battle, 440-446
bloody sign of b., 446
even play of b., 442
fearful b. renewed, 6997
few die well in b., 441
here pitch our b., 962

I saw him in b. range, 2567
noise of b. hurtled, 5097
rushed into bowels of b., 861
Saint Alban's b., 444
when b.'s lost and won, 6573
Battles of Lord of Hosts, 443
fight last of many b., 440
Bauble: idiot holds b. for god, 5063
Bawcock: king is a b., 3877
Bawd: blind muffled b., 4995
  ever your powder'd b., 7102
  I remember him, a b., 5550
  one wouldst be a b., 3941
Bawds: pious b., 6962
Bay-trees are wither'd, 5941
Be: I had as lief not be, 4131
  stoutly say, so be it, 3357
  to be or not to be, 1847
Be-all and end-all, 1932
Beacon of the wise, 2169
Bead: you b., you acorn, 2250
Beadle, hold thy hand, 7101
  b. to humorous sigh, 1714
Beadsman: be thy b., 1795
Beaks: turn b. with gale, 5716
Beam do find in each, 4812
Beams of watery moon, 1716
  sun's transparent b., 6273
Bear, 449-452
  afraid to see b. loose, 4596
  approach like Russian b., 5879
  bay'd b. with hounds, 4864
  b. that lives like lamb, 7281
  cub-drawn b. would couch, 4975
  exit, pursued by a b., 452
  head-lugg'd b. would lick, 1808
  how easy is bush supposed b., 3705
  I am as ugly as a b., 6812
  more can I b., 5008
  one b. will not bite another, 351
  one must b., 6869
  run into Russian b., 3311
  thou'ldst shun a b., 449
  whose hand b. licks, 4178
Bear-baiting: dancing and b., 6685
  out of favour about a b., 454
Bear-baitings: he haunts b., 455
Bear-herd: valour turned b., 6934
Bear-like, I must fight the course, 6232
Bear-ward: manacle the b., 453
Bear-whelp: like unlick'd b., 4266
Beard, 456-479
  b. be shook with danger, 464
  b., fair health, honesty, 472
  b. like paring-knife, 474
  b. neglected, 4249
  b. of formal cut, 7466
  b. of general's cut, 468
  b. was not cut well, 4091
  black b. will turn white, 7361
  brave thee, b. thee too, 463
  by my old b., 456
  by this white b., 478
  comest thou to b. me, 463
  had white hairs in b., 2724
  hair less in his b., 5499
  have b. grow in palm, 466
  have you not white b., 7578
  he hath but little b., 458
  he that hath b. more than youth, 475

his b. was grizzled, 461
his b. was sable silver'd, 461
his b. white as snow, 462
I b. thee to thy face, 463
I could not endure husband with b., 475
if you wore b., I'd shake it, 471
ignobly pluck me by b., 470
I'll hide my b. in beaver, 467
Jove send thee a b., 479
meet him b. to b., 459
no b., less than a man, 475
no man but I'll b. him, 463
plucks off my b., 1634
priest, beware your b., 469
thy father's b. turned white, 465
we met b. to b., 459
what a b. hast thou got, 473
whose b. the silver hand of peace, 467
yellow b., Cain-coloured b., 474
you had more b., 460
younger by loss of a b., 476
Bearded like a pard, 7466
Beards: kiss as many as had b., 3917
  merry in hall when b. wag all, 4657
  old men have grey b., 143
  wear b. of Hercules, 4210
  white b. have armed, 478
  your b. deserve not honourable grave,
    1201
  your b. forbid me, 7319
Bears: affable wolves, meek b., 5155
  b. are tied by the neck, 4061
  b. betrayed with glasses, 2723
  b. will not bite one another, 450
  call hither my brave b., 453
  we'll bait thy b. to death, 453
Beast, 480-489
  any strange b. makes man, 2339
  b. that wants discourse, 481
  b. with many heads, 4831
  familiar b., signifies love, 217
  ill-beseeming b., 4534
  let b. be lord of beasts, 482
  little better than a b., 4500
  love makes a b. a man, 4292
  many a b. in city, 4512
  no b. so fierce but knows pity, 488
  play noble b. in love, 974
  rough b. obeys appetite, 486
  she would have me a b., 1360
  that incestuous b., 5861
  thou owest b. no hide, 4494
  unkindest b. kinder than mankind, 489
  very gentle b., 485
  what is a man, a b., 4488
  wildest b. hath not heart, 483
Beasts, fishes, fowls, 4483
  b. that meet me run, 6812
  b. tremble at thy din, 1745
  here come two noble b., 484
  let b. bear gentle minds, 487
  lion and a king of b., 4192
  nature teaches b., 480
  pair of very strange b., 2796
Beat 'em into bench-holes, 490
  b. him like a dog, 5470
  more you b. me, more I'll fawn, 6151
Beaten black and blue, 492
  b. into all colours, 492
  I'ld have b. him like a dog, 491

Beatrice like a lapwing runs, 4003
Beauteous thou art, 527
Beauties : examine other b., 6551
  one that composed your b., 6551
Beautified is a vile phrase, 5256
Beautiful, therefore to be woo'd, 7362
  more b. than beauteous, 508
Beauty, 494-536
  b. and honour in her mingled, 504
  b. blemished forever lost, 516
  b. bought by judgement of eye, 506
  b. brief in goodness, 3076
  b. confounds the tongue, 501
  b. doth of itself persuade, 517
  b. doth varnish age, 510
  b. I never knew thee, 3216
  b. is a flower, 534
  b. is a witch, 2931
  b. is but doubtful good, 516
  b. lives with kindness, 5953
  b. making beautiful old rhyme, 531
  b. my prize is, 1989
  b. no stronger than flower, 528
  b. of a woman's face, 6293
  b. of this sinful dame, 560
  b. oft makes women proud, 503
  b. provoketh thieves, 495
  b. purchas'd by weight, 511
  b. should not be wasted, 526
  b. starved cuts off posterity, 519
  b. that tyrant oft reclaims, 502
  b. too rich for use, 522
  b., wit, high birth, 6945
  b.'s ensign crimson, 1984
  could b. have commerce, 494
  dedicate his b. to sun, 1075
  fresh b. made for use, 6828
  he hath a daily b. in his life, 515
  her b. and brain go not together, 499
  her b. makes vault light, 524
  holiday-time of my b., 4083
  honour and b. weakly fortress'd, 3552
  I ne'er saw true b. till this night, 522
  I saw sweet b. in her face, 533
  I swear b. is black, 1467
  in b. as first of May, 513
  infect her b., you fogs, 1740
  let b. be her dower, 2172
  like Eve's apple doth thy b. grow, 530
  more doth b. beauteous seem, 6779
  my b. can not please his eye, 497
  my b. needs not flourish, 506
  no honour where there is b., 3536
  power of b. transforms honesty, 494
  smother up his b., 6317
  so seems this gorgeous b., 501
  thy b. made me effeminate, 523
  thy b. is proposed my fee, 6675
  'tis b. truly blent, 2473
  turn b. into thoughts of harm, 2532
  unmask her b. to the moon, 4461
  were b. under twenty locks, 535
  what though you have no b., 496
  why should b. seek roses, 5136
  your b. did haunt me, 1143
  your b. was the cause, 1143
Because, woman's reason, 5579
Bed, 537-554
  b., dear repose for limbs, 551
  best turn i' the b., 6790

big enough for b. of Ware, 4102
come, Kate, we'll to b., 552
conquer'd my maiden b., 538
convey me to my b., 5894
die upon b. father died, 165
every man hence to his b., 544
go home to b., 3568
go to b. to work, 7325
I have forsworn his b., 546
I was in love with my b., 4351
in your b. find fortune, 537
laid in b. majestical, 6021
make b. with the defunct, 4901
make bridal b. in monument, 4775
royal b. of Denmark, 542
run as to a lover's b., 1837
steal out of wholesome b., 5926
strangle her in b., 5358
thrice-driven b. of down, 1754
thy b., lust-stained, 549
to go to b. after midnight, 554
tumble on b. of Ptolemy, 539
wed her, b. her, 7372
which b., press it to death, 553
wrong to truant with b., 5985
you've stole from my b., 545
Bedchamber : in b. barr'd of rest, 3365
Bedfellow, 555-561
  allot thee for his b., 561
  but soft ! no b., 557
  go, you wild b., 555
  grieve to leave sweet b., 559
  I'll have that doctor for my b., 7021
  man that was his b., 6710
  princes seek her as b., 560
  tie him not to be b., 556
Bed-fellows : misery has strange b., 4742
Bed-presser : this b., 1456
Bed-right : no b. paid, 1245
Bed-room : no b. me deny, 547
Bed-swerver : she's a b., 99
Bed-time : consort till b., 541
  I would 'twere b., 541
Bed-work : they call this b., 5539
Bedlam : to B. with him, 4448
Beds i' the east are soft, 540
  died holily in their b., 6976
  he hides him in soft b., 540
  let their b. be soft, 6010
  make our b. of roses, 5706
  millions in unproper b., 548
  they love men in b., 4866
Bee, 562-570
  b., culling from flower, 6084
  b. doth leave comb, 562
  some say the b. stings, 565
  where the b. sucks, 569
Bee-hives : drones rob b., 2210
Beef : great eater of b., 7254
  what say you to b., 2789
Beer, 571-573
  chronicle small b., 573
  felony to drink small b., 572
  poor creature small b., 571
  vile to desire small b., 571
Bees care not who they sting, 564
  kill the b. that yield, 7017
  leave Hybla b. honeyless, 7385
  like b., murdered, 6084
  old b. die, 568

Beetle, 574-576
poor b. we tread upon, 576
shard-borne b., 1936
sharded b., 574
three-man b., 575
Before and after, 4488
Beg of Hob and Dick, 1748
I am bound to b., 587
to b. will not become me, 577
you taught me to b., 583
Beggar, 577-585
b. and the king, 585
b. begs that never begged, 585
b. in his drink, 7107
b. that I am, 6507
begging prince b. pities, 5431
fond b. to touch crown, 584
how b. should be answered, 583
king is b., play done, 3869
mouth with a b., 582
not furnished like b., 577
while b., I will rail, 580
Beggar-maid : Copethua loved b., 1723
Beggar-man : is it a b., 581
Beggars in poorest things, 4941
b. mounted run horse to death, 579
but b. that count worth, 7508
silly b. in the stocks, 6566
speaking is for b., 6186
when b. die, no comets seen, 1863
Beggary hangs upon thy back, 2524
b. in love reckon'd, 4242
b. is valiant, 578
impotent b., 1964
no vice but b., 580
Begging sixteen years, 1623
trouble poor with b., 588
young knave and b., 589
Beginning, 590-601
b. of feast, keen guest, 2619
end unknown to b., 593
I will tell you the b., 592
sweet b., unsavoury end, 4365
true b. of our end, 598
Beginnings : weak b., 3482
Beguiled me to heart of loss, 1220
Behaviour, 602-610
b. of country mockable, 1602
b. of young gentleman, 610
his b. vain, ridiculous, 1206
practising b. to own shadow, 609
there is fair b. in thee, 608
this loose b. I throw off, 5595
very gross kind of b., 5146
what an unweighed b., 607
your b. hath struck her, 603
Behaviours : dedicated b. to love, 4299
Behold : ere man can say b., 4157
Belch : eat and b. us, 4510
Beldams do prophesy, 4782
Bell, 611-617
b. book and candle, 615
b. invites me, 616
hear surly sullen b., 4822
let's mock midnight b., 611
live no longer than b. rings, 4774
midnight b. did sound, 611
silence that dreadful b., 617
startle you worse than sacring b., 614

sullen b. tolling, 954
warning b. sings heavy music, 613
Bellman gives good-night, 5125
Bellows blows up sin, 2721
b. to cool gipsy's lust, 4426
Bells : bid merry b. ring, 3109
like sweet b. jangled, 4681
ring, b., aloud, 612
why ring not out the b., 612
you are b. in parlours, 7325
Belly, 618-621
an I but had a b., 619
body rebelled against b., 618
fair round b., 7466
have increasing b., 7578
lie upon back to defend b., 7336
my b. is as cold, 620
no barricado for a b., 621
somewhat a round b., 660
wears his wit in his b., 7252
Belmont : run as far as B., 4987
Beloving : more b. than beloved, 4243
Bench-holes : beat 'em into b., 490
Benediction of heavens, 689
out of heaven's b., 5804
Benedick, 622-625
B., the married man, 623-625
if he hath caught the B., 622
let B. consume in sighs, 1882
Benefits, 626-627
b. forgot, 626
disable b. of country, 6706
we are born to do b., 2917
when b. shall prove, 627
Bequest : nature's b., 4919
Bermoothes : still-vexed B., 628
Berries : two b. on one stem, 6819
wholesome b. thrive best, 6285
Besonian : die by vile b., 630
under which king, B., 629
Best, 631-639
all done well, you b., 637
all is for the b., 635
b. for the worst, 636
b. in this kind, shadows, 3706
b. sometimes forget, 2838
b. that ever I heard, 636
created of every creature's b., 7335
I'll do my b., 634
let each man do his b., 634
make the b. of it, 633
men dare bite the b., 2349
of many good I think him b., 638
turn all to the b., 639
we did it for the b., 632
Bestial : what remains is b., 5626
Bethumped with words, 7430
Better, 640-641
be b. at thy leisure,.5891
b. for being bad, 2594
b. is by evil made b., 3701
b. said than done, 6169
do b. than well, 640
I took thee for thy b., 1785
striving to b., oft we mar, 641
Bettering thy loss, 1743
dedicate to b. of mind, 4695
Betters : give b. way, 643
see b. bearing woes, 644
your b., sir, 642

Bias : assays of b., 3715
  my fortune runs against b., 5747
Bibble babble : vain b.b., 6036
Bidding : finished with b., 5067
Bier : bore him on b., 3106
Big-bellied with wind, 5783
Biggen : with homely b. bound, 1677
Bigger : run till I am b., 2672
Bilberry : blue as b., 2475
Billow : swell b., 3308
Bind : fast b., fast find, 5462
Bird, 645-654
  am I your b., 654
  b. better than beast, 6670
  b. of dawning singeth, 1395
  b. of night sit hooting, 5123
  b. that hath been limed, 651
  b. that will revenge, 648
  I heard a b. so sing, 647
  I saw Jove's b., eagle, 2256
  I would I were thy b., 653
  if thou be eagle's b., 2257
  no further than wanton's b., 5169
  obscure b., clamour'd, 4982
  poor b., never fear, 652
  she is alone Arabian b., 500
  thou art a summer b., 646
  what b. hath done to nest, 645
  who would give b. the lie, 1706
Bird-bolt : thumped with b., 1715
Birds never limed no bushes fear, 652
  b. of selfsame feather, 650
  melodious b. sing, 5706
  of their feather many b., 649
  sweet b., oh how they sing, 186
  we will sing like b., 5438
  when b. sing, hey ding, 4401
Birnam Wood shall come, 655
Biron like envious frost, 2933
  B. they call him, 7233
Birth, 656-671
  at my b. earth shaked, 659
  bring monstrous b. to light, 670
  prodigious b. of love, 4377
  since b. of Cain, 3400
  some glory in their b., 4329
  subject to his b., 657
  violent b., poor validity, 5472
  why joy in abortive b., 2933
Birthrights : bearing b., 2878
Births : at b. good stars opposite, 669
Bis coctus, 3693
Biscuit : dry as remainder b., 885
Bit : gimmel b. lies foul, 3771
Bitch : heir of mongrel b., 3941
Biting : his b. is immortal, 7496
Bits to headstrong wills, 6255
  dainty b. make rich ribs, 2546
Bitter as colonquintida, 2784
  b. past more welcome, 6379
  b. to look into happiness, 3255
  b. to me as death, 6535
Bitterness of galls, 7578
Blab heart's malice, 672
Blabbed them with eloquence, 673
  why have I b., 674
Blabs : when my tongue b., 675
Black : as b. as Acheron, 680
  as b. as hell, 532, 3407
  as b. as ink, 4968

as b. as smeared in hell, 678
as gross as b. and white, 6772
beaten b. and blue, 492
b. as ebony, 679
b., coal-b. as jet, 678
b. is badge of hell, 679
b. men pearls, 5223
dye makes whitest b., 3739
fool him b. and blue, 677
hung be heavens with b., 1415
if she be b. and hath a wit, 7245
in b. my lady's brows, 679
is b. so base a hue, 682
make b. white, 3066
pinch us b. and blue, 5287
put on sullen b., 4821
smear'd b. as Vulcan, 2474
swear beauty is b., 1467
though ne'er so b., 2731
we mourn in b., 4819
Blackness, 676-683
  find white that b. fits, 681
  raven chides b., 5561
Bladder : blows man up like b., 5931
Bladders full of imposthume, 1747
  swim on b., 2492
Blade : bloody blameful b., 6402
  let fall b. on vulnerable crests, 666
Blame : worthy b., 2763
  you were to b., 5324
Blanch : Lady B., 4270
Blasphemy : in soldier b., 1091
Blastments most imminent, 1070
Blasts upon thee, 1739
  they that stand high have b., 3128
  unruly b. wait on spring, 6223
Blazes giving more light, 707
Bleat : you have his b., 974
Bleed : we must b. for it, 2093
Bleeding piece of earth, 1031
Blemish : no b. but the mind, 685
Blemishes : forget my b., 686
  read not my b., 684
Bless thee from whirlwinds, 694
Blessedness of being little, 1204
  lives in single b., 6922
Blesseth him that gives, 4642
Blessing, 687-699
  b. of your heart, 185
  double b. is double grace, 690
  honour, marriage-b., 696
  I feel too much thy b., 4287
  kneel and take my b., 2739
  never b. of God, 1284
  steal immortal b., 4202
  thrift is b., 6576
  when thou ask b., 5438
Blessings on him, 692
  dews fall thick in b., 689
  flow, you b. on her, 688
  heavenly b. follow, 4684
  pack of b. on thy back, 695
  thousand thousand b., 2297
  world of earthly b., 3340
Blind is his love, 4394
  knows me as b. knows cuckoo, 6951
  strucken b. cannot forget, 5939
  you strike like b. man, 701
Blind-worms do no wrong, 2478

Bliss : all poets feign of b., 1679
  b. in our brows' bent, 2352
Blister : sets a b. there, 38
Blithe and bonny, 4506
Block-head : wit wedged in b., 7227
Blood, 702-745
  am I not of her b., 745
  art thou of b. and honour, 5552
  bathe hands in Cæsar's b., 1028
  b. and judgement mingled, 2861
  b. and revenge hammering, 5655
  b. had been shed ere now, 724
  b. hath bought b., 721
  b. he lost for country, 706
  b. is hot, 7445
  b. is their argument, 441
  b. like sacrificing Abel's, 736
  b. made dull with act of sport, 44
  b. more stirs to rouse lion, 1787
  b. of English manure ground, 49
  b. of our natures, 5576
  b. of youth burns not, 7216
  b. should sprinkle me, 737
  b. thou art b., 729
  b. untainted still red, 735
  b. which runs up veins, 4618
  b. will have b., 725
  b. will I draw on thee, 2028
  Christ's b. shed for sins, 5594
  civil b. makes hands unclean, 740
  comes not b. as evidence, 761
  contaminated b., 715
  corrupted b. watery token, 735
  cursed be b. that let b., 1741
  daub lips with children's b., 6994
  dearest-valued b. of France, 7526
  dip napkins in his b., 6503
  does it curd thy b., 702
  drizzled b. upon Capitol, 5097
  drop my b. for drachmas, 4762
  drop of b. that's calm, 432
  drunk with innocents' b., 739
  examine well your b., 6922
  for my country shed b., 706
  freeze thy young b., 6417
  from face to foot b., 705
  gave b. to lime stones, 3629
  he forfeits his own b. that spills another, 742
  helmet to spur all b., 705
  her blue b. changed to black, 734
  here's smell of b., 3225
  heyday in b. is tame, 708
  hood my unmann'd b., 4998
  I am in b. so far, 726
  I am so far in b., 726
  I scarce ever looked on b., 704
  I smell b. of British man, 5743
  I'll not shed her b., 5993
  in sea of b. my boy died, 716
  is your b. so madly hot, 743
  lay bathed in maiden b., 4794
  let forth my foul-defiled b., 6050
  lift your b. up, 5235
  maiden b. cry for vengeance, 3807
  make thick my b., 702
  makest my b. cold, 5241
  many swoon when look on b., 704
  mind to feed on your b., 1176
  most noble b. of world, 1029

  my b. begins guides to rule, 732
  my b. hath been too cold, 709
  my b. shall wash slander, 733
  my b. upon your heads, 718
  my mother's b. in dexter cheek, 1257
  no more b. in belly than will sup flea, 1168
  no sure foundation set on b., 2879
  now could I drink hot b., 4673
  now is mad b. stirring, 741
  o'er shoes in b., 730
  old man had so much b. in him, 727
  one drop of b. from country's bosom, 714
  our b. to our b. born, 5736
  painted with spots of b., 3218
  prove whose b. reddest, 1467
  quick b., spirited with wine, 709
  red b. reigns in winter's pale, 1757
  repast them with my b., 2904
  rich b. of kings, 4476
  she reigns in my b., 2654
  shed my dear b., 710
  so much b. as clog foot of flea, 4212
  some of her b. pure, 734
  some of king's b. spilt, 711
  steeps safety in true b., 5779
  strange, unusual b., 3079
  such b. o' the grape, 7186
  summon up the b., 7013
  swallow up king's b., 2269
  swills warm b. like wash, 772
  that b. is Cæsar's homage, 753
  their b. is caked, 163
  their b. upon thy head, 719
  thoughts that thick my b., 6569
  thrice-blessed that master b., 6922
  thy b. is cold, 5879
  thy brother's b. earth drunk, 720
  thy son's b. cleaving to my blade, 717
  time hath not dried b., 5648
  treason of the b., 6720
  tricked with b. of fathers, 705
  up to the ears in b., 6995
  when b. burns, tongue vows, 707
  when b. is nipp'd, ways foul, 5124
  who else must be let b., 1029
  whose b. is snow-broth, 728
  why does my b. muster, 729
  why mourn we not in b., 4819
  wisdom and b. combatting, 731
  with b. to win your right, 5690
  with king's b. stained land, 711
  with man's b. paint ground, 7007
  young b. doth not obey old decree, 722
Blood-stained with combatants, 4809
Blood-suckers : damned b., 738
Bloods : our b. now in calm, 744
  our b. would confound distinction, 703
  we'll mingle b. in earth, 2272
Bloody, bold and resolute, 806
  b. thou art, b. thy end, 1744
  b. with spurring, 3290
Bloom that promiseth fruit, 872
Blossom passing fair, 4278
  b. that hangs on bough, 569
Blossoms of my sin, 3709
  thus are my b. blasted, 1073
Blot : mark'd with a b., 5060
Blots : full of unpleasing b., 6811
  look into b. of right, 3828

Blow, 746-751
b., b., thou winter wind, 3722
have at thee with downright b., 748
make it a word and a b., 7393
remember thy swashing b., 751
there was b. for b., 746
Blows and buffets of world, 7479
b. and revenge for me, 7069
b. have answer'd b., 721
fall to b., 747
fortune's b. struck home, 2856
good words better than bad b., 7385
how many bear shameful b., 749
let thy b. fall like thunder, 750
our b. malicious mockery, 7539
tame to fortune's b., 5376
words before b. 7385
Blue : as b. as bilberry, 5288
black and b., 677
laced with b. of heaven, 2406
Blunt as fencer's foils, 7244
b., but passing wise, 1210
I am too b. and saucy, 3954
Bluntness : praised for b., 5322
Blush at speeches rank, 759
b. doth thaw snow, 3067
b. in thinking kisses sin, 4202
b. modest as morning, 766
canst thou say this and never b., 765
come, what need you b., 767
her b. is guiltiness, 761
I assay to make thee b., 757
maiden b. bepaint my cheek, 763
we b. that thou shouldst choose, 752
wherefore b. you now, 756
with safety of pure b., 4246
Blushed extempore, 755
Blushes in thy cheeks whisper, 752
b. that banish what they sue for, 760
cool b., and Parolles live, 5313
put off your maiden b., 7361
Blushing : betray with b., 764
Boar, 769-775
angels guard thee from b.'s annoy, 5682
angry-chafing b., 773
b. knows no pity, 774
does old b. feed in old frank, 769
fly b. before b. pursues, 770
urchin-snouted b., 775
wretched, usurping b., 772
Boar-pig : Bartholomew b., 2510
Boar-spear : where is b., 771
Board, 776-780
b. her, woo her, assail her, 780
I will b. her, tho she chide, 779
will to grapple as to b., 777
Boarded her in wanton way, 776
he would never have b. me, 778
Boarding, call you it, 778
Boasting show their scars, 5814
no b. like a fool, 1939
Boat, 781-784
hazard all in one b., 2777
her b. hath a leak, 782
my b. sails freely, 781
rotten carcase of a b., 783
Boats that are not steer'd, 2858
light b. sail swift, 784
Bob : senseless of the b., 2794

Bode : I would b., 5556
what should that b., 4302
Bodements : sweet b., 655
Bodes : I wonder what it b., 7354
Bodged : we b. again, 6363
Bodies : our b. are gardens, 793
our b. soft and weak, 3670
Bodkin : quietus make with b., 1847
Body, 785-799
before b. I throw shield, 2343
b. fill'd, vacant mind, 6021
b. to cover in priestly guards, 4215
b. yet distemper'd, 3911
commit my b. to your mercies, 789
deck my b. in ornaments, 3396
endanger b. for a girl, 3007
foul b. of infected world, 4680
from her b. never babe, 7344
her b. sleeps in Capels' monument, 799
his b. couched in curious bed, 5899
I must yield my b. to earth, 1148
leaving his b. as a paradise, 1519
little b. with mighty heart, 2328
make less thy b. hence, 2513
motion toward common b., 786
my b. or soul, which dearer, 798
my b. shall pay recompense, 795
my little b. is a-weary, 791
my poor b. requires it, 2017
my well-known b. to anatomize, 788
patch up old b. for heaven, 2510
Thersites' b. good as Ajax', 5656
this b., consecrate to thee, 4427
this b. hath a tail, 6409
this common b., 785
thou hadst power over b., 797
'tis mind makes b. rich, 4694
twine arms about that b., 787
undeck the b. of a king, 6471
what bequeath save b., 1431
what is b. when head is off, 790
when b. did contain spirit, 3617
who cannot abuse b. dead, 794
yield my b. up to shame, 1238
young b. with old head, 7584
Bog : o'er b. and quagmire, 1407
Boggle : you b. shrewdly, 2624
Bohemia, a desert country, 801
deserts of B., 802
Bohemian born, 800
Boil : thou art a b., 1806
Boiling in leads or oils, 6700
Boils plaster you o'er, 1734
Bold : faint dares not be b., 808
Bold-beating oaths, 3548
Boldness, 803-808
b. be my friend, 803
what b. brought thee, 807
you call b. sauciness, 804
Bolingbroke : out-faced by B., 2468
sun of B., 3905
Bolt : according to fool's b., 2797
fool's b. is soon shot, 2797
mark'd I where b. of Cupid fell, 1716
thy sharp, sulphurous b., 6587
'twas but a b. of nothing, 5028
Bolting-hatch of beastliness, 2512
Bombard : cloud like b., 1388
Bombast : creature of b., 3955
Bona terra, mala gens, 4014

Bond, 809-812
b. gives thee no blood, 2743
b. of board and bed, 3674
b. which keep me pale, 4981
cancel his b. of life, 5678
I crave forfeit of my b., 812
I'll take a b. of fate, 6348
let him look to his b., 809
no b. but just ones, 5869
Bondage, 813-815
b. is hoarse, 2284
doting on obsequious b., 3943
I begin to find idle b., 814
into b. brought my ear, 3274
most welcome, b., 813
Bondman : every b. bears power, 4132
who so base would be b., 1032
Bondmen : make your b. tremble, 1313
Bond-slaves shall statesmen be, 75
Bonds : rotten parchment b., 2324
Bone-ache : incurable b., 1747
Bones, 816-823
bare-pick'd b. of majesty, 7001
beat not b. of the buried, 818
broke b. with industry, 6084
covered with dead men's b., 819
did these b. cost no more, 816
fill thy b. with aches, 1745
how my b. ache, 820
I feel 't upon my b., 823
leave valiant b. in France, 3541
let's have tongs and b., 4863
my b. would rest, 5633
my old b. ache, 822
of his b. coral made, 2576
strike her b. with lameness, 1740
thy b. are hollow, 3320
thy b. are marrowless, 5879
within my tent his b. lie, 817
would thou hadst my b., 820
Bonfire : primrose way to b., 7033
Bonfires clear and bright, 612
command citizens to make b., 612
nothing but b., 4969
Bonum quo antiquius, eo melius, 6095
Book, 824-832
beggar's b. outworths noble's blood, 826
bloody b. of law, 4039
b. and volume of my brain, 4625
b. where men read strange matters, 2465
damn'd in b. of heaven, 5060
enroll'd in Jove's own b., 5728
from b. of honour razed, 7015
I'll drown my b., 832
I'll note you in my b. of memory, 4627
I will unclasp a secret b., 825
my b. of songs and sonnets, 828
painfully pore upon a b., 6775
read the b. of fate, 2550
sour misfortune's b., 4745
that b. doth share glory, 830
this precious b. of love, 830
tire with b. of words, 4404
unclasp'd b. of my soul, 825
upon some b. I love, I'll pray, 4347
was ever b. so fairly bound, 1917
Book-men : you two are b., 827
Books : authority from others' b., 6291
b., arts, academes, 2428
b. in the running brooks, 4117

fitter are my b., 5152
keeps his b. uncross'd, 4121
knowing I loved my b., 831
let my b. be eloquence, 4327
no b. but score and tally, 5435
not in your b., 829
O, put me in thy b., 829
these trees shall be my b., 6730
Boot, 833-835
and rich east to b., 6899
appliances and means to b., 6019
I'll give you b., 5078
look upon his b. and sing, 4611
there is no b., 833
what an exchange without b., 835
Booties : drops b. in my mouth, 3519
Bootless make housewife churn, 2477
Boots and spurs and all, 2121
liquor b. with me, 1650
over b. in love, 4347
Bores : fill b. of hearing, 4379
Born : better lowly b., 667
b. about three in afternoon, 660
b. to make black fair, 679
b. to speak all mirth, 669
b. under a hedge, 661
I was b. so high, 671
not b. under rhyming planet, 669
we were b. to die, 1846
would thou hadst ne'er been b., 7061
you were b. in merry hour, 669
Borrower of the night, 4983
neither b. nor lender be, 836
Borrowing dulls edge of husbandry, 836
b. only lingers it out, 5477
Borrows in God's name, 839
Bosom, 841-847
bared b. to thunder-stone, 4156
b. black as death, 6127
b. of good old Abraham , 1
b. of perilous stuff, 4689
he did in general b. reign, 844
he's in Arthur's b., 2515
I know you are of her b., 843
lie in your sweet b., 1143
my b. shall lodge thee, 7522
shook b. of my conscience, 1508
so hot a summer in my b., 6314
stall this in your b., 841
swell, b., with thy fraught, 846
you have your father's b., 847
Bosoms : brassy b., 4235
broken b. that to me belong, 845
double b. wear one heart, 2921
emptying b. of counsel, 7357
I am in their b., 842
Botches : no b. in work, 5746
Bottom of the deep, 3537
finds b. in the deeps, 5466
I see not b. of it, 4696
if b. were deep as hell, 2212
my ventures not in one b., 6856
O B., thou art changed, 1192
to b. search my wound, 7520
Bottoms : draw huge b., 5780
Bough : wing to wither'd b., 6798
Boughs shake against cold, 6638
shade of melancholy b., 6608
Bought golden opinions, 5105
mad to be b. and sold, 4438

you are b. and sold, 5587
Bounce: smoke and b., 4825
Bound: nothing but hath b., 4483
Bountiful as mines of India, 2970
Bounty, 848-856
  b. makes gods, 856
  for his b., no winter in't, 849
  let your b. take a nap, 1627
  magic of b., 853
  my b. is boundless as sea, 852
  my hand has open'd b., 850
  our largest b. may extend, 851
  pity b. had not eyes behind, 854
  tuned his b. to happiness, 2123
  with b. overplus, 848
Bourn no traveller returns, 1847
  I'll set a b. how far, 4242
Bow, 857-860
  b. is bent and drawn, 857
  handles b. like crow-keeper, 858
  I swear by Cupid's b., 6966
  love's b. shoots buck and doe, 4340
  love's weak childish b., 1722
  no woodman doth bend b., 859
  swifter than arrow from Tartar's b., 6385
  Tartar's b. of lath, 6185
Bow-string: cut Cupid's b., 1721
Bow-strings: hold or cut b., 860
Bow-wow: dogs bark b., 2159
Bowels, 861-863
  b. of the battle, 861
  b. of the commonwealth, 2137
  b. of the land, 861
  b. of the Lord, 861
  fatal b. of the deep, 3094
  my b. crumble to dust, 6314
  no more weight than b., 4050
  thine own b. curse gout, 862
  thou thing of no b., 863
Bower: pleached b., 3524
Bowls: fill our b., 4970
  we'll play at b., 5747
Boxes: beggarly account of empty b., 267
Boy, 864-882
  beardless b., 874
  b., half French, 7361
  b. has grace in him, 768
  b. is fair, 868
  b. was staff of my age, 875
  disgrace to be called b., 1713
  dishonest paltry b., 1646
  foolish, idle b., 865
  I scorn thee, peevish b., 865
  lily-liver'd b., 2612
  look on the b., 870
  naked blind b., 4391
  not young enough for a b., 880
  O, 'tis a parlous b., 878
  parlous b., too shrewd, 878
  proud insulting b., 864
  proud, scornful b., 864
  purblind, wayward b., 1714
  rash and unbridled b., 864
  that blind rascally b., 1712
  this b. is forest-born, 869
  thought to be b. eternal, 881
  'tis a very pretty b., 868
  'tis but a peevish b., 865
  when that I was little tiny b., 5536

yon green b. shall have no sun, 872
you are a saucy b., 879
Boys, apes, braggarts, 6902
  b. are not to kiss, 4482
  b. with women's voices, 877
  dimpled b., like Cupids, 866
  fashion-monging b., 876
  wanton b. that swim on bladders, 2492
Brabble will undo us, 5501
Brabbler: spend mouth like B., 5455
Brach: lady b., 6774
Brag: Cæsar's thrasonical b., 1037
Braggards: break jests as b. blades, 3789
Braggart found an ass, 5313
  play b. with my tongue, 7320
Braggarts, milksops, 6902
Braid: Frenchmen are b., 5048
Brain, 883-898
  beauty and b. go not together, 499
  b. barren as banks of Libya, 896
  b. dry as biscuit, 885
  b. full of fiery shapes, 5764
  b. may devise laws, 6490
  b. of foolish-compounded clay, 7228
  b. that nourishes our nerves, 884
  have I laid my b. in sun, 893
  his pure b. doth foretell, 890
  I wear not motley in b., 4770
  live within volume of my b., 4625
  mine Italian b., 886
  mint of phrases in his b., 6707
  my b. I'll prove female, 895
  my b. weaves snares, 889
  no more b. than a stone, 5553
  no more b. than in elbows, 897
  not so much b. as ear-wax, 898
  this b. hunts not policy, 887
  wash my b., fouler, 883
  women's gentle b., 7296
Brains: broke b. with care, 6084
  cudgel thy b. no more, 888
  drink till his b. turn, 2208
  if man be beaten with b., 894
  I'll have my b. buttered, 892
  put enemy into mouths to steal b., 7184
  rock his b. in cradle, 6019
  unhappy b. for drinking, 2205
  when b. out, man would die, 724
  with crutch beat out b., 1697
Brainsickly: think b., 6550
Brake virtue must go through, 5315
Brakes of vice, 5965
Bran: meal and b. together, 3996
  nature hath meal and b., 4899
Branches: lop superfluous b., 6733
Branchless: yours so b., 3529
Brand from heaven, 900
  fatal b. Althæa burn'd, 899
Brands calumny doth use, 1054
  senseless b. sympathize, 1460
Brass eternal slave to mortal rage, 6636
  can face of b. hold out, 5229
Brave not me, 2472
  that's a b. man, 1198
Bravery of his grief, 5172
  hiding b. in rotten smoke, 1387
Brawl between red rose and white, 5732
Brawling: what b., 5547
Brawns of Hercules, 4485

Breach : more honour'd in the b., 1749
  once more into the b., 901
  to the b., to the b., 902
Bread : bitter b. of banishment, 413
  cramm'd with distressful b., 6021
  honest as ever broke b., 3511
  humour of b. and cheese, 3649
  one half-pennyworth of b., 5763
Break-vow : that daily b., 1443
Breaker of proverbs, 2023
Breakfast, 903-905
  be at b. of enemies, 2923
  eat b. on lip of lion, 2733
  he kills Scots at a b., 3608
  I will bestow a b., 903
  I would have been a b., 905
  not a relation for b., 1331
  not worth a b., 1241
  thou livedst but as a b., 904
Breast, 906-908
  boiling bloody b., 6402
  ease b. with panting, 906
  he has a loyal b., 907
  my b. can brook dagger, 7429
  my b. I'll burst, 1595
  sheathed in b. a knife, 3961
  thy b. encloseth my heart, 5702
  truth hath a quiet b., 6778
  what b. forges tongue vents, 1202
  who has b. so pure, 908
Breasts : cherish'd in b., 6053
  come to my woman's b., 2950
  if snow white, her b. dun, 4749
  plant courage in quailing b., 1597
Breath, 909-919
  age's b. is short, 7585
  ah, balmy b., 914
  although thy b. be rude, 3722
  b. is gone whereof praise, 5391
  b. not so long as tale, 926
  b. of bitter words, 6688
  b. of garlic-eaters, 910
  b. of worldly men, 3899
  b. reeks of rotten fens, 4834
  b. terrible as terminations, 913
  b. that from mistress reeks, 4749
  b. thou art, servile, 1874
  b. which heart would deny, 4136
  contagious b., 917
  fly away, fly away, b., 1902
  foul b. is noisome, 7440
  free b. of sacred king, 3887
  heaven's b. smells wooingly, 912
  hold hard the b., 7013
  how art thou out of b., 916
  let your b. cool yourself, 3288
  lips parted with sugar b., 4197
  O for b. to utter, 1456
  stop this b. with dust, 1868
  such dulcet b., 4654
  such is the b. of kings, 7392
  superfluous b., 3264
  sweet b. of flattery, 2717
  sweeten with b. this air, 3821
  that b. wilt thou lose, 915
  uttered stinking b., 5527
  vows are but b., 6964
  wanton with her b., 5273
  we are to utter sweet b., 910

with her b. perfume air, 911
  your b. kindled coal of war, 7002
Breathe not where princes are, 5352
  b. truth that b. in pain, 7446
Breathers of world dead, 4776
Breathing perfumes chamber, 911
  tyrannous b. of north, 2558
Breathless and faint, 4225
Breaths that I defied not, 3917
  poor suitors, strong b., 909
  thick b., rank, 6007
Bred i' the wars, 3996
Breeches may carry them, 7546
  his b. cost but a crown, 5420
  most master wear no b., 4568
  what fashion make your b., 3191
Breed for barren metal, 2930
  b. of greatness, 4899
  this happy b. of men, 2324
Breed-hate : no b., 6487
Breeder of sinners, 5037
Breeding, 920-922
  consider what is b., 922
  his b. at my charge, 6087
  much is b., 921
  of good capacity and b., 610
  put you to height of b., 920
Brevity soul of wit, 923
  imitate Romans in b., 923
Bribe you not with gold, 5402
  take b. to pay my sword, 928
Bribes : contaminate fingers with b., 929
Bride : encounter darkness as a b., 1800
  he took b. about the neck, 3927
  ripe to be b., 1283
  take possession of the b., 590
Bride-bed to have deck'd, 6375
Bridegroom : die bravely like b., 1837
  fresh as a b., 4225
  I will be b. in death, 1837
  sounds creep into b.'s ear, 4861
Bridge, 931-933
  Cade has gotten London b., 931
  set London b. on fire, 932
  what need b. broader than flood, 933
Brief : be curst and b., 2953
  better b. than tedious, 925
  b. as lightning in collied night, 4157
  b. as woman's love, 924
  I will be b., 926
  we must be b., 1964
Briers bear scarlet hips, 6984
  b. will have leaves, 6312
  how full of b. this world, 981
Brightness of her cheeks, 1264
Brimstone : fire and b., 2697
  put b. in your liver, 6845
Brine : eye-offending b., 4343
  stew'd in brine, 1733
Britain, 934-937
  B. is a world by itself, 934
  B.'s harts die flying, 937
  hath B. all the sun, 936
British : called B. reveller, 4718
  I smell blood of B. man, 5743
Briton laughs from free lungs, 4019
Britons strut with courage, 4219
Broad as the casing air, 2167
Broils : delight in b., 1338

Broker breaks path of faith, 1443
  crafty knave needs no b., 3939
  play b. in own behalf, 3835
Broker-lackey : hence, b., 5896
Brokers not of that dye, 6962
  vows b. to defiling, 6963
Brokers-between, Pandars, 5145
Brook candied with ice, 6356
  drowned in the b., 2795
  she fell in weeping b., 1851
  smooth runs water where b. is deep, 7022
Broth : my wind cooling my b., 7175
Brothels : keep foot out of b., 2660
Brother, 938-944
  better it were b. died, 940
  b. should a b. dare, 1167
  b. to a leash of drawers, 3643
  from his arm puff'd his b., 1081
  I am sworn b. to necessity, 4934
  I had rather my b. die, 941
  mildew'd ear blasting b., 5272
  more than b. is chastity, 1238
  my b. is in Elysium, 944
  my b. wears thee not, 4169
  our firebrand b. burns us, 5163
  primal curse, b.'s murder, 5084
  who sheds blood with me, my b., 3540
  you call'd me b., 939
  your b. and lover have embraced, 7345
  your b. and my sister no sooner met, 4387
  your b. is legitimate, 7133
Brothers : all b. of father's house, 7339
  are we not b., 938
  forty thousand b. could not, 4264
  O, my gentle b., 939
  sworn b. in filching, 6517
  twinn'd b. of one womb, 943
Brow, 945-951
  arched beauty of the b., 948
  black b. of night, 6974
  b. with biggen bound, 1677
  chaste unsmirched b., 432
  outface b. of horror, 43
  she kissed his b., 601
  she strikes at the b., 3487
  some b. will bless it, 5603
  this man's b. foretells, 946
Brown as hazel nuts, 6978
  too b. for fair praise, 5389
Browner than Judas's, 3192
Brownist as politician, 5366
Brows : beetle b. shall blush, 949
  bind my b. with iron, 3622
  black b. become women, 950
  b. full of discontent, 2069
  b. like to Achilles' spear, 947
  my queen's square b., 7142
  'tis not your inky b., 945
Brush : through b., through brier, 2476
Brute : et tu B., 956
Brutus, 952-959
  B. bastard hand stabbed, 630
  B. had rather be villager, 954
  B. is an honourable man, 1033
  B. is noble, wise, 957
  B. says he was ambitious, 1033
  B., thou art noble, 955
  B. was Cæsar's angel, 1033
  I am no orator, as B. is, 1033
  I am thy evil spirit, B., 5241

I should do B. wrong, 7541
  poor B., with himself at war, 953
  there was a B. once, 954
  vanities outside of B., 6849
  well-beloved B. stabbed, 1033
  when B. grows so covetous, 1626
  woman B. took to wife, 7312
Bubbles in disturbed stream, 6198
Bubukles : face all b., 2457
Buck of the first head, 1953
  divide me like bribe b., 1954
Bucket full of tears, 1686
Buckets filling one another, 1686
Bucklersbury : smell like B., 6040
Buckram : two rogues in b., 2674
Bud bit with envious worm, 1075
  forward b. eaten by canker, 1077
Budge, 960-964
  b. says the fiend, 1570
  he will not b. a foot, 964
  hence we will not b., 962
  I'll not b. an inch, 964
  I will not b., 964
  you shall not b., 961
Budger : let first b. die, 960
Buds : canker sweetest b. love, 6875
  shakes b. from growing, 2558
Buffets and rewards equal, 2860
  I could go to b., 5712
Bug that fear'd us all, 967
  b. which would fright me, 970
Bugbear take him, 969
Bugs : fear boys with b., 968
  mortal b. o' the field, 965
  such b. in my life, 966
Build : when we mean to b., 971
Buildings left without roof, 972
  rail against great b., 3630
Builds stronger than mason, 3107
Bull leap'd father's cow, 974
  he thinks upon savage b., 974
  pluck off b.'s horns, 973
  savage b. bears yoke, 973
  thou wast b. for Europa, 3811
  where b. and cow milk-white, 683
Bull-beeves : fat b., 2331
Bullet : golden b. beats it down, 3065
Bullets : paper b. of brain, 3650
Bulls : wild as young b., 3613
Bully : I love the lovely b., 3877
Bully-knight, Sir John, 3604
Bully-rook : what says b., 3601
Bulwark : water-walled b., 2334
Bum, 975-978
  b. greatest thing about you, 975
  then slip I from her b., 976
Bum-baily : like a b., 978
Bums : jutting out of b., 977
Bunch : I am b. of radish, 2674
Bung : filthy b., away, 5549
Bunting : took lark for b., 4004
Burdock : crown'd with b., 4453
Burgomasters, great oneyers, 6756
Burgonet of men, 3586
  wear aloft my b., 1146
Burgundy : milk of B., 6915
Burial : Christian b., 979
Buried in king's highway, 3902
Burier of dead, 7472
Burr : I am kind of b., 982

Burrs are in my heart, 981
  they are b., they'll stick, 7377
Burthen too heavy for man, 3543
  grievous b. was thy birth, 1209
  I bear a b. like an ass, 3595
  leave the b. on thee, 4939
Burthens : why sweat under b., 6010
Bush, 984-988
  fear each b. an officer, 986
  good wine needs no b., 5328
  how easy is b. supposed bear, 3705
  I mean to shift my b., 654
  myself have limed b., 984
  shape every b. a devil, 988
Business, 989-1001
  b. asketh silent secrecy, 4841
  b. of this man looks out, 990
  b. that seeks dispatch, 997
  b. which I bear i' the state, 6617
  do b. in veins of earth, 1001
  do such bitter b., 4673
  every man has b., 992
  every man to his b., 993
  full of careful b., 1000
  groan under b., 3562
  heavy b. hath my lord, 994
  it was a gentle b., 996
  like man to b. bound, 5401
  my b. is to the court, 1601
  no feeling of his b., 1751
  shake all b. from age, 1103
  slubber not b. for my sake, 999
  sodden b., a phrase, 5259
  tell the clock to any b., 6311
  this swift b., 5443
  this weighty b., 995
  'tis not sleepy b., 991
  to b. we love we rise betimes, 989

turn b. of soul to surprises, 3779
what's the b., 998
you as b. shall point you, 5166
you smell this b., 6043
Buss me as thy wife, 1868
Busy : too b. is some danger, 1785
But Yet : I do not like b. y., 1002
Butcher of a silk button, 2681
  b. with an axe, 2364
  lamb entreats b., 3991
  like to b. bent to kill, 6390
Butchers : sacrificers, not b., 5769
Butt : here is my b., 3809
Butt-shaft : blind boy's b., 1892
  Cupid's b., 1713
Butter : subject to heat as b., 4502
Butterwoman mouth, 6654
Butter-women's rank, 5666
Butterflies show mealy wings, 3120
  pluck wings from b., 1005
  we'll laugh at gilded b., 5438
Butterfly, 1003-1005
  difference between grub and b., 1004
  run after gilded b., 1003
  your b. was a grub, 1004
Buttock : broad b., 3598.
  b. of night, 1200
Button : on fortune's cap not b., 2859
Button-hole : take you b. lower, 1168
Buy and sell with you, 2282
  b. lads, or lasses cry, 1007
  dispraise things you b., 1006
  I'ld have you b. and sell, 5981
Buzzard take thee, 6797
Buzzing : stolen their b., 7385
By and by easily said, 1009
  I'll see you b. and b., 1008

C

Cabin hanged with care, 4992
  willow c. at your gate, 4344
Cabin'd, cribb'd, confined, 2167
Cables of toughness, 2913
Cacodemon : thou c., 1970
Cadmus : Hercules and C., 4864
Cælo, sky, welkin, 1953
Cæsar, 1010-1036
  angry spot on C.'s brow, 1023
  as C. loved me, I weep, 1032
  as for C., kneel down, 1014
  bathe hands in C.'s blood, 1028
  broad-fronted C., 1011
  C. beast without heart, 1026
  C. grew fat feasting, 1013
  C. is more dangerous, 1026
  C. is Jupiter of men, 1014
  C., Keisar, Pheezar, 1035
  C. living, die slaves, 1032
  C. refused the crown, 5527
  C. said "Darest thou, Cassius", 1020
  C. was mighty, bold, 957
  C. whose remembrance lives, 1016
  C.'s spirit cry "Havoc", 1031
  C.'s thrasonical brag, 1037
  carried queen to C., 1013
  do C. what he can, 1840
  enter C. in his nightgown, 1025

ghost of C. hath appear'd, 2993
how many times shall C. bleed, 1028
I come to bury C., 1033
I did enact Julius C., 64
I did love thee, C., 1030
imperious C., dead, 1017
Julius C. was a famous man, 1036
kind of conquest C. made, 1038
kiss dead C.'s wounds, 6503
mock the luck of C., 4418
morsel on C.'s trencher, 4802
no bending knee will call thee C., 1018
not that I loved C. less, 1032
O Julius C., mighty yet, 1034
O mighty C., dost thou lie so low, 1029
scarce-bearded C., 1010
shall C. send a lie, 1027
she made C. lay sword to bed, 1012
soldier fit to stand by C., 6075
spake you of C., the nonpareil, 5017
speak in C.'s funeral, 1033
strike, as thou didst at C., 1761
'tis paltry to be C., 1015
upon what meat does C. feed, 1022
what, did C. swound, 1024
when C. says "Do this", 1019
with C. paragon again, 6480

Cæsars : jades compare with C., 5128
many C. ere another Julius, 1016
Cage : in c. of rushes, 4249
Cain, first male child, 3400
  month old at C.'s birth, 4784
  spirit of first-born C., 7427
Cake, 1041-1044
  have c. tarry grinding, 1044
  my c. is dough, 1043
  our c. is dough, 1042
Cakes : look for ale and c., 1041
Calamity, 1045-1047
  makes c. of long life, 1847
  no true cuckold but c., 1047
  thou art wedded to c., 1046
  why c. full of words, 7448
  you are transported by c., 1045
Calendar, find moonshine, 4783
  high tides in c., 3494
  he's a c. of gentry, 2969
Calf much like to you, 974
  coal-black c., 683
  never answer c., 1280
Calf's-skin kill'd for prodigal, 5445
  hang c. on limbs, 4184
  he that goes in c., 1048
  will not c. stop mouth, 1049
Caliban has a new master, 1050
  C., thy foot-licker, 2828
Callet : laid terms upon c., 7107
Calumny, 1051-1054
  back-wounding c., 1053
  c. will scar virtue itself, 1054
  petty brands c. doth use, 1054
  thou shalt not escape c., 1052
Cambyses : King C. vein, 55
Came, saw, overcame, 1037
Camel : hard for c. to thread postern, 1056
Camels in the war, 1055
Camomile, more trodden, 7559
Canakin : let c. clink, 6074
Canaries : into such a c., 1057
  you have drunk too much c., 7180
Canary : brought into a c., 1057
  make you dance c., 4601
Candle, 1058-1069
  here burns my c. out, 1059
  hold c. to my shames, 1065
  how far that little c. throws its beams,
    1067
  out, out, brief c., 1064
  out went the c., 1061
  this c. burns not clear, 1060
  thus hath c. singed moth, 1066
  wassail c., all tallow, 1058
  without c. go dark to bed, 496
  you are as a c., 1058
Candle-holder : be a c., 5464
Candle-wasters : drunk with c., 3155
Candles : blessed c. of night, 1068
  night's c. are burnt out, 1832
  their c. are all out, 1063
Candlesticks : like fixed c., 3771
Candy deal of courtesy, 1614
Canker, 1070-1077
  c. death eats plant, 3078
  c. galls infants of spring, 1070
  c. of ambitious thoughts, 1072
  c. sweetest buds loves, 6875
  forward bud eaten by c., 1077

in sweetest bud c. dwells, 1077
lothsome c. in sweetest bud, 1096
now will c. sorrow eat, 1074
Cankers of calm world, 6064
Cannibals each other eat, 4305
Cannon : battering c., 1080
  c. to clouds shall tell, 1078
  carry c. by our sides, 5257
  I have seen the c., 1081
  thunder of c. heard, 1079
Cannon-shot : like c., 7425
Cannoneer begot this lusty, 4825
Cannons have bowels full, 1079
Canon against self-slaughter, 5855
Canonize : fame c. us, 3438
Canonized : thou shalt be c., 4449
Canons : religious c. are cruel, 7007
Canopy : dwell under c., 1354
  excellent c., the sky, 2268
Canstick : brazen c. turn'd, 5348
Canterbury : pilgrims to C., 5280
Cantle of world is lost, 3915
Cantons of contemned love, 4344
Canvass thee between sheets, 2510
Cap and knee slaves, 5155
  on fortune's c. not button, 2859
  wear c. with suspicion, 389
  wear selves in c. of time, 1157
Cap-a-pe : arm'd c., 2560
Capacity as the sea, 4343
Caparisoned like a man, 1462
Caper, 1082-1084
  c. for thousand marks, 7578
  faith I can cut a c., 1084
  he offered to cut a c., 1083
  I have seen him c., 1082
Capers in lady's chamber, 7005
  he c., he dances, 6039
  lovers run into strange c., 4248
Capitol : against C. I met lion, 4181
  drizzled blood on C., 5097
Capon : belly with c. lined, 7466
  c. burns, pig falls, 4597
  carve a c. and eat it, 4925
Capons : minutes were c., 6615
Caps applaud to clouds, 1087
  made shower with their c., 1086
  they threw their c., 1085
Captain, 1088-1091
  art not ashamed to be called c., 1090
  c. I'll be no more, 5313
  c. there drops bloody sweat, 6374
  in c. but a choleric word, 1091
  our great c.'s c., 1089
  who does more than c., 1089
Captivate : sent husbands c., 6800
Captives bound to car, 4819
Captivity : power to cancel c., 4132
Car : guide heavenly c., 5240
Carbuncle : thou art a c., 1806
Carcanet : jewels in c., 2622
Carcass : hew him as a c., 2099
  shakes c. of death, 1867
Carcasses of unburied men, 4834
Card : as sure c. as ever won, 1094
  faced with c. of ten, 5633
  we must speak by the c., 6164
Cardinal virtues, 6937
Cards : best c. for game, 1093
  she pack'd c. with Cæsar, 1092

Care, 1095-1099
c. and labour of mind, 4683
c. is an enemy to life, 1099
c. is no cure, 1095
c. keeps his watch, 1098
c. killed a cat, 1096
c., mistrust waits, 5899
golden c. that keeps ports of slumber
  open, 1677
keeps on windy side of c., 3389
killing c. and grief of heart, 5119
my c. is loss of c., 1097
past cure is past c., 1729
what loss to be rid of c., 3914
where c. lodges sleep will never lie, 1098
your c. is gain of c., 1097
Career of humour, 3650
down hill he holds c., 7115
Cares and joys abound, 1101
c. I give I have, 1104
his c. are now all ended, 1100
'tis our intent to shake c., 1103
why heap these c. on me, 1105
your c. do not pluck my c. down, 1104
Carnal, unnatural acts, 6165
Carnation ribbon buy, 5613
Carnations and gillyvors, 2767
Carol they began that hour, 4119
Carp of truth, 2496
use c. as you may, 3936
Carpenter : it is some c., 7355
Carpet hang upon grave, 2762
Carpet-mongers : quondam c., 4303
Carriage caught as diseases, 1454
of a most noble c., 2511
Carrion : green-sickness c., 7533
Carry-tale told our intents, 6737
Cart : become c. as well as another, 3240
c. draws the horse, 343
I cannot draw a c., 7459
Carthage : burn'd C. queen, 6966
waft her love to C., 4987
Carve : a' can c. too, 1617
he may not c. for himself, 657
Carver : be his own c., 5696
Casca : what a rent C. made, 1033
Case, 1106-1109
but the c. is alter'd, 1109
my c. past help of law, 314
rotten c. abides no handling, 1108
'tis a plain c., 1107
what a c. am I in, 1106
what c. stand I in, 1106
Casement : woman's wit out at c., 7226
Cashiered : when he sold, c., 3943
Casques that affright air, 5040
Cassibelan made Lud's-town, 4219
Cassio, I love thee, 5094
I will question C., 4023
Cassius has lean and hungry look, 2581
C. is aweary of world, 2908
C., you are much condemn'd, 5139
hath C. lived to be but mirth, 241
help me, C., or I sink, 1020
in this space ran C. dagger, 1033
Castle : my old lad of the, 3605
strongest c., tower, town, 3065
this c. hath a pleasant seat, 179
your c. is surprised, 1289
Casualty in force of c., 4839

Cat, 1110-1117
as vigilant as c. to steal cream, 1113
c. will mew, 1112
c. with eyen of burning coal, 1115
endure anything but a c., 1110
if the c. be after kind, 1111
like poor c. in adage, 1645
mad if they behold a c., 120
our c. wringing her hands, 2162
part to tear a c. in, 6809
playing mouse in absence of c., 5822
purr of fortune's c., 2123
take suggestion as c. laps milk, 6311
thou owest c. no perfume, 4494
thrice brindled c. hath mewed, 1114
Cat-a-mountain looks, 3548
Cataian : I will not believe C., 1118
my lady's a C., 1119
Catalogue : in c. ye go for men, 4496
Cataplasm : no c. can save, 6814
Cataracts and hurricanes spout, 7174
Catastrophe, 1120-1123
c. and heel of pastime, 1120
c. is a nuptial, 1123
c. of the old comedy, 5185
I'll tickle your c., 1121
Catch draw three souls, 7087
I am dog at a c., 7087
Catechism : so ends my c., 3539
Caterpillar, 1124-1129
for every graff send c., 1127
Caterpillars eat my leaves, 1125
c. of the commonwealth, 1128
herbs swarming with c., 1129
scholars they call c., 1126
whoreson c., 7558
Cates : feed on c., 6431
Cato : soldier to C.'s wish, 6062
well-reputed, C.'s daughter, 7312
Cats that can judge so fitly, 5525
drown c. and blind puppies, 2214
good king of c., 1117
more than prince of c., 1116
Cattle of that colour, 1130
he blasts tree and takes c., 1131
poor men's c. break necks, 1132
Caucasus : frosty C., 6115
Caudle thy morning taste, 6356
Cauldron : fire burn, c. bubble, 6748
Cause, 1133-1141
as thy c. is right, 1138
c. is in my will, 1136
c. of night lack of sun, 4971
c. on foot lives in hope, 3566
c. that fills eyes with tears, 1996
c. that hath no dependence, 1141
find out c. of this effect, 1142
for that c. worthy to live, 5564
hear me for my c., 1032
hearing c. between orange-wife, 1201
his c. being just, 1135
I have savage c., 431
I to my fortunes commit my c., 1140
if c. be not good, 1135
it is the c., the c., 1137
our c. is just, 1034
report me and my c. aright, 1133
what is c. of thunder, 6586
Cave where Echo lies, 2284
Cavern dark enough, 1520

Caveto be counsellor, 5051
Caviarre to the general, 5329
Cavil on ninth part of a hair, 421
Cavilling : stand c. here, 2676
Cawdor shall sleep no more, 6024
Cedar, 1144-1150
  c. stoops not to shrub, 1149
  flourish like mountain c., 1147
  from c. lopped branches, 1144
  lofty c. personates thee, 1145
  on mountain top c. shows, 1147
  yields c. to axe's edge, 1148
Celerity, 1151-1152
  c. never more admired, 1151
  hence hath offence quick c., 5091
  she has c. in dying, 1835
  swift c. of his death, 1152
Cellarage : fellow in c., 6369
Cement : broken glass no c., 3009
Censure, 1153-1156
  c. me by what you were, 1154
  how blest in my just c., 1156
  no greatness can c. 'scape, 1053
  take each man's c., 1153
Censures : carping c. of world, 1155
Centaurs : from waist, C., 7317
Cerberus : fell asleep as C., 3275
Ceremonies : all c. minister'd, 6924
  I never stood on c., 1159
Ceremony, 1157-1161
  appurtenance is fashion and c., 7078
  bid c. give thee cure, 1158
  c. devised to set a gloss, 1161
  c., show me but thy worth, 1158
  love useth an enforced c., 4269
  no c. that to great ones 'longs, 4638
  perfect c. of love's rite, 4327
  sauce to meat is c., 1160
  use a more spacious c., 1157
  what have kings save c., 1158
  you saw the c., 5933
Ceres' blessing is on you, 696
Certain as I know sun is fire, 1163
  is it most c., 1163
  I was c. o'er incertainty, 1166
Certainties are past remedies, 1164
Chafed : why are you c., 6492
Chaff and corn fly asunder, 5074
Chain : about neck like usurer's c., 2961
  rub your c. with crums, 2116
Chair : barber's c. fits all buttocks, 246
Chalice for the nonce, 2201
  ingredients of poison'd c., 3846
Challenge, 1167-1173
  by north pole I c. thee, 1168
  God bless me from a c., 1170
  hear c. urged modestly, 1167
  I c. thee to trial, 1169
  I have a roisting c. sent, 1171
  I'll write thee a c., 1172
Challenger on mount of age, 5986
Challengers : a style for c., 6295
Cham : hair off C's beard, 5875
Chamber : get you to my lady's c., 7549
  I'll show you a c., 553
Chambers : keep their c., 5928
Chameleon, 1174-1176
  c. can feed on air, 4352
  he is a kind of c., 1176

I can add colours to c., 1681
I eat the c.'s dish, air, 1174
Champains rich'd with rivers, 4586
Champion, 1177-1181
  c. that dost never fight, 1180
  like bold c. I assume lists, 2658
  most complete c. ever I heard, 1178
  stouter c. never handled sword, 1177
Champions : hardy c., 1179
  his c. are the prophets, 3496
  Rome's readiest c., 1181
Chance, 1182-1187
  c. may crown me, 1184
  consider the c. of war, 6993
  fall off by c. of war, 4809
  if c. will have me king, 1184
  in reproof of c. lies proof, 1186
  main c., father, you mean, 1183
  slaves of c., 1187
  you must take your c., 1185
Chances : against ill c. men merry, 1182
  common c. men could bear, 2401
  I spake of disastrous c., 4305
  secure from worldly c., 1181
Change : all things c., 1193
  bolts up c., 1920
  c. of fourteen years, 1283
  kiss lips of unacquainted c., 1191
  lamentable c., 7503
Changed into another man, 1188
  O Bottom, thou art c., 1192
Changes fill cup of alteration, 1190
  follow c. of moon, 3779
Chanticleer : crow like c., 1194
  strain of strutting c., 1195
Chaos of well-seeming forms, 4376
  vast sin-concealing c., 4995
  when I love thee not, c., 4308
Chap-fallen : quite c., 7549
Chape of his dagger, 6991
Chapels had been churches, 7401
Chapless, knocked about, 4583
Chaplet of summer buds, 5832
Chapmen : do as c. do, 1006
  sale of c.'s tongues, 506
Character, 1196-1215
  in barks my thoughts I'll c., 6730
Characters of brass, 1984
  without c., fame lives long, 4593
  written with c. of age, 7578
Charge too heavy for my strength, 3306
  once again cry 'Charge', 4223
Chariot empty hazel-nut, 4434
Chariots : triumphant c., 6745
Charity, 1216-1218
  c. chased by rancour's hand, 6935
  c. itself fulfills the law, 1219
  c. of a penny cord, 3237
  c. renders good for bad, 1217
  do poor Tom some c., 6651
  hand open as day for c., 1203
  rob in behalf of c., 6522
  thou hast not so much c., 1218
  who can sever love from c., 1216
  you know no rules of c., 1217
Charm ache with air, 3156
  never c. come lady nigh, 1224
  no c. for tooth-ache, 6695
  this c. hath beguiled me, 1220
Charmer : she was a c., 1229

Charms, 1219-1229
  all the c. of love, 1219
  all the c. of Sycorax, 1745
  c. by which youth abused, 1227
  mumbling of wicked c., 1222
  practised with foul c., 1228
  prevailed with hellish c., 1225
  unchain spirits with spelling c., 1221
  you have c., la, 1226
  your spells provide your c., 1223
Charnel-house : shut in c., 819
Charon : be thou my C., 6147
Charter : as large c. as wind, 4085
Charybdis : fall into C., 5968
Chase : run wild-goose c., 7258
  seek out some other c., 3652
Chased : with more spirit c., 5481
Chaste : be thou c. as ice, 1052
  c. as is the bud, 5845
  c. as may be in world, 1247
  c. as the icicle, 1231
  c. as unsunned snow, 1235
  c. in very thought, 3807
  I will die c. as Diana, 1239
  more c. than ladies of France, 1232
  my life has been c., 1250
  stubborn-c. against all suit, 1246
  sworn that she live c., 1243
Chastity, 1230-1255
  c. is rifled of her store, 1255
  despite of fruitless c., 1249
  force virgin's c., 5052
  he praised cold c., 1237
  in proof of c. arm'd, 1722
  lamenting some enforced c., 4789
  more c. than brother is c., 1238
  my c. is jewel of my house, 1251
  my stole of c. I daff'd, 1253
  not c. enough in language, 3997
  peevish c. not worth breakfast, 1241
  there's a palm presages c., 5138
  thy sons pillage her c., 5244
  touches soft conquer c., 1240
  upon grave thou vow'dst c., 1248
  very ice of c., 3916
  wakened c. he wounded, 1234
Chat : palmer's c. makes short, 2077
Cheap : as c. as lies, 6455
Cheapest ten groats too dear, 4745
Cheater : abominable c., 1090
  I will be c. to them, 2378
Cheek, 1256-1264
  affliction may subdue c., 5458
  bear'st a c. for blows, 4209
  bid c. be ready with blush, 766
  c. by jole, 1262
  c. of two pile, 1257
  have you not a yellow c., 7578
  his right c. worn bare, 1257
  lean c. you have not, 4249
  leaning c. to c., 5034
  make pale our c., 2946
  she leans c. upon hand, 1264
  sinister c. bounds father, 1257
  villain with smiling c., 6136
  why is your c. so pale, 1261
  your c. of cream, 945
Cheeks : blushing c. by faults, 2590
  brightness of c. shame stars, 1264
  I thy amiable c. do coy, 1263

linen c. counsellors to fear, 2612
natural ruby of your c., 5935
nicely-gawded c., 1258
no such roses in her c., 4749
strain c. to merriment, 4618
thy c. blush for shame, 1259
wet c. with artificial tears, 6045
your c. counterfeit roses, 1259
Cheer, 1265-1268
  be of good c., 1773
  have a better c., 1265
  I have not c. of mind, 1268
  pray God our c. may answer, 7076
  receive what c. you may, 4985
  show a merry c., 1267
  small c., great welcome, 7076
  we will make good c., 2281
  you are so far from c., 2140
Cheerer of the heart, 6914
Cheerful : be c., 2489
Cheese, 1269-1272
  choked with piece of c., 3022
  it will toast c., 3756
  live with c. and garlic, 6431
  mouse-eaten dry c., 1272
  pippins and c. to come, 1270
  you Banbury c., 1269
Cheese-paring : made of c., 4489
Cherishing : kill with c., 653
Cherries : thy lips kissing c., 4199
Cherry : as like as c. to c., 4162
  grew like a double c., 6819
Cherry-pit : play c. with Satan, 2046
Cherubim : heaven's c., 5304
Cherubin thou wast, 1274
  for all her c. look, 7109
  young, rose-lipp'd c., 1273
Cherubins : fears make devils of c., 2617
  quiring to young-eyed c., 3273
Chest : ten-times-barr'd-up c., 6202
Chestnut the only colour, 3192
Cheval volant, 3590
Cheveril glove to wit, 7454
  c. stretches from inch to ell, 7258
Chew upon this, 6549
Chickens : all my pretty c., 1289
  eat c. in the shell, 2288
Chiding : better c. than heart-break, 1275
  I am a child to c., 1276
  never did I hear such c., 4864
Chien retourné à vomissement, 2150
Child, 1277-1283
  as much as c. e'er loved, 4271
  be a c. o' the time, 1277
  c. begotten of my body, 3658
  c. of grandmother Eve, 7318
  c. that guided dotards, 2373
  God lent us this only c., 1281
  if you hear a c. cry, 1280
  ill to teach c. such words, 7103
  indeed 'tis a noble c., 1278
  let c. wake her with crying, 1280
  my c. is yet a stranger, 1283
  old man is twice a c., 144
  thankless c., 1279
  this is a c., a dwarf, 2248
  went as any christom c., 2515
  wise father knows own c., 2571
  with c. by tyrant war, 5755
  woe to land governed by c., 1282

Childhood fears painted devil, 1288
Childish-foolish : too c., 1970
Childishness : second c., 7466
Children, 1284-1293
aery of c., eyases, 1286
as c. but one step below, 3097
as indifferent c. of earth, 1285
fools make ill-favour'd c., 5898
free your c. from sword, 1293
good hearing when c. toward, 7334
if c. predecease progenitors, 1291
my c. shall be comfort, 1292
my c. too, my pretty ones, 1289
not good that c. know wickedness, 1290
sins of father laid on c., 5968
thou hast comfort of c., 4816
unbridled c., headstrong, 6568
were all thy c. kind, 2328
your c. were vexation, 1292
your c.'s c. quit it, 1293
Chimes at midnight, 4675
Chimney : fly out at c., 7226
Chimney-sweepers come to dust, 2240
Chimneys were blown down, 4982
Chin, 1294-1297
alas, poor c., many a wart is richer, 1297
c. enriched with one hair, 1295
his Amazonian c., 1294
his c. new reap'd, 4225
is his c. worth a beard, 458
is not your c. double, 7578
small show of man upon c., 1296
Chinks : he shall have c., 4766
Chisel : what c. could cut breath, 919
Chivalry : truant to c., 3614
Choice, 1298-1302
c. breeds native slip, 4896
I stuck my c. upon her, 1299
I'd rather be this c., 1298
let's have first c., 1302
on his c. depends the state, 657
reserved quantity of c., 4444
small c. in rotten apples, 1301
thou art most c. forsaken, 5680
well content with any c., 1300
Choirs where birds sang, 6638
Choler, 1303-1313
aggravate your c., 1306
digest c. on enemies, 1308
engenders c., planteth anger, 4600
let's purge this c., 1310
plunge him into more c., 1304
put him to c. straight, 1303
throw cold water on my c., 1309
touched with c., hot, 1307
what, drunk with c., 1305
Choleric : are you so c., 1312
go show your slaves how c., 1313
lest it make you c., 1311
Chop-logic : how now, c., 6512
Chorus to this history, 1315
you are good as a c., 1314
Christ, 1316-1318
as far as to sepulchre of C., 1316
C., under whose cross, 1316
C.'s blood shed for sins, 5594
fought for Jesu C., 1318
gave his soul to captain C., 1318
in the name of Jesu C., 1317
you shall sup with Jesu C., 1317

Christendom : by my c., 4660
summer-house in C., 6431
Christian, 1319-1328
as I am a C., 7106
as I am a C. faithful man, 4996
he hath made me a C., 1322
I hate him for he is a C., 4068
much in a bare C., 1324
my husband hath made me C., 5968
no more wit than a C., 7254
not worth name of C., 1323
she defies me like Turk to C., 6295
spoke as a C. ought to speak, 6177
there will come C. by, 1321
Christian-like : a C. fear, 1327
C. laments his death, 1326
plant C. accord, 1325
virtuous C. conclusion, 1328
Christians raise price of hogs, 1322
we were C. enow before, 1322
what these C. are, 1320
Christmas : at C. desire rose, 2933
Chronicle, 1329-1332
c. of day by day, 1331
c. of wasted time, 531
let me embrace thee, good old c., 1332
make c. rich with praise, 5387
whose c. thus writ, 1329
Chroniclers : time's doting c., 147
Chronicles of the time, 62
fill c. in time to come, 1330
I have read in the c., 1330
look in the c., 5717
Chrysolite : world of one c., 7478
Chuck : dearest c., 1936
Church, 1333-1337
be champion of our c., 1335
get thee to c. Thursday, 1336
I live by the c., 1343
in best array bear her to c., 1337
let c. breathe her curse, 1335
ne'er to c. thou goest, 1334
see c. by daylight, 2433
what inside of c. made of, 1333
Church-door : wide as c., 3655
Churches : he must build c. then, 4626
Churchman, 1338-1343
ambitious c., 1340
art thou a c., 1343
c. bears bounteous mind, 1341
meekness becomes c., 1342
Churchmen so hot, 1339
holy c. delight in broils, 1338
Churchyards yawn, 4673
Churlish as the bear, 1211
Cicatrice, emblem of war, 1256
c. the palm keeps, 2404
Cincture can hold out tempest, 1369
Cinders of my spirits, 6205
Cinna : I am C. the poet, 6865
Cinque-pace : measure c., 7369
Cipher of a function, 2591
Circe : with C. change my shape, 7268
you have drunk of C.'s cup, 1710
Circuit : golden c. on my head, 6273
Circumstance, 1344-1348
bombast c., 1347
by no drift of c., 1344
c. I'll tell you, 1346
c. of glorious war, 2533

c. of place, time, 1348
without more c. at all, 5166
Circumstances : if c. lead, 6770
Citizens cast by ornaments, 1351
c. forsake their homes, 931
civil c. kneading honey, 563
snorting c., 1350
you fat and greasy c., 1349
City, 1352-1356
c. on whom plenty held, 1355
hear c. abused extremely, 5334
in c. of kites and crows, 1354
that is way to lay c. flat, 1353
what is c. but the people, 1352
Civet : give me ounce of c., 3704
Civil as an orange, 1358
he is sad and c., 1359
Civility not seen from other, 3750
in c. thou seem'st empty, 1357
show of smooth c., 1357
Claim : no sinister c., 1361
such c. as to your horse, 1360
Clamour of two eager tongues, 7445
Clamours of jealous woman, 7299
soul-fearing c., 1080
Clap : shall we c. to 't, 6091
Clapper-clawing one another, 2678
Clarence : perjured C., 2186
Claw no man in his humour, 1207
Clay and c. differs, 938
compounded am with c., 4822
foolish-compounded c., 7228
men are but painted c., 5627
now a king, now c., 3889
temper c. with blood, 3851
Clean as sheep's heart, 4206
c. enough to spit upon, 1363
Cleanly : neat and c., 4925
not neat, but c., 4926
Cleopatra : salt C., 1219
swallows in C.'s sails, 6359
Clients : good counsellors lack no c., 1575
Clifford vows to fight, 5693
how he singled C., 2597
well hath C. play'd orator, 5115
Climate delicate, 181
Climbing : bought c. dear, 1366
man and birds fain of c. high, 1365
Clip your wives, friends, 1367
O let me c. ye, 1368
Cloak, 1369-1372
c. of night pluck'd, 6325
I have night's c. to hide, 4319
make me travel without c., 1387
night's all-hiding c., 1372
old c. makes new jerkin, 6444
take thine auld c. about thee, 5420
'tis not my inky c., 5843
what colour is his c., 5589
whose c. can hold out tempest, 1369
Cloaks : wise men put on c., 1387
Clock, 1373-1376
c. gives me my cue, 1707
c. hath strucken twelve, 4597
c. upbraids me with waste, 1376
fought by Shrewsbury c., 2675
made me his numbering c., 6632
no c. in the forest, 1373
tell c. to any business, 6311

unhappy was the c., 1375
woman like a German c., 7134
Clock-setter : time, the c., 6620
Clocks tongues of bawds, 6615
Clod : all thou seest is c., 3373
c. of wayward marl, 3665
motion to become a c., 1876
Clog : here comes my c., 7123
stealing away with c., 7123
Cloister : in shady c. mew'd, 6922
steal egg out of c., 1197
Cloistress : like c. walk, 4343
Closet : I'll to my c., 6279
Closet-war : they call this c., 5539
Cloten was a fool, 2800
Cloth : by painted c. kept in awe, 5806
Cloth-of-gold of tissue, 1977
Clothes : know'st me by my c., 6412
she has excellent c., 5487
soul of man is his c., 6125
those c. make thee, 6412
through tatter'd c. small vices, 6871
up he rose, donn'd his c., 6832
Clotpoles : hanged like c., 5686
Cloud, 1377-1389
black c. looks like bombard, 1388
black-faced c. doth threat, 1385
c. takes all away, 4350
every c. engenders not storm, 1383
he has a c. in his face, 1378
I spy a suspicious c., 1384
one c. of winter showers, 5391
sometimes hath brightest day a c., 1101
we see c. that's dragonish, 1380
yond c. cannot choose but fall, 1388
yonder c. in shape of camel, 1381
Clouds : base contagious c., 6317
checquering eastern c., 4799
c. and dangers come, 6321
c. in bosom of ocean buried, 7203
c. o'ertake me in my way, 1387
c. stain both moon and sun, 1076
c. would open, show riches, 2190
coal-black c. that shadow, 1389
dissolve, thick c., 1379
distracted c. give way, 1377
filthy c. of heady murder, 3088
give way, c., to curses, 1742
he would be above the c., 1382
uglier seem c. that fly, 1386
when c. appear wise men put on cloaks, 1387
when c. in autumn crack, 779
Cloudy : foul when you are c., 7053
Clown, 1390-1392
c. shall make those laugh, 1391
most simple c., 1392
roynish c., 1390
Clowns : let c. speak no more, 54
Clubs cannot part them, 4387
Clyster-pipes for your sake, 2687
Coal-black as jet, 678
c. better than other hue, 682
never beget c. calf, 683
some will mourn in c., 4820
Coals : all eyes dead c., 2431
men would carry c., 6517
throw c. of vengeance, 6999
Coasts and hedges, 3425

Coats : glittering in golden c., 3613
  in gold c. spots, 2476
  silken c. and caps, 5638
  they have lined their c., 3943
Cobbler : I am a c., 5912
Cobweb : I desire acquaintance, C., 1393
Cobwebs : entrap gnats in c., 3199
Cock, 1394-1398
  by c., they are to blame, 6832
  c. that is trumpet to morn, 1395
  c. that treads them, 7330
  crow, c., with comb on, 1394
  go up and down like a c., 1394
  he walks till first c., 2661
  meet me at first c. crow, 1397
  second c. hath crow'd, 1397
  village c. done salutation, 1397
  you are c. and capon too, 1394
Cock-a-diddle-dow, 1195
Cock-a-hoop : set c., 1398
Cockatrice hatch'd to world, 7346
Cockle hat and staff, 4262
  nourish c. of rebellion, 5584
  sow'd c. reap'd no corn, 1549
Cockpit : can this c. hold, 169
Cocks : country c. crow, 1396
  his c. win the battle, 2954
Coctus : bis c., 5954
Codling when 'tis apple, 880
Codpiece : have with a c., 3191
Codpieces : king of c., 1714
Cod's head for salmon's tail, 7212
Cœur-de-lion : trick of C., 5675
Coffers : shall c. be emptied, 6715
Coffin : my heart is in c., 1033
  not a flower on my c., 1902
  upon a wooden c. we attend, 4819
Cog and flout, 876
  deceive and c., 2726
  I cannot c. or prate, 1400
  I'll c. their hearts, 1399
  since you can c., 1399
  you hear him c., 1401
Coil : shuffled off mortal c., 1847
  what a c. is here, 977
Coinage of brain, 2286
Coiner made me counterfeit, 432
Colbrand : I am not C., 1700
Cold, 1402-1409
  catch c. and starve, 1404
  c. as any stone, 2515
  c. as if I'd swallowed snowballs, 1406
  c. as snowball, 1406
  c. never let grass grow, 1737
  comfort me with c., 1426
  dangerous to take c., 1788
  endure c. as sword, 3756
  felt c. as over shoes, 2641
  I found her wondrous c., 1402
  I have caught extreme c., 1409
  icy c., 1405
  it is indifferent c., 1405
  lest he catch c. on's feet, 1404
  nipping c., 1405
  taller man than I take c., 1409
  thou'lt catch c. shortly, 1404
  'tis bitter c., 1405
  Tom's a-c., 1409
  you are c. and stern, 1403
  you will catch c., 1404

Cold-hearted toward me, 3328
Coldest ever turned ace, 7199
Colic : with c. pinch'd, 4906
Collier : bang him, foul c., 2046
Collop of my flesh, 2739
Colonquintida : bitter as c., 2784
Colossus : bestride world like C., 1021
Colour : cast nighted c. off, 1846
  do you change c., 1176
  what c. is his cloak, 5589
  your c. is red, 5588
Colours : add c. to chameleon, 1681
  mocking the air with c., 874
Colt, 1410-1414
  c. that's burdened young, 1414
  hobby-horse but a c., 3491
  what mean ye to c. me thus, 1410
Colted : she hath been c. by him, 1410
  thou art not c., 1410
Colts : like unbacked c., 1413
  wanton herd of youthful c., 1411
  young hot c., 1412
Columbine : that c., 2760
Co-mates in exile, 4117
Come : before you say c., 2430
  c. what c. may, 6623
  if it be not to c., 5562
Comeliness : his c. plucked gaze, 7555
Comedy : lamentable c., 5335
  like a Christmas c., 6737
Comely envenoms him, 7465
Comer : grasps the c., 6642
Comes : look, who c. here, 3111
Comet, 1415-1418
  gaze as if they saw c., 1418
  gazed on like a c., 1417
  like c. wonder'd at, 1416
Comets, brandish tresses, 1415
Comfit-maker : swear like c.'s wife, 6370
Comfort, 1419-1435
  be c. to my age, 1420
  cold c., 1426
  c. forswear me, 6823
  c. is in heaven, 1450
  c. me with cold, 1426
  c., my sovereign, 1422
  c. when misery could beguile, 7532
  entreats you to take c., 1425
  here comes a man of c., 2068
  I have c. from this fellow, 3245
  I take my c. of thy worth, 1433
  I'll hate him bids me be of c., 1432
  is this your c., 1424
  is thy c. shut in tomb, 1423
  my c. is that heaven will take, 3409
  not another c. like this, 1429
  of c. no man speak, 1431
  receives c. like cold porridge, 1434
  speak c. to that grief, 3156
  that c. comes too late, 1425
  thou art all the c., 1421
  well, here's my c., 1435
  what c. have we now, 1432
Comforter : no c. delight ear, 1569
  sleep is a c., 6035
Comfortless as frozen water, 3928
Comforts false, worse, 5755
  c. we despise, 1419
  I dote in mine own c., 1429

lay c. to your bosom, 1427
make c. of our losses, 4232
now I am past all c., 1425
our c. should increase, 1429
thy c. do me no good, 1428
Command, 1436-1438
c. where I adore, 5948
correspondent to c., 1437
great c. o'ersways order, 980
not born to sue but to c., 1436
Commander : I was world's c., 190
Commandment on pulse of life, 4807
thy c. alone shall live, 4625
Commandments : leave my ten c. in your face, 4883
to sea with Ten C., 6257
Commend what we sell, 1006
Commendation with woman, 6846
Commendations : good at c., 1439
mere satiety of c., 1441
my c. great, 1440
Commiseration : pluck c. from bosoms, 4235
Commission to blank of danger, 1794
from whom this c., 3828
Commodity, bias of the world, 1443
c. lose gloss with lying, 1442
tickling c., 1443
why rail I on this c., 1443
Common : as c. as the way, 3864
Common-hackney'd in eyes of men, 5104
Commons like hive of bees, 564
let c. hear this testament, 6503
Commutual in sacred bands, 3675
Companion to the streets, 3876
God send prince better c., 1444
scall, clogging c., 3603
Companions that waste time, 1447
I abhor point-devise c., 1446
prince but studies his c., 1445
Company, 1448-1455
best when least in c., 198
choose your own c., 1450
c. thou keepest defiles, 5296
c., villanous c., 1453
discharge yourself of our c., 2110
entreat thy c. to see world, 7574
have your c. in hell, 2044
I thank you for your c., 1452
keeping such vile c., 1453
let men take heed of their c., 1454
let us not lack your c., 1449
misery doth part c., 4738
stale in vulgar c., 5104
steal me from mine own c., 6030
we shall not have his c., 1448
wherefore gaze this c., 1418
your c. hath beguiled, 1455
your friends woo your c., 1451
Compare : belied with false c., 4749
Comparisons are odorous, 1457
full of c. and flouts, 6668
tired thyself in base c., 1456
Compass : my life is run his c., 6619
within c. of man's wit, 7247
Compassion, 1458-1461
in c. weep fire out, 1460
make mine eyes sweat c., 1458
melting with kind c., 1461

Compassionate : be c., 1459
boots not to be c., 1459
melt at tears, be c., 6270
Competency lives longer, 3258
Complexion, 1462-1468
all foul that my c. lack, 1467
best thing is his c., 1463
discolours c. of my greatness, 7047
good my c., 1462
his c. perfect gallows, 3245
how near to c. of goose, 4292
let all of his c. choose me, 5685
mislike me not for my c., 1467
of what c., 1467
oft is his gold c. dimm'd, 6316
one of my c., 1468
somewhat of that jealous c., 1358
soul of your c., 3076
what c. is she of, 1464
whose c. affliction alters, 5458
Complexions : all c. meet, 1465
c. that liked me, 3917
one of the four c., 1464
soft as our c. are, 7321
Compliment, 1469-1472
farewell c., 1471
feigning was called c., 1472
sans c., what news, 4965
that they call c., 1469
time will not allow c., 1470
valour melted into c., 4538
Complots of mischief, 4855
Composition : no c. in news, 4960
Compost : spread c. on weeds, 7056
Composture from excrement, 6520
Compt : we shall meet at c., 6140
Compulsion : give reason upon c., 5571
Compunctious visitings, 5612
Comrade with wolf and owl, 4929
new-hatch'd, unfledged c., 2902
Concave as covered goblet, 5269
Concealment feed on her cheek, 7339
Conceit, 1473-1481
c. brags of his substance, 1478
c. in weakest bodies strongest, 1475
c. my comfort, injury, 1474
dress'd in gravity, c., 5106
how c. may rob, 1477
infusing him with vain c., 3901
my earthly-gross c., 1473
no more c. than mallet, 1476
Conceitless to be seduced, 1479
Conceits are poisons, 1481
their c. have wings, 6667
Conception is a blessing, 1804
swelling evil of my c., 5403
Conceptions by mis-dread, 5178
Conclusion, 1482-1485
bald c., 1482
false c., 1485
foregone c., 1484
lame and impotent c., 1483
Conclusions : preposterous c., 5576
Concord, 1486-1488
c. of sweet sounds, 4862
c. of this discord, 2072
c. of well-tuned sounds, 1487
c. with harsh descant, 1488
sweet milk of c., 1486
Concubine : too good to be c., 5509

Condition : hard c. for a maid, 4391
  hard c. twin-born, 3880
  my c. smooth as oil, 5848
Condolement : obstinate c., 2561
Confess yourself to heaven, 1489
  I c. here on my knee, 1489
  I'll c. the truth, 1491
  to c. and be hanged, 1493
Confessed is not redressed, 1492
Confession, 1489-1494
  fairest excuse is c., 1490
  riddling c., riddling shrift, 1494
Confident against world in arms, 3615
Confirmations strong as holy writ, 6743
Confirmer of false reckonings, 4399
Confusion: 1495-1497
  c. made masterpiece, 1496
  c.'s cure lives not in c., 1497
  heaping c. on own heads, 4732
  vast c. waits, 1495
  whole swallowed in c., 4237
  why he puts on this c., 1344
Congregation of vapours, 2268
Conjecture : on eyelids c. hang, 2532
Conjure thee by all saints, 5800
  c. thee by Rosalind's eyes, 264
  my way is to c. you, 577
Conjurers and sorcerers, 5326
Conqueror : death made of conquest of
  this c., 1036
  I am c. of myself, 2100
  we came in with Richard C., 5717
Conquerors : brave c., 1498
Conquest : better c. never make, 1499
  c. for prince to boast of, 5441
  have I in c. stretched, 1027
  kind of c. Cæsar made, 1038
  outlook c., win renown, 5616
  peace is of nature of a c., 5212
Conquests : thy c. shrunk, 1029
Consanguineous : am I not c., 745
Conscience, 1500-1517
  almost against my c., 1503
  best c. not to leave 't undone, 7141
  c. but word cowards use, 1515
  c. devised to keep strong in awe, 1515
  c. is born of love, 4337
  c. makes cowards of us all, 1847
  c. makes man a coward, 1513
  c. 'tis a tender place, 1507
  c. to profoundest pit, 1768
  c. with injustice corrupted, 5493
  coward c., how dost thou, 1514
  Don Worm, his c., 6763
  dregs of c. yet within me, 1513
  his c. crept near another lady, 4561
  I'll catch c. of the king, 5330
  let not c. inflame too nicely, 1511
  my c. hath thousand tongues, 1514
  my c. says budge not, 1510
  my c., thou art fetter'd, 1500
  my c. will serve me, 1510
  quiet of my wounded c., 1506
  shook bosom of my c., 1508
  still and quiet c., 1509
  stuff of c. to do no murder, 4851
  thou hast a thing called c., 1517
  what you speak is in c. wash'd, 6167
  worm of c. shall begnaw soul, 1512
  your c. must acquittance seal, 1502

Consent : given my soul's c., 6471
  I will wink on her to c., 7189
Consequence : trammel up the c., 1932
Consideration like angel came, 1519
  let's drown c., 1518
Conspiracy against me, 1521
  c., shamest to show brow, 1520
  open-eyed c., 1522
Conspirant 'gainst prince, 6725
Constable : justle a c., 1524
  most fit man for c., 1523
  night-watch c., 1714
Constance : my name is C., 4449
Constancies expire before fashions, 4114
Constancy, 1525-1527
  c., be strong upon my side, 1526
  fellow of plain c., 7361
  keep c. in plight, 7337
Constant as northern star, 1527
  c. you are, but yet woman, 7305
  they are c. being won, 7377
  to one thing c. never, 4506
  were man but c., perfect, 4525
Constant-qualified : more c., 1232
Constantinople : go to C., 7361
Construction : mind's c., 2464
Consummation devoutly to be wish'd, 1847
Consumption : no remedy against c., 5477
Consumptions sow in bones, 7110
Contagion : all c. of south, 1734
  breathes c. to the world, 4673
  dare vile c. of night, 5926
Contemplation makes turkey-cock, 1528
  sweet is zealous c., 1528
Contempt, 1529-1532
  c. and anger of his lip, 5819
  c. and clamour my knell, 5338
  c., farewell, 5419
  c. hangs upon thy back, 2524
  c. will kill speaker's heart, 1532
  he did solicit in free c., 1530
  his c. shall not be bruising, 1530
  let foul'st c. shut door, 1532
  nature hath c. and grace, 4899
  what our c. doth often hurl, 1529
Content, 1533-1540
  clothe me in a forced c., 194
  commends me to own c., 1534
  c. is our best having, 1537
  c. to make virtue of necessity, 4933
  c. with my harm, 3979
  cry c. with that which grieves, 1681
  desire is got without c., 1538
  fulness of my heart's c., 1536
  he that wants c. without friend, 4760
  light upon low c., 1533
  make c. with fortunes fit, 7231
  my crown is called c., 3884
  poor and c. rich enough, 5379
  thoughts tending to c., 6566
  well c., 1535
  worse than worst, c., 2071
Contentless : best state c., 2071
Contention hath broke loose, 6646
  feed c. in lingering act, 7472
  no quarrel but a slight c., 5494
Continent melt into the sea, 2550
  orbed c., 6371
Contract : no joy of this c., 4158
Contumely : proud man's c., 1847

Contusions: aged c., 4177
Conversation: my c. coped, 3842
  your c. would infect my brain, 1201
Convey him to the Tower, 1540
  c. the wise it call, 1539
Conveyors are you all, 1540
Cony: so doth c. struggle, 7358
Cony-catching: full of c., 1409
Cook helps to make gluttony, 1543
  ill c. cannot lick fingers, 1543
Cookery: his neat c., 1542
  your fine Egyptian c., 1013
Cookoo-birds: ere c. sing, 7365
Cooks: Epicurean c., 1541
Cophetua: illustrate king C., 1545
  let C. know truth, 4955
  when king C. loved beggar, 1723
Copulation: let c. thrive, 95
  get living by c. of cattle, 5958
Copulatives: country c., 4555
Copy: nature's c. not eterne, 5821
Coral more red than lips', 4749
  of his bones c. made, 2576
Corantos: teach swift c., 1778
Cord: give me c., or knife, 2801
Cordelia: fairest C., 5680
Cordial ye bring lady, 1424
Cords too intrinse to unloose, 5716
Core: in my heart's c., 5171
Corinthian: no Jack, but C., 1547
Coriolanus: deeds of C., 6835
  my name is C., 4887
Corioli: holding C., 3138
Cork: take c. out of mouth, 6595
Cormorant: insatiate c., 6850
Corn, 1548-1551
  chaff and c. fly asunder, 5074
  c. to make your bread, 1548
  first thresh the c., 1551
  gods sent not c. for rich only, 5459
  like to autumn's c., 2320
  our c. is to reap, 1550
  our c. shall seem light, 7171
  shall of a c. cry woe, 1552
  sow'd cockle reap'd no c., 1549
  want ye c. for bread, 1548
Corn-fields: o'er green c., 4401
Corner in thing I love, 4562
  sits the wind in that c., 7170
Corners: all c. of earth, 5440
  come three c. of world in arms, 2337
Corns: she hath c., 1553
Corollary: bring a c., 6204
Coronet: adorn temples with c., 5878
Correctioner: filthy c., 5714
Correspondent to command, 1437
Corrival: without c., 3537
Corrupters of my faith, 3462
Corruption, 1554-1557
  c. inhabits our blood, 3726
  c. wins not more than honesty, 1555
  foul sin break into c., 5974
  I have seen c. boil, 1557
  rank c., mining all within, 1554
  take c. from that fault, 1955
  what c. in this life, 1556
Corse: before dead Henry's c., 4051
  dead c. in complete steel, 4780
  I'll make a c. of him, 1559

ne'er part till one drop a c., 3613
  regarded as most noble c., 1558
Corslet: pierce c., 2405
Core: most putrified c., 280
Cost: ask for one penny c., 4809
  avoid c. and encounter it, 1561
  command what c. your heart, 1450
  how little is the c., 1560
  it will c. you dear, 1562
  proud c. of buried age, 6636
Costard broken on a shin, 311
  my good knave, C., 5613
  rational hind, C., 4274
Coster-monger times, 6934
Cottages had been palaces, 7401
Couch for damned incest, 542
  c. of lasting night, 1868
  flinty c. of war, 1754
Cough or cry hem, 3450
Counsel, 1563-1573
  all too late comes c., 1570
  bosom up my c., 1564
  c. may stop awhile, 1568
  friendly c. cuts off foes, 1563
  give me present c., 3963
  hard for women to keep c., 7313
  I can keep honest c., 1566
  I hold little c. with fear, 3538
  I pray thee, cease thy c., 1569
  ill c. of a desert place, 4758
  liberal of your c., 1565
  my c. is my shield, 1964
  need your use and c., 2108
  skip o'er good c., 7566
  stay'd to hear good c., 4057
  take c. of their friends, 1575
  take c. of wiser head, 1572
  their c. turns to passion, 3156
  to c. deaf, not flattery, 2729
  two may keep c., one away, 1571
  when wise man gives better c., 1567
Counsellor, 1574-1581
  can he be a good c., 1574
  Caveto be thy c., 5051
  good c. lacks no clients, 1575
  grave and noble c., 1579
  his own affections' c., 1580
  love admits not reason for his c., 4382
  love's c. fills bores of hearing, 4379
  meet to be emperor's c., 1581
Countenance, 1582-1585
  evil wrapt up in c., 2370
  his c. enforces homage, 3590
  his c., like richest alchemy, 5088
  his c. likes me not, 1584
  making you c. you are, 6706
  my c. makes others fly, 1583
  out of c., 1585
  put thee in c., 1585
  turn from me that noble c., 1582
  turn my c. upon myself, 6747
Counter-caster: this c., 324
Countercheck Quarrelsome, 4091
Counterpoised: man cannot be c., 6835
Counterfeit grossly with slave, 3116
  downy sleep, death's c., 6026
  I am no c., 1587
  never call true gold c., 1586
  to c. dying is no c., 1587
  'twas time to c., 1587

Counters : lock c. from friends, 1626
Country, 1588-1592
alas, poor c., 5823
bleed, bleed, poor c., 1591
disable benefits of own c., 6706
for my c. I shed blood, 706
how can we for c. pray, 1590
I love my c.'s good, 1589
march to assault thy c., 1590
my c. shall have more vices, 1592
our c. sinks beneath yoke, 1591
undiscovered c., 1847
Couples coming to ark, 2795
Courage, 1593-1599
c., father, fight it out, 1593
c. mounteth with occasion, 1598
cry c., and away, 1593
cry c. to the field, 1593
full of haughty c., 3966
greater should c. be, 1791
lack c. of a woman, 2100
my breast I'll burst with c., 1595
my c. try by combat, 1594
plant c. in quailing breasts, 1597
screw c. to sticking-place, 1599
soft c. makes followers faint, 1596
where is your ancient c., 2401
with c. heart did lend, 3208
Couriers : sightless c. of air, 5304
Course : bear-like fight c., 6232
c. of true love never smooth, 4294
I must stand the c., 6231
prodigal c. like sun's, 5448
Courses : by bad c., 2362
Court, 1601-1608
all's savage but at c., 1604
base c. where kings grow base, 1607
c. is a learning place, 1600
c. it with words, 7376
c., whose top to climb, 1603
emperor's c. house of fame, 1608
friend i' c. better than penny, 2905
get you from our c., 2105
I was trained in English c., 5348
our c. is haunted, 6707
our c. shall be Academe, 7353
retire to c. of his eye, 605
this is English not Turkish c., 1605
wast ever in c., shepherd, 4540
who would live turmoil'd in c., 1606
Court-odour : receives c., 1625
Courtesan : night to cool c., 4978
Courtesans : dallying with c., 5432
Courtesies : debtor to you for c., 1610
laid strange c. upon me, 1609
outward c. would proclaim, 1611
Courtesy, 1612-1619
c. your cradle promised, 1613
dissembling c., 1612
duck with apish c., 2726
I am king of c., 1615
I am very pink of c., 1618
I scant this breathing c., 7081
kiss'd hand away in c., 1617
mirror of all c., 1616
not the flower of c., 1619
use devil himself with c., 2048
what a candy deal of c., 1614
Courtier, 1620-1625
do not c.'s hands sweat, 1620

English c. may be wise, 1622
I am a c., 1625
I am yet a c. beggarly, 1623
not a c. hath a heart, 1621
Courtiers are free, 1624
c. they call caterpillars, 1126
our c. say all's savage, 2393
Courtship : employ thoughts to c., 4661
Covenant : your hand ; a c., 422
Coventry : march through C., 6064
Cover of salt hides salt, 3202
they have a good c., 277
Covet : those that c. gain, 2949
Covetous would have chain, 2020
when Brutus grows so c., 1626
Covetousness : age and c., 7579
sin of c., 1627
Cow : curst c. short horns, 1629
like a c. in June, 1628
that I would not for c., 1700
Coward, 1630-1647
am I a c., 1634
c. that I am, 1644
c. worse than cup of sack, 1638
damned ere I call thee c., 1638
devout c., religious in it, 1646
either a c. or flatterer, 1651
foul-spoken c., 7405
he excels brother for c., 1630
he's a notorious c., 1196
I think him solely a c., 4109
let him that is no c. dare, 5732
live c. in own esteem, 1645
made c. turn terror, 2372
more c. than a hare, 1646
now thou seem'st a c., 1632
play c. with thy indenture, 3428
this sanguine c., 1456
was there ever man a c., 5768
we took him for a c., 2049
what a c., 1635
Coward-like with terror, 2614
Cowardice : bootless when c. pursues, 6 ,90
I hold it c., 1648
liver white badge of c., 4207
patience is cold c., 1649
Cowardly : I find it c., 1643
Cowards : conscience does make c. of
   us all, 1847
c. die many times, 1642
c. fight when they can fly no further,
   1641
c. have livers white as milk, 4210
mannish c. that outface, 1631
plenty and peace breeds c., 1633
true-bred c., 1635
Cowslip, burnet, clover, 4585
in c.'s bell I lie, 569
Cowslips tall her pensioners, 2476
Coxcomb of frize, 3023
set nothing by bloody c., 3656
Coy as haggerds of rock, 6211
Coystrill : he's a c., 2208
Cozen him that would unjustly win, 5956
Cozenage : full of c., 7267
Cozened and beaten, 1650
Cozeners : devil take c., 1614
Crab : as like as c. to apple, 4164
c., my dog, 2162
like a c. go backwards, 143

Crabbed : too c. that way, 4075
Crab-tree : graft with c., 433
Crack of doom, 4170
  when 'a was a c., 1278
Cracker : what c. is this, 3264
Cracking warrant of an oath, 5060
Cradle of imperious surge, 6019
  rough c. for little ones, 382
Cradle-clothes, 6081
Cradles : thoughts unveil in c., 5466
Craft : fish with c. for opinion, 6781
Cramp : he has c., 1630
Cramps : plagued with c., 4737
  rack thee with old c., 1745
  to-night thou shalt have c., 1745
Crare might harbor in, 4615
Creaking of shoes betray heart, 2660
Creation : bodiless c., 2286
  men their c. mar, 7321
Creature that bore shape of man, 4501
  fair c., kill'd too soon, 5222
  I am not a sickly c., 7160
  my sweet c. of bombast, 3955
  plainest c. that breathed, 6728
  poor c. of earth, 2661
  world hath not sweeter c., 7327
Creatures : call these delicate c. ours, 4562
  c. of another place, 3640
  c. that teach act of order, 563
  from fairest c. desire increase, 525
  guilty c. sitting at a play, 5330
  you nickname God's c., 5135
Credit : compact of c., 7298
  my c. stands on slippery ground, 1651
  one ne'er got me c., 4886
  though c. be asleep, 6468
  try what my c. can do, 1651
Creditor : glory of c., 4914
Credulous to false prints, 7321
Cressid : fly to C., 6147
  I cannot come to C. but by Pandar, 5144
  where C. lay that night, 4987
  why was C. hard to win, 7197
Cressids : all false women C., 5145
Crestfallen as dried pear, 1650
Crests : they fall their c., 2480
Crete : in C. they bay'd, 4864
  what fool that of C., 2806
Crib shall stand at king's mess, 482
Cricket to chimney leap, 2475
Crickets : as merry as c., 4656
  I heard c. cry, 1933
Crime : flashes into c., 1654
  forbid thee heinous c., 6634
  if you bethink of any c., 1657
Crimes, 1653-1658
  capital c., 1653
  c. not inherited, 1658
  c. unwhipp'd of justice, 3845
  foul c. done in days of nature, 6196
  make me know nature of c., 1656
  men cover c. with bold looks, 4532
  mightier c. laid unto you, 1653
  undivulged c., 1655
  with his c. broad blown, 2562
Crimson : virgin c. of modesty, 4464
Cripple can find a halt, 1660
  good counsel, the c., 7566
  restore c. to his legs, 1659
Crispian : feast of C., 3540

Crispin Crispian shall ne'er go by, 3540
Crispin Crispianus, 171
Critic : I that have been a c., 1714
Critical : nothing if not c., 1662
  satire, keen and c., 1661
Crocodile : each drop a c., 6468
  mournful c., 1665
  what thing is c., 1664
Crop : plenteous c. to glean, 4252
  rich c. of sea and land, 4484
Cropped : he ploughed, she c., 1012
Cross : bear offence's c., 5092
Crosses, cares, grief, 1430
  impatient to bear c., 4067
Crotchets : duke has c. in him, 1666
  these are c. he speaks, 1668
  thou hast c. in thy head, 1667
Crow, 1669-1676
  c., cock, with comb on, 1394
  c. doth sing as sweetly, 1675
  c. makes wing to wood, 4981
  c. may bathe in mire, 1676
  c. o' the same nest, 1669
  c. that flies in heaven's air, 529
  c. without feather, 1670
  go borrow me a c., 1670
  make thee think swan a c., 6367
  we'll pluck a c. together, 1670
  yield the c. a pudding, 1672
Crow-flowers, nettles, 2959
Crow-keeper ; handles bow like c., 858
  scaring ladies like c., 6185
Crown, 1677-1690
  c. no bigger than thy head, 1685
  c. or glorious tomb, 1680
  c. that seldom kings enjoy, 3884
  c. will find an heir, 1690
  from c. of head to sole of foot, 4724
  he bids you deliver c., 861
  here, cousin, seize the c., 1686
  hide c., he'll rake for it, 1678
  hollow c. that rounds temples, 3901
  how sweet to wear c., 1679
  I know not how to get c., 1681
  I will divide my c., 3805
  my c. is called content, 3884
  my c. is in my heart, 3884
  strike c. into hazard, 4754
  thine eyes beat on a c., 3395
  thrice presented him a c., 1033
  torment myself to catch c., 1681
  uneasy lies head that wears c., 6019
  upon my head placed c., 1683
  win a new world's c., 1688
  with my hands give c., 1687
  yield c. and throne, 4373
Crowner's quest law, 4027
Crowns for convoy, 3540
  c. in my purse I have, 7490
  fearless minds climb soonest unto c., 1682
  give c. like pins, 3481
  sedged c., 5038
  we must have crack'd c., 4265
  with cunning gild copper c., 6781
Crows are fatted with flock, 1674
  c. to peck the eagles, 1671
  executors, knavish c., 1672
  leaving thy trunk for c., 1673
  our c. shall fare the better, 1672

Cruel only to be kind, 1691
let me be c., not unnatural, 4946
Cruelty, 1691-1694
c. to load falling man, 2491
farewell, fair c., 1694
fill me full of direst c., 1692
get thee to yond c., 1694
to do worse were fell c., 1693
Crum : nor crust nor c., 6982
Crums : rub chain with c., 2116
Crust : keeps nor c., 6982
Crutch, 1695-1698
gives c. cradle's infancy, 510
I'll lean upon one c., 1695
pluck c. from limping sire, 1697
Crutches : time goes on c., 4298
Cry like a woman, 7292
Crying : we came c. hither, 668
Crystal is muddy, 2411
Crystals : clear thy c., 2411
Cub : dissembling c., 7589
Cubs : pluck c. from bear, 2053
Cuckold, 1699-1703
cries c. to my father, 432
c. and c.-maker, 1702
c., devil hath not name, 1702
c. or c.-maker, 1700
do not recompense making me c., **1701**
fate ordaining he be c., 1702
if I be his c., he's my drudge, 1699
make husband c., 3668
no true c. but calamity, 1047
that c. lives in bliss, 3779
Cuckold-mad : not c., 4437
Cuckolds ere we deserved it, 1701
peace great maker of c., 7009
there have been c. ere now, 1703
Cuckoo, 1704-1706
as c. is in June, 3876
c. buds of yellow hue, 1705
c. builds not for himself, 1704
c. mocks married men, 1705
c., O word of fear, 1705
hedge-sparrow fed c., 1704
knows me as blindman c., 1951
maintained by the c., 7202
plain-song c. gray, 1706
ungentle gull, c.'s bird, 1704
your c. sings by kind, 1699
Cuckoo-flowers : crown'd with c., 4453
Cuckoos hatch in sparrows' nests, 7501
Cucullus non facit monachum, 4769
Cue, 1707-1709
clock gives me my c., 1707
every one according to c., 1708
my c. is melancholy, 4619
remember you your c., 1707
speak, 'tis your c., 1709
when my c. comes, call, 1708
you come upon your c., 1709
Cues : you speak c. and all, 1708
Cuisses on his thighs, 3613
Cunning of the scene, 5330
c. as fast and loose, 425
have more c. to be strange, 763
hence bashful c., 3672
in sports my c. faints, 2954
so c. and so young, 7569
unfold what c. hides, 6621

virtue and c. endowments, 6942
with c. gild copper crowns, 6781
Cup : crush c. of wine, 7185
c. of wine that's brisk, 3387
c. that's stored unto brim, 1710
drunk of Circe's c., 1710
every inordinate c. unbless'd, 7184
fill the c., 1710
sour c. of prosperity, 5457
Cupboarding the viand, 618
Cupid, 1711-1724
C. all arm'd, 1716
C. grant all maidens here, 553
C. hath clapp'd him, 1711
C. is good hare-finder, 3767
C. is knavish lad, 1717
C. is no longer archer, 1718
C.'s butt shaft hath, 1711
from C.'s shoulder pluck wings, 6147
he cut C.'s bow-string, 1721
I swear by C.'s bow, 6866
little C.'s crafty arrow, 1719
mark'd I where bolt of C. fell, 1716
no C. hoodwink'd with scarf, 6185
not hit with C.'s arrow, 1722
rhymes guards on C.'s hose, 5667
see C.'s fiery shaft, 1716
some C. kills with arrows, 1720
sweet C. hast thumped him, 1715
therefore hath C. wings, 4323
this giant-dwarf Dan C., 1714
weak wanton C., 1724
wing'd C. painted blind, 4393
young Adam C. shot so trim, 1723
Cups : in flowing c. remember'd, 3540
Cur, 1725-1728
butcher's c. venom-mouth'd, 1725
cruel-hearted c., 2162
impenetrable c., 1726
this carnal c. preys, 1727
Curbs to headstrong wills, 6255
Curds : shepherd's homely c., 5899
Cure, 1729-1730
c. fit for a king, 1506
mortal to cut, to c. easy, 2089
past c. am I, 1730
past c. is past care, 1729
past c., past help, 7075
such a one were past c., 1730
to strange sores strain the c., 6098
you are not past c., 1729
Curfew : he begins at c., 2661
Curiosity : mocked for c., 2402
Curls : Hyperion's c., 5272
Currance : with steady c., 5596
Current, 1731-1732
c. with murmur glides, 1732
like impediment in c., 1731
o'er-walk a c. roaring loud, 825
take c. when it serves, 6591
Currents : corrupted c. of world, 5084
their c. turn awry, 1847
Curs shall take each other, 1720
c. that like not peace, 7008
foolish c. run winking, 3311
like to village c., 2321
shall dung-hill c. confront Helicons, 4955
small c. not regarded, 4176
you common cry of c., 4834

Curse, 1733-1747
common c. of mankind, 1746
c. away winter's night, 1737
c. of kings to be attended, 3888
c. shall light upon men, 1031
mother's c. on revolting son, 1335
my profit is I know to c., 3999
O c. of marriage, 4562
primal eldest c., 5084
serpent's c., 3512
take with thee my c., 1744
teach me how to c., 1743
teach thee how to c., 1743
that's the c. of Rome, 1738
we have c. in having her, 1281
what meanest thou to c., 1747
wherefore should I c., 1737
woundings of father's c., 1739
yet I needs must c., 1745
Curses : can c. pierce clouds, 1742
c. be darted on thee, 1736
c. not loud but deep, 4136
these c. recoil upon thyself, 1737
well skill'd in c., 1743
with c. in her mouth, 3297
would c. kill, I'd invent, 1737
Cursing : a-c. like a drab, 341
Curtain : draw the c., 2473
such man drew Priam's c., 7100
Curtains of thine eye, 2446
Curvet of Mars's steed, 6990
Custard : leaped into c., 2121

Custom, 1748-1754
as the c. is, 1337
c. calls me to 't, 1748
c. is angel yet in this, 1750
c. made it easiness, 1751
c. made this life sweet, 4117
c. more honour'd in breach, 1749
c. stale her variety, 140
if c. hath not brass'd it, 3332
my c. of the afternoon, 3709
that monster, c., 1750
think of this as a c., 1753
tyrant c. made flinty couch, 1754
we are strong in c., 6341
what c. wills, we do 't, 1748
Customs : new c. are follow'd, 1752
nice c. curtsy to kings, 1751
Cut : unkindest c. of all, 1033
Cut-purse of the empire, 1755
I remember him, a c., 5550
nimble hand for c., 1756
Cut-throats : best o' c., 5019
Cyclops' hammers fall, 5610
Cygnet to this faint swan, 6364
Cygnets : so swan c. save, 6362
Cynthia : by eye of C. she vow'd, 4216
Cypress black as crow, 1007
in c. let me be laid, 1902
sweetest shade c. trees, 1737
Cytherea in sedges hid, 5273
sweeter than C.'s breath, 2767

D

Dace bait for old pike, 4907
Dad : call'd brother's father d., 7430
Dædalus, Icarus, Minos, 2806
Daffed me to cabin hanged with care, 4992
Daffodils come before swallow, 1758
when d. begin to peer, 1757
Dagger, 1759-1765
beat thee with d. of lath, 3875
hath no d. point for me, 1764
he hacked it with his d., 6391
I have same d. for myself, 1032
I wear not d. in my mouth, 7417
is this a d. that I see before me, 1762
my breast can brook d., 7429
my d. muzzled, 882
O happy d., 1765
pare nails with wooden d., 4881
there is my d., here my breast, 1761
this d. hath mista'en, 1765
this is the air-drawn d., 1762
Daggers thou hast whetted, 1760
give me the d., 5474
I will speak d. to her, 1759
there's d. in men's smiles, 1763
these words, like d., 7420
thou hidest thousand d., 1760
Dainties made to taste, 6828
fed of d. bred in book, 3693
I hold your d. cheap, 7076
Daintiest : regreet d., 2309
Daisies : when d. pied, 1705
Dalliance : give d. rein, 6924
primrose path of d., 5187

silken d. in wardrobe, 7561
wanton d. with paramour, 5152
Dam : she is devil's d., 5799
unnatural d., 5728
Damask : red and d., 4194
Dames : chaste d. meet reproach, 4604
Damn : God d. me, 1767
Damnation, 1766-1775
botch and bungle up d., 2027
d. of his taking off, 6939
I dare d., 1768
'twere d. to think so base, 1772
wickedness is sin, sin d., 4540
Damned for never king's son, 1769
d. like ill-roasted egg, 1602
I'll see her d. first, 1770
more deep d. than Lucifer, 1771
thou art d. to hell, 1775
truly, I think thou art d., 1773
truly, thou art d., 1766
Damp of night disponge, 4779
Dams : no more d. I'll make, 1050
Dance barefoot on wedding-day, 263
let's have a d., 1779
make you d. canary, 4601
shall we d. Bacchanals, 1776
when you d. I wish you, 1784
which will deny to d., 1553
Dances : she d. goddess-like, 5979
Dancing, 1776-1784
d. shoes with nimble soles, 1781
for other than d. measures, 1777
no d., girl, 1780
past our d. days, 1783

Dancing-schools: English d., 1778
Danger, 1785-1796
  d. deviseth shifts, 1796
  d. knows Cæsar more dangerous, 1026
  daring an opposite to d., 5683
  foretold d. lurks within, 1793
  I must go meet d., 1789
  if ever d. environ thee, 1795
  in d. of her former tooth, 6054
  out of nettle d., 1788
  send d. from east to west, 1787
  to be too busy is d., 1785
  we are in great d., 1791
  worthy d. and death, 4375
Dangerous when baser nature, 4905
  something in me d., 1786
Dangers of days newly gone, 1790
  loved me for d. I had passed, 4305
  men mistrust ensuing d., 3752
Daniel come to judgement, 1797
  second D., a D., Jew, 1798
Dare: how you d., with what you d., 1170
  I d. do all that may become a man, 1645
  I d. meet Surrey, 4099
  letting I d. not wait upon I would, 1645
  what man d. I d., 5879
Darius: coffer of D., 3805
Dark needs no candles, 1062
  here stood he in the d., 1222
  so d. I could not see hand, 1799
  we are for the d., 1816
Darkling of the sun, 3423
  we were left d., 1061
Darkness, 1799-1801
  d. burier of the dead, 7472
  d. does face of earth entomb, 1821
  d. like a drunkard reels, 4799
  encounter d. like a bride, 1800
  following d. like a dream, 1801
  jaws of d. devour it, 4157
  light in d. lies, 4153
  no d. but ignorance, 3697
  prince of d. gentleman, 5427
  send to d. all that stop me, 2669
  to d. fleet souls, 6126
  to thy d. hie thee, 5800
Darlings: curled d. of nation, 1802
  eat those little d., 1803
Darnel, and idle weeds, 4453
Dart of chance, 4917
Date of such prolixity, 6185
  their d. is out, 1504
Daughter, 1804-1814
  call you me d., 1814
  Cato's d., 7312
  have you a d., 1804
  he says he loves my d., 4367
  how speed you with my d., 6191
  I am d. to his blood, 1809
  I think this is your d., 1811
  king's d. is found, 4969
  my d. is afeard, 2287
  my d. is my flesh, 2752
  my d., O my ducats, 2232
  my d. will run mad, 7129
  one fair d. and no more, 1805
  piece of tender air, thy d., 7128
  still harping on my d., 3277
  taught of your chaste d., 1236
  they say owl was baker's d., 5122

thou art my flesh, my d., 1806
  your d. made revolt, 1812
Daughters of my father's house, 7339
  he curses all Eve's d., 1810
  nothing subdued nature but d., 1807
  Philip's d. were like thee, 3743
  this flesh begot those d., 1807
Dauphin is so pleasant, 4754
Daw: no wiser than a d., 4030
Dawning may bare raven's eye, 2175
Day, 1815-1834
  alack, the heavy d., 3905
  babbling, remorseful d., 1822
  breathing time of d., 1819
  bright d. brings forth adder, 84
  bright d. is done, 1816
  busy d. hath roused crows, 1833
  by d., when goose is cackling, 5003
  by the clock, 'tis d., 1827
  d. begins to break, 1821
  d. dapples drowsy east, 1830
  d. longer than wonder lasts, 7352
  d. serves not light, 2659
  for ever and a d., 4554
  hold d. with the Antipodes, 4988
  I have seen d. of wrong, 2082
  it is my d., my life, 1143
  it is not yet near d., 4008
  it sufficeth d. will end, 2307
  jocund d. stands tiptoe, 1832
  makes July's d. short, 1834
  merrier d. did never greet Rome, 1818
  merry as d. is long, 4660
  no d. without a deed, 2297
  not a d. of season, 1377
  on a d., alack the d., 4278
  our d. is gone, 6321
  promise such a beauteous d., 1387
  proud d. too wanton, 6322
  shall I compare thee to summer's d., 6316
  sleep d. out of countenance, 1815
  so foul and fair a d., 1826
  so great a d. cheaply bought, 1828
  so tedious is this d., 1831
  such a d. came not till now, 1820
  survive my well-contented d., 1898
  they sat live-long d., 1823
  what hath this d. deserved, 3494
Day-bed: lewd d., 5432
Daylight: night but d. sick, 4988
  we burn d., 1829
  welcome daylight with ditty, 5242
Days: abridge my doleful d., 1856
  halcyon d., 6313
  I hope for quiet d., 4432
  I hope good d. to see, 2876
  look'd on better d., 2984
  my d. are past the best, 4335
  my salad d., 5789
  one of these d., 5513
  past our dancing d., 1783
  shorten my d. thou canst, 4143
  since old d. of Adam, 3646
  these d. are dangerous, 6935
  we have seen better d., 1817
  welcome these pleasant d., 4128
  what dark d. have I seen, 1408
  winding up d. with toil, 6021
  you have look'd on better d., 1817
Dead: better be with the dead, 1872

d. as a doornail, 1857
d. as nail in door, 1857
d., for a ducat, d., 1848
he is d. and gone, lady, 4262
he's d. and rotten, 1867
sheeted d. did squeak, 5095
sleeping and d. but as pictures, 6025
spirits o' the d. may walk, 6214
when I am d. and gone, 1859
would I were d., 7274
Deaf as the sea, 6265
like the adder waxen d., 83
Deafness : your tale would cure d., 6425
Dear : farewell, thou art too d., 2536
it will cost thee d., 1562
Dearth of daughters, sons, 1249
d. that I have pined in, 2790
if d. or foison follow, 5004
make d. in this land, 6569
untimely storms expect d., 6275
Death, 1835-1905
apprehends d. no more, 1877
at point of d. made merry, 1893
bad d. argues monstrous life, 1860
be absolute for d., 1874
beg d. upon my knee, 2844
better cherish'd, nearer d., 6716
better d. than mocks, 1882
blindfold d., 1886
brave d., when princes die, 4127
canker d. eats plant, 3078
come away, come away, d., 1902
contrive my d. with plots, 1225
d., a grave, 873
d. and destruction dog thee, 1891
d. doth front thee, 2008
d. ends a mortal woe, 1887
d. for his ambition, 1032
d. gives her fame, 6000
d. hath not struck so fat a deer, 2508
d. is a fearful thing, 1876
d. is a great disguiser, 1878
d. is certain to all, 1846
d. is fairest cover, 2555
d. is in my hand, 5655
d. is most in apprehension, 1875
d. is the end of all, 1846
d. like untimely frost, 1897
d. lines chaps with steel, 1866
d. made no conquest, 1036
d. made proud with beauty, 1869
d. of dear friends made sad, 5174
d. of each day's life, 6024
d. rock me asleep, 1856
d. should be like mirror, 1885
d. sucked honey of thy breath, 1894
d. umpire of miseries, 1858
d. unloads thee, 1874
d. will come when it will, 1863
d. will have his day, 1888
d. will seize doctor too, 4602
d. with slower foot, 1157
d.'s approach so terrible, 1860
d.'s destroying wound, 1889
d.'s pale flag, 1894
destined to drier d., 3245
die the d., 6922
done to d. by slanderous tongues, 6000
doting d. is near, 3110
double d. to drown in ken of shore, 2215

downy sleep, d.'s counterfeit, 6026
drowned, a d. I abhor, 2213
earthy hand of d., 3617
fell sergeant, d., 1852
forgets he heard name of d., 1202
give him d. by inches, 1844
grim d., how foul, 6034
grossly fear'st thy d., 6028
guiltless d. I die, 1884
hath d. lain with thy wife, 1897
have I not hideous d., 1870
he shall die flea's d., 1881
I here importune d., 1838
I would fain die dry d., 1900
I'll make d. love me, 2669
in sleep of d. what dreams, 1847
keeper back of d., 3572
kill me with living d., 2436
kill'd by d.'s sharp sting, 5222
let d. sit in thy cheek, 752
love-devouring d., 4703
make d. proud to take us, 1839
not guilty of d., 4027
not wish fairer d., 6072
nothing can we call our own but d., 1431
now boast thee, d., 1842
O amiable lovely d., 1868
O proud d., what feast, 1853
pain of d. would die, 4135
pull'd wretch to muddy d., 1851
resolved for d. or dignity, 1861
secret house of d., 1839
seeking for Richmond in throat of d., 5683
she shall die the d., 1836
sight of d. is as a bell, 1896
snatch'd out of jaws of d., 1903
speak me fair in d., 1880
spits forth d., 4825
strange that d. should sing, 6364
stroke of d. as lover's pinch, 1841
studied in d. to throw away, 1871
sure physician, d., 1845
swift celerity of his d., 1152
that churl d., 1898
then is d. a benefit, 1864
there is mettle in d., 1835
this way I fall to d., 3342
thou owest God a d., 1855
through hollow eyes of d., 4144
till d., that winter, kill, 4415
unburthen'd crawl toward d., 1103
unsubstantial d. is amorous, 1894
upon my d. French can little boast, 4233
way to dusty d., 4137
we owe God a d., 1855
what ugly sights of d., 2216
when d. is our physician, 2214
where art thou, d., 1840
within keeps d. his court, 3901
Death-bed : go to thy d., 1849
on d. play ruffian, 3956
thou art on thy d., 5232
Death-counterfeiting sleep, 6029
Deaths put on by cunning cause, 6165
thousand d. would die, 1904
Debate of commonwealth affairs, 1908
d. our trivial difference, 1906
d. question of this straw, 1907
Debonair as bending angels, 1624

Debt that sleep doth owe, 6110
d. to their salt sovereign, 6286
what d. in all humanity, 7144
what he speaks is in d., 5452
Debtor to you for courtesies, 1610
die not my master's d., 2877
no d. but cord, 3237
Debts : he that dies pays all d., 1901
our d. lay on the king, 3880
words pay no d., 7406
Decay of lust through realm, 2341
d. of wrested pomp, 1495
Deceit, 1909-1917
fairest show means d., 1915
good d. that intends d., 1911
oh that d. should dwell, 1917
oh that d. steal gentle shapes, 1916
shape that means d., 1912
your words' d., 1473
Deceits : tongues full of d., 1910
Deceive more slily than Ulysses, 5114
December when they wed, 7360
D.'s bareness everywhere, 8
rain and wind beat dark D., 6160
Deck : keep him above d., 778
Decorum : athwart goes d., 4087
Decrees : hot temper leaps o'er cold d., 6490
Dedicate to war, 6999
Deed, 1918-1951
as good d. as to drink, 1172
bloody d. is done, 1944
blow horrid d. in every eye, 5304
by d. acquire high fame, 1918
d. of dreadful note, 1936
d. whereat valour weeps, 1923
d. without a name, 1938
d. you undertake is damnable, 5594
do the d. of darkness, 1943
good d. to say well, 7395
I have done the d., 1933
if one good d., I repent, 1948
make ugly d. look fair, 5150
no day without a d., 2297
not more ugly than my d., 7397
one good d. dying tongueless, 1950
place dignified by doer's d., 6928
poor instrument may do noble d., 1919
so shines good d. in naughty world, 1067
this d. I'll do, 1939
what rash and bloody d., 1925
Deedless in his tongue, 1212
Deeds : better d. than words, 6782
cherish such high d., 6838
do d. make heaven weep, 1942
doing d. of hospitality, 5897
foul d. will rise, 1924
grace age with noble d., 3614
he looks through d. of men, 5565
I talk of abominable d., 4855
I'll endeavor d. to match words, 7408
ill d. doubled with evil word, 1921
ill d. make d. ill done, 1921
let d. express their words, 7396
my d. upon my head, 812
our d. are done, 6321
renowned for their d., 2324
rewards is with doing, 1922
these d. must not be thought, 1934
those scraps are good d. past, 6642

'tis d. must win prize, 1945
unnatural d. breed troubles, 1940
with d. requite gentleness, 6515
words are no deeds, 7395
words pay no debts, give d., 7406
words to d. cold breath gives, 7400
your speeches may d. approve, 7398
Deep of night crept upon talk, 4908
not so d. as a well, 3655
Deep-divorcing vow, 2145
Deep-search'd with saucy looks, 6291
Deer, 1952-1954
art thou my d., 1954
death hath not struck so fat a d., 2508
d. was sanguis, 1953
I must hunt this d., 3652
I will count you my d., 344
let stricken d. go weep, 7469
stall'd d. thou shouldst strike, 1572
unruly d. breaks pale, 1952
what shall he have that kill'd d., 3580
yield d. to stealer, 3057
Defacer of God's handiwork, 7347
Defeatures : strange d., 3144
Defect quarreled with grace, 7335
stamp of one d., 1955
Defects : faint d. of age, 164
our d. prove commodities, 1956
Defence : stand in your d., 4282
Defiler of Hymen's bed, 3067
Deformed, unfinished, 666
I know that D., 1957
none d. but the unkind, 1957
Deformity not so horrid, 7316
d. to mock my body, 4266
Defunct : bed with d., 4901
Delight : find d. writ there, 2469
weighing d. and dole, 3816
Degree, 1959-1960
d. being vizarded, 1959
observe d., priority, 1959
take d. away, discord, 1960
thou art of low d., 5420
when d. is shaked, 1960
Deities : humbling d. to love, 3055
Deity : I feel not d. in bosom, 1516
Delay, 1961-1965
d. leads beggary, 1964
if we use d., winter, 1963
in d. lies no plenty, 4751
in d. we waste our lights, 1965
one inch of d. more, 1961
who would bear law's d., 1847
Delays have dangerous ends, 1962
Delicates : prince's d., 5899
Delights : all d. are vain, 1966
besotted in your d., 5164
violent d. have violent ends, 1967
Demerits speak unbonneted, 4142
Demi-Atlas of this earth, 3586
Demi-devil : demand that d., 2038
Demon that hath gull'd, 1969
thy d., thy spirit, 1968
Den : murkiest d., 4432
Denis : on Saint D. cry, 3805
Saint D. and Saint George, 7361
Denmark is a prison, 5437
it may be so in D., 6044
something rotten in D., 5742
Dependency of thing on thing, 4454

Depths and shoals of honour, 6450
Deputy elected by the Lord, 3899
  this outward-sainted d., 2031
Deputy-elect, 3903
Descant : harsh d., 1488
Descent below thy foot, 6725
Description, 1977-1981
  d. cannot suit itself, 1977
  he went to bed to her d., 1981
  her person beggar'd all d., 1977
  maid that paragons d., 1980
  your wondrous rare d., 1979
Desdemona : divine D., 1980
  to D. hath caroused, 5372
Desert : use every man after his d., 1983
  why should this a d. be, 6684
  your d. speaks loud, 1984
Deserve : they d. to have, 1985
Deserver : love linked to d., 1982
Desire, 1986-1992
  deep d. hath none, 1992
  d. is got without content, 1538
  d. my pilot is, 1989
  die by drops of hot d., 4054
  it provokes the d., 2204
  miserable d., that's glorious, 1987
  my d., more sharp than steel, 1991
  satiate yet unsatisfied d., 7151
  strange that d. outlives performance,
    1988
Desires like cruel hounds, 1990
  thy d. are wolvish, 5483
  your heart's d. be with you, 1986
Desmesnes that adjacent lie, 264
Desolation : demonstrating d., 4249
  my d. makes better life, 1993
  where thou art not is d., 7146
  you have lived in d., 1994
Despair, 1995-1997
  hits where d. most fits, 2387
  I'll join with black d., 1997
  purge this black d., 1995
  rash-embraced d., 4287
  whence springs this d., 1996
Destinies as the D. decree, 1998
  D. cut thread of life, 2000
  D. will curse thee, 2001
  mark'd by D. to be avoided, 1999
Destiny, 2002-2006
  d., that hath to instrument, 2006
  he brings his d. with him, 6051
  let determined things to d., 2002
  'tis d. unshunnable, 4562
  unavoided is doom of d., 2005
Destroyers : courteous d., 5155
Destruction, 2007-2014
  by d. dwell in doubtful joy, 1538
  cry woe, d., ruin, 1888
  death and d. dog thee, 1891
  d. fang mankind, 2014
  d. shall dog them, 2012
  gallop to her d., 2010
  hemm'd about with d., 2009
  incenses them to send d., 5096
  into d. cast him, 2007
  pale d. meets thee, 2008
  swooning d., 3823
  winning leap'd into d., 3565
  you woo your own d., 2011
Determine : what we d. we break, 5472

Detractions to mending, 1663
Device : dull not d., 2015
  O excellent d., 2016
Devices : our d. overthrown, 7152
Devil, 2017-2049
  an d. come to him, 3421
  an you speak ill of d., 2046
  as like as d. to dam, 4163
  can the d. speak true, 2029
  childhood fears painted d., 1288
  curb this cruel d., 4038
  d. can cite Scripture, 2032
  d. damn thee black, 2030
  d. hath power to assume pleasing shape,
    2021
  d. knew not what he did, 2043
  d. on whose nature, 2042
  d. or d.'s dam, 2028
  d. rides upon fiddlestick, 2024
  d. shall have his bargain, 2023
  d. take mocking, 4752
  d. take such cozeners, 1614
  d. understands Welsh, 2025
  d. will have no shepherds, 1766
  d. will not eat a woman, 7291
  d. will not have me damned, 2034
  d. would have him about women, 7307
  fit for d.'s grace, 5442
  give the d. his due, 2023
  got by d. upon thy dam, 6012
  he needs must that d. drives, 2017
  he's a very d. 2047
  how agrees d. with thee, 2023
  I can teach thee to shame d., 2026
  I can teach you to command d., 2026
  if d. have him not, 6987
  if d., I cannot kill thee, 2037
  if d., you are fair, 5021
  let d. and dam haunt you, 2036
  let the d. wear black, 2022
  let us call thee d., 7184
  long spoon to eat with d., 2019
  make a moral of d. himself, 3074
  make puritan of the d., 5469
  master d., or throw him out, 6828
  mortal eyes cannot endure d., 2039
  no man means evil but d., 2033
  now shall d. be shamed, 1521
  prince of darkness, alias d., 2018
  see thyself, d., 7316
  seek redemption of the d., 5592
  shape every bush a d., 988
  she is the d.'s dam, 5799
  sugar o'er d. himself, 2050
  take the d. in thy mind, 2041
  tell truth and shame d., 2026
  there is a d. haunts me, 2512
  this is a d., no monster, 2019
  thou, merry d., didst rob, 3631
  though d. lead measure, 1157
  trunks o'erflourish'd by d., 6946
  use d. with courtesy, 2048
  very d. incardinate, 2049
  virtue profaned in such a d., 6943
  what, defy the d., 2046
  would I were a d., 2044
  you the blacker d., 226
Devils : all the d. are here, 3444
  fears make d. of cherubins, 2617
  more d. than hell can hold, 3705

other d. botch damnation, 2027
some d. ask but parings, 2020
they were d. incarnate, 7307
they will fight like d., 4589
we are d. to ourselves, 2045
when d. will sins put on, 2035
whip me, ye d. 6140
whoreson d. do harm, 7291
wonderful when d. tell truth, 2040
you are d. being offended, 7325
Devotion : in d. spend latter days, 2051
  with d.'s visage, 2050
Dew : before d. of evening, 5961
  d. will rust bright swords, 6403
  fetch d. from Bermoothes, 628
  honey-heavy d. of slumber, 6022
  morning's silver-melting d., 3259
  resolve itself into a d., 2736
  tears virginal as d. to fire, 6460
  vain d. shall dry your pities, 7075
  wicked d. drop on you, 1745
Dew-drop from lion's mane, 1724
Dew-drops : go seek d., 2477
Dews of heaven fall thick, 689
  his d. fall every where, 1341
  water'd with d. of flattery, 2718
Diadem : precious d., 1755
Dial shows how minutes waste, 4712
  drew d. from poke, 2793
  my d. goes not true, 4004
Dialect : he had the d., 6665
  speechless d., 7565
Dialogue : so skipping a d., 4795
  to hear the wooden d., 67
Dials : carve out d., 4710
Diamonds : not deck'd with d., 3884
Dian : as D. had hot dreams, 1236
  D., from thy altar do I fly, 4239
  my mother seem'd the D., 432
  she hath D.'s wit, 1722
  thaw snow on D.'s lap, 3067
  you seem to me as D., 5845
Diana's lip is not more smooth, 4204
  die as chaste as D., 1239
  let us be D.'s foresters, 4781
  live like D.'s priest, 1233
  makes D.'s ranger false, 3057
  she'll wear D.'s livery, 4216
  weep like D. at fountain, 7067
Dice, 2052-2055
  d. loved I dearly, 1205
  he chides the d., 2052
  keep gamester from d., 2054
  over-lusty French play at d., 2895
  very d. obey him, 2954
Dick the shepherd blows his nail, 5124
  some D. told our intents, 6737
Dickens : what the d. his name is, 4892
Dickon thy master is bought, 2323
Dictynna, goodman Dull, 4784
Did : thou canst not say I d. it, 1937
Dido with a willow, 4987
Die : all that lives must d., 1846
  d. a good old man, 4610
  d. all, d. merrily, 1854
  d., but not for love, 7361
  d. by drops of hot desire, 4054
  d. contented in king's company, 1135
  d. men like dogs, 3481
  d. the death, 1836

d. the death or abjure society, 6922
d. thou, and d. our fear, 967
d. two months ago, 4626
d. with harness on back, 1873
few d. well in battle, 441
I will d. in thy lap, 3353
if I d., no soul pity me, 4314
if I d. tomorrow, 4704
if it were now to d., 1883
if we are mark'd to d., 3540
live how we can,.d. we must, 4130
man can d. but once, 1855
that we shall d. we know, 1864
to d. is to be counterfeit, 1587
when we drink we d., 4915
Died holily in their beds, 6976
  had I but d. before, 4808
  he d. fearing God, 1204
  he that d. o' Wednesday, 3539
  we d. at such a place, 1135
Dies this year, quit for next, 1855
  he d. and makes no sign, 1860
  he that d. pays all debts, 1901
Diet : gods will d. me, 1421
  kept very good d., 1730
Dieted like mules, 2331
Difference between red and damask, **4194**
  d. between wake and sleep, 3417
  d. of man and man, 4495
  d. twixt amorous and villanous, 1236
  wear your rue with a d., 5750
Differences : full of excellent d., 2969
Difficulties easy when known, 2056
Digestion, 2057-2058
  for your d.'s sake, 2063
  good d. to you all, 2057
  good d. wait on appetite, 2058
  things sweet in d. sour, 6382
Dignity : let none wear undeserved **d., 4651**
  not a thought but on d., 6548
Diligence : best of me is d., 1566
Din to fright monster, 2060
  little d. can daunt, 2059
Dine with us, 2282
Dined : hath he d., 2062
Ding, dong, bell, 2526, 2576
  hey d. a d. d., 4401
Dinner : at d. of friends, 2923
  not speak till after d., 2062
Dinners and suppers excepted, 5666
Diomed has got sleeve, 2350
Direness cannot start me, 2613
Dirge of her certain ending, 6366
  with d. in marriage, 3816
Disasters : make sun of d., 6245
  weary with d., 7479
Discomfort guides my tongue, 2065
  d. you it nothing must, 2140
  from spring d. swells, 2064
Discontent, 2066-2071
  brawling d., 2068
  content you in my d., 2070
  heart's d. and affliction, 1737
  what's more miserable than d., **2066**
  winter of our d., 7203
  wrought out of our d., 2067
  your brows full of d., 2069
Discord : age of d., 4559
  find concord of this d., 2072

I never heard so musical a d., 4864
melodious d., 2073
Discords : harsh d., 4008
Discourse, 2074-2077
bid me d., I will enchant, 2079
d. is heavy, fasting, 2075
d. the freezing hours away, 6160
excellent dumb d., 2078
his d. is peremptory, 1206
list his d. of war, 6997
no d. of reason, 743
sweet and voluble is his d., 7233
voluble and sharp d., 2074
wench of excellent d., 7088
what means this d., 2076
with incorporal air hold d., 2410
your fair d. as sugar, 2077
Discourses : woes serve for d., 7280
Discretion, 2080-2083
better part of valour is d., 2080
common for young to lack d., 7575
covering d. with coat of folly, 6849
goose for his d., 4189
he had good d., 3895
led by some d., 2081
let d. be your tutor, 54
little hole of d., 2082
not to outsport d., 2083
old folks have d., 1290
pigeon-egg of d., 5225
valour cannot carry his d., 4189
Disdain, 2084-2087
d. and scorn ride sparkling, 2085
do not press with d., 2086
he pouted in a dull d., 288
is it possible d. should die, 2084
my dear lady D., 2084
sour-eyed d., 6924
trampling on thy d., 2087
Disease, 2088-2096
appliance which d. requires, 6492
before curing of d., 2094
d. of not listening, 2092
d. that must be cut away, 2089
d. that's in my flesh, 1806
fee bestow upon foul d., 5265
hang on him like a d., 622
like owner of foul d., 2090
make him by inch-meal a d., 1745
the d. is incurable, 5477
Diseased : we are all d., 2093
Diseases desperate grown, 2091
I'll bequeath you my d., 2096
rank d. grow near heart, 3911
rheumatic d. do abound, 4788
rotten d. of the south, 1747
subject to the same d., 3797
we do lance d., 2088
Disgrace is to be called boy, 1713
when in d. with fortune, 4328
Disgraced : I am d., 6003
Dish, 2097-2099
d. fit for the gods, 2099
d. for the gods, 2098
d. that I love, 2789
here's a d. I love not, 6671
to his Egyptian d. again, 2097
woman is d. for the gods, 7291
Dishclout : Romeo is d., 2979
Dishes : so many strange d., 7439

Dishonour, 2100-2103
bring burthen of d. home, 2102
d. in thine age, 2101
I have lived in such d., 2100
never did d. blur our name, 2103
Dismay : much much more d., 3457
Disorder is such as war, 2118
d. wounds where it should guard, 2119
fear framed d., 2119
most admired d., 2120
Displeasure, 2121-2127
everlasting d. of king, 2122
lest your d. enlarge, 2127
poor and private d., 2125
private d. against monarch, 3879
run into my lord's d., 2121
run to meet d. farther, 2126
smell of her strong d., 2846
unclean fishpond of d., 2123
Displeasures to ourselves unjust, 2124
Disposition, 2128-2134
d. would have come to truth, 7438
entertain a cheerful d., 3418
he is of a melancholy d., 2133
her d. addicted to melancholy, 2133
I fear your d., 2132
I know our country d. well, 7141
in a more coming-on d., 2128
lay goatish d. to a star, 6245
let this d. have scope, 2131
O well-divided d., 5772
of so blessed a d., 2134
Dispositions : put away these d., 2130
Disputation : that's a feeling d., 3919
Dissemble with my nature, 2136
Dissembled with outward show, 7330
Dissembler : arise, d., 2386
Dissemblers : all men d., 4514
Dissembling : scene of d., 2135
Dissension, 2137-2139
civil d. viperous worm, 2137
I feel such sharp d., 2139
on d. of a doit, 2921
this d. will break out, 2138
Distemper : heat of thy d., 5191
madness tameness to his d., 4455
Distemperatures : pale d., 4614
Distinction of place, 5656
lose d. in my joys, 3823
Distress : thorny point of d., 1357
Distribution undo excess, 2375
Distrust : breed d., 2141
so sick I d. you, 2140
Ditch in Egypt be grave, 1840
Ditties sung by queen, 3919
sing no more d., 2234
Ditty : many an English d., 5348
Dive into bottom of deep, 3537
Divided : must we be d., 5168
Divine : good d. follows own instructions, 7401
more needs she d. than physician, 4687
Divinity doth hedge a king, 3874
d. in odd numbers, 4423
d. of hell, 2035
d. that shapes our ends, 2142
hear him reason in d., 2143
Divorce, 2144-2147
d. between me and you, 2144
d. 'twixt son and sire, 3067

hateful d. of love, 1905
he counsels a d., 2147
I here d. myself from bed, 2146
long d. of steel falls, 229
Do that I shall be sorry for, 1931
if to do were easy, 7401
I'll do, and I'll do, 5782
know not what they do, 1928
O, what men dare do, 1941
that we would do we should do, 1926
this I will not do, 586
we will yet do well, 5796
what men may do, 1941
what you do betters what is done, 1951
Dobbin : more hair than D., 473
d.'s tail grows backward, 6410
Doctor : death will seize d., 4602
Doctors say no month to bleed, 1310
Doctrine of ill-doing, 881
Doe : unseasonable d., 859
who comes here, my d., 1954
Doers : talkers no good d., 7403
Dog, 2148-2162
as true a d. as ever fought, 2161
away, unpeaceable d., 2160
be damn'd, inexecrable d., 5483
circumcised d., 2156
d. in madness, 1205
d. is obeyed in office, 2153
d. that brings me food, 4745
d. to worry lambs, 7347
d. will have his day, 1112
farmer's d. bark at beggar, 2153
fly, like d., heels of ass, 2160
had been d. that howled, 6954
hold-fast is the only d., 5051
hope is a curtal d., 3571
I had rather be a d., 929
I wish thou wert a d., 4520
I'ld beat him like a d., 5470
like a black d., 765
live to say, d. is dead, 5678
mine enemy's d. though he bit me, 2154
no more pity than a d., 6271
not a word to throw at a d., 7378
not have stone to throw at d., 6268
rather hear d. bark at crow, 4296
showed me d. and bush, 4792
since I am d., beware fangs, 2155
sourest-natured d., 2162
staff quickly found to beat a d., 5460
thou call'dst me d., 2155
thus I would teach a d., 6451
trust d. that seems sleeping, 3095
truth is a d. must to kennel, 6774
when I ope lips, let no d. bark, 5112
why should d. have life, 2810
you call me cut-throat d., 6830
Dog-apes : encounter of d., 1469
Dog-hole : France is a d., 2891
Dog-weary : I am d., 7049
Dog's-leather : make d. of, 5992
Dogs : curs go by name of d., 4496
d. bark at me as I halt, 2157
d. easily won to fawn, 6905
d. spend their mouths, 2149
d. that are beat for barking, 2148
down, down, d., faitors, 1770
glutton's d. licked sores, 6064
knowing nought, like d., 5716

let slip d. of war, 1031
little d. bark at me, 2152
set d. to bay me, 6266
they said d. must eat, 5459
Doing : he will still be d., 1927
Doit : not give d. to beggar, 2339
on dissension of a d., 2921
Dole : happy man be his d., 4421
Dolour others have endured, 4744
Dolphin-chamber : my D., 4558
Dolphin-like : delights d., 256
Done that you be sorry for, 1931
I have d. the deed, 1933
if it were d. when 'tis d., 1932
what he bids be d., 5067
what's d. cannot be amended, 1935
what's d. cannot be undone, 1935
what's d. is d., 1935
what's to be d., 1936
wish things d. undone, 1930
Doom : crack of d., 4170
d. of destiny, 2005
Doomsday is near, 1854
his houses last till d., 3107
if she lives till d., 7089
then is d. near, 4964
Door : bar d. upon liberty, 2903
Doornail : dead as a d., 1857
Doors : clap to the d., 7019
d. open upon woman's wit, 7226
let d. be shut upon him, 2803
Dormouse valour, 6845
Dotage : I speak not like d., 138
lose myself in d., 2649
that scope d. gives it, 2131
Dotes in idolatry, 3686
d., yet doubts, 3779
Double-dealer : be a d., 2164
make thee a d., 2163
Double-dealing : that would be d., 2164
Doublet and hose courageous, 7292
I have a d. and hose, 1462
make thy d. of taffeta, 4698
wearing new d. before Easter, 5499
Doublets : no more d. than backs, 5531
Doubt, 2165-2169
d. that stars are fire, 4258
end one d. by death, 2166
I'll see before I d., 3779
modest d. beacon of wise, 2169
sag with d., 4688
to be in d., resolved, 3779
Doubting things go ill, 2165
Doubts by time clear'd, 2854
d. of my decay, 4992
littlest d. are fear, 4259
our d. are traitors, 2168
saucy d. and fears, 2167
Douglas : my name is D., 2171
O, D., hadst thou fought, 2171
that sprightly Scot, D., 2170
Dove pursues the griffin, 6190
d. trooping with crows, 522
d. will peck the estridge, 2943
mild as a d., 4311
roar as gently as d., 4187
seems he a d., 2628
valiant as wrathful d., 6839
who will not change raven for d., 5558
Dove-cote : like eagle in d., 2255

Doves peck in safeguard of brood, 7498
nimble-pinion'd d. draw love, 4323
simplicity of Venus' d., 6966
so d. peck the falcon, 1641
Dower, 2172-2174
I'll pay thy d., 2173
let her beauty be her d., 2172
mine honesty be my d., 3503
modesty, jewel in my d., 4759
thy truth be thy d., 2172
virtue and she her d., 2172
Dowlas, filthy d., 5906
Down : cygnet's d. is harsh, 3229
Down-feather : swan's d., 6656
Dowry : she is herself a d., 2174
Doxy over the dale, 1757
Drachmas : drop blood for d., 4762
Draff : eating d. and husks, 6064
still swine eats all the d., 6389
Dragon, 2175-2177
come not between d. and wrath, 2176
did ever d. keep so fair cave, 1917
of a d. and finless fish, 6421
Dragonish : cloud that's d., 1380
Dragons : death-like d., 2177
go great with d., 7349
night's swift d. cut clouds, 6237
you d. of the night, 2175
Dram : no d. of a scruple, 5825
Drawers : leash of d., 3643
Dread of something after death, 1847
Dream, 2178-2193
as a d. doth flatter, 3908
d. itself is but shadow, 2179
d. past wit of man, 2183
empty from d. of mercy, 2322
ever d. of such a thing, 2184
I did d. of money-bags, 2182
I do despise my d., 2513
if I do d., my wealth, 2191
if it be to d., let me sleep, 2192
my d. lengthened after life, 2186
new-risen from a d., 2189
rarest d. that sleep, 2185
short as any d., 6384
'tis still a d., 2178
to sleep, perchance to d., 1847
when I waked, I cried to d., 2190
Dreamer : he is a d., 3680
Dreaming : past size of d., 256
Dreams : bad d., 2179
d., children of idle brain, 2187
in sleep of death what d., 1847
my d. presage joyful news, 2188
night full of ghastly d., 4996
such stuff as d. are made on, 4147
thoughts are but d., 6565
which d. are ambition, 2179
wicked d. abuse sleep, 2181
Dregs of conscience, 1513
Drench : give horse a d., 3608
Drift, 2194-2197
be homely in thy d., 1494
by no d. of circumstance, 1344
I'll tell you my d., 2197
understand my d., 2196
we know your d., 2195
what is d. of compact, 2194
Drones, 2209-2211
d. hive not with me, 2209

d. rob bee of honey, 2211
d. suck not eagles' blood, 2210
purge land of d., 2211
Drop seeks another d., 7467
d. would prove a crocodile, 6468
Drops of women's rheum, 6455
liquid d. of tears, 6472
ruddy d. visit my heart, 7132
Dross : my love admits no d., 4341
Drown : double death to d. in ken of
shore, 2215
d. for love of guinea-hen, 2214
incontinently d. myself, 2214
what pain it was to d., 2216
Drowned, a death I abhor, 2213
d. with salt water, 2217
Drowning : no d. mark upon him, 3245
pox of d. thyself, 2214
Drowns for want of skill, 6387
Drink of Severn's flood, 4809
d. poured out of a cup, 5659
d. provoker of nose-painting, 2204
d. sooner than pray, 6756
d. that for me, 2207
d. till his brains turn, 2208
d. with harness on throats, 3129
hold thee that to d., 2643
I can d. with any tinker, 2202
I do not speak in d., 2511
I d. to joy of whole table, 7183
I will not d. with you, 2282
leave thy d. and whore, 604
thin d. doth over-cool blood, 2203
thin d. out of bottle, 5899
we'll teach you to d. deep, 2200
when we d. we die, 4915
Drinking, 2198-2208
d. deep, dyeing scarlet, 2202
heat my liver with d., 2198
made night light with d., 1815
they were red-hot with d., 6844
unhappy brains for d., 2205
Drudge : he's my d., 1699
Drum, 2218-2222
at chamber door I'll d., 2222
beat thou the d., 5276
follow thy d., 7007
let the d. strike, 2220
lover of d., 4369
no music in him but d., 4865
spirit-stirring d., 2533
start an echo with d., 2221
strike up the d., 1593
strike up the d. towards Athens, 2220
when you hear the d., 2665
Drummer, strike up, 2220
Drumming : I'll no more d., 2218
Drums demurely wake sleepers, 2219
then strike up d., 2220
your d. will cry out, 2221
Drunk : bid those d. to bed, 2226
do not think I am d., 2227
d. out of five sentences, 2225
d. with innocents' blood, 739
he's d. an hour agone, 2231
he's d. nightly, 2208
that hath made them d., 805
Drunkard : one d. loves another, 5892
tell me I am a d., 2228
Drunken : what's d. man like, 2230

Dry with rage and toil, 4225
Ducats: O, my d., 2232
Ducdame, ducdame, 2233
Duck with French nods, 2726
I can swim like a d., 6388
Duello he regards not, 1713
Dues: nature craves d., 7144
Dug: never palates the d., 1920
Dugs: kissing of cow's d., 4248
Duke: I made you a d., 1701
tyrant d. to brother, 6049
Dukedom: my library was d., 4088
Duller than weed on Lethe, 7055
Dulness of the fool, 2792
Dumb: taught dumb to sing, 2442
Dumps, 2234-2238
distress likes d., 2235
d. so dull and heavy, 2236
how now, in your d., 2237
step out of these dreary d., 2238
when doleful d. mind oppress, 4870
Duncan is in his grave, 1872
Dungeon: airless d., 6200
Dunghill for unguem, 4016
d. shall be my grave, 1673
thou hast it at d., 4016
Dunghills: buried in d., 3541
Dupped the chamber door, 6832
Durance: he is now in d., 69
Dust, 2239-2240
all must come to d., 2240
blows d. in others' eyes, 6874
compound me with d., 3109
d. and damn'd oblivion, 3527
d. and injury of age, 4332
d. below thy foot, 6725

d. on antique time, 1748
d. that did offend it, 2239
d. that is a little gilt, 5036
from d. of oblivion raked, 1361
make d. our paper, 1431
mean and mighty have one d., 5656
not worth d. wind blows, 7507
overmastered with valient d., 3665
Dutchman: as the D. says, 6690
Duty, 2241-2247
d. never wants his meed, 2247
d. shall have dread, 2243
every subject's d. is king's, 6300
fleet-wing'd d., 2246
I hold my d. as hand, 2241
I owe him little d., 2242
I perceive divided d., 2245
lay my d. on your hand, 3205
let haste commend your d., 3283
my d. pricks me on, 2244
such d. as subject owes prince, 3670
trimm'd in forms of d., 3943
Dwarf, 2248-2251
child, a silly d., 2248
follow him like a d., 2249
get you gone, you d., 2250
stirring d., 2251
Dwelling: goodly d. and a rich, 2254
Dwelling-house: soul's d., 890
Dwindle, peak and pine, 6023
Dye makes whitest black, 3739
Dyer: subdued like d.'s hand, 4920
Dying: fearing d. pays death, 2615
I am d., Egypt, d., 1838
no more d. then, 1899

E

Eagle, 2254-2260
e. hath not so fair an eye, 2979
e. suffers little birds, 2260
full-winged e., 574
I chose e., not puttock, 2254
if thou be e.'s bird, 2257
Jove's bird, Roman e., 2256
like e. in a dove-cote, 2255
lover's eyes gaze e. blind, 4402
pity that e. be mewed, 2259
with an e. inspired, 3743
Eagles: bated like e., 3613
e. gazed upon with every eye, 2258
wrens prey where e. dare not, 7530
Ear, 2261-2263
box o' the e., 2262
bruised heart pierced through e., 7441
cleave e. with speech, 63
e. of man hath not seen, 2183
e. quick of apprehension, 4990
eye interprets to the e., 5938
give every man thine e., 2261
his e. is stopp'd, 2263
honest words pierce e. of grief, 7432
I cannot scratch mine e., 5138
I have good e. in music, 4863
I will enchant thine e., 2079
in e. durst not stick rose, 2461
knavish speech sleeps in foolish e., 6163
like mildew'd e., 5272

lover's e. hears lowest sound, 4402
makest e. stranger to thoughts, 2914
mine e. can take no greater wound, 6430
mine e. is open, 3914
open e. of youth, 2263
she hangs upon e. of night, 522
shot through e. with love-song, 1892
tying e. to no tongue but own, 2805
Ear-wax: not so much brain as e., 898
Earing: our ills as our e., 7054
Earnest: your jest is e., 3786
Ears: aged ears play truant, 7233
by e. our hearts oft tainted, 3356
by the e., 2264
deafs e. with breath, 3264
e. more deaf than adders, 4343
glean broken e. after man, 4252
go shake your e., 5470
God give him e., 5234
grafted them in e., 7409
he hears with e., 2266
kiss thy fair large e., 1263
mad men have no e., 2266
men's e. grow to his tunes, 407
men's e. to counsel deaf, 2729
mine e. art stopt, 4963
o'er head and e., 3316
open your e., 5755
pitchers have e., 5299
she starves e. she feeds, 7142

stop e. against mermaid's song, 4653
stuffing e. with false reports, 5755
up to the e. in blood, 6995
warlike e. could never brook, 2267
we request your kindest e., 786
Earth, 2268-2274
behold, e. hath roots, 6984
canst work in e. so fast, 6369
dear e., I do salute thee, 3912
e. affords no joy to me, 1681
e. can have but e., 2274
e. could teem with tears, 6468
e., gape open wide, 2269
e. gapes, hell burns, 5678
e. had not hole to hide deed, 1869
e. hath bubbles, 2270
e. hath swallow'd hopes, 2273
e., sea, air too little, 4827
e. sings when he touches it, 3590
e. that kept world in awe, 1017
e. was feverous, 4982
face of whole dungy e., 3516
find out new heaven, new e., 4242
give him a little e., 149
glance from e. to heaven, 3705
lards lean e. as he walks, 6373
lay her i' the e., 2737
let e. be drunken with blood, 720
let e. hide thee, 5879
made happy e. thy hell, 2039
make base e. proud, 3958
make e. devour her brood, 6634
make e. my hell, 1209
mingle bloods in e., 2272
most peerless piece of e., 5434
no better than e. he lies upon, 942
oft e. with colic pinch'd, 4906
on e. where nothing lives but grief, 1430
our dungy e. feeds beast, 3910
shakes old beldame e., 4906
sinful e., 6145
the little O, the e., 256
this e. of majesty, 2324
this e. that bears thee dead, 3617
this goodly frame, the e., 2268
when e. is baked with frost, 1001
Earth-treading stars, 2620
Earthquake: din to make e., 2060
good woman born at e., 7287
Earthquakes: mountains removed with e., 2900
Ease: heart's e. kings neglect, 3880
of sufferance comes e., 6306
some come to take their e., 5334
take mine e. in inn, 2275
Eases: I'll seek for e., 2096
East, Juliet the sun, 6328
wander from e. to occident, 4567
Eastcheap: all lads in E., 1547
Easter: new doublet before E., 5499
Easy, 2276-2279
e. as cannon shoots, 2278
e. as lying, 5331
e. as set dogs on sheep, 2276
e. as thanks, 2279
Eat and drink as friends, 4024
e. and make good cheer, 2281
e. rest of his anatomy, 4212
e. under influence of star, 1151

e. when I have stomach, 1207
every man e. in safety, 2297
I earn what I e., 3979
I will e. and drink, 5313
I will not e. my word, 7380
I will not e. with you, 2282
to e. of habitation of devil, 2282
Eaten out of house and home, 2280
Eater of broken meats, 3941
Ebb and flow by the moon, 5438
e. and flow like the sea, 4781
in as low e. as foot, 4781
Ebony: black as e., 679
is e. like her, wood divine, 679
Echo: cave where E. lies, 2284
double like voice and e., 5756
E. replies as if chase, 2285
Echoes: he e. me, 2283
Eclipse of sun and moon, 3627
Eclipses portend no good, 6245
e. stain moon and sun, 1076
Ecstasy, 2286-2287
creation e. is cunning in, 2286
e. hath overborne her, 2287
lie in restless e., 1872
nor sense to e. so thrall'd, 4444
this is very e. of love, 4257
unmatch'd form blasted with e., 4681
Eden: this other E., 2324
Edward and Richard, 3140
God take King E., 7486
this prince is not an E., 5432
Edge of doom, 4333
e. of war, 6994
Edifice: I have lost my e., 4291
Eel-skin: thrust into e., 4489
Eel-skins: my arms e., 2461
Effect: cause of title e., 1142
e. defective comes by cause, 1142
e. of love in idleness, 4388
Effects: good e. from words, 7398
Egg, 2288-2289
as addle as an e., 5499
damned like ill-roasted e., 1602
esteem an addle e., 2288
not worth an e., 6735
steal e. out of cloister, 1197
think him a serpent's e., 5862
Eggs: as like as e., 4166
sucks her princely e., 5822
take e. for money, 2289
Eglamour, a gentleman, 2981
Eglantine out-sweetened, 2758
musk-roses and e., 2761
Egypt: I am dying, E., 1838
rail against first-born of E., 6016
Roman to great E. sends, 5221
Egyptian puppet shown in Rome, 6007
Elbow, 2290-2292
E. is your name, 2291
he's out at e., 2291
I am at thy e., 2292
one rubbed his e. thus, 6174
pluck him by the e., 2290
Elbow-room: my soul hath e., 6132
Eld: palsied e., 7582
Elder than thy looks, 3831
Judas hanged on an e., 3826
Elder-gun: shot out of e., 3879

Election : before we make e., 2295
I prophesy e. lights, 2294
popp'd in between e., 2293
Elegancy of poesy, 5349
Element shows to him, 3878
I am not of your e., 3247
Elements be kind to thee, 2528
e. of fire and water, 2700
e. so mixed in him, 5725
my other e. to baser life, 3707
Elephant hath joints, 2296
slow as the e., 1211
Elephants betrayed with holes, 2723
Elf-locks : bakes e. in hairs, 4435
Elf-skin : you e., 1456
Elizabeth, mighty princess, 2297
Elm : thou art e., I vine, 6913
Eloquence with sighs mixed, 5116
his e. parcel of reckoning, 7421
more e. in sugar touch, 4195
saucy and audacious e., 5955
Eloquent in my behalf, 6423
e. and full of invention, 2953
Elsinore : in E., 6574
Elves, list your names, 2475
Elysium : my brother is in E., 944
within circle is E., 1679
Embarquements of all fury, 3296
Embassage : do e. to Pigmies, 5875
Ember-eves and holy-ales, 6095
Emperor : lie by e.'s side, 7327
thou'rt an e., Cæsar, 1035
your e. continues a Jove, 848
Empery : fasten'd to e., 3986
Employment : hand of little e., 3211
is not there e., 589
Empty-hearted : nor are they e., 3344
Emulation hath thousand sons, 2299
gory e., 2300
out of teeth of e., 6938
pale and bloodless e., 2298
Enacts and counsels of heart, 764
Encounter of our wits, 7257
e. of two dog-apes, 1469
Encounters of lascivious men, 3191
End, 2301-2312
and there an e., 2312
e. crowns all, 2305
e. is the renown, 2301
e. of life cancels all bands, 4125
e. of war is uncertain, 6992
e. purposed by gods, 2553
e. unknown to beginning, 593
e. where he was to begin, 594
harm done to great good e., 2308
he made a good e., 2303
he makes a swan-like e., 4861
heaven has an e. in all, 3398
here is my journey's e., 3809
I'll e. where I begin, 590
know e. of day's business, 2307
let e. try the man, 2304
let this e. where it begun, 599
make e. most sweet, 2309
make e. of which I begun, 591
orderly to e. where I begun, 595
respect your e., 2302
there's an e., 6941
time will one day e. it, 2305
where I begin there e., 596

you e. ere you begin, 600
you may see the e., 592
End-all : be-all and e., 1932
Endeavour : setting e. in motion, 5068
Ender : my origin and e., 597
Ending : my e. is despair, 2311
Endowments greater than riches, 6942
Ends : all's well that e. well, 2301
delays have dangerous e., 1962
divinity that shapes our e., 2142
let all thy e. be thy country's, 2306
more are men's e. marked, 6673
neglecting worldly e., 4695
odd e. stolen from holy writ, 2032
where she e. she doth begin, 601
Endymion : moon sleeps with E., 4785
Enemies bay'd about with e., 6230
he shall have skins of e., 5992
left naked to mine e., 3027
man to love his e., 2925
my weak-hearted e., 2314
our e. have beat us, 7475
thou madest e. shake, 6062
you have many e., 2321
your father's e., 2318
Enemy, 2315-2323
be able for thine e., 2315
cunning e., to catch saint, 5787
e. comes on in gallant show, 446
flatter e. in bower, 2316
follow e. in fiery gulf, 2316
held a rancorous e., 2726
he's an e. to mankind, 2046
I have been smooth with e., 1199
I must love a loathed e., 4377
my nearest and dearest e., 2317
no e. but winter, 201
put e. into mouths, 7184
seasons him his e., 2922
thing devised by the e., 2323
to myself become an e., 1997
weigh e. more mighty, 2319
what e. commends fame blows, 5397
Enfeoffed to popularity, 3876
Engine of her thoughts, 673
hand that made the e., 5539
he moves like an e., 6973
Enginer hoist with own petar, 5634
Engines, whose rude throats, 2533
England, 2324-2339
eagle E. being in prey, 5822
E. all Olivers bred, 2332
E. bound with triumphant sea, 2324
E. breeds valiant creatures, 2330
E. hath made conquest of itself, 2324
E. hedged in with main, 2334
E. is safe, if true, 2333
E. keep my bones, 3401
E. model to greatness, 2328
E. most potent in potting, 2338
E. never at foot of conqueror, 2337
E.'s ground, farewell, 2325
E.'s lawful earth, 2995
from E. add thus much, 2335
God for E., 3139
if E. do rest but true, 2337
mad and sent into E., 2326
never merry world in E., 2971
nor can E. look on double reign, 6242
sleeping E. watched, 2965

swear truth out of E., 6391
this realm, this E., 2324
were I in E. now, 2339
wish not a man from E., 3540
your dear mother, E., 2336
English : abusing of king's E., 2340
drive E. forth of France, 3804
E. not Turkish court, 1605
famish'd E., like ghosts, 2331
fly, noble E., 5587
I can speak E. as well as you, 5348
low-rated E., 2895
make fritters of E., 2341
my native E. I must forego, 3998
Englishman : is E. so expert, 2206
true-born E., 2325
Enjoyed no sooner but despised, 4431
Enmity : covert e. wounds, 5755
e. under smile of safety, 5755
friends break out to e., 2921
wage against e. of air, 4929
Enobarbus did repent, 4779
Enough : damn'd that cries e., 2343
each man should have e., 2375
e. I may call her mine, 4703
e. with over-measure, 2342
he hath e., 5461
pauca, that's e., 2343
Ensign : beauty's e., 1894
e. of Christian cross, 1318
Enskyed and sainted, 6921
Entail him and his heirs, 5859
Enterprise that hath stomach, 6262
Enterprises of pith and moment, 1847
Entertainment, 2344-2346
do not dull palm with e., 2902
e. my bosom likes not, 5142
I spy e. in her, 4289
if love or gold can buy e., 2344
let us devise some e., 2345
some e. of time, 2345
strain his e., 2346
Entrails were hairs, 3590
Entrance of this soil, 6994
Entreatments at higher rate, 4462
Envy, 2347-2350
advanced beyond pale e., 2350
here no e. dwells, 1181
keenness of thy sharp e., 6137
lean-faced e. in her cave, 1737
men that make e. nourishment, 2349
of coarse metal moulded, e. 2348
thou damnable box of e., 1747
when e. breeds division, 2347
Epicurean cooks, 1541
E. rascal, 5551
Epilogue : good play needs no e., 5328
it is e. of discourse, 5792
Epitaph : waxen e., 3483
Epitaphs : let's talk of e., 1431
Epithets of war, 1347
Equinox : vice to virtue e., 6881
Equity is exiled, 6935
there's no e. stirring, 1636
Equivocation will undo us, 6164
Equivocator : here's an e., 4111
Ercles : I could play E., 55
this is E. vein, 6809
Erebus : dark as E., 4862
not E. were dim enough, 1520

with E. and tortures vile, 1770
Erection : rate cost of e., 971
Eringoes : hail e., 1954
Eros : valiant E., 5005
Errand : go on slightest e., 5875
sleeveless e., 2350½
Errands : sent on e., 4493
Error of eye directs mind, 7338
hateful e., melancholy's child, 2351
if this be e. upon me proved, 4333
it is e. of the moon, 4790
many an e. will rush in, 5408
mountainous e. heapt, 1748
O e., soon conceived, 2351
what e. but some sober brow, 5603
Errors by opinion bred, 6628
e. of the blood, 5090
smother'd in e., 1473
Eruption : bodes strange e., 5102
Eruptions : break forth in e., 4906
Escapes of wit, 5317
Eschewed : what cannot be e., 2313
Esperance : O, e., 3589
things stand still in e., 7503
Essence : his glassy e., 4498
Estate : in preposterous e., 4424
though my e. be fallen, 5623
wish e. of world undone, 6323
Estridge : dove will peck e., 2943
Estridges : plumed like e., 3613
Eternity, 2352-2354
e. was in our lips, 2352
he wants nothing but e., 2354
passing through nature to e., 1846
time's progress to e., 6639
who sells e. to get a toy, 4727
Ethiope words blacker, 7296
Juno but an E. were, 5964
rich jewel in E.'s ear, 522
Eunuch, 2355-2358
her e. and her guard, 6985
no pleasure in aught e. has, 2356
voice of unpaved e., 2358
woman with e. play'd, 2357
Eunuchs : to make e. of, 2355
Europa : bull for thy E., 3811
E. will rejoice at thee, 974
Evasion of whore-master man, 6245
Eve : child of grandmother E., 7318
he curses E.'s daughters, 1810
witty piece of E.'s flesh, 7255
Even or odd, 5077
give e. or give none, 5078
that's the e. of it, 2514
you are odd, and he e., 5078
Evened with him, 5649
Evening : how still the e. is, 2360
made e. at noontide, 2359
this e. must I leave, 7305
Events never fall out good, 2362
high e. strike those, 2361
many e. in womb of time, 6626
strange e. are welcome, 1419
Ever : for e. and a day, 4554
Everlasting fix'd canon, 5855
Evidence : give true e., 2363
there action to give e., 5084
where are the e., 2365
Evil, 2366-2371
beauteous e. empty trunks, 6946

e. of my conception, 5403
e. that men do live after them, 1033
e. to him who thinks e., 2371
forget your e., forgive self, 3414
no e. lost is wail'd, 2367
unfold e. here wrapp'd up, 2370
unlook'd-for e., 6943
Evil-eyed : find me e., 5998
Evils : by night e. free, 1520
e. laid to charge of women, 7294
e. that take leave, 2368
e. to darken his goodness, 2584
oppress'd with two weak e., 2366
Ewe : black ram is tupping e., 3377
e. will not hear her lamb, 1280
made e. bleat for lamb, 3798
Ewes and rams together, 5958
milk my e. and weep, 2193
my e. breed not, 5538
see my e. graze, 3979
Example : by e. made coward, 2372
lose present pains upon e., 5134
so hot speed doth want e., 2374
things done without e., 1929
Excellence : constant in wondrous e., 4331
e. angels love men with, 2147
she a fair divided e., 4530
Excellencies : crammed with e., 1215
Excess : distribution undo e., 2375
profit of e. is surfeit, 2376
wasteful and ridiculous e., 2375
Exchange without boot, 835
Exchequer : rob me the e., 2377
thanks, e. of the poor, 6511
you have e. of words, 2379
Exchequers : they shall be e., 2377
Excrement : composture from e., 6520
Excuse, 2380-2383
cover with e., 2382
e. that thou dost make, 2383
e. what cannot be amended, 2380
never e., 2381
speech be spoke for e., 6185
teach us some fair e., 1490
this admits no e., 594
you patch'd up your e., 5489
your play needs no e., 2381
Execution : do e. on my flesh, 2753
Executioner first begs pardon, 2384
I will not be e., 2386
think'st thou I am e., 2385
Executions : cease these e., 1737
Executors : choose e., 1431
their e., knavish crows, 1672
Exercise : dare to gentle e., 1167
starved for want of e., 4827
Exile hath more terror, 416
Exits : they have their e., 7466
Expectancy of fair state, 4681
Expectation fainted, 2388
e. whirls me round, 2391
he hath bettered e. 2390
mock e. of the world, 2389
oft e. fails, 2387
opens eyes of e., 5454
Expedition of my love, 4381
fiery e. be my wing, 1964
have I e. of thought, 6547
Expense of spirit, 4431

Experience, 2392-2397
e. be a jewel, 2395
e. by industry achieved, 2396
e. disprovest report, 2393
home where small e. grows, 7176
how hast thou purchased e., 2394
I have gained my e., 2392
years young, e. old, 2397
your e. makes you sad, 2392
Exploit : close e. of death, 930
Exploits : ripe for e., 7560
Exposition hath been sound, 3830
e. of sleep upon me, 6031
Expositor : conceit's e., 7233
Expostulate : I'll not e., 5358
Exsufflicate surprises, 3779
Extempore, from mother-wit, 7250
you may do it e., 4187
Extenuate : nothing e., 1208
Exterior nor inward man, 1188
Extremes : break not into e., 2400
e. of hot and cold, 5772
e. will not feed selves, 2398
grow into e. 2399
Extremity, 2401-2402
e. of both ends, 2402
e. of griefs make men mad, 3172
e., trier of spirits, 2401
in e. of great and little, 3422
smiling e. out of act, 5201
Eyas-musket : how now, e., 5710
Eyases : little e., 1286
Eye, 2403-2449
all places e. of heaven visits, 7214
auspicious and dropping e., 3816
bear welcome in your e., 7080
bend your e. on vacancy, 2410
blue e. and sunken, 4249
by e. of Cynthia she vow'd, 4216
dishonour not your e., 3847
downward e. looketh for grave, 775
every e. in forest looks, 6730
e. interprets to the ear, 5938
e. like Mars to threaten, 5272
e. of childhood fears painted devil, 1288
e. of heaven is out, 4994
e. of man hath not heard, 2183
e. sees not itself, 2419
e. whose bend doth awe world, 4196
friendly e. never see faults, 2908
full e. will wax hollow, 7361
have you not a moist e., 7578
he squints the e., 2661
heavenly rhetoric of e., 5662
her e. discourses, 2427
his e. begets occasion for wit, 7233
his e. being big with tears, 5167
his e. did heal it up, 2403
his e. is ambitious, 1206
how can love's e. be true, 2444
I have a good e., uncle, 2433
in her e. I find wonder, 2420
in my mind's e., Horatio, 4486
inviting e., right modest, 2434
let every e. negotiate for self, 2931
let thine e. look like friend, 1846
looking with lack-lustre e., 2793
looks with threatening e., 2867
mine e. hath play'd painter, 2441
more peril in thine e., 2438

my e. is too quick, 2417
not learning more than e. doth teach, 4839
nothing situate under heaven's e., 4483
one e. thou hast, 2414
pity dwells not in this e., 5308
poet's e. in frenzy rolling, 3705
present e. praises present, 5036
scarf up tender e. of day, 4981
searching e. of heaven, 6325
sorrow's e., glazed, 3165
stabbed with wench's black e., 1892
still-soliciting e., 2421
stop e. of Helen's needle, 7252
study how to please e., 4153
thine e. hath chose dame, 1572
things in motion catch e., 2447
to what shall I compare e., 2411
too hot e. of heaven shines, 6316
unthread e. of rebellion, 5587
what an e. she has, 2434
wonder in a mortal e., 2427
Eyeballs in vaulty brows, 1868
upon thy e., tyranny, 2416
your bugle e., 945
Eye-beams when their rays, 2426
Eyebrow: ballad to mistress' e., 7466
Eyebrows: what colour your e., 951
Eye-drops: wash'd knife with e., 6799
Eyelids will no longer wag, 2673
no more weigh e. down, 6019
on my e. conjecture hang, 2532
on your e. god of sleep, 3417
Eyes: all e. blind, 5034
all e. else dead coals, 2431
asleep with e. wide open, 5622
best use of e., 2408
close his e., 4605
e., look your last, 1895
e., that are softest things, 2404
fools' e. drop tears, 4677
from her e. fair messages, 2429
from women's e. this doctrine, 2428
get thee glass e., 5365
had I as many e. as wounds, 1030
hath noble lustre in e., 2412
have rich e., poor hands, 2392
he has e. of youth, 6039
her e. as jewel-like, 7142
her e. grey as glass, 2432
her e. stream bright, 2437
his e. blab heart's malice, 672
his e. green as leeks, 2432
his e. were set at eight, 2231
I will be buried in thy e., 3353
if our e. had authority, 6523
if thou hast e. to see, 1913
lend me ten thousand e., 6477
look with thine e., 2423

make e. blind with tears, 6121
men's e. made to look, 2439
millions of false e. stuck, 5317
mine e. are full of tears, 6471
mine e. are grey, bright, 2432
mine e. are turn'd to fire, 4054
mine e. do itch, 2435
mine e. hurt thee not, 2404
mine e. tell tales of me, 6478
mine e. were not in fault, 498
mortal e. cannot endure devil, 2039
my e. can look as swift, 4748
my mistress' e. nothing like sun, 4749
no e. in your head, 2423
one whose e. drop tears, 1208
opens e. of expectations, 5454
our e. are sometimes blind, 2407
outstare sternest e., 2053
pale to see thine e. so red, 3347
pitch-balls for e., 6985
play woman with mine e., 7320
say e. are murderers, 2404
scarce hath e. treasure, 4737
seal up ship-boy's e., 6019
seel father's e. close, 1914
spurn thine e. like balls, 1733
their e. purging thick amber, 143
there is no force in e., 2404
these e. now are dimm'd, 2418
these e. wax dim, 2415
they have changed e., 2446
thine e. are wounding, 2416
thine e. have added feathers, 2442
those e. have drawn tears, 2436
those e. the break of day, 3920
those holes where e., 2216
thou dost infect my e., 2436
thou hast hazel e., 5499
through hollow e. of death, 4144
thy e. are set in thy head, 5767
thy e. start from spheres, 6417
to hear with e., 4327
turn your e. toward napes, 5416
turn'st e. into my soul, 2409
use e. for water-pots, 2424
what e. hath love put, 2444
whither do you follow e., 1972
will you put out mine e., 3759
wise men have no e., 2266
with rainy e. write sorrow, 1431
your e. are lode-stars, 2431
your e. in heavy case, 2423
your e., where I o'erlook, 5575
Eyesight: dearer than e., 4271
treasure of e. lost, 5939
Eyesore: be e. in my coat, 2450
e. to our festival, 2451

F

Fable: but that's a f., 2037
Fabric of this vision, 5639
Face, 2452-2474
can f. of brass hold out, 5229
compare her f. with some, 6367
do thou amend thy f., 2455.
f. not me, 2472
f. not worth sunburning, 2458

f. of whole dungy earth, 3516
f. without a heart, 2564
fair f. will wither, 7361
frame f. to all occasions, 1681
from f. to foot the blood, 705
God has given you one f., 5135
he hath but a wee f., 474
hid with flowering f., 1917

his f. is a f.-royal, 466
his f. is all bubukles, 2457
his f. subdued to shame, 5886
his f. was as the heavens, 256
his f. worst thing about him, 2467
I never beheld that f., 2471
in thy f. map of honour, 2459
let his f. steel thy heart, 870
look him in the f., 5066
look in the lady's f., 2420
mind's construction in f., 2464
ne'er look you in f., 3134
never fair woman has true f., 2453
never look me in f., 1336
never look upon thy f. again, 1744
O that f. were not full of O's, 5042
paint your f., 5016
sad f., reverend carriage, 5983
sell your f. for five pence, 2461
she has a good f., 5487
show sunshine of your f., 6339
smile his f. into lines, 6047
tartness of f. sours grapes, 2454
that f. I remember well, 2474
thy f. bears a command, 269
trick of Cœur-de-lion's f., 5675
true f., good conscience, 1504
was this a f. to be opposed, 2463
was this f. that faced follies, 2468
was this fair f. the cause, 7287
we never saw your f., 5658
with thine angel's f., 3280
woman's f. with Nature's own hand
    painted, 2470
you have a February f., 974
your f. is as a book, 2465
your f. is valanced, 460
Faced : neither f. nor braved, 2472
Faces : all men's f. true, 2453
bid them wash their f., 1362
f. it out, 4208
I have seen better f., 2462
make f. vizards to hearts, 2466
no f. truer than so washed, 6467
say they have angels' f., 2731
women's f., faults' books, 4532
ye have angels' f., 2460
Faction : leave f. of fools, 5686
Faculty : infinite in f., 4487
Fair : as f. as day, 509
call you me f., 512
ever f. from f. declines, 6316
ever f., never proud, 514
f., chaste, unexpressive she, 6730
f. is foul, foul is f., 6573
f. is my love, 4311
f. she scarce makes honest, 494
f. without f. within, 2712
I have sworn thee f., 532
if she be f. and wise, 7245
passing f., 520
so lovely f., so sweet, 7061
that thou art f. infallible, 508
thou art f., dear boy, 505
where f. is not, praise cannot mend, 507
Fair-spoken and persuading, 1204
Fairer than tongue can name, 509
one f. than my love, 521
Fairies, black, grey, 2475
from f. guard me, 3048

Fairy : night-tripping f., 6081
Faith, 2479-2482
better none than plural f., 2482
corrupters of my f., 3462
few words to fair f., 7450
he wears f. as fashion of his hat, 2481
made of f. and service, 4254
makest me waver in my f., 5483
no f., no honesty in men, 4514
no tricks in simple f., 2480
O where is f., 2479
play fast and loose with f., 2543
welcome home discarded f., 5587
you would break f. and troth, 5146
Faithful : day serves not light more f., 2659
Faithfulness and courage, 2658
Faiths are wafer-cakes, 5051
Faitors : down, f., 1770
Falchion : his purple f. painted, 2483
murderous f. smoking, 2485
my good biting f., 2484
Falcon as the tercel, 2488
f., towering in pride, 2486
my f. now is sharp, 2487
Falconer : O for f.'s voice, 6956
Fall, 2489-2495
f. and bruise to death, 2494
f. like bright exhalation, 2490
if he f. in, good night, 825
if they f., dash to pieces, 3128
if you f., there's an end, 1672
O, what a f. was there, 1033
thou wilt f. backward, 2495
we will f. for it, 2493
Falling : cruelty to load f. man, 2491
fear's as bad as f., 1603
press not f. man too far, 2491
Falling-off : what a f., 5861
Falls : he f. as I do, 2492
some f. are means the happier, 2489
when he f., he f. like Lucifer, 5426
False as air, water, wind, 2506
f. as Cressid, 2506
f. as dicers' oaths, 2499
f. as o'er-dyed blacks, 2507
f. as stairs of sand, 4210
f. face must hide f. heart, 2500
hide the f. seems true, 5574
if she be f. or swerve, 2506
if she be f., then, 2501
if she play'd f., fault hers, 7133
never say I was f. of heart, 2505
not play f., yet wrongly win, 4911
she was f. as water, 2503
thou art f. as hell, 2502
thou canst not be f. to any man, 6758
Falser than vows made in wine, 2498
Falsehood, 2496-2497
bait of f. takes carp of truth, 2496
f. f. cures, 3716
f. worse in kings, 4092
let memory upbraid my f., 2506
unmask f., bring truth to light, 6628
what goodly outside f. hath, 2497
Falseness cannot come from thee, 2504
Falstaff, 2508-2515
F. he is dead, 2515
F. sweats to death, 6373
F. white-bearded Satan, 2512
F. will learn humour of age, 6577

I remember his name is F., 2511
if I be not Jack F., 2509
Sir John [F.] sack and sugar, 5611
there is virtue in that F., 2511
what, a coward, Sir John [F.], 1635
Fame, 2516-2520
f. cannot better be held, 2516
f. in time canonize us, 3438
f. may cry you loud, 3526
he lives in f., 1036
his f. folds in this orb, 2517
know nought but f., 6291
let f., that all hunt, 2518
my f. is shrewdly gored, 5628
sword and shield win f., 6394
Familiar : be thou f., 2521
f. as his garter, 5263
f. as household words, 3540
we have been f., 2833
Familiarity : upon f. contempt, 2522
Famine is in thy cheeks, 2524
f. makes nature valiant, 2523
he was very genius of f., 4489
Famous by their birth, 2324
Fan : brain him with f., 5712
f. of your fair sword, 5337
f. to cool gipsy's lust, 4426
Fancies : our f. more giddy, 3673
rack thee in their f., 5317
thick-coming f., 4689
Fancy, 2525-2526
f. dies in cradle, 2526
let f. my sense in Lethe steep, 2192
see f. outwork nature, 1977
sweet and bitter f., 2525
tell me where is f. bred, 2562
Fancy-free : in maiden meditation f., 4607
Fang of winter's wind, 4117
Fantasies which care draws, 6022
Fantastical : are ye f., 275
it alone is high f., 4343
Fantasticoes : pox of f., 2527
Fantasy : begot of f., 2187
fie on sinful f., 4428
to be all made of f., 4254
Fardels : who would f. bear, 1847
Fardingales : ruffs, cuffs, f., 5638
Farm : keep f. and carters, 2537
Farmer that hanged himself, 2538
Farewell, 2528-2536
f. All-hallown summer, 2529
f. for all and ever, 2534
f. goes out sighing, 7082
f. honest soldier, 6063
f. my dearest sister, 2528
f. the plumed troop, 2533
f. the tranquil mind, 2533
f. thou art too dear, 2536
f. thou latter spring, 2529
f. till soon, 2535
f. till we meet again, 2531
f. to all my greatness, 2492
for ever, f., Cassius, 2530
most foul, most fair, f., 2532
our everlasting f. take, 2530
sweets to the sweet, f. 6375
Farewells : as many f. as stars, 6643
Fartuous modest wife, 7137
Fashion, 2539-2542
carving f. of new doublet, 2540

do it after proud Roman f., 1839
f. is the f., 2541
f. of world to avoid cost, 1561
f. of your garments, 2539
f. wears out more apparel, 2541
glass of f., mould of form, 4681
hang quite out of f., 5233
I will put the f. on, 6103
in world's new f. planted, 6707
let's hear in what f., 5982
not f. for maids to kiss, 1751
not for f. of times, 5872
this passion is my f., 5170
what a deformed thief f. is, 6531
wit would be out of f., 7253
Fashion-mongers, 2527
Fashions : old f. please best, 2542
study f. to adorn body, 3010
Fast : at f. and loose, 1220
but a three years' f., 2546
confined to f. in fires, 6196
f. bind, f. find, 5462
I will f., being loose, 2544
now can I break my f., 4353
play f. and loose, 2543
thou shalt f. for offences, 2547
Fastolfe play'd coward, 1639
Fasts : broke f. today, 2545
punish'd with bitter f., 4353
Fat as butter, 2579
he's f., scant of breath, 2578
if f. is to be hated, 2512
let me have men that are f., 2581
make us f. as tame things, 5393
melt me out of my f., 1650
one is f. and grows old, 4537
Fate, 2548-2557
do not please sharp f., 2548
f. held his hand, 1702
f. o'er-rules one man, 5058
f., take not away hand, 2555
I am mistress of my f., 2557
I'll take a bond of f., 6348
my f. cries out, 2549
our f. hid in auger-hole, 2554
read the book of f., 2550
'tis but the f. of place, 5315
who can control his f., 2556
Fates : according to F., 3403
f., know your pleasures, 1864
make and mar foolish F., 4479
men are masters of f., 2552
what f. impose, men abide, 2551
wills and f. contrary run, 7152
Father, 2558-2577
comes in my f., 2558
decrepit f. takes delight, 1433
f. and mother man and wife, 4529
f. at nuptial of his son, 2577
f. gracious aged man, 1808
f. to so blest a son, 6081
fathom five my f. lies, 2576
happy to be f. unto sons, 2568
he took my f. grossly, 2562
her f. loved me, 4305
his f. had never a house, 661
his f. loves him not, 5354
his f., so his mother says, 2575
I am thy f.'s spirit, 6196
I had it from my f., 6435

I'll be f. and brother, 2565
loyal f. of treacherous son, 2574
make thee f. of idle dreams, 5317
methinks I see my f., 4486
my f. was no traitor, 6721
my true-begotten f., 2570
no more like my f. than I to Hercules, 4556
our right valiant f., 2567
rude son strike f. dead, 6290
seek for thy f. in dust, 2559
seel f.'s eyes close as oak, 1914
she did deceive her f., 1914
she did print your f. off, 4818
she has deceived her f., 1913
sins of f. laid upon children, 5968
so rare a wonder'd f., 5148
surfeit f. of much fast, 6353
thou hast thy f. much offended, 2563
was my f. a traitor, 6726
was your f. dear to you, 2564
who should succeed f. but son, 6085
who would be a f., 2573
wise f. knows own child, 2571
your f. got husbands, 3666
your f. lost a f., 2561
your f. should be as a god, 2572
Fathered husbanded, 7312
Fathers that bear bags, 2569
f. that wear rags, 2569
f. trust not daughters, 1813
foolish over-careful f., 6084
Fathom five my father lies, 2576
Fathom-line touch ground, 3537
Fatness of these pursy times, 6879
Fault, 2582-2600
condemn f. and not actor, 2591
every f. condemn'd ere done, 2591
every f. seeming monstrous, 7294
every man has his f., 2595
excusing f. makes f. worse, 2588
f. against the dead, 2561
f. done in form of beast, 3811
f. is not in our stars, 2587
f. on hazards of husbands, 7133
f. unknown is thought unacted, 2586
flint and hardness of my f., 4779
headstrong potent f. it is, 2600
his worst f. prayer, 2595
make her f. husband's occasion, 7295
nobody but has his f., 2595
pattern'd by thy f., 5973
some condemned for a f., 5965
some say thy f. is youth, 2599
something reproves my f., 2600
'tis a f. to heaven, 2561
you must amend this f., 4542
Faults: abstract of all f., 2584
all f. are woman's, 7301
all men make f., 2598
best men moulded out of f., 2594
call f. of fools folly, 2776
chide him for f., 1203
f. lie open to the laws, 2491
f. that are rich are fair, 2596
from f. or f. from seeming, 2592
give us f. to make us men, 2585
her f. will ne'er be known, 2590
his f. as spots of heaven, 2584
his f. lie gently on him, 1862

his f. set in note-book, 2908
I do not like your f., 2908
in our f. by lies we flatter'd be, 4335
kills for f. of own liking, 2593
little f. not wink'd at, 1653
men's f. seldom to selves appear, 2597
petty f. to f. unknown, 2586
rash f. make trivial price, 2582
taunt my f. with license, 2583
teeth and forehead of f., 5084
thou makest f. graces, 2599
vile ill-favoured f., 2596
whip own f. in other men, 2593
whip cover f., shame derides, 2589
Favour to the youth, 6845
sickness is catching, O were f. so, 5927
to this f. she must come, 7549
Favourite: great man down, f. flies, 2922
Favourites made proud by princes, 3524
Favours: cloy'd with gracious f., 558
f. that keep within, 1611
fly f. of so good a king, 864
he that depends upon f., 4828
neither beg nor fear f., 6622
rhyme selves into ladies' f., 5672
wretched to hang on princes' f., 5426
Fawn: more you beat, I f., 6151
Fawning: thrift may follow f., 2719
Fear, 2601-2618
beside themselves with f., 2607
blind f. that reason leads, 2617
distill'd to jelly with f., 2601
extreme f. can neither fight, 2614
f. and be slain, 2615
f. doth teach divination, 2618
f. frames disorder, 2119
f. is as bad as falling, 1603
f. oppresseth strength, 2615
frighted out of f., 2943
leaving f. of God on left, 3548
let f. keep with mean-born men, 2605
not f. where most mistrust, 4365
of passions f. accursed, 2604
over-red thy f., 2612
pale with agued f., 1734
pale-faced f., 2605
part of men to f., 3049
possess them not with f., 3030
put fetters upon this f., 2650
submit selves to unknown f., 4714
surprised with uncouth f., 2616
tell pale-hearted f. it lies, 2610
Fears by pale white shown, 2590
f. he would not know, 6357
f. make devils of cherubins, 2617
forgot the taste of f., 2613
little f. great, 4259
more f. than women have, 5426
our f. make us traitors, 2611
present f. less than imaginings, 2609
sick and capable of f., 2608
Feast, 2619-2623
beginning of a f., 2619
f. and banquet in streets, 612
gives f., takes stomach, 2863
great f. of languages, 7431
hold an old accustomed f., 2620
small cheer, great welcome makes a merry f., 7076
this day is f. of Crispian, 3540

we'll f. until our stars, 6247
what f. is toward, 1853
Feast-won, fast-lost, 5391
Feasts are too proud, 2623
  therefore are f. so solemn, 2622
Feather, 2624-2633
  best f. of our wing, 2625
  birds of self-same f., 650
  blow this f. from my face, 2629
  brush'd with raven's f., 1745
  every f. starts you, 2624
  every f. sticks in own wing, 2632
  f. of lead, 4376
  f. will turn the scale, 2631
  I am f. for each wind, 2633
  I am not of that f., 2916
  not a f. in our host, 2627
  of their f. many more birds, 649
  was ever f. so lightly blown, 4837
Feathers: added f. to wing, 2442
  his f. are but borrowed, 2628
  set f. to thy heels, 3285
  what plume of f. is he, 2630
Feats: do all fell f. enlink'd, 6998
  f. of broil and battle, 6181
Fed: highly f. and lowly taught, 920
Fee bestow upon disease, 5265
Fee-simple: entering f., 4226
  f. of the tetter, 1747
  have him not in f., 6987
Feeble: most forcible F., 6839
  not enough to help f. up, 3445
Feed: bring us where we may f., 2344
  those that f. grow full, 7345
  we shall f. like oxen, 6716
Feeder of my riots, 2513
Feeding food doth choke, 2787
Feeling: love's f. is more soft, 4281
  no f. of his business, 1751
Fees: supple knees man's f., 3959
Feet: blessed f. nailed on cross, 1316
  fall his princely f. before, 4186
  his f. were cold as stone, 2515
  I look towards his f., 2037
  more f. than verses bear, 6862
  sometime more f. than shoes, 5531
  stairs kiss his f., 6376
  subjects' f. trample on head, 3902
Feigning called compliment, 1472
Felicity: absent thee from f., 1133
Fell of hair would rouse, 2613
Fellow, 2634-2644
  barren-spirited f., 2639
  each takes f. for officer, 6526
  f. damn'd in a fair wife, 7140
  f. of good respect, 3545
  f. of no mark or likelihood, 2636
  f. of infinite jest, 7549
  f. of uncoined constancy, 7361
  f. that hath had losses, 4236
  f. that will take rewards, 3206
  f. with best king, 2638
  French song, fiddle no f., 6093
  he was a wise f., 3895
  honest f. enough, 898
  honest willing kind f., 6487
  hook-nosed f. of Rome, 1039
  I am a woodland f., 2018
  most active f. in Europe, 618
  paltry f., milksop, 2641

snipt-taffeta f., 2635
such a f. not for court, 1601
superficial, ignorant f., 2640
tall f. of thy hands, 2644
that mad f. of the north, 3609
thou art a good f., 2644
to be your f. deny me, 3672
what blunt f. is this, 5748
Fellows: learned, authentic f., 2634
  nature framed strange f., 4916
  one of those f. that claps sword, 4942
  there be good f. in world, 2642
  these f. of infinite tongue, 7361
Fellowship, 2645-2648
  all titles of good f., 2647
  fears f. to die with us, 3540
  f. in woe doth woe assuage, 7275
  great men's f., 2645
  half-faced f., 2646
  soul of sound good f., 2648
  sour woe delights in f., 7275
  sweet f. of shame, 5892
  when bearing hath f., 6309
Female: a f., or woman, 7318
  son of f. shadow of male, 6083
Females: men masters to f., 4483
Fence with his shadow, 4500
  whip you from foining f., 2680
Fens: reek o' rotten f., 4834
Fenton: what say you to F., 6039
Fern-seed: receipt of f., 4973
Fertility: suck soil's f., 7063
Fervour placed in contempt, 1694
Festival: this day kept f., 3494
Festivals: sung at f., 6095
Fetlocks shag and long, 3598
Fetters put upon this fear, 2650
  these Egyptian f. I must break, 2649
Fever, 2651-2654
  after life's fitful f., 1872
  brought into burning f., 2093
  f. reigns in my blood, 2654
  f. seethe blood to froth, 7186
  f. that hath troubled me, 2653
  fiery f. will go out, 2652
  grows to an envious f., 2298
  so great a f. on goodness, 4966
  tyrant f. burns me up, 2653
  what's f. but a fit of madness, 2651
  white hand of lady f., 3207
Few: we f., we happy f., 3540
Fickle: be f., fortune, 2875
Fickleness: fortune's f., 6068
Fico for the phrase, 1539
Fiction: for thy f., natural, 2655
  improbable f., 2656
Fiddle: song and f. no fellow, 6093
Fiddlestick: devil rides f., 2024
Fidele is my name, 2657
Fie, foh, and fum, 5743
  f. on him, 6187
Field: tented f., 6181
Field-bed is too cold, 550
Fields: babbled of green f., 2515
  f. where I may wallow, 6147
Fiend, 2660-2664
  beat away busy f., 1995
  defy the foul f., 2660
  f. gives me counsel, 1510
  f. is at mine elbow, 1510

f. is rough, 2046
f. like thee bear soul, 2663
foul f. Flibbertigibbet, 2661
foul f. led through fire, 6651
out, hyperbolical f., 2664
take heed o' the foul f., 2660
thou art a f., 7316
thou marble-hearted f., 3723
Fiends : be juggling f., 2662
beneath is all the f., 7317
f. roar, saints pray, 5678
Fife : ear-piercing f., 2533
wry-necked f., 2665
Fig for Peter, 2668
f. of Spain, 2667
Fight : do not f. by sea, 5902
f. and die is death, 2615
f. it out, 2676
f. till the last gasp, 2676
f. upon this theme, 2673
f. when I cannot choose, 5844
f. with hearts more proof, 2671
he that will not f., 3568
I'll f. maliciously, 2669
I'll f. with thee tomorrow, 478
let's f. with gentle words, 7447
try fortune in f., 3614
we come to see thee f., 2679
would they'd f. in fire, 2670
you denied to f. with me, 2982
you shall f. hearts out, 2488
Fighter : dull f., 2619
Fighting : when wilt thou leave f., 2510
Fights : all on foot he f., 5683
he f. as you sing, 2681
Figo for thy friendship, 2667
Figs : love life better than f., 4116
Figure : baby f. of mass, 6538
f. for time of scorn, 133
f. like your father, 2560
f. of God's majesty, 3903
it is a f. in rhetoric, 5659
key-cold f. of holy king, 3907
thou art an O without a f., 5041
thou hast no f., 6022
Filching like unskilful singer, 6518
sworn brothers in f., 6517
File : right-hand f., 5687
Filling : one is f. still, 4743
Filth : his f. being cast, 2031
Filths savour but themselves, 6889
Fin couronne les œuvres, 2305
Finch, sparrow, lark, 1706
Find-faults : mouths of f., 1751
Finder of occasions, 3944
Fine is the crown, 2301
Finem : respice f., 2302
Finger, 2682-2689
between f. and thumb, 2683
but wag a f. at thee, 2685
f. of a throned queen, 3801
I had as lief break neck as f., 4935
I'll break thy little f., 2682
I'll never put f. in fire, 2686
lay my f. on lips, 2687
let our f. ache, 2688
my f. like a dial's point, 6632
no pie freed from his f., 2684
not break back to heal f., 2689
point her unmoving f. at, 133

put f. in eye and weep, 2798
put f. in the eye, 2070
Fingers : alike as f. to f., 4161
at my f. ends, 3791
barky f. of the elm, 3763
contaminate f. with bribes, 929
maids dead men's f. call, 2959
ring these f. with worms, 1868
shaking bloody f. of foes, 1030
take thy f. from my throat, 1786
thou hast it at f. ends, 4016
to be pinching f., 5142
your f. to your lips, 2687
Finisher : of works f., 4705
Fins of lead, 4828
Finsbury : further than F., 6351
Firago : such a f., 2047
Fire, 2689-2704
against f. do I shrink up, 6314
against love's f., fear's frost, 4313
as soon kindle f. with snow, 4356
be f. with f., 43
be he f., I'll be water, 2700
blow f. to quench it, 3158
burn in everlasting f., 2044
die like f. and powder, 1967
f. and brimstone, 2697
f. burn, cauldron bubble, 6748
f. drives out f., 2690
f. i' flint shows not, 2702
f. of lust melted him, 5647
f. of youth, 4771
f. that mounts liquor, 2694
f. that severs night from day, 6371
f. that's closest burns, 2703
f. us hence like foxes, 900
f. which burn'd Carthage queen, 6966
f. will burn, 4152
frighted with false f., 2691
hasty as f., 6265
heretic that makes the f., 3468
I always loved a great f., 2018
I am f. and air, 3707
led through f. and flame, 6651
little f. in wild field, 2696
little f. quickly trodden out, 2692
love's f. heats water, 4338
make mighty f. with straws, 2695
no surer than f. upon ice, 4828
oaths straw to f. in blood, 5062
one f. burns out another, 2699
one f. drives out one f., 2690
property of f. is to burn, 5533
put f. in your heart, 6845
quench f. of passion, 5572
quenched them, given me f., 805
right Promethean f., 2428
shunn'd f. for fear of burning, 2704
this f. is now too huge, 7002
this spark prove raging f., 6153
touch f., weather cold, 808
wash me in gulfs of f., 6140
who can hold f. in his hand, 6115
won as towns with f., 6292
ye blew f. that burns ye, 5636
Fire-new from the mint, 3793
Fire-shovel : stole a f., 6517
Fires : huge f. abide, 2698
if f. be hot, knives sharp, 6923
little f. grow great, 2701

thought-executing f., 6585
violent f. soon burn out, 2699
where two raging f. meet, 2701
Firing: fetch f. at requiring, 1051
Firmament: o'erhanging f., 2268
First-born: rail against f., 6016
Firstlings of my heart, 1939
Fish, 2705-2712
 eat no f., 5844
 eat of f. that fed of worm, 7497
 f. hangs in the net, 2711
 f. lives in the sea, 2712
 f. not with melancholy bait, 5106
 f. with craft for opinion, 6781
 for f. without fin, 1670
 froze them as f. in pond, 5586
 man or f., he smells like f., 6042
 no more than f. loves water, 7410
 of a dragon and finless f., 6431
 this f. will bite, 2708
 'tis well thou art not f., 2745
Fisher meddle with pencil, 5913
Fishermen appear like mice, 3476
Fishes: how f. live in sea, 2710
Fishified: how art thou f., 2746
Fishmonger: you are a f., 2707
Fist: give me thy f., 3212
Fit: before curing, f. strongest, 2094
 then comes my f. again, 2167
Fitness: woman's f. by fits, 7302
Fits: cope him in sullen f., 4574
Five: there's f. to one, 5082
Flag: death's pale f., 1894
 I must show f. of love, 4372
 like vagabond f., 785
Flame: as near as f. to smoke, 5971
 break out into a f., 2138
 f. of sovereignty, 6149
 live after f. lacks oil, 4114
 sulphurous, tormenting f., 3620
 very f. of love, 4263
Flames: array'd in f., 6998
Flap-dragon easier swallowed, 7431
Flat: that's f., 2713, 6064
Flatter: do not think I f., 2719
 f. and praise, commend, 2731
 f. me, for love delights in praises, 4354
 he cannot f., he, 5322
 I cannot f., 2720
 I cannot f. and speak fair, 2726
 think not I f., 2981
 'tis sin to f., 2721
 would not f. Neptune, 1202
Flattered me like a dog, 2724
 he that loves to be f., 2728
 I have f. a lady, 1199
Flatterer: he is a f., 3572
 this man's a f., 2730
 worthy of a f., 2728
Flatterers: betrayed with f., 2723
 f. sit within crown, 1685
 I tell him he hates f., 2723
Flattering woman's part, 7301
Flattery, 2716-2731
 f. conquers strife, 2717
 f. is bellows blows up sin, 2721
 I come not to hear f., 1439
 monarch's plague, f., 2727
 seduced by thy f., 1479
 soft and tender f., 2725

there is f. in friendship, 2929
to counsel deaf, not f., 2729
water'd with dews of f., 2718
what drinkst thou but f., 1158
words let none think f., 2722
Flaw: this mad-bred f., 6273
Flaws and starts imposters, 4497
Flax-wench that puts to, 7145
Flaying: what f., boiling, 6700
Flea: die a f.'s death, 1881
 f. on lip of lion, 2733
 f. upon Bardolph's nose, 2732
Fleece: won the f., 6304
Fleeces: shear the f., 5897
Flesh, 2734-2746
 as if f. were impregnable, 3901
 as pretty a piece of f., 2744
 buy ladies' f. at million, 2735
 collop of my f., 2739
 could not this f. keep life, 2508
 devour them f. and fell, 7071
 exchange f. with loved, 7343
 f. cheap, females dear, 2281
 f., how art thou fishified, 2746
 hearken after the f., 2740
 her fair unpolluted f., 2737
 I am driven by the f., 2017
 I am pretty piece of f., 2745
 makes f. a deity, 3685
 man and wife is one f., 4529
 more f. than another man, 2738
 mousing f. of men, 1866
 my f. is soft and plump, 2747
 my gross f. sinks downward, 6142
 O that this too solid f. would melt, 2736
 pound of f. nearest heart, 2742
 sweet ounce of man's f., 3796
 take thy pound of f., 2743
 this f. begot daughters, 1807
 this huge hill of f., 1456
 this world-wearied f., 1895
 thou didst eat strange f., 2734
 thou wilt not take his f., 809
 weight of carrion f., 2741
 witty piece of Eve's f., 7255
Flesh and Blood, 2748-2754
 as true as f. and b., 2750
 do execution on f. and b., 2753
 I will be f. and b., 5250
 men are f. and b., 4492
 my daughter is my f. and b., 2752
 none of your f. and b., 2754
 our f. and b. vile, 2749
 see him in f. and b., 2751
 thou art my f., my b., 1806
 wicked as all f. and b., 2748
 your f. and b. has not offended, 2754
Flies: as f. to wanton boys, 2769
 f. of every wind that blows, 1187
 honest as summer f., 3513
 like f. at Bartholomew-tide, 7189
 time's f., 5155
 winter kills the f., 2770
Flibbertigibbet: fiend F., 2661
Flight: untread steps of f., 5076
Flights of angels sing thee, 3371
Flint: as f. to rain, 6476
 being incensed he's f., 1203
 f. and hardness of my fault, 4779
 rough heart of f., 4235

Flirt-gills : none of his f., 3945
Flock : like f. of wild-geese, 3875
  so many hours I tend my f., 3624
Flocks : my f. feed not, 5538
Flood, 2755-2757
  bid f. bate usual height, 3798
  I pass'd melancholy f., 2757
  never came reformation in a f., 5596
  no f. raining slaketh, 2756
  taken at f., leads to fortune, 6591
  there is a f. toward, 2796
  through f., through fire, 2476
Flood-gate : my grief is of so f., 3157
Floodgates of her eyes, 5505
Floods from simple sources, 2755
  f. of Sala and Elbe, 3727
  to bathe in fiery f., 1876
Floor of heaven inlaid, 3273
Flourish set on youth, 6635
  f. when subjects bow, 4861
Flout 'em and scout 'em, 6553
Flouting : we shall be f., 7260
Flouts : full of wounding f., 6668
Flow : high f. as gallows, 4781
Flower : every f. did weep, 3420
  fell upon little western f., 1716
  f. deflowered by him, 1897
  f. that dies when bud, 516
  f. that smiles on every one, 6483
  f. that's like thy face, 2758
  fresh uncropped f., 2173
  he is not f. of courtesy, 1619
  I am that f., that mint, 2760
  inveigh against wither'd f., 2763
  look like innocent f., 5864
  not a f. on my coffin, 1902
  summer's f. to summer sweet, 2765
  sweetest f. of the field, 1897
Flower-de-luce being one, 2767
  my fair f., 7361
Flowers, 2758-2767
  away to sweet beds of f., 4343
  bruise f. with armed hoofs, 6994
  fair f. rot and consume, 2766
  fairest f. o' the season, 2767
  feed on f., poison breed, 5866
  f. are slow, weeds haste, 7064
  .f. distill'd leese but show, 2764
  f. like pleasures of world, 2759
  f. with frost beat down, 6600
  my unblown f., sweets, 383
  strew thy green with f., 2762
  these are f. of summer, 2767
  weeds take root with f., 7062
Fluellen : I know F. valiant, 1307
Fly, 2768-2771
  but as f. by eagle, 2768
  f. does lecher in my sight, 95
  how if that f. had father, 2771
  I have but kill'd a f., 2771
  I never hurt a f., 3654
Foam : plough'st the f., 3068
Foamed : he f. at mouth, 1024
Foe : heat not furnace for f., 5635
  met my dearest f. in heaven, 6574
  to fear f. weakness, 2615
Foemen : valiant f. mow'd down, 2320
Foes : do I tell of f., 2317
  fellest f. grow friends, 2921

mongst f., friend worst, 2927
  strangers and f. sunder, 6281
Fog as black as Acheron, 680
Fogs : blasts and f., 1739
  infect her, fen-suck'd f., 1740
Foil : no f. to set it off, 5595
  one f. never breed distrust, 2141
Foin : come to see thee f., 2679
  he will f. like any devil, 4734
Foining : when wilt leave f., 2510
  whip you from f. fence, 2680
Foison plenty, 696
  if dearth or f. follow, 5004
Folks : old f. have discretion, 1290
  to beguile old f., 7587
Follies lovers cannot see, 4392
  one eye upon my f., 2779
  your f. fight against self, 2615
Follow : he will never f., 2773
  I'll f. thee through world, 4320
Follower : be diligent f. of mine, 2772
  you were wont to be a f., 2774
Folly, 2775-2782
  all's brave that f. guides, 7552
  call faults of fools but f., 2776
  cold wisdom waiting on f., 7215
  covering discretion with f., 6849
  curse of mankind, f., 1746
  f. controlling skill, 367
  f. in fools not strong, 7216
  f. in wisdom hatch'd, 7216
  f. that he wisely shows, 2822
  gate that let my f. in, 2778
  her f. help'd to an heir, 514
  how short his time of f., 6629
  most galled with my f., 4085
  nature will betray its f., 4924
  remove fabric of his f., 5830
  slightest f. that ever love, 4247
  to do good accounted f., 3268
  too much f. is it, 2777
  uses f. like stalking-horse, 2775
  what f. to hazard life, 7547
  why should f. lurk, 2780
  with thy f. burn world, 5240
Fond : in truth I am too f., 763
Food, 2783-2790
  fed with same f., 3797
  f. as luscious as locusts, 2784
  f. for fortune's tooth, 4342
  f. for his rage, 4186
  f. for powder, 5382
  f. for worms, 3617
  f. of sweet and bitter fancy, 2525
  f. of us that trade in love, 4858
  f. to make misfortune live, 4745
  go and beg my f., 586
  gold, hard f. for Midas, 3060
  his looks are my soul's f., 2790
  pines beholding f., 2786
  to thoughts as f. to life, 2788
  who wanteth f. and will not, 2785
  with eager feeding f. doth choke, 2787
Fool, 2791-2823
  better witty f., 7259
  call me not f., 2793
  dost thou call me f., 2808
  dulness of f. whetstone of the wits, 2792
  every f. can play upon word, 7390
  every f. can tell that, 2804

f. doth think he is wise, 2818
f. me to top of my bent, 1381
f. slides o'er the ice, 2814
f.'s bolt is soon shot, 2797
f.'s play, by heaven, 5337
he that a f. doth hit, 2794
how ill white hairs become a f., 2513
I am fortune's f., 2809
I met a f. i' the forest, 2793
I think him a great f., 4109
I was seeking for a f., 2795
learned pate ducks to f., 2813
more knave than f., 3940
most credulous f., 2801
my f. usurps my body, 4495
my poor f. is hang'd, 2810
natural f. of fortune, 2809
no longer will I be a f., 2798
not holiday f., 2339
O noble f., worthy f., 2793
play f. in own house, 2803
put down with ordinary f., 5553
rash, intruding f., 1785
rather have f. to make merry, 2392
say the f. is the f., 2541
she will breed it like a f., 7295
so yoked by a f., 4348
thou art death's f., 1874
transformed into strumpet's f., 2791
wasp-stung, impatient f., 2805
what a f. honesty is, 3517
what peevish f. of Crete, 2806
why should I play Roman f., 6400
wise enough to play f., 2822
wit's grace to learned f., 7216
Foolery: by f. thrive, 5313
f. does walk orb, 2782
f. in the wise, 7216
thrown in holiday f., 981
Fooling: in admirable f., 2781
wit put me into good f., 7259
Foolish: never f. that was fair, 514
Foolish-witty: love is f., 4364
Fools: at f. I laugh, 2819
come to this stage of f., 668
f. are as like husbands, 2816
f. are not mad folks, 2799
f. as gross as ignorance, 5802
f. by compulsion, 6245
f. make ill-favour'd children, 5898
f. may not speak wisely, 2817
f. with varnish'd faces, 2665
f. would fain have drink, 2811
how many f. serve jealousy, 3776
in all tongues called f., 2796
let f. do good, 6146
let f. use their talents, 2821
loyalty to f. makes folly, 4413
make f. laugh in alehouse, 5149
none but f. do wear it, 4218
old f. are babes again, 2807
play f. with time, 2820
suckle f., chronicle small beer, 573
these tedious old f., 2802
thus credulous f. caught, 4604
what f. these mortals be, 2812
wise men give f. money, 2824
wishers were ever f., 7218
wits very often prove f., 7259
you f. of fortune, 5155

Foot, 2824-2828
all on f. he fights, 5683
better f. before, 3285
f. it featly, 5795
from crown to sole of f., 4724
from thy head to thy f., 6725
his f. Mercurial, 4485
horsing f. on f., 5034
I will kiss thy f., 2827
I will set this f. of mine, 2824
keep f. out of brothels, 2660
nay, her f. speaks, 4000
noiseless f. of time, 6604
one f. in sea, one on shore, 4506
so light a f. will never, 2826
wishing f. equal with eye, 6148
Football: like f. you spurn me, 2829
Football-player: you base f., 2829
Foot-licker: for aye thy f., 2828
Footing: nymphs in country f., 5921
set no f. on this shore, 5820
unsteadfast f. of a spear, 825
Footstool of security, 5839
Foppery of freedom, 2831
f. of the world, 6245
let not f. enter, 2832
Fops got between wake and sleep, 438
For: we are f. you, 6091
Forage: from f. to play, 4186
Forbearance from so foul a wrong, 5011
she pray'd me oft f., 1235
Force entangles with strength, 3978
f. of heaven-bred poesy, 5350
f. of merit makes way, 4650
there is no f. in eyes, 2404
Ford: through f., whirlpool, 6651
Fore-foot to me give, 3212
Forehead of married honourable, 387
f. of the morning, 1200
from my f. wipe perjured note, 3699
teeth and f. of faults, 5084
with unbashful f. woo, 141
Foreheads villanous low, 265
Foreskirt: longer than f., 3542
Forest: this is f. of Arden, 6705
who can impress the f., 655
Foresters: Diana's f., 4781
Forever and a day, 4554
I am yours f., 4366
Forfeits in barber's shop, 4036
Forge that stithied Mars, 3861
f. working-house of thought, 4222
Forget: best sometimes f., 2838
f. and forgive, 2843
f., forgive, conclude, 1310
f. myself to be myself, 2837
f. what I have been, 2840
f. your evil, forgive self, 3414
teach me how I can f., 6551
teach me to f. myself, 2834
'tis like I f. myself, 4449
you f. yourself, 2836
Forgetfulness, 2833-2841
blind f. and oblivion, 2841
ingrate f. shall poison, 2833
steep my senses in f., 6019
Forgive: forget, f., 1310
f. and forget, 2843
Forgiven and forgotten, 2842
Forgiveness: I'll ask f., 5438

Forgot : I had f. myself, 3900
not f. which ne'er remember, 2839
Forgotten and forgiven, 2842
Form : dwell on f., 763
I am a scribbled f., 6314
in f. how admirable, 4487
Fornications : given to f., 5378
Forsworn in will, 5230
I am f. for thee, 5964
I am f. on mere necessity, 4931
Forthright : hedge from f., 2299
Fortinbras : election on F., 2294
Fortitude of soul, 2314
Fortress built by nature, 2324
Fortressed from the world, 3552
Fortune, 2845-2878
all is but f., 4517
arrows of outrageous f., 1847
at flood leads on to f., 6591
bear your f. like a man, 4512
despite thy fire-new f., 6725
exclaim on f.'s fickleness, 6068
fallen out with f., 3130
flies f. when it follows, 3006
f. and Antony part here, 2851
f. brings in some boats, 2858
f. cannot recompense me, 2877
f. fall in love with thee, 2855
f. is good wench, 2872
f. is merry, 2866
f. is painted blind, 2864
f. knows we scorn her, 2850
f. made havoc of my means, 5648
f. may grow out at heels, 2868
f. men call fickle, 2875
f. of us moon's men, 4781
f. shows herself more kind, 2874
f., that arrant whore, 2870
f., turn thy wheel, 2869
f.'s blows struck home, 2856
f.'s minion and her pride, 6081
giddy f.'s fickle wheel, 2864
giglot f., 2857
here is a purr of f., 2123
he's but f.'s knave, 1015
hold your f. for your bliss, 2873
housewife f. break wheel, 2852
I am f.'s fool, 2809
I am his f.'s vassal, 5066
laugh away his f., 2848
made lame by f.'s spite, 1433
made tame to f.'s blows, 5376
man f. cruelly scratched, 2846
mock good housewife f., 2853
muddied in f.'s mood, 2846
my f. lives for me, 2876
my f. runs against the bias, 5747
not first of f.'s slaves, 6566
on f.'s cap not button, 2859
our f. is out of breath, 2849
out of suits with f., 2854
out, thou strumpet f., 2860
out-frown f.'s frown, 2871
pipe for f.'s finger, 2861
rail'd on Lady F., 2793
si f. me tormente, 2862
since this f. falls to you, 2873
so be thy f. in this fight, 1138
thou poutest upon thy f., 695
though f.'s malice overthrow, 2865

try f. in single fight, 3614
wash'd his father's f., 6337
what cannot be preserved f. takes, 5199
what counts harsh f. cast, 2847
when f. means most good, 2867
who shall go to cozen f., 4651
will f. never come, 2863
wisdom and f. combating, 7206
yield not neck to f.'s yoke, 4938
Fortune-tell : I'll f. you, 7271
Fortune-teller : juggler and f., 6893
Fortunes : all my f. at thy foot, 4320
hazard of new f., 2878
many their f. seek, 2877
my f. will ever after droop, 6239
not nature can bear great f., 4922
sold their f. at home, 2878
to my f. commit my cause, 1140
Fosset-seller, 1201
Foster-nurse of nature, 5620
Fought by Shrewsbury clock, 2675
Foul : fair is f., f. is fair, 6573
f. as Vulcan's stithy, 3703
f. is most f., being f., 4251
nothing f. to those that win, 7193
Foundation, 2879-2881
f. of earth shaked, 659
God save the f., 2880
no sure f. set on blood, 2879
Foundations I build upon, 2881
Founded as the rock, 2167
Fount : you are the f., 2882
Fountain : by paved f., 4587
f. from which current runs, 133
immaculate and silver f., 2574
like f. did run blood, 2180
mud not the f., 2883
woman moved like f. troubled, 7333
Fountains : emptied f. in my well, 845
silver f. have mud, 5739
stray where pleasant f. lie, 4205
Foutre for the world, 7473
Fowl without feather, 1670
Fox, 2884-2887
as false as f. to lamb, 2506
f., ape, humble-bee, 6572
f. barks not when he steal, 2884
f. carries the goose, 4189
f. in stealth, 1205
f. shepherd of lambs, 2887
f. have trick of ancestors, 6716
lion is f. for his valour, 4189
make f. surveyor of fold, 2885
seek lamb of the f., 3992
wake wolf bad as to smell f., 7282
when f. hath got in nose, 2886
you will eat no grapes, f., 3098
Foxes : fire us hence like f., 900
where find you f., geese, 4828
Frail : in our natures f., 2889
ten times f., 7321
Frailty, 2888-2890
f., thy name is woman, 2888
have we not f. as men, 3671
more f. than another man, 2738
organ-pipe of f. sings, 6364
our f. is cause, not we, 2890
out of f., want of wisdom, 2889
tempt f. of our powers, 2045
Frame : I holp to f. thee, 7014

Frampold : leads f. life, 3663
France, 2891-2896
  bear swords as far as F., 5081
  F. and England look pale, 2893
  F., fickle wavering nation, 2894
  F. is a dog-hole, 2891
  F. is a stable, 2891
  garden of world, fertile F., 5213
  my thoughts bend toward F., 2892
  Salique land realm of F., 3727
  vines of F., 6915
Frank, she lends to free, 4919
Fraught of aspics' tongues, 846
Fray : latter end of f., 2619
Freckles : in f. savours, 2476
Free-footed : goes too f., 2650
Freeze thou bitter sky, 626
Freezings : what f. have I felt, 8
French can well on horseback, 3588
  F. song has no fellow, 6093
  over-lusty F., 2895
  submission, 'tis F. word, 6302
  subtle-witted F., 5326
Frenchman : none like a F., 2896
Frenchmen are so braid, 5048
Frenzy : melancholy nurse of f., 4621
Fresh as a bridegroom, 4225
Fret : you can f. me, 5331
Friar : Chartreaux F., 2897
  f. of orders grey, 2898
  Robin Hood's fat f., 3909
Friend, 2899-2927
  conspire against thy f., 2914
  dearest f. to me, 2911
  f. i' court better than penny, 2905
  f. should bear f.'s infirmities, 2908
  f. that dips in same dish, 2919
  happier he no f. to feed, 2924
  he is your f. for ever, 6786
  he was my f., faithful, 1033
  I have been politic with f., 1199
  I have chid away my f., 2909
  I have professed me thy f., 2913
  I never love what f. hates, 2912
  I to myself am dearer than f., 2920
  if I think on thee, dear f., 5608
  keep thy f. under life's key, 2899
  not a f. greet my corpse, 1902
  shake off f. when he needs me, 2916
  who not needs never lacks f., 2922
Friends : advertised by loving f., 2906
  by f. well advertised, 2906
  desperate to threat f., 6571
  destroy f. and weep dust, 2124
  eat and drink as f., 4042
  fellest foes grow dear f., 2921
  f. fall away like water, 2907
  f. fast sworn break to enmity, 2921
  f. kill f., 2118
  f., Romans, countrymen, 1033
  f. that purpose merriment, 4722
  hard for f. to meet, 2900
  have f. for wife's sake, 1699
  I am wealthy in my f., 2918
  my bad life reft me of f., 5648
  my f. poor but honest, 5373
  no f. by, men praise selves, 5396
  our f. true and constant, 5345
  rejoice at f. newly found, 2910
  remembering my good f., 2915

  those f. thou hast, 2902
  to his f. I'll ope my arms, 2904
  to wail f. lost not profitable, 2910
  trust f. if I should need, 3095
  'twixt f. few words suffice, 7450
  we shall know f. in heaven, 3400
  what need we have f., 2917
  what viler things that f., 2925
  without three good f., 4760
  worse for my f., 2926
Friendship, 2928-2932
  f. is constant in all other things, 2931
  f. is full of dregs, 2932
  most f. is feigning, 2930
  there is flattery in f., 2929
  when did f. take metal, 2930
  where true f. no ceremony, 1161
Frighted with false fire, 2691
Fringe upon a petticoat, 2252
Fritters : makes f. of English, 2341
Frog : eats the swimming f., 6652
Froissart, a countryman, 2332
Front of Jove himself, 5272
Frontier of a servant brow, 4475
Frost : envious sneeping f., 2933
  f. as actively doth burn, 5888
  third day comes a f., 2492
Frosts will bite them, 3566
  hoary-headed f. fall, 5832
Froth : come, Master F., 6443
Froward by nature, 6829
Frown, 2934-2937
  bandy f. for f., 3670
  dies in tempest of f., 2937
  fear no more f. of great, 2240
  I f., yet he loves me, 2935
  out-frown fortune's f., 2871
  smile recures wounding of f., 6048
Frowned : so f. he once, 2934
Frowning : he parted f., 4180
Frowns more upon humour, 3888
  f. must not repel lover, 4411
  f. teach smiles skill, 2933
  put off these f., 2936
Fruit, 2938-2941
  earliest f. i' the country, 2938
  f. known by the tree, 6732
  f. maids call medlars, 4394
  f. maintain'd with beauty's sun, 4267
  f. unripe sticks on tree, 5472
  golden f., but dangerous, 3474
  hang like f., my soul, 7127
  ripest f. falls first, 2939
  tree known by f., 2511
  tree yields bad f., 2938
  weakest f. drops earliest, 2939
Fruitfulness and liberal, 3233
Fruits that blossom first, 2940
Fuel : add f. to your fire, 2693
Fugitive : master-leaver and f., 4779
Full-gorged : not be f., 2487
Fullam : gourd and f., holds, 3187
Fulvia : shrill-tongued F., 753
Fume needs no spurs, 2010
Fumiter : crown'd with f., 4453
Funeral baked meats, 6574
  obscure f., no trophy, 1850
  see your father's f., 6574
  with mirth in f., 3816
Furious is to be frighted, 2943

Furlongs of sea, 1900
Furnace: heat not f. for foe, 5635
Furrow: come from the f., 5921
Fury, 2942-2946
  calm f. of this flaw, 6273
  chasing blood with f., 2946
  dizzy-eyed f., 2944

fire-eyed f. be my conduct, 4076
I understand a f. in your words, 7443
like f. crown'd with snakes, 2942
men ne'er spend f. on child, 2945
unreasonable f. of a beast, 4534
Fust: reason to f. in us, 4488
Fustilarian: away, you f., 1121

G

Gaberdine: spit upon my g., 6830
Gain, 2947-2949
  despair to g. doth traffic, 2949
  drown our g. in tears, 4232
  g. be my lord, 2947
  that which seeks for g., 2948
Gait: my g. measure of court, 1625
  with iron g. walk world, 1969
Gale: what g. blows you, 7176
Gall, 2950-2953
  choking g., preserving sweet, 4315
  convert to bitter g., 2951
  deadly g., these of scorns, 2952
  g., daintiest they taste, 1737
  g. enough in thy ink, 2953
  his g. coins slander, 6014
  take my milk for g., 2950
  tie g. in slanderous tongue, 1053
  you have honey, these g., 5164
Gallant in brow of youth, 4177
  this g. had witchcraft, 3588
  this g. will command sun, 6330
Gallants, hearts of gold, 2647
Gallimaufry: he loves g., 7365
Gallop: false g. of verses, 2938
  g. to her destruction, 2010
Gallowglasses and kerns, 330
  kerns and g., 3852
Gallows: bring thee to g., 3840
  from g. did his soul fleet, 5483
  gallops with thief to g., 6609
  high flow as ridge of g., 4781
  his complexion perfect g., 3245
  marry a g., 2996
  shall there be g. standing, 4028
Gallows-maker, outlives tenants, 3107
Galls: bitterness of your g., 7578
  soldiers, they have g., 1624
  steep'd g. in honey, 2318
  we have g., and revenge, 3671
Gambol in his eyes, 3867
Gambols: where are your g., 7549
Game, 2954-2956
  g. is afoot, 3139
  g. is up, 2955
  he knows the g., 2956
  I'll warrant her full of g., 6218
  play at any g., lose, 2954
Games: play at subtle g., 5980
Gamesome: I am not g., 6199
  none so merry and g., 4718
  thou art g., courteous, 2986
Gamester: gentler g. winner, 4072
  keep g. from the dice, 2054
Garbage: longs after g., 7151
  lust will prey on g., 6931
Garden of world, France, 5213
  our sea-walled g., 1129

unweeded g. goes to seed, 7468
  weeds will o'ergrow g., 7058
Gardeners hide roots, 6849
Gardens: Adonis' g., 5450
Gargantua's mouth, 7379
Garland, 2957-2961
  call him vile that was g., 4828
  comes third time with g., 2958
  green willow be my g., 7166
  I'll wear a willow g., 7163
  make a g. for my head, 3561
  make him a g., 7164
  Marcius wears war's g., 2957
  wear g. of the realm, 1689
  what fashion wear g., 2961
  wither'd is g. of war, 6061
Garlands: charge horns with g., 3659
  fantastic g., 2959
  g. of crow-flowers, 2959
  put g. on thy head, 6745
  they brought me g., 2960
Garlic: eat no onions nor g., 910
  rather live with g., 6431
  she smelt bread and g., 582
Garlic-eaters: breath of g., 910
Garment nobler than that it covers, 824
  g. out of fashion, 3773
  here's a g. for 't, 6258
Garments heavy with drink, 1851
  g. new-fangled ill, 4329
  our g. shall be poor, 4694
  strange g. cleave not, 3563
  stuffs out his vacant g., 3153
Garter: familiar as his g., 5563
  knights of the g., 3966
  see to g. hose, 4351
Garters: he wears cruel g., 4061
  heir-apparent g., 3239
Gash: give me a g., 3820
  perilous g., 5925
Gasp: fight till last g., 2676
  follow thee to last g., 4414
Gate: broad g., great fire, 2962
  climb o'er house to unlock g., 6292
  g. that let folly in, 2778
  I am for house with narrow g., 2962
  open thy g. of mercy, God, 6129
  this g. instructs you, 2963
Gates of monarchs high, 2963
  g. of steel time decays, 6637
  shut g. on atomies, 2404
Gaudy: rich, not g., 3189
Gaunt am I for grave, 2965
  g. in being old, 2965
  how is 't with aged G., 2965
  I am not John of G., 1635
  old John of G., 2964
  talks of John a Gaunt, 6432

Gawds : all praise new-born g., 5036
  wanton and full of g., 6322
Gazers : slay more g. than basilisk, 1681
Gear : soon-speeding g., 5361
Geese : since I plucked g., 493
  spring near when g. breed, 6221
  where find you foxes, g., 4828
Gelidus timor occupat artus, 2606
General : caviarre to the g., 5329
  g. is disdain'd, 2298
  g. of trotting 'paritors, 1714
  I attend here on the g., 7326
  what miscarries g.'s fault, 2516
Genitive : what is g. plural, 7103
Genius : very g. of famine, 4489
Gentile and no Jew, 4286
Gentle : as g. and jocund, 2677
  g. as zephyrs blowing, 4900
  g. thou art and to be won, 527
  he was g. but unfortunate, 129
  I find you passing g., 2986
  I'll warrant him g. as lamb, 1619
  more g. than father, 4750
  we must be g., 2982
  wherefore are you g., 6920
Gentleman, 2966-2983
  absolute g., 2969
  as you are a g., 5158
  g. of excellent breeding, 2974
  g. of very first house, 2681
  g. that loves to hear self, 4633
  g., valiant, wise, 2981
  goes up and down like a g., 6531
  he bears him like portly g., 2978
  he is a worthy g., 2970
  he's a lovely g., 2979
  I know you a g. born, 2982
  keeping for g. of my birth, 2967
  my master hath been g., 2966
  prince of darkness is a g., 5427
  since every Jack became g., 2977
  so stout a g., 3617
  sweeter and lovelier g., 2976
  true g. may swear it, 2983
  true-born g., 5732
  when g. disposed to swear, 6368
  when this lusty g. was got, 435
  you are g. and gamester, 2972
Gentlemen : be gentle, now g., 2982
  g. in England now abed, 3540
  g. of the shade, 4780
  no ancient g. but gardeners, 2968
  we are g. neither envy the great, 2975
  young g. would be sad, 5773
Gentleness, 2984-2986
  g. of gods go with you, 698
  I have not from you g., 2985
  I will requite thy g., 6515
  let g. my enforcement be, 2984
  your g. shall force more, 2984
George, I'll call him Peter, 3546
  Saint Denis and Saint G., 7361
  Saint G. swinged dragon, 5786
German from waist downward, 2988
  how like you the young G., 4500
Germans are honest men, 2987
  g. spill at once, 6585
Germany, Salique land, 3727
Get : surest way to g., 1985
  what cannot g., deal for, 2004

Ghost, 2989-2995
  gave up the g., 2992
  g. of Cæsar hath appear'd, 2993
  grim-grinning g., 1905
  make g. of him that lets me, 2889
  needs no g. to tell us, 6895
  never do his g. the wrong, 3530
  poor mortal living g., 2995
  seen a timely-parted g., 2991
  towards design moves like g., 4848
  vex not his g., 2994
  yield the g., 2990
Ghosts break up their graves, 7269
  g. squeal about streets, 5097
  g. troop to churchyards, 6237
  haunted by g. they deposed, 3901
  we'll make the g. gaze, 5503
Giant : dwarf before sleeping g., 2251
  excellent to have g.'s strength, 6289
Giant-dwarf, Dan Cupid, 1714
Giantess under Mount Pelion, 6796
Giants may jet through, 2963
Gib-cat : melancholy as g., 4617
Gibes : where are your g., 7549
Gibbet : I am no g. for you, 2997
Gibbets : beget young g., 2996
Giddy thinks world turns, 7492
Gift, 2998-3002
  g. doth stretch itself, 2998
  g. which heaven gives, 4650
  have g. of a grave, 1213
  make my g. more delay'd, 4256
  new-year's g., 892
  no g. but breeds return, 5523
  this is a g. I have, 6201
  woman's g. to rain tears, 6475
Gifts appertinent to man, 6934
  he hath g. of nature, 1213
  love g. and snatch them, 3054
  meets such golden g., 2999
  men take women's g., 3002
  of nature's g. thou boast, 505
  rich g. wax poor, 3002
  she has good g., 3001
  win her with g., 3803
Giglot fortune, 2857
Gild it with happiest terms, 4096
Gillyvors, bastards, 2767
Gilt o'er-dusted, 5036
  in g. they mocked thee, 2402
Ging against me, 1521
Ginger : lying as knapped g., 3081
  of the heat of the g., 3590
Gingerbread : penny to buy g., 5225
Gipsies : like two g. on horse, 6091
Gipsy : like a right g., 1220
Girdle : beachy g. of ocean, 2550
  but to g. do gods inherit, 7317
  he knows how to turn g., 3004
  put g. round the earth, 3003
  salt-water g., 934
Girl : endanger life for a g., 3007
  this it is to be peevish g., 3006
  unlesson'd g., 3005
Girls : between two g., merriest eye, 4030
Gis : by G. and Saint Charity, 6832
Give it or take it, 7394
  more I g., more I have, 852
  unapt to g. or forgive, 2061

Givers: rich gifts poor when g unkind, 3000
Gives: what he has he g., 1212
Glamis hath murder'd sleep, 6024
Glass, 3008-3010
  broken g., no cement, 3009
  brighter than g., yet brittle, 4311
  crack g. of her virginity, 6927
  give me the g., 2468
  g. of fashion, 4681
  g. that feated them, 2373
  g. wherein youth did dress, 3618
  made mouths in the g., 7315
  methinks you are my g., 7554
  not live running of one g., 4213
  O flattering g., 2468
  pilot's g. told minutes, 4709
  thou art thy mother's g., 4817
  'tis not her g. that flatters, 5898
  you go not till I set g., 3008
Glean broken ears after man, 4252
Gleek upon occasion, 4383
Glendower: great G., 4809
  irregular and wild G., 3011
  met devil as well as G., 3012
  oft he hears G. spoke of, 3610
  what call you him, G., 3013
Glimpses of the moon, 4780
Glisters: all g. not gold, 3059
Globe: affrighted g., 3627
  great g. shall dissolve, 5639
Glories: my g. and state depose, 3166
Glory, 3014-3017
  brittle g. shineth in face, 2468
  g. is like circle in water, 3014
  his g. is to subdue men, 1713
  I see thy g. like a star, 3015
  let it be your g., 6476
  like madness is g. of life, 3016
  made g. base, 6471
  no g. lives behind back, 5419
  she false-played my g., 1092
  so greater g. dims less, 1067
  some g. in their birth, 4329
  time's g. is to calm kings, 6628
  uncertain g. of April day, 4359
  vain pomp and g. of world, 5368
  wretchedness that g. brings, 3017
Glose: youth taught to g., 6673
Gloss: newest g., 5105
  set g. on faint deeds, 1161
Glove: cheveril g. to good wit, 7454
  O, that I were a g., 1264
Gloves as sweet as roses, 1007
  wore g. in my cap, 1205
Glow-worm shows matin, 3018
Glow-worms shall lanterns be, 3019
Gluttony: cook helps make g., 1543
Gnat: king transformed to g., 3891
Gnats: entrap g. in cobwebs, 3199
  foolish g. make sport, 3020
  g. are unnoted, 2258
  g. which make a sound, 5428
  is sun dimm'd that g. fly, 6334
  whither fly g. but to sun, 3021
Go, get thee hence, 2114
Goal: get g. for g. of youth, 884
Goat: exchange me for a g., 3779
  luxurious mountain g., 3022
  ridden with Welsh g., 3023

Goats: as prime as g., 5802
  g. ran from the mountains, 659
  wanton as youthful g., 3613
Goblet: covered g., 5269
  swear on parcel-gilt g., 4558
Goblin: be thou g. damned, 6195
Goblins: such g. in my life, 966
God, 3024-3045
  art thou g. to shepherd turn'd, 3024
  art thou some g., 5241
  as G. shall mend me, 6370
  awake the g. of day, 1395
  back'd with G. and seas, 2333
  chide G. for making you, 6706
  cry G. for Harry, England, 3139
  from a g. to a bull, 3026
  G. and good angels fight, 235
  G. and his angels guard, 3027
  G. and our good cause, 1139
  G. and Saint George for us, 2220
  G. be at your table, 3025
  g. bears celestial liquor, 6227
  G. befriend us, 1134
  G. best maker of marriages, 3032
  G. bids us do good for evil, 2032
  G. damn me, 7090
  G. defend but G. should go, 3039
  G. defend the right, 5689
  G. for his mercy, 7278
  G. forbid, 4560
  G. forgive sins of all, 5961
  G. fought for us, 3021
  G. give thee spirit of persuasion, 5234
  G. gives light in darkness, 3033
  G. guard your sacred throne, 6580
  G. has given you one face, 5135
  G. have mercy upon souls, 3045
  G. help the while, 4537
  G. help thee, shallow man, 1766
  G. is a good man, 3038
  G. is above all, 3041
  G. is to be worshipped, 3028
  G. keep all vows unbroke, 5061
  G. knows I loved my niece, 6902
  G. made him, 4500
  G. make incision in thee, 1766
  G. may finish it when he will, 466
  g. of my idolatry, 3044
  G. pardon all oaths broke, 5061
  G. reward me for it, 2455
  G. save the foundation, 2880
  G. save the king, 3904
  G. save the mark, 4225
  G. send him well, 1600
  G. sends curst cow short horns, 1629
  G. shall be my hope, 3035
  G. the widow's champion, 3042
  G.'s arm strike with us, 5082
  had I but served my G., 3037
  he died fearing G., 1204
  he sits like a descended g., 3533
  how near g. to goose, 4292
  I prithee, be my g., 2827
  idiot holds bauble for a g., 5063
  in great hand of G., 3028
  just, true-disposing G., 1727
  leaving fear of G. on left, 3548
  no man cried, G. save him, 66
  no wings to fly from G., 3029
  not serve G. if devil bid, 3040

now G. be praised, 3033
O G. of battles, 3030
O G., thy arm was here, 3031
O thou dull g., 6019
one that would circumvent G., 5364
praise G. for merry year, 2281
take it, G., it was thine, 442
they hope they serve G., 3029
thou owest G. a death, 1855
thou visible g., 3067
we are in G.'s hand, 3028
what a g. is gold, 3068
what kind of g. art thou, 1158
whom G. hath joined, 4560
you have grace of G., 5461
God-den to your worships, 1201
Goddess : fair g., Fortune, 2855
  g. I forswore not, 6964
  g. on whom airs attend, 2446
  I never saw a g. go, 4749
  like a thrifty g., 4914
  that g. blind, 2864
  thou, nature, art my g., 4909
Godfather can give a name, 6291
Godfathers of heaven's lights, 6291
  have two g., 3840
Godhead laid apart, 3024
Godheads : were g. to borrow, 840
Gods, 3046-3055
  draw near nature of the g., 4646
  false to thy g., 6725
  g. are deaf to peevish vows, 6968
  g. are just, 3052
  g. are quick of ear, 5404
  g. begin to mock me, 587
  g. doom him after, 960
  g. kill us for their sport, 2769
  g. look down and laugh, 3047
  g. mean to strike me dead, 3815
  g. sent not corn for rich, 5459
  g. taken shapes of beasts, 3055
  g. themselves do weep, 1379
  g. throw stones of sulphur, 6267
  g. to-day stand friendly, 3050
  g. who freely give, 5428
  hot-blooded g. assist me, 3053
  if the great g. be just, 3046
  immortal g., I crave no pelf, 3095
  mighty g. send heralds, 3049
  now the good g. forbid, 5728
  O you g. why make us love, 3054
  revenging g. 'gainst parricides, 3051
  swear to g. winter kills, 2770
  that dwells with g. above, 4384
  throw sceptre at injurious g., 5815
  when g. have hot backs, 3053
  worship dirty g., 4761
  you g. in general synod, 2860
  you g., look down, 699
Goers-between, Pandars, 5145
  pitiful g., 5145
Going : stand not upon order of g., 2111
Gold, 3056-3069
  all that glisters not g., 3059
  corrupting g. would tempt, 930
  fond shekels of tested g., 5402
  gild refined g., 2375
  g. and silver becks me, 615
  g. and silver turn to dirt, 4761
  g. as good as twenty orators, 3062

g. bides still tester, 3056
g. cannot come amiss, 3058
g. doing more murders, 3064
g. hard food for Midas, 3060
g. makes leprosy adored, 3066
g. makes true man kill'd, 3057
g. put to use g. begets, 5762
g. thou king-killer, 3067
g. will corrupt him, 927
g. worse poison to souls, 3064
hearts of g., 2647
hoard of g. kept by devil, 4055
I am not covetous of g., 3540
knows Plutus' g., 5466
often-touching will wear g., 3056
plate sin with g., 5963
play infirmities for g., 6855
saint-seducing g., 3063
this is fairy g., 3069
'tis g. buys admittance, 3057
try if thou be current g., 3061
what a god is g., 3068
yellow, glittering g., 3066
Goliath : I fear not G., 4503
Gondola : swam in a g., 6706
Gone does not mean away, 2731
  you are g. both ways, 5968
Good : as g. as my word, 7383
  captive g., captain ill, 3074
  chief g. but to sleep, 4488
  do g. against evil, 3071
  finds g. in every thing, 4117
  glad of other men's g., 3979
  g. alone is g. without name, 3070
  g. enough to toss, 5382
  g. for nothing, 7506
  g. oft interred with bones, 1033
  g. things should be praised, 3080
  make bad g., g. provoke, 4860
  never repent for doing g., 3077
  one g. in ten, 7287
  opposite to every g., 3075
  some g. comes tomorrow, 1182
  that's g. that's gone, 4241
  thy overflow of g. converts, 2574
  time is breeder of all g., 6645
  to do g. accounted folly, 3268
  too much of a g. thing, 3072
Good-fellowship : neither manhood nor g., 3507
Good-year : what the g., 3481
Good-years shall devour them, 7071
Goodness, 3070-3080
  God's g. hath been great, 3034
  g. dare not check thee, 6803
  g. growing to plurisy, 3073
  g. is never fearful, 6940
  g. that is cheap in beauty, 3076
  some soul of g. in evil, 3074
  undone by g.,3079
  wisdom, g. to vile seem vile, 6889
Goods : she is my g., 4570
Goose : boy sold him g., 425
  complexion of a g., 4292
  g. carries not the fox, 4189
  g. for his discretion, 4189
  makes green g. a goddess, 3685
  until g. came out of doors, 6572
  when every g. is cackling, 5003
Gooseberry : not worth a g., 6834

Goose-pen : write with g., 2953
Goose-quills : afraid of g., 5542
Gorboduc : niece of King G., 7256
Gordian knot he will unloose, 3972
  slippery as G. knot, 3971
Gorge : cracks his g. 6193
Gormandizing : leave g., 2513
Gosling : never be such a g., 3749
Gossamer that idles in air, 4407
Gossip, 3081-3083
  as lying a g. in that, 3081
  babbling g. of the air, 4344
  long-tongued, babbling g., 3083
  my good g., Report, 3081
Gossips : smatter with g., 3082
Gourd and fullam holds, 3187
Gout : curse the g., serpigo, 862
  g. galls the one, 7579
  rich that hath not g., 6609
Gouts : plagued with g., 4737
Government keep in one consent, 3084
  g. makes women seem divine, 3085
  we be men of good g., 4781
Gown : black g. of big heart, 3502
Gowns : one hath two g., 4236
Grace, 3086-3095
  both g. and faults loved, 2599
  given g. double majesty, 2442
  g. and rude will, 3078
  g. is g. despite controversy, 3090
  g. me no g., 3093
  g. of heaven enwheel thee, 3092
  g. soul of your complexion, 3076
  g. thou wilt have none, 3087
  let fair men call for g., 6146
  mickle is g. that lies, 3078
  momentary g. of men, 3094
  our g. is only in heels, 1778
  so full of g. it flows, 3086
  some say thy g. is youth, 2599
  thy g. cures disgrace, 6964
  what g. was on this brow, 5272
  when g. is saying, hood eyes, 606
  when g. we have forgot, 2091
  wit's g. to g. a learned fool, 7216
  word g. is but profane, 3093
  you have g. of God., 5461
Graces : all princely g., 2297
  extol their g., 2731
  g. serve them as enemies, 6930
  g. will appear, 6941
  imitate g. of the gods, 3532
  in fresh numbers number g., 2440
  king-becoming g., 3089
  lead g. to the grave, 2473
  till g. be in one woman, 7323
Gracious if observed, 1203
Graff : for every g., caterpillar, 1127
  g. it with a medlar, 2938
Grain, dust, gnat, 4811
  see which g. will grow, 6622
  'tis in g., sir, 2473
Grandam : authorized by g., 4497
  g.'s name less in love, 3097
  might ha' been g., 3096
  soul of g. inhabit bird, 5484
  studied to please his g., 606
Grandfather : who is thy g., 6412
Grandmother : child of g. Eve, 7318
Grand-jury-men since Noah, 3841

Grand-jurors : you are g., 7558
Grandsire cut in alabaster, 4721
Grant : fairest g., necessity, 933
Grape : for g. who vine destroy, 4727
  subtle blood o' the g., 7186
Grapes were made to eat, 3099
  purple g., green figs, 3867
  you will eat no g., fox, 2098
Grapple them to thy soul, 2902
  willing to g. as to board, 777
Grass, 3100-3103
  foul with chew'd g., 3771
  g. beat down with storms, 6600
  g. stoops not, 3103
  how lusty the g. looks, 3102
  I have not skill in g., 3100
  never eat g. more, 1857
  while g. grows, 3101
Grass-green turf, 4262
Gratis : endanger my soul g., 6138
Gratitude enroll'd in Jove's book, 5728
Grave, 3104-3115
  almost no g. allow'd me, 6816
  be my g. my peace, 3112
  dig my g. thyself, 3109
  either victory or a g., 6885
  g. gapes thrice wider, 2513
  g. shall have monument, 4773
  g. unto a soul, 3111
  g. whose hollow womb, 2965
  here I measure my g., 3104
  in his g. rained tear, 3106
  little g., obscure g., 3902
  little kingdom of g., 3729
  my g., wedding bed, 3113
  not have strew'd thy g., 6375
  not mother but our g., 5823
  on every g. a lying trophy, 3527
  our g. shall have mouth, 3483
  renowned be thy g., 3105
  wash him from g. with tears, 3169
  we need no g. to bury honesty, 3516
  wrong to take me out of g., 7540
  you find me a g. man, 3655
Grave-maker lasts till doomsday, 3107
Grave-making : sings at g., 1751
Grave-stone : let g. be oracle, 3115
Graved in hollow ground, 1889
Gravel i' the back, 1747
Graves : find dishonourable g., 1021
  fretted us a pair of g., 6469
  g. gaping wide, 4674
  g. have waked sleepers, 3114
  g. have yawned, 5097
  g. stood tenantless, 5095
  let's talk of g., 1431
Gravity, 3116-3119
  buried in his g., 3118
  g.'s revolt to wantonness, 7216
  how ill agrees it with g., 3116
  my g. wherein I take pride, 3119
  not for g. to play, 2046
  utter g. o'er gossip's bowl, 3082
  what doth g. out of bed, 3117
Graybeards : tell g., 1027
Graze on my lips, 4205
Grease : melted him in own g., 5647
Great : envy g. nor low despise, 2975
  extremity of g. and little, 3422
  g. man down, favourite flies, 2922

g. men have reaching hands, 3123
g. men jest with saints, 3125
g. men should drink with harness, 3129
g. ones eat little ones, 2710
I seek not to wax g., 1606
if I grow g., grow less, 5657
nature and fortune join'd to make thee
  g., 505
rightly to be g., 3121
some are born g., 3132
wear out packs of g. ones, 5438
what g. do prattle of, 3131
Greatest in Christian world, 6349
Greatness, 3120-3133
abuse of g. is remorse, 3124
be not afraid of g., 3132
breed of g., 4899
farewell to all my g., 2492
g. fall'n out with fortune, 3130
g. knows itself, 3122
g. was no guard to bar, 3897
have g. thrust upon them, 3132
no g. can censure scape, 1053
O place and g., 5317
rive not more than g. going, 3120
some achieve g., 3132
thinks g. is a-ripening, 2492
touch'd highest point of g., 2490
Grecian : captive G. falls, 5337
Grecians are prompt, 5980
why the G. sacked Troy, 7287
Greedy to confound a man, 4501
Greek : forego this vantage, G., **3423**
it was G. to me, 3134
Green in judgement, 5789
g. is colour of lovers, 3137
his eyes g. as leeks, 2432
how g. you are and fresh, **3135**
look so g. and pale, 3570
of sea-water g., 1464
Green-eyed monster, 3779
Green-sickness : male g., 2203
Green-Sleeves, 7438
tune of G., 1954
Green-sward : ran o'er g., 536
Greenly : you have done g., 3136
Grey : her eyes g. as glass, 2432
Greybeards call divine, 4268
Greyhound : like g. in the leash, **3138**
quick as g.'s mouth, 7244
slipp'd me like his g., 3141
this fawning g. offered, 1614
Greyhounds : like g., in slips, 3139
Grief, 3142-3176
as fond of g. as of child, 3153
as full of g. as age, 154
each g. hath twenty shadows, 3165
every one can master g., 3154
excessive g. enemy to living, 3994
great g. grieves most, 3161
g. bears such emphasis, 3147
g. boundeth where it falls, 3162
g. fills the room up, 3153
g. has so wrought, 3171
g. has vanquished my powers, 1340
g. hath changed me, 3144
g. hath kept tedious fast, 2965
g. hath two tongues, 3175
g. is perfect that I taste, 3174
g. is proud, 3152

g. makes one hour ten, 3163
g. makes wild g. tame, 4885
g. nor law nor limit knows, 3161
g. pleased with g.'s society, 3160
g. softens the mind, 3149
g. that does not speak, 6109
g. that smites my heart, 3143
g. that's beauty's canker, 3170
g. would have tears, 3142
hard-favoured g., 6746
honest words pierce g., 7432
honourable g. which burns, 7075
I was journeyman to g., 3164
medicines to cure this g., 5644
much g. shows want of wit, 3169
my g. is so flood-gate, 3157
my g. is so great, 3152
my g. lies all within, 3167
my heart drowned with g., 3148
no g. did come so near, 1248
now is vessel full of g., 3151
one g. cures with another's languish, 3168
patch g. with proverbs, 3155
perked up in glistering g., 667
reason to be fond of g., 3153
some g. shows much of love, 3169
speak comfort to g., 3156
to weep less depth of g., 7069
too heinous respect of g., 3153
true g. is testy, 3159
what g. set jaundice, 3173
what's past help, past g., 3176
when g. hath mates, 6309
when griping g. heart doth wound, 4870
Griefs : deny g. to friend, 2903
drinking my g., 1686
ease them of their g., 3868
extremity of g., 3172
great g. medicine less, 3146
I am sick of many g., 3150
some g. are med'cinable, 3145
still my g. are mine, 3166
suffer'st mortal g., 1158
tales of others' g., 3158
Grievance : commend thy g. to my prayers,
  1795
Griffin : clip-wing'd g., 6431
dove pursues the g., 6190
Grinding : tarry the g., 1044
Grinning : mock your own g., 7549
Grise of fortune smooth'd, 2813
pity not a g. to love, 5312
Grissel : second G., 5203
Grizzle : time hath sow'd g., 7589
Groan : kill as doth mandrake's **g.**, **1737**
twice for one step I'll g., 7037
Groans stretch leathern coat, 6228
heart cool with g., 4721
rejoice to hear my g., 5526
Groats : ten g. too dear, 4745
Gross as a mountain, 4094
g. as black and white, 6772
Ground : beat g. for kissing feet, 6844
England's g., farewell, 2325
gain little patch of g., 3177
g. shrinks before his treading, 6973
I affect g. her shoe treads, 3178
let us sit upon the g., 3901
we'll shift our g., 6369
Groundlings : split ears of g., 54

Grub and butterfly, 1004
Grudge : feed fat ancient g., 3478
Grudges : here grow no g., 1181
Guard thee well, 3861
Guardage to sooty bosom, 4470
Gudgeon : this fool g., 5106
Guest, 3179-3181
  dull fighter, keen g., 2619
  g. that best becomes table, 2577
  I have invited many a g., 2620
  make yourself my g., 3179
  shakes parting g. by hand, 6642
  to-night we will be your g., 3180
  triumph is ale-house g., 6746
Guests welcomest when gone, 3181
  what g. were in her eyes, 6338
  woeful brooks not merry g., 3606
Guiana : region in G., 4289
Guile : dissembling g., 6712
  with vizard hide foul g., 1916
Guilt, 3182-3186
  g. defeats my strong intent, 5401
  g. like poison begins to bite, 3186
  g. within bosom, 3416
  murderous g. shows not, 4385
  so full of jealousy is g., 3183
  whose g. within bosoms lie, 3185

Guiltiness will speak, 3184
Guilty : be g. to self-wrong, 4653
  started like g. thing, 3182
Guinea-hen : love of g., 2214
Guinover : Queen G., 5805
Gules : head to foot total g., 705
  paint the ground g., 7007
Gulf of forgetfulness, 2841
  like a g. it did remain, 618
Gulfs of liquid fire, 6140
Gull him into a nayword, 5470
  I should think this a g., 3950
  left a naked g., 2632
  thin-faced knave, a g., 3948
  ungentle g., cuckoo's bird, 1704
Gum : drop medicinal g., 1208
  g. down-roping from eyes, 3571
Gunpowder : hot as g., 1307
Gun-stones : balls to g., 4754
Guns : but for vile g., 4225
Gurnet : I am a soused g., 6064
Gusts : extreme g. will blow, 2701
Guts : let vultures gripe g., 3187
  sheeps' g. hale souls, 3188
  sure as g. of puddings, 5646
  wears his g. in his head, 7252
Gyves : in twisted g., 5169

H

Habit, 3189-3191
  costly thy h. as purse can buy, 3189
  how use doth breed h., 6827
  in what h. will you go, 3191
  put on a sober h., 606
  put this sour-cold h. on, 3190
  scan outward h. by inward man, 5108
  with h. wrench awe from fools, 5316
Habitation giddy, 4835
Hacks on his helmet, 3421
Hag that presses maids, 4435
Haggerds of the rock, 6211
Hags : secret, black h., 1938
Hai : ah, the h., 2681
Hail : cried all h., 3825
  from cold heart engender h., 3328
  men did cry all h., 3904
Hailstone : no surer than h., 4828
Hailstones : vanish like h., 6577
Hair, 3192-3202
  beg a h. of him, 6503
  chin enriched with one h., 1295
  cutting smaller h., 6667
  each h. to stand on end, 6417
  excellent head of h., 6685
  fetch h. off Cham's beard, 5875
  h. less in his beard, 5499
  his h. of dissembling colour, 3192
  his h. of good colour, 3192
  horrid image unseats h., 6310
  if my h. tickle I scratch, 345
  makest my h. to stare, 5241
  many hath more h. than wit, 3193
  more h. on chin than Dobbin, 473
  my fell of h. would rouse, 2613
  never wear h. on my face, 3875
  no time to recover h., 6611
  scanted men in h., 3193
  she hath more h. than wit, 3202

  swerve a h. from truth, 2506
  this h. I tear is mine, 4449
  'tis not your black h., 945
  to a h.'s breadth, 3200
  weight of h. turn scales, 3195
  white h. is my father, 3201
  with h. up-staring, 3444
  your bedded h. starts up, 3194
Hair-breadth scapes, 4305
Hairs : had his h. been lives, 5651
  had white h. in beard, 2724
  how ill white h. become a fool, 2513
  if h. be wires, black wires, 4749
  in her h. painter plays, 3199
  silver h. purchase opinion, 3197
  spread thy golden h., 4653
  two and fifty h. on chin, 3201
Hairy : marvelous h., 345
Halcyon days, 6313
Half : lose h. with patience, 4237
Half-caps, 5947
Half-kirtles : forswear h., 5714
Half-moon made with pen, 950
Halfpenny purse of wit, 5225
  thanks too dear a h., 6507
Half-workers : women be h., 4528
Hall : merry in h., 4657
Halter : strangled with a h., 3240
Hamlet : adieu ; H., remember me, 4625
  H., cast nighted colour off, 1846
  H., he that is mad, 2326
  O H., speak no more, 2409
Hammer : I'll h. it out, 5439
  saw smith stand with h., 4958
Hammers : Cyclops' h., 5610
Hamstring : conceit lies in h., 67
Hand, 3203-3230
  by brother's h. dispatched, 3709
  chop this h. off, 3215

cursed be the h., 1741
each render me bloody h., 3217
fairest h. I ever touch'd, 3216
give me your h., 2874, 3232
give my h. against heart, 7375
giving h. shall have praise, 3221
h. as fruitful as land, 1341
h. from h., 5168
h. instrumental to mouth, 6578
h. of little employment, 3211
h. on her bosom, 7165
h. open as day for charity, 1203
h. that kings have lipp'd, 3203
h. that made the engine, 5539
h. that made you fair, 3076
h. which writ his honour, 3208
have you not a dry h., 7578
he put his h. behind him, 5167
he wrung Bassanio's h., 5167
her h., all whites are ink, 3229
her lily h., 3227
here's my h., 3236, 3672
his heart and h. open, 1212
in faith, 'tis a fair h., 3226
in faith, your h. is out, 3222
in h. of God I stand, 3028
in right h. carry peace, 5214
keep h. out of plackets, 2660
kiss his h., say nothing, 1601
let me kiss that h., 3219
man's h. not able to taste, 2183
my h. is ready ; may it do him ease, 3670
my playfellow, your h., 3206
offence's gilded h., 5084
own h. strike honour down, 1498
pawn'd open h., 1648
profane with unworthiest h., 3925
right h. perjured to bosom, 6767
sign of brave mind, hard h., 3214
subdued like dyer's h., 4920
that phraseless h., 3223
this h. is a maiden h., 3218
this h. is moist, 3233
this h. thicker with blood, 3210
this is my right h., 2227
thou hast an open h., 3230
thrust thy h. into purse, 5456
time's deformed h., 3144
'tis a good h., 3233
to her h. commend counsel, 3220
'twas that h. gave heart, 3233
we forget office of our h., 5522
we know the sweet Roman h., 3226
we'll h. in h., 5503
white h. of lady, 3207
whose h. forest bear licks, 4178
whose h. threw pearl away, 1208
wide o' the bow h., 3222
wilt thou lay h. on me, 6892
with bloody h. cancel, 4981
with h. I seal heart's love, 3235
woe to h. shed this blood, 1031
write it in a martial h., 2953
you give h. that is mine, 4552
your mother's h. shall right wrongs, 697
¹Handicrafts-men : virtue in h., 5009
Hands : clapped chopped h., 5527
come with both h. full, 2863
courtier's h. are perfumed, 1620
do it with unwashed h., 2377

great men have reaching h., 3123
h. tremble upon a lute, 3228
her pretty chopt h., 4248
heraldry is h., 3233
here do we shake h., 2851
join h., with h., hearts, 3231
lay no h. on me, 5594
lay not thy h. on me, 3213
leave wringing of your h., 3332
my h. are of your colour, 3224
place h. below husband's foot, 3670
shake h. and part, 5166
tall fellow of thy h., 2644
tall man of his h., 6252
these h. are not more like, 4160
these h. lack nobility, 3204
they shook h., 3688
wash my h. of murder, 5279
will h. ne'er be clean, 3225
wring from h. of peasants, 4762
Handsaw : I know hawk from h., 4442
my sword hacked like h., 6391
Handsome in three hundred pounds, 2596
Handy-dandy, which is justice, 6527
Hang : go h. yourselves all, 3247
h. him with pen and ink-horn, 7536
h. it first, draw it after, 6695
h. me up in chains, 1840
h. no more about me, 2997
h. themselves in own straps, 3246
h. thyself in garters, 3239
teaches me to h. myself, 4449
Hang-dog Latin for bacon, 393
Hanged : be h. for his labour, 1493
born to be h., 3245
h. because they could not read, 5564
h. betimes in the morning, 3243
I'll see thee h. first, 3238
I'll see you h. like clotpoles, 5686
man never undone until h., 3250
must all be hanged that lie, 6726
well h. needs fear no colours, 3248
Hanging, 3237-3250
good h. prevents bad marriage, 3249
h. and wiving by destiny, 3244
h. is the word, sir, 3237
· h. is too good, 3240
h. of thy nether lip, 6082
stand fast, Fate, to his h., 3245
Hangings in homely house, 7155
Hangman dare not shoot, 1721
h. is penitent trade, 3242
Hap : more blessed h. ne'er befall, 3251
more direful h. betide, 3253
our h. is loss, 3252
what h. may, 3254
what h., what hope of good, 3252
when thou meet good h., 3260
Happiness, 3255-3260
dead h. with living woe, 1743
good day and h., Rosalind, 6863
h. courts in best array, 695
h. enjoyed but of a few, 3259
h., honour keep with you, 697
h. that both receive, 4869
h. that madness hits on, 4441
I envy no man's h., 3979
look into h. through other man's eyes, 3255
no mean h. seated in mean, 3258

society is h. of life, 6060
sorrow abides, h. takes leave, 6749
they promised eternal h., 2960
wish me partaker of thy h., 3260
Happy : by coming made you h., 6817
earthlier h. is rose distill'd, 6922
h. man be his dole, 3256
h. thou art not, 3257
little h. if say how much, 5946
then h. low, lie down, 6019
Harbinger : virtue's h., 6878
yonder shines Aurora's h., 6237
Harbingers of blood, 6762
Harbour : dark h. for defame, 4995
where shall it find h., 2479
Hard, 3261-3263
as h. as steel, 3263
h. as palm of ploughman, 3229
he was too h. for him, 3261
it shall go h., 6911
it will go h. with Antonio, 3262
more h. than stones, 3263
'twill go h. with you, 3262
you are too hard for me, 3261
Hard-favoured : thou wert h., 3504
Hard-handed men that work, 4504
Hard-hearted : men grow h., 839
Hardiment : changing h., 4809
Hardness of hardiness is mother, 1633
Hardy as Nemean lion, 2549
Hare, 3264-3265
an old h. hoar, 3265
hang me for poulter's h., 3429
h. is madness the youth, 7566
h. of whom proverb goes, 3264
having flying h. in sight, 3140
unless a h. in lenten pie, 3265
Harebell : azured h., 2758
Hare-brained Hotspur, 3616
Harelip : he makes the h., 2661
Hares : he finds you h., 4828
voice of lions, act of h., 7407
Harfleur : you men of H., 3088
Harlot : brands h. even here, 432
h.'s cheek, beautied, 7397
trust h. for her weeping, 3095
Harm : I have done no h., 3268
little h. done to good end, 2308
never h. come our lady nigh, 1224
not half power to do h., 3269
to do h. often laudable, 3268
Harmony, 3271-3275
h. of their tongues, 3274
heard the heavenly h., 3275
hush'd to grace h., 2360
lest deceiving h. should run, 3365
ravish like enchanting h., 6707
such h. is in immortal souls, 3273
that celestial h. I go to, 3272
touches of sweet h., 3273
what hope of h., 6263
Harms : cure h. by wailing, 3270
take away the h. I fear, 3267
thousand h. idleness hatches, 3266
we beg often our own h., 5399
Harness : die with h. on, 1873
drink with h. on throat, 3129
Harp not on that, 3278
h. on it still shall I, 3279

h. not on that string, 3279
I framed to h. a ditty, 5348
Harping on what I am, 3276
still h. on my daughter, 1804
Harpy : like the h., 3280
Harry : cry God for H., 3139
H. of England, I am thine, 7361
H. succeeds H., 1605
H. the king, Bedford, 3540
H. to H. shall meet, 3613
I saw H. with beaver on, 3613
Harshness : composed of h., 4750
Hart : here bay'd, brave h., 1030
let h. ungalled play, 7468
turned into h., 1990
Harts : Britain's h. die flying, 937
Harvest of his wits, 4737
make thee curse the h., 1548
man main h. reaps, 4252
right, as snow in h., 6057
wit is come to h., 5570
Harvest-home : at h., 4225
Haste, 3281-3291
affair cries h., 3287
dispatch you with h., 2105
fiery-red with h., 3290
h. still pays h., 3286
in h., post-h., come, 3284
let h. commend duty, 3283
let's make h. away, 1183
nay, but make h., 3285
requires h., post-h., 3284
sweaty h., 3281
woo'd in h., 7375
Hasty and tinder-like, 1200
h. as fire, 6265
Hat : cockle h. and staff, 4262
he brushes h. o' mornings, 4302
lay head to man's h., 5055
ne'er pull h. upon brows, 6109
Hatches : come under my h., 778
Hatchment : no h. o'er bones, 1856
Hate, 3292-3299
barren h. bestrew union, 6924
h. I bear thee, 3298
here's much to do with h., 4376
I do h. thee worse, 3295
I h., from h., away, 3299
I h. him as hell-pains, 4372
I have more cause to h., 4371
I owe no man h., 3979
let not h. encounter love, 4368
man of my soul's h., 3294
nought I did in h., 4853
O loving h., 4376
sourest, most deadly h., 4374
take her in extremest h., 3297
thankful even for h., 6512
we h. that which we fear, 3292
yield to tyrannous h., 4373
Hated are grown to love, 4370
h. by one he loves, 2908
Hates any man the thing he would not
kill, 3857
Hats : rye-straw h., 5921
Haud credo, 1954
Haunch : in h. of winter, 646
Haunt : all the h. be ours, 5503
Have more than thou showest, 604
they deserve to h., 1985

to h. is to h., 5659
what we h. we prize not, 7508
Havings : pared present h., 850
Havoc: 3300-3301
cry h. and let slip, 1031
cry h., kings, 3301
do not cry h., 3300
tear and h., 5822
Hawk : know h. from handsaw, 4442
Hawking or spitting, 6091
Hawks : between two h., 4030
Hawthorn : through h. wind, 3303
Hawthorn-buds : lisping h., 1400
when h. appear, 6669
Hawthorn-bush gives shade, 3302
Hay : bottle of h., 3305
butter'd his h., 3304
good h. hath no fellow, 3305
lie tumbling in the h., 4010
winter mars wished-for h., 1963
Hazard, 3306-3309
all is on the h., 3308
extremest edge of h., 3306
h. all in one boat, 2777
h. of doubtful hour, 3307
h. of new fortunes, 2878
h. of spotted die, 2055
make h. of my head, 3336
men that h. all in hope, 4691
Hazel-nut : her chariot a h., 4434
Hazel-twig straight, 6978
He : I am that unfortunate he, 4249
Head, 3310-3316
banish'd from frosty h., 2479
bring thy h. to ground, 2101
broke h. against post, 3310
change cod's h., 7212
crown of h. to sole of foot, 4724
cutt'st h. with golden axe, 416
from h. to foot, 6725
h. bare till merit crown, 4652
h. fantastically carved, 4489
h. native to the heart, 6578
h. to foot total gules, 705
here is h. of traitor, 6728
hid crisp h. in bank, 4809
his h. unmellow'd, 2397
hop without thy h., 3312
I hang my h. and perish, 6815
I hang h. as flowers, 6600
I'll have thy h. for this, 4031
is his h. worth a hat, 458
lay h. to man's hat, 5055
lay thy h. in Furies' lap, 4955
let my h. stoop to block, 3313
never broke any h. but own, 3310
o'er h. and ears, 3316
off with his h., 3314
rest h. upon her lap, 3417
small h., nostril wide, 3598
stuff my h. with ill news, 4957
thy h. beaten addle as egg, 5499
uneasy lies h. wears crown, 6019
wiser h., neither too young, 1572
young body with old h., 7584
Head-piece : house good h., 3630
Heads : beast with many h., 4831
h. crushed like rotten apples, 3311
hide h. like cowards, 4282
houseless h., unfed sides, 7531

lose h. to gild horns, 2952
men whose h. grow beneath shoulders,
4305
they shake their h., 7097
Health, 3317-3321
be thou spirit of h., 6195
have care of your h., 7577
have mind upon your h., 3319
h. consort your grace, 7221
h. shall live free, 3317
h. with youthful wings flows, 3318
importing h. and graveness, 7576
no h. that Denmark drinks, 1078
no news but h. hear, 3321
so long, h., 744
to you all, good h., 7079
Healths to my niece, 2208
Healthy : not h., 3320
Hear : ever h. the like, 3325
Hearer : tire h. with words, 4404
Hearers : wonder-wounded h., 3147
Hearing, 3322-3326
bestow sense of h., 3324
good h. when children toward, 7334
make passionate sense of h., 3322
no more offend sense of h., 3322
pays h. double recompense, 4990
Hearings ravished, 7233
Hearsay : wounds by h., 1719
Heart, 3327-3390
athwart h. of his lover, 1198
betray thy h. to woman, 2660
break, h., hold tongue, 4556
break, h., I prithee, 3376
buildeth on vulgar h., 4835
burn h. to cinders, 6119
cheer your h., 3327
cold h. engender hail, 3328
cursed be h. that had h., 1741
cut lace, that my pent h., 3359
did my h. love till now, 522
easily win a woman's h., 4182
eat h. in market-place, 3352
faint not, faint h., 3357
false h. never sound legs, 2932
fare thee well, great h., 3617
fret till proud h. break, 2372
gentler h. never did sway, 6067
give hand ; my h. too, 3232
goes thy h. with this, 7563
good h. is sun and moon, 7361
good h. is worth gold, 3337
good h. never changes, 3338
he was great of h., 3355
head native to the h., 6578
h. as big as thine, 7417
h. be wrathful still, 6395
h. cool with groans, 4721
h. crack thy frail case, 3370
h. dearer than Plutus mine, 1761
h. death makes hard, 2384
h. dies in tempest of frown, 2937
h. from h., 5163
h. full of sorrows, 3363
h. hath treble wrong, 4410
h. I bear shall never sag, 4688
h. is drown'd in cares, 1996
h. is not confederate, 3234
h. of stone, 3386
h. pierced through ear, 7441

h. replete with thankfulness, 3340
h. sound as a bell, 3351
h. unspotted not daunted, 3341
h. with strings of steel, 3331
heavy h. bears not nimble tongue, 3345
heavy h., why sigh'st, 3379
his captain's h., 4426
his flaw'd h. burst, 3375
his h. and hand both open, 1212
his h. as far from fraud, 6249
his h. is fracted, 2514
his h. is his mouth, 1202
hold, hold, my h., 3330
how he takes it at h., 2046
how ill all's about my h., 3335
how weak the h. of woman, 7314
I am pale at mine h., 3347
I cannot heave h. into mouth, 3343
I feel my h. new open'd, 5368
I had rather coin my h., 4762
I have one h., 3362
I have too grieved a h., 5685
I saw his h. in his face, 3367
I shall be out of h., 5618
I will ease my h., 3336
I will live in thy h., 3353
if h. great 'twould burst, 3368
it does a man's h. good, 3421
just as high as my h., 6251
kind h. he hath, 3348
king is h. of gold, 3877
leave to afflict my h., 1340
let me wring your h., 3332
let thy tongue equal h., 6661
light h. lives long, 3388
made my h. too great, 3329
make his h. of flint, 1694
make my h. her vassal, 2847
make my seated h. knock, 6310
merry h. goes all the day, 3390
merry h. lives long-a, 3387
mine own h. was free, 3346
my hand, and my h. in it, 3236
my h. accordeth with tongue, 6168
my h. dances, 3366
my h. dropped love, 850
my h. fly to your service, 4389
my h. hath one string, 3373
my h. is drowned with grief, 3148
my h. is exceeding heavy, 3667
my h. is heavy, 3142
my h. is in the coffin, 1033
my h. is purged from hate, 3235
my h. is true as steel, 3349
my h. is turn'd to lead, 4054
my h. is turn'd to stone, 3381
my h. longs not to groan, 3365
my h. must break with silence, 3378
my h. no measure keeps, 1780
my h. o'erweens too much, 2417
my h. stands armed, 3365
my h. suspects more, 3361
my h. unto yours is knit, 547
my h. will break, 6677
my little h. undone, 3365
my old h. is crack'd, 3374
my proud h. sues, 6675
nature never framed h. prouder, 3350
never at h.'s ease, 2581
no matter from the h., 7418

no woman's h. so big, 7339
nor can h. inform tongue, 6656
nothing so full of h., 1624
now cracks a noble h., 3371
O h., lose not thy nature, 4946
O, my h. is sick, 2653
O that my h. would burst, 6420
on my h. they tread, 3902
one h., one bed, 547
outbrave h. most daring, 2053
persuade h. to perjury, 5662
pluck out h. of mystery, 5331
pure unspotted h. I send, 3339
raven's h. within dove, 3993
repose come to thy h., 5621
revengeful h. cannot forgive, 2844
rocky h. will not wear, 6465
seek to soften Jewish h., 3798
serpent h., hid with flowering face, 1917
set not h. on proud array, 2660
she hath h. of fine frame, 4343
show me thy humble h., 3358
tackle of my h. crack'd, 3373
take my h. with thee, 3342
taming my wild h., 4301
tears pierce marble h., 7309
then burst his mighty h., 1033
this blows my h., 3369
this h. break ere I weep, 7070
thou hast cleft my h., 3333
throw my h. against hardness, 4779
thy flinty h., more hard, 3380
thy h. as hard as steel, 3263
tiger's h. in woman's hide, 7308
wear h. so white, 3224
wear him in my h. of h., 5171
wear my h. upon sleeve, 3354
what h. thinks tongue speaks, 3351
whetted on thy stone-hard h., 3962
with h. as willing, 3692
yet do they ease the h., 7448
you have a merry h., 3389
your h. is burst, 3377
your h. is cramm'd with arrogancy, 4609
Heart-ache flesh is heir to, 1847
Heart-blood breathed poison, 6003
Heart-break: better chiding than h., 1275
Heart-string: from h. I love, 3877
Heart-strings: harp till h. break, 3279
Heart-whole: I'll warrant him h., 1711
Hearts: all h. use own tongues, 2931
by ears our h. oft tainted, 3356
cause makes hard h., 3384
cherish h. that hate thee, 5851
gentle h. change to bloody, 2336
he sits high in people's h., 5088
h. create of duty, 2318
h. false as stairs of sand, 4210
h. more proof than shields, 2671
h. of gold, 2647
h. of old gave hands, 3233
h. of princes kiss obedience, 5425
heaven knows your h., 2460
I kept h. in liveries, 3346
lighten our own h., 1779
make faces vizards to h., 2466
neither in h. nor eyes, 2975
O you hard h., 3383
steel my soldiers' h., 3030
stir your h. to mutiny, 7541

stone him with harden'd h., 3385
those you give your h. to, 2907
women's waxen h., 2890
your h. are mighty, 5766
your h. full of sorrow, 2069
your high-swoln h., 5541
Heat : as subject to h. as butter, 4502
fear no more h. of sun, 2240
measure h. of our livers, 7578
one h. another h. expels, 4355
rash h. wrapp'd in cold, 3393
she knows h. of luxurious bed, 761
Heaven, 3394-3410
airs from h., 6195
brightest h. of invention, 4856
civil strife in h., 6493
confess yourself to h., 1489
damn'd in the book of h., 5060
did h. look on, 1289
either in h. or in hell, 2515
find out new h., 4242
gentleman is gone to h., 3403
glance from h. to earth, 3705
hast dropp'd from h., 4792
he wisheth you in h., 3610
heard as from h. to earth, 1850
heard h.'s artillery, 6588
h. and honour be witness, 3431
h. divides state of man, 5068
h. forgive you and us, 6986
h. had part in this maid, 3406
h. hath my empty words, 5403
h. in my mouth, 5403
h. in your cheek pleads, 2448
h. is above all yet, 3399
h. keeps part in life, 3406
h. knows thou art false, 2502
h. knows your hearts, 2459
h. me such uses send, 398
h. prosper the right, 5689
h. send prosperous life, 2297
h. shall move about her, 2297
h. still guards the right, 227
h. such grace doth lend, 5953
h. take my soul, 3401
h. was full of fiery shapes, 659
h. will take our souls, 3409
h. with us as torches, 3402
high hope for a low h., 3569
his heels kick at h., 3407
I from h. banish'd, 6727
if h. would make a world, 7478
if not to h., to hell, 3410
I'll make my h. to dream, 3408
know friends in h., 3400
leave her to h., 4814
let h. cry shame, 6183
let h. kiss earth, 3394 ✧
let h. requite with curse, 3512
look how the floor of h., 3273
make face of h. so fine, 4998
make my h. in lady's lap, 3396
make my h. to dream, 1681
means that h. yields, 3404
met my dearest foe in h., 6574
nor h. peep through blanket, 4980
nor of h. nor earth, 5619
selfsame h. that frowns on me, 3405
shun h. that leads to hell, 4431

thank h. fasting for love, 4251
then h. mocks itself, 2501
this villain send to h., 5641
thy h. is on earth, 3395
trouble deaf h. with cries, 4328
wants but h. to throne in, 2354
will of h. be done, 3397
you may as well strike at h., 5727
Heavens, 3411-3414
do as the h. have done, 2845
h. are angry and frown, 5996
h. are just, 3411
h. blaze death of princes, 1863
h. do lour upon you, 3413
h. hold walls of honour, 3534
h. observe degree, 1959
h. thee guard and keep, 691
h. threaten bloody stage, 1827
h. were all on fire, 659
hung be h. with black, 1415
I must be patient till h. look, 5327
let the h. give him defence, 3412
Heavier by weight of a man, 3667
Heaviness, 3415-3418
burthen with h. that's gone, 5609
charming with pleasing h., 3417
h. foreruns good event, 1182
h. within my bosom, 3416
lay aside life-harming h., 3418
our strength gone into h., 3415
sorrow's h. heavier grow, 6110
Heavy weighs my lord, 3415
Hebrew : thou art an H., 1323
Hecate : black H.'s summons, 1936
Hector, 3419-3424
art thou for H.'s matching, 5552
H. dead, no more to say, 3424
H. shall have good catch, 7252
H. was not clean-timbered, 3419
H. whose patience is fix'd, 3420
H. will challenge him, 1168
look, H., sun begins to set, 3423
manly as H., 1212
that's H., there's a fellow, 3421
valiant as H., 6838
valorous as H. of Troy, 2510
valour excells in H., 3422
Hecuba : cruses H. gave, 1736
H. laughed till eyes ran, 4679
what's H. to him, 63
Hedge : born under a h., 661
h. aside from forthright, 2299
I am fain to h., 3548
I will but look upon h., 3427
Hedge-hogs : thorny h., 2478
Hedge-pig whined, 1114
Hedge-sparrow fed cuckoo, 1704
Heed : take h., 695
Heel : I'll begin at thy h., 863
Heels, 3428-3433
at her h. infectious troop, 4614
betake me to my h., 3431
hang me up by the h., 3429
his h. may kick at heaven, 3407
I am almost out at h., 3433
I will lay ye by the h., 3432
lighten our wives' h., 1778
made of Atalanta's h., 7225
one woe upon another's h., 7273

punish you by the h., 3430
show a fair pair of h., 3428
Hefts: cracks with h., 6193
Heifer and calf called neat, 1364
who finds the h. dead, 2364
Heifers: kin as parish h., 3864
Heigh-ho: cry h. for husband, 3666
sing h., 2928
Height: urged her h., 6253
Heir of mongrel bitch, 3941
her ashes create an h., 5254
Heirs: careless h. darken, 6942
h. of all eternity, 2519
marry them to your h., 6010
orphan h. of destiny, 2475
rich-left h., 4772
Helen, 3434-3438
H., mother of Constantine, 3743
H. must needs be fair, 3435
H. so blushed, 3201
H. was a sweet creature, 456
H. with Paris sleeps, 3434
H.'s beauty in brow of Egypt, 3705
stop eye of H.'s needle, 7252
Helicanus, strike me, 3820
Helicons: curs confront H., 4955
Hell, 3439-3444
account this world but h., 3408
all h. shall stir for this, 3439
as low as h. from heaven, 6494
blasts from h., 6195
he wishes you in h., 3610
heaven that leads to h., 4431
h. and night must bring, 670
h. breathes out contagion, 4673
h. burns, fiends roar, 5678
h. is empty, all devils here, 3444
h. is murky, 3442
h.'s black intelligencer, 5678
hie thee to h. for shame, 1970
I live in h., 3440
if not to heaven, then to h., 3410
keep the gate of h., 3443
rebellious h., 7556
she's gone to burning h., 226
there's h., there's darkness, 7317
what a h. of witchcraft, 6465
what hole in h. hot enough, 4648
you've passed a h. of time, 6824
Hell-fire: burning in h., 2732
Hell-hound hunts us to death, 7347
Hell-kite: O h., 1289
Hell-pains: hate him as h., 4372
Hellespont: Propontic and H., 4692
Helm: we will not from h., 7026
Helmet to spur all blood, 705
what hacks on his h., 3421
Help feeble up, 3445
much I need to h., 4943
past h., past grief, 3176
study h. for that, 3446
Helter-skelter have I rode, 4955
Hem: cry h., 3447
h. and stroke thy beard, 3451
Hemlocks foul as hell, 6474
Hempen home-spuns, 3499
Hempseed; thou h., 5713
Hems and beats her heart, 3448
Henry is dead, 4819
King H. throws away crutch, 1696

Hens: short-legged h., 3854
Herald: bold h. of tongue, 1299
silence h. of joy, 5946
Heraldry is hands, 3233
Heralds: love's h. thoughts, 4323
Herb: she was h. of grace, 5788
Herb-grace: call it h., 5750
Herbs made for smell, 6929
h. swarming with caterpillars, 1129
small h. have grace, 7064
Hercules, 3452-3458
brawns of H., 4485
for valour love a H., 4281
go, H., live thou, 3457
he is as valiant as H., 4538
H. did shake mellow fruit, 3454
H. must yield to odds, 3455
I was with H. and Cadmus, 4864
if H. and Lichas play, 2053
if you had been wife of H., 3453
leave that labour to H., 3984
let H. do what he may, 1112
made H. turn spit, 3458
no more like than I to H., 4556
not H. could knock brains, 2800
present H. in minority, 3456
see H. whipping a gig, 3891
'tis the god H., 3452
too hard for H.' club, 1713
wear beards of H., 4210
well done, H., 3456
Herd: wild and wanton h., 4862
Here, there, everywhere, 3459
neither h. nor there, 3460
we cannot be h. and there, 3461
Heresies hated most, 3463
Heresy: scriptures turn'd to h., 3462
strange without h., 5582
Heretic, 3464-3468
ever an obstinate h., 3467
he is a most arch h., 3465
h. that makes the fire, 3468
revolt from h., 3466
there is sprung up an h., 3464
Heritage: service no h., 5871
Hermes: more musical than H., 3590
Hermit: old h. of Prague, 7256
wither'd h. five score, 510
Hermitage: palace for h., 3902
Herod, 3469-3472
H. of Jewry, 3469
H.'s head I'll have, 3470
it out-herods H., 54
what H. of Jewry is this, 3472
Herring: I am a shotten h., 4537
Hesperides: fair H., 3474
still climbing trees in H., 4281
Hey, ho, wind and rain, 7231
h. non, nonny, 3106
h. nonny, nonny, 4506
with a h. and a ho, 4401
Hey-dey in blood is tame, 708
Hic et ubique, 6369
Hide: thou wear lion's h., 4184
tiger's heart in woman's h., 7308
vengeance on withered h., 5653
Hiems: bold H. icy crown, 5832
this side is H., 7202
High and low beguiles, 3187
Highly: what wouldst h., 4911

High-stomach'd both, 6265
Highway : buried in king's h., 3902
Hilding for a livery, 6008
Hill, 3475-3477
　come to top of this h., 3476
　heaven-kissing h., 5272
　over h., over dale, 2476
Hills : high h. draw out miles, 2077
　h. whose heads touch heaven, 4305
　if h. be dry, stray lower, 4205
　to climb steep h., 3475
　who digs h. because aspire, 3477
Him, O wondrous h., 3618
Hind speeds to catch tiger, 6190
　h. that would be mated by lion, 4171
　tiger hath seized gentle h., 6601
　you are a cowardly h., 1637
Hindmost : leave you h., 2299
Hinges : crook h. of knee, 2719
Hip : catch him upon h., 3478
　have Cassio on the h., 3480
　now I have you on the h., 1798
Hips : briers bear scarlet h., 6984
　too wide for Nature's h., 2550
Hire : this is h. and salary, 5641
Hiren : have we H. here, 3481
Hiss me to my grave, 5338
History, 3482-3484
　if I should tell my h., 3484
　our h. shall speak freely, 3483
　there is h. in men's lives, 3482
　what's her h., 7339
Hit or miss, 3488
　h., very palpable h., 3485
　thou canst not h. it, 3487
　you have h. it, 2170
Hither : come h., come h., 6729
Hoarding went to hell, 3489
Hoarse : we are h., 6091
Hob : beg of H. and Dick, 1748
　h. nob is his word, 7394
Hobby-horse is but a colt, 3491
　h. is forgot, 3490
　my wife's a h., 7145
Hobgoblin call you, 2477
　h. make fairy oyes, 2475
Hog in sloth, 1205
Hogs : shall I keep h., 5444
Hogshead : bear huge h., 6869
Hold-fast is the only dog, 5051
Hole to keep wind away, 1017
　what h. in hell hot enough, 4648
Holidame : by my h., 2495
Holiday, 3492-3495
　be merry, make h., 5921
　he speaks h., 6039
　in a h. humour, 3645
　this blessed day a h., 3494
　this little one make h., 3494
　with h. and lady terms, 4225
Holiday-time of my beauty, 4083
Holidays : if year were h., 3492
Holily : that wouldst thou h., 4911
Holiness : mind bent to h., 3496
Holla : cry h. to tongue, 6657
Holland of eight shillings, 5906
Hollander : swag-bellied H., 2338
Hollowness : low sound no h., 3344
　not with empty h., 3162
Holly : heigh-ho unto green h., 2928

Holmedon : at H. met, 3607
Holy : be h. as severe, 6401
　h., fair, wise is she, 5953
　man divine and h., 3497
　my tears prove h. water, 6456
　so h. is my love, 4252
Holy-ales : ember-eves, h., 6095
Holy-water better than rain-water, 7023
Homage : what instead of h., 1158
Home, 3498-3501
　at h. I was in a better place, 6705
　go thou toward h., 3498
　he speaks h., madam, 6182
　h. art gone and ta'en wages, 2240
　h. where small experience grows, 7176
　lie not a night from h., 7021
　men are merriest from h., 4658
　speak to me h., 6655
　spend youth at h., 3501
　thou liest warm at h., 3670
Home-keeping youth, 7574
Homely in thy drift, 1494
Home-spuns : hempen h., 3499
Homo name common to all, 4890
Honest as any man living, 3511
　h. as skin between brows, 3511
　h. he is and hates slime, 3514
　h. in deed and word, 5347
　h. maid as broke bread, 4472
　h. makes ill-favouredly, 494
　h. man can speak for self, 3508
　h. soul as broke bread, 3511
　I durst wager she is h., 3512
　I hope lord esteems me h., 3513
　I pray gods make me h., 3504
　if she be less than h., 3510
　if she be not h., 3512
　if you be h. and fair, 494
　my friends poor but h., 5373
　sometimes h. by chance, 3518
　to be direct and h., 3515
　to be h., one in thousand, 3506
　where not h. never valiant, 3509
　would you not have me h., 3504
Honesty, 3502-3519
　arm'd so strong in h., 6570
　corruption wins not more than h., 1555
　h. coupled to beauty, 3504
　h. is a fool and loses, 3515
　h. is his fault, 3515
　h. should admit no discourse, 494
　make h. a vice, 3515
　mine h. be my dower, 3503
　neither h. nor manhood, 3507
　no legacy so rich as h., 3503
　rich h. dwells like miser, 3505
　there's no h. in men, 4514
　though h. be no puritan, 3502
　thy h. doth mince matter, 4578
　we need no grave to bury h., 3516
　what a fool h. is, 3517
　why should honour outlive h., 3550
Honey, 3520-3523
　feed on such sweet h., 7017
　h. and milk and sugar, 7388
　h. guarded with a sting, 3522
　h., sauce to sugar, 3504
　our mouths packed with h., 6084
　suck'd h. of his vows, 4681
　suck'd h. which bee kept, 7016

sweet as h. of Hybla, 3605
sweetest h. is loathsome, 3521
they surfeited with h., 3520
wax nor h. bring home, 4114
we may gather h. from weed, 3074
ye have h. ye desire, 3523
you have h., these gall, 5164
Honey-bags from humble-bees, 566
Honey-bees: so work the h., 563
Honey-comb: thick as h., 5290
Honey-heavy dew of slumber, 6022
Honey-mouthed: prove h., 6683
Honey-seed: thou art a h., 5713
Honey-stalks: more sweet than h., 7453
Honeysuckles, ripen'd by sun, 3524
Honi soit qui mal y pense, 2371
Honorificabilitudinitatibus, 7431
Honour, 3525-3559
  aged h. cites virtuous youth, 3525
  art thou of blood and h., 5552
  believe me for mine h., 1032
  best ward of h. rewarding, 5613
  can h. set a leg, 3539
  depths and shoals of h., 6450
  fewer men, greater h., 3540
  fine strains of h., 3532
  from book of h. razed, 7015
  give me staff of h., 3556
  he hath a kind of h., 3533
  he wears h. in a box, 6990
  heavens and h. witness, 3431
  hiding h. in necessity, 3426
  hold your h. more precise, 3530
  h. and policy grow together, 3531
  h. bates scythe's edge, 2518
  h. for his valour, 1032
  h. forgets men's names, 3546
  h. hath no skill in surgery, 3539
  h. is a mere scutcheon, 3539
  h. is essence not seen, 3549
  h. more precious-dear than life, 3558
  h. no better than picture-like, 5614
  h. now or never, 1593
  h. of a maid is her name, 3503
  h. peereth in meanest habit, 3554
  h. pricks me on, 3539
  h., riches, blessing, 696
  h. travels in strait, 3557
  h. weakly fortress'd, 3552
  h.'s train longer, 3542
  how if h. pricks me off, 3539
  I love h. more than fear death, 3544
  I should do so in h., 2136
  if h. bid me on, 3538
  if it be sin to covet h., 3540
  it is a dropsied h., 6928
  jealous in h., 7466
  laid h. too unchary out, 3386
  let it look like h., 2135
  let us die in h., 5889
  lose h. I lose myself, 3529
  mine h. is my life, 3553
  mine h. keeps weather, 3558
  never melt h. into lust, 4432
  no h. where there is beauty, 3536
  not a man hath any h., 3564
  not profit that leads h., 3528
  not to woo h., but to wed, 3526
  on her virgin h., 4216
  outward h. for inward toil, 5430

own hand may strike h., 1498
perseverance keeps h. bright, 5233
pluck bright h. from moon, 3537
pluck drowned h. by locks, 3537
rake h. from me, life done, 3553
set h. in one eye, 3544
set mine h. at stake, 3559
so h. cross it from north, 1787
stands on h. of his birth, 5732
take the h., 6742
they smack of h. both, 7434
thou mayst in h. come off, 4245
thy life hath smatch of h., 3545
to plainness h. is bound, 3547
too much h. a burden, 3543
what is h., a word, 3539
what loss h. may sustain, 1252
when h. is at stake, 3121
who bates mine h., 3555
who hates h. hates gods, 3551
why should h. outlive honesty, 3550
you stand upon your h., 3548
Honours, 3560-3564
  bears blushing h. thick, 2492
  budding h. on thy crest, 3561
  but honour for these h., 3564
  drawing h. up to heaven, 3541
  gave h. to world again, 1862
  h. thrive from our acts, 3527
  h. titles but of scorn, 3560
  new h. come upon him, 3563
  planted h. in their eyes, 3734
  sell large h. for trash, 929
Hoodman-blind: cozened at h., 708
Hoods make not monks, 4768
Hoodwinked: Cupid h., 6185
Hoof more musical, 3590
  plod away o' the h., 6577
Hook: bait the h., 2708
  hold h. and line, 1770
Hook-nosed fellow of Rome, 1039
Hooking right and wrong, 4826
Hoop: admiration did not h., 6718
  with age grown into h., 7272
Hooping: out of all h., 7350
Hoops of steel, 2902
Hop in his walks, 3867
  h. without thy head, 3312
Hope, 3565-3578
  at enmity with h., 3572
  entertain him with h., 5647
  false h. lingers in extremity, 3572
  he lined himself with h., 3565
  here I will put off h., 3575
  high h. for low heaven, 3569
  hits where h. is coldest, 2387
  h. gives not warrant, 3566
  h. is a curtal dog, 3571
  h. is a lover's staff, 3578
  h. to joy is little less, 3573
  I see some sparks of h., 6155
  our h. but sad despair, 3252
  past h., past cure, 7073
  puts forth leaves of h., 2492
  true h. is swift, 3574
  was h. drunk, 3570
Hopes dash selves to pieces, 3567
  in you all h. are lost, 4233
  there my h. lie drowned, 3576
  who builds h. on air, 3094

Horam, harum, horum, 7103
Horatio : thrift, H., 6574
Horn of abundance, 5838
  h. to laugh to scorn, 3580
  no scorn to wear h., 3580
Horn-beasts, 3579
Horn-mad : I'll be h., 3581
  my master is h., 4437
  thou wouldst be h., 4437
  young man would be h., 4427
Horned man is monster, 4512
Horning : goodly gift in h., 3582
Hornpipes : sings to h., 5471
Horns: 3579-3582
  as h. are odious, 3579
  charge h. with garlands, 3659
  curst cow short h., 1629
  h. beholding to wives for, 6051
  h. o' the moon, 1085
  if I have h. to make mad, 3581
  know him by his h., 2033
  leather skin and h., 3580
  leave h. without a case, 6052
  lose heads to gild h., 2952
  my h. I bequeath to husbands, 1954
  pluck off the bull's h., 973
  tender h. of cockled snails, 4281
  we'll tip thy h. with gold, 974
Horror, tongue cannot name, 3583
  on h.'s head h. accumulate, 3584
Horrors : supp'd full with h., 2613
Horse, 3585-3598
  an two men ride h., 4508
  give me another h., 3596
  give my roan h. a drench, 3608
  happy h. to bear Antony, 3586
  his h. is slain, 5683
  h. full of high feeding, 6646
  h. of that colour, 5475
  h. seized by leopard, 4078
  h. that doth untread, 3593
  I am a brewer's h., 1333
  I have h. will follow game, 6361
  I was not made a h., 3595
  I will not change my h., 3590
  is he on his h., 3586
  let me taste my h., 3613
  like Trojan h. stuff'd, 5903
  my kingdom for a h., 3597
  nothing but talk of h., 3592
  O, for a h. with wings, 3587
  she is my h., my ox, 4570
  snorting like a h., 6018
  spur a forward h., 3594
  spurs h. but on one side, 1198
  that which is now a h., 1380
  what h., a roan, 3589
  what h. should have, 3598
  would my h. had speed, 6670
Horseback : runs h. up a hill, 2170
Horseback-breaker : this h., 1456
Horsemanship : noble h., 3613
Horsemen like candlesticks, 3771
Horse-stealer : not be h., 5269
Horses are tied by heads, 4061
  h. neigh, men groan, 5097
  h. of the sun, 3585
  like h. hot at hand, 2480
  those that tame wild h., 3591

Hose : see to garter h., 4351
  your h. ungartered, 249
  youthful h. too wide, 7466
Hospitality : deeds of h., 5897
Host, 3599-3604
  call'st thou me h., 3599
  it is thine h., 3604
  mine h. of the Garter, 3601
  play the humble h., 3600
  ranting h. of the Garter, 3602
  time like fashionable h., 6642
Hostess of the tavern, 3605
  woeful h. brooks not, 3606
Hot : be not so h., 3392
  h. as molten lead, 4050
  h. as monkeys, 5802
  h. because meat is cold, 4597
  thou art as h. a Jack, 5499
Hotspur : gallant H., 3607
  hare-brain'd H., 3616
  H., Mars in swathling, 3611
  H. of the north, 3608
Hound licking of wound, 7524
Hounds go by name of dogs, 4496
  like fell and cruel h., 1990
  my h. Spartan kind, 4864
Hour, 3619-3628
  from h. to h. we ripe, 2793
  I know my h. is come, 2993
  insupportable, heavy h., 3627
  make coming h. o'erflow, 3813
  my h. is almost come, 3620
  no h. so fit as Cæsar's, 1029
  ragged'st h. time dare bring, 3622
  sixth h., when beasts graze, 6342
  third h. of drowsy morning, 1396
  this pernicious h., 3626
  thy h. is not yet come, 3623
  time and the h., 6623
  you come upon your h., 3619
Hours : careful h. have written, 3144
  carve not with h. love's brow, 6634
  creeping h. of time, 6608
  discourse the h. away, 6160
  entertain with quiet h., 4126
  happy h. attend you, 2531
  h. for necessities, 3625
  h. unregister'd in fame, 6491
  I'll not be tied to h., 4081
  let the h. be short, 3621
  lovers' h. long, 4412
  make use of thy salt h., 7110
  sad h. seem long, 3628
  so many h. tend my flock, 3624
  unless h. were cups of sack, 6615
House, 3629-3632
  break bloody h. of life, 3888
  cannot keep wealth, keep h., 7040
  climb o'er h. to unlock gate, 6292
  eaten out of h. and home, 2280
  fair h. on another's ground, 4291
  he carries h. on his head, 6051
  h. is good head-piece, 3630
  I will not ruinate father's h., 3629
  my h. stands by church, 1343
  no h. to put his head in, 3630
  our h. in perplexity, 2162
  our h. is hell, 3631
  secret h. of death, 1839
  she is my h., 4570

snail has h. to put head, 6052
this mortal h. I'll ruin, 1840
war no strife to dark h., 7122
who lets fair h. decay, 3632
worse than a smoky h., 6431
you take my h., 4140
Houses last till doomsday, 3170
  plague o' both your h., 5320
Housewife : bounteous h. nature, 6984
  false h. fortune, 2852
  h. by selling desires, 4023
  I play the noble h., 6603
  mock good h. fortune, 2853
Housewifery : players in h., 7325
Housewives in your beds, 7325
Howling, 3633-3637
  h. after music, 3637
  imagine h., 1876
  like h. of Irish wolves, 3633
  plague upon such h., 3636
Howlings attend it, 3635
Hue : add h. to rainbow, 2375
  h. of dungeons, 679
  native h. of resolution, 1847
Hugger-mugger to inter, 3136
Hulks : greater h. deep, 784
Hum : his h. a battery, 6429
Humanity : change h. with baboon, 2214
  h. must prey on itself, 3639
  h. thou never knewest, 2402
  seem to lack h., 3638
Humble : all h. kiss rod, 4349
  h. as ripest mulberry, 3642
Humble-bee : ape and h., 6572
  merrily h. doth sing, 570
  red-hipped h., 567
Humble-bees : steal from h., 566
Humble-mouthed : meek, h., 4609
Humidity : from earth h., 6333
Humility, 3640-3644
  dress'd myself in h., 3644
  fawn on rage with h., 4192
  making proud of his h., 3640
  modest stillness and h., 7013
  napless vesture of h., 3641
  plant in tyrants mild h., 4281
  sounded base-string of h., 3643
Humorous as winter, 1203
Humour, 3645-3651
  awe man from career of h., 3650
  cold and drowsy h., 5468
  every h. hath pleasure, 3651
  here's a fellow frights h., 3649
  his h. is lofty, 1206
  h. of bread and cheese, 3649
  h. of it is too hot, 3648
  I am in a holiday h., 3645
  I like not h. of lying, 3649
  learn h. of the age, 6577
  say it is my h., 2741
  that's the h. of it, 3647
  unyoked h. of idleness, 3684
Humours : I am of all h., 3646
  king hath run bad h., 2514
  suck up h. of morning, 5926
  unsettled h. of land, 2878
Hundredth Psalm, 7438
Hungarian wight, 6444
Hunger broke stone walls, 5459
  h. till he famish, 2785

Hungry when most she satisfies, 140
  they said they were h., 5459
Hunt is up, 3653
Hunter : ring h.'s peal, 3653
Hurly-burly done, 6573
Hurt past all surgery, 5626
  I never did her h., 3654
  I never h. you, 3656
  what, art thou h., 3655
Hurts : had he his h. before, 6072
Husband, 3657-3673
  cry heigh-ho for h., 3666
  get thee a good h., 3657
  heavier for a h., 3667
  her h. will be from home, 3663
  here is your h., 5272
  h., be not so disquiet, 4600
  h.'s fault if wives fail, 3671
  I am h. for your turn, 4565
  I that kill'd her h., 3297
  in second h. accurst, 3661
  light wife makes heavy h., 7136
  make h. cuckold, 3668
  my h. made me Christian, 5968
  my h. was a merry man, 2495
  never get thee a h., 3664
  no worse h. than best, 3660
  not endure h. with beard, 475
  O, that I knew this h., 3659
  play good h. at home, 3669
  saved your h. sweat, 3453
  second time kill h. dead, 3661
  see you fitted with h., 3665
  son ere h. for bed, 6087
  thy h. is thy lord, 3670
  wept for death of h., 3081
Husbandry must uphold, 3632
  in lieu of thy h., 5872
  like as h. in war, 3420
  there's h. in heaven, 1063
Husbands : hazards of all h., 7133
  let h. know wives have sense, 3671
  pranks they not show h., 7141
  why have my sisters h., 3662
  your father got h., 3666
Husks : eating draff and h., 6064
  keep hogs, eat h., 5444
Hybla bees honeyless, 7385
  sweet as honey of H., 3605
Hydra : many mouths as H., 2228
Hydra-headed wilfulness, 7153
Hyen : laugh like a h., 4018
Hymen, 3674-3676
  defiler of H.'s bed, 3067
  H. did our hands unite, 3675
  H. god of every town, 3674
  H. hath bride to bed, 3676
  H.'s lamps light you, 6924
  till H.'s torch be lighted, 1245
  'tis H. peoples every town, 3674
Hymn : chants h. to own death, 6364
Hymns : chanting h. to moon, 6922
  sings h. at heaven's gate, 4328
Hyperboles : three-piled h., 7363
Hyperion to a satyr, 3871
  H.'s curls, 5272
Hypocrite : done like h., 1617
Hyrcan : like H. tiger, 5879
Hyrcania : tigers of H., 7308
Hysterica passio, down, 6104

I

I am I, howe'er begot, 7194
Iago : the pity of it, I., 5306
Icarus : my poor boy, I., 2806
Ice, 3677-3679
  break i. and do feat, 3677
  cold brook candied with i., 6356
  hot i., strange snow, 2072
  piece of i., 3679
  thick-ribbed i., 1876
  thou art all i., 3677
  to smooth the i., 2375
  very i. of chastity, 1230
Icicle curdied by frost, 1231
Icicles hang by the wall, 5124
Ides : beware the i. of March, 3680
  i. of March are come, 3681
  i. of March remember, 3682
Idiot holds bauble for god, 5063
  play the i. in her eyes, 4522
  tale told by an i., 4137
Idleness : harms i. doth hatch, 3266
  love in i., 4388
  mar brother with i., 4477
  sterile with i., 793
  take you for i. itself, 3683
  'tis labour to bear i., 3683
  unyoked humour of your i., 3684
  wear out youth with i., 7574
Idolatry : love be call'd i., 4331
  pure, pure i., 3685
  she dotes in i., 3686
If is your only peacemaker, 3688
  much virtue in if, 3688
Ifs : tellest me of ifs, 3689
Ignobly : not i. have I given, 855
Ignominy sleep with thee, 3617
Ignomy pursue life, 5896
Ignorance, 3690-3697
  curse of mankind, i., 1746
  his i. was wise, 3692
  i., how deformed thou look, 3693
  i. is made my gaoler, 3695
  i. is the curse of God, 3691
  if he have power, vail i., 4071
  let me not burst in i., 3690
  no darkness but i., 3697
  set afire by thine own i., 7249
  such a valiant i., 3696
  taught i. aloft to fly, 2442
Ilion : cloud-kissing I., 6753
  Troy nor I. stand, 5163
Ill, 3698-3702
  destined i. she must assay, 5407
  i. deserve by doing well, 3698
  i., to example i., 3699
  in venturing i. we leave, 3700
  nothing i. can dwell, 3702
  nought shall go i., 5463
  O benefit of i., 3701
  some i. a-brewing, 2182
  what care I who calls me i., 5810
Ill-favoured thing, 4555
  that will be i., 3191
Ills : bear i. we have, 1847
  i. we do i. instruct, 3671
Illyria : what should I do in I., 944

Image doth unfix my hair, 6310
  like waxen i. 'gainst fire, 4355
  make my i. alehouse sign, 1423
  true i. of life, 1587
Images : his loves brazen i., 3496
  none of Pygmalion's i., 7322
Imagination, 3703-3706
  are of i. all compact, 3705
  as i. bodies forth, 3705
  beyond i. is the wrong, 7538
  great i. proper to madmen, 3565
  if i. amend them, 3706
  such tricks hath strong i., 3705
  sweeten my i., 3704
Imaginations : my i. foul, 3703
Imaginings : fears less than i., 2609
Imbecility : lord of i., 6290
Immortal part with angels, 799
  lost i. part of myself, 5626
  thou must be made i., 3708
Immortality attends virtue, 6942
Imp of flame, 3877
  most royal i. of fame, 691
Impatience becomes dog, 5190
Impeach : intricate i., 1710
Impediment in the current, 1731
Impediments of filial fear, 4284
  let me not admit i., 4333
  made way through i., 7044
Imperator of 'paritors, 1714
Imperfections on head, 3709
Impiety made feast of thee, 3320
  thou pure i., 2532
Implorators of suits, 6962
Importunity : vehement i., 2346
Impossible : make not i., 3713
  nothing is i., 3714
  strive with things i., 3712
Impossibility : murdering i., 3711
  what i. would slay, 3710
Impudence : take gifts for i., 3002
Impudency : audacious without i., 5582
Impurity doth not pollute, 5228
In : who's in, who's out, 5438
In-a-door : keep i., 604
Incense : gods throw i., 5770
Inch : every i. a king, 3890
  my i. of taper burnt, 1886
  not an i. further, 7305
  stretches from i. to ell, 7258
Inch-meal : by i., 1745
Inch-thick, knee-deep, 3316
Inches : would I had thy i., 6250
Incision for your love, 1467
Inconstancy falls off, 4525
Incontinent before marriage, 4387
Incorpsed and demi natured, 3588
Increase : earth's i., 696
Ind : east to western I., 3799
Indenture : coward with i., 3428
Index of direful pageant, 5512
  thunders in the i., 38
Indexes things to come, 6538
Indian threw pearl away, 1208
  lay out ten to see dead I., 2339

Indies: map with I., 6074
my East and West I., 4289
our king has I. in his arms, 7311
Indignation: spit forth i., 1079
Indignities you laid on me, 2834
Indirections find directions, 3715
i. grow direct, 3716
wring vile trash by i., 4762
Indiscretion: offence i. finds, 3718
our i. serves us well, 3717
Industry: broke bones with i., 6084
i. is up-stairs, down-stairs, 7421
manured with i., 793
sweat of i. would dry, 6372
Inexorable: more i. than tigers, 3755
Infamy will arise, 6704
Infancy techy and wayward, 1209
Infant mewling and puking, 7406
Infants: first-born i., 2933
i. prattle of thy pride, 7116
Infections that sun sucks, 1745
Infidel, I have thee on hip, 3479
pagan rascal, an i., 5548
Infirmities: play with i. for gold, 6855
Infirmity, 3719-3721
God send you speedy i., 3720
i. doth neglect office, 3719
i. that decays the wise, 3720
i. waits upon worn times, 3721
Influence of received star, 1157
Influences: servile to skyey i., 1874
Ingener: tire the i., 1980
Ingratitude, 3722-3726
filial i., 3724
hate i. more than lying, 3726
i. is monstrous, 4829
i., marble-hearted fiend, 3723
i., more strong than traitors' arms, 1033
not so unkind as man's i., 3722
sin of i. heavy on me, 3725
Ingratitudes: monster of i., 6642
Ingredient is a devil, 7184
present i. to his eye, 6193
Ingredients of poison'd chalice, 3846
Inhabitants o' the earth, 2270
Inheritance to daughter, 3728
i. of this poor child, 3729
small i. my father left, 1606
Inhuman: more i. than tigers, 7308
Iniquity, 3730-3732
draw not sword to guard i., 6405
I lack i. sometimes, 3731
i.'s throat cut like calf, 5960
like the formal vice, i., 4593
that grey i., father ruffian, 3730
what virtue breeds, i. devours, 6944
wholesome i. have you, 3732
Injuries they themselves procure, 3735
i. written in our flesh, 3733
Injury: ingrateful i., 3724
patience her i. mockery, 5199
Injustice: plague i. with pains, 3409
with i. corrupted, 5493
Ink: fallen into pit of i., 1281
he hath not drunk i., 3693
i. temper'd with love's sighs, 4281
Ink-horn: hang him with i., 7536
Inkle: price of this i., 5613
Inn: take ease in mine i., 2275
thou most beauteous i., 6746

Innocence, 3736-3742
by i. I swear, 3362
dallies with i. of love, 6097
i. make accusation blush, 3742
it will help nothing to plead i., 3739
prompt me, holy i., 3672
take the sense of my i., 547
trust is in my i., 3738
we changed i. for i., 881
Innocency: rivers of i., 6463
Innocent as grace itself, 6721
i. as sucking lamb, 3737
i. of the knowledge, 1936
play the pious i., 3741
sweetest i. that e'er did lift up eye, 3859
Innocents 'scape not thunderbolt, 3736
Inoculate our old stock, 6932
Insinuate to make thee sigh, 2041
Insolence of office, 1847
Inspiration of celestial grace, 3807
Inspirations: good i., 3745
Inspired: every man thing i., 3744
was Mahomet i. by dove, 3743
Instances: modern i., 7466
Instant: at unseasonable i., 3748
take i. by forward top, 3746
upon that i., 3747
Instinct, 3749-3752
by divine i. men mistrust, 3752
hath by i. knowledge, 6357
I was coward on i., 3751
i. is a great matter, 3751
I'll never obey i., 3749
wonder i. should frame them, 3750
you ran away upon i., 5759
Instruction: better the i., 6911
Instructions: follows own i., 7401
we teach bloody i., 5637
Instrument: call me what i. you will, 5331
his tongue a stringless i., 6674
poor i. may do noble deed, 1919
such an i. I was to use, 1762
Instruments of darkness, 2029
Insurrection: nature of i., 40
Intellect not replenished, 3693
it rejoiceth my i., 7236
Intelligencer: hell's i., 5678
Intemperant: more i. than Venus, 5845
Intent: overtake bad i., 3734
Intents: be thy i. wicked, 6195
ere I can perfect i., 6349
i. but merely thoughts, 3754
my i. are fix'd, 3753
my i. are savage-wild, 3755
Interior: pries not to i., 4839
Interpretation will misquote, 6716
Interrogatories: what name to i., 3887
Intertissued robe of gold, 6021
Intrusion convert to gall, 2951
Inundation of the eyes, 6465
Invention: age eat up my i., 5648
giant-rude i., 7296
Inventions: true rules for old i., 2542
Inventor: plague i., 5637
Inventory of thy shirts, 5908
take i. of all I have, 5224
Invisible: we walk i., 4973
Invitation: leer of i., 4289
Invocation: Greek i., 2233
Invulnerable as the air, 7539

Ira furor brevis est, 244
Ire : full of i., 6265
Irish : now for I. wars, 3853
Iron, 3756-3760
  eat i. like an ostrich, 3757
  forswear to wear i., 6408
  i. may hold with her, 3760
  I'll wink and hold out my i., 3756
  more stubborn-hard than i., 3759
  strike or else i. cools, 3758
  this i. age, 3759
  whilst i. on anvil cool, 4958
Irons : with hot i. burn, 3859
Is : that that is, is, 7256
  what is or is not, 5151
Isabel, live chaste, 1238
Islanders from other lands, 2334
Islands far away, 3501

Isle : frights i. from propriety, 617
  i. is full of noises, 2190
  this scepter'd i., 2324
Isles : western i. of kerns, 3852
Issue : have i. of my body, 1284
  I hope for fair i., 4432
  preys on i. of mother, 1727
Issueless : heavens left me i., 5977
Issues : touch'd to fine i., 6210
Italian : writ in choice I., 6278
Italy : retired to I., 1318
Itch from head to foot, 3762
  poor i. of your opinion, 5101
  scratch her where she i., 3761
Iteration : damnable i., 5784
Ivy : female i. so enrings, 3763
  he was i. which had hid, 3764

J

Jack, 3765-3769
  as hot a J. as any, 5499
  banish plump J., 2512
  go thy ways, old J., 4537
  here comes lean J., 3955
  I am no proud J., 1547
  if I be not J. Falstaff, 2509
  J. hath not Jill, 7364
  J. o' the clock, 3766
  J. out of office, 3765
  J. shall have Jill, 5463
  play the flouting J., 3767
  poor J., farewell, 2508
  since J. became gentleman, 2977
  wed to a swearing J., 1814
  when I kissed the J., 4419
Jack-a-Lent : made J., 7240
  you little J., 3766
Jackanapes must take me up, 6368
Jacksauce : as arrant a J., 5625
Jack-slave hath bellyful, 1394
Jacks : apes, braggarts, J., 6902
  be J. fair within, 3769
  sly, insinuating J., 2726
Jade, 3770-3772
  how like a j. he stood, 3772
  I know he'll prove a j., 6439
  j. hath eat bread, 3595
  let the galled j. wince, 3770
  poor j., wrung in withers, 3770
Jades : give j. the bots, 3770
  j. lob down their heads, 3771
  pamper'd j. of Asia, 5128
January : not till hot J., 4456
Jasons : we are the J., 6304
Jaundice : creep into j., 4721
  grief set j. on cheek, 3173
Jaws of danger, 7003
  j. of darkness, 4157
  out of j. of death, 1903
Jay more precious than lark, 3774
  some j. betray'd him, 3773
Jealous : as j. as Ford, 3778
  each j. of the other, 3777
  is not this man j., 3780
  j. as stung are of adder, 3777
  j. for they are j., 3780
  j. souls not answer'd so, 3780

more j. than cock-pigeon, 3775
one not easily j., 1208
Jealousy, 3775-3783
  beware, my lord, of j., 3779
  fond fools serve mad j., 3776
  green-eyed j., 4287
  he's very j. man, 3663
  j., affection's sentinel, 3783
  j. gives false alarms, 3783
  j., green-eyed monster, 3779
  love is full of j., 3781
  self-harming j., 3776
  waited on with j., 4365
Jelly : distill'd to j., 2601
  out, vile j., 2422
Jenny : vengeance of J., 7103
Jeopardy : thou art in j., 7526
Jephthah, judge of Israel, 1805
Jerkin : buff j., sweet robe, 3605
  old cloak makes new j., 6444
  wear it like leather j., 5109
  what have I to do with j., 3605
Jerusalem : die but in J., 3784
  meet with joy in J., 3785
Jessica steal from Jew, 4987
Jest, 3786-3794
  break j. upon company, 3790
  dry j., sir, 3791
  I thank thee for that j., 6258
  j. unseen, inscrutable, 3794
  j. savour shallow wit, 4754
  j. with a sad brow, 4097
  j.'s prosperity lies in ear, 3788
  mirth-moving j., 7233
  Nestor swear j. laughable, 4916
  now your j. is earnest, 3786
  reply not with fool-born j., 2513
  that's a pretty j., 7160
  to j., tongue far from heart, 6921
Jester : how ill white hairs become j., 2513
Jesters oft prove prophets, 3787
  shallow j., bavin wits, 3876
Jests : break j. as blades, 3789
  excellent j., fire-new, 3793
  mood on whom he j., 3792
  most sweet j., 7235
Jet : between j. and ivory, 2752
  j. upon innocent throne, 6804

Jets : how he j., 1528
  see how he j., 6784
Jew, 3795-3798
  hath not a J. eyes, hands, 3797
  I am a J., Ebrew J., 3795
  I thank thee, J., 1798
  J. may claim pound of flesh, 2742
  my incony J., 3796
  thou art an Hebrew, a J., 1323
  you question with the J., 3798
Jewel, 3799-3803
  basest j. well esteemed, 3801
  hangeth like j. in ear, 1953
  I am rich in such a j., 3802
  immediate j. of their souls, 4894
  j. in barr'd-up chest, 6202
  j. lock'd in wofull'st cask, 3342
  j. purchased at infinite rate, 2395
  j. suffer'd under praise, 1441
  j. that we find we take, 3800
  like j. hung about neck, 2147
  mend j. by wearing it, 6847
  modesty, j. in my dower, 4759
  no j. is like Rosalind, 3799
  rich j. in Ethiope's ear, 522
Jewels : give j. for beads, 3902
  j. are made to wear, 6828
  j. for prince to buy, 2425
  j. in carcanet, 2622
  j. oft move woman, 3803
  unvalued j. scattered, 2216
Jewish : soften J. heart, 3798
Jig, measure, cinque pace, 7369
  you j., you amble, 5135
Jig-maker : your only j., 4655
Jill : Jack shall have J., 5463
Jills : be J. fair without, 3769
Joan doth keel the pot, 5124
  some love lady, some J., 4276
Joan (of Arc), 3804-3807
  J. by whom day is won, 3805
  J. of Arc, virgin, 3807
  J. shall be France's saint, 3805
Job : poor as J., not so patient, 5374
  poor as J., wicked as wife, 5378
Jockey of Norfolk, 2323
Jocund, apt, willingly, 1904
  j. as to jest, 2677
Jog on, j. on, 3390
Jogging : you may be j., 1976
John sack and sugar, 5611
Joined : whom God hath j., 4560
Joint-labourer with day, 3281
Jointure : better j., 6051
Jole : cheek by j., 1262
Jollity for apes, 6703
Journey : fashion'd for j., 4921
  here is my j.'s end, 3809
  I have j. shortly to go, 3808
Journeyman to grief, 3164
Journeymen : nature's j., 54
Journeys end in lovers meeting, 4751
Jove, 3810-3812
  at lovers' perjuries J. laughs, 4399
  bull J. had an amiable low, 974
  could men thunder as J., 6587
  forget that thou art J., 3812
  front of J. himself, 5272
  if J. stray, who dare say ill, 3893
  J. send thee a beard, 479

J. shield your husband, 3582
J. sometimes went disguised, 3810
J. turning mortal for love, 5964
J. wast bull for Europa, 4292
J. would infringe an oath, 5146
made J. to humble him, 533
makes rain as well as J., 6452
my king, my J., 2513
rifted J.'s stout oak, 6590
she is sport for J., 6218
tell tales of J., 5891
thou for whom J. would swear, 5964
would not flatter J., 1202
your emperor continues a J., 848
Joy, 3813-3824
  beheld one j. crown another, 3824
  better to weep at j., 7072
  good j., my lord and lady, 3817
  hour's j. wrecked, 6118
  I drink to j. of whole table, 7183
  I have no j. of this contract, 4158
  if thy j. be heap'd like mine, 3821
  in measure rein thy j., 4287
  j. and fresh days of love, 3819
  j. delights in j., 3822
  j. little less in j., 3573
  j. too fine for my powers, 3823
  make hour o'erflow with j., 3813
  never more have j., 4217
  scarce any j. did long live, 6124
  strike me with j., 3815
  their j. waded in tears, 3824
  why j. in abortive birth, 2933
  with a defeated j., 3816
Joys : briefly die their j., 3814
  hourly j. be upon you, 696
  I speak of Africa and golden j., 7473
  j. of heaven on earth, 3818
  lose distinction in my j., 3823
  this great sea of j., 3820
Judas : his kisses are J., 3916
  J. was hanged on an elder, 3826 •
  so J. did to Christ, 3904
  so J. kiss'd his master, 3825
Judases : three J., 6905
Judge, 3827-3832
  forbear to j., 1860
  had I been j., 3840
  j. how deep I am in love, 1712
  j. no king can corrupt, 3399
  j. robbed, prisoner dies, 3832
  j. you as you are, 3829
  noble to be upright j., 5011
  O wise and upright j., 3831
  O wise young j., 1797
  that supernal j., 3828
  you are a worthy j., 3830
Judgement, 3833-3838
  green in j., 5789
  He, which is top of j., 3829
  his j. ripe, 2397
  I am old only in j., 7578
  in choosing you showed j., 3835
  j. hath repented o'er doom, 3838
  j. is oft cause of fear, 3834
  j. of the heavens, 3837
  j. only belongs to Thee, 3026
  O j., thou art fled, 1033
  our j. sits five times, 4591
  reserve thy j., 1153

what j. dread, 4641
young in limbs, in j. old, 7583
Judgements : accidental j., 6165
eyes like j. blind, 2407
j. fathers of their garments, 4114
men's j. are parcel, 3833
Judges : thieves have authority when
  j. steal, 6528
when j. have been babes, 377
Judicious : make the j. grieve, 54
Juggled : I'll not be j. with, 1768
Juggler : basket-hilt j., 5549
  threadbare j., 6893
Jugglers deceive the eye, 7267
Juliet is the sun, 6328
Julius : mightiest J. fell, 5095
July's day short as December, 1834
Jump the life to come, 1932
Juno : as J. had been sick, 1542
  in pace another J., 7142
  J. but an Ethiope were, 5964
  J. does command, 5038
  J. sings blessings on you, 696
  like J.'s swans, coupled, 6818
  sweeter than J.'s eyes, 2767
  wedding is J.'s crown, 3674
Jupiter became a bull, 3055
  you were, J., a swan, 4292
Jure : we'll j. ye, faith, 7558
Jurors : spots j. on thy life, 4078

Jury passing on prisoner, 3839
Just, 3842-3850
  arms fair when bearing j., 3843
  be j. and fear not, 3844
  deceiving when most j., 4365
  thou art as j. a man, 3842
Justice, 3845-3850
  as thou urgest j., have j., 3848
  crimes unwhipp'd of j., 3845
  even-handed j., 3846
  for thy life j. accused, 5483
  heard me and given me j., 3847
  in j. none see salvation, 4642
  j. feasting, widow weeps, 3849
  j. in fair round belly, 7466
  j. of it pleases, 5358
  j., verity, temperance, 3089
  liberty plucks j. by nose, 4087
  no j. in earth nor hell, 3850
  offence's hand shove by j., 5084
  persuade J. to break sword, 914
  sad-eyed j., 563
  see how yond j. rails, 6527
  send j. to wreck wrongs, 3850
  strong lance of j. breaks, 5963
  time is the old j., 6610
  which is j., which thief, 6527
Justices : seven j. could not, 3638
  we be j., doctors, 7567
Justle a constable, 1524

K

Kate : come, K., your song, 6370
  go thy ways, K., 7131
  I care not for thee, K., 4265
  kiss me, K., 4565
  K. like the hazel-twig, 6978
  none of us cared for K., 6679
  why report K. doth limp, 6978
Katherine : fair K., 6065
  K. the curst, 4473
Keech, the butcher, 6916
Keen as is razor's edge, 6667
  let us be k., 2494
Keenness of thy envy, 6137
Keisar : Cæsar, K., 1035
Kernel : how like to k., 882
  no k. in this nut, 6125
  nut with no k., 7252
Kernels : sweeter than k., 6978
Kerns and gallowglasses, 3852
  those rough rug-headed k., 3853
  uncivil k. of Ireland, 3851
Kersey : honest k. noes, 7363
Key : in what k. take you, 6094
  k. of villanous secrets, 7105
Key-cold figure of king, 3907
Key-hole : out at k., 7226
Kibe put me to slipper, 1516
Kibes : in danger of k., 891
  let k. ensue, 3433
Kickshaws : any little k., 3854
Kickshawses : good at k., 3855
Kicky-wicky : hugs his k., 6990
Kidney : man of my k., 4502
Kill : in peaceful hour cry k., 3783
  k. him in the shell, 5862
  k. thee a hundred ways, 3856

k. thee every where, 3861
k. things they do not love, 3857
let's k. him boldly, 2099
to k. in defence just, 3860
to k. is sin's extremest gust, 3860
Killing myself, die upon kiss, 3924
nine years a-k., 3858
Kin, 3862-3864
  honour of my k., 5975
  little more than k., 3863
  no more k. to me, 3862
  such k. as parish heifers, 3864
Kind : be k. and courteous, 3867
  is she k. as she is fair, 5953
  k. is my love to-day, 4331
  more than kin, less than k., 3863
Kindness, 3865-3868
  I will some k. to them, 3868
  kill a wife with k., 7143
  kind overflow of k., 6467
  k. in women wins my love, 7332
  k. nobler than revenge, 3865
  milk of human k., 4911
  this k. merits thanks, 6513
  thy k. freezeth, 3677
  woman's k. over-ruled, 3866
  you know road to his k., 2061
Kindred made my eyes water, 4880
Kine : Pharaoh's lean k., 2512
King, 3869-3909
  best k. of good fellows, 2638
  divinity doth hedge a k., 3874
  doth not k. lack subjects, 589
  every inch a k., 3890
  farewell k., 3901
  God save the k., 3904

great K. of kings, 4854
happy k., name of good, 3896
he hath kill'd my k., 2293
he was a goodly k., 4486
if thou be k., where is crown, 3884
in sleep a k., 3908
key-cold figure of holy k., 3907
kill k. and marry brother, 1925
k. doth wake to-night, 1749
k. enacts more wonders, 5683
k. finger'd from deck, 3885
k. for our wild faction, 3909
k. has Indies in his arms, 7311
k. is a bawcock, 3877
k. is a beggar, play done, 3869
k. is but a man, 3878
k. of codpieces, 1714
k. of infinite space, 2179
k. of shreds and patches, 3872
k. Stephen was worthy peer, 5420
k. your mote did see, 4812
k.'s misdeeds not hid, 3898
k.'s name tower of strength, 3900
k.'s name twenty thousand, 3900
let k. tempt you to bed, 3873
lion and k. of beasts, 4192
mockery k. of snow, 3905
never alone did k. sigh, 4474
no tyrant, Christian k., 6806
now a k., now is clay, 3889
plain k. that sold farm, 7361
power that made you k., 5384
presence of k. engenders love, 3881
see k. transformed to gnat, 3891
seek k. sun never set, 6320
skipping k. ambled, 3876
so excellent a k., 3871
sometimes k., then beggar, 3906
subject long'd to be k., 3882
substitute shines as k., 3892
they have a k., 563
undeck the body of a k., 6471
wash balm from anointed k., 3899
what, is old k. dead, 1857
what k. so strong, 1053
what must the k. do now, 3902
King-killer : gold, thou k., 3067
Kingdom, 3910-3918
beat thee out of k. with lath, 3875
for k. oath may be broken, 5053
give my k. for a grave, 3902
is my k. lost, 3914
k. for a stage, 4856
k. too small a bound, 3617
little k. of a forced grave, 3729
my k. for a horse, 3597
my k. sick with blows, 3912
our k., how foul it is, 3911
stand upon my k. again, 3913
Kingdoms are clay, 3910
kissed away k., 3915
live to join our k., 5984
measure k. with feeble steps, 5281
mused of taking k. in, 3205
never two such k. contend, 713
Kings : beget happy race of k., 234
curse of k. to be attended, 3888
had k. for messengers, 3870
k. are earth's gods, 3893
k. are makers of manners, 1751

k. hope makes gods, 3574
k. like gods should govern, 3894
k. that fear treachery, 3302
men may talk of k., 3884
nice customs curtsy to k., 1751
no word like pardon for k., 5161
rich blood of k., 4476
scorn to change state with k., 4328
serve where k. command, 5781
setter up of k., 3883
some k. break faith, 2947
stories of death of k., 3901
task breath of sacred k., 3887
time's glory is to calm k., 6628
turn'd crown'd k. to merchants, 3436
two opposed k. encamp, 3078
we live to tread on k., 4127
what have k. save ceremony, 1152
what heart's ease k. neglect, 3880
Kinsman to grim despair, 4614
Kinsmen digged their graves, 6469
Kinswoman of my master's, 3864
Kiss, 3915-3932
all humble k., the rod, 4349
cheapen a k. of her, 5469
claim her with loving k., 2873
come k. me, sweet, 4751
die upon a k., 3924
give him parting k., 2558
giving k. to every sedge, 1732
I k. his dirty shoe, 5910
I will k. thy bones, 1868
I will k. your lips, 1751
k. as many as had beards, 3917
k. dead Cæsar's wounds, 6503
k. distasted with tears, 6643
k. long as my exile, 3918
k. me Kate, 4565
k. on k., she vied, 4940
k. sweet as my revenge, 3918
k. the rod and fawn, 4192
k. you take better, 3930
let's k. and part, 3929
men k. by own direction, 4526
not half a k. to choose, 4367
palm to palm palmers' k., 3925
seal with a righteous k., 1895
sovereign k., 7522
stairs k. his feet, 6376
stop his mouth with a k., 3921
strangers sunder, not k., 6281
sweet k. sun gives not, 2326
take occasion to k., 4575
that k. is comfortless, 3928
thus will I k. I die, 268
touch with tender k., 3925
unauthorized k., 3923
you k. by the book, 3925
you ride us with k., 3932
Kissed : curtsied when you k., 5795
I k. thee ere I kill'd thee, 3924
k. away kingdoms, 3915
k. with clamorous smack, 3927
not to be k. fasting, 918
she k. his brow, 601
Kisses : as if he plucked up k., 3922
blush in thinking k. sin, 4202
but my k. bring again, 3920
for a pair of reechy k., 3873
he that k. my wife, 1699

his k. are Judas's own, 3916
I understand thy k., 3919
I'll smother thee with k., 3931
nun k. not more religiously, 3916
of many k. the poor last. 1838
Phœbus' burning k., 1258
ten k. short as one, 3931
were k. all joys in bed, 3926
Kissing : his k. sanctity, 3916
in k. render or receive, 3930
k. with golden face, 4800
k. with inside lip, 5034
Kissing-comfits : hail k., 1954
Kite with unbloodied beak, 2364
when k. builds look to linen, 3935
Kites : carrion k., crows, 3934
fatted all the region k., 3933
k. and buzzards prey, 2259
Kitten : be k. and cry mew, 5348
Knapped ginger, 3081
Knave, 3936-3948
beetle-headed k., 3947
crafty k. needs no broker, 3939
duteous, knee-crooking k., 3943
he looks like rascally k., 3936
he's but Fortune's k., 1015
I am a scurvy railing k., 5552
I know thee for a k., 3941
k. not able to speak, 3508
lily-livered k., 3941
more k. than fool, 3940
ne'er a villain but arrant k., 6895
pestilent complete k., 3944
rascally yea-forsooth k., 5838
slipper and subtle k., 3944
swear that I am a k., 457
thank God, you are rid of k., 1523
thin-faced k., a gull, 3948
this k. came into world, 6087
'tis base k. that jars, 3946
what, a young k. begging, 589
worsted-stocking k., 3941
Knavery : arrant piece of k., 3949
k. cannot hide himself, 3950
k.'s plain face never seen, 3951
such juggling, such k., 3952
Knaves : bacon-fed k., 7558
he call'd them untaught k., 4225
k. come to do for me, 1699
little better than false k., 3942
none but k. follow, 1567
these kind of k. I know, 5322
three k. in Kendal green, 3938
we are arrant k. all, 3937
whip me such honest k., 3943
Knee, 3953-3959
crook hinges of k., 2719
hath thy k. forgot to bow, 3956
here's my k., 3954
how long since sawest k., 3955
no bending k. will call thee Cæsar, 1018
thy k., whose duty is false, 3358
you debase your princely k., 3958
Knees : bow, stubborn k., 3331
down on your k., 4251
I cannot be lower than k., 3957

k. kissed Cretan strand, 533
may my k. grow to earth, 5160
on his k. at meditation, 5432
shame him with our k., 3953
supple k. feed arrogance, 3959
Knell : contempt be my k., 5338
he talks like a k., 6429
his k. is knoll'd, 6072
k. that summons thee, 616
let us ring fancy's k., 2526
sea-nymphs ring his k., 2576
Knife, 3960-3964
hardest k. loseth edge, 3964
he would have dropt his k., 3275
murderous k. was dull, 3962
my k. sees not wound it makes, 4980
sheathed in breast harmful k., 3961
short k. and a thong, 2997
this bloody k. shall umpire, 3963
wash'd k. with eye-drops, 6799
what means that bloody k., 3960
Knight, 3965-3968
arise a k., 3967
base Assyrian k., 4955
bully k., bully Sir John, 3604
dub me k., Samingo, 3965
he is k., dubbed, 3968
k. of the burning lamp, 2455
k. that swore by honour, 5049
Phœbus, wandering k., 5476
true k., not yet mature, 1212
Knighthoods titles of scorn, 3560
Knights of garter noble, 3966
Knitters in the sun, 6097
Knocks are too hot, 902
k. go and come, 902
Knot, 3969-3973
confirm amity with nuptial k., 213
Gordian k. he will unloose, 5363
knit hearts with unslipping k., 211
slippery as Gordian k., 3971
this k. intrinsicate untie, 3969
too hard k. for me to untie, 3973
unknit k. of abhorred war, 6996
unknit noble k. he made, 3970
Knot-grass : minimus of k., 2250
Knots : blunt wedges rive k., 3973
Know : I know thee not, 2513
I k. what I k., 3976
mistress, k. thyself, 4251
not utter what dost not k., 7305
they k. not what they do, 1928
too much to k. is to k. nought, 6291
we k. what we are, 3977
what you k. you k., 2038
Knowledge, 3974-3977
be innocent of the k., 1936
ensconsing selves in k., 4714
hath by instinct k., 6357
he is very great in k., 3975
his k. is not infected, 6193
his k. must prove ignorance, 3692
I desire more k. of you, 7464
k. set up against mortality, 3974
k. talks with dearer love, 4285
k. wing we fly to heaven, 3691

L

Labour, 3978-3984
  all l. mars what it does, 3978
  I have had l. for travail, 3982
  l. be his meed, 3980
  l. delight in them sets off, 2310
  l. for own preferment, 3981
  l. for the realm, 3981
  l. refresh self with hope, 5874
  l. we delight in physics pain, 3983
  l. when I wash brain, 883
  leave that l. to Hercules, 3984
  sweating l. to bear such idleness so near,
    3683
  with l. swim against tide, 6363
  you do but lose your l., 3982
Labourer : I am a true l., 3979
Labours : makes l. pleasures, 4750
Lace : cut my l. in sunder, that my pent
    heart, 3359
Lack-beard : my Lord L., 477
Lack-brain : what l. is this, 1637
Lad of life, 3877
  l. of mettle, 1547
  my old l. of the castle, 3605
Ladder of high designs, 1960
Lade : he'll l. it dry to have his way, 6148
Ladies : fair l. mask'd, 3990
  good night, sweet l., 4972
  if l. be young and fair, 3985
  l. call him sweet, 4188
  lion among l. dreadful, 4188
Lads : golden l. and girls, 2240
  good l., how do you, 1285
  l. to be boy eternal, 881
  lusty l. roam here, 2281
Lady, 3985-3990
  hail to thee, l., 3092
  hopeful l. of my earth, 2273
  I find no rhyme for l., 5668
  l. doth protest too much, 3988
  l. hath a thing to grant, 3989
  l. so fair, fasten'd to empery, 3986
  l. so tender of rebukes, 3987
  l. that subdues lord, 5388
  my l. sweet, arise, 4005
  she's a most exquisite l., 5227
  some love l., some Joan, 4276
  swear like a l., 6370
  'twas a good l., 5788
  why did you throw your wedded l. from
    you, 7127
Lady-smocks silver-white, 1705
Lag-end of my life, 1535
Lake : Pluto's damned l., 1770
Lamb, 3991-3993
  I'll sacrifice l. I love, 3993
  I'll warrant him gentle as l., 1619
  in figure of l., feats of lion, 2390
  in peace never l. more mild, 4191
  is he a l., skin lent him, 7284
  l. baes like a bear, 7281
  l. entreats the butcher, 3991
  l. environed by wolves, 5778
  l. that standest as prey, 4186
  ravening l. longs after for the **garbage**,
    7151
  seek l. of the fox, 3992

when lion fawns l. follows, 4179
you are yoked with a l., 241
Lambs might betray wolf, 7286
  we were as twinned l. that did frisk i' the
    sun, 881
Lame : made l. to leap, 4716
Lameness : strike her with l., 1740
Lamentation : give no help in l., 3995
  hear your mother's l., 383
  moderate l. right of dead, 3994
Lammas-tide : how long to L., 5077
Lamp and flames of love, 7337
  my oil-dried l. extinct, 1886
  our l. is spent, 1839
Lamps : he wastes l. of night, 2584
  Hymen's l. light you, 6924
  like l. by day, 1965
  like l. whose oil is spent, 2415
  my l. some glimmer left, 142
Lancaster : time-honour'd L., 2964
Lance : braver never couched l., 6067
  l. of justice breaks, 5963
Lances : our l. are but straws, 3670
Land : buy l. cheap as mackerel, 465
  he that ears my l., spares my team, 1699
  this dear, dear l., 2324
  this sickly l., 5754
  upon this l. blessings, 693
  woe to l. governed by child, 1282
Land-rakers : no l., 6756
Land-rats and water-rats, 5295
Lands : of my l. nothing left, 4130
  thy l. confiscate, 2743
Language, 3996-4000
  ill school'd in bolted l., 3996
  l. I have learn'd, 3998
  not chastity enough in l., 3997
  there's l. in her eye, 4000
  you taught me l., 3999
Languages : feast of l., 7431
Lantern : bear you the l., 1523
  bearest l. in poop, 2455
  l. to my feet, 3035
Lap : I will die in thy l., 3353
  rest your head on her l., 3417
Lapwing : far from nest l. cries, 4001
  like l. close to ground, 4003
  this l. runs with shell, 4002
  with maids to seem l., 6921
Lards the lean earth, 6373
Largesse universal like sun his liberal eye
  doth give, 2413
  promised l., 3577
Lark, 4004-4010
  gentle l., weary of rest, 4009
  her lays tuned like l., 5242
  I do hear the morning l., 4006
  I took l. for a bunting, 4004
  it was nightingale, not l., 4008
  l. and toad change eyes, 4008
  l. at break of day arising, 4328
  l. at heaven's gate sings and Phoebus
    'gins arise, 4005
  l. gives sweet tidings, 5560
  l. herald of morn, 4008
  l. sings so out of tune, 4008
  l. that tirra-lyra chants, 4010

more tunable than l., 6669
morn to l. less welcome, 7077
raven doth not hatch a l., 5559
raven sing so like l., 5560
some say l. makes division, 4008
stir with l. tomorrow, 4007
Lass unparallel'd, 1842
  prettiest low-born l., 536
Late: better soon than l., 4012
  glad I was up so l., 4011
  never too l., 4013
  to be up l. is to be up l., 4011
Late-walking: decay of l., 2341
Lath glued within sheath, 6396
  sword though of l., 6396
  Tartar's bow of l., 6185
Latin, 4014-4017
  away, he speaks L., 4014
  hang-dog L. for bacon, 393
  I smell false L., 4016
  L. for three farthings, 5613
  what he 'leges in L., 4017
Laud: more l. than gilt, 5036
Laugh: easy for you to l., 5775
  I must l. when merry, 1207
  I will l. like hyen, 4018
  l. like parrots, 4916
  l. myself to death, 4025
  l. yourself into stitches, 4026
  make her l. at that, 7549
  make the weeper l., 6665
  they l. that win, 7196
Laugher: make the l. weep, 6665
Laughing: there was such l., 3201
  waked herself with l., 6816
  were't not for l., 6373
Laughing-stocks to others, 4022
Laughs and weeps in a breath, 4361
Laughter, 4018-4026
  I am stabb'd with l., 4020
  invent anything tends to l., 7228
  l. for a month, 306
  passion of loud l., 6466
  present mirth hath present l., 4751
  refrain from excess of l., 4023
  stopping l. with sigh, 5034
  that idiot, l., 4618
  wild l. in throat of death, 4021
  with l. let wrinkles come, 4721
Launcelot and I are out, 5496
Laus Deo, bene intelligo, 4015
Lavender, mints, savory, 2767
Lavolt: heel high, l., 5980
Lavoltas: teach l. high, 1778
Law, 4027-4045
  bidding l. make curt'sy, 4826
  bite l. by the nose, 4035
  bloody book of l., 4039
  crowner's quest l., 4027
  do as adversaries in l., 4042
  frame l. unto my will, 4029
  I charge you by the l., 3830
  I crave the l., 812
  I have been truant in l., 4029
  if l. and power deny not, 3262
  in l. what plea so tainted, 4037
  is the l. of our side, 4041
  keep on windy side of l., 4044
  keeps you from blow of l., 4044
  l. hath not been dead, 4034

l. on my side, 5498
l. which is past depth, 4043
lawful l. bar no wrong, 4032
let the l. go whistle, 4045
make scarecrow of the l., 4033
no l. to make thee rich, 7587
old father antic, the l., 4028
pity is virtue of the l., 5310
poor man's right in l., 2711
quillets of the l., 4030
rigour of the l., 4031
tables of the l., 4854
take the l. of our sides, 4041
to l. my services bound, 4909
who would bear l.'s delay, 1847
wicked prize buys l., 5084
wrest l. to your authority, 4038
you know the l., 3830
Lawful that law bar no wrong, 4032
Lawn white as driven snow, 1007
Laws: civil l. are cruel, 7007
  l. for all faults, 4036
  l. prove an idle scorn, 5055
  loath to break country's l., 4040
  we have most biting l., 6255
Lawyer: breath of unfeed l., 4048
  may not that be skull of l., 4046
Lawyers in the vacation, 6609
  l. they call caterpillars, 1126
  let's kill all the l., 4047
Lazarus: as ragged as L., 6064
Lead, 4049-4054
  as hot as molten l., 4050
  as swift as l., 4052
  God keep l. out of me, 4050
  heavy heart's l., melt, 4054
  is l. slow fired from gun, 4052
  let us be l. within bosom, 4053
  love, I am full of l., 4049
  make him burst his l., 4051
  my heart is turn'd to l., 4054
Leader: now you are a l., 2774
Leaf: sere, the yellow l., 4136
League: continue this l., 6820
  keep a l. till death, 4934
  make a l. with me, 5075
Leander cross'd Hellespont, 4347
  L. the good swimmer, 4303
Leanness is all gaunt, 2965
Leaping-houses: signs of l., 6615
Learn more than thou trowest, 604
Learning, 4055-4058
  l. deceased in beggary, 4857
  l. is a mere hoard of gold, 4055
  l. is an adjunct to self, 4056
  O this l., what a thing, 4058
  O, what l. is, 4057
  where we are, l. likewise is, 4056
Leave: I'll take my l., 1973
  what is 't to l. betimes, 5562
  you have l. to l. us, 2108
Leave-taking: dainty in l., 6519
Leaves will wither, 5293
  tender l. of hope, 2492
  yellow l., or few, do hang, 6638
Lecher: like l.'s heart, 2696
Lechery: lenity to l., 4075
  young limbs and l., 7579
Leda: swan for love of L., 4292
Leer of invitation, 4289

Lees left to brag of, 7182
Leets and law-days, 908
Leg, 4059-4063
  good l., good foot, 7368
  good l. will fall, 7361
  have you decreasing l., 7578
  he cannot make a l., 1601
  I know shape of 's l., 4485
Legacy : bequeathing rich l., 6503
  no l. so rich as honesty, 3503
Legerity : move with fresh l., 5134
Legitimate : prove it l., 3841
Legs : his l. are for necessity, 2296
  his l. bestrid the ocean, 256
  I came into world l. forward, 665
  l., arms chopped off, 1135
  l. two riding-rods, 2461
  my l. can keep no measure, 1780
  my l. understand me, 4063
  over-lusty at l., 4061
  shape my l. unequal, 4266
  taste your l., sir, 4063
  turn swan's l. white, 682
  use your l., run away, 1510
  with leaden l., 6029
  your l. are young, 4059
  your l. did better service, 4060
Leisure, 4064-4066
  have l. to make good, 4065
  how has he l. to be sick, 5925
  I have no superfluous l., 4066
  l. answers l., 3286
  wait for no man's l., 1207
  when thou hast l., prayers, 4064
Leman : drink unto l., 3387
  searched for wife's l., 3778
Lend : I neither l. nor borrow, 837
  I will l. thee money, 840
  if thou wilt l. this money, 4069
  I'll l. you something, 4070
  l. less than thou owest, 604
  l. me thousand pound, 4067
  l. nothing for God's sake, 839
  l. to each man enough, 840
  l. where sure to lose, 5301
  you neither l. nor borrow, 838
Lender : keep pen from l.'s books, 2660
  neither borrower nor l. be, 836
Lends money gratis, 4068
Lengths of seas, 435
Lenity, 4071-4076
  awake your dangerous l., 4071
  away to heaven, l., 4076
  l. must be laid aside, 4073
  little more l. to lechery, 4075
  use l., sweet chuck, 447
  what makes robbers bold but l., 4074
  when l. and cruelty play, 4072
L'envoy : take l. for salve, 5792
Leopard german to lion, 4078
  seized by the l., 4078
Leopards : lions make l. tame, 4077
Leprosy : gold makes l. adored, 3066
Lesson : effect of l. keep, 4079
  hard l. do thee good, 4080
Lessons : learn l. as I please, 4081
Lethe : crimson'd in l., 1030
  fat weed on L. wharf, 7055
  may this be wash'd in L., 2834
  steep'd sense in L., 7178

Letter too long by mile, 4082
  zed, unnecessary l., 4084
Letters : in golden l. set, 3494
Level : nothing l. in natures, 6912
  steal by line and l., 6258
Leviathan : ere l. swim league, 3003
Leviathans forsake deeps, 5121
Lewdness in shape of heaven, 6931
Lewdsters and lechery, 6713
Liar, 4109-4113
  good men hate foul l., 4113
  he's an endless l., 1196
  I am sorry he approves l., 4110
  I do despise a l., 4112
  I know him a notorious l., 4109
  measureless l., 3329
  turned the greatest l., 2352
Liars and swearers fools, 6726
Liberal as the north, 6183
  something too l., 5749
  you are l. in offers, 583
Libertine : charter'd l., 6166
  puff'd, reckless l., 5187
  thyself hast been a l., 5957
Liberty, 4085-4087
  all corners let l. use, 5440
  bar door upon your l., 2903
  cry peace, freedom, l., 1028
  I must have l., 4085
  l., freedom, enfranchisement, 4086
  l. plucks justice by nose, 4078
  lust and l. creep in youth, 7571
  man is master of l., 4483
  translate l. into bondage, 3856
  try if they can gain l., 1221
Library : my l. was dukedom, 4088
  take choice of all my l., 4089
License of ink, 2953
Licentious : I were l., 2145
Lick : let me l. thy shoe, 5910
Lid : by God's l., 3421
Lids : her l., azure laced, 2406
Lie, 4090-4108
  credit his own l., 4101
  give me the l., do, 2982
  gives me l. in throat, 1634
  he will l. with volubility, 1197
  I do nothing but l., 4106
  I l. with her, she with me, 4335
  I love to hear him l., 6707
  if I l., spit on me, 4094
  if l. may do thee grace, 4096
  l. and do no harm by it, 4093
  l. circumstantial, l. direct, 4091
  l. seven times removed, 4091
  l. with a light oath, 4097
  shall I tell you a l., 4112
  tells a l. and swears it, 4538
  that l. shall l. so heavy, 4099
  that's a l. in thy throat, 4105
  upon my soul a wicked l., 4098
  you l. in your throat, 4104
  you l. up to hearing of gods, 4090
  you told l., odious l., 4098
Lie-giver : thou the l., 4099
Liege of all loiterers, 1714
Lies : as cheap as l., 6455
  as many l. as lie, 4102
  he l. to the heart, 4098
  I say he l. and l., 4099

l. steel'd with arguments, 4100
these l. are open, 4094
what l. I have heard, 1604
Life, 4114-4151
believe thy living is l., 2369
better brook loss of l., 3617
break bloody house of l., 3888
cancel his bond of l., 5678
end l. when I end loyalty, 4417
end of l. cancels all bands, 4125
entertain lag-end of l., 4126
except my l., 1973
fie upon this quiet l., 3608
folly to hazard l. for ill, 7547
for l. to come, I sleep, 4151
for thy l. let justice, 5483
happy l. to be no better, 4710
here my l. must end, 5793
his l. was gentle, 5725
how like you shepherd's l., 4118
I bear a charmed l., 666
I love l. better than figs, 4116
I spy l. peering, 4144
I will lead a private l., 2051
if of l. you keep a care, 1522
in l. lie hid deaths, 1874
in l. so lifeless, 1978
it is a good l., 4118
jump the l. to come, 1932
let l. be short, 5889
l. better ended by hate, 4319
l. consists of eating 4149
l. consists of four elements, 4149
l. disdain'd in reporting, 3484
l. every man holds dear, 3558
l. from men of royal siege, 4142
l. I never held but as pawn, 4134
l. I prize not a straw, 4150
l. is a shuttle, 4141
l. is better l. past fearing, 4139
l. is but a span, 6074
l. is but a walking shadow, 4137
l. is but breath, 1885
l. is tedious, 4133
l. is time's fool, 3617
l. looks through, 4683
l. more sweet than pomp, 4117
l. never lacks power to dismiss itself, 4132
l. rebel to my will, 4779
l. ride upon dial's point, 4127
l. that died with shame, 6000
l. that I have desired, 6444
l. that late I led, 4128
l. was but a flower, 4119
l. which bleeds away, 1870
l.'s uncertain voyage, 3868
make a l. of jealousy, 3779
man's l. cheap as beast's, 4941
man's l. no more than to say one, 4124
more l. in one of your eyes, 2443
most loathed l. a paradise, 1876
my bad l. reft me of friends, 5648
my l. in his dishonour lies, 2574
my l. is fall'n into sere, 4136
my l. is run his compass, 6619
my l., my joy, my food, 6086
my l. not esteem'd, 7135
no l. achieved by death, 2879
nothing in l. became him, 1871
our l. finds tongues in trees, 4117

our l. rounded with sleep, 4147
prefer noble l. before a long, 4120
promise me l., 1491
reason thus with l., 1874
send prosperous l., 2297
set l. at a pin's fee, 4123
set my l. on any chance, 7479
set my l. upon a cast, 3309
shepherd's l. is naught, 4118
so out of love with l., 4138
take my l. and all, 4140
this l. is richer, 4121
time of l. is short, 4127
translate l. into death, 3856
web of l. of mingled yarn, 4115
wine of l. is drawn, 7182
you take my l., 4140
Life-blood from my heart, 7426
Life-weary fall dead, 5361
Light, 4152-4154
darts l. through every hole, 6325
had she been l., like you, 3096
I can thy l. restore, 4154
let me give l., not be l., 7136
l. and lust are enemies, 4430
l. seeking l. doth l. beguile, 4153
more l. than heat, 707
put out the l., 4154
seek the l. of truth, 6775
time-bewasted l., 1886
we need more l., 4591
what l. through window breaks, 6328
your l. grows dark, 4153
Lightness of his wife, 5838
more betray than woman's l., 4756
O heavy l., serious vanity, 4376
such is l. of men, 2629
Lightning, 4155-4159
as l. in eyes of France, 1079
brief as l. in night, 4157
he'll outstare the l., 4155
it is too like the l., 4158
l. before death, 1893
l. which doth cease to be, 4157
quick, cross l., 2465
secure of l. flash, 5841
when blue l. seem'd to open, 4156
Lightning-flash : fear no l., 2240
secure of l., 5841
Lightnings : Jove's l., 4159
l., dart into her eyes, 1740
Lights that mislead morn, 3920
small l. soon blown out, 2698
waste our l. in vain, 1965
Like : as l. as devil to dam, 4163
as l. as eggs, 4166
as l. as half-pence, 7294
as l. as pilchards to herrings, 2816
as l. as rain to water, 4163
as l. this as a crab, 4164
as l. you as cherry to cherry, 4162
did you ever hear the l., 3325
I shall not look upon his l., 4486
l. doth quit l., 3286
these hands are not more l., 4160
Likelihood : lay it in l., 6305
Likelihoods, forms of hope, 3566
Lilies that fester, 2765
Lily, 4168-4169
like l., hang my head, 6815

O sweetest, fairest l., 4169
thou fresh l., 4168
to paint the l., 2375
unspotted l., 2297
Lily-liver'd boy, 2612
Limb that has disease, 2089
Limbeck : reason a l., 4629
Limbo : he talked of L., 5798
Limbs : young in l., 7583
Limehouse : limbs of L., 7562
Lime-kilns i' the palm, 1747
Limit of becoming mirth, 7233
Limits : stony l. cannot hold love, 4318
Line : steal by l. and level, 6258
  will l. stretch out to doom, 4170
Lineament : examine every l., 2469
Linen on every hedge, 5907
Linguist : manifold l., 1110
Lion, 4171-4193
  against Capitol met a l., 4181
  better fits l. than man, 4647
  better to fall before l., 5381
  blood stirs to rouse l., 1787
  couching l., 6431
  doing as lamb feats of l., 2390
  eat breakfast on lip of l., 2733
  had I been seized by l., 905
  hardy as Nemean l., 2549
  have you l.'s part written, 4187
  he bore him as doth l., 2567
  he is l. I am proud to hunt, 4173
  hear the Nemean l. roar, 4186
  hind mated by the l., 4171
  hold chafed l. by paw, 5863
  in war was never l. raged, 4191
  let me play the l. too, 4187
  like an overgrown l., 6255
  l. among ladies dreadful, 4188
  l. and belly-pinched wolf, 4975
  l. and king of beasts, 4192
  l. dying thrusteth paw, 4192
  l. endure have paws pared, 4193
  l. in prey, 1205
  l. is fox for valour, 4189
  l. will not touch prince, 4174
  man that sell l.'s hide, 4175
  men tremble when l. roars, 4176
  mock l. when he roars, 2053
  no l. were not Romans hinds, 7285
  not more fearful wild-fowl than l., 4188
  now the hungry l. roars, 4674
  plucks dead l. by beard, 3264
  Richard that robb'd l., 5677
  seek l. in his den, 4185
  so look l. upon huntsman, 4180
  that winter l. who forgets, 4177
  thou wear a l.'s hide, 4184
  tremble, you hear l. roar, 4183
  well roared, l., 4190
  when l. fawns upon lamb, 4179
Lion-mettled : be l., 655
Lion-sick, of proud heart, 5929
Lioness whelped in streets, 5097
Lions : have I not heard l. roar, 2059
  he that robs l. of hearts, 4182
  l. cast gentle looks, 4178
  talks familiarly of l., 4825
  voice of l., act of hares, 7407
  we are two l. litter'd, 1026

where find you l., 4828
you are l. too, 5759
Lip, 4194-4205
  contempt and anger of l., 5819
  Diana's l. not more smooth, 4202
  hanging of thy nether l., 6082
  my l. hath virgin'd it, 3918
  pretty redness in her l., 4194
  why gnaw you nether l., 5177
Lips : bestow'd his l., 3205
  daub her l. with blood, 6994
  drove bristled l. before him, 1294
  graze on my l., 4205
  here are sever'd l., 4197
  his l. blow at nose, 2457
  his l. did from colour fly, 4196
  I saw her coral l. move, 911
  l. is parcel of the mouth, 4198
  l. parted with sugar breath, 4197
  l. they use in prayer, 3925
  l. were made to open, 3099
  my l. freeze to teeth, 5370
  my l., two blushing pilgrims, 3925
  no world to tilt with l., 4265
  seal up your l., 4841
  steal blessing from l., 4202
  take, O, take l. away, 3920
  take winter from thy l., 4203
  teach not thy l. such scorn, 4200
  their l., four red roses, 4201
  thy l., kissing cherries, 4201
  when I ope l., no dog bark, 5112
  you have witchcraft in l., 4195
Liquor : celestial l., 6227
  here's yet some l. left, 1133
  there is l. in his pate, 3602
Lisp : carve and l., 1617
  l. and wear strange suits, 6706
Little : blessedness of being l., 1204
  l. more than l. too much, 3520
  too l. for great praise, 5389
Live : let me l. here ever, 5148
  l. cleanly as nobleman, 5657
  l. how we can, die we must, 4130
  l. like old Robin Hood, 6606
  l. loathed and long, 5155
  l. no longer than widow weeps, 4774
  l. to be snuff of younger, 4114
  we'll l., and pray, 5438
Lived : I have l. long enough, 4136
Liver, 4206-4213
  heat l. with drinking, 2198
  let l. heat with wine, 4721
  l. white and pale, 4207
  no motion of l., 7339
  put brimstone in your l., 6845
  so much blood in his l., 4212
  wash your l. clean, 4206
  were wife's l. infected, 4213
  white l. badge of cowardice, 4207
Liver-vein : this is l., 3685
Livers : dirt-rotten l., 1747
  make l. pale, 5578
  measure heat of our l., 7578
  range with humble l., 667
  spotted l. in sacrifice, 6968
  there's l. out of Britain, 936
Livery, 4214-4218
  cunning l. of hell, 4215
  endure l. of a nun, 6922

he gives a frock or l., 1750
her vestal l. is but sick, 4218
l. of burnish'd sun, 1467
she wears thy silver l., 4214
she will wear Diana's l., 4216
silver l. of advised age, 4214
vestal l. will I take, 4217
youth becomes careless l., 7576
youth's proud l., 7586
Lives : I have no case of l., 902
one of your nine l., 1117
slave had thousand l., 5650
Living : enforce thievish l., 586
l. by copulation of cattle, 5958
Living-dead man, 6893
Load would sink a navy, 3543
Loads : ease selves of divers l., 3562
Loaf : of cut l. steal shive, 6259
Loam : men are gilded l., 5627
Loan oft loses friend, 836
Loathing to stomach brings, 6355
Loathness to depart, 5165
Loaves : seven half-penny l., 572
Lock : I have pick'd the l., 3535
Locks : golden l. dowry, 511
gray l., pursuivants of death, 3196
her l. hang on temples, 3198
never shake gory l. at me, 1937
open, l., whoever knocks, 6581
thy knotted l. to part, 6417
Locusts : luscious as l. 2784
Lode-stars : your eyes l., 2431
Lofty and sour, 1204
Loggats : play at l., 816
London, 4219-4223
I hope to see L. ere I die, 4221
L. doth pour out citizens, 4222
to L. will we march amain, 4223
Long-tail : cut and l., 6411
Longings : immortal l., 3707
Look how we can, 6715
l. upon his like again, 4486
of a cheerful l., 2511
stern l., gentle heart, 2909
sunny l. would repair, 1952
this l. will hurl soul, 6140
Looker-on here in Vienna, 1557
Looking before and after, 4488
Looking-glass : charges for l., 3010
smiles in l., 5142
Looks : bloody l., 4809
coy l., 4348
frowning l., 7413
her l. do argue, 4755
his l. my soul's food, 2790
interpretation misquote l., 6716
meagre were his l., 267
puts on his pretty l., 3153
saucy l., 6291
thy grim l., 6062
thy l. be sour, 6383
thy l. humble, 6955
your cat-a-mountain l., 3548
Loon : cream-faced l., 2030
Loose : you be not l., 1565
Loquitur : qui pauca l., 6173
Lord, 4224-4231
beef-witted l., 4230
blunt-witted l., 4229
certain l., trimly dress'd, 4225

commend me to my kind l., 1884
filthy, scurvy l., 4224
hate a l. with my heart, 4228
he shall be l. of Imogen, 130
heavens, that I were a l., 4228
her l., her governor, 3005
l. of folded arms, 1714
l. of the soil, 4226
l. of this fair mansion, 5700
l. of thy presence, 4227
my bosom's l. sits lightly, 3360
my wedded l., 4217
no man l. of any thing, 4231
O, L., that lends me life, 3340
remember what L. hath done, 3034
sodden-witted l., 4230
we may glorify L., 1346
what do to win my l., 7200
you scurvy l., 4224
Lords of the wide world, 4483
revelling like l., 5294
Lorenzo swear he loved, 4987
Lose : they that l. half, 4237
thou art sure to l., 2954
Loser : give l. leave to chide, 4234
Losers will have leave to speak, 4234
l. will have leave, 4234
thus l. part, 5685
Loss, 4232-4238
most patient man in l., 7199
never widow had so dear l., 4238
no l. is known to me, 4233
what l. to be rid of care, 3914
wise men ne'er wail l., 7209
your l. is great, 4233
Losses : all l. restored, 5608
fellow that had l., 4236
l. huddled on back, 4235
make comforts of our l., 4232
Lots : if we draw l., 2954
Lottery : each drop by l., 6801
Louses become old coat, 217
Lout : so vile a l., 2420
Louvre : never see L., 1622
Love, 4239-4412
against l.'s fire, frost, 4313
alas l. should be tyrannous, 4316
away with l., 3779
beggary in l. reckon'd, 4242
beshrew me but I l. her, 4286
blind is his l., 4394
bought mansion of a l., 4325
burn'd with l., as straw, 4310
chameleon l. feed on air, 4352
choose l. by another's eyes, 4295
clap thyself with l., 4366
course of true l. never smooth, 4294
die, but not for l., 7361
do not presume upon my l., 1931
effect of l. in idleness, 4388
eternal l. in l.'s case, 4332
fair is my l., 4311
fall, when l. please, 4747
feel what 'tis to l., 4360
feigned ashes of forced l., 2138
for valour l. a Hercules, 4281
him I l. more than life, 4346
how deep I am in l., 1712
how should I your true l. know, 4262
how sweet is l. possess'd, 4326

how wayward is this l., 4349
I have been l.'s whip, 1714
I know not l., quoth he, 4361
I l. favour and form, 5076
I l. him not nor hate him, 4371
I l. prize, honour you, 4389
I l. that country girl, 4274
I l. thee against my will, 4304
I l. thee better than myself, 5976
I l. you more than words, 4271
I must l. a loathed enemy, 4377
I post from l., 4279
I think my l. as rare, 4749
I was in l. with bed, 4351
if ever thou shalt l., 4409
if he be not in l., 4302
if it be l., tell me, 4242
if l. be blind, agrees with night, 4395
if l. be blind, l. cannot hit, 4394
if l. be honourable, 4320
if l. be rough, be rough, 4317
if l. sought birth, 4270
if lusty l. go in quest, 4270
if no l. in beginning, 4288
if you l. you cannot see, 4396
I'll lock up gates of l., 2532
in a twink won me to l., 4940
in l. heavens guide state, 4293
innocence of l., 6097
is l. a tender thing, 4317
kind is my l. to-day, 4331
know inly touch of l., 4356
let me but bear your l., 2565
let not l. be call'd idolatry, 4331
let thy l. be younger, 3673
let your l. with life decay, 4822
l. adds seeing to eye, 4280
l. admits not reason, 4282
l. all, trust a few, 602
l. alters not, 4333
l. becomes churchman, 1340
l. chased sleep from my eyes, 4353
l. comforteth like sunshine, 4433
l. delights in praises, 4354
l. deserves dark house, 4250
l. doth approach disguised, 4282
l. doth to her eyes repair, 5953
l. forswore me in womb, 4266
l. goes toward l.,4321
l. greybeards call divine, 4268
l. him as angels l., 2147
l. him that is honest, 5844
l. is a familiar, 4275
l. is a fire sparkling in eyes, 4315
l. is a mighty lord, 4353
l. is a sea, 4315
l. is a smoke, 4315
l. is a spirit, 4363
l. is all truth, 4433
l. is begun by time, 4263
l. is blind and enforces, 4391
l. is blind, lovers cannot see, 4392
l. is crowned, 4119
l. is food for fortune's tooth, 4342
l. is full of jealousy, 3781
l. is full of strains, 4283
l. is like a child, 4357
l. is merely a madness, 4250
l. is my sin, 4336
l. is not l. when mingled, 2174

l. is not l. which alters, 4333
l. is wise in folly, 4364
l. is your master, 4348
l. keeps his revels, 4362
l. like a shadow flies, 4290
l. lives not immured, 4280
l. looks not with eyes, 4393
l. make his heart flint, 1694
l. make your fortunes, 4240
l. makes a beast a man, 4292
l. makes young men thrall, 4364
l. me and leave me not, 5701
l. moderately, 4287
l. never linked to deserver, 1982
l. no man in good earnest, 4246
l. nothing but l., 4340
l. of wicked men converts, 4375
l. set on thy horns, 4292
l. sought is good, 4385
l. surfeits not, 4433
l. talks with knowledge, 4285
l. taught me to rhyme, 4277
l. that comes too late, 4241
l. that makes breath poor, 4271
l. that would be hid, 4385
l. they to live that l., 5894
l. thrives not in heart, 4312
l. thyself last, 5851
l. too young to know, 4337
l. transforms me to oyster, 4300
l. turn'd wrong side out, 5372
l. whose month is ever May, 4278
l. whose view is muffled, 4316
l. will creep in service, 4358
l. will not be spurr'd, 4378
l.'s arms are peace, 4284
l.'s best habit soothing tongue, 4309
l.'s bow shoots buck, 4340
l.'s counsellor fill bores, 4379
l.'s feeling is more soft, 4281
l.'s fire heats water, 4338
l.'s heralds, thoughts, 4323
l.'s night is noon, 4385
l.'s not time's fool, 4333
l.'s reason's without reason, 4380
l.'s spring fresh, 4433
l.'s stories written, 5575
l.'s tongue proves Bacchus gross, 4281
mad that trusts boy's l., 4451
making l. over nasty sty, 543
men have died, but not for l., 4253
muffle your false l., 5985
my former l. forgotten, 4355
my honey l. we will return, 5638
my l. admits no dross, 4341
my l. is deep as sea, 852
my l. is most immaculate, 4273
my l. is richer than tongue, 4272
my l. more noble than world, 4345
my l. shall in verse live, 6634
my only l. sprung from hate, 4377
my true l. is grown, 4324
nature is fine in l., 4903
never doubt I l., 4258
no evil angel but l., 4275
no l. where there's another, 3536
now my l. is thaw'd, 4355
O brawling l., 4376
O cunning l.,2444
O l., be moderate, 4287

O most false l., 4344
O most potential l., 4284
O spirit of l., 4343
omnipotent l., 4292
our own l. waking cries, 2124
over shoes in l., 4347
presage ruin of your l., 5700
prick l. for pricking, 4317
quench fire of l. with words, 4356
reason and l. keep little company, 4383
ruin'd l., when built anew, 4334
she burn'd out l., as straw, 4310
she never told her l., 7339
she shall be my l., 4755
show flag and sign of l., 4372
since thou lovest, l. still, 7574
so holy is my l., 4252
so much in l., 4249
some l. my lady, some Joan, 4276
speak low if you speak l., 4297
stony limits cannot hold l., 4318
suffer l., a good epithet, 4304
swear l. was eternal plant, 4267
sweet l. turns to hate, 4374
tell youth what 'tis to l., 4254
thank heaven for good man's l., 4251
that l. is merchandised, 4330
their l. call'd appetite, 7339
their l. lies in purses, 5479
they are in wrath of l., 4387
they do not l. that do not show l., 4330
they l. least that let men know, 4330
things base l. can transpose, 4393
this is the ecstasy of l., 4257
this l. I feel, 4376
though l. use reason, 4282
thy l. is better than high birth, 4329
thy l. is black as ebony, 679
thy l. such wealth brings, 4328
to be in l. where scorn, 4348
to be wise and l., 4384
to l. do my sighs stream, 4239
true l. cannot speak, 6782
we cannot fight for l., 7367
well, I will l., write, 4276
what is l., 'tis not hereafter, 4751
what l. can do dares l. attempt, 4318
what l. women to men owe, 7339
when I l. thee not chaos, 4308
when in l. I broke my sword, 4248
when l. begins to sicken, 4269
when my l. swears, 4335
where l. great, doubts, 4259
where l. reigns, jealousy, 3783
whether l. lead fortune, 4260
who can sever l. from charity, 1216
whom best I l. I cross, 4256
with l.'s light wings, 4318
women cannot l. where beloved, 4359
yield up, O l., thy crown, 4373
you are over boots in l., 4347
you cannot see because l. is blind, 4396
you once did l. me, 4261
young men's l. lies in eyes, 4322
your l. impression fill, 5810
your true l.'s coming, 4751
Love-broker : no l. in world, 6846
Love-gods : we are only l., 1717
Love-in-idleness, 1716
Love-letters : 'scaped l., 4083

Love-prate : sex in l., 645
Love-shaft : loosed his l., 1716
Love-shaked : I am so l., 4249
Love-song : shot with l., 1892
Love-suit : plead his l., 6065
Love-thoughts lie rich, 4343
Loved not wisely but too well, 1208
l. when I am lack'd, 4255
no sooner looked but l., 4387
she l. me for dangers, 4305
thou art most l. despised, 5680
who ever l. that l. not at first sight, 4386
Lover, 4397-4412
as true l. as ever sigh'd, 4397
I as your l. speak, 2814
I slew my best l., 1032
it was a l. and his lass, 4401
l. may bestride gossamer, 4407
l. of thy drum, 4369
l. sees Helen's beauty, 3705
l. sighing like furnace, 7466
l.'s eyes gaze eagle blind, 4402
oath of a l. no stronger, 4399
resolve propositions of l., 4398
since I cannot be a l., 6906
thou wilt be like a l., 4404
Lovers : all l. come to dust, 2240
as I am all true l. are, 4409
at l. perjuries Jove laughs, 4399
journeys end in l. meeting, 4751
l. are given to poetry, 5347
l. break not hours, 4403
l. can see to do rites, 4395
l. cannot see pretty follies, 4392
l. ever run before clock, 4403
l. hours are long, 4412
l. say heart hath wrong, 4410
l. swear more performance, 4408
l. to bed, 'tis fairy time, 4676
pair of star-cross'd l., 4405
sight of l. feedeth love, 4400
silver-sweet sound l. tongues, 4406
sweet l. love the spring, 4401
true l. run into capers, 4248
Loves : bind l. in holy band, 4301
he that l. himself no valour, 6999
no creature l. me, 4314
our l. with fortunes change, 4260
two l. I have, 236
whose l. I prize, 4834
Loving goes by haps, 1720
most l. mere folly, 2928
pardon for too much l. you, 5159
Loving-jealous of liberty, 653
Low : how l. am I, 6253
l. as hell from heaven, 6494
then happy l., lie down, 6019
too l. for a high praise, 5398
Lowliness is young ambition's ladder, 204
Lown : called tailor l., 5420
Loyalty, 4413-4417
end life when I end l., 4417
I follow thee with l., 4414
I nothing render but l., 4415
l. well held to fools, 4413
my l. ever growing, 4415
O, where is l., 2479
persevere in course of l., 4416
Lubber : this l. the world, 7495
Lucentio slipp'd me, 3141

Luces : dozen l. in coat, 217
Lucifer : he falls like L., 5426
  L. sounds well, 1702
  L. take all, 5143
  more damn'd than L., 1771
Luck, 4418-4424
  as good l. would have it, 4422
  good l. lies in odd numbers, 4423
  if it be my l., so, 4421
  mock the l. of Cæsar, 4418
  no ill l. stirring, 4420
  planets of good l., 5326
  they shall have good l., 2477
  was ever man had such l., 4419
Lucrece for her chastity, 1244
  silence, like L. knife, 5948
Lud's-town : made L. bright, 4219
  on gates of L. set heads, 4220
  on L. set your heads, 1836
Lump : foul undigested l., 663
  indigested, deformed l., 664
Luna, the moon, 4784
Lunacy is so ordinary, 4250
Lunatic, lover and poet, 3705
Lungs and rotten ones, 190
  l. tickle o' the sere, 1391
  my l. began to crow, 1194
  speak from thy l., 3604
Lupercal : on the L., 1033
Lust, 4426-4433
  by ruffian l. contaminate, 4427
  decay of l. through realm, 2341
  fie on l. and luxury, 4428
  let l. join with beauty, 1219
  light and l. enemies, 4430
  l. and rank thoughts, 7301
  l. creeps in youth, 7571
  l. doth play, loathes, 4425

l. is but bloody fire, 4428
l. is full of lies, 4433
l. like a glutton dies, 4433
l. melted him in own grease, 5647
l. poorer than before, 1255
l. will prey on garbage, 6931
l.'s effect, tempest after sun, 4433
l.'s winter comes ere summer, 4433
near to l. as flame to smoke, 5971
never melt honour into l., 5649
not out of absolute l., 5649
served l. of my mistress, 1205
slept in contriving of l., 1205
tears harden l., 4429
till action, l. perjured, 4431
to cool a gypsy's l., 4426
won to his l. my queen, 5861
Lustihood : bloom of l., 7560
  make l. deject, 5578
Lustre in your eye pleads, 2448
  noble l. in your eyes, 2412
  where is thy l. now, 2422
Lusts : cool unbitted l., 5576
Lusty : I am strong and l., 141
Lute : lascivious pleasing of l., **7005**
  l. should be like case, 278
  musical as Apollo's l., 4281
  Orpheus' l., 5121
  play on l., towns burn, 4948
Lutes : iron may hold, never l., **3760**
Lutheran : spleeny L., 5601
Luxury : heart-wished l., 1237
Lying : as easy as l., 5331
  how subject old men to l., 146
  how world is given to l., 4095
  I like not humour of l., 3649
  l. becomes tradesmen, 4103
  l. is the woman's part, 7301

M

M.O.A.I. sway my life, 5948
Mab hath been with you, 4434
  this is that very M., 4435
Macbeth does murder sleep, 6024
  M. shall live lease of nature, 655
  M. shall never vanquished be, 655
  M. shall sleep no more, 6024
Macduff : lay on, M., 2343
  M. from womb ripped, 666
Machiavel : set M. to school, 5114
Mackerel : stinking m., 465
Mad : has the man grown m., **4448**
  he's m. that trusts wolf, 4451
  I am not m., 4449
  if m., I should forget, 4449
  it will make us m., 1934
  m. as a buck, 4438
  m. as sea and wind, 4446
  m. as the vex'd sea, 4453
  m. north-north-west, 4442
  sure he is stark m., 4437
  thou art essentially m., 1586
  though m., I will not bite, 4436
  what, are men m., 4484
  you will never run m., 4456
  your noble son is m., 4439
Madeira : cup of M., 2023

Madman : bound more than m., 4457
  he speaks nothing but m., 6187
  weapons in m.'s hands, 7042
Madmen : such stuff as m. tongue, **2178**
  when m. lead the blind, 4452
Madness, 4436-4458
  fetter m. in silken thread, 3156
  happiness that m. hits, 4441
  her m. hath sense, 4454
  like m. is glory of life, 3016
  love is m. most discreet, 4315
  m. in great ones, 4443
  m. rules in brain-sick men, **4447**
  m. seemed tameness, 4455
  m. would not err, 4444
  m., yet method in 't, 4440
  midsummer m., 4458
  my m. speaks, 4445
  not m. that I utter'd, 4445
  riotous m., 6960
  that way m. lies, 4450
  true m. what is 't, 4439
Madrigals : birds sing m., 5706
Maggot ostentation, 7363
Magic of bounty, 853
Mahomet inspired with dove, 3743
Mahu : Modo and M., 5427

Maid, 4459-4463
chariest m. prodigal enough, 4461
fiery-eyed m. of war, 6995
he preached pure m., 1237
holy m. hither I bring, 3804
honest m. as ever broke bread, 4472
honour of m. her name, 3503
how like a m. she blushes, 761
I am a simple m., 4459
I live and die a m., 5048
if you be m. or no, 2446
is there m. with child, 4466
let in a m. that out a m., 6832
m. might do shrewd turn, 6785
m. not vendible, 5945
m. paragons description, 1980
m. rosed with modesty, 4464
m. so tender would run, 4470
neither m., widow, wife, 4468
once a day behold m., 5440
sad brow and true m., 4752
she shall not be m. long, 4465
slain by fair cruel m., 1902
such passion as m. that milks, 7288
thou her m. are more fair, 6328
title for m. of all worst, 4473
trots hard with young m., 6609
you saw mistress, I the m., 4748
Maid-child called Marina, 4214
Maiden : be scanter of m. presence, 4462
in m. meditation, 1716
m. never bold, 4471
m. no tongue but thought, 4469
no m., but a monument, 4771
Maiden-tongued he was, 6666
Maidenhead : as secret as m., 5837
by my troth and m., 5510
get a pottle-pot's m., 756
venture m. for it, 5510
Maidenheads : buy m. by hundred, 465
wear your m. growing, 2767
Maidenhoods : stainless m., 4998
Maidens : cause if m. fall, 4463
frights m. of villagery, 2477
when m. sue, men give, 4467
Maidhood, honour, truth, 4385
Maids : free m. that weave, 6097
m. are May when m., 4460
m. as think not on sins, 5289
m. blind though have eyes, 7189
m. in modesty say no, 7328
m. whose minds are dedicate, 5402
when m. lie on their backs, 4435
Main : look unto the m., 1183
m. chance you meant, 1183
set so rich a m., 3307
Main-top : struck m., 4485
Majestas : ah, sancta m., 612
Majesty, 4474-4476
awake, coward m., 3900
bare-pick'd bones of m., 7001
figure of God's m., 3903
flow in formal m., 712
I am unfit for m., 1105
made proud m. a subject, 6471
m. dies not alone, 4474
m. high thy glory towers, 4476
m. might never yet endure, 4475
when m. stoops to folly, 3547
words clad with wisdom's m., 7427

Make and mar foolish fates, 4479
what m. you here, 4477
Makes him and mars him, 4478
m. us or mars us, 4480
Mal : honi soit qui m., 2371
Malady of not marking, 2092
where greater m. is fixed, 2095
Malcontents : Mars of m., 5645
Malefactions : proclaimed m., 5330
Malice : fortune's m., 2865
good uncle, hide such m., 1339
m. makes deep incision, 1310
m. of this age, 6934
nor set down aught in m., 1208
our m. remains in danger, 6054
spend my m. in breath, 1200
Malignancy of my fate, 6248
Malkin : held a m., 7510
Malleable : make m., 6927
Mallecho : miching m., 4729
Malmutius made our laws, 935
Malt-worms : purple-hued m., 6756
Mammets : play with m., 4265
Man, 4482-4535
are you a m., 4497
art thou a m., 4534
as I am Christian m., 4996
as if m. were author, 3749
away, slight m., 3319
bold, bad m., 4490
cannot a plain m. live, 2726
creature bore shape of m., 4501
do you know what m. is, 4521
drunken m. like drowned m., 2230
ebb'd m. ne'er loved, 6448
even such a m., so faint, 7100
every m. a thing inspired, 3744
every m. has his fault, 2595
every m. is odd, 5078
every m. shift for rest, 4517
fond m. remember wife, 5153
foolish-compounded clay, m., 7228
foremost m. of the world, 929
give world assurance of a m., 5272
go before you like a m., 2249
goodly, portly m., 2511
happy m. be his dole, 2289, 4421
he is every m. in no m., 4500
he is half part of a m., 4530
he is little worse than a m., 4500
he is m. worth any woman, 4527
he proved best m. i' field, 5046
he was a m., 4486
heavier by weight of a m., 3667
here comes a m. of comfort, 2068
honest m. speak for self, 3508
horned m. is monster, 4512
I am foolish fond old m., 156
I am not a double m., 2509
I cannot be m. with wishing, 3352
I could have spared better m., 2508
I hate a proud m., 5422
I smell blood of British m., 5743
I was m. i' the moon, 4792
is m. no more than this, 4494
let him pass for a m., 4500
let no m. care for self, 4517
let no such m. be trusted, 4862
like a m. he died, 6072
like plain-dealing m., 7536

living-dead m., 6893
love makes a m. a beast, 4293
made me think m. a worm, 581
m. and m. should be brothers, 938
m. and wife is one flesh, 4529
m. can die but once, 1855
m. delights not me, 4487
m. drest in brief authority, 4498
m. fain of climbing, 1365
m. fit to be sent errands, 4493
m. hath his desires, 4553
m. haunts the forest, 4249
m. in new fashion planted, 6707
m. is a forked animal, 4494
m. is enemy to virginity, 6925
m. is master of liberty, 4483
m. made of cheese-paring, 4489
m. may rot even here, 5704
m. might ne'er be wretched, 854
m. more sinn'd against, 5962
m. never undone till hanged, 3250
m. not passion's slave, 5171
m. of action called on, 4649
m. of feeble temper, 1021
m. of my kidney, 4502
m. of my soul's hate, 3294
m. of parts, 2424
m. replete with mocks, 6668
m. shall have his mare, 5463
m. should take his own, 5463
m. that fortune's buffets, 2861
m. that hath no music, 4862
m. that makes his toe, 1552
m. that sold lion's hide, 4176
m. that's of woman born, 6399
m. to business bound, 5401
m. when Pepin was a boy, 5805
m. whom waters and wind, 5413
m. wish'd to love enemies, 2925
m.'s life cheap as beast's, 4941
merrier m. I never spent, 7233
milk-liver'd m.,4209
no less than a stuffed m., 4505
no m. has what he leaves, 5562
no m. is lord of any thing, 4231
no m., of m.'s complexion, 4526
not old enough for a m., 880
old m. broken with storms, 149
old m. is twice a child, 144
one m. plays many parts, 7466
point-devise the very m., 4524
press not falling m., 2491
proper m. as ever went, 4491
proper m. as one shall see, 4491
rapier and dagger m., 5544
scan outward habit by inward m., 5108
slight unmeritable m., 4493
small show of m. on chin, 1296
strain of m. is bred out, 4518
take up this good old m., 2937
tempt not a desperate m., 6501
that m. that hath a tongue, 6682
that's a brave m., 1198
this is m. of that quirk, 4502
this is the m. I seek, 3423
this is the state of m., 2492
this m. hath robbed many, 1211
this spotted inconstant m., 3686
this was a m., 5725
'tis not a year shows m., 4510

true m. that gallops so, 4279
turns m. wrong side out, 4531
understand a plain m., 5325
was ever m. thus beaten, 7112
were m. but constant, perfect, 4525
what a piece of work is m., 4487
what is m. if his chief good, 4488
what manner of m., 2511
what may m. within him hide, 4499
what's a drunken m. like, 2230
why should m. sit like grandsire, 4721
wise m. knows himself fool, 2818
you are an odd m., 5078
you are a properer m., 5898
you have undone a m., 165
young m. married, marred, 4551
Man-at-arms : maidenly m., 756
Man-monster drowned, 5767
Man-queller : thou art a m., 5713
Manager is in love, 4275
Mandragora : give me m., 6015
  not poppy nor m., 6032
Mandrake : kill as m.'s groan, 1737
Manes : plats m. of horses, 4435
Manhood, 4536-4538
  guilt takes off m., 3416
  if m. be not forgotten, 4537
  m. is call'd foolery, 4536
  m. melted into courtesies, 4538
  neither m. or fellowship, 3507
Manhoods : hold m. cheap, 3540
Mankind : how beauteous m., 4516
  unkindest beast kinder than m., 489
Manna : drop m. in the way, 2783
Manner of his speech, 6158
  pretty and sweet m., 6459
  to the m. born, 1749
  what m. of man, 4523
Manners, 4539-4545
  crooked in m. as shape, 663
  defect of m., 4542
  evil m. live in brass, 4543
  external m. of laments, 3167
  frame m. to the time, 4544
  good m. at court, 1602
  good m. be your speed, 4542
  here's a million of m., 4545
  if God hath lent man m., 1601
  kings are makers of m., 1751
  near m. of my mother, 6478
  sharp occasions lay m. by, 4539
  thou never sawest good m., 1602
  thy m. must be wicked, 4540
  you put me to forget m., 4541
Manor : sold m. for a song, 4611
  your m. of Pickt-hatch, 2997
Mansion : bought m. of a love, 4325
  leave not m. tenantless, 9
  made his everlasting m., 3115
  what a m. have vices got, 6876
Mantle of standing pool, 6652
Mantuan : good old M., 4546
Manured with industry, 793
Many : mutable m., 4832
Many-headed multitude, 4830
Map of honour, truth, 2459
  m. with Indies, 6047
Mappery : call this m., 5539
Mar brother with idleness, 4477

Marble wears with raining, 4429
much rain wears m., 5534
not m. shall outlive this rhyme, 5669
whole as the m., 2167
Marble-constant: I am m., 7289
Marcius: blame M. for being proud, 5416
M. wears war's garland, 2957
Mardian: thou eunuch, M., 2356
Mare: man shall have his m., 5463
tired m. she will plod, 5194
whose m. is dead, 4571
Margaret be paramour, 5153
M. must strike her sail, 5781
Margent of his eyes, 2469
Marigold to bed with sun, 2767
Marigolds: violets and m., 2762
Marina: maid-child M., 4214
Mark, 4547-4550
ever-fixed m., 4333
fair m. soonest hit, 4550
God bless the m., 4549
God save the m., 4225
hast thou m. to thyself, 7536
he was m., glass, copy, 3618
let m. have prick in 't, 4548
m. but that m., 4548
m. marvellous well shot, 4548
no drowning m. upon him, 3245
thy m. is feeble age, 1905
you have hit the m., 4547
Mark-man: a right good m., 4550
Market-place: eat heart in m., 3352
sit at noonday in m., 5123
Markets: not for all m., 5856
Marks: none of my uncle's m., 4249
Marl: clod of wayward m., 3665
Marred: too soon m., 4481
young man married, m., 4551
Marriage, 4551-4566
curse of m., 4562
hanging prevents bad m., 3249
hasty m. seldom well, 4560
if thy purpose m., 4320
is not m. honourable, 3667
m. binds, blood breaks, 4555
m. is matter of worth, 4559
m. of true minds, 4333
m. with brother's wife, 4561
pair of stairs to m., 4387
second m., thrift, 3661
with dirge in m., 3816
your m. comes by destiny, 1699
Marriage-pleasure, 560
Marriages: God maker of m., 3032
we will have no more m., 4557
Married: best m. dies young, 4563
m. to no man but me, 4565
we three are m., 552
we will be m. o' Sunday, 4565
what, are you m., 4468
will you be m., motley, 4553
young man m., marred, 4551
Marrow: my m. burning, 2747
spending his manly m., 6990
Marrows of our youth, 7571
Marry: he swore to m. me, 5048
I shall never m., 3662
I'll m. her at your request, 4288
if thou wilt m., m. a fool, 4557
m. them to your heirs, 6010

they are fools that m., 388
thou didst swear to m. me., 4558
will you, nill you, I will m. you, 4565
Mars: beards of frowning M., 4210
curvet of M.'s steed, 6990
eye like M. to threaten, 5272
forge that stithied M. helm, 3861
it makes him and m. him, 4478
it makes us or m. us, 4480
M. in swathling clothes, 3611
M. of malcontents, 5645
M. shall on his altar sit, 6995
M. 's armour forged for proof, 5610
this seat of M., 2324
Mart: venture on desperate m., 4633
Martin: Saint M.'s summer, 6313
Martlet builds in weather, 4839
Mary: blessed M.'s Son, 2324
Mary-buds ope their eyes, 4005
Mask of night on my face, 763
Masks for faces, noses, 1007
Masons: singing m. building, 563
Masques: delight in m., 3855
what m., what dances, 5336
Mass: giant m. of things, 6538
Mast: upon giddy m., 6019
what though m. be blown, 5282
Master, 4567-4570
I will be m. of mine own, 4570
man is m. of his liberty, 4483
m. ever keeps good fire, 2018
m. wear no breeches, 4568
my m. calls me, 3808
my m. is churlish, 5897
never such another m., 4567
see m. with pleach'd arms, 5886
tongue shakes m.'s undoing, 6653
you are music's m., 4867
Master-leaver, fugitive, 4779
Master-mistress of my passion, 2470
Masterpiece: confusion his m., 1496
Masters: men m. of fates, 2552
men m. to their females, 4483
no more such m., 4567
we cannot all be m., 4569
Mastiff, greyhound, 2152
Mastiffs of courage, 2330
tarre the m. on, 1728
Match: make m. with tears, 6469
m. play'd for crown, 1093
to lose winning m., 4998
Mate: lack-linen m., 4599
Mates: grief hath m., 6309
Mathematics fall to them, 6294
Matron: sober-suited m., 4998
Matter, 4571-4579
dislike m., but manner, 6158
give less m. better ear, 4572
gravelled for lack of m., 4575
I see no m., 5936
it is no m., 3335, 6022
make the m. savoury, 5790
m. should feed this fire, 7002
mince the m., 4578
more m. for May morning, 4579
more m. with less art, 4576
no m. from the heart, 7418
no m. in the phrase, 5790
pour out m. to mine ear, 6594
put m. to present push, 4577

ravel all this m. out, 3873
read m. deep and dangerous, 825
then he's full of m., 4574
what's the m., 4571, 5101
why, what's the m., 974
Matters point to rich ends, 2310
small to greater m. give way, 4573
Maugre all thy pride, 4385
Maw : cram m., clothe back, 2369
your m. be your clock, 4597
Maxim : this m. I teach, 5482
May, 4580-4582
his M. of youth, 7560
love, whose month is M., 4278
matter for M. morning, 4579
nettle against M., 7074
observance to morn of M., 4580
observe rite of M., 4581
wish snow in M.'s mirth, 2933
May-day : sleep M. morning, 4582
May-morn : in M. of youth, 7560
Mazzard : knock you o'er m., 4584
knock'd about the m., 4583
Mead that brought forth, 4585
Meadows : paint m. with delight, 1705
Meal and bran together, 3996
nature hath m. and bran, 4899
Meals : give them great m., 4589
unquiet m., ill digestions, 4588
Mean and mighty have one dust, 5656
none so m. and base, 2412
Meaner than myself, 3204
Meaning, 4590-4593
folded m. of your deceit, 1473
lawful m. in lawful act, 5344
take our good m., 4592
what's your dark m., 4591
Meanings : I have fair m., 4590
moralize two m., 4593
Means : ability in m., 5648
m. for every man alive, 5313
m. how things perfected, 4714
m. that heaven yields, 3404
m. to do ill deeds, 1921
m. whereby I live, 4140
my extremest m. unlocked, 5478
proffer'd m. of succor, 3404
true, save m. to live, 4136
wicked m. in lawful deed, 5344
your m. are very slender, 7018
Measure : I have trod a m., 1199
m. for m. answered, 4594
m. in every thing, 4595
m. still for m., 3286
reasonable m. in strength, 6288
we'll m. them a m., 1781
Meat, 4596-4600
cold m. in the cave, 281
here's money for my m., 4761
I am m. for your master, 4599
it is m. and drink to me, 4596
made worms' m. of me, 3655
man loves m. in youth, 285
m. cold because you come not, 4597
m. sauced with upbraidings, 4598
m. was made for mouths, 5459
m. was well, 4600
sauce to m. is ceremony, 1160
upon what m. does Cæsar feed, 1022
who abstains from m., gaunt, 2965

Meats : eater of broken m., 3941
funeral baked m., 6574
Mechanic slaves, 6007
Meddle you must, certain, 6408
Meddler : not a temporary m., 3497
Medea gather'd herbs, 4987
Medice, teipsum, 5264
Medicine, 4601-4604
by m. life prolonged, 4602
give preceptorial m., 2156
m. that breathes life, 4601
m. thee to sweet sleep, 6032
miserable have no m. but hope, 4740
no m. can do thee good, 6853
patiently receive my m., 4680
restored with little m., 3911
work on, my m., work, 4604
Medicines : make m. of revenge, 5644
m. to make me love him, 4603
Meditating with two divines, 5432
Meditation : in maiden m., 1716
let us all to m., 4605
on his knees at m., 4605
swift as m., 5640
Meditations : leave you to m., 4606
Mediterranean : wave of M., 7236
Medlar : graff it with a m., 2938
now will it sit under m., 4394
that's virtue of the m., 2938
Medlars : maids call m., 4394
Meed bound with oak, 5046
thanks is honourable m., 6514
Meek and humble-mouth'd, 4609
m. have no other cause, 4608
Meekness : put m. in thy mind, 4610
Meet little as we can, 6282
we ne'er shall m. again, 2534
well, we may m. again, 2534
when shall we three m. again, 6573
Meeting bare without ceremony, 1160
Melancholy, 4611-4621
dull-eyed m., 4620
green and yellow m., 7339
he is m. without cause, 1211
m. as a gib cat, 4617
m. compounded of simples, 4613
m. is nurse of frenzy, 4621
my cue is villanous m., 4619
my young lord very m., 4611
O m., who could sound, 4615
solemn mistress of true m., 4779
something o'er his m. sits, 4616
that surly spirit m., 4618
turn m. forth to funerals, 4723
you may call it m., 5929
Memory, 4622-4630
beg hair of him for m., 6503
begot in ventricle of m., 4628
divorce his m. from his part, 1532
great man's m. may outlive, 4626
it comes o'er my m., 4630
it presses to my m., 415
let m. upbraid falsehood, 2506
made such sinner of m., 4101
m. warder of the brain, 4629
m. written on the earth, 1790
note you in book of m., 4627
of brother m. be green, 4623
pluck from m. rooted sorrow, 4689
riveted in my m., 4622

'tis in my m. lock'd, 4624
while m. holds a seat, 4625
Men : all m. and women players, 7466
all m. have like oaths, 5048
an two m. ride horse, 4508
are you good m. and true, 4507
base m. being in love, 4307
best m. moulded of faults, 2594
black m. pearls, 5223
fewer m., greater honour, 3540
give me the spare m., 2580
glad to learn of noble m., 6070
great m. drink with harness, 3129
great m. great losses, 1865
great m. have reaching hands, 3123
great m. jest with saints, 3125
great m. tremble when lion roars, 4176
hard-handed m. that work, 4504
heavens, what some m. do, 4522
hollow m. make gallant show, 2480
holy m. at death, 3745
holy m. I thought ye, 6937
how subject old m. to lying, 146
I wonder m. trust selves with m., 4519
in catalogue ye go for m., 4496
m. April when they woo, 7360
m. are as the time is, 6398
m. are but gilded loam, 5627
m. are flesh and blood, 4492
m. are masters of fates, 2552
m. are m., 2838
m. are not gods, 4511
m. are to mell with, 4482
m. are turned into tongue, 4538
m. can cover crimes, 4532
m. have died, not for love, 4253
m. have marble minds, 4693
m. kiss by own direction, 4526
m. like butterflies, 3130
m. masters to their females, 4483
m. merriest when from home, 4658
m. must endure going hence, 5704
m. of few words best m., 7423
m. of good government, 4781
m. of other metal, 3665
m. of royal siege, 4142
m. prize thing ungain'd, 5482
m. should be what they seem, 5847
m. shut doors against setting sun, 6332
m. so noble find respect, 5629
m. their creation mar, 7321
m. were deceivers ever, 4506
m. whose visages do cream, 5106
mortal m., mortal m., 5382
no honesty in m., 4514
not in roll of common m., 659
not three good m. unhanged, 4537
old m. forget, 3540
poor, despised old m., 155
proper m. as ever trod, 4491
rich m. sin, I eat root, 3095
since m. prove beasts, 487
some m. creep in fortune's hall, 4522
such m. are dangerous, 2581
they are honourable m., 7541
they are thrifty honest m., 5911
they love m. in arms, 4866
young m. must live, 7558
young m. unfit to hear philosophy, 7572
young m. will do 't, 7557

Men-children : bring forth m., 1287
Menelaus : gored by M.'s horn, 5162
ravished Helen, M.'s queen, 3434
Menenius : old and true M., 6454
Merchant, 4631-4634
m. of great traffic, 4632
now I play m.'s part, 4633
press royal m. down, 4235
what saucy m. was this, 4631
Merchants show foulest wares, 4634
m. venture trade, 563
Mercurial : his foot m., 4485
Mercury : be M., set feathers, 3285
Jove's M. and herald, 1964
littered under M., 6744
rise like feather'd M., 3613
station like herald M., 5272
words of M. harsh, 7433
Mercy, 4635-4647
beyond the reach of m., 1771
cry the man m., 4251
empty from dream of m., 2322
how hope for m., 4641
I cry you m., 4637
lawful m. nothing kin, 4640
lie within m. of your wit, 6668
m. bade thee run away, 5976
m. but murders, pardoning, 4643
m. is above sceptred sway, 4642
m. nobility's true badge, 4646
m. not that oft looks so, 4638
m. of wild beasts, 483
my m. dried their tears, 5303
no ceremony becomes as m., 4639
no more m. than milk, 4635
nothing emboldens sin so much as m.,
   4645
open thy gates of m., 6129
quality of m. not strain'd, 4642
steals away, no m. left, 6519
turn my m. out o' doors, 4644
we do pray for m., 4642
when m. seasons justice, 4642
whereto serves m., 4636
you have a vice of m., 4647
Meridian of my glory, 2490
Merit, 4648-4652
go without stamp of m., 4651
got without m., 5626
head bare till m. crown it, 4652
his m. makes his way, 4650
if men were saved by m., 4648
men of m. sought after, 4649
Merlin and his prophecies, 6431
Mermaid on dolphin's back, 4654
stop ears against m.'s song, 4653
train me not, sweet m., 4653
Mermaid-like bore her, 1851
Merops : thou art M.' son, 5240
Merrier : I have been m., 5773
Merriest : men m. from home, 4658
Merrily shall I live now, 569
Merriment : friends that purpose m., 4722
nature's tears, reason's m., 4918
strain cheeks to idle m., 4618
your flashes of m., 7549
Merry, 4655-4662
be m., employ your thoughts, 4661
be m., my wife has all, 4657
m. against the hair, 1211

m. as crickets, 4656
m. as day is long, 4660
m. as good company can make, 4659
m. as when nuptial day done, 1368
m. because you are not sad, 5775
m. in hall when beards wag all, 4657
never m. when I hear music, 4862
none so m. and gamesome, 4718
not m., not my friend, 7079
therefore be m., coz, 1182
though m., yet honest, 1210
'twas m. when we wager'd, 2705
what, shall we be m., 2647
what should man do but be m., 4655
Mesh to entrap hearts, 3199
Message : deliver plain m. bluntly, 1566
give to gracious m. tongues, 4951
Messages : speechless m., 2429
Messala : we must die, M., 1865
Messenger : baleful m., out, 2416
Messina : pretty flesh as any in M., 2744
Met : exceedingly well m., 5613
Metal, 4663-4666
here's m. more attractive, 4663
like bright m., 5595
no m. can bear keenness, 6137
of self-same m. as sister, 4664
more test made of my m., 4665
thy m. may be wrought, 955
thy m. should compose males, 1287
touch'd and found base m., 4666
Metals : a word, good m., 6152
Metaphysics, 6294
Meteors fright the stars, 5941
Method : fall into slower m., 7257
madness, yet m. in 't, 4440
Metre of antique song, 6096
Metres : lascivious m., 2263
Mettle, 4667-4671
he has m. in his belly, 4670
I see there's m. in thee, 4671
make promise of their m., 2480
man of this m., 4668
m. enough to kill care, 1096
m. of your pasture, 4669
of unproved m., 4667
of your m., your blood, 3097
there is m. in death, 1835
Mewling in nurse's arms, 7466
Mice : like drowned m., 2331
m., rats, such small deer, 6652
Midas : hard food for M., 3060
Midnight, 4672-4676
iron tongue of m., 4676
to be up after m. early, 554
we heard chimes at m., 4675
Midsummer madness, 4458
Midwife : fairies' m., 4434
like aqua-vitae with m., 7461
m. to my woe, 7277
Might : right overcome m., 5688
Mightier man, m. thing, 3127
Mightiest in the m., 4642
Mild as a dove, 4311
Mildews white wheat, 2661
Mile : go thirty m. a day, 5128
Militarist : gallant m., 5255
Military : speak m., 3604
Milk comes frozen home, 5124
m. in a male tiger, 4635

m. of Burgundy, 6915
m. of human kindness, 4911
mother's m. scarce out, 880
such a dish of skim m., 5712
sweet m. of concord, 1487
would m. had been ratsbane, 2739
Milk-liver'd man, 4209
Milk-sop never in life, 2641
Milksops : apes, m., 6902
Milk-white : bull and cow m., '683
flower, before m., now purple, 1716
Mill : more sacks to m., 5765
Miller : more water than wots m., 7025
Milliner : perfumed like a m., 4225
Million : play pleased not m., 5329
Millstones : he will weep m., 4678
her eyes run with m., 4679
your eyes drop m., 4677
Mince not general tongue, 6655
m. the matter, 4578
no ways to m. in love, 7361
Mind, 4680-4698
alone suffers most in m., 6309
an all men were of my m., 7253
base ignoble m., 1365
bettering of my m., 4695
body fill'd, vacant m., 6021
farewell the tranquil m., 2533
full of scorpions is my m., 5821
furnished with m. so rare, 500
golden m. stoops not to dross, 4691
honest m. and plain, 5322
I am not in perfect m., 156
I'll bear no base m., 2637
in my m.'s eye, Horatio, 4486
leave to speak my m., 4680
let m. ride in triumph, 4938
m. free, body delicate, 4686
m. growing more corrupt, 627
m. I sway by never sag, 4688
m. is youthful as your blood, 3135
m. like fountain stirr'd, 4696
m. much sufferance o'erskips, 6309
m. quicken'd, organs move, 5134
m. shall banquet, body pine, 2546
m. sway'd by eyes, 7338
m. that envy could not call but fair, 4697
m. that suits with character, 608
m.'s construction in face, 2464
minister to m. diseased, 4689
mote to trouble m.'s eye, 4810
my m. as big as yours, 3670
my m. exceeds the compass, 2865
my wooing m. express'd, 7363
ne'er disclose her m., 573
no blemish but the m., 685
noble m. is here o'erthrown, 4681
policy of m., 5648
refresh m. of man, 4872
sign of brave m., hard hand, 3214
suspicion haunts guilty m., 6358
taint not thy m., 4814
that temple, thy fair m., 3534
thy m. is a very opal, 4698
'tis m. makes body rich, 4694
'tis with my m. as tide, 4682
you bear a gentle m., 4684
you do change a m., 4828
your m. may change, 4692
your m. tossing on ocean, 4690

Minds : fearless m. climb soonest, 1682
 infected m. discharge secrets, 4687
 men have marble m., 4693
 m. dedicate to nothing temporal, 5402
 never labour'd in m. till now, 4504
 noble m. keep with likes, 4685
 noblest m. to basest ends, 2925
 when quick m. lie still, 7054
Mine, 4699-4704
 I may but call her m., 4703
 if whilst I live she be m., 4704
 m. and m. I loved, 4702
 m. own and not m. own, 4701
 m. will now be yours, 4699
 she shall have me and m., 4700
 what's m. is yours, 4699
Mineral : like poisonous m., 5649
Mingle : O heavenly m., 5772
Minime, honest master, 4052
Minimus of knot-grass, 2250
Minion : fortune's m., 6081
Minions : go, rate thy m., 864
 m. of the moon, 4781
Minister, 4705-4708
 avaunt, thou m. of hell, 4707
 does them by weakest m., 4705
 flaming m., 4154
 foul m. of hell, 4706
 m. to mind diseased, 4689
Ministers : these are my m., 4708
 you blessed m. above, 2370
 you murdering m., 2950
Minnows : Triton of the m., 5884
Minos, that denied course, 2806
Mint : fire-new from m., 3793
 m. of phrases in brain, 6707
 that m., that columbine, 2760
Minute : not a m. thou canst give, 5143
 not a m. without pleasure, 5339
Minute-jacks : vapours, m., 5155
Minutes, 4709-4712
 how thy precious m. waste, 4712
 see the m. how they run, 4710
 so do m. hasten to end, 4711
 thievish m. how they pass, 4709
 unless m. were capons, 6615
 what damned m. tells he, 3779
Miracle : done a m., 4716
 I have 'scaped by m., 6391
 nature's m., 6362
 O m. of men, 3618
 that m. of gems, 4345
Miracles, 4713-4716
 m. are ceased, 4715
 m. are past, 4714
 m. have been denied, 4713
 nothing sees m. but misery, 4739
 work m. on earth, 3807
 you have done more m., 4716
Mire : cast m. upon me, 6266
Mirror : command m. hither, 2468
 hold m. up to nature, 54
Mirth, 4717-4728
 all m. and no matter, 669
 awake spirit of m., 4723
 be large in m., 4720
 he is all m., 4724
 he was disposed to m., 6543
 how well m. becomes labour, 4725
 I have lost all my m., 4719

if in m., I am sick, 5771
I'll use you for my m., 3372
is he disposed to m., 4718
limit of becoming m., 7233
m. becomes a feast, 4726
m. cannot move soul in agony, 4021
m. fate turns to sadness, 6122
present m. hath present laughter, 4751
put on boldest suit of m., 4722
then is there m. in heaven, 4717
with m. in funeral, 3816
with m. let wrinkles come, 4721
you have displaced m., 2120
Misanthropos : I am M., 4520
Misbeliever : call me m., 6830
Mischance go along with you, 1737
 never come m. between us, 6017
 ride in triumph over m., 4938
Mischief, 4729-4735
 he cares not what m., 4730
 m. and despair drive you, 4937
 m. thou art afoot, 4733
 mourn m. that is past, 4734
 O m., thou art swift, 4735
 pray his voice bode no m., 6954
 this means m., 4729
 what m. hath been enacted, 4731
Mischiefs : have in hearts m., 6230
 what m. work the wicked, 4732
Misdeeds : kings' m. not hid, 3898
Misdoubt to resolution, 6560
Miser in poor house, 3505
Miserable no medicine but hope, 4740
Misery, 4738-4744
 m. acquaints with strange bedfellows,
   4742
 m. had worn him to bones, 267
 m. makes sport to mock self, 4741
 m. outlives uncertain pomp, 4733
 m. parts flux of company, 4738
 nothing sees miracles but m., 4739
 state of hellish m., 1560
Misfortune : food to make m. live, 4745
 writ in sour m.'s book, 4746
Misfortunes : bearing m. on back, 6566
 make m. drunk, 3155
Mishap : curse planets of m., 5326
Misleader of brain-sick son, 3956
 villanous m. of youth, 2512
Misprison : in m. shackle, 864
Mistakings : I made no m., 5876
Mistress, 4747-4751
 I am m. of my fate, 2557
 m. I serve quickens, 4750
 m. to this theoric, 4129
 my m. eyes are nothing like sun, **4749**
 my m. showed me thy dog, 4792
 my m. treads on the ground, 4749
 O m. mine, where roaming, 4751
 show me m. passing fair, 520
 sovereign m. of melancholy, 4779
 to each a virtuous m., 4747
 you saw m., I beheld maid, 4748
Mists : foul and ugly m., 6317
Mock : as much in m., 4036
 m. expectation of world, 2389
 m. housewife fortune, 2853
 m. mothers from sons, 4754
 m. with fairest show, 2500

to show scars a m. due, 5814
what a m. is this, 2408
Mocked and wondered at, 3568
  m. for curiosity, 2402
Mockery king of snow, 3905
  monumental m., 5233
  patience a m. makes, 5199
  trust m. of slumbers, 770
  unreal m., hence, 5879
Mocking : the devil take m., 4752
Mocks : afflict me with m., 4753
  man replete with m., 6668
Modest as justice, 2504
Modesty, 4755-4759
  allay with m. thy spirit, 4757
  do not impeach your m., 4758
  in pure and vestal m., 4202
  know more than maiden m., 4509
  lie further off, in human m., 547
  m. may betray our sense, 4756
  m. of fearful duty, 5955
  my m., jewel in my dower, 4759
  o'erstep not m. of nature, 54
  replete with m., 4755
  win souls with m., 1342
Modo he's call'd, 5427
Module of royalty, 3373
Moldwarp and the ant, 6431
Mole : blind m. casts hills, 7499
  blind m. hear foot-fall, 6979
  vicious m. of nature, 1955
  well said, old m., 6369
Mollis aer, mulier, 7128
Momentany as a sound, 6384
Momentary : more m. were not, 4159
Monachum : cucullus non facit m., 4769
Monarch : becomes m. better than crown, 4642
  come thou m. of the vine, 386
  I was morsel for a m., 4801
  sole m. of universal earth, 5895
Money, 4760-4767
  he lends out m. gratis, 4068
  he that wants m. without friends, 4760
  here's m. for thy meat, 4761
  if m. goes before, all ways open, 4764
  make all the m. thou canst, 4765
  m. buys lands, 4293
  m. enough in his purse, 7368
  m. is a good soldier, 4764
  put m. in thy purse, 4765
  you owe me m., 5906
Money-bags : I dream of m., 2182
Monkey : baboon and m., 4518
  more giddy than a m., 258
Monkeys : as hot as m., 5802
  m. are tied by loins, 4061
Monks : hoods make not m., 4768
Monster : be m. like thyself, 1868
  green-eyed m., jealousy, 3779
  horned man is m., 4512
  laugh at puppy headed m., 4025
  make m. of multitude, 4829
  make m. of you, 4183
  many a civil m. in city, 4512
  m. begot upon itself, 3780
  m. of ingratitudes, 6642
  m. too hideous to be shown, 2283
  m. with uncounted heads, 5755
  there would m. make man, 2339

Monsters : teem with new m., 7349
  wise men know what m., 4557
Montant : see thy m., 2679
Month old at Cain's birth, 4784
  this is no m. to bleed, 1310
Monument, 4771-4777
  let fathers lie without m., 4772
  live no longer in m., 4774
  sat like patience on a m., 7339
  that dim m. where Tybalt lies, 4775
  this grave shall have living m., 4777
  this m. five hundred years, 4777
  you are no maiden, but m., 4771
  your m. shall be my verse, 4776
Mood : break into woman's m., 2805
  unused to melting m., 1208
Moody, give him scope, 1203
Moon, 4778-4795
  be witness, blessed m., 4779
  by yonder m. I swear, 4786
  chaste mistress, the m., 4781
  ebb and flow by the m., 5438
  envious m., pale with grief, 6328
  flying between m. and earth, 1716
  follow changes of m., 3779
  four days bring in m., 4787
  glimpses of the m., 4780
  go by m. and stars, 5476
  govern'd by watery m., 3995
  how slow old m. wanes, 4787
  I was man i' the m., 4792
  minions of the m., 4781
  m. clouded, is miss'd, 4791
  m. comes nearer earth, 4790
  m. governess of floods, 4788
  m. is an arrant thief, 6520
  m. like silver-bow, 4787
  m. looks with watery eye, 4789
  m. month old when Adam, 4784
  m. no planet is of mine, 7289
  m. shines bright, 4987
  m. sleeps with Endymion, 4785
  never gazed m. upon water, 4367
  not that time o' the m., 4795
  our terrene m. eclipsed, 4778
  pale shone m. on Pyramus, 4794
  pale-faced m. looks bloody, 5941
  rather be dog and bay m., 929
  scarr'd m. with splinters, 787
  though night, m. shines, 4783
  title to Phœbe, the m., 4784
  when m. shone, no candle, 1067
Moon-calf, speak once, 4793
Moonbeams : fan m. from eyes, 1005
Moonlight : how sweet m. sleeps, 3273
Moons : five m. seen, 4782
  not many m. gone by, 3870
Moonshine : find out m., 4783
Moor : batten on this m., 5272
  clasps of lascivious M., 1812
  I did love the M., 4306
  I suspect the lusty M., 5649
  look to her, M., 1913
Moral : make m. of devil, 3074
  m. of my wit is plain, 6781
Morality or imprisonment, 2831
More I give, m. I have, 852
  there is no m. to say, 3424
Morisco : like wild M., 1082

Morn : grey-eyed m., 4799
m. and dew of youth, 1070
m. in russet mantle clad, 4797
m. to lark less welcome, 7077
red m. that betoken'd wrack, 5591
Morning, 4796-4800
full many a glorious m., 4800
many a m. hath he been seen, 6473
m., like spirit of youth, 4796
night at odds with m., 4984
see how m. opes her gates, 4798
'tis almost m., 653
wakes m., from whose breast, 4009
Morrow : give not windy night rainy m.,
4999
good m., fool, quoth I, 2793
not lend a m., 4143
Morsel, 4801-4805
how doth my dear m., 4804
I found you a m. cold, 4802
I was a m. for a monarch, 1011
now comes the sweetest m., 4803
to perpetual wink put m., 4805
Mortal : all m. in nature, 4248
Mortality, 4806-4808
foretell ending of m., 890
here on my knee I beg m., 4806
it smells of m., 3219
knowledge set against m., 3974
nothing serious in m., 4808
o'erbear shores of m., 3820
sad m. o'ersways power, 528
we cannot hold m.'s hand, 4807
Mortals : what fools these m. be, 2812
Mortimer : noble M. taken, 3011
revolted M., 4809
so much she doteth on M., 7129
Mote : but a m. in yours, 4811
m. to trouble mind's eye, 4810
m. will turn balance, 4813
you found his m., 4812
Mother, 4814-4818
all my m. came into eyes, 6459
amazement on thy m. sits, 6128
contrive against thy m., 4814
doting title of a m., 3097
gasping, new-deliver'd m., 7277
he hath whored my m., 2293
he is all the m.'s, 878
heaven shield m. play'd fair, 4815
he'll think your m. chides, 241
his m. played false, 3592
kill'st m. that engender'd, 2351
my m. seemed the Dian, 432
my m. weeping, 2162
never m. had so dear a loss, 4238
not our m. but our grave, 5823
sins of m. visited upon me, 5968
so loving to my m., 3871
this m. swells my heart, 6104
thou art a m., 4816
thou art thy m.'s glass, 4817
thy m. felt more than m.'s pain, 664
thy m. took some churl, 433
thy m. was piece of virtue, 1811
witty m., witless son, 7250
your m. true to wedlock, 4818
Mother-wit : extempore from m., 7250
Motion : her m. blush'd, 4471
m. of schoolboy's tongue, 7363

m. toward common body, 786
no m. of liver, 7339
no m. that tends to vice, 7301
scoured with perpetual m., 5761
things in m. catch eye, 2447
warm m. to become clod, 1876
Motions of his spirits dull, 4862
Motive of the post-haste, 3282
Motley is the only wear, 2793
wear not m. in my brain, 4770
will you be married, m., 4553
Mould of form, 4681
Mountain on my back, 4266
on m. leave to feed, 5272
set m. between heart, 1526
throws down one m., 3477
Mountain-tops : flatter m., 4800
Mountains : make m. level, 2550
m. removed with earthquakes, 2900
on m. let him starve, 7615
spits forth m., rocks, 4825
Mountebank : bought of m., 6814
I'll m. their loves, 1399
m. and fortune-teller, 6893
Mourn : come, m. with me, 4821
no longer m. for me, 4822
some will m. in ashes, 4820
we m. in black, 4819
Mouse, 4823-4824
fear the smallest m., 4824
call you his m., 3873
I never kill'd a m., 3654
m. in absence of cat, 5822
not a m. stirring, 4823
Mousing flesh of men, 1866
Mouth, 4825-4827
be m. black or white, 2152
borrow Gargantua's m., 7379
familiar in m. as household words, 3540
hand instrumental to m., 6578
he will spend his m., 5455
he would m. with a beggar, 582
here's a large m. indeed, 4825
I wear not dagger in m., 7417
in world's m. scandalized, 5808
match'd in m. like bells, 4864
m. of Russian bear, 3311
m. tear hand, 3723
m. that spits forth death, 4825
my m. be parliament, 6254
my m. engaol'd my tongue, 6672
one blast of minikin m., 5900
quick as greyhound's m., 7244
stop his m. with a kiss, 3921
with open m., 4958
Mouth-honour, breath, 4136
Mouthed, last swallowed, 261
Mouths : as many m. as Hydra, 2228
m. of wisest censure, 4893
never woman but made m., 7315
our m. packed with honey, 6084
perilous m., 4826
put enemy into m., 7184
stop their m. with bits, 3591
then do they spend m., 2285
these m. now starved, 4827
Much : cloy'd with m., 5681
I do not ask you m., 1426
more by m. too m., 3520

too m. of a good thing, 3072
too m. to know, 6291
Mud : on Nilus' mud lay me, 1840
Mudded : there lie m., 6089
Muddied in fortune's mood, 2846
Muddy, ill-seeming, 7333
Mulberry : humble as m., 3642
Mulier is constant wife, 7128
Mulieres ne succedant, 3727
Multitude, 4828-4840
blown to and fro as m., 4837
fool m. that choose, 4839
for m. to be ingrateful, 4829
many-headed m., 4823
see how giddy m. point, 4836
wavering m., 5755
Multitudes : barbarous m., 4840
Multitudinous seas, 3224
Mum, 4841-4844
give no words but m., 4841
hold thy tongue, m., 4842
m. then, and no more, 4844
well said, master, m., 4843
Murder, 4845-4855
commit m. in healing, 1906
do not contrived m., 4851
forgive me my foul m., 5401
heady m., spoil, villany, 3088
how easily m. discovered, 4850
I can m. whiles I smile, 1681
m. as near to lust, 5971
m. cannot be hid long, 4850
m. in mine eye, 2404
m. is out of tune, 4852
m. most foul, 4845
m. though it have no tongue, 5330
m. will speak, 5330
primal curse, brother's m., 5084
sacrilegious m., 4849
thou shalt do no m., 4854
treason and m., 6718
wash my hands of m., 5279
wither'd m. like ghost, 4848
Murdered for our pains, 6084
Murderer : an honourable m., 4853
egregious m., thief, 2801
out on thee, m., 2771
Murders : black stage for m., 4995
I must talk of m., 4855
m. stand bare and naked, 6325
m. too terrible for ear, 724
unseen in m., outrage, 6325
'dure : wrought m. so thin, 4683
Muse : O for a M. of fire, 4856
Muses : thrice three M., 4857
Music, 4858-4874
battle render'd in m., 6997
beholding for your m., 4867
ear's deep-sweet m., 2073
give me some m., 6097
how irksome is this m., 6263
I have good ear in m., 4863

I will die in m., 6365
if m. be food of love, 4874
in sweet m. is such art, 5119
let m.'s tongue unfold, 4869
lifted noses as smelt m., 1413
like softest m. to ears, 4406
loud m. harsh for ladies, 4866
makes m. with enamell'd stones, 1732
man that hath no m., 4862
most heavenly m. nips me, 4868
much m. in this organ, 5331
m. crept by me, 4873
m. doth change nature, 4862
m. frightful as serpent's hiss, 1737
m. hath pleasing sound, 4749
m. is as the flourish, 4861
m. moody food of love, 4858
m. of his own tongue, 6707
m. of men's lives, 6632
m. of the spheres, 4868
m. oft hath such charm, 4860
m. use to quicken you, 6294
m. when time is broke, 6632
m. with her silver sound, 4870
my pulse makes healthful m., 5467
never merry when I hear m., 4862
no m. in him but drum, 4865
no m. in nightingale, 5952
setting sun and m., at close, 6324
shamest m. of sweet news, 4961
slander m. more than once, 6953
swan-like fading in m., 4861
where should this m. be, 4873
why m. was ordain'd, 4872
wilt thou have m., hark, 4871
you are m.'s master, 4867
Musical as Apollo's lute, 4281
Musicians sound for silver, 5951
those m. hang in air., 4859
Musk-roses and eglantine, 2761
stick in thy head, 1263
Must, 4875-4879
needs m. I like it, 4877
things m. be as they may, 2004
thither I m., against will, 4875
what m. be shall be, 4878
whither I m., I m., 7305
you m. perforce, 4879
Mustard too hot a little, 2789
swore m. was naught, 5049
thick as Tewkesbury m., 7229
Mustardseed : Master M., 4880
Mutability and variation, 2864
Mutable, rank-scented many, 4832
Mutations make me hate, 7477
Mutine in matron's bones, 7556
Mutiny : stir hearts to m., 7541
Muzzle : power to m., 1725
Myself to m. not mine, 4702
Mystery of things, 5438
pluck out heart of m., 5331

N

Nail : dead as n. in door, 1857
one n. drives out another, 4355
one n. drives out one n., 2690

Nails, 4881-4885
come near beauty with n., 4883
every one pare his n., 4881

like mad lad, pare thy n., 4881
my n. anchor'd in thine eyes, 4885
my n. can reach eyes, 6253
my n. stronger than eyes, 4882
plough thy visage with n., 4882
these n. tear a passage, 6566
too late to pare her n., 4881
with her n. she'll flay, 4884
Naked on mountain top, 1737
n. though lock'd in steel, 5493
strip your sword n., 6408
Nakedness : appears in n., 2382
in n. but a man, 3878
Name, 4886-4896
deny father, refuse thy n., 4895
every godfather can give n., 6291
fairer n. than French crown, 5613
give n. to every fixed star, 6291
good n. in man or woman, 4894
halloo your n. to hills, 4344
hath not the n. of valour, 6999
he that filches my good n., 4894
homo common n. to men, 4890
I can write my n., 7536
I throw n. against stones, 2087
king's n. thousand names, 3900
king's n. tower of strength, 3900
lose the n. of action, 1847
my n. be blotted, 6727
my n. lost by treason, 4891
n. as rank as flax-wench, 7145
n. unmusical to ears, 4887
odious is the n., 7365
set n. in scroll of youth, 7578
shame live with thy n., 5896
shepherds give grosser n., 2959
that's the dog's n., 2158
thou hast stolen my n., 4886
thy n. well fits thy faith, 2657
what the dickens his n., 4892
what wounded n. shall live, 4888
what's in a n., 4895
your n. is great, 4893
your n. shall flight abuse, 5615
Names : commodity of n., 4889
n. familiar in his mouth, 3540
now subscribe your n., 1498
Napes : turn eyes toward n., 5416
Napkins : dip n. in blood, 6503
Narcissus in face, 2452
Narines de feu, 3590
Nativity : at my n., 659
be out of love with your n., 6706
cursed be time of thy n., 2739
in their n. truth appears, 6967
my n. under Ursa Major, 656
Natural : I do it more n., 2781
something more than n., 5247
Nature, 4896-4924
all n. in love mortal, 4248
allow not n. more, 4941
baser n. comes between, 4905
bounteous housewife n., 6984
compunctious visiting of n., 5612
corrupt n. with bribe, 4266
disguise fair n., 7013
draw near n. of gods, 4646
fond n. bids us lament, 4918
foster-nurse of n., repose, 5620
hard to hide sparks of n., 4898

hath n. given them eyes, 4484
he bow'd his n., 4897
his n. is too noble, 1202
his royalty of n. reigns, 4913
if thou and n. part, 1841
in n. no blemish but mind, 685
n. abhors to make his bed, 4901
n. and fortune join'd, 505
n. as it grows toward earth, 4921
n. can bear great fortunes, 4922
n. cannot choose his origin, 658
n. commands mind to suffer, 3719
n. craves dues be render'd, 7144
n. dear goddess hear, 7344
n. does not grow in thews, 4902
n. falls into revolt, 6084
n. hath framed strange fellows, 4916
n. hath meal and bran, 4899
n. her custom holds, 4904
n. is above art, 4910
n. is fine in love, 4903
n. might stand up, 5725
n. must obey necessity, 4908
n. never framed heart prouder, 3350
n. never lends scruple, 4914
n. of bad news infects teller, 4950
n. ofttimes breaks forth, 4906
n. passion could not shake, 4917
n. requires preservation, 6617
n. stands on very verge, 153
n. subdued to that it works in, 4920
n. teaches beasts, 480
n. which contemns its origin, 2132
n. will betray its folly, 4924
n.'s bequest gives nothing, 4919
n.'s book of secrecy, 5833
n.'s copy's not eterne, 5821
n.'s tears, 4918
O thou divine n., 4900
O worthiness of n., 4899
o'er half-world n. dead, 4912
one touch of n., 4923
thou, n., art my goddess, 4909
thoughts n. gives way to, 6562
through n. to eternity, 1846
thy n. did commence, 6307
thy n. too full of kindness, 4911
when n. framed this piece, 6793
yet do I fear thy n., 4911
Natures : men's n. wrangle, 2688
our n. pursue evil, 4918
Navarre wonder of the world, 7353
Nave : bowl round n. down, 2860
Nay : answer n. and take it, 7328
woman's n. stand for nought, 7328
Nayword : gull him into n., 5470
Nazarite : your prophet, N., 2282
Near as flame to smoke, 5971
Neat : calf call'd n., 1364
n. and cleanly, 4925
not n. but cleanly, 4926
trod on n.'s leather, 4491
we must be n., 1364
Nebuchadnezzar : great N., 3100
Necessities : art of n., 4930
there be hours for n., 3625
Necessity, 4928-4934
fairest grant is n., 933
forsworn on mere n., 4931
hiding honour in my n., 3426

make a virtue of n., 4933
nature must obey n., 4908
n. commands me name self, 4887
n. of time commands, 4928
no virtue like n., 4932
sworn brother to grim n., 4934
teach n. to reason thus, 4932
Neck, 4935-4940
about n. like usurer's chain, 2961
as lief break n. as finger, 4935
bending his corrigible n., 5886
break his n. or hazard mine, 4936
break your own n. down, 260
halter'd n. hangman thanks, 431
here I slip my weary n., 4939
she hung about my n., 4940
thrust n. into a yoke, 4938
thy n. bears half my yoke, 4939
yield not n. to fortune's yoke, 4938
Necks: break n. or hang, 4937
Need, 4941-4945
God send no n. of thee, 4944
much I n. to help you, 4943
n. and oppression starveth, 2524
reason not with n., 4941
there's no n. of thee, 4943
we may never n. you, 4942
Needle: postern of n.'s eye, 1056
stop eye of Helen's n., 7252
Needles change to lances, 2336
Needs: immediate are my n., 4945
Negligent: celerity by n., 1151
Neigh like bidding of monarch, 3590
Nell, if thou dost love, 1072
nor shall N. keep lodgers, 3599
Nemean: hardy as N. lion, 2549
hear N. lion roar,4186
Neptune: all N.'s ocean, 3224
flatter N. for trident, 1202
N. became a ram, 3055
o'er green N.'s back, 2100
siege of watery N., 2324
your isle as N.'s park, 934
Nero, 4946-4949
let not soul of N. enter, 4946
like N. play on lute, 4947
N. angler in lake of darkness, 4949
Neroes: you bloody N., 2336
Nerves: firm n. never tremble, 5879
Nervil: he overcame N., 1033
Nessus: he parallels N., 1197
shirt of N. is upon me, 5904
Nest: crow o' same nest, 1669
Nestor: mouse-eaten cheese, N., 1272
N. aged in age of care, 3196
N. play at push-pin, 3891
N. swear jest laughable, 4916
now play me N., 3451
play orator as well as N., 1681
Nether-socks: wooden n., 4061
Nettle against May, 7074
out of this n. danger, 1788
we call n. but a n., 2776
New: all but n. disdain, 4114
New-fangled than ape, 258
though n. ill, 4329
New-lighted on hill, 5272
New-risen from a dream, 2189
News, 4950-4963
bad n. infects the teller, 4950

blackest n. ever heard'st, 4968
bringer of unwelcome n., 4954
I bring happy n., 4955
if summer n., smile, 4952
my ears cannot hear good n., 4963
never good to bring bad n., 4951
n. called true, old tale, 4969
n. is not so tart, 4959
n. is old enough, 4966
no composition in these n., 4960
no n. but health, 3321
shall good n. be baffled, 4955
stuff my head with ill n., 4957
such n. as never heard, 4962
swallowing tailor's n., 4958
these n. full of grief, 4956
this n. made thee ugly, 6811
though n. sad, tell merrily, 4961
villanous n. abroad, 4953
what n. abroad in world, 4966
what n. in our state, 1689
what n. on the Rialto, 4967
what n. with you, 5710
what's the n., 4964
you have heard n. abroad, 310
Newts and blind-worms, 2478
Nicety: lay by all n., 760
Nicholas: Saint N., 5785
Nick-name for her heir, 1723
you n. virtue, 6865
Niece: I loved my n., 6902
Night, 4970-5001
borrowed of the n., 4983
brave n. to cool courtesan, 4978
bring in cloudy n., 4997
calmest, most stillest n., 6019
cause of n. lack of sun, 4971
civil n., 4980
come, seeling n., 4981
come, thick n., 4980
comfort-killing n., 4995
dark n., silent of n., 7269
dark n. strangles lamp, 1827
dead vast and middle of n., 4672
dismal-dreaming n.,5242
doom'd to walk the n., 6196
dragon-wing of n., 5001
good n., as sweet repose, 5621
good n., good rest, 4992
good n., sweet ladies, 4972
good n., sweet prince, 3371
heavy middle of n., 4672
I have pass'd miserable n., 4996
if he fall in, good n., 825
in such a n. as this, 4987
in the n., some fear, 3705
last out a n. in Russia, 4986
let's have one gaudy n., 4970
love-performing n., 4997
love's n. is noon, 4385
loving, black-brow'd n., 4998
made n. light with drinking, 1815
make n. joint-labourer, 3281
making n. hideous, 4780
misty n. covers shame, 4994
naughty n. to swim in, 4979
n. at odds with morning, 4984
n. flies grasps of love, 5000
n. hangs upon mine eyes, 5633
n. has been unruly, 4982

n. is but daylight sick, 4988
n. is fled whose mantle, 1821
n. of dew that on cheeks, 2426
n. pities neither wise nor fool, 4977
n. that from eye function takes, 4990
n. that never finds day, 4985
n. to owl less welcome, 7077
n. when Troy was fired, 7269
n. will hide our joys, 1833
n.'s black agents, 4981
not n. when I see your face, 4989
now comes in sweet o' n., 4974
sable n., mother of dread, 4993
say good n. till tomorrow, 5169
she bade good n., 4992
things that love n., 4976
think n. chain'd below, 4432
this is n. that makes me, 4991
though n., yet moon shines, 4783
trusting defiles pitchy n., 4425
ugly n. comes breathing, 3423
when sun sets, look for n., 4971
windy n. rainy morrow, 4999
witching time of n., 4673
world in love with n., 4998
yet hath n. of life memory, 142
Night-caps : threw up n., 5527
Night-crow cried, 662
Night-owl : rouse n., 7087
Night-owls shriek, 1607
Night-raven : heard n., 6954
Night-shriek : hear n., 2613
Night-tapers : for n. crop, 566
Night-tripping fairy, 6081
Night-watch constable, 1714
Nightingale, 5002-5003
it was the n., not lark, 4008
n. if she sing by day, 5003
n. we have beat to beds, 5002
no music in the n., 5952
roar as 'twere any n., 4187
sings as sweetly as n., 7374
Nightingales : caged n. do sing, 4871
Nights : four n. will dream away, 4787
in winter's n. by fire, 6422
pluck n. from me, 4143
Nile : flow of N., 5004
where's my serpent of N., 5860
Nilus : higher N. swells, 5004
on N.' mud lay me, 1840
pretty worm of N., 7496
Nine : among n. one good, 7287
ten times better than n., 2510
Niobe : like N., all tears, 6457
Niobes : make N. of maids, 3424
No : maids in modesty say no, 7328
Noah : since N. was a sailor, 3841
Nob : not be sir N., 2461
Nobility, 5005-5012
farewell n., 5010
I sin in envying his n., 5006
n. more than is native, 4307
n. think scorn in aprons, 5009
true n. exempt from fear, 5008
Noble : call him n., 4828
enough n. to be judge, 5011
glad to learn of n. men, 6070
scarce worth a n., 5012
Nobleness : got upon me n., 5005
greater than n., riches, 6942

Nobler sir ne'er lived, 5007
thrice n. than myself, 5005
Noblesse learn forbearance, 5011
Noblest of men, woo't die, 4
Nod : insinuating n., 5013
will he give you the n., 5014
Noddle : comb n. with stool, 5016
Noddles : smite his n., 5015
Nods : duck with French n., 2726
Noes : honest kersey n., 7363
Noise : didst hear a n., 1933
dreadful n. of waters, 2216
n. of battle hurtled, 5097
Nonino : with a hey n., 4401
Nonny : hey non, n., 3106
Nonpareil, 5017-5021
he calls her a n., 5020
my wife seem'd n., 5018
spake you of Cæsar, the n., 1014
thou art n. of cut-throats, 5019
you are n. of beauty, 5012
Noon : love's night is n., 4385
Noon-day in market-place, 5123
North-north-west : mad n., 4442
Nose, 5022-5026
against rose stop n., 5731
dead man's n., 6043
good n. is requisite, 1756
his n. sharp as pen, 2515
innocent n., 6228
invisible as n. on face, 3794
lady's n. been blue, 951
led by the n., 5026
my n. fell a-bleeding, 5025
n. like coal of fire, 2457
not n. but can smell, 5024
to hear by the n., 917
tweaks me by the n., 1634
when fox hath got in n., 2886
why n. stands in middle, 5024
Nose-painting : provoker of n., 2203
Noses : all that follow n., 5024
others have crooked n., 1016
pay nothing for wearing n., 5022
we must have bloody n., 4265
Nostril : stretch n. wide, 7013
Note : not a n. worth noting, 313
one pleasing n. do sing, 1487
take but good n., 2791
turn his merry n., 6729
Notes of sorrow, 6100
our jarring n. agree, 7006
Nothing, 5027-5034
bolt of n. shot at n., 5028
can you make use of n., 5033
covering sky is n., 5034
do n. but speak n., 5030
gives to airy n., 3705
having n., n. can he lose, 5032
he speaks deal of n., 5583
I am n., or if not n., 5029
left n. in the middle, 7230
n. can content my soul, 5649
n. if not critical, 1662
n. will come of n., 5032
say n., do n., have n., 5027
scoured to n., 5761
seen much, have n., 2392
yet art thou good for n., 7506

Nourisher in life's feast, 6024
Nourishment : make envy n., 2349
  n. call'd supper, 6342
Novelty only in request, 5035
Now : if it be not n., 5562
  n. or never, 6560
Nought : come to n., 399
Numbers : good luck in odd n., 4423
  in book of N. writ, 3728
  in fresh n. number graces, 2440
Nun : endure livery of n., 6922
  n. of winter's sisterhood, 3916
Nunnery : get thee to a n., 5037
Nuns : self-loving n., 1249

Nurse : beggar's n., 1920
  dear n. of arts, 5213
  if I were thy n., 5161
  my n., that bears me yet, 2325
  you must call to n., 1280
Nurture can never stick, 2042
Nut : fusty n., no kernel, 7252
  sweetest n. sourest rind, 6380
  worm-eaten n., 5269
Nutmeg : colour of n., 3590
Nutshell : bounded in n., 2179
Nym and Bardolph, 6517
Nymph, in thy orisons, 5400
Nymphs : fresh n. encounter, 5921
  n., call'd Naiads, 5038

O

O, 5039-5043
  an O without a figure, 5041
  cram within wooden O, 5040
  face not full of O, 5042
  fall into deep O, 5043
  little O, the earth, 256
Oak, 5044-5047
  brow-bound with the o., 5046
  his brows bound with o., 5045
  many strokes fell the o., 5047
  o. whose boughs mossed, 5044
  rifted Jove's stout o., 6590
  unwedgeable and gnarled o., 6587
Oaks : hews o. with rushes, 4828
  o. bear mast, 6984
  winds rived knotty o., 6493
Oars : golden o. silver stream, 2709
Oath, 5048-5065
  any o. may be broken, 5053
  bound by solemn o., 5052
  by o. remove his folly, 5830
  confounding o. on o., 5058
  cracking warrant of o., 5060
  good mouth-filling o., 6370
  I have an o. in heaven, 5057
  idiot keeps o., 5063
  I'll not ask thine o., 5059
  Jove would infringe an o., 5146
  lose o. to win paradise, 6964
  never trust man on o., 3095
  o. gives manhood approbation, 5064
  o. of lover no stronger, 4399
  protesting o. on o., 4940
  sin to keep sinful o., 5052
  sworn too hard an o., 5054
  terrible o. sharply twanged, 5064
  where learned you that o., 5049
  your eye breaks my o., 6965
Oaths : all men have like o., 5048
  as if I borrowed my o., 6368
  false as dicers' o., 2499
  God pardon all o. broke, 5061
  he swears brave o., 1198
  his o. are oracles, 6249
  in breaking o. stronger, 1197
  not many o. makes truth, 6959
  o. are straws, 5051
  o. must have their course, 5050
  o. of judgement, 3841
  standers-by curtail o., 6368
  strongest o. straw, 6924
  swearing with o. of love, 5056

swore as many o. as I, 1205
these o. an idle scorn, 5055
thousand o. a welcome, 5065
your bold-beating o., 3548
your o. are pass'd, 1498
Oats : I cannot eat o., 7459
  much your dry o., 3305
Obdurate : art thou o., 3263
Obedience, 5066-5070
  an aim or butt, o., 5068
  hearts of princes kiss o., 5435
  I hourly learn o., 5066
  you have o. scanted, 5070
Obey that know not to rule, 5069
Obligation of our blood, 2300
Oblivion : alms for o., 6642
  blind o. swallow'd cities, 2506
  damn'd o. is the tomb, 3527
  formless ruin of o., 5181
  from dust of o. raked, 1361
  gulf of dark o., 2841
  razure of o., 1984
Observance to morn in May, 4580
  use all o. of civility, 606
Observants : twenty silly o., 5322
Observation : crammed with o., 885
  doth not smack of o., 437
Observed of all observers, 4681
Observer : he is a great o., 5565
Obstacle : no o. between, 5825
Obstacles : full of o., 1513
Obstruction : lie in cold o., 1876
Occasion, 5071-5076
  catch this good o., 5070
  form of this fair o., 5076
  mellowing of o., 4628
  o. smiles upon leave, 5072
  see o. in good quarrel, 5498
  thief of o. will rob you, 5071
  withhold thy speed, o., 5075
Occasions : all o. inform, 5073
  goaded with sharp o., 4539
  o. why and wherefore, 7114
  on the wing of o., 7188
Occupation : Othello's o.'s gone, **2533**
  'tis my o. to be plain, 5322
Occupations perish, 1735
Occupy, excellent word, 1090
Ocean : all Neptune's o., 3224
  I have seen o. swell, 5096
Oceans : drinking o. dry, 6447

O'clock : what is it o., 1373
   what o. I say, 6330
Octavia : bound unto O., 6790
Odd : every man is o., 5078
   you are o., he even, 5078
   you're an o. man, 5078
Odds, 5079-5083
   five to one fearful o., 5082
   he beats thee 'gainst o., 2954
   Hercules must yield to o., 3455
   I am content he take o., 3614
   I shall win at the o., 7192
   I will lay o., 5081
   o. for high and low alike, 5083
   o. is gone, nothing left, 6061
   stay'd o. by adding four, 6572
   that makes o. all even, 1874
   'tis o. beyond arithmetic, 5079
   your grace hath laid o., 5080
Odour : stealing, giving o., 4874
   sweet o., that doth live, 5735
Œillades : judicious o., 4289
O'er-green : you o. my bad, 5810
Offal : fatted with o., 3933
Offence, 5084-5092
   all's not o. that dotage, 3718
   confront visage of o., 4636
   dismiss'd o. would gall, 5305
   every o. is not a hate, 3857
   faster than tongue made o., 2403
   hence hath o. celerity, 5091
   him that bears o.'s cross, 5092
   make o. a skill, 5086
   not meet every o. comment, 5089
   O, my o. is rank, 5084
   o.'s gilded hand shove justice, 5084
   that would appear o. in us, 5088
   way to make o. gracious, 3456
   what is my o., 2365
   where o. is let axe fall, 5085
Offences come from heart, 5087
   o. errors of the blood, 5090
Offend : none o. when all dote, 3699
Offender's sorrow weak relief, 5092
Offer : heaven's o. we refuse, 3404
Office : dog obeyed in o., 2153
   forget o. of our hand, 5522
   o. and affairs of love, 2931
   o. opposite Saint Peter, 3443
   thy princely o. how fulfil, 5973
   time's o. is to fine, 6628
Officer : art thou o., 5093
   each takes fellow for o., 6526
   every petty o. thunder, 6587
   never more be o. of mine, 5094
Offices : holy o., 6617
Offspring : we their o., 1291
Oil : bring o. to fire, 5716
   o. and fire too strong, 7550
   o. in me set hell on fire, 2034
Old : if o. and merry be sin, 2512
   not o. till wise, 152
   not so o. but she may learn, 3005
   o. consider not young, 774
   o. folks feign as dead, 160
   o. have ingratitude hereditary, 163
   o. only in judgement, 7578
   why art o. and not wise, 152
   you are o. and reverend, 152
   you never can be o., 161

Oldest hath borne most, 7581
Olive : bear the o. freely, 5209
   peace puts forth her o., 5209
Olivers and Rowlands bred, 2332
Olivia : let O. plough visage, 4882
   make air cry out O., 4344
   when eyes did see O., 1990
Olympus : climbeth O' top, 2349
   high as huge O., 2908
Olympus-high : hills O., 6494
Omission seals commission, 1794
Omittance no quittance, 5521
One, 5098-5100
   all's o. to me, 5099
   do not wish o. more, 3540
   grieved I had but o., 1281
   how many is o. thrice told, 6441
   it's all o., 3421
   no more than to say o., 5124
   o. for all, all for o., 5100
   o. good in ten, 7287
   o. is o. too many, 5098
   o. is o. too much, 1281
   o. is too weak, 5650
   o. more, most welcome, 2620
   o. on his side fights, 6447
   o., two, third in bosom, 2681
   that's all o., 5907
   'tis all o. to me, 5099
One-trunk-inheriting slave, 6009
Oneyers : burgomasters, o., 6756
Onion will do as well, 6475
   tears live in an o., 6453
Onion-eyed : I am o., 7066
Onions : eat no o., 910
Ooze : my son in o. bedded, 6089
   o. and bottom of the sea, 5387
   o. to show what coast, 4615
Opal : thy mind is o., 4698
Ophelia : I loved O., 4264
   the fair O., nymph, 5400
Opinion, 5101-5109
   dress'd in o. of wisdom, 5106
   errors by o. bred, 6628
   fish for great o., 6781
   hold o. with Pythagoras, 5483
   how blest in my true o., 1156
   in the gross of my o., 5102
   itch of your o., 5101
   learned without o., 5582
   o. did help me to crown, 5104
   o. is but a fool, 5108
   o. mistress of effects, 5107
   plague of o., 5109
   quite from main o., 6340
   raze out rotten o., 2389
   this fool gudgeon, o., 5106
   what is o. of Pythagoras, 5484
Opinions : bought golden o., 5105
   fond and winnowed o., 5103
Opportunity, thy guilt great, 5110
   trust o. of night, 4758
Opposite to every danger, 5683
Oppugnancy : meets in o., 1960
Oracle : I am Sir O., 5112
   o. is fulfilled, 4969
Oracles hardly understood, 5111
Orange-wife, fosset-seller, 1201
Orator, 5113-5117
   be not tongue shame's o., 6658

I am no o. as Brutus is, 1033
play o. as well as Nestor, 1681
text old, o. too green, 5117
well hath Clifford play'd o., 5115
Orators : gold good as o., 3062
  o. dumb when beauty pleadeth, 518
  o. when out, will spit, 5113
Oratory adds grace, 5116
  prevail with o., 3866
Orb : small o. of one tear, 6465
  smallest o. like angel sings, 3276
  walk about o. like sun, 2782
Orchard : sleeping in my o., 3709
Order : let o. die, 3394
  stand not upon o. of going, 2111
  temperate o. wants example, 2374
Ordure : with o. hide roots, 6849
Organ : every o. of her life, 7508
  much music in this o., 5331
  sound within o. weak, 6194
  speak with miraculous o., 5330
Organ-pipe : dreadful o., 6589
  o. of frailty sings, 6364
Organs break up grave, 5134
  o. of increase, 7344
Orient : from o. to west, 5755
Origin : my o. and ender, 597
Orisons : in thy o. be my sins re-
  membered, 5400
Orlando : run, run, O., 6730
  will you, O., have to wife, 4554
Orleans : we lie near O., 2331
Ornament : gave tongue o., 5348
  o. is but guiled shore, 5118
  o. of beauty is suspect, 529
  o. of his cheek, 476
  o. to shape and love, 7249
  o. which truth doth give, 6779
  world deceived with o., 5118
Ornaments : deck body in o., 3396
Orphan : reave o. of patrimony, 5052
Orphans : each morn o. cry, 6108
  o. had so dear a loss, 4238
Orpheus, 5119-5121
  O. drew trees, stones, 4862
  O.' lute strung with poets' sinews, 5121
  O. with his lute made trees, 5119
  Pluto winks while O. plays, 5120
Orthography : turned o., 6179
Orts : beggar's o. to crave, 195
  one that feeds on o., 2639
Ostentation : maggot o., 7363
  no funeral o., 1850
  o. of our love, 4245
  o. of sorrow, 1453

Ostents : fair o. of love, 4661
Ostrich : eat iron like o., 3757
Othello's occupation's gone, 2533
  O.'s visage in his mind, 4306
Ounce of man's flesh, 3796
Ourselves that we are thus, 5849
Out : Launcelot and I are o., 5496
Out-faced by Bolingbroke, 2468
Out-paramoured the Turk, 1205
Out-talk us all, 6439
Out-venoms worms of Nile, 5999
Out-wall : more than my o., 272
Outlaw in castle keeps, 5729
Outrage : do desperate o., 2287
Outroar the horned herd, 431
Outrun by swiftness, 5760
Outside : stubborn o., 2566
  swashing and martial o., 1631
  thy o. looks so fair, 273
  what goodly o. falsehood hath, 2497
  you look but on o., 271
Outwards : by o. commended, 274
Oven stopp'd burneth hotly, 6123
Over-earnest : when you are o., 241
Over-flow of kindness, 6467
Over-leather : toes look through o., 5531
Over-measure : enough with o., 2343
Over-red thy fear, 2612
Over-running : lose by o., 5760
Overthrow heaped happiness, 1204
  plotted our glory's o., 5326
Owl, 5122-5127
  clamorous o. that hoots, 5126
  I heard the o. scream, 1933
  it was the o. shrieked, 5125
  like o. by day mocked, 3568
  maintained by the o., 7202
  nightly sings staring o., 5124
  o., night's herald, shrieks, 5127
  o. shrieked at my birth, 662
  o. was a baker's daughter, 5122
Ox : both ox and ass, 344
  o. hath his bow, 4553
  stalling of o., 2967
Ox-beef : giant-like o., 4880
Ox-head to lion's hide, 4183
Oxen : feed like o., 6716
Oxlips : bold o., 2767
  o. and nodding violet, 2761
Oyster : as apple doth o., 4167
  pearl in foul o., 3505
  transform me to o., 4300
  treasure of an o., 5221
  world's mine o., 7482

P

Paces : two p. of earth enough, 3617
Pack of blessings, 695
  p. when it begins to rain, 2948
  seek shelter, p., 6577
  time to p. and be gone, 1971
Pack-horse in his affairs, 5129
  p., pamper'd jades, 5128
Packing : I'll send him p., 2109
  I'll send some p., 2109
  send me p., 2109
Paddle with palm of hand, 5140

Paddling in your neck, 3873
Pagans : chase p. from holy fields, 1216
Page : ah, sweet Anne P., 6377
  myself and skirted p., 6577
Pageant : index of direful p., 5512
  this insubstantial p., 5639
Paid : well p., well satisfied, 5207
Pain, 5130-5131
  how light my p. seems, 5130
  p. lessen'd by another's, 5131
  p. of death hourly die, 4135

pity-wanting p., 2086
put me to present p., 3820
what p. it was to drown, 2216
with p. inherit p., 1966
Pains, 5132-5134
good to love present p., 5134
how we lose our p., 5132
I have taken great p., 6188
my p. all lost, 2042
thank you for your p., 5480
Paint an inch thick, 7549
p. your face, 5016
Painter plays the spider, 3199
wrought better than p., 5274
Painting of a sorrow, 2564
p. thy outward walls gay, 6145
why should p. imitate cheek, 5136
Paintings : I've heard of your p., 5135
Palace : give p. for hermitage, 3902
p. for truth to dwell, 2504
p. full of tongues, eyes, 1608
soul's p. is a prison, 6130
Palate : no motion but p., 7339
Palates : let p. be season'd, 6010
never p. more the dug, 1920
p. for sweet and sour, 3671
Palestine : fought holy wars in P., 5677
Palfreys : prince of p., 3590
Palm, 5138-5142
bear the p. alone, 1021
dull p. with entertainment, 2902
hard as p. of ploughman, 3229
have itching p., 5139
he takes her by the p., 5140
oily p. not fruitful, 5138
paddle with p. of hand, 5140
p. presages chastity, 5138
p. to p. is palmers' kiss, 3925
see him a p. in Athens, 5141
virginalling upon his p., 5142
Palms : paddling p., 5142
Palter in double sense, 2662
Pancakes : were good p., 5049
Pandar : come to Cressid by P., 5143
P. to provide their gear, 553
Pandars : brokers-between P., 5145
goers-between P., 5145
employer of P., 4303
Pandarus from Cupid, 6147
Sir P. of Troy, 5143
Pangs of despised love, 1847
Pansies for thoughts, 5607
Pantaloon : slipper'd p., 7466
Pantler, not so eminent, 6008
Pap : thumped under p., 1715
Paper : hath not eat p., 3693
p. bullets of brain, 3650
p. made to write whore, 7106
Paper-mill : built a p., 5435
Paradise, 5146-5148
fool's p., 5146
for p. break faith, 5146
lose oath to win p., 6964
p. to fear of death, 1876
rare wife makes this place p., 5148
Paradox : this was a p., 494
too strict a p., 5149
Paradoxes : stuff to make p., 5151
these are old fond p., 5149

Paragon : an earthly p., 220
p. of animals, 4487
you must say p., 5154
Parallel : whom world cannot p., 3437
Parallels in beauty's brow, 6635
Paramour, 5152-5154
he is a p. for voice, 5154
how can Margaret be p., 5153
keeps thee to be his p., 1894
p. is a thing of naught, 5154
wanton dalliance with p., 5152
Parasites : detested p., 5155
Parchment : drawn upon p., 6314
p. should undo a man, 565
p. with seal of Cæsar, 6503
skin of lamb made p., 565
Pard : bearded like a p., 7466
false as p. to hind, 2506
Pardon, 5156-5161
give me your p., sir, 5158
how royal 'twas to p., 5156
I beseech you of your p., 5159
like p. after execution, 1425
like p. slowly carried, 4241
no word like p. for kings, 5161
p., as you are gentleman, 5158
p. ere I rise or speak, 5160
p. is nurse of second woe, 4638
p. is the word for all, 5157
p. should be the first word, 5161
Parent : their p. and grave, 6627
Parents : obey thy p., 2660
p. of so fair a child, 561
Parings of one's nails, 2020
Paris, 5162-5164
let P. bleed, 5162
our brother P. burns us, 5163
P. gored with Menelaus' horn, 5162
P. returned home hurt, 5162
P. speaks like one besotted, 5164
read o'er volume of P.' face, 2469
which of these hairs is P., 3201
Parish-top : turn like p., 2208
Park : over p., over pale, 2475
Parle : in an angry p., 2934
Parley of provocation, 2434
Parliament : my mouth be, 6254
Parmaceti for inward bruise, 4245
Parricides : 'gainst p. thunders, 3051
Parrot : fewer words than p., 7421
Parrot-teacher : rare p., 6670
Parrots : laugh like p., 4916
Parsley : to garden for p., 4566
Part : lion's p., 4187
must we p., 5168
p. to tear a cat in, 6809
p. whose issue hiss me, 59
shake hands and p., 5166
so he plays his p., 7466
Partaker of thy happiness, 3260
Parted : and so they p., 5167
Parthian : like P. flying fight, 803
Parting, 5165-5169
p. is such sweet sorrow, 5169
such p. were too petty, 5165
this p. was well made, 2530
Partition make, 4484
Partridge in puttock's nest, 2364
Parts : examined his p., 5675
Pass : an excellent p., 6258

Passado : ah, immortal p., 2681
p. he respects not, 1713
Passage to remorse, 5612
Passenger : never did p. thirst, 6794
Passion, 5170-5178
 all made of p., **4254**
 as oft as any p., 4257
 beating of so strong p., 7339
 bloody p. shakes frame, 5177
 his words from p. fly, 7456
 it did relieve my p., 6097
 man not p.'s slave, 5171
 my p. hungry as the sea, 7339
 nature p. could not shake, 4917
 never heard p. so confused, 2232
 p. assays to lead the way, 5175
 p. ending doth purpose lose, 5472
 p. is catching, 5173
 p. of loud laughter, 6466
 p. would make man look sad, 5174
 quench the fire of p., 5572
 smooth every p., 5716
 such p. as maid that milks, 7288
 tear a p. to tatters, 54
 this shepherd's p. my fashion, 5170
 what in p. we propose, 5472
 whose every p. strives, 5502
 wit nor reason can p. hide, 4385
 with p. shake the world, 6663
Passionate : make p. my hearing, 3323
Passions : catching all p., 6665
 his p., like a whale, 1203
 how all other p. fleet, 4287
 of all p. fear accursed, 2604
 p. of the mind, 5178
Passport shall be made, 3540
Past, 5179-5181
 p. and to come best, 5180
 things p. are done, 5179
 what's p. and to come, 3804
 what's p. strew'd with husks, **5181**
Paste and cover to bones, 1431
Pasterns : on four p., 3590
Pastime to harder bosoms, 4924
Pastors : do not as p. do, 5187
Pasture, 5182-5183
 good p. makes fat sheep, 5182
 p. lards rother's sides, 5183
 show mettle of your p., 4669
Pat : it will fall p., 5186
 now might I do it p., 5641
 p. he comes like catastrophe, 5185
Patchery : his gross p., 1401
 such p., such juggling, 3952
Patches set upon breach, 2588
Pate : breaks my p. across, 1634
 chop away that p., 4448
 curled p. will grow bald, 7361
 learned p. ducks to fool, 2813
 p. of a politician, 5364
Path : keep then the p., 3557
 p. smooth to danger, 5139
 p. thou shalt ne'er return, 5188
 primrose p. of dalliance, 5187
Patience, 5190-5204
 abusing of God's p., 2340
 all p. and impatience, 4254
 arming myself with p., 1643
 as little p. as another, 5196
 do not press p., 2086

for p. a second Grissel, 5203
God grant us p., 3569
I know your p. well, 4880
I oppose my p. to fury, 5197
I will be pattern of p., 5195
keep me in p., 2370
like p. on a monument, 7339
men's office to speak p., 5198
on distemper sprinkle p., 5191
p. doth lesser blench, 5204
p. gazing on kings' graves, 5201
p. injury a mockery makes, 5199
p. is cowardice in noble breasts, **1649**
p. is sottish, 5190
p. is stale, 5202
poor that have not p., 5200
rob you of p., 5071
though p. be a tired mare, 5194
with what p. have I sat, 3891
you tread upon my p., 5193
Patient : be p., gentle Nell, 2835
 how does your p., doctor, 4689
 p. as female dove, 5192
 p. dies, physician sleeps, 5268
 p. must minister to self, 4689
Patines of bright gold, 3273
Patrimony : reave of p., 5052
Pattern of celestial peace, 4559
 p. of nature, 4154
 p. of patience, 5195
 p. to all princes, 2297
Pauca, there's enough, 2342
Paucas pallabris, 7488
Paunches : fat p. lean pates, 2546
Pause for a reply, 1032
 p. where I shall begin, 5401
Pauser : outrun p., reason, 4381
Pawn against enemies, 4134
Paws : princely p. pared, 4193
Pay nothing for wearing noses, 5022
 word is pitch and p., 5051
 you p. too dear, 5208
Payment for foul words, 507
 too little p. for debt, 3670
Pays : base is slave that p., 5206
Peace, 5209-5218
 be at p., 4731
 cankers of a long p., 6064
 cry p., freedom, 1028
 drawn, and talk of p., 5217
 I bequeath a happy p., 7161
 I do but keep the p., 5217
 I pray thee, p., 5250
 I speak of p., 5755
 in p. and honour rest, 1181
 in p. never lamb more mild, 4191
 little bless'd with p., 6181
 long p. dishonourable, 1071
 love's arms are p., 4284
 may honourable p. attend, 1859
 naked, mangled p., 5213
 not hard for old to keep p., 5218
 our p. will grow stronger, 5211
 p. above all dignities, 1509
 p. breeds cowards, 1633
 p. dear nurse of arts, 5213
 p. dwell in thy breast, 6033
 p. getter of bastards, 7009
 p. is a very apoplexy, 7009
 p. is maker of cuckolds, 7009

p. is nothing but to rust, 7009
p. it bodes, love, 7354
p. of heaven is theirs, 5215
p. of nature of conquest, 5213
p. puts forth her olive, 5209
p. shall sleep with Turks, 49
p. should not dull kingdom, 7012
petition prays for p., 6073
still in right hand carry p., 5214
universal p. is near, 5209
uproar the universal p., 1486
weak piping time of p., 5216
would I were sleep and p., 6033
wound of p. is surety, 6352
Peacemakers : blessed are p., 5209
Peacock : fly pride, says p., 5415
like p., sweeps tail, 5219
stalks like a p., 5220
Peal : ring hunter's p., 3653
rung night's yawning p., 1936
Pearl, 5221-5223
as p. in foul oyster, 3505
black orient p., 5222
hang p. in cowslip's ear, 2476
Indian threw p. away, 1208
p. hath launched ships, 3436
transform'd to orient p., 6472
Pearls : black men are p., 5223
p. are fair, 5223
p. from diamonds dropp'd, 6338
p. that were his eyes, 2576
Peas and beans dank, 3770
Peascod : squash before p., 880
Peat : a pretty p., 2070
Pebble-stone : he is a p., 6271
Pedantical : figures p., 7363
Peddler : he is wit's p., 7237
Peep : thou darest not p., 22
Peerless : you so p., 7335
Peevish : creep into being p., 4721
something p. that way, 2595
Pegasus, narines de feu, 3590
wind fiery P., 3613
Pelf : I crave no p., 3095
Pelican : life-rendering p., 2904
Pelion : under Mount P., 6796
Pell-mell : to 't p., 3410
Pelting of this storm, 7531
Pen : draw no lines with p., 6634
drawn with p. on parchment, 6314
keep p. from lender's books, 2660
mar young clerk's p., 7021
never saw p. and ink, 7256
Penalty : exact the p., 4069
feel but p. of Adam, 4117
Penance for contemning love, 4353
Penitence : by p. wrath appeased, 5619
Penned : well p., 6188
Penny, 5224-5225
an I had but one p., 5225
friend better than p., 2905
not a p., not a p., 4067
p. of observation, 2394
to the last p., 5224
Pennyworths of pillage, 5294
Pent-house lid, 6023
Penury : come to such p., 5444
crushing p. persuades, 3906
People : common p. swarm, 3021
his p. shall revolt, 1191

my p. enfeebled, 2329
our slippery p., 1982
p. are the city, 1352
why do p. love you, 6930
you heavy p., circle me, 5698
Pepin : when P. was a boy, 5805
Pepper : vinegar and p. in it, 1173
Pepper-gingerbread, 6370
Peppercorn : I am a p., 1333
Peppered for this world, 3655
p. two of them, 2674
Percy : not yet of P.'s mind, 3608
P. stands on high, 3612
P., thou art dust, 3617
that mad fellow, P., 3609
young Harry P., 3607
Perdition catch my soul, 4308
Perdona-mi's : these p., 2527
Peregrinate : too p., 1206
Perfect : I had else been p., 2167
so p. and so peerless, 7335
Perfection, 5226-5228
her fullness of p., 4530
no p. is so absolute, 5228
seasoned to true p., 5831
she is indeed p., 5227
Perfections : her p. challenge, 4755
p. of that lovely dame, 5226
Performance : desire outlives p., 1988
his p. nothing, 5453
p. is a kind of will, 5454
Performances : words, p. no kin, 7402
Perfume for lady's chamber, 1007
p. of a minute, 6918
thou owest cat no p., 4494
throw p. on the violet, 2375
Perfumed like a milliner, 4225
Perfumes : all p. of Arabia, 3225
in some p. more delight, 4749
Peril : full of peril, spirit, 825
more p. in thine eyes, 2438
Period : puts p. from place, 5116
Periods : make p. in sentences, 5955
Perjured : all p., 4514
nor God delights in p. men, 6965
Perjuries : lovers' p., 4399
Perjury, 5229-5232
lay p. upon my soul, 5057
persuade my heart to p., 5662
pour down plagues for p., 5229
take heed of p., 5232
this is flat p., 5231
to p. we add terror, 5230
Peroration with circumstance, 2076
Perpend : learn of wise, p., 7207
Perpetual motion, 5761
Persecutor thou art, 2385
Perseverance keeps honour bright, 5233
Person : her p. beggar'd description, 1977
p. suspected, 7324
set thy p. forth to sell, 6676
Persons : philosophical p., 4714
Persuade : well she can p., 5236
Persuasion : lift blood with p., 5235
spirit of p., 5234
Perturbation : polish'd p., 1677
Pestilence : infectious p., 1733
now the red p. strike, 1735
p. that infects land, 3465

she purged air of p., 1990
sooner caught than p., 622
Petar : hoist with own p., 5634
Peter : office opposite P., 3443
Petition prays for peace, 6073
Petitions : all p. theirs, 4467
Petticoat, 5237-5239
doublet courageous to p., 7292
made two holes in p., 5238
you might have worn p., 5239
your old smock brings new p., 5237
Phaethon : down come like P., 1607
P. Merops' son, 5240
P. tumbled from car, 2359
such a waggoner as P., 4997
Phantasimes : fanatical p., 1446
Pharaoh's lean kine, 2512
Phebes : she P. me, 6805
Pheeze : I'll p. you, 5717
Philip : kneel down, P., 5676
P. sparrow, 6156
Saint P.'s daughters, 3743
Philippi : see thee at P., 5241
Philomel in summer's front, 5243
P. must lose her tongue, 5244
Philomela sits and sings, 5242
Philosopher endure toothache, 6696
prove the weeping p., 5249
such a one a natural p., 5245
Philosophy, 5245-5252
adversity's milk, p., 5251
hang up p., 5251
hast any p. in thee, 5245
if p. could find it out, 5247
more than dreampt on in p., 5246
of p. you make no use, 5248
p. that treats of happiness, 6294
preach p. to make me mad, 4449
suck sweets of p., 5252
unfit to hear moral p., 7572
Phœbe, Luna, moon, 4784
Phœbus : gallop toward P.' lodging, 4997
golden P. never beheld, 1842
P.' amorous pinches, 676
P. 'gins rise, 4005
P.' steeds are foundered, 4432
P., wandering knight, 5476
P.' burning kisses, 1258
thirty times hath P.' cart, 3675
Phœnix : burn p. in blood, 6634
my ashes, as the p., 648
p., bird of wonder, 5254
p. down began to appear, 1296
p. shall make France afeard, 5253
Phrase, 5255-5259
I know not the p., 7381
little bless'd with p., 6181
p. is to the matter, 5258
p. would be more german, 5257
proverb'd with grandsire p., 5464
that was his own p., 5255
that's an ill p., 5256
there's a stewed p., 5259
Phrases : mint of p., 6707
red-lattice p., 3548
taffeta p., silken terms, 7363
Phrygian : base P. Turk, 4863
Physic, 5260-5263
brings p. after death, 5261
I will not cast away p., 5260

in poison there is p., 5355
p. bitter to sweet ends, 5263
p. for it there is none, 1703
p. given in time, had cured, 1425
throw p. to the dogs, 5262
Physical to walk unbraced, 5929
Physician, 5264-5268
cured by sure p., death, 1845
kill p., and fee bestow, 5264
patient dies, p. sleeps, 5268
p. heal thyself, 5264
p. that should be patient, 5267
trust not the p., 5266
use reason for p., 4282
when death is our p., 2214
Physicians : health from p., 3321
Pia-mater : womb of p., 4628
Pibble pabble : no p., 6433
Pick-axe and a spade, 3108
Pick-purse : at hand, quoth p., 5270
I think he is not a p., 5269
Pick-purses in love, 5271
Picked : he is too p., 1206
Pickers and stealers, 4261
Picking teeth, 3133
Pickle : how camest in this p., 2229
I have been in such a p., 6750
smarting in lingering p., 1733
Pickle-herring : plague o' p., 2980
Pickt-hatch : manor of P., 2997
Picture, 5272-5274
how likest this p., 5274
look upon this p., 5272
Picture-like : no better than p., 5614
Pictures : dost thou love p., 5273
p. out of doors, 7325
sleeping and dead but p., 6025
Pie : no man's p. free, 2684
Pies in discord sung, 662
Pig falls from spit, 4597
some men love not p., 120
Pigeon-egg of discretion, 5225
Pigeon-livered lack gall, 1634
Pigeons : as p. bill, 4553
pecks up wit as p. pease, 7237
Pigmies : embassage to P., 5875
Pike : trail'st puissant p., 5277
Pikes : revenge with our p., 5275
trail your steel p., 5276
Pilate : with P. wash hands, 5278
Pilates have delivered me, 5278
Pilchards : as p. to herrings, 2816
Pilcher : pluck sword out of p., 6407
Pilgrim, you wrong your hand, 3925
true-devoted p. not weary, 5281
Pilgrimage : undergo maiden p., 6922
Pilgrims to Canterbury, 5280
Pillage of her chastity, 5244
p. they bring home, 563
Pillar of world transformed, 2791
well-deserving p., 3830
Pillow : cozening p. of kiss, 3227
fair thoughts be fair p., 6567
sigh'd upon midnight p., 4397
sloth finds down p. hard, 7046
Pillows discharge secrets, 4687
Pilot : I am no p., 5283
yet lives our p., 5282
Pin : not care a p., 5284
not worth a p., 5285

scratch with p., scar, 2404
very p. of heart cleft, 1892
with a little p. bores, 3901
Pinch, 5286-5291
P., hungry villain, 6893
p. maids blue as bilberry, 2475
p. more stinging than bees, 5292
p. them, arms, legs, 5289
p. wanton on your cheek, 3873
stroke of death lover's p., 1841
there cannot be p. in death, 1841
they'll p. black and blue, 5289
Pinched thick as honeycomb, 5290
Pinches : fill skins with p., 5291
with amorous p. black, 676
Pine : bark peel'd from p., 5293
this p. is bark'd, 5292
Pines : fires tops of eastern p., 6325
forbid mountain p., 3798
p. beholding food, 2786
Pink of courtesy, 1618
Pinnace : sail my p., 6577
Pins of steel, 1007
Pint-pot : peace, p., 5505
Pioneer : a worthy p., 6369
Pipe for fortune's finger, 2861
thy small p., 6957
will you play upon this p., 5331
Pippins and cheese to come, 1270
Pirate : sanctimonious p., 6257
Pirates make cheap pennyworths, 5294
water-thieves, p., 5295
Pistol : how now, P., 3599
I am thy P., 4955
P., discharge yourself, 2110
P., lay head in Furies' lap, 4955
Pit : fallen into p. of ink, 1281
fill p. as well as better, 5382
p. of clay to be made, 3108
there's sulphurous p., 7317
Pitch : I am toiling in p., 5297
pour down stinking p., 7029
thing known by name of p., 5296
touch p., defiled, 5298
word is p. and pay, 5051
Pitch-balls in face, 6985
Pitchers have ears, 5299
Pitfall : never fear the p., 652
Pith : feed on p. of life, 2090
Pitiful : wondrous p., 4305
Pity, 5301-5312
as small p. as wren's eye, 5302
give p. to her, 5301
leave the hermit p., 5311
my p. hath been balm, 5303
no more p. than a dog, 6271
p. drives out p., 2690
p. is degree to love, 5312
p. is virtue of the law, 5310
p. like new-born babe, 5304
p. me not, 4753
p. must be laid aside, 4073
p. of it, Iago, 5306
p. those I do not know, 5305
pregnant to good p., 5376
soft p. enters at iron gate, 5307
tear-falling p., 5308
the more the p., 4383
'tis p. and p. 'tis 'tis true, 4439

Pizzle : you bull's p., 1456
Place, 5313-5318
bestow this p. on us, 2107
braver p. hath no man, 2720
buys p. next to the king, 4650
fellow, give p., 2113
fit in his time and p., 5673
from lowest p. virtuous things, 6928
give p., by heaven, 5753
give us the p. alone, 2107
he stands on slippery p., 6037
I know my p., 5318
I will ask him for my p., 2228
in world I fill a p., 5314
keeps p. with thought, 5466
no respect of p. in you, 5631
nor time nor p. did then adhere, 6625
O p. and greatness, 5317
O p., O form, 5316
p. below the first, 2516
p. dignified by doer's deed, 6928
p. for every man alive, 5313
this p. is dangerous, 2127
'tis the fate of p., 5315
Places eye of heaven visits, 7214
Plackets : dread prince of p., 1714
keep hand out of p., 2660
Plague, 5319-5320
drink up monarch's p., 2727
feel p. of each calamity, 4449
p. of all cowards, I say, 1638
p. of sighing and grief, 5931
p. on both your houses, 5320
p. upon you all, 5319
p. when madmen lead blind, 4452
private pleasure, public p., 5342
quickly may one catch p., 4390
'tis the p. of great ones, 4562
what p. could have come, 6954
Plague-sore : thou art a p., 1806
Plagues : all p. that in air, 1807
p. that thee alone obey, 3068
thus pour stars down p., 5229
Plain : honest mind and p., 5322
I must be p. with you, 5324
I was always p. with you, 5323
moral of my wit is, 6781
p. and bluntly, 6296
p. and not honest, 6299
p. as bald head of Time, 5321
p. as way to church, 7111
p. man in p. meaning, 5325
'tis my occupation to be p., 5322
Plain-song of it, 3648
Plaining comes too late, 1459
Plainness : in p. harbour craft, 5322
to p. honour's bound, 3547
Planet, 5326-5327
born under rhyming p., 5668
some p. strike me down, 2191
there's some ill p. reigns, 5327
this is a bawdy p., 1703
Planets of good luck, 5326
p. of mishap, 5326
Planks : trust not to rotten p., 5902
Plantagenet : arise P., 5676
Edward P., arise a knight, 3967
Plaster : bring the p., 6099
gainst sores sovereign p., 7524

Plautus cannot be too light, 61
Play, 5328-5338
  fair p., fool's p., 5337
  go p., boy, p., 59
  good p. needs no epilogue, 5328
  guilty, sitting at a p., 5330
  I p. so disgraced a part, 5338
  I will p. no more to-night, 3261
  is there no p. to ease anguish, 5336
  no boy's p. here, 5333
  our p. lamentable comedy, 5335
  p. on lute, towns burn, 4948
  p. out the p., 5332
  p. pleased not the million, 5329
  p.'s the thing, 5330
  this p. can never please, 5334
  thus p. I many people, 3906
  will you p. upon this pipe, 5331
  you cannot p. upon me, 5331
  you rise to p., 7325
  your p. needs no excuse, 2381
Player : monstrous that this p., 63
  poor p. that struts, 4137
  strutting p. whose conceit, 67
Players : all men and women p., 7466
  doth it like harlotry p., 5505
  see the p. well bestowed, 62
Playfellow : my p., your hand, 3206
  p. in marriage-pleasure, 560
  p. to keep you company, 1737
Playhouse : thunder at p., 7562
Playing with lion's whelp, 4172
Plea : what p. so tainted, 4037
Pleasant without scurrility, 5582
Pleasing : lascivious p. of lute, 7005
Pleasure, 5339-5343
  every humour has p., 3651
  I speak not in p., 2511
  me of my lawful p. she restrained, 1235
  no p. of his gain, 4737
  no profit where no p. ta'en, 6294
  not a minute without p., 5339
  p. and action make hours short, 5341
  p. and revenge more deaf, 5343
  p. drown the brim, 3813
  present p. becomes opposite, 5340
  private p., public plague, 5324
  spoils p. of the time, 1753
  use her at thy p., 6927
  what p. find we in life, 4122
Pleasures : idle p., 6906
  p. of the world, 6322
  so to your p., 1777
Pledge you a mile, 1710
Plentitude of subtle matter, 759
Plenty breeds cowards, 1633
Plod away o' the hoof, 2109
Plodders : small p. ever won, 6291
Plot, 5344-5346
  let us assay our p., 5344
  our p. is a good p., 5345
  p. against my life, 5346
  we first survey the p., 971
Plots broke their sleep, 2921
  p. of damned witchcraft, 1225
  when our deep p. pall, 3717
Ploughed : he p. her, 1012
  p. for, sow'd, 5584
  she shall be p., 6927

Ploughman : cheer p. with crops, 6628
  hard as palm of p., 3229
  heavy p. snores, 4674
Pluck one another down, 6038
Plucker down of kings, 3883
Plum : like a green p., 5222
  mellow p. doth fall, 2941
Plume : change for idle p., 3119
  what p. of feathers, 2630
Plumes : jets under his p., 6784
  we'll pull his p., 5219
Plummet : deeper than p., 832
Pluto winks, 5120
  to P.'s damned lake, 1770
Pocket up these wrongs, 7546
Pocketing up of wrongs, 7545
Poesy : golden cadence of p., 5349
  much is force of p., 5350
  p. use to quicken you, 6294
Poet's eye in frenzy rolling, 3705
Poetical : gods made thee p., 5347
Poetry, 5347-5350
  lovers given to p., 5347
  mincing p., 5348
  truest p. most feigning, 5347
Poignard : give me my p., 5697
Poignards : she speaks p., 6178
Poins : no valour in P., 1636
Point-blank : shoot p., 2278
Point-device in accoutrements, 4249
Point-devise the very man, 4524
Pointing-stock : made a p., 7351
Points of mighty opposite, 4905
  touch sourest p., 1906
Poison, 5351-5361
  deal in p. with thee, 3856
  do it not with p., 5358
  feed on flowers yet p. breed, 5866
  give me some p., Iago, 5358
  hide not p. with sugar'd words, 5356
  I feed myself with p., 5351
  I have drunk p., 6180
  in p. there is physic, 5355
  let me have dram of p., 5361
  never hung p. on fouler toad, 5360
  p. be their drink, 1737
  p. hands of sin, 5971
  p. it in the source, 3328
  p. o'ercrows my spirit, 5353
  p. us, do we not die, 3797
  steel nor p. touch him, 1872
  such stuff as well might p. p., 6855
  sweet p. for age's tooth, 5357
  they love not p. that p. need, 5359
  thou gavest me p., fellow, 5352
  within rind p. hath residence, 3078
  would it were mortal p., 5360
Poisoned by their wives, 3901
  p., forsook, cast off, 6314
  p. with a pot of ale, 5354
Poisons more deadly, 7299
  p. scarce found to distaste, 1481
Poking-sticks of steel, 1007
Polacks : smote sledded P., 2934
Poland : burn a P. winter, 7089
Pole : painted upon a p., 6808
  soldier's p. is fall'n, 6061
Polecat : out, you p., 7271

Policy, 5362-5363
base and rotten p., 5362
honour and p. grow together, 3531
p. of mind, 5648
turn him to any cause of p., 3972
Politician, 5364-5366
as lief be Brownist as p., 5366
it might be pate of a p., 5364
like a scurvy p., 2423
p. would circumvent God, 5364
Poll : flaxen was his p., 462
Pomegranate-tree : sings in p., 4008
Pomewater : ripe as p., 1953
Pomp, 5367-5369
candied tongue lick p., 2719
misery outlives p., 4743
more sweet than painted p., 4117
take physic, p., 5369
tide of p. that beats, 6021
too little for p. to enter, 2962
vain p. of this world, 5368
what is p. but dust, 4130
Pompey laughs away fortune, 2848
Pond : cream like standing p., 5106
his p. fish'd by neighbour, 1703
p. as deep as hell, 2031
Pontic sea whose current, 4692
Poop was beaten gold, 429
Pooped : she p. him, 7500
Poor : as p. as Job, 5378
fortune ne'er turns key to p., 2870
he fears he shall be p., 5379
how apt p. to be proud, 5381
my friends p. but honest, 5373
none so p. to do him reverence, 1033
p. advanced make friends, 2922
p. and content rich enough, 5379
p. man made tame, 5376
p. that have not patience, 5200
sends p. well pleased, 1606
trouble p. with begging, 588
why should p. be flatter'd, 2719
Poppy : not p., mandragora, 6032
Popular : art thou common, p., 5093
Popularity : enfeoff'd to p., 3876
Pork : to smell p., 2282
Pork-eaters : be p., 1322
Porpentine : quills upon p., 6417
Porridge : comfort like cold p., 1434
they want their p., 2331
Portance in travels' history, 4305
Portcullised with teeth, 6672
Portents : these are p., 5177
Portia is Brutus' harlot, 7132
P. is dead, 1865
this is the voice of P., 6951
Portion : prodigal p. spent, 5444
Ports and happy havens, 7214
Posies : fragrant p., 5706
Possession : loyal to p., 5104
virtue p. would not show, 7508
yield p. to my prayers, 5800
Possibilities : speak with p., 2400
Possible : never thought it p., 4388
Post : I am no fee'd p., 5480
you'll beat the p., 701
Post-horse : wind my p., 5755
Posterior of the day, 2345
Posteriors of this day, 1825

Postern of needle's eye, 1056
Posters of sea and land, 5987
Posy : is this p. of a ring, 924
p. like cutler's poetry, 5701
Pot : greasy Joan keels p., 5124
little pot soon hot, 5370
three-hooped p., 572
Potations : forswear thin p., 5764
p. pottle-deep, 5372　.
Potatoes : let sky rain p., 1954
Potent in potting, 2338
Potions : what p. have I drunk, 6474
Potting : potent in p., 2338
Pottle-pot's maidenhead, 756
Pouch : tester in p., 4763
Poultice for my bones, 821
Pouncet-box : he held a p., 4225
Pound of flesh, 2742
Pout upon the morning, 2061
Poverty, 5373-5381
in such p. of grace, 4252
my p. consents, 5380
she scorns our p., 5375
steeps me in p. to lips, 133
view an age of p., 2874
Powder : fire and p. kiss, 1967
food for p. 5382
like p. in soldier's flask, 7249
violently as p. fired, 5361
which will break to p., 4779
Power, 5383-5384
I have not p. to muzzle, 1725
if he have p. vail ignorance, 4071
laugh to scorn p. of man, 806
no p. in Venice can alter, 5408
not half p. to do me harm, 3269
p. hath not tomb so evident, 5383
p. that made you king, 5384
p. to cancel his captivity, 4132
when p. to flattery bows, 2243
with a puissant p., 330
Pox pinches the other, 7579
p. upon him for me, 1110
what a p. have I to do, 3605
Prabbles : given to p., 5412
Prague : old hermit of P., 7256
Praise, 5385-5398
breath whereof p. is made, 5391
cram us with p., 5393
devours deed in p., 5398
I will p. any man, 5385
make chronicle rich with p., 5387
means found to buy p., 5391
no friends by, men p. selves, 5396
no wise man will p. self, 5395
p. cannot mend the brow, 507
p. us as we are tasted, 5392
p. we afford to any lady, 5388
she will outstrip all p., 5390
sing her endless p., 3805
take p. with thee to heaven, 3617
this p. doth nourish agues, 5386
too brown for a fair p., 5389
Praises are our wages, 5393
p. self but in deed, 5398
Pranks : pestiferous p., 7116
p. they dare not show husbands, 7141
Prater : a speaker but a p., 7361

Prattle out of fashion, 1429
p. without practice, 6438
thinking his p. tedious, 66
Prawls : keep out of p., 4670
Prawns : good dish of p., 6916
Pray can I not, 5401
watch to-night, p. to-morrow, 7019
when I would p. and think, 5403
Prayed that never p. before, 5406
Prayer, 5399-5406
he is given to p., 2595
p. assaults mercy itself, 2311
require space for p., 5404
what form of p. can serve, 5401
Prayer-books in pocket, 606
Praying to enrich his soul, 5432
p. to purse-taking, 6947
that's past p. for, 2674
Prayers : fall to thy p., 2513
find profit by losing p., 5399
going where p. cross, 6497
he scorns to say his p., 7423
I'll bribe you with true p., 5402
parted with p. for provider, 4761
p. from preserved souls, 5402
true p. that shall rise, 5402
when leisure, say p., 4064
Prays : he p. but faintly, 5405
Precedence : obscure p., 5792
Precedent : recorded for a p., 5408
who ever shunn'd by p., 5407
Precepts in thy memory, 5410
p. of stale example, 4284
you load me with p., 5409
Precursors of thunder-claps, 4159
Preferment goes by letter, 5871
p. goes not by gradation, 5871
put sons to seek p., 3501
Pregnant : how p. his replies, 4441
p. to good pity, 5376
Prelate of the church, 5729
Preparations : warlike p., 2974
Prerogative of age, 138
Presagers of my breast, 4327
Presages be not vain, 2534
Prescription to die, 2214
Presence : be scanter of maiden p., 4464
lavish of my p. been, 5104
lord of thy p., 4227
p. of king engenders love, 3881
show a fair p., 2936
Present for any emperor, 4927
take the p. time, 4119
Presentment of two brothers, 5272
Preservation : times of p., 6617
Pretty : all my p. ones, 1289
p. and witty, 7088
Prey for carrion kites, 3934
Preys make men thieves, 6532
Priam : drew P.'s curtain, 7100
had P. check'd his son, 6754
P. found the fire, 7100
Pyrrhus' sword falls on P., 5610
was this King P.'s joy, 7287
word will P. turn to stone, 3424
Pribbles : given to p., 5412
leave p. and prabbles, 5411
Price : falls into low p., 4343
trivial p. of serious things, 2582
what's p. of this inkle, 5613

Prick us, do we not bleed, 3797
Prick-song : sing p., 2681
Pricket : princess prick'd p., 5433
'twas a p., 1953
Pricking of my thumbs, 6581
Prickles : rose have p., 5740
Pride, 5413-5424
drawn to blast her p., 1740
fly p., says peacock, 5415
maiden p., adieu, 5419
maugre all thy p., 4385
mow'd in tops of p., 2320
my high-blown p. broke, 2492
my p. fell with my fortunes, 5413
one man eats another's p., 5424
p. hath no glass but p., 5423
p. is fasting in wantonness, 5424
p. is his own glass, 5422
p. must have a fall, 3595
p. must tarre mastiffs, 1728
p. of kingly sway, 1687
p. pomp, circumstance, 2533
p. pulls country down, 5420
p. went before, 5418
p. which taints happy man, 5417
proud, yet p. becomes him, 7553
sick of p., 5929
stand condemn'd for p., 5419
who cries out on p., 5414
you talk of p., 5416
Priest : live like Diana's p., 1233
no Italian p. shall tithe, 2335
p., beware your beard, 469
p. that lacks Latin, 6609
Priests and fanes that lie, 6100
p. pray for enemies, 6395
p. shall sing her praise, 3805
Prig : out upon his, p., 455
Prime : as p. as goats, 5802
love crowned with p., 4119
p. of manhood daring, 1209
Primrose : pale p., 2758
p. way to everlasting bonfire, 7033
Primrose-beds : upon p. to lie, 7357
Primroses that die unmarried, 2767
Prince, 5425-5432
begging p. what beggar pities not, 5431
conquest for p. to boast of, 5441
dread p. of plackets, 1714
from p. to prentice, 3026
God send p. better companion, 1444
good night, sweet p., 3371
how might p. forget, 2834
I can serve black p., 2018
lion will not touch true p., 4174
nimble-footed P. of Wales, 3613
present services to new p., 5513
p. hath outgrown me, 7065
p. of darkness, alias devil, 2018
p. of darkness is gentleman, 5427
p. of the world, 2018
p. studies his companions, 1445
this p. is not an Edward, 5432
you P. of Wales, 3875
Princes : breathe not where p. are, 5352
p. are like to gnats, 5428
p. are the glass, book, 5429
p. have but titles, 5430

p. should be free, 5506
p. should live like gods, 5428
sweet aspect of p., 5426
Princess: his p. with him, 5434
preyful p. prick'd pricket, 5433
she shall be aged p., 2297
Print: in p. I found it, 5436
wear p. of it, 4938
Printing: caused p. used, 5435
Priscian a little scratched, 4015
Prison, 5437-5440
come, let's away to p., 5438
compare p. unto world, 5439
goodly p. with many wards, 5437
she sends you to p., 5437
space enough in such a p., 5440
vile p. of afflicted breath, 3111
Prison-house: secrets of p., 6417
Prisoner: keeping them p., 6362
like p. in twisted gyves, 653
Prisons: make not thoughts p., 6555
Private: let me enjoy my p., 2117
Privilege of age to brag, 138
p. of antiquity upon thee, 138
p. of a private man, 5878
rotten p. and custom, 3296
Prize, 5441-5443
goodly p., fit for devil, 5442
is not this a gallant p., 5441
light winning makes p. light, 5443
p. of precious you, 6866
war's p. to take vantages, 7000
wicked p. buys out law, 5084
Prizer: precious as is p., 6848
Prizes accident oft as merit, 3564
Procreants: leave p. alone, 2112
Prodigal, 5444-5449
calf killed for the P., 5445
calf's skin killed for P., 1048
how like a p., 5447
p. course is like sun's, 5448
what p. portion have I spent, 5444
Prodigality of nature, 2976
Prodigals from swine-keeping, 5446
tattered p., 6064
Prodigious: like p. son, 5449
Prodigy: soul brought forth p., 7277
Profanation: foul p., 3125
Profession: Adam's p., 2968
Proffers not took reap thanks, 6504
Profit: no p. where no pleasure, 6294
p. by losing our prayers, 5399
p. is I know to curse, 3999
p. of excess is to surfeit, 2376
p. of their shining nights, 6291
'tis not p. leads honour, 3528
Profitless as water in sieve, 1569
Progenitors: predecease p., 1291
Progeny of kings, 3807
Prognostication: fruitful p., 5138
Progress: time's p. to eternity, 6639
Prohibition so divine, 5854
Prolixity: date out of p., 6185
Prologue: is this a p., 924
no without-book p., 6185
p. to egg and butter, 3087
p. to omen coming on, 5095
p. to some great amiss, 3183
what's past is p., 51

Prologues to a bad voice, 6091
Promethean fire, 2428
that P. heat, 4154
Promise, 5450-5455
beyond p. of age, 2390
he will spend mouth and p., 5455
keep word of p. to ear, 2662
to p. is courtly, 5454
Promise-breaker: hourly p., 1196
worse than p., 3295
Promise-crammed: eat air, p. 1174
Promise-keeping: precise in p., 5451
Promises: his p. fly beyond his state, 5452
his p. were mighty, 5453
thy p. like Adonis' gardens, 5450
Promising, air of the time, 5454
Promontory: I sat upon a p., 4654
one that stands on p., 6148
sterile p., 2268
Promotion: sweat for p., 5872
Promotions to ennoble, 5012
Prompter: spoke after p., 6185
Proof: curb it upon others' p., 5801
in reproof true p. of men, 1186
in strong p. of chastity, 1722
p. and bulwark against sense, 3332
Prop that sustains house, 4140
Proper-false: easy for p., 2890
Property by what it is, 3070
p. of youth and maidhood, 1227
Prophecy: spirit of deep p., 3804
Prophesy: O, I could p., 3617
over thy wounds I p., 1031
p. with a near aim, 3482
Prophets: jesters oft prove p., 3787
lean-look'd p. whisper, 5941
Propontic and Hellespont, 4692
Proportion: received my p., 5449
Propositions of a lover, 4398
Prosperity, 5456-5458
hate and terror to p., 1868
jest's p. lies in ear, 3788
p. is the bond of love, 5458
thrust hand into purse of p., 5456
welcome sour cup of p., 5457
Protector: am I not p., 5729
p., protect yourself, 5264
Proteus: change shapes with P., 1681
stars did govern P.' birth, 6249
welcome to my P., 5065
Proud: he seems p., 3276
how apt poor are to be p., 5381
I hate a p. man, 5422
p. can I never be, 6512
p. eats up himself, 5422
p. in heart and mind, 1205
p. me no prouds, 6512
why should man be p., 5422
Provand for bearing burdens, 1055
Provender: peck of p., 3305
p. tied to mouths, 2331
wears out his time for p., 3943
Proverb, 5459-5464
ancient p. well affected, 5460
country p. known, 5463
hare of whom p. goes, 3264
let p. go with me, 3581
old p. very well parted, 5461

p. is something musty, 3101
p. never stale, 5462
Proverbed with grandsire phrase, 5464
Proverbs : breaker of p., 2023
  patch grief with p., 3155
  they sigh'd forth p., 5459
Providence in fall of sparrow, 5465
  p. in watchful state, 5466
Provinces : kissed away p., 3915
Provoked : not soon p., 1212
Prudence : this Sir P., 4805
Prunes : lived upon mouldy p., 1090
Psalm : hundredth p., 7438
Psalms : I could sing p., 7470
  sings p. to hornpipes, 5471
Publican : like a fawning p., 4068
Pucelle be France's saint, 3805
  P. they term so pure, 3806
Puck : call you sweet P., 2477
Pudding : yield crow a p., 1672
Puddings : guts made of p., 5446
Pudency so rosy, 1235
Puisny : as a p. tilter, 1198
Pulpits : common p., 4086
Pulse : let me feel your p., 3209
  my p. doth keep time, 5467
  no p. shall keep progress, 5468
Punish : I will p. home, 3724
Punishment that women bear, 7297
Punto : pass thy p., 2679
Punto reverso : ah, the p., 2681
Pupil-like take correction, 4192
Pupilage of this present, 3646
Puppet : Egyptian p., 6007
Puppies : drown blind p., 2214
Puppy-dogs : talks of p., 4825
Purchase of his lustful eye, 7120
  p. to make men glorious, 6095
Pure : as p. as sin, 6167
  p. as snow, 1052
Purgation consist in words, 6721
  put him to his p., 1304
Purgatory : venture p., 3668
Purge and leave sack, 5657
Puritan, 5469-5471
  but one p. among them, 5471
  he is a kind of p., 5470
  make a p. of the devil, 5469
  though honesty be no p., 3502

Purity : all p., deservings, 4254
  in p. of manhood stand, 2730
  thou impious p., 2532
Purple with love's wound, 1716
Purples : long p., 2959
Purpose, 5472-5475
  flighty p. never o'ertook, 1939
  infirm of p., 5474
  my p. is horse of that colour, 5475
  my p. would not fail, 7220
  passion ending doth p. lose, 5472
  p. is slave to memory, 5472
  p. makes strong the vow, 6938
  p. you undertake dangerous, 1788
  shake my fell p., 5612
  speak to the p., 6179
  whet thy blunted p., 5473
Purposes mistook, 3716
Purr of fortune, 2123
Purse, 5476-5480
  consumption of the p., 5477
  empty p., no money, 2800
  for foreign p. sell sovereign, 6710
  halfpenny p. of wit, 5225
  keep your p., 5480
  my p. unlock'd, 5478
  p. of rich prosperity, 5456
  put money in thy p., 4765
  she bears the p., 4289
  who steals my p. steals trash, 4894
Purse-taking : praying to p., 6947
Purses : our p. shall be proud, 4694
  their love in their p., 5479
  we that take p. by moon, 5476
Pursuit where no chase, 770
Pursuivants of death, 3196
Push : made p. at chance, 5250
  put matter to present p., 4577
Push-pin : play at p., 3891
Puttock : I did avoid a p., 2254
  partridge in p.'s nest, 2364
Pygmalion : P.'s images, 7322
Pyramids : make p. my gibbet, 1840
Pyramis to her I'll rear, 3805
Pyramus : shine moon on P., 4794
Pyramus and Thisbe, comedy, 5335
Pyrrhus' bleeding sword falls, 5610
Pythagoras : hold opinion with P., 5483
  what is opinion of P., 5483

Q

Quagmire : o'er bog and q., 6651
Quailing : there is no q., 1597
Quails : one that loves q., 898
Quake and tremble, 6207
Qualities : has she any q., 5487
  vicious q., 3807
Quality, 5485-5487
  give us taste of your q., 5485
  q. of mercy is not strain'd, 4642
  you are not of our q., 5486
Quantity of life, 1870
Quarrel, 5488-5501
  beware of entrance to q., 5491
  find q. in a straw, 3121
  find q. on seventh cause, 4091
  full of q. and offence, 5490

good q. to draw factions, 318
holy seems the q., 5488
in false q. no true valour, 5497
no q., but contention, 5494
patch a q., 5489
pick a q. to beguile me, 5906
q., ho, already, 5701
q. with man for cracking nuts, 5499
see occasion in good q., 5498
sudden and quick in q., 7466
thrice arm'd that hath q. just, 5493
Quarreler : he's a great q., 1213
Quarrelled for coughing, 5499
Quarrelling is valour misbegot, 5500
  tutor me from q., 5499
Quarrelous as the weasel, 5490

Quarrels : best q. are cursed, 5495
busy minds with foreign q., 5492
thy head as full of q., 5499
Quart d'ecu : for q., sell, 927
Quartered in her heart, 2420
Queen, 5502-5513
carried q. to Cæsar, 1013
come not near fairy q., 2478
convey my tristful q., 5515
ere you q., husband king, 5129
fairest q. ever king received, 5507
fie, wrangling q., 5502
fire burn'd Carthage q., 6966
Grecian q., whose youth, 3436
I come, my q., stay, 5503
I was q. o'er myself, 5700
I would not be a q., 5510
I'll q. it no inch farther, 2193
jealous q. of heaven, 3918
our q. hates sluts, 2475
poor shadow painted q., 5512
q. crowned with infamy, 5508
q. mother rounds apace, 5513
q. of curds and cream, 536
q. of earthly queens, 7131
q. worth many beggars, 1840
rather serving-maid than q., 5511
remembrance of weeping q., 5751
she shall be my q., 4755
sung by fair q. to lute, 3919
to be q. in bondage, 5506
tongue-tied our q., 6689
weep not, sweet q., 5505
who had seen mobled q., 5504
won to his lust my q., 5861
Quern : labour in the q., 2477

R is dog's name, 2158
Rabbit-sucker : hang me for r., 3429
Rabble : follow'd with r., 5526
r. unroof'd the city, 5524
'twas you incensed the r., 5525
Rabblement hooted, 5527
Rack, 5528-5530
I live upon the r., 5529
leave not a r. behind, 5639
r. of this tough world, 2994
thou hast set me on the r., 5530
to the r. with him, 5528
you speak upon the r., 5529
Rackets : matched r. to balls, 4754
Radish : I am bunch of r., 2674
like a forked r., 4489
Rage : disguise nature with r., 7013
fawn on r., 4192
great r. of heart, 2944
in r. deaf as the sea, 6265
r. be his, whilst on earth I rain, 2700
r. whose heat nothing allay, 7526
replete with r., 4327
stop the r. betime, 7516
thy r. shall burn thee, 7526
Raggedness : window'd r., 7531
Rags : arm it [sin] in r., 5963
her r. will burn, 7089
r. under shelter of honour, 3548
Raiment : ne'er ask what r., 5531

Quest have given verdict, 2365
Questant : bravest q. shrinks, 3526
Question left yet to prove, 4260
q. with wicked tongue, 2563
Quick, 5514-5517
I am struck to the q., 5515
I have touch'd thee to the q., 5517
I'll tent him to the q., 5515
q. as greyhound's mouth, 7244
touch thee to the q., 7244
Quid for Quo, 4637
Quiddities : quips and q., 3605
where be his q., 4046
Quiet as a lamb, 5519
q. as father's skull, 5520
q. of my wounded conscience, 1506
Quietness, sick of rest, 5518
Quietus make with bodkin, 1847
Quillets how to cheat devil, 6735
q. of the law, 4030
where be his q., 4046
Quills upon porpentine, 6417
Quinapalus : what says Q., 7259
Quintessence of dust, 4487
Quip Modest : called Q., 4091
Quips and sentences, 3650
Quire of enticing birds, 984
Quiring to cherubins, 3273
Quirk : man of that q., 4502
Quirks of blazoning pens, 1980
Quit me of them thoroughly, 5648
Quittance : exceeding all q., 5528
omittance is no q., 5521
q. of desert and merit, 5522
Quoifs and stomachers, 1007
Quotidian of love, 4249

R

took immodest r., 5532
vouchsafe me r., food, 153
wear them like r., 7547
Rain, 5533-5537
gentle r. from heaven, 4642
hey, ho, wind and r., 5536
is there not r. enough, 3210
like as r. to water, 4163
makes r. as well as Jove, 6452
much r. wears the marble, 5534
pack when it begins to r., 2948
property r. is to wet, 5533
r. added to river rank, 5537
r. and wind beat December, 6160
r. came to wet me once, 5535
r. it raineth every day, 7231
stone at r. relenteth, 6272
sunshine and r. at once, 6338
Rain-water : holy water better than r.,
7023
Rainbow : add hue to r., 2375
Raining : marble wear with r., 4429
Rakes : pikes ere become r., 5275
Ram is tupping your ewe, 3377
r. that batters down wall, 5539
Rampalian : away, you r., 1121
Ramps : vaulting variable r., 1233
Rams : my r. speed not, 5538
Rancour of your hearts, 5541
r. will out, 5540

Rank-scented many, 4832
Ranks : our r. are broke, 3252
Ransom : world's r., Mary's Son, 2324
Rapes parallels Nessus, 1197
Rapier, 5542-5545
 dubbed with unhatched r., 3968
 gave you a dancing r., 6571
 r. and dagger man, 5544
 rust, r., 4275
 scour you with my r., 5543
 wear thy r. bare, 5545
Rapiers : wearing r. afraid, 5542
Rapine and murder, 4708
Rarities of nature, 6635
Rascal, 5546-5553
 away, you cut-purse r., 5549
 dull, muddy-mettled r., 5546
 I cannot endure fustian r., 5549
 no, no, I am a r., 5552
 peace, ye fat-kidneyed r., 5547
 takes delight in barren r., 5553
 this is a counterfeit r., 5550
 what a damned Epicurean r., 5551
 what pagan r. is this, 5712
Rascals : I never see such r., 5382
 lash the r. naked, 6002
 O you pandarly r., 1521
Rash : as r. as fire, 2503
 it is too r., 4158
Rasher : no r. on the coals, 1322
Rat : house troubled with r., 2741
 like r. without a tail, 5782
Rat-catcher : you r., 1117
Rats : land r., water r., 5295
 r. bite cords atwain, 5716
 r. ravin down bane, 4915
 very r. have quit it., 783
Ratsbane : milk had been r., 2739
 put r. in my mouth, 5838
Ravel all this matter out, 3873
Raven, 5556-5561
 change r. for a dove, 5558
 comes as r. o'er infected house, 4630
 did ever r. sing like lark, 5560
 disposed as hateful r., 2628
 I would croak like r., 5556
 r. chides blackness, 5561
 r. doth bellow for revenge, 5556
 r. doth not hatch lark, 5559
 r. himself is hoarse, 5557
 r. rooked on chimney top, 662
 r.'s heart within dove, 3993
 waits as doth a r., 1495
Ravens : he that doth r. feed, 1420
Ravisher : war a r., 7009
Razor : keen as r.'s edge, 6667
Razors to my heart, 7452
Razure of oblivion, 1984
Read : could not r., hanged, 5564
 exceedingly well r., 2970
 he is well r. in poetry, 5567
 r. what love hath writ, 4327
 to r. comes by nature, 5568
Readiness : put on manly r., 5563
 r. is all, 5562
Realms dropped from his pocket, 256
Reap : like to r. proper man, 5570
 they that r. must sheaf, 5569
Reason, 5571-5579
 ask me no r. why, 4382

blind r. stumbling, 2617
do not banish r., 3278
give no man r., 5571
godlike r. to fust in us, 4488
how noble in r., 4487
in r. nothing, 5673
it fits not to ask r. why, 5577
let your r. serve, 5574
let's r. with the worst, 7502
love admits not r., 4382
love's r. is without r., 4380
make will Lord of r., 7149
men have lost their r., 1033
neither rhyme nor r., 7112
no other but woman's r., 5579
noble and sovereign r., 4681
now r. is past care, 1730
one r. to poise another, 5576
outrun the pauser, r., 4381
past r. hunted, 4431
r. and love keep little company, 4383
r. and respect make livers pale, 5578
r. marshal to my will, 5575
r. not with need, 4941
r. panders will, 5888
r. says you are worthier, 5575
r. themselves out, 5672
r. thus with r. fetter, 4385
r. to cool raging motions, 5576
reasonable produces r., 4449
receipt of r. limbeck only, 4629
root takes r. prisoner, 5573
tell me r. why, 2017
'tis you that have the r., 5674
will of man by r. swayed, 5575
wit nor r. can my passion hide, 4385
your r., Jack, your r., 5571
Reasoning with yourself, 5674
Reasons, 5580-5583
 good r. give place to better, 5580
 his r. two grains of wheat, 5583
 if r. were plentiful, 5571
 strong r. make strong actions, 5581
 your r. have been sententious, 5582
Rebel : what is she but r., 3670
Rebellion, 5584-5587
 ever did r. find rebuke, 5585
 r. shall lose sway, 5585
 r.'s head rise never, 655
 that same word, r., 5586
 unthread the rude eye of r., 5587
 we nourish cockle of r., 5584
Rebels need soldiers, 589
 r. wound thee with hoofs, 3913
Rebuke : rebellion find r., 5585
 r. me not, 6965
Reckless what I do, 7479
Reckoning : I am ill at r., 6441
 no r. made, 3709
 O weary r., 5
 thou hast called her to r., 3605
Recompense : for r. praised vile, 6867
 my r. is thanks, 6510
 r. slow to overtake thee, 3725
 study's god-like r., 6291
Recreation : sweet r. barr'd, 4614
Red, 5588-5591
 as r. as any rose, 5588
 as r. as blood, 5589

as r. as fire, 5590
like a r. morn, 5591
Red-hot with drinking, 6844
Red-lattice phrases, 3548
Rede : recks not own r., 5187
Redemption : condemned to r., 6901
 damn'd without r., 6905
 mercy nothing kin to r., 4640
 r. by Christ's dear blood, 5594
 seek r. of the devil, 5592
Redress : good night to r., 392
 past r., past care, 4040
Redressed : confessed, not r., 1492
Reek of rotten fens, 4834
Reflection : small r. of wit, 499
Reformation : never came r. in flood, 5596
 r. glittering o'er fault, 5595
Regard : deep r. beseem sage, 7213
Regent of love-rhymes, 1714
Region of thick-ribbed ice, 1876
 r. seem'd one cry, 4864
Register : dim r. of shame, 4995
Regreet daintiest last, 2309
Reguerdoned with thanks, 5658
Rein : master'd with leathern r., 3772
 what r. can hold wickedness, 7115
Relief : for this r. much thanks, 5598
 my r. must not be toss'd, 4945
 wherever sorrow is, r., 5597
Religion, 5599-5603
 I see you have r., 5599
 in r. what damned error, 5603
 r. makes rhapsody of words, 5600
 r. makes vows kept, 5602
 thou hast sworn against r., 5603
Religious : thou art r., 1517
Relish : imaginary r. sweet, 2391
 r. of saltness of time, 7577
Remarkable beneath moon, 6061
Remedies in ourselves lie, 5604
 r. past, griefs ended, 5605
Remedy : he found the r., 6135
 is there no r., 4811
 no r. against consumption, 5477
 r. indeed to do me good, 6050
 without r., without regard, 1935
Remember : pray, love, r., 5607
Remembrance, 5606-5609
 keep this r., 428
 let us not burthen our r., 5609
 praising lost makes r. dear, 5606
 rain r. with mine eyes, 3618
 r. of a weeping queen, 5751
 r. of these valiant dead, 6840
 rosemary, that's for r., 5607
 thanks as fits king's r., 6506
 writ in r., 6324
Remorse, 5610-5612
 abandon all r., 6001
 fall with less r., 5610
 rivers of r., 6463
 stop up passage to r., 5612
 what says Monsieur R., 5611
Remover : with r. to remove, 4333
Remuneration : let not virtue seek r.,
 6945
 r., Latin for three farthings, 5613
Renege, affirm, turn beaks, 5716
Renown, 5614-5616
 if r. made it not stir, 5614

outlook conquest, win r., 5616
 r. and grace is dead, 4808
 thou never hadst r., 5615
Rents : what are thy r., 1158
Repasture for his den, 4186
Repent : I'll r., and suddenly, 5618
 never r. for doing good, 3077
 no strength to r., 5618
 r. what's past, 1489
 when one cannot r., 5617
Repentance, 5617-5619
 r. falls into cinque-pace, 7369
 try what r. can, 5617
 who by r. is not satisfied, 5619
Replication prompt, 6665
 what r. should be made, 6215
Replies : how pregnant his r., 4441
Reply : I pause for a r., 1032
 this called R. Churlish, 4091
Report : I find r. a liar, 2986
 my good gossip R., 3081
Reports : false r., 5755
Repose, 5620-5622
 foster-nurse of nature is r., 5620
 sweet r. and rest, 5621
 this is a strange r., 5622
Reproach and everlasting shame, 5889
Reproof of chance proof of men, 1186
 this is called R. Valiant, 4091
Repulse : take no r., 2731
Reputation, 5623-5628
 his r. is as a villain, 5625
 I have lost my r., 5626
 I have offended r., 5624
 my r. is at stake, 5628
 purest treasure is spotless r., 5627
 put r. in staining act, 5623
 r. got without merit, 5626
 r. is idle imposition, 5626
 seeking bubble r., 7466
 you will lose your r., 1168
Requital to hair's breadth, 3200
Residence : forted r., 1984
 to everlasting r. fleet, 5961
Resolutes : lawless r., 6262
Resolution : be brief, lest r. drop, 6462
 change misdoubt to r., 6560
 native hue of r., 1847
 no want of r. in me, 3431
Respect, 5629-5631
 men noble should find r., 5629
 no r. of place in you, 5631
 nothing good without r., 5630
 r. make livers pale, 5578
 too much r. upon world, 7480
Respective and sociable, 3546
Respice finem, 2302
Rest, 5632-5633
 here will I set my r., 1895
 life's preserving r., 4588
 man's sense repairs by r., 5632
 my bones would r., 5633
 r. me his minim r., 2681
 r., r., perturbed spirit, 6197
 r. thy unrest on England, 2995
 so many hours take r., 3624
 sweet r. come to thy heart, 5621
 thy best of r. is sleep, 6028
Restoratives : read for r., 6095
Retire, if Warwick bid stay, 6336

Retort Courteous, 4091
Retreat : in r. he outruns lackey, 1630
let us make honourable r., 400
Returning were as tedious, 726
Revel bravely as the best, 5638
wastes night in r., 2584
Reveller : British r., 4718
Revellers : moonshine r., 2475
Revelling like lords, 5294
Revels : love keeps his r., 4362
what r. are at hand, 5336
Revenge, 5640-5655
blows and r. for me, 7069
capable and wide r., 4692
I may sweep to my r., 5640
make medicines of r., 5644
my r. had stomach, 5651
partly led to diet my r., 5649
r. has ears more deaf, 5343
r. is hammering in my head, 5655
r. should have no bounds, 5642
rouse r. from ebon den, 5643
shall we not r., 3797
spur my dull r., 5073
sweet r. grows harsh, 4852
think on r., 3149
this is hire, not r., 5641
to r. is no valour, 5654
too weak for my r., 5650
wilt thou r., 5645
Revenged : how shall I be r., 5646
so am I r., 5641
Revenges : time brings r., 6644
Revenue : no r. but good spirits, 2719
withering young man's r., 4787
Revenues : she bears duke's r., 5375
Reverence : lay r. by, 1169
none so poor to do him r., 1033
r., angel of the world, 5656
those I r. I fear, 2819
Revolts : ingrate r., 2336
Revolution of the times, 2550
Reward, 5657-5658
he that rewards me, God r. him, 5657
never have you tasted our r., 5658
reap thanks for their r., 6504
Rewarder of his friends, 5129
Rhapsody : r. of words, 5600
Rhetoric, 5659-5663
fie, painted r., 5661
heavenly r. of thine eye, 5662
it is a figure in r., 5659
practise r. in your talk, 5663
sweet smoke of r., 5660
Rheum : drops of women's r., 6455
how now, foolish r., 6462
villany not without r., 6463
Rheumatic as two dry toasts, 5664
Rhinoceros : approach like r., 5879
Rhyme, 5666-5669
find no r. to lady, 5668
I cannot show love in r., 5668
I'll r. you eight years, 5666
love taught me to r., 4277
neither r. nor reason, 7112
neither r. nor reason can express, 4249
never will I woo in r., 7363
not marble shall outlive this r., 5669
r. is but a ballad, 7361

r. selves into ladies' favours, 7361
something then in r., 5673
Rhyme and reason, 5670-5674
Rhymers : scald r., 403
Rhymes : in love as r. speak, 4249
r. guards on Cupid's hose, 5667
Rhyming : nay, I was r., 5674
not born under r. planet, 5668
Rialto : in R. you rated me, 6830
what news on the R., 4967
Riband in cap of youth, 7576
Ribbon : carnation r., 5613
Ribs : call in r., 2224
dainty bits make rich r., 2546
flinty r. of this world, 6566
over-weather'd r., 5447
seated heart knock at r., 6310
Rich : all of her most r., 500
art thou r., so so, 5679
as r. as twenty seas, 3802
if r., thou'rt poor, 1874
poor and content r. enough, 5379
poorly r., so wanteth, 5681
r. men sin, I eat root, 3095
r. not gaudy, 3189
she is r. in beauty, 519
thou art r., being poor, 5680
when old and r. no heat, 7582
Richard, 5675-5678
arise sir R., 5676
his parts are perfect R., 5675
R. robb'd lion of his heart, 5677
R. yet lives, 5678
upright judge with R., 5011
we came in with R. Conqueror, 5717
Riches, 5679-5681
endowments greater than r., 6942
I bequeath my r. to earth, 7161
nothing to make r. pleasant, 7582
r. is poor as winter, 5379
r. of thyself room at, 7366
r. point to misery, 7041
r. strewed in streets, 1355
thou bear'st r. but a journey, 1874
Richmond, 5682-5684
R. is on the seas, 4211
seeking for R., 5683
sleep, R., sleep in peace, 5682
Richmonds : six R. in field, 5684
Riddance : gentle r., 5685
good r., 5686
Riddle : much upon this r., 6776
Ridges with clouds contend, 7030
Riding forth to air, 5165
Riding-rods : legs two r., 2461
Right, 5687-5692
God defend the r., 5689
heaven prosper the r., 5689
I'll win our ancient r., 5691
pray that r. may thrive, 5689
r. as snow in harvest, 6057
r. should overcome might, 5688
when r. with r. wars, 5692
with blood to win your r., 5690
Right and Wrong, 5693-5699
be title r. or wrong, 5693
do him r., answering wrong, 5694
hooking both r. and wrong, 4826
I swear to right your wrongs, 5697

r. and wrong lose names, 5699
to do great r., do little wrong, 4038
Right-hand: of r. file, 5687
Rights by r. falter, 2690
Rigol: golden r., 6020
Rigour of the law, 4031
  r. of the statute, 6256
Rind of this flower, 3078
  sweetest nut, sourest r., 6380
Ring, 5700-5703
  get r. upon my finger, 3658
  hoop of gold, paltry r., 5701
  I give with this r., 5700
  r. encompasseth finger, 5702
  runs fastest gets r., 5703
  spring time, r. time, 4401
  when r. parts from finger, 5700
Rings: we will have r., 4565
Riot: drown themselves in r., 7571
  r. and dishonour stain brow, 6081
  r. is thy care, 3912
Riots: superfluous, r., 1356
Ripe: from hour to hour we r., 2793
  reeling r., 2229
Ripeness is all, 5704
Riping of the time, 999
River: rain added to r., 5537
  r. dry fill with tears, 6479
  r. in Macedon, 5705
  r. stayed swelleth, 6123
Rivers as sweet fish, 2706
  r. of remorse, 6463
  shallow r., to whose falls, 5706
Rivo says the drunkard, 2224
Road to his kindness, 2061
Roam thither, then, 5729
Roan shall be my throne, 3589
Roar as 'twere nightingale, 4187
  r. gently as sucking dove, 4187
Roared: well r., lion, 4190
Roarers: what care r., 7028
Roast: rules the r., 5752
Roast-meat for worms, 7500
Robbed that smiles steals, 5708
Robbers range abroad, 6325
  what makes r. bold but lenity, 4074
Robbery shook down my leaves, 6731
Robe: intertissued r. of gold, 6021
  like giant's r. on thief, 6650
Robes: old r. worn out, 5237
Robin: bonny sweet R., 5709
  here comes little R., 5710
Robin Goodfellow, sprite, 2477
Robin Hood, Scarlet, John, 4955
  live like old R., 6606
  R.'s fat friar, 3909
Rock: founded as the r., 2167
Rocks: I could hew up r., 239
  r. not so stout, 6637
  splitting r. in sands, 3380
Rod: all humble kiss r., 4349
  kiss the r. and fawn, 4192
Roe: without r., 2746
Rogue, 5711-5717
  blue-bottle r., 5714
  busy insinuating r., 6002
  frosty-spirited r., 5712
  honey-seed r., 5713
  I am very filthy r., 5552
  not more cowardly r., 1647

super-serviceable r., 5715
what a r. am I, 5711
you mouldy r., away, 4599
you sweet little r., 2510
Roguery: nothing but r. found, 1638
Rogues as these, like rats, 5716
  Slys are no r., 5717
  two r. in buckram suits, 2674
Roll of common men, 659
Romage in the land, 3282
Roman, 5718-5725
  after proud R. fashion, 1839
  as you are R., tell true, 5723
  firm R. to Egypt sends, 5221
  I am more R. than Dane, 5720
  like a R. bear the truth, 5723
  noblest R. of them all, 5725
  rather be dog than such a R., 929
  R. by R. vanquished, 5718
  R. thought struck him, 6543
  R. with R. heart can suffer, 5719
  we know the sweet R. hand, 3226
  who would not be a R., 5722
  why play the R. fool, 6400
Romans: friends, R., 1033
  last of all the R., 5724
  lusty R. came smiling, 2180
  R. are but sheep, 7285
  R., countrymen, lovers, 1032
  R. now have thews, 5721
  stoop, R., stoop, 1028
  yet two R. living, 5724
Rome, 5726-5730
  cruel men of R., 3383
  impossible R. should breed, 5724
  let R. in Tiber melt, 5726
  loved R. more, 1032
  move stones of R. to rise, 1033
  now it is R. indeed, 5730
  palmy state of R., 5095
  R. but wilderness of tigers, 417
  R. shall remedy this, 5729
  R. should eat up her own, 5728
  shake R. about your ears, 3454
  sun of R. is set, 6321
  that's the curse of R., 1738
  thou shalt be shown in R., 6007
  window'd in great R., 5886
Romeo: alas, poor R., 1892
  come, night, give me my R., 4998
  R. is dishclout to him, 2979
  R., thou art a villain, 3298
  R. without his roe, 2746
  rosemary and R. one letter, 2158
  wherefore art thou Romeo, 4895
  why, R., art thou mad, 4457
Ronyon: out, you r., 7271
  rump-fed r., 7270
Roof: bring r. to foundation, 1353
  cleave to r. within mouth, 5160
  majestical r. fretted, 2268
  swearing till my r. was dry, 5056
Roofs: I abjure all r., 4929
Root: eaten of insane r., 5573
  impossible you take r., 7052
  r. fix'd in virtue's ground, 4267
Roots: behold, earth hath r., 6984
  cuts our r. in characters, 1542
Rope-tricks: rail in r., 6739

Ropery : full of r., 4631
Rosalind : carving R., 4249
  I will be your R., 2128
  no jewel is like R., 3799
Roscius : what hath R. to act, 55
Rose, 5731-5740
  against blown r. stop nose, 5731
  as red as any r., 5588
  beauty's r. might never die, 525
  earthlier happy is r. distill'd, 6922
  hath not thy r. a canker, 5732
  he wears r. of youth, 7551
  I know thorns r. defends, 6542
  in ear I durst not stick r., 2461
  pluck white r. with me, 5732
  r. by any other name as sweet, 4895
  r. look fair, but fairer, 5735
  sweet r., fair flower, 5734
  takes r. from forehead, 38
  what though r. have prickles, 5740
  when I have pluck'd the r., 5733
Rosemary and bays, 1242
  r. and Romeo one letter, 2158
  r. and rue, 2767
  r. for remembrance, 5607
Roses : by r. of spring, 4385
  four red r. on a stalk, 4201
  how r. there do fade, 1261
  I have seen r. damasked, 4749
  morning r. wash'd in dew, 7374
  r. have thorns, 1076
  seek r. of shadow, 5136
Rot from hour to hour, 2793
Rother : pasture lards r., 5183
Rotten ere half ripe, 2938
  something r. in Denmark, 5742
Rottenness : sound r., 1868
Rotundity : smite r., 6585
Rough as rudest wind, 4900
Rough-hew them how we will, 2142
Roughness : affect saucy r., 5322
Round : golden r., 6208
  r. and top of sovereignty, 1684
Rouse : king's r., 1078
Rout : all is on the r., 2119
Rowland to dark tower came, 5743
Rowlands : Olivers and R., 2332
Royal 'twas to pardon, 5156
Royalty : frame them to r., 3750
  mingled r. with fools, 3876
  r. of nature reigns, 4913
Roynish clown, 1390
Rub, 5744-5747
  ay, there's the r., 1847
  every r. is smoothed, 5745
  r. in your fortunes, 2907
  what r. there is, 5213
Rubs : leave no r. nor botches, 5746
  world is full of r., 5747
Ruby : natural r. of cheeks, 5935

Rude am I in my speech, 6181
  thou art too r., 5749
Rudeness is sauce to wit, 5748
Rudesby : mad-brain r., 7375
Rue, 5750-5751
  I'll set a bank of r., 5751
  r., even for ruth, 5751
  r., sour herb of grace, 5751
  there's r. for you, 2767
  wear r. with a difference, 5750
Ruffian : on deathbed play r., 3956
  r. that will swear, 5959
  that father r., 3730
  wed to madcap r., 1814
Ruffs and cuffs, 5638
Ruin : bury all in r., 1353
  fall to cureless r., 7239
  formless r. of oblivion, 5181
  r. leap'd from his eyes, 4180
  r. of your love, 5700
  r. taught to ruminate, 6636
  weigh thee down to r., 4053
Ruins of noblest man, 1031
Rule, 5752-5754
  all done by r., 684
  obey that know not to r., 5069
  seek r., supremacy, 3670
  thou shalt r. no more, 5733
  to be ruled, not to r., 5754
  what is r. but dust, 4130
Ruler : created for thy r., 5753
Rules the roast, 5752
  true r. for old inventions, 2542
Ruminate : ruin taught to r., 6636
Rumination wraps me, 4613
Rumour, 5755-5758
  from R.'s tongues, 5755
  hold r. from what we fear, 5758
  R. doth double numbers, 5756
  R. pipe blown by surmises, 5755
  stop hearing when R. speaks, 5755
  this from R.'s tongue, 5757
  who but R. make fearful, 5755
Run : I ran when others r., 5759
  r. as fast as thou canst, 5759
  they stumble that r. fast, 3291
Runagate : white-liver'd r., 4211
Runaways : lofty r., 1778
Ruptures : guts-griping r., 1747
Rush be beam to hang thee, 1771
Rushes : hews oaks with r., 4828
  tickle senseless r., 1782
Russet yeas, kersey noes, 7363
Russia : last out night in R., 4986
Russian : like R. bear, 5879
  run into R. bear, 3311
Rust : eaten with r., 5761
  foul-cankering r., 5762
Rustling in silk, 4121
Ruttish : very r., 865
Rye-straw : your r. hats, 5921

S

Sables : age becomes his s., 7576
  I'll have suit of s., 2022
Sack, 5763-5768
  addict themselves to s., 5764
  drown'd his tongue in s., 5767

  drunk so much s. as I., 5768
  good sherris-s. ascends, 5764
  if s. and sugar be a fault, 2512
  I'll purge and leave s., 5657
  intolerable deal of s., 5763

let a cup of s. be my poison, 404
let burnt s. be the issue, 5766
thou stolest a cup of s., 755
what says Sir John S., 5611
Sacks: more s. to mill, 5765
Sacrifice lamb I love, 3993
Sacrificers, not butchers, 5769
Sacrifices: come like s., 6995
  upon s. incense, 5770
Sad: be'st s. or merry, 5772
  find him s., I'm dancing, 5771
  he was not s. nor merry, 5772
  I know not why I am so s., 5774
  nobody be s. but I, 5773
  s. as night for wantonness, 5773
  s. because not merry, 5775
  s. when I have cause, 1207
Sadness: full of s. in youth, 5249
  want-wit s. makes of me, 5774
Safe and sound aboard, 5776
Safety, 5776-5779
  best s. lies in fear, 5777
  find but bloody s., 5779
  s. finds the lamb, 5778
  steeps his s. in blood, 5779
  we pluck this flower, s., 1788
Saffron: villanous s., 2635
Sag with doubt, 4688
Sage: regard beseem s., 7213
Said: better s. than done, 6169
  O, let it not be s., 4185
  so s., so done, is well, 7404
  well s., very well s., 6161
Sail, 5780-5783
  bear so low a s., 3215
  in a sieve I'll thither s., 5781
  Margaret must strike s., 5781
  proud s. of his verse, 6866
  she hoists s. and flies, 1628
  will you hoist s., sir, 2115
Sailor: drunken s. on mast, 3094
Sailors: half our s. in flood, 5282
  I'll drown more s., 1681
  s. are but men, 5295
Sails: behold threaden s., 5780
  laugh'd to see s. conceive, 5783
  purple the s., perfumed, 429
Saint, 5784-5787
  able to corrupt a s., 5784
  England and S. George, 3139
  is she not a heavenly s., 220
  S. Denis and S. George, 7361
  S. George that swinged dragon, 5786
  S. Martin's summer, 6313
  seems s. when most a devil, 2032
  teach sin carriage of s., 6878
  to catch s. with saints bait, 5787
  worshippest S. Nicholas, 5785
Saints: great jest with s., 3125
  have not s. lips, 3925
  I conjure thee by all s., 5800
  she call'd s. to surety, 6350
  with s. bait thy hook, 5787
Salad: my s. days, 5789
  sweet-marjoram of s., 5788
Salads: pick a thousand s., 5788
Salamander: maintained a s., 2455
Salary: this is hire and s., 5641
Salicam: in terram S., 3727
Salique: in S. land, 3727

Salisbury, that winter lion, 4177
Sallets: no s. in lines, 5790
Salmon's tail, 7212
Salmons in both, 5705
Salt: as s. as wolves, 5802
  cover of s. hides the s., 3202
  distasted s. of tears, 6643
  make use of thy s. hours, 7110
  s. of unrighteous tears, 4556
  spice and s. season man, 4521
  we have s. of youth, 7567
Salt-fish: hang s. on hook, 2705
Salt-petre: villanous s., 4225
Salt-water: our s. girdle, 934
Saltness of time, 7577
Salutation to the morn, 1397
Salutations from mouths, 3644
Salvation: none see s., 4642
  suffer s., body and soul, 796
  wilfully seeks own s., 979
Salve: is not l'envoy a s., 5792
  provide s. for any sore, 5791
  see s. makes wound ache, 7518
Samphire: one gathers s., 3476
Sample to the youngest, 2373
Samson: I am not S., 1700
  who was S.'s love, 1464
Sanctity: full of s., 3916
Sand: false as stairs of s., 4210
Sands, 5793-5795
  come unto these yellow s., 5795
  his task is numbering s., 6447
  if all their s. were pearl, 3802
  now our s. are almost run, 5793
  s. numbered that make life, 5793
Sans teeth, s. eyes, 7466
Sap in it yet, 2669
  there's s. in this, 5797
  with s. of reason quench, 5572
Sarcenet surety, 6351
Satan, 5798-5800
  as slanderous as S., 5378
  he talked of S., 5798
  I charge thee, S., yield, 5800
  is this Mistress S., 5799
  play at cherry-pit with S., 2046
  S., avoid, I charge thee, 5799
  that white-bearded S., 2512
Satchel and morning face, 7466
Satiety of commendations, 1441
Satire: care for a s., 625
  s. keen and critical, 1661
Satisfaction, 5801-5803
  make any possible s., 1504
  nor gives it s. to our blood, 5801
  what s. canst have tonight, 5803
  where is s., 5802
Satisfied: well paid, well s., 5207
Saturn: born under S., 656
  might have warmed old S., 1235
Sauce: I'll s. her, 7413
  it is a most sharp s., 7258
  no s. can be devised, 7380
  s. to his good wit, 5748
  s. to meat is ceremony, 1160
  sharpen with cloyless s., 1541
Saucy: I am too s., 3954
Savage-wild: my intents s., 3755
Savageness out of a bear, 5978
Savagery this is wildest s., 4847

Saved by my husband, 1322
Saviour's birth celebrated, 1395
Savory, marjoram, 2767
Savour of tar nor of pitch, 3761
Savoury: what's homely s., 6261
Saw: I find thy s. of might, 4386
  the common s., 5804
  who fears old man's s., 5906
Saws: full of wise s., 7466
  holy s. of sacred writ, 3496
  I'll wipe away all s., 4625
Say: no more to s., 3424
Saying, 5804-5807
  ancient s. no heresy, 3244
  come with an old s., 5805
  I can tell where s. was born, 5807
  reputed wise for s. nothing, 7211
  there's a s. old and true, 5822
Scab: loathsomest s. in Greece, 3762
Scabs: make yourselves s., 5101
Scale: in equal s. weighing, 3816
  one s. to poise another, 5576
Scales: hair will turn s., 3195
Scalp of fat friar, 3909
Scandal on greatest state, 5809
  s. stamp'd upon brow, 5810
Scandalized and foully, 5808
Scanned: that would be s., 5641
Scar, 5811-5814
  s. nobly got good livery, 5811
  show me one s., 5812
  'tis a s. to scorn, 5162
Scarcity shall shun you, 696
Scarecrow of law, 4033
Scarecrows: such s., 6064
Scarf: hoodwink'd with s., 6185
  like lieutenant's s., 2961
Scarfs and fans, 5638
Scene: last s. of all, 7466
  my dismal s. I act alone, 58
  our s. is altered, 585
Sceptre, 5815-5819
  give s. for palmer's staff, 3902
  give s. from my hand, 1687
  put barren s. in my gripe, 1683
  s. must come to dust, 2240
  s. or earthly sepulchre, 1680
  s. shows force of power, 4642
  s. snatch'd with unruly hand, 5817
  s. to control the world, 3556
  with s. strucken down, 584
Sceptres in children's hands, 5816
Scholar: breeching s., 4081
  more soldier than s., 6182
  s., ripe and good one, 1204
Scholars, caterpillars, 1126
  worst of all her s., 4867
School: creeping like snail to s., 7466
  erecting a grammar s., 5435
School-days frightful, 1209
Schoolboy with his satchel, 7466
Schoolboys: as s. from books, 4321
Schoolmasters: injuries, s., 3735
Scoffer: foul to be s., 4251
Sconce: show unbarbed s., 4876
Scope turns to restraint, 6353
  s. which dotage gives, 2131
Scorn, 5818-5819
  become s. by falling in love, 4299
  curse Dauphin's s., 4754

honour's s. challenges self, 3527
salt s. of her eyes, 5818
s. is bought with groans, 4348
s. makes after-love more, 7340
teach not thy lips such s., 4200
weapons I laugh to s., 6399
what s. looks beautiful, 5819
Scorns of time, 1847
Scorpion: seek not s.'s nest, 5820
Scorpions: full of s. my mind, 5821
Scot: paid me s. and lot, 1587
  sprightly S. of Scots, 2170
  that hot termagant S., 1587
  weasel S. comes sneaking, 5822
Scotch jig, cinque pace, 7369
Scotched the snake, 6053
Scotches: room for six s., 490
Scotland, 5822-5823
  no such word in S., 2602
  stands S. where it did, 5823
  with S. first begin, 5822
Scots: kills S. at breakfast, 3608
Scout 'em and flout 'em, 6553
  s. him for me at orchard, 978
Scraps are good deeds past, 6642
  they have stolen the s., 7431
Scratch: ay, a s., 3655
Screech-owls cry, 7269
Scrip and scrippage, 400
Scripture: piece of s., 2032
Scriptures turn'd to heresy, 3462
Scruple: nature never lends s., 4914
  no s. of a s., 5825
  not bate thee a s., 5824
Scullion: away, you s., 1121
Scurrility: without s., 5582
Scut: doe with black s., 1954
Scutcheon: honour a s., 3539
Scylla: shun S., 5968
Scythe: contend with s., 2669
  nothing for s. to mow, 6635
Sea, 5826-5830
  chides s. that sunders, 6148
  doth not s. wax mad, 5828
  drench'd me in s., 2704
  float upon a wild s., 5758
  flow as hugely as s., 5414
  forbid s. to obey moon, 5830
  in that s. of blood, 716
  lost him on dangerous s., 3412
  on full s. afloat, 6591
  rude s. grew civil, 4654
  s. being smooth, boats dare, 5829
  s. hath bounds, 1992
  s. hath too few drops, 1281
  s. mounting to welkin, 7029
  s. receives rain still, 5827
  s. shall suck thee dry, 2882
  s. works high, 6341
  stone set in silver s., 2324
  to s. with Ten Commandments, 6257
  'twixt green s. and vault, 6331
  when s. calm, boats alike, 5826
Sea-change: suffer a s., 2576
Sea-mark of utmost sail, 3809
Sea-monster: hideous s., 3723
Sea-nymphs ring his knell, 2576
Seals of love, 3920
Seamy side without, 7248

Seas : great s. have dried, 4713
multitudinous s., 3224
s. breed monsters, 2706
s. for fence impregnable, 2333
Season : by s. seasoned are, 5831
s. of all natures, sleep, 6027
s. of Saviour's birth, 1395
Seasoned to true perfection, 5831
Seasons : make glad the sorry s., 6637
s. alter, 5832
Seat : this s. of Mars, 2324
thy s. is on high, 6124
Secrecy, 5833-5837
for s. no lady closer, 7305
in dreadful s. impart, 5834
nature's book of s., 5833
Secret as maidenhead, 5837
'tis s. must be locked, 5835
Secrets of my prison-house, 6417
villanous s., 7105
Sects newly born, 5500
Secure of thunder's crack, 5841
Security, 5838-5841
he may sleep in s., 5838
made footstool of s., 5839
s. is mortals' enemy, 5840
s. makes fellowship accurst, 6775
stand upon s., 5838
Sedges play with wind, 5273
Seduced : who cannot be s., 4685
Seeds of time, 6632
Seeing : well worth s., 5933
Seeks and will not take, 6414
Seem : be no less than I s., 5844
men be what they s., 5847
Seemest : not what thou s., 5846
Seeming, 5842-5847
good s. put on for villany, 5842
I beguile thing I am by s., 4662
s. I will write against, 5845
s. worn as bait for ladies, 5842
steal dead s. of hue, 5136
tie wiser souls to s., 5316
write me down after my s., 2389
Seems, I know not s., 5843
Self : forget s. to be s., 2836
I have turned away former s., 2513
I to s. am dearer, 2920
I will be my s., 5848
infusing him with s., 3901
Self-love, 5850-5853
dedicate to war no s., 6999
s. is not so vile a sin, 5850
sin of s. possetheth eye, 5852
you are sick of s., 5853
Self-neglecting : vile as s., 5850
Self-slaughter : against s., 5854
canon 'gainst s., 5855
Sell when you can, 5856
Semblance of my soul, 1560
s. very dogs disdained, 270
Sender : to s. sour offence, 4241
Seneca cannot be too heavy, 61
Sense : above s. of s., 6667
in common s., s. saves, 3710
man's o'erlaboured s., 5632
nor s. to ecstasy thrall'd, 4444
s. cold as dead nose, 6043
s. of hearing, 3322

Senses : all s. lock'd in eye, 2325
his s. human, 3878
my s. would have cool'd, 2613
steep s. in forgetfulness, 6019
Sensual as brutish sting, 5957
Sentence but cheveril glove, 7454
who pronounced bitter s., 2365
Sentences : out of five s., 2225
sweet and honey'd s., 6166
Sententious : swift and s., 2797
Sentinel : alarum'd by s., 4848
Septentrion : south to s., 3075
Sepulchre : make thy s., 5859
s. hath oped jaws, 5858
s. of Christ, 1316
s. of stubborn Jewry, 2324
s. wherein inurn'd, 5858
warns my age to s., 1896
Sere, the yellow leaf, 4136
Sergeant : fell s., death, 1852
Sermons in stones, 4117
Serpent, 5860-5867
be the s. under it, 5864
have s. sting thee twice, 3857
he is a s. in my way, 873
hold s. by the tongue, 5863
not Afric owns a s., 3295
s. did sting father, 5851
sharper than s.'s tooth, 1279
take a s. by the tongue, 6902
there the grown s. lies, 5865
think him as s.'s egg, 5862
trust s. when he hisses, 6766
where's my s. of old Nile, 5860
who 'scapes s.'s sting, 4178
who sees s. steps aside, 5867
your s. of Egypt, 1664
Serpent-like : most s., 6664
Serpigo : curse the s., 862
dry s. on subject, 3952
Servant : fit s. for prince, 1578
good s. does not all, 5869
I had rather be their s., 5868
Servant-maid : country s., 5511
Servants to deceitful men, 5065
sort you with my s., 5870
Serve bravely, 5873
s. truly 5844
Service, 5871-5876
command me any service, 5875
do me true s., 6894
done thee worthy s., 5876
how paid my better s., 848
inward s. of mind, 4902
it did me yeoman's s., 7535
make s. greater than god, 3687
poorest s. repaid with thanks, 6513
s. is no heritage, 5871
s. of antique world, 5872
s. shall with sinews toil, 5874
'tis the curse of s., 5871
weary and old with s., 2492
your faithful s., toil, 5658
Services : necessity commands s., 4928
present s. to new prince, 5513
Serving-man : been a s., 1205
withered s., 6444
Servitor to dull delay, 1964
Sessions of sweet silent thought, 5608
Setter up of kings 3883

Setting : I haste to my s., 2490
Severn : S.'s sedgy bank, 4809
Sex : ah, poor our s., 7338
  I exceed my s., 1594
  misused s. in love-prate, 645
  no stronger than my s., 7312
Sexton : bald s. time, 6620
Shade of cypress trees, 1737
  s. of melancholy boughs, 6608
  trip after night's s., 4006
  under s. a lion slept, 1148
Shaded : too timely s., 5222
Shadow, 5877-5883
  at own s. thief run mad, 5882
  fence with his own s., 4500
  hence, horrible s., 5879
  I am but s. of myself, 5877
  life's but a walking s., 4137
  must he be s. of himself, 5878
  saw lion's s. ere himself, 4987
  see my s. as I pass, 3010
  s. like an angel, 2186
  s. of a dream, 2179
  s. of myself in her eye, 2420
  s. of wings, 2260
  son of female s. of male, 6084
  swift as a s., 6384
Shadows : afraid of s., 5883
  best in this kind but s., 3706
  he takes s. for substances, 3171
  s. and shows of men, 5586
  s. have struck more terror, 5883
  s. to the unseen grief, 3167
  some that s. kiss, 5881
Shaft : lost one s., 333
Shake : feel how I s., 2603
  first I s. with you, 3217
Shall : mark his absolute s., 5884
  s., what villain spake, 5885
Shallow, I owe you, 2513
  S., whose son art thou, 6083
Shallows : bound in s., 6591
Shambles : summer-flies in s., 3513
Shame, 5886-5896
  alack and fie for s., 6832
  expense of spirit waste of s., 4431
  he was not born to s., 5895
  hide from open s., 6391
  his face subdued to s., 5886
  is it worse s. to beg, 589
  let heaven cry s., 6183
  let s. come when it will, 5891
  let s. say what it will, 4904
  life short, else s. long, 5889
  live in thy s., 5894
  mail'd up in s., 5526
  O s., where is thy blush, 5888
  safest in s., being fool'd, 5313
  s. and confusion, 2119
  s. doth thy death attend, 1744
  s. folded up in night, 5893
  s. hath a bastard fame, 5887
  s. him with our knees, 3953
  s. in disguise of love, 5532
  s. is a baby, 767
  s. live with thy name, 5896
  s., nothing but s., 5889
  s. pursue thy life, 5896
  s. sleeps out afternoon, 2124
  s. spoil'd world's taste, 5890

s. that follows delight, 4994
s. to him whose striking, 2593
s. to thy silver hair, 3956
sweet fellowship of s., 5892
targets to put off s., 5971
this is the bloodiest s., 4847
treble s. on Angelo, 6873
upon his brow s., 5895
Shames : thousand innocent s., 3740
Shank : hose too wide for s., 7466
Shape that means deceit, 1912
  comest in questionable s., 6195
  thy noble s. but wax, 7031
Shapes : change s. with Proteus, 5114
  full of strange s., 4283
Shards : they are his s., 1014
Sharp : more s. than steel, 1991
Sharper than serpent's tooth, 1279
She : cruellest s. alive, 2473
  unexpressive s., 6730
She-wolf of France, 6662
Sheaf : they that reap s., 5569
Shears : bear s. of destiny, 4807
  pair of s. between us, 3090
Sheep : good pasture, fat s., 5182
  he sees Romans are s., 7285
  s. are gone to fold, 5127
  s. run not so treacherous, 1640
  s. very often stray, 5901
  shepherd seeks s., 5901
  thou owest s. no wool, 4494
  thou wolf in s.'s array, 7283
  thy s. be in the corn, 5900
  thy s. take no harm, 5900
Sheeps' guts hale souls, 3188
  two hot s., marry, 777
Sheet bleaching on hedge, 186
Sheets : canvas thee between s., 2510
  live betwixt cold s., 1233
  my traffic is s., 3925
  post to incestuous s., 4556
  whiter than the s., 4168
  your s. privy to wishes, 7217
Shekels of tested gold, 5402
Shelter to avoid the storm, 6495
Shepherd, 5897-5901
  dead s., I find thy saw, 4386
  Dick the s. blows his nail, 5124
  I am s. to another man, 5897
  if s. be a while away, 5901
  s. blowing of his nails, 445
  s. seeks the sheep, 5901
  s.'s life is naught, 4118
  sleepest or wakest, jolly s., 5900
  you foolish s., 5898
Shepherds give grosser name, 2959
  s. looking on silly sheep, 3302
Shield : seven-fold s. of Ajax, 3370
  sword and s. win fame, 6394
Shields : put s. before hearts, 2671
Shift : let us s. away, 6519
Shifts : not live by s., 2999
Shins : break my s., 7224
Ship : save s. from wreck, 3245
Ship-boy : seal s.'s eyes, 6019
Ship-tire, tire-valiant, 948
Ships are but boards, 5295
  s. stored with corn, 5903
Shirt, 5904-5908
  but a s. and half, 5907

I advise you to shift s., 5905
s. of Nessus is upon me, 5904
Shirts : I bought dozen s., 5906
inventory of thy s., 5908
Shive : easy to steal a s., 6259
Shoal : this s. of time, 1932
Shoe : kiss his dirty s., 3877
let me lick thy s., 5910
Shoemaker meddle with yard, 5913
Shoes : creaking of s., 2660
no more s. than feet, 5531
not see to wipe my s., 4351
o'er s. in blood, 730
over s. in love, 4347
over s. in snow, 2641
surgeon to old s., 5912
tying new s. with riband, 5499
wear nothing but high s., 5909
Shog : will you s. off, 1874
Shoon : by his sandal s., 4262
go in clouted s., 5911
Shop : disfigure not his s., 5667
every s. yields work, 7463
Shore : far-off s., 6148
high s. of the world, 6021
s. that now lies foul, 6593
that white-faced s., 2334
vast s. wash'd with sea, 5285
Shores : undream'd s., 5797
Short : not so s. as sweet, 5161
s. as any dream, 6384
Short and Long, 5914-5918
s. and long is, I serve, 5915
s. and long is, our play, 5918
that's the s. and long, 5916
this is the s. and long, 5917
Shortness : spend s. basely, 4127
Shot : never welcome till s. paid, **7083**
s. of accident, 4917
s. out of elder-gun, 3879
Shoulder : from s. to heel, 3679
Shoulder-clapper, 2901
Shoulders : straight in s., 1638
Show : fairest s. means deceit, **1915**
outward s. seldom jumpeth, 279
s. and gaze o' the time, 6808
s. in posterior of day, 2345
that within which passeth s., 5843
Shower : made s. with caps, 1086
makes s. as well as Jove, 6452
s. of commanded tears, 6475
sunshine brew'd a s., 6337
Showers : as s. to ground, 2788
faster than spring-time s., 6548
see what s. arise, 5919
s. made lasting spring, 5119
small s. last long, 5920
Shows : heavenly s., 2035
Shreds : king of s., patches, 3872
Shrewsbury clock, 2675
Shrift : riddling s., 1494
Shrimp : writhled s., 2248
Shroud : my s. of white, 1902
white his s. as snow, 7099
Shrove-tide : merry S., 4657
Shrubs wither at cedar's root, 1149
we are s., no cedars, 1150
Shrug : borne with patient s., 6830
s., the hum or ha, 1054
Shuffle, hedge and lurch, 3426

Shuffled off mortal coil, 1847
Shuffling : above there is no s., 5084
Shuttle : life is a s., 4141
Sibylla : as old as S., 1239
Sibyls : nine s. of Rome, 3804
Sick : be s., great greatness, 1158
grievous s., 5925
he is not s., 5929
I am not very s., 5924
I am s. at heart, 1405
is Brutus s., 5926
leisure to be s., 5925
many not s. keep chambers, 5928
s. of proud heart, 5929
s. that surfeit, 6354
s. with working of thoughts, 2139
testy s. men, 3321
you are so s. of late, 2140
Sicklemen : sunburnt s., 5921
Sickness, 5922-5929
he hath the falling s., 1024
s. is catching, 5927
s. shall freely die, 3317
this s. infects enterprise, 5929
troubled with green s., 5922
warms s. in my heart, 3334
with s. much enfeebled, 2329
your father's s. a maim, 5925
Side : seamy s. without, 7248
wrong s. turned outward, 7454
Side-stitches pen breath, 1745
Sides : can my s. hold, 4019
O, cleave my s., 3370
Siege : envious s. of Neptune, 2324
men of royal s., 4142
remove s. from my heart, 3364
s. unto wretch's soul, 1995
Sieve : in a s. I'll sail, 5782
Sigh, 5930-5932
he raised s. so piteous, 5930
like a spendthrift s., 1926
s. lack of many a thing, 5608
s. like Tom o' Bedlam, 4610
s. mort o' the deer, 5142
s. no more, ladies, 4506
Sighed : no sooner loved but s., 4387
Sighing : a plague of s., 5931
Sighs : call her winds s., 6452
count thy way with s., 7037
coy looks, heart-sore s., 4348
daily heart-sore s., 4353
drive boat with my s., 5932
her s. make a battery, 7309
made of s. and tears, 4254
no s. but of my breathing, 4420
she gave me world of s., 4305
thousand s. to save, 1902
Sight, 5933-5939
blind s., dead life, 2995
get thee from my s., 2106
hence, and avoid my s., 2106
hence, from my s., 2106
I cannot brook thy s., 6811
s. of lovers feedeth, 4400
this is a sorry s., 5933
Sight-holes : stop all s., 301
Sights : now you behold s., 5935
to see sad s. moves, 5938
Sign of a brave mind, 3214
s. of battle is hung out, 446

s. that he will look sad, 5940
what a s. of evil life, 1860
Signal of bloody day, 6326
Significants proclaim thoughts, 6689
Signs forerun death of kings, 5941
  s. have marked me, 659
Signum : ecce s., 6391
Silence, 5942-5949
  be check'd for s., 5942
  be tenable to your s., 5943
  my gracious s., hail, 7125
  no noise, but s., 1181
  out of s. I pluck'd welcome, 5955
  s. is herald of joy, 5946
  s. is only commendable, 5945
  s. like a Lucrece knife, 5948
  s. of innocence persuades, 5949
  the rest is s., 5944
  they froze me into s., 5947
Silk : owest worm no s., 4494
  rustling in unpaid-for s., 4121
Silks : rustling in s., 2660
Silliness to live, 2214
Silly-stately : s. style, 6297
Silver hath sweet sound, 5951
Silver-sweet sound lovers, 4406
Silver-voiced : as s., 7142
Silvia, 5952-5953
  except I be by S., 5952
  what joy if S. be not by, 5952
  who is S., what is she, 5953
Simpleness and duty, 5955
  s. and merit purchaseth, 4531
Simplicity, 5954-5955
  prove by wit worth in s., 7216
  simple truth miscall'd s., 6780
  s. of Venus' doves, 6966
  such is s. of man, 2740
  tongue-tied s., 5955
  twice-sod s., bis coctus, 3693
  with truth catch mere s., 6781
Sin, 5956-5977
  arm s. in rags, 5963
  by that s. fell the angels, 203
  can cunning s. cover itself, 5969
  cut off in blossoms of my s., 3709
  do not call it s. in me, 5964
  foul s. in chiding s., 5957
  foul s. may say, 5973
  foul s. shall break, 5974
  goad us to s., 6499
  I have done s., 5977
  if it be s. to covet honour, 3540
  man's worst s., 3079
  no longer guilty of this s., 1456
  no s. but to be rich, 580
  no s. to cozen him, 5956
  nothing emboldens s. as mercy, 4645
  one s. another doth provoke, 5971
  plate s. with gold, 5963
  pure as s. with baptism, 6167
  put not another s. upon my head, 5976
  rich men s., I eat root, 3095
  s. clear'd with absolution, 5972
  s. had his reward, 3897
  s. is damnation, 1602
  s. is patched with virtue, 6883
  s. of ingratitude heavy, 3725
  s. of self-love, 5852
  s. struck down like ox, 5960

s. to keep sinful oath, 5052
s. to match my kindred, 3665
s. to rush into death, 1839
s. to swear unto a s., 5052
s. will pluck on s., 726
some rise by s., 5965
teach s. carriage of saint, 6878
that is simple s. in you, 5958
thy s. is not accidental, 5967·
'tis my familiar s., 6920
'tis s. to flatter, 2721
to strike him dead not s., 5975
water cannot wash your s., 5278
what heinous s. it is, 1809
wickedness is s., 4540
Sincerity : bashful s., 6500
  talk'd with in s., 6921
Sinews : knit s. to mine, 5456
  my s. grow not old, 3330
  s. of new-born babe, 3331
  stiffen the s., 7013
  your wit lies in your s., 7252
Sing : I cannot s., 5980
  s. both high and low, 4751
  s. savageness out of a bear, 5978
  we two will s. like birds, 5438
  when you s., I'ld have you, 5981
Singe : s. yourself, 5635
Singing-man of Windsor, 4558
Sings faster than tell money, 407
  s. like one immortal, 5979
  s. sweetly as nightingale, 7374
Singularity : more than s., 5982
  trick of s., 6740
Sink : or s. or swim, 825
Sinking : alacrity in s., 2212
  s. where treasure lies, 1989
Sinner : be so much a s., 2164
  made such s. of memory, 4101
  too weak to be a s., 7024
Sinners : we are s. all, 1860
  wouldst be breeder of s., 5037
Sinning : more sinn'd against than s., 5962
Sinon : like S. take Troy, 5114
Sins : cardinal s., 6937
  commit oldest s. newest ways, 5959
  compell'd s., 5966
  few love to hear s., 5970
  God forgive s. of all, 5961
  in thy orisons be my s. remembered, 5400
  let all my s. lack mercy, 4509
  s. of fathers upon children, 5968
Siren : potions of s. tears, 6474
  sing, s., for thyself, 4653
Sister, 5984-5989
  live a barren s., 6922
  self-same metal as my s., 4664
  s. driven into desperate terms, 5986
  s. I bequeath you, 5984
  wed my s. for her wealth, 5985
Sisters Three, 3403
  to the weird s., 5988
  untwine the S. Three, 7515
  weird s., hand in hand, 5987
Six and seven : at s. and s., 5990
Sixpence all too dear, 5420
  take s. in earnest, 263
Skains-mates : none of his s., 3945
Skies look grimly, 5996
  wrathful s., 4976

Skill : drowns for want of s., 6387
  show our simple s., 598
  some glory in their s., 4329
  touching point of human s., 5575
Skillful enough to have lived, 3974
Skimble-skamble stuff, 6431
Skin, 5991-5993
  calf's s. for prodigal, 5445
  his s. laced with blood, 723
  my s. hangs about me, 5991
  s. of lamb made parchment, 565
  whiter s. than snow, 5993
Skins : have s. of enemies, 5992
  your s. are whole, 5766
Skip : I would have made s., 2484
Skirmish of wit, 7241
Skirts of the forest, 2252
Skull : quiet as father's s., 4099
  s. that bred in sepulchre, 511
Skulls : dead men's s., 2216
Sky, 5994-5996
  excellent canopy, the s., 2268
  fair and crystal is s., 1386
  freeze, thou bitter s., 626
  judge by complexion of s., 5995
  s. changes when wives, 4460
  s. pour down stinking pitch, 7029
  so foul s. clears not, 5994
Slander, 5997-6005
  coins s. like a mint, 6014
  fear not s., censure, 2240
  no s. in allowed fool, 2815
  no s. they steal hearts, 2453
  no s. which is truth, 6004
  pierced with s.'s spear, 6003
  s. her never pray more, 6001
  s. lives upon succession, 5997
  s. of most stepmothers, 5998
  s. sharper than sword, 5999
  s. whose sting is sharper, 5999
  s.'s mark ever the fair, 6005
Slandered by villains, 6902
Slanderous as Satan, 5378
  s. to thy mother's womb, 6811
Slanders : upon tongues s. ride, 5755
Slaughter : 'twas he made s., 2364
Slaughters : casual s., 6165
Slave, 6006-6014
  base is s. that pays, 5206
  base s., a hilding, 6008
  being your s., what do, 6011
  most perfidious s., 6006
  one-trunk-inheriting s., 6009
  poisonous s., got by devil, 6012
  s. had forty thousand lives, 5640
  s. whose coins slanders, 6014
  sleep so soundly as s., 6021
  that s. should wear sword, 6397
  what a s. art thou, 6391
  yellow s. breaks religions, 3066
  you have many purchased s., 6010
Slaves : cap and knee s., 5155
  mechanic s., 6007
  not first of fortune's s., 6566
  show your s. how choleric, 1313
  shrinking s. of winter, 1613
  s. apes would beat, 1734
  s. as ragged as Lazarus, 6064
  s. that take humours, 3888
  we are s. of chance, 1187

Slays more than you rob, 5266
Sleave : sleep knits up s., 6024
Sleek-headed men, 2581
Sleep, 6015-6036
  after-dinner's s., 1874
  between wake and s., 3417
  broke s. with thoughts, 6084
  by s. end heart-ache, 1847
  chief good but to s., 4488
  death-counterfeiting s., 6029
  debt that s. doth owe, 6110
  endeavour thyself to s., 6036
  exposition of s. upon me, 6031
  flattering truth of s., 2188
  forbear to s. the nights, 1743
  gentle s., nature's nurse, 6019
  I am tamer than s., 7039
  I heard a voice cry s. no more, 6024
  I must s. when drowsy, 1207
  I will s. soft as captain, 1088
  I'll go s., if I can, 6016
  in s. a king, 3908
  in s. of death what dreams, 1847
  love chased s. from my eyes, 4353
  Macbeth does murder s., 6024
  medicine thee to s., 6032
  men walked in their s., 6976
  partial s., give thy repose, 6019
  season of natures, s., 6027
  she doth talk in her s., 6440
  s. an act or two, 5334
  s., death's counterfeit, 6026
  s. dwell upon thine eyes, 6033
  s. in spite of thunder, 2610
  s. is a comforter, 6035
  s. neither night nor day, 5023
  s. out this gap of time, 6015
  s. rock thy brain, 6017
  s. seldom visits sorrow, 6035
  s. soundly as a slave, 6021
  s. that knits up sleave, 6024
  s. that shuts sorrow's eye, 6030
  s. upon the dead, 4901
  slumber in eternal s., 2191
  some must watch, some s., 7469
  still-waking s., 4376
  such men as s. o' nights, 2581
  this s. is sound indeed, 6020
  thy best of rest is s., 6028
  to s., perchance to dream, 1847
  turn his s. to wake, 1552
  where care lodges s. will never lie, 1098
  winding up nights with s., 6021
  would I were s. and peace, 6033
Sleepest or wakest thou, 5900
Sleeping and dead but pictures, 6025
  s. to engross his body, 5432
  s. within my orchard, 3709
Sleeps, feels not tooth-ache, 6694
  s. while it s. alone, 3365
Sleeve : fasten on s. of thine, 6913
  show us the s., 7298
  wear my heart upon s., 3354
Slime sticks on filthy deeds, 3514
Slings and arrows of fortune, 1847
Slippery standers, 6038
  stands upon s. place, 6037
Slips of wilderness, 7147
Sloth finds down pillow hard, 7046
Slough : move with casted s., 5134

Slubber not business, 999
Sluggardized at home, 7574
Sluiced in his absence, 1703
Slumber : honey-heavy dew of s., 6022
  keeps ports of s. open, 1677
  shake off s. and beware, 1522
  thick s. hangs upon eyes, 4868
Sluts and sluttery, 2475
Smack : kiss'd with clamorous s., 3927
Smatch of honour, 3545
Smell, 6039-6043
  ancient and fish-like s., 6042
  compound of villanous s., 6041
  here's s. of blood still, 3225
  they s. like Bucklersbury, 6040
  what man cannot s. out, spy, 5023
  you s. this business, 6043
Smells : he s. April and May, 6039
  he s. like a fish, 6042
  it s. to heaven, 5084
Smile, 6044-6048
  I can s. and murder, 1681
  if we do meet, we'll s., 2530
  loose s. I'll live upon, 4252
  moved to s. at anything, 6046
  show teeth in way of s., 4916
  s. and be a villain, 6044
  s. and murder whiles I s., 1681
  s. as the wind sits, 1404
  s. at no man's jests, 1207
  s. at scapes overblown, 7006
  s. his face into lines, 6047
  s. in men's faces, 2726
  s. recures wounding of frown, 6048
  some that s. have mischiefs, 6230
  that s. he would aspire to, 5426
  who durst s. when Warwick, 3886
Smiles : making practised s., 5142
  seldom he s., 6046
  s. and tears were like, 6338
Smilets play'd on her lips, 6338
Smock : old s., new petticoat, 5237
  pale as thy s., 6149
Smoke, 6049-6050
  fly out with s. at chimney, 7226
  from s. into smother, 6049
  helpless s. of words, 6050
  pall thee in s. of hell, 4980
  sweet s. of rhetoric, 5660
Smooth as alabaster, 5993
Smooth-pates : whoreson s., 5838
Smother : from smoke into s., 6049
Smothering of the sense, 4379
Snail : be wooed of a s., 6051
  creeping like s., 7466
  why s. has a house, 6052
Snails : horns of cockled s., 4281
Snake, 6053-6054
  fell Alecto's s., 5643
  s. in flowering bank, 1665
  we have scotch'd the s., 6054
  you but warm starved s., 6053
Snakes in heart-blood warm'd, 6095
  s. with double tongue, 2478
Snapper-up of trifles, 6744
Snare : from s. uncaught, 6929
Snares : my brain weaves s., 889
Snatch would serve turns, 6789
Snatches of old tunes, 1851
Snores out watch of night, 1677

Snoring : you here do s. lie, 1522
Snorting like a horse, 6018
Snow, 6055-6057
  bring s. to colder moods, 716
  if s. white, breasts dun, 4749
  little s. becomes mountain, 6056
  right, as s. in harvest, 6057
  sap-consuming winter's s., 142
  s. melts with sun's beams, 6055
  thaw s. on Dian's lap, 3067
  wallow in December s., 6115
  wash it white as s., 3210
  wish s. in May's mirth, 2933
Snow-broth : blood is s., 728
Snowball : cold as a s., 1406
Snowballs : swallowed s., 620
Snuff : nose took it in s., 4225
  s. of younger spirits, 4114
  s. that will abate love, 4263
Snug, the joiner, 4187
So so is good, very good, 5679
Society, 6058-6060
  abjure s. of men, 6922
  of very soft s., 2969
  ourself will mingle with s., 3600
  s. is happiness of life, 6060
  s. no comfort to not sociable, 6058
  this is worshipful s., 6059
Soft as our complexions, 7321
Soil : fattest s. to weeds, 7057
Soldier, 6061-6079
  armipotent s., 1110
  braver s. never couched lance, 6067
  die s. as I lived king, 5691
  farewell, honest s., 6063
  fie, a s. and afeard, 6071
  God's s. be he, 6072
  greatest s. of the world, 2352
  I said elder s., 6070
  I speak to thee plain s., 7361
  in s. flat blasphemy, 1091
  let no s. fly, 6999
  may s. recreant prove, 6079
  money is a good s., 4764
  not a s. prays for peace, 6073
  relish him more in s., 6182
  say s. lies, is stabbing, 6077
  s. abler than yourself, 6070
  s. even to Cato's wish, 6062
  s. fit to stand by Cæsar, 6075
  s. full of strange oaths, 7466
  s. is better accommodated, 7381
  s. is but a man, 6074
  s. unapt to weep, 6068
  s.'s life to be waked, 6076
  s.'s pole is fall'n, 6061
  some stain of s. in you, 6925
  take a s., take a king, 7361
  vouchsafe to teach a s., 6065
  why let a s. drink, 6074
  you say a better s., 6070
  your son paid s.'s debt, 6072
Soldiers : good s., tall fellows, 1774
  here none but s. repose, 4777
  I be not ashamed of my s., 6064
  s. bore bodies by, 4225
  s. brook wrongs as gods, 6078
  s.'s stomachs serve well, 6066
  they are s., witty, 6069
  when s., they have galls, 1624

Sole : from crown to s., 4724
  not on thy s., but soul, 6137
Soles : mender of bad s., 5912
Solidares : here's three s., 7191
Solomon tune a jig, 3891
  yet was S. so tempted, 4275
Solus : have you s., 1974
Son, 6080-6089
  art thou a woman's s., 4360
  blessed Mary's S., 2324
  frail s. amongst brethren, 6617
  he talks who never had s., 3153
  is this your s., my lord, 6087
  let's smother my damned s., 6688
  like the prodigious s., 5449
  misleader of brain-sick s., 3956
  my s. in ooze is bedded, 6089
  my s. spends all at university, 3669
  prize to be his s., 2567
  rude s. strike father, 6290
  sole s. of my queen, 2254
  s. for cradle ere husband, 6087
  s. of dear father murdered, 341
  s. of female shadow of male, 6083
  s. of mongrel bitch, 3941
  s. that can astonish mother, 6080
  s. who is theme of honour's tongue, 6081
  s. whose father hoarding, 3489
  taught s. office of fowl, 2806
  that thou art my s., I have thy
    mother's word, 6082
  thy mother's s., 6083
  who succeed father but s., 6085
  your noble s. is mad, 4439
  your s. had but the corpse, 5586
  your s. paid soldier's debt, 6072
Song, 6090-6097
  come, sit, and a s., 6091
  French s. has no fellow, 6093
  have you no s. for this, 6090
  she had a s. of willow, 7165
  sing a s. that old was sung, 6095
  sing a s. that pleaseth, 3417
  sing me a bawdy s., 6092
  sold manor for a s., 4611
  stop ears against mermaid's s., 4653
  stretched metre of antique s., 6096
  suck melancholy out of a s., 4612
  that old and antique s., 6097
Songs : merry s. of peace, 2297
  s. of Apollo, 7433
  summer s. for me, 4010
Sons : Adam's s. my brethren, 3665
  as many s. as hairs, 6072
  good wombs, bad s., 6088
  s. to seek preferment, 3501
  we be s. of women, 7567
Soon : better too s., 4012
Sooth : it is silly s., 6097
  not mine, in good s., 6370
Soothers : tongues of s., 2720
Sop of moonshine, 4783
Sophister : traitor needs no s., 6724
Sorcerers : dark-working s., 7267
Sore : salve for any s., 5791
  you rub the s., 6099
Sores : all s. lay siege, 4922
  rained s. on my bare head, 133
  to strange s. strain cure, 6098

Sorrow, 6100-6124
  bad trade plays fool to s., 6105
  bid s. wag, cry hem, 3155
  concealed s., 6123
  do obsequious s., 2561
  down, thou climbing s., 6104
  eighty years of s. seen, 6118
  give s. words, 6109
  gnarling s. has less power, 6115
  hath s. made no wounds, 2468
  how slow time goes in s., 6629
  lest s. lend me words, 2086
  lost s. to wail lost, 6117
  more in s. than in anger, 6101
  no s. but kill'd itself, 6124
  notes of s. out of tune, 6100
  now will s. eat my bud, 1074
  offender's s. weak relief, 5092
  pluck from memory rooted s., 4689
  seek for s. with spectacles, 3956
  set thee down, s., 6106
  show an unfelt s., 6107
  sit thee down, s., 5457
  sleep seldom visits s., 6035
  s. abides, happiness leaves, 6749
  s. bids me speak, 3142
  s. breaks seasons, 6116
  s. brings heir, 6111
  s. conceal'd burns heart, 6119
  s. conjures wandering stars, 3147
  s. couch'd in gladness, 6122
  s. ebbs, blown with wind, 6112
  s. ends not when it seemeth done, 6114
  s. flouted is double death, 6120
  s. go along with you, 1737
  s. is an enemy, 6121
  s. makes noontide night, 6116
  s. on love shall attend, 4365
  s. so royally in you appears, 6103
  s. to s. join'd, 7277
  s. to the shepherds, 5591
  s. vanquish'd my powers, 1340
  s. wept to take leave, 3824
  s.'s eye, glazed with tears, 3165
  s.'s heaviness heavier grows, 6110
  s.'s tooth never rankle more, 6115
  sudden s. serves to say, 1182
  tears will water s., 6453
  wear a golden s., 667
  wherever s. is, relief, 5597
  wring under load of s., 5198
  write s. on bosom of earth, 1431
  your s. too sore laid on, 6124
Sorrows : each morn s. strike, 6108
  full of s. as sea of sands, 3363
  give tongue-tied s. leave, 6687
  here I and s. sit, 3152
  instruct s. to be proud, 3152
  s. come in battalions, 6102
  s. overwhelmed his wits, 7266
  swallows other s., 3157
Soul, 6125-6147
  Aaron will have s. black, 6146
  black s. burning in hell, 2732
  call upon my s., 4344
  endanger my s. gratis, 6138
  ensnared my s. and body, 2038
  every subject's s. his own, 6300
  evil s. producing holy witness, 6136
  from gallows did s. fleet, 5483

gave his pure s. unto Christ, 1318
give s. to him thou servest, 2028
harrow up thy s., 6417
hear my s. speak, 4389
heaven take my s., 3401
his s. as black as hell, 3407
his s. stand sore charged, 4754
his s. thou canst not have, 797
honest s. as ever broke bread, 3511
hurl my s. from heaven, 6140
I have a s. of lead, 1781
joy's s. lies in doing, 1949
lay down my s. at stake, 3512
lay not that unction to your s., 4445
let not s. of Nero enter, 4946
let s. forth that adoreth, 2844
lift my s. to heaven, 229
like s. upon Stygian banks, 6147
limed s., struggling to be free, 6127
may his s. rot, 4098
most offending s. alive, 3540
mount, mount, my s., 6142
my body or s., which dearer, 798
my s., a thing immortal, 4123
my s. and fortunes consecrate, 4306
my s. brought forth prodigy, 7277
my s. flies through wounds, 6129
my s. hates nothing more, 3293
my s. is full of woe, 737
my s. shall manifest me, 6139
my s. to heaven, 718
my s.'s palace is prison, 6130
never win a s. so easy, 1969
no English s. stronger, 5572
no s. shall pity me, 4314
nor let thy s. contrive, 4814
not on thy sole, but s., 6137
nothing can content my s., 5649
now my s. hath elbow-room, 6132
O my prophetic s., 5861
poor s., centre of earth, 6145
secure in s., 2895
sigh'd s. toward Grecian tents, 4987
sings s. to lasting rest, 6364
sluiced out his innocent s., 736
s. and body rive not, 3120
s. as even as a calm, 6489
s. lends the tongue vows, 707
s. of good fellowship, 2648
s. of goodness in evil, 3074
s. of grandam inhabit bird, 5484
s. of this man his clothes, 6125
s. would give you thanks, 6133
stealing her s. with vows, 4987
step between her and her s., 6128
take my s., my body, 795
these fellows have some s., 3943
thou art a s. in bliss, 7094
thy s. thou soldest devil, 2023
unlettered, small-knowing s., 6134
within wall of flesh, a s., 6131
you have lost half your s., 3377
Souls : all s. forfeit once, 6135
blow thousand s. to heaven, 6273
draw three s. out of weaver, 7087
heaven will take our s., 3409
I will not vex your s., 6141
jealous s. not answer'd, 3780
sad s. slain in company, 3160
send a thousand s. to death, 5732

s. of animals infuse selves, 5483
s. of men full of dread, 6143
s. that fly backwards, 6126
suppler s. than in fasts, 2061
their s. topfull of offence, 2067
there be s. must be saved, 3041
tie wiser s. to seeming, 5316
where s. couch on flowers, 5503
win straying s. with modesty, 1342
you s. of geese, 1734
your s. must part your bodies, 6141
Sound : full of s. and fury, 4137
low s. reverbs no hollowness, 3344
momentany as a s., 6384
powerful s. within organ, 6194
s. as a bell, 3351
s. as things hollow, 3320
s. that breathes on violets, 4874
that bears a frosty s., 6596
Sounds : deep s. make lesser noise, 6112
dulcet s. in break of day, 4861
unprofitable s., 7444
Sour : looks s., 6383
prove in digestion s., 6382
Sours : sweets turn to s., 6381
South : foggy s. puffing, 5898
wing'd from spongy s., 2256
South-sea of discovery, 1961
South-west blister you, 1745
Sovereign : anointed s. of sighs, 1714
hath he forgot his s., 6296
pay debt to salt s., 6286
treason to my s., 6719
Sovereignty, 6148-6149
aspiring flame of s., 6149
her perfections challenge s., 4755
I do but dream on s., 6148
made s. a slave, 6471
round and top of s., 1684
Space : here is my s., 5726
Spaces : s. cannot parallel, 3437
Spaniel : I am your s., 6151
you play the s., 6150
Spaniel-like, she spurns, 4358
Spare neither man, woman, 4730
Sparing makes waste, 1243
Spark, 6152-6155
s. will prove raging fire, 6152
small s., all rest cold, 2696
Sparks : good s. and lustrous, 6152
hide s. of nature, 4898
I see s. of better hope, 6155
s. that are like wit, 6154
Sparrow : caters for s., 1420
Philip s., 6156
providence in fall of s., 5465
with pistol kills s., 2170
Sparrows are lecherous, 6157
s. must not build, 6157
Speak : I love to hear her s., 4749
I never thought to hear you s., 7219
I s. to thee plain soldier, 7361
I'll s. in a little voice, 6952
leave to s. my mind, 4680
not to s. it profanely, 54
s. and purpose not, 7399
s. from lungs military, 3604
s. less than thou knowest, 604
s. liberal as the north, 6183
s. low, if you s. love, 4297

s. me fair in death, 1880
s. more in a minute, 4631
s. of me as I am, 1208
s. plain to the purpose, 6179
s. sad brow, true maid, 4752
s. scholarly and wisely, 3601
s. sooner than drink, 6756
s. sweetly, 6383
s. to me home, 6655
s. to unknowing world, 6165
s. what we feel, 6172
spoke as Christian ought to s., 6177
this I s. in print, 5436
we must s. by the card, 6164
we s. not wnat we mean, 6175
what s. of when old, 6160
what you s. is wash'd, 6167
when I think, I must s., 7293
you s. his very heart, 847
you s. upon the rack, 5529
Speaker is but a prater, 5672
Speakest wiser than aware, 6159
Speaking : little s., 2703
silence when s. fails, 5949
s. is for beggars, 6186
Speaks : he s. home, 6182
he s. nothing but madman, 6187
he s. plain cannon fire, 4825
she s. poniards, 6158
she s. small like a woman, 6176
Spear : Achilles s., 947
pierced with slander's s., 6003
Spectacles : see without s., 5936
seek for sorrow with s., 3956
s. on nose, 7466
Speculation : no s. in eyes, 5879
Speech, 6158-6188
be never tax'd for s., 5942
better s. never spoke, 6174
free s. and fearless, 6184
how smart lash that s., 6162
knavish s. in foolish ear, 6163
loath to cast away my s., 6188
manner of his s., 6158
mend your s. a little, 6171
pardon first word of s., 5161
rude am I in my s., 6181
runs not this s. like iron, 6180
shall this s. be spoke, 6185
speak the s. trippingly, 54
to penn'd s. no grace, 1532
where study this goodly s., 7250
Speeches : trust to s. penn'd, 7363
your s. may deeds approve, 7398
Speed, 6189-6191
as much s. as to fly death, 6189
bend you with dearest s., 6189
bootless s., 6190
fool's s., 3980
happy be thy s., 7373
how s. you with my daughter, 6191
most wicked s., 4556
so hot s. wants example, 2374
s. must answer it, 3287
time shall teach me s., 3285
withhold thy s., 5975
would my horse had s., 6670
Spells provide your charms, 1223
Spend this for me, 5480
Spendthrift of his tongue, 6678

Spent : nought's had, all's s., 1538
Sperato me contento, 2862
Spheres : music of the s., 4868
Sphinx : subtle as S., 4281
Spice and salt season man, 4521
Spider, 6192-6193
in cup a s. steep'd, 6193
painter plays the s., 3199
s. like he gives me note, 6192
thread that s. twisted, 1771
Spies : God's s., 5438
Spigot : wouldst s. wield, 6444
Spinsters and knitters, 6097
Spirit, 6194-6204
allay thy skipping s., 4757
an unaccustom'd s. lifts me, 3360
awake pert s. of mirth, 4723
be thou s. of health, 6195
bend every s. to full height, 7013
best-conditioned s., 2911
blushing shamefast s., 1513
bold s. in loyal breast, 6202
Cæsar's s. cry "Havoc", 1031
dauntless s. of resolution, 43
erring s. hies to confine, 1395
expense of s. is a waste of shame, 4431
flesh his s. in warlike soil, 874
foolish extravagant s., 6201
full of s. as month of May, 3613
gallant s. aspired clouds, 6203
her gentle s. commits itself, 3005
holding eternal s., 3111
I am thy evil s., Brutus, 5241
I am thy father's s., 6196
I lack that quick s., 6199
if ill s. have fair house, 3702
if thy s. look upon me, 1030
in thee blessed s. speaks, 6194
invisible s. of wine, 7184
my s. better part of me, 2274
my uncle's s., 3401
nimble, stirring s., 3096
no s. dare stir abroad, 1395
poison o'ercrows my s., 5353
rarer s. never did steer, 2585
rest, rest, perturbed s., 6369
retentive to strength of s., 6200
s. hath been at war, 6198
s. of a tapster, 6441
s. of deep prophecy, 3804
s. of first-born Cain, 7472
s. of love, how fresh, 4343
s. of the time, 3285
s. to curse thine enemy, 1737
suffer with quietness of s., 5197
thy currish s. govern'd, 5483
thy s. is noble, high, 1968
thy s. walks abroad, 1034
weep my s. from eyes, 2908
with more s. chased, 5481
worser s. a woman, 236
Spirits, 6205-6214
call s. from vasty deep, 6206
cheer up your s., 1596
choice of dauntless s., 2878
cull'd these fiery s., 7003
entame my s. to worship, 945
her s. are as coy, 6211
her wanton s. look out, 4000
how weary are my s., 7045

I have thousand s. in one breast, 6213
master s. of this age, 1029
not jump with common s., 4840
pour my s. in thine ear, 6208
show cinders of my s., 6205
s. are not finely touch'd, 6210
s. at midnight wilder, 997
s. o' the dead may walk, 6214
s. of wise mock us, 2820
s. that tend on thoughts, 1692
s. thy power hath conjured, 853
this hath dash'd your s., 6212
thy s. are most tall, 3212
time when s. walk, 7269
to stubborn s. swell, 5425
unchain your s. now, 1221
with my vex'd s., 6207
your s. are attentive, 4862
your s. shine through you, 6209
Spit : never s. white, 3391
orators, when out, s., 5113
s. and throw stones, 6266
s. at him he'd run, 1647
s. at me and spurn, 2145
s. in the hole, man, 3946
s. on me, call me horse, 4094
s. upon my gaberdine, 6830
why dost thou s. at me, 5360
Spite : cursed s., 6614
Spleen : abate over-merry s., 2399
conceived of s., 1712
govern'd by a s., 3616
Spleens : fierce dragons' s., 2878
Splenitive : I am not s., 1786
Split : part to make all s., 6809
Spoil : honourable s., 5441
Spokes : break s. from wheel, 2860
Sponge : married to a s., 6216
take you me for a s., 6215
to be demanded of a s., 6215
Spoon : I have no long s., 2019
long s. to eat with devil, 2019
Sport, 6217-6220
good s. at his making, 6087
have we not desires for s., 3671
holy s. to be a little vain, 2717
misery makes s. to mock, 4741
now for our mountain s., 4059
she is s. for Jove, 6218
s. royal, 6220
s. to have the enginer, 5634
swift his time of s., 6629
that s. best pleases, 6217
to s. as tedious as work, 3492
what s. shall we devise, 6219
Sports : in s. my cunning faints, 2954
some s. are painful, 2310
Spot : angry s. on Cæsar's brow, 1023
out, damned s., 3225
Spots : not change his s., 4077
s. of kindred jurors, 4078
Spouse : commit not with man's s., 2660
Spring, 6221-6223
apparell'd like the s., 6222
from s. whence comfort, 2064
it is love's s., 295
love's gentle s., 4433
purest s. not free from mud, 6719
short summers, forward s., 6315
s. near when geese breed, 6221

s. summer, autumn, 5832
s. time, ring time, 4401
strew green lap of s., 6919
sweet lovers love the s., 4401
this s. of love resembleth, 4350
thy hasty s. still blasts, 3393
unruly blasts wait in s., 6223
welcome as s. to earth, 7084
Springe : as woodcock to s., 6225
if s. hold, cock's mine, 6226
Springes to catch woodcocks, 6224
Springs : all s. reduce currents, 3995
four wanton s., 7392
s. on chaliced flowers, 4005
within mile hundred s., 6984
Sprites : if they be not s., 6227
Spruce : he is too s., 1206
Spur : endure bloody s., 2480
s. a forward horse, 3594
s. to valiant deeds, 3438
with s. we heat acre, 3932
Spur-gall'd and tired, 3595
Spurns that merit takes, 1847
Spurring : bloody with s., 3290
Spurs : tires that s. too fast, 3298
Square : kept my s., 684
Squash : as s. before peascod, 880
how like this s., 882
Squealing of wry-necked fife, 2665
Squire : such s. he was, 7248
Squires of night's body, 4781
Stabbing : say soldier lies is s., 6077
Stabs looked like breach, 723
Staff : breaks s. like goose, 1198
no s. more reverend than horn, 7139
s. of honour for age, 3556
s. quickly found to beat dog, 5460
Stag : I am a windsor s., 6229
poor sequester'd s., 6228
take him for a s., 3582
Stage : all the world's a s., 7466
black s. for tragedies, 4995
drown the s. with tears, 63
played upon s., 2656
s. to feed contention, 7472
s. where every man must play, 7480
this great s. of fools, 668
Stains : full of sightless s., 6811
Stair-work, trunk-work, 7462
Stairs kiss his feet, 6376
s. to marriage, 4387
Stake, 6230-6232
I am tied to the s., 6231
they tied me to the s., 6232
we are at the s., 6230
Stale : I am but his s., 1952
it grows s. with me, 5170
poor I am s., 3773
s. and cheap, 5104
Stalking-horse, 2775
Stall : not s. together, 6241
Stalling of ox, 2967
Standers : slippery s., 6038
Standers-by : not for s., 6368
Star, 6233-6239
born under charitable s., 656
constant as northern s., 1527
give name to fixed s., 6291
influence of received s., 1157
like shooting s. fall, 3015

love a particular s., 6233
moist s. was sick, 6235
most auspicious s., 6239
she would infect north s., 913
s. is fallen, 6234
s. to wandering bark, 4333
there was a s. danced, 669
unfolding s. calls shepherd, 6236
Star-blasting : bless from s., 694
Star-chamber matter, 5836
Star-crossed lovers, 4405
Stars, 6240-6249
cut him out in little s., 4998
doubt that s. are fire, 4258
earth-treading s., 2620
go by moon and seven s., 5476
let all the s. give light, 687
little s. may hide them, 4791
my good s. have left, 6240
my s. shine darkly, 6248
our s. unreconcilable, 6241
pour s. down plagues, 5229
scourge the revolting s., 1415
seven s. no more than seven, 6243
s. above us govern, 6246
s. shot from spheres, 4654
s. will kiss the valleys, 5083
truer s. did govern, 6249
two s. keep not motion, 6242
we have seen seven s., 6243
what s. spangle heaven, 2445
wilt thou reach s., 5240
you chaste s., 1137
Starting-hole : what s. find, 6391
Starve : on mountains let him s., 6715
we'll see 'em s. first, 7071
Starve-lackey : Master S., 5544
Starveling : you s., 1456
State : cons s. without book, 1215
greatest scandal greatest s., 5809
I am unfit for s., 1105
palmy s. of Rome, 5095
taught us from primal s., 6448
then his s. empties, 3892
this is the s. of man, 2492
thou art in a parlous s., 4540
States : in s. unborn, 1028
mighty s. grated to nothing, 2506
Station like herald Mercury, 5272
Statists : hole it, as s. do, 7535
Statua : erect s. and worship it, 1423
she dreamt she saw my s., 2180
Statues : make s. of youth, 3424
Stature, 6250-6253
her s. to an inch, 7142
what s. is she of, 6251
Statures : compare our s., 6253
Statute : rigor of the s., 6254
Statutes : biting s., 6254
s. stand like forfeits, 4036
we have strict s., 6255
Staves : amaze welkin with s., 7086
Steal : of cut loaf s. shive, 6259
s. by line and level, 6258
s. egg out of cloister, 1197
s. single ten, 3855
thou shalt not s., 6257
Stealers : pickers and s., 4261
Stealth of nature, 438

Steed : farewell neighing s., 2533
Mars' fiery s., 6990
Steeds : bestride foaming s., 4223
gallop, fiery-footed s., 4997
Steel : by my side wear s., 5143
my heart true as s., 3349
naked though lock'd in s., 5493
s. nor poison touch him, 1872
s. to the very back, 7548
Steeples : drench'd s., 7174
topples s. and towers, 4906
Steerage : he that hath s., 2043
Stelled in table of heart, 2441
Stench : odoriferous s., 1868
Step grows to fever, 2298
Stepdame : false as s. to son, 2506
like to a s., 4787
Stephen : King S. worthy peer, 5420
S. Sly, John Naps, 4515
Stepmothers : slander of s., 5998
Steps : hear not my s., 2271
untread s. of flight, 5076
Stern : thou art s., flinty, 7308
Sticking-place : screw courage to s., 1599
Stile : merrily hent the s., 3390
Still-stand : tide makes s., 4682
Stillness and the night, 3273
willful s. entertain, 5106
Sting : death's sharp s., 5222
thy s. is not so sharp, 626
who 'scapes serpent's s., 4178
Stings : cool carnal s., 5576
wanton s. of sense, 728
Stinking and fly-blown, 6649
Stirring : be s. as the time, 43
Stitches : laugh into s., 4026
Stock and honour of my kin, 5975
Stockfish : make s. of thee, 4644
you s., 1456
Stockings : no more s. than legs, 5531
Stockish : nought so s., 4862
Stocks : pair of s., 5717
Stole : white s. of chasity, 1253
Stolen what we fear to keep, 6521
Stomach, 6260-6265
cram words against s., 7451
deepest loathing to s., 6355
do it on full s., 2547
enterprise that hath s., 6261
fall to as you find s., 6294
gives men s. to digest, 5748
gives s. and no food, 2863
he hath an excellent s., 6264
it goes against my s., 6909
my knightly s. is sufficed, 6482
my revenge had s. for all, 5651
no s. to this fight, 3540
you have no s., 4597
Stomachers to my heart, 3462
Stomachs : ease s. with tongues, 4234
our s. will make savoury, 6261
soldiers' s. serve well, 6066
they are s., we food, 4510
vail your s., 3670
winds high, so your s., 6263
your s. are too young, 15
Stone : at his heels a s., 4262
first s. drop in my neck, 3328
he is a s., pebble-s., 6271
if no harder than s., 1459

my heart is turn'd to s., 3381
precious s. set in silver sea, 2324
set this s. a-rolling, 5636
s. at rain relenteth, 6272
s. him with harden'd hearts, 3385
Stone-cutter made him, 6413
Stones, 6266-6272
are there no s. in heaven, 6269
give her no token but s., 3263
gods throw s. of sulphur, 6267
I will cut his two s., 6268
more hard than s., 3263
spit and throw s., 6266
s. dissolved in water, 6270
s. have been known to move, 725
s. whose rates are rich, 5402
waste s. with water-drops, 6628
Stool : three-legged s., 5016
Stools : push us from s., 724
Stop : honourable s., 2083
Stops : you know my s., 5331
Store-house of body, 618
Stories : love's s. written, 5575
sad s. in times of old, 6279
sad s. of death of kings, 3901
their s. without audience, 6280
Storm, 6273-6275
hideous s. that follow'd, 3744
I will stir up black s., 6273
leave thee in the s., 2948
now begins a second s., 6275
pelting of pitiless s., 7531
s. is up, all on hazard, 3308
s. of robbery shook, 6731
Storms : broken with s. of state, 149
greater s. than almanacs, 6452
grow terrible as s., 5425
shipwrecking s., 2064
sudden s. are short, 5920
untimely s. expect dearth, 6276
Story, 6277-6280
demand thee of thy s., 2075
earns a place i' the s., 4413
let us this s. know, 6277
locks in the golden s., 830
shallow s. of deep love, 4347
s. extant in choice Italian, 6278
s. is no less in pity, 2361
woman's s. at winter's fire, 4497
Strain of chanticleer, 1195
s. of man is bred out, 4518
that s. again, 4874
Strand : knees kiss'd Cretan s., 533
Strange : passing s., 4305
this is wondrous s., 6283
Stranger, 6281-6284
as a s. give it welcome, 6283
count the world a s., 6767
extravagant, wheeling s., 1812
Strangers : be better s., 6282
means that make us s., 6284
s. and foes do sunder, 6281
Strangle her in her bed, 5358
Strangled with a halter, 3240
Strappado : at the s., 5571
Stratagems : fit for s., 4862
Straw : after burn the s., 1551
as s. out-burneth, 4310
find quarrel in a s., 3121
I prize it not a s., 4150

pigmy's s. doth pierce it, 5963
start at wagging of a s., 57
strongest oaths s., 6924
Strawberry underneath nettle, 6285
Straws : begin fire with s., 2695
spurns enviously at s., 3448
Stray : seize me for a s., 4226
Stream : strive against s., 6287
which way s. of time, 6616
Streams pay daily debt, 6286
Strength, 6288-6290
excellent to have giant's s., 6289
I have no s. in measure, 6288
I'll have no s. to repent, 5618
maugre thy s., 6725
spend s. with waves, 6363
s. gone into heaviness, 3415
s. lord of imbecility, 6290
s. match'd with s., 721
s. of limb, 5648
unbend your noble s., 6550
Strengths by s. do fall, 2690
Strife : civil s. in heaven, 6493
civil s. shall cumber Italy, 1031
Strike me to death with joy, 3815
s. not, but perish, 6495
s. or else iron cools, 3758
s. sooner than speak, 6756
Strikers : sixpenny s., 6756
String husband to another, 1487
untune that s., 1960
Strings : silken s. delight to kiss, 3228
when s. jar, what harmony, 6264
Stripling : proper s., 7570
Strive mightily, 4042
Stroke : bloodless s., 5948
nimble s. of lightning, 2463
s. of death as lover's pinch, 1841
Strokes fell great oaks, 5047
wail inevitable s., 2003
Strong upon stronger side, 1645
Struck : oft s. them dead, 3123
Strumpet : are you not a s., 7106
I've heard I am a s., 6430
s.'s plague to beguile, 7104
Stubble-land at harvest-home, 4225
Stubborn-chaste against all suit, 1246
Stubborn-hard : more s. than iron, 3759
Stubbornness : impious s., 2561
Student : keep s. from book, 2054
Study, 6291-6294
fitter is my s., 5152
ground of s.'s excellence, 6293
his s. is his tilt-yard, 3496
I am slow of s., 4186
I s. virtue and philosophy, 6294
I would burn my s., 829
s. evermore is overshot, 6292
s. is like heaven's sun, 6291
s. what you most affect, 6294
that is s.'s recompense, 6291
to s. now it is too late, 6292
what is the end of s., 6291
Stuff : made of penetrable s., 3332
silliest s. ever I heard, 3706
skimble-skamble s., 6431
s. which weighs on heart, 4689
such s. as dreams, 4147
such s. as madmen tongue, 2178
such s. might poison poison, 6855

Stumble that run fast, 3291
Stygian : soul upon S. banks, 6147
Style, 6295-6299
  boisterous and cruel s., 6295
  he hath changed his s., 6296
  here is silly-stately s., 6297
  his large s. agrees not, 6298
  plain is too harsh a s., 6299
  s. for challengers, 6295
  Turk writes not tedious s., 6297
  writ the s. of gods, 5250
Subject, 6300-6301
  I'll swear myself thy s., 2827
  never s. long'd to be king, 3882
  puny s. strikes at thy glory, 3900
  s.'s duty is king's, 6300
  s.'s soul is his own, 6300
  what s. can sentence king, 3903
Subjects : I speak to s., 3903
  none of prince's s., 6301
Submission : dishonourable s., 6303
  s. a mere French word, 6302
Subornation : foul s., 6935
Substance : my s. not here, 5877
  put all my s. into belly, 2280
Substitute shines as king, 3892
Subtle as Sphinx, 4281
Subtle-potent : too s., 3823
Subtleties : world's false s., 4335
Suburbs : dwell I in s., 7132
Success, 6304-6305
  catch with surcease s., 1932
  he will be glad of s., 6304
  never o'ertake pursued s., 3143
  s. or loss serves as staff, 5151
  s. strew'd before your feet, 6884
  s. will fashion the event, 6305
Succour : proffer'd means of s., 3404
Such as made of, s. we be, 2890
Sucking dove, 4187
Sudden as flaws congealed, 1203
Sue : not born to s., 1436
Sued : I never s., 6675
Sufferance, 6306-6307
  corporal s., 576
  lesser blench at s., 5204
  mind s. doth o'erskip, 6309
  of s. comes ease, 6306
  s. badge of our tribe, 6830
  thy nature commence in s., 6307
Suffering all, suffers nothing, 6308
Suffers : who s. s. in mind, 6309
Sufficiency : no man's s., 5198
Suffolk : doth S. comfort me, 1422
  S., that rules the roast, 5752
Sugar o'er devil himself, 2050
Suggestion as cat laps milk, 6311
  why yield to that s., 6310
Suggestions : loose s., 1499
Suit : first s. is hot, 7369
Suitors : poor s. strong breaths, 909
  see s. following, 573
Suits of solemn black, 5843
Sulphur : burn like mines of s., 1481
  charge thy s. with bolt, 6583
  gods throw stones of s., 6367
  roast me in s., 6140
Sulphurous fires, 6585
  s. tormenting flame, 3620
Sum : giving s. of more, 6502

Summer, 6312-6316
  after s. succeeds winter, 1101
  expect Saint Martin's s., 6313
  farewell All-hallown s., 2529
  made s. by sun of York, 7203
  shall I compare thee to s.'s day, 6316
  so hot a s. in my bosom, 6314
  s.'s lease too short a date, 6316
  swallow follows not s., 6360
  take heed ere s. comes, 7365
  thy s. shall not fade, 6316
  time leads s. to winter, 6633
  time will bring on s., 6312
  why should s. boast, 2933
Summer-flies have blown me, 7363
Summer-house in Christendom, 6431
Summers : let two s. wither, 1283
  short s., forward spring, 6315
Sun, 6317-6335
  arise fair s., 6328
  as plays s. upon stream, 501
  as s. breaks through clouds, 3554
  as when s. salutes morn, 2350
  bedimm'd noontide s., 6331
  better parch in Afric s., 5818
  blessed breeding s., 6333
  doubt that s. doth move, 4258
  gorgeous as s. at midsummer, 3613
  hath Britain all the s., 936
  herein will I imitate s., 6317
  I 'gin to be a-weary of s., 6323
  is s. dimm'd that gnats fly, 6334
  men shut doors against setting s., 6332
  O setting s., 6321
  O s., thy uprise I shall see, 2851
  out of benediction to warm s., 5804
  pay no worship to garish s., 4998
  setting s., and music, 6324
  show descent by gazing gainst s., 2257
  s. hath made golden set, 6326
  s. hides not from cottage, 6335
  s. is a thief, 6520
  s. is in his heaven, 6322
  s. looks on all alike, 6335
  s. made lasting spring, 5119
  s. of Rome is set, 6321
  s. peer'd forth window, 6327
  s. sees not itself, 6329
  s. shall usher honours, 6320
  s. shines bright, 7361
  s. shines hot, 1963
  s. that shines on court, 6335
  s. vieweth world, 2414
  s.'s transparent beams, 6273
  suspect the s. with cold, 6988
  that s. that warms you, 412
  that will be ere set of s., 6573
  this gallant will command s., 6330
  when s. sets, look for night, 4971
  worse than s. in March, 5386
Sunburning : not worth s., 2458
Sunday : divide S. from week, 6446
Sunday-citizens, 6370
Sundays : sigh away S., 4938
Sunshine, 6336-6339
  live to see a s. day, 6336
  see s. and hail in him, 1377
  show s. of your face, 6339
  s. brew'd shower for him, 6337
  you have seen s., 6338

Sup : I s. upon myself, 238
s. with Jesu Christ, 1317
Superfluity : one for s., 5908
s. comes sooner by white hairs, 3258
Superfluous : why be so s., 6615
Supernatural : things s., 4714
Superscription : churlish s., 6296
Superstition : that's your s., 6341
Superstitious grown of late, 6340
Supper : let's to s., 1518
nourishment called s., 6342
you'll come to s. to-night, 6343
Suppliance of a minute, 6918
Supply : my needs must find s., 4945
Supporter : no s. but earth, 3152
Surcease : with s. success, 1932
Sure : as s. as bark on tree, 6345
as s. as day, 6370
as s. as death, 6346
as s. as guts made of puddings, 5646
as s. as I live, 6347
make assurance double s., 6348
Surety, 6349-6352
greatest shall be my s., 6349
she call'd saints to s., 6350
what s. of the world, 3889
wound of peace is s., 6352
you give sarcenet s., 6351
Surfeit, 6353-6356
cure thy o'er-night's s., 6356
suffer s., cloyment, 7339
s. is father of much fast, 6353
s. of the sweetest things, 6355
s. with too much, 6354
Surfeit-swell'd : so s., 2513
Surfeiting and wanton hours, 2093
s., appetite may sicken, 4874
Surgeon : defy the s., 3732
s. to old shoes, 5912
Surgery : hurt past all s., 5626
Surplice of humility, 3502
Surprises : exsufflicate s., 3779
Survey : make s. of selves, 5416
Surveyor of the fold, 2885
Suspect : if my s. be false, 3026
s. the sun with cold, 6988
s. where no cause of fear, 4365
Suspects, yet strongly loves, 3779
Suspicion, 6357-6358
bid s. double-lock door, 3782
s. haunts guilty mind, 6358
s. stuck full of eyes, 6716
swept s. from our seat, 5839
what ready tongue s. hath, 6357
Swaddling-clouts : not out of s., 144
Swain : shepherd s., 3807
Swains commend her, 5953
true s. in love, 6761
Swallow follows not summer, 6360
you think me a s., 6547
Swallows : run like s., 6361
s. in Cleopatra's sails, 6359
Swan, 6362-6367
cygnet to this s., 6364
pale s. in watery nest, 6366
play s. and die, 6365
snow-white s., 1676
s. for the love of Leda, 4292
s. her cygnets saves, 6362
s. swim against the tide, 6363

s.'s down-feather, 6656
think thy s. a crow, 6367
turn s.'s legs to white, 682
Swan-like end, 4861
Swans : like Juno's s., 6919
Swart, like my shoe, 1464
Swashing, martial outside, 1631
Swear : all traitors that s., 6726
by yonder moon I s., 4786
I s. by Cupid's bow, 6966
s. but now and then, 606
s. by my sword, 6369
s. by your beards, 457
s., drink, dance, revel, 5959
s. in both the scales, 4111
s. me, Kate, like a lady, 6370
s. not by the moon, 4786
s. on parcel-gilt goblet, 4558
s. truth out of England, 6391
to s. and to forswear, 4555
when disposed to s., 6368
when I s., irrevocable, 7384
you s. like comfit-maker's wife, 6370
Swearers are fools, 6726
Swearing, 6368-6371
damned to hell for s., 1774
s. till my roof was dry, 5056
take me up for s., 6368
Swearings will I keep, 6371
Sweat : beads of s. on brow, 6198
captain drops bloody s., 6374
chilling s. o'erruns joints, 2616
rank s. of enseamed bed, 543
s. of industry, 6372
s. under a weary life, 1847
why s. they under burthens, 6010
Sweats : Falstaff s. to death, 6373
Sweet, 6375-6383
ah, s. Anne Page, 6377
be as s. as sharp, 6312
bitter 'past, welcome s., 6379
kiss me, s. and twenty, 4751
ladies call him s., 6376
more s. than baits to fish, 7453
more s. than painted pomp, 4117
not so short as s., 5161
now comes s. o' the night, 4974
so s. was ne'er so fatal, 914
s. and commendable, 2561
s. as ditties highly penn'd, 3919
s. as honey of Hybla, 3605
s. as spring-time flowers, 2986
s. as summer, 1204
sweets to the s., 6375
then comes s. o' the year, 1757
things s. to taste, 6382
whence didst steal thy s., 6920
Sweet-marjoram of salad, 5788
Sweeter than Cytherea's breath, 2767
Sweetest things turn sourest, 2765
Sweeting : thy wit a bitter s., 7258
trip no further, pretty s., 4751
Sweetly : speak s., man, 6383
Sweetness : drown me with s., 3820
loathe the taste of s., 3520
O, our lives' s., 4135
tuned too sharp in s., 3823
Sweets : last taste of s. sweetest, 6324
s. grown common lose delight, 6378
s. of sweet philosophy, 5252

s. that seem so good, 5801
s. to the sweet, farewell, 6375
s. turn to sours, 6381
s. with s. war not, 3822
Swerving: unnoble s., 5624
Swift: as s. as lead, 4052
  more s. than thought, 5000
  s. as a shadow, 6384
  too s. arrives as tardy, 6386
Swifter than arrow, 6385
  s. than moon's sphere, 2476
Swiftness: outrun by violent s., **5760**
Swim: or sink or s., 825
  s. like a duck, 6388
Swimmer: unpractised s., 6387
Swine: churlish s., 6390
  still s. eats the draff, 6389
Swine-keeping: come from s., 5446
Swoop: at one fell s., 1289
Sword, 6391-6408
  awake sleeping s. of war, 6393
  base and boisterous s., 586
  broke s. upon a stone, 4248
  despite thy victor s., 6725
  draw not s. to guard iniquity, 6405
  draw thy s. in right, 3967
  every whipster gets my s., 6404
  flesh'd thy maiden s., 6392
  get s. though of lath, 6396
  he hath a quiet s., 6659
  I'll make thee swallow my s., 3757
  lend thee sharp-pointed s., 2844
  my s. hacked like hand-saw, 6391
  pluck s. out of pilcher, 6407

rest, s., thou hast thy fill, 3423
rust, s., cool blushes, 5313
strip your s. naked, 6408
s. and shield win fame, 6394
s., hold thy temper, 6395
s. is an oath, 5050
s. of heaven will bear, 6401
that slave should wear s., 6397
this arm and a good s., 7044
'tis not the s., mace, 6021
upon your s. sit victory, 6884
valour eats s. it fights with, 6834
what tongue speaks, s. prove, 6406
whilst I can shake s., 3498
why die on my own s., 6400
wind of your fair s., 5337
with my s. quarter'd world, 2100
with s. wiped away blot, 2103
Sword-and-buckler Prince, 5354
Sworder: Roman s., 630
Swords: bear s. far as France, 5081
  keep up your bright s., 6403
  lift s. in just war, 5215
  sheathed s. for lack of argument, 307
  s. I smile at, 6399
  s. made rich with blood, 1029
  s. of soldiers are fangs, 1866
  turn s. into own entrails, 1034
  we measured s. and parted, 4091
Sycamore: sat by s. tree, 7165
Sycorax: charms of S., 1745
  foul witch s., 7272
Syllable: last s. of time, 4137
Syrups: drowsy s. of world, 6032

T

Table: set t. on a roar, 7549
  t. of her eye, 2420
  t. of my heart, 2441
  t. of my memory, 4625
Table-talk: serve for t., 6437
Tables of the law, 4854
  when he plays at t., 2052
  wipe the t. clean, 6484
Tabor: live by thy t., 1343
  rather hear t., 4865
Tackle of heart cracked, 3373
Tadpole: eats the t., 6652
Taffeta: changeable t., 4698
  flame-coloured t., 6615
  t. phrases, silken terms, 7363
Tag: before t. returns, 4833
Tail: cut and long t., 6411
  Dobbin's t. grows backward, 6410
  thereby hangs a t., 6416
  this body hath a t., 6409
Tailor, 6412-6413
  fall out with a t., 5499
  he called t. lown, 5420
  no, nor thy t., rascal, 6412
  t. falls into cough, 976
  t. make a man, 6413
  t. make thy doublet, 4698
  t. meddle with his last, 5913
  t. might scratch her, 3761
Tailors: undone three t., 1199
Taint of vice, 3726

Take: both t. and give, 3920
  every man t. his own, 5463
  seeks and will not t., 6414
Taking: what a t., 6415
Talbot: if T. but thunder, 6584
  let frantic T. triumph, 5219
Tale, 6416-6428
  every t. condemns me, 1514
  honest t. speeds best, 6423
  I could a t. unfold, 6417
  in his t. lie death, 6768
  in plain terms tell my t., 6299
  lamentable t. of me, 6422
  like an old t. still, 6428
  list a brief t., 6420
  mar curious t. in telling, 1566
  not so long as tedious t., 926
  plain t. will put you down, 6418
  round unvarnish'd t., 6421
  sad t. best for winter, 6427
  strangest t. ever I heard, 6419
  t. full of sound and fury, 4137
  t. told by an idiot, 4137
  tedious as twice-told t., 4133
  tell t. in lady's ear, 6424
  thereby hangs a t., 2793
  your t. would cure deafness, 6425
Tales: I will tell no t., 6426
  t. of others' griefs, 3158
  t. of woeful ages, 6422
  tell t. to thee of Jove, 5891

Talk, 6431-6440
he loves to hear himself t., 4631
how you do t., 6436
I cannot sweeten t., 5980
let's t. of graves, 1431
night crept upon our t., 4908
practise rhetoric in t., 5663
she doth t. in her sleep, 6440
sleep not in her t., 6440
smooth not with filed t., 6676
t. a little wild, 6435
t. thy tongue weary, 6430
'tis no time to t., 6435
what sad t. was that, 3501
Talkers are no good doers, 7403
Talking : he will be t., 6678
I wonder you still be t., 2084
Talks : he t. like a knell, 6429
t. familiarly of lions, 4826
t. of Arthur's death, 4838
Tall man of his hands, 6252
Tallow-face : out, you t., 7533
Talon : not eagle's t. in waist, 3955
Talons : seize with eagle's t., 3280
Tamora : now climbeth T., 2350
Tang : let thy tongue t., 6681
she had tongue with a t., 6679
Tanlings : summer's t., 1613
Tantalus : like T. he sits, 4737
Taper : how ill this t. burns, 5241
my inch of t. done, 1886
Taper-light heaven to garnish, 2375
Tapers burn'd to bedward, 1368
Tapster, 6441-6444
fitteth spirit of a t., 6441
I'll be your t. still, 6442
poor widow's t., 6443
t. is a good trade, 6444
Tardy : an you be so t., 6051
too swift arrives as t., 6386
Targets to put off shame, 5971
Tarpeian : rock T., 2007
Tarquin did press the rushes, 1234
T.'s ravishing strides, 4848
Tarre the mastiffs on, 1728
Tarsus, city of plenty, 1355
T., whose towers kiss clouds, 6701
Tart : news is not so t., 4959
Tartar : arrow from T.'s bow, 6385
return to vasty T., 1969
T.'s bow of lath, 6185
Tartness of face sours grapes, 2454
Task, 6445-6447
long day's t. is done, 6445
t. does not divide Sunday, 6446
t. is numbering sands, 6447
thou thy t. hast done, 2240
weary t. foredone, 4674
Tassel-gentle : lure t., 6956
Taste : alter not his t., 6286
caudle thy morning t., 6356
early pluck'd sour to t., 2941
forgot the t. of fears, 2613
give us t. of your quality, 5485
in t. confounds appetite, 3521
last t. of sweets sweetest, 6324
things sweet to t. prove sour, 6382
Taught : highly fed, lowly t., 920
Taunted and baited at, 5511
Taurus : born under T., 656

Tax any private party, 5414
Teach me how to think, 6449
t. twenty what were good, 7401
thus I would t. a dog, 6451
Team : heavenly-harness'd t., 2417
Tear, 6452-6479
for thy sake many a t., 2739
he hath a t. for pity, 1203
here did she fall a t., 5751
in his grave rained t., 3106
not think to shed a t., 6461
orb of one particular t., 6465
weaker than woman's t., 7039
Tears : blind with tributary t., 6121
burns worse than t., 7075
call her waters t., 6452
despised t., 6469
did he break into t., 6467
drop t. fast as trees, 1208
eyes draw salt t., 2436
fill with prophetic t., 6477
gave me up to t., 6459
glory to see your t., 6486
her t. pierce marble heart, 7309
his eye big with t., 5167
his t. pure messengers, 6249
I forbid my t., 6458
I'll spring up in his t., 7074
if you have t., prepare to shed them, 1033
like Niobe, all t., 6457
liquid drops of t., 6472
made of sighs and t., 4254
match with shedding t., 6469
melt at my t., 6270
mine eyes full of t., 6471
more merry t. never shed, 6466
my t. prove holy water, 6456
my t. scald like lead, 7094
nature's t., 4918
no t. but of my shedding, 4420
plenteous t. to drown world, 395
punish'd me with nightly t., 4353
rejoice to see my t., 5526
river dry, fill it with t., 6479
salt of unrighteous t., 4556
say t. belong to Egypt, 2135
shower of commanded t., 6475
t. augmenting morning's dew, 6473
t. coursed down nose, 6228
t. do stop floodgates, 5505
t. live in an onion, 6453
t. of it are wet, 1664
t. of soft remorse, 4847
t. shall drown the wind, 5304
t. show their love, 6470
t. then for babes, 7069
t. virginal as dew, 6460
teem with women's t., 6468
tender womanish t., 6462
there is t. for his love, 1032
thy t. are saltier, 6454
thy t. are venomous, 6454
thy t. are womanish, 4534
trickling t. are vain, 5505
wash him from grave with t., 3169
wet cheeks with artificial t., 1681
what potions of Siren t., 6474
with own t. wash away balm, 1687
with t. keep'st me blind, 2444
Tearsheet : Doll T., 3864

Techy and wayward infancy, 1209
Tedious : be not t., 5404
  brief and t. of it, 5914
  t. as tired horse, 6431
  t. as twice-told tale. 4133
Tediousness : taste of t., 3631
  t. of my travel, 1455
Teen : joy wrecked with t., 6118
Teeth, 6480-6483
  bid them keep t. clean, 1362
  give them bloody t., 6480
  I'll set my t., 2669
  know him by picking t., 3133
  locked between t. and lips, 5835
  pick his t. and sing, 4611
  pluck t. from tiger's jaws, 6634
  sans t., sans eyes, 7466
  set my t. on edge, 5348
  set t., stretch nostril, 7013
  show t. in way of smile, 4916
  t. and forehead of faults, 5084
  t. as white as whale's bone, 6483
  t. hadst thou when born, 662
  tell him to his t., 3334
  then I suck my t., 6482
  unless his t. be pulled, 6254
Tell-tale, 6484-6487
  keep no t. to memory, 6484
  no t. nor breed-hate, 6487
  that is no fleering t., 6485
Tell-tales : we are no t., 6486
Tellus : rob T. of weed, 2762
Temper, 6488-6490
  dauntless t., of his mind, 4913
  his t. be well observed, 1203
  hot t. leaps over cold decree, 6390
  sword, hold thy t., 6395
  you have a gentle t., 6489
  you keep a constant t., 6488
Temperance : ask God for t., 6492
  guess what t. should do, 6491
  reined to t., 1303
  tender and delicate t., 4146
Temperate : lovely and t., 6315
Tempest, 6491-6493
  after t. comes calms, 6494
  hear fearful t. sing, 6495
  t. doth take all feeling, 4686
  t. dropping fire, 5096
  t. of provocation, 1954
  t. shall not cease to rage, 6273
  t. shook down trees, 662
  t. to the field, 5591
  windy t. of heart, 5919
Tempests : greater t. than almanacs
    report, 6452
  I have seen t. rive oaks, 5096
  looks on t., never shaken, 4333
  t. omit their mortal natures, 1980
Temple : as t. waxes service grows, 4902
  baser t. than where swine, 3068
  broke ope Lord's t., 4849
  keep unshak'd that t., 3534
  no t. but the wood, 3579
  nothing ill in such a t., 3702
Tempt not a desperate man, 6501
Temptation, 6496-6501
  I am going to t., 6497
  that t. that goads us on, 6499

Tempted : I never t. her, 6500
  one thing to t., 6496
  tempter or t., who sins most, 6498
Ten : faced with card of t., 5653
  t. to one no impeach, 7000
  t. to one this play, 5334
Ten Commandments : to sea with
    T. C., 6257
Tender-minded does not become
    sword, 6398
Tenderness : melting with t., 1461
  more t. than may become man, 7068
  my conscience received t., 1508
Tenders : ta'en t. for pay, 379
Tennis-balls, my liege, 4754
Tennis-court : vast t., 4513
Tens : two t. and a score, 604
Tent that searches to bottom, 2169
Tenures : where be his t., 4046
Tercel : falcon as the t., 2488
Termagant : o'erdoing t., 54
Terminations : terrible as t., 913
Terms : bitter-searching t., 1737
  holiday and lady t., 4225
  t. will enter lady's ear, 6065
Terra : bona t., mala gens, 4014
Terram Salicam, 3727
Terror : coward-like with t., 2614
  full of t. was the time, 4996
  no t. in your threats, 6570
  thou t. to prosperity, 1868
  to perjury we add t., 5230
Terrors : make trifles of t., 4714
Tertian : quotidian t., 2514
Test of my metal, 4665
Testament : let commons hear t., 6503
  performance is a t., 5454
  poor deer, makest a t., 6502
  purple t. of bleeding war, 7004
  t. of a good conscience, 1504
Tester I'll have in pouch, 4763
Tewkesbury mustard, 7229
Text : approve it with a t., 5603
  t. old, orator too green, 5117
  that's a certain t., 4878
Thankings : thank me no t., 6512
Thanks, 6504-6516
  doth she not give us t., 6512
  he renders me beggardly t., 1469
  I am even poor in t., 6507
  I can no answer make but t., 6516
  I can render nothing but t., 6509
  my recompense is t., 6510
  my t. are too dear, 6507
  my treasury is but t., 6511
  proffers not took reap t., 6504
  reguerdoned with t., 5658
  service repaid with t., 6513
  such t. as fits king, 6506
  take his t. that hath nothing else, 6508
  t., exchequer of the poor, 6511
  t. I give is I am poor of t., 6505
  t. in part of desert, 6515
  t. is honourable meed, 6514
Thanksgiving before meat, 6073
Theatre : this universal t., 7466
Theban : I'll talk with T., 7386
Theft most base, 6521
  warrant in that t., 6519

Thefts : his t. too open, 6518
  use violent t. and rob, 6522
Theme : she is t. of honour, 3438
  t. of all our scorns, 2952
  t. of honour's tongue, 6081
Theoric : bookish t., 6438
  mistress to t., 4129
  whole t. of war, 6991
Thersites as good as Ajax, 5656
Thews : grow in t. and bulk, 4902
Thick as Tewkesbury mustard, 7229
Thief, 6323-6532
  every man's apparel fits t., 6529
  gallops with t. to gallows, 6609
  if you meet t. suspect him, 6530
  in sworn twelve have t., 3839
  sun's a t., robs sea, 6520
  t. brags of own attaint, 6524
  t. doth fear each bush, 986
  t. guiltier than him they try, **3839**
  t. of occasion will rob, 5071
  true man or t., 4279
  vile t. this seven year, 1957
  what a t. fashion is, 6531
  yond justice rails upon t., 6527
Thievery : example with t., 6520
Thieves : rich preys make t., 6532
  so triumph t. upon booty, 7358
  t. are all scattered, 6526
  t. are not judged, 3903
  t. breathe out invectives, 1641
  t. cannot be true, 6525
  t. do foot by night, 7365
  t. for robbery have authority, 6528
  t. of the day's beauty, 4781
  t. range abroad, 6325
  water t. and land t., 5295
  we are not t. but men, 6984
Thighs packed with wax, 6084
Thimbles into gauntlets, 2336
Thing, 6533-6539
  beguile t. I am by seeming, 4662
  every t. that heard him, 5119
  foolish t. but a toy, 5536
  good t. comes tomorrow, 1182
  I had a t. to say, 6170
  I told you a t. yesterday, 7074
  ill-favoured t., but mine own, 4555
  make good t. too common, 2327
  outrageous t. wiped away, 3898
  presume not I am t. I was, 2513
  started like guilty t., 3182
  t. bitter as death, 6535
  t. that ends all deeds, 1920
  thou art the t. itself, 4494
  too much of a good t., 3072
  unworthy t. you make of me, **5331**
  what one t., what another, 6539
Things : abhorred t. amend, 2801
  all but new t. disdain, 4114
  ask you how t. go, 6533
  base t. sire base, 4899
  can such t. be, 6537
  construe t. after fashion, 6536
  earthly t. atone together, 4717
  good t. should be praised, 3080
  leaving free t. behind, 6309
  make t. supernatural, 4714
  make vile t. precious, 4930
  more t. in heaven and earth, 5246

small t. make base men proud, **6741**
  so quick bright t. come, 4157
  these t. beyond all use, 5097
  t. bad begun make strong, 397
  t. base and vile, 4393
  t. but done by chance, 3733
  t. done well exempt selves, 1929
  t. familiar to us, 7011
  t. growing are not ripe, 5575
  t. growing to themselves, 6828
  t. ill-got bad success, 3489
  t. in motion catch eye, 2447
  t. must be as they may, 2004
  t. of day begin to droop, 4981
  t. out of hope, 6858
  t. outward draw inward, 3833
  t. past redress past care, 4040
  t. rank and gross, 7468
  t. spoke, seldom meant, 6168
  t. sweet to taste sour, 6382
  t. that love night, 4976
  t. to come at large, 6538
  t. won are done, 1949
  to t. of sale seller's praise, 5757
  wish t. done undone, 1930
  worse than senseless t., 3383
  you are idle shallow t., 3247
  you shall hear how t. go, 6533
Think : I t. and pray, 5403
  I t. him so because I t. him so, **5579**
  teach me to forget to t., 6551
  t. as every man thinks, 6546
  what I t. I utter, 1200
  when I t., I must speak, 7293
Thinking makes it so, 6545
Thinkings are below moon, 6561
Thinks : he t. too much, 2581
  what he t. he shows, 1212
This : come to t., 3871
Thisbe : Pyramus and T., 5336
  T. fearfully o'ertrip dew, 4987
Thorn, 6540-6542
  can so young t. prick, 6541
  this t. doth to our rose, 5736
  withering on virgin t., 6922
Thorns : leave t. to prick, 5737
  mow down t. that annoy, 6540
  roses have t., 5739
  t. and dangers of world, 7035
  t. that in her bosom lodge, 4814
  what t. rose defends, 5738
Thought, 6543-6553
  be it t. and done, 1939
  begot of t., 1712
  damnation to think so base a t., 1772
  drive away t. of care, 6219
  faster comes t. on t., 6548
  fly like t., 3285
  have expedition of t., 6547
  if swift t. break it not, 3369
  impair t. with breath, 1212
  in our course of t., 1345
  in this t. find ease, 6566
  more swift than t., 5000
  never t. keeps road better, 6546
  not a t. but on dignity, 6548
  pale cast of t., 1847
  Roman t. struck him, 6543
  sessions of sweet silent t., 5608
  t. can jump sea and land, 6552

t. doth gnaw my inwards, 5649
t. is a slave of life, 3617
t. is free, 6553
t. runs before actions, 6544
unproportion'd t., 6556
working-house of t., 4222
your t. abuses your bosom, 3512
Thoughts, 6554-6569
all t. are winged, 6544
all unmuzzled t., 3559
apt t. of men, 2351
avouch t. of your heart, 7361
banish ambitious t., 1072
bloody t. ne'er look back, 4692
crown my t. with acts, 1939
cursed t. nature gives, 6562
employ t. to courtship, 4661
fair t. attend you, 2531
fair t. be your pillow, 6567
give thy t. no tongue, 6556
give worst of t. words, 6563
gracious words revive t., 6687
heavenly t. counsel her, 2297
his t. immaculate, 6249
I have bloody t., 6558
in significants proclaim t., 6686
love's heralds should be t., 4323
lust and rank t., 7301
make me like my t., 4369
make not t. prisons, 6555
my t. are minutes, 6632
my t. as food to life, 2788
my t. be bloody, 6558
my t. I'll character, 6730
my t. remain below, 7419
our t. are ours, 6557
she could read t., 1229
sick with working of t., 2139
steel thy fearful t., 6560
t. are but dreams, 6565
t. are no subjects, 3754
t. like unbridled children, 6568
t. tending to ambition, 6566
t. tending to content, 6566
t. that would thick blood, 6569
t. unveil in their cradles, 5466
t. whirled like potter's wheel, 6559
unstain'd t. seldom dream, 6564
words without t. never to heaven, 7419
worser t. heaven mend, 6554
Thrasonical : behaviour t., 1206
Thread of verbosity, 312
t. will strangle thee, 1771
with silk t. pluck back, 5169
Threat before you sting, 7385
Threats : no terror in t., 6570
Three : being but t., 6572
I'll give t. for one, 834
we t. here part, 2534
when shall we t. meet again, 6573
Three-farthings goes, 2461
Three-farthings : stumble at t., 1793
Thrice-blessed they, 6922
Thrift, 6574-6577
French t., you rogues, 6577
how, i' the name of t., 6575
t. is blessing, 6576
t. may follow fawning, 2719
t.. t.. Horatio, 6574

Throat : iniquity's t. cut, 5960
laughter in t. of death, 4021
seeking in t. of death, 5683
took by t. circumcised dog, 2156
you lie in your t., 4104
Throne, 6578-6580
fore whose t. kneel, 6349 ·
God guard your sacred t., 6580
immediate to our t., 6579
innocent and aweless t., 6804
my t. bid kings bow, 3152
this royal t. of kings, 2324
t. of Denmark, 6578
t. where honour crown'd, 5895
yield hearted t. to hate, 4373
Throng : I'll to the t., 5889
Throstle : if t. sing, 4500
t. with note so true, 7529
Thrush : heigh, t. and jay, 4010
Thumb : do you bite your t., 6582
Thumb-ring : alderman's t., 3955
Thumbs : pricking of my t., 6581
Thunder, 6583-6590
chide as loud as t., 779
could great men t. as Jove, 6587
deep dread-bolted t., 2463
every officer would t., 6587
heaven's artillery t., 6588
I never heard such t., 4864
if Talbot t. rain follows, 6584
in t., lightning, or in rain, 6573
made t. with their shouts, 1086
mock deep-mouthed t., 2221
no stones but serve for t., 6269
our t. from the south, 1079
re-speaking earthly t., 1078
secure of t.'s crack, 5841
sleep in spite of t., 2610
tear with t. cheeks o' air, 6583
thou all-shaking t., 6585
t. deep and dreadful, 6589
t. of my cannon, 1079
t. to tune of Green Sleeves, 1954
to dread rattling t., 6590
what is cause of t., 6586
Thunder-bearer : bid t. shoot, 5891
Thunder-claps : precursors of t., 4159
Thunder-darter of Olympus, 3812
Thunder-stone : all-dreaded t., 2240
bared bosom to t., 4156
Thunderbolt : bear me like t., 3613
Thunderbolts : oak-cleaving t., 6585
t. dash him to pieces, 1626
Thundered with thy tongue, 7405
Thyme : bank where wild t. blows, 2761
Tiber : no allaying T., 7179
Tick : I had rather be a t., 3696
Tickle us, do we not laugh, 3797
Tickle-brain : peace, t., 5505
Tickled : she's t. now, 2010
Tickling : die with t., 1882
trout caught with t., 6752
Tiddle taddle : no t., 6433
Tide, 6591-6593
float upon swelling t., 2878
he moves wind and t., 6275
lackeying the varying t., 785
like t. they rush by, 2299
my t. turns not, 6592
parted at turning of t., 2515

resist wind and t., 2551
swim against the t., 6363
t. in affairs of men, 6591
t. of blood in me, 712
t. of pomp, 6021
t. that makes still-stand, 4682
t. will fill the shore, 6593
Tides : high t. in calendar, 3494
spurns ocean's roaring t., 2334
Tidings, 6594-6600
fruitful t., 6594
good t., Lord Hastings, 6598
I may drink thy t., 6595
joyful t., 6597
let ill t. tell themselves, 4951
sad t. I bring you, 6599
sweet t. of sun's uprise, 5560
these t. nip me, 6600
t. I bring and lucky joys, 4955
t. of slaughter, 6599
what good t. comes, 6597
worst t. I hear of yet, 6596
Tiger, 6601-6602
approach like Hyrcan t., 5879
hind speeds to catch t., 6190
hold t. by the tooth, 5863
imitate action of the t., 7013
milk in a male t., 4635
t. hath seized hind, 6601
t. will be mild, 7309
t.'s heart in woman's hide, 7308
t.'s young teach dam, 6602
Tigers : go great with t., 7349
more inexorable than t., 3755
more inhuman than t., 7308
t., not daughters, 1808
touch could make t. tame, 5121
Tillage of thy husbandry, 7348
Tillyvally, 745
Tilt-yard : his study is t., 3496
saw him once in t., 6432
Tilter : a puisny t., 1198
Time, 6603-6645
backward abysm of t., 6640
be not troubled with t., 3327
bid t. return, 6631
breathing t. of day, 1819
by t.'s fell hand defaced, 6636
cormorant devouring T., 2518
creeping hours of t., 6608
devouring t., 6634
envious, calumniating t., 6945
every t. serves, 6605
fit in t. and place, 5673
for holy offices a t., 6617
gates of steel t. decays, 6637
hand in hand with t., 1332
help t. furrow me with age, 4143
high t. that I were hence, 6612
how short his t. of folly, 6629
I have no t. to spend, 6010
I wasted t., now t. wastes me, 6632
injurious t., 6643
let t. try, 6610
long t. lies in one word, 7392
look into seeds of t., 6622
many a t. and oft, 6830
many events in womb of t., 6626
never-resting t., 6633
no t. so miserable, 6760

noiseless foot of t., 6604
nor t. nor place adhere, 6625
old common arbitrator, t., 2305
old t., the clock-setter, 6620
perfected by course of t., 2396
play housewife with t., 6603
relish of saltness of t., 7577
residence against tooth of t., 1984
short t. seems long, 6113
spring t., only ring t., 4401
stream of t. doth run, 6616
swift-footed t., 6634
take the present t., 4119
that bald sexton t., 6620
that t. of year behold, 6638
there's a t. for all things, 6611
they fleet t. carelessly, 6606
t. and the hour, 6623
t. comes stealing on, 6613
t. doth transfix flourish, 6635
t. goes on crutches, 4298
t. hath a wallet, 6642
t. hath done injuries, 6647
t. hath made thee hard, 6307
t. hath sow'd grizzle, 7589
t. himself is bald, 6611
t. is at his period, 6234
t. is breeder of good, 6645
t. is come around, 6619
t. is king of men, 6627
t. is like fashionable host, 6642
t. is out of joint, 6614
t. is the old justice, 6610
t. is their master, 4483
t. made me his clock, 6632
t. must friend or end, 6641
t. must have a stop, 3617
t. must untangle this, 3973
t. of life is short, 4127
t. of universal peace, 5209
t. qualifies spark of love, 4263
t. shall bring to ripeness, 2297
t. shall not be of age, 5974
t. shall unfold cunning, 6621
t. suppresseth wrongs, 3411
t. to mark how slow it goes, 6629
t. to think upon business, 6617
t. travels in divers paces, 6609
t. tutor to good and bad, 6630
t. when screech-owls cry, 7269
t. will bring on summer, 6312
t. will bring to light, 2586
t. will have bald followers, 6611
t. will take my love, 6636
t.'s glory to calm kings, 6628
t.'s office to fine hate, 6628
t.'s thievish progress, 6639
weak piping t. of peace, 5216
wears out his t., 3943
what t. of day is it, 6615
when t. is old, 2506
whirligig of t., 6644
willingly waste my t., 6607
wit depends on dilatory t., 7246
witching t. of night, 4673
you've passed a hell of t., 6824
Time-pleaser : a t., 1215
Times, 6646-6648
brisk and giddy-paced t., 6097
construe t. to necessities, 6647

cruel are the t., 5758
fatness of pursy times, 6879
golden t., 4955
rotten t., 215
these coster-monger t., 6934
these naughty t., 6648
t. are wild, 6646
t. to repair nature, 3625
Timon hath made mansion, 3115
T. laugh at toys, 3891
T. will be left gull, 2632
T. will to the woods, 489
Timor : gelidus t., 2606
Tinder-like upon motion, 1200
Tinker : drink with any t., 2202
Tip of his subduing tongue, 6665
Tip-toe : stand a t., 3540
Tires betimes that spurs, 3289
Tirra-lyra chants, 4010
Titan's fiery wheels, 4799
Tithe : our t. is to sow, 1550
Title, 6649-6650
  be thy t. right or wrong, 5693
  farced t. running 'fore king, 6021
  guard t. that was rich, 2375
  this t. honours me, 4700
  t. hangs loose upon him, 6650
  t. of all titles worst, 4473
Title-leaf foretells volume, 946
Titles : magnifiest with t., 6649
  other t. given away, 2808
  princes have but t., 5430
  t. blown from adulation, 2652
Toad : I'd rather be a t., 4562
  lark and t. change eyes, 4008
  t. wears precious jewel, 104
Toads : cistern for foul t., 133
  engendering of t., 5422
Toasts : rheumatic as dry t., 5664
Today o'erthrows my joys, 6631
Toe to crown fill skins, 5291
Toes : my t. look through, 5531
  t. unplagued with corns, 1553
Toge : this wolvish t., 1748
Toil : unapt to t., 3670
  weary with t., 551
  winding up days with t., 6021
Token : no t. but stones, 3263
Tom, 6651-6652
  poor T. that eats frogs, 6652
  T. bears logs into hall, 5124
  T., Dick and Francis, 3643
  T. will make them weep, 2152
  T.'s a-cold, 1407
  who gives to poor T., 1407
Tom o' Bedlam : sigh like T., 4619
Tomb : erect his own t., 4774
  t. evident as a chair, 5383
  t. where never scandal slept, 218
Tomboys : partner'd with t., 3986
Tombs : gilded t. worms enfold, 3059
Tomorrow : good night till t., 5169
  t., and t., and t., 4137
Tongs and bones, 4863
Tongue, 6653-6683
  barr'd aidance of the t., 4410
  be not t. shame's orator, 6658
  bird of my t. better, 6670
  chastise with valour of t., 6208
  credit her false-speaking t., 4335

cry holla to thy t., 6657
double t. mortal touch, 87
every t. brings tale, 1514
faster than t. made offence, 2403
fellows of infinite t., 7361
gave t. helpful ornament, 5348
had t. at will, 514
he hath a killing t., 6659
he wears t. in 's arms, 6186
heavy heart bears not nimble t., 3345
her t., most serpent-like, 6664
her t. will not obey, 6656
his t., conceit's expositor, 7233
his t. is filed, 1206
his t. is the clapper, 3351
his t. stringless instrument, 6674
his t. sullen bell, 4954
hold your t., prudence, 3082
I cannot endure Lady T., 6671
I have not gift of t., 5235
I must hold t., 4556
iron t. of midnight, 4676
keep good t. in head, 6680
knave's t. begins to double, 6660
let candied t. lick pomp, 2719
let music's t. unfold, 4869
let my t. blister, 6683
let thy t. tang, 6681
let t. equal heart, 6661
love's best habit soothing t., 4309
love's t. proves Bacchus gross, 4281
make airy t. hoarse, 2284
men are turned into t., 4538
mince not the general t., 6655
motion of schoolboy's t., 7363
mouths bear self-same t., 4826
murder have no t., 5330
music of his own t., 6707
my heart accordeth with t., 6168
my heart prompts t., 6675
my t. cleave to my roof, 5160
my t. hath tale to say, 5995
my t. learn smoothing words, 6675
my t. shall tell anger, 6677
my t.'s use no more, 6672
neat's t. dried, 5945
nurse thy t. to teach, 5161
one t. for all wounds, 4809
play braggart with my t., 7320
put t. in every wound, 1033
rattling t. of eloquence, 5955
she had a t. with a tang, 6679
she struck me with her t., 6664
smooth not t. with filed talk, 6676
so shrewd of thy t., 3664
speak'st with every t., 3067
speaks with t. of enemy, 1574
spendthrift of his t., 6678
take her without her t., 7226
take serpent by the t., 6902
talk thy t. weary, 6430
that man that hath a t., 6682
they want use of t., 2078
this from Rumour's t., 5757
thundered with thy t., 7405
thy t. makes Welsh sweet, 3919
tip of his subduing t., 6665
t. doubly portcullis'd, 6672
t. far from heart, 6921
t. I am glad I have not, 2421

t. in thunder's mouth, 6663
t. more poisons than adder, 6662
t. not able to conceive, 2183
t. outvenoms worms of Nile, 5999
t. put you into mouth, 6654
t. shakes master's undoing, 6653
torment you with my t., 2044
tying ear to no t. but own, 2805
understanding but no t., 5943
wag thy t. in noise, 38
what heart thinks t. speaks, 3351
what ready t. suspicion hath, 6357
what t. speaks sword proves, 6406
when t. blabs let eyes not see, 675
with base t. give heart lie, 4876
with doubler t. never adder, 85
with iron t., brazen mouth, 611
with t. he cannot win woman, 6682
with wagging t. win me, 6150
within mouth engaol'd my t., 6672
world's large t., 6668
would my horse had speed of t., 6670
yes, I will hold my t., 4842
you dried neat's t., 1456
Tongue-tied : be not t., 6688
give t. sorrows leave, 6687
my t. patience, 2086
t. and loath to speak, 6686
t., our queen ; speak you, 6689
Tongues, 6684-6685
bestowed time in the t., 6685
bitter clamour of two t., 7445
cloven t. hiss me, 89
defy t. of soothers, 2720
done to death by slanderous t., 6000
fraught is of aspics' t., 846
silver-sweet sound lovers' t., 4406
t. applaud it to the clouds, 1087
t. I'll hang on every tree, 6684
t. in trees, 4117
t. of dying men, 6673
t. of men full of deceits, 1910
t. of mocking wenches, 6667
t. to be your being shall rehearse, 4776
traduced by ignorant t., 5315
upon t. continual slanders, 5755
Tooth, 6690-6693
by treason's t. bare-gnawn, 4891
his venom t. will rankle, 6693
how sharper than serpent's t., 1279
in danger of her former t., 6054
ne'er a t. in her head, 6690
poisons more than mad dog's t., 7299
residence 'gainst t. of time, 1984
set my pugging t. on edge, 186
sorrow's t. never rankle, 6115
sweet poison for age's t., 5357
thy t. is not so keen, 3722
t. that poisons if it bite, 2152
whilst I have t. in head, 6690
your colt's t. not cast, 6691
Tooth-ache, 6694-6696
endure t. patiently, 5250
he that sleeps feels not t., 6694
I have the t., 6695
no charm for the t., 6695
what, sigh for the t., 6695
Toothpicker : fetch a t., 5875
Top : bow'd his eminent t., 3640
this is the very t., 4847

Top-branch overpeer'd, 1148
Tops of eastern pines, 6325
Torches : as we with t. do, 3402
teach t. to burn bright, 522
t. are made to light, 6928
Torment : from t. I free myself, 1681
t. that it cannot cure, 4737
Tormentors : words my t. be, 5894
Torments : what studied t. hast, 6700
Torrent of occasion, 6616
Torture, 6697-6700
deep t. call'd a hell, 6699
on t. of mind to lie, 1872
t. me to leave unspoken, 6698
turning t. out of door, 6462
what old or newer t., 6700
with t. let life be ended, 6697
Touch : I know no t. of it, 5331
now do I play the t., 3061
one t. of nature, 4923
softest t. smart as stings, 1737
their t. affrights me, 3213
Touches ne'er touch'd, 2440
t. still conquest chastity, 1240
Touse you joint by joint, 5528
Tower : burn down the T., 932
let him to the T., 4448
look back unto the T., 382
nor stony t. nor walls, 6200
Tower-hill : tribulation of T., 7562
Towers : cloud-capp'd t., 5639
lofty t. down-razed, 6636
topples down moss-grown t., 4906
t. bore heads kiss'd clouds, 6701
t. whose tops buss clouds, 6702
yond t. must kiss own feet, 6702
Town : take pity of your t., 3088
walled t. worthier, 387
Towns : won as t. with fire, 6292
you made whole t. fly, 4716
Toy, 6703-6704
each t. seems prologue, 3183
foolish thing was but t., 5536
for a t. of no regard, 6704
who sells eternity to get t., 4727
Toys : all is but t., 4808
lamenting t. jollity, 6703
shall we fall for t., 7085
there's t. abroad, 6156
Trade : bad is t. plays fool, 6105
I will t. to them both, 4289
in t. of war I have slain, 4851
some way of common t., 3902
what t. are you of, 6443
you need not change t., 6442
Traders riding to London, 5280
Trading : have good t., 465
Traffic : merchant of great t., 4632
my t. is sheets, 3936
Traffickers : petty t., 4690
Tragedian : counterfeit t., 57
Tragedies : stage for t., 4995
Traitor, 6721-6728
arrant t. as any, 6723
every t. must be hanged, 6726
graceless t. to her lord, 3670
here is head of ignoble t., 6727
himself love's t., 2420
I find myself a t., 6471
if ever I were t., 6727

kissing t., Judas, 3826
my father was no t., 6721
subtle t. needs no sophister, 6724
thou art a t., false, 6725
toad-spotted t., 6725
t. lives, true man's put to death, 2574
t. stands in worse case, 6722
unless king calls me t., 4107
what is a t., 6726
Traitors : be all t., 6726
brief when t. brave field, 1964
guard these t. to block, 6717
men's vows women's t., 6961
our fears make us t., 2611
Transformed : I am t., 338
Transgression : rude t., 1490
Transgressions they smother, 2597
Translated : thou art t., 1192
Transportance : quick t., 6147
Transported : he is t., 1192
Trap to take my life, 6711
Trappings and suits of woe, 5843
Trash : steals purse, steals t., 4894
wring from peasants vile t., 4762
Traveller, 6705-6709
Monsieur T., look you lisp, 6706
now spurs lated t. apace, 6708
refined t. of Spain, 6707
Travellers must be content, 6705
t. ne'er did lie, 6709
Traverse, go, 4765
to see thee t., 2679
Tray, Blanch, 2152
Treachery, 6710-6714
for thy t., manifest, 6711
he is framed of t., 6714
kill'd with mine own t., 6225
monstrous t., can this be, 6712
sell sovereign's life to t., 6710
those that betray do no t., 6713
t., seek it out, 6908
Tread : a' shall not t. on me, 2672
pray you, t. softly, 6979
Treason, 6715-6720
betray'd feel t. sharply, 6722
block of death, t.'s bed, 6717
bloody t. flourished, 1033
by t.'s tooth bare-gnawn, 4891
here lurks no t., 1181
search t. of world, 2418
shall we buy t., 6715
t. and murder ever together, 6718
t. are hands of sin, 5971
t. but trusted like fox, 6716
t. can but peep, 3874
t. has done his worst, 1872
t. is not inherited, 6721
t. mingled with your love, 5529
t. of the blood, 6720
ugly t. of mistrust, 5529
Treasons : fit for t., 4862
my followers' base t., 3431
t. make me beggar, 3906
t. stand bare and naked, 6325
Treasure : precious t. of eyesight, 5939
purest t. is reputation, 5627
rust hidden t. frets, 5762
scarce hath eyes t., 4737
taken t. of her honour, 3535
this t. of an oyster, 5221

what a t. hadst thou, 1805
when t. is the meed, 2949
who fears sinking where t. lies, 1989
your chaste t. open, 1252
Treasures : pour our t. into foreign laps, 3671
t. of your body, 1254
Treasury : my t. is thanks, 6511
rob the t. of life, 1477
t. of everlasting joy, 3395
Treble : childish t., 7466
the t. jars, 3946
Tree, 6729-6734
carve on every t., 6730
I have a tree grows here, 6734
my t. felt the axe, 6734
prunest a rotten t., 5872
t. bend with fruit, 6731
t. known by fruit, 2511
t. yields bad fruit, 2938
under the greenwood t., 6729
Trees in Hesperides, 4281
t. shall be my books, 6730
Tremble, hear lion roar, 4183
Tremor cordis : have t., 3366
Trencher : scrape t., 1050
Trencher-friends, 5155
Trencher-knight, 6737
Trencher-man valiant, 6264
Trenches : dig t. in beauty, 7586
Trespass : not your t. speaks, 4445
Trial of a woman's war, 7445
t. of kingdom's king, 5961
Tribulation of Tower-hill, 7562
Tribute : no t. but love, 3670
Trick, 6735-6740
I see the t. on't, 6737
t. not worth an egg, 6735
t. of Cœur-de-lion's face, 5675
t. of our English nation, 2327
t. of singularity, 5983
t. of voice I remember, 3890
t. to lay down ladies, 6093
t. worth two of that, 6736
villanous t. of eye, 6082
what t. canst find, 6391
wild t. of his ancestors, 6716
Tricks : no t. in simple faith, 2480
plays fantastic t., 4498
such t. hath imagination, 3705
t. as make angels weep, 4498
t. he hath in him, 2966
t. how to cheat devil, 6735
t. that in them lurk, 7330
Trifle : a t., a t., 3608
throw away as 'twere a t., 1871
Trifler : away, you t., 4265
Trifles : dispense with t., 6742
in our t. I shall win, 7198
make t. of terrors, 4714
snapper-up of t., 6744
t. light as air, 6743
win us with honest t., 2029
Trinculo is reeling ripe, 2229
Triton of the minnows, 5884
Triumph is ale-house guest, 6746
Triumphs for nothing, 6703
Troilus : I'll show you T., 5014
they call him T., 1212

T., employer of pandars, 4303
T. mounted Trojan walls, 4987
Troiluses : constant men T., 5145
Trojan : each T. to field, 6757
T. horse stuffed within, 5903
Trojans : there are other T., 6756
Tromperies : pleines de t., 1910
Trophies of affections hot, 597
Trot with ne'er a tooth, 6690
Troth : and not break t., 5054
fate o'er-rules t., 5058
virtue never breaks t., 6965
you break faith and t., 5146
Troth-plight, 7145
Trouble, 6747-6750
double, toil and t., 6748
never came t. to my house, 6749
pains for purchasing t., 5133
t. gone, comfort remains, 6749
t. of my countenance, 6747
you come to meet t., 6749
Troubles : raze t. of brain, 4689
take arms against sea of t., 1847
Trout caught with tickling, 6752
Trouts : groping for t., 6751
Trowel : laid on with t., 2716
Troy, 6753-6757
half his T. was burnt, 7100
in T. lies the scene, 3434
like Sinon take T., 1681
night T. was set on fire, 7269
scare T. out of itself, 3424
T. bright with fame, 6754
T. in our weakness stands, 6755
T. must not be, 5163
why Grecians sacked T., 7287
worn stones of T., 2506
Troyan : false T. under sail, 6966
Truant : been t. in law, 4029
I have t. been to chivalry, 3614
I will never be a t., 3919
wrong to t. with bed, 5985
Truckle-bed : I'll to t., 550
Trudge : 'tis time to t., 1971
t., plod away o' the hoof, 2109
True, 6758-6761
all's t. that's mistrusted, 5346
as t. as flesh can be, 2750
as t. as I live, 6370
as t. as iron to adamant, 6761
as t. as plantage to moon, 6761
as t. as steel, 6759
as t. as sun to day, 6761
as t. as Troilus, 6761
as t. as turtle to mate, 6761
if t. or false I know not, 5757
I'll be sworn 'tis t., 7074
look thou be t., 6924
neither t. nor trusty, 4311
no time but man be t., 6760
O she was heavenly t., 2503
'tis t., 'tis pity, 4439
to thine own self be t., 6758
t. or else I am a Turk, 7325
who tells me t., 6768
Truepenny : art there, t., 6369
Truie lavée au bourbier, 2150
Trumpet : hideous t. calls, 998
never to my anger be t., 6683
now let the t. blow, 7474

till the last t., 980
t. of his own virtues, 6763
Trumpet-tongued, 6939
Trumpets : make t. speak, 6762
Trunk : ivy hid my t., 3764
t. discharged of breath, 5361
Trunks o'erflourish'd by devil, 6946
Trust, 6764-6767
built absolute t., 6765
I never t. thee more, 6767
not t. that you see, 5937
so far will I t. thee, 7305
there's no t. in men, 4514
t. him when he leers, 6766
t. I have is innocence, 3738
t. none, 5051
t. not broken faith, 6764
t., very simple gentleman, 3517
Trusted : who should be t., 6767
Trusting : no use for t., 1909
saucy t. of thoughts, 4425
Truth, 6768-6782
breathe t. in pain, 7446
bring t. to light, 6628
doubt t. to be a liar, 4258
fear not my t., 6781
find where t. is hid, 6770
he in twelve found t., 3904
he must speak t., 5322
is not the t. the t., 6771
make t. appear where hid, 5574
make t. in pleasure flow, 6277
no t. where semblance, 3536
not oaths make t., 6959
ornament t. doth give, 6779
resolved of your t., 5658
scarce t. enough alive, 6776
seek the light of t., 6775
sickens to speak a t., 6006
simple t. miscall'd simplicity, 6780
swear t. out of England, 6391
tell t. and shame devil, 2026
thy t. be thy dower, 2172
truer than t. itself, 508
t. and plainness I wear, 6781
t. doth falsely blind, 6775
t. doth lack gentleness, 6099
t. hath a quiet breast, 6778
t. hath better deeds, 6782
t. is a dog to kennel, 6774
t. is t. to end, 6771
t. loves open dealing, 6773
t. never confirm'd enough, 6777
t. of girls and boys, 3814
t. of it stands gross, 6772
t. shall nurse her, 2297
t. should be silent, 6769
t. will come to light, 4850
with t. catch simplicity, 6781
wonderful when devils tell t., 2040
Tub fill'd and running, 7151
Tub-fast and the diet, 7110
Tufts : write in emerald t., 2371
Tun : this t. of treasure, 4754
t. of man my companion, 2512
Tunable : more t. than lark, 6669
Tune : heavenly t., 2073
no matter how it be in t., 6090
Tuners : new t. of accents, 2527

Turf : by head grass-green t., 4262
one t. serve as pillow, 547
Turk : base Phrygian T., 4763
defies me like T., 6295
malignant, turban'd T., 2156
out-paramoured the T., 1205
send them to the T., 2355
take T. by the beard, 7361
true, or else I am a T., 7325
T. writes not so tedious, 6297
Turkey-cock : makes rare t., 1538
swelling like a t., 6783
Turn, 6785-6794
best t. i' the bed, 6790
do a good t., 6791
do her shrewd t., 6785
do my Lord a shrewd t., 6786
for what good t., 6790
I never did ill t., 3654
I owe you a good t., 6792
she can t. and t., 6788
she meant a good t., 6793
walk a t. together, 6787
Turns : count the t., 321
good t. shuffled off, 6516
snatch would serve t., 6789
Turpitude : sway'd by t., 7338
t. dost crown with gold, 848
Turtle : I, an old t., 6798
O slow-winged t., 6797
Turtle-doves : pair of t., 6795
Turtles : lascivious t., 6796
Tutor both to good and bad, 6630
t. of my riots, 2513

Tu-whit, tu-who, 5124
Twelve : in t. found truth, 3904
Twice-sod simplicity, 3693
Twink : in a t. she won me, 4940
with a t., 2430
Twinkling of an eye, 2430
Two may keep counsel, 1571
Tybalt, you rat-catcher, 1117
why, what is T., 1116
Tyke : bobtail t., 2152
Tyranny, 6799-6804
by t. wasted our country, 6800
insulting t. begins to jet, 6804
let high-handed t. range, 6801
t. and rage of spirit, 5197
t. I can shake off, 4132
t. lay thy basis sure, 6803
t. never quaff'd but blood, 6799
t. of the night's rough, 6802
Tyrant, 6805-6810
grand t. of the earth, 7347
hard-favour'd t., ugly, 1905
here you may see the t., 6808
how fine t. can tickle, 1612
my chief humour is for a t., 55
this is a t.'s vein, 6809
thou art past t.'s stroke, 2240
tread upon t.'s head, 1592
t. duke to t. brother, 6049
we are no t., 6805
Tyrants : how can t. govern, 6808
none but t. use law, 5310
plant in t. humility, 4281
time to fear when t. kiss, 6810

U

Ugly and slanderous, 6811
u. as a bear, 6812
Ulysses : deceive more than U., 5114
Umpire : play the u., 3963
u. of men's miseries, 1858
Unbonneted : speak u., 4142
Unbreached : saw myself u., 882
Unburthen'd crawl toward death, 1103
Uncle : I am no traitor's u., 3093
my prophetic soul, my u., 5861
u. me no uncles, 3093
Unclew me quite, 1441
Unction : bought u., 6814
lay not that flattering u. to your soul,
4445
Underlings : we are u., 2587
Understanding : for thy u., 7318
give it u., no tongue, 5943
wooing fit for thy u., 7361
Undertakings : desperate u., 4257
Undeserver : poor u., 6509
u. may sleep, 4649
Undo : I'll u. myself, 1687
Undone : better leave u., 1918
not u., but unknown, 7141
Uneasy lies the head, 6019
Unguem : dunghill for u., 4016
Unlettered soul, 6134
Unhair : I'll u. thy head, 1733
Unhappiness : dreamed of u., 6816
Unhouseled, unaneled, 3709
Unicorns may be betrayed, 2723

Unity, 6818-6820
confound all u., 1486
happy in your u., 6820
Universities : studious u., 3501
University : son spends all at u., 3669
Unkind : none deformed but u., 1958
Unkindness, 6821-6824
bury all u., 6821
by my u. shaken, 6824
drink down all u., 6822
unjust u., impediment, 1731
u. blunts more than marble, 2074
u. may defeat my life, 6823
u. may do much, 6823
Unknown : too early seen u., 4377
Unmatchable : high, u., 1968
Unsatisfied : leave me u., 5803
Unsecret to ourselves, 674
Unstaid in all motions, 4409
Unsure : what's to come, 4751
Unswayable : rough, u., 4897
Untender : young and so u., 7563
Unthrifts : none but u., 3632
Unwieldy, slow, heavy, 160
Unwisely have I given, 855
Up-cast : upon u. to be hit, 4419
Up-stairs, down-stairs, 7421
Ursa Major : under U., 656
Usance : rate of u., 4068
Usances : rated me about my u., 6830
Use, 6825-6828
come to deadly u., 6826

fresh beauty for u., 6828
how u. doth breed habit, 6827
need your u. and counsel, 2108
out of u. and staled, 2639
u. can change stamp of nature, 6825
u. make of what they hate, 4425

Uses : to what base u., 187
Usurer : pernicious u., 6829
wont to call me u., 809
Usurpation : witness'd u., 946
Usurpers sway rule awhile, 3411
Usury : use not forbidden u., 6831

V

Vacancy : bend eye on v., 2410
Vaded : soon v., 5734
Vagrom men, 1523
Valanced : your face v., 460
Vale of years, 158
Valentine : maid to be v., 6832
Saint V. is past, 6932
to-morrow is V.'s day, 6832
Valiant : as v. as Hector, 6837
as v. as Hercules, 4538
as v. as the lion, 1211
as v. as wrathful dove, 6839
less v. than virgin, 7039
remembrance of v. dead, 6930
thou little v., 1645
to be v. is no praise, 5164
truly v. that can suffer, 7547
v. in a better cause, 1632
v. taste of death but once, 1642
you are gentle, v., 6930
Validity : of poor v., 5472
Valorous as Hector, 2510
Valour, 6834-6846
adieu, v. ; rust, rapier, 4275
awake your dormouse v., 6845
better part of v. is discretion, 2080
bootless speed when v. flies, 6190
deed whereat v. weep, 1923
for v. is not love a Hercules, 4281
full of v. as kindness, 6841
guide v. to act in safety, 4913
he hath not name of v., 6999
his v. did enrich his wit, 1036
his v. upon our crests, 6838
in false quarrel no v., 5497
more v. than habits show, 6836
no more v. than duck, 1636
so full of v. they smote air, 6844
ten to one no impeach of v., 7000
to revenge is no v., 5654
true v. true respect, 6843
v. cannot carry discretion, 4189
v. dignifies the haver, 6835
v. eats the sword, 6834
v. is chiefest virtue, 6835
v. is turned bear-herd, 6934
v. melted into compliment, 4538
v. of a man, 7031
v. of my tongue, 6208
v. plucks dead lions, 3264
what v. when cur grins, 6842
when v. preys on reason, 6834
Value : like v. prized, 6847
v. dwells not in will, 6848
Valued : aught but as v., 6848
Vanities : his v. but outside, 6849
Vanity, 6949-6850
light v., cormorant, 6850
so light is v., 4407

that v. in years, 3730
world's mass of v., 7108
Vantage : forego this v., Greek, 3423
Vantages : take v., 7000
Vantbrace : in v. brawn, 467
Vapour of dungeon, 4562
Vapours : dries all crudy v., 5764
foul congregation of v., 2268
v., minute-jacks, 5155
v. that strangle him, 6317
Variety : her infinite v., 140
Varletry : show me to v., 1840
Varnish of a complete man, 2972
Vassal : I am fortune's v., 5066
Vassals : God's v. drop, 902
Vaunt-couriers to thunderbolts, 6585
Vaunting : make v. true, 6070
Vaward of our youth, 7578
Veil : beauty's v. covers blot, 6876
dimm'd with death's v., 2418
Vein : finds his v., 6851
not in giving v. today, 6852
this is Ercles' v., 6809
Veins : bluest v. to kiss, 3203
I'll empty these v., 710
v. bound richer blood, 4270
v. unfill'd, blood cold, 2061
Velvet-guards, 6370
Venetia, chi non te vede, 4546
Vengeance : arise, black v., 5650
can v. be pursued further, 5652
cry for v. at gates of heaven, 3807
render v. and revenge, 4099
take v. of such men, 4708
throw hot coals of v., 6999
v. is in my heart, 5655
v. of Jenny's case, 7103
v. on your withered hide, 5653
v. ride upon our swords, 5311
Vengeances of heaven, 1740
Veni, Vidi, Vici, 1037-1040
Venice : at V. gave bond, 1318
in V. let heaven see pranks, 7141
no power in V. can alter, 5408
traveller of V., 4546
Venison pasty to dinner, 6822
Venom : digest v. of spleen, 3372
live like v., 3853
partake no v., 6193
v., do thy work, 6853
Venom-mouth'd : cur is v., 1725
Ventricle of memory, 4628
Venture on desperate mart, 4633
Ventured like wanton boys, 2492
Ventures, 6855-6858
diseased v. that play, 6855
have all his v. fail'd, 6857
my v. not in one bottom, 6856
Venue : quick v. of wit, 7236

Venus, 6859-6860
more intemperant than V., 5845
o'er-picturing that V., 1977
simplicity of V.' doves, 6966
speak to my gossip V., 1723
that bastard of V., 1712
V., heart-blood of beauty, 6860
V. smiles not in tears, 6859
what V. did with Mars, 2356
Venuto : alla nostra casa ben v., 4017
Ver : this side is V., 7202
Verbal : being so v., 4541
Verbosity : thread of v., 312
Verdict unto frowning judge, 2365
Verdure : suck'd my v. out, 3764
Verge of salt sea flood, 3115
Verily, V., by your V., 6861
Verity in suspicion, 4969
Verona brags of him, 2978
Verse, 6862-6867
blank v. shall not halt, 6864
full sail of his great v., 6866
love in v. live ever, 6634
thy v. swells so fine, 2655
v. which sings the good, 6867
you talk in blank v., 6863
Verses : false gallop of v., 2938
hangs v. on the trees, 4249
he writes brave v., 1198
hear these v., 6962
more feet than v. bear, 6862
put me to v. undid me, 7361
tear him for bad v. 6865
Vessel, 6868-6870
can empty v. bear hogshead, 6969
comfort the weaker v., 7292
emptier v., 6869
empty v., greatest sound, 6870
nature's fragile v., 3868
now is v. full of grief, 3151
preserve v. for my lord, 7106
this bravest v. in world, 4485
thou show'st a noble v.. 269
you are the weaker v., 6869
Vessels : women, weaker v., 7292
Vestal : ne'er touch'd v., 6980
v. throned by west, 1716
Vestals : love-lacking v., 1249
Vesture : muddy v. of decay, 3273
napless v. of humility, 3641
Vexing ear of drowsy man, 4133
Vials : from v. pour graces, 699
where be the sacred v., 4244
Viands sparkling in golden cup, 5899
Vice, 6871-6883
apparel v. like virtue, 6878
canker v. buds doth love, 6875
clothe from such filthy v., 2369
daub'd his v. with virtue, 6728
duteous to v. of mistress, 6898
his v. to virtue equinox, 6881
in v. their law's their will, 3893
no motion tends to v., 7301
no v. but assumes virtue, 6880
no v. but beggary, 580
run from brakes of v., 5965
v. by action dignified, 6882
v. inhabits blood, 3726
v. like wandering wind, 6874
v. that most I do abhor, 6872

v. you should have spoke, 6965
virtue itself turns v., 6882
virtue of v. pardon beg, 6879
weed my v., let his grow, 6873
you have a v. of mercy, 4647
Vices : bolder v., 6877
pleasant v. instruments, 3052
small v. appear, 6871
what a mansion have v. got, 6876
Victory, 6884-6888
death's dishonourable v., 4819
either v. or a grave, 6885
harder match'd, greater v., 6887
to whom God will the v., 6886
upon your sword sit v., 6884
v. is twice itself, 6888
Vigilant as cat to steal, 1113
Vile : be he ne'er so v., 3540
better v. than v. esteemed, 6890
liest with v. in beds, 6019
nought so v. on earth, 3078
v. will not love country, 1032
wisdom, goodness to v. v., 6889
Vileness is so, 3070
Villain, 6891-6907
arrant v. and Jacksauce, 5625
base dunghill v., 4031
bloody bawdy v., 6896
determined to prove a v., 6906
he's a v. and traitor, 7536
hungry lean-faced v., 6893
I am v. of the earth, 6891
I would not be a v., 6899
ne'er a v. but he's knave, 6895
play the v., 6904
remorseless v., 6896
smile and be a v., 6044
smiling damned v., 6044
thou art a v., 3298
thou art a wicked v., 3090
unnatural brutish v., 6897
v. and he be miles apart, 6907
v. kills my father, 5641
v., thou wilt be condemned, 6901
v. with smiling cheek, 6136
which is the v., 6903
who calls me v., 1634
whoreson valiant v., 2510
you are a v., I jest not, 1170
Villains : flesh'd v., dogs, 1461
rich v. need poor ones, 6900
slandered by v., 6902
stony-hearted v., 7169
v. by necessity, 6245
v., vipers, damned, 6905
Villany, 6908-6912
no visor becomes black v., 2725
nothing level but v., 6912
O v., let door be locked, 6908
there is v. abroad, 6910
thus I clothe my v., 2032
v. goes against stomach, 6909
v. I bid thee do perform, 6894
v. I'll prove on his body, 2680
v. is not without rheum, 6463
v. you teach I'll execute, 6911
Vine : eat under own v., 2297
her v. unpruned dies, 6914
thou art elm, I the v., 6913

Vinegar : borrow mess of v., 6916
of such v. aspect, 4916
v. and pepper in it, 1173
Vines of France, 6915
Viol-de-gamboys : plays v., 1213
Violation : hot forcing v., 4463
Violence may trumpet to world, 4306
v. of action, 5905
v. thee becomes, 5772
Violet, 6918-6920
forward v. did I chide, 6920
throw perfume on the v., 2375
v. in youth of nature, 6918
v. smells to him as to me, 3878
where nodding v. grows, 2761
Violets : bank of v., 4874
daisies pied, v. blue, 1705
from flesh may v. spring, 2737
purple v., marigolds, 2762
v. sweeter than Cytherea, 2767
who are the v. now, 6919
Vipers, damn'd, 6905
Vir sapit qui pauca loquitur, 6173
Virgin, 6921-6924
less valiant than v., 7039
never v. got till virginity lost, 6925
on her v. honour, 4216
v. crimson of modesty, 4464
v. from tender infancy, 3807
withering on v. thorn, 6922
yet a v. she shall pass, 2297
yield my v. patent up, 6922
young budding v., 561
Virgin-knot : break her v., 6924
untied my v. shall keep, 6923
Virginal : tears v., 6460
Virginalling upon palm, 5142
Virginity, 6925-6927
are you meditating on v., 6925
ask if he had my v., 6926
crack the glass of her v., 6927
he had not my v., 6926
loss of v. is increase, 6924
man is enemy to v., 6925
never virgin till v. lost, 6925
rich worth of your v., 4758
Virgins : play with all v., 6921
Virtue, 6928-6946
apparel vice like v., 6878
assume a v. if you have it not, 6933
brake v. must go through, 5315
calumny whitest v. strikes, 1053
can v. hide itself, 6931
change to v., worthiness, 5089
daub'd vice with show of v., 6728
forgive me this my v., 6879
gainst stream of v. strive, 7571
goad to sin in loving v., 6499
he died in v.'s cause, 2520
his vice is to v. equinox, 6881
I see v. in his looks, 2511
I study v. and philosophy, 6294
infinite v., comest smiling, 6929
let not v. seek remuneration, 6945
let virtue be as wax, 7556
no vice but assumes v., 6880
no v. like necessity, 4932
rise by sin, by v. fall, 5965
see thy v. witness'd, 6730
untainted v. of your years, 279

v. accident could not pierce, 4917
v. and cunning endowments, 6942
v. and she is her dower, 2172
v. breeds, iniquity devours, 6944
v. cannot inoculate our stock, 6932
v. in handicrafts-men, 5009
v. is beauty, 6946
v. is bold, 6940
v. is choked with ambition, 6935
v. is patched with sin, 6883
v. itself turns vice, 6882
v. makes women admired, 6936
v. never breaks troth, 6965
v. never seen in you, 5348
v. never will be moved, 6931
v. of so little regard, 6934
v. of the medlar, 2938
v. of vice must pardon beg, 6879
v. of your eye breaks oath, 6865
v. out of emulation, 6938
v. profaned in such a devil, 6943
v. scapes not calumnious strokes, 1051
you nickname v., 6965
Virtues : for several v. liked several
women, 7335
his v. plead like angels, 6939
our v. proud, 4115
two cardinal v., 6937
v. that attend good, 2297
v. we write in water, 4543
world to hide v. in, 7494
Virtuous : I suppose him v., 1214
one woman is v., 7323
v. to be constant, 5035
why are you v., 6930
Visage : devotion's v., 2050
I saw Othello's v., 4306
mask thy monstrous v., 1520
she'll flay thy v., 4884
v. of offence, 4636
Visages do cream and mantle, 5106
Vision : baseless fabric of v., 5639
v. sent from heaven, 3804
Visitings of nature, 5612
Visor : no v. like flattery, 2725
Vizard : never come in v., 7363
virtuous v. hide guile, 1916
Vizards : faces v. to hearts, 2466
Vocation : labour in thy v., 6948
no sin to labour in v., 6947
Voice, 6949-6958
bad v. bode no mischief, 6954
double like v. and echo, 5756
give few thy v., 2261
he has my dying v., 2294
he knows me by bad v., 6951
her v. was ever soft, 6950
I heard a v. cry sleep no more, 6024
is not your v. broken, 7578
manly v. turning to treble, 7466
mellifluous v., 6958
monstrous little v., 6952
no more v. than dogs, 2148
O for a falconer's v., 6956
paramour for sweet v., 5154
season'd with gracious v., 4037
tax not so bad a v., 6953
this is v. of Portia, 6951
thou art too bold of v., 5749
v. of gods make heaven drowsy, 4281

v. of lions, act of hares, 7407
v. of unpaved eunuch, 2358
v. propertied as tuned spheres, 256
v. thunder, looks humble, 6955
Voices: buy men's v., 3197
thank you for your v., 6949
v. would make me sleep, 2190
Volscians: flutter'd V., 2255
Volume of enticing lines, 5226
v. of Paris' face, 2469
Volumes I prize above dukedom, 831
Votaress: imperial v. passed on, 1716
Vow, 6959-6969
deep-divorcing v., 2145
my v. was earthly, 6964
plain v. vow'd true, 6959
solemn v. to rob a man, 5052
v. nor space hath sting, 4284
when I v., I weep, 6967
Vows: do not believe his v., 6962
God keep all v. unbroke, 5061
gods deaf to peevish v., 6968
his v. are brokers, 6962
men's v. women's traitors, 6961

mouth-made v. break, 6960
much in v., little in love, 7339
religion makes v. kept, 5602
suck'd honey of his music v., 4681
unheedful v. may be broken, 6969
v. are but breath, 6964
v. brokers to defiling, 6963
v. for thee broke, 6964
v. made in wine, 2498
v. men have broke, 6966
v. of faith, 4987
v. of women of no bondage, 7300
v. to every purpose not hold, 6968
v. to the blackest devil, 1768
you give away heaven's v., 4552
Voyage: life's uncertain v., 3868
v. of their life, 6591
Vulcan: foul as V.'s stithy, 3703
V. is a rare carpenter, 3767
Vulgar, 6970-6972
base and obscure v., 1040
drive v. from the streets, 6971
v. drench their limbs, 6971
Vultures gripe thy guts, 3187

W

Wafer-cakes: faiths are w., 5051
Wag: bid sorrow w., 3449
how now, mad w., 3605
shall we w., 1975
Wages: ere thy w. spent, 1533
home art gone, ta'en thy w., 2240
Waggon-spokes of slippers' legs, 4434
Waggoner a small gnat, 4434
Waist: from w. Centaurs, 7317
girdled with w. of iron, 2009
I would my w. slenderer, 7018
not eagle's talon in w., 3955
Waiting-gentlewoman: like a w., 4225
make him my w., 475
Wake: between w. and sleep, 3417
Wakes: w. and wassails, 7237
Wales: madcap Prince of W., 3613
Prince of W. joins world, 3614
sword-and-buckler Prince of W., 5354
you Prince of W., 3875
Walk: I am yours for the w., 6977
let her not w. in sun, 1804
let me see thee w., 6978
men must not w. too late, 6975
w. a turn together, 6787
w. about orb like sun, 2782
w. before me toward sea-side, 3427
w. in absence of the sun, 4988
w. in black brow of night, 6974
with fern-seed w. invisible, 4973
Walked: Banquo w. too late, 6974
w. in their sleep, 6976
Walks till first cock, 2661
w. up and down with me, 3153
when he w. he moves like engine, 6973
Wall: close w. with dead, 901
patch w. to expel winter's flaw, 1017
weaker vessels thrust to w., 7292
weakest goes to the w., 7038
Wallet: time hath w. at back, 6642
Walls: painting outward w., 6145
w. of beaten brass, 6200

Walnut: searched w. for leman, 3778
Wand-like straight, 7142
Wanderers of the dark, 4976
Want, 6980-6984
he shall w. some, 6982
in w. friend doth try, 2922
w. will perjure vestal, 6980
what I w. boots not, 6983
why w., 6984
worth the w. you wanted, 5070
you w. much of meat, 6984
Wanted, more wonder'd at, 6317
Wanton: cocker'd silken w., 874
how w. ye appear, 2348
lip w. in secure couch, 6989
play w. with your woes, 6469
too w. and full of gawds, 6322
w. as a child, 4283
w. as youthful goats, 3613
w. dalliance with paramour, 5152
w. more than beseems a man, 6829
w. with a velvet brow, 6985
your worship is a w., 6986
Wantonness, 6985-6989
gravity's revolt to w., 7216
make w. your ignorance, 5135
pride is fasting in w., 5424
sad as night for w., 5773
suspect thee with w., 6988
w. is scared out of him, 6987
Wantons: let w. tickle rushes, 1782
Wants: supply w. of friend, 837
War, 6990-7015
at w. 'twixt will and will not, 6872
circumstance of glorious w., 2633
consider the chance of w., 6993
dedicate to w. no self-love, 6999
dogged w. bristles crest, 7001
edge of w. no more shall cut, 6994
end of w. uncertain, 6992
fall off my chance of w., 4809
gallant head of w., 7003

grim-visaged w., 7005
he had whole theoric of w., 6991
impious w., array'd in flames, 6998
in w. I have slain men, 4851
in w. was never lion raged, 4191
laws cruel, what w. be, 7007
let me have w., say I, 7009
list his discourse of w., 6997
never w. ceased ere bloody, 7010
no more w. channel fields, 6994
stuffed with epithets of w., 1347
to a cruel w. I sent him, 5045
trial of a woman's w., 7445
unknit knot of w., 6996
w. and lechery confound, 3952
w. exceeds peace, 7009
w. is his beadle, 3029
w. no strife to detested wife, 7122
w. nor quarrel in question, 7012
w. of lilies and roses, 762
w. of red and white, 762
w. of white and damask, 1258
w. or peace familiar, 7011
w. said to be a ravisher, 7009
w., thou son of hell, 6999
w.'s prize to take vantages, 7000
with child by tyrant w., 5755
Warble, child, 3323
Ward : best w. of honour, 5613
one knows not at what w., 7336
Wardrobe : dalliance in w., 7561
Wards : lock it in w. of bosom, 1984
Ware : bed of W., 4102
Wares : show our foulest w., 4634
Warming-pan : office of w., 2456
Warrant for thy death, 3708
w. in that theft, 6519
w. of an oath, 5060
Warrener : fought a w., 6252
Warrior : thou art my w., 7014
w. famoused for fight, 7015
Warriors fought upon clouds, 5097
Wars : bred i' the w., 3996
is not there w., 589
now for our Irish w., 3853
thinking of civil w., 2566
to the w., to the w., 6990
to w. to try fortune, 3501
w. that make ambition virtue, 2533
Wart : many a w. richer, 1297
Warwick : retire, if W. bid stay, 6336
smile when W. bent brow, 3886
W. bug that fear'd us all, 967
Wash : I will go w., 754
w. it white as snow, 3210
Wasp : in thy hive a w., 7016
let not the w. outlive, 3523
Wasp-stung, impatient fool, 2805
Waspish : when you are w., 3372
Wasps : injurious w., 7017
Wassail : king keeps w., 1749
Wassails : at w., markets, 7237
Waste : beauty's w. hath end, 526
your w. is great, 7018
Watch : some must w., some sleep, 7469
w. me like Argus, 7021
w. night in storms, 3670
w. thou and wake, 7020
w. tonight, pray tomorrow, 7019
winding up w. of his wit, 7251

Watch-case or 'larum bell, 6019
Watching breeds leanness, 2965
Watchman to my heart, 4079
Water, 7022-7025
be he fire, I'll be w., 2700
can w. decoct cold blood, 709
drop of w. seeks another, 7467
fall away like w., 2907
honest w. ne'er left man in mire, 7024
indistinct as w. in w., 1380
more w. glideth by mill, 7025
my tears prove holy w., 6456
not all w. in rough sea, 3899
put little w. in a spoon, 1771
rocky heart to w. will not wear, 6465
salt w. blinds them, 6471
smooth runs w. brook deep, 7022
throw cold w. on thy choler, 1309
too much of w. hast thou, 6458
too weak to be sinner, honest w., 7024
virtues we write in w., 4543
w. cannot wash away sin, 5278
w. cools not love, 4338
w. her chamber round, 4343
w. swells a man, 2213
world of w. shed, 7129
Water-drops : melt in w., 3905
waste stones with w., 6628
when w. have worn, 2506
women's weapons, w., 6464
Water-flies blow me, 1840
Water-pots : eyes for w., 2424
Water-spaniel : more qualities than w., 1324
Water-thieves, land-thieves, 5295
Watering : breathe in your w., 2202
Waters : call her w. tears, 6452
put wild w. in roar, 7029
trust not w. of his eyes, 6463
unpath'd w., 5797
w. I would have stopp'd, 6459
Wave : salt w. of Mediterranean, 7236
w. of the sea, 1784
Waves : as good chide w., 7026
w. make toward pebbled shore, 4711
wild w. whist, 5795
wild w. with clouds contend, 7030
yesty w. swallow navigation, 7027
Wawl : we w. and cry, 668
Wax : bleeds as forms of w., 1870
but as a form in w., 2572
nor w. nor honey bring, 4114
softer than w., 4311
then her w. must melt, 5590
thighs packed with w., 6084
thy shape is but w., 7031
'tis the bee's w. stings, 565
what w. but dissolves, 7032
Way, 7033-7037
count thy w. with sighs, 7037
flowery w. to great fire, 2962
I have lost my w. among thorns, 7035
I have lost my w. forever, 7034
longest w. shall have moans, 7037
make their w. seem short, 1455
making hard w. sweet, 2077
piece w. with heavy heart, 7037
plain as w. to church, 7111
primrose w. to bonfire, 7033
surest w. to get, 1985

take the instant w., 3557
that's the eftest w., 7036
there lies your w., 7092
thorny w. to heaven, 5187
thou didst teach the w., 5973
w. is but short, 4052
w. to dusty death, 4137
w. to kill a wife with kindness, 7143
Ways : go thy w., 2104
money go before, all w. open, 4764
Waywarder : wiser the w., 7225
Waywardness years bring, 150
Weak heart of woman, 7314
Weaker than a woman's tear, 7039
Weakest goes to the wall, 7038
Weakness : cannot avoid, w. to fear, 2313
w. married to stronger, 6913
Wealth, 7040-7041
be from w. exempt, 7041
cannot sum up half my w., 4324
I seek not to gather w., 1606
let man outlive w., 2874
show w. of thy wit, 7238
some glory in their w., 4329
thy father's w. was motive, 7266
w. ran in my veins, 2973
who cannot keep w., 7040
Wealthy in my friends, 2918
Weapon, 7042-7044
behold, I have a w., 7044
kill with w., not words, 7429
with w. nothing perform, 7405
Weapons : hurt with same w., 3797
men broken w. use, 7043
put w. in madman's hands, 7042
w. I laugh to scorn, 6399
women's w., water-drops, 6464
Weariness, 7045-7049
w. can snore upon flint, 7046
w. durst not attach high blood, 7047
Weary : how w. are my spirits, 7045
I am dog-w., 7049
I am exceeding w., 7047
was ever man so w., 7048
w., stale, flat, 7468
Weasel : quarrelous as w., 5490
w. hath not such spleen, 262
Weather, 7050-7053
builds in w. on wall, 4839
fair w. you make yourself, 7052
foul w. when you're cloudy, 7053
I must make fair w., 7050
left me bare to w., 6731
make foul w. with tears, 6469
many can brook the w., 7051
no enemy but rough w., 6729
two women make cold w., 7310
Weathercock : invisible as w., 3794
what w. is he, 2630
Weaver : draw souls out of w., 7087
would I were a w., 7470
Web : gives w. and pin, 2661
his self-drawing w., 6192
w. of life of mingled yarn, 4115
Wed : none w. second but kill'd first, 3661
w. to one half lunatic, 1814
Wedding is Juno's crown, 3674
w. is mannerly-modest, 7369
Wedding-bed : grave to be w., 3113
Wedding-ring : from hand cut w., 2145

Wedges : blunt w. rive knots, 3973
w. of gold, anchors, 2216
Wedlock : as pigeons bill, w. nibbling, 4553
high w. shall be honoured, 3674
what is w. forced but a hell, 4559
your mother true to w., 4818
Wednesday : he that died o' W., 3539
W. in Wheeson week, 4558
Weed, 7054-7065
basest w. outbraves dignity, 2765
fat w. roots on Lethe, 7055
gather honey from w., 3074
thou w. art so lovely, 7061
Weeder-out of adversaries, 5129
Weeding : lets grow the w., 7060
Weeds : he w. the corn, 7060
idle w. fast in growth, 7064
idle w. grow in our corn, 4453
lilies smell worse than w., 2765
root away noisome w., 7063
spread compost on w., 7056
subject is fattest soil to w., 7057
unwholesome w. take root, 7062
we bring forth w., 7054
w. are shallow-rooted, 7058
w. do grow apace, 7064
w. make haste, 7064
w. that beseem page, 3191
what cherishes w. but air, 7059
Week : what, keep a w. away, 5
Weep : better to w. at joy, 7072
come w. with me, 7073
ere they shall make us w., 7071
I am soldier, unapt to w., 6068
I'll w. for nothing, 7067
I'll w. what's left away, 497
look, they w., 7066
O lady,w. no more, 7068
she can w., sir, w., 6788
so dear I loved, I must w., 6728
to w. is to make less grief, 7069
w. as 'twere a man born, 7074
would it not make one w., 7107
you think I'll w., 7070
Weeper : make the w. laugh, 6665
Weeping, 7066-7075
does that bode w., 2435
evermore w. for cousin, 3169
I am not prone to w., 7075
I have full cause of w., 7070
wondering fall to w., 7427
Weigh : you w. equally, 2631
Weight : heavy w. from head, 1687
need no w. than bowels, 4050
w. of carrion flesh, 2741
w. of hair turn scales, 3195
w. of this sad time, 6172
Welcome, 7076-7084
appurtenance of w., 7078
as stranger give it w., 6283
at first and last hearty w., 3600
bear w. in your eye, 7080
morn to lark less w., 7077
never w. till shot paid, 7083
out of silence I picked w., 5955
sir, you are very w., 7081
small cheer great w., feast, 7076
to me w. you are, 4040
w. as is the spring, 7084

w. ever smiles, 7082
w. these pleasant days, 4128
w. which comes to punish, 2548
you're w., my fair guests, 7079
Welcomes : premeditated w., 5955
Welkin, 7085-7087
amaze w. with staves, 7086
by w. and her star, 5645
let the w. roar, 7085
rattle the w.'s ear, 2221
shall we make w. dance, 7087
starry w. cover thee anon, 680
threatening w. with face, 5828
Well : all shall be w., 5463
all yet seems w., 6379
all's w. that ends w., 2301
not so deep as a w., 3655
w. that owes two buckets, 1686
Well-favoured gift of fortune, 5568
Welsh : devil understands W., 2025
no man speaks better W., 659
thy tongue makes W. sweet, 3919
Wench, 7088-7091
brown w. lay kissing, 614
fair hot w. in taffeta, 6615
God make me a light w., 7090
good w. for this gear, 2872
ill-starr'd w., pale, 6140
kitchen w. all grease, 7089
misbehaved sullen w., 695
stabbed with w.'s black eye, 1892
w. married in afternoon, 4566
w. of excellent discourse, 7088
Wenches : light w. will burn, 4152
marry, they get w., 2203
Wept like two children, 1561
West : there your way, due w., 7092
w. glimmers with streaks of day, 6708
Westward-ho : then w., 7092
Wether : tainted w. of flock, 1879
Whale : like a w. on ground, 1203
very like a w., 1381
w. plays and tumbles, 4736
What : I tell thee w., 1336
I'll tell thee w., 625
Wheat : mildews the w., 2661
two grains of w., 5583
when w. is green, 6669
Wheel, 7093-7095
bound upon w. of fire, 7094
dry w. grate on axle-tree, 5348
fortune, turn thy w., 2869
fortune's fickle w., 2864
great w. that goes up-hill, 7093
let go when w. runs downhill, 7093
massy w. fix'd on summit, 4474
thoughts whirled like potter's w., 6559
w. is come full circle, 7095
Whelp : playing with lion's w., 4172
Where : I know not w. I am, 6559
Wherefore : why and w., 5671
Whetstone of the wits, 2792
Whip : I have been love's w., 1714
put in every hand a w., 6002
Whipped with wire, 1733
Whippers are in love, 4250
Whipping : who should scape w., 1983
Whips : keen w. I'll wear, 1238
w. and scorns of time, 1847
Whipster : every w. gets sword, 6404

Whirligig of time, 6644
Whirlpool : ford and w., 1407
Whirlwinds : bless thee from w., 694
Whisper, 7096-7098
never admitted private w., 7096
w. one another in ear, 7097
Whispering : is w. nothing, 5034
Whisperings : foul w. abroad, 7098
Whistle : let law go w., 4045
worth the w., 7507
White : made of w. and red, 2590
wash it w. as snow, 3210
w. as driven snow, 7099
w. as whale's bone, 6483
w. that shall blackness fit, 681
White-livered and red faced, 4208
w. runagate, 4211
Whiteness in thy cheek is apter, 7100
Whiter than paper, 3226
w. than the sheets, 4168
Whites : all w. are ink, 3229
Whither away, 512, 1972
Whole as the marble, 2167
w. swallowed in confusion, 4237
Whore, 7101-7110
be a w. still, 7110
common w. of mankind, 3066
cunning w. of Venice, 7106
ever your fresh w., 7102
he call'd her w., 7107
I cannot say w., 7108
leave thy drink and thy w., 604
like w. unpack my heart, 341
mad that trusts w.'s oath, 4451
never name her if she be w., 7103
talked of w. of Babylon, 5665
this fell w. of thine, 7109
this is a subtle w., 7105
why lash that w., 7101
why should he call her w., 7107
Whored : he w. my mother, 2293
Whoremaster : is w. I deny, 2512
Whoresons have trick, 6093
Why, 7111-7114
every w. has a wherefore, 7112
in w. and wherefore, 5671
w. and wherefore in all things, 7114
w. is plain as way to church, 7111
w. is this, wherefore, 7113
Wick or snuff abate it, 4263
Wicked : I have been w., 2748
something w. comes, 6581
Wickedness : children know w., 1290
thy audacious w., 7116
what rein can hold w., 7115
w. is sin, 1602
Wide as church-door, 3655
Widow, 7117-7121
be a w. maker, 7119
distressed w., 7120
enforce a poor w., 7117
he'll have a lusty w., 7121
how content this w. lady, 7118
I am poor w. of Eastcheap, 7117
lady w. of Vitruvio, 7118
makes wappen'd w. wed, 3066
neither maid, w., nor wife, 4468
never w. had so dear a loss, 4238
no longer than w. weeps, 4774
so came I a w., 3618

thou art a w., 4816
wring w. from her right, 5052
Widow-comfort : my w., 6086
Widower : he'll prove a w., 7163
Widows : each morn w. howl, 6108
many w. shall this mock, 4754
Wife, 7122-7145
  damn'd in a fair w., 7140
  evened w. for w., 5649
  fartuous modest w., 7137
  get thee a w., 7139
  I am your w., if you will, 3672
  I sue, I seek a w., 7134
  kill a w. with kindness, 7143
  kisses my w. is my friend, 1699
  lie with neighbour's w., 1513
  light w., heavy husband, 7136
  look to your w., 7141
  make me lady thy w., 4558
  man and w. one flesh, 4529
  mulier is this constant w., 7128
  my true honourable w., 7132
  my w. is a hobby-horse, 7145
  my w. is shrewish, 7124
  my w. seem'd the nonpareil, 5018
  my w. was like this maid, 7142
  neither maid, widow nor w., 4468
  rare w. makes paradise, 5148
  remember thou hast a w., 5153
  reports he has better w., 7131
  tedious as a railing w., 6431
  thy w. holds thee in awe, 7130
  time to corrupt man's w., 7126
  war no strife to detested w., 7122
  what nearer debt than w., 7144
  w. and babes slaughtered, 1289
  w. as dear as life, 7135
  w., gracious silence, hail, 7125
  w. of such wood felicity, 679
  w. with such a wit, 7226
  w.'s wit to neighbour's bed, 7226
  your w. is like to reap, 5570
Wight : base Hungarian w., 6444
  w. of high renown, 5420
Wights : venomous w., 5000
Wild-cats in your kitchens, 7325
Wild-duck : valour than w., 1636
Wild-fowl : more fearful w., 4188
Wild-geese : if w. fly, 7201
Wild-goose chase, 7258
Wilderness : live in this w., 4933
  thou wilt be w. again, 3912
  warped slip of w., 7147
  w. is populous enough, 7146
Wiles that women work, 7330
  wit to defend my w., 7336
Wilful-blame : too w., 4542
Wilfulness : Hydra-headed w., 7153
Will, 7148-7162
  at war 'twixt w. and w. not, 6872
  bid sick man make his w., 7162
  cloyed w. longs after garbage, 7151
  his w. in feeble body, 7155
  his w. is not his own, 657
  I did it on my free w., 7148
  I ne'er made my w. yet, 7160
  ill w. never said well, 7154
  made his w. and read it, 7159
  make his w. his act, 3126
  make his w. lord of reason, 7149

make my w. as sick do, 7161
my good w. is great, 6510
what I w. I w., 7158
what is your w., 7160
whoever hath wish, thou hast W., 7157
w. hears no heedful friends, 7156
w. mutiny with wit's regard, 1570
w. of heaven be done, 3397
w. of man by reason sway'd, 5575
w. to die by himself, 1843
w. you, nill you, 4565
Willow, 7163-7166
  I'll wear a w. garland, 7163
  offered my company to a w., 7164
  sing all a green w., 7165
  w. grows aslant a brook, 2959
Wills : blest that have w., 7150
  let's talk of w., 1431
  mention it in their w., 6503
  w. and fates contrary run, 7152
Win : furious when you w., 7199
  I shall w. at the odds, 7192
  I shall w. of you, 7198
  nothing foul to those that w., 7193
  they laugh that w., 4024
  unjustly w.,5956
  what shall I do to w., 7200
  why so hard to w., 7197
  w. me and wear me, 7195
  wrongly w., 4911
Wind, 7165-7177
  as large charter as the w., 4085
  beggar'd by strumpet w., 5447
  blow, w., come, wrack, 1873
  blow w., swell billow, 3308
  borne with invisible w., 5780
  embraced by strumpet w., 5447
  endure w. and weather, 2473
  foul w. but foul breath, 7440
  hey, ho, w. and rain, 5536, 7231
  how true he keeps the w., 2956
  I shall break my w., 7169
  if w. and fuel be brought, 6153
  ill w. blows no man good, 7172
  ill w. that profits nobody, 7173
  is not your w. short, 7578
  is the w. in that door, 7170
  making w. my post-horse, 5755
  moves both w. and tide, 6275
  my w. cooling my broth, 7175
  pass me as the idle w., 6570
  resist w. and tide, 2551
  run upon sharp w. of north, 1001
  sits the w. in that corner, 7170
  something in the w., 7167
  such w. as scatters young men, 7176
  sweet w. did kiss trees, 4987
  unruly w. within womb, 4906
  what w. blew you hither, 7172
  w. is northerly, 1405
  w. sits in shoulder of sail, 7168
  w. sore upon our sails, 6495
  w. takes mountain pine, 4900
  w. to make me chatter, 5535
  winnow'd with rough w., 7171
  words are but w., 7415
Wind-instruments : these w., 6416
Winding-sheet : for a w., 3108
Windlasses and assays, 3715
Windmill : with cheese in w., 6431

Window of the east, 6327
Windowed in great Rome, 5886
Windows : downy w. close, 1842
her two blue w., 2449
it would not out at w., 6132
Winds : blow me about in w., 6140
blow, w., crack cheeks, 7174
call w. and waters sighs, 6432
call'd forth mutinous w., 6331
if w. rage, sea wax mad, 5828
rough w. shake buds of May, 6316
w. blow till wakened death, 6494
w. grow high, so stomachs, 6263
w. rived knotty oaks, 6493
w. were love-sick, 429
Windy side of the law, 4044
Wine, 7178-7186
crush a cup of w., 7185
cup of w., brisk and fine, 3387
cup of w. with no Tiber, 7179
give me a bowl of w., 6821
give me w., fill full, 7182
good w. is a good creature, 7184
good w. needs no bush, 5328
he drinks no w., 7181
let liver heat with w., 4721
marvellous searching w., 7180
spirited with w., 709
stuff'd with w., 2061
thou invisible spirit of w., 7184
w. hath steep'd sense, 7178
w. loved I deeply, 1205
w. of life is drawn, 7182
Wing : dragon w. of night, 5001
on the w. of occasions, 7188
Wings : flies with swallow's w., 3574
from Cupid pluck his w., 6147
no w. to fly from God, 3029
pluck w. from butterflies, 1005
w. fleeter than arrows, 6667
w. more swift than thought, 5000
w. of protector's grace, 7187
w. swift as meditation, 5640
with batty w., 6029
with love's w. o'erperch, 4318
Wink : when most I w., best see, 7190
w. at me and say, 7191
w. on her to consent, 7189
yet do they w. and yield, 4391
you to perpetual w., 4805
Winking : consent w., 7189
on w. of authority, 3888
w., leap'd to destruction, 3565
Winners : beshrew the w., 4234
Winning : light w., prize light, 5443
w. puts man into courage, 7199
Winnowed : thoroughly w., 5074
Winter, 7201-7205
barren w., nipping cold, 1101
biting w. mars our hay, 1963
burn a Poland w., 7089
chide rough w., 2763
cooled by the same w., 3797
how like w. thy absence, 8
lust's w. comes ere summer, 4433
no enemy but w., 6729
take w. from your lips, 4203
this side is Hiems, w., 7202
when leaves fall, w. at hand, 7204
w. is not gone yet, 7201

w. of our discontent, 7203
w. tames man, woman, beast, 7205
Winterly keep countenance, 4952
Winters : four lagging w., 7392
six w. are quickly gone, 3163
when forty w. shall besiege, 7586
worn so many w. out, 3905
Wires : if hairs be w., 4749
Wisdom, 7206-7214
by w. make prince servant, 1578
censure me in your w., 1032
cold w. waiting on folly, 7215
dress'd in w., gravity, 5106
folly in w. hatch'd, 7216
God give them w., 2821
in w. never was so frail, 7212
we of w. and reach, 3715
w. and blood combatting, 731
w. and fortune combatting, 7206
w. and goodness to vile, 6889
w. cries in the streets, 7208
w. of the world, 6776
w. subject to fears, 2608
w. that doth guide valour, 4913
w. wishes to appear bright, 7210
Wise : be w. and circumspect, 7428
converse with w., 5844
exceeding w., 1204
I know you w., 7305
learn of the w., perpend, 7207
not one w. will praise self, 5395
reputed w. for saying nothing, 7211
she is w. if I can judge, 4286
to be w. and love, 4384
to w. ports, happy havens, 7214
who can be w., amazed, 4381
w. enough to play fool, 2822
w. man knows self a fool, 2818
w. men give fools money, 2823
w. men have no eyes, 2266
w. men ne'er wail woes, 7279
w. men taint their wit, 2822
w. so young never live long, 7568
Wisely and slow, 3291
Wiser, the waywarder, 7226
Wish, 7217-7223
at high w., 4743
best I w. thee, 7223
thy w. I w. thee, 7221
w. father to that thought, 7219
w. of happy years, 7222
Wishers were ever fools, 7218
Wishes : if w. could prevail, 7220
your sheets privy to w., 7217
Wit, 7224-7256
better witty fool than foolish w., 7259
cause w. is in other men, 7228
halfpenny purse of w., 5225
hath w. to lose his hair, 3193
he is w.'s peddler, 7237
he that has tiny w., 7231
her words show her w., 4755
his eye begets occasion for w., 7233
his w. makes valour live, 1036
his w. thick as mustard, 7229
if black and hath a w., 7245
keep where there is w., 5686
lie on w. to defend wiles, 7336
moral of my w. is plain, 6781
more hair than w., 3193

most incony vulgar w., 7235
ne'er ware of my own w., 7224
no more w. than Christian, 7254
not so much w. as will stop eye, 7252
pared thy w. o' both sides, 7230
pecks up w. as pigeons pease, 7237
prove by w. worth, 7216
quick venue of w., 7236
repair thy w., 7239
she had a green w., 7232
she hath Dian's w., 1722
show thy w. in instant, 7238
skirmish of w., 7241
sparks that are like w., 6154
take little w. from them, 3812
that does harm to my w., 7254
thousand escapes of w., 5317
thy w. a bitter sweeting, 7258
thy w. quick as greyhound, 7244
thy w. set afire by ignorance, 7249
to play fool craves w., 2822
wants w. that wants will, 6969
we work by w., 7246
wears w. in his belly, 7252
what w. could w. have, 7226
when w. is come to harvest, 5570
wife with such a w., 7226
winding up watch of his w., 7251
w. depends on time, 7246
w. enough to keep self warm, 7242
w. enough to lie straight, 5470
w. made Jack-a-Lent, 7240
w. nor reason can passion hide, 4385
w. of cheveril stretches, 7258
w. put me into fooling, 7259
w. shall not go unrewarded, 6258
w. that fools have silenced, 2817
w. turn'd fool, 7216
w. waits on fear, 1796
w. wedged in blockhead, 7227
w., whither wilt, 7226
w. will not hurt a woman, 7244
w. would be out of fashion, 7253
w.'s grace to grace fool, 7216
with witchcraft of his w., 5861
within compass of man's w., 7247
woman's w. will out, 7226
you have a nimble w., 7225
your w. ambles well, 7243
your w. is too hot, 7234
your w. lies in sinews, 7252
Wit-crackers: college of w., 625
Witch, 7267-7270
aroint thee, w., 7270
foul w. Sycorax, 7272
out of my door, you w., 7271
see how w. doth bend, 7268
thou art a w., 2028
w. ladies with my words, 3396
Witchcraft: he thought 'twas w., 1914
let w. join with beauty, 1219
pots of damned w., 1225
this gallant had w., 3588
this is only w. I used, 4305
we work by wit, not w., 7246
what a hell of w. lies, 6465
with w. of his wit, 5861
you have w. in your lips, 4195
Witches: soul-killing w., 7267
Withers: our w. are unwrung, 3770

wrung in the w., 3770
Witness: be w., blessed moon, 4779
bleeding w. of her hatred, 3297
evil producing holy w., 6136
Witnesses: you w. above, 4346
Wits, 7257-7266
bless thy five w., 6651
dainty bits bankrupt w., 2546
have good w. to answer for, 7260
his w. are gone, 7264
his w. are not so blunt, 3511
his w. begin to unsettle, 7263
his w. lost in calamities, 7265
home-keeping youth have homely
    w., 7574
keen encounter of w., 7257
my w. begin to turn, 7262
not in his perfect w., 7261
shallow jesters, bavin w., 3876
sorrows overwhelmed his w., 7266
thy w. run wild-goose chase, 7258
w. do often prove fools, 7259
Witty: cry that's w., 5334
not only w. in myself, 7228
w., courteous, liberal, 6069
w. mother, witless son, 7250
w. piece of Eve's flesh, 7255
w. without affection, 5582
Wive it wealthily, 4564
Wives: have revolted w., 1703
poison'd by their w., 3901
sky changes when w., 4460
w. are sold by fate, 4293
w. merry yet honest too, 7138
Wiving goes by destiny, 3244
Wizards know their times, 7269
Woe, 7273-7280
cry w., destruction, 1888
fellowship in w., 7275
midwife to my w., 7277
my soul is full of w., 737
one w. treads upon another, 7273
sour w. delights in fellowship, 7275
what is but grief and w., 7274
w. doth heavier sit, 7276
w. is me, 4681
w. to land governed by child, 1282
w. to w. join'd, 7277
w. unto the birds, 5591
Woes: attorneys to me, 7448
what tide of w. comes, 7278
wise men ne'er wail w., 7279
with old w. wail waste, 5608
w. I am bound to bear, 6854
w. roll forward like flood, 3161
w. serve for discourses, 7280
Wolf, 7281-7286
be comrade with the w., 4929
belly-pinched w., 4975
false as w. to calf, 2506
he would not be a w., 7285
I will hunt this w., 3652
inclined as ravenous w., 7284
mad that trusts in w., 4451
many lambs might w. betray, 7286
question with the w., 3798
wake not a sleeping w., 7282
who does the w. love, 7281
w. behowls the moon, 4674
w. hang'd for slaughter, 5483

w. in greediness, 1205
w. in sheep's array, 7283
w. where lamb may get, 5110
w. who's howl'd his watch, 4846
Wolsey trod ways of glory, 6450
Wolves : affable w., 5155
as salt as w. in pride, 5802
better fall to lion than w., 5381
howling of w. against moon, 3633
peopled with w., 3912
they will eat like w., 4589
Wolvish, bloody, 5483
Woman, 7287-7343
an excellent thing in w., 6950
be a w., 7321
be w. to feed her lamp, 7337
clamours of a jealous w., 7299
constant, but yet a w., 7305
devil will not eat a w., 7291
die a w. with grieving, 3352
do you not know I am a w., 7293
easily win a w.'s heart, 4182
fine w., fair w., 7327
for thy understanding, a w., 7318
forced me to play the w., 6461
frailty, thy name is w., 2888
good w. born at earthquake, 7287
goodliest w. that ever lay by man, 7311
honest w. given to lie, 7290
honest w. of her word, 3081
how weak the heart of w., 7314
I am no w., I'll not swoon, 4965
I could cry like a w., 7202
I could play the w., 7320
I grant I am a w., 7312
less than an honest w., 3510
let w. take an elder, 3673
love w. for singing, 7580
man delights not me, nor w., 4487
man that's of w. born, 6399
most unhappy w. living, 6815
never fair w. but made mouths, 7315
never fair w. has true face, 2453
no more but e'en a w., 7288
no other but w.'s reason, 5579
no w. in Salique land, 3727
none of w. born shall harm Macbeth, 806
nothing of w. in me, 7289
O perjured w., 5232
one good w. in ten, 7287
one that was a w., 7304
one w. fair, yet I am well, 7323
one w. not in my grace, 7323
poor lone w., 7306
speaks small like a w., 6176
sweet w. leads ill life, 3663
tiger's heart in w.'s hide, 7308
unseemly w. in seeming man, 4534
was ever w. in this humour won, 7362
when a w. woos, 7371
who is 't can read a w., 7303
win any w. in the world, 7368
with tongue win a w., 6682
w. Brutus took to wife, 7312
w. conceived me, 390
w. I forswore, 6964
w. is dish for the gods, 7291
w. is like German clock, 7134
w. lost among ye, 1424
w. mannish grown, 4535

w. more worth than any man, 5434
w. moved, fountain troubled, 7333
w. naturally born to fears, 2608
w. scorns what best contents, 7340
w. therefore may be won, 7362
w. to be pitied much, 7309
w. turned into cold fish, 7343
w. well-reputed, 7312
w. when Guinover was wench, 5805
w. with eunuch play'd, 2357
w. with maid by him, 4466
w. would run through fire, ·3348
w.'s fitness comes by fits, 7302
w.'s nay stand for nought, 7328
w.'s shape doth shield thee, 7316
w.'s thought before actions, 6544
yet the w. will be out, 6458
Woman-queller : thou art a w., 5713
Womaned : see me w., 7326
Womb, 7344-7349
accursed w., bed of death, 7346
divorce me from w., 97
ensear thy fertile w., 7349
from earth's dark w., 1385
from kennel of thy w., 7347
from w. untimely ripped, 666
her w. expresseth his tilth, 7345
into her w. sterility, 7344
love forswore me in w., 4266
making their tomb the w., 6866
many events in w. of time, 6626
my w., my w. undoes me, 619
nourished in w. of pia mater, 4628
ripping up w. of England, 2336
slanderous to mother's w., 6811
teeming w. of kings, 2324
thy w. let loose, 7347
tread on thy mother's w., 1590
unear'd w. disdains tillage, 7348
unruly wind within her w., 4906
Wombs : good w., bad sons, 6088
Women : alas, poor w., 7298
framed to make w. false, 7324
hard for w. to keep counsel, 7313
harsh when w. froward, 7334
he did indeed handle w., 7307
I liked several w., 7335
kindness in w. wins my love, 7332
no newly made w. to be had, 7322
O that w. had men's privilege, 7367
other w. cloy appetites, 140
punishment that w. bear, 7297
she is rarest of all w., 5434
teem with w.'s tears, 6468
tell-tale w. rail, 7329
transform us not to w., 7066
two w. make cold weather, 7310
virtue makes w. admired, 6936
vows of w. of no bondage, 7300
wiles and guiles w. work, 7330
w. are angels, wooing, 7360
w. are as roses, 3673
w. are frail as glasses, 7321
w. are made to bear, 7331
w. are shrews, 4657
w. are soft, mild, 7308
w. cannot love where beloved, 4359
w. change shapes, 4525
w. have waxen minds, 4693
w. fall in love with him, 4371

w. fall when no strength, 4533
w. must be half-workers, 4528
w. not in fortunes strong, 6980
w. simple to offer war, 3670
w. the weaker vessels, 7292
w. thrust to the wall, 7292
w. were devils incarnate, 7307
w. will say any thing, 7342
w., yet your beards, 7319
w.'s gentle brain, 7296
w.'s weapons water-drops, 6464
Women-kind : go way of w., 1242
Won : well w. is well shot, 7194
w. as towns with fire, 6292
w. with the first glance, 7197
Wonder, 7350-7354
here is a w., 7354
no w., but certainly maid, 2446
such w. is broke out, 4969
ten days' w. at least, 7352
w. and pointing-stock, 7351
w. in a mortal eye, 2427
w. in extremes, 7352
w. lurketh in men's ears, 6166
w. of the world, 7353
Wonderful, w., most w. w., 7350
w. when angels are angry, 2040
Wondering : from w. fall to weeping, 7427
Wonders : see w. of the world, 7574
Woo : I w. not like babe, 7373
men April when they w., 7360
never will I w. in rhyme, 7363
we were not made to w., 7367
well mayst thou w., 7373
when I come to w., I fright, 2566
w. her, wed her, bed her, 7372
w. her with spirit, 7374
w. in festival terms, 7370
w. those would mischief me, 2925
Wood, 7355-7357
he talks of w., carpenter, 7355
in w. of Crete they bay'd, 4864
in w. where you and I, 7357
lost in thorny w., 1681
yonder stands thorny w., 7356
Wood-birds begin to couple, 6833
Woodbine : lusty w., 2761
Woodcock is near the gin, 7359
w. strives with the gin, 7358
w. to mine own springe, 6225
w., what an ass it is, 4058
Woodcocks : springes to catch w., 6224
Woodman that doth bend bow, 859
Woods more free from peril, 4117
Wooed : as lief be w. of snail, 6051
beautiful, therefore to be w., 7362
I loved you, but w. not, 7367
long ere they are w., 7377
was ever woman in this humour w., 7362
w. and wedded in a day, 7121
w. in haste, wed at leisure, 7375
Wooer : fresh, delicate w., 3067
Wooers : smooth-faced w., 472
Wooes : he w. high and low, 7365
when a woman w., 7371
Wooing, 7360-7377
my w. mind express'd, 7363
our w. not like old play, 7364
women are angels, w., 7360

w. fit for understanding, 7351
w. thee of more value, 7366
w., wedding, repenting, 7369
Wool-sack : how now, w., 1638
Woolen : lie in the w., 475
Word, 7378-7408
answer me in one w., 7379
as good as my w., 7383
bandy w. for w., 3670
damned use w. in hell, 3635
every fool play upon w., 7390
every w. stabs, 6178
he owes for every w., 5452
his w. was Fie, foh, fum, 5743
hob nob is his w., 7394
hopeless w. of never to return, 412
I hate the w. as hell, 5217
I may call back w., 7389
I never spake bad w., 3654
I never will speak w., 2038
I will not eat my w., 7380
I would have kept my w., 7384
I'll take thy w., 5059
I'll talk a w. with Theban, 7386
if my w. be sterling, 2468
ill deeds doubled with evil w., 1921
ill w. empoisons liking, 7391
immodest w. look'd upon, 7282
keep thy w. justly, 2660
keep w. of promise to ear, 2662
lightest w. would harrow soul, 6417
long time in little w., 7392
make it a w. and a blow, 7393
make w. odious, 1090
never sell out this w., 5613
no w. like pardon, 5161
not a w. to throw at a dog, 7378
not such w. as fear, 2602
one sweet w. with thee, 7388
pardon first w. of speech, 5161
pardon is the w. for all, 5157
soldier-like w., 7381
some w. that murder'd me, 415
speak a w. in your ear, 1170
submission mere French w., 6302
this w. froze them up, 5586
this w. shall speak for me, 4931
what, gone without a w., 6782
will you eat your w., 7380
w. debosh'd on every tomb, 3527
w. ill-urged to one ill, 7162
w. is pitch and pay, 5051
w. is well-culled, 7387
w. not short as sweet, 5158
w. of good command, 7381
w. short but sweet, 5161
w. too great for mouth, 7379
w. will Priam turn to stone, 3424
Words, 7409-7457
alms-basket of w., 7431
apt and gracious w., 7233
believe me my w., 7424
bethump'd with w., 7430
better deeds than w., 6782
breath of bitter w., 6688
breathe w. in pain, 7446
court it with w., 7376
cram w. into mine ear, 7451
dally with w., wanton, 7454
deeds to match w., 7408

digest w. with appetite, 5748
dressing old w. new, 7449
envenom him with w., 6854
Ethiope w., blacker, 7296
fair w. in foulest letters, 2863
familiar as household w., 3540
few w. to fair faith, 7450
fewer w. than parrot, 7421
foul w. but foul wind, 7440
foul w. must not repel, 4411
fury in your w., 7443
good w. better than blows, 7385
gracious w. revive thoughts, 6687
haughty w. have batter'd me, 7425
he speaks brave w., 1198
he w. me, girls, 7412
heaven hath my empty w., 5403
her w. all ears took captive, 7411
her w. do show her wit, 4755
his w. are bonds, 6249
his w. are fantastical banquet, 7439
his w. from passion fly, 7456
I hope for high w., 3569
I love not many w., 7409
idle w., servants to fools, 7444
if purgation consist in w., 6721
kill me not with w., 7429
let deeds express w., 7396
let not smoothing w. bewitch, 7428
let not w. accuse zeal, 7445
let's fight with gentle w., 7447
men of few w. best, 7423
mere w., no matter, 7418
my w. fly up, 7419
never learn smoothing w., 6675
not that we love w., 7385
plain w. best pierce ear, 7432
plausive w., 7409
poison with sugar'd w., 5356
purge himself with w., 7416
quench fire of love with w., 4356
sauce her with bitter w., 7413
smoke of w. doth no right, 6050
speak not in w., but woes, 2511
teach a child such w., 7103
these are bitter w., 7422
these w. are razors, 7452
these w. draw life-blood, 7426
these w., like daggers, 7420
these w. my tormentors, 5894
thy w. are bigger, 7417
thy w. become thee, 7434
tire hearer with w., 4404
to be slow in w. virtue, 7341
'twixt friends few w., 7450
unpack my heart with w., 341
unpleasant'st w., 7457
volley of w. quickly shot, 7457
weigh'st thy w., 7442
what care I for w., 7414
why calamity full of w., 7448
w. and performances no kin, 7402
w. are but wind, 7415
w. are no deeds, 7395
w. are strokes, 3987
w. are very rascals, 7455
w. are w., 7441
w. before blows, 7385
w. clad with wisdom, 7427
w. do well, 7414

w. express my pain, 2086
w. expressly are a pound of flesh, 2743
w. let none think flattery, 2722
w. more sweet than baits, 7453
w. of Mercury harsh, 7433
w. of smooth-faced wooers, 472
w. pay no debts, 7406
w. scarce, seldom spent, 7446
w. so false to reason, 7455
w. that should be howl'd, 7435
w. to deeds cold breath, 7400
w. too precious to be cast away, 7378
w. will make thee dumb, 6189
w. without thoughts, 7419
w., w., w., 7418
you but waste your w., 7436
you have exchequer of w., 2379
your w. rob Hybla bees, 7385
Work, 7458-7463
canst w. in earth so fast, 6369
damned and bloody w., 74
does it w. upon him, 7461
every shop yields w., 7463
filthy piece of w., 5274
go to bed to w., 7325
good day's w., 7460
if man's w., I'll do it, 7459
know you of this fair w., 1771
now is my day's w. done, 3423
stair-w., trunk-w., 7462
there's other w. in hand, 7458
Working-day world, 981
Working-house of thought, 4222
World, 7464-7495
account this w. but hell, 3408
all the w. mourn her, 2297
all the w.'s a stage, 7466
all this the w. knows, 4431
as if w. were feverous, 6062
as in the golden w., 6606
as is our fangled w., 824
bad w., I say, 7470
bad w. the while, 3729
brave new w., 4516
cankers of a calm w., 6064
come abroad to see the w., 7490
compare prison unto w., 5439
confident against w. in arms, 3615
count the w. a stranger, 6767
daff'd the w. aside, 3613
fled from this vile w., 4822
foul body of infected w., 4680
foutre for the w., 7473
get start of majestic w., 1021
giddy thinks w. turns round, 7492
give w. assurance of a man, 5272
give w. to beasts, 7493
he doth bestride the w., 1021
here's a good w., 1771
how fresh in this old w., 3125
how goes the w., 7491
how weary all this w., 7468
how w. is given to lying, 4095
I am in this earthly w., 3268
I hold w. but as w., 7480
I to w. am drop of water, 7467
I with sword quarter'd w., 2100
I'll tell the w., 7471
in a better w. than this, 7464
in the universal w., 6723

in w. draw breath in pain, 1133
in w. I fill a place, 5314
in w.'s mouth scandalized, 5808
it is a reeling w., 1689
it is a w. to see, 7485
leave w. to bustle in, 7486
let me tell the w., 7471
let the vile w. end, 7474
let the w. slide, 7488
let the w. slip, 7489
let the w. take note, 6579
let w. no longer be a stage, 7472
little of w. can I speak, 6181
mad w., mad kings, 7476
my life, my all the w., 6086
never merry w. in England, 2971
no w. to play with mammets, 4265
no w. without Verona, 416
O monstrous w., 3515
O slanderous w., 6978
O what a w. is this, 7465
O w., thy slippery turns, 2921
o'er half w. nature dead, 4912
old folks know the w., 1290
reckless to spite the w., 7479
see how the w. wags, 2793
see wonders of w. abroad, 7574
smite rotundity o' the w., 6585
so runs the w. away, 7469
speak to unknowing w., 6165
this great lubber, the w., 7495
this working-day w., 981
this w. I do renounce, 131
thou seest w., how it goes, 7475
three-nook'd w., 5209
what do with the w., 7493
what in w. but grief, 7274
where thou art, there the w., 7146
wicked, wicked w., 7481
wish estate of w. undone, 6323
with passion shake the w., 6663
w. affords no law, 7487
w. and all in it nothing, 5034
w. furnished with men, 4492
w. has grown honest, 4964
w. hath not sweeter creature, 7327
w. is broad and wide, 416
w. is cheered by sun, 1143
w. is full of rubs, 5747
w. is mine oyster, 7482
w. is not for aye, 4260
w. is not thy friend, 7487
w. knows not which is which, 5832
w. must be peopled, 7484
w. no better than a sty, 4
w. of blessings to my soul, 3340
w. of faults looks handsome, 2596
w. of one chrysolite, 7478
w. of water shed, 7129
w. six thousand years old, 4253
w., thy mutations, 7477
w. to hide virtues in, 7494
w. too saucy with gods, 5096
you see how w. goes, 2423
Worldings : foutre for w., 7473
make testament as w. do, 6502
Worm, 7496-7501
Don W., conscience, 6763
earth's w., 1905
I trod upon a w., 3654

like a w. in the bud, 7339
made me think man a w., 581
no goodness in the w., 7490
pretty w. of Nilus, 7496
smallest w. will turn, 7498
thou owest w. no silk, 4494
viperous w., 2137
w. doth die for it, 7499
w. is emperor for diet, 7497
w. of conscience, 1512
w. that eat of a king, 7497
w. that's fled hath nature, 5865
Worm-holes of vanished days, 1361
Worms : convocation of w., 7497
dust and food for w., 3617
froward and unstable w., 3670
give that unto the w., 3109
let's talk of w., 1431
made worms' meat of me, 3655
men died, w. eaten them, 4253
ring fingers with w., 1868
roast-meat for w., 7500
with vilest w. to dwell, 4822
Worse than a smoky house, 6431
w. than the worst, 2071
Worser : throw away w. part, 3333
Worship : pay no w. to sun, 4998
Worst, 7502-7505
give w. of thoughts w. of words, 6563
know by w. means w., 5988
let's reason with the w., 7502
not first who incurred w., 7504
this is the w., 7503
to fear w. cures w., 2617
w. is worldly loss, 3914
w. returns to laughter, 7503
w. that man can breathe, 7547
w. which on hopes depended, 5605
Worth, 7506-7510
but beggars that count w., 7509
it was well w. seeing, 5933
longer kept, less w., 1442
my w. unknown, 4233
not w. a breakfast, 1241
not w. a gooseberry, 6934
not w. a pin, 5285
not w. an egg, 6735
not w. dust wind blows, 7507
not w. the search, 5583
not w. the time of day, 7510
not w. wagging of beards, 1201
scarce w. a noble, 5012
scarce w. taking up, 7506
w. a Jewess' eye, 1321
w. of your virginity, 4758
w. the whistle, 7507
Worthiness of nature, 4899
w. of praise, 5394
Worthy to inlay heaven, 689
Would and w. not, 3091
you cannot as you w., 4879
Wound, 7511-7524
death's destroying w., 1889
ear can take no greater w., 6430
gall a new-healed w., 7514
he jests at scars that never felt a w., 5813
hound licking of his w., 7524
knife sees not w., 4980
private w. is deepest, 7523
salve makes w. ache more, 7518

searching of thy w., 7512
show me w. of this news, 4965
show w. eye hath made, 2404
to bottom search my w., 7520
what w. heal but by degrees, 7517
with a w. I must be cured, 7511
w. green, hope of help, 7516
w. of peace is surety, 6352
Wounding : deep-sore w., 2073
Woundings of father's curse, 1739
Wounds : bind up my w., 3596
dead Henry's w. open, 7519
ghastly, gaping w., 7515
kiss dead Cæsar's w., 6503
sweet Cæsar's w., 1033
these w. on Crispin's day, 3540
working with deadly w., 5362
w. heal ill men give selves, 7521
w. invisible love's arrows, 7513
w. like dumb mouths, 1031
w. valiantly he took, 4809
Wrack : blow, wind, come, w., 1873
w. to the seaman, 5591
Wrath, 7525-7527
come not within my w., 7527
gods assuage thy w., 7525
I am burn'd with w., 7526
in very w. of love, 4387
to flaming w. be oil, 502
wall-eyed w., 4847
Wreaks : his w., his fits, 7266
Wreck : out of w. to rise, 6450
sunken w., treasuries, 5387
Wrecks : thousand w., 2216
Wren, 7528-7539
no better musician than w., 5003
w. goes to it, 95
w. will fight against owl, 7528
w. with little quill, 7528
Wrens make prey, 7530
Wretch, 7531-7534
come, thou mortal w., 3969
disobedient w., 7533
inhuman w., 2322
needy hollow-eyed w., 6893
pretty w. left crying, 2495
pulled w. to muddy death, 1851
sly frantic w., 7534
Wretchedness deprived benefit, 7532
w. that glory brings, 3017

Wretches : feel what w. feel, 5369
poor naked w., 7531
w. fetter'd in prisons, 6806
Wrinkle : hanged in w. of brow, 2420
stop no w. in pilgrimage, 4143
Wrinkled deep in time, 5286
Wrinkles : let old w. come, 4721
no deeper w. yet, 2468
Wrist : gripe the hearer's w., 7097
Writ : holy w., 377
Write : baseness to w. fair, 7535
I can w. my name, 7536
to w. comes by nature, 5568
why should I w. this, 4622
w. it in a martial hand, 2953
w. with a goose-pen, 2953
Wrong, 7537-7542
answering one foul w., 5694
be it my w., 7437
beyond imagination is w., 7538
do a little w., 5695
do w. to none, 602
he hath done me w., 7540
I should do Brutus w., 7541
I've done you w., 5158
make w. right, 3066
oppressor's w., 1847
persist in doing w., 7542
we do it w., 7539
w. myself and you., 7541
w. not w. with contempt, 7537
w. to truant with bed, 5985
w. us, shall we not revenge, 3797
you do me w., 7540
you offer him a w., 478
you w. me every way, 6070
Wronged my innocent child, 1169
Wrongs, 7543-7548
by day and night he w. me, 1654
brook little w. as gods, 6078
feeling of my cousin's w., 5696
honourable to remember w., 7543
I pocket up these w., 7546
if w. be evils, 7545
make his w. his outsides, 7547
plain pocketing-up of w., 7545
wrung with w., 7548
your w. scandal my sex., 7367
Wrought he not well, 5274

Y

Yard : draw clothier's y., 858
Yare about him, 431
Yarn : life of mingled y., 4115
Year : big y., swoln, 5755
praise God for merry y., 2281
'tis not a y. shows a man, 4510
Years : cut off twenty y., 1864
good y. shall devour them, 7071
his y. but young, 2397
I have y. on my back, 7580
thou hast many y. to live, 4143
Yeas : russet y., 7363
Yeoman : did me y.'s service, 7535
Yeomen made in England, 4669
Yerked him under ribs, 3731

Yesterday : call back y., 6631
y. word of Cæsar stood, 1033
Yesterdays have lighted fools, 4137
Yoke : golden y., 207
now thy neck bears y., 4939
savage bull doth bear y., 973
thrust neck into a y., 4938
yield not thy neck to y., 4938
y. of inauspicious stars, 1895
Yoke-devils sworn, 6718
Yorick : alas, poor Y., 7549
York : sun of Y., 7203
Y. is most unmeet, 2295
Young : capacities of y., 7578
not so y. to love for singing, 7480

so cunning and so y., 7569
so wise y. never live long, 7568
so y. and so untender, 7563
we y. never live so long, 7581
y. body with old head, 7584
y. in limbs, 7583
y. lack discretion, 7575
y. ripe not to reason, 5575
y. unfit to hear philosophy, 7572
Younger : we shall ne'er be y., 7489
y. by loss of a beard, 476
Younker : how like a y., 5447
y. prancing to his love, 4798
Youth, 7550-7589
all is brave y. mounts, 7552
banged y. into dumbness, 3793
blood of y. burns, 7216
corrupted y. of realm, 5435
crabbed age and y., 7585
done i' the blaze of y., 7550
fairest y. made eyes swerve, 7555
feature of blown y., 4681
fresh and stainless y., 1214
hare is madness the y., 7566
he has eyes of y., 6039
he wears rose of y., 7551
his May of y., 7560
home-keeping y. homely wits, 7574
I am a sweet faced y., 7554
if y. light not your mind, 4771
in May-morn of his y., 7560
in vaward of our y.,7578
in y. a speechless dialect, 7565
in y. I never did apply, 141
it is a pretty y., 7553
know of your y., 6922
liquid dew of y., 1070
nips y. i' the bud, 2031

not clean past your y., 7577
riband in cap of y., 7576
rose-cheeked y., 7110
set name in scroll of y., 7578
think me untutored y., 4335
thou hast nor y. nor age, 1874
thou hast robb'd me of y., 3617
thy fault is y., 2599
thy y. doth beg alms, 7582
to flaming y. let virtue be as wax, 7556
transfix flourish set on y., 6635
unbaked and doughy y., 2635
violet in y. of nature, 6918
we have some salt of y., 7567
wear out y. in idleness, 7574
well-govern'd y., 2978
wit and y. come to harvest, 5570
y. a stuff will not endure, 4751
y. and comeliness, 7555
y. and ease, 6673
y. becomes careless livery, 7576
y., I do adore thee, 7585
y. in ladies' eyes, 7588
y. is bought more oft, 7573
y. is full of sport, 7585
y. is hot and bold, 7585
y. is nimble, age lame, 7585
y. is wild, age tame, 7585
y. like summer morn, 7585
y. makes stale morning, 3436
y. of England on fire, 7561
y. so apt to pluck a sweet, 7564
y. that means to be of note, 4796
y. wasted sooner wears, 7559
y.'s proud livery, 7586
Youths and wildness, 3118
y. no audience endure, 7562
y. that thunder at playhouse, 7562

Z

Zeal : let not words accuse z., 7445
Zed : thou whoreson z., 4084

Zenith : my z. doth depend, 6239
Zephyrs : gentle as z., 4900